Library of Congress Cataloging-in-Publication Data

Carter, T. Barton.
    The First Amendment and the fifth estate : regulation of
electronic mass media / by T. Barton Carter, Marc A. Franklin, Jay
B. Wright. — 3rd ed.
        p.   cm.
    Includes index.
    ISBN 1–56662–039–2
    1. Broadcasting—Law and legislation—United States.   2. Cable
television—Law and legislation—United States.   3. Press law—
United States.   I. Franklin, Marc A.   II. Wright, Jay B.
III. Title.
KF2805.C37   1993
343.73'0994—dc20
[347.303994]   92–35662

C., F. & W. First Amend. Fifth Estate 3rd Ed. F.P.

THE FIRST AMEND

AND

THE FIFTH ESTAT

REGULATION OF ELECTRONI MASS MEDIA

By

T. BARTON CARTER
Associate Professor of Mass Communication
College of Communication
Boston University

MARC A. FRANKLIN
Frederick I. Richman Professor of Law
Stanford University

JAY B. WRIGHT
Professor of Journalism
S.I. Newhouse School of Public Communications
Syracuse University

THIRD EDITION

Westbury, New York
THE FOUNDATION PRESS, INC.
1993

For Alison, Jonathan, and Richard

*

PREFACE TO THE THIRD EDITION

The shared power in the English Parliament of the three estates of the realm—the Lords Spiritual, the Lords Temporal and the Commons—was long ago recognized as being in some ways matched by the special powers of the Reporters' Gallery. Journalism thus came to be known as the Fourth Estate. *Broadcasting & Cable* magazine and others have referred to the world of the electronic mass media as the Fifth Estate.

It was in recognition of the special importance and influence of the electronic mass media that we wrote the first edition of this book—a companion to our earlier book, *The First Amendment and the Fourth Estate*.

Since the last edition four years ago, electronic mass media regulation has continued its rapid change and development. During that time, Congress has passed the Children's Television Act of 1990 and the Cable Television Consumer Protection and Competition Act of 1992. Meanwhile, the Supreme Court has upheld license preferences for minorities, and the Federal Communications Commission has set up guidelines for the introduction of high definition television.

This Third Edition continues to reflect our belief that a proper understanding of this subject is possible only through examination of the opinions and decisions of the governmental bodies most directly responsible for the laws and regulations that apply to the electronic mass media: Congress, the Federal Communications Commission and the courts.

The book is divided into three parts. Chapters I and II serve as an introduction to the legal, technological and economic structure that has produced our system of electronic media regulation. Chapters III through X detail the laws and regulations that apply specifically to the electronic media. Finally, Chapters XI through XIV outline some of the more important laws applicable to *both* print and electronic media.

We have used the earlier editions of the book in teaching undergraduate, graduate, and law students and have incorporated what we have learned from that experience, but we welcome, of course, comments about ways of using the book or improving it.

Thanks are due to the American Law Institute for excerpts from the *Restatement (Second) of Torts* and to B.M. Owen, J.H. Beebe and W.G. Manning, Jr. for the chart from their book, *Television Economics*. Lisa Berman, Simon Miller, Aaron Pollack and Jodi Wolfman deserve special thanks for their work in preparing the index to this edition.

T. Barton Carter
Marc A. Franklin
Jay B. Wright

March, 1993

*

SUMMARY OF CONTENTS

SUMMARY OF CONTENTS

APPENDICES

*

TABLE OF CONTENTS

TABLE OF CONTENTS

*

TABLE OF CASES

Principal cases are in italic type. Non-principal cases
are in roman type. References are to Pages.

TABLE OF CASES

THE FIRST AMENDMENT

AND

THE FIFTH ESTATE

———

REGULATION OF ELECTRONIC MASS MEDIA

*

Chapter I

INTRODUCTION

The rapidly changing law and regulation of electronic media in the United States presents a challenge both to communications students and to law school students. This casebook surveys the law and regulation with which both types of students need to become familiar.

Law school students will typically have had such courses as constitutional law, contracts, torts and civil procedure before they undertake the more specialized study of electronic media law. They need to know the specialized law in this area if they, as practicing attorneys, are to give advice to media clients.

Most students in communications schools, on the other hand, will be *consumers* of legal advice. They will need to know when to ask for such advice and how to be guided by it. Presumably, an intelligent professional in any aspect of communications should know enough about law and public policy to make on-the-spot judgments. This is particularly true in the electronic media, where deadline pressures often require quick decision-making. The competent professional also needs to know enough to alert a superior when a potential legal problem is spotted and should know, particularly after reaching management level, how to use an attorney's advice in arriving at a decision.

With some experience, the consumer of legal advice learns how to take the attorney's advice. Some attorneys are much more cautious than others, and they will tend to give advice discouraging clients from airing some controversial materials that could lead to law suits. Other attorneys, particularly those who represent major media, may be much more daring and may say to a client, "Air what you need to. You're the journalist, and you know best what you think has to be aired. If you get sued, it will be my responsibility to defend you."

Newcomers are sometimes surprised to discover how unclear the law seems to be. Many questions have never been anticipated by legislators nor been answered by the courts. This is especially true with the electronic media, where technological developments are constantly raising new issues. Sometimes in two similar cases in different parts of the country, different courts have reached different conclusions. Bright attorneys disagree when they predict the outcomes of cases. Judges—even the nine justices of the Supreme Court of the United States—frequently disagree with one another and arrive at split decisions based on 5–4 or 6–3 votes. Newcomers to the law may be surprised to find, after they have read the opinion of the majority of the Court and agreed with it, that they also agree with points made in the dissenting opinion. It should not be quite so surprising that frequently there are good arguments on *both* sides of a dispute that has reached the Supreme Court.

Textbooks like this one give heavy emphasis to opinions of the Supreme Court because those opinions influence the application of the law in the courts below and they influence out-of-court settlements made on a much less formal basis. They also, of course, have an impact on rules and regulations imposed on electronic media by the Federal Communications Commission. It should be recognized, however, that a case that reaches the Supreme Court is an unusual case rather than a typical one. If, for example, we were to examine 1,000 instances in which the electronic media had aired something erroneous about individuals, we would probably find that most of the resulting "disputes" were resolved by the media's retracting the erroneous statements or by the unhappy individuals' being advised that they did not have libel cases because they really suffered no reputational harm as a result of the errors, or by the individuals' deciding that they did not have the time, inclination, or money to file a lawsuit. Even if 100 of those disputes resulted in lawsuits, the odds would still favor an out-of-court settlement or a decision by a trial court without getting into the appellate courts. If a single one of those 100 lawsuits reached the Supreme Court it would be surprising.

If Supreme Court cases are so relatively rare, one might ask, why not study the "ordinary" cases instead? The answer, of course, is that the way communications professionals and attorneys assess their chances of winning or losing a suit, and thereby decide whether to pursue it in court or to settle out of court, is by applying the principles from decisions in the major cases.

In this chapter we look not just at the Supreme Court cases but at a variety of sources of law in America and at the way legal cases proceed.

A. THE LAW

Law has always been an important force in American life—and courts have always been at the center of our legal system. All state constitutions created state court systems. The United States Constitution established the Supreme Court of the United States and empowered Congress to create lower federal courts. Many critical national questions have been addressed and resolved in court, from sedition questions after the Revolutionary War to the treatment of blacks after the Civil War, from school desegregation beginning in the 1930s, '40s, and '50s to questions of Presidential behavior in office in the 1970s. Hindsight shows that not all judicial decisions over 200 years have been correct, nor have they all been popular. But the overall respect Americans have for the legal system, even when they may disagree with particular decisions or dislike particular judges, has allowed the country to solve most major problems without violent upheavals. In general terms, the law is a system of rules of conduct that individuals and institutions are expected to follow, rules given force by a community's decision to punish those who violate them.

1. SOURCES AND STRUCTURE OF LAW AND THE LEGAL PROCESS

a. *Sources of Law*

In the United States, laws and sanctions for disobeying them come from four major sources: constitutions, statutes, administrative decisions and the judge-made law called the common law.

Constitutions. Although much of our legal system was borrowed from Great Britain, that country has no written constitution. This important form of law was developed in the United States. Not only is there a federal constitution, but each state has one. These documents decree governmental organization, describe the duties and responsibilities of governmental branches and officials and frequently specify certain individual rights, such as freedom of expression.

A constitution is written to allow flexibility as social conditions change. As new questions arise courts must ascertain whether the document permits or requires certain conduct. For instance, the First Amendment to the United States Constitution reads in part: "Congress shall make no law . . . abridging the freedom of speech, or of the press . . .." As simple as this seems, our study of electronic media law will show the complexity of these words.

Statutes. Another source of law is the array of statutes passed by Congress, state legislatures, and city and county governments. The law we inherited from Great Britain generally served as basic authority in the early days of the United States. After that, statutes adopted by legislative bodies began to be more important than judicially developed law. Today, statutes are the dominant form of lawmaking. Much judicial time is spent interpreting these laws and deciding how they apply to specific situations. Statutes are general in scope and prospective in operation.

Statutes are also used to create administrative agencies, specifying exactly how much authority they have. For example, the Communications Act of 1934 created the Federal Communications Commission. All criminal laws in this country are now statutory. Crimes must be described carefully so that people know precisely what is forbidden. Case law could rarely provide sufficient guidance.

Administrative Regulations and Decisions. Much law comes from decisions of administrative agencies. These were first developed by Congress as a way to bring expertise to bear on areas under the legislature's responsibility. The first administrative agency was the Interstate Commerce Commission, but today such agencies are numerous. The Federal Communications Commission, the Federal Trade Commission and the Copyright Royalty Tribunal, all of which affect electronic media law, are just a few of the federal agencies. Administrative agencies also exist on the state and city levels. Much more law is created by these agencies through their delegated lawmaking powers than by all the courts in the country. We will return to administrative law and some of these agencies later in this chapter.

Common Law. The term "common law" is sometimes used to distinguish the Anglo–American legal system from the "civil law" systems of continental Europe. More commonly, the term refers to those areas of law in which no statutes exist and, thus, in which courts are expected to chart their own decisional course without legislative direction. The product of this process, law based on cases alone, is called common law. It is the ever growing result of specific but principled decisions in individual disputes rather than a written body of prospective general rules set down by a legislature.

The common law came from England, where the term first was used to distinguish law made by the King's courts from that made by ecclesiastical courts. But if the law were made by courts, not following a written statute, could not each court—each judge—decide similar cases in different ways? Not only would this cause consternation among citizens who would not know how to act, but judges might totally reconsider whole areas of law as each case arose. The concept of *stare decisis* emerged from these concerns. This is the doctrine of precedent under which judges refer to previous decisions involving basically similar legal issues and facts in order to decide the case at hand. It is then possible to look at previous cases and decisions to see how a court is likely to decide future cases. However, courts are not strictly bound by *stare decisis*. They can "distinguish" a current case from previous cases and refuse to follow the guidance of the past if they find the facts sufficiently different. Or, in an unusual situation, a court can overrule precedents and explicitly embark on a new approach to the legal area. In general, though, judges work within the boundaries of *stare decisis*.

Although the common law was dominant at the time of the Revolution, the increasing complexity of our society and other factors have brought legislation in almost all areas—and a consequent reduction in the role of the common law. It still retains importance for us, however, in the areas of defamation and privacy.

b. Hierarchy

There is a hierarchy among these four sources of law. Within a state the state constitution is dominant. If a question is not answered in the constitution, an appropriate statute, as interpreted by the courts, will be the final word. But a statute in conflict with the constitution will be struck down by the courts.

Within the spheres of their statutory authority, administrative agency rulings have the force of a statute and will be upheld by courts unless the ruling violates the constitution, the agency has violated its own rules in making the decision or the agency is arbitrary and capricious. Courts examine decisions by zoning commissions and public utility commissions according to these criteria.

When no constitution or statute or administrative agency ruling controls, courts will apply common law principles to decide a dispute.

c. Federalism

The hierarchy just discussed applies within a single state. But the federal structure of the United States creates a second hierarchy of legal sources that must be explored. When the United States Constitution was written, most space was devoted to creating the three branches of government—Legislature in Article I, Executive in Article II and Judiciary in Article III. Those articles dealt only with how the federal government should conduct its internal affairs. In this respect, the federal government's structure resembled that of a state government.

But the nature of federalism required that some attention be paid to the relationship between the existing state governments and the new federal government. This was addressed in Article VI, Section 2, the Supremacy Clause, which provides that:

> This Constitution, and the Laws of the United States which shall be made in pursuance thereof ... shall be the supreme Law of the Land; and the Judges in every State shall be bound thereby, any Thing in the Constitution or Laws of any State to the Contrary notwithstanding.

This aspect of federalism becomes important because some of our cases involve claims that state laws are invalid because they conflict with some federally protected right. Notice also that state court judges are obligated to declare state laws invalid if they conflict with federal provisions.

Finally, notice how important the courts are at every stage of the legal system. Although courts act only to resolve specific disputes that the parties cannot settle, the judicial power permeates every layer of the two hierarchies. When a constitutional provision is relied upon by one of the parties to the dispute, the court must interpret the provision's meaning and its application to the dispute before it. When one party relies upon a statute, the court may have to interpret it—and may also have to decide whether it is consistent with the state's constitution. When an administrative ruling is involved in the dispute, the court must decide whether the agency acted constitutionally, acted within its statutory authority, followed its own rules, and acted without being arbitrary or capricious. When none of these sources appears to have a bearing on the litigation, the court turns to common-law decisionmaking.

When federalism is involved, state and federal courts are obligated to assure that in cases of conflict proper scope is given to the federal provisions in resolving the case before them.

d. Litigation

The judicial system must deal with several kinds of controversies.

Some of the controversies begin as administrative proceedings. For example, the Federal Communications Commission makes decisions on license applications by would-be broadcasters. It makes rules and regulations. It decides whether broadcasters have violated those rules and regulations. Like the decisions of other regulatory agencies, FCC decisions are subject to appeal, and appellate courts may be called upon to decide whether the FCC acted appropriately. These matters are normally civil; that is, there is usually no allegation of criminal behavior on the part of the broadcaster.

A variety of other civil matters are also addressed by the judicial system. When one party sues another for breach of contract, it is a civil case. When a decision must be made as to whether a journalist is protected from having to divulge secret sources or other confidential information, it is a civil matter. When one party sues another because the second party somehow harmed the first, the party suing is alleging that the defendant committed a *tort*—a civil wrong or injury. Libel, slander and several kinds of invasion of privacy are examples of torts for which plaintiffs can bring civil lawsuits that must be decided by the judicial system. If one party were to go to court and ask for an order to stop the other party from doing something, that action (i.e., seeking an injunction), is also a civil matter. If one thought that a statute were unconstitutional, one could initiate a lawsuit to have the statute so declared; that, too, would be a civil matter. Or, one might go to court to seek an injunction to stop government authorities from enforcing such a law; that, too, would be a civil matter.

The judicial system also, of course, concerns itself with criminal law—cases in which defendants are alleged to have committed crimes. Although there are certainly instances in which people in the media commit crimes, such cases are obviously much less frequent than the civil cases in which people in the media find themselves. In criminal law, facts are disputed: can the victim accurately identify the defendant or is the jury persuaded by the defendant's alibi witnesses? In conventional criminal cases, the parties agree on the legal rules but they disagree about the facts—and a trial is needed to determine the facts governed by these rules.

In most of the cases in this book, and most First Amendment cases generally, the crucial questions that will determine the outcome do not depend on disputed facts. Rather, the parties usually disagree over what legal rule applies to an accepted set of facts. Such a dispute raises legal questions to be resolved by a judge, often with no need for a trial.

The dispute will be brought in one of two court systems—state or federal. Before the United States Constitution was adopted, each state had its own court system—with trial and appellate courts. These systems survived. As a result of the adoption of the United States Constitution, and early action of Congress, a second court system—the federal system—was created.

When one party sues another party in the same state, under state libel law, for example, the trial—if there is one—will take place in a state court. When the parties are individuals or corporations in different states, questions beyond our present concerns arise about whether the litigation will take place in a state or federal court. Regardless, the trial will provide the opportunity for the presentation of evidence, including testimony by witnesses. Usually a jury would hear the case, but in some instances the trial judge will decide the case alone.

If there has been a trial, or if the judge has made a legal ruling on a motion on an agreed upon set of facts, either or both of the parties may be dissatisfied. They may believe that errors were made—either errors in procedure or errors in substantive law. If they choose to appeal to a higher (appellate) court, they will submit a transcript of the lower court proceedings and a *brief,* a document explaining the alleged errors to the appellate court. Virtually every system permits the right to one appeal. But, although one is entitled to one's "day in court" and even a second day in an appellate court, higher courts often do not have to take cases for review unless they choose to do so.

Depending on the size of the state and the complexity of the state system, state judgments might be appealed to one or more levels of appellate courts before reaching the highest court in the state—typically, but not always, called the supreme court. In the federal system, decisions from the trial court, called the U.S. District Court, are appealed to a regional court of appeals and then to the Supreme Court of the United States. Federal administrative agency decisions are appealed directly to a court of appeals.

The Supreme Court performs two distinct roles. As the final appellate court for litigants who have lost cases in *federal* courts, it is the apex of the federal system. As such, it construes federal statutes just as state courts construe state statutes. In the chapter on obscenity and indecency, for example, we will encounter cases in which defendants have been prosecuted for violating *federal* statutes. Some other cases are tried in federal courts because the parties in the case are from different states; when such a *diversity of citizenship* exists, the federal court may provide a more neutral forum for the resolution of the dispute than a state court might. The second distinct role that the Supreme Court performs is in hearing appeals on cases from the *state* courts: states and state courts have obligations imposed upon them by the United States Constitution, and the Supreme Court is sometimes called upon to decide if those obligations have been met. For example, Article I, Section 10, of the Constitution states Article I, Section 10, that no state may adopt an *ex post facto* law or coin its own currency. Other limitations are imposed by the Supremacy Clause of Article VI, Section 2, which declares that when federal and state law conflict, the federal law is supreme—and the judges of the state courts are required to recognize that supremacy. The Supreme Court of the United States has the power to review the actions of state courts to assure that states are complying with federal obligations.

Some of the cases we consider have come to the Supreme Court from the state courts. The losing party has usually claimed that the decision of the state courts has incorrectly interpreted the First Amendment—which applies to the states because of the Fourteenth Amendment, as explained shortly. Although state courts may render decisions interpreting the First and Fourteenth Amendments, the Supreme Court is the *final* authority on the meaning of the United States Constitution.

If a case poses an important question involving the First Amendment or some other part of the United States Constitution, it can wind up in the Supreme Court whether it starts in the state courts or in the federal courts.

In most instances the Supreme Court has been given discretion by Congress to choose what cases it will hear, and of the many thousands of cases that are brought each year, the Court accepts fewer than 200 for hearing and decision. To seek review by the Supreme Court, the litigant who lost the case in the lower court files what is called a "petition for *certiorari*" stating the nature of the dispute, the decision below, and the reasons why the Court should review this case. Since a case usually reaches the Supreme Court only after several lower courts, state or federal, have considered it, it rarely suffices for the petitioner to allege that the judges below made a mistake—a better reason is necessary. A serious claim that a state law violates the First Amendment is such a reason.

After the petition for *certiorari* is filed, the party who won below will usually file a memorandum trying to persuade the Court either that the case is not important, that there is no conflict with other decisions or that the decision is clearly correct in light of previous Supreme Court cases. In deciding whether or not to grant a petition for *certiorari*, all the justices will meet in conference and vote. The Court follows the so-called "rule of four" under which, if four justices believe the case should be heard, the petition for *certiorari* will be granted.

If the Supreme Court decides not to hear the case, it will usually not state its reasons and will issue an order that says simply "The petition for *certiorari* is denied." In this book that procedure is indicated when "*certiorari* denied" is part of the citation. Although this outcome favors the party that won in the lower court, the legal effect is different from having the Supreme Court listen to the case on the merits and decide to affirm the decision of the lower court. When the Supreme Court denies *certiorari*, all that is clear is that the Court did not think the case worthy of full consideration. This does not mean that the Court believes that the case was correctly decided below. It may mean only that the Court does not think the issue is important enough to justify further attention.

When the Supreme Court decides it will listen to a case, it will generally issue an order "granting" the petition for *certiorari* and directing the parties to file formal briefs arguing the merits of the controversy. The losing party below, the petitioner, prepares a brief, trying to persuade the Court to decide the case on the merits in petitioner's favor. The respondent's brief seeks to persuade the Court to affirm the result reached by the lower court.

The Court will schedule oral arguments at which the attorneys representing both parties have a limited period of time before the justices of the Court to make the best arguments they can for their clients and to answer questions posed by the justices. Because new evidence is not presented at the appellate level, and witnesses are not heard, the parties to the case need not even be present. In a sense, the discussion is about whether errors have been made in the trial court below, and it is not necessary to hear from the witnesses. The witnesses' testimony and other evidence is already reflected in the transcripts of the case filed with the Court, so the oral argument should, as the name suggests, focus on the attempts to persuade the justices as to the outcome of the case.

Following the oral arguments in the case, the justices meet privately to discuss the case and to indicate how they expect to vote. In the Supreme Court, if the Chief Justice is a member of the majority, he may assign the writing of the majority opinion to himself or to any of the other justices in the majority. Similarly, the senior justice among the dissenters may assign the dissenting opinion. When the Chief Justice is dissenting, the senior justice among the majority assigns the majority opinion. Drafts of opinions, written by the justices and their clerks, are circulated privately among the justices. Agreement is reached where possible, but the justices may publish their own opinions if they choose. In the "Pentagon Papers" case (see discussion of New York Times Co. v. United States later in this chapter), to use a most unusual example, all nine justices wrote opinions.

A single opinion that has the support of a majority of the participating justices is denominated an "opinion of the Court." As such it becomes binding on the Court, establishing a precedent for subsequent decisions (unless later overruled by the Court itself). Sometimes, however, while a majority of the Court agree on the outcome of a case, they do so for different reasons. For example, six of the nine justices might vote to affirm a lower court decision, but four could be doing so for one reason and two could be doing so for a different reason. In such a case, the opinion written by the four justices is a "plurality" opinion, not a majority opinion. Such an opinion is entitled to substantially less precedential value than an opinion of the Court. The first line of the reported decision will indicate the nature of the opinion—a named justice either delivers the "opinion of the Court" or announces "the judgment of the Court and an opinion joined by" up to three other justices. The "judgment of the Court" means the bare result, such as affirmance or reversal. The reasons for the judgment are found in the opinions.

2. READING THE LAW

Supreme Court decisions obviously are not written for readers who are totally unfamiliar with legal language. Typically, they refer to, or *cite,* earlier cases that you may or may not have to read. Not surprisingly, some of the justices are better writers than others. The meaning of some paragraphs may be perfectly clear, but some confuse even the best lawyers and require subsequent cases to resolve the confusion. Although reading Supreme Court decisions may seem difficult at first, it usually becomes easier as you become more familiar with the language and gradually develop some background in reading the law.

As you read the cases, note the names. When the losing party in the lower court files a petition for *certiorari*, the petitioner's name comes first in the title of the case. The initial plaintiff thus may later become the *respondent* and be listed second in the title in the Supreme Court. A few other appellate courts follow the practice of putting the losing party's name first. As you read the appellate cases in this book, do not assume that the party named first in the title was the original plaintiff.

On a related point, every title of a case is followed by a group of numbers and abbreviations called a "citation." This tells which volumes in the law library contain the full report of the opinions in the case. For example, the citation to Cox Broadcasting Corp. v. Cohn, 420 U.S. 469, 95 S.Ct. 1029, 43 L.Ed.2d 328, 1 Med.L.Rptr. 1819 (1975), means that the case can be found in volume 420 of the official *United States Reports* at page 469, and also in volume 95 of the *Supreme Court Reporter* at page 1029, and also in volume 43 of *United States Supreme Court Reports (Lawyers' Edition, 2d Series)* at page 328 and also in volume 1 of *Media Law Reporter* at page 1819. Opinions of the United States Court of Appeals are found in the *Federal Reporter Second Series* (F.2d). Decisions of the United States District Courts are found in the *Federal Supplement* (F.Supp.). State decisions usually have two citations: one to a state reporter and one to a private service that groups state decisions in regional volumes. Thus, in Taylor v. KTVB, 96 Idaho 202, 525 P.2d 984 (1974), the first reference is to volume 96 of the official *Idaho Reports* at page 202, and the second is to volume 525 of the *Pacific Reporter, Second Series*, page 984, where the Idaho case will also be found.

In addition to citing judicial opinions, we will cite the *U.S. Code Annotated* (U.S.C.A.), an unofficial publication of federal statutes. The comparable official publication is the *U.S. Code* (U.S.C.) but U.S.C.A. includes useful comments and references to judicial decisions. We will also cite the *Code of Federal Regulations* (C.F.R.), which contains rules and regulations of the federal regulatory agencies, including the FCC.

There are certain reporting services of special importance to electronic media regulation. The FCC's official reports from 1986 and earlier, the *FCC Reports*, are referred to by volume number, F.C.C. or F.C.C.2d, followed by page number. Beginning with materials from October 1986, the Commission's official record, including decisions, reports, public notices and other documents, is the *FCC Record*. It is cited by volume number, F.C.C.Rcd. and the page number. When the Commission proposes rules for possible adoption, formal notice of the pending action must be given to the public. This is done through the *Federal Register* (Fed.Reg. or F.R.). The register is organized chronologically and covers all federal agencies and departments. An unofficial service, *Pike and Fischer's Radio Regulation,* reports Commission rulemaking actions and case decisions as well as court decisions. The name of this service is abbreviated as R.R. or R.R.2d, and sometimes as P & F Radio Reg. Note that the name *Radio Regulation* is deceptive: the service includes television decisions as well as telephone and other common carrier decisions. Another unofficial service, *Media Law Reporter,* (Med.L.Rptr.) reports judicial decisions in mass media law but does not include FCC decisions and covers fewer electronic media cases than does *Pike & Fischer.*

The foregoing discussion of litigation and the role of the Supreme Court has necessarily been general and abstract. As we turn to actual cases, you should review this information if some aspect of a case puzzles you. Any unusual matters will be discussed in the introduction to the case or in the notes that follow the opinions.

Some of the terms used in the texts, particularly the Latin ones, may be unfamiliar to you at first. Although there are a variety of legal dictionaries published, some in paperback, you will probably find most of the terms defined in any good collegiate dictionary. As you see them used in the cases, they will become part of your legal vocabulary.

B. THE FIRST AMENDMENT

In the United States, regulation of the mass media is different from the regulation of any other industry. What distinguishes it is the First Amendment to the Constitution of the United States: "Congress shall make no law . . . abridging the freedom of speech, or of the press . . .." A brief examination of the historical roots of the First Amendment and its interpretation by the courts is necessary for an understanding of electronic mass media regulation.

1. Introduction to Freedom of Expression

a. *The English Background*

In England repression of ideas antithetical to the government was in operation by the 13th century. In 1275 and again in 1379, Parliament made it criminal to speak against the state. Later known as "seditious libel," words that questioned the crown in any way were punished by the King's Council sitting in the "starred chamber." Ecclesiastical laws forbidding heresy already existed, thus making it dangerous to say anything in opposition to the Church or the state.

With the advent of printing, around 1500, the government became even more concerned about statements that questioned the secular powers. To prevent the wider dissemination that the printing press made possible, the Crown established a system of censorship, similar to the one already used by the Church, for all publications. This repression lasted until almost 1700. The core of the censorship system was licensing. Unlicensed publication could lead to severe punishment and to charges of criminal libel.

In addition to criminal prosecutions for libel, the English government found taxation to be an effective way to control the press. The purpose of the Stamp Act of 1711 and later laws was to reduce the circulation of newspapers. Half of England's newspapers went out of business in the first year of the Act.

Despite such measures, it was possible for Great Britain still to contend that freedom of the press existed. Sir William Blackstone, the most famous compiler of the common law, wrote in the late 1760s:

> [w]here blasphemous, immoral, treasonable, schismatical, seditious, or scandalous libels are punished by the English law . . . the liberty of the press, properly understood, is by no means infringed or violated. The liberty of the press is indeed essential to the nature of a free estate; but this consists in laying no previous restraints upon publications, and not in freedom from censure for criminal matter when published. Every freeman has an undoubted right to lay what sentiments he pleases before the press: to forbid this is to destroy the freedom of the press: but if he publishes what is improper, mischievous, or illegal, he must take the consequences of his own temerity . . ..

W. Blackstone, 4 Commentaries on the Laws of England 151–52 (1765–69).

Blackstone is central to this analysis because he was a major influence on English and American legal thinking in the period when our Constitution was taking shape. His definition of freedom of the press as the absence of "previous restraints upon publications," and the distinction between liberty thus defined, and licentiousness, for which punishment was considered legitimate, made clear that freedom of expression meant, as a minimum, rejection of prior restraint. Uncertainty remains as to the legitimacy of subsequent punishment for seditious libel, and as to what types of expression constitute punishable "licentiousness."

b. The Colonial Experience

Those who drafted and adopted the United States Constitution and the Bill of Rights were well aware of this background of repression in Great Britain. They also knew of, and had experienced, similar restrictions on freedom of expression imposed by Britain on the colonies. The British Stamp Act of 1765 was directed specifically against the colonies and was meant to offset "the expense of defending, protecting and securing" the colonies. In fact, the Act served more to anger colonists than to raise revenue. The colonists saw the Act as "taxation without representation" and rebelled against it.

Prior to that, however, laws that applied to the press in England during the 17th and 18th centuries were also applied to the emerging colonial press, and the licensing of presses in the colonies closely paralleled the English practice. The colonies saw printers jailed and their books burned for publishing without permission.

In 1734 John Peter Zenger, who printed the *Weekly Journal,* was charged with seditious libel by the Governor General of New York, whom Zenger had criticized. Zenger spent almost a year in jail awaiting trial. By the traditional common law standards he was surely guilty because he had published the articles in question and the law did not recognize truth as a defense. Zenger's lawyer, Andrew Hamilton, convinced the jury that the only question in the case involved the liberty to write the truth, and the jury, despite the judge's instructions, acquitted Zenger. Although the verdict set no precedent (because a jury verdict is not a ruling on the law), it did signal a change in the political climate.

After the American Revolution, the governments of the former colonies sought to come together to form a nation. Even before the war was ended, the colonies had attempted to form a national government under the Articles of Confederation, devised in 1783. This document allowed the states to retain much power, leaving little for the central government. The Articles contained no mention of freedom of expression, but many argued such a clause was not necessary. Because the federal government had no power to interfere with citizens, there was no need to forbid it from exercising power it did not have. Additionally, most states had some form of bill of rights in their own constitutions.

The new Constitution, formulated at the Constitutional Convention of 1787, created the national government with three branches. Some states in their own constitutions had protected citizens against state government action, but the federal Constitution was not primarily concerned with that problem. The omission led some critics to oppose ratification because the new government might itself threaten the freedom of citizens of the new country.

Although the records of the Constitutional Convention are sketchy, it is known that discussion of a bill of rights did not take place until the last few days of the meeting. That short-lived debate was inconclusive. The Constitution was promulgated without a bill of rights and sent to the states for ratification.

During ratification debates there was much enthusiasm for freedom of the press but no clear idea of exactly how it should be protected or how far it should extend.

Even though 13 states ratified the Constitution, five expressed concern that a bill of rights had been omitted.

As a result of this dissatisfaction, James Madison introduced a set of amendments to the Constitution when the First Congress met. The House of Representatives approved an amendment that protected freedom of speech and press from infringement "by any state." The Senate struck the provision limiting the powers of the states and the final version provided that "Congress shall make no law . . . abridging the freedom of speech, or of the press . . .." This was the third of 12 amendments submitted to the states for ratification. When the first two failed at that time, this became the First Amendment to the United States Constitution. (One of the two "failed" amendments would have prohibited mid-term pay raises for the members of Congress. First proposed 203 years earlier, that amendment was approved by Michigan, the 38th state to approve it, in May 1992; Congress voted overwhelmingly two weeks later to endorse the amendment. Because in recent years Constitutional amendments to the constitution have had to be ratified within seven years, some Constitutional scholars have questioned whether 203-year process of ratifying the 27th Amendment meets the requirements of Article V of the Constitution with regard to the amending process. The Archivist of the United States, meanwhile, went ahead and published the amendment in the *Federal Register.*)

Although it was later argued that the Bill of Rights was intended to protect citizens against invasions by the state as well as the federal government, this was rejected in Barron v. Baltimore, 32 U.S. (7 Pet.) 243 (1833) when the Supreme Court decided that the Bill of Rights applied solely against the federal government. Constraints on the states were those specified in Article I, Section 10 and in such other provisions as the Supremacy Clause.

Though on its face the First Amendment appears to bind only the Congress, it is well established today that the prohibitions of the First Amendment extend to all branches of both the federal and state governments by way of the "due process" clause of the Fourteenth Amendment. The First Amendment guarantees, the Supreme Court has held, are a fundamental element of the "liberty" protected by the Fourteenth Amendment. Gitlow v. New York, 268 U.S. 652 (1925).

As a result, what Congress may not do because of the First Amendment, a state may not do because of the Fourteenth Amendment. The Constitution restrains only governments, not private individuals from interfering with the exercise of freedom of expression.

In Free Speech in the United States (1941), Professor Zechariah Chafee, Jr. acknowledging that little was said at the time about the meaning of freedom of speech, reviewed some contemporary statements that suggest that in the years before the First Amendment "freedom of speech was conceived as giving a wide and genuine protection for all sorts of discussion of public matters." He argued that "such a widely recognized right must mean something," and that merely reaffirming the freedom of the press from previous censorship would have been pointless. During the 18th century, besides the narrow legal meaning of liberty of the press, there existed "a definite popular meaning: the right of unrestricted discussion of public affairs," and Chafee thought the framers were aware of basic differences between Great Britain and the former colonies.

2. BASES FOR FREEDOM OF COMMUNICATION

Professor Thomas I. Emerson, in The System of Freedom of Expression 6–9 (1970), asserted that "the system of freedom of expression in a democratic society" is based on four premises:

(1) freedom of expression facilitates self-fulfillment,

(2) it is an essential tool for advancing knowledge and discovering truth,

(3) it is a way to achieve a more stable and adaptable community, and

(4) it permits individuals to be involved in the democratic decision-making process.

Perhaps the most powerful judicial statement of the justifications for free expression is that of Justice Louis Brandeis, concurring in Whitney v. California, 274 U.S. 357, 375–77 (1927):

> Those who won our independence believed that the final end of the State was to make men free to develop their faculties; and that in its government the deliberative forces should prevail over the arbitrary. They valued liberty both as an end and as a means. They believed liberty to be the secret of happiness and courage to be the secret of liberty. They believed that freedom to think as you will and speak as you think are means indispensable to the discovery and spread of political truth; that without free speech and assembly discussion would be futile; that with them, discussion affords ordinarily adequate protection against the dissemination of noxious doctrine; that the greatest menace to freedom is an inert people; that public discussion is a political duty; and that this should be a fundamental principle of the American government.

They recognized the risks to which all human institutions are subject. But they knew that order cannot be secured merely through fear of punishment for its infraction; that it is hazardous to discourage thought, hope and imagination; that fear breeds repression; that repression breeds hate; that hate menaces stable government; that the path of safety lies in the opportunity to discuss freely supposed grievances and proposed remedies; and that the fitting remedy for evil counsels is good ones. Believing in the power of reason as applied through public discussion, they eschewed silence coerced by law—the argument of force in its worst form. Recognizing the occasional tyrannies of governing majorities, they amended the Constitution so that free speech and assembly should be guaranteed.

How many of Emerson's premises do you find in the Brandeis view?

Each of these explanations has been used, to a greater or lesser extent, by the Supreme Court to justify the high value placed on freedom of speech in our constitutional scheme of government. Each may justify different notions of the breadth and depth of the First Amendment freedom and each may apply with peculiar force in particular contexts.

These fundamental justifications for protecting speech tend to divide into two main groups: those that stress the values to the individual and those that stress the values to the society of freedom of speech. The emphasis on value to the individual, contained in what are variously called the self-fulfillment or self-realization models, is on the importance of expression as a route to individual development and fulfillment.

a. For Individuals

A concept of "natural law" was actively discussed for a century before the Constitution was adopted. In attempting to reconcile government's role with individual rights, certain personal freedoms were seen as inviolable. They were "natural rights" of individuals, rights that official persons or bodies had no power to affect. Among these rights was freedom of expression.

This concept derived in large part from the 17th century English philosopher John Locke, who contended that government's purpose was to use its power to protect life, liberty and property, natural rights to which each individual was entitled. Locke's views influenced the language of the First Amendment with the notion of free speech as a natural right, and the Fifth Amendment ("No person shall . . . be deprived of life, liberty, or property, without due process of law. . . .").

Locke discussed the origin of society in terms of a social contract. He believed the pre-social status was one of freedom. Private property was recognized, but no security existed. To achieve security, people surrendered a certain amount of freedom to establish a government. But the government rested on the consent of the governed, who would control the government rather than vice versa. A government that encroached on an individual's rights should be abolished or changed.

Several commentators believe that even with this Lockean philosophy to draw on, the framers had no clear concept of the First Amendment's purpose. No matter what the framers might have had in mind, however, they could not have foreseen the many changes in media technology and society generally. Thus, more expansive views of freedom of communication became necessary.

b. For Society

Neither disputing nor relying upon the assertion that we as individuals profit from freedom of speech, the society-centered reasons offered for protection explain why we as a people are better for having First Amendment freedoms.

Marketplace of Ideas. The seminal view that freedom of expression enhances the social good came from John Milton's *Areopagitica* in 1644. Milton, an English poet and essayist, wanted a divorce and wrote an essay he hoped would lower the strict legal barriers prohibiting it. He was chastised for publishing without a license and wrote *Areopagitica* to induce Parliament to allow unlicensed printing. Milton argued that licensing was unworkable and an affront to those who had views to express. But more, he said, it was harmful to society, since people are better able to function as citizens if they are knowledgeable and exposed to different points of view. Attempting to assuage official fears that the Crown's views would be overwhelmed if unlicensed printing were allowed, Milton wrote: "And though all the winds of doctrine were let loose to play upon the earth, so Truth be in the field, we do injuriously by licensing and prohibiting to misdoubt her strength. Let her and Falsehood grapple; who ever knew Truth put to the worse, in a free and open encounter?"

English philosopher and economist John Stuart Mill, who wrote 200 years after Milton, believed more in full and free discussion than did Milton. Mill thought that society could function well only with such freedom. He saw freedom of thought, discussion and investigation as "goods in their own right" but, more importantly, thought that society benefits from an exchange of ideas. People could trade their false notions for true ones, but only if they could hear the true ones. Such open discussion would necessarily mean that false as well as true ideas would be expressed.

The concept of the marketplace of ideas, first enunciated by Milton, was recognized in American law by Justice Oliver Wendell Holmes. It was later developed by Mill, who was more skeptical about the ultimate emergence of truth in the marketplace. In Patterson v. Colorado, 205 U.S. 454, 462 (1907), Justice Holmes observed that the First Amendment prevents all "previous restraints upon publications," but allows "the subsequent punishment of such as may be deemed contrary to the public welfare. . . . The preliminary freedom extends to the false as well as to the true; the subsequent punishment may extend as well to the true as to the false." He took a broader view in Abrams v. United States, 250 U.S. 616 (1919). Abrams and others had been accused of publishing pamphlets that criticized Pres. Woodrow Wilson's sending of troops to help counter the Russian revolution. The pamphlets also advocated a strike against American munitions plants. A majority of the Supreme Court ruled that publishing such pamphlets during wartime was not protected by the First Amendment. In dissent, Justice Holmes, joined by Justice Brandeis, argued that the pamphlets did not attack the form of the United States government, and thus did not violate the sedition statute as charged.

The marketplace of ideas approach has been criticized from several sides. In a Marxist attack, American philosopher Herbert Marcuse disagreed with the basic premise of the marketplace notion, that rational beings engage in a free interchange of opinions and information. People are not rational because government and mass media manipulate them—each for its own purposes, he said. In an essay entitled "Repressive Tolerance" in *A Critique of Pure Tolerance* (1965), he started from the premise that "the people must be capable of deliberating and choosing on the basis of knowledge." He was appalled by the broadcaster's reporting of the momentous and the mundane in the same monotone: "It offends against humanity and truth by being calm where one should be enraged, by refraining from accusation where accusation is in the facts themselves."

Marcuse said the "concentration of economic and political power" allows "effective dissent" to be blocked where it could freely emerge, and the "monopolistic media" prejudge "right and wrong, true and false . . . wherever they affect the vital interest of the society." The situation was so dangerous, Marcuse believed, that he recommended "suspension of the right of free speech and free assembly" so that "spurious objectivity" is replaced by "intolerance against movements from the Right, and toleration of movements from the Left."

Another group adopted a quite different approach. In the mid–1940s, the Commission on Freedom of the Press was organized to study the press in America. Funded primarily by Time Inc. and Encyclopedia Britannica, Inc., and chaired by Robert M. Hutchins, the Commission was composed of philosophers, historians, law professors and others. No media professionals were included on the panel, but some were called to share their views with Commission members. The Commission found that press freedom was not seriously threatened in mid–20th century America. The press had, however, despite the enforcement of antitrust laws, become increasingly concentrated in the hands of fewer individuals. Media owners, in fact, were reasonably free from government interference, but the First Amendment had little direct application to most people.

One Commission member, Professor Chafee, stated that the press could not play its proper part in society in the "mere absence of governmental restrictions." Rather, "affirmative action by the government or others," would be needed. Chafee started with Justice Holmes's formulation, "The best test of truth is the power of the thought to get itself accepted in the competition of the market." *Abrams,* p. 18, *supra.* But how, Chafee asked, could views compete in a market constricted because of a lack of media outlets? He answered that "a free market requires regulation, just as a free market for goods needs law against monopoly . . .. The government can lay down the rules of the game which will promote rather than restrict free speech." Such laws might require "essential facilities accessible to all," methods to assure that communication channels remain open, and measures directed at particular communication industries "intended to promote freedom, improve content, or otherwise make them perform their proper function in a free society." Z. Chafee, 2 Government and Mass Communications 471 ff. (1947).

Later law professor Jerome A. Barron adopted the same approach. He said the marketplace is an antiquated and impractical concept because of changes in the media and society since 1791. It is difficult for a person to begin a broadcast service because of limits in spectrum allocation or to begin a newspaper because of the prohibitive cost. Barron found censorship by media because they limit the views they disseminate and permit few new or unpopular ideas to be heard widely. Barron concluded that those who do not control media should be able to express their views through the mass media. "At the very minimum," Barron wrote, "the creation of two remedies is essential—(1) a nondiscriminating right to purchase editorial advertisements in daily newspapers, and (2) a right of reply for public figures and public officers defamed in newspapers." J. Barron, Freedom of the Press for Whom? 6 (1973). See also, Barron, Access to the Press—A New First Amendment Right, 80 Harv.L.Rev. 1641 (1967).

Safety Valve. When a government permits freedom of expression, it not only allows society to be exposed to a wide range of ideas, it also brings about a stable and adaptable community, according to Professor Thomas Emerson. T. Emerson, The System of Freedom of Expression, 11–14 (1970). Substituting force for logic, which is what happens when freedom of expression is suppressed, makes it impossible to come to rational decisions. In addition, coercion is ineffective in changing thoughts and beliefs. Instead, stifling expression breeds discontent that focuses not on the issues being suppressed, but on the act of suppression itself.

Emerson's argument is that freedom of expression will not cause society to become fragmented, to divide into opposing camps. Rather, suppression of communication will do that. Freedom of speech and press will allow dissidents to express their ideas "in a release of energy, a lessening of frustration and a channeling of resistance into courses consistent with law and order."

Self-governance. A third reason that freedom of communication is valuable in a democratic society is that such a society is based on self-governance, on an informed citizenry that will intelligently elect its representatives. James Madison believed that the people, not the government, were sovereign, and that the main purpose of freedom of speech was to allow citizens to govern themselves in a free society.

In the late 1940s, Professor Alexander Meiklejohn agreed that self-governance was the most important concern of the First Amendment. He advocated distinguishing between two kinds of expression. Speech concerning the self-governing process was "political speech" and deserved absolute protection from governmental interference. Speech that was nonpolitical in character, "private speech," was protected only by the due process clause of the Fifth Amendment, which permits the government some leeway for regulation.

Meiklejohn drew this distinction between political and private speech because he believed the central purpose of the First Amendment is to give citizens the greatest opportunity to discuss and hear about society's problems, the very information one must have to function in a self-governing society.

Meiklejohn's emphasis on self-government might have suggested that the First Amendment would protect only what we conventionally regard as political speech. His vagueness on this point in his 1948 edition was criticized by Chafee, who was concerned about what types of speech were being relegated to the Fifth Amendment's protection. Chafee observed that "there are public aspects to practically every subject." If Meiklejohn intended this broad view of the First Amendment, then Chafee wondered how there could be any limitations in such traditionally regulated areas as obscenity and libel. If, however, Meiklejohn were to place scholarship and the arts in the category of private speech, Chafee would regard it as "shocking to deprive these vital matters of the protection of the inspiring words of the First Amendment." Book Review, 62 Harv.L.Rev. 891, 900 (1949).

3. THE FIRST AMENDMENT AND THE INSTITUTIONAL PRESS

"Congress shall make no law . . . abridging the freedom of speech, or of the press . . .."

The lack of a broad consensus concerning the philosophical underpinnings of the majestic words of the First Amendment does not mean that the courts and legislatures of the United States are released from the obligation to obey the Amendment's dictates. To the contrary, our nation's lawmaking bodies have clearly acknowledged that the Amendment represents a constitutional bar to government action in numerous situations.

An appreciable and important fraction of these situations involves the institution of "the press," including the electronic press. This chapter sketches some of those elements of First Amendment doctrine that apply most directly to the press. Students interested in a more comprehensive exposition of First Amendment doctrine might consult M. Nimmer, Nimmer on Freedom of Speech (1984).

a. Restriction on Government Power

Liberty protected under the Fourteenth Amendment against encroachments of state governments is protected to the exact same extent that the First Amendment itself protects the freedoms of speech and press from the federal government. Lawyers and judges have developed the shorthand expression "incorporation" to express this idea. Since the First Amendment has been "incorporated" into the Fourteenth Amendment, its prohibitions are no less specific by virtue of such incorporation. This means that branches of the state governments are bound, to the same extent as the federal government, to respect the guarantees of the First Amendment.

Despite the considerable expansion of the field of operation of the First Amendment as a result of the incorporation doctrine, it is important to remember that the First Amendment is a bar only to abridgments by government. Private parties are free to "abridge" another's exercise of the speech and press clauses at will so long as they do not violate some other valid law in the process. For example, it is established that a right to distribute printed material is part and parcel of the First Amendment freedoms and the government is prohibited from interfering with such distribution. Lovell v. Griffin, 303 U.S. 444 (1938). On the other hand, private owners of properties may prohibit such distributions from taking place on their own property without running afoul of the First Amendment. See PruneYard Shopping Center v. Robins, 447 U.S. 74 (1980).

b. The Protected Sphere

Speech v. Conduct. More difficult than determining who is prohibited from interfering with protected expression is determining what forms of expressive activity fall within the protected category. Perhaps the most basic line between the protected and the unprotected is suggested by the distinction between "speech" and "conduct." Presumptively, at least, all oral and written communication falls within the protected sphere, and non-verbal conduct remains outside the domain of the First Amendment. Difficulties abound when verbal and non-verbal elements—"symbolic speech"—are mixed into a single expressive activity, such as labor picketing, protest marches or the wearing of armbands.

Consider, for example, United States v. O'Brien, 391 U.S. 367 (1968). *O'Brien* resulted from the burning, on the steps of the South

Boston Courthouse, of Selective Service registration certificates by David Paul O'Brien and three companions during the Vietnam War. O'Brien did not deny burning his certificate; he told the jury he did so to influence others to adopt his antiwar beliefs. Appealing his conviction ultimately to the Supreme Court, O'Brien maintained that his burning of the certificate was "symbolic speech" protected by the First Amendment.

Chief Justice Warren, in the opinion for the Court, wrote:

> This Court has held that when "speech" and "nonspeech" elements are combined in the same course of conduct, a sufficiently important governmental interest in regulating the nonspeech element can justify incidental limitations on First Amendment freedoms. . . . [W]e think it clear that a governmental regulation is sufficiently justified if it is within the constitutional power of the government; if it furthers an important or substantial governmental interest; if the governmental interest is unrelated to the suppression of free expression; and if the incidental restriction on alleged First Amendment freedom is no greater than is essential to the furtherance of that interest.

Finding that the statute under which O'Brien was convicted met all of the requirements, the Court upheld O'Brien's conviction.

O'Brien is, of course, not a media case, but it has taken on particular importance for the electronic media because the requirements set forth in it have been used to determine the constitutionality of cable regulation in such cases as Home Box Office Inc. v. Federal Communications Commission (1977), Quincy Cable TV, Inc. v. Federal Communications Commission (1985) and Century Communications v. Federal Communications Commission (1987) all discussed in Chapter IX.

Another example of symbolic speech is found in Tinker v. Des Moines Independent School District, 393 U.S. 503 (1969), which established that public students' First Amendment rights, including the wearing of armbands, could be limited only if their exercise would cause material and substantial interference with school operations or a collision with the rights of others.

Protection for symbolic speech stirred public opinion in June 1989 when the Supreme Court decided 5–4 that a Texas flag-desecration law was unconstitutional because of the First Amendment. Texas v. Johnson, 491 U.S. 397 (1989). The decision led to widespread calls for a Constitutional amendment and to the Federal Flag Protection Act of 1989, Congress's own attempt to protect the American flag from being burned or defaced. In two cases decided a year later, the Court, with the same 5–4 split, found the federal statute constitutionally flawed in the same way as the Texas statute because it suppressed expression. United States v. Eichman and United States v. Haggerty, 496 U.S. 310 (1990). Public opinion polls made clear that the First Amendment is not always popular; a NewYork Times/CBS News poll that year found that 83 percent of respondents thought flag burning should be against the law, and 59 percent would favor a constitutional amendment if it were the only way to make flag destruction illegal. New York Times, June 12, 1990, at p. B7. Critics said that making such an exception to the First Amendment would set a dangerous precedent.

Non-protected Speech. Though speech *generally* is a protected activity, the Supreme Court has long placed certain categories of words outside the First Amendment's protection. In 1942 the Court asserted, in Chaplinsky v. New Hampshire, 315 U.S. 568 (1942), that certain classes of expression might be subject to legal sanctions. Chaplinsky had been arrested for calling a town marshal a "God-damned racketeer and a damned Fascist." The Supreme Court characterized the expression as "fighting words . . . likely to cause violence." The words were not protected expression because they invited a violent response by the person to whom they were directed. The Court then observed that other types of speech, including obscenity and libel, were similarly outside the protection of the First Amendment. Many people presumed that "hate speech" was similarly unprotected, but the Court ruled in a 1992 case, R.A.V. v. City of St. Paul, Minn., 112 S.Ct. 2538 (1992) that the First Amendment prohibits the government from "silencing speech on the basis of its content." A St. Paul ordinance made it a crime to engage in speech or behavior likely to arouse "anger or alarm" on the basis of "race, color, creed, religion or gender." A white teenager was accused of violating the law by burning a cross on the lawn of a black family's house. Justice Scalia, writing for a 5-member majority of the court, said "St. Paul has not singled out an especially offensive mode of expression. . . . It has not, for example, selected for prohibition only those 'fighting words' that communicate ideas in a threatening, as opposed to merely obnoxious manner." The other four justices found the St. Paul ordinance to be unconstitutional on the basis of overbreadth—thinking that there was too great a risk that it might deter speech or expression that deserved constitutional protection. Although "hate speech" (as we see from the St. Paul case) and some libels (as we shall see in Chapter XII) are protected by the First Amendment, obscenity continues to remain outside of First Amendment protection.

Distribution. Freedom of speech and press have been held to imply more than the freedom only to speak and write. The First Amendment guarantees include the right to disseminate the words produced after creating them. In a milestone case, a city ordinance in Griffin, Ga., prescribed criminal penalties for distributing printed material without permission. The Court found the ordinance was overly broad because it included all "literature," making no distinction between that which the First Amendment does and does not protect. Also, the ordinance gave the city manager unbridled censorship powers since he was given no criteria for decision and was not obligated to explain why he refused permission to distribute. Lovell v. Griffin, 303 U.S. 444 (1938).

In 1988 the Supreme Court overturned portions of a newsrack ordinance in Lakewood, Ohio, that had given the mayor and an architectural review board unlimited discretion in denying permits for placement of newsracks on city property. A majority of the sitting justices held that distribution of newspapers is conduct related to expression and is therefore protected by the First Amendment. City of Lakewood v. Plain Dealer Publishing Co., 486 U.S. 750, 15 Med.L.Rptr. 1481 (1988).

A federal appeals court subsequently held that a Cincinnati ordinance prohibiting the newsrack distribution of "commercial" publications (such as magazines listing real estate for sale), but allowing such distribution of "non-commercial" publications (including newspapers) was a *content-based* restriction that violated the First Amendment. "The ordinance treats newsracks differently on the basis of the commercial content of the publications distributed," the court said. Discovery Network, Inc. v. City of Cincinnati, 946 F.2d 464, 19 Med.L.Rptr. 1449 (6th Cir.1991).

Gathering. The "right to gather" information from willing private sources began to take shape in 1972 with two cases. In Kleindienst v. Mandel, 408 U.S. 753 (1972), American scholars sought to invite Mandel, a Belgian Marxist economist, to attend conferences and to speak at several American universities. Congress had barred visas for aliens who advocated "the economic, international and governmental doctrines of world communism or the establishment in the United States of a totalitarian dictatorship." After concluding that Mandel, as an alien, had no constitutional right of entry, the Court turned to the rights claimed by the scholars:

> The Government . . . suggests that the First Amendment is inapplicable because [the scholars] have free access to Mandel's ideas through his books and speeches, and because "technological developments," such as tapes or telephone hookups, readily supplant his physical presence. This argument overlooks what may be particular qualities inherent in sustained, face-to-face debate, discussion and questioning. . . . We are loath to hold on this record that existence of other alternatives extinguishes altogether any constitutional interest on the part of the [scholars] in this particular form of access.

The Court, however, concluded that this interest was overcome by the government's longstanding power to make rules for excluding aliens.

The second case to provide some indirect support for protection of gathering was Branzburg v. Hayes, 408 U.S. 665, 1 Med.L.Rptr. 2617 (1972). Although the Court held that the reporters had no First Amendment right to refuse to testify before a grand jury, the majority acknowledged that the Court was not suggesting "that news gathering does not qualify for First Amendment protection; without some protection for seeking out the news, freedom of the press could be eviscerated." The case is discussed in Chapter XIV. For a detailed discussion of First Amendment protection for news gathering, see S. Helle, The News–Gathering/Publication Dichotomy and Government Expression, 1982 Duke L.J. 1.

Refusal to Speak. Most freedom of communication questions concern whether the government can prevent a person from, or punish a person for, speaking. In Chapter III we will see that another question is whether individuals can be forced to speak against their will. In the latter situation the broadcast media and the print media are treated quite differently.

c. Abridgment Defined

Determining whether the press is engaged in protected speech represents only half the question in evaluating whether a constitutional issue has been raised under the First Amendment. Courts must also determine whether an abridgment has taken place.

Prior Restraints. In the traditional view, prior restraints represented the quintessential, indeed exclusive, abridgments of speech. "Prior restraint" meant that rather than punishing the publisher by criminal or civil sanctions for what had been published, the government barred the publication from occurring in the first place. This is, of course, the essence of censorship. In English history the censor was an administrative official, who administered the licensing system. Recall the view of Blackstone, p. 12, *supra.*

Although it might have been argued that only administrative or executive branch behavior could constitute a prior restraint, it has become clear in this country that judicial orders that bar publications are also analyzed as prior restraints. Nonetheless, court orders imposing prior restraints are thought somewhat less objectionable than similar administrative actions because of a perception that administrators may cut procedural corners and otherwise be unfair in executing their obligations. Even so, some administrative prior restraints are permitted even today. The most obvious example is that the Supreme Court has permitted states to license motion pictures. Under such a system, it is a crime to exhibit a film that has not been approved in advance, even if the film is totally unobjectionable on any ground. This type of licensing system was upheld in Freedman v. Maryland, 380 U.S. 51, 1 Med.L.Rptr. 1126 (1965), so long as the administrative decision was subject to swift judicial review.

The deep-seated antagonism to prior restraint is seen in the Supreme Court's decision in Near v. Minnesota, 283 U.S. 697, 1 Med. L.Rptr. 1001 (1931), the first case in which the Court invalidated a state law because it violated the First and Fourteenth Amendments to the United States Constitution. More specifically, *Near* involved a Minnesota statute allowing officials to stop publication of "malicious, scandalous, and defamatory" newspapers and periodicals. Once stopped, publication could be resumed only on order of a judge, who would have to approve the content before allowing continued printing. The country attorney had brought an action to stop publication of a Minneapolis newspaper, *The Saturday Press*. The newspaper had accused certain government officials of being involved in bootlegging and gambling that it said were controlled by a "Jewish gangster."

The Supreme Court of the United States reversed the state court. Chief Justice Charles Evans Hughes, writing for the 5–4 majority, noted that Blackstone's observation that "[t]he liberty of the press . . . consists in laying no *previous* restraints upon publications . . ." was too broad. Although prior restraint is presumed to be unconstitutional, "the protection . . . is not absolutely unlimited." The Court then suggested some areas in which such restraints might be upheld:

> No one would question but that a government might prevent actual obstruction to its recruiting service or to the publication of sailing dates of transports or the number and location of troops. On similar grounds, the primary requirements of decency may be enforced against obscene publications. The security of the community life may be protected against incitements to acts of violence and the overthrow by force of orderly government. The constitutional guaranty of free speech does not "protect a man from an injunction against uttering words that may have all the effect of force." [ ]

Because the defendant's charges in the Near case did not come within any of these categories, prior restraint was impermissible.

The Court similarly struck down a Rhode Island system for reviewing publications for possible obscenity in Bantam Books, Inc. v. Sullivan, 372 U.S. 58, 1 Med.L.Rptr. 1116 (1963), a prior restraint on distribution of leaflets critical of a Chicago real estate agent in Organization for a Better Austin v. Keefe, 402 U.S. 415, 1 Med.L.Rptr. 1021 (1971), and a restraint on publication of the "Pentagon Papers" in New York Times Co. v. United States, 403 U.S. 713, 1 Med.L.Rptr. 1031 (1971). In these decisions, the Court has said that "Any system of prior restraints of expression comes to this Court bearing a heavy presumption against its constitutional validity," and that the party seeking a restraint "carries a heavy burden of showing justification for the imposition of such a restraint."

A federal district judge in Wisconsin issued a preliminary injunction in 1979 restraining *The Progressive* magazine from publishing an article by Howard Morland about the H-bomb. Some people in communications law feared that the case could become the first Supreme Court case in which a prior restraint against the news media would be upheld, but the so-called "secret of the H-bomb" was published in other media before that ever happened, and the government withdrew its request for an injunction. The government might have gone ahead with criminal proceedings but did not. *The Progressive* published its article.

In 1980 Public Broadcasting Service broadcast a "documentary drama" portraying a love affair between a Saudi princess and a commoner, and their subsequent execution. The program also dwelt on some aspects of Saudi Arabian life that the Saudi government asserted were totally misrepresented. The program was patterned on a true story.

If the Saudi government had made a credible threat to cut off all oil shipments to the United States immediately upon the presentation of the program, and if the best evidence had been that such a cutoff would cripple the American economy, would the government have been able to obtain an injunction against the showing of the program? Is it crucial that no "secret" is involved?

A different aspect of the problem will be seen in Muir v. Alabama Educational Television Commission, discussed in Chapter VIII.

A publisher was enjoined in August 1989 from publishing *Spy Notes*, a book created by *Spy* magazine to look and feel like *Cliff's Notes* study guides with their trademarked yellow and black diagonal striped design. The action sought trademark protection under the Lanham Act. A federal district court rejected the assertion that *Spy Notes* was merely a parody and found a "profound" likelihood of confusion between the study guides and *Spy Notes*. Cliff's Notes, Inc. v. Bantam Doubleday Dell Publishing Group, Inc., 718 F.Supp.1159, 16 Med. L.Rptr. 2025 (S.D.N.Y.1989). The U.S. Court of Appeals for the Second Circuit vacated the injunction a month later, holding that the public interest in free expression must be weighed against public interest in avoiding consumer confusion. The court thought *Spy Notes* was a parody and that the risk of confusion was slight. Cliffs Notes, Inc. v. Bantam Doubleday Dell Publishing Group, Inc., 886 F.2d 490, 16 Med.L.Rptr. 2289 (2d Cir.1989).

Several restraints were imposed in 1990, but all were short-lived. The syndicated news program "Inside Edition" was temporarily restrained in January 1990 from broadcasting a videotape of a physician allegedly engaged in malpractice. The doctor claimed that "Inside Edition" had violated a statute prohibiting interception and disclosure of wire communications or oral communications (18 U.S.C.A. § 2511). The order was vacated 11 days later by the court of appeals, which held that § 2511 "in no way provides for a prior restraint of the press in their exercise of first amendment rights, even if the press's conduct clearly violates" the section. In re King World Productions, Inc., 898 F.2d 56, 17 Med.L.Rptr. 1531 (6th Cir.1990).

Lifetime Cable was briefly subjected to an order restraining it from showing "Hilary in Hiding," a British Broadcasting Corp. film about the battle between Eric Foretich and Elizabeth Morgan over custody of their child. The order was issued April 6, 1990, after the father said irreparable harm would come to the child if the scenes of her describing alleged sexual abuse were shown. It was vacated the same day by the U.S. Court of Appeals for the District of Columbia. The latter held that any rights the father and child have must be redressed in legal actions "that do not require a prior restraint in derogation of the First Amendment." In re Lifetime Cable, 17 Med.L.Rptr. 1648 (D.C.Cir. 1990). See also Broadcasting, April 16, 1990, at 73.

In another case, the government of Israel tried to stop distribution of Victor Ostrovsky's book, *By Way of Deception: A Devastating Insider's Portrait of the Mossad.* Faced with the argument that Israeli intelligence agents would be killed if the book were distributed, a judge in New York temporarily restrained publication, but the order was overturned the next day because, although the book had been restrained in Canada, approximately 1,500 wholesalers and book reviewers had already received copies of the book, and 17,000 books had already been shipped to stores. State of Israel v. St. Martin's Press, Inc., 166 A.D.2d 251, 560 N.Y.S.2d 450 (1st Dept. 1990).

In remarks at a communications law seminar in November 1990, prominent attorney Floyd Abrams remarked that "The near-total ban on prior restraints we used to talk about seems secure but in a rather insecure way," noting the several prior restraint attempts during the year. "The reasons for prior restraint *always* sound pretty good," Abrams said, "and the potential for damage to First Amendment rights *always* sounds minimal, yet appellate courts have reversed consistently and quickly."

That same month the issue of a prior restraint to protect a defendant's fair trial rights arose again in the case of former Panamanian leader Manuel Noriega, and the restraint was not so quickly overturned. Cable News Network (CNN) had obtained tape recordings of Noriega talking to members of his defense team. Normally, of course, attorney-client conversations are confidential. Fearing that Noriega's future trial could be prejudiced by CNN's playing of the tapes, the U.S. district Court for the Southern District of Florida issued a temporary restraining order barring their playing. The U.S. Court of Appeals for the Eleventh Circuit affirmed the ruling, and the Supreme Court of the United States, without a written opinion, refused to overrule the lower courts or to review the order. Cable News Network, Inc. v. Noriega, 498 S.Ct. 976, 18 Med.L.Rptr. 1358 (1990). Justices Thurgood Marshall and Sandra Day O'Connor dissented. The Supreme Court's action would not necessarily have precluded their considering the prior restraint later, but the trial court subsequently lifted the restraint and essentially ended the dispute.

Journalists subjected to restraining orders they believe to be unconstitutional have sometimes disobeyed those orders. The question has always been whether a subsequent finding that the restraining order was unconstitutional serves as a defense against a contempt citation for disobeying the order. In United States v. Dickinson, 465 F.2d 496 (5th Cir.1972), a federal judge ordered the media not to publish any testimony taken at a hearing for fear it might prejudice an upcoming state trial. Two reporters violated the order, were cited for criminal contempt and were fined $300 each. The court of appeals held the order unconstitutional but ruled that it had to be obeyed until overturned on appeal. The court held that such orders must be followed unless there is "a showing of 'transparent invalidity' or patent frivolity surrounding the order . . .." The Supreme Court denied *certiorari*. 414 U.S. 979 (1973).

In the case titled In re Providence Journal Co., 820 F.2d 1342, 13 Med.L.Rptr. 1945 (1st Cir.1986), rehearing en banc 820 F.2d 1354, 14 Med.L.Rptr. 1029 (1987), a federal district court had held *The Providence Journal* and its executive editor in contempt of court for publishing truthful information obtained under the Freedom of Information Act while it was under a temporary restraining order (TRO) not to do so. The TRO was sought by a person who claimed the government had obtained the information in the first place by means that violated the person's constitutional right to privacy—and that its release was improper. The judge offered to decide the merits in the next day or two after the TRO was entered. The newspaper asked the judge to defer for another day, during which it published the information.

Although the judge later denied the preliminary injunction, he found the newspaper in contempt. The basis for requiring obedience to the TRO was that a court "ought to have time to determine legal issues presented to it, and has the right in the meantime to preserve the *status quo*." The judge rejected the newspaper's argument that the plaintiff's claim was frivolous, and sentenced the newspaper to a fine of $100,000 and the executive editor to 18 months probation and 200 hours of public service.

On appeal, the court reversed, holding that the district court's original restraining order was transparently invalid and that it constituted a presumptively unconstitutional prior restraint on pure speech by the press. The court held that the requisite heavy burden of proof necessary to justify such a restraint was not met and that the newspaper and editor should have been allowed to challenge its constitutionality at the contempt proceedings and that the order could not serve as the basis for a contempt citation.

A petition for rehearing *en banc* was granted, and the court added to, and modified, the panel opinion in a *per curiam* opinion holding that in such a case the publisher must make a good faith effort to seek emergency relief from the appellate court, and may proceed to publish and challenge the constitutionality of the order in the contempt proceedings only if timely access to the appellate court is not available or if timely decision is not forthcoming.

Although the Supreme Court of the United States granted *certiorari* in the case in 1987, it dismissed the case because of a procedural issue: the Court held that because the court-appointed special prosecutor had not obtained the solicitor general's authorization before filing for *certiorari*, he lacked authority to appear on behalf of the United States. 485 U.S. 693, 15 Med.L.Rptr. 1241 (1988).

Subsequent Sanctions. Though far less compelling from an historical point of view, it is quite clear that sanctions imposed after publication may be like prior restraints, in that they may prevent would-be speakers and writers from publishing protected speech. Such sanctions, whether they are penal in nature, such as imprisonment or fines, or civil damage awards or the denial of some privilege, generally raise precisely the same issues as prior restraints on publication. Recall Justice Holmes's comment in Patterson v. Colorado, p. 17, *supra,* that the First Amendment prevents all "previous restraints upon publications" but allows "the subsequent punishment of such as may be deemed contrary to the public welfare." Holmes' view that it was possible to make such a distinction so sharply has given way to a different view, as exemplified in a case involving *The Virginia Pilot.*

The *Virginia Pilot,* a newspaper published by Landmark Communications, Inc., was found guilty of a misdemeanor and fined $500 plus costs after it accurately reported that a named judge was under investigation by a state commission in a confidential proceeding. Chief Justice Burger delivered the opinion of the Court, reversing the decision of the Supreme Court of Virginia: "We conclude that the publication Virginia seeks to punish under its statute lies near the core of the First Amendment, and the Commonwealth's interests advanced by the imposition of criminal sanctions are insufficient to justify the actual and potential encroachments on freedom of speech and of the press which follow therefrom." Landmark Communications, Inc. v. Virginia, 435 U.S. 829, 3 Med.L.Rptr. 2153 (1978).

In Smith v. Daily Mail Publishing Co., 443 U.S. 97, 5 Med.L.Rptr. 1305 (1979), the Supreme Court was faced with a statute that made it a crime for a newspaper to publish a juvenile offender's name unless the paper had obtained the prior written approval of a court. The paper argued that the prior approval requirement acted in "operation and effect" like a licensing scheme. The Court decided the case in favor of the newspaper but avoided the question of whether the system had operated as a prior restraint:

> . . . [E]ven when a state attempts to punish publication after the event it must nevertheless demonstrate that its punitive action was necessary to further the state interests asserted [citing *Landmark*]. Since we conclude that this statute cannot satisfy the constitutional standards defined in *Landmark Communications, Inc.,* we need not decide whether, as argued by respondents, it operated as a prior restraint.

Neutral Regulation. The great proportion of government regulation of the press has never been considered to be abridgment so long as it is fairly applied, despite the considerable costs such regulation may exact from the press. Thus, for example, one may not operate a broadcasting station without obeying local building codes, the income tax laws and other tax statutes, the antitrust laws, the Occupational

Safety and Health Act, or any of the myriad other bodies of general regulatory law administered by local, state and federal governments.

4. APPLYING THE FIRST AMENDMENT

An "abridgment" of protected speech is not, despite the apparently unqualified language of the First Amendment, necessarily unconstitutional.

a. *Balancing*

Most frequently, the Supreme Court has used a "balancing test" to determine the propriety of a restraint on freedom of expression. The test involves weighing two interests—the government's concern about protecting a particular interest, such as national security or individual reputation, and the individual's and society's interests in expression.

Professor Chafee, an early advocate of balancing, expressed the virtues of that approach in his Free Speech in the United States (1941) at 31 as follows:

> Or to put the matter another way, it is useless to define free speech by talk about rights. The agitator asserts his constitutional right to speak, the government asserts its constitutional right to wage war. The result is a deadlock. . . . To find the boundary line of any right, we must get behind rules of law to human facts. In our problem, we must regard the desires and needs of the individual human being who wants to speak and those of the great group of human beings among whom he speaks. That is, in technical language, there are individual interests and social interests, which must be balanced against each other, if they conflict, in order to determine which interest shall be sacrificed under the circumstances and which shall be protected and become the foundation of a legal right. It must never be forgotten that the balancing cannot be properly done unless all the interests involved are adequately ascertained, and the great evil of all this talk about rights is that each side is so busy denying the official's claim to rights that it entirely overlooks the human desires and needs behind that claim.

Most freedom of expression cases are decided by balancing interests. The Supreme Court, without always explaining its approach, will use one of two variations of the balancing test. Focusing on the interests at stake in the individual case is commonly characterized as "ad hoc" balancing: the specific interests applicable to the facts of the particular case are considered crucial. The court attempts to identify the state's interest in limiting or preventing the speech in question and the would-be speaker's and society's interests in having the speech permitted.

At other times, a more general process, called "definitional" or "categorical" balancing, is used. Here the interests analyzed transcend the merits of a particular case. Rather than asking, for example, whether the value of speech in a particular case outweighs the arguments for proscribing it, the Court might generalize and consider the values of that category of speech, or that category of speaker, and develop a more general analysis. Recall *Chaplinsky*, p. 23, *supra.*

b. *Preferred Position*

A basic tenet of constitutional law calls upon courts to presume that enactments of legislative bodies are constitutional. If the legislation has a rational basis, courts will generally hold it constitutional. In United States v. Carolene Products Co., 304 U.S. 144 (1938), involving the validity of a federal economic regulation, Justice Stone, writing for the majority, restated this generally accepted view of deference to legislatures. But in one of the Court's most famous footnotes, footnote 4, Justice Stone wrote:

> There may be narrower scope for operation of the presumption of constitutionality when legislation appears on its face to be within a specific prohibition of the Constitution, such as those of the first ten amendments, which are deemed equally specific when held to be embraced within the Fourteenth.. . . .
>
> It is unnecessary to consider now whether legislation which restricts those political processes which can ordinarily be expected to bring about repeal of undesirable legislation, is to be subjected to more exacting scrutiny under the general prohibitions of the Fourteenth Amendment than are most other types of legislation. . . .

Justice Stone was suggesting that legislation that inhibits political freedoms, such as freedom of communication, must survive more "exacting judicial scrutiny" than other legislative acts. Instead of having a presumption of constitutionality, such legislation might be presumed to inhibit a basic freedom and the government might have to show an overriding need for it, not simply a rational basis. As a result of some cases that built on this footnote, freedom of communication became a "preferred freedom," one that courts would not allow the legislature to restrict without a compelling state interest.

c. *Clear and Present Danger*

The balance between speech and anti-speech interests is struck in a wide variety of issues affecting mass media. In defamation, for example, speech interests are balanced against the individual's interest in reputation. In other cases, speech interests must be balanced against privacy interests, property interests, security interests, public safety and morals, and even countervailing speech interests, to name only a few. The balance struck in each situation differs as the countervailing interests vary in weight and as the value of the speech interest itself changes in various contexts.

One important example of the balancing process is the evolution of the "clear and present danger" test originally framed by Justice Oliver Wendell Holmes in such cases as *Abrams*, p. 18, *supra*, and Schenck v. United States, *infra*. These cases represent the struggle of the courts to accommodate both the federal government's interest in maintaining the integrity of its effort to wage war and the dissenters' free speech rights. The Espionage Act banned attempts to cause insubordination in the armed forces or to obstruct military recruiting or to conspire to achieve these results. Most of these cases, which confronted the Court from 1919 until the mid–1920s, involved radical speakers who opposed the war effort and criticized the political and economic structure of the country.

Based on his marketplace of ideas approach, Justice Holmes saw the clear and present danger test as being least intrusive on freedom of expression in a society in which absolute freedom was impractical. In Schenck v. United States, 249 U.S. 47 (1919), Justice Holmes said that expression could be punished when "the words used are used in such circumstances and are of such a nature as to create a clear and present danger that they will bring about the substantive evils that Congress has a right to prevent. It is a question of proximity and degree."

Schenck involved a prosecution under the Espionage Act for publishing a leaflet that interfered with recruiting by urging young men to violate the draft law. Justice Holmes, writing for the majority, found that the leaflet could be closely connected with violations of the Conscription Act (proximity) and that this was a serious danger to the country's security (degree).

In *Abrams*, p. 18, *supra*, the Supreme Court upheld convictions in a case involving pamphlets calling for a strike of munitions workers. And six years later the Court upheld a conviction under a New York criminal statute that barred advocating overthrow of the government by violence. Gitlow v. New York, 268 U.S. 652 (1925).

The curious case of Dennis v. United States, 341 U.S. 494 (1951), involved prosecution of 11 leading members of the Communist Party for conspiring to advocate the forcible overthrow of the government of the United States. Although a plurality of the Court recognized that the Holmes–Brandeis position had evolved to become a majority view, the plurality refused to apply it to this case. The plurality observed that each case confronting Justices Holmes and Brandeis involved "a comparatively isolated event, bearing little relation in their minds to any substantial threat to the safety of the community. . . . They were not confronted with any situation comparable to the instant one—the development of an apparatus designed and dedicated to the overthrow of the Government, in the context of world crisis after crisis."

The Court adopted the test framed by Judge Learned Hand in the lower court: "In each case [courts] must ask whether the gravity of the 'evil,' discounted by its improbability, justifies such invasion of free speech as is necessary to avoid the danger." That statement "takes into consideration those factors which we deem relevant, and relates their significances. More we cannot expect from words." The plurality found that the requisite danger existed.

The status of clear and present danger remained unclear until Brandenburg v. Ohio, 395 U.S. 444 (1969), involving prosecution of a Ku Klux Klan member for advocating racial and religious bigotry. The Court pointed out that its decisions had "fashioned the principle that the constitutional guarantees of free speech and free press do not permit a State to forbid or proscribe advocacy of the use of force or of law violation except where such advocacy is directed to inciting or producing imminent lawless action and is likely to incite or produce such action." Because the criminal syndicalism statute under which Ohio proceeded permitted punishment of advocacy with no requirement of a showing that imminent lawless action was likely to follow, the convictions could not stand.

Despite the extended period during which the clear and present danger test has been discussed in the Supreme Court, its importance and utility must not be overstated.

d.   The Literalist Interpretation of the First Amendment

Some have argued that the First Amendment allows no room for interpretation because its language is absolute: "Congress shall make no law . . . abridging the freedom of speech, or of the press . . .." They have concluded that the federal government "is without any power whatever under the Constitution to put any type of burden on speech and expression of ideas of any kind." Ginzburg v. United States, 383 U.S. 463, 476, 1 Med.L.Rptr. 1409, 1414 (1966) (Black, J., dissenting). Justice Black strongly criticized the balancing approach to First Amendment questions because the test could be used to justify a judge's predilections, but he did not believe that action should be protected to the same extent as speech.

Justice Black's distinction between speech and action provided the escape hatch for his absolutist view. For instance, he would not have required states to allow public high school students to wear black arm bands to protest the Vietnam war. Recall Tinker v. Des Moines Independent School District, p. 22, *supra*, (Black, J., dissenting). He called the behavior "action," not speech, and thus not protected by the First Amendment.

In his book, *The System of Freedom of Expression* 17 (1970), Professor Thomas Emerson drew a similar distinction, believing, with Justice Black, that expression should be absolutely protected by the First Amendment.

Recall Meiklejohn, too, believed in an absolute approach to the First Amendment—but only for "political speech." As with Justice

Black and Emerson, his distinction narrows the types of expression to be afforded absolute protection, leaving to the courts the problem of defining "political speech" and differentiating it from unprotected or less protected expression.

5. "OR OF THE PRESS"

Until this point we have used the terms "freedom of speech" and "freedom of the press" interchangeably. Some have argued, however, that the speech and press guarantees have independent and distinct significance. Are some types of activity protected under the press clause not protected under the speech clause? Or are some activities, though they constitute protected speech, outside the press guarantee?

The most prominent proponent of the theory that the press clause is of different scope than the speech clause was Justice Potter Stewart, who contended, in a speech at Yale Law School reprinted in 26 Hastings Law Journal 631 (1975), that the press clause, unlike the speech guarantee, was a *structural* provision of the Constitution. Stewart relied heavily on the notion that the institutional press has a special role in our constitutional scheme as an additional check on the power of government officials. He asserted that because of this special role the institutional press in certain situations had rights of access and immunities growing out of the press clause to which the general citizenry could not lay claim.

Chief Justice Burger rejected this analysis. Concurring in First National Bank of Boston v. Bellotti, 435 U.S. 765, 3 Med.L.Rptr. 2105 (1978), he contended that the press clause of the First Amendment does not give the "institutional press" a special status. The Chief Justice thought the framers did not contemplate special privileges for the press, and he foresaw difficulty in defining what was and was not included in the "institutional press" if it were to be accorded special status.

Regardless of how the issue of special protection is resolved, it is true as a practical matter that certain First Amendment issues arise in connection with the institutional press, while others are generally raised in the context of individual speech.

C. ADMINISTRATIVE LAW

Congress usually creates administrative agencies when the task at hand requires continuing supervision, extensive technical considerations, or the development of expert skills, or all of these. The thought is that a group devoting full attention to such a problem may do a better job than Congress might do in sporadic legislative forays into an area. In 1927 Congress did not have the ability or time or desire to unravel the mess that had developed on the airwaves. The basic decision for Congress, in retrospect, was whether to decree a system of private ownership for the airwaves and to allow the courts to unravel the matters through lawsuits invoking property law, to opt for outright public ownership or to create an administrative body to develop and enforce an allocation system that would bring order from the chaos. As we will see in Chapter II, Congress chose the last of these.

All agencies must function within the direction that the legislature gives them by statute. Here, Congress had no specific idea how the Federal Radio Commission and its successor, the Federal Communications Commission (FCC), should proceed. Instead, Congress provided in § 303 of the Communications Act of 1934 that "Except as otherwise provided in this Act, the Commission from time to time, as public convenience, interest, or necessity requires shall . . .." The list that followed included powers to assign bands of frequencies to the various classes of radio stations and assign individual frequencies; decide the times each station may operate; establish areas to be served by any station; regulate the apparatus used with respect to the sharpness of the transmissions; take steps to prevent interference; suspend licenses upon a showing that a licensee has violated any statute or regulation or transmitted obscene communications; make rules and regulations that are necessary to carry out the other provisions of the statute; and require licensees to keep records the FCC may deem desirable.

Notice that all these powers are conditioned on a showing that "public convenience, interest, or necessity requires" the regulation. This is a vague standard, and, as we shall see, the FCC has rarely been barred from acting on the ground that Congress did not authorize the particular regulation.

An administrative agency such as the FCC usually functions in a variety of ways. Within its statutory authorization it may issue rules or regulations that have the virtual effect of statutes. At other times, it may have to choose between two applicants for a broadcasting license in what resembles a judicial proceeding. At still other times, it performs executive branch functions, as when it seeks out broadcasters or ham operators who are violating their licenses by using excessive power or unauthorized frequencies.

This variety of regulatory patterns may not comport with traditional understandings about the separation of powers, but these multifunction agencies have been with us for so long that little concern is voiced about their structure. As we shall see, however, questions are continually raised about whether the agency followed the statutory requirements in performing its functions, whether it followed its own rules, whether its decision was arbitrary and capricious and whether its processes met constitutional requirements.

An administrative agency like the FCC makes public announcements of possible changes in rules, through published Notices of Proposed Rulemaking (NPRMs), and similar announcements of inquiries, through Notices of Inquiry (NOIs). The public in general—and in particular those affected by the rules or inquiries—then have opportunity to voice their opinions for or against the proposed changes. In this way, such an agency is behaving as a quasi-legislature, providing room for debate before acting.

The rules or regulations adopted by the agency are, of course, binding on the people or businesses under its regulatory jurisdiction, but Congress always has the authority to create or change statutes, thus in effect overruling the administrative agencies.

There are literally hundreds of administrative agencies. Only a few of these are important to the electronic mass media. We turn now to a brief look at those particular agencies.

1. THE FEDERAL COMMUNICATIONS COMMISSION

In 1927 Congress created a five-member Federal Radio Commission to rationalize the radio spectrum and make allocations. In 1934 the agency was expanded to seven members, given jurisdiction over telephone and telegraph communication as well, and renamed the Federal Communications Commission. In 1982 Congress voted to return to a five-member commission. Each member is appointed by the President for a five-year term subject to Senate confirmation. No more than three members may be from the same political party. The terms are staggered so that no more than one expires in any year. If a member resigns in the middle of a term, the new appointment is only for the unexpired portion of that term. One consequence is that many of those appointed do not have the independence of beginning with a five-year term. The Chairman, chosen by the President, is the chief executive officer and has major administrative responsibilities, including the setting of the agenda. A chart showing the organization of the Commission is presented in Appendix C.

Of the agency's several offices and bureaus for its various functions, the most important for our purposes is the Mass Media Bureau, formed by the 1982 merger of the Broadcast Bureau and the Cable Bureau, which receives all applications for licenses, renewals and transfers. Under delegated authority from the Commission, the Bureau's staff is authorized to issue some licenses and renew others. In cases in which it has no such power, it may still recommend to the Commissioners which applications to grant and which to deny, thus assuming the position of an advocate within the agency. In addition, complaints of violations of the equal opportunities provision of § 315 are processed through the Mass Media Bureau.

When an adjudicatory hearing is required, usually in a licensing case, it is conducted by an Administrative Law Judge (ALJ), formerly called a Hearing Examiner, who is an independent employee of the Commission. The Mass Media Bureau may also appear before the Administrative Law Judge to argue in favor of or against an applicant. The judge renders an initial decision which will become effective unless appealed. The appeal will be either to the Commission itself or to the

Review Board. This Board, composed of senior employees of the Commission, sits in panels of three and reviews the initial decisions. The Commission chooses whether to accept appeals from the Review Board.

Within the Commission the Mass Media Bureau takes positions and makes recommendations. But once the Commission renders a decision, the Bureau's role ceases. The General Counsel then takes over to represent the Commission in any litigation that results from the Commission's decision. The General Counsel may also advise the Commission as it prepares to promulgate rules. Sometimes one part of the agency may disagree with another. For example, during reconsideration of the *1974 Fairness Report*, which we will discuss in Chapter VI, the General Counsel's office proposed that complaints that a licensee had not sufficiently covered issues of public importance should be considered only at renewal time. The Bureau opposed the proposal and the Commissioners agreed with the Bureau.

2. The Federal Trade Commission

The Federal Trade Commission (FTC) was established by the Federal Trade Commission Act (FTCA) in 1914. The Commission was initially charged with prohibiting "unfair methods of competition in commerce." As originally conceived, this phrase was intended to allow the FTC to enforce antitrust laws, laws that courts had viewed with some hostility. The agency also concerns itself with the Clayton Act of 1914, which outlaws specific practices recognized as instruments of monopoly. Soon the FTC tried to regulate deceptive advertising as a form of "unfair competition." In 1938 Congress passed the Wheeler–Lea Amendments to the FTCA explicitly giving the FTC the authority to regulate unfair or deceptive advertising.

Overseeing advertising is just one FTC task—though the most important for the media. The agency is composed of five commissioners, including the chairman, appointed by the President and confirmed by the Senate for five-year terms. It has an annual budget of about $83 million (compared with $100 *billion* spent on advertising annually). Its other responsibilities include laws concerning antitrust violations, warranties, granting of credit, and label laws.

As an administrative agency, acting quasi-judicially and quasi-legislatively, the Commission deals with trade practices on a continuing and corrective basis. The FTC has no authority to punish; its function is to "prevent," through cease-and-desist orders and other means, those practices condemned by the law of federal trade regulation. However, court-ordered civil penalties up to $10,000 may be obtained for each violation of a Commission order or trade regulation.

Cases before the Commission may originate through a complaint by a consumer or a competitor, the Congress or from federal, state or municipal agencies.

3. NATIONAL TELECOMMUNICATIONS AND INFORMATION ADMINISTRATION

The National Telecommunications and Information Administration (NTIA) was established in 1978 as part of the Commerce Department, and NTIA is headed by the Assistant Secretary for Communications and Information. The reorganization that established NTIA combined within the new unit the former Office of Telecommunications Policy, which had been part of the Executive Office of the President, and the Office of Telecommunications of the Commerce Department. There had been concern about excessive Presidential influence on the Office of Telecommunications Policy during the Nixon administration.

In essence, NTIA is the telecommunications policy research department of the government. It does long-term studies into the effects of and need for telecommunication regulation. NTIA also advises the President on telecommunications policy issues.

NTIA's role is to formulate policies to support the development and growth of telecommunications, information and related industries; to further the efficient development and use of telecommunications and information services; to provide policy and management for federal use of the electromagnetic spectrum; and to provide telecommunications facilities grants to public service users.

4. THE COPYRIGHT ROYALTY TRIBUNAL

The Copyright Royalty Tribunal (CRT) was created by the Copyright Act of 1976, which took effect Jan. 1, 1978. Among its duties is overseeing the compulsory licensing scheme governing cable retransmission of broadcast signals. Under this scheme money is collected from cable systems and distributed to motion picture producers, program syndicators, broadcasters, sports teams, etc. We will examine this licensing mechanism in Chapter IX.

The Tribunal also makes determinations concerning the adjustment of copyright royalty rates for records and jukeboxes. It also establishes, and makes determinations concerning, terms and rates of royalty payments for the use by public broadcasting stations of published nondramatic compositions and pictorial, graphic and sculptural works.

Tribunal decisions take into account existing economic conditions, impact on copyright owners and users and the industry involved, and the need to maximize the availability of creative works to the public. Recognizing the right of copyright owners to receive a return, the Tribunal ensures them access to information about the use of their works.

5. Equal Employment Opportunity Commission

The Equal Employment Opportunity Commission (EEOC), as might be imagined, is charged with enforcing the equal employment opportunity laws. Issues of illegal discrimination have become increasingly important for the electronic media, which are obligated to bear them in mind in making hiring or promotion decisions.

The EEOC was created by the Civil Rights Act of 1964 in an attempt to eliminate discrimination based on race, color, religion, sex or national origin in hiring, promoting, firing, wages, testing, training, apprenticeship and all other conditions of employment.

The Commission is a major publisher of data on the employment status of minorities and women.

Although the EEOC has primary responsibility for equal employment opportunities, broadcasters must also comply with requirements in this area placed on them by the FCC. Initially the FCC required that licensees file employment reports at the time of license renewals. (We will examine the importance of equal opportunity in the licensing process in Chapter IV.) Subsequently the FCC imposed a requirement of annual reports on full-time and part-time employees from licensees with more than four employees.

In 1985 the Federal Communications Commission proposed an easing of broadcasters' requirements for equal opportunity reporting— saying that it was concerned primarily with a licensee's overall EEO *efforts* as opposed to the numerical composition of its work force. The changes were adopted in April 1987 and released in June 1987. Under the new rules, licensees with no more than five employees are exempted from the requirements and new reporting forms have been issued. EEO remains an important part of the license renewal process.

6. National Labor Relations Board

The National Labor Relations Board (NLRB) was created by the National Labor Relations Act (NLRA) of 1935 (Wagner Act), as amended by the acts of 1947 (Taft–Hartley Act), 1959 (Landrum–Griffin Act), and 1974.

The Board has two principal functions: preventing and remedying unfair labor practices by employers and labor organizations or their agents and conducting secret ballot elections among employees in appropriate collective-bargaining units to determine whether or not they desire to be represented by a labor organization.

The electronic media are heavily unionized today with most management decisions affected to at least some extent by the various union contracts in effect.

D. INTERNATIONAL REGULATION OF ELECTRONIC MEDIA

Radio and television signals obviously do not stop at international borders, so neighboring countries' telecommunications concerns overlap. This is true whether one is talking about Western Europe, where a country has several nearby neighbors, or the United States, where we share a long border with Canada and a shorter one with Mexico.

The concern is not a new one. Napoleon III called a conference in Paris in 1865 to take some collective action to deal with technical standards, codes and tariffs for telegraph. Out of that conference came the International Telegraph Union, which has been called "the first genuine international, intergovernmental organization to see the light of day." Delegates to the conference adopted the international Morse code and agreed on the interconnection of important cities, hours of reception for telegrams, and the obligation to deliver messages from abroad.

Today's International Telecommunications Union (ITU) is a direct descendant of the group formed in Paris, but its interests go far beyond the "electric telegraph." Much of the technology of today and tomorrow—communications satellites, sea cables, fiber optics, dynamic radio systems, mass data storage and processing facilities—has and will have international implications. The constitution, statutes, administrative rules and regulation and case law of any single country obviously cannot govern the international traffic of messages, and international agreements are of increasing importance.

A reflection of that is the growth of the ITU. With more than 156 member nations today, it is headquartered in Geneva. Among its varied activities are the registration and management of frequencies and the collection and dissemination of massive amounts of information concerning telecommunications throughout the world.

The ITU Convention, which sets forth its rules of procedure, permits world and regional administrative conferences. A World Administrative Radio Conference (WARC) may have the authority to revise most of the regulations or may have jurisdiction only in a limited area. Such conferences in Geneva in 1959 and 1979 and in Atlantic City in 1974 had very broad jurisdiction. For WARC 79 in Geneva, delegates from 140 member countries met to work on 14,000 proposals that had been submitted to amend the Radio Regulations. Examples of WARCs with more limited jurisdiction include the Broadcasting Satellite WARC, the WARC on the Aeronautical Mobile, and the WARC for Space Telecommunications.

Regional Administrative Radio Conferences (RARCs) have regional jurisdiction. For the purpose of radio frequency management, the world is divided into three general regions. Region 1 includes Europe and Africa; Region 2 includes the Americas; and Region 3 includes Asia and Oceania.

More than 900 delegates from 120 countries gathered in Geneva in 1988, for a Space WARC session. Despite concerns that it would be unable to produce a plan for international coordination of fixed-satellite services, the session did just that. The delegation from the United States was generally pleased with the outcome, including an agreement on "multilateral planning meetings that are flexible" as a means of resolving conflicts among existing and proposed systems in the conventional fixed-satellite-service bands. Representatives of U.S. corporations that operate satellites were particularly happy with the agreement for informal rather than rigid structure for the coordination process. The United States and other developed countries made large investments in time and resources to prepare for the conference, where they had to deal with developing countries' fears that, before they had the means to launch satellites of their own, orbital capacity would be gobbled up by developed countries. Broadcasting, Oct. 10, 1988 at 10.

A WARC in Torremolinos, Spain, early in 1992, laid the foundation for the introduction of a powerful new competitor to AM and FM radio, allocating spectrum space for satellite or terrestrial digital audio broadcasting for most countries and recognizing the use of 50 mhz of S band spectrum for Digital Radio Broadcasting (DAB) in the U.S. Broadcasting, March 9, 1992 at 40.

When the radio broadcasting committee of the InterAmerican Telecommunications Conference (CITEL) meet in Mexico City in August 1992, the broadcast satellite program manager for Voice of America and representatives of the National Association of Broadcasters and the National Telecommunications and Information Administration encouraged others present to give in-band digital audio broadcasting a chance over the next couple of years, but the U.S. delegation faced aggressive attempts to defeat in-band, particularly from Canadians. The group is scheduled to meet again in the spring of 1993. Broadcasting, Sept. 14, 1992 at 32.

Quite different international implications were raised by Radio Marti, a radio facility which went on the air in 1985, created by the Reagan administration in an attempt to break what the administration considered the Castro government's monopoly on news available to Cubans. Radio Marti was established within the Voice of America following the controversial legislation authorizing it. Voice of America's charter prohibits it from disseminating propaganda. The station was named after Cuban patriot-writer Jose Marti.

The Radio Broadcasting to Cuba Act, 22 U.S.C.A. § 1465, authorizes compensation for stations modifying facilities to lessen effects of responsive Cuban interference. The FCC Mass Media Bureau found Susquehanna Broadcasting Co. eligible for more than $714,000 in compensation for expenses for its Miami station, WQBA. Broadcasting, Oct. 13, 1986 at 78.

Funds for a television version, TV Marti, were approved by the Senate Appropriations Committee in 1988, much to the displeasure of the National Association of Broadcasters (NAB). The NAB expressed concerns that the proposed station would cause interference to stations in the U.S. Plans were for the station to transmit from a tethered blimp about three miles above the Florida Keys, and costs for TV Marti through fiscal 1989 were estimated to be about $25 million. By April 1990, $47 million had been spent on TV Marti, but the Cuban government had successfully jammed its broadcast virtually since it went on the air. Nearly all of TV Marti's programs have been aired between 3 a.m. and 6 a.m. The Washington Post, Apr. 16, 1992 at A1.

Chapter II

THE SPECTRUM AND ITS UTILIZATION

A. THE NATURE OF THE SPECTRUM

The electromagnetic spectrum is a unique natural resource. Utilization does not use it up or wear it out. It does not require continual maintenance to remain usable. It is subject to pollution (interference), but once the interference is removed the pollution totally disappears. The value of the spectrum lies primarily in its use for conveying a wide variety of information at varying speeds over varying distances: in other words, for communication.

All electromagnetic radiation is a form of radiant energy, similar in many respects to heat, light or X-radiation. All of these types of radiation are considered by physicists to be waves resulting from the periodic oscillations of charged subatomic particles. All radiation has a measurable frequency, or rate of oscillation, which is measured in cycles per second, or hertz. One thousand cycles per second equals one kilocycle per second (1 kHz); 1,000 kilocycles per second equals one Megacycle per second (1 MHz); and 1,000 Megacycles per second equals one Gigacycle per second (1 GHz). The frequencies of electromagnetic radiation that comprise the radio spectrum span a wide range, from 10 kHz to 3,000,000,000,000 cycles per second (3,000 GHz), all of which are nearly incomprehensibly rapid. Present technology allows use of the spectrum only up to around 40 GHz.

The radio spectrum resource itself has three dimensions: space, time and frequency. Two spectrum users can transmit on the same frequency at the same time, if they are sufficiently separate physically; the physical separation necessary will depend on the power at which each signal is transmitted. They then occupy different parts of the spectrum in the spatial sense. Similarly, the spectrum can be divided in terms of frequency, dependent on the construction of the transmitting and receiving equipment; or in a temporal sense, dependent largely on the hours of use.

The spectrum is subject to the phenomenon of interference. One radio signal interferes with another to the extent that both have the same dimensions. That is, two signals of the same frequency that occupy the same physical space at the same time will interfere with each other (co-channel interference). Signals on adjacent channels may also interfere with each other. Interference usually obscures or destroys any information that either signal is carrying: the degree to which two signals occupy the same physical space depends on the intensity of the radiated power at a given point, which in turn depends on the construction of the transmitting equipment and antenna.

44

The spectrum is divided into numbered bands, extending from Very Low Frequencies (VLF) to Very, Ultra, Super and Extremely High Frequencies (EHF) and beyond. The lower frequencies of the radio spectrum are used for "point-to-point" communications and for navigational aids. AM radio is located in the range between 300 and 3,000 kHz, known as the Medium Frequency band (MF). FM radio and VHF television (channels 2–13) are in the Very High Frequency band (VHF), from 30 to 300 MHz. The Ultra High Frequency band, from 300 to 3,000 MHz, is the location of UHF television (channels 14–69). Still higher frequencies are used for microwave relays and communication satellites.

The effective limitations on use of the radio spectrum are defined by (1) the propagation characteristics of the various frequencies and (2) the level of interference. Low frequency radio waves are best suited to long distance communications. In the lowest frequency bands the radio waves propagate primarily along the ground or water and follow the curvature of the earth. The attenuation of these "ground waves" generally increases with frequency; VLF waves may be propagated for thousands of miles, which explains their value for point-to-point communication. Ground waves in the HF band below VHF can propagate no more than a few hundred miles and above that band they become unimportant. Sky wave propagation is important up to the start of the VHF band. These radio waves tend to depart from the earth's surface and are reflected by the ionosphere, an electrically charged region of the atmosphere 35 to 250 miles above the earth. The amount of reflection depends on the level of daily solar activity, the time of day, the season, geographical location, the length of the signal path and the angle at which the waves strike the ionosphere. The reflection of sky waves is much greater at night, when they may be transmitted over great distances. Above 30 MHz, radio waves tend to pierce the ionosphere rather than to be reflected, and line-of-sight transmission becomes increasingly necessary. As frequency increases above 30 MHz, surface objects absorb radiation at an increasing rate until at 1 GHz a clear unobstructed line of sight becomes necessary. In the very highest frequencies, the waves are subject to substantial absorption by water vapor and oxygen in the atmosphere and cannot be used for communication.

Interference constitutes the second major limitation on the use of the electromagnetic spectrum. As noted above, interference results when two signals attempt to occupy the same spectrum in all three of its dimensions. Even if two users wish to transmit on the same frequency, interference can be avoided by sufficient geographical separation between transmitters, limitations of the power radiated by each transmitter, limitations on antenna height, or separation of the signals in time. The first three techniques cause spatial differentiation; the last affects the temporal dimension.

Standard (AM) broadcasting propagates its waves by "amplitude modulation." The sound waves vary in power, producing variations in the height of the waves that are transmitted. The receiving unit decodes these height variations, reproducing the original sounds. AM transmissions occur in the MF band and thus have a long range primary service through ground waves, particularly near the lower end of the band. AM also can utilize sky waves to provide a secondary service at night.

FM broadcasting utilizes "frequency modulation" rather than "amplitude modulation." In this system the height of the wave is held constant, but the frequency of the waves transmitted is varied. This type of broadcasting provides higher-quality service with less interference than does AM, but it serves smaller areas, because the waves of the VHF band do not follow the surface of the earth and are not reflected by the ionosphere. This also means that FM service is unaffected by skywave interference at night.

Television utilizes separate signals for the visual and the sound components. The picture is transmitted by amplitude modulation and the sound by frequency modulation. Because the transmissions are either in the VHF or UHF bands, the range of the signal is short and television cannot utilize either long ground waves or sky waves.

B. ALLOCATION OF THE SPECTRUM

The method of dividing the spectrum resource among prospective users is enormously complex and highly controversial. The general term "allocation policy" includes three separate but not always distinct processes, each of which involves both technical and nontechnical considerations. The allocation process is the division of the spectrum into blocks of frequencies to be used by specified services or users. Thus, the television service is allocated certain frequencies in the VHF and UHF bands, microwave users are allocated certain frequencies in the UHF and SHF bands, and so on. The second process, allotment, involves the distribution of spectrum rights within allocated bands to users in various geographical areas. Assignment, the third process, denotes the choice among potential individual users of allocated and allotted channels or frequency bands. We usually refer to all three processes under the general label of "allocation policy."

Perhaps the most important objective consideration in formulating an allocation policy is the technical usability of the spectrum itself. Technical usability is dependent primarily on three factors: the propagation characteristics of each frequency range, interference problems and their resolution, and limitations imposed by the communications system itself, especially the transmitting and receiving equipment. In other words, it is dependent on the physics of radio waves, other users of the spectrum and the technical state of the electronics industry. Frequency characteristics themselves seldom pose significant problems, for although there are optimal frequency ranges for various services, these tend to be broad ranges. Consequently, there is usually considerable flexibility in the initial choice of a frequency for a given service except for whatever priority is given to those already utilizing the space.

Several forms of interference may present problems since interference can be caused by an overcrowded frequency, insufficient geographical separation or unduly strong power levels.

The third constraint on spectrum allocation involves the technology of the communications system used, especially the antenna system and the transmitting and receiving equipment. Any major change in receivers might create economic problems for the public and thus for the industry as a whole.

The problem of crowding in the broadcasting industry began early in the 1920s. The episode is recounted by Justice Frankfurter in his opinion for the Court in National Broadcasting Co. v. United States, 319 U.S. 190 (1943), a case to which we return later:

> Federal regulation of radio begins with the Wireless Ship Act of June 24, 1910, 36 Stat. 629, which forbade any steamer carrying or licensed to carry fifty or more persons to leave any American port unless equipped with efficient apparatus for radio communication, in charge of a skilled operator. The enforcement of this legislation was entrusted to the Secretary of Commerce and Labor, who was in charge of the administration of the marine navigation laws. But it was not until 1912 when the United States ratified the first international radio treaty, 37 Stat. 1565, that the need for general regulation of radio communication became urgent. In order to fulfill our obligations under the treaty, Congress enacted the Radio Act of August 13, 1912, 37 Stat. 302. This statute forbade the operation of radio apparatus without a license from the Secretary of Commerce and Labor; it also allocated certain frequencies for the use of the Government, and imposed restrictions upon the character of wave emissions, the transmission of distress signals and the like.
>
> The enforcement of the Radio Act of 1912 presented no serious problems prior to the World War. Questions of interference arose only rarely because there were more than enough frequencies for all the stations then in existence. The war accelerated the development of the art, however, and in 1921 the first standard broadcast stations were established. They grew rapidly in number, and by 1923 there were several hundred such stations throughout the country. The Act of 1912 had not set aside any particular frequencies for the use of private broadcast stations; consequently, the Secretary of Commerce selected two frequencies, 750 and 833 kilocycles, and licensed all stations to operate upon one or the other of these channels. The number of stations increased so rapidly, however, and the situation became so chaotic, that the Secretary, upon recommendation of the National Radio Conferences which met in Washington in 1923 and 1924, established a policy of assigning specified frequencies to particular stations. The

entire radio spectrum was divided into numerous bands, each allocated to a particular kind of service. The frequencies ranging from 550 to 1500 kilocycles (96 channels in all, since the channels were separated from each other by 10 kilocycles) were assigned to the standard broadcast stations. But the problems created by the enormously rapid development of radio were far from solved. The increase in the number of channels was not enough to take care of the constantly growing number of stations. Since there were more stations than available frequencies, the Secretary of Commerce attempted to find room for everybody by limiting the power and the hours of operation of stations in order that several stations might use the same channel. The number of stations multiplied so rapidly, however, that by November, 1925, there were almost 600 stations in the country, and there were 175 applications for new stations. Every channel in the standard broadcast band was, by that time, already occupied by at least one station, and many by several. The new stations could be accommodated only by extending the standard broadcast band, at the expense of the other types of services, or by imposing still greater limitations upon time and power. The National Radio Conference which met in November, 1925, opposed both of these methods and called upon Congress to remedy the situation through legislation.

[During 1926 courts held that the Secretary of Commerce lacked the power to stem the tide, and his pleas for self-regulation went unheeded by the burgeoning new industry.]

From July, 1926, to February 23, 1927, when Congress enacted the Radio Act of 1927, 44 Stat. 1162, almost 200 new stations went on the air. These new stations used any frequencies they desired, regardless of the interference thereby caused to others. Existing stations changed to other frequencies and increased their power and hours of operation at will. The result was confusion and chaos. With everybody on the air, nobody could be heard.

1. THE FEDERAL COMMUNICATIONS COMMISSION

As we noted in Chapter I, the Radio Act of 1927 and the Communications Act of 1934 rejected the idea of a market system of spectrum allocation and of any property rights in the spectrum resource. The Federal Communications Commission has the sole power to allocate the radio spectrum, to establish general standards of operations and to license persons to use designated parts of the spectrum.

Many services must be placed, but some critics of Commission policies charge undue reliance on the bloc allocation concept, which calls for allocating discrete frequency bands to classes of users essentially without regard to geographical location and maintaining a relatively strict segregation among allocations. This can lead to such anomalous results as marine bands in Nebraska and forestry bands in New York

City. These problems are exacerbated by the general administrative difficulty of changing an allocation once made: the start-up costs are so great and the capital investment is usually so heavy that there is a strong economic incentive not to move users from one frequency band to another. Thus, as new uses develop, they are allocated higher and higher frequencies, with little consideration of which frequencies are technically best suited for which services. For example, location of radio broadcasting in the AM band (535–1605 kHz) may be inefficient. Local broadcasting might be moved to the current FM band (88–108 MHz), which is much better suited technically to local radio, and long distance broadcasting might be moved to frequencies below 500 kHz to take advantage of the long distance ground wave propagation characteristics at those frequencies.

Another claim is that area coverage by broadcasting stations would require less spectrum if the Commission were to drop its so-called "local station goal." High-power stations in major urban centers could serve the entire country in only one-third the spectrum space presently used. Yet local stations are important; they are outlets for local news and forums for local citizens to express their views, they serve local advertisers, and they provide such local services as weather reports (which might be critical in areas subject to flash flooding or sudden tornadoes or storms).

2. RADIO ALLOCATION

a. *AM Allocation*

AM broadcasting occupies slightly more than 1 MHz of spectrum in the Medium Frequency band between 535 kHz and 1605 kHz. This is divided into 107 assignable channels each with a bandwidth of 10 kHz. AM stations are divided into four major classes. Class I "clear channel" stations are high-power stations designed to provide primary (groundwave) service to a metropolitan area and its environs and secondary nighttime (skywave) service to an extended rural area. Class II stations also operate on clear channels with primary service areas limited by interference from Class I stations. A Class II station must usually avoid causing interference within the normally protected service areas of Class I or other Class II stations. Class III stations are medium powered and are designed to provide service primarily to larger cities and contiguous rural areas. Class IV stations are low powered and operate on local channels to provide service to a city or town and contiguous areas.

The 1927 Act creating the Federal Radio Commission had charged the Commission to provide "fair, efficient, and equitable radio service" to all areas of the country. The Commission then proceeded by establishing general engineering constraints such as maximum interference standards, and by allocating each of the 107 frequencies to a class of stations. Within these general constraints, the Commission adopted a first-come-first-served approach. An applicant who could find a promising community could apply for a license to serve that community if it could find a channel that would satisfy the various general constraints. An applicant had to show that it would not interfere excessively with the signals of existing stations nor expose too many of its new listeners to interference beyond certain acceptable limits.

Clear Channels. As noted earlier, because of the skywave phenomenon, powerful AM stations can be received at great distances at night. In the 1940s, with an estimated 20 million persons uncovered by local radio service at night, the FCC created a group of 25 powerful stations operating at 50 kw. Each station shared its daytime channel frequency with other stations around the country. But at sundown all the others left the air so that the channel was clear except for the powerful station, which could reach distant and remote areas of the country.

With the development of FM radio and a surge in interest in AM radio, some argued that the clear channel stations should have their protections reduced to allow more diversity. In response, the clear channel stations argued that their power should be increased to 750 kw so that they could provide additional service. The FCC faced the issue in 1961 but reached no conclusion. In a compromise, it ordered that 13 of the 25 frequencies be shared with one or two other stations, but left the remainder fully protected while it continued to consider the problem.

In 1980 the Commission acted decisively. The number of persons unserved by nighttime local radio was down to 4 million, and applicants were clamoring for space on the AM spectrum. The Commission decided to end the clear channel concept but to protect those stations from interference for a radius of 750 miles. This still permits them to reach larger areas than ordinary stations but it also permits an additional 125 stations to broadcast at night.

The new stations are limited in power to 1 kw except in special cases. At the same time, the FCC explicitly refused to allow the clear channel stations to raise their power above 50 kw. (In the 1930s an experiment permitted a Cincinnati station to broadcast at 500 kw. The experiment was terminated, and a limit of 50 kw imposed for all stations.)

Similarly, in 1985 the Commission voted to allow full-time stations to use frequencies previously reserved for foreign clear channel stations. These channels were available as a result of new agreements negotiated with Canada, Mexico and the Bahamas. AM Broadcast Stations (Nighttime Operations on Canadian, Mexican and Bahamian Clear Channels), 101 F.C.C.2d 1, 58 R.R.2d 655 (1985).

Expanding the Band. A second way to increase the number of AM stations is to expand the part of the spectrum available for such broadcasting. This occurred in 1979, when the World Administrative Radio Conference decided to increase the AM band in the Western Hemisphere so that it will run from 525 to 1705 kHz.

Agreements reached at subsequent Regional Administrative Radio Conferences (RARC) limit stations in the new section of the band to 10 kw. The Commission has decided to use the expanded band to reduce congestion in the existing AM band. By allowing existing AM licensees to operate new stations in the expanded band, and then, after a transition period, shut down their old stations, the Commission hopes to reduce interference and improve signal quality. The FCC will limit the entire expanded band to these migrating AM stations. AM Improvement, 6 F.C.C.Rcd. 6273, 69 R.R.2d 1395 (1991). The new stations could go on the air as early as 1993.

b. FM Allocation

FM broadcasting, which began around 1940, is located in the VHF band. It occupies the frequencies between 88 and 108 MHz, which are excellent for aural broadcast service and allow an effective range of 30 to 75 miles. That spectrum space is divided into 100 assignable channels, each 200 kHz wide. The lowest 20 channels are reserved for noncommercial educational stations; the remaining 80 are given over to commercial use. Commercial FM channels were originally divided into three classes: A, B and C. Class A channels are designed for use by low-power stations serving relatively small communities and the surrounding area. Class B channels are for medium-power stations intended to serve a sizable city or town or the principal city of an urbanized area. Class C channels are used by high-power stations serving a city and large surrounding areas. Commercial FM assignments are based on a Table of Assignments, in which communities are assigned a specific number of FM stations of specified power and on specific channels. Licenses are given only for stations within the communities listed in the Table of Assignments or within a 15 mile radius—unless an application to change the table is granted.

In the late 1970s the demand for FM licenses increased dramatically as FM outlets started to overcome the traditional dominance of AM stations. The superior quality of the FM signal and the availability of stereo were the keys to this change.

In an effort to meet the increased demand for FM stations, the FCC initiated a drop-in rulemaking allowing new FM stations to be started without interfering with present broadcasters. FM Broadcast Stations (Additional Commercial Allocations), 53 R.R.2d 1550 (1983). 47 C.F.R. § 73.202 (1983). This ongoing rulemaking created three new intermediary classes of commercial licenses: B1, C1 and C2. In addition, Class A licenses are now permitted on channels previously set aside for Class B and Class C licenses.

In 1984 the FCC approved a list of 689 locations, an initial step in the omnibus rulemaking process. Most of the new availabilities were Class A licenses in the southeast. The Commission initiated the application process in 1985 but staggered the applications for different channels over the next three years. Some of these stations are already on the air. Others, however, are tied up in comparative hearings. We will discuss comparative license hearings in Chapter IV.

c. *Beneficiaries*

Who are the likely beneficiaries of these attempts to increase the number of broadcast outlets? In radio, daytime AM broadcasters have argued forcefully that they deserve the opportunity to obtain fulltime outlets. Meanwhile, the Commission has long been concerned that minority groups are woefully underrepresented among the owners of broadcast licenses. Although minority ownership does not necessarily mean that a station's programming will take minority tastes into special account, the FCC believes that minority ownership itself is important—and that the other may follow. Other demonstrations of the FCC's concern about minorities in broadcasting are discussed elsewhere in this and later chapters.

In the FM drop-in rulemaking, *supra,* the Commission voted to give preference both to AM daytime broadcasters and to minority applicants. FM Broadcast Assignments, 101 F.C.C.2d 638, 57 R.R.2d 1607 (1985), reconsidered in part, 59 R.R.2d 1221, reconsideration denied, 2 F.C.C.Rcd. 481, 61 R.R.2d 1704 (1986). The preference was affirmed. National Black Media Coalition v. Federal Communications Commission, 822 F.2d 277 (2d Cir.1987).

In contrast, the Commission specifically rejected petitions requesting preference for minority and non-commercial applicants for the new stations authorized for either domestic or foreign clear channels, p. 50, *supra.* Deletion of AM Acceptance Criteria, 102 F.C.C.2d 548, 59 R.R.2d 521 (1985); AM Broadcast Stations (Nighttime Operations on Clear Channels), 3 F.C.C.Rcd. 3597, 64 R.R.2d 1475 (1988), recon. denied, AM Broadcast Stations (Nighttime Operations on Canadian, Mexican and Bahamian Clear Channels), 66 R.R.2d 1049 (1989).

In a separate action, the Commission temporarily froze all applications for new AM daytime stations and indicated it would seek through rulemaking procedure to make the freeze permanent. AM Daytime Applications (Temporary Freeze), 1 F.C.C.Rcd. 1264, 61 R.R.2d 1067 (1986). The Commission believes it can find ways to expand service for current daytimers but would be unable to help any new daytime stations. One method will be allowing AM daytimers to participate in the migration to the expanded band, p. 50, *supra.* Note that in 1990, as part of its inquiry into improving AM radio, the Commission instituted a freeze on all AM broadcast applications. AM Improvement, 5 F.C.C.Rcd. 4381.

3. TELEVISION ALLOCATION

The first licensing of television stations in this country occurred in 1941 and involved 18 channels. The first assignment plan was developed in 1945, based solely on the VHF channels. It involved the assignment of about 400 stations to 140 major market centers. Early comers quickly preempted the 100 choice assignments. In 1948, because of unexpected problems with tropospheric interference and concern that the 1945 assignment plan could cause problems, the Commission ordered a freeze on channel assignments.

The freeze ended with the issuance of the Sixth Report and Order on Television Allocations, 17 Fed.Reg. 3905, 1 R.R. 91:601 (1952), creating the Table of Assignments. The Commission rejected the idea of moving all television to the UHF band. Instead, 12 VHF channels were retained, and 70 new UHF channels were added, so that the Table provided for about 620 VHF and 1400 UHF stations. Television uses an enormous amount of spectrum compared to radio. One VHF channel uses six MHz—six times more than the entire AM band.

The Commission generated the Table of Assignments from its hierarchy of priorities: (1) to provide at least one television service to every part of the United States; (2) to provide each community with at least one television station; (3) to provide a choice of at least two television services to all parts of the U.S.; (4) to provide each community with at least two television stations; and (5) to assign remaining channels to communities on the basis of population, geographical location and the number of television services already available to that community. Note the emphasis on "local" outlets. Is this a sound hierarchy?

In making these assignments the Commission decided to "intermix" VHF and UHF channels as a single service in the same markets. Many observers warned that the newer UHF channels could not survive, but the Commission apparently believed that the demand for VHF would overflow into the UHF band, and it also feared that failure to intermix would relegate UHF stations to markets overshadowed by VHF outlets in nearby metropolitan areas, or to remote rural areas. In any event, the Table of Assignments called for combined VHF and UHF channels in the following pattern: six to 10 for cities with population over 1 million; four to six for cities with 250,000 to 1,000,000; two to four for those with populations between 50,000 and 250,000; and one to two for communities under 50,000.

Because the Table tended to allot three VHF stations to most markets with only a few getting more than three, the three major networks could now program almost entirely through VHF affiliates. This gave them strong audience and advertiser support. (In 1971, for example, 108 of the nation's 207 television markets, covering 58 percent of the nation's television households, could receive the three networks but no VHF independent stations. R. Noll, M. Peck and J. McGowan, Economic Aspects of Television Regulation 168 (1973)). Without adequate set penetration, UHF stations found it difficult if not impossible to secure advertising revenues and network affiliation. By the end of 1956, there were 395 VHF stations and 96 UHF stations on the air. By this time Dumont, a fourth network, had collapsed. By 1960 only 75

(15 percent) of the 575 commercial stations on the air were UHF, even though 70 percent of the total channel assignments were UHF.

The Commission recognized that intermixture was not working. In 1956, while considering broader solutions such as the transfer of all television to the UHF band, the Commission adopted deintermixture as an "interim" measure in several communities, making them all-UHF. In 1961 the Commission planned to deintermix eight more communities. This time, however, the opposition from established VHF stations was formidable. After a fierce battle, Congress entered the fray and enacted a compromise: the All Channel Receiver Act of 1962. The Act, which became § 303(s) of the Communications Act, authorized the Commission to order that all sets shipped in interstate commerce be capable of receiving both VHF and UHF signals. The VHF interests gave their support for the proposal in exchange for the Commission's indefinite suspension of deintermixture proposals. The Commission did require "all-channel" receivers and declared a moratorium on most pending deintermixture proposals. The Commission's regulation came too late for many of the UHF pioneers of the 1950s. (In 1971 the Commission began steps to require detent ("click") dialing on all UHF receivers.)

The continued underutilization of UHF spots led the FCC to begin to reallocate frequencies to competing uses of the airwaves. Channels 70 to 83 were reassigned for land mobile use. In some cities Channels 14 to 20 are being used by land mobile operators and are being shared elsewhere. In 1980, 63 percent of the television assignments were UHF. The vacancy rates were as follows: 61 of the 578 commercial VHFs; 266 of the 648 commercial UHFs; 23 of the 136 noncommercial VHFs; and 374 of the 570 noncommercial UHFs. In the top 100 markets, vacancies existed on 86 UHF channels but on no commercial VHF. In the top 200 markets, the comparable figures were 176 and six.

In addition to the intermixture problem, UHF stations are also more expensive to operate because it takes 10 times as much power for a UHF transmitter to reach the same area as a VHF transmitter. Because of the inferior wave-propagation qualities of UHF signals compared with VHF signals, UHF stations are permitted to operate at a power of 5,000 kw compared with 100 or 316 kw for VHF stations. But the energy costs are so high that few UHF stations operate at maximum permitted power.

Since most network programs, the most popular, were on VHF stations, viewers in intermixed communities had little incentive to seek out UHF, even though by 1983, 96 percent of all homes with television could receive UHF. Until "click" dialing became common, some viewers trying to use UHF found it difficult to tune in the desired station.

During 1979 the future of UHF suddenly brightened. Applicants sought stations that had gone begging since 1952, existing stations were sold at increasingly higher prices and major broadcast owners became interested in UHF for the first time. The change in climate was apparently due to a variety of independent factors coming into play at the same time. Viewers were finding "click" dialing or newer digital dialing systems more attractive; cable television was improving the reception of the UHF stations. Another temporary boost came from the introduction of Subscription Television (STV), an over-the-air pay television system in which viewers who wish to buy the service are supplied decoders that unscramble the signal being transmitted. Although little original programming was being provided, the prospect of uncut motion pictures without commercials was sufficiently attractive to make the venture appear profitable.

However, due to increasing cable penetration, piracy of signals and increasing interest in Multi-channel Multipoint Distribution Service (MMDS, which will be discussed in Chapter X), STV is apparently no longer viable. As of 1991 there were no STV stations in operation.

A few UHF stations have become profitable as the result of developments in cable television. Because of changes in FCC rules governing cable systems, it became possible for a single television station, in effect, to become a network by supplying its programs by satellite to cable systems throughout the country. The operation of these "superstations" is described more extensively in the discussion of cable television in Chapter IX.

Arguing that the UHF spectrum is under-utilized, representatives of the land mobile radio industry petitioned the FCC to reallocate portions of the UHF spectrum for their use. In response the Commission issued a NPRM proposing allocation of up to six additional UHF channels (some were previously reallocated in 1972) in eight major metropolitan areas to land mobile. Further Sharing of the UHF Television Band, 50 Fed.Reg. 25,587 (June 25, 1985). The proposal has been vigorously opposed by members of the broadcast industry who contend that UHF television is in a period of tremendous growth and that, due in part to FCC-mandated improvements in television receivers, this growth and a concomitant increase in demand for UHF spectrum space are likely to continue.

In addition, broadcasters argue that the development of a new television service, high definition television (HDTV), discussed at p. 56, *infra*, makes it necessary to retain the currently unused UHF spectrum. The Commission has delayed any further action on the land mobile petition pending decisions on HDTV.

a. New Television Outlets

In 1982 the FCC approved the start of a new television service of perhaps as many as 4,000 low-power television (LPTV) stations throughout the country. These stations operate at a power sufficient to reach viewers within a radius of 10–15 miles. It is up to the applicant to find spots on the VHF and UHF bands in which such stations will not interfere with existing stations.

LPTV operators are permitted to join together by satellite to set up networks. Neither the duopoly nor the one-to-a-market rules, which we will discuss in Chapter V, apply to LPTV. There is no limit set on the number of LPTV licenses one entity can have. Programming restrictions are also minimal. The fairness doctrine and § 315 of the Communications Act (see Chapter VI) apply only to licensee-originated programming.

A lottery procedure for initial licensing of LPTV was approved by the Commission in March 1983. Selection from Among Competing Applications Using Random Selection or Lotteries Instead of Comparative Hearings, 48 Fed.Reg. 27,182 (1983). This procedure was necessitated by the great number of applications. Applications for LPTV licenses were frozen in September 1983 and the lottery disposed of competing applications at a rate of 250–350 each month. By 1987 the backlog was reduced to the point where the Commission was able to resume accepting applications. The first window produced more than 1,500 applications. (Under new FCC procedures, a period of time—a "window"—is set during which applications for specified channels and locations will be accepted.) In 1988 a second window produced almost 1,000 more applications.

On the same day it authorized LPTV, the Commission, 4–3, approved four drop-ins on specific VHF channels in specific cities. These would be full-power stations that the Commission decided would provide enough new service to viewers to outweigh any loss of service to some persons in areas near existing stations on the same channel. The drop-in is required to reduce its power in the direction of existing stations, but it would be far more powerful than a low-power station.

b. High Definition Television

HDTV is television with approximately twice as many scan lines as the current United States standard of 525 lines. Coupled with a change in the aspect ratio (the ratio between the width and height of the picture) HDTV delivers vastly superior picture quality. Proponents of the new service claim that it is equivalent in quality to 35 mm. film.

When first proposed, however, HDTV required a bandwidth greater than 6 MHz. Initially, two methods of getting around this problem were proposed. One used two adjacent UHF channels to deliver a single HDTV signal. In 1986 an experimental broadcast using this system was transmitted over channels 58 and 59 in Washington. Another system used non-adjacent channels. This would have allowed a current VHF station to transmit HDTV by transmitting the remainder of the signal over a UHF channel in the same market.

The possibility of HDTV indicated a potential need for future UHF spectrum. On the other hand, HDTV was only a possibility. Standards had not been established and no method of delivery had been agreed upon. Thus, as noted above, the Commission has to balance a current need claimed by the land mobile industry and a potential need claimed by broadcasters.

The suggestion that the Commission set an HDTV standard points out another problem faced by the Commission in allocating spectrum for new services. Should the Commission determine the technical standards for such a service or leave it to the marketplace to decide? In the past the Commission has tried both approaches. For example, in 1953 the Commission chose the National Television System Committee (NTSC) standard for color television. Amendment of the Commission's Rules Governing Color Television Transmissions, 41 F.C.C. 658 (1953).

In contrast, in 1982 the FCC authorized AM radio stations to broadcast in stereo but refused to choose from among five incompatible systems. Licensees were free to use any of the five systems. AM Stereophonic Broadcasting, 51 R.R.2d 1 (1982). Six years later the FCC again refused to choose among the two remaining systems or to mandate that all AM stereo receivers be capable of decoding the signals produced by both systems. AM Stereophonic Broadcasting, 64 R.R.2d 516 (1988).

What factors should influence the Commission's decision on setting a standard for a new service? In the case of AM stereo, is it relevant that after six years only 10 percent of AM stations broadcast in stereo? What about the fact that eventually one became the *de facto* standard?

In 1988 the Commission issued a tentative decision and further NOI involving Advanced Television (ATV). Advanced Television Systems and Their Impact on the Existing Television Broadcast Service, 3 F.C.C.Rcd. 6520, 65 R.R.2d 295 (1988). The Commission defined ATV as "any system that results in improved television audio and video quality, whether the methods employed improve the existing NTSC transmission system or constitute an entirely new system." Included within this definition are HDTV—"systems that provide quality approaching that of 35mm. film"—and Enhanced Definition Television (EDTV)—"systems that perform better than NTSC but not on a par with 35mm. film."

The Commission started by concluding that ATV "can be brought to the public best and most rapidly by utilizing the existing television broadcast allocations." According to the FCC, attempting to identify additional unused spectrum space with propagation characteristics appropriate for ATV would only delay the development of ATV.

The Commission also decided that "service must be continued to the public's existing NTSC receivers, at least during the transition period to ATV." This could be accomplished either by transmitting an ATV signal compatible with NTSC receivers or by "simulcasting NTSC and incompatible ATV signals on separate channels." Regardless, ATV signals will be limited to 6 MHz. Note that these restrictions would apply only to terrestrial broadcasting. The Commission specifically declined to set any restrictions on ATV delivered by Direct Broadcast Satellite (DBS) or nonbroadcast media such as cable.

In its NOI the Commission requested comments on three specific options for implementing ATV: "(a) provide ATV within existing 6 MHz assignments; (b) provide to each broadcaster an additional 3 MHz for an augmentation signal; or (c) provide to each broadcaster an additional 6 MHz for either an augmentation signal or for a dual non-compatible ATV signal. The FCC also sought comments "on how standards should be established for ATV and whether we should relax or repeal the NTSC standard."

In 1990 the Commission announced that it intends to select a simulcast HDTV system. No further consideration will be given to augmentation systems. Although the Commission did not envision selecting an EDTV system prior to the selection of an HDTV system, it left open the possibility that such a system could be selected at some time in the future.

The FCC gave several reasons for the rejection of augmentation systems in favor of simulcast. First, simulcast systems, able to use all new technology, "offer the potential for significantly greater improvement in the quality of television picture and audio performance" than augmentation systems, which have to incorporate the now antiquated NTSC technology.

A simulcast system also will be spectrum efficient and facilitate the implementation of ATV service. Such a system will transmit the increased information of an HDTV signal in the same 6 Mhz channel space used in the current television channel plan. This ultimately will minimize the amount of spectrum needed for HDTV service and simplify the HDTV channel allocation process. . . . In addition, a simulcast system will provide consumers with the greatest degree of initial improvement in the quality of television picture and audio service. Finally, our selection of a simulcast system will eliminate confusion for consumers about which type of receiver to purchase. This latter factor can be expected to speed the growth of HDTV receiver penetration.

The Commission also noted that existing spectrum restrictions would force many stations to transmit their primary signal in the VHF band and their augmentation channel in the UHF band. Because signals in these two bands have different propagation characteristics, there would be additional technical problems for augmentation systems resulting in more expensive receivers. Advanced Television Systems, 68 R.R.2d 167 (1990).

In 1992 the Commission decided a number of additional issues. These included limiting initial eligibility for ATV licenses to existing TV licensees and adopting an initial two-year deadline for broadcasters to apply for ATV licenses (to be paired with their original licenses) and a three-year deadline for construction of ATV facilities, once assigned. In addition, once ATV becomes the prevalent medium, broadcasters will be forced to convert to ATV by surrendering one of each of their paired broadcast channels and ceasing to broadcast in NTSC. The

Commission also announced its intention to adopt a 100 percent simulcasting requirement at the earliest appropriate date. Advanced Television Systems, 57 Fed.Reg. 21,744 (May 8, 1992).

In its order, the Commission suggested that the date for conversion to ATV should be "15 years from either selection of an ATV system or the date a Table of ATV Allotments is effective, whichever is later." The FCC also proposed that the 100 percent simulcasting requirement go into effect no later than four years after the application/construction period has passed. Meanwhile, the six proposed ATV systems were tested in 1992. The Commission is expected to choose a system in 1993.

Broadcasters have indicated some concern over the FCC's plan. The same digital technology that allows HDTV to be compressed into 6 MHz may allow an improved NTSC signal. Even if it doesn't equal the quality of HDTV, it may be good enough to deter consumers from investing in more expensive HDTV sets. At the same time digital NTSC will permit compressing several NTSC signals into a single 6 MHz channel (multichannel NTSC). If broadcasters are locked into HDTV and consumers choose digital NTSC, the broadcasters will be at a serious competitive disadvantage with cable and other media that have the capability of transmitting both. Broadcasting, Aug. 24, 1992 at 3.

C. A NOTE ON THE ECONOMICS OF TELEVISION

The basic unit in the broadcasting system is the individual station that receives the license from the Federal Communications Commission. As of August 1992, 1,691 full-power television stations were authorized to operate in the United States. These included 698 VHF and 993 UHF. Of the total authorized, 662 VHF and 716 UHF were actually in operation, with the remainder either under construction or off the air for financial or technical reasons. Of the operating stations, 1,140 were commercial (557 VHF and 583 UHF), and the remainder were noncommercial.

Because of multiple ownership limitations to be discussed, the ownership of the commercial stations is widely distributed. Prior to the 1985 relaxation of the multiple ownership rules, there were several group owners whose holdings included the maximum five VHFs. Among these group owners were the three major networks. Each owned and operated one VHF in New York City, Los Angeles and Chicago. The fourth and fifth VHFs were located in six different cities. These 15 O & Os (owned and operated) were a major source of profit for the television networks. The O & Os realized 90 percent of their revenue from non-network sales because of their desirable frequencies in major cities.

As a result of changes in regulation and competition from newer technologies, especially cable, it appears that major changes in the economics and structure of the television industry will be taking place during the next few years. However, exactly what form these changes will take is not yet clear.

For example, with the relaxation of the multiple ownership rules, the networks acquired additional O & Os. At the same time Fox Television has started a fourth network. As of late 1992, Fox was supplying prime-time programming for Wednesday through Sunday nights as well as non-prime-time programming for other nights.

The majority of the commercial stations are "affiliated" with one or more networks by contractual arrangements. Of the 1,140 commercial stations, more than 200 are affiliated with each of the three major networks. As a general rule, unaffiliated VHFs are located in markets that have more than three commercial VHFs so no major network affiliation is available. UHF stations generally can secure a major network affiliation only in markets in which there are fewer than three commercial VHFs. Group owners, other than the networks, may produce some programs for their group or may treat their stations as individual facilities with each one affiliated with a different network or no network.

The following chart, from B. Owen, J. Beebe and W. Manning, Jr., Television Economics 7 (1974), gives an understanding of the structure and economics of the television industry and of television program procurement and production: *

* Reprinted by permission of the author, from *Television Economics* by Bruce M. Owen, Jack H. Beebe and Willard G. Manning, Jr. (Lexington Books, D. C. Heath and Co., 1974).

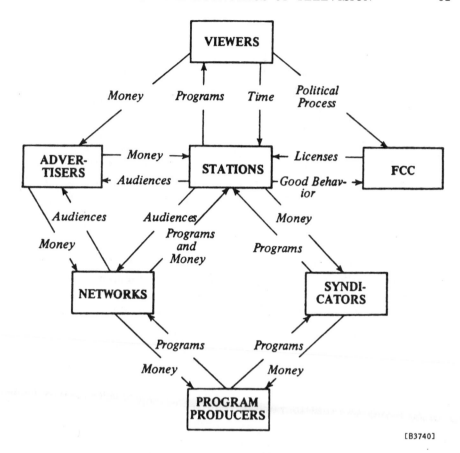

[B3740]

The station would seem to be central, and its economic relationships are complex. Although it would have been possible for stations to develop their own programming and sell time to advertisers or to have the advertisers prepare programming and place it on individual stations, the industry has developed differently. The most important feature from the outset has been the role of the networks. It would have been possible for a network to own no stations and to perform no function other than as a broker between individual stations and national advertisers with no involvement in programming, or it could have arranged for the distribution of programs, often simultaneously, over common carrier interconnections. Instead, networks emerged as group owners who each controlled stations in five of the largest cities in the country. These have been profitable in their own right and have formed a solid base of guaranteed viewers.

To make the brokering function simpler and to maximize the audiences they can deliver, networks seek affiliates in each of the 200–odd market areas. A station, owned individually or by a group, will seek affiliation. The station will be relieved from having to create or purchase much of its programming because the network will supply programs to the affiliates and the profit will be more than it could make by remaining independent. The affiliate will be able to sell advertising for some spots in and around the network programming. Moreover, the network may pay fees ("compensation") to affiliates depending upon how much network programming they carry in excess of about 20 hours per week. The result is that the station clears time for the most popular programs without charge in order to be able to sell the available commercial time for these features, and is persuaded to clear for the next tier of programs by receiving a fee. To obtain these advantages, the station turns its audience over to the network for the agreed-upon programming and gives up most of its independent efforts. Occasionally, the relationship is discontinued.

Reduced revenues due to declining shares of the audience have caused the three major networks to consider reducing compensation to their affiliates. There are, however, several risks involved in doing so. First, the affiliates may find it more attractive to replace less successful network programming with syndicated programming. Second, the affiliates may balk at renewing their affiliation agreements. For example, CBS had to modify a recent proposed reduction in affiliate compensation under pressure from its affiliates. Broadcasting, July 6, 1992 at 3.

Program production is generally thought to fall into two categories: the production of news, documentaries and public affairs programs, and the production of entertainment programming. Although news programming has not always been remunerative and could be left to local stations, the fact that so much of the news is national or international has led the networks themselves to undertake much of the production responsibility for these programs. Although the networks could contract with independent producers for this programming, they have uniformly decided to develop their own news and public affairs organizations and to produce all of their own programs in this category. Moreover, some networks will not buy documentaries from independent producers. The probable explanation is that the networks want total editorial control over this sensitive area to protect their stations from complaints and charges that may arise.

The considerations in entertainment programming are obviously quite different. In the earlier days of television, advertisers developed their own programming, perhaps through independent producers, and bought time to present the program and related commercials. The network simply sold time and access to the O & Os and affiliates in a single deal. As television developed, networks became more aware of the importance of continuity throughout the evening's entertainment programming, so that one show would link with the next to produce the largest loyal audiences. This required considering what the other networks were programming. Advertiser-initiated programming could aim for demographically discrete groups but could not accommodate all these concerns. By now advertiser-prepared programs have virtually disappeared and network productions play a minor role due at least in part to the financial interest and syndication rules to be discussed in

Chapter V. The independent producer pattern has become dominant. This entails interdependence of independent producers, local stations, advertisers and the networks.

Independent stations must operate in a totally different pattern because they must provide all their own programs. Independents tend to exist in markets with more than four stations and thus compete not only with each other but also with network affiliates. If one of the networks did not have an affiliate in a market, it would make sense for the network to obtain an affiliate to increase the audience it can provide advertisers, and for the station to become an affiliate because network programming is more popular than alternatives, and affiliates are generally much more profitable than independents. If the network alternative is unavailable, the independents produce some inexpensive local programming and purchase programming from syndicators, who negotiate with individual stations rather than networks. The stations generally bargain for exclusive local rights for a period of time. Some programs are prepared by producers specially for syndication, but others have previously run on networks ("off-network programs") and are now being offered to the independents—or to affiliates who want to fill open time. Occasionally, independents join together to form an impromptu network for simultaneous showing of a sporting event or other single feature, but that is unusual and is likely to involve a program that the four networks have rejected.

Rerun syndications are generally preferred to original syndications because they are proven commodities. Station managers will be able to predict how successful a rerun of specific material will be in their viewing area. Also, off-network syndications may be less expensive because most of the original creative costs have been returned by the network runs, whereas a first-run syndication must return its costs all at once. To reduce this differential, first-run syndications were traditionally less expensive shows that did not compete with the types of off-network programs that are most commonly and successfully syndicated; first-run syndications moved out of the situation comedy-mystery-detective script situation into game shows and talk shows. Independent stations have "stripped" some of the syndicated programs by presenting them at the same viewing time five days each week. The original program may have been shown on the network once a week, but enough backlog has been developed so that a station using syndication programming may be able to show the program daily and thereby build a loyal audience on a day-by-day basis. This helps the independent's quest for advertising.

The success during the 1987–1988 season of "Star Trek: The Next Generation" has led to an increase in the number of first-run syndicated shows that appear directly competitive with both off-network syndicated shows and current network programs.

Advertisers may deal at one of several levels. National advertisers may work through networks as well as in specific local markets through "national spot" advertising. Local advertisers will deal directly with local stations, both affiliates and independents. In all cases the rates are determined by the size and characteristics of the audience that can be delivered to the advertiser.

As noted above, the television industry appears to be entering a period of great change. Although the three major networks still dominate, their power is waning. The networks' share of the market has declined from 90 percent in 1969 to less than 65 percent in 1992. Independents, Fox Television and various cable services have all contributed to this decline.

To keep matters in perspective, perhaps it is well to realize that television accounted for 53 percent of mass media advertising expenditures in 1991. By comparison, newspapers carried 20 percent of the total, magazines 17 percent, radio 5 percent, billboards 2 percent, and cable television 3 percent.

Chapter III

JUSTIFICATIONS FOR GOVERNMENT REGULATION

A. "PUBLIC INTEREST" AND GOVERNMENT REGULATION

We have just been considering the special nature of the spectrum and various actions that the FCC has taken to regulate the behavior of those who use part of the spectrum. We turn now to the legal question of what justifies the Commission in undertaking these forms of regulation, plus other types of regulation that we consider later. Although a few cases challenged this power early in the life of the FCC, the first major case to address the problem was National Broadcasting Co. v. United States, 319 U.S. 190 (1943).

After conducting a study of business practices and ownership patterns of radio networks in 1941, the Federal Communications Commission concluded that the major networks (NBC and CBS) exerted too much control over the broadcast industry through control over local station programming. To correct this situation, the Commission issued the Chain Broadcasting Regulations, which defined permissible relationships between networks and stations in terms of affiliation, network programming of affiliates' time and network ownership of stations. These regulations were aimed at dissuading individual licensees from entering contracts that gave the networks the power to exert such control over licensees. NBC challenged the Commission's authority to adopt regulations controlling licensee behavior not related to technical and engineering matters. We will return to the substance of these regulations in Chapter V.

The first claim was that Congress had not authorized the FCC to adopt these regulations. Section 303 of the Act provided that the Commission "as public interest, convenience, or necessity requires, shall . . . have authority to make special regulations applicable to radio stations engaged in chain broadcasting." NBC argued that the "public interest" language was to be read as limited to technical and engineering aspects of broadcasting—and that these were not the basis for the FCC's regulations in this case.

The Court noted that several sections of the Act authorized the FCC in furtherance of the "public interest, convenience, or necessity" to do such things as "study new uses for radio, . . . and generally encourage the larger and more effective use of radio in the public interest" and to provide a "fair, efficient and equitable distribution [of licenses] among the states." Building from these several grants of power, the Court rejected NBC's claim:

The Act itself establishes that the Commission's powers are not limited to the engineering and technical aspects of regulation of radio communication. Yet we are asked to regard the Commission as a kind of traffic officer, policing the wave lengths to prevent stations from interfering with each other. But the Act does not restrict the Commission merely to supervision of the traffic. It puts upon the Commission the burden of determining the composition of that traffic. The facilities of radio are not large enough to accommodate all who wish to use them. Methods must be devised for choosing from among the many who apply. And since Congress itself could not do this, it committed the task to the Commission.

. . .

... The Commission's licensing function cannot be discharged, therefore, merely by finding that there are no technological objections to the granting of a license. If the criterion of "public interest" were limited to such matters, how could the Commission choose between two applicants for the same facilities, each of whom is financially and technically qualified to operate a station? Since the very inception of federal regulation by radio, comparative considerations as to the services to be rendered have governed the application of the standard of "public interest, convenience, or necessity." [   ]

. . .

These provisions, individually and in the aggregate, preclude the notion that the Commission is empowered to deal only with technical and engineering impediments to the "larger and more effective use of radio in the public interest." We cannot find in the Act any such restriction of the Commission's authority. Suppose, for example, that a community can, because of physical limitations, be assigned only two stations. That community might be deprived of effective service in any one of several ways. More powerful stations in nearby cities might blanket out the signals of local stations so that they could not be heard at all. The stations might interfere with each other so that neither could be clearly heard. One station might dominate the other with the power of its signal. But the community could be deprived of good radio service in ways less crude. One man, financially and technically qualified, might apply for and obtain the licenses of both stations and present a single service over the two stations, thus wasting a frequency otherwise available to the area. The language of the Act does not withdraw such a situation from the licensing and regulatory powers of the Commission, and there is no evidence that Congress did not mean its broad language to carry the authority it expresses.

The Court then considered NBC's claims that if Congress did authorize the FCC to do this, the statute was unconstitutional. The first argument was that the phrase "public interest" was too vague a standard for delegating functions to the FCC. The Court disagreed and relied on an earlier broadcasting case in which it had said that the phrase "is as concrete as the complicated factors for judgment in such a field of delegated authority permit." The phrase is not to be interpreted as giving the FCC "unlimited power." Next, the Court rejected NBC's First Amendment claim:

> We come, finally, to an appeal to the First Amendment. The Regulations, even if valid in all other respects, must fall because they abridge, say the appellants, their right of free speech. If that be so, it would follow that every person whose application for a license is denied by the Commission is thereby denied his constitutional right of free speech. Freedom of utterance is abridged to many who wish to use the limited facilities of radio. Unlike other modes of expression, it is subject to governmental regulation. Because it cannot be used by all, some who wish to use it must be denied. But Congress did not authorize the Commission to choose among applicants upon the basis of their political, economic or social views, or upon any other capricious basis. If it did, or if the Commission by these Regulations proposed a choice among applicants upon some such basis, the issue before us would be wholly different. The question here is simply whether the Commission, by announcing that it will refuse licenses to persons who engage in specified network practices (a basis for choice, which we hold is comprehended within the statutory criterion of "public interest"), is thereby denying such persons the constitutional right of free speech. The right of free speech does not include, however, the right to use the facilities of radio without a license. The licensing system established by Congress in the Communications Act of 1934 was a proper exercise of its power over commerce. The standard it provided for the licensing of stations was the "public interest, convenience, or necessity." Denial of a station license on that ground, if valid under the Act, is not a denial of free speech.

Notes and Questions

1. The origin of the phrase, "public interest, convenience and necessity," § 309(a), or "public convenience, interest or necessity," § 307(a), is unclear from legislative documents. A former chairman of the Commission, Newton Minow, suggested the origin in Equal Time 8–9 (1964): Sen. Clarence C. Dill, who had played a major part in the early legislation, told Minow that the drafters had reached an impasse in attempting to define a regulatory standard for this new, uncharted activity. A young lawyer who had been loaned to the Senate by the Interstate Commerce Commission proposed the words because they were used in other federal statutes.

Judge Henry Friendly, in *The Federal Administrative Agencies* 54–55 (1962), commented on the standard:

> The only guideline supplied by Congress in the Communications Act of 1934 was "public convenience, interest, or necessity."

The standard of public convenience and necessity introduced into the federal statute book by Transportation Act, 1920, conveyed a fair degree of meaning when the issue was whether new or duplicating railroad construction should be authorized or an existing line abandoned. It was to convey less when, as under the Motor Carrier Act of 1935, or the Civil Aeronautics Act of 1938, there would be the added issue of selecting the applicant to render a service found to be needed; but under those statutes there would usually be some demonstrable factors, such as, in air route cases, ability to render superior one-plane or one-carrier service because of junction of the new route with existing ones, lower costs due to other operations, or historical connection with the traffic, that ought to have enabled the agency to develop intelligible criteria for selection. The standard was almost drained of meaning under section 307 of the Communications Act, where the issue was almost never the need for broadcasting service but rather who should render it.

2. The Radio Commission's first obligation was to clear the airwaves to avoid destructive interference. It decided in 1928 that "as between two broadcasting stations with otherwise equal claims for privileges, the station which has the longest record of continuous service has the superior right." Great Lakes Broadcasting Co., 3 F.R.C.Ann.Rep. 32 (1929), modified on other grounds 37 F.2d 993 (D.C.Cir.1930), certiorari dismissed 281 U.S. 706 (1930). In that case, involving three competing stations, the Commission also stated, however, that if there was a "substantial disparity" in the services being offered by the stations, "the claim of priority must give way to the superior service." The Commission was soon evaluating service in terms of program content. In *Great Lakes*, the Commission contented itself with noting that stations using formats that appeal to only a "small portion" of the public were not serving the public interest because each member of the listening public is entitled to service from each station in the community.

3. In its early years the Radio Commission showed no hesitation in denying renewal of licenses because of the content of the speech uttered over the station. Section 29 of the 1927 Act, reenacted as § 326 of the 1934 Act, provided in relevant part:

> Nothing in this Act shall be understood or construed to give the licensing authority the power of censorship over the radio communications or signals transmitted by any radio station, and no regulation or condition shall be promulgated or fixed by the licensing authority which shall interfere with the right of free speech by means of radio communication.

In 1930 the Commission denied renewal of a license to KFKB on the ground that the station was being controlled and used by Dr. J.R. Brinkley to further his personal interest. Dr. Brinkley had three half-hour programs daily in which he answered anonymous inquiries on health and medicine and usually recommended several of his own tonics and prescriptions that were known to the public only by numerical designations. Druggists paid a fee to Dr. Brinkley for each sale they made.

In affirming the denial of renewal, KFKB Broadcasting Association v. Federal Radio Commission, 47 F.2d 670 (D.C.Cir.1931), the court rejected the station's argument that the Commission had censored in violation of § 29:

> This contention is without merit. There has been no attempt on the part of the commission to subject any part of appellant's broadcasting matter to scrutiny prior to its release. In considering the question whether the public interest, convenience, or necessity will be served by a renewal of appellant's license, the commission has merely exercised its undoubted right to take note of appellant's past conduct, which is not censorship.

In Trinity Methodist Church, South v. Federal Radio Commission, 62 F.2d 850 (D.C.Cir.1932), certiorari denied 288 U.S. 599 (1933), the controlling figure was the minister of the church, Dr. Shuler, who regularly defamed government institutions and officials, and attacked labor groups and various religions. The Commission's denial of renewal was affirmed. The court concluded that the broadcasts "without facts to sustain or to justify them" might fairly be found not to be within the public interest:

> If it be considered that one in possession of a permit to broadcast in interstate commerce may, without let or hindrance from any source, use these facilities, reaching out, as they do, from one corner of the country to the other, to obstruct the administration of justice, offend the religious susceptibilities of thousands, inspire political distrust and civic discord, or offend youth and innocence by the free use of words suggestive of sexual immorality, and be answerable for slander only at the instance of the one offended, then this great science, instead of a boon, will become a scourge and the nation a theater for the display of individual passions and the collusion of personal interests. This is neither censorship nor previous restraint, nor is it a whittling away of the rights guaranteed by the First Amendment, or an impairment of their free exercise. Appellant may continue to indulge his strictures upon the characters of men in public office. He may just as freely as ever criticize religious practices of which he does not approve. He may even indulge private malice or personal slander—subject, of course, to being required to answer for the abuse thereof—but he may not, as we think, demand, of right, the continued use of an instrumentality of commerce for such purposes, or any other, except in subordination to all reasonable rules and regulations Congress, acting through the Commission, may prescribe.

4. The Supreme Court did not again consider the FCC's power until 26 years after *NBC*. Because this case, Red Lion v. Federal Communications Commission, affects everything else that follows, we consider it at the outset of our exploration of broadcasting law. The case deals fairly closely with the personal attack part of the broader fairness doctrine. The case also refers to the "equal opportunities" rule (sometimes incorrectly called the "equal time" rule), which applies during election campaigns. Although we look at each of these doctrines in detail in Chapter VI, including the FCC's 1987 decision eliminating much, if not all, of the fairness doctrine, we must introduce each one now so that *Red Lion* can be fully understood.

As part of the first Communications Act, Congress passed what is now § 315, which requires any broadcaster who sells or gives time for a candidate's use to treat all other candidates for the same office equally. This means, for example, that a broadcaster who sells a candidate for Congress 15 minutes of prime time, must be prepared to sell each opponent of that candidate 15 minutes of prime time at the same price.

The fairness doctrine, on the other hand, was not imposed by Congress. Developed by the Commission on its own in the 1940s, the doctrine has two separate parts. One part requires the broadcaster to air issues that "are so critical or of such great public importance that it would be unreasonable for a licensee to ignore them completely." Much more attention has been paid to the second part of the doctrine—that if a broadcaster does cover a "controversial issue of public importance" it must take steps to assure that important contrasting views are also presented. These views may be presented by the licensee itself or by speakers chosen by the licensee.

The personal attack aspect of the fairness doctrine emerged in decisions in which the FCC ordered stations that had broadcast programs attacking a person's character during a discussion of a controversial issue of public importance to inform the person and offer him time to present his side. The Red Lion case arose from such a situation.

While the Red Lion case was being litigated, the FCC decided to promulgate a formal rule to make the personal attack doctrine more precise and more readily enforceable. The personal attack rule applied when "during the presentation of views on a controversial issue of public importance, an attack is made upon the honesty, character, integrity, or like personal qualities of an identified person or group." Notice and an opportunity to respond were required.

At the same time the FCC decided to promulgate a formal political editorial rule providing that when a licensee editorially endorsed a candidate for political office, other candidates for the same office were to be advised of the endorsement and offered a reasonable opportunity to respond. The same opportunity was to be extended to any candidate who was attacked in an editorial.

As soon as these two formal rules were announced, the Radio Television News Directors Association (RTNDA) sued to declare the rules unconstitutional. The court of appeals agreed and held that the rules violated the First Amendment. The Supreme Court heard both cases together and decided them in the same opinion.

RED LION BROADCASTING CO. v. FEDERAL COMMUNICATIONS COMMISSION

Supreme Court of the United States, 1969.
395 U.S. 367, 89 S.Ct. 1794, 23 L.Ed.2d 371, 16 R.R.2d 2029, 1 Med.L.Rptr. 2053.

MR. JUSTICE WHITE delivered the opinion of the Court.

The Federal Communications Commission has for many years imposed on radio and television broadcasters the requirement that discussion of public issues be presented on broadcast stations, and that each side of those issues must be given fair coverage. This is known as the fairness doctrine, which originated very early in the history of broadcasting and has maintained its present outlines for some time. It is an obligation whose content has been defined in a long series of FCC rulings in particular cases, and which is distinct from the statutory requirement of § 315 of the Communications Act that equal time be allotted all qualified candidates for public office. Two aspects of the fairness doctrine, relating to personal attacks in the context of controversial public issues and to political editorializing, were codified more precisely in the form of FCC regulations in 1967. The two cases before us now, which were decided separately below, challenge the constitutional and statutory bases of the doctrine and component rules. *Red Lion* involves the application of the fairness doctrine to a particular broadcast, and *RTNDA* arises as an action to review the FCC's 1967 promulgation of the personal attack and political editorializing regulations, which were laid down after the *Red Lion* litigation had begun.

I.

A.

The Red Lion Broadcasting Company is licensed to operate a Pennsylvania radio station, WGCB. On November 27, 1964, WGCB carried a 15–minute broadcast by the Reverend Billy James Hargis as part of a "Christian Crusade" series. A book by Fred J. Cook entitled "Goldwater—Extremist on the Right" was discussed by Hargis, who said that Cook had been fired by a newspaper for making false charges against city officials; that Cook had then worked for a Communist-affiliated publication; that he had defended Alger Hiss and attacked J. Edgar Hoover and the Central Intelligence Agency; and that he had now written a "book to smear and destroy Barry Goldwater." When Cook heard of the broadcast he concluded that he had been personally attacked and demanded free reply time, which the station refused. After an exchange of letters among Cook, Red Lion, and the FCC, the FCC declared that the Hargis broadcast constituted a personal attack on Cook; that Red Lion had failed to meet its obligation under the fairness doctrine as expressed in Times–Mirror Broadcasting Co.,

24 P & F Radio Reg. 404 (1962), to send a tape, transcript, or summary of the broadcast to Cook and offer him reply time; and that the station must provide reply time whether or not Cook would pay for it. On review in the Court of Appeals for the District of Columbia Circuit, the FCC's position was upheld as constitutional and otherwise proper. [   ]

. . .

C.

Believing that the specific application of the fairness doctrine in *Red Lion,* and the promulgation of the regulations in *RTNDA,* are both authorized by Congress and enhance rather than abridge the freedoms of speech and press protected by the First Amendment, we hold them valid and constitutional, reversing the judgment, below in *RTNDA* and affirming the judgment below in *Red Lion.*

II.

The history of the emergence of the fairness doctrine and of the related legislation shows that the Commission's action in the *Red Lion* case did not exceed its authority, and that in adopting the new regulations the Commission was implementing congressional policy rather than embarking on a frolic of its own.

A.

Before 1927, the allocation of frequencies was left entirely to the private sector, and the result was chaos. It quickly became apparent that broadcast frequencies constituted a scarce resource whose use could be regulated and rationalized only by the Government. Without government control, the medium would be of little use because of the cacophony of competing voices, none of which could be clearly and predictably heard. Consequently, the Federal Radio Commission was established to allocate frequencies among competing applicants in a manner responsive to the public "convenience, interest, or necessity."

Very shortly thereafter the Commission expressed its view that the "public interest requires ample play for the free and fair competition of opposing views, and the commission believes that the principle applies . . . to all discussions of issues of importance to the public." . . . After an extended period during which the licensee was obliged not only to cover and to cover fairly the views of others, but also to refrain from expressing his own personal views, Mayflower Broadcasting Corp., 8 F.C.C. 333 (1940), the latter limitation on the licensee was abandoned and the doctrine developed into its present form.

There is a twofold duty laid down by the FCC's decisions and described by the 1949 Report on Editorializing by Broadcast Licensees, 13 F.C.C. 1246 (1949). The broadcaster must give adequate coverage to public issues, [   ], and coverage must be fair in that it accurately reflects the opposing views. [   ] This must be done at the broadcaster's own expense if sponsorship is unavailable. [   ] Moreover, the duty must be met by programming obtained at the licensee's own initiative if available from no other source. . . .

When a personal attack has been made on a figure involved in a public issue, both the doctrine of cases such as *Red Lion* and *Times Mirror Broadcasting Co.*, 24 P & F Radio Reg. 404 (1962), and also the 1967 regulations at issue in *RTNDA* require that the individual attacked himself be offered an opportunity to respond. Likewise, where one candidate is endorsed in a political editorial, the other candidates must themselves be offered reply time to use personally or through a spokesman. These obligations differ from the general fairness requirement that issues be presented, and presented with coverage of competing views, in that the broadcaster does not have the option of presenting the attacked party's side himself or choosing a third party to represent that side. But insofar as there is an obligation of the broadcaster to see that both sides are presented, and insofar as that is an affirmative obligation, the personal attack doctrine and regulations do not differ from the preceding fairness doctrine. The simple fact that the attacked men or unendorsed candidates may respond themselves or through agents is not a critical distinction, and indeed, it is not unreasonable for the FCC to conclude that the objective of adequate presentation of all sides may best be served by allowing those most closely affected to make the response, rather than leaving the response in the hands of the station which has attacked their candidacies, endorsed their opponents, or carried a personal attack upon them.

B.

The statutory authority of the FCC to promulgate these regulations derives from the mandate to the "Commission from time to time, as public convenience, interest, or necessity requires" to promulgate "such rules and regulations and prescribe such restrictions and conditions . . . as may be necessary to carry out the provisions of this chapter. . . ." 47 U.S.C. § 303 and § 303(r). The Commission is specifically directed to consider the demands of the public interest in the course of granting licenses, 47 U.S.C. §§ 307(a), 309(a); renewing them, 47 U.S.C. § 307; and modifying them. Ibid. Moreover, the FCC has included among the conditions of the Red Lion license itself the requirement that operation of the station be carried out in the public interest, 47 U.S.C. § 309(h). This mandate to the FCC to assure that broadcasters operate in the public interest is a broad one, a power "not niggardly but expansive," National Broadcasting Co. v. United States, 319 U.S. 190, 219 (1943), whose validity we have long upheld. [ ] It is broad enough to encompass these regulations.

The fairness doctrine finds specific recognition in statutory form, is in part modeled on explicit statutory provisions relating to political candidates, and is approvingly reflected in legislative history.

In 1959 the Congress amended the statutory requirement of § 315 that equal time be accorded each political candidate to except certain appearances on news programs, but added that this constituted no exception *"from the obligation imposed upon them under this Act to operate in the public interest and to afford reasonable opportunity for their discussion of conflicting views on issues of public importance."* Act of September 14, 1959, § 1, 73 Stat. 557, amending 47 U.S.C. § 315(a) (emphasis added). This language makes it very plain that Congress, in 1959, announced that the phrase "public interest," which had been in the Act since 1927, imposed a duty on broadcasters to discuss both sides of controversial public issues. In other words, the amendment vindicated the FCC's general view that the fairness doctrine inhered in the public interest standard. Subsequent legislation declaring the intent of an earlier statute is entitled to great weight in statutory construction. And here this principle is given special force by the equally venerable principle that the construction of a statute by those charged with its execution should be followed unless there are compelling indications that it is wrong, especially when Congress has refused to alter the administrative construction. Here, the Congress has not just kept its silence by refusing to overturn the administrative construction, but has ratified it with positive legislation. Thirty years of consistent administrative construction left undisturbed by Congress until 1959, when that construction was expressly accepted, reinforce the natural conclusion that the public interest language of the Act authorized the Commission to require licensees to use their stations for discussion of public issues, and that the FCC is free to implement this requirement by reasonable rules and regulations which fall short of abridgment of the freedom of speech and press, and of the censorship proscribed by § 326 of the Act.

The objectives of § 315 themselves could readily be circumvented but for the complementary fairness doctrine ratified by § 315. The section applies only to campaign appearances by candidates, and not by family, friends, campaign managers, or other supporters. Without the fairness doctrine, then, a licensee could ban all campaign appearances by candidates themselves from the air and proceed to deliver over his station entirely to the supporters of one slate of candidates, to the exclusion of all others. In this way the broadcaster could have a far greater impact on the favored candidacy than he could by simply allowing a spot appearance by the candidate himself. It is the fairness doctrine as an aspect of the obligation to operate in the public interest, rather than § 315, which prohibits the broadcaster from taking such a step.

. . .

In light of the fact that the "public interest" in broadcasting clearly encompasses the presentation of vigorous debate of controversial issues of importance and concern to the public; the fact that the FCC has rested upon that language from its very inception a doctrine that these issues must be discussed, and fairly; and the fact that Congress has acknowledged that the analogous provisions of § 315 are not preclusive in this area, and knowingly preserved the FCC's complementary efforts, we think the fairness doctrine and its component personal attack and political editorializing regulations are a legitimate exercise of congressionally delegated authority. . . .

III.

The broadcasters challenge the fairness doctrine and its specific manifestations in the personal attack and political editorial rules on conventional First Amendment grounds, alleging that the rules abridge their freedom of speech and press. Their contention is that the First Amendment protects their desire to use their allotted frequencies continuously to broadcast whatever they choose, and to exclude whomever they choose from ever using that frequency. No man may be prevented from saying or publishing what he thinks, or refusing in his speech or other utterances to give equal weight to the views of his opponents. This right, they say, applies equally to broadcasters.

A.

Although broadcasting is clearly a medium affected by a First Amendment interest, United States v. Paramount Pictures, Inc., 334 U.S. 131, 166 (1948), differences in the characteristics of new media justify differences in the First Amendment standards applied to them. [ ] For example, the ability of new technology to produce sounds more raucous than those of the human voice justifies restrictions on the sound level, and on the hours and places of use, of sound trucks so long as the restrictions are reasonable and applied without discrimination. [ ]

Just as the Government may limit the use of sound-amplifying equipment potentially so noisy that it drowns out civilized private speech, so may the Government limit the use of broadcast equipment. The right of free speech of a broadcaster, the user of a sound truck, or any other individual does not embrace a right to snuff out the free speech of others. Associated Press v. United States, 326 U.S. 1, 20 (1945).

When two people converse face to face, both should not speak at once if either is to be clearly understood. But the range of the human voice is so limited that there could be meaningful communications if half the people in the United States were talking and the other half listening. Just as clearly, half the people might publish and the other half read. But the reach of radio signals is incomparably greater than the range of the human voice and the problem of interference is a massive reality. The lack of know-how and equipment may keep many from the air but only a tiny fraction of those with resources and intelligence can hope to communicate by radio at the same time if intelligible communication is to be had, even if the entire radio spectrum is utilized in the present state of commercially acceptable technology.

It was this fact, and the chaos which ensued from permitting anyone to use any frequency at whatever power level he wished, which made necessary the enactment of the Radio Act of 1927 and the Communications Act of 1934, as the Court has noted at length before. National Broadcasting Co. v. United States, 319 U.S. 190, 210–214 (1943). It was this reality which at the very least necessitated first the division of the radio spectrum into portions reserved respectively for public broadcasting and for other important radio uses such as amateur operation, aircraft, police, defense, and navigation; and then the subdivision of each portion, and assignment of specific frequencies to individual users or groups of users. Beyond this, however, because the frequencies reserved for public broadcasting were limited in number, it was essential for the Government to tell some applicants that they could not broadcast at all because there was room for only a few.

Where there are substantially more individuals who want to broadcast than there are frequencies to allocate, it is idle to posit an unabridgeable First Amendment right to broadcast comparable to the right of every individual to speak, write, or publish. If 100 persons want broadcast licenses but there are only 10 frequencies to allocate, all of them may have the same "right" to a license; but if there is to be any effective communication by radio, only a few can be licensed and the rest must be barred from the airwaves. It would be strange if the First Amendment, aimed at protecting and furthering communications, prevented the Government from making radio communication possible by requiring licenses to broadcast and by limiting the number of licenses so as not to overcrowd the spectrum.

This has been the consistent view of the Court. Congress unquestionably has the power to grant and deny licenses and to eliminate existing stations. FRC v. Nelson Bros. Bond & Mortgage Co., 289 U.S. 266 (1933). No one has a First Amendment right to a license or to monopolize a radio frequency; to deny a station license because "the public interest" requires it "is not a denial of free speech." National Broadcasting Co. v. United States, 319 U.S. 190, 227 (1943).

By the same token, as far as the First Amendment is concerned those who are licensed stand no better than those to whom licenses are refused. A license permits broadcasting, but the licensee has no constitutional right to be the one who holds the license or to monopolize a radio frequency to the exclusion of his fellow citizens. There is nothing in the First Amendment which prevents the Government from requiring a licensee to share his frequency with others and to conduct himself as a proxy or fiduciary with obligations to present those views and voices which are representative of his community and which would otherwise, by necessity, be barred from the airwaves.

This is not to say that the First Amendment is irrelevant to public broadcasting. On the contrary, it has a major role to play as the Congress itself recognized in § 326, which forbids FCC interference with "the right of free speech by means of radio communication." Because of the scarcity of radio frequencies, the Government is permitted to put restraints on licensees in favor of others whose views should be expressed on this unique medium. But the people as a whole retain their interest in free speech by radio and their collective right to have the medium function consistently with the ends and purposes of the First Amendment. It is the right of the viewers and listeners, not the right of the broadcasters, which is paramount. See FCC v. Sanders Bros. Radio Station, 309 U.S. 470, 475 (1940); FCC v. Allentown Broadcasting Corp., 349 U.S. 358, 361–362 (1955); 2 Z. Chafee, Government and Mass Communications 546 (1947). It is the purpose of the First Amendment to preserve an uninhibited marketplace of ideas in which truth will ultimately prevail, rather than to countenance monopolization of that market, whether it be by the Government itself or a private licensee. Associated Press v. United States, 326 U.S. 1, 20 (1945); New York Times Co. v. Sullivan, 376 U.S. 254, 270 (1964); Abrams v. United States, 250 U.S. 616, 630 (1919) (Holmes, J., dissenting). "[S]peech concerning public affairs is more than self-expression; it is the essence of self-government." Garrison v. Louisiana, 379 U.S. 64, 74–75 (1964). See Brennan, The Supreme Court and the Meiklejohn Interpretation of the First Amendment, 79 Harv.L.Rev. 1 (1965). It is the right of the public to receive suitable access to social, political, esthetic, moral, and other ideas and experiences which is crucial here. That right may not constitutionally be abridged either by Congress or by the FCC.

B.

Rather than confer frequency monopolies on a relatively small number of licensees, in a Nation of 200,000,000, the Government could surely have decreed that each frequency should be shared among all or some of those who wish to use it, each being assigned a portion of the broadcast day or the broadcast week. The ruling and regulations at issue here do not go quite so far. They assert that under specified circumstances, a licensee must offer to make available a reasonable amount of broadcast time to those who have a view different from that which has already been expressed on his station. The expression of a political endorsement, or of a personal attack while dealing with a controversial public issue, simply triggers this time sharing. As we have said, the First Amendment confers no right on licensees to prevent others from broadcasting on "their" frequencies and no right to an unconditional monopoly of a scarce resource which the Government has denied others the right to use.

In terms of constitutional principle, and as enforced sharing of a scarce resource, the personal attack and political editorial rules are indistinguishable from the equal-time provision of § 315, a specific enactment of Congress requiring stations to set aside reply time under specified circumstances and to which the fairness doctrine and these constituent regulations are important complements. That provision, which has been part of the law since 1927, Radio Act of 1927, § 18, 44 Stat. 1170, has been held valid by this Court as an obligation of the licensee relieving him of any power in any way to prevent or censor the broadcast, and thus, insulating him from liability for defamation. The constitutionality of the statute under the First Amendment was unquestioned. Farmers Educ. & Coop. Union v. WDAY, 360 U.S. 525 (1959).

Nor can we say that it is inconsistent with the First Amendment goal of producing an informed public capable of conducting its own affairs to require a broadcaster to permit answers to personal attacks occurring in the course of discussing controversial issues, or to require that the political opponents of those endorsed by the station be given a chance to communicate with the public.[18] Otherwise, station owners and a few networks would have unfettered power to make time available only to the highest bidders, to communicate only their own views on public issues, people and candidates, and to permit on the air only those with whom they agreed. There is no sanctuary in the First Amendment for unlimited private censorship operating in a medium not open to all. "Freedom of the press from governmental interference under the First Amendment does not sanction repression of that freedom by private interests." Associated Press v. United States, 326 U.S. 1, 20 (1945).

C.

It is strenuously argued, however, that if political editorials or personal attacks will trigger an obligation in broadcasters to afford the opportunity for expression to speakers who need not pay for time and whose views are unpalatable to the licensees, then broadcasters will be irresistibly forced to self-censorship and their coverage of controversial public issues will be eliminated or at least rendered wholly ineffective. Such a result would indeed be a serious matter, for should licensees actually eliminate their coverage of controversial issues, the purposes of the doctrine would be stifled.

At this point, however, as the Federal Communications Commission has indicated, that possibility is at best speculative. The communications industry, and in particular the networks, have taken pains to present controversial issues in the past, and even now they do not assert that they intend to abandon their efforts in this regard. It would be better if the FCC's encouragement were never necessary to induce the broadcasters to meet their responsibility. And if experience with the administration of these doctrines indicates that they have the net effect of reducing rather than enhancing the volume and quality of coverage, there will be time enough to reconsider the constitutional

---

18. The expression of views opposing those which broadcasters permit to be aired in the first place need not be confined solely to the broadcasters themselves as proxies. "Nor is it enough that he should hear the arguments of adversaries from his own teachers, presented as they state them, and accompanied by what they offer as refutations. That is not the way to do justice to the arguments, or bring them into real contact with his own mind. He must be able to hear them from persons who actually believe them; who defend them in earnest, and do their very utmost for them." J. Mill, On Liberty 32 (R. McCallum ed. 1947).

implications. The fairness doctrine in the past has had no such overall effect.

That this will occur now seems unlikely, however, since if present licensees should suddenly prove timorous, the Commission is not power-less to insist that they give adequate and fair attention to public issues. It does not violate the First Amendment to treat licensees given the privilege of using scarce radio frequencies as proxies for the entire community, obligated to give suitable time and attention to matters of great public concern. To condition the granting or renewal of licenses on a willingness to present representative community views on contro-versial issues is consistent with the ends and purposes of those constitu-tional provisions forbidding the abridgment of freedom of speech and freedom of the press. Congress need not stand idly by and permit those with licenses to ignore the problems which beset the people or to exclude from the airways anything but their own views of fundamental questions. The statute, long administrative practice, and cases are to this effect.

Licenses to broadcast do not confer ownership of designated fre-quencies, but only the temporary privilege of using them. 47 U.S.C. § 301. Unless renewed, they expire within three years. 47 U.S.C. § 307(d). The statute mandates the issuance of licenses if the "public convenience, interest, or necessity will be served thereby." 47 U.S.C. § 307(a). In applying this standard the Commission for 40 years has been choosing licensees based in part on their program proposals. In FRC v. Nelson Bros. Bond & Mortgage Co., 289 U.S. 266, 279 (1933), the Court noted that in "view of the limited number of available broadcast-ing frequencies the Congress has authorized allocation and licenses." In determining how best to allocate frequencies, the Federal Radio Commission considered the needs of competing communities and the programs offered by competing stations to meet those needs; moreover, if needs or programs shifted the Commission could alter its allocations to reflect those shifts. Id., at 285. . . .

D.

The litigants embellish their First Amendment arguments with the contention that the regulations are so vague that their duties are impossible to discern. Of this point it is enough to say that, judging the validity of the regulations on their face as they are presented here, we cannot conclude that the FCC has been left a free hand to vindicate its own idiosyncratic conception of the public interest or of the require-ments of free speech. . . .

We need not and do not now ratify every past and future decision by the FCC with regard to programming. There is no question here of the Commission's refusal to permit the broadcaster to carry a particu-lar program or to publish his own views; of a discriminatory refusal to require the licensee to broadcast certain views which have been denied access to the airwaves; of government censorship of a particular program contrary to § 326; or of the official government view dominating public broadcasting. Such questions would raise more serious First Amendment issues. But we do hold that the Congress and the Commission do not violate the First Amendment when they require a radio or television station to give reply time to answer personal attacks and political editorials.

E.

It is argued that even if at one time the lack of available frequencies for all who wished to use them justified the Government's choice of those who would best serve the public interest by acting as proxy for those who would present differing views, or by giving the latter access directly to broadcast facilities, this condition no longer prevails so that continuing control is not justified. To this there are several answers.

Scarcity is not entirely a thing of the past. Advances in technology, such as microwave transmission, have led to more efficient utilization of the frequency spectrum, but uses for that spectrum have also grown apace. Portions of the spectrum must be reserved for vital uses unconnected with human communication, such as radio-navigational aids used by aircraft and vessels. Conflicts have even emerged between such vital functions as defense preparedness and experimentation in methods of averting midair collisions through radio warning devices. "Land mobile services" such as police, ambulance, fire department, public utility, and other communications systems have been occupying an increasingly crowded portion of the frequency spectrum and there are, apart from the licensed amateur radio operators' equipment, 5,000,000 transmitters operated on the "citizens' band" which is also increasingly congested. Among the various uses for radio frequency space, including marine, aviation, amateur, military, and common carrier users, there are easily enough claimants to permit use of the whole with an even smaller allocation to broadcast radio and television uses than now exists.

Comparative hearings between competing applicants for broadcast spectrum space are by no means a thing of the past. The radio spectrum has become so congested that at times it has been necessary to suspend new applications. The very high frequency television spectrum is, in the country's major markets, almost entirely occupied, although space reserved for ultra high frequency television transmission, which is a relatively recent development as a commercially viable alternative, has not yet been completely filled.[25]

The rapidity with which technological advances succeed one another to create more efficient use of spectrum space on the one hand, and to create new uses for that space by ever growing numbers of people on the other, makes it unwise to speculate on the future allocation of that space. It is enough to say that the resource is one of considerable and growing importance whose scarcity impelled its regulation by an agency authorized by Congress. Nothing in this record, or in our own researches, convinces us that the resource is no longer one for which

---

25. See note 25 on page 81.

there are more immediate and potential uses than can be accommodated, and for which wise planning is essential. This does not mean, of course, that every possible wavelength must be occupied at every hour by some vital use in order to sustain the congressional judgment. The substantial capital investment required for many uses, in addition to the potentiality for confusion and interference inherent in any scheme for continuous kaleidoscopic reallocation of all available space may make this unfeasible. The allocation need not be made at such a breakneck pace that the objectives of the allocation are themselves imperiled.

Even where there are gaps in spectrum utilization, the fact remains that existing broadcasters have often attained their present position because of their initial government selection in competition with others before new technological advances opened new opportunities for further uses. Long experience in broadcasting, confirmed habits of listeners and viewers, network affiliation, and other advantages in program procurement give existing broadcasters a substantial advantage over new entrants, even where new entry is technologically possible. These advantages are the fruit of a preferred position conferred by the Government. Some present possibility for new entry by competing stations is not enough, in itself, to render unconstitutional the Government's effort to assure that a broadcaster's programming ranges widely enough to serve the public interest.

25. In a table prepared by the FCC on the basis of statistics current as of August 31, 1968, VHF and UHF channels allocated to and those available in the top 100 market areas for television are set forth:

Commercial

Market Areas	Channels Allocated		Channels On the Air, Authorized, or Applied for		Available Channels	
	VHF	UHF	VHF	UHF	VHF	UHF
Top 10	40	45	40	44	0	1
Top 50	157	163	157	136	0	27
Top 100	264	297	264	213	0	84

Noncommercial

Market Areas	Channels Reserved		Channels On the Air, Authorized, or Applied for		Available Channels	
	VHF	UHF	VHF	UHF	VHF	UHF
Top 10	7	17	7	16	0	1
Top 50	21	79	20	47	1	32
Top 100	35	138	34	69	1	69

1968 FCC Annual Report 132–135.

In view of the scarcity of broadcast frequencies, the Government's role in allocating those frequencies, and the legitimate claims of those unable without governmental assistance to gain access to those frequencies for expression of their views, we hold the regulations and ruling at issue here are both authorized by statute and constitutional.[28]   The judgment of the Court of Appeals in *Red Lion* is affirmed and that in *RTNDA* reversed and the causes remanded for proceedings consistent with this opinion.

It is so ordered.

Not having heard oral argument in these cases, MR. JUSTICE DOUG-LAS took no part in the Court's decision.

Notes and Questions

1.   The Court states that the differences among the technical aspects of media warrant different regulatory treatment.   Compare Jackson, J., concurring, in Kovacs v. Cooper, 336 U.S. 77, 97 (1949): "The moving picture screen, the radio, the newspaper, the handbill, the sound truck and the street corner orator have differing natures, values, abuses and dangers.   Each, in my view, is a law unto itself."

2.   The Court states that only a tiny fraction of those who want to broadcast are able to do so "even if the entire radio spectrum is utilized."   Who decided how much of the spectrum to allocate to radio?   Could a niggardly or inefficient allocation of radio space justify government exercise of its regulatory power?   The notion of "scarcity" plays a major role in the Court's analysis.   What does the term appear to mean in the opinion?

Consider whether scarcity is present in the following contexts: (a) all three radio outlets allocated to a community are being used; (b) of the five radio outlets allocated, three are being used; (c) all 40 radio outlets allocated to an urban area are being used; (d) seven of the 40 outlets are vacant.

3.   Does Justice White's next-to-last paragraph suggest that the reality of scarcity in the past will be enough to justify continuing regulation even if it were determined that no scarcity exists today?

4.   Justice White says that "It is the right of the viewers and listeners, not the right of the broadcasters, which is paramount.   [   ]   It is the

---

28. We need not deal with the argument that even if there is no longer a technological scarcity of frequencies limiting the number of broadcasters, there nevertheless is an economic scarcity in the sense that the Commission could or does limit entry to the broadcasting market on economic grounds and license no more stations than the market will support. Hence, it is said, the fairness doctrine or its equivalent is essential to satisfy the claims of those excluded and of the public generally. A related argument, which we also put aside, is that quite apart from scarcity of frequencies, technological or economic, Congress does not abridge freedom of speech or press by legislation directly or indirectly multiplying the voices and views presented to the public through time sharing, fairness doctrines, or other devices which limit or dissipate the power of those who sit astride the channels of communication with the general public. Cf. Citizen Pub. Co. v. United States, 394 U.S. 131 (1969).

purpose of the First Amendment to preserve an uninhibited market-place of ideas in which truth will ultimately prevail, rather than to countenance monopolization of that market, whether it be by the Government itself or a private licensee." What philosophical strands are being brought together here?

When Justice White says that the "right" involved in the case belongs to "the public" and that this "right may not constitutionally be abridged either by Congress or by the FCC," is he suggesting that the absence of governmental control of broadcasters' programming would deny the public's constitutional right to "receive suitable access to social, political, esthetic, moral and other ideas and experiences?"

5. There is reason to believe that Fred Cook's demand for reply time was part of a broader effort to use the fairness doctrine to soften attacks on the Kennedy administration by right-wing political commentators. The plan was to monitor right-wing programs and then to demand balance under the general fairness doctrine. F. Friendly, The Good Guys, The Bad Guys and the First Amendment (1976). If the result was that licensees cancelled several right-wing commentators, would that affect your reaction to the *Red Lion* decision? Did Cook misuse the doctrine?

6. By concentrating on the scarcity issue and declaring that the rights of the listeners were paramount, the Court seemed to be agreeing with scholars like law professor Jerome Barron, who argued that the development of mass media had reduced the "marketplace of ideas" to a romantic fantasy. Reasoning that increased concentration in media ownership had resulted in a marketplace failure, Barron contended that a government-created right of access to the media was not just allowed, but indeed required by the First Amendment.

Barron did not limit this to broadcasting, however. Due to economic as opposed to technological scarcity, the number of daily newspapers in this country had been reduced to the point where he felt the same arguments should apply. It was not very long before he had his chance to argue this point before the Supreme Court. Miami Herald Publishing Co. v. Tornillo, 418 U.S. 241, 1 Med.L.Rptr. 1898 (1974), involved a Florida right-of-reply statute which provided a political candidate attacked by a newspaper space to respond.

The Court unanimously ruled the statute unconstitutional under the First Amendment. The Court argued that requiring a newspaper to print replies interfered with the editorial discretion of the publisher and had a "chilling effect" on the publisher's First Amendment rights. "Faced with the penalties that would accrue to any newspaper that published news or commentary arguably within the reach of the right-of-access statute, editors might well conclude that the safe course is to avoid controversy. Therefore, under the operation of the Florida statute, political and electoral coverage would be blunted or reduced."

What was especially interesting about the case, however, was that there were no references to *Red Lion*. Are the two cases in any way contradictory? Is it relevant that there are approximately seven to eight times as many radio stations in this country as there are daily newspapers? Or that there are fewer than 40 cities in the entire country with more than one daily newspaper? Is there a difference between technological and economic scarcity?

7. Aside from the spectrum scarcity arguments there are intrinsic differences between print and broadcast media. There is a physical limit to the number of words that can be uttered intelligibly over a broadcasting facility during a 24–hour day. Based on an estimate of about 200,000 words, using normal speaking patterns, one author suggests that a newspaper is the equivalent of between one and three 24–hour programs. But newspaper readers can at any time go directly to what interests them and skim or ignore the rest. In broadcasting, the choice is made for the listener by the broadcaster; the speed, content and sequence are fixed. Baxter, Regulation and Diversity in Communications Media, 64 Am.Econ.Rev. 392 (1974). Might such differences justify greater regulation of broadcasting?

On the other hand, broadcasting is an inelastic medium. In order to carry a response by the subject of a personal attack, the broadcaster must drop other programming. In contrast, a newspaper does have the option of adding pages. Does this mean that the chilling effect of forced access is greater for the broadcast media?

8. Other differences between the print and electronic media emphasize the greater impact of broadcasting in conveying certain types of information. The vivid telecasts during the Vietnam War are thought to have been a strong factor in the shift of public attitude against that war, beyond the potential of any verbal journalism. Another major difference is the role of sound in broadcasting, which makes it possible to use songs and jingles effectively in advertising. During the discussion of the broadcast advertising of cigarettes, one court observed:

> Written messages are not communicated unless they are read, and reading requires an affirmative act. Broadcast messages, in contrast, are "in the air." In an age of omnipresent radio, there scarcely breathes a citizen who does not know some part of a leading cigarette jingle by heart. Similarly, an ordinary habitual television watcher can *avoid* these commercials only by frequently leaving the room, changing the channel, or doing some other such affirmative act. It is difficult to calculate the subliminal impact of this pervasive propaganda, which may be heard even if not listened to, but it may reasonably be thought greater than the impact of the written word.

Banzhaf v. Federal Communications Commission, 405 F.2d 1082, 1100–01, 14 R.R.2d 2061, 1 Med.L.Rptr. 2037 (D.C.Cir.1968), certiorari denied 396 U.S. 842 (1969). Does this suggest an additional basis for regulating some aspects of broadcasting?

Does the *Banzhaf* view of broadcasting imply a "captive audience" comparable to the addressees of sound trucks in residential neighborhoods or political advertisements in mass transit vehicles? Is turning off the program like averting your eyes from offensive wording on someone's jacket? Is it relevant to this aspect of the discussion that most television sets and radios are in private homes? These questions are the focus of Federal Communications Commission v. Pacifica Foundation, which is discussed in Chapter VII.

9. The Supreme Court returned to the question of forced access once again in Columbia Broadcasting System, Inc. v. Democratic National Committee, 412 U.S. 94, 27 R.R.2d 907, 1 Med.L.Rptr. 1855 (1973). The Court decided that broadcasters were not obligated to accept paid advertisements from "responsible" individuals and groups. The majority relied upon *Red Lion.*

Justice Stewart, in a separate concurring opinion, stated, "I agreed with the Court in *Red Lion,* although with considerable doubt, because I thought that that much Government regulation of program content was within the outer limits of First Amendment tolerability."

In another concurring opinion, Justice Douglas stated of *Red Lion:* "I did not participate in that decision and, with all respect, would not support it. The Fairness Doctrine has no place in our First Amendment regime." He argued that the uniqueness of the spectrum was "due to engineering and technical problems. But the press in a realistic sense is likewise not available to all. Small or 'underground' papers appear and disappear; and the weekly is an established institution. But the daily papers now established are unique in the sense that it would be virtually impossible for a competitor to enter the field due to the financial exigencies of this era. The result is that in practical terms the newspapers and magazines, like TV and radio, are available only to a selected few."

10. The most recent extended discussion of the bases for regulating broadcasting occurred in Federal Communications Commission v. League of Women Voters of California. The three plaintiffs were the League, which wished to persuade public noncommercial educational broadcasters to take editorial positions; a listener who wished to hear such editorials; and a noncommercial broadcaster that wished to take editorial stands. The impediment was § 399 of the Public Broadcasting Act of 1967, as amended in 1981:

> No noncommercial educational broadcasting station which receives a grant from the Corporation for Public Broadcasting under subpart C of this part may engage in editorializing. No noncommercial educational broadcasting station may support or oppose any candidate for public office.

The case in fact centered on the first sentence of the section, which most of the justices thought severable from the second sentence. The core of the decision, centering on the nature of "public broadcasting," is reprinted in Chapter VIII. Here we focus on the majority's background discussion of the bases for regulating broadcasting.

The issue arose in the context of determining the "appropriate standard of review." The trial court, whose judgment of unconstitutionality was on direct review, had held that § 399 could survive constitutional scrutiny only if it served a "compelling" governmental interest. The FCC argued that a less demanding standard was appropriate. It based this argument in part on the "special characteristic" of spectrum scarcity and in part on the unique role of noncommercial broadcasting in this country.

The response of the five-member majority follows.

FEDERAL COMMUNICATIONS COMMISSION v. LEAGUE OF WOMEN VOTERS OF CALIFORNIA

Supreme Court of the United States, 1984.

468 U.S. 364, 104 S.Ct. 3106, 82 L.Ed.2d 278, 56 R.R.2d 547, 10 Med.L.Rptr. 1937.

[After setting forth the facts discussed in the introduction to this case, *supra*, and reviewing the history of noncommercial broadcasting, Justice Brennan addressed the appropriate standard of review in the following passage:]

JUSTICE BRENNAN delivered the opinion of the Court.

.   .   .

At first glance, of course, it would appear that the District Court applied the correct standard. Section 399 plainly operates to restrict the expression of editorial opinion on matters of public importance, and, as we have repeatedly explained, communication of this kind is entitled to the most exacting degree of First Amendment protection. [ ] Were a similar ban on editorializing applied in newspapers and magazines, we would not hesitate to strike it down as violative of the First Amendment. E.g., Mills v. Alabama, 384 U.S. 214 (1966). But, as the Government correctly notes, because broadcast regulation involves unique considerations, our cases have not followed precisely the same approach that we have applied to other media and have never gone so far as to demand that such regulations serve "compelling" governmental interests. At the same time, we think the Government's argument loses sight of concerns that are important in this area and thus misapprehends the essential meaning of our prior decisions concerning the reach of Congress' authority to regulate broadcast communication.

The fundamental principles that guide our evaluation of broadcast regulation are by now well established. First we have long recognized that Congress, acting pursuant to the Commerce Clause, has power to regulate the use of this scarce and valuable national resource. The distinctive feature of Congress' efforts in this area has been to ensure through the regulatory oversight of the FCC that only those who satisfy the "public interest, convenience and necessity" are granted a license to use radio and television broadcast frequencies. 47 U.S.C. § 309(a).[11]

Second, Congress may, in the exercise of this power, seek to assure that the public receives through this medium a balanced presentation of information on issues of public importance that otherwise might not be addressed if control of the medium were left entirely in the hands of those who own and operate broadcasting stations. Although such governmental regulation has never been allowed with respect to the print media, [*Tornillo*, p. 83, *supra*], we have recognized that "differences in the characteristics of new media justify differences in the First Amendment standards applied to them." [*Red Lion*, p. 71, *supra*]. The fundamental distinguishing characteristic of the new medium of broadcasting that, in our view, has required some adjustment in First Amendment analysis is that "[b]roadcasting frequencies are a scarce resource [that] must be portioned out among applicants." Columbia Broadcasting System, Inc. v. Democratic National Committee, 412 U.S. 94, 101 (1973). Thus, our cases have taught that, given spectrum scarcity, those who are granted a license to broadcast must serve in a sense as fiduciaries for the public by presenting "those views and voices which are representative of his community and which would otherwise, by necessity, be barred from the airwaves." *Red Lion*, supra, at 389. As we observed in that case, because "[i]t is the purpose of the First Amendment to preserve an uninhibited marketplace of ideas in which truth will ultimately prevail, . . . the right of the public to receive suitable access to social, political, esthetic, moral and other ideas and experiences [through the medium of broadcasting] is crucial here [and it] may not constitutionally be abridged either by the Congress or the FCC." Id., at 390.

Finally, although the government's interest in ensuring balanced coverage of public issues is plainly both important and substantial, we have, at the same time, made clear that broadcasters are engaged in a vital and independent form of communicative activity. As a result, the First Amendment must inform and give shape to the manner in which Congress exercises its regulatory power in this area. Unlike common carriers, broadcasters are "entitled under the First Amendment to exercise 'the widest journalistic freedom consistent with their public [duties].'" Columbia Broadcasting System, Inc. v. FCC, 453 U.S. 367, 395 (1981) (quoting Columbia Broadcasting System, Inc. v. Democratic National Committee, supra, at 110). See also FCC v. Midwest Video Corp., 440 U.S. 689, 703 (1979). Indeed, if the public's interest in

---

11. [ ].

The prevailing rationale for broadcast regulation based on spectrum scarcity has come under increasing criticism in recent years. Critics, including the incumbent Chairman of the FCC, charge that with the advent of cable and satellite television technology, communities now have access to such a wide variety of stations that the scarcity doctrine is obsolete. See, e.g., Fowler & Brenner, A Marketplace Approach to Broadcast Regulation, 60 Tex. L.Rev. 207, 221–226 (1982). We are not prepared, however, to reconsider our longstanding approach without some signal from Congress or the FCC that technological developments have advanced so far that some revision of the system of broadcast regulation may be required.

receiving a balanced presentation of views is to be fully served, we must necessarily rely in large part upon the editorial initiative and judgment of the broadcasters who bear the public trust. See Columbia Broadcasting System, Inc. v. Democratic National Committee, supra, at 124–127.

Our prior cases illustrate these principles. In *Red Lion*, for example, we upheld the FCC's "fairness doctrine"—which requires broadcasters to provide adequate coverage of public issues and to ensure that this coverage fairly and accurately reflects the opposing views—because the doctrine advanced the substantial governmental interest in ensuring balanced presentations of views in this limited medium and yet posed no threat that a "broadcaster [would be denied permission] to carry a particular program or to publish his own views." Id., at 396.[12] Similarly, in Columbia Broadcasting System, Inc. v. FCC, supra, the Court upheld the right of access for federal candidates imposed by § 312(a)(7) of the Communications Act both because that provision "makes a significant contribution to freedom of expression by enhancing the ability of candidates to present, and the public to receive, information necessary for the effective operation of the democratic process," id., at 396, and because it defined a sufficiently *"limited* right of 'reasonable' access" so that "the discretion of broadcasters to present their views on any issue or to carry any particular type of programming" was not impaired. Id., at 396–397 (emphasis in original). Finally, in Columbia Broadcasting System, Inc. v. Democratic National Committee, supra, the Court affirmed the FCC's refusal to require broadcast licensees to accept all paid political advertisements. Although it was argued that such a requirement would serve the public's First Amendment interest in receiving additional views on public issues, the Court rejected this approach, finding that such a requirement would tend to transform broadcasters into common carriers and would intrude unnecessarily upon the editorial discretion of broadcasters. 412 U.S., at 123–125. The FCC's ruling, therefore, helped to advance the important purposes of the Communications Act, grounded in the First Amendment, of preserving the right of broadcasters to exercise "the widest journalistic freedom consistent with [their] public obligations," and of guarding against "the risk of an enlargement of Government control over the broadcast discussion of public issues." 412 U.S., at 110, 127.[13]

12. We note that the FCC, observing that "[i]f any substantial possibility exists that the [fairness doctrine] rules have impeded, rather than furthered, First Amendment objectives, repeal may be warranted on that ground alone," has tentatively concluded that the rules, by effectively chilling speech, do not serve the public interest, and has therefore proposed to repeal them. Notice of Proposed Rulemaking In re Repeal or Modification of the Personal Attack and Political Editorial Rules, 48 Fed.Reg. 28295, 28298, 28301 (June 21, 1983). Of course, the Commission may, in the exercise of its discretion, decide to modify or abandon these rules, and we express no view on the legality of either course. As we recognized in *Red Lion*, however, were it to be shown by the Commission that the fairness doctrine "has the effect of reducing rather than enhancing" speech, we would then be forced to reconsider the constitutional basis of our decision in that case. 395 U.S., at 393.

13. This Court's decision in FCC v. Pacifica Foundation, 438 U.S. 726 (1978), upholding an exercise of the Commission's authority to regulate broadcasts containing "indecent" language as applied to a partic-

Thus, although the broadcasting industry plainly operates under restraints not imposed upon other media, the thrust of these restrictions has generally been to secure the public's First Amendment interest in receiving a balanced presentation of views on diverse matters of public concern. As a result of these restrictions, of course, the absolute freedom to advocate one's own positions without also presenting opposing viewpoints—a freedom enjoyed, for example, by newspaper publishers and soapbox orators—is denied to broadcasters. But, as our cases attest, these restrictions have been upheld only when we were satisfied that the restriction is narrowly tailored to further a substantial governmental interest, such as ensuring adequate and balanced coverage of public issues. [ ] Making that judgment requires a critical examination of the interests of the public and broadcasters in light of the particular circumstances of each case. E.g., FCC v. Pacifica Foundation, supra.

[Justice Brennan then turned to a consideration of the specifics of this case. His discussion of this issue, and the opinions of the dissenting justices are reprinted in Chapter VIII.]

Notes and Questions

1. Opponents of content regulation of broadcasting took footnotes 11 and 12 as a sign that the Court was willing to reconsider the First Amendment status of broadcasters. The *1985 Fairness Report,* to be discussed in Chapter VI, was considered by many to be a specific response to these footnotes.

2. In 1986 the scarcity rationale was sharply criticized by the court of appeals. Telecommunications Research and Action Center v. Federal Communications Commission, 801 F.2d 501, 61 R.R.2d 330, 13 Med. L.Rptr. 1881, rehearing denied 806 F.2d 1115, 61 R.R.2d 1342, 13 Med.L.Rptr. 1896 (D.C.Cir.1986), certiorari denied 482 U.S. 919 (1987). The case was an appeal of the Commission's refusal to apply the political broadcast rules to teletext and is discussed in Chapter X. The court acknowledged that it was bound by *Red Lion,* but questioned the Supreme Court's reliance on scarcity as a rationale for distinguishing between the broadcast and print media:

ular afternoon broadcast of a George Carlin monologue, is consistent with the approach taken in our other broadcast cases. There, the Court focused on certain physical characteristics of broadcasting—specifically, that the medium's uniquely pervasive presence renders impossible any prior warning for those listeners who may be offended by indecent language, and, second, that the ease with which children may gain access to the medium, especially during daytime hours, creates a substantial risk that they may be exposed to such offensive expression without parental supervision. Id., at 748–749. The governmental interest in reduction of those risks through Commission regulation of the timing and character of such "indecent broadcasting" was thought sufficiently substantial to outweigh the broadcaster's First Amendment interest in controlling the presentation of its programming. Id., at 750. In this case, by contrast, we are faced not with indecent expression, but rather with expression that is at the core of First Amendment protections, and no claim is made by the Government that the expression of editorial opinion by noncommercial stations will create a substantial "nuisance" of the kind addressed in FCC v. Pacifica Foundation.

. . . The basic difficulty in this entire area is that the line drawn between the print media and the broadcast media, resting as it does on the physical scarcity of the latter, is a distinction without a difference. Employing the scarcity concept as an analytic tool, particularly with respect of new and unforeseen technologies, inevitably leads to strained reasoning and artificial results.

It is certainly true that broadcast frequencies are scarce but it is unclear why that fact justifies content regulation of broadcasting in a way that would be intolerable if applied to the editorial process of the print media. All economic goods are scarce, not least the newsprint, ink, delivery trucks, computers, and other resources that go into the production and dissemination of print journalism. Not everyone who wishes to publish a newspaper, or even a pamphlet, may do so. Since scarcity is a universal fact, it can hardly explain regulation in one context and not another. The attempt to use a universal fact as a distinguishing principle necessarily leads to analytical confusion.

Neither is content regulation explained by the fact that broadcasters face the problem of interference, so that the government must define usable frequencies and protect those frequencies from encroachment. This governmental definition of frequencies is another instance of a universal fact that does not offer an explanatory principle for differing treatment. A publisher can deliver his newspapers only because government provides streets and regulates traffic on the streets by allocating rights of way. Yet no one would contend that the necessity for these governmental functions, which are certainly analogous to the government's function in allocating broadcast frequencies, could justify regulation of the content of a newspaper to ensure that it serves the needs of citizens.

There may be ways to reconcile *Red Lion* and *Tornillo* but the "scarcity" of broadcast frequencies does not appear capable of doing so. Perhaps the Supreme Court will one day revisit this area of the law and either eliminate the distinction between print and broadcast media, surely by pronouncing *Tornillo* applicable to both, or announce a constitutional distinction that is more usable than the present one.

How convincing is the court's critique? What constitutional distinction might the court find more usable than the scarcity rationale?

B. IS BROADCASTING "GOVERNMENT ACTION"?

The issues raised in *NBC, Red Lion* and *League of Women Voters* revolve around the broadcaster's claim that the First Amendment protects it from government regulation. Sometimes claims in the name of the First Amendment are made by private citizens against the media. In *Tornillo,* the citizen's claim failed. But when such a claim is made against broadcast media a new element enters the picture. When government undertakes to provide a forum for discussion, or a street for parades, it must not discriminate among prospective users according to their views. Government must be neutral in such situations. If too many want to parade or use the forum, government might develop a lottery system or queuing system; but it could not prefer those views it liked. Some have argued that this analysis applies to broadcasters—that they are so closely related to, and regulated by, government that their actions are government action, and, thus, bound by the neutrality principle.

The Supreme Court avoided this question in *Columbia Broadcasting System, Inc.*, p. 85, *supra.* The DNC wanted to buy commercial time to urge financial support for the party. Another group Business Executives' Move for Peace (BEM) sought to buy time to oppose the war in Vietnam. The broadcasters refused to sell time to either group because the proposed commercials did not fit into the type of programming the broadcasters wanted to present. The DNC and BEM asked the FCC to order the broadcasters to take their commercials—at least as long as they were taking commercials from other sources. The FCC refused. The Supreme Court upheld the FCC's refusal.

The DNC–BEM claim that the broadcasters should be treated as government fragmented the Court badly. Three justices met it head on and rejected it. They were concerned that the "concept of journalistic independence could not co-exist with a reading of the challenged conduct of the licensee as government action" because a government medium could not exercise editorial judgment as to what content should be carried or excluded.

The three observed, however, that even if the First Amendment applied to this case, the groups were not entitled to access. Here, they relied on Meiklejohn's theme that the essential point was "not that everyone shall speak, but that everything worth saying shall be said." Congress and the Commission might reasonably conclude that the "allocation of journalistic priorities should be concentrated on the licensee rather than diffused among many. This policy gives the public some assurance that the broadcaster will be answerable if he fails to meet its legitimate needs. No such accountability attaches to the private individual."

Three other justices agreed that even if government action were involved in the case, there was no violation of the groups' rights under the First Amendment. They therefore refused to pass on the question of government involvement.

Justice Douglas, concurring, did not decide the question. He noted that if a licensee were to be considered a federal agency it would "within limits of its time be bound to disseminate all views." If a licensee was not considered a federal agency, "I fail to see how constitutionally we can treat TV and radio differently than we treat newspapers." He agreed that "The Commission has a duty to encourage a multitude of voices but only in a limited way, viz., by preventing monopolistic practices and by promoting technological developments that will open up new channels. But censorship or editing or the screening by Government of what licensees may broadcast goes against the grain of the First Amendment."

In dissent Justice Brennan, with whom Justice Marshall concurred, disagreed:

> Thus, given the confluence of these various indicia of "governmental action"—including the public nature of the airwaves, the governmentally created preferred status of broadcasters, the extensive Government regulation of broadcast programming, and the specific governmental approval of the challenged policy—I can only conclude that the Government "has so far insinuated itself into a position" of participation in this policy that the absolute refusal of broadcast licensees to sell air time to groups or individuals wishing to speak out on controversial issues of public importance must be subjected to the restraints of the First Amendment.

The dissenters then concluded that the absolute refusal did violate the First Amendment. "The retention of such *absolute* control in the hands of a few Government licensees is inimical to the First Amendment, for vigorous, free debate can be attained only when members of the public have *some* opportunity to take the initiative and editorial control into their own hands." The emergence of broadcasting as "the public's prime source of information," has "made the soapbox orator and the leafleteer virtually obsolete."

The case, however, indicates only that the Constitution does not create a right of access to broadcasting. It does not address the question of whether Congress might enact a statute requiring broadcasters as a condition of their licenses to give a certain period of time per day or week to members of the public. How might those who wish to speak be selected? Would such a statute be valid? Might the Commission issue a rule to the same effect? Even if such a statute or rule would be constitutional, would it be sound? What does this controversy say about the "agenda-setting" role of media?

In the DNC–BEM case, much of the majority's approach was based on the power to enforce the broadcaster's responsibility to program in the public interest because of the two prongs of the fairness doctrine. It is ironic that the fairness doctrine, resisted by the broadcasters in *Red Lion,* also shielded them from having to give unlimited access to their broadcasting facilities. As a broadcaster, which would you find a greater interference with your freedom—the fairness doctrine or a rule requiring you to give some persons or groups access to your facilities? This issue as it pertains to Public Broadcasting is discussed in Chapter VIII in Muir v. Alabama Educational Television Committee.

Chapter IV

BROADCAST LICENSING

In this chapter we consider the substantive and procedural aspects of the licensing activities of the Federal Communications Commission. As we have seen, the Commission was charged with reducing interference on the airwaves, which eventually, in the name of the public interest, involved licensing. We follow this process through from the initial stage of awarding a vacant spot to the conditions for transferring a license.

A. INITIAL LICENSING

1. The Administrative Process at Work

First we must examine the process by which the Commission grants licenses to applicants. To seek a license for a broadcast frequency, an applicant first asks the Commission for a construction permit to build the facility. If the construction permit is granted, the license will then follow almost automatically if the facility is constructed on schedule.

The application is filed initially with the part of the FCC called the Mass Media Bureau. Its staff reviews the papers to identify any deficiency. If the case is a routine one, the Commissioners have authorized the staff of the Mass Media Bureau to issue the license. But if the application raises any fact questions or legal questions, then a more complex procedure is required.

Section 309(a) of the Communications Act provides that if after examining an application the Commission concludes that the "public interest, convenience, and necessity" will be served it shall grant the application. But subsection (e) provides that "if a substantial and material question of fact is presented or the Commission for any reason is unable to make the finding specified in [subsection (a)], it shall formally designate the application for hearing . . . and shall forthwith notify the applicant . . . of such action and the grounds and reasons therefor, specifying with particularity the matters and things in issue. . . ."

The "hearing" mentioned in the statute is conducted by a member of the FCC's staff called an Administrative Law Judge (ALJ) who functions much as a regular judge presiding over a trial—except that there is no jury and the issues to be explored at the hearing are prescribed, or designated, in advance by the Commission. For example, if the application seems to raise no problem except the question of

93

whether the applicant is adequately financed for the initial period, the Commission will order the ALJ to conduct a hearing limited to that fact question.

Does the applicant have an adversary at the hearing? The answer is that if the Mass Media Bureau has raised a question about the applicant's answers, the Mass Media Bureau itself may take part in the hearing to oppose the applicant. If the fact dispute is resolved in favor of the applicant, and the rest of the application is proper, the ALJ may grant the permit. If the Mass Media Bureau thinks the ALJ has made a mistake, it may appeal within the agency—sometimes to a "review board" that serves as an appellate decision-making body and sometimes to the Commissioners themselves. By the same token, if the judge's ruling favors the Bureau, the unhappy applicant may appeal within the agency.

If the Commission eventually decides against issuing a license or a construction permit, the unhappy applicant may then appeal to the courts—usually to the United States Court of Appeals for the District of Columbia Circuit. In this situation, the adversary is the Commission itself, represented by its general counsel's staff. However the court of appeals may decide, the losing side may seek Supreme Court review by filing a petition for a writ of *certiorari*.

An indication of how the court views its role in reviewing broadcast licensing is found in Greater Boston Television Corp. v. Federal Communications Commission, 444 F.2d 841, 850–53, 20 R.R.2d 2052, 1 Med.L.Rptr. 2003 (D.C.Cir.1970), certiorari denied 403 U.S. 923 (1971), to which we return shortly for its substantive part (footnotes citing a wealth of authorities have been omitted):

> Assuming consistency with law and the legislative mandate, the agency has latitude not merely to find facts and make judgments, but also to select the policies deemed in the public interest. The function of the court is to assure that the agency has given reasoned consideration to all the material facts and issues. This calls for insistence that the agency articulate with reasonable clarity its reasons for decision, and identify the significance of the crucial facts, a course that tends to assure that the agency's policies effectuate general standards, applied without unreasonable discrimination. . . .

> Its supervisory function calls on the court to intervene not merely in case of procedural inadequacies or bypassing of the mandate in the legislative charter, but more broadly if the court becomes aware, especially from a combination of danger signals, that the agency has not really taken a "hard look" at the salient problems, and has not genuinely engaged in reasoned decision-making. If the agency has not shirked this fundamental task, however, the court exercises restraint and affirms the agency's action even though the court would on its own account have made different findings or adopted different standards. Nor will the

court upset a decision because of errors that are not material, there being room for the doctrine of harmless error. . . .

This posture of judicial self-restraint would apply to review of actions of administrative agencies generally.

This brief description assumes that it is possible for the Commission, or its Bureau, to deny an application for a vacant frequency or channel—even though no one else has applied for it. Although this may seem surprising, it does happen.

But the most complex cases before the Commission are those in which more than one applicant seeks a single vacant frequency or channel. These are called "mutually exclusive" applications because only one can be granted. These cases almost always raise serious fact questions that must be resolved in a hearing. These hearings can be extremely time-consuming because each of two or more parties not only attempts to present arguments showing why it should get the spot, but also may present evidence attacking each of the other applicants.

In these cases there may be specific questions, such as whether one of the applicants is an alien, or whether another is inadequately financed or proposes to use inadequate engineering equipment. But even if all the applicants meet every basic qualification, a hearing would still be needed to determine which qualified applicant should get the award.

We might note now that the same hearing process may be required at other stages in the licensing process. When a licensee applies for a renewal, if claims are made that the licensee has misbehaved in some way or should not get the license renewed, any fact questions that need to be resolved will be explored at a similar hearing conducted by an ALJ.

In the interests of simplicity, the foregoing description of the administrative process assumes that when the FCC decides to grant or renew a license to an applicant who has no competitors that is the end of the process. If the applicant has beaten out challengers they can carry the fight into the courts. But if the applicant has no challenger and the Commission decides in its favor, the Bureau—even if it has disagreed with that result—cannot attack the decision of its agency.

Standing for Competitors. Other parties, however, do have a right to participate ("standing"). For example, existing licensees can object to the granting of a new license on the grounds that it will cause technical interference with existing stations. A more difficult question is raised when a competitor wishes to argue that there is not enough potential advertising revenue in the community to support an additional station. Initially, the Commission was receptive to these economic injury arguments. Then, in the late 1930s, the FCC decided that economic injury was no longer a ground for denying license applications. On appeal the court held that the Commission's failure to make findings on the issue of economic injury rendered its decision arbitrary and capricious. Sanders Brothers Radio Station v. Federal Communications Commission, 106 F.2d 321 (D.C.Cir.1939). The Supreme Court disagreed and upheld the Commission's position. 309 U.S. 470 (1940).

The FCC read *Sanders* as holding that there were no situations where economic injury arguments had to be given consideration. This overly expansive reading of *Sanders* continued until 1958, when the court of appeals announced its interpretation of *Sanders.* Carroll Broadcasting Company v. Federal Communications Commission, 258 F.2d 440, 17 R.R. 2066 (D.C.Cir.1958):

> . . . As we have just said, we think it is not incumbent upon the Commission to evaluate the probable economic results of every license grant. Of course, the public is not concerned whether it gets service from A or from B or from both combined. The public interest is not disturbed if A is destroyed by B, so long as B renders the required service. The public interest is affected when service is affected. We think the problem arises when a protestant offers to prove that the grant of a new license would be detrimental to the public interest. The Commission is equipped to receive and appraise such evidence. If the protestant fails to bear the burden of proving his point (and it is certainly a heavy burden), there may be an end to the matter. If his showing is substantial, or if there is a genuine issue posed, findings should be made.

In 1988 the Commission eliminated the *Carroll* doctrine. Policies Regarding Detrimental Effects of Proposed New Broadcast Stations on Existing Stations, 3 F.C.C.Rcd. 638, 64 R.R.2d 583 (1988). The FCC began by noting the rigorous standards required for obtaining a *Carroll* hearing:

> [A] petitioner seeking a hearing on the *Carroll* issue must plead specific factual data sufficient to make out a *prima facie* case that the economic consequences of a grant of the challenged application will lead to an overall derogation of service to the public. Specifically, the petitioner must raise substantial and material questions of fact as to whether: (1) the revenue potential of the market is such that a grant will cause the petitioner to suffer a significant loss of income; (2) the effect of this loss will be to compel the petitioner to eliminate some or all of its public service programming; and (3) this loss of programming will not be offset by the increased nonnetwork programming proposed to be offered by the applicant. Since these three aspects of the *Carroll* issue are essentially interdependent, a failure to satisfy any one of the three is likely to be dispositive of the petitioner's claim to a hearing.

The Commission also noted that in 30 years not one proposed new service had been rejected on *Carroll* grounds. Thus, in the Commission's view, the policy had not yielded any public interest benefits. "Rather, it appears that, to the extent such claims have had any effects on the public interest, those effects have been negative. Resolution of claims of *Carroll* injury by the Commission takes time. Where the

Commission determines that an authorization of a new station will not result in *Carroll* injury, as it consistently has in the cases on record involving such issues, the public is disserved by the delay in the initiation of the service of the new station."

Looking at changes in the electronic media marketplace since *Carroll*, the Commission concluded that the possibility of a *Carroll* injury was "virtually nonexistent. Even if a *Carroll* injury were to occur, the multiplicity of media voices that now exists makes the amount of harm that would result minimal."

The Commission cited WNCN Listeners Guild v. Federal Communications Commission (discussed later in this chapter) for the authority to abolish the judicially imposed *Carroll* doctrine. In *WNCN Listeners Guild*, the Supreme Court had approved the Commission's decision to rely on the marketplace, rather than on regulatory intervention, to determine entertainment formats in radio.

Standing for Listeners. For many years the Commission firmly rejected all efforts of listeners or citizen groups to take a formal part in the licensing process. Formally stated, the FCC denied outsiders standing to participate.

In 1966, however, the court of appeals ordered that citizen groups be allowed to participate in these proceedings. In Office of Communication of United Church of Christ v. Federal Communications Commission, 359 F.2d 994, 7 R.R.2d 2001 (D.C.Cir.1966), the opinion by then Circuit Judge Warren Burger said in part:

> The argument that a broadcaster is not a public utility is beside the point. True it is not a public utility in the same sense as strictly regulated common carriers or purveyors of power, but neither is it a purely private enterprise like a newspaper or an automobile agency. A broadcaster has much in common with a newspaper publisher, but he is not in the same category in terms of public obligations imposed by law. A broadcaster seeks and is granted the free and exclusive use of a limited and valuable part of the public domain; when he accepts that franchise it is burdened by enforceable public obligations. A newspaper can be operated at the whim or caprice of its owners; a broadcast station cannot. After nearly five decades of operation the broadcast industry does not seem to have grasped the simple fact that a broadcast license is a public trust subject to termination for breach of duty.

> . . .

> Public participation is especially important in a renewal proceeding, since the public will have been exposed for at least three years to the licensee's performance, as cannot be the case when the Commission considers an initial grant, unless the applicant has a prior record as a licensee. In a renewal proceeding, furthermore, public spokesmen, such as Appellants here, may be the only objec-

tors. In a community served by only one outlet, the public interest focus is perhaps sharper and the need for airing complaints often greater than where, for example, several channels exist. Yet if there is only one outlet, there are no rivals at hand to assert the public interest, and reliance on opposing applicants to challenge the existing licensee for the channel would be fortuitous at best. Even when there are multiple competing stations in a locality, various factors may operate to inhibit the other broadcasters from opposing a renewal application. An imperfect rival may be thought a desirable rival, or there may be a "gentleman's agreement" of deference to a fellow broadcaster in the hope he will reciprocate on a propitious occasion.

He also noted that the fears of regulatory agencies that they will be flooded with applications have rarely been borne out.

In the period since this case, the feared flood has not developed, though citizen groups are playing a more active part in the regulatory processes of the Commission than before. The role of citizen groups is extensively discussed in D. Guimary, *Citizens' Groups and Broadcasting* (1975). Their most common legal action is the filing of a petition to deny a renewal application on the ground that the applicant has failed to meet the required level of public service.

Negotiation and Agreement. Another possibility is to negotiate. In order to avoid the expense of defending against petitions to deny renewals, broadcasters will sometimes enter into agreements with citizen groups that challenge their license applications or renewals. In return for withdrawal of the challenge, a broadcaster typically undertakes to make certain changes in its station's operation. The broadcaster may promise to change its employment policies, to support local production of broadcast programming, or to attempt to expand certain types of programming.

The Commission generally allows broadcasters to enter into the agreements if they maintain responsibility at all times for determining how best to serve the public interest. Agreements Between Broadcast Licensees and the Public, 57 F.C.C.2d 42 (1975). Does recognition of these private agreements serve the public interest? Does it allow a broadcaster to "buy off" citizen groups who may be in the best position to point out programming deficiencies? The Commission recently examined these issues as part of a more general inquiry into abuses of the comparative renewal process. We will discuss this in more detail later in this chapter.

2. INTRODUCTION TO BASIC QUALIFICATIONS

In the 1934 Act, Congress empowered the Federal Communications Commission to grant licenses to applicants for radio stations for periods of up to three years "if public convenience, interest, or necessity will be served thereby." § 307(a). Section 307(b) requires the Commission to make "such distribution of licenses, frequencies, hours of operation, and of power among the several states and communities as to provide a fair, efficient, and equitable distribution of radio service to each of the same."

As we have seen, the Commission responded by allocating a portion of the spectrum for standard (AM) radio service and then subdividing that space further by requiring very powerful stations to use certain frequencies and weaker stations to utilize others and some stations to leave the air at sundown. The Commission used its rulemaking powers to develop these allocations and then set engineering standards of separation and interference. The 1934 Act empowered the Commission to promulgate "such rules and regulations and prescribe such restrictions and conditions, not inconsistent with law, as may be necessary to carry out the provisions of this chapter." § 303(r). The Commission did not allocate the AM frequencies to particular cities. Instead, it left it to those interested in broadcasting to determine whether they could organize an AM broadcast facility in a given location that complied with the various allocation and interference rules. With FM and television, the Commission utilized rulemaking to allocate particular frequencies to particular cities. An applicant for one of these licenses must apply for the assigned frequency in the listed, or a nearby, community or must seek to change the frequency assignments through an amendment of the rules.

In addition to requiring proof that a grant will serve the "public convenience, interest, or necessity," § 307(a), the Act also requires that each applicant demonstrate that it meets basic "citizenship, character, and financial, technical, and other qualifications," § 308(b). An applicant who fails to satisfy any one of the following "basic qualifications" is ineligible to receive a license.

a. *Legal Qualifications.* An applicant for a license must comply with the specific requirements of the Communications Act and the Commission's rules. For example, there are restrictions on permitting aliens to hold radio and broadcast licenses. § 310(b). Prior revocation of an applicant's license by a federal court for an antitrust violation precludes grant of a new application. § 313. An application will be denied if its grant would result in violation of the Commission's multiple ownership or crossownership rules or its chain broadcasting regulations. (We will discuss these in Chapter V.)

b. *Technical Qualifications.* An applicant for a broadcast station must also comply with the Commission's standards for transmission. These standards include such issues as interference with existing or allocated stations and efficiency of operation, gains or losses of service to affected populations, structure, power and location of the antenna, coverage and quality of the signal in the areas to be served, and studio location and operating equipment utilized.

c. *Financial Qualifications.* Although the applicant must show it has an adequate financial base to commence operations, it need not demonstrate that it can sustain operations indefinitely. The test applied by the Commission is that the applicant must have sufficient funds to operate a broadcast station for three months without advertising revenue. The Commission may also inquire into the applicant's estimates of the amounts that will be actually required to operate the station and the reliability of its proposed sources of funds, such as estimated advertising revenues.

d. *Character Qualifications.* Until the mid–1980s character issues considered by the Commission included past criminal convictions of the applicant, trafficking in broadcast licenses, failure to keep the Commission informed of changes in the applicant's status and other situations that raised questions as to the integrity or reliability of the applicant in the broadcasting function. In 1986, in keeping with the move toward deregulation, the Commission narrowed the scope of character examinations. The Commission confined its interest to three areas: misconduct involving violations of the Act or Commission rules, misrepresentations or lack of candor before the Commission and fraudulent programming.

Other than those issues, the Commission would consider as relevant only criminal fraud convictions, adjudicated cases of broadcast-related antitrust or anticompetitive misconduct and felony convictions substantially related to operating as a broadcaster in a manner consistent with Commission rules and policies. Character Qualifications in Broadcast Licensing, 102 F.C.C.2d 1179, 59 R.R.2d 801 (1986). The policy statement was upheld on appeal. National Association for Better Broadcasting v. Federal Communications Commission, 830 F.2d 270 (D.C.Cir.1987).

Several years later the Commission expanded the scope of character examinations to include any felony conviction, regardless of whether it was broadcast related or not. The FCC's rationale for this expansion was that "[b]ecause all felonies are serious crimes, any conviction provides an indication of an applicant's or licensee's propensity to obey the law." The FCC also expanded consideration of antitrust violations to cover all mass-media-related violations instead of just broadcast-related ones.

With regard to both felony convictions and antitrust violations the Commission will, however, continue to take into consideration mitigating factors such as "the willfulness of the misconduct, the frequency of the misconduct, the currentness of the misconduct, the seriousness of the misconduct, the nature of the participation (if any) of managers or owners, efforts made to remedy the wrong, overall record of compliance with FCC rules and policies, and rehabilitation." The Commission also reiterated its willingness to condition license grants on the outcome of allegations being adjudicated in courts or other agencies. Character Qualifications Policy, 5 F.C.C.Rcd. 3252, 67 R.R.2d 1107 (1990).

On reconsideration, the FCC clarified its position with regard to misdemeanor convictions. They do not have to be reported to the

Commission, but in appropriate cases serious misdemeanor convictions may be considered in evaluating the character qualifications of an applicant. Character Qualifications Policy, 69 R.R.2d 279 (1991).

e. The final category of basic qualifications, "other," has been interpreted to refer primarily to character issues, but it may also overlap with public interest considerations.

3. SUBSTANTIVE CONSIDERATIONS

Assuming an applicant has met the basic qualifications, such as citizenship and financial security, how does the Commission decide if granting the application will serve the "public interest, convenience and necessity"? In this section we will take an extensive look at the substantive considerations in the process, starting with the single applicant for the single vacancy.

As noted earlier, even though an applicant has met the basic qualifications and is the only applicant for the license, that applicant may not get the license. Given that the FCC was created in large part to reduce crowding and eliminate chaos, what role may it play when only one applicant seeks an available spot? A first answer may be found in *NBC*, where the Court recognized that the FCC may act beyond its policeman's role and may consider the public interest. Sometimes the public interest might be better served by leaving a vacancy that a good applicant might later fill rather than by taking the first comer.

But this, of course, requires that the FCC be able to distinguish a "good" applicant from a lesser one. From the beginning the Commission has confronted the tension between using criteria that directly address programming considerations and the concern that too close a look at proposed programming may amount to government control.

The Commission believed that the "entire listening public within the service area of a station, or of a group of stations in one community, is entitled to service from that station or stations." Specialized stations were entitled to little or no consideration. In the Commission's opinion, "the tastes, needs, and desires of all substantial groups among the listening public should be met, in some fair proportion by a well-rounded program, in which entertainment, consisting of music of both classical and lighter grades, religion, education and instruction, important public events, discussions of public questions, weather, market reports and news, and matters of interest to all members of the family find a place." Recognizing that communities differed and that other variables were relevant, the Commission did not erect a "rigid schedule."

In 1946 the Commission issued a report entitled Public Service Responsibility of Broadcast Licensees (known generally as the "Blue Book"). The Commission stressed that although licensees bore the primary responsibility for program service, the Commission would still play a part: "In issuing and in renewing the licenses of broadcast stations, the Commission proposes to give particular consideration to four program service factors relevant to the public interest." One category was the carrying of "sustaining" (unsponsored) programs during hours "when the public is awake and listening." This would provide balance by allowing the broadcast of certain types of programs that did not lend themselves to sponsorship, including experimental programs. Second, the Commission called for local live programs to encourage local self-expression. Third, the Commission expected "programs devoted to the discussion of public issues." Finally, the Commission, expressing concern about excessive advertising, announced that "in its application forms the Commission will request the applicant to state how much time he proposes to devote to advertising matter in any one hour."

In 1960 the Commission changed direction. In Report and Statement of Policy Re: Commission En Banc Programming Inquiry, 25 Fed.Reg. 7291, 20 R.R. 1901 (1960), the FCC asserted that "the principal ingredient of the licensee's obligation to operate his station in the public interest is the diligent, positive and continuing effort . . . to discover and fulfill the tastes, needs and desires of his service area, for broadcast service." Broadcasters were advised to meet this obligation in two ways: they were to consult with members of the listening public who could receive the station's signal and with a variety of community leaders. The distinction between sustaining and sponsored programs was explicitly abandoned.

In 1971 the Commission elaborated upon and clarified the applicant's obligation. The Primer on Ascertainment of Community Problems by Broadcast Applicants, 27 F.C.C.2d 650, 21 R.R.2d 1507 (1971), standardized the Commission's policy with respect to ascertainment of, and programming for, community needs. It placed specific ascertainment requirements upon all commercial applicants for new broadcast stations, modification of existing facilities and renewals. The Primer required that an applicant determine the economic, ethnic and social composition of the communities it proposed to serve and that principals or management-level employees consult with leaders from each significant community group. The applicant was also to consult with a random sample of members of the general public. Finally, the applicant had to set forth in its license application, program proposals designed to meet community problems identified. The ascertainment had to take place within six months of the application.

The courts readily accepted the Commission's emphasis on the importance of the ascertainment process. In Henry v. Federal Communications Commission, 302 F.2d 191 (D.C.Cir.), certiorari denied 371 U.S. 821 (1962), Suburban Broadcasters filed the sole application for a permit to construct the first commercial FM station in Elizabeth, N.J. Although Suburban was found legally, technically and financially qualified, the Commission found that Suburban had made no inquiry into the characteristics or programming needs of Elizabeth and was "totally without knowledge of the area." Suburban's program proposals for Elizabeth were identical to those submitted in its application for an AM station in Berwyn, Ill., and in the application of two of its principal stockholders for an FM station in Alameda, Calif. Although acknowledging the community's "presumptive need" for its first FM service, the Commission denied the permit, finding that a grant would not serve the public interest.

On appeal, the Commission's denial was upheld on the ground that an applicant may be required to "demonstrate an earnest interest in serving a local community by evidencing a familiarity with its particular needs and an effort to meet them."

In 1976 the FCC amended the ascertainment regulations to require interviews "within the following [19] institutions and elements commonly found in a community." The list included agriculture, business, charities, religion, and organizations of elderly, youth and women. "A licensee is permitted to show that one or more of these institutions or elements is not present in its community. At its option it may also utilize the 'other' category to interview leaders in its elements not found on the checklist." Other groups, particularly from the gay community, soon claimed that broadcasters were not using the "other" category to interview them, and asked to be added to the list of 19. The FCC rejected that approach because its studies did not indicate that gay (or handicapped) persons were significant elements in all or most communities. Instead, it declared that broadcasters must ascertain unlisted groups if the groups first bear the burden of getting in touch with the broadcasters to let them know of the group's needs and problems. Amendment of the Primers on Ascertainment of Community Problems, 76 F.C.C.2d 401, 47 R.R.2d 189 (1980).

The ascertainment process was designed to allow the FCC to consider proposed programming from the standpoint of the nature of the community rather than the Commission's own ideas of what is "good" programming. It was part of the Commission's continued emphasis on localism.

In 1981 the FCC adopted, 6–1, a set of proposals reducing the regulations affecting commercial radio licensees. Deregulation of Radio, 84 F.C.C.2d 968, 49 R.R.2d 1 (1981). The underlying rationale was that with over 8,000 radio stations on the air, the Commission could rely on competition in the market to provide appropriate service. Among the changes was the elimination of the formal ascertainment requirements. The Commission's order deleting formal ascertainment procedures for all radio broadcasters was upheld in Office of Communication of the United Church of Christ v. Federal Communications Commission, 707 F.2d 1413, 53 R.R.2d 1371 (D.C.Cir.1983).

In 1984 the Commission adopted a similar set of changes in the regulations for commercial television. Formal ascertainment was eliminated because, according to the Commission, the administrative costs outweighed the benefits. Deregulation of Commercial Television, 98

F.C.C.2d 1076, 56 R.R.2d 1005 (1984). We will return to the changes brought about by these proceedings in the section on renewals.

4. THE COMPARATIVE PROCEEDING

If two or more applicants file for use of the same or interfering facilities, the Commission must proceed by way of comparative hearing among all qualified applicants to determine which will best serve the public interest. An applicant in a comparative proceeding not only must meet minimum qualifications but also must prevail when judged on the Commission's comparative criteria. These criteria, which involve considerations other than those applied in the non-comparative proceeding, evolved through adjudication rather than rulemaking.

POLICY STATEMENT ON COMPARATIVE BROADCAST HEARINGS

Federal Communications Commission, 1965.
1 F.C.C.2d 393, 5 R.R.2d 1901.

By the Commission: Commissioners Hyde and Bartley dissenting and issuing statements; Commissioner Lee concurring and issuing a statement.

[The Commission noted that choosing one from among several qualified applicants for a facility was one of its primary responsibilities. The process involved an extended hearing in which the various applicants were compared on a variety of subjects. The "subject does not lend itself to precise categorization or to the clear making of precedent. The various factors cannot be assigned absolute values." Moreover, the membership of the Commission is continually changing and each member has his or her own idea of what factors are important. Thus, the statement is not binding and the Commission is not obligated to deal with all cases "as it has dealt with some that seem comparable." Nonetheless, it is "important to have a high degree of consistency of decision and of clarity in our basic policies." The statement was to "serve the purpose of clarity and consistency of decision, and the further purpose of eliminating from the hearing process time-consuming elements not substantially related to the public interest." The Commission declared that this statement "does not attempt to deal with the somewhat different problems raised where an applicant is contesting with a licensee seeking renewal of license." The Commission then turned to the merits and identified "two primary objectives": "best practicable service to the public" and "maximum diffusion of control of the media of mass communications."]

Several factors are significant in the two areas of comparison mentioned above, and it is important to make clear the manner in which each will be treated.

1. *Diversification of control of the media of mass communication.*—Diversification is a factor of primary significance since, as set forth above, it constitutes a primary objective in the licensing scheme.

2. *Full-time participation in station operation by owners.*—We consider this factor to be of substantial importance. It is inherently desirable that legal responsibility and day-to-day performance be closely associated. In addition, there is a likelihood of greater sensitivity to an area's changing needs, and of programing designed to serve these needs, to the extent that the station's proprietors actively participate in the day-to-day operation of the station. This factor is thus important in securing the best practicable service. It also frequently complements the objective of diversification, since concentrations of control are necessarily achieved at the expense of integrated ownership.

We are primarily interested in full-time participation.

Attributes of participating owners, such as their experience and local residence, will also be considered in weighing integration of ownership and management. While, for the reasons given above, integration of ownership and management is important per se, its value is increased if the participating owners are local residents and if they have experience in the field. Participation in station affairs on the basis described above by a local resident indicates a likelihood of continuing knowledge of changing local interests and needs. . . .

. . .

3. *Proposed program service.*—. . . The importance of program service is obvious. The feasibility of making a comparative evaluation is not so obvious. Hearings take considerable time and precisely formulated program plans may have to be changed not only in details but in substance, to take account of new conditions obtaining at the time a successful applicant commences operation. Thus, minor differences among applicants are apt to prove to be of no significance.

. . .

Decisional significance will be accorded only to material and substantial differences between applicants' proposed program plans. [ ] Minor differences in the proportions of time allocated to different types of programs will not be considered. Substantial differences will be considered to the extent that they go beyond ordinary differences in judgment and show a superior devotion to public service. . . .

In light of the considerations set forth above, and our experience with the similarity of the program plans of competing applicants, taken with the desirability of keeping hearing records free of immaterial clutter, no comparative issue will ordinarily be designated on program plans and policies, or on staffing plans or other program planning elements, and evidence on these matters will not be taken under the standard issues. The Commission will designate an issue where examination of the applications and other information before it makes such action appropriate, and applicants who believe they can demonstrate significant differences upon which the reception of evidence will be useful may petition to amend the issues.

No independent factor of likelihood of effectuation of proposals will be utilized. The Commission expects every licensee to carry out its proposals, subject to factors beyond its control, and subject to reasonable judgment that the public's needs and interests require a departure from original plans. If there is a substantial indication that any party will not be able to carry out its proposals to a significant degree, the proposals themselves will be considered deficient.

4. *Past broadcast record.*—This factor includes past ownership interest and significant participation in a broadcast station by one with an ownership interest in the applicant. It is a factor of substantial importance upon the terms set forth below.

A past record within the bounds of average performance will be disregarded, since average future performance is expected. Thus, we are not interested in the fact of past ownership per se, and will not give a preference because one applicant has owned stations in the past and another has not.

We are interested in records which, because either unusually good or unusually poor, give some indication of unusual performance in the future. . . .

. . .

5. *Efficient use of frequency.*—In comparative cases where one of two or more competing applicants proposes an operation which, for one or more engineering reasons, would be more efficient, this fact can and should be considered in determining which of the applicants should be preferred. . . .

6. *Character.*—The Communications Act makes character a relevant consideration in the issuance of a license. See section 308(b), 47 U.S.C. § 308(b). Significant character deficiencies may warrant disqualification, and an issue will be designated where appropriate. Since substantial demerits may be appropriate in some cases where disqualification is not warranted, petitions to add an issue on conduct relating to character will be entertained. In the absence of a designated issue, character evidence will not be taken. Our intention here is not only to avoid unduly prolonging the hearing process, but also to avoid those situations where an applicant converts the hearing into a search for his opponents' minor blemishes, no matter how remote in the past or how insignificant.

7. *Other factors.*—As we stated at the outset, our interest in the consistency and clarity of decision and in expedition of the hearing process is not intended to preclude the full examination of any relevant and substantial factor. We will thus favorably consider petitions to add issues when, but only when, they demonstrate that significant evidence will be adduced.[13]

13. Where a narrow question is raised, for example on one aspect of financial qualification, a narrowly drawn issue will be appropriate. In other circumstances, a broader inquiry may be required. This is a matter for ad hoc determination.

DISSENTING STATEMENT OF COMMISSIONER HYDE

. . .

The proposed fiat as to the weight which will be given to the various criteria—without sound predication of accepted data and when considered only in a vacuum and in the abstract—must necessarily result in a degree of unfairness to some applicants and in the fashioning of an unnecessary straightjacket for the Commission in its decisional process. How can we decide in advance and in a vacuum that a specific broadcaster with a satisfactory record in one community will be less likely to serve the broadcasting needs of a second community than a specific long-time resident of that second community who doesn't have broadcast experience? How can we make this decision without knowing more about each applicant? . . .

. . .

DISSENTING STATEMENT OF COMMISSIONER ROBERT T. BARTLEY

I believe that our comparative hearings should be expedited by eliminating what has amounted to extensive bickering in the record over minutiae.

As I see it, however, the Commission majority is attempting the impossible here when it prejudges the decisional factors in future cases. My observation is that there are no two cases exactly alike. There are so many varying circumstances in each case that a factor in one may be more important than the same factor in another. Broadcasting—a dynamic force in our society—experiences constant change. I have expressed it differently on occasions by saying, "There's nothing static in radio but the noise." If we are to encourage the larger and more effective use of radio in the public interest, we must avoid becoming static ourselves.

CONCURRING STATEMENT OF COMMISSIONER ROBERT E. LEE

Even though I recognize the policy statement adopted by the Commission to be the result of a sincere effort to clarify the historical process of selecting a winner in comparative broadcast hearings, I am concurring with considerable reluctance. . . .

Over the years I have participated in decisions in hundreds of "comparative proceedings" and candor compels me to say that our method of selection of the winning applicant has given me grave concern. I realize, of course, that where we have a number of qualified applicants in a consolidated proceeding for a single facility in a given community, it is necessary that we grant one and deny the others. The ultimate choice of the winner generally sustains the Commission's choice despite the recent rash of demands from the court. Thus, it would appear that we generally grant the "right" application. However, I am not so naive as to believe that granting the "right application" could not, in some cases, be one of several applications.

The criteria that the Commission now says will be decisive— assuming all other things are substantially equal—in choosing among qualified applicants for new broadcast facilities in comparative broadcast hearings are not new. However, the policy statement does tend to restrict the scope somewhat of existing factors and if undue delay is thus prevented, some good will have been accomplished.

I wish to make clear that my concurrence here does not bind me with respect to the weight I might see fit to put upon the various criteria in a given case. . . .

Historically, a prospective applicant hires a highly skilled communications attorney, well versed in the procedures of the Commission. This counsel has a long history of Commission decisions to guide him and he puts together an application that meets all of the so-called criteria. There then follows a tortuous and expensive hearing wherein each applicant attempts to tear down his adversaries on every conceivable front, while individually presenting that which he thinks the Commission would like to hear. The examiner then makes a reasoned decision which, at first blush, generally makes a lot of sense—but comes the oral argument and all of the losers concentrate their fire on the "potential" winner and the Commission must thereupon examine the claims and counterclaims, "weigh" the criteria and pick the winner which, if my recollection serves me correctly, is a different winner in about 50 percent of the cases.

The real blow, however, comes later when the applicant that emerged as the winner on the basis of our "decisive" criteria sells the station to a multiple owner or someone else that could not possibly have prevailed over other qualified applicants under the criteria in an adversary proceeding. It may be that there is no better selection system than the one being followed. If so, it seems like a "hell of a way to run a railroad," and I hope these few comments may inspire the Commission to find that better system even if it requires changes in the Communications Act.

Notes and Questions

1. The *1965 Policy Statement* eliminated three specific criteria—staffing and related plans, likelihood of effectuation of proposals, and proposed studios and equipment—that had formerly been used for comparison.

2. In 1986 the Commission eliminated character as a comparative criterion. Recall it is still a basic qualification. Character Qualifications in Broadcast Licensing, 102 F.C.C.2d 1179, 59 R.R.2d 801 (1986).

3. Does choosing licensees on the basis of proposed programming violate either the First Amendment or § 326 of the Communications Act? How far can the Commission go in examining applicants' programming proposals? These questions were answered in Johnston

Broadcasting Co. v. Federal Communications Commission, 175 F.2d 351, 359 (D.C.Cir.1949):

> As to appellant's contention that the Commission's consideration of the proposed programs was a form of censorship, it is true that the Commission cannot choose on the basis of political, economic or social views of an applicant. But in a comparative consideration, it is well recognized that comparative service to the listening public is the vital element, and programs are the essence of that service. So, while the Commission cannot prescribe any type of program (except for prohibitions against obscenity, profanity, etc.) it can make a comparison on the basis of public interest and, therefore, of public service. Such a comparison of proposals is not a form of censorship within the meaning of the statute. . . .

4. When is a comparative hearing required? In Ashbacker Radio Corp. v. Federal Communications Commission, 326 U.S. 327 (1945), the Commission had held a hearing on an application for a construction permit while an application for license modification in a nearby community was pending. The grant of the construction permit precluded the license modification. The Court held that the second applicant was denied its § 309(e) right to a hearing by the granting of the first application. As a result, the *Ashbacker* doctrine requires that whenever mutually exclusive applications are pending, the Commission must hold a single comparative hearing on all of the applications before granting any of them.

5. We consider Commissioner Lee's point about the transferability of licenses at p. 108, *infra.*

6. Although the Commission has emphasized localism, there has always been an undercurrent of doubt. In the early 1960s, when the Commission appeared to favor not only local programs but also live presentations, Judge Friendly observed, "I wonder also whether the Commission is really wise enough to determine that live telecasts, so much stressed in the decisions, e.g., of local cooking lessons, are always 'better' than a tape of Shakespeare's Histories." Friendly, The Federal Administrative Agencies: The Need for Better Definition of Standards, 75 Harv.L.Rev. 1055, 1071 (1962). This concern was restated in a different context by a former chairman of the Commission:

> [T]he automatic preference accorded local applicants disregards the possibility that, depending on the facts of a particular case, a competitor's proposed use of a professional employee-manager from outside the community might very well bring imagination, an appreciation of the role of journalism, and sensitivity to social issues far exceeding that of a particular local owner-manager.

Hyde, FCC Policies and Procedures Relating to Hearings on Broadcast Applications, 1975 Duke L.J. 253, 277.

In the mid–1970s, the Chairman of the House Communications Subcommittee estimated that local television averaged 80 percent non-local programming and "maybe that's the way the viewers want it." He was suggesting that Congress might reconsider the desirability of localism. See Broadcasting, Nov. 22, 1976 at 20.

7. *Minority Ownership.* New issues may reflect changes in licensing policy. In TV 9, Inc. v. Federal Communications Commission, 495 F.2d 929 (D.C.Cir.1973), rehearing en banc denied (1974), Comint Corp., Mid–Florida Television Corporation and six other applicants sought a construction permit for Channel 9 in Orlando, Fla. In making the award to Mid–Florida, the Commission rejected Comint's contention that it was entitled to special consideration because two of Comint's principals were local black residents and 25 percent of those to be served by Channel 9 were black. The Commission's position was that the Communications Act was "color blind" and did not permit considerations of color in the award of licenses. The court disagreed and ruled that the ownership interests and participation of the two black residents gave Comint an edge in providing "broader community representation and practicable service to the public by increasing diversity of content, especially of opinion and viewpoint." We will examine the issue of minority preferences in more detail in Chapter V.

8. In 1978 the Commission began granting women a preference in comparative proceedings. In 1992 the court of appeals struck down a license award based in part on such a preference. Lamprecht v. Federal Communications Commission, 958 F.2d 382, 70 R.R.2d 658 (D.C.Cir.1992). *Lamprecht* is discussed in more detail in Chapter V.

9. Previously, the Commission had refused to grant preferences to women applicants in the lotteries being held to award LPTV licenses. Lottery Selection (Preference for Women), 58 R.R.2d 1077 (1985), affirmed sub nom. Pappas v. Federal Communications Commission, 807 F.2d 1019, 61 R.R.2d 1398 (D.C.Cir.1986).

10. The "recent rash of remands from the court" referred to by Commissioner Lee was caused by the revelation in the late 1950s that an FCC Commissioner had been bribed to vote in certain ways in licensing proceedings. Since the outcomes of these comparative hearings were not readily predictable, it was relatively easy for a Commissioner to vote one way in a particular case without being embarrassed by previous votes he might have cast in other licensing cases. The incentive to offer bribes was due to the fact that a license is awarded without charging the applicant the value of the part of the spectrum being licensed. In addition, due in part to the fact that renewals have been virtually automatic, television channels in large cities have acquired great value—some are worth more than $500 million.

After the bribes came to light, the court of appeals remanded virtually every licensing decision the FCC had recently made for a second look by what was then an FCC with some new faces.

11. The 1965 Policy Statement that has controlled comparative licensing for 27 years is suddenly in doubt. The process began in Bechtel v. Federal Communications Commission, 957 F.2d 873, 70 R.R.2d 397

(D.C.Cir.1992), in which three parties were seeking a license. Bechtel was eliminated on the ground that the other two were proposing integration of ownership and management whereas Bechtel was proposing to hire a full-time manager. This overcame whatever advantages Bechtel might have had over the others.

On Bechtel's appeal from the grant to one of the other parties, the court vacated and remanded on the ground that the FCC had never come to grips with Bechtel's challenge to the significance being given to the integration factor. The Commission had simply followed its past practices without explanation. In passing, the court noted that Bechtel had challenged the other parties and the Commission to show a single case in the last 10 years "in which a licensee prevailed in a comparative hearing based upon its integration proposal and then actually constructed and operated the station in conformity with that proposal for a period substantially exceeding one year." According to the court, no example was produced.

In addition, the court cited one episode alleged by Bechtel in which an integrated applicant won a license and then within five months had contracted to sell it for $4 million to a group broadcaster.

On remand, the Commission concluded that the integration criterion was still valid. Bechtel had asserted that two rule changes adopted by the Commission since the integration criterion was first applied to comparative licensing proceedings had undermined its validity. The first of these two was the Commission's decision to exclude passive investors (e.g., limited partners and non-voting stockholders) from the calculation of the integration credit. Anax Broadcasting, Inc., 87 F.C.C.2d 483, 49 R.R.2d 1589 (1981). The second was the reduction of the required holding period for licenses obtained in a comparative proceeding from three years to one year. Transfer of Broadcast Facilities, 52 R.R.2d 1081 (1982). (We will discuss this in more detail later in this chapter). Bechtel alleged that the combination of these two rule changes had encouraged passive investors to seek out people who would propose to run a station fulltime, thus qualifying for 100 percent integration credit, and then, only one year after building the station, to sell it to a nonintegrated entity.

The FCC rejected this argument, claiming that it rigorously examines license proposals and denies integration credit to those it finds unreliable or in bad faith. Furthermore, the Commission concluded that even the one-year holding period was a sufficient deterrent to the type of speculation Bechtel had argued was being encouraged. With regard to the challenge, *supra,* to cite successful examples of the application of the integration criterion, the Commission simply noted that Bechtel, not the Commission, had the burden of proof. Thus, the Commission concluded that it did not have to cite any examples. Anchor Broadcasting Limited Partnership, 70 R.R.2d 1569 (1992).

The Commission also responded to the remand in *Bechtel* by issuing a notice of proposed rulemaking aimed at reconsidering the entire 1965 statement. Reexamination of the Policy Statement on Comparative Broadcast Hearings, 7 F.C.C.Rcd. 2664 (1992). The Commission has asked for comments on whether to retain each of the factors set out in that statement. It has also suggested awarding a "finder's preference" for applicants who persuade the Commission to allot a new frequency, and for a "service continuity preference" designed "to enhance the public interest in the comparative process by encouraging comparative applicants to retain the stations they are attempting to secure through the comparative hearing for a certain period of time."

The Commission is also considering whether to accord definite weights or points for each factor used in the process, whether to define precisely when such points are awarded, and whether to provide a "tie breaker" procedure to resolve cases in which no applicant "receives a dispositive preference under the comparative criteria."

The Commission also expressed the belief that any proposed action here would be fully consistent with preferences given to minority applicants.

12. Although the following is technically a renewal case, it is appropriately considered here because, for reasons to be seen at p. 138, *infra*, the court of appeals remanded an earlier decision in this matter to the Commission. On this remand, the Commission treated the incumbent, Simon Geller, as though he were competing for a new station. Discussion of Geller's past record at WVCA–FM might be treated as though it was addressed to his performance at some other station he owned—and used for whatever predictive value it might have on his qualifications for this new license. The case is useful here as a short checklist of the current status of the comparative factors. The competitors are Geller and Grandbanke Corp.

APPLICATION OF SIMON GELLER

Federal Communications Commission, 1985.
102 F.C.C.2d 1443, 59 R.R.2d 579.

By the Commission:

. . .

11. The Court of Appeals affirmed the Commission's denial of a renewal expectancy to Geller. Accordingly, that finding will not be revisited on remand, and Geller will receive no renewal expectancy in the overall comparative analysis.

PROPOSED PROGRAMMING

12. Geller proposes to continue his present format, broadcasting 99.52% symphonic music, no news, 0.24% public affairs, and 0.24% other nonentertainment programming. Grandbanke proposes to devote 16.9% of its broadcast time to news, 5.9% to public affairs, and 5.9% to other nonentertainment programming, with 55% of its news to be local and regional. Unlike Geller, Grandbanke proposes that its informa-

tional programming will be directly related to ascertained community needs and interests. Whereas Geller proposed a 44–hour 27–minute-a-week program schedule, Grandbanke proposes to broadcast 136 hours of programming a week.

13. The Commission concluded that Grandbanke deserved a substantial preference for proposed programming for its demonstrated superior devotion to public service. This preference arose from Grandbanke's superior attention to presenting informational programming responsive to ascertained community needs and interests and was enhanced by the significant discrepancy between the applicants' proposed hours of operation and the relative restrictiveness of Geller's programming.

14. As it did with respect to the renewal expectancy, the court affirmed the award of a substantial preference to Grandbanke for its proposed programming.

EFFICIENT USE OF FREQUENCY

15. Because of differences between their engineering proposals, Grandbanke's facilities will have greater coverage than Geller's. Grandbanke's 1 mV/m contour will cover more than 300 square miles, providing a signal to nearly 360,000 people, as opposed to Geller's 73 square miles and 43,000 people. All relevant areas are served by at least five other aural signals.

16. The Commission awarded Grandbanke a slight preference based on the superiority of its coverage. Only a slight preference was warranted since the areas in question are already well served by at least five other aural signals.

17. The court did not specifically address this issue. Grandbanke will therefore continue to receive a slight preference.

INTEGRATION OF OWNERSHIP INTO MANAGEMENT

18. Geller is WVCA–FM's sole owner and employee and will devote full time to the operation of the station. He has been a resident of Gloucester for 13 years. Grandbanke proposes that its 66% owner Edward Mattar will serve as the station's general manager. Mattar has had 3 years of broadcast experience and proposes to move to Gloucester in the event Grandbanke's application is granted.

19. The Commission previously held that despite Geller's technical advantages under the integration criterion, Geller merited only a slight preference over Grandbanke. The Commission reasoned that the rationale of the integration proposal was that an integrated owner would tend to be more sensitive to an area's changing needs and that Geller's poor past broadcast record detracted from these assurances.

20. The court criticized the Commission's conclusions in this regard. In the court's view, the Commission had failed to reconcile its integration analysis in this case with past precedent. . . . The court noted that the Commission did not make, as it usually does, an explicit

analysis of the quantitative and qualitative aspects of integration. Moreover, the court noted that the Commission does not customarily reduce the merit accorded for a quantitative integration advantage unless the applicant has committed misconduct. The court speculated that the Commission may have engaged in the type of "functional analysis" of the essentially structural characteristic of integration, which was previously disapproved by the court. . . .

. . .

22. Having reexamined the integration aspect of this case pursuant to the court's remand, we conclude that our prior treatment of this issue constituted the type of functional analysis previously criticized by the court.[27] We will therefore reevaluate the integration criterion using our ordinary analytical approach. This approach encompasses a weighing of the customary quantitative and qualitative factors, without attempting to factor in other considerations. . . .

23. Turning first to the quantitative aspect of integration, we agree with Grandbanke that, consistent with precedent, an applicant proposing 100% integration deserves a moderate preference over an applicant proposing 66% integration. Qualitatively, Geller's integration is enhanced by his long term local residence, which outweighs Grandbanke's proposal that Mattar will move to Gloucester prospectively and Mattar's limited broadcast experience. Geller will therefore receive a qualitatively enhanced moderate integration preference to be taken into account in the overall comparative analysis.

DIVERSIFICATION OF MEDIA OWNERSHIP

24. Geller owns no media interests other than WVCA. On the other hand, Grandbanke's principals have interests in other broadcast stations. Edward Mattar, Grandbanke's 66% owner, has a 100% interest in station WINQ–FM, Winchendon, Massachusetts. Stockholders with a 34% interest in Grandbanke have a 100% interest in Station WNCS–FM, Montpelier, Vermont.

25. The Commission awarded Geller a moderate preference for diversification. In the Commission's view, based on the degree of media ownership alone, Geller would have been entitled to a substantial preference. However, the Commission believed that Geller's preference should be diminished because of his failure to present substantial amounts of informational programming. The Commission reasoned that the rationale of diversification was to present the public with diverse and antagonistic points of view. Since Geller had virtually abandoned his role as an information source, the Commission concluded that he did not qualify as a diverse and antagonistic voice or deserve full credit for diversification.

27. Central Florida Enterprises, Inc. v.   dismissed, 441 U.S. 957 (1979).
FCC, 598 F.2d 37, 56 (D.C.Cir.1978), cert.

26. The court rejected the Commission's analysis. The court held that the crux of the diversification issue is ownership, based on the probability that diverse ownership will lead to a diversity of views. Moreover, the court held that a direct evaluation of the content of a broadcaster's views would be questionable under the First Amendment. In this vein, the court indicated that there was no basis for inferring that the amount of informational programming presented necessarily represented the broadcaster's as a diverse voice. On remand, the court required, at minimum, that the Commission adequately explain its apparent departure from established principles.

. . .

28. Having reexamined our diversification analysis pursuant to the court's mandate, we conclude that it must be revised. As in the case of integration, we believe that our prior discussion relied on an improper functional analysis. In accordance with the court's ruling, we will not look behind the presumption that underlies the diversification criterion. Our prior conclusion that, based on considerations of media ownership alone, Geller deserves a substantial preference stands una-bridged. In line with the court's views, no other considerations are relevant in this assessment. Accordingly, Geller will receive a substan-tial preference for diversification.

OVERALL COMPARATIVE ANALYSIS

. . .

30. In his comments, Geller maintains that once his integration and diversification preferences are given their proper weights, undimin-ished by "multiple counting" of his past broadcast record, these advan-tages are decisive. Grandbanke, which considers Geller's integration and diversification advantages to be moderate, submits on the other hand that its advantages for proposed programming and efficient use of frequency are dispositive. Grandbanke continues to assert that Geller's failure to provide substantial amounts of informational programming responsive to local needs and interests should weigh heavily in the comparative balancing.

31. The framework for the comparative evaluation of broadcast applicants is provided by the Commission's 1965 Policy Statement on Comparative Broadcast Hearings. There, the Commission enunciated two primary objectives: (1) best practicable service to the public, and (2) diversification of control of the media of mass communications. The former objective encompasses several factors of which those relevant here are: (1) integration of ownership into management, (2) proposed programming, and (3) efficient use of frequency. Under the best practicable service criterion, we have concluded that Grandbanke de-serves a substantial preference for proposed programming and a slight preference for efficient use of frequency, while Geller deserves an enhanced moderate preference for integration. On balance, we believe Grandbanke should receive a moderate preference for best practicable

service. As to diversification, the other primary criterion, Geller receives a substantial preference. Thus, we are faced with a situation in which each applicant is superior to the other with respect to one of the primary objectives of the comparative process. However, the substantial preference awarded to Geller for diversification clearly outweighs the moderate preference awarded to Grandbanke for best practicable service. For this reason, we believe that Geller is ultimately the preferred applicant.

. . .

Notes and Questions

1. How are the various pluses compared?

2. In 1988 Simon Geller sold his station to someone other than Grandbanke for $1 million. Does this change your opinion as to the correctness of the FCC's decision? Should it?

3. The bribery episode noted earlier raises the question of whether there are better ways to decide comparative cases than through the approach developed in the Policy Statement. Is it that Congress gave the FCC a difficult, if not impossible, task?

Some critics have suggested that the Commission emphasize one or two factors, such as diversity, and use these as the major bases for decision. Others have suggested using more factors but giving each a preannounced weight, so that the result would be more predictable than it is now.

Still another suggestion is to award the license to the winner of a lottery among equally qualified applicants. The theory of this approach is that sometimes there simply is no superior applicant and it is unrealistic, if not dishonest, to announce a single winner on the merits. The lottery idea might be applied to all applicants who met the basic tests and also had offered maximum diversification or some other added criteria.

In 1980 the FCC voted, 4–3, to order its staff to prepare a decision that would award the license by lottery to one of two applicants who were both judged superior to a third but equal to each other. Two dissenters complained that one applicant should win on the merits because of the full-time participation of a black woman who was a 5-percent owner. The third dissenter argued that the action was "an impermissible abdication of the Commission's statutory responsibilities and an improper denial of the hearing rights of the applicants." The FCC had an obligation to make "public-interest judgments" rather than use lotteries. Broadcasting, June 9, 1980 at 30. In early 1981 the FCC abandoned the idea of a lottery, but shortly thereafter Congress amended § 309 of the Communications Act to authorize the use of lotteries.

In response to that amendment, the Commission developed lottery procedures for some licensing proceedings including LPTV. These procedures gave preferences (additional chances) for minority ownership and diversity. Then, in 1984, the Commission decided that even though the lottery statute did not authorize the use of lotteries to resolve ties in comparative proceedings, the general public interest standard gave the FCC the authority to adopt such a system. Thus, where the Commission finds applicants who "are in true equipoise on comparative factors" it will use a lottery to decide which applicant will be awarded the license. Lottery Selection Among Applicants, 57 R.R.2d 427 (1984). On appeal the court held that the order would not be ripe for review until the lottery procedure was actually used. The National Latino Media Coalition v. Federal Communications Commission, 816 F.2d 785, 62 R.R.2d 1552 (D.C.Cir.1987).

4. As part of a continuing effort to cut down on such abuses as filing sham applications for the sole purpose of extracting money from legitimate applicants in return for withdrawal of the application, the Commission imposed new limitations on settlement payments in comparative proceedings for new broadcast stations. Settlement payments are limited to legitimate and prudent out-of-pocket expenses. Comparative Broadcast Hearings (Settlement Agreement Payments), 68 R.R.2d 960 (1990).

Initially, even payments for legitimate and prudent expenses were to be permitted only until the trial phase of the hearing. From that point on, no settlement payments of any kind were to be permitted. However, on reconsideration, the Commission concluded that the legitimate-and-prudent-expenses limitation was sufficient to deter sham applications and that prohibiting any settlement payments after the start of a trial would only serve to deter parties from settling. This result would be contrary to the primary purpose of new station proceedings, that of facilitating the expeditious delivery of new service to the public. Therefore, settlement payments for legitimate and prudent expenses will be permitted at any point of new broadcast station proceedings. Comparative Broadcast Hearings (Settlement Agreement Payments), 69 R.R.2d 175 (1991).

B. RENEWAL OF LICENSES

1. INTRODUCTION

The initial license period was limited to three years by § 307(d), and the Commission considered renewal applications from about one-third of all licensees each year. In 1981 Congress changed license terms to five years for television and seven years for radio. At the outset, as it sought to unclutter the AM spectrum, the Commission frequently denied renewals, but after the initial flurry, denials were rare unless the broadcaster's behavior fell far below par. A study of denials and reasons for them is discussed at p. 122 *infra*. With the large number of renewal applications now filed annually, the FCC staff cannot fully investigate the performance of each applicant. Instead, the Commission has relied increasingly on informal complaints from citizens or citizen groups, and on petitions to deny renewal that became possible after the United Church of Christ case, p. 97, *supra*. Section 307(d) authorizes renewals only on the same terms as initial grants— public interest, convenience and necessity.

Traditionally, members of the public who wished to challenge a station's renewal could obtain a great deal of information from the licensee itself. Broadcast licensees were required to keep detailed program logs and show them to the public on request. Commercial TV licensees were also required to submit a composite week log. (The "composite week" referred to a practice by which the Commission each year identified one Sunday, one Monday, etc. from the prior year by which to judge whether licensees had honored their obligations. This avoided the necessity of considering an entire year's data at renewal time.)

In addition, broadcasters were required to place the results of their formal ascertainment in their public file—a collection of material available for inspection by anyone wishing to see it. Also in the public file are almost all applications filed with the FCC—including any accompanying documents, all written citizen agreements, ownership reports, network contracts, all documents relating to present or future ownership of the station, a manual on the public file prepared by the FCC, all requests for broadcast time by candidates for political office and the station's response, annual employment reports and a model EEO program, letters from the public pertaining to station operation, certification of pre- and post-filing announcements, and documents relating to sponsorship identification of political or public controversy programming.

In *Deregulation of Radio*, p. 103, *supra*, the Commission eliminated the requirement that commercial radio licensees keep program logs. Instead each radio station would have to list between five and 10 issues of public importance in its community that it had addressed in its programming. There was no requirement that this programming be produced locally. It was this failure to require local production that brought forth the sole dissent on the Commission.

A specialized station would be able to adhere to its special focus and allow other stations in the market to serve other needs. A classical music station need no longer present national or world news, but might emphasize artistic and cultural news and events. A station presenting black programming in an urban area, might no longer need to worry about presenting programs that would be of interest to other segments of the community. The FCC expected that the array of stations would, one way or another, meet the varied needs and interests of the community's audience.

As a result of the appellate court remand of *Deregulation of Radio*, the Commission changed the annual issues/programs list to a quarterly list and specified that a minimum of five issues must be listed.

When the revised issues/program list was challenged on appeal, the court rejected the revised list as inadequate to provide someone filing a petition to deny sufficient information to make a *prima facie* case. Office of Communication of United Church of Christ v. Federal Communication Commission, 779 F.2d 702, 59 R.R.2d 895 (D.C.Cir. 1985). In 1986 the Commission revised the regulation to require a list of programs that have provided the station's most significant treatment of community issues during the preceding three-month period. Deregulation of Radio, 104 F.C.C.2d 505, 60 R.R.2d 789 (1986).

At the same time, in response to a petition for reconsideration the Commission modified its order deregulating television to require the quarterly issues/program list, but otherwise affirmed its decision. Programming and Commercialization Policies (Reconsideration), 104 F.C.C.2d 357, 60 R.R.2d 526 (1986). Action for Children's Television (ACT) and Black Citizens for a Fair Media both filed appeals in *Deregulation of Television.* ACT's appeal centered on the elimination of commercial guidelines; Black Citizens for a Fair Media's appeal focused on the lack of program reporting requirements in renewal applications. In 1987 the court of appeals affirmed the Commission's actions with one exception. The court held that, given the previous special treatment accorded children's television by the Commission, it had presented inadequate justification for its elimination of commercial guidelines for children's television. We will discuss children's television in more detail in Chapter VII.

In 1981 the Commission drastically shortened and simplified the application forms that renewal applicants must use. All commercial radio renewal applicants and 95 percent of the commercial television renewal applicants fill out short five-question forms. The other randomly chosen five percent had to complete longer forms similar to the old 21–page forms. This "postcard renewal" process was affirmed on appeal. The court of appeals rejected the contention that the duty to award renewals based on the public interest was violated by the absence of any questions concerning licensees' nonentertainment programming. "Although the FCC has deleted from the application many questions which previously supplied substantial information, we believe that it was not arbitrary or capricious for the Commission to conclude, in the exercise of its discretion, that it still has sufficient information to make the 'public interest' determination." Black Citizens for a Fair Media v. Federal Communications Commission, 719 F.2d 407, 54 R.R.2d 1151 (D.C.Cir.1983), certiorari denied 467 U.S. 1255 (1984).

In *Deregulation of Television, supra,* the Commission eliminated the requirement that 5 percent of commercial television renewal applicants fill out the longer renewal application forms. As a result, all commercial radio and television renewal applicants now use the five-question short form.

The FCC has been generally reluctant to deny renewals except in egregious cases. The reason is the size of the penalty that denial of renewal inflicts on the licensee in a world in which VHF stations may be worth $500 million or more, and even radio stations may be worth tens of millions of dollars.

Penalties and Short Renewals. Before 1960 the Commission had few weapons for dealing with misbehavior, since Congress assumed that denial of renewal would suffice in most cases, with revocation during the term to handle the most serious violations. But the Commission came to view denial of renewal as too harsh for all but the most serious violations of rules or other misbehavior. In the 1960 amendments to the Communications Act, Congress explicitly authorized shorter renewals by amending § 307(d), but this could not be utilized until the end of the license period. To fill this gap, Congress responded with §§ 503(b) et seq. to provide the Commission with "an effective tool in dealing with violations in situations where revocation or suspension does not appear to be appropriate." Under § 503(b), the Commission can impose a fine, called a forfeiture, against a licensee who has violated a specific rule.

Responding to the Commission's repeated requests for the authority to levy heavier forfeitures—the maximum fine was $2,000 per violation—Congress amended § 503(b)(2) in late 1989. Broadcasters and cable operators may now be assessed forfeitures of $25,000 per violation for each day of a continuing violation up to a maximum of $250,000 for any single act or failure to act. The Commission quickly adopted the new higher limits. Forfeitures, 67 R.R.2d 1193 (1990).

The added array of sanctions reduced the likelihood that the denial of renewal would be used for what the Commission perceived to be lesser transgressions of the rules. The Commission has in the past resorted extensively to the short-term renewal. The expectation is that if the licensee performs properly during that period it will then return to the regular renewal cycle. In addition to the probationary impact, a short renewal imposes burdens of legal expenses and administrative effort in preparing and defending the application.

Single instances of fraudulent behavior toward advertisers or conducting rigged contests, traditionally led to forfeitures or short-term renewals. Among the most common types of fraud are billing advertisers for commercials that were never actually broadcast and the practice of "double-billing." This latter involves cooperative advertising in which a national manufacturer promises to share advertising expenses with its local retailers. The retailer gets a discount for volume, but the station sends it two bills—one for the actual discounted amount due and a second based on a higher non-discounted rate to be forwarded to the national manufacturer as the basis for the sharing.

After many years of warning against the practice and punishing violators with forfeitures and other penalties, the Commission, in the 1970s, began to deny license renewals to violators. The courts upheld the FCC. See White Mountain Broadcasting Co., Inc. v. Federal Communications Commission, 598 F.2d 274, 45 R.R.2d 681 (D.C.Cir.1979) (upholding denial of renewal where the practice had continued for five and one-half years with full knowledge of the president and sole shareholder of licensee). In the 1980s, however, the Commission again changed its attitude toward enforcing these regulations. In 1986, as part of an ongoing attempt to reduce overly restrictive regulations as well as those that duplicate other federal or state law, the Commission eliminated the rules on fraudulent billing. Elimination of Unnecessary Broadcast Regulation (Business Practices), 59 R.R.2d 1500 (1986). We will return to these "regulatory underbrush" proceedings in Chapter VII.

2. SUBSTANTIVE GROUNDS FOR NONRENEWAL

a. *Non-speech Considerations*

Just as the Commission may deny an uncontested application for a vacant channel, it may deny renewal when no other applicant seeks the spot and even when no complaint has been made. The Mass Media Bureau may argue against renewals when it believes that they would not serve the public interest.

Lying to the Commission may be the clearest basis for denying renewal. In its early years the FCC did not treat dishonesty toward the Commission with heavy sanctions. This led to more examples of such behavior. Finally the Commission denied the renewal of a station whose general manager, for 12 years, had concealed from the Commission the fact that a vice-president of a network secretly owned 24 percent of the station's stock. The station appealed on the grounds, among others, that the harsh treatment came without warning and that there was no indication that the FCC would not have renewed the station's application even if it had known the truth.

The Supreme Court upheld the denial of renewal. The fact that the FCC had previously dealt more mildly with similar cases did not prevent it from changing course without warning. Also, the "fact of concealment may be more significant than the facts concealed. The willingness to deceive a regulatory body may be disclosed by immaterial and useless deceptions as well as by material and persuasive ones." The fact that stockholders of a majority of the shares had no knowledge of the dishonesty did not bar the FCC from acting—"the fact that there are innocent stockholders cannot immunize the corporation from the consequences of such deception." Stockholders often suffer from the misdeeds of their chosen officers. Federal Communications Commission v. WOKO, Inc., 329 U.S. 223 (1946).

Sometimes the Commission has held that the manager's deceit is the licensee's responsibility because of its failure to exercise adequate control and supervision consistent with its responsibilities as a licensee. Renewal was denied and the court affirmed in such a case. Continental Broadcasting, Inc. v. Federal Communications Commission, 439 F.2d 580, 20 R.R.2d 2126 (D.C.Cir.), certiorari denied 403 U.S. 905 (1971).

Because the license is issued to the licensee, the licensee must meet the standards of the Communications Act and the FCC. Misbehavior of the officers may show that the licensee knew of the misbehavior or a serious failure to control the station. In an appropriate situation, either may justify denial of renewal. We will consider such a case, RKO v. Federal Communications Commission, later in this chapter.

However, in 1980 the Commission unanimously renewed the license of a Westinghouse broadcasting station despite claims that the licensee's parent corporation had engaged in criminal misrepresentations to federal agencies. Because the licensee was "virtually autonomous," the parent's misdeeds did not reflect on the licensee's qualifications. Westinghouse Broadcasting Co., 75 F.C.C.2d 736, 46 R.R.2d 1431 (1980).

In response to the Anti–Drug Abuse Act of 1988, the Commission announced a new ground for possible non-renewal or revocation. "[A]bsent extenuating or mitigating circumstances, the Commission intends promptly to take all appropriate steps, including initiation of license revocation proceedings, where information comes to our attention that FCC licensees or their principals have been convicted of drug trafficking." Drug Trafficking Policy, 66 R.R.2d 1617 (1989).

b. Speech Considerations

As you will recall, p. 117, supra, in its early days the Commission was not hesitant about denying renewals when it disapproved of the speech being uttered. The potential implications of that practice were not tested because the situation eased after the famous Mayflower Broadcasting Corp. case, 8 F.C.C. 333 (1940), in which the Commission renewed a license but appeared to criticize the licensee for editorializing: "A truly free radio cannot be used to advocate the causes of the licensee. . . . In brief, the broadcaster cannot be an advocate." The case apparently deterred controversial discussion and therefore reduced the need for the Commission to judge speech directly. The situation changed after the Commission's Report on Editorializing by Broadcast Licensees, 13 F.C.C. 1246, 1 R.R. pt. 3, § 91.21 (1949), which directed licensees to devote a reasonable portion of their broadcast time to the discussion of controversial issues of public importance and to encourage the presentation of various views on these questions. This has also affected renewal cases.

One study indicated that 64 radio and television licenses were revoked or not renewed between 1970 and 1978, compared with 78 during the years from 1934 to 1969. Weiss, Ostroff & Clift, Station License Revocations and Denials of Renewal, 1970–1978, 24 J. Broadcasting 69 (1980). The authors analyzed the grounds for revocation or nonrenewal in the 64 cases. Since multiple grounds were common, 110 reasons were listed. The most common were misrepresentations to the FCC (18), failure to pursue the renewal procedure (16), fraudulent billing practices (11), departure from promised programming (11) and unauthorized transfer of control by the licensee (10).

Few of the 64 involved speech grounds. Even those that did were commonly combined with other derelictions because the Commission has been reluctant to single out a speech basis for nonrenewal. For example, although the study shows that four licenses were lost for "news slanting," all four of these stations were also listed under "misrepresentations to the Commission," three were listed under character qualifications, and the fourth was also listed under failure to prosecute renewal. Similarly, although three cases listed "fairness" violation as grounds for nonrenewal, one of these was also one of the group of four listed above and had four separate reasons for nonrenewal. A second was also listed for misrepresentation. The third, the Brandywine case, is discussed shortly.

The situation is not surprising. First, a station that senses that it may be doing something wrong may seek to hide the matter without realizing that misrepresentation to the Commission may be much more serious than its substantive misbehavior. Recall the WOKO case. Second, misbehavior sometimes occurs because the licensee has not exerted sufficient control over management or employees. In such a case, the FCC combines the misbehavior with inadequate supervision as grounds for the denial of renewal. Third, the posture of the courts has not encouraged the FCC to deny renewals on pure speech grounds—as a few examples will make clear.

In one case, the FCC found that a disc jockey had been using vulgar and suggestive language. When the FCC began to investigate, the licensee denied all knowledge of the offending conduct. Because of the history of complaints, the Commission found that denial not credible, which raised a question about the licensee's character qualifications. After renewal was denied, the court affirmed but did so explicitly on the character ground, refusing to pass on whether the speech alone would have justified nonrenewal. Robinson v. Federal Communications Commission, 334 F.2d 534, 2 R.R.2d 2001 (D.C.Cir.1964), certiorari denied 379 U.S. 843 (1964).

In Walton Broadcasting, Inc., 78 F.C.C.2d 857, 47 R.R.2d 1233 (1980), the Commission denied renewal to a station that had tried to build upon the popularity of a new disc jockey by having him disappear and reporting that he had been kidnapped. Listeners jammed telephone lines to the police and the radio station. The licensee was an absentee owner who took no steps to rectify the matter until after the FCC began investigating. The renewal was denied because the licensee failed to exercise adequate control over the station's operations:

> The misconduct in this case, the hoax broadcast of news and the false announcement about the kidnapping or disappearance in a non-news context over a 4–day period, was designed to shock and alarm KIKX's listening public. The misconduct can be traced directly to the licensee's failure to require promotion formats be

approved, its failure to transmit and emphasize the substance of its policies to its station manager, its failure to insure that the manager understood its policies, its failure to check to see if he transmitted the information to on-the-air personnel, and its failure to understand and inculcate the most elementary principle of public trusteeship.

The licensee was also found responsible for six technical violations of the logging rules and 12 engineering violations. Because the control was inadequate and the resulting misconduct was quite serious, the penalty of nonrenewal was justified.

Another kind of deception was attempted by a minister whose initial efforts to acquire a station for his seminary were challenged by groups who believed that his past record showed that he would not honor the fairness doctrine (see Chapter VI) or his other obligations. The prospective licensee responded by promising to provide balanced programming. Within 10 days of obtaining the license, the licensee began drastically altering its format and groups complained that the licensee was not living up to its obligations. The Commission denied renewal on two grounds: alleged violations of the fairness doctrine and deception practiced on the Commission in obtaining the license. On appeal, the court affirmed, 2–1. Two judges agreed on the deception ground, but the dissenter found that ground "too narrow a ledge" for decision. He thought that the Commission had really denied renewal because of the speech uttered on the station, and he concluded that this was impermissible. Brandywine–Main Line Radio, Inc. v. Federal Communications Commission, 473 F.2d 16, 25 R.R.2d 2010, 1 Med. L.Rptr. 2067 (D.C.Cir.1972), certiorari denied 412 U.S. 922 (1973), Douglas, J. dissenting.

In United Television Co., 55 F.C.C.2d 416, 34 R.R.2d 1465 (1975), the Commission denied renewal to a station accused of violating 18 U.S.C.A. § 1304 by broadcasting information concerning lotteries. This was done by ministers who "broadcast programs offering three-digit scripture citations in return for monetary donations." The licensee conceded that the language used in the broadcasts referred to numbers games. The Commission, rejecting the claim that freedom of religion was involved, stated that it had the power to determine whether asserted beliefs are "sincerely held" and whether the ministers were in "good faith." Since the numbered references were not part of any creed and "the representations of the ministers concerning financial blessings defy belief," the Commission concluded that no First Amendment problem was involved. There was no specific reference to the speech and press parts of the First Amendment. This behavior alone was held to warrant denial and to bar United from a comparative hearing. In addition to this misbehavior, the licensee was found to have engaged in false and misleading advertising as well as violations of technical rules.

United's appeal failed. United Broadcasting Co. v. Federal Communications Commission, 565 F.2d 699 (D.C.Cir.1977). The court, however, refused to accept the speech ground. It noted that the FCC's order cited several independent reasons for nonrenewal, including technical violations: "In our view, the long history of persistent violations of those rules was a sufficient reason for disqualification. The Commission's decision is therefore affirmed on the basis of its discussion of this issue, and we reach no other question tendered by this appeal." *Certiorari* was denied, 434 U.S. 1046 (1978).

In Trustees of the University of Pennsylvania, 69 F.C.C.2d 1394, 44 R.R.2d 747 (1978), the Commission denied a renewal application from a university. Listeners had complained for some time that announcers on the station had frequently used obscenity and that entire programs had been obscene. The University took few steps to meet the problem until after the FCC began inquiries and ordered a hearing on the renewal application. The Commission denied renewal exclusively on the ground that the licensee had totally abdicated its control over the station's management. The Commission explicitly indicated that the ALJ had denied renewal because of lack of control "and it is that conclusion which we today affirm." The FCC refused to accept the argument that noncommercial licensees should not be held to the same level of accountability as commercial licensees. Finally, "corrective action taken by the licensee cannot mitigate its unsatisfactory performance . . . because remedial steps which were taken came only after months of critical deficiencies in supervision and control of the station and, moreover, they occurred after it became clear the station's license was in jeopardy."

A dissenting Commissioner argued for a short-term renewal on the ground that the FCC had been renewing university stations for years although it knew that they "were not as tightly controlled as commercially operated stations." He was distressed that the University and the community should suffer because of the actions of a "few immature, irresponsible students" who "should have been spanked long ago and the matter ended there."

The most dramatic nonrenewal on speech grounds involved the station in Jackson, Miss., that was the subject of the United Church of Christ case discussed at p. 97, *supra*. Strangely, the case did *not* involve a Commission decision not to renew. Groups claimed that the station had violated the fairness doctrine, had failed to air contrasting viewpoints on racial matters, had given blacks inadequate exposure, had generally been disrespectful to blacks, had discriminated against local Catholics and had given inadequate time to public affairs. Blacks constituted 45 percent of the population of the station's primary service area. The FCC gave the licensee a short renewal and ordered it to honor its obligations.

After the FCC had been ordered to allow the citizen groups to participate and to reconsider the case, it decided that the station deserved renewal because the allegations had not been proven.

On a second appeal, the court reversed on the ground that the FCC's decision was not supported by substantial evidence. The FCC's errors included placing the burden of proof on the citizen groups rather than on the renewal applicant and failing to accept uncontradicted testimony about the station's practices, including cutting off national programs that showed blacks in a favorable light or discussed racial issues. Sometimes the licensee falsely blamed technical difficulties for the interruptions in service. Office of Communication of United Church of Christ v. Federal Communications Commission, 425 F.2d 543, 16 R.R.2d 2095 (D.C.Cir.1969).

Rather than remand again, the court itself vacated the license and ordered the FCC to invite applications for the now vacant channel—and to provide for interim operation of the facility. Finally, the station was taken over by a different licensee.

Surely the most widescale nonrenewal occurred when the Commission refused to renew licenses for eight educational stations in Alabama as well as an application for a construction permit for a ninth. Alabama Educational Television Commission, 50 F.C.C.2d 461, 32 R.R.2d 539 (1975). The Commission found that "blacks rarely appeared on AETC programs; that no black instructors were employed in connection with locally-produced in-school programs; and that unexplained decisions or inconsistently applied policies caused the preemption of almost all black-oriented network programming." The Commission concluded that the "licensee followed a racially discriminatory policy in its overall programming practices and, by reason of its pervasive neglect of a black minority consisting of approximately 30 percent of the population of Alabama, its programming did not adequately meet the needs of the public it was licensed to serve." Although a station need not meet minority needs by special programming, the licensee "cannot with impunity ignore the problems of significant minorities in its service areas." Two dissenters argued that the improvements in the last few years should justify more lenient treatment. The majority used that improvement, which came only after the challenges to renewal, to waive its usual rule that an applicant who is denied renewal is ineligible to reapply for that same station. The state agency here was permitted to reapply but it did so on equal footing with the other applicants.

Generally, however, a licensee runs no risk of losing its license because of what it broadcasts so long as the content is not obscene or otherwise proscribed, as discussed in Chapter VII. The clearest judicial exposition of this view occurred when a petition to deny renewal was filed against a radio station that had broadcast several programs that "made offensive comments concerning persons of the Jewish faith, equating Judaism with Socialism and Socialism with Communism." The Commission granted renewal without a hearing. The court of appeals affirmed. Anti–Defamation League of B'Nai B'Rith v. Federal Communications Commission, 403 F.2d 169, 14 R.R.2d 2051 (D.C.Cir. 1968), certiorari denied 394 U.S. 930 (1969).

The court approvingly quoted from the Commission's opinion in the case:

> The Commission has long held that its function is not to judge the merit, wisdom or accuracy of any broadcast discussion or commentary but to insure that all viewpoints are given fair and equal opportunity for expression and that controverted allegations are balanced by the presentation of opposing viewpoints. Any other position would stifle discussion and destroy broadcasting as a medium of free speech. To require every licensee to defend his decision to present any controversial program that has been complained of in a license renewal hearing would cause most—if not all—licensees to refuse to broadcast any program that was potentially controversial or offensive to any substantial group. More often than not this would operate to deprive the public of the opportunity to hear unpopular or unorthodox views.

The court rejected the petitioner's main contention that "recurrent bigoted appeals to anti-Semitic prejudice" was a basis for denial of renewal. Here it quoted extensively from the opinion of a concurring Commissioner:

> It is not only impractical—and impossible in any ultimate sense—to separate an appeal to prejudice from an appeal to reason in this field, it is equally beyond the power or ability of authority to say what is religious or racial. There are centuries of bloody strife to prove that man cannot agree on what is or is not "religion."
>
> . . .
>
> Nevertheless these subjects will and must be discussed. But they cannot be freely discussed if there is to be an official ban on the utterance of "falsehood" or an "appeal to prejudice" as officially defined. All that the government can properly do, consistently with the right of free speech, is to demand that the opportunity be kept open for the presentation of all viewpoints. Yet this would be impossible under the rule espoused by the ADL. . . . If what the ADL calls "appeals to racial or religious prejudice" is to be classed with hard-core obscenity, then it has no right to be heard on the air, and the only views which are entitled to be broadcast on matters of concern to the ADL are those which the ADL holds or finds acceptable. This is irreconcilable with either the Fairness Doctrine or the right of free speech.
>
> Talk of "responsibility" of a broadcaster in this connection is simply a euphemism for self-censorship. It is an attempt to shift the onus of action against speech from the Commission to the broadcaster, but it seeks the same result—suppression of certain views and arguments. . . . Attempts to impose such schemes of self-censorship have been found as unconstitutional as more direct censorship efforts by government. [   ]

Promise v. Performance. If the Commission "encourages" promises of certain types of programs, how should the Commission treat disparities between the promises and the actual performance? The Commission's general reluctance to deny renewals originally led it to overlook disparities. The subject is discussed extensively in Moline Television Corp., 31 F.C.C.2d 263, 22 R.R.2d 745 (1971), dealing with an assertion that an applicant obtained a station by lavish promises and failed to carry them out. The Commission noted that it had "not awarded a preference to any applicant based on proposed programming. The door to a sorry episode has been firmly closed."

In 1976 the Commission adopted a quantitative guideline for the "promise versus performance" issue in renewals. Matter of Revision of FCC Form 303, Application for Renewal of Broadcast Station Licenses, 59 F.C.C.2d 750, 37 R.R.2d 1 (1976). The Commission's guideline was that "an actual decrease of 15% in any of the three nonentertainment program categories or a 20% decrease overall should be explained to the Commission. This refers to decreases between the composite week performance and the amount promised in the applicant's last renewal application."

In West Coast Media, Inc., 79 F.C.C.2d 610, 47 R.R.2d 1709 (1980), a petition to deny renewal was filed against a San Diego FM station for failing to comply with its promises to the FCC. After a hearing, the FCC denied renewal. The Commission stressed that it had not set minimum program requirements to qualify for renewal. Instead, the licensee is obliged to comply substantially with its promises for future performance. "Insubstantial variations do not raise a question of the licensee's ability" to serve the public interest. Here the licensee fell far below its promises. In such cases "the Commission confines its review of programming performance to a determination of whether the licensee made reasonable and good faith efforts to effectuate its proposal. Moreover, the licensee must show that its programming has been appropriately responsive to community problems, needs and interests."

After reviewing the case, including the licensee's explanations for the substantial disparity, the Commission concluded that the record showed that the licensee failed to make "reasonable and good faith efforts to effectuate its proposal." This order was upheld in West Coast Media, Inc. (KDIG) v. Federal Communications Commission, 695 F.2d 617, 52 R.R.2d 1295 (D.C.Cir.1982), certiorari denied 464 U.S. 816 (1983).

In *Deregulation of Television,* p. 103, *supra,* the Commission eliminated quantitative programming guidelines including those dealing with promise versus performance. This action was based on studies showing that commercial television stations were carrying non-entertainment programming greatly in excess of the percentages set up by the Commission.

3. COMPARATIVE RENEWAL PROCEEDINGS

In the early years of regulation of each medium, except perhaps for AM, so many vacant frequencies existed that few applicants tried to oust incumbents. When such a challenge did occur, the Commission undertook the difficult comparison of the incumbent's actual performance and the challenger's proposed operation. In a major case involving renewal of the license of a Baltimore AM station, the Commission's analysis included some factors favoring the incumbent and others favoring the challenger. Hearst Radio, Inc. (WBAL), 15 F.C.C. 1149, 6 R.R. 994 (1951). Although the incumbent had not integrated ownership and management this did not matter because its actual performance was now available for review. Similarly, although the incumbent also controlled an FM station, a television station and a newspaper in Baltimore, it had not abused its power so this was not a serious problem. The Commission found little difference in programming despite the challenger's strong assertions to the contrary, and concluded:

> We have found that both of the applicants are legally, technically, and financially qualified and must therefore choose between them as their applications are mutually exclusive. We have discussed at some length why the criteria which we may sometimes consider as determining factors when one of the applicants is not operating the facilities sought and where the applicants have not proved their abilities, are not controlling factors in the light of the record of WBAL. The determining factor in our decision is the clear advantage of continuing the established and excellent service now furnished by WBAL and which we find to be in the public interest, when compared to the risks attendant on the execution of the proposed programming of Public Service Radio Corporation, excellent though the proposal may be.

This decision was thought to give renewal applicants such an advantage that prospective challengers began to seek entry by other means, such as buying an existing facility or seeking available, though less desirable, vacant frequencies. In its *1965 Policy Statement on Comparative Broadcast Hearings*, p. 104, *supra*, the Commission noted that it was not attempting to deal with "the somewhat different problems raised where an applicant is contesting with a licensee seeking renewal of a license." Yet, later that year, in a case in which two applicants were challenging the incumbent, the Commission stated that, on further consideration, it had "concluded that the policy statement should govern the introduction of evidence in this and similar proceedings where a renewal application is contested. . . . However, we wish to make it clear that the parties will be free to urge any arguments they may deem applicable concerning the relative weights to be afforded the evidence bearing on the various comparative factors." Seven (7) League Productions, Inc., 1 F.C.C.2d 1597 (1965).

Although the Commission might have developed a special set of standards governing renewal cases, it has found it quite difficult to do so. This was not a serious problem so long as few applicants challenged renewal applicants. But in the 1960s and early 1970s, those who wished to get into broadcasting were faced with virtually no vacancies on the spectrum (except UHF) and greatly increasing prices for existing stations. Despite the warning of *Hearst,* applicants began increasingly to challenge incumbents. Whether because the incumbents were superior—or at least equal—or because the denial of renewal imposed a serious financial penalty, the Commission continued to favor renewal applicants.

The WHDH Case. But in a complex case that dragged on 15 years, the Commission rendered a decision that shocked the broadcast industry. In 1954, four mutually exclusive applicants began a contest for Channel 5 in Boston. After hearings, the FCC selected WHDH, Inc., which was wholly owned by the *Boston Herald–Traveler* newspaper. While the losers appealed, WHDH began broadcasting. During the appeals, it was learned WHDH's president, Robert Choate, had had private meetings with the FCC chairman in what was later described as a "meaningful and improper, albeit subtle, attempt to influence the Commission." * The FCC reopened the case in 1960, and WHDH again was selected—but given only a four-month license because of the misbehavior. Appeals were again taken. When WHDH filed for renewal, the FCC invited competing applications.

As a result of a new hearing in 1966, the FCC found WHDH's past record within the bounds of average performance and thus not entitled to special credit. On diversification grounds, WHDH fared badly because of its newspaper connection. In 1969 the FCC awarded BBI the license. When WHDH argued that it should benefit from the *Hearst* decision, the FCC responded that this was not an ordinary renewal case because of its "unique events and procedures." Even though WHDH had been operating for 12 years, all but four months of that had been on temporary licenses and its only permanent license had been very short because of the misbehavior.

On appeal, the court affirmed the FCC's grant of the license to BBI instead of WHDH. *Greater Boston Television Corp.,* p. 94, *supra.* If renewal criteria had been applied, the relationship between WHDH and the newspaper would not have been considered—and WHDH would have gotten the benefits of *Hearst* and might well have gotten the license. The court recognized that the FCC had put this case into a special category and had not treated WHDH as a renewal applicant, which it found entirely appropriate given the peculiar history of the case.

---

* Once a proceeding is underway, parties are generally prohibited from meeting with Commission personnel outside the presence of other parties to the proceeding. The rationale for the prohibition on "ex parte" contacts is that opponents would not have the opportunity to rebut statements made at these meetings because they would be unaware of them.

The court recognized that in ordinary cases renewal expectancies "are provided in order to promote security of tenure and to induce efforts and investments, furthering the public interest, that may not be devoted by a licensee without reasonable security." But that did not apply here.

Even before the court's decision in *Greater Boston,* the industry mobilized to overturn what it saw as a retreat from *Hearst.* The FCC sought to forestall Congressional action by adopting a Policy Statement on Comparative Hearings Involving Regular Renewal Applicants. 22 F.C.C.2d 424, 18 R.R.2d 1901 (1970). Briefly, that policy stated that in any hearing between an incumbent and a challenger, the incumbent would obtain a controlling preference by demonstrating substantial past performance without serious deficiencies. The FCC would never get to consider the merits of the challenger if the incumbent's record met the non-comparative renewal standard.

The new Policy Statement was challenged in Citizens Communication Center v. Federal Communications Commission, 447 F.2d 1201, 22 R.R.2d 2001 (D.C.Cir.1971). At issue was whether the Policy Statement violated § 309(e) of the Communications Act and the *Ashbacker* doctrine. Section 309(e) states in part, "If, in the case of any application to which subsection (a) of this section applies, . . . the Commission for any reason is unable to make the finding specified in such subsection, it shall formally designate the application for hearing on the ground or reasons then obtaining . . .. Any hearing subsequently held upon such application shall be a full hearing in which the applicant and all other parties in interest shall be permitted to participate . . .."

The court of appeals decided that the Policy Statement did violate § 309(e) and the *Ashbacker* doctrine despite the Commission's inclusion of all competing applicants in the renewal proceeding:

> To circumvent the *Ashbacker* strictures, however, [the Commission] adds a new twist: the Policy Statement would limit the "comparative" hearing to a single issue—whether the incumbent licensee had rendered "substantial" past performance without serious deficiencies. If the examiner finds that the licensee has rendered such service, the "comparative" hearing is at an end and, barring successful appeal, the renewal application must be granted. Challenging applicants would thus receive no hearing at all on their own applications, contrary to the express provisions of Section 309(e) which requires a full hearing.

In *Ashbacker* the Commission had promised the challenging applicant a hearing on his application after the rival application was granted. The Supreme Court in *Ashbacker* said that such a promise was "an empty thing." At least the Commission here must be given credit for honesty. It does not make any empty promises. It simply denies the competing applicants the "full hearing" promised them by Section 309(e) of the Act. Unless the renewal applicant's past performance is found to be insubstantial or marred by serious deficiencies, the competing applications get no hearing at all. The proposition that the 1970 Policy Statement violates Section 309(e), as interpreted in *Ashbacker,* is so obvious it need not be labored.

The court did not, however, rule that superior performance by a licensee should be ignored. "At the same time, *superior* performance should be a plus of major significance in renewal proceedings. Indeed, as *Ashbacker* recognizes, in a renewal proceeding, a new applicant is under a greater burden to 'make the comparative showing necessary to displace an established licensee.' "

Thus, some renewal expectancy was clearly allowed but its exact role in the renewal process still needed clarification. *Citizens Communications Committee* stated it could never reach the level of a controlling preference. But just how much weight should renewal expectancy be given and how good did the licensee's performance have to be to earn it?

During the early 1970s broadcasters sought legislation clarifying the position of licensees in the renewal process. Their reliance on the Commission had been shaken by their perception of the WHDH case, and the Commission's efforts to reassure them failed when the 1970 *Policy Statement* was upset. The pressure on Congress was aimed mainly toward obtaining a renewal standard that avoided the comparative treatment for an incumbent that had generally been acceptable during the prior period. In 1974 the broadcasters nearly succeeded. Different bills passed the House, 379–14, and the Senate, 69–2, but a conference was never held because the Chairman of the House Interstate Commerce Committee refused to name conferees. He was angry because he believed the broadcasters had reneged on a deal by maneuvering on the floor of each house to raise the term of the license to five years from the Committee's proposed four years. The concern about the length of the term was felt most strongly by smaller broadcasters who were hoping to avoid the paperwork and legal expenses that occurred every three years. These broadcasters were also not usually subject to challenges. The holders of licenses in the large urban areas cared more about the standards to be utilized in renewal cases and less about the length of the term. The result of the maneuvering was that neither group got anything at that time.

Throughout the 1970s, the Commission continued to grant renewals except in cases of serious licensee misconduct. While the Commission purported not to be, it appeared to be giving incumbent licensees a controlling preference for "superior" or even "substantial" service. One such case involved the application by Cowles Florida Broadcasting, Inc., for renewal of the license for its Daytona Beach, Fla., television station. The administrative law judge, in recommending renewal, characterized Cowles's performance as "thoroughly acceptable." The Commission granted renewal, 4–3; but the majority, after its own study of the record, concluded that the performance was "superior" and warranted renewal even though the challenger, Central Florida Enterprises, Inc., had gained advantages on several other issues, including diversification, integration and minority participation, as well as the incumbent's having moved its main studio location in violation of an FCC regulation. The majority also chose to disregard mail fraud allegations against other subsidiaries of Cowles's parent company.

One dissenter thought that the majority had distorted the record to find "superior" service. He thought it only "solid" and would have held that enough to justify renewal but felt constrained to dissent because the court of appeals had set a higher standard. Another dissenter followed much the same path and urged alternative licensing techniques such as lotteries and auctions.

In an order "clarifying" its earlier opinion, a majority of the Commission explained that its previous use of "superior" was not meant to suggest "exceptional when compared to other broadcast stations" in the area or elsewhere. Rather, the intention was to distinguish "between the two situations—one where the licensee has served the public interest but in the least permissible fashion still sufficient to be renewed in the absence of competing applications, and the other where the licensee has done so in a solid, favorable fashion." The licensee was said to be in the second group. The majority shifted from "superior" to "substantial."

The court of appeals reversed the renewal and remanded. Central Florida Enterprises, Inc. v. Federal Communications Commission, 598 F.2d 37, 44 R.R.2d 345 (D.C.Cir.1978). The court's final position (after an original opinion, an order amending that opinion, and a supplemental opinion denying a petition for rehearing) rejected the Commission's entire approach to comparative renewal proceedings—and found inadequacies in its dealings with specific issues. The Commission purported to be following its *1965 Policy Statement* in conducting a full hearing. The court observed:

> It found favorably to Central [the challenger] on each of diversification, integration, and minority participation, and adversely to Cowles on the studio move question. Then simply on the basis of a wholly noncomparative assessment of Cowles' past performance as "substantial," the Commission confirmed Cowles' "renewal expectancy." Even were we to agree (and we do not agree) with the Commission's trivialization of each of Central's advantages, we still would be unable to sustain its action here. The Commission nowhere even vaguely described how it aggregated its findings into the decisive balance; rather, we are told that the conclusion is based on "administrative 'feel.'" Such intuitional forms of decision-making, completely opaque to judicial review, fall somewhere on the distant side of arbitrary.

On remand the Commission again awarded the license to Cowles. Central Florida appealed once more.

CENTRAL FLORIDA ENTERPRISES, INC. v. FEDERAL COMMUNICATIONS COMMISSION

United States Court of Appeals, District of Columbia Circuit, 1982.
683 F.2d 503, 51 R.R.2d 1405.
Certiorari denied 460 U.S. 1084, 103 S.Ct. 1774, 76 L.Ed.2d 346 (1983).

Before ROBINSON, CHIEF JUDGE, WILKEY, CIRCUIT JUDGE, and FLANNERY, DISTRICT JUDGE for the District of Columbia.

WILKEY, CIRCUIT JUDGE:

. . .

In its decision appealed in *Central Florida I* the FCC concluded that the reasons undercutting Cowles' bid for renewal did "not outweigh the substantial service Cowles rendered to the public during the last license period." Accordingly, the license was renewed. Our reversal was rooted in a twofold finding. First, the Commission had inadequately investigated and analyzed the four factors weighing against Cowles' renewal. Second, the process by which the FCC weighed these four factors against Cowles' past record was never "even vaguely described" and, indeed, "the Commission's handling of the facts of this case [made] embarrassingly clear that the FCC [had] practically erected a presumption of renewal that is inconsistent with the full hearing requirement" of the Communications Act. We remand[ed] with instructions to the FCC to cure these deficiencies.

On remand the Commission has followed our directives and corrected, point by point, the inadequate investigation and analysis of the four factors cutting against Cowles' requested renewal. The Commission concluded that, indeed, three of the four merited an advantage for Central Florida, and on only one (the mail fraud issue) did it conclude that nothing needed to be added on the scale to Central's plan or removed from Cowles'. We cannot fault the Commission's actions here.

We are left, then, with evaluating the way in which the FCC weighed Cowles' main studio move violation and Central's superior diversification and integration, on the one hand, against Cowles' substantial record of performance on the other. This is the most difficult and important issue in this case, for the new weighing process which the FCC has adopted will presumably be employed in its renewal proceedings elsewhere. We therefore feel that it is necessary to scrutinize carefully the FCC's new approach, and discuss what we understand and expect it to entail.

For some time now the FCC has had to wrestle with the problem of how it can factor in some degree of "renewal expectancy" for a broadcaster's meritorious past record, while at the same time undertaking the required comparative evaluation of the incumbent's probable future performance versus the challenger's. As we stated in *Central Florida I,* "the incumbent's past performance is some evidence, and perhaps the best evidence, of what its future performance would be."

And it has been intimated—by the Supreme Court in FCC v. National Citizen's Committee for Broadcasting (NCCB) and by this court in Citizens Communications Center v. FCC and *Central Florida I*—that some degree of renewal expectancy is permissible. But *Citizens* and *Central Florida I* also indicated that the FCC has in the past impermissibly raised renewal expectancy to an irrebuttable presumption in favor of the incumbent.

We believe that the formulation by the FCC in its latest decision, however, is a permissible way to incorporate some renewal expectancy while still undertaking the required comparative hearing. *The new policy, as we understand it, is simply this: renewal expectancy is to be a factor weighed with all the other factors, and the better the past record, the greater the renewal expectancy "weight."*

> In our view [states the FCC], the strength of the expectancy depends on the merit of the past record. Where, as in this case, the incumbent rendered substantial but not superior service, the "expectancy" takes the form of a comparative preference weighed against [the] other factors . . . .. An incumbent performing in a superior manner would receive an even stronger preference. An incumbent rendering minimal service would receive no preference.

This is to be contrasted with the Commission's *1965 Policy Statement on Comparative Broadcast Hearings*, where "[o]nly unusually good or unusually poor records have relevance."

If a stricter standard is desired by Congress, it must enact it. We cannot: the new standard is within the statute.

The reasons given by the Commission for factoring in some degree of renewal expectancy are rooted in a concern that failure to do so would hurt broadcast *consumers.*

> The justification for a renewal expectancy is three-fold. (1) There is no guarantee that a challenger's paper proposals will, in fact, match the incumbent's proven performance. Thus, not only might replacing an incumbent be entirely gratuitous, but *it might even deprive the community of an acceptable service and replace it with an inferior one.* (2) Licensees should be encouraged through the likelihood of renewal to make investments *to ensure quality service. Comparative renewal proceedings cannot function as a "competitive spur" to licensees if their dedication to the community is not rewarded.* (3) Comparing incumbents and challengers as if they were both new applicants could lead to a haphazard restructuring of the broadcast industry especially considering the large number of group owners. *We cannot readily conclude that such a restructuring could serve the public interest.*

We are relying, then, on the FCC's commitment that renewal expectancy will be factored in for the benefit of the public, not for incumbent broadcasters. . . . . As we concluded in *Central Florida I,* "[t]he only legitimate fear which should move [incumbent] licensees is the fear of their own substandard performance, and that would be all to the good."

There is a danger, of course, that the FCC's new approach could still degenerate into precisely the sort of irrebuttable presumption in favor of renewal that we have warned against. But this did not happen in the case before us today, and our reading of the Commission's decision gives us hope that if the FCC applies the standard in the same way in future cases, it will not happen in them either. The standard is new, however, and much will depend on how the Commission applies it and fleshes it out. Of particular importance will be the definition and level of service it assigns to "substantial"—and whether that definition is ever found to be "opaque to judicial review," "wholly unintelligible," or based purely on "administrative 'feel.' " [27]

In this case, however, the Commission was painstaking and explicit in its balancing. The Commission discussed in quite specific terms, for instance, the items it found impressive in Cowles' past record. It stressed and listed numerous programs demonstrating Cowles' "local community orientation" and "responsive[ness] to community needs," discussed the percentage of Cowles' programming devoted to news, public affairs, and local topics, and said it was "impressed by [Cowles'] reputation in the community. Seven community leaders and three public officials testified that [Cowles] had made outstanding contributions to the local community. Moreover, the record shows no complaints . . .." The Commission concluded that "Cowles' record [was] more than minimal," was in fact " 'substantial,' i.e., 'sound, favorable and substantially above a level of mediocre service which might just minimally warrant renewal.' "

The Commission's inquiry in this case did not end with Cowles' record, but continued with a particularized analysis of what factors weighed against Cowles' record, and how much. The FCC investigated fully the mail fraud issue. It discussed the integration and diversification disadvantages of Cowles and conceded that Central had an edge on these issues—"slight" for integration, "clear" for diversification. But it reasoned that "structural factors such as [these]—of primary importance in a new license proceeding—should have lesser weight compared

---

27. Id. at 50 (quoting earlier proceeding, 60 F.C.C.2d 372, 422 (1976)). We think it would be helpful if at some point the Commission defined and explained the distinctions, if any, among: substantial, meritorious, average, above average, not above average, not far above average, above mediocre, more than minimal, solid, sound, favorable, not superior, not exceptional, and unexceptional—all terms used by the parties to describe what the FCC found Cowles' level of performance to have been. We are especially interested to know what the standard of comparison is in each case. "Average" compared to all applicants? "Mediocre" compared to all incumbents? "Favorable" with respect to the FCC's expectations? We realize that the FCC's task is a subjective one, but the use of imprecise terms needlessly compounds our difficulty in evaluating what the Commission has done. We think that we can discern enough to review intelligently the Commission's actions today, but if the air is not cleared or, worse, becomes foggier, the FCC's decisionmaking may again be adjudged "opaque to judicial review."

with the preference arising from substantial past service." [31]　　Finally, with respect to the illegal main studio move, the FCC found that "licensee misconduct" in general "may provide a more meaningful basis for preferring an untested challenger over a proven incumbent." The Commission found, however, that here the "comparative significance of the violation" was diminished by the underlying facts . . .. The FCC concluded that "the risk to the public interest posed by the violation seems small when compared to the actuality of depriving Daytona Beach of Cowles' tested and acceptable performance."

Having listed the relevant factors and assigned them weights, the Commission concluded that Cowles' license should be renewed. We note, however, that despite the finding that Cowles' performance was " 'substantial,' i.e., 'sound, favorable and substantially above a level of mediocre service,' " the combination of Cowles' main studio rule violation and Central's diversification and integration advantages made this a "close and difficult case." Again, we trust that this is more evidence that the Commission's weighing did not, and will not, amount to automatic renewal for incumbents.

We are somewhat reassured by a recent FCC decision granting for the first time since at least 1961, on *comparative* grounds the application of the challenger for a radio station license and denying the renewal application of the incumbent licensee.[38] In that decision the Commission found that the *incumbent deserved no renewal expectancy* for his past program record and that his application was inferior to the challenger's on comparative grounds. Indeed, it was the *incumbent's* preferences on the diversification and integration factors which were overcome (there, by the challenger's superior programming proposals and longer broadcast week). The Commission found that the incumbent's "inadequate [past performance] reflects poorly on the *likelihood of future service in the public interest.*" Further, it found that the incumbent had no "legitimate renewal expectancy" because his past performance was neither "meritorious" nor "substantial."

---

31. . . .

Here we have a caveat. We do not read the Commission's new policy as *ignoring* integration and diversification considerations in comparative renewal hearings. In its brief at page 6 the Commission states that "an incumbent's meritorious record should outweigh in the comparative renewal context a challenging applicant's advantages under the structural factors of integration and diversification." Ceteris paribus, this may be true—depending in part, of course, on how "meritorious" is defined. But where there are weights on the scales other than a meritorious record on the one hand, and integration and diversification on the other, the Commission must afford the latter two *some* weight, since while they alone may not outweigh a meritorious

record they may tip the balance if weighed with something else. See *Citizens,* 447 F.2d at 1208–09 n. 23.

That, of course, is precisely the situation here, since the main studio move violation must also be balanced against the meritorious record. The Commission may not weigh the antirenewal factors separately against the incumbent's record, eliminating them as it goes along. It must weigh them all simultaneously. . . .

38. In re Applications of Simon Geller and Grandebanke Corp., FCC Docket Nos. 21104–05 (Released 15 June 1982). We intimate no view at this time, of course, on the soundness of the Commission's decision there; we cite it only as demonstrating that the Commission's new approach may prove to be more than a paper tiger.

We have, however, an important caveat. In the Commission's weighing of factors the scale mid-mark must be neither the factors themselves, nor the interests of the broadcasting industry, nor some other secondary and artificial construct, but rather the intent of Congress, which is to say the interests of the listening public. All other doctrine is merely a means to this end, and it should not become more. If in a given case, for instance, the factual situation is such that the denial of a license renewal would not undermine renewal expectancy *in a way harmful to the public interest,* then renewal expectancy should not be invoked.[40]

Finally, we must note that we are still troubled by the fact that the record remains that an incumbent *television* licensee has *never* been denied renewal in a comparative challenge. American television viewers will be reassured, although a trifle baffled, to learn that even the worst television stations—those which are, presumably, the ones picked out as vulnerable to a challenge [42]—are so good that they never need replacing. We suspect that somewhere, sometime, somehow, some television licensee *should* fail in a comparative renewal challenge, but the FCC has never discovered such a licensee yet. As a court we cannot say that it must be Cowles here.

We hope that the standard now embraced by the FCC will result in the protection of the public, not just incumbent licensees. And in today's case we believe the FCC's application of the new standard was not inconsistent with the Commission's mandate. Accordingly the Commission's decision is

Affirmed.

Notes and Questions

1. Ironically, less than a year later, when the court was presented with the case alluded to in *Central Florida II* where the Commission awarded a radio license to a new applicant rather than the incumbent, the court did not approve. Simon Geller had operated a one-man classical music FM station in Gloucester, Mass., since the early 1960s. In 1981 Grandebanke Corporation filed a competing application. The Commission held that because less than one percent of the station's programming was of a nonentertainment nature and the station broadcast no news, editorials, or locally produced programming, Geller was not entitled to the benefit of renewal expectancy. Simon Geller, 91 F.C.C.2d 1253, 52 R.R.2d 709 (1982).

---

40. Thus, the justifications given by the Commission for renewal expectancy, [ ] should be remembered by the FCC in future renewal proceedings and, where these justifications are in a particular case attenuated, the Commission ought not to chant "renewal expectancy" and grant the license.

42. Counsel for the FCC conceded at oral argument, "I grant you, [competitors] wouldn't challenge the [incumbent] they thought was exceptional or far above average." The dissent from the Commission's decision declared it a "readily apparent fact that competing applicants file against only the ne'er-do-wells of the industry." 86 F.C.C.2d at 1055 n. 99.

On appeal, the FCC's action was vacated and the case remanded. The court began by characterizing it as "yet another meandering effort by the [FCC] to develop a paradigm for its license renewal hearings."

> For years this court has urged the FCC to put some bite into its comparative hearings. [citing *Central Florida I*] Indeed, we have too long hungered for just one instance in which the FCC properly denied an incumbent's renewal expectancy. Unfortunately, in the process of seeking to respond to this court's signals with regard to renewal expectancy, the FCC ignored its own precedents as to the other factors that must be considered in conducting a comparative analysis.

The court of appeals agreed that Geller was entitled to no renewal expectancy because his programming did not even attempt to respond to ascertained community needs and problems. The FCC then properly turned to the comparative criteria. Here, however, the court concluded that the FCC had improperly diminished the value of Geller's obvious advantages of diversification and integration of ownership and management because it tied each to its view of Geller's programming. The FCC thus failed to accord to Geller the importance it had usually attached to diversification and integration in prior cases. The case was remanded for further consideration. Geller v. Federal Communications Commission, 737 F.2d 74 (D.C.Cir.1984). As discussed previously, p. 112, *supra*, the Commission granted Geller's application for renewal.

2. Is the latest Commission explanation of its comparative renewal standards clear? Exactly how much renewal expectancy is there? Has the Commission adequately justified the need for a strong renewal expectancy? Some would argue that it is impossible to devise an adequate system of comparing incumbents and new applicants and that comparative renewals should be eliminated. Would this eliminate the incentive for licensees to serve the public interest?

3. The extension of license terms, p. 117, *supra*, meant that there were no renewal applications for two years. With a new round of applications came renewed criticism of the comparative criteria as well as complaints that challengers were abusing the system. The most frequent claim was that challengers were using the system to extort money from existing broadcasters. In response, the Commission issued an NOI/NPRM aimed at reforming the comparative renewal process. Among the proposed changes were limits on the amount of money that challengers can receive in return for withdrawing applications and/or petitions to deny and stricter ownership and financial disclosure requirements. The Commission also proposed to clarify the comparative licensing criteria, questioned the heavy weight given diversification of media as a criterion, and requested comments on both the weight that should be accorded renewal expectancy and the bases for awarding it. Formulation of Policies and Rules Relating to Broadcast Renewal Applicants, Competing Applicants, and Other Participants to the Com-

parative Renewal Process and to the Prevention of Abuses of the Renewal Process, 3 F.C.C.Rcd. 6019 (1988).

In 1989 the FCC took some initial steps towards curbing abuse of the license renewal process. First, the Commission adopted a prohibition on "all payments to competing applicants (other than the incumbent licensee) for the withdrawal of an application prior to the Initial Decision stage of a comparative hearing. Thereafter, we will approve settlements that do not exceed the withdrawing party's legitimate and prudent expenses for filing and litigating the competing application."

The Commission reasoned that this would weed out weak applications filed for the purpose of extracting settlement payments. The cost of staying in until an initial decision would be too great for a non *bona fide* applicant. Further, an applicant that lost in the initial decision stage would have very little leverage, especially if the initial decision was in the incumbent's favor.

At the same time allowing recovery of legitimate and prudent expenses after the initial decision provides "an efficient way to resolve comparative licensing proceedings, preserve funds for service to the public, and allow us to conserve our limited administrative resources."

The Commission also placed a legitimate and prudent expense limitation on settlements of petitions to deny:

> 41. We believe that a legitimate and prudent expense limitation on settlement payments of petitions to deny strikes the appropriate balance between deterring abuse and not discouraging the filing of such petitions. By prohibiting payments in excess of legitimate and prudent expenses we are removing the profit motive for filing petitions to deny. This should help ensure that petitions are filed for legitimate public interest purposes. By permitting recovery of legitimate and prudent expenses, we are preserving the petition to deny process as a monitoring and regulatory tool. It is more likely that individuals or public interest groups will perform their function of informing us of licensee deficiencies if they can maintain hope of recovery of the expenses they incur. To preserve the private attorney general function of petitions to deny, we believe we should provide for the possibility that a petitioner can be made economically whole.

The FCC also announced that it would review all future citizens' agreements—contracts in which licensees agree to "implement a nonfinancial reform such as a programming or an employment initiative" in return for the dismissal of a petition to deny. In determining whether an agreement furthers the public interest the Commission:

> . . . will presume that any agreement with a petitioner that calls for the *petitioner*, or any person or organization related to the petitioner, to carry out for a fee, any programming, employment or other "nonfinancial" initiative does not further the public interest and hence will be disapproved. As discussed above, this type of

arrangement is particularly susceptible to abuse. In contrast, a licensee's agreement with a petitioner to make changes in operations or programming, either *by itself* or through *disinterested third parties* without further participation by the petitioner, will likely be approved. For example, we will regard an agreement to increase minority employment by using, for a fee, the services of *petitioner* or any person or organization related to petitioner, as presumptively contrary to the public interest, and it will likely be disapproved. In contrast, we will regard an agreement to increase the pool of minority applicants for employment by contracting with a third party, completely independent from petitioner, as consistent with the public interest, and it will likely be approved.

The Commission will allow these presumptions to be rebutted by clear and convincing evidence that they are incorrect as applied to a specific citizens' agreement. Broadcast Renewal Applicants (Abuses of Comparative Renewal Process), 66 R.R.2d 708 (1989).

Various petitions for reconsideration were denied, 67 R.R.2d 1515 (1990). At the same time, the Commission adopted similar rules governing petitions to deny and citizens' agreements for new stations, license modification, and transfer applications. Abuses of the Broadcast Licensing and Allotment Processes, 67 R.R.2d 1526 (1990).

4. If the purpose of renewal expectancy is to encourage licensees to serve the public interest by rewarding those who do, is there any justification for granting renewal expectancy to licensees who provide subscription television service? The Commission decided that the standards for STV stations should be essentially the same as those for conventional stations. Video 44, 103 F.C.C.2d 408, 60 R.R.2d 21 (1986).

Subsequently, the Review Board reversed an ALJ decision denying Video 44 a renewal expectancy. The Board held that the ALJ had placed disproportionate weight on the less than one half year during which the station operated as an STV station. More importantly, the ALJ had only considered locally produced programming in deciding the renewal expectancy question. The Board held that renewal expectancy must be based on institutional and syndicated programming, as well as locally produced programming. Video 44, 3 F.C.C.Rcd. 3587, 64 R.R.2d 1517 (Rev.Bd.1988).

The Commission upheld the Review Board's action and awarded Video 44 a renewal expectancy. The FCC argued that it should not give too much weight to the drop in non-entertainment programming at the end of the license term because that drop resulted in large part from Video 44's "experimentation" with an STV format. Video 44, 4 F.C.C.Rcd. 1209, 65 R.R.2d 1512 (1989).

The court of appeals reversed the renewal expectancy award as arbitrary and capricious. The court quoted its opinion in *Central Florida II* that the primary argument for renewal expectancy is that "the incumbent's past performance is some evidence, and perhaps the best evidence, of what its future performance would be." Given that there was no evidence that the switch to STV was temporary, the station's performance under that format was better evidence than its performance under a previous format of what its future service to the public would be. The court remanded the case to the Commission "with instructions to focus on the downward trend in Video 44's non-entertainment programming through the latter stages of the previous license period in order to predict Video 44's likely performance in the license period at issue here." Monroe Communications Corp. v. Federal Communications Commission, 900 F.2d 351, 67 R.R.2d 843 (D.C.Cir. 1990).

On remand, the Commission found that Video 44's late term performance did not justify any renewal expectancy. With the elimination of Video 44's renewal expectancy preference, Monroe's preferences for integration and diversity became controlling. Video 44, 68 R.R.2d 503 (1990).

C. TRANSFER OF LICENSES

In part because of the Commission's renewal policies, radio and television licenses have acquired substantial value. When a licensee decides to leave broadcasting altogether or to switch services or locations at the end of a license period, the licensee has no opportunity to reap profit. To reap profits, the licensee must seek renewal and, during the term, sell the facilities and goodwill and assign the license to a prospective buyer. In some ways this "transfer" procedure resembles the sale of any business, but the Commission's rules substantially affect the transaction.

Section 310(d) of the Communications Act requires the Commission to pass on all transfers and find that "the public interest, convenience, and necessity will be served thereby." But it also provides that in deciding whether the public interest would be served by the transfer the Commission "may not consider whether the public interest . . . might be served by the transfer . . . to a person other than the proposed transferee or assignee." Why might Congress have imposed this limitation?

When a transferee applies for its first full term, should it be judged as an original applicant who must compete in a comparative hearing without any advantage of incumbency or as a renewal applicant? What are the justifications for each view?

Despite the possible objections to transfer applications, most are granted, usually with little or no delay. This kind of turnover suggests a problem for the Commission. If licenses acquire substantial value a tendency may develop to build up stations and then sell them at a profit. This might be viewed as undermining the "public interest" philosophy of the licensing process. On the other hand, the public may benefit from someone's building up a station, even though that person's motive is to sell it for a profit.

In 1962 the Commission adopted a rule prohibiting licensees from transferring a broadcast license during the first three years after acquisition unless a hardship waiver—usually upon a showing of financial loss—was granted. The rationale for this rule was a belief that it took three years for a licensee to learn the needs and interests of the community and institute programming responsive to those needs and interests. Frequent changes in ownership were viewed as disruptive and thus contrary to the public interest. Applications for Voluntary Assignments or Transfer of Control, 32 F.C.C. 689 (1962).

Twenty years later the Commission reversed its position on this issue after concluding that a willing buyer was more likely to serve the public interest than an unwilling owner prohibited from selling the station. Although the three-year rule was abolished, a one-year limitation was instituted for licenses acquired through the comparative hearing process. Applications for Voluntary Assignments or Transfer of Control, 52 R.R.2d 1081 (1982). Subsequently the one-year rule was extended to licenses obtained through the minority ownership policy. We will discuss this policy in Chapter V.

1.　Format Changes

Until 1970 the foregoing summary would have covered most of the major problems related to transfers, but then the question of format change arose, plaguing the courts and the Commission for a decade until the Supreme Court decided the issue. The problem arose when a prospective transferee of a radio license proposed to change the station's distinctive programming format.

FEDERAL COMMUNICATIONS COMMISSION
v. WNCN LISTENERS GUILD

Supreme Court of the United States, 1981.
450 U.S. 582, 101 S.Ct. 1266, 67 L.Ed.2d 521, 49 R.R.2d 271, 5 Med.L.Rptr. 1449.

Mr. Justice White delivered the opinion of the Court.

Sections 309(a) and 310(d) of the Communications Act of 1934, 48 Stat. 1064, as amended, 47 U.S.C. § 151 et seq. (Act), empower the Federal Communications Commission to grant an application for license transfer or renewal only if it determines that "the public interest, convenience, and necessity" will be served thereby. The issue before us is whether there are circumstances in which the Commission must review past or anticipated changes in a station's entertainment programming when it rules on an application for renewal or transfer of a radio broadcast license. The Commission's present position is that it may rely on market forces to promote diversity in entertainment programming and thus serve the public interest.

This issue arose when, pursuant to its informal rulemaking authority, the Commission issued a "Policy Statement" concluding that the public interest is best served by promoting diversity in entertainment formats through market forces and competition among broadcasters and that a change in entertainment programming is therefore not a material factor that should be considered by the Commission in ruling on an application for license renewal or transfer. Respondents, a number of citizens groups interested in fostering and preserving particular entertainment formats, petitioned for review in the Court of Appeals for the District of Columbia Circuit. That court held that the Commission's Policy Statement violated the Act. We reverse the decision of the Court of Appeals.

I

Beginning in 1970, in a series of cases involving license transfers, the Court of Appeals for the District of Columbia Circuit gradually developed a set of criteria for determining when the "public-interest" standard requires the Commission to hold a hearing to review proposed changes in entertainment. Noting that the aim of the Act is "to secure the maximum benefits of radio to all the people of the United States, [ ], the Court of Appeals ruled in 1974 that "preservation of a format [that] would otherwise disappear, although economically and technologically viable and preferred by a significant number of listeners, is generally in the public interest." [ ] It concluded that a change in format would not present "substantial and material questions of fact" requiring a hearing if (1) notice of the change had not precipitated "significant public grumbling"; (2) the segment of the population preferring the format was too small to be accommodated by available frequencies; (3) there was an adequate substitute in the service area for the format being abandoned; or (4) the format would be economically unfeasible even if the station were managed efficiently. The court rejected the Commission's position that the choice of entertainment formats should be left to the judgment of the licensee, stating that the Commission's interpretation of the public-interest standard was contrary to the Act.

In January 1976, the Commission responded to these decisions by undertaking an inquiry into its role in reviewing format changes. In particular, the Commission sought public comment on whether the public interest would be better served by Commission scrutiny of entertainment programming or by reliance on the competitive marketplace.

Following public notice and comment, the Commission issued a Policy Statement pursuant to its rulemaking authority under the Act. The Commission concluded in the Policy Statement that review of format changes was not compelled by the language or history of the Act, would not advance the welfare of the radio-listening public, would pose substantial administrative problems, and would deter innovation in radio programming. In support of its position, the Commission quoted from FCC v. Sanders Brothers Radio Station, 309 U.S. 470, 475 (1940): "Congress intended to leave competition in the business of broadcasting where it found it, to permit a licensee . . . to survive or succumb according to his ability to make his programs attractive to the public." The Commission also emphasized that a broadcaster is not a common carrier and therefore should not be subjected to a burden similar to the common carrier's obligation to continue to provide service if abandonment of that service would conflict with public convenience or necessity.

The Commission also concluded that practical considerations as well as statutory interpretation supported its reluctance to regulate changes in formats. Such regulation would require the Commission to categorize the formats of a station's prior and subsequent programming to determine whether a change in format had occurred; to determine whether the prior format was "unique"; and to weigh the public detriment resulting from the abandonment of a unique format against the public benefit resulting from that change. The Commission emphasized the difficulty of objectively evaluating the strength of listener preferences, of comparing the desire for diversity within a particular type of programming to the desire for a broader range of program formats and of assessing the financial feasibility of a unique format.

Finally, the Commission explained why it believed that market forces were the best available means of producing diversity in entertainment formats. First, in large markets, competition among broadcasters had already produced "an almost bewildering array of diversity" in entertainment formats. Second, format allocation by market forces accommodates listeners' desires for diversity within a given format and also produces a variety of formats. Third, the market is far more flexible than governmental regulation and responds more quickly to changing public tastes. Therefore, the Commission concluded that "the market is the allocation mechanism of preference for entertainment formats, and . . . Commission supervision in this area will not be conducive either to producing program diversity [or] satisfied radio listeners."

The Court of Appeals, sitting en banc, held that the Commission's policy was contrary to the Act as construed and applied in the court's prior format decisions. [ ] The court questioned whether the Commission had rationally and impartially re-examined its position and particularly criticized the Commission's failure to disclose a staff study on the effectiveness of market allocation of formats before it issued the Policy Statement. The court then responded to the Commission's criticisms of the format doctrine. First, although conceding that market forces generally lead to diversification of formats, it concluded that the market only imperfectly reflects listener preferences [23] and that the Commission is statutorily obligated to review format changes whenever there is "strong prima facie evidence that the market has in fact broken down." [ ] Second, the court stated that the administrative

---

23. The court observed . . . that because broadcasters rely on advertising revenue they tend to serve persons with large discretionary incomes. [ ] The dissenting opinion noted that the Commission had not rejected this assumption. [ ]

problems posed by the format doctrine were not insurmountable. Hearings would only be required in a small number of cases, and the Commission could cope with problems such as classifying radio format by adopting "a rational classification schema." [ ] Third, the court observed that the Commission had not demonstrated that the format doctrine would deter innovative programming. Finally, the court explained that it had not directed the Commission to engage in censorship or to impose common carrier obligations on licensees: *WEFM* did not authorize the Commission to interfere with licensee programming choices or to force retention of an existing format; it merely stated that the Commission had the power to consider a station's format in deciding whether license renewal or transfer would be consistent with the public interest. [ ]

Although conceding that it possessed neither the expertise nor the authority to make policy decisions in this area, the Court of Appeals asserted that the format doctrine was "law," not "policy," and was of the view that the Commission had not disproved the factual assumptions underlying the format doctrine. Accordingly, the court declared that the Policy Statement was "unavailing and of no force and effect." [ ]

II

Rejecting the Commission's reliance on market forces to develop diversity in programming as an unreasonable interpretation of the Act's public-interest standard, the Court of Appeals held that in certain circumstances the Commission is required to regard a change in entertainment format as a substantial and material fact in deciding whether a license renewal or transfer is in the public interest. With all due respect, however, we are unconvinced that the Court of Appeal's format doctrine is compelled by the Act and that the Commission's interpretation of the public-interest standard must therefore be set aside.

It is common ground that the Act does not define the term "public interest, convenience, and necessity." The Court has characterized the public-interest standard of the Act as "a supple instrument for the exercise of discretion by the expert body which Congress has charged to carry out its legislative policy." [ ] Although it was declared in National Broadcasting Co. v. United States, supra, that the goal of the Act is "to secure the maximum benefits of radio to all the people of the United States," [ ], it was also emphasized that Congress had granted the Commission broad discretion in determining how that goal could best be achieved. The Court accordingly declined to substitute its own views on the best method of encouraging effective use of the radio for the views of the Commission. [ ] Similarly, in FCC v. National Citizens Committee for Broadcasting, 436 U.S. 775 (1978), we deemed the policy of promoting the widest possible dissemination of information from diverse sources to be consistent with both the public-interest standard and the First Amendment, [ ], but emphasized the Commission's broad power to regulate in the public interest. We noted that the

Act permits the Commission to promulgate "such rules and regulations, . . . not inconsistent with law, as may be necessary to carry out the provisions of [the Act]," and that this general rule-making authority permits the Commission to implement its view of the public-interest standard of the Act "so long as that view is based on consideration of permissible factors and is otherwise reasonable." [   ] Furthermore, we recognized that the Commission's decisions must sometimes rest on judgment and prediction rather than pure factual determinations. In such cases complete factual support for the Commission's ultimate conclusions is not required since " 'a forecast of the direction in which future public interest lies necessarily involves deductions based on the expert knowledge of the agency.' "

The Commission has provided a rational explanation for its conclusion that reliance on the market is the best method of promoting diversity in entertainment formats. . . . The Court of Appeals places great value on preserving diversity among formats, while the Commission emphasizes the value of intraformat as well as interformat diversity. Finally, the Court of Appeals is convinced that review of format changes would result in a broader range of formats, while the Commission believes that government intervention is likely to deter innovative programming.

. . .

Our opinions have repeatedly emphasized that the Commission's judgment regarding how the public interest is best served is entitled to substantial judicial deference. [   ] Furthermore, diversity is not the only policy the Commission must consider in fulfilling its responsibilities under the Act. The Commission's implementation of the public-interest standard, when based on a rational weighing of competing policies, is not to be set aside by the Court of Appeals, for "the weighing of policies under the 'public interest' standard is a task that Congress has delegated to the Commission in the first instance." [   ] The Commission's position on review of format changes reflects a reasonable accommodation of the policy of promoting diversity in programming and the policy of avoiding unnecessary restrictions on licensee discretion. As we see it, the Commission's Policy Statement is in harmony with cases recognizing that the Act seeks to preserve journalistic discretion while promoting the interests of the listening public.

. . .

III

. . .

A major underpinning of its Policy Statement is the Commission's conviction, rooted in its experience, that renewal and transfer cases should not turn on the Commission's presuming to grasp, measure, and weigh the elusive and difficult factors involved in determining the acceptability of changes in entertainment format. To assess whether the elimination of a particular "unique" entertainment format would serve the public interest, the Commission would have to consider the benefit as well as the detriment that would result from the change. Necessarily, the Commission would take into consideration not only the number of listeners who favor the old and the new programming but also the intensity of their preferences. It would also consider the effect of the format change on diversity within formats as well as on diversity among formats. The Commission is convinced that its judgments in these respects would be subjective in large measure and would only approximately serve the public interest. It is also convinced that the market, although imperfect, would serve the public interest as well or better by responding quickly to changing preferences and by inviting experimentation with new types of programming. Those who would overturn the Commission's Policy Statement do not take adequate account of these considerations.

. . .

IV

Respondents contend that the Court of Appeals' judgment should be affirmed because, even if not violative of the Act, the Policy Statement conflicts with the First Amendment rights of listeners "to receive suitable access to social, political, esthetic, moral, and other ideas and experiences." Red Lion Broadcasting Co. v. FCC, 395 U.S. 367, 390 (1969). *Red Lion* held that the Commission's "fairness doctrine" was consistent with the public-interest standard of the Communications Act and did not violate the First Amendment, but rather enhanced First Amendment values by promoting "the presentation of vigorous debate of controversial issues of importance and concern to the public." [   ] Although observing that the interests of the people as a whole were promoted by debate of public issues on the radio, we did not imply that the First Amendment grants individual listeners the right to have the Commission review the abandonment of their favorite entertainment programs. The Commission seeks to further the interests of the listening public as a whole by relying on market forces to promote diversity in radio entertainment formats and to satisfy the entertainment preferences of radio listeners. This policy does not conflict with the First Amendment.

Contrary to the judgment of the Court of Appeals, the Commission's Policy Statement is not inconsistent with the Act. It is also a constitutionally permissible means of implementing the public-interest standard of the Act. Accordingly, the judgment of the Court of Appeals is reversed, and the case is remanded for further proceedings consistent with this opinion.

So ordered.

[Justice Marshall joined by Justice Brennan dissented, arguing that the Commission's failure to include a waiver provision in the Policy Statement made it too inflexible:

The Policy Statement completely forecloses any possibility that the Commission will reexamine the validity of its general policy on format changes as it applies to particular situations. Thus, even when it can be conclusively demonstrated that a particular radio market does not function in the manner predicted by the Commission, the Policy Statement indicates that the Commission will blindly assume that a proposed format change is in the "public interest." This result would occur even where reliance on the market to ensure format diversity is shown to be misplaced, and where it thus appears that action by the Commission is necessary to promote the public interest in diversity. This outcome is not consistent with the Commission's statutory responsibilities.

Justice Marshall argued that although the court of appeals might have gone too far in providing specific guidelines for handling unique formats, it was well within its authority when it held that the lack of any "safety valve" in the Policy Statement was a violation of the Commission's public interest obligations.]

Notes and Questions

1. *WNCN Listeners Guild,* like many of the cases involving the Commission, revolves around the problem of defining "public interest, convenience and necessity." Is a clear definition possible? If not, how much deference should the Commission be given in applying the standard?

2. In his dissent, Justice Marshall argued that it was not impossible for the Commission to define formats. He noted two suggestions by the court of appeals for dealing with this issue. One was to develop "a format taxonomy which, even if imprecise at the margins, would be sustainable so long as not irrational." Alternatively, the Commission could avoid defining formats altogether "by simply taking the existence of significant and bona fide listener protest as sufficient evidence that the station's endangered programming has certain unique features for which there are no ready substitutes."

Are these two suggestions in any way contradictory? The first emphasizes treating the format as a whole, and the latter focuses on individual features within a format. What are the pros and cons of each approach?

3. The Policy Statement at issue in *WNCN Listeners Guild* dealt only with renewals and transfers. Assuming that the Commission should review at least some format changes, is it practical to do so only with regard to applications for transfer or renewal? Under these restrictions review of a format change might not be possible until six years after the change takes place.

4. In 1985 a citizen group again tried to get the Commission to hold a hearing on a transfer involving a format change. The group alleged that because the station in question was simulcasting programming on its AM and FM stations 25 percent of the time and running similar

formats the rest of the time, it was clear that competition in the marketplace was not producing diversity and therefore the Policy Statement should not apply. The Commission refused to hold a hearing, reaffirming its position of non-intervention in format controversies. WEAM Radio, Inc., 58 R.R.2d 141 (1985).

The court of appeals affirmed the Commission's decision not to hold a hearing. Citing *WNCN Listeners Guild,* the court held that the Commission can rely on the Policy Statement unless presented with persuasive evidence that the rationale of the Policy Statement is not applicable to the market in which the station in question is located. Committee to Save WEAM v. Federal Communications Commission, 808 F.2d 113, 61 R.R.2d 1444 (D.C.Cir.1986).

5. However, in another format case, a Commission decision to dismiss a petition to deny and grant renewal without a hearing was reversed by the court of appeals. The petition to deny was filed by Citizens for Jazz on WRVR, Inc. The court felt that there was sufficient evidence that the licensee, Viacom, Inc., misrepresented its programming intentions in its transfer application. Citizens for Jazz on WRVR, Inc. v. Federal Communications Commission, 775 F.2d 392, 59 R.R.2d 249 (D.C.Cir. 1985).

2. THE RKO CASE

Perhaps the most complex and longest-running licensing controversy involves the stations owned by RKO General, Inc. Although most of the controversy has been tied to renewal applications for the various stations, transfer applications have also been involved. Overall, this continuing soap opera highlights many issues raised by the licensing process.

The first RKO license to be challenged was that of KHJ, Channel 9, Los Angeles, in 1966. The examiner recommended denial of renewal and granting of the license to the challenger, Fidelity Television, Inc. He criticized KHJ's past programming, particularly its concentration on old films and its ignoring of community criticism of excessive violence in the movies. The Commission reversed the examiner and granted the renewal. In comparing the various factors, the Commission concluded that RKO's programming and community relations, though not "unusually good" or "superior," were also not "insubstantial" or "unusually poor." Thus, the "record must be deemed to be within the bounds of average performance expected of all licensees" and warranted neither a merit nor a demerit. After reviewing all the factors the Commission concluded that the two applicants were essentially equal and that the outcome rested on a decision that "credit must be given in a comparative renewal proceeding, when the applicants are otherwise equal, for the value to the public in the continuation of the existing service."

The challenger's appeal was rejected, Fidelity Television, Inc. v. Federal Communications Commission, 515 F.2d 684, 32 R.R.2d 1607, rehearing denied 34 R.R.2d 419 (D.C.Cir.), certiorari denied 423 U.S. 926 (1975). One ground of appeal concerned the Commission's refusal to consider programming proposals even though Fidelity proposed to offer 22 percent less entertainment and twice as much educational and news programming as KHJ. The court observed that the Commission's refusal to consider this on the ground that differences were only judgmental, might be questionable, but found that the refusal was also based on the defensible ground of the challenger's inadequate ascertainment. The court then upheld the determination that KHJ's performance was "average" because it was not "bereft of the support of substantial evidence." The court stressed that this was not a situation in which a "superior applicant is denied a license because to give it to him would work a 'forfeiture' of his opponent's investment." Rather, the incumbent's performance, was enough to "withstand the competition of a 'nothing' competitor."

While this case was progressing through the Commission and court of appeals, two other RKO General stations were challenged when they applied for license renewal. In 1969 two challengers, Community Broadcasting of Boston, Inc., and The Dudley Station Corp., filed applications for the license of WNAC–TV, Channel 7, Boston, and in 1974 Multi-state Communications, Inc. filed an application for the license of WOR–TV, Channel 9, New York City.

Among the issues that were raised in the WNAC–TV proceeding were allegations that RKO and its parent company, General Tire and Rubber Co., had engaged in anticompetitive practices and that RKO had violated the sponsorship identification requirements of § 317 during its broadcasts of the "Della Reese Show." (We will discuss sponsorship identification in Chapter VII.) In 1974 the ALJ awarded the license to RKO after concluding that RKO had not knowingly engaged in anticompetitive practices and that the violations that occurred with respect to the "Della Reese Show" were cause for a comparative demerit as opposed to disqualification.

In early 1975 the Securities and Exchange Commission started investigating General Tire with respect to illegal bribes of foreign public officials and illegal foreign bank accounts. Then, in late 1975, before the full FCC had heard oral argument on WNAC–TV's license renewal, Community filed a petition to reopen the record and enlarge the issues. The petition, accompanied by 640 pages of exhibits, alleged that General Tire had engaged in illegal and unethical conduct in both the United States and foreign countries and that RKO had violated the FCC's rules and "exhibited a lack of candor" by failing to disclose ongoing investigations into General Tire's conduct.

Meanwhile, the ongoing SEC investigation uncovered several examples of misconduct by General Tire. Finally, an SEC complaint was filed on May 10, 1976, covering among others, all the misconduct detailed in the 1975 Community petition. On the same day, General Tire entered into a consent decree that prohibited "the concealment of any of the misconduct alleged in the SEC complaint including, *inter alia,* unlawful political contributions, unlawful payments to foreign government officials and the overbilling of affiliates and subsidiaries." The decree also set up a Special Review Committee to further investigate General Tire's conduct and file a report with the SEC and the court. On May 14, 1976, RKO advised the FCC of the SEC inquiry and the consent decree for the first time.

On June 29, 1976, oral argument on the ALJ's renewal award to RKO was held before the FCC, *en banc,* and the Commission decided that any action should be delayed until the submission of the Review Committee's report. While the parties awaited the filing of the report, further issues surfaced. During the years 1972–1976, RKO had knowingly failed to properly complete the barter and trade portion of the financial report (form 324) that was required at that time. Community filed a further petition raising this issue in April 1977.

When the Special Review Committee's report was finally filed in July 1977, it confirmed most of Community's allegations. Among the Review Committee's findings were the following: "(a) General Tire and certain of its subsidiaries engaged in various schemes and practices that resulted in improper domestic political contributions; (b) Aerojet, an RKO subsidiary, gave gratuities to military and other government-connected personnel having dealings with Aerojet; (c) General Tire and its affiliates maintained and used improper secret and unrecorded funds designed to avoid foreign currency exchange and tax laws; (d) General Tire and its affiliates paid bribes to foreign agents and officials not only to do business in a country but also to keep competitors out; (e) through the use of secret bank accounts, General Tire systematically overbilled its foreign affiliates; and (f) RKO did not maintain adequate records concerning the amount or use of consideration resulting from its barter and trade transactions."

In 1978, before the FCC had taken further action on the renewal application, Community and Dudley filed another petition seeking approval of the transfer of WNAC–TV's license to New England Television Corporation—formed by the merger of Community and Dudley— for $54 million. The sale was contingent on the FCC's granting RKO's renewal application. The petition was opposed by Fidelity Television, Inc. and Multi–State Communications, Inc., challengers for RKO's Los Angeles and New York television licenses respectively. Those proceedings had by this time been conditioned on the outcome of the Boston proceeding.

In 1980 the Commission denied the RKO application for renewal of the WNAC–TV license:

> In general the evidence is clear and convincing that RKO has engaged in a variety of misconduct which renders it unfit to be a Commission licensee for Channel 7 in Boston. RKO has engaged in an improper reciprocal trades program that was anticompetitive, it has knowingly filed false financial statements with this Commis-

sion, and it has not been entirely honest and forthcoming in its dealings with the Commission in these proceedings. Our concern here is heightened by the misconduct engaged in by RKO's parent, General Tire. General Tire not only controls RKO as a legal matter; the record also demonstrates that General Tire has exercised practical control over RKO operations in certain respects and has involved the broadcast operations in serious misconduct. It is that close legal and practical relationship that further taints RKO's qualifications. This record thus compels the conclusion that we cannot trust RKO to operate Channel 7 in the future in a manner consistent with the public interest.

The Commission also denied RKO's renewal applications for the Los Angeles and New York stations reasoning that RKO was equally unfit to hold those licenses. However, the Commission delayed any final action on the one other TV license and 12 radio licenses held by RKO.

Commissioners Lee and Quello filed separate dissents, each arguing that the punishment—potentially the loss of all 16 licenses—was gross overkill. Commissioner Lee entitled his dissent "Capital Punishment." Commissioner Washburn dissented separately on the grounds that there was insufficient connection between General Tire's conduct and the ability of RKO to operate its stations in the public interest to justify the penalty. An appeal was taken.

RKO v. FEDERAL COMMUNICATIONS COMMISSION

United States Court of Appeals, District of Columbia Circuit, 1981.
670 F.2d 215, 50 R.R.2d 821.
Certiorari denied, 457 U.S. 1119, 102 S.Ct. 2931, 73 L.Ed.2d 1331 (1982).

Before TAMM, MIKVA and EDWARDS, CIRCUIT JUDGES.

MIKVA, CIRCUIT JUDGE:

. . .

II. INVALID BASES OF THE FCC DECISION

At the outset, we hold that the FCC has stated at least three independent grounds for its ultimate finding that RKO should be disqualified as a broadcast licensee in Boston. The Decision states that RKO's reciprocal dealings "alone" require disqualification, [ ], that RKO's "willful and repeated [financial] misrepresentation warrants disqualification by itself," [ ], and that perhaps of greatest importance, RKO has demonstrated a persistent lack of candor with the Commission in these proceedings. . . .

. . .

A. *Reciprocal Trade Practices*

There are several reasons to doubt that reciprocal trade practices during the early 1960s can justify out-right disqualification of RKO as a broadcast licensee in 1980. First and foremost, the conduct of RKO at issue has been found to be clearly improper only in retrospect. Although it has been understood since the 1930s that "coercive" reciprocity was anticompetitive, it was not until the late 1960s that a series of judicial decisions began to cast increasing doubt on the legality and propriety of unleveraged "mutual patronage" agreements. Even then, however, questions remained. As late as 1979, the FCC itself recognized that a *per se* rule was probably inappropriate . . .. The FCC unquestionably has the authority and even the duty to change its mind as to the degree of anticompetitive practices that are not in the public interest. [ ] Such a finding may not be applied retroactively, however, to conduct that ceased almost fifteen years ago. [ ]

We are particularly concerned that in retroactively applying its "greater appreciation" for the adverse effects of reciprocal trading, the FCC has abruptly reversed its decision to the contrary in RKO General, Inc. (KHJ–TV), 44 F.C.C.2d 149 (1969), aff'd sub nom. Fidelity Television, Inc. v. FCC, 515 F.2d 684. That case held that essentially the same conduct was neither disqualifying nor ground even for a comparative demerit. Failure to explain the reversal of a directly controlling precedent is unlawful. [ ] . . . Although the FCC conditioned its first decision on RKO's reciprocal dealings on the possibility that significant new evidence might be introduced in the subsequent WNAC proceeding, such evidence never appeared. Additional evidence of reciprocal trading was heard in that second proceeding, but the bulk related to nonbroadcast activities by General Tire rather than RKO, and the remainder was merely cumulative of evidence in the first proceeding.

Finally, we doubt the Commission's claim that it can predict RKO's future character and performance from evidence concerning conduct that took place between 1961 and 1964. Only the unusual nature of these proceedings allows the FCC to argue that such evidence is at all relevant. FCC precedents consider a licensee's behavior during the preceding license term relevant to renewal requests for the following term. Central Florida Enterprises, Inc. v. FCC, 598 F.2d 37, 43 (D.C.Cir.1978), cert. dismissed, 441 U.S. 957 (1979); Citizens Communications Center v. FCC, 447 F.2d 1201, 1208 (D.C.Cir.1971). RKO sought renewal for the 1969–1972 term, and the FCC has failed to allege acts of reciprocity during the earlier term from 1966 to 1969. But RKO's renewal application for KHJ concerned the 1965–1968 term, thereby giving the FCC an excuse for claiming that conduct from 1962 to 1965 "is precisely the conduct at issue." [ ] Even so, the FCC acknowledges that the recency of misconduct is an important factor for purposes of character evaluation. [ ] The Commission has not paid sufficient heed to that principle here.

. . .

B. *Financial Misrepresentations*

The Commission's finding that RKO submitted intentionally false financial reports is equally insufficient to support RKO's disqualification. The Decision states that "RKO knowingly certified to the Commission that certain financial reports were complete and accurate when RKO knew otherwise." [ ]   The FCC's conclusion presumes that RKO's inaccuracies were either deliberate and intentionally deceptive, [ ], or that RKO's reports were made with such "wanton, gross, and callous" disregard for their truth as to reflect the equivalent of such an "affirmative and deliberate intent." [ ]   Despite the fact that RKO had consistently denied acting with such intent or disregard, the FCC brushed aside proffered RKO affidavits to that effect and drew adverse inferences without allowing RKO to defend itself in a hearing. Such a procedure is not lawful.

. . .

The Special Report does demonstrate a pervasive failure to maintain adequate records at RKO stations, a failure that does nothing to recommend RKO as a broadcast licensee. But it is a far leap from this to the finding that RKO intentionally or knowingly misrepresented financial information to the Commission. Section 309 of the Communications Act, 47 U.S.C. § 309(e) (1976), requires the Commission to hold a hearing in cases where "a substantial and material question of fact is presented," and to specify "with particularity the matters and things in issue but not including issues or requirements phrased generally." Whether RKO submitted inaccurate reports knowingly and with intent to mislead the Commission remains an unresolved and material question of fact, and it was therefore error for the Commission to disqualify RKO without following the procedures outlined by the statute.

C. *General Tire's Nonbroadcast Misconduct*

The FCC found it unnecessary to reach the question of whether RKO would have been disqualified had the only adverse character evidence been that relating to General Tire's nonbroadcast misconduct. [ ]   Instead, the Commission found that General Tire's misconduct had "an adverse effect on RKO's qualifications" and lent "substantial weight" to the Commission's decision to disqualify RKO on each of the other grounds. [ ]   We find nothing unlawful in this approach, although it raises other questions.

As General Tire's own admissions in the Special Report illustrate, its conduct in nonbroadcast fields hardly enhances RKO's character assessment. . . .   Were RKO's owner a single individual as opposed to a corporation, it appears that a far lesser showing of character flaws would support disqualification. [ ]   For reasons that are far from clear, however, the FCC seems to distinguish between misconduct by individual owners and misconduct by corporate entities. [ ]

It is difficult to discern any legitimacy for such differential treatment of individuals as opposed to corporate owners. It is to be hoped that pending FCC efforts to clarify the character standards to be applied in comparative hearings will cast more light on this point. See Policy Regarding Character Qualifications in Broadcast Licensing: Notice of Inquiry, 87 F.C.C.2d 836 (1981). In any event, the FCC has not tried in this appeal to increase the significance attached to corporate misconduct in nonbroadcast areas, [ ], nor could it have done so without first serving notice that its policy had changed. . . .

In short three of the four areas on which the FCC focused in its Decision will not serve as a basis for RKO's outright disqualification, at least on this record. It is not necessary to underscore our criticism too pointedly, however. We uphold the Commission's disqualification of RKO in the Boston proceeding because we conclude that the Decision's ultimate basis, RKO's lack of candor before the FCC, fully and independently supports that judgment.

III.   RKO's LACK OF CANDOR

The Commission found that three instances demonstrated RKO's lack of candor before the agency during a period from 1975 to 1977. First, RKO failed to inform the FCC that there was a factual basis to the allegations first made against General Tire by Community in late 1975. [ ]   Second, RKO failed to report the initiation of a formal SEC investigation of General Tire in February 1976. [ ]   Finally, RKO failed to concede that it had inaccurately reported trade and barter revenues when pressed to do so by Community in April 1977, despite the indication in General Tire's 1976 Annual Report that there might be some problems with these accounts. [ ]

A.   The Merits of the FCC's Finding

The record fully supports the Commission's finding that RKO did not display full candor before the Commission during the period from late 1975 to July 1976. Uncontroverted documentary evidence shows that General Tire responded to the initial phase of the SEC's inquiry regarding overseas operations in May 1975. [ ]   As the SEC investigation progressed, RKO's competitors began pressing the FCC to reopen the Boston proceeding, alleging facts that were similar or identical to the admissions later made by General Tire in the consent decree and its Special Report. RKO's first response was to seek an extension of time in which to respond, citing the need to consult with "persons who may have knowledge of the pertinent facts." [ ]   More than a month later, in January 1976, RKO clearly decided to stonewall the opposition and the FCC. This seems the only explanation for RKO's decision to file a document opposing the suggestion that the Boston proceeding be reopened on the ground that "there is no factual or legal foundation for this pyramid of charges," that "the charges, as we show below, are groundless," and that other charges were "essentially unsupported."

RKO contends that these statements were technically correct. [ ] It adds that because the burden lay on Community to establish grounds for reopening the proceeding, RKO's pleadings "in context" merely claimed that this burden had not been met. Both arguments are irrelevant, because the question before the FCC was not so much what RKO said as what it had failed to say.

Section 1.65 of the Commission's Rules requires applicants to inform the Commission within thirty days whenever "there has been a substantial change" regarding any matter that may be "of decisional significance in a Commission proceeding involving the pending application." 47 C.F.R. § 1.65 (1979). This requires that an applicant inform the Commission "of *all* facts, whether requested in [renewal] Form 303 or not, that may be of decisional significance so that the Commission can make a realistic decision based on all relevant factors." [ ] Unlike a private party haled into court, or a corporation such as General Tire facing an investigation by the SEC, RKO had an affirmative obligation to inform the Commission of the facts the FCC needed in order to license broadcasters in the public interest. As a licensing authority, the Commission is not expected to "play procedural games with those who come before it in order to ascertain the truth," [ ], and license applicants may not indulge in common-law pleading strategies of their own devise.

The Decision and the record on which it is based demonstrate irrefutably that RKO did not meet these standards, and that RKO's conduct thus threatened "the integrity of the Commission's processes." RKO General, Inc., 82 F.C.C.2d 291, 306 (1980). In spite of an SEC investigation that was rapidly gathering steam, and in spite of the fact that its qualifications as a licensee were at issue before the FCC, RKO failed to come forward with a candid statement of relevant facts. RKO did not inform the FCC that the SEC had issued a formal order of investigation in February 1976, even though this suggested the seriousness of the charges against General Tire. RKO did not advise the FCC of the SEC's preliminary findings until May 14, 1976, despite the fact that General Tire had advised its stockholders of these preliminary findings in February when it released its 1975 Annual Report. RKO did not advise the FCC until May 1976 that General Tire's own internal investigation demonstrated that many of the SEC concerns were valid, even though Community had submitted General Tire's 10–K Report the previous March. RKO never once attempted to amend or supplement its earlier pleadings with the FCC, despite a growing awareness of the facts that General Tire would later admit in its Special Report. These instances involve a lack of candor through omission. Whether or not RKO would have had an obligation to come forward with these facts under other circumstances, it could not have doubted their relevance once the filings and petitions of the intervenors put these questions before the Commission. We need not decide whether RKO's pleadings were affirmatively misleading—it is enough to find that they did not state the facts.

. . . It is . . . unnecessary to show that RKO officials had actual knowledge in early 1976 of the improprieties and illegalities to which General Tire later admitted, or that RKO officials willfully intended to misrepresent these facts to the FCC. Whether RKO sought to protect its parent, or whether the parent withheld information from the subsidiary in order to protect itself, the result is the same. We cannot improve on the language of FCC counsel: "It is obvious that where a complete disclosure of facts will militate against the interests of this organization, the Commission will be deprived of that information. It is irrelevant where in the RKO–General Tire organizational structure this breakdown in candor first occurs. In the end, RKO, as the public trustee, is responsible for the reliability of the information and representations furnished by it to the Commission." [ ]

[The court next addressed the various defenses asserted by RKO. The lack of evidence that the Commission was in fact misled by RKO's failure to disclose was found irrelevant since it was the attempt to mislead that indicated a lack of fitness to hold the license. A claim that RKO's actions were on advice of counsel was dismissed since it was long settled that "advice of counsel cannot excuse a clear breach of duty by a licensee." Finally, the court turned to the issue of whether RKO was denied a hearing on the "lack of candor" issue. Given that the lack of candor was clearly proven by documents submitted by RKO in the renewal hearing itself, the court concluded that no purpose would be served by holding a separate hearing on that issue.]

Our decision to affirm the FCC's action should not be read to include situations not covered by this unique record. The Commission concedes that "this case is unprecedented," [ ], and we expect that successors if any will be rare. Before the FCC can take action of this sort in the future, we believe that at least three conditions must be met in order to protect the parties. First, not only must the misconduct occur directly before the agency, but it should be of such a blatant and unacceptable dimension that its existence cannot be denied. The FCC has satisfied itself that this is the case with regard to RKO, whose lack of candor "is abundantly clear." [ ] Second, although formal notice may not always be necessary, it should be evident that the party has some form of actual notice of the conduct said to be at issue, and must not be prejudiced by surprise. Finally, the party must be given an "opportunity to speak in [its] own behalf . . .." [ ] The procedure adopted by the FCC in this case satisfies these requirements, at least insofar as the Boston renewal is concerned. RKO does not contend that it was prejudiced by the lack of notice, for it undoubtedly had actual notice of the candor issue, as the pleadings filed prior to the Commission's decision demonstrate. [ ] . . . RKO had a full opportunity to speak on its own behalf, and exercised it in pleadings, proffers of proof, and oral argument before the Commission. We cannot say that the FCC abused its discretion by not giving RKO a formal hearing on issues arising from RKO's conduct during the initial proceeding. Section 309 was not intended by Congress to reward delay and concealment that disserves the public interest. "Congress did not intend by this section of the statute to require the formality of Commission consideration of and [re]hearing on an application in which the signatory obviously fails in major material respects to abide the regulations." [ ] ("We do not think Congress intended the Commission to waste time on applications that do not state a valid basis for a hearing.") The FCC's denial of the Boston license renewal must therefore be affirmed.

IV. THE LOS ANGELES AND NEW YORK CITY PROCEEDINGS

The narrow basis of our decision concerning RKO's Boston license illustrates why the FCC may not deny license renewals in Los Angeles and New York City simply because it happened to condition those proceedings on the Boston outcome. RKO's lack of candor during the Boston proceeding justifies its disqualification there because the misconduct took place directly before the trier of fact and has bearing on its general character, but the same cannot be said of the Los Angeles and New York City proceedings. The latter was conditioned on the Boston outcome in order to avoid making the parties "relitigate those issues" that had already been specified with regard to Boston. [ ] By contrast, the former had been conditioned on the reciprocity issue only, in order to "enable the Commission to proceed with the Los Angeles matter and bring it to a conclusion with no risk to the public interest." RKO General, Inc. (KHJ–TV), 31 F.C.C.2d 70, 74 (1971). The FCC could not have known, when it conditioned either of these proceedings as it did, that the Boston outcome would turn on a lack of candor issue that had not even been designated in the Boston proceeding. RKO's misconduct did not occur directly before the trier of fact in either the Los Angeles or New York City proceedings. Accordingly, these decisions must be remanded to the Commission for further consideration as it deems appropriate.

. . .

CONCLUSION

This opinion will not close a sorry chapter in the history of American communications law. We must remand the Los Angeles and New York City proceedings because the FCC has not yet provided a principled explanation for RKO's disqualification as a licensee of those stations. The FCC's findings that RKO intentionally misrepresented financial information and engaged in unlawful reciprocal trade practices cannot stand, for one was reached without notice or hearing and the other constitutes an ex post facto application of new standards to conduct that is long past.

We affirm the Commission's decision in the Boston proceeding, however, because the Commission's finding that RKO displayed an egregious lack of candor in that proceeding does not suffer from either of these infirmities. During an administrative review that had already lasted for years, the FCC suddenly was confronted by documentary evidence establishing beyond doubt that RKO had been less than candid with the Commission in the very proceeding under way. The FCC could observe all material facts for itself, simply by comparing the documents that had already been submitted with those that were now before it.

The denial of a license renewal to a major licensee in a major market is of manifest moment and financial impact. The FCC's decision has not been reviewed callously, and we have tried not to lose sight of the difficult issues in this case by sweeping the reasoning of the Commission under a rug of agency expertise or administrative convenience. The record presented to this court shows irrefutably that the licensee was playing the dodger to serious charges involving it and its parent company. The Commission was entitled to ask whether such conduct, however convenient for corporate purposes, was consistent with the candor required of an applicant for a license to the public airwaves. We believe the Commission's answer is not open to doubt. The disqualification of RKO as a licensee of WNAC in Boston is affirmed.

It is so ordered.

Notes and Questions

1. While the New York proceeding was pending, Congress amended the Communications Act (adding § 331) to require that the Commission renew the license of any VHF commercial licensee willing to relocate to a state with no VHF commercial television stations. After RKO notified the FCC in September, 1982, that it would move WOR–TV from New York City to Secaucus, N.J., its license was renewed. RKO General, Inc. (WOR–TV), 53 R.R.2d 469 (1983). In addition, RKO was granted a temporary waiver of the main studio rule, which permitted the use of the station's existing New York studio facilities while the Commission's renewal order was on appeal. Otherwise, RKO would have been required to expend large sums of money on studio construction in New Jersey during a period when the station's relocation was uncertain. RKO General, Inc., 54 R.R.2d 853 (1983). The grant of the five-year license to RKO without a hearing, pursuant to § 331, was unanimously affirmed in Multi–State Communications, Inc. v. Federal Communications Commission, 728 F.2d 1519, 55 R.R.2d 911 (D.C.Cir. 1984), certiorari denied 469 U.S. 1017 (1984).

2. In *Character Qualifications in Broadcast Licensing*, p. 100, *supra*, the Commission adopted a rule prohibiting applicants and licensees from making any written "misrepresentation or willful material omission[s] bearing on any matter within the jurisdiction of the Commission." 47 C.F.R. § 73.1015. In *Character Qualifications Policy*, p. 100, *supra*, the FCC amended Part I of its rules in order to emphasize that this requirement applies to all FCC applicants, licensees and permittees, not just those involved in broadcasting. 47 C.F.R. § 1.17.

3. In addition to WOR and KHJ, RKO owned one other TV station and twelve radio stations. In 1983, acting under an order from the court of appeals, the Commission started accepting competing applications for the other 13 RKO stations. More than 160 applications were filed. Initially, no action on these applications was to be taken until the character issue in the KHJ case was decided. In 1985, however, the

Commission decided to start comparative proceedings among the applicants. Broadcasting, Mar. 4, 1985 at 75.

4. Compounding RKO's difficulties were allegations of fraud and over-billing by the two RKO radio networks. In 1984 RKO announced that there was truth to some of these allegations. Despite the subsequent sale of the networks to United Stations, the question of network fraud was designated as an issue in the KHJ case.

5. In late 1985 Westinghouse Broadcast and Cable (Group W) agreed to purchase KHJ–TV from RKO for $313 million. Technically, the proposal called for RKO to dismiss its application for renewal and sell KHJ's physical assets to Group W for $215 million. As a result of RKO's withdrawal of its application, Fidelity would be awarded the license. Fidelity would then sell its stock to Group W for $95 million. Group W would also pay Fidelity's current liabilities, approximately $3.25 million.

When the deal had not been approved after more than a year, Westinghouse withdrew. The withdrawal caused a major uproar because, as an outgrowth of the proposed deal, the Commission had suggested a way to settle the proceedings involving the other RKO properties. The Commission requested that for each property interested parties enter into purchase negotiations with all the applicants. The hope was that all properties could be disposed of in this fashion, providing a quick end to all litigation while removing RKO from the broadcasting business. The various proceedings were suspended to allow for these negotiations.

After several months agreements appeared likely for only a minority of the properties. The suspensions in the various proceedings were therefore ended. Meanwhile, Disney Co. negotiated a deal for KHJ similar to the earlier Westinghouse proposal.

The ALJ then found RKO unfit to hold a license and stripped it of all its remaining licenses. The finding was based on RKO's conduct with regard to the barter and trade agreements between 1971–1975, especially its destruction of a 1974 internal audit and subsequent efforts to conceal that destruction and the circumstances surrounding it. The ALJ also found RKO Networks guilty of fraudulent practices that altered audience ratings reports and fraudulent billing:

> 512. If RKO had been able to establish that its dishonesty would not recur, its claims of equity, based on its programming and broadcast history, would take on meaning. But the Commission is obligated by the Communications Act to license only those persons or entities that are of good character. No case ever before decided by this Commission presents dishonesty comparable to RKO's. There is not a single case of fraudulent billing practices investigated and reviewed by this Commission which exhibits as many practices affecting as many advertisers over as many years. During the time consumed by this proceeding, RKO repeatedly misrepresented the truth and engaged in dishonest broadcasting activities.

These findings lead to the conclusion that RKO cannot be trusted to act as a fiduciary of the public interest; RKO General, Inc. is unqualified to continue as a broadcast licensee.

RKO General, Inc. (KHJ–TV), 63 R.R.2d 866 (A.L.J.1987).

In 1988 the Commission voted 2–1 to allow RKO to transfer its Los Angeles TV station and Memphis radio station.

The settlement agreement called for Disney to pay $218,625,000 to RKO and $105,375,000 to Fidelity Television. The Commission declined to decide the issue of RKO's qualifications as a licensee. Instead, likening the transfers to its minority distress sale policy (to be discussed in Chapter V), the Commission argued that approval would "further the public interest by helping to bring service to the public expeditiously by an unquestionably qualified licensee and will also preserve the Commission's objective of deterring licensee misconduct." The deterrence would come from limiting RKO's compensation to 75 percent of fair market value. The Commission also asserted that the public interest would be served by avoiding countless years of further regulation.

Commissioner Dennis dissented. Noting that the ALJ had found that "RKO had engaged in a pervasive, continuous pattern of deceit— even after the Boston license was revoked," she argued that a Commission determination as to RKO's qualifications was absolutely necessary. If RKO was unfit, it should lose its licenses without compensation. If it was fit, then it should be free to either keep its stations or sell them at fair market value. Dennis expressed concern that the decision "sends the wrong signal to station licensees—that the way to avoid license revocation is to prolong a proceeding until the Commission loses its will to litigate further." RKO General, Inc. (KHJ–TV), 3 F.C.C.Rcd. 5057, 65 R.R.2d 192 (1988).

The Commission subsequently approved similar settlement agreements for the other RKO stations. A settlement agreement for the last of the RKO stations was approved in early 1991. The terms were similar to the other RKO settlement agreements with RKO receiving significantly less than 75 percent of the station's fair market value. RKO General, Inc. (KFRC), 68 R.R.2d 1341 (1991).

3. HOSTILE TAKEOVERS OF CORPORATIONS

Up until now we have been looking at cases where the incumbent licensee wishes to transfer the license. In the last decade, the Commission has found itself faced with a different sort of problem: hostile takeovers of corporations with broadcast properties. The leading example was Ted Turner's unsuccessful attempt in 1985 to take over CBS. How should the Commission treat cases like this?

What if existing shareholders wish to replace a corporation's board of directors? Does this constitute a transfer of control and, if so, is it the same as an attempt by outsiders to take over a corporation? The Commission faced this issue for the first time in Committee for Full Value of Storer Communications, Inc., 57 R.R.2d 1651 (1985). The Committee for Full Value of Storer Communications, Inc. was a group of dissident Storer stockholders who wished to sell all the assets of Storer and distribute the proceeds to the stockholders. Because the incumbent board of directors opposed this plan, the dissidents announced that they would stage a proxy contest to elect a board of directors that would implement their plan. The scheme raised several important questions for the Commission.

Under § 309(b) of the Communications Act, applications for a transfer of control of a broadcast licensee are subject to a public notice requirement and a 30–day waiting period. The purpose of these requirements is to give members of the public who feel that the proposed transfer is not in the public interest an opportunity to file a petition to deny. However, § 309(c) contains an exception to these requirements for cases where the transfer of control is not substantial. Thus, the Commission had to determine whether election of a new board of directors, absent any significant change in stock ownership, constitutes a transfer of control, and if so is it a substantial transfer of control.

The Mass Media Bureau concluded that ownership of the corporation resides in the stockholders, and thus there is no transfer of control, substantial or otherwise. The Commission disagreed, holding that electing a new board of directors is a transfer of control, but since the ultimate control of any corporation rests with the stockholders, the transfer of control is not a substantial one. The practical effect of this decision was that the Committee did have to file an application for transfer of control, but the application was not subject to the public notice and 30–day waiting period requirements.

The Commission's decision was affirmed on appeal. The court of appeals reasoned that the Commission had not abused its discretion in resolving a case with competing policy considerations. Although a change in directors might indeed result in a major change in the working control of the corporation, determining what constitutes a "substantial" change was a complex task best resolved by the Commission. Also, there was the danger that requiring public notice and a 30–day waiting period in any such proxy fight would allow incumbent boards of directors to use the Commission to insulate them from challenges since the added delay and cost that would occur might well discourage such challenges. Storer Communications, Inc. v. Federal Communications Commission, 763 F.2d 436, 58 R.R.2d 244 (D.C.Cir. 1985).

Despite the favorable ruling, the Committee for Full Value of Storer Communications, Inc. was unable to elect a majority of the board of directors.

In 1986 the Commission affirmed its previous policies on proxy contests and tender offers. In most proxy contests, a short form application with certain additional information concerning the basic qualifications of the candidates for board of directors will be sufficient. In the case of hostile takeover attempts, a long form application will be required. Pending review of the long form application, a special temporary authorization (STA) will be issued to a trustee approved by the Commission. Tender Offers and Proxy Contests, 59 R.R.2d 1536 (1986).

The court of appeals rejected an appeal by the Office of Communication of the United Church of Christ, Action for Children's Television and the National Organization for Women, holding that the Commission's Policy Statement was not ripe for review. According to the court, there were too many ambiguities and unanswered questions in the Policy Statement. The court thought it was necessary to await the application of the Statement to a specific case. Office of Communication of United Church of Christ v. Federal Communications Commission, 826 F.2d 101, 63 R.R.2d 1065 (D.C.Cir.1987).

One difficult question for the Commission is determining when a *de facto,* as opposed to *de jure,* transfer of control has occurred. In CBS Management Changes (Transfer of Control Allegations), 2 F.C.C.Rcd. 2274, 62 R.R.2d 852 (1987), Fairness in Media alleged that there was an unauthorized *de facto* transfer of control to Loews Corp. and its chairman, Laurence A. Tisch. Loews had purchased almost 25 percent of CBS common stock and subsequently Tisch was appointed chief executive officer of CBS. Despite statements by Robert Preston Tisch, President of Loews, various CBS directors and others that Laurence Tisch intended to take control of CBS, the Commission determined that a *de facto* transfer of control had not taken place. The Commission noted that there was no evidence that Laurence Tisch had sufficient influence on the shareholders unassociated with Loews to constitute a *de facto* transfer of control. Also, some of Tisch's proposals to change CBS had been rejected by the board of directors, indicating that he did not control the board.

Chapter V

MEDIA CONCENTRATION

As we saw when considering the NBC case, the Commission has long been concerned about excessive concentration of control over the process of deciding what programs to present. There are several ways to attack the problem. One, utilized in that case, is to prevent the networks from imposing their power on the licensees. Another is to order licensees to obtain their programs from non-network sources for certain periods of the day. Still another, which gets at this problem indirectly but also attacks other problems, is to attempt to diversify the ownership of broadcast facilities. In this chapter we consider these various methods of limiting concentration of control.

The Commission has used its rulemaking powers primarily to handle technical and engineering matters, which can be addressed in quantitative terms—and which are more likely to lend themselves to uniform treatment without the need for exceptions.

The Commission has also used rulemaking to achieve diversity of control—again perhaps because the material lends itself to quantitative expression, such as how many stations a person should be allowed to control in a particular area. It is important to realize, however, that even though the Commission may choose to adopt specific rules to meet a problem, it must always consider requests for waivers of that rule if the public interest would be furthered by the waiver. The 1934 Act grants the Commission powers to act in the public interest and, although a rule may operate in the public interest most of the time, some exceptions may be in the public interest.

In 1980, for example, a radio station licensee in Alaska sought a license for a vacant television channel in the same community. A rule barred the same licensee from controlling radio and VHF stations in the same community. The community had three vacant VHF frequencies. If the FCC adhered to its rule, the community might not get any television service for several years. The Commission granted a waiver of its rule to meet the needs of the situation.

Note, however, that the Commission might be able to argue in some situations that the overriding public interest may be better served by rigorous adherence to a firm rule that all know will be followed, than by granting waivers that seriously undercut the thrust of a vitally important main rule.

165

A. LOCAL CONCENTRATION

1. DUOPOLY

Local concentration of control of mass media facilities has been a problem for the Commission at least since 1938, when it received an application for a standard broadcasting station in Flint, Mich., from applicants who already controlled another corporation that operated a standard broadcasting station in the same area. Although there were no rival applicants, the Commission refused to grant the second facility without a compelling showing that the public interest would be served in such a situation.

This was the beginning of the so-called "duopoly" rule, which the Commission formalized in a general rule that it would not grant a license to any applicant who already held a similar facility or license so located that the service areas of the two would overlap.

In the 1960s the Commission returned to this subject and recognized that the dwindling number of American newspapers made the impact of individual broadcasting stations "significantly greater." This reinforced the need for diversity in the broadcast media and led the Commission to announce that it would never again grant a duopoly.

During this period, however, the Commission was granting to the same applicant one AM, one FM and one television station in the same locality because this was not a duplication of facilities in the same service area. In 1970 the Commission moved the next step and proposed the "one-to-a-customer" rule. Rules Relating to Multiple Ownership, 22 F.C.C.2d 306, 18 R.R.2d 1735 (1970). Under this rule licensees would be limited to one broadcast station in any given market, regardless of the type of broadcast service involved. The Commission viewed this as a logical extension of its earlier diversification rules:

> 21. Application of the principles set forth above dictates that one person should not be licensed to operate more than one broadcast station in the same place, and serving substantially the same public, unless some other relevant public interest consideration is found to outweigh the importance of diversifying control. It is elementary that the number of frequencies available for licensing is limited. In any particular area there may be many voices that would like to be heard, but not all can be licensed. A proper objective is the maximum diversity of ownership that technology permits in each area. We are of the view that 60 different licensees are more desirable than 50, and even that 51 are more desirable than 50. In a rapidly changing social climate, communication of ideas is vital. If a city has 60 frequencies available but they are licensed to only 50 different licensees, the number of sources for ideas is not maximized. It might be the 51st licensee that would become the communication channel for a solution to a severe social crisis. No one can say that present licensees are

broadcasting everything worthwhile that can be communicated. We see no existing public interest reason for being wedded to our present policy that permits a licensee to acquire more than one station in the same area.

The Commission rejected an argument "that the good profit position of a multiple owner in the same market results in more in-depth informational programs being broadcast and thus, in more meaningful diversity. We do not doubt that some multiple owners may have a greater capacity to so program, but the record does not demonstrate that they generally do so. The citations and honors for exceptional programming appear to be continually awarded to a very few licensees—perhaps a dozen or so multiple owners out of a total of hundreds of such owners."

The Commission was persuaded, however, that UHF stations presented a special problem in that they were still weak competitively and few would go on the air unless affiliated with an established radio station. Therefore, the Commission refused to adopt a firm rule against radio-UHF combinations but again indicated that it would review those on a case-by-case basis. Finally, the Commission announced that the rules would be prospective only and no divestitures would be required, due to the large number of existing combinations and a sense that ordering divestiture for such a large group might very well create instability.

The rules as originally adopted would have banned not only VHF-radio combinations, but also AM–FM combinations, even though traditionally FM had been weak as a competitive force, and indeed the Commission during the 1950s had encouraged AM stations to acquire FM stations. On reconsideration the Commission decided that although FM stations were becoming more powerful competitors and increasingly profitable, most AM–FM combinations might still be "economically and/or technically interdependent." Concerned that the rules as originally adopted might hinder the development of FM service, the FCC modified them to permit the formation of new AM–FM combinations. Multiple Ownership of Standard, FM and TV Broadcast Stations, 28 F.C.C.2d 662, 21 R.R.2d 1551 (1971). Thus, only VHF-radio combinations were banned by the new rules.

In late 1988 the FCC modified the duopoly rule to allow greater overlap between commonly-owned AM or commonly-owned FM stations. The change reduces the minimum spacing required between such stations. The FCC also announced that it would be inclined to grant waivers of the one-to-a-market rule in those top 25 markets that have at least 30 broadcast voices.

A few years later, the FCC announced a further relaxation of the duopoly rules for radio. Arguing that the marked increase in competition had produced an extremely fragmented radio marketplace in which radio licensees would experience increasingly severe economic and financial stress, the Commission concluded that increased economies of scale were necessary for these licensees. The FCC decided to allow owners to own more stations in any single market. The exact number depended on the total number of stations in the market. The Commission also imposed a cap of 25 percent on the combined audience share of all stations owned by the one licensee as of the filing date of the application to acquire a new station. Radio Multiple Ownership Rules, 7 F.C.C.Rcd. 2755, 70 R.R.2d 903 (1992).

The relaxation of the duopoly rules, as well as changes in the multiple ownership rules, discussed later in this chapter, produced an extremely negative reaction by Congress. In response to this, the Commission modified the new duopoly rules. Licensees in markets with fewer than 15 radio stations are permitted to own up to three stations as long as the number owned is less than 50 percent of the total number of stations in the market. In markets with 15 or more stations, licensees are permitted to own up to four stations. No more than two can be in the same service. In addition, the Commission imposed an audience share cap of 25 percent. Radio Multiple Ownership Rules, Recon., 7 F.C.C.Rcd. 6387, 71 R.R.2d 227 (1992).

The FCC has also issued an NPRM proposing various ways to relax the duopoly rules for television. Among the alternatives proposed are allowing common ownership of one AM, one FM and one TV station, allowing only TV–AM combinations, or deleting the one-to-a-market rule. Review of the Commission's Regulations Governing Television Broadcasting, 7 F.C.C.Rcd. 4111 (1992).

2. Crossownership

When the Commission adopted its one-to-a-customer rules, it also proposed the adoption of another set of rules that would proscribe common ownership of newspapers and broadcast facilities serving the same area and require divestiture of prohibited combinations. Although the Commission had flirted with such a regulation in the early 1940s, it had abandoned the attempt. The basis for the Commission movement in 1970 was an awareness that 94 television stations were affiliated through common control with newspapers in the same city. In addition, of course, "some newspapers own television stations in other cities, which also serve the city in which the newspaper is located." The Commission thought this situation was very similar to the joint ownership of two television stations in the same community, something the Commission has never permitted. "The functions of newspapers and television stations as journalists are so similar that their joint ownership is, in this respect, essentially the same as the joint ownership of two television stations." After extensive consideration, the Commission adopted rules in 1975 that prohibit granting a license for a television or radio station to any applicant who already controls, owns or operates a daily newspaper serving part of the same area.

FEDERAL COMMUNICATIONS COMMISSION v. NATIONAL CITIZENS COMMITTEE FOR BROADCASTING

Supreme Court of the United States, 1978.
436 U.S. 775, 98 S.Ct. 2096, 56 L.Ed.2d 697, 43 R.R.2d 152, 3 Med.L.Rptr. 2409.

MR. JUSTICE MARSHALL delivered the opinion of the Court.

. . .

I

A

. . .

In setting its licensing policies, the Commission has long acted on the theory that diversification of mass media ownership serves the public interest by promoting diversity of program and service viewpoints, as well as by preventing undue concentration of economic power. See, *e.g., Multiple Ownership of Standard, FM and Television Broadcast Stations,* 45 F.C.C. 1476, 1476–1477 (1964). . . .

. . .

Diversification of ownership has not been the sole consideration thought relevant to the public interest, however. The Commission's other, and sometimes conflicting, goal has been to ensure "the best practicable service to the public." [ ] To achieve this goal, the Commission has weighed factors such as the anticipated contribution of the owner to station operations, the proposed program service, and the past broadcast record of the applicant—in addition to diversification of ownership—in making initial comparative licensing decisions. [ ] Moreover, the Commission has given considerable weight to a policy of avoiding undue disruption of existing service. As a result, newspaper owners in many instances have been able to acquire broadcast licenses for stations serving the same communities as their newspapers, and the Commission has repeatedly renewed such licenses on findings that continuation of the service offered by the common owner would serve the public interest. [ ]

B

Against this background, the Commission began the instant rulemaking proceeding in 1970 to consider the need for a more restrictive policy toward newspaper ownership of radio and television broadcast stations. [ ] Citing studies showing the dominant role of television stations and daily newspapers as sources of local news and other information, [ ], the notice of rulemaking proposed adoption of regulations that would eliminate all newspaper-broadcast combinations serving the same market, by prospectively banning formation or transfer of such combinations and requiring dissolution of all existing combinations within five years, [ ]. The Commission suggested that the proposed regulations would serve "the purpose of promoting competition among the mass media involved, and maximizing diversification of service sources and viewpoints." [ ] At the same time, however, the Commission expressed "substantial concern" about the disruption of service that might result from divestiture of existing combinations. [ ] . . .

. . .

. . . While recognizing the pioneering contributions of newspaper owners to the broadcast industry, the Commission concluded that changed circumstances made it possible, and necessary, for all new licensing of broadcast stations to "be expected to add to local diversity." [ ] In reaching this conclusion, the Commission did not find that existing co-located newspaper-broadcast combinations had not served the public interest, or that such combinations necessarily "spea[k] with one voice" or are harmful to competition. [ ] In the Commission's view, the conflicting studies submitted by the parties concerning the effects of newspaper ownership on competition and station performance were inconclusive, and no pattern of specific abuses by existing cross-owners was demonstrated. [ ] The prospective rules were justified, instead, by reference to the Commission's policy of promoting diversification of ownership: Increases of diversification of ownership would possibly result in enhanced diversity of viewpoints, and, given the absence of persuasive countervailing considerations, "even a small gain in diversity" was "worth pursuing." [ ]

With respect to the proposed across-the-board divestiture requirement, however, the Commission concluded that "a mere hoped-for gain in diversity" was not a sufficient justification, [ ]. Characterizing the divestiture issues as "the most difficult" presented in the proceeding, the Order explained that the proposed rules, while correctly recognizing the central importance of diversity considerations, "may have given too little weight to the consequences which could be expected to attend a focus on the abstract goal alone." [ ] Forced dissolution would promote diversity, but it would also cause "disruption for the industry and hardship for individual owners," "resulting in losses or diminution of service to the public." [ ]

The Commission concluded that in light of these countervailing considerations divestiture was warranted only in "the most egregious cases," which it identified as those in which a newspaper-broadcast combination has an "effective monopoly" in the local "marketplace of ideas as well as economically." [ ] The Commission recognized that any standards for defining which combinations fell within that category would necessarily be arbitrary to some degree, but "[a] choice had to be made." [ ] It thus decided to require divestiture only where there was common ownership of the sole daily newspaper published in a community and either (1) the sole broadcast station providing that entire community with a clear signal, or (2) the sole television station encompassing the entire community with a clear signal. [ ]

The Order identified 8 television-newspaper and 10 radio-newspaper combinations meeting the divestiture criteria. [ ] Waivers of the divestiture requirement were granted *sua sponte* to 1 television and 1 radio combination, leaving a total of 16 stations subject to divestiture. The Commission explained that waiver requests would be entertained in the latter cases, but, absent waiver, either the newspaper or the broadcast station would have to be divested by January 1, 1980, [ ].

. . .

C

. . .

. . . [T]he Court of Appeals affirmed the prospective ban on new licensing of co-located newspaper-broadcast combinations, but vacated the limited divestiture rules, and ordered the Commission to adopt regulations requiring dissolution of all existing combinations that did not qualify for a waiver under the procedure outlined in the order. [The court concluded that the Commission had no rational basis for banning prospective combinations while grandfathering most existing combinations. The court was also unable to find a rational basis for distinguishing between the 16 egregious cases that had to be divested and the remaining grandfathered combinations. The Commission, NAB, ANPA and some of the cross-owners who had been grandfathered under the Commission's order petitioned the Supreme Court for review.]

II

. . .

A

Section 303(r) of the Communications Act, [ ], provides that "the Commission from time to time, as public convenience, interest, or necessity requires, shall . . . [m]ake such rules and regulations and prescribe such restrictions and conditions, not inconsistent with law, as may be necessary to carry out the provisions of [the Act]." [ ] As the Court of Appeals recognized, [ ], it is now well established that this general rulemaking authority supplies a statutory basis for the Commission to enact regulations codifying its view of the public interest licensing standard, so long as that view is based on consideration of permissible factors and is otherwise reasonable. If a license applicant does not qualify under standards set forth in such regulations, and does not proffer sufficient grounds for waiver or change of those standards, the Commission may deny the application without further inquiry. [ ]

This Court has specifically upheld this rulemaking authority in the context of regulations based on the Commission's policy of promoting diversification of ownership. In United States v. Storer Broadcasting Co., [ ], we sustained the portion of the Commission's multiple ownership rules placing limitations on the total number of stations in each broadcast service a person may own or control. [ ] And in National

Broadcasting Co. v. United States, [   ], we affirmed regulations that, *inter alia,* prohibited broadcast networks from owning more than one AM radio station in the same community, and from owning " 'any standard broadcast station in any locality where the existing standard broadcast stations are so few or of such unequal desirability . . . that competition would be substantially restrained by such licensing.' " [   ]

Petitioner NAB attempts to distinguish these cases on the ground that they involved efforts to increase diversification within the boundaries of the broadcasting industry itself, whereas the instant regulations are concerned with diversification of ownership in the mass communications media as a whole. NAB contends that, since the Act confers jurisdiction on the Commission only to regulate "communication by wire or radio," 47 U.S.C. § 152(a), it is impermissible for the Commission to use its licensing authority with respect to broadcasting to promote diversity in an overall communications market which includes, but is not limited to, the broadcasting industry.

This argument undersells the Commission's power to regulate broadcasting in the "public interest." In making initial licensing decisions between competing applicants, the Commission has long given "primary significance" to "diversification of control of the media of mass communications," and has denied licenses to newspaper owners on the basis of this policy in appropriate cases. [   ] As we have discussed on several occasions, [   ], the physical scarcity of broadcast frequencies, as well as problems of interference between broadcast signals, led Congress to delegate broad authority to the Commission to allocate broadcast licenses in the "public interest." And "[t]he avowed aim of the Communications Act of 1934 was to secure the maximum benefits of radio to all the people of the United States." [   ] It was not inconsistent with the statutory scheme, therefore, for the Commission to conclude that the maximum benefit to the "public interest" would follow from allocation of broadcast licenses so as to promote diversification of the mass media as a whole.

Our past decisions have recognized, moreover, that the First Amendment and antitrust values underlying the Commission's diversification policy may properly be considered by the Commission in determining where the public interest lies. "[T]he 'public interest' standard necessarily invites reference to First Amendment principles," Columbia Broadcasting System, Inc. v. Democratic National Committee, 412 U.S. 94, 122 (1973), and, in particular, to the First Amendment goal of achieving "the widest possible dissemination of information from diverse and antagonistic sources," Associated Press v. United States, supra, 326 U.S., at 20. See Red Lion Broadcasting Co. v. FCC, supra, at 385, 390. See also United States v. Midwest Video Corp., 406 U.S. 649, 667–669, and n. 27 (1972) (plurality opinion). And, while the Commission does not have power to enforce the antitrust laws as such, it is permitted to take antitrust policies into account in making licensing decisions pursuant to the public interest standard. See, e.g., United

States v. Radio Corp. of America, 358 U.S. 334, 351 (1959); National Broadcasting Co. v. United States, supra, at 222–224. . . .

(2)

It is thus clear that the regulations at issue are based on permissible public interest goals and, so long as the regulations are not an unreasonable means for seeking to achieve these goals, they fall within the general rulemaking authority recognized in the *Storer Broadcasting* and *National Broadcasting* cases. Petitioner ANPA contends that the prospective rules are unreasonable in two respects: first, the rulemaking record did not conclusively establish that prohibiting common ownership of co-located newspapers and broadcast stations would in fact lead to increases in the diversity of viewpoints among local communications media; and second, the regulations were based on the diversification factor to the exclusion of other service factors considered in the past by the Commission in making initial licensing decisions regarding newspaper owners, [ ]. With respect to the first point we agree with the Court of Appeals that, notwithstanding the inconclusiveness of the rulemaking record, the Commission acted rationally in finding that diversification of ownership would enhance the possibility of achieving greater diversity of viewpoints. As the Court of Appeals observed, "[d]iversity and its effects are . . . elusive concepts, not easily defined let alone measured without making qualitative judgments objectionable on both policy and First Amendment grounds." [ ] Moreover, evidence of specific abuses by common owners is difficult to compile; "the possible benefits of competition do not lend themselves to specific forecast." [ ] In these circumstances, the Commission was entitled to rely on its judgment, based on experience, that "it is unrealistic to expect true diversity from a commonly owned station-newspaper combination. The divergency of their viewpoints cannot be expected to be the same as if they were antagonistically run." [ ]

As to the Commission's decision to give controlling weight to its diversification goal in shaping the prospective rules, the Order makes clear that this change in policy was a reasonable administrative response to changed circumstances in the broadcasting industry. [ ] The Order explained that, although newspaper owners had previously been allowed, and even encouraged to acquire licenses for co-located broadcast stations because of the shortage of qualified license applicants, a sufficient number of qualified and experienced applicants other than newspaper owners was now readily available. In addition, the number of channels open for new licensing had diminished substantially. It had thus become both feasible and more urgent for the Commission to take steps to increase diversification of ownership, and a change in the Commission's policy toward new licensing offered the possibility of increasing diversity without causing any disruption of existing service. In light of these considerations, the Commission clearly did not take an irrational view of the public interest when it decided to impose a prospective ban on new licensing of co-located newspaper-broadcast combinations.

B

Petitioners NAB and ANPA also argue that the regulations, though designed to further the First Amendment goal of achieving "the widest possible dissemination of information from diverse and antagonistic sources," Associated Press v. United States, supra, 326 U.S. at 20, nevertheless violate the First Amendment rights of newspaper owners. We cannot agree, for this argument ignores the fundamental proposition that there is no "unabridgeable First Amendment right to broadcast comparable to the right of every individual to speak, write, or publish." Red Lion Broadcasting Co. v. FCC, supra, 395 U.S. at 388.

. . .

In the instant case, far from seeking to limit the flow of information, the Commission has acted, in the Court of Appeals' words, "to enhance the diversity of information heard by the public without ongoing government surveillance of the content of speech." [ ] The regulations are a reasonable means of promoting the public interest in diversified mass communications; thus they do not violate the First Amendment rights of those who will be denied broadcast licenses pursuant to them. Being forced to "choose among applicants for the same facilities," the Commission has chosen on a "sensible basis," one designed to further, rather than contravene, "the system of freedom of expression." T. Emerson, The System of Freedom of Expression 663 (1970).

III

After upholding the prospective aspect of the Commission's regulations, the Court of Appeals concluded that the Commission's decision to limit divestiture to 16 "egregious cases" of "effective monopoly" was arbitrary and capricious within the meaning of the Administrative Procedure Act (APA), § 10(e), 5 U.S.C. § 706(2)(A). We agree with the Court of Appeals that regulations promulgated after informal rulemaking . . . may be invalidated by a reviewing court under the "arbitrary or capricious" standard if they are not rational and based on consideration of the relevant factors. [ ] Although this review "is to be searching and careful, [t]he court is not empowered to substitute its judgment for that of the agency." [ ]

In the view of the Court of Appeals, the Commission lacked a rational basis, first, for treating existing newspaper-broadcast combinations more leniently than combinations that might seek licenses in the future; and, second, even assuming a distinction between existing and new combinations had been justified, for requiring divestiture in the "egregious cases" while allowing all other existing combinations to continue in operation. We believe that the limited divestiture requirement reflects a rational weighing of competing policies, and we therefore reinstate the portion of the Commission's order that was invalidated by the Court of Appeals.

A

(1)

The Commission was well aware that separating existing newspaper-broadcast combinations would promote diversification of ownership. It concluded, however, that ordering widespread divestiture would not result in "the best practicable service to the American public," [ ], a goal that the Commission has always taken into account and that has been specifically approved by this Court, FCC v. Sanders Bros. Radio Station, 309 U.S. 470, 475 (1940); [ ]. In particular, the Commission expressed concern that divestiture would cause "disruption for the industry" and "hardship to individual owners," both of which would result in harm to the public interest. Order, at 1078. Especially in light of the fact that the number of co-located newspaper-broadcast combinations was already on the decline as a result of the prospective rules, the Commission decided that across-the-board divestiture was not warranted. [ ]

The Order identified several specific respects in which the public interest would or might be harmed if a sweeping divestiture requirement were imposed: the stability and continuity of meritorious service provided by the newspaper owners as a group would be lost; owners who had provided meritorious service would unfairly be denied the opportunity to continue in operation; "economic dislocations" might prevent new owners from obtaining sufficient working capital to maintain the quality of local programming; and local ownership of broadcast stations would probably decrease. [ ] We cannot say that the Commission acted irrationally in concluding that these public interest harms outweighed the potential gains that would follow from increasing diversification of ownership.

In the past, the Commission has consistently acted on the theory that preserving continuity of meritorious service furthers the public interest, both in its direct consequence of bringing proven broadcast service to the public, and in its indirect consequence of rewarding—and avoiding losses to—licensees who have invested the money and effort necessary to produce quality performance. Thus, although a broadcast license must be renewed every three years, and the licensee must satisfy the Commission that renewal will serve the public interest, both the Commission and the courts have recognized that a licensee who has given meritorious service has a "legitimate renewal expectanc[y]" and should not be destroyed absent good cause. [ ] Accordingly, while diversification of ownership is a relevant factor in the context of license renewal as well as initial licensing, the Commission has long considered the past performance of the incumbent as the most important factor in deciding whether to grant license renewal and thereby to allow the existing owner to continue in operation. Even where an incumbent is challenged by a competing applicant who offers greater potential in terms of diversification, the Commission's general practice has been to go with the "proven product" and grant renewal if the incumbent has rendered meritorious service. [ ] In the instant proceeding, the Commission specifically noted that the existing newspaper-broadcast cross-owners as a group had a "long record of service" from the outset. [ ] Notwithstanding the Commission's diversification policy, all were granted initial licenses upon findings that the public interest would be served thereby, and those that had been in existence for more than three years had also had their licenses renewed on the ground that the public interest would be furthered. The Commission noted, moreover, that in terms of percentage of time devoted to several categories of local programming, these stations had displayed "an undramatic but nonetheless statistically significant superiority" over other television stations. [ ] An across-the-board divestiture requirement would result in loss of the services of these superior licensees, and—whether divestiture caused actual losses to existing owners, or just denial of reasonably anticipated gains—the result would be that future licensees would be discouraged from investing the resources necessary to produce quality service.

At the same time, there was no guarantee that the licensees who replaced the existing cross-owners would be able to provide the same level of service or demonstrate the same longterm commitment to broadcasting. And even if the new owners were able in the long run to provide similar or better service, the Commission found that divestiture would cause serious disruption in the transition period. Thus, the Commission observed that new owners "would lack the long knowledge of the community and would have to begin raw," and—because of high interest rates—might not be able to obtain sufficient working capital to maintain the quality of local programming. [ ]

The Commission's fear that local ownership would decline was grounded in a rational prediction, based on its knowledge of the broadcasting industry and supported by comments in the record, [ ], that many of the existing newspaper-broadcast combinations owned by local interests would respond to the divestiture requirement by trading stations with out-of-town owners. It is undisputed that roughly 75% of the existing co-located newspaper-television combinations are locally owned, [ ], and these owners' knowledge of their local communities and concern for local affairs, built over a period of years, would be lost if they were replaced with outside interests. Local ownership in and of itself has been recognized to be a factor of some—if relatively slight— significance even in the context of initial licensing decisions. [ ] It was not unreasonable, therefore, for the Commission to consider it as one of several factors militating against divestiture of combinations that have been in existence for many years.

In light of these countervailing considerations, we cannot agree with the Court of Appeals that it was arbitrary and capricious for the Commission to "grandfather" most existing combinations, and to leave opponents of these combinations to their remedies in individual renewal proceedings. In the latter connection we note that, while individual renewal proceedings are unlikely to accomplish any "overall restructuring" of the existing ownership patterns, the Order does make clear that existing combinations will be subject to challenge by competing applicants in renewal proceedings, to the same extent as they were prior to the instant rulemaking proceedings. [ ] That is, diversification of ownership will be a relevant but somewhat secondary factor. And, even in the absence of a competing applicant, license renewal may be denied if, *inter alia*, a challenger can show that a common owner has engaged in specific economic or programming abuses. [ ]

(2)

In concluding that the Commission acted unreasonably in not extending its divestiture requirement across-the-board, the Court of Appeals apparently placed heavy reliance on a "presumption" that existing newspaper-broadcast combinations "do not serve the public interest." [ ] The Court derived this presumption primarily from the Commission's own diversification policy, as "reaffirmed" by adoption of the prospective rules in this proceeding, and secondarily from "[t]he policies of the First Amendment," [ ], and the Commission's statutory duty to "encourage the larger and more effective use of radio in the public interest." 47 U.S.C. § 303(g). As explained in Part II above, we agree that diversification of ownership furthers statutory and constitutional policies, and, as the Commission recognized, separating existing newspaper-broadcast combinations would promote diversification. But the weighing of policies under the "public interest" standard is a task that Congress has delegated to the Commission in the first instance, and we are unable to find anything in the Communications Act, the First Amendment, or the Commission's past or present practices that would require the Commission to "presume" that its diversification policy should be given controlling weight in all circumstances.

Such a "presumption" would seem to be inconsistent with the Commission's long-standing and judicially approved practice of giving controlling weight in some circumstances to its more general goal of achieving "the best practicable service to the public." Certainly, as discussed in Part III–A(1) above, the Commission through its license renewal policy has made clear that it considers diversification of ownership to be a factor of less significance when deciding whether to allow an existing licensee to continue in operation than when evaluating applicants seeking initial licensing. Nothing in the language or the legislative history of § 303(g) indicates that Congress intended to foreclose all differences in treatment between new and existing licensees, and indeed, in amending § 307(d) of the Act in 1952, Congress appears to have lent its approval to the Commission's policy of evaluating existing licensees on a somewhat different basis than new applicants. Moreover, if enactment of the prospective rules in this proceeding itself were deemed to create a "presumption" in favor of divestiture, the Commission's ability to experiment with new policies would be severely hampered. One of the most significant advantages of the administrative process is its ability to adapt to new circumstances in a flexible manner, [ ], and we are unwilling to presume that the Commission acts unreasonably when it decides to try out a change in licensing policy primarily on a prospective basis.

The Court of Appeals also relied on its perception that the policies militating against divestiture were "lesser policies" to which the Commission had not given as much weight in the past as its divestiture policy. [ ] This perception is subject to much the same criticism as the "presumption" that existing co-located newspaper-broadcast combinations do not serve the public interest. The Commission's past concern with avoiding disruption of existing service is amply illustrated by its license renewal policies. In addition, it is worth noting that in the past when the Commission has changed its multiple ownership rules it has almost invariably tailored the changes so as to operate wholly or primarily on a prospective basis. . . .

The Court of Appeals apparently reasoned that the Commission's concerns with respect to disruption of existing service, economic dislocations, and decreases in local ownership necessarily could not be very weighty since the Commission has a practice of routinely approving voluntary transfers and assignments of licenses. [ ] But the question of whether the Commission should compel proven licensees to divest their stations is a different question from whether the public interest is served by allowing transfers by licensees who no longer wish to continue in the business. . . .

The Court of Appeals' final basis for concluding that the Commission acted arbitrarily in not giving controlling weight to its divestiture policy was the Court's finding that the rulemaking record did not adequately "disclose the extent to which divestiture would actually threaten" the competing policies relied upon by the Commission, [ ]. However, to the extent that factual determinations were involved in the Commission's decision to grandfather most existing combinations, they were primarily of a judgmental or predictive nature—e.g., whether a divestiture requirement would result in trading of stations with out-of-town owners; whether new owners would perform as well as existing cross-owners, either in the short run or in the long run; whether losses to existing owners would result from forced sales; whether such losses would discourage future investment in quality programming; and whether new owners would have sufficient working capital to finance local programming. In such circumstances complete factual support in the record for the Commission's judgment or prediction is not possible or required; "a forecast of the direction in which future public interest lies necessarily involves deductions based on the expert knowledge of the agency." [ ]

B

We also must conclude that the Court of Appeals erred in holding that it was arbitrary to order divestiture in the 16 "egregious cases" while allowing other existing combinations to continue in operation. The Commission's decision was based not—as the Court of Appeals may have believed, [ ]—on a conclusion that divestiture would be more harmful in the grandfathered markets than in the 16 affected markets, but rather on a judgment that the need for diversification was especially great in cases of local monopoly. This policy judgment was certainly not irrational, [ ], and indeed was founded on the very same assumption that underpinned the diversification policy itself and the prospective rules upheld by the Court of Appeals and now by this Court—that the greater the number of owners in a market, the greater the possibility of achieving diversity of program and service viewpoints.

As to the Commission's criteria for determining which existing newspaper-broadcast combinations have an "effective monopoly" in the "local marketplace of ideas as well as economically," we think the standards settled upon by the Commission reflect a rational legislative-type judgment. Some line had to be drawn, and it was hardly unreasonable for the Commission to confine divestiture to communities in which there is common ownership of the only daily newspaper and either the only television station or the only broadcast station of any kind encompassing the entire community with a clear signal. [ ] It was not irrational, moreover, for the Commission to disregard media sources other than newspapers and broadcast stations in setting its divestiture standards. The studies cited by the Commission in its notice of rulemaking unanimously concluded that newspapers and television are the two most widely utilized media sources for local news and discussion of public affairs; and, as the Commission noted in its Order, [ ], "aside from the fact that [magazines and other periodicals] often had only a tiny fraction in the market, they were not given real weight since they often dealt exclusively with regional or national issues and ignored local issues." Moreover, the differences in treatment between radio and television stations, [ ], were certainly justified in light of the far greater influence of television than radio as a source for local news. [ ]

The judgment of the Court of Appeals is affirmed in part and reversed in part.

It is so ordered.

MR. JUSTICE BRENNAN took no part in the consideration or decision of these cases.

Notes and Questions

1. As in *WNCN Listeners Guild*, the primary issue in this case is the scope of the appellate court's power to review Commission decisions. How does the Supreme Court's view of this differ from the appellate court's?

2. During the time between the appellate court decision and the Supreme Court decision, *The Washington Post* and the *Detroit Evening News* exchanged their locally-owned television stations to achieve com-

pliance with the crossownership rule. If most crossowners had engaged in similar swaps, would requiring divestiture have served the public interest? As the Supreme Court noted, one obvious effect of such transactions would be to reduce local ownership of broadcast stations.

3. One important question for the application of the various FCC ownership rules concerns the level of ownership necessary to invoke the application of one of these rules. For example, should someone who buys five shares of stock in each of several publicly held corporations, be considered in violation of an FCC ownership rule because the combined holdings of those corporations would violate that rule? Obviously, such a stock holding would not raise the concentration concerns underlying these rules. Furthermore, such an extreme reading of the rules would be unenforceable. The Commission has therefore set minimum ownership percentages for what it calls "cognizable" interests. Only cognizable interests subject the owner to the FCC ownership rules.

The current minimum ownership levels required to constitute cognizable interests were set in 1984. The basic level is 5 percent. However, for passive investors such as banks, investment companies and insurance companies, the level is 10 percent. Multiple Ownership Rules, 55 R.R.2d 1465 (1984).

4. When approval of an application for a new license or a license transfer would result in a violation of one of the Commission's media concentration rules, the new licensee is usually granted a temporary waiver of the rule. This gives such licensees a reasonable period of time to sell whatever is necessary to bring themselves into compliance. For example, when Rupert Murdoch's News America Corporation purchased six television stations from Metromedia, the Commission granted it a two-year waiver from the cross-ownership rule as applied to his properties in New York and Chicago. The two-year waiver was upheld on appeal. Health and Medicine Policy Research Group v. Federal Communications Commission, 807 F.2d 1038, 61 R.R.2d 1450 (D.C.Cir. 1986).

The Commission granted a similar waiver when News America bought channel 25 in Boston. Twentieth Holdings Corp., 1 F.C.C.Rcd. 1201, 61 R.R.2d 1484 (1986). As of December 1987 the company had sold only the Chicago newspaper, and for months stories had been circulating that he planned to ask for a permanent waiver for the New York and Boston newspapers. Boston Business Journal, June 22, 1987 at 1. However, in December 1987 Congress included a provision in the FCC's budget authorization prohibiting the Commission from either altering the cross-ownership rules or extending temporary waivers. (The only two existing waivers were held by News America.)

News America appealed the FCC's subsequent denial of its petition for an extension of the temporary waivers. Noting that the continuing budget resolution struck at "Murdoch with the precision of a laser beam," the court of appeals found it fatally underinclusive. News

America Publishing, Inc. v. Federal Communications Commission, 844 F.2d 800, 64 R.R.2d 1309, 15 Med.L.Rptr. 1161 (D.C.Cir.1988).

In the meantime News America had sold the *New York Post.* Although the court decision gave News America the option of seeking an extension of the waiver for the Boston newspaper and television station, the company decided instead to to sell the television station. It was purchased by the Boston Celtics.

5. The Commission has also established limitations on broadcast-cable crossownership. We will discuss these in Chapter IX.

B. NATIONAL CONCENTRATION

The Commission has proven equally concerned about the effects of concentration of ownership across different markets. Are the issues raised by national concentration different from those presented by local concentration? How is the marketplace of ideas in one city affected by a company's media holdings in other cities? Are there any potential benefits of a company owning stations in other communities?

1. MULTIPLE OWNERSHIP RULES

Beginning in 1940 the Commission adopted rules limiting the number of stations that might be held by a single owner. In 1953 the Commission resolved that the rules should prohibit the ownership or control, directly or indirectly, by any party of more than seven AM stations, seven FM stations and seven television stations of which not more than five could be VHF. The Commission explained its position as follows:

> The vitality of our system of broadcasting depends in large part on the introduction into this field of licensees who are pre- pared and qualified to serve the varied and divergent needs of the public for radio service. Simply stated, the fundamental purpose of this facet of the multiple ownership rules is to promote diversifica- tion of ownership in order to maximize diversification of program and service viewpoints as well as to prevent any undue concentra- tion of economic power contrary to the public interest. In this connection, we wish to emphasize that by such rules diversification of program services is furthered without any governmental en- croachment on what we recognize to be the prime responsibility of the broadcast licensee. (See Section 326 of the Communications Act.)

The Commission chose an equal number of AM and FM stations because at that time 538 of the 600 FM stations were owned by AM licensees, the result of a conscious Commission policy to encourage AM stations to put FM stations on the air since most of those operating FM stations alone were finding it extremely unprofitable. The number seven was chosen "in order that present holdings of such stations be not unduly disrupted." Few owners had holdings in excess of seven, and the Commission planned to hold a divestiture hearing for each of them. Rules and Regulations Relating to Multiple Ownership, 18 F.C.C. 288 (1953).

This limitation rule was challenged immediately by a group owner who claimed that the Commission was illegally using the rulemaking procedure to foreclose the right of an applicant to a hearing as to whether the license would be in the public interest, by making a categorical judgment linking the public interest with a given maximum concentration of holdings. The rules were upheld in United States v. Storer Broadcasting Co., 351 U.S. 192, 1 Med.L.Rptr. 1983 (1956). The Court rejected Storer's argument that § 309 of the Communications Act always requires a full hearing to determine whether granting additional licenses to the applicant would be in the public interest:

> We do not read the hearing requirement, however, as withdrawing from the power of the Commission the rule-making authority necessary for the orderly conduct of its business. As conceded by Storer, "Section 309(b) does not require the Commission to hold a hearing before denying a license to operate a station in ways contrary to those that the Congress has determined are in the public interest." The challenged Rules contain limitations against licensing not specifically authorized by statute. But that is not the limit of the Commission's rulemaking authority.

> This Commission, like other agencies, deals with the public interest. [ ] Its authority covers new and rapidly developing fields. Congress sought to create regulation for public protection with careful provision to assure fair opportunity for open competition in the use of broadcasting facilities. Accordingly, we cannot interpret § 309(b) as barring rules that declare a present intent to limit the number of stations consistent with a permissible "concentration of control." It is but a rule that announces the Commission's attitude on public protection against such concentration.

The opinion did state, however, that the Commission's responsibility to behave in the public interest required it to grant a hearing to an applicant who had already reached the maximum number of stations but nonetheless asserted sufficient reasons why the rule should be waived in its particular case.

In 1984 the Commission voted to expand the limits on multiple ownership from 7–7–7 to 12–12–12 with a six-year sunsetting provision (eliminating the rules entirely at the end of six years). Multiple Ownership, 100 F.C.C.2d 17, 56 R.R.2d 859 (1984). The new rule made no distinction between VHF and UHF television stations. Faced with mounting criticism of the new rule and threatened Congressional action, the Commission delayed implementation of the television portion of the order and reconsidered it. The revised order contained several new provisions:

33. After reviewing the petitions for reconsideration filed in this proceeding, we now find it appropriate to modify certain aspects of our Report and Order. In this regard, we now find our modification of the rule should be revised to better account for the effect that this relaxation will have on population penetration. We also find that the Report and Order should be revised to take cognizance of the limitations inherent in UHF broadcasting and to promote our traditional policy of facilitating minority ownership. In addition, we find that a more appropriate approach is to eliminate the automatic sunset provision contained in our previous decision.

. . .

36. On reconsideration, we have become increasingly aware of the limitations of proceeding solely with a numerical multiple ownership limit in the event that there is a rapid expansion of group ownership in the wake of our relaxing of the national multiple ownership rules. As various parties have argued throughout this proceeding, a numerical approach may not give appropriate consideration to wide discrepancies in population coverage because a station in the largest market is deemed equivalent to a station in the smallest market for purposes of ownership regulation. As a consequence, relaxing the numerical cap from seven stations to twelve stations may provide an opportunity for a single group owner to increase its audience base substantially, particularly if acquisitions are made in the largest markets. A numerical cap does not affect this type of restructuring. While there is no evidence in the record that would lead us to believe that such an eventuality would necessarily have an adverse result, we now believe that the potential for this type of restructuring warrants a more cautious approach. To this extent, we now believe it is advisable to adopt an additional ownership limit based on audience reach.

The Commission settled on a 25 percent limit on audience reach. This limited the growth of the largest group owners without requiring any divestiture or grandfathering. (Metromedia had the largest combined reach at 23.89 percent.)

The FCC then turned to requests for special treatment for both UHFs and minorities. Due to the physical limitations inherent in the UHF band, UHF stations cannot compete on an equal basis. The original rules' stricter limitation on VHF ownership was part of the Commission's longstanding efforts to foster the development of UHF. There were no incentives for minorities in the original rules, but the Commission has adopted several other policies designed to increase minority ownership:

44. While we agree with the petitioners' assessment as to the need for a UHF incentive within the context of the audience reach

limit, we do not believe that the incentive should be structured so as to merely increase the reach cap. Such an approach would not accurately represent the physical handicaps confronting UHF television. Consistent with the diversity objectives expressed in our ownership rules, we believe that a more appropriate indicator of the reach handicap of UHF stations is one that measures the actual coverage limitation inherent in the UHF signal. Therefore, with respect to the audience reach limit adopted herein, we believe that owners of UHF stations should be attributed with only 50 percent of an ADI market's theoretical audience reach to account for this disparity. For example, the theoretical ADI audience reach of the New York market comprises 7.72 percent of all television households. Under the system adopted today, the owner of a UHF station in the New York market would be attributed with an audience reach of only 50 percent of this amount which equals 3.86 percentage points. We find that the discount system adopted herein properly reflects the Commission's historical concern with UHF television. Furthermore, the discount approach provides a measure of the actual voice handicap and is therefore consistent with our traditional diversity objectives.

(b) Minority Incentives

45. In the Report and Order, we observed that the national multiple ownership rules were not primarily intended to function as a vehicle for promoting minority ownership in broadcasting. In this regard, we noted that the Commission has instituted various policies such as tax certificates, distress sale benefits and lottery preferences to promote minority ownership in communications. We continue to believe that these policies, as opposed to our multiple ownership rules, should serve as the primary mechanisms to promote minority ownership in television and radio broadcasting. We recognize, however, that our national multiple ownership rules may, in some circumstances, play a role in fostering minority ownership. Thus, while it would be inappropriate to retain multiple ownership regulations for the sole purpose of promoting minority ownership, we now believe that a minority incentive should be included in the rules adopted by our action today. Accordingly, we are adopting rules today which permit group owners of television and radio stations to utilize a maximum numerical cap of 14 stations provided that at least two of the stations in which they hold cognizable interests are minority controlled. Group owners having a cognizable interest in at least one minority controlled television or radio station may utilize a maximum numerical cap of 13 stations. Extending this policy to the audience reach limit for television, we believe that a group owner having cognizable interests in minority controlled television stations should be allowed to reach a maximum of 30 percent of the national audience, provided that at least five percent of the aggregate reach of its stations is contributed by minority controlled stations.

Commissioners Dawson and Patrick each wrote separate statements to express disagreement with using the multiple ownership rules to promote minority ownership. Commissioner Dawson stated that she did not see how national "concentration is in any way ameliorated by the race of [an] entity's owners." Commissioner Patrick similarly observed, "If the public interest is threatened by concentrating ownership of 14 stations in a single owner, how is that threat obviated by the race of that owner?" Multiple Ownership (12–12–12 Reconsideration), 100 F.C.C.2d 74, 57 R.R.2d 967 (1985). The rules have been appealed by the National Association of Black-owned Broadcasters.

Both Commissioners seem to be taking the position that any specific rule must serve only one interest. But remember the newspaper-broadcast crossownership case. Is the Commission allowed to apply rules differently to various groups as long as it can provide a rational basis for the unequal treatment?

At the same time the FCC relaxed the duopoly rules for radio, it also relaxed the multiple ownership rules. In Radio Multiple Ownership Rules, p. 168, *supra,* the Commission decided to permit licensees to own up to 30 AM and 30 FM stations nationwide. This was modified on reconsideration to 18 AM and 18 FM stations. This will be raised to 20 AM and 20 FM after two years. Licensees may acquire an attributable interest in an additional three AM and three FM stations as long as they are controlled by either minorities or small business (total revenues of less than $500,000 and total assets of less than $1,000,000.) *Radio Multiple Ownership Rules, Recon.,* p. 168, *supra.* The Commission has also proposed relaxing the multiple ownership rules. *Review of the Commission's Regulations Governing Television Broadcasting,* p. 168, *supra.*

2.   CONGLOMERATES IN BROADCASTING

Occasionally the problem has been raised, not in terms of multiple ownership of competing media, but in terms of concern about other businesses in which a prospective licensee is engaged. The prime example is a merger that was proposed between ABC, which, in its capacity as group owner, owned 17 broadcasting stations, and International Telephone and Telegraph, a vast conglomerate with manufacturing facilities, telecommunication operations and other activities in 66 countries throughout the world.

Critics were concerned that ITT would use the broadcasting facilities to further the interests of the parent corporation in ways that might include distorting the news and making editorial decisions on grounds other than professional journalism criteria. The Commission rejected these concerns on the ground that "it is too late in the day to argue that such outside business interests are disqualifying. . . . We cannot in this case adopt standards which when applied to other cases would require us to restructure the industry unless we are prepared to undertake that task. We could not, in good conscience, forbid ABC to merge with ITT without instituting proceedings to separate NBC from RCA, both of which are bigger than the respective principals in this case." The Commission granted the application for transferring of the 17 licenses by a 4 to 3 vote. ABC–ITT Merger, 7 F.C.C.2d 245, 9 R.R.2d 12 (1966).

While an appeal by the Justice Department on antitrust grounds was pending, the parties abandoned their proposed merger. Would there be any problem if, for example, General Motors sought to acquire a television station in Detroit? Are different questions raised if a book publisher or motion picture producer seeks a television license?

The Gannett–Combined Communications Merger. In 1979 the FCC approved what was at that time the largest deal in broadcasting history. The parties were Gannett, which at the time published 77 daily and 32 weekly newspapers and owned WHEC–TV in Rochester, N.Y., and Combined Communications Corp. which at the time owned newspapers in Cincinnati and Oakland, plus five VHF, two UHF, six AM and six FM stations. In addition, Gannett owned Louis Harris and Associates, the polling firm, and Combined was a major supplier of outdoor advertising. The deal called for $370 million in Gannett stock to go to Combined. After spin-offs to meet the FCC's cross-ownership policies, Gannett had 79 daily newspapers, seven television stations and 12 radio stations.

The final result, because of the spin-offs, violated no concentration rule. Nonetheless, the Commission considered whether granting the applications to transfer ownership of the stations would be in the "public interest." The majority concluded that the deal was not likely to affect competition adversely or raise antitrust concerns.

The First Amendment issue, however, raised harder questions. The FCC noted that Gannett had represented that "local autonomy will be the touchstone for the operation of each newspaper and broadcast property" and that the newspapers would operate separately from the broadcast properties. For example, Gannett asserted that in 1976, of its 35 papers that made endorsements, 22 endorsed Gerald Ford and 13 endorsed Jimmy Carter. Decentralized operation was the goal, although everyone recognized that under § 310 of the 1934 Act, Gannett had to retain ultimate control of its stations.

Some were concerned about the possibility that the size of the combination would lead advertisers and stock market investors to exercise more control over management than would occur with less centralized control. They feared that a large communications entity might "harm diversity of information and opinion through its institutional pressures rather than by any intentional acts of its corporate leadership."

The FCC stressed countervailing considerations: "Media chains may have more freedom and might be inclined to take more risks in their reporting of news and opinion because their financial health allows a degree of independence from the political views of their major advertisers." The size of the organization might permit more coverage of national news in competition with the wire services, the television networks, and the largest newspapers and magazines.

Because all of these newspapers and stations face "substantial local mixed-media competition," even if a "Gannett" view entered a new market, it was not eliminating other views available in that market. Affirmatively, the Commission noted that the deal had resulted in the break-up of cross-ownership interests in Phoenix and St. Louis, as well as sale of WHEC–TV to a buyer controlled by a minority group. This made WHEC–TV the first network-affiliated major market television station controlled by a minority group. The merger was approved 5–1.

The dissenter was greatly concerned by the "trend" toward placing "organs of information and news and opinion in this country in fewer and fewer hands. This is an unhealthy thing for a democracy: absentee ownership, on a vast scale, of newspapers and broadcasting stations. . . . Where are the William Allen Whites of 1979? Too many of them have been bought out, one by one, by the chains. They've been made offers they could not refuse."

In 1985 Gannett reached an agreement to purchase the Evening News Association, expanding both its newspaper and its broadcast holdings. As a result of the purchase, the audience reach of Gannett's television stations was increased from 6 to 10 percent.

The Capital Cities Communications–American Broadcasting Companies Merger. In 1985 Capital Cities Communications (CCC) announced plans to acquire American Broadcasting Companies, Inc. (ABC) for $3.5 billion. This transaction, larger by far than any previous broadcast sale or merger, resulted in the formation of a new company, Capital Cities/ABC, Inc. (CC/ABC).

To meet the various FCC ownership rules, CC/ABC had to sell more than $1 billion worth of properties. Although CCC and ABC owned only 12 AM stations, 12 FM stations and 12 TV stations between them, the total reach of the TV stations was 28.59 percent. To bring that figure down to the 25 percent maximum allowed by the new multiple ownership rules, CCC sold WKBW–TV, Buffalo, and WTNH(TV), New Haven.

The latter was also necessary because of a signal overlap between WTNH and WABC–TV, New York. A similar overlap between WABC–TV and WPVI–TV in Philadelphia did not necessitate selling one of those stations because the Commission granted them a waiver of the duopoly rule. However, a number of radio stations had to be sold to comply with the duopoly rule. Record prices were paid for many of these properties.

Soon after the modifications in the duopoly rule, p. 167, *supra*, were announced, the Commission ruled on an additional waiver request.

The CC/ABC merger had produced ownership of TV–AM–FM combinations in New York City, Chicago, and Los Angeles and of an AM–FM combination in San Francisco. The FCC granted permanent waivers in all four cases because all four cities were in the top 25 television markets and each had over 30 separately owned and operated broadcast stations after the proposed waivers. The FCC found 94 separate licensees in New York, 105 in Chicago, 79 in Los Angeles and 57 in San Francisco. The Commission did not scrutinize each proposal for economic efficiencies because it had already concluded that such efficiencies generally exist. Allowing the combinations would not undermine the benefits that flow from the "Commission's traditional pro-competitive and diversity policies."

Commissioner Dennis concurred separately. She had suggested a two-tier approach in lieu of the 25 market–30 licensee approach. She would have restricted waivers to markets with at least 10 television stations, 45 separate owners and 65 broadcast stations. "In all other markets, we should not only retain the rule, but enforce it strictly." Because the four markets involved here met even her tighter requirements, she concurred. Capital Cities/ABC, Inc., 66 R.R.2d 1146 (1989).

Several CCC newspapers were also subject to divestiture requirements. *The Oakland (Mich.) Press* and *The Daily Register* are published in suburbs of cities in which ABC broadcast outlets are located. Finally, CC/ABC had to sell all the cable properties owned by CCC. Another FCC media concentration rule prohibits network ownership of cable. *The Washington Post* purchased the cable properties.

The Commission approved the merger. There was not much concern with the more general media concentration issues addressed in the Gannett case.

3. MINORITY OWNERSHIP

One of the FCC's concerns in recent years has been the dearth of minority broadcasters. The FCC has developed several policies aimed at increasing minority ownership. In addition to the minority preference in comparative licensing proceedings, p. 110, *supra,* these policies include the distress sale policy and the tax certificate policy.

In 1978 in an effort to meet two concerns at once, the Commission announced steps to allow licensees whose renewals might be in jeopardy to sell their stations to minority groups for more than the value of the buildings and equipment but less than the going concern value. Statement of Policy on Minority Ownership of Broadcast Facilities, 68 F.C.C.2d 979, 42 R.R.2d 1689 (1978). The Commission announced that it would permit "licensees whose licenses have been designated for revocation hearings, or whose renewal applications have been designated for hearing on basic qualification issues . . . to transfer or assign their licenses at a 'distress sale' price to applicants with a significant minority ownership interest, assuming the proposed assignee or transferee meets our other qualifications." The distress price was expected to be "somewhat greater than the value of the unlicensed equipment, which could be realized even in the event of revocation."

In a clarifying statement, the Commission stated that the opportunity for distress sales applied only when no competing applicant was involved in the hearing.

The distress sale option has been attractive to licensees who are ordered to hearings. The fact that allegations have been thought serious enough to warrant a hearing is a dangerous warning. To litigate and lose the renewal would leave the licensee with nothing except the buildings and equipment that it owns. The distress sale may yield the owner as much as 75 percent of the fair appraised value of a viable business.

The immediate social result of the distress sale policy has been to allow minority groups to enter the broadcasting industry in greater numbers. If the FCC's efforts to develop new stations, discussed in Chapter II, work as expected, many minority broadcasters will use that route and the relatively limited distress sale route will become less important.

The distress sale policy explicitly limited "minority" to specific ethnic groups but indicated that "other clearly definable groups, such as women, may be able to demonstrate that they are eligible for similar treatment." But in Minority Ownership of Broadcast Facilities, 69 F.C.C.2d 1591, 44 R.R.2d 1051 (1978), the Commission ruled that although it had on occasion recognized female involvement as a merit in comparative proceedings, it would not extend the minority policy to women because it had "not concluded that the historical and contemporary disadvantagement suffered by women is of the same order, or has the same contemporary consequences" as those involving groups covered in the original policy statement.

In 1985 the Commission similarly refused to extend the minority preference in lottery proceedings. The FCC concluded that it did not have the authority and that, furthermore, extending it to women was inappropriate. Lottery Selection (Preference for Women), 58 R.R.2d 1077 (1985). The Commission's refusal to extend the preference to women was affirmed. Pappas v. Federal Communications Commission, 807 F.2d 1019, 58 R.R.2d 1463 (D.C.Cir.1986).

The FCC has developed other techniques for encouraging minority entry into broadcasting. In the *1978 Policy Statement*, the Commission also announced that it would grant tax certificates, permitting a seller to defer payment of capital gains taxes, to owners who sell their stations to groups controlled by members of minority groups. Recall also the preference awarded minorities applying for the new FM licenses recently created by the Commission.

In 1987, as a result of a court of appeals decision and the Commission's subsequent actions, all of the minority and female preference policies appeared to face possible elimination. The case was the appeal of the FCC's decision to grant an FM construction permit to Dale Bell in a comparative hearing. The primary factor in the decision was a female preference awarded to Bell.

The court of appeals held 2–1 that the Commission had exceeded its authority by adopting the female preference policy. The court subsequently granted Bell's petition for rehearing *en banc* and asked the parties to file briefs addressing two questions: "(1) whether the FCC has statutory authority to grant a limited preference for integrated ownership-management by women applicants in comparative licensing proceedings, and (2) whether such a grant is constitutional." The Commission's brief took many people by surprise:

> The racial and gender preference policies employed by the FCC in comparative licensing proceedings since 1978 are discriminatory classifications by government that are inherently suspect, presumptively invalid and subject to stringent scrutiny under the equal protection guarantee implicit in the due process clause of the Fifth Amendment. See Wygant v. Jackson Bd. of Educ., 476 U.S. 267 (1986); Lehr v. Robertson, 463 U.S. 248, 265–66 (1983). . . .
>
> . . .
>
> It has been suggested that one aspect of the justification for both the gender and race preference policies is that they serve as a remedy for past discrimination. . . .
>
> Yet in a recent Supreme Court decision it was emphasized that "[t]his Court never has held that societal discrimination alone is sufficient to justify a racial classification. Rather, the Court has insisted upon some showing of prior discrimination by the governmental unit involved before allowing limited use of racial classifications in order to remedy such discrimination." *Wygant,* 476 U.S. at 274 (opinion of Powell, J.). There has never been a finding, nor so far as we know even an allegation, that the FCC engaged in prior discrimination against racial minorities or women in its licensing process. The general societal discrimination alluded to in some opinions is hence inadequate to support licensing preferences imposed by the FCC to remedy such general societal discrimination. Thus, there has been a clear failure to meet applicable constitutional standards to justify use of racial and gender licensing preferences as a remedy for prior discrimination.

The Commission did not go so far as to argue that the use of racial and gender licensing preferences to enhance diversity of programming was *per se* unconstitutional. Rather, it claimed that the requirement of strict scrutiny prohibited such preferences in the absence of a record demonstrating: (1) "that a race- or gender-based preference scheme to increase minority and female ownership is essential to achieving" diversity, and (2) "that a nexus exists between an owner's race or gender and program diversity." The Commission therefore asked the court to remand the case for further proceedings to determine whether "exceedingly persuasive justification" for the preferences could be established. The court granted the Commission's motion. Steele v. Federal Communications Commission, 806 F.2d 1126 (1986).

The Commission's other policies aimed at increasing minority ownership also came under attack. For example, in Faith Center, Inc., 57 R.R.2d 1185 (1984), an application for approval of a distress sale was challenged in part on the grounds that the distress sale policy is unconstitutional. The application was granted, and Shurberg Broadcasting of Hartford, Inc. appealed. After the remand in *Steele* was granted, the Commission requested a similar remand in Shurberg Broadcasting of Hartford, Inc. v. Federal Communications Commission, 876 F.2d 902 (D.C.Cir.1989). Although the remand request was initially denied, the court subsequently did remand *Shurberg* with instructions to decide it in accordance with the court's decision in *Steele*.

Following the remand in *Steele*, the Commission issued an NOI addressing these issues. Reexamination of the Commission's Comparative Licensing, Distress Sales and Tax Certificate Policies Premised on Racial, Ethnic or Gender Classifications, 1 F.C.C.Rcd. 1315 (1986).

In December 1987 Congress included a provision in the Omnibus Spending Bill prohibiting the Commission from repealing or continuing its reexamination of the minority ownership policies. In accordance with that mandate, the Commission terminated its proceedings and notified the court of appeals of its action. Pub. L. 100–202 (1987).

In 1988 a tentative settlement was reached in *Steele*. Despite the settlement in *Steele*, the court of appeals soon found itself addressing the issues raised in that case. In Winter Park Communications Inc., v. Federal Communications Commission, 873 F.2d 347, 66 R.R.2d 575 (D.C.Cir.1989), the court upheld the minority preference policy. In Shurberg v. Federal Communications Commission, 876 F.2d 902, 66 R.R.2d 261 (D.C.Cir.1989), a different panel of the court found that the distress sale policy violated the equal protection clause of the Fifth Amendment. The Supreme Court granted *certiorari* in both cases.

METRO BROADCASTING, INC. v. FEDERAL COMMUNICATIONS COMMISSION

Supreme Court of the United States, 1990.
497 U.S. 547, 110 S.Ct. 2997, 111 L.Ed.2d 445, 67 R.R.2d 1353.

JUSTICE BRENNAN delivered the opinion of the Court.

The issue in these cases, consolidated for decision today, is whether certain minority preference policies of the Federal Communications Commission violate the equal protection component of the Fifth Amendment. The policies in question are (1) a program awarding an enhancement for minority ownership in comparative proceedings for new licenses, and (2) the minority "distress sale" program, which permits a limited category of existing radio and television broadcast stations to be transferred only to minority-controlled firms. We hold that these policies do not violate equal protection principles.

I

A

The policies before us today can best be understood by reference to the history of federal efforts to promote minority participation in the broadcast industry.[1] . . . Although for the past two decades minorities have constituted at least one-fifth of the United States population, during this time relatively few members of minority groups have held broadcast licenses. In 1971, minorities owned only 10 of the approximately 7,500 radio stations in the country and none of the more than 1,000 television stations, [ ]; in 1978, minorities owned less than 1 percent of the Nation's radio and television stations, [ ]; and in 1986, they owned just 2.1 percent of the more than 11,000 radio and television stations in the United States. [ ] . . . Moreover, these statistics fail to reflect the fact that, as late entrants who often have been able to obtain only the less valuable stations, many minority broadcasters serve geographically limited markets with relatively small audiences.

The Commission has recognized that the viewing and listening public suffers when minorities are underrepresented among owners of television and radio stations:

> "Acute underrepresentation of minorities among the owners of broadcast properties is troublesome because it is the licensee who is ultimately responsible for identifying and serving the needs and interests of his or her audience. Unless minorities are encouraged to enter the mainstream of the commercial broadcasting business, a substantial portion of our citizenry will remain underserved and the larger, non-minority audience will be deprived of the views of minorities." [ ]

The Commission has therefore worked to encourage minority participation in the broadcast industry. The FCC began by formulating rules to prohibit licensees from discriminating against minorities in employment. The FCC explained that "broadcasting is an important mass media form which, because it makes use of the airwaves belonging to the public, must obtain a federal license under a public interest standard and must operate in the public interest in order to obtain periodic renewals of that license." [ ] Regulations dealing with employment practices were justified as necessary to enable the FCC to satisfy its obligation under the Communications Act to promote diversity of programming. [ ] The United States Department of Justice, for example, contended that equal employment opportunity in the broad-

---

1. The FCC has defined the term "minority" to include "those of Black, Hispanic Surnamed, American Eskimo, Aleut, American Indian and Asiatic American extraction." Statement of Policy on Minority Ownership of Broadcasting Facilities, 68 F.C.C.2d 979, 980, n. 8 (1978). . . .

cast industry could " 'contribute significantly toward reducing and ending discrimination in other industries' " because of the " 'enormous impact which television and radio have upon American life.' " [ ]

Initially, the FCC did not consider minority status as a factor in licensing decisions, maintaining as a matter of Commission policy that no preference to minority ownership was warranted where the record in a particular case did not give assurances that the owner's race likely would affect the content of the station's broadcast service to the public. [ ] [This position was overruled in *TV 9*, p. 110, *supra.*]

. . . [T]he FCC adopted in May 1978 its *Statement of Policy on Minority Ownership of Broadcasting Facilities*, 68 F.C.C.2d 979. After recounting its past efforts to expand broadcast diversity, the FCC concluded:

> "[W]e are compelled to observe that the views of racial minorities continue to be inadequately represented in the broadcast media. This situation is detrimental not only to the minority audience but to all of the viewing and listening public. Adequate representation of minority viewpoints in programming serves not only the needs and interests of the minority community but also enriches and educates the non-minority audience. It enhances the diversified programming which is a key objective not only of the Communications Act of 1934 but also of the First Amendment." [ ]

Describing its actions as only "first steps," [ ], the FCC outlined two elements of a minority ownership policy.

First, the Commission pledged to consider minority ownership as one factor in comparative proceedings for new licenses. [Here, the Court outlined the six comparative criteria used for mutually exclusive license applications, p. 104, *supra.*] In the Policy Statement on Minority Ownership, the FCC announced that minority ownership and participation in management would be considered as a "plus" to be weighed together with all other relevant factors. [ ] The "plus" is awarded only to the extent that a minority owner actively participates in the day-to-day management of the station.

Second, the FCC outlined a plan to increase minority opportunities to receive reassigned and transferred licenses through the so-called "distress sale" policy. [ ] As a general rule, a licensee whose qualifications to hold a broadcast license come into question may not assign or transfer the license until the FCC has resolved its doubts in a noncomparative hearing. The distress sale policy is an exception to that practice, allowing a broadcaster whose license has been designated for a revocation hearing, to assign the license to an FCC-approved minority enterprise. [ ] The assignee must meet the FCC's basic qualifications, and the minority ownership must exceed 50 percent or be controlling.[6] The buyer must purchase the license before the start of

---

6. In 1982, the FCC determined that a limited partnership could qualify as a minority enterprise if the general partner is a minority who holds at least 20 percent interest and who will exercise "complete control over a station's affairs." [ ]

the revocation or renewal hearing, and the price must not exceed 75 percent of fair market value. These two Commission minority owner-ship policies are at issue today.

B

1

. . . [P]etitioner Metro Broadcasting, Inc. (Metro) challenges the Commission's policy awarding preferences to minority owners in com-parative licensing proceedings. Several applicants, including Metro and Rainbow Broadcasting (Rainbow), were involved in a comparative proceeding to select among three mutually exclusive proposals to con-struct and operate a new UHF television station in the Orlando, Florida, metropolitan area. . . . [The Commission's Review Board considered] Rainbow's comparative showing and found it superior to Metro's. In so doing, the Review Board awarded Rainbow a substantial enhancement on the ground that it was 90 percent Hispanic-owned, whereas Metro had only one minority partner who owned 19.8 percent of the enterprise. The Review Board found that Rainbow's minority credit outweighed Metro's local residence and civic participation advan-tage. [ ] The Commission denied review of the Board's decision largely without discussion, stating merely that it "agree[d] with the Board's resolution of this case." [ ]

[The court of appeals affirmed the decision, 2–1, and petitions for rehearing were denied.]

2

[The other case] emerged from a series of attempts by Faith Center, Inc., the licensee of a Hartford, Connecticut television station, to execute a minority distress sale. In December 1980, the FCC designat-ed for a hearing Faith Center's application for renewal of its license. [ ] [Faith Center obtained FCC approval for a distress sale, but the sale fell through due to financing problems. A second attempt at a distress sale was approved, this time over the objections of Alan Shurberg. The second sale also fell through due to financing problems.]

In December 1983, respondent Shurberg Broadcasting of Hartford, Inc. (Shurberg) applied to the Commission for a permit to build a television station in Hartford. The application was mutually exclusive with Faith Center's renewal application, then still pending. In June 1984, Faith Center again sought the FCC's approval for a distress sale, requesting permission to sell the station to Astroline Communications Company, Limited Partnership (Astroline), a minority applicant. Shur-berg opposed the sale to Astroline on a number of grounds, including that the FCC's distress sale program violated Shurberg's right to equal protection. Shurberg therefore urged the Commission to deny the distress sale request and to schedule a comparative hearing to examine the application Shurberg had tendered alongside Faith Center's renewal request. In December 1984, the FCC approved Faith Center's petition for permission to assign its broadcast license to Astroline pursuant to the distress sale policy. [ ] The FCC rejected Shurberg's equal protection challenge to the policy as "without merit." [ ]

[The court of appeals, 2–1, held that the distress sale policy was unconstitutional. The majority found that the policy "unconstitutionally deprives Alan Shurberg and Shurberg Broadcasting of their equal protection rights under the Fifth Amendment because the program is not narrowly tailored to remedy past discrimination or to promote programming diversity."]

II

It is of overriding significance in these cases that the FCC's minority ownership programs have been specifically approved—indeed mandated—by Congress. . . .

. . . We hold that benign race-conscious measures mandated by Congress—even if those measures are not "remedial" in the sense of being designed to compensate victims of past governmental or societal discrimination—are constitutionally permissible to the extent that they serve important governmental objectives within the power of Congress and are substantially related to achievement of those objectives.

. . .

We hold that the FCC minority ownership policies pass muster under the test we announce today. First we find that they serve the important governmental objective of broadcast diversity. Second, we conclude that they are substantially related to the achievement of that objective.

A

Congress found that "the effects of past inequities stemming from racial and ethnic discrimination have resulted in a severe underrepresentation of minorities in the media of mass communications." [ ] Congress and the Commission do not justify the minority ownership policies strictly as remedies for victims of this discrimination, however. Rather, Congress and the FCC have selected the minority ownership policies primarily to promote programming diversity, and they urge that such diversity is an important governmental objective that can serve as a constitutional basis for the preference policies. We agree.

We have long recognized that "[b]ecause of the scarcity of [electromagnetic] frequencies, the Government is permitted to put restraints on licensees in favor of others whose views should be expressed on this unique medium." [*Red Lion*] The Government's role in distributing the limited number of broadcast licenses is not merely that of a "traffic officer," [*NBC*]; rather it is axiomatic that broadcasting may be regulated in light of the rights of the viewing and listening audience and that "the widest possible dissemination of information from diverse and antagonistic sources is essential to the welfare of the public." [*AP*]

Safeguarding the public's right to receive a diversity of views and information over the airwaves is therefore an integral component of the FCC's mission. We have observed that " 'the "public interest" standard necessarily invites reference to First Amendment principles,' " [NCCB], and that the Communications Act has designated broadcasters as "fiduciaries for the public." [League of Women Voters]. "[T]he people as a whole retain their interest in free speech by radio [and other forms of broadcast] and their collective right to have the medium function consistently with the ends and purposes of the First Amendment," and "[i]t is the right of the viewers and listeners, not the right of the broadcasters, which is paramount." [Red Lion] "Congress may . . . seek to assure that the public receives through this medium a balanced presentation of information on issues of public importance that otherwise might not be addressed if control of the medium were left entirely in the hands of those who own and operate broadcasting stations." [League of Women Voters]

Against this background, we conclude that the interest in enhancing broadcast diversity is, at the very least, an important governmental objective and is therefore a sufficient basis for the Commission's minority ownership policies. . . . The benefits of such diversity are not limited to the members of minority groups who gain access to the broadcasting industry by virtue of the ownership policies; rather, the benefits redound to all members of the viewing and listening audience. . . .

B

We also find that the minority ownership policies are substantially related to the achievement of the Government's interest. One component of this inquiry concerns the relationship between expanded minority ownership and greater broadcast diversity; both the FCC and Congress have determined that such a relationship exists. Although we do not " 'defer' to the judgment of the Congress and the Commission on a constitutional question," and would not "hesitate to invoke the Constitution should we determine that the Commission has not fulfilled its task with appropriate sensitivity" to equal protection principles, [CBS v. DNC], we must pay close attention to the expertise of the Commission and the factfinding of Congress when analyzing the nexus between minority ownership and programming diversity. With respect to this "complex" empirical question, ibid, we are required to give "great weight to the decisions of Congress and the experience of the Commission." Id., at 102.

1

. . .

Furthermore, the FCC's reasoning with respect to the minority ownership policies is consistent with longstanding practice under the Communications Act. From its inception, public regulation of broadcasting has been premised on the assumption that diversification of ownership will broaden the range of programming available to the broadcast audience. . . . The Commission has never relied on the market alone to ensure that the needs of the audience are met. Indeed, one of the FCC's elementary regulatory assumptions is that broadcast content is not purely market-driven; if it were, there would be little need for consideration in licensing decisions of such factors as integration of ownership and management, local residence, and civic participation. . . .

2

[The Court then reviewed the various actions Congress had taken in support of the minority ownership policies. Most recently, for the past three years, Congress "specifically required the Commission, through appropriations legislation, to maintain the minority ownership policies without alteration."]

C

The judgment that there is a link between expanded minority ownership and broadcast diversity does not rest on impermissible stereotyping. Congressional policy does not assume that in every case minority ownership and management will lead to more minority-oriented programming or to the expression of a discrete "minority viewpoint" on the airwaves. Neither does it pretend that all programming that appeals to minority audiences can be labeled "minority programming" or that programming that might be described as "minority" does not appeal to nonminorities. Rather, both Congress and the FCC maintain simply that expanded minority ownership of broadcast outlets will, in the aggregate, result in greater broadcast diversity. A broadcasting industry with representative minority participation will produce more variation and diversity than will one whose ownership is drawn from a single racially and ethnically homogenous group. . . .

Although all station owners are guided to some extent by market demand in their programming decisions, Congress and the Commission have determined that there may be important differences between the broadcasting practices of minority owners and those of their nonminority counterparts. This judgment—and the conclusion that there is a nexus between minority ownership and broadcasting diversity—is corroborated by a host of empirical evidence. Evidence suggests that an owner's minority status influences the selection of topics for news coverage and the presentation of editorial viewpoint, especially on matters of particular concern to minorities. "[M]inority ownership does appear to have specific impact on the presentation of minority images in local news," inasmuch as minority-owned stations tend to devote more news time to topics of minority interest and to avoid racial and ethnic stereotypes in portraying minorities. In addition, studies show that a minority owner is more likely to employ minorities in managerial and other important roles where they can have an impact on station policies. If the FCC's equal employment policies "ensure that . . . licensees' programming fairly reflects the tastes and view-points of minority groups," [ ], it is difficult to deny that minority-owned stations that follow such employment policies on their own will also contribute to diversity. While we are under no illusion that members of a particular minority group share some cohesive, collective viewpoint, we believe it a legitimate inference for Congress and the Commission to draw that as more minorities gain ownership and policymaking roles in the media, varying perspectives will be more fairly represented on the airwaves. The policies are thus a product of " 'analysis' " rather than a " 'stereotyped reaction' " based on " '[h]ab-it.' "

. . .

D

We find that the minority ownership policies are in other relevant respects substantially related to the goal of promoting broadcast diver-sity. First, the Commission adopted and Congress endorsed minority ownership preferences only after long study and painstaking consider-ation of all available alternatives. [ ] . . .

. . .

Moreover, the considered nature of the Commission's judgment in selecting the particular minority ownership policies at issue today is illustrated by the fact that the Commission has rejected other types of minority preferences. For example, the Commission has studied but refused to implement the more expansive alternative of setting aside certain frequencies for minority broadcasters. [ ] In addition, in a ruling released the day after it adopted the comparative hearing credit and the distress sale preference, the FCC declined to adopt a plan to require 45–day advance public notice before a station could be sold, which had been advocated on the ground that it would ensure minori-ties a chance to bid on stations that might otherwise be sold to industry insiders without ever coming on the market. [ ] . . .

The minority ownership policies, furthermore, are aimed directly at the barriers that minorities face in entering the broadcasting indus-try. The Commission's Task Force identified as key factors hampering the growth of minority ownership a lack of adequate financing, paucity of information regarding license availability, and broadcast inexperi-ence. [ ] The Commission assigned a preference to minority status in the comparative licensing proceeding, reasoning that such an enhance-ment might help to compensate for a dearth of broadcasting experience. Most license acquisitions, however, are by necessity purchases of exist-ing stations, because only a limited number of new stations are avail-able, and those are often in less desirable markets or on less profitable portions of spectrum, such as the UHF band. Congress and the FCC therefore found a need for the minority distress sale policy, which helps to overcome the problem of lack of information by providing existing licensees with an incentive to seek out minority buyers. The Commission's choice of minority ownership policies thus addressed the very factors it had isolated as being responsible for minority underrepresentation in the broadcast industry.

. . .

Finally, we do not believe that the minority ownership policies at issue impose impermissible burdens on nonminorities. Although the nonminority challengers in these cases concede that they have not suffered the loss of an already-awarded broadcast license, they claim that they have been handicapped in their ability to obtain one in the first instance. But just as we have determined that "[a]s part of this Nation's dedication to eradicating racial discrimination, innocent persons may be called upon to bear some of the burden of the remedy," [ ] we similarly find that a congressionally mandated benign race-conscious program that is substantially related to the achievement of an important governmental interest is consistent with equal protection principles so long as it does not impose *undue* burdens on nonminorities. [ ]

In the context of broadcasting licenses, the burden on nonminorities is slight. The FCC's responsibility is to grant licenses in the "public interest, convenience, or necessity," 47 U.S.C. §§ 307, 309 (1982 ed.), and the limited number of frequencies on the electromagnetic spectrum means that "[n]o one has a First Amendment right to a license." *Red Lion*, [ ]. Applicants have no settled expectation that their applications will be granted without consideration of public interest factors such as minority ownership. Award of a preference in a comparative hearing or transfer of a station in a distress sale thus contravenes "no legitimate firmly rooted expectation[s]" of competing applicants. [ ]

. . .

III

The Commission's minority ownership policies bear the imprimatur of longstanding congressional support and direction and are substantially related to the achievement of the important governmental objective of broadcast diversity. The judgment in [*Metro*] is affirmed, the judgment in [*Shurberg*] is reversed, and the cases are remanded for proceedings consistent with this opinion.

JUSTICE STEVENS, concurring.

Today the Court squarely rejects the proposition that a governmental decision that rests on a racial classification is never permissible except as a remedy for a past wrong. [ ] I endorse this focus on the future benefit, rather than the remedial justification, of such decisions.

I remain convinced, of course, that racial or ethnic characteristics provide a relevant basis for disparate treatment only in extremely rare situations and that it is therefore "especially important that the reasons for any such classification be clearly identified and unquestionably legitimate." [ ] The Court's opinion explains how both elements of that standard are satisfied. Specifically, the reason for the classification—the recognized interest in broadcast diversity—is clearly identified and does not imply any judgment concerning the abilities of owners of different races or the merits of different kinds of programming. Neither the favored nor the disfavored class is stigmatized in any way. In addition, the Court demonstrates that this case falls within the extremely narrow category of governmental decisions for which racial or ethnic heritage may provide a rational basis for differential treatment. The public interest in broadcast diversity—like the interest in an integrated police force, diversity in the composition of a public school faculty or diversity in the student body of a professional school— is in my view unquestionably legitimate.

Therefore, I join both the opinion and judgment of the Court.

JUSTICE O'CONNOR, with whom THE CHIEF JUSTICE, JUSTICE SCALIA, and JUSTICE KENNEDY join, dissenting.

At the heart of the Constitution's guarantee of equal protection lies the simple command that the Government must treat citizens "as *individuals*, not 'as simply components of a racial, religious, sexual or national class.'" [ ] Social scientists may debate how peoples' thoughts and behavior reflect their background, but the Constitution provides that the Government may not allocate benefits and burdens among individuals based on the assumption that race or ethnicity determines how they act or think. To uphold the challenged programs, the Court departs from these fundamental principles and from our traditional requirement that racial classifications are permissible only if necessary and narrowly tailored to achieve a compelling interest. This departure marks a renewed toleration of racial classifications and a repudiation of our recent affirmation that the Constitution's equal protection guarantees extend equally to all citizens. The Court's application of a lessened equal protection standard to congressional action finds no support in our cases or in the Constitution. I respectfully dissent.

I

As we recognized last Term, the Constitution requires that the Court apply a strict standard of scrutiny to evaluate racial classifications such as those contained in the challenged FCC distress sale and comparative licensing policies. [ ] . . .

. . .

Nor does the congressional role in prolonging the FCC's policies justify any lower level of scrutiny. As with all instances of judicial review of federal legislation, the Court does not lightly set aside the considered judgment of a coordinate branch. Nonetheless, the respect due a coordinate branch yields neither less vigilance in defense of equal protection principles nor any corresponding diminution of the standard of review. . . .

. . .

II

Our history reveals the most blatant forms of discrimination have been visited upon some members of the racial and ethnic groups identified in the challenged programs. Many have lacked the opportunity to share in the Nation's wealth and to participate in its commercial enterprises. It is undisputed that minority participation in the broadcasting industry falls markedly below the demographic representation of those groups, [   ], and this shortfall may be traced in part to the discrimination and the patterns of exclusion that have widely affected our society. . . .

. . .

III

Under the appropriate standard, strict scrutiny, only a compelling interest may support the Government's use of racial classifications. Modern equal protection doctrine has recognized only one such interest: remedying the effects of racial discrimination. The interest in increasing the diversity of broadcast viewpoints is clearly not a compelling interest. It is simply too amorphous, too insubstantial, and too unrelated to any legitimate basis for employing racial classifications. The Court does not claim otherwise. Rather, it employs its novel standard and claims that this asserted interest need only be, and is, "important." . . .

An interest capable of justifying race-conscious measures must be sufficiently specific and verifiable, such that it supports only limited and carefully defined uses of racial classifications. . . .

. . . The [asserted] interest [in this case] is certainly amorphous: the FCC and the majority of this Court understandably do not suggest how one would define or measure a particular viewpoint that might be associated with race, or even how one would assess the diversity of broadcast viewpoints. . . . [T]he interest would support indefinite use of racial classifications, employed first to obtain the appropriate mixture of racial views and then to ensure that the broadcasting spectrum continues to reflect that mixture. We cannot deem to be constitutionally adequate an interest that would support measures that amount to the core constitutional violation of "outright racial balancing." [   ]

The asserted interest would justify discrimination against members of any group found to contribute to an insufficiently diverse broadcasting spectrum, including those groups currently favored. [We have previously] rejected as insufficiently weighty the interest in achieving role models in public schools, in part because that rationale could as readily be used to limit the hiring of teachers who belonged to particular minority groups. [ ] The FCC's claimed interest could similarly justify limitations on minority members' participation in broadcasting. It would be unwise to depend upon the Court's restriction of its holding to "benign" measures to forestall this result. Divorced from any remedial purpose and otherwise undefined, "benign" means only what shifting fashions and changing politics deem acceptable. Members of any racial or ethnic group, whether now preferred under the FCC's policies or not, may find themselves politically out of fashion and subject to disadvantageous but "benign" discrimination.

Under the majority's holding, the FCC may also advance its asserted interest in viewpoint diversity by identifying what constitutes a "Black viewpoint," an "Asian viewpoint," an "Arab viewpoint," and so on; determining which viewpoints are underrepresented; and then using that determination to mandate particular programming or to deny licenses to those deemed by virtue of their race or ethnicity less likely to present the favored views. Indeed, the FCC has, if taken at its word, essentially pursued this course, albeit without making express its reasons for choosing to favor particular groups or for concluding that the broadcasting spectrum is insufficiently diverse. [   ]

. . .

Even considered as other than a justification for using race classifications, the asserted interest in viewpoint diversity falls short of being weighty enough. The Court has recognized an interest in obtaining diverse broadcasting viewpoints as a legitimate basis for the FCC, acting pursuant to its "public interest" statutory mandate, to adopt limited measures to increase the number of competing licensees and to encourage licensees to present varied views on issues of public concern. See, *e.g.*, [*NCCB*]; [*Red Lion*]; [*Storer Broadcasting*]; [*AP*]; [*NBC*]. We have also concluded that these measures do not run afoul of the First Amendment's usual prohibition of Government regulation of the marketplace of ideas, in part because First Amendment concerns support limited but inevitable Government regulation of the peculiarly constrained broadcasting spectrum. [*Red Lion*] But the conclusion that measures adopted to further the interest in diversity of broadcasting viewpoints are neither beyond the FCC's statutory authority nor contrary to the First Amendment hardly establishes the interest as important for equal protection purposes.

The FCC's extension of the asserted interest in diversity of views in this case presents, at the very least, an unsettled First Amendment issue. The FCC has concluded that the American broadcasting public receives the incorrect mix of ideas and claims to have adopted the challenged policies to supplement programming content with a particular set of views. Although we have approved limited measures designed to increase information and views generally, the Court has never upheld a broadcasting measure designed to amplify a distinct set of views or the views of a particular class of speakers. Indeed, the Court has suggested that the First Amendment prohibits allocating licenses to further such ends. See [*NBC*] ("But Congress did not authorize the Commission to choose among [license] applicants on the basis of their political, economic or social views, or upon any other capricious basis. If it did, or if the Commission by these Regulations proposed a choice among applicants upon some such basis, the [First Amendment] issue before us would be totally different"). Even if an interest is determined to be legitimate in one context, it does not suddenly become important enough to justify distinctions based on race.

IV

Our traditional equal protection doctrine requires, in addition to a compelling state interest, that the Government's chosen means be necessary to accomplish and narrowly tailored to further the asserted interest. [ ] . . .

1

The FCC claims to advance its asserted interest in diverse viewpoints by singling out race and ethnicity as peculiarly linked to distinct views that require enhancement. The FCC's choice to employ a racial criterion embodies the related notions that a particular and distinct viewpoint inheres in certain racial groups, and that a particular applicant, by virtue of race or ethnicity alone, is more valued than other applicants because "likely to provide [that] distinct perspective." [ ] The policies directly equate race with belief and behavior, for they establish race as a necessary and sufficient condition of securing the preference. . . .

The FCC assumes a particularly strong correlation of race and behavior. The FCC justifies its conclusion that insufficiently diverse viewpoints are broadcast by reference to the percentage of minority owned stations. This assumption is correct only to the extent that minority owned stations provide the desired additional views, and that stations owned by individuals not favored by the preferences cannot, or at least do not, broadcast underrepresented programming. Additionally, the FCC's focus on ownership to improve programming assumes that preferences linked to race are so strong that they will dictate the owner's behavior in operating the station, overcoming the owner's personal inclinations and regard for the market. . . .

. . . The Court embraces the FCC's reasoning that an applicant's race will likely indicate that the applicant possesses a distinct perspective, but notes that the correlation of race to behavior is "not a rigid assumption about how minority owners will behave in every case." [ ] The corollary to this notion is plain: individuals of unfavored racial and ethnic backgrounds are unlikely to possess the unique experiences and background that contribute to viewpoint diversity. Both the reasoning and its corollary reveal but disregard what is objectionable about a stereotype: the racial generalization inevitably does not apply to certain individuals, and those persons may legitimately claim that they have been judged according to their race rather than upon a relevant criterion. [ ] Similarly disturbing is the majority's reasoning that different treatment on the basis of race is permissible because it is efficacious "in the aggregate." [ ] . . . This reliance on the "aggregate" and on probabilities confirms that the Court has abandoned heightened scrutiny, which requires a direct rather than approximate fit of means to ends. We would not tolerate the Government's claim that hiring persons of a particular race leads to better service "in the aggregate," and we should not accept as legitimate the FCC's claim in this case that members of certain races will provide superior programming, even if "in the aggregate." The Constitution's text, our cases, and our Nation's history foreclose such premises.

2

Moreover, the FCC's selective focus on viewpoints associated with race illustrates a particular tailoring difficulty. The asserted interest is in advancing the Nation's different "social, political, esthetic, moral, and other ideas and experiences," *Red Lion*, [ ], yet of all the varied traditions and ideas shared among our citizens, the FCC has sought to amplify only those particular views it identifies through the classifications most suspect under equal protection doctrine. Even if distinct views could be associated with particular ethnic and racial groups, focusing on this particular aspect of the Nation's views calls into question the Government's genuine commitment to its asserted interest. [ ]

. . . The policy is overinclusive: many members of a particular racial or ethnic group will have no interest in advancing the views the FCC believes to be underrepresented, or will find them utterly foreign. The policy is underinclusive: it awards no preference to disfavored individuals who may be particularly well versed in and committed to presenting those views. The FCC has failed to implement a case-by-case determination, and that failure is particularly unjustified when individualized hearings already occur, as in the comparative licensing process. [ ] . . .

Moreover, the FCC's programs cannot survive even intermediate scrutiny because race-neutral and untried means of directly accomplishing the governmental interest are readily available. The FCC could directly advance its interest by requiring licensees to provide programming that the FCC believes would add to diversity. The interest the FCC asserts is in programming diversity, yet in adopting the challenged policies, the FCC expressly disclaimed having attempted *any* direct efforts to achieve its asserted goal. [ ] . . . The FCC and the Court suggest that First Amendment interests in some manner should exempt the FCC from employing this direct, race-neutral means to achieve its asserted interest. They essentially argue that we may bend our equal protection principles to avoid more readily apparent harm to our First Amendment values. But the FCC cannot have it both ways: either the First Amendment bars the FCC from seeking to accomplish indirectly what it may not accomplish directly; or the FCC may pursue the goal, but must do so in a manner that comports with equal protection principles. And if the FCC can direct programming in any fashion, it must employ that direct means before resorting to indirect race-conscious means.

Other race-neutral means also exist, and all are at least as direct as the FCC's racial classifications. The FCC could evaluate applicants upon their ability to provide and commitment to offer whatever programming the FCC believes would reflect underrepresented viewpoints. If the FCC truly seeks diverse programming rather than allocation of goods to persons of particular racial backgrounds, it has little excuse to look to racial background rather than programming to further the programming interest. Additionally, if the FCC believes that certain persons by virtue of their unique experiences will contribute as owners to more diverse broadcasting, the FCC could simply favor applicants whose particular background indicates that they will add to the diversity of programming, rather than rely solely upon suspect classifications. Also, race-neutral means exist to allow access to the broadcasting industry for those persons excluded for financial and related reasons. The Court reasons that various minority preferences, including those reflected in the distress sale, overcome barriers of information, experience, and financing that inhibit minority ownership. [ ] Race-neutral financial and informational measures most directly reduce financial and informational barriers.

. . .

The FCC has posited a relative absence of "minority viewpoints," yet it has never suggested what those views might be, or what other viewpoints might be absent from the broadcasting spectrum. It has never identified any particular deficiency in programming diversity that should be the subject of greater programming, or that necessitates racial classifications.

. . .

The FCC seeks to avoid the tailoring difficulties by focusing on minority ownership rather than the asserted interest in diversity of broadcast viewpoints. The Constitution clearly prohibits allocating valuable goods such as broadcast licenses simply on the basis of race. [ ] Yet the FCC refers to the lack of minority ownership to support the existence of a lack of diversity of viewpoints, and has fitted its programs to increase ownership. [ ] This repeated focus on ownership supports the inference that the FCC seeks to allocate licenses based on race, an impermissible end, rather than to increase diversity of viewpoints, the asserted interest. And this justification that links the use of race preferences to minority ownership rather than to diversity of viewpoints ensure's that the FCC's programs . . . "cannot be tailored to any goal, except perhaps outright racial balancing." [ ]

3

Three difficulties suggest that the nexus between owners' race and programming is considerably less than substantial. First, the market shapes programming to a tremendous extent. Members of minority groups who own licenses might be thought, like other owners, to seek to broadcast programs that will attract and retain audiences, rather than programs that reflect the owner's tastes and preferences. [ ] Second, station owners have only limited control over the content of programming. The distress sale presents a particularly acute difficulty of this sort. Unlike the comparative licensing program, the distress sale policy provides preferences to minority owners who neither intend nor desire to manage the station in any respect. [ ] Whatever distinct programming may attend the race of an owner actively involved in managing the station, an absentee owner would have far less effect on programming.

Third, the FCC had absolutely no factual basis for the nexus when it adopted the policies and has since established none to support its existence. . . .

. . .

4

Finally, the Government cannot employ race classifications that unduly burden individuals who are not members of the favored racial and ethnic groups. [ ] The challenged policies fail this independent requirement, as well as the other constitutional requirements. The comparative licensing and distress sale programs provide the eventual licensee with an exceptionally valuable property and with a rare and unique opportunity to serve the local community. The distress sale imposes a particularly significant burden. The FCC has at base created a specialized market reserved exclusively for minority controlled applicants. There is no more rigid quota than a 100% set-aside. . . . The Court's argument that the distress sale allocates only a small percentage of all license sales, [ ], also misses the mark. This argument readily supports complete preferences and avoids scrutiny of particular programs: it is no response to a person denied admission at one school, or discharged from one job, solely on the basis of race, that other schools or employers do not discriminate.

The comparative licensing program, too, imposes a significant burden. The Court's emphasis on the multifactor process should not be confused with the claim that the preference is in some sense a minor one. It is not. The basic nonrace criteria are not difficult to meet, and, given the sums at stake, applicants have every incentive to structure their ownership arrangement to prevail in the comparative process. Applicants cannot alter their race, of course, and race is clearly the dispositive factor in a substantial percentage of comparative proceedings. Petitioner Metro asserts that race is overwhelmingly the dispositive factor. In reply, the FCC admits that it has not assessed the operation of its own program, [ ], and the Court notes only that

"minority ownership does not guarantee that an applicant will prevail."
[ ]

. . . . I respectfully dissent.

JUSTICE KENNEDY, with whom JUSTICE SCALIA joins, dissenting.

[Justice Kennedy compared this case with Plessy v. Ferguson, in which the Court found constitutional a Louisiana law requiring "equal but separate accommodations" for railroad passengers of different races.]

. . . All that need be shown under the new approach . . . is that the future effect of discriminating among citizens on the basis of race will advance some "important" governmental interest.

Once the Government takes the step, which itself should be forbidden, of enacting into law the stereotypical assumption that the race of the owners is linked to broadcast content, it must decide which races to favor. While the Court repeatedly refers to the preferences as favoring "minorities," [ ], and purports to evaluate the burdens imposed on "nonminorities," [ ], it must be emphasized that the discriminatory policies upheld today operate to exclude the many racial and ethnic *minorities* that have not made the Commission's list. The enumeration of the races to be protected is borrowed from a remedial statute, but since the remedial rationale must be disavowed in order to sustain the policy, the race classifications bear scant relation to the asserted governmental interest. The Court's reasoning provides little justification for welcoming the return of racial classifications to our Nation's laws.

. . .

. . . Perhaps the Court can succeed in its assumed role of case-by-case arbiter of when it is desirable and benign for the Government to disfavor some citizens and favor others based on the color of their skin. Perhaps the tolerance and decency to which our people aspire will let the disfavored rise above hostility and the favored escape condescension. But history suggests much peril in this enterprise, and so the Constitution forbids us to undertake it. I regret that after a century of judicial opinions we interpret the Constitution to do no more than move us from "separate but equal" to "unequal but benign."

Notes and Questions

1. What effect does *Metro Broadcasting* have on the ongoing debate over the continuing viability of the scarcity rationale?

2. The *Metro Broadcasting* decision had stated that the FCC's "gender preference policy is not before us today." That issue was decided by the court of appeals in Lamprecht v. Federal Communications Com'n, 958 F.2d 382, 70 R.R.2d 658 (D.C.Cir. 1992). The court, 2–1, in an opinion by Thomas, Circuit Justice, recognized that Congress had ordered the Commission to continue granting gender preferences. Since it was impossible to find the Commission's action beyond statuto-

ry authorization, the court turned to constitutional questions—and concluded that the practice was unconstitutional on equal protection grounds. The government's methods were held not to be "substantially related" to the goal it hoped to achieve—more diverse programming if women were granted a preference in the licensing process.

The court understood that the Supreme Court had used a standard of "intermediate scrutiny" in situations such as *Metro.* This meant that "not only [must] sex-based generalizations be 'supported,' but [the support must] be strong enough to advance 'substantially' the legitimating government interest." Under that standard, the court could not find sufficient evidence in the FCC record to show that preferring women would have anything like the effect that the evidence in *Metro* suggested would occur if racial minority groups were granted preferences. There was no strong showing that women owners would program differently from men. The court concluded:

> When a government treats people differently because of their sex, equal-protection principles at the very least require that there be a meaningful factual predicate supporting a link between the government's means and its ends. In this case, the government has failed to show that its sex-preference policy is substantially related to achieving diversity on the airwaves. We therefore hold that the policy violated the Constitution.

The Commission decided not to seek further review, and has ended preferences for women applicants. Broadcasting, April 27, 1992 at 18.

C. NETWORKS

Concentration of control problems are not limited, however, to ownership issues. Because broadcast networks supply much of the programming in the country, their influence extends far beyond the stations they own. The two primary legal avenues available to control or limit the actions of the networks are application of the antitrust laws and FCC regulation.

1. ANTITRUST LAW

In its discussions of the various media concentration rules, the Commission often makes reference to antitrust concerns. The goals of American antitrust law were set in 1890, with the enactment of the Sherman Antitrust Act, 15 U.S.C.A. §§ 1 and 2. Section 1 states a desire to "protect trade and commerce against unlawful restraints and monopolies," and then declares illegal "every contract, combination in the form of trust or otherwise, or conspiracy, in restraint of trade, or commerce." Section 2 provides that "Every person who shall monopolize, or attempt to monopolize, or combine or conspire with any other person or persons, to monopolize any part of the trade or commerce . . . shall be guilty of a misdemeanor."

The quoted provisions of the Sherman Act have been applied against business enterprises engaged in manufacturing or marketing tangible products. In the early 1940s the Supreme Court decided that the First Amendment did not bar antitrust actions against media organizations. Associated Press v. United States, 326 U.S. 1 (1945). However, the special regulatory status of broadcasting under the Communications Act of 1934 raised two other important questions, both dealing with jurisdiction.

Since the antitrust laws are enforced by the Justice Department and the Federal Trade Commission, the first question was whether the Federal Communications Commission was barred from issuing regulations based on antitrust principles. In *NBC*, which we first considered in Chapter III and which we will examine further in this chapter, the Supreme Court concluded that the FCC was entitled to use antitrust principles in determining what constitutes the public interest.

The second jurisdictional question, whether an FCC ruling in a specific case barred action by other agencies, was raised in United States v. Radio Corporation of America, 358 U.S. 334 (1959). NBC, a wholly owned subsidiary of RCA, reached an agreement with Westinghouse to exchange NBC's Cleveland VHF television station plus $3 million for Westinghouse's Philadelphia VHF television station. Despite allegations that NBC had forced the transaction by threatening to withhold network affiliation from all Westinghouse stations, the FCC approved the transfer.

The Justice Department then filed an antitrust action against RCA and NBC asking among other things that NBC be forced to divest itself of the Philadelphia station. RCA argued that the FCC's approval of the sale had decided the antitrust questions, barring the government from bringing a separate antitrust action. The Supreme Court disagreed:

> . . . Appellees, like unregulated business concerns, made a business judgment as to the desirability of the exchange. Like unregulated concerns, they had to make this judgment with knowledge that the exchange might run afoul of the antitrust laws. Their decision varied from that of unregulated concern only in that they also had to obtain the approval of a federal agency. But [the] scope of that approval in the case of the FCC was limited to the statutory standard, "public interest, convenience, and necessity." . . . The monetary terms of the exchange were set by the parties, and were of concern to the Commission only as they might have affected the ability of the parties to serve the public. Even after approval, the parties were free to complete or not to complete the exchange as their sound business judgment dictated. In every sense, the question faced by the parties was solely one of business judgment (as opposed to regulatory coercion), save only that the Commission must have found that the "public interest" would be served by their decision to make the exchange. . . .

This is not to imply that federal antitrust policy may not be considered in determining whether the "public interest, convenience, and necessity" will be served by proposed action of the broadcaster, for this Court has held to the contrary. National Broadcasting Co. v. United States, 319 U.S. 190, 222–224. Moreover, in a given case the Commission might find that antitrust considerations alone would keep the statutory standard from being met, as when the publisher of the sole newspaper in an area applies for a license for the only available radio and television facilities, which, if granted, would give him a monopoly of that area's major media of mass communication. [   ]

In 1972 the Justice Department, concerned with excessive network control over the market for television prime-time programming, filed antitrust suits against the three major networks. Six years later NBC entered into a consent decree that prohibited acquisition of syndication rights from independent producers and reciprocal dealings with the other networks and placed other limitations on dealings with independent producers. Subsequently the other networks signed similar consent decrees.

In 1992 the networks sought judicial review of the consent decrees. The district court denied motions to intervene brought by several parties opposing any change in the rules. The only remaining parties, the networks and the Justice Department, favor repeal of the consent decrees. Broadcasting, Nov. 9, 1992 at 8.

2. THE CHAIN BROADCASTING RULES

By the late 1930s the three national network companies (NBC, CBS and Mutual) had almost half of the entire broadcast business in the country. In 1938, deeply concerned by this concentration of control, the Commission began an inquiry into the need for special regulations to curb the power of the networks by prohibiting certain common network practices. In 1941, after extensive public hearings at which nearly 100 witnesses testified, the Commission adopted a series of regulations pertaining to chain broadcasting.

The networks then brought suit to enjoin enforcement of the chain broadcasting rules. We examined the arguments concerning the Commission's authority to regulate broadcasting at p. 65, *supra*. We now turn to the Court's consideration of the rules themselves.

NATIONAL BROADCASTING COMPANY v. UNITED STATES
Supreme Court of the United States, 1943.
319 U.S. 190, 63 S.Ct. 997, 87 L.Ed. 1344.

MR. JUSTICE FRANKFURTER delivered the opinion of the Court.

.   .   .

The Commission recognized that network broadcasting had played and was continuing to play an important part in the development of

radio. "The growth and development of chain broadcasting," it stated, "found its impetus in the desire to give widespread coverage to programs which otherwise would not be heard beyond the reception area of a single station. Chain broadcasting makes possible a wider reception for expensive entertainment and cultural programs and also for programs of national or regional significance which would otherwise have coverage only in the locality of origin. Furthermore, the access to greatly enlarged audiences made possible by chain broadcasting has been a strong incentive to advertisers to finance the production of expensive programs. . . . But the fact that the chain broadcasting method brings benefits and advantages to both the listening public and to broadcast station licensees does not mean that the prevailing practices and policies of the networks and their outlets are sound in all respects, or that they should not be altered. The Commission's duty under the Communications Act of 1934 is not only to see that the public receives the advantages and benefits of chain broadcasting, but also, so far as its powers enable it, to see that practices which adversely affect the ability of licensees to operate in the public interest are eliminated."
[ ]

The Commission found that eight network abuses were amenable to correction within the powers granted it by Congress:

Regulation 3.101—Exclusive affiliation of station. The Commission found that the network affiliation agreements of NBC and CBS customarily contained a provision which prevented the station from broadcasting the programs of any other network. The effect of this provision was to hinder the growth of new networks, to deprive the listening public in many areas of service to which they were entitled, and to prevent station licensees from exercising their statutory duty of determining which programs would best serve the needs of their community. The Commission observed that in areas where all the stations were under exclusive contract to either NBC or CBS, the public was deprived of the opportunity to hear programs presented by Mutual. To take a case cited in the Report: In the fall of 1939 Mutual obtained the exclusive right to broadcast the World Series baseball games. It offered this program of outstanding national interest to stations throughout the country, including NBC and CBS affiliates in communities having no other stations. CBS and NBC immediately invoked the "exclusive affiliation" clauses of their agreements with these stations, and as a result thousands of persons in many sections of the country were unable to hear the broadcasts of the games.

"Restraints having this effect," the Commission observed, "are to be condemned as contrary to the public interest irrespective of whether it be assumed that Mutual programs are of equal, superior, or inferior quality. The important consideration is that station licensees are denied freedom to choose the programs which they believe best suited to their needs; in this manner the duty of a station licensee to operate in the public interest is defeated. . . . Our conclusion is that the disadvantages resulting from these exclusive arrangements far outweigh any advantages. A licensee station does not operate in the public interest when it enters into exclusive arrangements which prevent it from giving the public the best service of which it is capable, and which, by closing the door of opportunity in the network field, adversely affects the program structure of the entire industry." [ ] . . .

Regulation 3.102—Territorial exclusivity. The Commission found another type of "exclusivity" provision in network affiliation agreements whereby the network bound itself not to sell programs to any other station in the same area. The effect of this provision, designed to protect the affiliate from the competition of other stations serving the same territory, was to deprive the listening public of many programs that might otherwise be available. If an affiliated station rejected a network program, the "territorial exclusivity" clause of its affiliation agreement prevented the network from offering the program to other stations in the area. For example, Mutual presented a popular program, known as "The American Forum of the Air," in which prominent persons discussed topics of general interest. None of the Mutual stations in the Buffalo area decided to carry the program, and a Buffalo station not affiliated with Mutual attempted to obtain the program for its listeners. These efforts failed, however, on account of the "territorial exclusivity" provision in Mutual's agreements with its outlets. The result was that this program was not available to the people of Buffalo.

The Commission concluded that "It is not in the public interest for the listening audience in an area to be deprived of network programs not carried by one station where other stations in that area are ready and willing to broadcast the programs. It is as much against the public interest for a network affiliate to enter into a contractual arrangement which prevents another station from carrying a network program as it would be to drown out that program by electrical interference." [ ]

Recognizing that the "territorial exclusivity" clause was unobjectionable in so far as it sought to prevent duplication of programs in the same area, the Commission limited itself to the situations in which the clause impaired the ability of the licensee to broadcast available programs. . . .

Regulation 3.103—Term of affiliation. The standard NBC and CBS affiliation contracts bound the station for a period of five years, with the network having the exclusive right to terminate the contracts upon one year's notice. The Commission, relying upon § 307(d) of the Communications Act of 1934, under which no license to operate a broadcast station can be granted for a longer term than three years, found the five-year affiliation term to be contrary to the policy of the Act: "Regardless of any changes that may occur in the economic, political, or social life of the Nation or of the community in which the station is located, CBS and NBC affiliates are bound by contract to continue broadcasting the network programs of only one network for 5 years. The licensee is so bound even though the policy and caliber of programs of the network may deteriorate greatly. The future necessities of the station and of the community are not considered. The station licensee is unable to follow his conception of the public interest until the end of the 5–year contract." [ ] The Commission concluded that under contracts binding the affiliates for five years, "stations become parties to arrangements which deprive the public of the improved service it might otherwise derive from competition in the network field; and that a station is not operating in the public interest when it so limits its freedom of action." [ ] . . .

Regulation 3.104—Option time. The Commission found that network affiliation contracts usually contained so-called network optional time clauses. Under these provisions the network could upon 28 days' notice call upon its affiliates to carry a commercial program during any of the hours specified in the agreement as "network optional time." For CBS affiliates "network optional time" meant the entire broadcast day. For 29 outlets of NBC on the Pacific Coast, it also covered the entire broadcast day; for substantially all of the other NBC affiliates, it included, 8½ hours on weekdays and 8 hours on Sundays. Mutual's contracts with about half of its affiliates contained such a provision, giving the network optional time for 3 or 4 hours on weekdays and 6 hours on Sundays.

In the Commission's judgment these optional time provisions, in addition to imposing serious obstacles in the path of new networks, hindered stations in developing a local program service. The exercise by the networks of their options over the station's time tended to prevent regular scheduling of local programs at desirable hours. The Commission found that "shifting a local commercial program may seriously interfere with the efforts of a [local] sponsor to build up a regular listening audience at a definite hour, and the long-term advertising contract becomes a highly dubious project. This hampers the efforts of the station to develop local commercial programs and affects adversely its ability to give the public good program service. . . . A station licensee must retain sufficient freedom of action to supply the program and advertising needs of the local community. Local program service is a vital part of community life. A station should be ready, able, and willing to serve the needs of the local community by broadcasting such outstanding local events as community concerts, civic meetings, local sports events, and other programs of local consumer and social interest. We conclude that national network time options have restricted the freedom of station licensees and hampered their efforts to broadcast local commercial programs, the programs of other national networks, and national spot transcriptions. We believe that these considerations far outweigh any supposed advantages from 'stability' of network operations under time options. We find that the optioning of time by licensee stations has operated against the public interest." [ ]

. . .

Regulation 3.105—Right to reject programs. The Commission found that most network affiliation contracts contained a clause defining the right of the station to reject network commercial programs. The NBC contracts provided simply that the station "may reject a network program the broadcasting of which would not be in the public interest, convenience, and necessity." NBC required a licensee who rejected a program to "be able to support his contention that what he has done has been more in the public interest than had he carried on the network program." Similarly, the CBS contracts provided that if the station had "reasonable objection to any sponsored program or the product advertised thereon as not being in the public interest, the station may, on 3 weeks' prior notice thereof to Columbia, refuse to broadcast such program, unless during such notice period such reasonable objection of the station shall be satisfied."

While seeming in the abstract to be fair, these provisions, according to the Commission's finding, did not sufficiently protect the "public interest." As a practical matter, the licensee could not determine in advance whether the broadcasting of any particular network program would or would not be in the public interest. "It is obvious that from such skeletal information [as the networks submitted to the stations prior to the broadcasts] the station cannot determine in advance whether the program is in the public interest, nor can it ascertain whether or not parts of the program are in one way or another offensive. In practice, if not in theory, stations affiliated with networks have delegated to the networks a large part of their programming functions. In many instances, moreover, the network further delegates the actual production of programs to advertising agencies. These agencies are far more than mere brokers or intermediaries between the network and the advertiser. To an ever-increasing extent, these agencies actually exercise the function of program production. Thus it is frequently neither the station nor the network, but rather the advertising agency, which determines what broadcast programs shall contain. Under such circumstances, it is especially important that individual stations, if they are to operate in the public interest, should have the practical opportunity as well as the contractual right to reject network programs. . . .

"It is the station, not the network, which is licensed to serve the public interest. The licensee has the duty of determining what programs shall be broadcast over his station's facilities, and cannot lawfully delegate this duty or transfer the control of his station directly to the network or indirectly to an advertising agency. He cannot lawfully bind himself to accept programs in every case where he cannot sustain the burden of proof that he has a better program. The licensee is obliged to reserve to himself the final decision as to what programs will best serve the public interest. We conclude that a licensee is not fulfilling his obligations to operate in the public interest, and is not operating in accordance with the express requirements of the Communications Act, if he agrees to accept programs on any basis other than his own reasonable decision that the programs are satisfactory." [   ]

. . .

Regulation 3.106—Network ownership of stations. The Commission found that NBC, in addition to its network operations, was the licensee of 10 stations, 2 each in New York, Chicago, Washington, and San Francisco, 1 in Denver, and 1 in Cleveland. CBS was the licensee of 8 stations, 1 in each of these cities: New York, Chicago, Washington, Boston, Minneapolis, St. Louis, Charlotte, and Los Angeles. These 18 stations owned by NBC and CBS, the Commission observed, were among the most powerful and desirable in the country, and were permanently inaccessible to competing networks. "Competition among networks for these facilities is nonexistent, as they are completely removed from the network-station market. It gives the network complete control over its policies. This 'bottling-up' of the best facilities has undoubtedly had a discouraging effect upon the creation and growth of new networks. Furthermore, common ownership of network and station places the network in a position where its interest as the owner of certain stations may conflict with its interest as a network organization serving affiliated stations. In dealings with advertisers, the network represents its own stations in a proprietary capacity and the affiliated stations in something akin to an agency capacity. The danger is present that the network organization will give preference to its own stations at the expense of its affiliates." [ ]

The Commission stated that if the question had arisen as an original matter, it might well have concluded that the public interest required severance of the business of station ownership from that of network operation. But since substantial business interests have been formed on the basis of the Commission's continued tolerance of the situation, it was found inadvisable to take such a drastic step. The Commission concluded, however, that "the licensing of two stations in the same area to a single network organization is basically unsound and contrary to the public interest," and that it was also against the "public interest" for network organizations to own stations in areas where the available facilities were so few or of such unequal coverage that competition would thereby be substantially restricted. Recognizing that these considerations called for flexibility in their application to particular situations, the Commission provided that "networks will be given full opportunity, on proper application for new facilities or renewal of existing licenses, to call to our attention any reasons why the principle should be modified or held inapplicable." [ ] . . .

Regulation 3.107—Dual network operation. [Because the Commission had indefinitely suspended this regulation, the Court did not consider it.]

Regulation 3.108—Control by networks of station rates. The Commission found that NBC's affiliation contracts contained a provision empowering the network to reduce the station's network rate, and thereby to reduce the compensation received by the station, if the station set a lower rate for non-network national advertising than the rate established by the contract for the network programs. Under this provision the station could not sell time to a national advertiser for less than it would cost the advertiser if he bought the time from NBC. In the words of NBC's vice-president, "This means simply that a national advertiser should pay the same price for the station whether he buys it through one source or another source. It means that we do not believe that our stations should go into competition with ourselves." [ ]

The Commission concluded that "it is against the public interest for a station licensee to enter into a contract with a network which has the effect of decreasing its ability to compete for national business. We believe that the public interest will best be served and listeners supplied with the best programs if stations bargain freely with national advertisers." [ ] . . .

. . .

In essence the Chain Broadcasting Regulations represent a particularization of the Commission's conception of the "public interest" sought to be safeguarded by Congress in enacting the Communications Act of 1934. The basic consideration of policy underlying the Regulations is succinctly stated in its Report: "With the number of radio channels limited by natural factors, the public interest demands that those who are entrusted with the available channels shall make the fullest and most effective use of them. If a licensee enters into a contract with a network organization which limits his ability to make the best use of the radio facility assigned him, he is not serving the public interest. . . . The net effect [of the practices disclosed by the investigation] has been that broadcasting service has been maintained at a level below that possible under a system of free competition. Having so found, we would be remiss in our statutory duty of encouraging 'the larger and more effective use of radio in the public interest' if we were to grant licenses to persons who persist in these practices."

We would be asserting our personal views regarding the effective utilization of radio were we to deny that the Commission was entitled to find that the large public aims of the Communications Act of 1934 comprehend the considerations which moved the Commission in promulgating the Chain Broadcasting Regulations. True enough, the Act does not explicitly say that the Commission shall have power to deal with network practices found inimical to the public interest. But Congress was acting in a field of regulation which was both new and dynamic. "Congress moved under the spur of a widespread fear that in the absence of governmental control the public interest might be subordinated to monopolistic domination in the broadcasting field." [ ] In the context of the developing problems to which it was directed, the Act gave the Commission not niggardly but expansive powers. It was given a comprehensive mandate to "encourage the larger and more effective use of radio in the public interest," if need be, by making "special regulations applicable to radio stations engaged in chain broadcasting." § 303(g)(i).

. . .

A totally different source of attack upon the Regulations is found in § 311 of the Act, which authorizes the Commission to withhold licenses from persons convicted of having violated the anti-trust laws. Two contentions are made—first, that this provision puts considerations relating to competition outside the Commission's concern before an applicant has been convicted of monopoly or other restraints of trade, and second, that, in any event, the Commission misconceived the scope of its powers under § 311 in issuing the Regulations. Both of these contentions are unfounded. Section 311 derives from § 13 of the Radio Act of 1927, which expressly commanded, rather than merely authorized, the Commission to refuse a license to any person judicially found guilty of having violated the anti-trust laws. . . . The Commission was thus permitted to exercise its judgment as to whether violation of the anti-trust laws disqualified an applicant from operating a station in the "public interest." We agree with the District Court that "The necessary implication from this [amendment in 1934] was that the Commission might infer from the fact that the applicant had in the past tried to monopolize radio, or had engaged in unfair methods of competition, that the disposition so manifested would continue and that if it did it would make him an unfit licensee." [ ]

That the Commission may refuse to grant a license to persons adjudged guilty in a court of law of conduct in violation of the anti-trust laws certainly does not render irrelevant consideration by the Commission of the effect of such conduct upon the "public interest, convenience, or necessity." A licensee charged with practices in contravention of this standard cannot continue to hold his license merely because his conduct is also in violation of the anti-trust laws and he has not yet been proceeded against and convicted. By clarifying in § 311 the scope of the Commission's authority in dealing with persons convicted of violating the anti-trust laws, Congress can hardly be deemed to have limited the concept of "public interest" so as to exclude all considerations relating to monopoly and unreasonable restraints upon commerce. Nothing in the provisions or history of the Act lends support to the inference that the Commission was denied the power to refuse a license to a station not operating in the "public interest," merely because its misconduct happened to be an unconvicted violation of the anti-trust laws.

Alternatively, it is urged that the Regulations constitute an *ultra vires* attempt by the Commission to enforce the anti-trust laws, and that the enforcement of the anti-trust laws is the province not of the Commission but of the Attorney General and the courts. This contention misconceives the basis of the Commission's action. The Commission's Report indicates plainly enough that the Commission was not attempting to administer the anti-trust laws:

"The prohibitions of the Sherman Act apply to broadcasting. This Commission, although not charged with the duty of enforcing that law, should administer its regulatory powers with respect to broadcasting in the light of the purposes which the Sherman Act was designed to achieve. . . . While many of the network practices raise serious questions under the antitrust laws, our jurisdiction does not depend on a showing that they do in fact constitute a violation of the antitrust laws. It is not our function to apply the antitrust laws as such. It is our duty, however, to refuse licenses or renewals to any person who engages or proposes to engage in practices which will prevent either himself or other licensees or both from making the fullest use of radio facilities. This is the standard of public interest, convenience or necessity which we must apply to all applications for licenses and renewals. . . . We do not predicate our jurisdiction to issue the regulations on the ground that the network practices violate the antitrust laws. We are issuing these regulations because we have found that the network practices prevent the maximum utilization of radio facilities in the public interest." [   ]

We conclude, therefore, that the Communications Act of 1934 authorized the Commission to promulgate regulations designed to correct the abuses disclosed by its investigation of chain broadcasting. There remains for consideration the claim that the Commission's exercise of such authority was unlawful.

The Regulations are assailed as "arbitrary and capricious." If this contention means that the Regulations are unwise, that they are not likely to succeed in accomplishing what the Commission intended, we can say only that the appellants have selected the wrong forum for such a plea. What was said in Board of Trade v. United States, 314 U.S. 534, 548, is relevant here: "We certainly have neither technical competence nor legal authority to pronounce upon the wisdom of the course taken by the Commission." Our duty is at an end when we find that the action of the Commission was based upon findings supported by evidence, and was made pursuant to authority granted by Congress. It is not for us to say that the "public interest" will be furthered or retarded by the Chain Broadcasting Regulations. The responsibility belongs to the Congress for the grant of valid legislative authority and to the Commission for its exercise.

. . .

Affirmed.

MR. JUSTICE BLACK and MR. JUSTICE RUTLEDGE took no part in the consideration or decision of these cases.

[Mr. Justice Murphy dissented on the grounds that the regulations went beyond the authority delegated to the Commission by Congress.]

Notes and Questions

1. The reason that the dual network provision was suspended was that NBC had sold its Blue Network, thus obviating the need for that provision. The Blue Network subsequently became ABC.

2. In 1977 the Commission re-examined the application of the Chain Broadcasting Regulations to radio and concluded that due to the high

degree of competition that now existed, most of the Regulations were no longer necessary. Consequently, they eliminated all but a modified version of the territorial exclusivity regulation for both AM and FM stations.

> § 73.132 Territorial exclusivity. No licensee of an AM broadcast station shall have any arrangement with a network organization which prevents or hinders another station serving substantially the same area from broadcasting the network's programs not taken by the former station, or which prevents or hinders another station serving a substantially different area from broadcasting any program of the network organization: provided, however, that this section does not prohibit arrangements under which the station is granted first call within its primary service area upon the network's programs. The term "network organization" means any organization originating program material, with or without commercial messages, and furnishing the same to stations interconnected so as to permit simultaneous broadcast by all or some of them. However, arrangements involving only stations under common ownership, or only the rebroadcast by one station of programming from another with no compensation other than a lump-sum payment by the station rebroadcasting, are not considered arrangements with a network organization. The term "arrangement" means any contract, arrangement or understanding, express or implied.

Section 73.232 applies the same restrictions to FM stations. 47 C.F.R. § 73.232.

As a result of the elimination of these rules several companies now operate more than one radio network. For example, ABC operates the Contemporary, Direction, Entertainment, FM, Information, Rock and Talkradio networks.

3. *The Prime Time Access Rule.* In 1965 the Commission issued a notice of proposed rulemaking in which it sought, among other things, to limit the networks' control over programming during prime time. After extensive comments and hearings, the Commission decided in 1970 to adopt a rule providing that after Sept. 1, 1971:

> . . . . no television station, assigned to any of the top 50 markets in which there are three or more operating commercial television stations, shall broadcast network programs offered by any television network or networks for a total of more than 3 hours per day between the hours of 7 p.m. and 11 p.m. local time, except that in the Central time zone the relevant period shall be between the hours of 6 p.m. and 10 p.m.

Competition and Responsibility in Network Television Broadcasting, 23 F.C.C.2d 382, 18 R.R.2d 1825 (1970). This prime time access rule (PTAR I) exempted fast-breaking news events, on-the-spot coverage of news events and political broadcasts by candidates.

The Commission presented several reasons for its action. Primarily, it was concerned that during the 1960s the number of first-run syndicated entertainment series had fallen. The role of "off-network" entertainment series (programs that had been on the networks earlier and were now being syndicated to other stations) had grown enormously, as had the role of the networks in preparing new programs. Even among independent stations, "which should be the backbone of the syndication market," first-run syndications were being replaced by off-network programs. Only 14 of the top 50 markets had at least one independent VHF station.

Finally, the financial involvement of the networks in evening programming had doubled during the 1960s, and the independently produced programs had fallen by 90 percent. The Commission deplored this "unhealthy situation" and asserted that the new rule would provide a "healthy impetus to the development of independent program sources, with concomitant benefits in an increased supply of programs for independent (and, indeed, affiliated) stations. The entire development of UHF should be benefitted."

A constitutional and statutory challenge to the rules was rejected in Mt. Mansfield Television, Inc. v. Federal Communications Commission, 442 F.2d 470, 21 R.R.2d 2087, 1 Med.L.Rptr. 2020 (2d Cir.1970). The court relied on *Red Lion's* observations that the peculiar qualities of each medium must be considered in deciding the application of the First Amendment. It also quoted from cases, such as *Associated Press,* that stressed the virtues of "the widest possible dissemination of information from diverse and antagonistic sources," and observed:

> When viewed in the light of these principles, the prime time access rule, far from violating the First Amendment, appears to be a reasonable step toward fulfillment of its fundamental precepts, for it is the stated purpose of that rule to encourage the "[d]iversity of programs and development of diverse and antagonistic sources of program service" and to correct a situation where "[o]nly three organizations control access to the crucial prime time evening schedule." The specific arguments raised by the petitions reflect basic misconceptions of that purpose and of the First Amendment principles outlined above.

> For example, petitioner Columbia Broadcasting System, Inc. attempts an analogy between the prime time access rule and an imaginary governmental edict prohibiting newspapers in the 50 largest cities from devoting more than a given portion of their news space to items taken from national news services. This analogy completely overlooks the essential fact that "[w]here there are substantially more individuals who want to broadcast than there are frequencies to allocate, it is idle to posit an unabridgeable First Amendment right to broadcast comparable to the right of every individual to speak, write, or publish." Red Lion Broadcasting Co., supra, 395 U.S. at 388.

To argue that the freedom of networks to distribute and licensees to select programming is limited by the prime time access rule, and that the First Amendment is thereby violated, is to reverse the mandated priorities which subordinate these interests to the public's right of access. The licensee is in many ways a "trustee" for the public in the operation of his channel. . . .

The Court found statutory authority to promulgate PTAR I in the power of the Commission to regulate in the public interest, citing *National Broadcasting Co.,* p. 65, *supra.* It also upheld the Commission's adoption of the syndication and financial interest rules, the first direct regulation of networks (rather than regulating licensees of stations), as within the Commission's statutory power because they were "reasonably ancillary to the effective performance of the Commission's various responsibilities for the regulation of television broadcasting." 442 F.2d at 481.

The Commission considered requests for waiver of the off-network programs to be presented during prime time without being counted toward the permissible three hours of network and off-network material each evening. What considerations might have led the Commission to grant waivers for "Wild Kingdom," "National Geographic," "Six Wives of Henry VIII" and "Animal World," but to deny waivers to "Lassie" and "Hogan's Heroes"?

4. Less than two years later, the Commission issued a Notice of Inquiry and a Notice of Proposed Rulemaking in which it announced its intention to consider whether to modify or repeal PTAR I. In 1973 the Commission adopted PTAR II, which modified PTAR I in several ways. The major change was to eliminate access time altogether on Sunday evenings and to reduce it to one half-hour other evenings. However, PTAR II was successfully challenged in court because the effective date did not allow sufficient time for independent producers to withdraw programs being produced in reliance on PTAR I. National Association of Independent Television Producers & Distributors v. Federal Communications Commission, 502 F.2d 249, 33 R.R.2d 995 (2d Cir.1974).

As a result, in January 1975 the Commission adopted PTAR III, effective September 1975. The provisions were similar to PTAR I, covering one hour per night, except for certain exemptions that reflected waivers regularly granted under PTAR I and new provisions for the use of feature films. Exemptions covered network or off-network "public affairs" programming, documentaries, and programs designed for children. The Commission also noted that it expected "that stations subject to the rule will devote an appropriate portion of 'cleared time' or at least of total prime time to material particularly directed to the needs or problems of the station's community . . ., including programming addressed to the special needs of minority groups." 50 F.C.C.2d at 852, 32 R.R.2d at 722.

It reaffirmed its view that the rule lessened network dominance by releasing a portion of prime time for licensees of individual stations to use to respond to their respective communities and by encouraging a new body of syndicated programming. It also denied that the rule led to a lack of diversity and to low quality programs, arguing that the rule had not yet been fully tested. Although the Justice Department argued that to assure stability the Commission should guarantee that PTAR III would remain in effect at least five years, the Commission refused to do so.

Another challenge followed. In National Association of Independent Television Producers & Distributors v. Federal Communications Commission, 516 F.2d 526, 33 R.R.2d 795 (2d Cir.1975), the court generally upheld PTAR III, but remanded it to the Commission for reconsideration of several aspects of the rule. The Commission responded and PTAR III became effective in September 1975. The court recognized that the rule's results had been mixed at best:

> The result has been, as could have been expected to some degree, that it is largely the cheaper productions, daytime fare, that have been put into cleared prime time slots. What was not anticipated by the Commission was the monotony of the product. A kind of Gresham's law seems to operate in first-run syndication—the cheaper tending to drive the dearer out of circulation. The fact is, as the Commission concedes, that the degree of diversity in programming for access time has been disappointing. In the entertainment area, the emphasis has largely been on game shows and animal shows, game shows constituting 41.9% of the 2,100 access half hours on 150 stations in one season. [ ] Comedies, dramas, and Westerns in access time have dropped significantly. Comedy has been virtually eliminated. The Commission notes a similar lack of diversity, however, with respect to the three networks themselves which all show a crime drama at the same hour in prime time, also giving the viewer no choice.

> On the other hand, as the Commission found, and as the public *amici* stress, programs of local interest, on matters of concern to the people served by local stations, have begun to obtain a foothold on commercial stations in the access time period. One may assume that in the long run game shows will pall to some extent and that independent producers will have to turn to more variegated fare if they wish to survive, but any prophecy on public taste, certainly by judges, would be hazardous indeed.

Under PTAR I, the Commission had to pass upon waivers for specific network programs, said to be in the public interest, that would preempt access time. As noted, these *ad hoc* decisions gave rise to contentions that the Commission was regulating program content in violation of the First Amendment. In PTAR III the Commission exempted public affairs, documentary and children's programs. This led to a major constitutional challenge to PTAR III. The court considered the problem at some length (516 F.2d at 536–38):

This is said to be in violation of the First Amendment. It is true that the Commission has never before considered what types of program may be played at particular times. And it may be that *mandatory* programming by the Commission even in categories would raise serious First Amendment questions. On the other hand, the general power of the F.C.C. to interest itself in the kinds of programs broadcast by licensees has consistently been sustained by the courts against arguments that the supervisory power violates the First Amendment.

. . .

The only way that broadcasters can operate in the "public interest" is by broadcasting programs that meet somebody's view of what is in the "public interest." That can scarcely be determined by the broadcaster himself, for it is an obvious conflict of interest. "There is no sanctuary in the First Amendment for unlimited private censorship operating in a medium not open to all." Red Lion, supra, 395 U.S. at 392. "It is the right of the viewers and listeners, not the right of the broadcasters, which is paramount." Id. at 390.

Since the public cannot through a million stifled yawns convey that their television fare, as a whole, is not in their interest, the Congress has made the F.C.C. the guardian of that public interest. All that the Commission can do about it is to encourage competitive fare. If a large segment of the public prefers game shows to documentaries, the Commission can hardly do more than admit paradoxically that taste *is* a matter for dispute. The Commission surely cannot do its job, however, without interesting itself in general program format and the kinds of programs broadcast by licensees. . . .

The Commission by this amendment of the rule is not ordering any program or even any type of program to be broadcast in access time. It has simply lifted a restriction on network programs if the licensee chooses to avail himself of such network programs in specified categories of programming. . . .

. . .

It is suggested that the Commission should have elected to force the stations to carve out *network* prime time for these programs. Whether or not the Commission could have done this— a course that would doubtless have evoked constitutional protests from the networks—it is not for this court to say. Nor is it for this court to say that the Commission had, in any event, no right to choose between reasonable alternatives.

5. In 1980, as part of a study of network power, the FCC staff reported that the prime time access rule had not increased local programming. Many major stations were "stripping" syndicated programs five nights

per week. (Four NBC O & Os were running "Family Feud" five nights each week at 7:30 p.m.) A few creative local programs, particularly "Evening Magazine" on Westinghouse stations (syndicated as "PM Magazine" to non-Westinghouse stations), had emerged, but these were the rare exceptions. The staff suggested that if the Commissioners wanted local programming they should order it directly.

There are, however, other justifications for the prime time access rule. In the top 50 markets, the network affiliates are banned from using off-network programs during the access period. This has allowed independent stations, primarily UHFs, to offer these popular programs as competition to the network affiliate offerings. As a result, the viability of the UHF stations has been strengthened considerably.

At the same time the network affiliates have come to appreciate the rule because they can make more money selling all the commercial availabilities in syndicated programming in contrast to the limited availabilities in network programming. Most affiliates now oppose any proposals to eliminate the prime time access rule.

6. *The Financial Interest and Syndication Rules.* At the same time it adopted PTAR I, the Commission adopted rules "designed to eliminate the networks from distribution and profit-sharing in domestic syndication and to restrict their activities in foreign markets to distribution of programs of which they are the sole producers." These rules were defended on the ground that networks had a conflict of interest in choosing programs. Independent producers who sought to exhibit their products on a network had to bargain with the networks, who were their "principal competitors in syndication and foreign sales." The Commission concluded that "networks do not normally accept new, untried packager-licensed programs for network exhibition unless the producer/packager is willing to cede a large part of the valuable rights and interests in subsidiary rights to the program to the network." There were also allegations of "warehousing," purchasing programs with no intention of showing them in order to keep them out of the marketplace.

In 1981, acting on a petition by CBS, Inc., the Commission ruled that the financial interest and syndication rules do not apply to nonbroadcast rights to television programs. The decision opened the way for the networks to enter the cable, video cassette and video disc markets. An appeal by Viacom International, Inc., a major program syndicator, was denied. Viacom International Inc. v. Federal Communications Commission, 672 F.2d 1034, 50 R.R.2d 1641 (2d Cir.1982).

In 1982 the Commission issued an NPRM aimed at eliminating the financial interest and syndication rules. The NPRM was based on a 1980 report by the FCC Network Inquiry Special Staff that concluded the rules were unnecessary and ineffective. A year later the Commission issued a Tentative Decision proposing the deletion of the financial interest rule and modifying the syndication rule. 54 R.R.2d 457 (1983). The reaction in Congress to the Tentative Decision was extremely negative. Congress barred the Commission from expending any funds to repeal or modify the rules prior to May 31, 1984. Meanwhile, Sen. Pete Wilson (R–Cal.) introduced a bill calling for a five-year moratorium.

Bowing to Presidential, as well as legislative, pressure, Chairman Fowler indicated that he would not bring the matter before the Commission. Meanwhile, years of negotiations between the networks and syndicators were unable to resolve the issue.

7. Since adoption of the original financial interest and syndication rules and PTAR the FCC had granted two permanent waivers. The first allowed the Christian Broadcast Network (CBN) to provide up to 30 hours of weekly programming without being subject to those rules. Christian Broadcasting Network, Inc., 87 F.C.C.2d 1076, 50 R.R.2d 359 (1981). The second exempted the Home Shopping Network (HSN) from the dual network rule and PTAR. Home Shopping, Inc., 4 F.C.C.Rcd. 2422, 66 R.R.2d 175 (1989). According to the Commission, the waivers were justified by the fact that neither CBN nor HSN was significantly involved in either the sale of national advertising or the production, acquisition or distribution of traditional entertainment programs to commercial stations for airing during the prime-time-access period.

8. The attempt by Fox Television to establish a fourth network, p. 60, *supra*, forced the Commission to return to the issue of the financial interest and syndication rules. The rules did not initially apply to Fox because its early programming was not sufficient to meet the existing FCC definition of a network, 47 C.F.R. § 73.658(j)(4), p. 232, *infra*. Although Fox was providing programming to more than 25 affiliates in more than 10 states, it was providing only nine hours a week of such programming. However, after announcing plans to increase its programming efforts to 18½ hours a week by the fall 1990 television season, Fox filed a petition asking the FCC to resume rulemaking in the financial interest and syndication rules proceeding.

In response the Commission terminated the old rulemaking proceeding as "stale" and issued a new NPRM on the financial interest and syndication rules. In the NPRM the Commission sought comment on five different options. The first was to make no change in either rule. The second was to eliminate the financial interest rule while leaving the syndication rule unchanged. The third suggested alternative was to eliminate the financial interest rule and amend the syndication rule to apply only to domestic syndication of prime-time series. A fourth possibility suggested was elimination of the financial interest rule while amending the syndication rule to permit network syndication of a certain number or percentage of programs or to share in profits of non-network syndicators. The final option on which comments were sought was to leave the rules themselves unchanged, but to provide an exception for "emerging networks." Evaluation of the Syndication and Financial Interest Rules, 5 F.C.C.Rcd. 1815 (1990).

The NPRM on the financial interest and syndication rules elicited thousands upon thousands of pages of comments. These comments presented "alternative views of the television programming world so starkly and fundamentally at odds with each other that they virtually defy reconciliation." The Commission itself was sharply divided on the issue. Although the commissioners all agreed that the video marketplace had changed dramatically in the 20 years since the original rules were adopted, they did not agree on the degree to which that change rendered those rules unnecessary. By a 3–2 vote, the Commission decided to retain the rules, but with substantial modifications which it summarized as follows:

17. In particular, by this *Report and Order*, we take the following actions to enhance the ability of existing and emerging networks to compete effectively in today's video marketplace, but not dominate it unfairly.

—The financial interest and syndication rules will no longer be applied to non-entertainment programming (*e.g.*, news and sports) in prime time, nor to any network programming outside of prime time. These rules, as modified, will continue to govern production, acquisition and syndication of network prime time entertainment programs and network participation in first-run syndication.

—A network may acquire financial interests, domestic syndication rights and foreign syndication rights in any outside productions aired on its prime time entertainment schedule, provided that (1) such rights are purchased pursuant to separate negotiations initiated no less than 30 days after execution of the network license fee agreement (and, where applicable, a pilot production agreement); and (2) the network certifies that access to its schedule was not conditioned on the acquisition of such rights.

—A network may produce up to 40 percent of its prime time entertainment schedule "in house" (*i.e.*, "solely produced" or co-produced" by the network, as defined herein), and it may retain financial interests and active syndication rights, both domestic and foreign, in those productions. Co-production arrangements between the network and a domestic producer may be initiated only by the outside producer, who shall be provided a 30–day cooling-off period before the arrangement becomes binding.

—Networks may not favor their affiliates nor unduly delay the syndication of those "in-house" productions they actively distribute in the domestic marketplace.

—A network may produce in-house an unlimited amount of prime time entertainment programming for airing or distribution on other broadcast networks or other broadcast outlets, and it may retain financial interests and foreign and domestic syndication rights in such programs. However, these programs may be syndicated domestically only through an independent syndicator subject to safeguards.

—Networks shall be allowed to engage in foreign distribution of programming free of any distribution safeguards.

—A network may produce first-run programming and retain financial interests and foreign syndication rights in such programming "solely produced" in-house, but may domestically distribute such programming only through an independent syndicator subject to safeguards. A network may not acquire any financial interests or syndication rights from outside producers of domestic first-run syndication programming.

—For purposes of these rules, a network will be defined as any entity providing more than 15 hours per week of prime time programming on a regular basis to interconnected affiliates that reach, in aggregate, at least 75 percent of television households nationwide.

—A new network's program ownership rights obtained prior to becoming a "network" shall be "grandfathered." A new network and its affiliates will have a transition period of 36 months to bring pre-existing contracts into compliance with the prime time access rule. A new network otherwise shall be required to comply immediately with the new rules.

—A network must maintain semi-annual reports in its owned and operated stations' public files. These reports must include network certification of its compliance with the instant rules and other specific information regarding prime time entertainment programs which it has produced or aired or in which it holds financial interests or syndication rights.

—These rules shall be reviewed by the Commission four years from their effective date.

The decision to limit the rules to prime-time programming and first-run syndication was based on the conclusion that this is the only programming for which strong syndication markets exist. Prime-time programming is defined as programming that "has network exhibition during the hours of 7 p.m. to 11 p.m. eastern time and pacific time, or 6 p.m. to 10 p.m. central time and mountain time."

With regard to the financial interest rule, the Commission concluded that although the networks no longer have the almost total dominance of 20 years ago, they still have sufficient power to extract rights from program producers in return for network exhibition. At the same time, the FCC determined that the existing financial interest rule was disserving "the public interest in diversity by limiting the funding of new, outside programming." The solution was to allow networks to obtain financial interests in prime-time entertainment programming subject to the "antiextraction" safeguards—separate negotiations 30 days apart and certification—noted above.

The 40 percent cap on in-house production also represents a balance between the recognition of the reduced power of the networks and a fear that sufficient power remains for the networks to engage in anticompetitive practices. More specifically, the cap was justified as serving three public interest goals. First, it will "curb potential network syndication abuses while at the same time assessing the actual impact of limited network involvement in that marketplace." Second, it would limit the ability of the networks "to coerce outside producers to produce programs in-house." Finally, allowing networks to produce their entire prime-time schedule in-house would reduce diversity of viewpoints.

The extraction concerns that led to the financial interest safeguards also convinced the Commission to apply the same safeguards to domestic syndication. In addition, to prevent networks from "warehousing" (unduly withholding programs from the syndication market) their product, the FCC imposed a requirement that networks must release programs into the syndication market "after four years or within six months following the end of the network run, whichever is sooner." However, the Commission did not have the same concerns regarding foreign syndication and thus, eliminated all restrictions on network participation in foreign syndication.

The two dissenters, Sykes and Quello, both felt that the Commission did not go nearly far enough in relaxing the rules. In separate dissents, each argued that the networks no longer have sufficient market power to exercise any significant control over the prime-time programming market. Thus, in their opinion, the Commission should have substantially, if not totally, repealed the rules. In support of his argument that the networks no longer have sufficient market power, Sykes cited the following comparative statistics:

> The video marketplace of 1991 bears not even a superficial resemblance to the marketplace that existed in 1970 when the rules were originally adopted. Even today's majority concedes this point. The number of television stations has grown by more than 500 since 1970, and television advertising revenues have increased from $3.6 billion to $26.9 billion. In 1970 there were only 65 independent stations; now there are 339. This expansion in the number of independent stations has provided a nucleus for a fourth television network, The Fox Network. Cable television, a negligible presence in 1970, has since become the means whereby the majority of American households view television. Cable now serves 59 percent of the national television audience, and is available to about 90 percent of it. As a result, the average American viewer can now access 30 channels of television, as opposed to 7 in 1970. Not surprisingly, yearly cable subscriber revenues have grown from $300 million in 1970 to $16.2 billion today, and cable advertising

revenues total $2.5 billion per year. It is estimated that cable revenues from local advertising and pay-per-view services will grow from 15 to 50 percent *each year*. The number of national cable program services has grown from zero in 1970 to 90 today. Today there are 3 million home satellite dish users and over 70 percent of American homes have VCRs; neither dishes nor VCRs were in use in 1970.

Financial Interest and Syndication Rules, 69 R.R.2d 341 (1991).

Numerous appeals were filed. The networks and their affiliates argued that the rules should have been eliminated rather than relaxed. Others, including Media Access Project and major studios, claimed that the rules were relaxed too much. In late 1992 the Seventh Circuit struck down the new financial interest and syndication rules. The court held that the FCC had given insufficient justification for the new rules. "Key concepts are left unexplained, key evidence is overlooked, arguments that formerly persuaded the commission and that time has only strengthened are ignored, contradictions within and among commission decisions are passed over in silence." The court stayed its order vacating the new rules for 30 days to allow the Commission to decide if it would attempt to rewrite the new rules and the FCC's rationale for them. The court also gave the parties 15 days to comment on whether the old rules, new rules or no rules should apply. Broadcasting, Nov. 9, 1992 at 4.

9. The following are the current Chain Broadcasting Regulations for television:

§ 73.658 Affiliation agreements and network program practices; territorial exclusivity in non-network program arrangements.— (a) Exclusive affiliation of station. No license shall be granted to a television broadcast station having any contract, arrangement, or understanding, express or implied, with a network organization under which the station is prevented or hindered from, or penalized for, broadcasting the programs of any other network organization. (The term "network organization" as used in this section includes national and regional network organizations. [ ])

(b) Territorial exclusivity. No license shall be granted to a television broadcast station having any contract, arrangement, or understanding, express or implied, with a network organization which prevents or hinders another broadcast station located in the same community from broadcasting the network's programs not taken by the former station, or which prevents or hinders another broadcast station located in a different community from broadcasting any program of the network organization. This regulation shall not be construed to prohibit any contract, arrangement, or understanding between a station and a network organization pursuant to which the station is granted the first call in its community upon the programs of the network organization. As employed in this paragraph, the term "community" is defined as the community specified in the instrument of authorization as the location of the station.

(c) Term of affiliation. No license shall be granted to a television broadcast station having any contract, arrangement, or understanding, express or implied, with a network organization which provides, by original terms, provisions for renewal, or otherwise, for the affiliation of the station with the network organization for a period longer than two years: provided, that a contract, arrangement, or understanding for a period up to two years may be entered into within six months prior to the commencement of such period.

(d) Station commitment of broadcast time. No license shall be granted to a television broadcast station having any contract, arrangement, or understanding, express or implied, with any network organization which provides for optioning of the station's time to the network organization, or which has the same restraining effect as time optioning. As used in this section, time optioning is any contract, arrangement, or understanding, express or implied, between a station and a network organization which prevents or hinders the station from scheduling programs before the network agrees to utilize the time during which such programs are scheduled, or which requires the station to clear time already scheduled when the network organization seeks to utilize the time.

(e) Right to reject programs. No license shall be granted to a television broadcast station having any contract, arrangement, or understanding, express or implied, with a network organization which, with respect to programs offered or already contracted for, pursuant to an affiliation contract, prevents or hinders the station from (1) rejecting or refusing network programs which the station reasonably believes to be unsatisfactory or unsuitable, or contrary to the public interest, or (2) substituting a program which, in the station's opinion, is of a greater local or national importance.

(f) Network ownership of stations. No license shall be granted to a network organization, or to any person directly or indirectly controlled by or under common control of a network organization, for a television broadcast station in any locality where the existing television broadcast stations are so few or of such unequal desirability (in terms of coverage, power, frequency, or other related matters) that competition would be substantially restrained by such licensing. (The word "control," as used in this section, is not limited to full control but includes such a measure of control as would substantially affect the availability of the station to other networks.)

(g) Dual network operation. No license shall be issued to a television broadcast station affiliated with a network organization which maintains more than one network of television broadcast stations: provided, that this section shall not be applicable if such networks are not operated simultaneously, or if there is no substantial overlap in the territory served by the group of stations comprising each such network.

(h) Control by networks of station rates. No license shall be granted to a television broadcast station having any contract, arrangement, or understanding, express or implied, with a network organization under which the station is prevented or hindered from, or penalized for, fixing or altering its rates for the sale of broadcast time for other than the network's programs.

(i) No license shall be granted to a television broadcast station which is represented for the sale of non-network time by a network organization or by an organization directly or indirectly controlled by or under common control with a network organization, if the station has any contract, arrangement, or understanding, express or implied, which provides for the affiliation of the station with such network organization: provided, however, that this rule shall not be applicable to stations licensed to a network organization or to a subsidiary of a network organization.

(j) Network syndication and program practices.

(1) Except as provided in subparagraph (3) of this paragraph, no television network shall:

(i) After June 1, 1973, sell, license, or distribute television programs to television station licensees within the United States for non-network television exhibition or otherwise engage in the business commonly known as "syndication" within the United States; or sell, license, or distribute television programs of which it is not the sole producer for exhibition outside the United States; or reserve any option or right to share in revenues or profits in connection with such domestic and/or foreign sale, license, or distribution; or

(ii) After August 1, 1972, acquire any financial or proprietary right or interest in the exhibition, distribution, or other commercial use of any television program produced wholly or in part by a person other than such television network, except the license or other exclusive right to network exhibition within the United States and on foreign stations regularly included within such television network; provided that if such network does not timely avail itself of such license or other exclusive right to network exhibition within the United States, the grantor of such license or right to network exhibition may, upon making a timely offer reasonably to compensate the network, re-acquire such license or other exclusive right to exhibition of the program.

(2) Nothing contained in subparagraphs (1) and (2) of this paragraph shall prevent any television network from selling or distributing programs of which it is the sole producer for television exhibition outside the United States, or from selling or otherwise disposing of any program rights not acquired from another person, including the right to distribute programs for non-network exhibition (as in syndication) within the United States as long as it does not itself engage in such distribution within the United States or retain the right to share the revenues or profits therefrom.

(3) Nothing contained in this paragraph shall be construed to include any television network formed for the purpose of producing, distributing, or syndicating program materials for educational, non-commercial, or public broadcasting exhibition or uses.

(4) For the purposes of this paragraph and paragraphs (k) and (*l*) of this section the term network means any person, entity or corporation which offers an interconnected program service on a regular basis for fifteen or more hours per week to at least twenty-five affiliated television licensees in ten or more states; and/or any person, entity or corporation controlling, controlled by or under common control with such person, entity or corporation.

(k) Effective September 8, 1975, commercial television stations owned by or affiliated with a national television network in the 50 largest television markets . . . shall devote, during the four hours of prime time (7–11 p.m. E.T. and P.T., 6–10 p.m. C.T. and M.T.), no more than three hours to the presentation of programs from a national network, programs formerly on a national network (off-network programs) other than feature films, or, on Saturdays, feature films; provided, however, that the following categories of programs need not be counted toward the three-hour limitations:

(1) On nights other than Saturdays, network or off-network programs designed for children, public affairs programs or documentary programs (see NOTE 2 to this paragraph for definitions).

(2) Special news programs dealing with fast-breaking news events, on-the-spot coverage of news events or other material related to such coverage, and political broadcasts by or on behalf of legally qualified candidates for public office.

(3) Regular network news broadcasts up to a half hour, when immediately adjacent to a full hour of continuous locally produced news or locally produced public affairs programming.

(4) Runovers of live network broadcasts of sporting events, where the event has been reasonably scheduled to conclude before prime time or occupy only a certain amount of prime

time, but the event has gone beyond its expected duration due to circumstances not reasonably foreseeable by the networks or under their control. This exemption does not apply to post-game material.

(5) In the case of stations in the Mountain and Pacific time zones, on evenings when network prime time programming consists of a sports event or other program broadcast live and simultaneously throughout the contiguous 48 states, such stations may assume that the network's schedule that evening occupies no more of prime time in these time zones than it does in the Eastern and Central time zones.

(6) Network broadcasts of an international sports event (such as the Olympic Games), New Year's Day college football games, or any other network programming of a special nature other than motion pictures or other sports events, when the network devotes all of its time on the same evening to the same programming, except brief incidental fill material.

. . .

NOTE 2. As used in this paragraph, the term "programs designed for children" means programs primarily designed for children aged 2 through 12. The term "documentary programs" means programs which are nonfictional and educational or informational, but not including programs where the information is used as part of a contest among participants in the program, and not including programs relating to the visual entertainment arts (stage, motion pictures or television) where more than 50% of the program is devoted to the presentation of entertainment material itself. The term "public affairs programs" means talks, commentaries, discussions, speeches, editorials, political programs, documentaries, forums, panels, roundtables, and similar programs primarily concerning local, national, and international public affairs.

Chapter VI

LEGAL CONTROL OF BROADCAST PROGRAMMING: POLITICAL SPEECH

In this chapter and the next we will consider direct regulation of content but not necessarily prohibitions on speech. In this chapter we will focus on political speech, including news. The next chapter will cover content regulation of other types of speech, which the FCC and courts have tended to treat as lower in the hierarchy of First Amendment values.

We begin this chapter with Congressional legislation to provide access and fairness in the electoral process. No speech is prohibited. Rather, broadcasters are told that they must allow certain candidates to use the station's facilities. In addition, if a candidate for an office is allowed to use the facilities, all other candidates for that office must be allowed equal opportunities.

We then turn to doctrines developed by the Commission itself that require broadcasters who have allowed certain types of comments to be made over their facilities to expose their listeners to contrasting viewpoints on that subject.

In each case, consider whether the regulations, although not prohibitory, may nonetheless indirectly influence broadcasters to air or not to air certain types of content.

A. EQUAL OPPORTUNITIES AND ACCESS IN POLITICAL CAMPAIGNS

1. Equal Opportunities—Section 315

In the Radio Act of 1927, § 18 provided:

> If any licensee shall permit any person who is a legally qualified candidate for any public office to use a broadcasting station, he shall afford equal opportunities to all other such candidates for that office in the use of such broadcasting station; . . . *Provided,* That such licensee shall have no power of censorship over the material broadcast under the provisions of this paragraph. No obligation is hereby imposed upon any licensee to allow the use of its station by any such candidate.

This became § 315 of the 1934 Act. Although the Commission has explicit rulemaking power to carry out the provisions of § 315(a), few rules have been promulgated. Most of the problems involve requests in the heat of an election campaign, and for this reason few decisions have been reviewed by the courts until recently.

a. General Application

One major limitation on the applicability of § 315 was defined in 1951, when it was held that the section did not apply to uses of a broadcast facility on behalf of a candidate unless the candidate appeared personally during the program. This meant that friends and campaign committees could purchase time without triggering § 315. Felix v. Westinghouse Radio Stations, 186 F.2d 1 (3d Cir.1950). This raised a separate set of problems discussed at p. 278, *infra*.

Section 315 applies only to "legally qualified" candidates for public office. According to § 73.1940(a) of the Commission's rules, a legally qualified candidate is one who:

（i) has publicly announced his or her intention to run for nomination or office;

（ii) is qualified under the applicable local, state or federal law to hold the office for which he or she is a candidate; and

（iii) has met the qualifications set forth in either paragraphs (a)(2), (3), or (4) below.

In essence, these other subparagraphs require the candidate either to have qualified for a place on the ballot or to have made a public commitment to seeking election by the write-in method as well as a substantial showing of being a bona-fide candidate for the office. Ways of making a substantial showing include "making campaign speeches, distributing campaign literature, issuing press releases, maintaining a campaign committee, and establishing campaign headquarters (even though the headquarters in some instances might be the residence of the candidate or his campaign manager)." 47 C.F.R. § 73.1940(a)(1–5).

Another basic question regarding § 315 was resolved in Farmers Educational & Cooperative Union v. WDAY, Inc., 360 U.S. 525 (1959), when the Court unanimously held that a licensee was barred from censoring the comments of a speaker exercising rights under § 315. The Court also held, 5–4, that the section preempted state defamation law and created an absolute privilege that protected the licensee from liability for statements made by such a candidate. Are these rulings sound? Because of the way the litigation arose, neither party challenged the constitutionality of § 315. Note, however, that although the station is protected from liability for defamation, the person who utters the statements is subject to liability under the general rules of defamation. We will examine these rules in Chapter XII.

Other content problems under § 315 are rare, but do arise. Among the candidates running in 1972 for the Democratic nomination for Senator from Georgia, one was broadcasting the following spot announcement:

I am J.B. Stoner. I am the only candidate for U.S. Senator who is for the white people. I am the only candidate who is against integration. All of the other candidates are race mixers, to one degree or another. I say we must repeal Gambrell's civil rights law. Gambrell's law takes jobs from us whites and gives those jobs to the niggers. The main reason why niggers want integration is because the niggers want our white women. I am for law and order with the knowledge that you cannot have law and order and niggers too. Vote white. This time vote your convictions by voting white racist J.B. Stoner into the run-off election for U.S. Senator. Thank you.

Several groups asked the Commission to rule that a licensee may, and has the responsibility to, withhold announcements under § 315 if they "pose an imminent and immediate threat to the safety and security of the public it serves." The groups alleged that the spot had created racial tension and that the Mayor of Atlanta had urged broadcasters not to air the advertisement. Letter to Lonnie King, 36 F.C.C.2d 635, 25 R.R.2d 54 (1972). The Commission refused to issue the requested order:

> The relief requested in your letter would amount to an advance approval by the Commission of licensee censorship of a candidate's remarks. By way of background, we note that Constitutional guarantees do not permit the proscription of even the advocacy of force or of law violation "except where such advocacy is directed to inciting or producing imminent lawless action and is likely to incite or produce such action." Brandenburg v. Ohio, 395 U.S. 444, 447 (1969). And a prior restraint bears a heavy presumption against its constitutional validity. Carroll v. President and Commissioners of Princess Anne, 393 U.S. 175, 181 (1968). While there may be situations where speech is "so interlaced with burgeoning violence that it is not protected," Carroll v. President and Commissioners of Princess Anne, 393 U.S. at 180 and while a similar approach might warrant overriding the no-censorship command of Section 315, we need not resolve that difficult issue here, for we conclude on the basis of the information before us that there is no factual basis for the relief you request. Despite your report of threats of bombing and violence, there does not appear to be that clear and present danger of imminent violence which might warrant interfering with speech which does not contain any direct incitement to violence. A contrary conclusion here would permit anyone to prevent a candidate from exercising his rights under Section 315 by threatening a violent reaction. In view of the precise commands of Sections 315 and 326, we are constrained to deny your requests.

The FCC has also received occasional complaints about political announcements that contain indecent language. The problem of indecent and obscene political announcements will be discussed in Chapter VII.

b. *Exemptions*

During its early years the statute apparently caused few serious problems. The advent of television, however, changed matters dramatically. In 1956 the Commission issued two major rulings during the presidential campaign. In one it ruled that presentation of Pres. Dwight Eisenhower's appearance in a two-to-three minute appeal on behalf of the annual drive of the United Community Funds would be a "use" of the facility by a candidate that would trigger the equal opportunities provision. The section carried no exception for "public service" nor did it require the appearance to be "political." Columbia Broadcasting System (United Fund), 14 R.R. 524 (F.C.C.1956). One week before the election, President Eisenhower requested and received 15 minutes of free time from the three networks to discuss the sudden eruption of war in the Middle East. The Democrats' request for equal time was granted by the networks, although the FCC later indicated that § 315 did not apply. Columbia Broadcasting System (Suez Crisis), 14 R.R. 720 (F.C.C.1956).

This response to an incumbent, speaking as President rather than as candidate, was unusual for the Commission, which had interpreted "use" very broadly. It did so, again, in 1959 when a third-party candidate for mayor of Chicago, Lar Daly, requested equal time on the basis of two series of television clips of his opponents, incumbent Mayor Richard Daley and the Republican challenger. One group of clips showed the two major candidates filing their papers (46 seconds), Mayor Daley accepting the nomination (22 seconds) and a one-minute clip asking the Republican why he was running. A second group of clips included "nonpolitical" activities such as a 29–second clip of Mayor Daley on a March of Dimes appeal and 21 seconds of his greeting President Frondizi of Argentina at a Chicago airport. The Commission, in a long opinion, ruled that both groups required equal time. Columbia Broadcasting System, Inc. (Lar Daly), 26 F.C.C. 715 (1959). It relied on the words "use" and "all" in the statute and thought the issue of who initiated the appearance (such as the March of Dimes, asking the Mayor to appear) to be irrelevant. Although formal campaigning was the most obvious way of putting forward a candidacy, "of no less importance is the candidate's appearance as a public servant, as an incumbent office holder, or as a private citizen in a nonpolitical role." Such "appearances and uses of a nonpolitical nature may confer substantial benefits on a candidate who is favored."

Congressional response was swift—and negative. Hearings began within days after the decision, and the result was an amended version of § 315:

> Sec. 315. (a) If any licensee shall permit any person who is a legally qualified candidate for any public office to use a broadcasting station, he shall afford equal opportunities to all other such candidates for that office in the use of such broadcasting station:

Provided, That such licensee shall have no power of censorship over the material broadcast under the provisions of this section. No obligation is hereby imposed upon any licensee to allow the use of its station by any such candidate.* Appearance by a legally qualified candidate on any—

(1) bona fide newscast,

(2) bona fide news interview,

(3) bona fide news documentary (if the appearance of the candidate is incidental to the presentation of the subject or subjects covered by the news documentary), or

(4) on-the-spot coverage of bona fide news events (including but not limited to political conventions and activities incidental thereto), shall not be deemed to be use of a broadcasting station within the meaning of this subsection. Nothing in the foregoing sentence shall be construed as relieving broadcasters, in connection with the presentation of newscasts, news interviews, news documentaries, and on-the-spot coverage of news events, from the obligation imposed upon them under this chapter to operate in the public interest and to afford reasonable opportunity for the discussion of conflicting views on issues of public importance.

Recall the significance of this episode to the Court in *Red Lion,* p. 71, *supra.*

In 1960 Congress suspended the operation of § 315 so that the stations could give time to national candidates without creating a § 315 obligation. This permitted the Kennedy–Nixon debates to be held without need to provide free time for the many minority candidates. There was no incumbent and no major third party candidate—two factors that made the debates politically possible.

Presidential election problems returned in 1964. First, the Commission ruled that coverage of an incumbent President's press conferences were not exempt under either § 315(a)(2) or (4). Nor were those of his main challenger. Columbia Broadcasting System (Presidential Press Conference), 3 R.R.2d 623 (F.C.C.1964). Then, two weeks before the election, the three networks granted Pres. Lyndon Johnson time to comment on two events that had just occurred: a sudden change of leadership was announced in Moscow, and China exploded a nuclear device. The Commission adhered to its 1956 ruling that this was not a "use." It also upheld a network claim that this program came within § 315(a)(4) as a bona fide news event. Republican National Committee (Dean Burch), 3 R.R.2d 647 (F.C.C.1964). An appeal of this ruling to the court of appeals led to an affirmance on a divided vote, 3–3, without opinion. A petition for *certiorari* was denied, Goldwater v. Federal Communications Commission, 379 U.S. 893 (1964), with Justice

---

* In 1971 Congress amended this sentence by adding "under this subsection" after the word "imposed." The reason for this is given when we consider § 312(a)(7) shortly.

Goldberg, joined by Justice Black, dissenting with opinion. They argued that the case presented substantial questions and that the Commission seemed not to be consistent in its own decisions.

In 1968 Sen. Eugene McCarthy announced early that he was a candidate for the Democratic nomination for President against the incumbent, Lyndon Johnson. During a traditional year-end interview with television reporters, President Johnson criticized Senator McCarthy and made several political statements. McCarthy sought "equal time" but the Commission denied the request on the ground that the President had not announced that he was a candidate for re-election and thus did not come within the statute or the Commission's rules on who is a "legally qualified candidate" for office. Eugene McCarthy, 11 F.C.C.2d 511, 12 R.R.2d 106 (1968). On appeal, the Commission's position was affirmed. McCarthy v. Federal Communications Commission, 390 F.2d 471, 12 R.R.2d 2003 (D.C.Cir.1968). Shortly thereafter President Johnson abruptly announced that he would not seek reelection.

In 1972 the problems centered around the Democratic nomination. Just before the crucial California primary, CBS held a joint session of "Face the Nation," expanded from its regular half-hour to one hour, featuring Senators Hubert Humphrey and George McGovern, the two leading candidates in the primary and for the nomination. The network claimed that this was a bona fide news interview and thus exempt under § 315(a)(2) from time requests by other Democratic candidates. Similar programs on other networks raised similar questions. The Commission found the changes did not deprive the programs of their bona fide character as interviews, and perceived and intended its opinion to accord "with the remedial purpose of the 1959 amendments to accord leeway to licensee journalistic decisions." Hon. Sam Yorty and Hon. Shirley Chisholm, 35 F.C.C.2d 572, 24 R.R.2d 447 (1972). On Chisholm's appeal, the FCC's ruling was vacated. Chisholm v. Federal Communications Commission, 24 R.R.2d 2061 (D.C.Cir.1972). The court thought the program more a debate than an interview. On remand, the Commission begrudgingly complied and ordered the networks to grant Chisholm one half-hour of prime time before the election. 35 F.C.C.2d 579, 24 R.R.2d 720 (1972).

The FCC has granted general exemptions under (a)(2) to such programs as "Today," "Donahue" and "Good Morning America." In determining whether a show falls under the (a)(2) exemption "the Commission considers the following factors: (1) whether it is regularly scheduled; (2) how long it has been broadcast; (3) whether the broadcaster produces and controls the program; (4) whether the broadcaster's decisions on the format, content and participants are based on its reasonable, good faith journalistic judgment rather than on an intention to advance the candidacy of a particular person; and (5) whether the selection of persons to be interviewed and topics to be discussed are based on their newsworthiness." CBS Inc., 63 R.R.2d 483 (M.Med.Bur. 1987).

The FCC changes course. Through the 1960s and 1970s, various proposals were made in Congress to amend or repeal § 315. Nothing came of any of them. But in 1975 the Commission responded dramatically to two petitions. It overruled its 1962 decisions that coverage of a debate did not come within the exemption for on-the-spot coverage of bona fide news events. The Commission said that it had misinterpreted legislative history when it required the appearance of the candidate to be incidental to the coverage of a separate news event. The Commission now concluded that in 1959 Congress intended to run the risks of political favoritism among broadcasters in an effort to allow broadcasters to "cover the political news to the fullest degree." Debates were exempt if controlled by someone other than the candidates or the broadcaster, and if judged to be bona fide news events under § 315(a)(4).

In a companion ruling, the Commission overruled its 1964 decision on press conference coverage. It decided that full coverage of a press conference by any incumbent or candidate would come within the exemption for on-the-spot coverage of a bona fide news event if it "may be considered newsworthy and subject to on-the-spot coverage." But the Commission refused to bring a press conference within the exemption for bona fide news interviews because the licensee did not "control" the format and the event was not "regularly scheduled." Petitions of Aspen Institute and CBS, Inc., 55 F.C.C.2d 697, 35 R.R.2d 49 (1975).

Appeals were taken against both parts of the Commission's 1975 rulings. The main contentions were that the Commission had not followed the Congressional mandate when it permitted the candidate to "become the event" under the (a)(4) exemption, and that the statute did not allow the Commission to uphold licensee decisions as long as they are in "good faith"—that it is for the Commission to make these judgments. By a vote of 2–1, the court affirmed both rulings, Chisholm v. Federal Communications Commission, 538 F.2d 349, 1 Med.L.Rptr. 2207 (D.C.Cir.1976). The opinions differed as to the significance of the complex legislative history, with the majority concluding that the Commission's interpretation was "reasonable." Rehearing *en banc* was denied. A petition for *certiorari* was denied 429 U.S. 890 (1976), White, J., dissenting.

Seizing on the Commission's rulings, the League of Women Voters set up "debates" between the two major Presidential candidates in 1976. They were held in auditoriums before invited audiences. The candidates were questioned by panelists selected by the League after consultation with the participants. Television was allowed to cover the events—but the League imposed restrictions against showing the audience or any audience reactions. Although the networks complained about the restrictions and about the way the panelists were selected, they did carry the programs live and in full.

Again in 1980 the League took steps to sponsor debates among the major candidates. It decided that John Anderson's showing in public opinion polls was sufficiently strong to warrant his inclusion in a three-way debate. When Pres. Jimmy Carter refused to participate in a debate with Anderson, the League went ahead anyway and staged an Anderson–Reagan debate. If networks decided to cover the event, as CBS and NBC did, the coverage would be exempt under (a)(4) because the networks and licensees were making the judgment it was a bona fide news event even without the President.

After Anderson's ratings fell to around 10 percent, the League invited Carter and Reagan to debate. Both accepted the invitation and held a single head-to-head debate a week before the election.

In 1980, just before the primaries began, President Carter, seeking renomination as Democratic candidate for President in a contest against Sen. Edward M. Kennedy, held a press conference that was carried live in prime time by the three commercial networks and the Public Broadcasting Service. Senator Kennedy, claiming that President Carter had used more than five minutes on that occasion to attack him and to misstate several of his positions, sought relief from the FCC.

In Kennedy for President Committee v. Federal Communications Commission, 636 F.2d 432, 47 R.R.2d 1537, 6 Med.L.Rptr. 1705 (D.C.Cir. 1980) (*Kennedy I*), the Senator asked for equal opportunities under § 315 to respond to the "calculated and damaging statements" and to "provide contrasting viewpoints." The FCC denied the request. On appeal, the court affirmed.

The press conference was exempt under § 315(a)(4) so long as the broadcasters reasonably believed that the conference was a "bona fide news event." The Commission said, in a passage approved by the court, that an incumbent President "may well have an advantage over his opponent in attracting media coverage" but "absent strong evidence that broadcasters were not exercising their bona fide news judgment, the Commission will not interfere with such judgments." The Senator was free to hold a press conference the next day to rebut the charges. Indeed, generally, Senator Kennedy was getting substantial media coverage.

The court traced the history of the exemptions to § 315 and adhered to its decision in *Chisholm* upholding the Commission's new approach to § 315. "The only inquiry now in order is whether there was anything so peculiar about the February 13 presidential press conference as to remove it from the ambit of *Aspen* and *Chisholm*. "The court found no reason to doubt the broadcasters' good faith. It also concluded that the actual content of the event could not control the question of exemption. Not only would the Commission and the courts have to make difficult judgments about content, context and impact, but also the goal of the exemptions would be defeated if broadcasters could not know until after an event whether it was exempt.

Senator Kennedy then argued that the First Amendment required that he be granted time to respond, even if the statute did not. The court rejected that contention on the basis of *CBS*, p. 85, *supra*:

From its inception more than a half-century ago, federal regulation of broadcasting has largely entrusted protection of that public right to short-term station licensees functioning under Commission supervision, and with liberty as well as responsibility to determine who may get on the air and when. The history of this era portrays Congress' consistent refusal to mandate access to the air waves on a non-selective basis and, contrariwise, its decision "to permit private broadcasting to develop with the widest journalistic experience consistent with its public obligations." [CBS] The Commission has honored that policy in a series of rulings establishing that a private right to utilize the broadcaster's facilities exists only when specially conferred. The net of these many years of legislative and administrative oversight of broadcasting is that "[o]nly when the interests of the public are found to outweigh the private journalistic interests of the broadcasters will government power be asserted within the framework of the Act."

The First Amendment permits Congress to enforce the public's primary interests by using broadcasters as public trustees, and CBS shows that no one has a constitutional right to broadcast his own views on any matter.

A more recent First Amendment attack on the application of (a)(4) to candidate debates was rejected in Johnson v. Federal Communications Commission, 829 F.2d 157, 63 R.R.2d 1492, 14 Med.L.Rptr. 1711 (D.C.Cir.1987). Sonia Johnson, who was running for President in 1984 as the nominee of the Citizens Party, and her running mate, Richard Walton, argued that "by 1984 the televised presidential and vice-presidential debates had become so institutionalized as to be a prerequisite for election." Thus, "their exclusion from the 1984 debates [restricted] their access to the ballot and impinge[d] upon associational choices protected by the First Amendment." Treating the claim as a demand for broadcast access, the court of appeals found Kennedy I and CBS v. DNC controlling. "In the present case, we find the First Amendment interests of candidates, broadcasters and the public adequately served by the adjustments made in the Communications Act, and perceive no basis for disturbing the Commission's denial of petitioners' complaint."

In Petitions of Henry Geller et al., 95 F.C.C.2d 1236, 54 R.R.2d 1246 (1983), the FCC reversed long-standing administrative decisions by permitting broadcasters themselves to sponsor debates between political candidates without having to provide uninvited candidates with equal broadcasting opportunities. Such debates may still fall within the § 315(a)(4) exemption. The Commission concluded that its previous interpretations neither represented the outer bounds of its legislated authority under the statute nor met the overriding Congressional mandate to encourage broadcast coverage of electoral issues. Third-party sponsorship was not the *sine qua non* of impartiality. For example, the risks of favoritism in the news interview format [§ 315(a)(2)] were thought to be no different from those in the debate format and therefore disparate treatment was not justified. The League of Women Voters' argument that this approach creates too great a risk of favoritism was rejected. The risks inherent in broadcaster-sponsored debates were no greater than the *Chisholm* court had understood the 1959 amendments to be willing to accept.

The Commission also noted that in many cases a broadcaster may be "the ideal, and perhaps the only, entity interested in promoting a debate between candidates for a particular office, especially at the state or local level." Exempting broadcaster-sponsored debates would therefore increase the number of debates and ultimately benefit the public. Finally, a debate's exempt status "should not be contingent upon whether a broadcaster is the sponsoring or controlling entity—for such control generally would not affect the program's news value." The Commission also made clear that this new interpretation of § 315(a)(4) did not authorize licensees to favor or disfavor any candidate. The League's expedited appeal was rejected without opinion. League of Women Voters v. FCC, 731 F.2d 995 (D.C.Cir.1984).

A debate between Gov. Michael Dukakis of Massachusetts and Rep. Richard Gephardt (D.–Mo.) presented the Commission with a slightly different question. Could a candidate-sponsored as opposed to a broadcaster-sponsored debate be considered exempt under § 315(a)(4)? In extending the exemption to candidate-sponsored debates, the Commission reemphasized its position that the identity of the sponsor is not a factor in determining if an event is newsworthy. As long as the broadcaster retains ultimate control over the amount and type of coverage, an event can qualify for exemption (a)(4). WCVB–TV, 63 R.R.2d 665 (M.Med.Bur.1987).

The "on the spot" language of § 315(a)(4) also has produced litigation. Groups afraid that an exempt program, such as a debate, might be recorded and replayed several times to the detriment of excluded candidates, have argued that the statute permits only one showing— and that it must be live. The FCC rejected this and allowed the broadcaster to tape the live event and to present it once during the next 24 hours. When that ruling was challenged, the court affirmed the Commission. The agency had authority to develop a balance between rigidly equal opportunities and the new freedom provided by the 1959 exemptions. There was no showing that the FCC had misconstrued the law, and it had fully explained what it was doing. Office of Communication of the United Church of Christ v. Federal Communications Commission, 590 F.2d 1062, 44 R.R.2d 261, 4 Med.L.Rptr. 1410 (D.C.Cir. 1978).

The one-day rule was eliminated in *Henry Geller, supra.* The reasonableness of a delayed broadcast will now be left to the broadcaster's good faith determination that the delay of more than one day after the occurrence of the exempt debate will better serve the community. Such delay, however, must be motivated by concerns of informing the public, and not in order to favor or disfavor any candidate.

The other subdivisions, (a)(1) and (a)(3), have given rise to fewer problems. In 1976 supporters of Ronald Reagan complained when a Miami television station broadcast six-minute interviews with Pres. Gerald Ford on five consecutive evening newscasts. The complaint asserted that the segments were from a single half-hour interview that had been broken up into five parts. The Commission held that even if the 30–minute interview would not have been exempt under § 315, inclusion of the segments within newscasts would not preclude "exempt status pursuant to § 315(a)(1) unless it has been shown that such a decision is clearly unreasonable or in bad faith." Even though this was broadcast during the last week of a primary campaign and might benefit President Ford, the complainants "have not shown that the licensee in deciding to air them, considered anything other than their newsworthiness." Citizens for Reagan, 58 F.C.C.2d 925, 36 R.R.2d 885 (1976). Does the statute's use of "bona fide" support the Commission's decision to leave the decision in the first instance with the licensee? If a program is exempt, that status is not lost simply because its timing may help one candidate more than another. The day before the Iowa caucus vote in 1980, President Carter was the guest on NBC's "Meet the Press," a program normally exempt under (a)(2) as a bona fide news interview program. One of his opponents argued that the program lost its exemption because of the impact just before the critical first voting of the 1980 primary process.

The FCC rejected the complaint. So long as the format remained the same and was controlled by the broadcaster, and the choice of guest was based on newsworthiness, the FCC would not intervene. The spirit of the *Aspen* decision was to leave judgments of newsworthiness to the professionals. In this case, because there was no showing that the incumbent's appearance would not be newsworthy, the timing was not controlling.

c. *Nonpolitical Appearances*

For many years the Commission defined "use" as "any positive appearance by a candidate by voice or picture." Thus, in United Way of America, 35 R.R.2d 137 (F.C.C.1975), which was decided at about the same time as the Aspen–CBS petitions, the Commission, 4–3, adhered to its earlier rulings that an appearance by candidate Ford opening an annual charity fund drive came within § 315. Similarly, the Commission consistently held that appearances by television personalities or film stars after they had announced their candidacy for office constituted a "use" under § 315. In Adrian Weiss, 58 F.C.C.2d 342, 36 R.R.2d 292 (1976), the Broadcast Bureau ruled that the showing of old Ronald Reagan films on television would require the offering of equal opportunities to other Republican presidential aspirants. The Bureau relied heavily on the claim that nonpolitical uses can be very effective. The Commission refused to review the Bureau's decision, with two Commissioners concurring separately and two dissenting. These four all thought that common sense dictated exempting movies made before Reagan actively entered politics, but the two concurring Commissioners thought that any change should be made by Congress.

In 1992, as part of an extensive review of its political broadcasting rules, the Commission narrowed its definition to "non-exempt candidate appearances that are controlled, approved, or sponsored by the candidate (or the candidate's authorized committee) after the candidate becomes legally qualified." This effectively overrules *Adrian Weiss* but not *United Way of America.* Codification of the Commission's Political Programming Policies, 7 F.C.C.Rcd. 4611, 70 R.R.2d 1331 (1992).

In Pat Paulsen, 33 F.C.C.2d 297, affirmed 33 F.C.C.2d 835, 23 R.R.2d 861 (1972), affirmed 491 F.2d 887, 29 R.R.2d 854 (9th Cir.1974), the Commission rejected a comedian's argument that applying § 315 would deprive him of due process and equal protection by forcing him to give up his livelihood in order to run for public office. Their interpretation was held permissible "to achieve the important and legitimate objectives of encouraging political discussion and preventing unfair and unequal use of the broadcast media."

In 1985 a California TV reporter raised similar objections to § 315 as it applied to him. He also argued that § 315 violated the First Amendment. In the alternative he asked that the Commission rule that appearing on the air as a journalist would not trigger § 315. The Commission denied his requests. William H. Branch, 101 F.C.C.2d 901 (1985).

On appeal, the court relied heavily on *Kennedy I* in affirming the Commission's actions.

BRANCH v. FEDERAL COMMUNICATIONS COMMISSION

United States Court of Appeals, District of Columbia Circuit, 1987.
824 F.2d 37, 63 R.R.2d 826, 14 Med.L.Rptr. 1465.
Certiorari denied 485 U.S. 959, 108 S.Ct. 1220, 99 L.Ed.2d 421 (1988).

Before BORK and STARR, CIRCUIT JUDGES, and McGOWAN, SENIOR CIRCUIT JUDGE.

BORK, CIRCUIT JUDGE:

. . .

Branch initially contends that the statute's "equal time" provisions do not apply to him because the statute exempts the television appearances of a newscaster candidate from their coverage. . . . Branch reads the statutory language to mean: the "equal opportunities" requirement applies only when there is a "use" of a broadcasting station; a candidate's appearance on a bona fide newscast does not constitute such a "use"; thus Branch's appearances on KOVR's bona fide news broadcasts are not subject to the "equal opportunities" requirement. The apparent simplicity of this argument, however, is misleading.

. . .

The legislative history of the 1959 amendments conclusively establishes three critical and overlapping points. First, Congress' central concern in taking action was to overrule the Commission's *Lar Daly* decision. . . .

Second, the purpose of overruling *Lar Daly* was to restore the understanding of the law that had prevailed previously. [ ] That understanding, as we have noted, required "equal opportunities" whenever any candidate appeared on the air, unless the candidate was the subject of "a routine news broadcast." . . .

Third, Congress objected to the imposition of "equal opportunities" obligations on any station that carried news coverage of a candidate, because it deterred the broadcast media from providing the public with full coverage of political news events, and many other news events as well. [ ] To the extent that Congress may have done more than reverse *Lar Daly,* by exempting broadcast coverage of news interviews and news documentaries in addition to newscasts and on-the-spot coverage of news events, it did so to protect a station's ability to exercise broad discretion in choosing which *newsworthy events* to present to the public. [ ]

Thus Congress' intent in enacting the amended section 315 is readily discernible. "Appearance by a legally qualified candidate," which is not "deemed to be use of a broadcasting station," is coverage of the candidate that is presented to the public as news. The "appearance" of the candidate is itself expected to be the newsworthy item that activates the exemption. "By modifying all four categories [not deemed to be 'use'] with the phrase 'bona fide,' Congress plainly emphasized its reliance on newsworthiness as the basis for an exemption." [ ]

The thrust of the language is brought out further in the third and fourth specific exemptions. The "news documentary" exemption applies only "if the appearance of the candidate is incidental to *the presentation of the subject or subjects covered by the news documentary.*" [ ] This passage relates the candidate's appearance to the subjects covered in the program. If the candidate's appearance has nothing to do with the subjects that are being covered as news—whether because the candidate is a regular employee on all such programs or, to take another example, because the candidate is being offered a gratuitous appearance that realistically is unrelated to the news content of the program—then the exemption does not apply. Similarly, the fourth exemption for "on-the-spot coverage" of news applies only to "coverage of bona fide news events." [ ] Here again the focus is on a news *event* that is being covered, with the candidate's appearance expected to occur as part of the event *being covered.*

When a broadcaster's employees are being sent out to cover a news story involving other persons, therefore, the "bona fide news event" is the activity engaged in by those other persons, not the work done by the employees covering the event. The work done by the broadcaster's employees is not a part of the event, for the event would occur without them and they serve only to communicate it to the public. For example, when a broadcaster's employees are sent out to cover a fire, the fire is the "bona fide news" event and the reporter does not become a part of that event merely by reporting it. There is nothing at all "newsworthy" about the work being done by the broadcaster's own employees, regardless of whether any of those employees happens also to be a candidate for public office.

. . .

Moreover, Congress' objection to *Lar Daly* was that it discouraged wide broadcast coverage of political news events by restricting a station's ability to determine which news *events* to present to the public. Congress solved this problem by exempting any on-air appearance by a candidate who is the *subject* of news coverage. It is irrelevant to that problem whether a station has broad discretion to determine which of its employees will actually present the news on the air. . . . At all times, the focus was not on preserving anyone's "right" to appear on the air, but on preserving broadcasters' ability to present to the public certain kinds of news programs and news events.

In opposition to that consistent approach, Branch asks this court to read the phrase "[a]ppearance by a legally qualified candidate on any [news program]" as exempting from the "equal opportunities" rule all on-air work done by newscaster candidates. We cannot do so. As we have already noted, such a reading would be at odds with the law before *Lar Daly,* which Congress explicitly sought to restore through the 1959 amendments. In addition, this reading would raise a station's news employees to an elevated status not shared by any of its other employees: although the work done on the air by any other employee on any other program would not be exempt, *see, e.g., [Paulsen],* the work done on the air by news employees would be. Yet this novel division was never endorsed, or even discussed by Congress.

. . .

IV.

We have determined that section 315 does not exempt newscaster candidates from the strictures of the "equal opportunities" rule. Branch challenges the statute, as so interpreted, on several constitutional grounds. . . .

A.

Branch's first objection is that the statute extinguishes his right to seek political office. That he has such a right is undeniable, though the Constitution and the Supreme Court's cases in the area do not pinpoint the precise grounds on which it rests. [ ] But whatever its source, the right is not implicated in this case. "In approaching candidate restrictions, it is essential to examine in a realistic light the extent and nature of their impact on voters." [ ] Here that impact is slight. The "equal opportunities" rule does not extinguish anyone's right to run for office. It simply provides that certain uses of a broadcast station by a candidate entitle other candidates for the same office to equal time. That the rule will affect some candidates favorably and others unfavorably is obvious. It may cause certain candidates to receive less time on the air than if the statute did not exist. But the Supreme Court has held that no individual has any right of access to the broadcast media. [*CBS v. DNC*]

The core of Branch's challenge on this point is that the statute imposes an undue burden on his ability to run for office because he cannot, during the time he is a candidate, do his normal work of reporting news on the air for station KOVR. But nobody has ever thought that a candidate has a right to run for office and at the same time to avoid all personal sacrifice. [   ] Even if the practicalities of campaigning for office are put to one side, many people find it necessary to choose between their jobs and their candidacies. The Hatch Act requires government employees to resign from work if they wish to run for certain political offices, [   ], and involves many more intrusive restrictions as well, yet the Supreme Court has upheld it against constitutional challenge. [   ] More recently, the Court upheld a Texas law that required certain public officials to resign from office if they wished to become candidates for certain other offices. [   ]

Indeed, the burdens Branch complains of are borne by all other radio and television personalities under section 315, though the exception he seeks would apply only to newscasters. In [*Paulsen*] those burdens were upheld against essentially the same objection made here. . . . Under established law, *Paulsen* was correct in finding the burdens imposed by section 315 justifiable as "both reasonable and necessary to achieve the important and legitimate objectives of encouraging political discussion and preventing unfair and unequal use of the broadcast media." *Id.* at 892.

B.

Branch's second constitutional objection to section 315 is that the "equal opportunities" rule violates the first amendment. He cites [*Miami Herald*], where the Supreme Court unanimously struck down a Florida law that gave political candidates a right to reply to criticisms and attacks published in newspapers. . . . The "equal opportunities" rule, in Branch's view, is identical to a right-of-reply statute in its impact.

The Supreme Court has expressly held, however, that the first amendment's protections for the press do not apply as powerfully to the broadcast media. In [*Red Lion*], the Court upheld the government's authority "to put restraints on licensees in favor of others whose views should be expressed on this unique medium." *Id.* at 390. What makes the broadcast medium unique, in the Court's view, is the scarcity of frequencies. *Id.* at 389–90.

While doubts have been expressed that the scarcity rationale is adequate to support differing degrees of first amendment protection for the print and electronic media, *see e.g.,* [TRAC]; [Meredith], it remains true nonetheless, that Branch's first amendment challenge is squarely foreclosed by *Red Lion.* . . . In the course of its opinion, the Court held that the statutory "equal opportunities" rule in section 315 and the Commission's own fairness doctrine rested on the same power to regulate "a scarce resource which the government has denied others the right to use". . . .

Nor can we adopt Branch's suggestion that this court would be justified in stepping away from *Red Lion.* The Supreme Court recently reaffirmed *Red Lion* and disavowed any intention "to reconsider our longstanding approach without some signal from Congress or the FCC that technological developments have advanced so far that some revision of the system of broadcast regulation may be required." [*League of Women Voters*] The Commission may now have sent just such a signal by issuing a report which concludes that section 315 is unconstitutional and should be abandoned. *See [1985 Fairness Report].* But unless the Court itself were to overrule *Red Lion,* we remain bound by it.

C.

Branch's final constitutional challenge to section 315 is that it impermissibly limits the discretion of broadcast stations to select the particular people who will present the news on the air to the public. Branch thus attempts to press the third-party rights of broadcasters who are not parties to this case. . . .

. . .

Nonetheless, the third-party challenge Branch advances is rebutted by *Red Lion.* A burden on the ability to present a particular broadcaster on the air, which applies to all broadcasters irrespective of the content of the news they present, is a much less significant burden than rules requiring the transmission of replies to personal attacks and political editorials, which were upheld in *Red Lion.* The latter provisions apply directly to political speech, and weigh more heavily on some messages than on others, depending on the precise content of the message conveyed. In contrast, the burdens on broadcasters that Branch asserts here do not "impair the discretion of broadcasters to present their views on any issue or to carry any particular type of programming." Columbia Broadcasting System, Inc. v. Federal Communications Commission, 453 U.S. 367, 396–97 (1981). Moreover, we note again that there is no right of any particular individual to appear on television. *See, e.g.,* [CBS v. DNC].

The petition for review is therefore,

Denied.

[Judge Starr concurred on the ground that although he agreed with Branch's interpretation of the statute, the Congressional intent was, in his view, "insufficiently clear to overturn the Commission's contrary reading."]

d. Lowest Unit Rate

In 1971, as part of legislation concerning election campaigning, Congress passed two statutes that affect broadcasting during political campaigns. One requires that candidates using broadcast facilities during the 45 days before a primary and the 60 days before a general election be charged rates not to exceed "the lowest unit charge of the station for the same class and amount of time for the same period. . . ." At all other times, the rates charged candidates are not to exceed "the charges made for comparable use of such station by other users thereof." 47 U.S.C.A. § 315(b). The major difference between the two quoted passages is that during the 45– and 60–day periods, the candidate pays the rate that the highest-volume advertiser would pay for that time. At other times, the candidate pays the rates charged to those who advertise as little or as much as the candidate does.

The lowest unit rate provision has caused great confusion among broadcasters. Most often a broadcaster will charge a candidate the lowest commercial rate for the number of spots he buys when the rule requires giving the candidate all volume and frequency discounts offered to any advertiser regardless of the number of spots the candidate purchases. However, this is not necessarily the lowest overall spot rate since the rule applies only to spots of the same class or type. Thus, a candidate buying prime time spots does not get the benefit of non-prime-time rates. Barter and per-inquiry spots are not applicable to the calculation of lowest unit rate.

Broadcasters are allowed to set certain conditions for political advertising—broadcast quality, prepayment, etc., but any discrimination in the application of these conditions to different candidates is strictly prohibited. For an example of the application of § 315(b), see Alpha Broadcasting Corporation, 57 R.R.2d 469 (1984).

As the 1988 general election got underway, the Commission found it necessary to address the application of § 315(b) to certain broadcast sales practices. Lowest Unit Charge Requirements, 65 R.R.2d 85 (1988). Causing the most concern were "the sale of commercial time on a preemptible only basis and the sale of commercials on a weekly rotation throughout dayparts rather than at a particular day and time." The latter, often referred to as "run-of-schedule spots," are placed in whatever time slots are available after the higher-priced "fixed-time spots" have been scheduled.

The FCC decided that preemptible spots—spots that can be preempted by other spots for which a higher rate is paid—and run-of-schedule spots each constitute a separate class of time for the purposes of § 315(b). With regard to preemptible spots, included in the calculation will be any "make good" spots that have aired in the same week as the candidate's spots. A make good is a spot offered to an advertiser whose original spot was preempted. Often make goods are sold at a lower rate than the original spot.

In July 1990 the Mass Media Bureau conducted an audit of 30 television and radio stations to determine the level of compliance with the political programming rules, particularly the lowest unit rate requirement. In September 1990 it issued a preliminary report on the results of its audit. The Bureau found that, "at sixteen of the twenty audited television stations (80%), candidates paid more for broadcast time than commercial advertisers in virtually every daypart or program time period analyzed. Indeed, candidates sometimes paid more than every commercial advertiser aired in the same dayparts. Candidates fared better on radio, paying more than commercial advertisers at only four of the eight audited stations that sold time to candidates."

The primary cause of the disparity was the fact that candidates tended to buy non-preemptible, fixed-time commercials. This assured that the candidates' commercials would not only run, but would do so at the exact times they wanted. In contrast, commercial advertisers tended to buy preemptible commercials. Because they were willing to risk that their commercials might be preempted if enough non-preemptible commercials were sold, they paid a lower rate. Technically, preemptible commercials are a different class of time, and thus, selling them at a lower rate is not a violation of the lowest unit rate requirement. However, the Bureau indicated a concern that candidates were not being given adequate information regarding the likelihood that a preemptible commercial would in fact be preempted and the availability of "make good" commercials in the event that preemptions did occur.

Based on its preliminary findings, the Bureau urged broadcasters to "disclose to candidates all rates and the availability of package options available to commercial advertisers. . . . This disclosure should specify all discount privileges, including every level of preemptibility, the approximate clearance potential of time purchased at current effective selling levels, and special package plans. The disclosure should also indicate the station's policies with respect to make goods and the availability of negotiating for time if that is the practice with commercial advertisers." Political Programming Audit, 68 R.R.2d 113 (M.M.Bur.1990).

The audit resulted in further questions from both candidates and broadcasters still seemingly confused over the exact requirements of the lowest unit rate provision of the Act. In mid–1991 the FCC issued an NPRM aimed at clearing up the confusion. Among the questions addressed in the NPRM were what constitutes a distinct class of time, how to "calculate the lowest unit charge when using a variety of different option privileges and discounts," and how much disclosure of the various option privileges and discounts should be made to political candidates.

The audit also proposed a stricter sponsorship identification requirement as a prerequisite for candidates availing themselves of the lowest unit rate. Under the proposal, sponsoring candidates' pictures would have to fill a minimum of 20 percent of the screen for at least six seconds. Broadcasting, June 17, 1991 at 21.

In *Codification of Commission's Political Programming Policies*, p. 245, *supra*, the FCC imposed a full disclosure requirement with regard to advertising rates on licensees. At a minimum this disclosure must include:

a) A description and definition of each class [of time] available to commercial advertisers which is complete enough to allow candidates to identify and understand what specific attributes differentiate each class;

b) A complete description of the lowest unit charge and related privileges (such as priorities against preemption and make goods prior to specific deadlines) for each class of time offered to commercial advertisers;

c) A description of the station's method of selling preemptible time based upon advertiser demand, commonly known as the "current selling level," with the stipulation that candidates will be able to purchase at these demand-generated rates in the same manner as commercial advertisers;

d) An approximation of the likelihood of preemption for each kind of preemptible time; and

e) An explanation of the station's sales practices, if any, that are based on audience delivery.

In the same proceeding, the Commission made several other decisions regarding lowest unit rate. Licensees are required to treat political candidates the same as their most-favored commercial advertiser, not only with regard to advertising rates but also to other sales practices including "make goods, preemption priorities and any other factors that enhance the value of a spot."

Licensees are now permitted to create more than one class of preemptible time, as long as the classes are distinguished by some demonstrable benefit to the advertiser, e.g. different levels of protection against preemption. Similarly, licensees can now have separate non-preemptible and fixed position classes of time. (Fixed position guarantees an exact time for the spot; non-preemptible guarantees only that the spot will run sometime during a particular day or time period.) Stations may not, however, create special classes of time for candidates only.

Stations that offer timely make goods to commercial advertisers for a specific class of time must offer similar make goods to political candidates. These make goods "must air before the election 'where the licensee would so treat its most-favored commercial advertiser where time is of the essence.'" Make goods must also be included in the calculation of lowest unit charge. Thus, where a make good is placed in a more valuable program or daypart, the cost of the make good must be included in the calculation of lowest unit charge for that program or daypart.

Another question raised during the 1990 elections involved jurisdiction over lowest-unit-rate disputes. Various Alabama and Georgia television stations had been sued for alleged violations of the lowest-unit-rate requirement. The cases had produced conflicting district court rulings on the question of whether the FCC has exclusive jurisdiction over lowest-unit-rate violations. The candidates had also filed complaints with the FCC. Broadcasting, July 8, 1991 at 52.

The FCC issued a declaratory ruling preempting any state cause of action involving § 315(b). At the same time it outlined the procedures for bringing a lowest-unit-rate complaint. Complainants are required to file a short, plain statement of the claim sufficient to show that the complainant is entitled to the relief requested. The complaint must be served on the station. The station will then be given ten days to answer. If the Mass Media Bureau determines that a *prima facie* case has been made, the parties will be given the choice of either mediation or evaluation and disposition by the Bureau. Lowest Unit Charge Requirements (Preemption of State Jurisdiction), 6 F.C.C.Rcd. 7511, 70 R.R.2d 1 (1991). Two petitions for reconsideration were denied. 7 F.C.C.Rcd. 4123, 70 R.R.2d 1355 (1992).

2. REASONABLE ACCESS—SECTION 312(A)(7)

In 1971, at the same time it passed the lowest unit rate provision, Congress adopted § 312(a)(7), providing that the Commission may revoke a license:

> (7) for willful or repeated failure to allow reasonable access to or to permit purchase of reasonable amounts of time for the use of a broadcasting station by a legally qualified candidate for Federal elective office on behalf of his candidacy.

The legislative history indicates that one purpose of the overall legislation was to "give candidates for public office greater access to the media so that they may better explain their stand on the issues and thereby more fully and completely inform the voters."

It was only in 1980 that cases involving the section began to reach the courts.

The first case raised the questions of when the campaign had begun and how requests should be treated. The Carter–Mondale Committee asked each major network to sell it 30 minutes of prime time in December 1979 (just after the formal announcement that President Carter was seeking renomination), in order to show a documentary on President Carter's first term. CBS offered two five-minute segments, one of which would be in prime time. ABC indicated that it would make time available beginning in January 1980. NBC said that it was "too early in the political season for nationwide broadcast time to be made available for paid political purposes." The Committee complained to the FCC, which found the stations in violation of § 312(a)(7), by a vote of 4–3. The court of appeals affirmed.

CBS, INC. v. FEDERAL COMMUNICATIONS COMMISSION

Supreme Court of the United States, 1981.
453 U.S. 367, 101 S.Ct. 2813, 69 L.Ed.2d 706, 49 R.R.2d 1191, 7 Med.L.Rptr. 1563.

CHIEF JUSTICE BURGER delivered the opinion of the Court.

[The Court agreed with the FCC that the section had "created an affirmative, promptly enforceable right of reasonable access to the use of broadcast stations for individual candidates seeking federal elective office" rather than simply codifying prior policies that the FCC had developed under the general public interest standard. The Court relied on the specific language of the statute itself, the legislative history and what the Court found to be the FCC's consistent administrative interpretation of the language since the statute's enactment. Perhaps the "most telling evidence" of Congressional intent was the contemporaneous change in § 315 from a statement that "No obligation is imposed upon any licensee to allow the use of its station by" a candidate to the statement that no such obligation "is imposed under this subsection [§ 315(a)]."]

III

A

Although Congress provided in § 312(a)(7) for greater use of broadcasting stations by federal candidates, it did not give guidance on how the Commission should implement the statute's access requirement. Essentially, Congress adopted a "rule of reason" and charged the Commission with its enforcement. . . . The Commission has issued some general interpretative statements, but its standards implementing § 312(a)(7) have evolved principally on a case-by-case basis and are not embodied in formalized rules. . . .

Broadcasters are free to deny the sale of air time prior to the commencement of a campaign, but once a campaign has begun, they must give reasonable and good faith attention to access requests from "legally qualified" candidates for federal elective office. Such requests must be considered on an individualized basis, and broadcasters are required to tailor their responses to accommodate, as much as reasonably possible, a candidate's stated purposes in seeking air time. In responding to access requests, however, broadcasters may also give weight to such factors as the amount of time previously sold to the candidate, the disruptive impact on regular programming, and the likelihood of requests for time by rival candidates under the equal opportunities provision of § 315(a). These considerations may not be invoked as pretexts for denying access; to justify a negative response, broadcasters must cite a realistic danger of substantial program disruption—perhaps caused by insufficient notice to allow adjustments in the schedule—or of an excessive number of equal time requests. Further, in order to facilitate review by the Commission, broadcasters must explain their reasons for refusing time or making a more limited counteroffer. If broadcasters take the appropriate factors into account and act reasonably and in good faith, their decisions will be entitled to deference even if the Commission's analysis would have differed in the first instance. But if broadcasters adopt "across-the-board policies" and do not attempt to respond to the individualized situation of a particular candidate, the Commission is not compelled to sustain their denial of access. [ ] Petitioners argue that certain of these standards are contrary to the statutory objectives of § 312(a)(7).

(1)

The Commission has concluded that, as a threshold matter, it will independently determine whether a campaign has begun and the obligations imposed by § 312(a)(7) have attached. [ ] Petitioners assert that, in undertaking such a task, the Commission becomes improperly involved in the electoral process and seriously impairs broadcaster discretion.

However, petitioners fail to recognize that the Commission does not set the starting date for a campaign. Rather, on review of a complaint alleging denial of "reasonable access," it examines objective evidence to find whether the campaign has already commenced, "taking into account the position of the candidate *and the networks* as well as other factors." . . . Such a decision is not, and cannot be, purely one of editorial judgment.

. . .

(2)

Petitioners also challenge the Commission's requirement that broadcasters evaluate and respond to access requests on an individualized basis. In petitioners' view, the agency has attached inordinate significance to candidates' needs, thereby precluding fair assessment of broadcasters' concerns and prohibiting the adoption of uniform policies regarding requests for access.

While admonishing broadcasters not to " 'second guess' the 'political' wisdom or . . . effectiveness" of the particular format sought by a candidate, the Commission has clearly acknowledged that "the candidate's . . . request is by no means conclusive of the question of how much time, if any, is appropriate. Other . . . factors, such as the disruption or displacement of regular programming (particularly as affected by a reasonable probability of requests by other candidates), must be considered in the balance." [ ] Thus, the Commission mandates careful consideration of, not blind assent to, candidates' desires for air time.

Petitioners are correct that the Commission's standards proscribe blanket rules concerning access; each request must be examined on its own merits. While the adoption of uniform policies might well prove more convenient for broadcasters, such an approach would allow personal campaign strategies and the exigencies of the political process to be ignored. A broadcaster's "evenhanded" response of granting only time spots of a fixed duration to candidates may be "unreasonable" where a particular candidate desires less time for an advertisement or a longer format to discuss substantive issues. . . . § 312(a)(7) assures a right of reasonable access to *individual* candidates for federal elective office, and the Commission's requirement that their requests be considered on an *individualized* basis is consistent with that guarantee.

[The Court concluded that the Commission's actions were a "reasoned attempt to effectuate the statute's access requirement, giving broadcasters room to exercise their discretion but demanding that they act in good faith." These ground rules were sufficiently clear in late 1979 to permit the FCC to rule that the networks had violated the statute by failing to grant "reasonable access."]

IV

Finally, petitioners assert that § 312(a)(7) as implemented by the Commission violates the First Amendment rights of broadcasters by unduly circumscribing their editorial discretion. . . .

. . .

The First Amendment interests of candidates and voters, as well as broadcasters, are implicated by § 312(a)(7). We have recognized that "it is of particular importance that candidates have the . . . opportunity to make their views known so that the electorate may intelligently evaluate the candidates' personal qualities and their positions on vital public issues before choosing among them on election day." [Buckley v. Valeo]. [ ] Indeed, "speech concerning public affairs is . . . the essence of self-government." [Garrison v. Louisiana]. The First Amendment "has its fullest and most urgent application precisely to the conduct of campaigns for public office." [Monitor Patriot Co. v. Roy]. Section 312(a)(7) thus makes a significant contribution to freedom of expression by enhancing the ability of candidates to present, and the public to receive, information necessary for the effective operation of the democratic process.

Petitioners are correct that the Court has never approved a *general* right of access to the media. [ ] Nor do we do so today. Section 312(a)(7) creates a *limited* right to "reasonable" access that pertains only to legally qualified federal candidates and may be invoked by them only for the purpose of advancing their candidacies once a campaign has commenced. The Commission has stated that, in enforcing the statute, it will "provide leeway to broadcasters and not merely attempt *de novo* to determine the reasonableness of their judgments. . . ." If broadcasters have considered the relevant factors in good faith, the Commission will uphold their decisions. See 629 F.2d, at 25. Further, § 312(a)(7) does not impair the discretion of broadcasters to present their views on any issue or to carry any particular type of programming.

Section 312(a)(7) represents an effort by Congress to assure that an important resource—the airwaves—will be used in the public interest. We hold that the statutory right of access, as defined by the Commission and applied in these cases, properly balances the First Amendment rights of federal candidates, the public, and broadcasters.

The judgment of the Court of Appeals is

Affirmed.

[Justice White, joined by Justices Rehnquist and Stevens, dissented on the grounds that the decision negated "the long-standing statutory policy of deferring to editorial judgments that are not destructive of the goals of the Act." Justice White also argued that the Commission had misinterpreted § 312(a)(7). His reading of the legislative history led him to believe that Congress intended only "to codify what it conceived to be the pre-existing duty of the broadcasters to serve the public interest by presenting political broadcasts."]

JUSTICE STEVENS, dissenting.

. . . The approach the Federal Communications Commission has taken in this case, now adopted by the Court, creates an impermissible risk that the Commission's evaluation of a given refusal by a licensee will be biased—or will appear to be biased—by the character of the office held by the candidate making the request.* Indeed, anyone who listened to the campaign rhetoric that was broadcast in 1980 must wonder how an impartial administrator could conclude that any presidential candidate was denied "reasonable access" to the electronic media. That wonderment is not dispelled by anything said in the opinions for the majority of the Commission in this case.

Notes and Questions

1. The relationship between § 312(a)(7) and § 315 was central to Kennedy for President Committee v. Federal Communications Commission, 636 F.2d 417, 47 R.R.2d 1521, 6 Med.L.Rptr. 1722 (D.C.Cir.1980) (*Kennedy II*). On March 14, 1980, President Carter made a 30–minute speech in the afternoon and held a press conference from 9 to 9:30 p.m. The three major commercial networks carried both programs live, except that ABC delayed the press conference for three hours. Senator Kennedy charged that these programs saturated the public with the President's views on the economy only four days before the Illinois primary. He asked for free time to reply under § 312(a)(7). The

---

* The possibility that Commission decisions under § 312(a)(7) may appear to be biased is well illustrated by this case. In its initial decision and its decision on the networks' petitions for reconsideration, the Commission voted 4–3 in favor of the Carter–Mondale Presidential Committee. [ ]

In both instances, the four Democratic Commissioners concluded that the networks had violated the statute by denying the Committee's request for access; the three Republican Commissioners disagreed. [ ]

networks denied the request, the Commission refused to order that time be granted, and the court affirmed.

The court began by noting that Congress, in 1971, enacted § 312(a)(7) and § 315(b)(1), requiring lowest charges to candidates using broadcast facilities, because Congress was concerned about the rising cost of candidates' televised appearances:

> It was believed that the informational and educational aspects of political broadcasting would be greatly enhanced by ensuring that more time would be made available to candidates at lower rates. This expectably would encourage less dependence on thirty- to sixty-second "spots"—necessarily little more than slogans—in favor of longer, more illuminating presentations; it would also enable more candidates to afford the television appearances so instrumental to present-day electioneering.

The court concluded that the "most straightforward reading" of § 312(a)(7) "is that broadcasters may fulfill their obligation thereunder either by allotting free time to a candidate *or* by selling the candidate time at the rates prescribed by Section 315(b)." Considering the legislative history, the FCC's consistent administrative interpretations and the apparent statutory scheme of the various provisions, the court concluded that § 312(a)(7), although seeking to assure federal candidates access to broadcasting, did not "confer the privilege of using the broadcaster's facilities without charge." The choice of giving or selling time is for the broadcaster:

> Should Section 312(a)(7) be construed as automatically entitling a candidate to responsive broadcast access whenever and for whatever reason his opponent has appeared on the air, Section 315(a)'s exemptions would soon become meaningless. Statutes are to be interpreted, if possible, to give operation to all of their parts, and to maintain them in harmonious working relationship.

Because Kennedy never claimed that he had not been given an opportunity to buy time, he could not invoke § 312(a)(7). Nor had he sought relief under § 315.

2. In 1981 the National Conservative Political Action Committee (NCPAC) petitioned the Commission for a ruling that an independent political action committee (PAC) had a right of reasonable access similar to that granted candidates for federal office by § 312(a)(7). The Broadcast Bureau rejected NCPAC's request, finding nothing in either the language of § 312(a)(7) or its legislative history that would support a right of access for anyone other than a candidate for federal office. The Commission upheld the Bureau's action, citing *CBS*, p. 85, *supra*. National Conservative Political Action Committee (NCPAC), 89 F.C.C.2d 626, 51 R.R.2d 233 (1982).

3. After *CBS*, the general rule for federal candidates is that broadcasters cannot establish across-the-board policies, but rather must consider the particular needs of each individual candidate. There is one excep-

tion to that, however. Stations may establish a policy of not selling any political advertisements during news programming. Commission Policy in Enforcing Section 312(a)(7), 68 F.C.C.2d 1079, 43 R.R.2d 1079 (1978). *In Codification of the Commission's Political Programming Policies*, p. 245, *supra*, the FCC decided to continue this policy. In addition, the Commission will now allow stations to treat news adjacencies (commercials aired immediately before or after a newscast) as a separate class of time for purposes of calculating lowest unit charge, p. 250, *supra*.

B. THE FAIRNESS DOCTRINE

1. IN GENERAL

Beginning in Chapter III with *Red Lion,* and at several points during the licensing discussion, we have had occasion to note the existence of, and to consider aspects of, the Commission-created fairness doctrine. As we shall discuss later in this chapter the Commission repealed the doctrine, at least in part, in 1987. However, legal challenges to that action and indications that Congress will attempt to codify the fairness doctrine leave open the possibility that the doctrine will be restored. Because understanding the many arguments for and against the reinstatement of the fairness doctrine requires knowledge of how the doctrine operated, and because there is at least a reasonable likelihood that it will in fact be reinstated, we begin by discussing the doctrine as it existed prior to 1987.

The Commission has been concerned with fairness and the exposure of varying views since its earliest days. Indeed, the Radio Commission in 1928 indicated as much in a discussion of the implications of the limited spectrum. It observed that there was not room "for every school of thought, religious, political, social, and economic, each to have its separate broadcasting station, its mouthpiece in the ether." Such ideas "must find their way into the market of ideas by the existing public-service stations, and if they are of sufficient importance to the listening public, the microphone will undoubtedly be available. If it is not, a well-founded complaint will receive the careful consideration of the commission in its future action with reference to the station complained of." Great Lakes Broadcasting Co., 3 F.R.C.Ann.Rep. 32 (1929), modified on other grounds 37 F.2d 993 (D.C.Cir.1930), certiorari dismissed 281 U.S. 706 (1930).

The doctrine evolved through case law until it became the subject of a major report in 1949. The doctrine has two separate parts. One part requires the broadcaster to air issues that "are so critical or of such great public importance that it would be unreasonable for a licensee to ignore them completely." Much more attention has been paid to the second part of the doctrine—that if broadcasters do cover "controversial issues of public importance" they must take steps to assure that important contrasting views are also presented. These views may be presented by the licensees themselves or by speakers chosen by the licensees.

In 1959, when § 315 was amended, p. 237, *supra*, many people interpreted the phrase, "nothing in the foregoing sentence shall be construed as relieving broadcasters . . . from the obligation under this chapter to operate in the public interest and to afford reasonable opportunity for the discussion of conflicting views on issues of public importance" as codifying the fairness doctrine in the Communications Act. This interpretation was the majority view until 1986, when the court of appeals held that the fairness doctrine was not codified in the Communications Act. *TRAC*, p. 89, *supra*. We will discuss the substance of this case—an appeal of the Commission's refusal to apply the fairness doctrine, as well as § 315 and § 312(a)(7), to teletext—in Chapter X.

IN THE MATTER OF THE HANDLING OF PUBLIC ISSUES UNDER THE FAIRNESS DOCTRINE AND THE PUBLIC INTEREST STANDARDS OF THE COMMUNICATIONS ACT (1974 FAIRNESS REPORT)

Federal Communications Commission, 1974.
48 F.C.C.2d 1, 30 R.R.2d 1261.

By the Commission: COMMISSIONER HOOKS concurring in part and dissenting in part and issuing a separate statement.

[The Commission first restated its commitment to the goal of "uninhibited, robust, wide open" debate on public issues and the need to recognize that achievement of this goal must be compatible with the public interest in "the larger and more effective use of radio" § 303(g). This included the fact that "ours is a commercially-based broadcast system" and that the Commission's policies "should be consistent with the maintenance and growth of that system." The Commission then quoted a critical passage from its Report on Editorializing, 13 F.C.C. 1246, 1249 (1949), in which the fairness doctrine was formally announced:

It is axiomatic that one of the most vital questions of mass communication in a democracy is the development of an informed public opinion through the public dissemination of news and ideas concerning the vital public issues of the day. . . . The Commission has consequently recognized the necessity for licensees to devote a reasonable percentage of their broadcast time to the presentation of news and programs devoted to the consideration and discussion of public issues of interest in the community served by the particular station. And we have recognized, with respect to such programs, the paramount right of the public in a free society to be informed and to have presented to it for acceptance or rejection the different attitudes and viewpoints concerning these vital and often controversial issues which are held by the various groups which make up the community. It is this right of the public to be informed, rather than any right on the part of the Government, any broadcast licensee or any individual member of the public to broadcast his own particular views on any matter, which is the foundation stone of the American system of broadcasting.

The *1974 Fairness Report* stressed that two basic duties were involved: "(1) the broadcaster must devote a reasonable percentage of time to coverage of public issues; and (2) his coverage of these issues must be fair in the sense that it provides an opportunity for the presentation of contrasting points of view." The Commission also noted that in 1970 it had described the two parts of the fairness doctrine "as the single most important requirement of operation in the public interest—the *sine qua non* for grant of a renewal of license." The Commission denied that imposition of these two duties could be inhibiting:

18. In evaluating the possible inhibitory effect of the fairness doctrine, it is appropriate to consider the specifics of the doctrine and the procedures employed by the Commission in implementing it. When a licensee presents one side of a controversial issue, he is not required to provide a forum for opposing views on that same program or series of programs. He is simply expected to make provision for the opposing views in his *overall programming.* Further, there is no requirement that any precisely equal balance of views be achieved, and all matters concerning the particular opposing views to be presented and the appropriate spokesmen and format for their presentation are left to the licensee's discretion subject only to a standard of reasonableness and good faith.

19. As a matter of general procedure, we do not monitor broadcasts for possible violations, but act on the basis of complaints received from interested citizens. These complaints are not forwarded to the licensee for his comments unless they present *prima facie* evidence of a violation. Allen C. Phelps, 21 F.C.C.2d 12 (1969). Thus, broadcasters are not burdened with the task of answering idle or capricious complaints. By way of illustration, the Commission received some 2,400 fairness complaints in fiscal 1973, only 94 of which were forwarded to licensees for their comments.

20. While there may be occasional exceptions, we find it difficult to believe that these policies add significantly to the overall administrative burdens involved in operating a broadcast station. . . . The Supreme Court has made it clear and it should be reemphasized here that "if present licensees should suddenly prove timorous, the Commission is not powerless to insist that they give adequate and fair attention to public issues." Red Lion Broadcasting Co. v. FCC, 395 U.S. at 393.

As to the first duty imposed, the Commission noted:

We have, in the past, indicated that some issues are so critical or of such great public importance that it would be unreasonable for a licensee to ignore them completely. [ ] But such statements on our part are the rare exception, not the rule, and we have no intention of becoming involved in the selection of issues to be discussed, nor do we expect a broadcaster to cover each and every important issue which may arise in his community.

26. We wish to emphasize that the responsibility for the selection of program material is that of the individual licensee. That responsibility "can neither be delegated by the licensee to any network or other person or group, or be unduly fettered by contractual arrangements restricting the licensee in his free exercise of his independent judgments." Report on Editorializing, 13 FCC at 1248. We believe that stations, in carrying out this responsibility, should be alert to the opportunity to complement network offerings with local programming on these issues, or with syndicated programming.

The Commission then turned to the second, and more frequently litigated, aspect of the fairness doctrine.]

2. *A Reasonable Opportunity for Opposing Viewpoints*

. . .

28. It has frequently been suggested that individual stations should not be expected to present opposing points of view and that it should be sufficient for the licensee to demonstrate that the opposing viewpoint has been adequately presented on another station in the market or in the print media. See WSOC Broadcasting Co., 17 P & F Radio Reg. 548, 550 (1958). While we recognize that citizens receive information on public issues from a variety of sources, other considerations require the rejection of this suggestion. First, in amending section 315(a) of the Communications Act in 1959, Congress gave statutory approval to the fairness doctrine, including the requirement that broadcasters themselves provide an opportunity for opposing viewpoints. See BEM, 412 U.S. at 110, note 8. Second, it would be an administrative nightmare for this Commission to attempt to review the overall coverage of an issue in all of the broadcast stations and publications in a given market. Third, and perhaps most importantly, we believe that the requirement that *each* station provide for contrasting views greatly increases the likelihood that individual members of the public will be exposed to varying points of view. . . .

a. *What is a "controversial issue of public importance"?*

29. It has frequently been suggested that the Commission set forth comprehensive guidelines to aid interested parties in recognizing whether an issue is "controversial" and of "public importance." However, given the limitless number of potential controversial issues and the varying circumstances in which they might arise, we have not been able to develop detailed criteria which would be appropriate in all cases. For this very practical reason, and for the reason that our role

must and should be limited to one of review, we will continue to rely heavily on the reasonable, good faith judgments of our licensees in this area.

30.　Some general observations, however, are in order.　First of all, it is obvious that an issue is not necessarily a matter of significant "public importance" merely because it has received broadcast or newspaper coverage.　"Our daily papers and television broadcasts alike are filled with news items which good journalistic judgment would classify as newsworthy, but which the same editors would not characterize as containing important controversial public issues."　Healey v. FCC, 460 F.2d 917, 922 (D.C.Cir.1972).　Nevertheless, the degree of media coverage is one factor which clearly should be taken into account in determining an issue's importance.　It is also appropriate to consider the degree of attention the issue has received from government officials and other community leaders.　The principal test of public importance, however, is not the extent of media or governmental attention, but rather a subjective evaluation of the impact that the issue is likely to have on the community at large.　If the issue involves a social or political choice, the licensee might well ask himself whether the outcome of that choice will have a significant impact on society or its institutions.　It appears to us that these judgments can be made only on a case-by-case basis.

31.　The question of whether an issue is "controversial" may be determined in a somewhat more objective manner.　Here, it is highly relevant to measure the degree of attention paid to an issue by government officials, community leaders, and the media.　The licensee should be able to tell, with a reasonable degree of objectivity, whether an issue is the subject of vigorous debate with substantial elements of the community in opposition to one another.　It is possible, of course, that "programs initiated with no thought on the part of the licensee of their possible controversial nature . . . will merit presentation of opposing views."　Report on Editorializing, 13 FCC at 1251.　In such circumstances, it would be appropriate to make provision for opposing views when the opposition becomes manifest.

b.　What specific issue has been raised?

32.　One of the most difficult problems involved in the administration of the fairness doctrine is the determination of the specific issue or issues raised by a particular program.　This would seem to be a simple task, but in many cases it is not. . . .

. . .

c.　What is a "reasonable opportunity" for contrasting viewpoints?

. . .

37.　The first point to be made with regard to the obligation to present contrasting views is that it cannot be met "merely through the adoption of a general policy of not refusing to broadcast opposing views where a demand is made of the station for broadcast time." Report on Editorializing, 13 FCC at 1251. The licensee has a duty to play a conscious and positive role in encouraging the presentation of opposing viewpoints.[13] . . .

38. In making provision for the airing of contrasting viewpoints, the broadcaster should be alert to the possibility that a particular issue may involve more than two opposing viewpoints. Indeed, there may be several important viewpoints or shades of opinion which warrant broadcast coverage.

. . .

41. In providing for the coverage of opposing points of view, we believe that the licensee must make a reasonable allowance for presentations by genuine partisans who actually believe in what they are saying. The fairness doctrine does not permit the broadcaster "to preside over a 'paternalistic' regime," BEM, 412 U.S. at 130, and it would clearly not be acceptable for the licensee to adopt a "policy of excluding partisan voices and always itself presenting views in a bland, inoffensive manner. . . ." . . .

42. This does not mean, however, that the Commission intends to dictate the selection of a particular spokesman or a particular format, or indeed that partisan spokesmen must be presented in every instance. We do not believe that it is either appropriate or feasible for a governmental agency to make decisions as to what is desirable in each situation. In cases involving personal attacks and political campaigns, the natural opposing spokesmen are relatively easy to identify. This is not the case, however, with the majority of public controversies. Ordinarily, there are a variety of spokesmen and formats which could reasonably be deemed to be appropriate. We believe that the public is best served by a system which allows individual broadcasters considerable discretion in selecting the manner of coverage, the appropriate spokesmen, and the techniques of production and presentation.

43. Frequently, the question of the reasonableness of the opportunity provided for contrasting viewpoints comes down to weighing the *time* allocated to each side. Aside from the field of political broadcasting, the licensee is not required to provide equal time for the various opposing points of view. Indeed, we have long felt that the basic goal of creating an informed citizenry would be frustrated if for every controversial item or presentation on a newscast or other broadcast the licensee had to offer equal time to the other side. . . . Similarly, we do not believe that it would be appropriate for the Commission to establish any other mathematical ratio, such as 3 to 1 or 4 to 1, to be

---

13. This duty includes the obligation defined in Cullman Broadcasting Co., 40 FCC 576, 577 (1963) . . ..

We do not believe that the passage of time since *Cullman* was decided has in any way since diminished the importance and necessity of this principle. If the public's right to be informed of the contrasting views on controversial issues is to be truly honored, broadcasters must provide the forum for the expression of those viewpoints at their own expense if paid sponsorship is unavailable.

applied in all cases. We believe that such an approach is much too mechanical in nature and that in many cases our preconceived ratios would prove to be far from reasonable. In the case of a 10–second personal attack, for example, fairness may dictate that more time be afforded to answer the attack than was given the attack itself.

. . .

e. Fairness and Accurate News Reporting

58. In our 1949 Report on Editorializing, we alluded to a licensee's obligation to present the news in an accurate manner:

> It must be recognized, however, that the licensee's opportunity to express his own views . . . does not justify or empower any licensee to exercise his authority over the selection of program material to distort or suppress the basic factual information upon which any truly fair and free discussion of public issues must necessarily depend. . . . A licensee would be abusing his position as public trustee of these important means of mass communication were he to withhold from expression over his facilities relevant news or facts concerning a controversy or to slant or distort the presentation of such news. No discussion of the issues involved in any controversy can be fair or in the public interest where such discussion must take place in a climate of false or misleading information concerning the basic facts of the controversy, 13 FCC at 1254–55.

It is a matter of critical importance to the public that the basic facts or elements of a controversy should not be deliberately suppressed or misstated by a licensee. But we must recognize that such distortions are "so continually done in perfect good faith, by persons who are not considered . . . ignorant or incompetent, that it is rarely possible on adequate grounds, conscientiously to stamp the misrepresentations as morally culpable. . . ." J.S. Mill, On Liberty 31 (People's ed. 1921). Accordingly, we do not believe that it would be either useful or appropriate for us to investigate charges of news misrepresentations in the absence of substantial extrinsic evidence or documents that on their face reflect deliberate distortion. See The Selling of the Pentagon, 30 FCC2d 150 (1971).

Notes and Questions

1. In 1976 the Commission denied reconsideration of the *1974 Fairness Report.* 58 F.C.C.2d 691, 36 R.R.2d 1021 (1976). Commissioner Robinson dissented because he doubted the value of the efforts involved and was concerned about the intrusion into editorial decisions. He noted that in 1973 and 1974, of 4,280 formal fairness complaints, only 19 resulted in findings adverse to the licensee. These included seven in the political editorial area, seven cases of personal attack and five general fairness complaints. Of the 19 violations, only eight resulted in tangible penalty to the licensee—seven political editorializing cases and one personal attack case involved forfeitures under § 503. Because

this sanction is available only for violations of formal rules, it is not available for violations of the uncodified general doctrine.

2. Commissioner Robinson asserted that so long as *Red Lion* was the law the Commission could not eliminate the fairness doctrine completely. He favored the suggestion made by the Committee for Open Media, under which a licensee might choose to meet its obligations under the fairness doctrine by allowing access to its facilities. The proposal was to allow 35 one-minute messages per week scheduled at different times, including prime time. Half the spots would be allocated on a first-come, first-served basis and the other half would use "a representative spokesperson" system. If an excessive number wanted to speak, Commissioner Robinson suggested that speakers might be chosen by lot or by queuing so as to minimize licensee bias. Efforts would be made to prevent monopolization by one outside group. Commissioner Robinson thought few licensees would choose to relinquish control in this way, but he thought it offered the Commission an opportunity to avoid judging content and he urged offering this alternative to licensees. For a study of the operation of Free Speech Messages in San Francisco, see Harris, Free Speech Messages: When the Public Gets Access, What Does It Say?, Access 34 at 20 (1976).

In a separate statement, Chairman Wiley attacked the access proposal on the grounds that it encouraged licensees to abdicate editorial control and emphasized a single programming technique—the access announcement: "In my opinion a more varied, interesting and informative coverage would be possible if professional journalists played a conscious and positive role in the process."

3. After the Commission's denial of reconsideration of the *1974 Fairness Report*, the court of appeals generally affirmed that ruling. National Citizens Committee for Broadcasting v. Federal Communications Commission, 567 F.2d 1095 (D.C.Cir.1977). The court upheld the Commission's decision to discontinue applying the fairness doctrine to most commercial advertisements—a result already reached in the snowmobile case, *infra*. The court did remand two issues to the Commission for additional consideration. One was the COM proposal, discussed *supra*. The other was a proposal that the Commission order each licensee to "list annually the ten controversial issues of public importance, local and national, which it chose for the most coverage in the prior year, set out the offers for response made, and note representative programming that was presented on each issue."

The parties who were dissatisfied with the commercial advertisement part of the decision sought Supreme Court review, but *certiorari* was denied. 436 U.S. 926 (1978).

On the remand, the Commission adhered to its earlier views. 74 F.C.C.2d 163, 46 R.R.2d 999 (1979). It rejected the COM proposal on the ground that "any system which has its emphasis on speakers rather than on ideas is at cross-purposes to that of the Fairness Doctrine. Since the goal of the Fairness Doctrine is to inform the public, any substitute means of compliance must do this." Studies of access usage in various cities provided no assurances that important and timely public issues would be discussed, that presentations on issues would be balanced, or that they would be informative and comprehensible. Even time assigned to spokespersons for issue-oriented groups might not be devoted to the discussion of important public issues.

Despite the acknowledged attractions of the access proposal, such as the opportunity for "true partisans" to express their views and the use of spot announcements "to reach larger and more diverse audiences than through program-length public affairs broadcasts," the defects were held to outweigh the potential gains.

Licensees who might choose to institute an access program must still comply with the fairness doctrine. "How the licensee achieves this mandate depends, as we have always stated, upon the journalistic discretion of each participating station."

The Commission again rejected the Geller proposal that television licensees be required to list annually the 10 community and national controversial issues of public importance that they chose for the most coverage in the prior year. The licensees would have been required to keep a record of their offers to the public for response, the representative programming that was devoted to each issue, the partisan speakers presented, and the sources and times of the broadcasts. Routine news coverage would have been excluded.

The Commission concluded that the added record keeping would not "necessarily enhance coverage" of controversial issues. The existing rules already required television licensees "to keep in their public inspection file a listing of no more than ten significant problems of the area served by the station during the preceding twelve months and to indicate typical and illustrative programming broadcast in response to those problems and needs." At renewal time the listings for the three prior years were sent to the Commission as part of the renewal process. In the absence of any showing that television licensees were not already covering controversial issues, the added burden was unwarranted.

Moreover, Geller's proposal was inconsistent with the goal of reviewing fairness doctrine complaints as they arose rather than waiting until renewal when the issues might have become stale.

4. In 1984, during "ABC World News Tonight," ABC broadcast allegations that the Central Intelligence Agency had participated in various illegal activities including a plot to assassinate an American citizen. Two months later ABC reported that efforts to substantiate the allegations had failed and that there was "no reason to doubt" the CIA's denials.

Both the CIA and the American Legal Foundation (ALF) filed complaints claiming deliberate news distortion and violations of the fairness doctrine and the personal attack rule. The Commission held that there was insufficient proof of deliberate news distortion. "The

Commission will initiate action in this area *only* when furnished with direct extrinsic evidence that a broadcaster possessed a deliberate intent to distort the news." Central Intelligence Agency, 58 R.R.2d 1544, 1549 [1985].

Turning to the fairness and personal attack complaints, the Commission found that the broadcasts did not deal with a controversial issue of public importance. The FCC rejected the CIA's contention that the controversial issue was, "Does the Central Intelligence Agency adhere to the mandate of American Law generally, and more particularly, does the CIA participate in or condone murder as a practice?" The Commission distinguished between an allegation of specific CIA misconduct and a statement that the CIA generally violates the law. "Under the Fairness Doctrine an issue must be addressed in an obvious and meaningful fashion so as to amount to advocacy on that particular issue. [ ] The Commission does not expect its licensees to present contrasting viewpoints on every statement or shade of opinion, or every possible inference to be drawn from individual statements or presentations."

The court of appeals rejected an appeal by ALF, holding that ALF lacked standing to bring the appeal. ALF could not claim associational standing because it did not have any members. ALF's failure to allege "injury in fact" precluded a finding of institutional standing. American Legal Foundation v. Federal Communications Commission, 808 F.2d 84, 61 R.R.2d 1694 (D.C.Cir.1987). The CIA had not appealed.

5. *The Affirmative Duty to Raise Issues.* The Commission refers to the fairness doctrine as having two parts. Virtually all the litigation and discussion have involved the second part: the requirement that a licensee who has presented one side of a controversial issue of public importance must present contrasting views.

In 1976, for the first time, the Commission applied the first part. A Congresswoman sent an 11–minute tape opposing strip mining to West Virginia radio stations to counter a presentation in favor of strip mining that had been distributed to many stations by the U.S. Chamber of Commerce. One station, WHAR, refused to play the tape because it had not presented the first program. Indeed, it had presented nothing on the issue except items on regular newscasts taken from the AP news service. Several persons and groups complained to the Commission contending that in this part of West Virginia at this time the question of strip mining was of primary importance. In its renewal application, WHAR had cited "development of new industry" and "air and water pollution" as issues of great concern to its listeners. In addition, bills on the subject were pending in Congress at the time, and local newspapers were extensively discussing the question. (Presentation of a five-minute tape by an outspoken foe of strip mining was not relevant because he did not discuss the economic or ecological aspects of strip mining or the pending legislation.)

The Commission asserted that although a violation of the first part "would be an exceptional situation and would not counter our intention to stay out of decisions concerning the selection of specific programming matter," this was such a case and demonstrated an "unreasonable exercise" of discretion. The Commission quoted the passage from *Red Lion* that "if the present licensees should suddenly prove timorous, the Commission is not powerless to insist that they give adequate and fair attention to public issues." The lack of any prior request to program on this subject was irrelevant because "it is the station's obligation to make an affirmative effort to program on issues of concern to its community." The role of the AP news items was minimal because it was not even clear which ones were aired. "Where, as in the present case, an issue has significant and possibly unique impact on the licensee's service area, it will not be sufficient for the licensee as an indication of compliance with the fairness doctrine to show that it may have broadcast an unknown amount of news touching on a general topic related to the issue cited in a complaint." The station was ordered to tell the Commission within 20 days how it intended to meet its fairness obligations. Rep. Patsy Mink, 59 F.C.C.2d 987, 37 R.R.2d 744 (1976).

What is the difference between saying (1) a station has an obligation to present programs on the need for good dental hygiene, even though the subject may not be controversial, and (2) a station must present programs on a controversial issue in the community? Are both covered by the fairness doctrine?

What is the justification for requiring each station in a community to present a range of views on controversial issues of public importance? Why is it not enough if the spectrum as a whole provides contrasting viewpoints? Is there more or less reason to require a station to raise important subjects when other stations in the community are doing so? Thus, in the strip mining case, should it matter that other broadcasters are devoting extensive coverage to the subject? What has this obligation to do with "fairness"?

6. *The Duty to Present Contrasting Views.* At one point the Commission quoted a court to the effect that not everything that is thought newsworthy by journalists necessarily presents a controversial issue of public importance. What are some examples of divergence between the two?

The Commission has never declared the fairness doctrine "applicable to issues involving the interpretation of religious doctrine." When a group complained that the program "In Search of Noah's Ark" presented one side of the issue of whether the Ark exists, and gave mistaken impressions about the attitudes of historians, archaeologists and scholars, the Broadcast Bureau responded: "While such issues may be widely and vigorously disputed in the religious community, they generally do not rise to the level of a controversial issue of public importance. . . . Although the issue has received media coverage in that the film itself was broadcast, you have not shown that government and community leaders have taken positions on the issue. Nor have you demonstrated that the issue has any particular impact on the community at large." The network's determination that the fairness doctrine did not apply was not unreasonable. Religion and Ethics Institute, Inc., 42 R.R.2d 1657 (Bd.Bur.1978).

7. *Defining the "Issue."* In American Security Council Educational Foundation v. Federal Communications Commission, 607 F.2d 438, 45 R.R.2d 1433, 5 Med.L.Rptr. 1193 (D.C.Cir.1979), ASCEF analyzed a full year's news programming of CBS. It transcribed all CBS news reports, broke them into sentences and then determined whether each was relevant to four topics: "United States military and foreign affairs; Soviet Union military and foreign affairs; China military and foreign affairs; and Vietnam affairs." Each relevant sentence was put into one of three categories: Viewpoint A was that the "threat to U.S. security is more serious than perceived by the government or that the United States ought to *increase* its national security efforts." Viewpoint B was that the government's perception is essentially correct, and viewpoint C was that the threat is less serious than perceived and national security efforts should be decreased. The ASCEF analysis put 3.54 percent of the content into viewpoint A; 34.63 percent into viewpoint B and 61.83 percent into viewpoint C. Based on these results and claimed similar disparities for later years, ASCEF filed a fairness complaint with the FCC asking that CBS be ordered to provide a reasonable opportunity for the expression of "A" viewpoints.

The FCC dismissed the complaint without calling for any response from CBS on the ground that the complaint did not identify "the particular issue of a controversial nature" that was involved. The court, 6–3, affirmed:

> We affirm the Commission's decision that ASCEF failed to base its complaint on a particular well-defined issue because (1) the indirect relationships among the issues aggregated by ASCEF under the umbrella of "national security" do not provide a basis for determining whether the public received a reasonable balance of conflicting views, and (2) a contrary result would unduly burden broadcasters without a countervailing benefit to the public's right to be informed.

Because the fairness doctrine is issue-oriented, it is essential that the "issue" be clearly identified. Here "national security" was an umbrella that held within it too many issues that were only tangentially related, such as detente with China, America's commitment to NATO, SALT and response to the Soviet Union's role in the Middle East.

The court suggested that a fairness complaint could be based on an issue that consists of separately identifiable subissues only if the main issue was well defined. If ASCEF had used single issues, it could have analyzed actual views "instead of superimposing artificial A, B, and C viewpoints on the broadcasts studied." Then the FCC could have determined the question of balance and, if necessary, framed a specific remedy.

Acceptance of ASCEF's approach would also burden broadcasters. "CBS could have had to review all of its news programming relevant to national security over at least a year's time. . . . It would have been virtually impossible to know which broadcasts should be included as relevant to national security, or how views discussed . . . should be tallied to measure 'balance' under the fairness doctrine."

Further burdens would fall on editors: "An editor preparing an evening newscast would be required to decide whether any of the day's newsworthy events is tied, even tangentially, to events covered in the past, and whether a report on today's lead story, in some remote way, balances yesterday's, last week's or last year's." *Certiorari* was denied, 444 U.S. 1013 (1980).

8. A potentially significant case involved a complaint that a network documentary about the failure of some private pension plans had been unfairly one-sided. The network responded that the program was about "some problems in some pension plans." The Commission concluded that the network had presented a one-sided program on the operation of the overall pension system and must provide balance. On appeal, the court, 2–1, reversed the Commission on the ground that the Commission was wrong in thinking that it was the proper body to decide the subject of the program. Instead, the court held that it was for the network to decide what the program was about and the Commission could reject the network's characterization only if it was found to be unreasonable. Because that was not the case here, the Commission's order could not stand.

The entire court voted to review the panel's decision *en banc*. But at that stage the Commission asked that the case be remanded to be dismissed. That occasioned another round of judicial opinions, but finally the case was remanded to the Commission and all decisions were vacated. All the action is reported in National Broadcasting Co., Inc. v. Federal Communications Commission, 516 F.2d 1101, 31 R.R.2d 551 (D.C.Cir.1974). An effort by the complainant, Accuracy in Media (AIM), to get the Supreme Court to reinstate the case failed when the Court denied AIM's petition for *certiorari*. 424 U.S. 910 (1976).

Although the "Pensions" case was mooted, subsequent cases have reiterated the court's finding that licensee discretion is central to fairness doctrine questions. The Commission is limited to judging the reasonableness of a licensee's determination. Thus, the Commission refused even to review a Broadcast Bureau ruling denying a fairness doctrine complaint in which the controversial issue of public importance was alleged to be whether or not the FBI was responsible for some of actress Jean Seberg's problems. The Bureau had accepted the licensee's assertion that the broadcasts did not concern a controversial issue of public importance. Accuracy in Media, Inc. v. CBS Television Network, 94 F.C.C.2d 501, 54 R.R.2d 518 (1983).

9. However, a San Francisco licensee's determination that programs advocating defeat of gay rights legislation elsewhere did not present a controversial question of public importance, was rejected by the Commission as unreasonable. The Commission stated that although the discussion was of "primary importance to the homosexual community . . ., the issue has had and continues to have a significant impact on the public at large." Council on Religion and the Homosexual, 68 F.C.C.2d 1500, 43 R.R.2d 1580 (1978).

The licensee had presented eight hours of programs (half original and half rebroadcasts) featuring Anita Bryant and others arguing against the proposed Dade County, Fla., ordinance barring discrimination on grounds of sexual preference. These programs were presented over a period of four months, with one and a half hours in prime time. The licensee presented a one-hour tape supporting gay rights, nine times over a period of four days, never in prime time. The complainants argued that this did not afford a reasonable opportunity for the presentation of opposing viewpoints. The Commission disagreed. It noted that the gay rights position had received more total time than the other side. Also, the licensee had advertised only the pro-gay talks in local newspapers.

When complainants objected to equating a single one-hour tape with more varied presentations on the other side, and four months on one side with four days on the other, the Commission noted that its role was "not to substitute our judgment for that of the licensee but merely to review that judgment for reasonableness." The Commission could not, and would not, "make the subjective determination of the relative impact of the pro or anti-gay rights programming presented on the station." The licensee's judgment could not be deemed unreasonable.

10. How helpful is the Commission's test for determining balance? Although it provides great flexibility, does it provide sufficient guidance? The absence of more specific guidelines has proved troubling for the Court of Appeals, District of Columbia Circuit, when it has been called upon to review Commission rulings on fairness complaints. For an extensive discussion of this problem, see Public Media Center v. Federal Communications Commission, 587 F.2d 1322, 44 R.R.2d 721, 4 Med.L.Rptr. 1634 (D.C.Cir.1978).

11. Occasionally entertainment programming may raise problems under the fairness doctrine. One typical example would be a story in which a character considers whether to seek an abortion. See Diocesan Union of Holy Name Societies, 41 F.C.C.2d 297, 28 R.R.2d 545 (1973) (involving a pro-abortion theme). Must contrasting views be presented? If so, must it be by other entertainment programming or will an interview program suffice? What about implicit presentations, such as a series featuring a happily married couple of different faiths? Must the licensee provide for contrasting views against interfaith marriages?

12. The owner of a station in the same county as WXUR, which was denied renewal in *Brandywine–Main Line,* p. 124, *supra,* wrote that his

station presented two guests on a call-in show on consecutive days. The first day, Dr. Carl McIntire, the principal figure behind WXUR, appeared. Every question called in was favorable to his position. The next day, the guest was an opponent, who believed strongly in the fairness doctrine and who attacked the operation of WXUR. He did not receive a single supportive call. The owner's point was that "liberal intellectuals" are most comfortable with each other and shy away from the less educated. When the "average liberal-intellectual" listens to radio he seeks out classical music or an all-news or educational station. "If he should tune in to a talk station and listen to some of the 'drivel' broadcast, he would become furious and switch to a station with which he is more at home." The conclusion was that if the liberal hopes to convert others to his viewpoint he must become a proselytizer, and call-in shows are an easy way to reach large numbers of voters. Tannen, Liberals and the Media, The Progressive, April, 1974 at 11. Is this report an accurate picture of "liberal" attitudes? If so, does that affect your view of the fairness doctrine?

13. *Commercials.* In the 1960s the Commission decided that advertisements for cigarettes required stations to present some programming on the dangers of smoking. This ruling was upheld in Banzhaf v. Federal Communications Commission, 405 F.2d 1082, 14 R.R.2d 2061, 1 Med.L.Rptr. 2037 (D.C.Cir.1968), certiorari denied 396 U.S. 842 (1969). Although the licensee could decide how to meet this requirement, most licensees presented material that had been prepared by the American Cancer Society and similar organizations. We trace the future of cigarette advertising in the next note.

The Commission attempted to treat the cigarette case as unique. Thus, when opponents of high-powered automobiles wanted the FCC to require licensees to present contrasting views on the value of such cars, the FCC refused. On appeal, the court of appeals could not distinguish the cigarette situation from the high-powered car situation and ordered the FCC to be consistent. Friends of the Earth v. Federal Communications Commission, 449 F.2d 1164, 22 R.R.2d 2145 (D.C.Cir.1971).

The Commission, in an omitted portion of its *1974 Fairness Report*, rethought the question of applying the fairness doctrine to commercials. It finally decided to divide commercials into those that simply try to sell products and those that present a "meaningful statement which obviously addresses, and advocates a point of view on, a controversial issue of public importance." The latter, also called "editorial" or "advocacy" advertisements, give rise to obligations under the fairness doctrine. If an advertisement is false or misleading, it might give rise to some action by the Federal Trade Commission or by competitors, but the fairness doctrine is not the appropriate way to handle commercials that do not address public issues.

This position was quickly challenged in the courts in a case involving a commercial for snowmobiles. Environmental groups complained that the commercials showed only one side of the controversial issue of the desirability of snowmobiles. The FCC rejected the complaint on the ground that, although the environmental effects of snowmobiles might involve a controversial issue of public importance, the commercials themselves were not devoted to an obvious or meaningful discussion of that issue.

The court of appeals affirmed. Public Interest Research Group v. Federal Communications Commission, 522 F.2d 1060, 34 R.R.2d 1375 (1st Cir.1975), certiorari denied 424 U.S. 965 (1976). The appellants argued that the FCC had no authority to retreat from its earlier rulings that selling commercials might invoke the fairness doctrine. The court disagreed. "In the absence of statutory or constitutional barriers, an agency may abandon earlier precedents and frame new policies." Congress had not frozen the fairness doctrine in any particular form. Nor was there any reason to require the FCC to apply the doctrine to all commercials or to none.

Finally, the appellants argued that the First Amendment itself required that the fairness doctrine be rigorously enforced so that the airwaves would be true public forums for the presentation of divergent views. The court rejected this argument. Although the *Red Lion* approach might be furthered by extending the fairness doctrine to all advertising, the court did "not view that question, in the short and long run, as so free from doubt that courts should impose an inflexible response as a matter of constitutional law. We believe that the first amendment permitted the Commission not only to experiment with full-scale application of the fairness doctrine to advertising but also to retreat from its experiment when it determined from experience that the extension was unworkable."

14. *Cigarettes.* After the *Banzhaf* decision, Congress moved into the picture. In 1969 it adopted 15 U.S.C.A. § 1335: "After January 1, 1971, it shall be unlawful to advertise cigarettes on any medium of electronic communication subject to the jurisdiction of the Federal Communications Commission."

The statute was challenged by broadcasters—but not by cigarette manufacturers. It was upheld by a three judge court in Capital Broadcasting Co. v. Mitchell, 333 F.Supp. 582 (D.D.C.1971), affirmed without opinion 415 U.S. 1000 (1972). The dissenting opinion in the lower court suggested that the cigarette manufacturers were not at all unhappy to be ordered to stop advertising on radio and television because it had become unprofitable.

The court rejected the argument that this amounted to censorship in violation of § 326 because licensees were still free to present pro-smoking messages—except to the extent that Congress had forbidden commercial messages. The Commission was leaving that decision to the licensees. Moreover, some aspects of anti-smoking messages might still be found to invoke the fairness doctrine—but health danger was not one of them. Also, it was permissible to consider at renewal time whether a licensee carried programs on the dangers of smoking—not because it was a controversial issue, but because one aspect of meeting the public interest is to warn about dangers to health and safety, even if they are obvious and non-controversial. What might the Commission do at renewal time if it found a licensee had presented several debates on cigarette smoking in which half the speakers argued that there was no health hazard in smoking? Is there a tension between saying that licensees are free to program pro-smoking material if they wish and that they will be judged at renewal time on how they have programmed on matters of health and safety?

2. Personal Attack Rules

As we saw in *Red Lion*, p. 71, *supra*, the personal attack part of the general fairness doctrine has been crystallized into a rule, 47 C.F.R.73.-123:

> (a) When, during the presentation of views on a controversial issue of public importance, an attack is made upon the honesty, character, integrity or like personal qualities of an identified person or group, the licensee shall, within a reasonable time and in no event later than 1 week after the attack, transmit to the person or group attacked (1) notification of the date, time and identification of the broadcast; (2) a script or tape (or an accurate summary if a script or tape is not available) of the attack; and (3) an offer of a reasonable opportunity to respond over the licensee's facilities.

> (b) The provisions of paragraph (a) of this section shall not be applicable (1) to attacks on foreign groups or foreign public figures; (2) to personal attacks which are made by legally qualified candidates, their authorized spokesmen, or those associated with them in the campaign, on other such candidates, their authorized spokesmen, or persons associated with the candidates in the campaign; and (3) to bona fide newscasts, bona fide news interviews, and on-the-spot coverage of a bona fide news event (including commentary or analysis contained in the foregoing programs, but the provisions of paragraph (a) of this section shall be applicable to editorials of the licensee).

The first point to note is that the episode must occur "during the presentation of views on a controversial issue of public importance." This limitation means that personal attacks unrelated to such a discussion do not invoke the rule—and presumably are left exclusively to defamation suits. Why is this distinction drawn?

Sometimes it is difficult to determine what constitutes "during the presentation of views on a controversial issue of public importance." In Straus Communications, Inc. v. Federal Communications Commission, 530 F.2d 1001, 35 R.R.2d 1649 (D.C.Cir.1976), a licensee's argument that time for reply was not justified because the attack did not take place during such a discussion was rejected by the Commission. On appeal, the court ruled that the Commission had used the wrong standard when stating that it "believed" that the comment was sufficiently related to an earlier discussion of a meat boycott to justify the conclusion that the personal attack occurred during a continuation of that discussion. The court concluded that the proper approach was for the Commission to judge "the objective reasonableness of the licensee's determination" that the meat boycott discussion had long since ended.

See also Polish American Congress v. Federal Communications Commission, 520 F.2d 1248, 34 R.R.2d 1359 (7th Cir.1975), certiorari denied 424 U.S. 927 (1976), in which the complainants had claimed that a skit of Polish jokes on television violated the personal attack part of the fairness doctrine. The Commission rejected the complaint. On appeal, the court stated that the order must be upheld "if the Commission properly determined that ABC's conclusion that the broadcast did not involve a controversial issue of public importance was not unreasonable or in bad faith." The court concluded that "the Commission was correct in ruling that ABC did not overstep its discretion in failing to find a controversial issue of public importance." This was true whether the issue was stated to be (1) whether "Polish Americans are inferior to other human beings in terms of intelligence, personal hygiene, etc." or (2) whether "promulgating" Polish jokes by broadcasting them is desirable. If the former, ABC could reasonably conclude that even if some people felt that way they had not generated enough support to raise a controversial issue of public importance. Even if they had, ABC could conclude that the skit presented did not constitute a "discussion" of this issue. If the issue was the latter, no controversy was shown.

Another issue raised in *Polish American Congress* (although it was not addressed due to the lack of a controversial issue of public importance) was the size of the group attacked. In defamation law, when a group is very large there is no identification (one of the requisite elements), and the individual plaintiff would have difficulty showing that his own personal reputation was harmed. Should the same analysis apply to the personal attack rule when the target is a large group rather than an individual or a small group? In Diocese of Rockville Centre, 50 F.C.C.2d 330, 32 R.R.2d 376 (1973), a licensee had broadcast a statement that perhaps an earlier writer was correct when he stated, "The Roman Church is filled with men who were led into it merely by ambition, who though they might have been useful and respectful as laymen, are hypocritical and immoral." The Commission ruled that the group is not sufficiently "identified" unless the licensee "could reasonably be expected to know exactly who or what finite group" is best able to inform the public of the contrasting viewpoint. The reference to "men" who fill the "Roman Church" was found too vague. Similarly, a personal attack claim was rejected where the complainant organization was one of several organizations discussed during a program. The program noted there were many differences among the groups and made no explicit allegations against complainant's church. The Commission concluded that the claimant had not met the burden of showing an attack on an identified person or group. Disciples of the Lord Jesus, 93 F.C.C.2d 7, 53 R.R.2d 319 (1983).

The Commission has also employed a narrow definition of what constitutes a personal attack. In *Straus,* the FCC decided that calling a Congressman a coward did not constitute a personal attack. Similarly, the rule was held inapplicable to remarks reflecting on a journalist's personal competence. Reverend Lester Kinsolving, 41 R.R.2d 573 (1977).

The Commission has made clear that attacks during discussions of controversial issues of public importance are not misbehavior, and wide-open debate is encouraged so long as the rules are followed.

3.　Fairness in Political Campaigns

The fairness doctrine enters into political issues in two ways. The first involves the use of broadcasting by the party in power, particularly the President, between political campaigns. The courts have taken the view that when the President speaks on an issue of national concern, the party out of power has no automatic right to reply. The only exception occurred when the President delivered five uninterrupted speeches during a seven-month period about the war in Indochina. Since broadcast coverage of that dispute had otherwise been roughly in balance, the FCC decided that the networks were obligated to provide free time for a spokesman from the other side of the issue.

But that instance aside, the courts have considered the speeches of a President just one factor to weigh in deciding whether the required rough balance in the presentation of contrasting views has been achieved. As usual, the FCC will generally defer to the views of the licensees, and the courts will generally defer to the views of the FCC. The subject is explored extensively in Democratic National Committee v. Federal Communications Commission, 481 F.2d 543 (D.C.Cir.1973) (unsuccessful attempt to obtain free reply time to counter President's speeches on economic policy). The official use of television and the response of the networks to official requests are discussed in N. Minow, J.B. Martin, and L.M. Mitchell, *Presidential Television* (1973).

The second role of the fairness doctrine in politics involves the campaign itself. Because § 315 was construed not to cover appearances by anyone other than candidates, and because the section also does not cover ballot propositions, many important political campaign broadcasts must be regulated under provisions much less precise than § 315. Not surprisingly, as television has become increasingly important in election campaigns, questions not covered by § 315 have arisen more frequently.

a. Uses by Supporters

Turning first to a close parallel situation, what are the controlling principles when Candidate A's friends or campaign committee purchase time to further his candidacy or to attack B, his opponent? In its Letter to Nicholas Zapple, 23 F.C.C.2d 707, 19 R.R.2d 421 (1970), the Commission stated that the 1959 amendment to § 315 had explicitly recognized the operation of the fairness doctrine when the candidate's own appearance was exempted from § 315. The doctrine was thought equally applicable here. Moreover, when a candidate is supported or his opponent attacked, although the licensee has the responsibility of identifying suitable speakers for opposing views, "barring unusual circumstances, it would not be reasonable for a licensee to refuse to sell time to spokesmen for or supporters of candidate B comparable to that previously bought on behalf of candidate A." But there was no obligation to provide B's supporters with free time. Although usually requiring that time be given away, if necessary, to get contrasting views before the public, the Commission thought this unsound in the political arena. To hold otherwise would require licensees, or other advertisers, to subsidize B's campaign. The rejection of subsidization meant that even if A's friends mounted a personal attack on B, B would not get free time. The Commission has adhered closely to the *Zapple* ruling, which is sometimes referred to as the "quasi equal opportunities" or "political party" corollary to the fairness doctrine.

In 1979 the Commission decided that Congress intended that "uses" under § 315 and *Zapple* were to be mutually exclusive of the fairness doctrine. The Commission concluded that licensees should not be responsible for "uses" since they have no control over them. As a result, the personal attack rule was rewritten to provide that it did not apply to personal attacks occurring during uses under § 315 or those occurring under *Zapple* situations.

More generally, the fairness doctrine was declared not to apply to issues raised during "uses." The Commission believed that issues raised during "uses" were likely to be of such public interest that other views would be aired in due course without the goad of the fairness doctrine. Personal Attacks and Applicability of the Fairness Doctrine to Section 315 "Uses," 78 F.C.C.2d 457, 45 R.R.2d 1635 (1979).

Recall that § 315 itself explicitly provides that the fairness doctrine applies to programs that are exempted from the equal opportunities provision of § 315.

A new problem emerged in 1980 involving groups organized by friends of Ronald Reagan but not controlled by the candidate. These groups are not bound by spending limits that may bind the candidates themselves. When these groups began to buy time on broadcast stations, the Carter campaign committee complained to the FCC that the stations selling time to these "independent expenditure groups" should be required to make equal, and free, opportunities available to the Carter campaign (and presumably to all other campaigns). These should be free, the Carter committee asserted, because it and the Reagan campaign were each limited to $29.4 million for campaigning because they agreed to accept federal funds. As a result, they could not match both the money Reagan was spending and that being spent by the independent groups.

The FCC rejected the claim on the ground that friends of Carter could start comparable groups to match the expenditures being made by the Reagan groups. To allow the Carter campaign free time would put the Commission in the position of benefitting one of the candidates at the expense of the other, whose friends had been required to pay for his time.

In an effort to apply the *Zapple* ruling outside campaign periods, CBS and others asked the FCC to declare that "when a licensee sells broadcast time for political advertisements by a political party, independent political committee or other supporters of a candidate, whether during or outside a campaign period, the *Cullman* doctrine does not apply and thus, the licensee has no obligation to provide free time to opposing groups." The FCC refused on the ground that Congress had shown that § 315 was to apply only during campaign periods and that *Zapple* was designed to supplement the statute only during the same periods. At other times, *Cullman* applied. CBS, Inc., 95 F.C.C.2d 1152 (1983). As a result, many licensees simply refuse to sell time for these political advertisements. Remember that Political Action Committees have no right of access under § 312(a)(7), *National Conservative Political Action Committee*, p. 258, *supra.*

In *Kennedy II*, p. 257, *supra*, after rejecting the candidate's claims under § 312 and § 315, the court turned to the role of the fairness doctrine in political campaigns. The Broadcast Bureau and the Commission had found three fatal flaws in Sen. Edward M. Kennedy's reliance on the fairness doctrine in this case—and the court agreed. First, he had failed to define the particular controversial issue involved with sufficient specificity. Second, there was no showing that the networks had failed to present contrasting viewpoints on the national economy in their overall programming. The fairness doctrine "does not operate with the dissective focus of" § 315(a). "Intelligent assessment of the nature and caliber of a broadcaster's overall programming obviously cannot be confined to one program, or even to one day's presentations, so a failure to show some fairness deficiency on the whole is necessarily fatal."

Even if imbalance were established, the third flaw was that Senator Kennedy had no "individual right to broadcast his views on the current economic crisis." Kennedy did not show that he was "uniquely and singularly qualified to represent those who dispute the President's economic leadership or strategies."

Finally, the fairness doctrine extends to political campaigns since the question of which candidate should be elected may be considered a "controversial issue of public importance." This means that even if no requests for time are made under § 315 or § 312, a broadcaster might be required to introduce the issue under the first part of the fairness doctrine. If some views are expressed about the forthcoming campaign during non-uses, the licensee would be obligated under the second part of the doctrine to provide coverage of contrasting views. In determining what views should get how much time, the licensee must make good faith judgments about the importance of the race and the significance of each candidate.

The Commission's dismissal of a fairness complaint alleging unbalanced coverage of economic matters was upheld in DNC v. Federal Communications Commission, 717 F.2d 1471, 54 R.R.2d 941 (D.C.Cir. 1983). Disparities approximating three to one and four to one in favor of the pro-Administration economic view occurred on the networks. Compliance with fairness doctrine obligations was to be measured by a standard of good faith and reasonableness, not by reference to "rough approximations of equality." Since the disparities were not "glaring," and the audiences were not shown to be very different in size, the Commission's dismissal of the complaint was reasonable. Although the court cited data showing that fairness complainants prevail in roughly 1 in 1,000 cases, the court rejected Commission statements that fairness complaints will inevitably be futile.

b.　Political Editorials

In a section of the personal attack rules, 47 C.F.R. § 73.123(c), the Commission covered political editorials:

> Where a licensee, in an editorial (i) endorses or (ii) opposes a legally qualified candidate or candidates, the licensee shall, within 24 hours after the editorial, transmit to respectively (i) the other qualified candidate or candidates for the same office or (ii) the candidate opposed in the editorial (1) notification of the date and the time of the editorial; (2) a script or tape of the editorial; and (3) an offer of a reasonable opportunity for a candidate or a spokesman of the candidate to respond over the licensee's facilities: *Provided, however,* That where such editorials are broadcast within 72 hours prior to the day of the election, the licensee shall comply with the provisions of this paragraph sufficiently far in advance of the broadcast to enable the candidate or candidates to have a reasonable opportunity to prepare a response and to present it in a timely fashion.

Be sure to note that a single editorial on behalf of one candidate creates an opportunity to respond for *each* opposing candidate. This is true regardless of the number of opposing candidates. Friends of Howard Miller, 72 F.C.C.2d 508, 45 R.R.2d 1142 (1979).

c. Ballot Propositions

In an omitted part of the *1974 Fairness Report*, the Commission reached the conclusion that such matters as referenda, initiative and recall propositions, bond proposals, and constitutional amendments were to be regulated under the fairness doctrine. The area was thought closer to general political discussion not involving elections than it was to the election of individuals to office. Thus, the *Cullman* doctrine requiring the licensee to present contrasting views, by the use of free time if necessary, was applicable. One argument against the *Cullman* doctrine was that some groups might spend their available money on non-broadcast media, wait for the other side to buy broadcast time, and then insist on free time under *Cullman* to counter their adversary. The Commission was not persuaded. First, this concern can always be raised against *Cullman*, but the Commission thought it most important that the public have access to contrasting views. On the tactical level, the Commission noted that the fairness doctrine does not guarantee equality of exposure of views nor who will be chosen as speakers. Those who rely solely on *Cullman* "have no assurance of obtaining equality by such means." Fairness Report, 48 F.C.C.2d 1, 33, 30 R.R.2d 1261, 1302 (1974).

4. THE ELIMINATION OF THE FAIRNESS DOCTRINE

As noted earlier, in 1987 the Commission eliminated the fairness doctrine. We now turn to the sequence of events that led to that decision, beginning with the *1985 Fairness Report*. Inquiry into Section 73.1910 of the Commission's Rules and Regulations Concerning the General Fairness Obligations of Broadcast Licensees, 102 F.C.C.2d 143, 58 R.R.2d 1137 (1985). In the report the Commission concluded that the doctrine was no longer justified. Although it did not question "the interest of the listening and viewing public in obtaining access to diverse and antagonistic sources of information," the FCC thought that the doctrine was neither a "necessary or appropriate means by which to effectuate this interest." The interest in "viewpoint diversity is fully served by the multiplicity of voices in the marketplace today." Moreover, "the intrusion by government into the content of programming occasioned by the enforcement of the doctrine unnecessarily restricts the journalistic freedom of broadcasters" and actually inhibits the presentation of controversial issues of public importance to the detriment of the public and in degradation of the editorial prerogatives of broadcast journalists."

On the scarcity point, the FCC asserted that since *Red Lion* there had been a 48 percent increase in radio outlets and a 44 percent increase in television outlets. By 1984, 96 percent of television households received five or more signals. During that period the networks' share of the market had declined from 90 percent to 76 percent, and the number of independent television stations had risen from 90 to 214.

Other electronic distribution systems, such as cable and multichannel multipoint distribution systems, had exploded. Finally, the FCC pointed to the continued availability of more than 1,700 daily newspapers and the increase in the number of periodicals from 6,960 in 1950 to 10,688 in 1982. The Commission concluded that "the dynamics of the information services marketplace overall insures that the public will be sufficiently exposed to controversial issues of public importance."

On the inhibition point, the Commission stressed that the fairness doctrine reduced the number of diverse views and the amount of controversial programming reaching the public. The reasoning began with the fact that enforcement of the first prong of the doctrine was virtually nonexistent. But the responsive programming requirement of the second prong came into play whenever a licensee undertook to present controversial programming even if beyond what was required under the first prong. The result was that broadcasters were being encouraged "to air only the minimal amount of controversial issue programming sufficient to comply with the first prong. By restricting the amount and type of controversial programming aired, a broadcaster minimizes the potentially substantial burdens associated with the second prong of the doctrine."

Broadcasters were burdened by being found in violation of the second prong because of the risks of being ordered to present programs without compensation or of having to defend against the charges and incurring legal expenses. The Commission cited the Spokane station that spent $20,000 in legal fees in successfully defending a fairness charge and NBC's expense of more than $100,000 in the "Pensions" case. The more remote risk of nonrenewal was an additional burden listed by the Commission.

The answer was not to enforce the first prong more rigorously because that "would increase the government's intrusion into the editorial decisionmaking process of broadcast journalists. It would enlarge the opportunity for governmental officials to abuse the doctrine for partisan political purposes."

The FCC also noted that it was inextricably involved in the "dangerous task of evaluating the merits of particular viewpoints" as it tried to distinguish statements that are "significant enough to warrant broadcast coverage" and those that "do not rise to the level of a major viewpoint of sufficient public importance that triggers responsive programming obligations."

If a responsive obligation was imposed, the Commission then had to consider the content offered by the licensee to show that it had met its obligation. In addition, the Commission noted how much of its staff time was needed to deal with inquiries and complaints related to the doctrine—6,787 hours in 1984. Finally, the Commission cited examples in which the fairness doctrine was misused by White House administrations intent upon gaining political advantage.

All of these costs were said to be unnecessary because of the recent increase in available information sources. To the argument that the doctrine was useful to provide broadcasters with a protection against outside pressures, the Commission responded that broadcasters were not asking for such protection and that print journalists did not need such protection.

Despite all the negative points made in the report, the Commission did not eliminate the doctrine. Instead, because of the "intense Congressional interest in the Fairness Doctrine" and uncertainty as to whether the doctrine was codified in § 315 of the Communications Act, the FCC deferred action until Congress had an opportunity to review the report—and announced that it would continue to enforce the doctrine.

However, during the 1980s a fairness complaint against Meredith Corporation's WTVH in Syracuse, N.Y., was working its way through the Commission and the court of appeals. Initially, the Commission found the station had violated the fairness doctrine. The court of appeals reversed and remanded. The Commission then decided that the doctrine was unconstitutional and that it disserved the public interest. The Commission's decision was appealed by the public interest group that had brought the original fairness complaint.

SYRACUSE PEACE COUNCIL v. FEDERAL COMMUNICATIONS COMMISSION

United States Court of Appeals, District of Columbia Circuit, 1989.
867 F.2d 654, 16 Med.L.Rptr. 1225.

Before Wald, Chief Judge, and Starr and Williams, Circuit Judges.

Williams, Circuit Judge.

Under the "fairness doctrine," the Federal Communications Commission has, as its 1985 Fairness Report explains, required broadcast media licensees (1) "to provide coverage of vitally important controversial issues of interest in the community served by the licensees," and (2) "to provide a reasonable opportunity for the presentation of contrasting viewpoints on such issues." [ ] In adjudication of a complaint against Meredith Corporation, licensee of station WTVH in Syracuse, New York, the Commission concluded that the doctrine did not serve the public interest and was unconstitutional. Accordingly it refused to enforce the doctrine against Meredith. Although the Commission somewhat entangled its public interest and constitutional findings, we find that the Commission's public interest determination was an independent basis for its decision and was supported by the record. We uphold that determination without reaching the constitutional issue.

I.

In the summer of 1982 Meredith ran a series of advertisements over WTVH arguing that the Nine Mile II nuclear power plant was a "sound investment for New York." Syracuse Peace Council complained to the Commission that Meredith had failed to give viewers conflicting perspectives on the plant and had thereby violated the second of the fairness doctrine's two requirements.

In its initial decision the Commission agreed with Syracuse that Meredith had failed to fulfill its obligations under the doctrine and demanded that the station within 20 days give notice of how it planned to meet those obligations. [ ]

Meredith filed a petition for reconsideration in which it argued that the fairness doctrine was unconstitutional. [ ] Before ruling on Meredith's petition, the Commission completed its 1985 Fairness Report, the culmination of a separate inquiry into both the wisdom and constitutionality of the fairness doctrine. [ ]

On the issue of whether the doctrine continued to promote the public interest, the 1985 Report said that the Commission was "firmly convinced that the fairness doctrine, as a matter of policy, disserves the public interest . . ." [ ] In reaching that conclusion the Commission invoked essentially the same grounds as it has in the present action—chiefly, that growth in the number of broadcast outlets reduced any need for the doctrine, that the doctrine often worked to dissuade broadcasters from presenting *any* treatment of controversial viewpoints, that it put the government in the doubtful position of evaluating program content, and that it created an opportunity for incumbents to abuse it for partisan purposes. Despite all this, it declined to eliminate the doctrine, expressing concern that it might be statutorily mandated. [ ]

The 1985 Report also raised serious doubts about the continuing constitutionality of the fairness doctrine, but, saying that it was "the province of the federal judiciary—and not this Commission—to interpret the Constitution," [ ], the Commission refused to make a constitutional ruling.

After issuing the 1985 Report, the FCC in due course considered Meredith's petition for reconsideration. In that context it again refused to address the constitutional issue—not on the ground that Meredith had raised the defense belatedly but solely on the theory that that issue should be left to Congress and the courts. It invoked its 1985 Report in support of this view. [ ]

On appeal, this court reversed and remanded the case to the Commission. [ ] We noted the principle that regulatory agencies cannot invalidate an act of Congress, [ ], but said that an agency could not blind itself to a constitutional defense to a "self-generated" policy. [ ] In the meantime, we observed, this court had in another decision found that the fairness doctrine was *not* mandated by statute. [*TRAC*] Thus on remand the Commission would have to resolve Meredith's constitutional defense, *unless* it determined in light of the 1985 Report that enforcement of the doctrine was contrary to the public interest. [ ] We explicitly noted that the 1985 Report had concluded that indeed the doctrine no longer served the public interest standard of the Communications Act, [ ], and that in the Report the Commission had "largely undermined the legitimacy of its own rule" and "eviscerate[d] the rationale" for the doctrine.

On remand, the Commission expanded the scope of the Meredith proceedings by soliciting comments from the public on the general questions whether "in light of the 1985 Fairness Report, enforcement of the fairness doctrine is constitutional and whether enforcement of the doctrine is contrary to the public interest." [ ] In its Memorandum Order and Opinion, [ ], the Commission ruled in favor of Meredith.

The FCC relied heavily on the conclusions drawn in the 1985 Fairness Report, and in fact incorporated that Report into the record and "reaffirm[ed] [its] findings and conclusions." [ ] After reciting and endorsing the 1985 Fairness Report's conclusions, the Commission declared that "the fairness doctrine chills speech and is not narrowly tailored to achieve a substantial government interest." [ ] Consequently, the FCC concluded "under existing Supreme Court precedent, as set forth in *Red Lion* and its progeny, that the fairness doctrine contravenes the First Amendment and thereby disserves the public interest." [ ]

II.

At no time during the long and intricate proceedings in this case has any party suggested that the fairness doctrine is constitutionally compelled. Nor can it be claimed here, in view of this court's TRAC decision, that the doctrine is statutorily mandated. Accordingly, the Commission has the authority to reject the doctrine if it concludes, without being arbitrary or capricious, that it no longer serves the public interest.

The Commission has slightly complicated the issue, however, by asserting that "the policy and constitutional considerations in this matter are inextricably intertwined." [ ] If that were true, we could resolve the case only by addressing the constitutional issue.

But it is an elementary canon that American courts are not to "pass upon a constitutional question . . . if there is also present some other ground upon which the case may be disposed of." See Ashwander v. Tennessee Valley Authority, 297 U.S. 288, 345–48 (1936) (Brandeis, J., concurring). . . .

Thus, if we are persuaded that the Commission would have found that the fairness doctrine did not serve the public interest even if it had forgone its ruminations on the constitutional issue, we must end our inquiry without reaching that issue. In fact, as we explain in part III, we have no doubt that even in the absence of constitutional problems the Commission would have reached the same outcome. We then turn in part IV to petitioners' objections to the Commission's policy decision, and in part V to issues relating to the Commission's withdrawal of the doctrine's "first prong," the requirement of coverage of controversial issues.

III.

It is quite true that the Commission at the outset of its opinion here asserted that the constitutional and policy issues were "inextricably intertwined," [   ], and at the end suggested that its policy conclusion was a mere consequence of its constitutional one, [   ] ("the fairness doctrine contravenes the First Amendment and *thereby* disserves the public interest") (emphasis added). Those who would have us grasp the constitutional nettle call our attention to these references. [   ]

But the Commission's reasoning behind its "intertwining" assertion belies any inference that its policy judgment *depends* upon its constitutional view. . . .

. . .

Happily the Commission's opinion is not written in exclusively constitutional terms. . . .

. . . The Commission's incorporation of the [1985] Report's reasoning here confirms our conclusion that the Commission would have made the same public interest finding if it had approached the issue free of "intertwining."

IV.

The FCC's decision that the fairness doctrine no longer serves the public interest is a policy judgment. There is no real dispute that fostering fair, balanced and diverse coverage of controversial issues is a good thing. Nor, so far as we can tell from the record or briefs, is there any question that discouraging any coverage at all, having government officials second-guess editorial judgments, or allowing incumbents an opportunity for abuse of power are things to be avoided, all other things being equal. The Commission's problem was to make predictive and normative judgments about the tendency of the fairness doctrine to produce each of these things, about how bad the bad effects were and how good the good ones, and ultimately about whether bad effects outweighed good.

In this situation, we owe great deference to the Commission's judgment. . . .

The Commission's factual judgments here are almost entirely predictive—statements about the overall effects of a policy on licensees and others. The Supreme Court has observed that "[I]n such cases complete factual support for the Commission's ultimate conclusions is not required since 'a forecast of the direction in which the future public interest lies necessarily involves deductions based on the expert knowledge of the agency.'" FCC v. WNCN Listeners Guild, [   ]. . . .

Of course, an agency can act arbitrarily or capriciously in the exercise of a policy judgment, and we must assure ourselves that that did not happen here. . . .

Before addressing those specific attacks, we must describe two core findings of the 1985 Report—that the fairness doctrine often operated to chill broadcaster speech on controversial issues and that recent increases in broadcasting outlets undercut the need for the doctrine— on which the Commission relied heavily in the present decision. It found that the doctrine produced chilling effects by placing burdens on stations which chose to air numerous programs on controversial issues—including the fear of denial of license renewal due to fairness doctrine violations, the cost of defending fairness doctrine attacks and of providing free air time to opposing views if a fairness violation is found, and the reputational harm resulting from even a frivolous fairness challenge. While the FCC recognized that to a degree the first prong of the fairness doctrine offset this effect by requiring broadcasters to present some controversial issues, it nonetheless found that broadcasters were encouraged[:]

> to air only the minimal amount of controversial issue programming sufficient to comply with the first prong. By restricting the amount and type of controversial programming aired, a broadcaster minimizes the potentially substantial burdens associated with the second prong of the doctrine while remaining in compliance with the strict letter of its regulatory obligations. Therefore, despite the first prong obligation, in net effect the fairness doctrine often discourages the presentation of controversial issue programming.

102 F.C.C.2d at 161.

The 1985 Fairness Report also noted that paradoxically the chilling effect often fell on the expression of unorthodox or "fringe" views on controversial issues. [ ] Since the doctrine compelled coverage only of "major" or "significant" opinions, the FCC claimed that in assessing fairness doctrine compliance, the Commission was called upon to evaluate broadcasters' decisions concerning the importance of given viewpoints. The Report expressed its fear that the fairness doctrine thus had the potential "to interject the government, even unintentionally, into the position of favoring one type of opinion over another." [ ]

In assessing whether any need for the doctrine persisted, the 1985 Report found a dramatic increase in broadcasting outlets since the 1974 Fairness Report, [ ]. This expansion in broadcasting capacity was found to have been spread widely across American society. The FCC found that by 1984 96% of television households received five or more over-the-air (non-cable) television signals, compared with 83% in 1972. [ ] Those receiving nine or more signals had tripled, from 21% of TV households in 1972 to 64% in 1984. [ ] Of course some signals may for one reason or another be unable to function as serious alternative sources. But the new signals are plainly not trivial in the aggregate, as they have driven the networks' audience share down from 90% in [1969] to 76% in 1984. [   ]

The Commission also found significant growth in radio outlets since the 1974 Fairness Report. The number of radio stations grew by 30% between 1974 and 1985. The subset of FM service increased during the same period by 60%, leading the FCC to proclaim that "there has also been a fundamental change in the structure of the radio market. Once predominantly an AM only service, radio is now composed of two very competitive services." [   ] The Commission noted that radio expansion impacted smaller communities as well as larger urban areas; "the number of radio voices available in each local market has grown." [   ]

Looking at substitute electronic media such as low power television, video cassette recorders, satellite master antenna systems, and so forth, the Commission found that the gains in radio and television accessibility and diversity actually understated the true development of broadcast media available to the viewing public. [   ] The Report also noted that print media coverage of controversial issues offered Americans exposure to the type of information which the fairness doctrine was designed to foster.

We now turn to the specific objections to the Commission's conclusions.

INSUFFICIENCY OF EVIDENCE TO SUPPORT FCC POSITION

Although there is some criticism of the 1985 Report's findings as to the growth of access to media signals, that commentary focuses largely on the point that some of the figures used by the Commission may exaggerate the significance of the alternative sources. But the Commission has included the figures on changes in audience shares, clearly reflecting its recognition that not all sources are equal. Some parties also assert that the FCC was overly concerned with aggregate or national figures at the expense of local data. Yet in looking at the Commission's finding concerning the number of households which receive five or more non-cable television signals—a whopping 96%—it seems to us that only a diminutive share of the population has been unaffected by the growth the Commission has recounted. Accordingly, we view these attacks as peripheral.

Several parties, however, have attacked the evidence of broadcaster chill and what they contend is the Commission's failure to respond adequately to the attacks. . . .

. . . It appears that numerically the main body of evidence comes from the comments submitted to the Commission by the National Association of Broadcasters ("NAB"), which presented 45 broadcaster accounts of the effects of the fairness doctrine on their industry and policies. It is clear, however, that the FCC also relied on important additional sources, including submissions by some *proponents* of the fairness doctrine. For example, it pointed to evidence from Public Media Center that after it had warned broadcasters that it would demand free response time from stations that accepted advertising on a specific controversy, more than two-thirds of those contacted had refused to sell advertising on the subject at all. [ ]

The 1985 Report responded substantially to the . . . attacks made on the NAB study. . . . We are persuaded that the self-interested character of the broadcasters' evidence did not bar the Commission from giving it substantial weight.

. . .

Third, the Commission made specific rebuttals of some . . . criticisms of NAB examples. . . . For example, one of the criticisms, twice invoked, was that the particular broadcaster need not have been deterred, since in the view of the critics the station's ordinary news coverage would have satisfied its obligations under the doctrine. In rebuttal, the Commission found the critic's observations highly speculative. [ ] Surely the FCC is right. The fairness doctrine applies to ordinary mortals who adjust their affairs on the basis of estimates of risk. The estimating process costs time and effort. It hardly disproves an alleged deterrent effect to suggest that by more careful research or analysis, or by greater brilliance, the deterred party might have come out the other way. This is typical of this line of critiques, and to avoid repetition we pass on to the remaining attacks.

. . .

Finally, [the United Church of Christ] attacks any reliance on the NAB study on the ground that it was "not based on a statistically valid sample of broadcasters' experiences, but rather, was merely a series of anecdotal accounts." [ ] The comment is quite valid, but in the absence of either any statistically valid evidence on the other side, or even a suggestion of how the Commission could have constructed a statistically valid study, we are perplexed as to what the Commission was supposed to have done. Editorial decisions are obviously driven by many factors. Isolation of causes in any scientific way seems virtually impossible. The fairness doctrine has been applicable in one form or another from 1949 until the present decision, so the Commission could not compare stations' practices under the rule with their conduct free of the rule. (Comparison to practice in other nations would encounter the usual cross-cultural difficulties.)

We note that when speaking of a state-enforced "right-of-reply" applicable to newspapers, the Supreme Court has taken it as self-evident that such a duty "*inescapably* 'dampens the vigor and limits the variety of public debate.' " Miami–Herald Publishing Co. v. Tornillo, [ ] (emphasis added). [ ] Of course we recognize that the fairness doctrine differs from the right-of-reply at issue in *Tornillo* and that *Red Lion* applies different constitutional standards to the broadcast media. But we think the Court's approach suggests that where a rule imposes potentially onerous and at least irksome consequences on the exercise of speech, there is nothing very startling about an inference that the rule will often deter speech. We think the Commission could properly find that effect from the evidence before it here.

FAILURE TO CONSIDER EVIDENCE OF DOCTRINE'S BENEFICENT EFFECTS

UCC also charges that the Commission ignored or discounted evidence of the benefits derived from the fairness doctrine. [ ] We think part of the problem here arises out of UCC's apparent assumption that the Commission believed that the fairness doctrine rarely (or never) increased diversity of expression. Indeed, the Commission only purported to find that "the overall NET effect of the doctrine is to reduce the coverage of controversial issues of public importance," [ ], a finding clearly consistent with a belief that the doctrine frequently produced its intended effects. We do not read the Commission's focus on the negative aspects as manifesting a blindness to unwelcome evidence but rather as a focus on what it viewed as novel or surprising. To say that a rule has often produced its intended effects is to tell a dog-bites-man story—not front-page stuff. The Commission was naturally more struck by evidence of unintended consequences—hardly in the man-bites-dog class, but closer.

.   .   .

We must confess, however, some perplexity at the Commission's insistence that the doctrine's overall "net effect [was] to reduce the coverage of controversial issues." [The court noted that *Red Lion* had said that if such a situation occurred "there will be time enough to reconsider the constitutional implications."] The Court then proceeded to declare, "[T]he fairness doctrine in the past has had no such overall effect." [ ] The Court did not explicate the basis for that finding.

We are frankly uncertain how anyone could be sure either way. The definitional problems alone are staggering. How could a court or agency persuasively define standards by which to evaluate the "quality" of coverage? Once it had done so, by what yardstick could it balance quality increments due to broadcasters' responding as intended against quality decrements due to the deterrent effects? The Commission does not explain. Nor do the challengers, who evidently are happy to weigh these unweighables but read the scales differently.

Despite this confusion, we believe we can "discern the path" followed by the Commission. [ ] It found itself confronted with evidence that it read as establishing that the doctrine has very substantial deterrent effects (and, as we have said, we believe that finding was permissible). It also quite plainly made the normative judgment that government decisions on program content and government forced expressions of ideas, together with the associated risks of partisan abuse, were anathema.   .   .   .   It was persuaded that the doctrine's deterrent effects were on the same scale as its expression-generating ones, and it plainly discounted the *value* of the latter as "governmentally-coerced speech." [ ] Accordingly, it rejected the doctrine as a matter of policy. That policy judgment seems to us by no means arbitrary or capricious. . . .

FAILURE TO CONSIDER ALTERNATIVES

Petitioners Geller and Lampert contest the FCC's refusal to adopt their proposed alternative to the elimination of the fairness doctrine. The two have repeatedly urged the Commission to review fairness matters only at license renewal, and to adopt a malice standard for this review.

The FCC has twice declined to return to its pre–1962 practice of resolving fairness doctrine complaints at renewal, first in its 1974 Fairness Report, [ ], affirmed by this court [ ], and then in its 1987 Alternatives Report, [ ]. The 1987 Report found . . . several specific defects . . . in the renewal review plan. First, by linking fairness evaluations with the renewal process, broadcasters would view the potential sanctions as being more threatening than those currently in effect, as loss of license or suspension would be seen as more likely. [ ] Second, the renewal plan deprives the broadcaster of a contemporaneous ruling on its behavior and chance to quickly rectify any imbalance in its programming. The FCC believed this could make broadcasters more conservative in coverage of controversial issues. [ ] Finally, it would only delay rather than diminish the government's meddling in the editorial process. [ ]

Geller and Lampert coupled their renewal-only suggestion with the idea that review would proceed under a "malice" standard such as that of New York Times Co. v. Sullivan, [ ], and with an alternative suggestion that the Commission continue to act case-by-case but under a malice standard. As to the first, the Commission agreed that such a standard would reduce the chilling effect, but judged that reduction inadequate to offset what it believed would be the increased chill from postponement to renewal. [ ] As to the second, the Commission in its reconsideration order in the present case expressed doubt whether a malice standard would substantially reduce the chilling effect when compared with the Commission's practice of deferring to broadcasters' reasonable judgments, [ ], and said that the difference in impact on licensees would be a matter of degree rather than of kind, [ ]. Although its discussion of the subject is more than usually framed in constitutional terms, we read it as concluding that the proposals only mildly mitigated the ill effects that drove the Commission to reject the fairness doctrine as previously enforced. That judgment seems well within its discretion, especially as the proposals would also appear to materially diminish the positive effects of the doctrine.

DEPARTURE FROM 1985 DECISION

Some parties complain that the present decision represents an unexplained abandonment of the Commission's 1985 decision to persist in enforcement of the doctrine. . . .

The 1985 Fairness Report had found that the doctrine disserved the public interest, but had refrained from dropping the doctrine on policy grounds only because of concern that perhaps it was statutorily mandated, [ ], and because of the intense congressional interest then brewing over the fairness doctrine, [ ]. This court's TRAC decision removed the first obstacle (except insofar as the Supreme Court might find otherwise); a successful presidential veto of Congress's attempt to mandate the fairness doctrine clearly diminished the second. Though we find no explicit reference to these reasons in the decision under review, they appear so obvious and compelling that a remand to extract the magic words from the Commission would be pure waste. [ ]

V.

Several parties attack the Commission's repeal of the so-called "first prong" of the fairness doctrine—the requirement that broadcasters provide coverage of important controversial issues of interest to the community they serve. First, they contend that they were not adequately notified of the Commission's intent to reconsider the first prong in this proceeding. Second, petitioners argue that the FCC's abandonment of the first prong was arbitrary and capricious.

NOTICE

[The court held the notice adequate.]

WHETHER RESCISSION OF THE FIRST PRONG WAS ARBITRARY AND CAPRICIOUS

[The court held inadequate the Commission's suggestion that the doctrine was a unified whole—so that if one part fell so did the other. The Commission had not explained why the parts were not severable.]

In other portions of its decision, however, the Commission went on to supply reasons for terminating the first prong. . . .

First, removal of the fairness doctrine's second requirement would reduce the need for the coverage requirement. With the chilling effects of the second requirement ended, the Commission expected that "coverage of controversial issues will be forthcoming naturally, without the need for continued enforcement of the first prong." . . .

Second, it viewed the coverage requirement as in significant part duplicative of its independent requirement that broadcasters cover issues "of importance" to their communities. [ ] While the FCC acknowledged on reconsideration that the two programming requirements were not identical, it saw sufficient similarity to believe that the community issues rule would fill any material regulatory gap. [ ]

Third, in its discussion of the fairness doctrine as a whole the Commission relied heavily on its view that government involvement in the editorial process was offensive. [ ] That judgment of course applies to the editorial decisions required for enforcement of the first prong, and the Commission made the point expressly: "[T]he doctrine requires the government to second-guess broadcasters' judgment on such sensitive and subjective matters as the 'controversiality' and 'public importance' of a particular issue. . . ." [ ] It also alluded to the offensive character of government first-prong decisions in distinguishing that part of the doctrine from the community issues requirement. . . .

While enforcement of the doctrine's first prong requires the government to judge, on a case-by-case basis, whether a specific issue is both controversial and of vital importance to mandate coverage by the broadcaster, enforcement of the issue responsive obligation requires a different level of government intervention in determining, at renewal time, whether broadcasters' *overall* programming covered the needs and interests of its community.

[ ] (emphasis in original). [ ]

We believe that these reasons, particularly in light of the Commission's background findings on the increased diversity of outlets and programming, adequately support its removal of the first prong.

CONCLUSION

We conclude that the FCC's decision that the fairness doctrine no longer served the public interest was neither arbitrary, capricious nor an abuse of discretion, and are convinced that it would have acted on that finding to terminate the doctrine even in the absence of its belief that the doctrine was no longer constitutional. Accordingly we uphold the Commission without reaching the constitutional issues. The petition for review is denied.

WALD, CHIEF JUDGE, concurring in part and dissenting in part.

I concur in Parts I–IV of Judge Williams' opinion, which uphold the FCC's decision to abrogate the second prong of the fairness doctrine as an exercise of its statutory authority to regulate in the public interest. I dissent, however, from Part V, which sustains the Commission's decision to eliminate the fairness doctrine's first prong. . . . I believe that this aspect of the Commission's decision is not supported by the record and was not adopted in compliance with the Administrative Procedure Act.

First, the agency failed to provide interested parties with notice, as required by the Administrative Procedure Act, that it proposed to eliminate the first as well as the second prong of the doctrine. . . .

. . .

But even if the Commission had provided adequate notice of its intentions, I do not believe that its decision could be sustained as reasoned decisionmaking. . . .

. . .

Neither can the Commission's action be justified by reference to the overlap between first prong obligations and the duty to cover issues of importance to the community. While a substantial overlap does exist, the requirements are by no means duplicative. The community issues requirement obliges broadcasters to devote reasonable air time to the coverage of issues important to the local community. The first prong of the fairness doctrine focuses on the broadcaster's obligation to cover *controversial* issues. It seems entirely foreseeable that some broadcasters might provide abundant coverage of community issues generally but might—perhaps from fear of incurring the displeasure of the public or of advertisers—steer clear of issues of a controversial nature. . . .

[Chief Judge Wald rejected the argument that the first prong could be repealed solely because it might no longer be a necessary spur for most broadcasters. There was no claim that it would be "counterproductive."]

Moreover, I do not believe that the FCC's obligation to identify the costs of an unwanted regulation could be satisfied by a bare showing that the rule would impinge on broadcasters' editorial freedom. I believe it is still the law that, in the regulation of electronic media, "[i]t is the right of the viewers and listeners, not the right of the broadcasters, which is paramount." [*Red Lion*] . . .

. . . [T]he Commission has made no effort whatsoever to explain how continued enforcement of the doctrine's first prong could induce broadcasters to alter their programming decisions in ways which would ultimately disserve the public interest.

. . . In eliminating prong one along with prong two of the fairness doctrine, the FCC appears to have been motivated primarily by a morbid fear that it might be accused of doing things halfway. This is deregulation running riot.

STARR, CIRCUIT JUDGE, concurring.

. . .

. . . With all respect to the court's view enunciated today, I am convinced that the record in this case simply will not, fairly read, yield the conclusion that the agency has based the specific decision before us independently on non-constitutional grounds. There is, therefore, no proper basis for skirting the Commission's constitutional analysis (unless we were to conclude, as I do not, that the Commission erred in even considering that issue); in short, the constitutional justifications for the Commission's action must, alas, be considered.

. . .

. . . There is no escaping this hard, cold fact: in the wake of the generously worded *Meredith* remand, the Commission has rendered a *Red Lion* decision. It has switched gears from three years ago and gone beyond the less heroic, public-interest reach of the 1985 Report.

. . .

. . . *Meredith* has unleashed *Red Lion*, and it will not do to pretend, with cheery *bravado*, that *Red Lion* is still secure in its pre-*Meredith* cage. *Red Lion* is now out on the streets, released by a deliberate and careful FCC decision.

For its part, the court airily treats this as just another case coming out of yet another agency here in town charged with making yet another broad public interest determination. This will not do. . . .

. . .

. . . Where, as here, the agency's policy judgment is wholly driven by its constitutional reasoning and conclusions, the reviewing court is obliged to analyse the case in those terms. . . .

. . . Indeed, the Supreme Court has expressly invited the FCC to examine whether the constitutional underpinnings of the doctrine remain viable. FCC v. League of Women Voters, 468 U.S. 364, 377 n.11 (1984). In view of the fairness doctrine's unique, constitutionally-charged history, it is hardly unreasonable for the FCC to view the public interest through First Amendment lenses.

. . .

In sum, as the FCC's decision is adequate in all respects and singularly unlikely to be altered on remand, I think the court is obliged to examine the FCC's decision—grounded in the Constitution—as it comes to us. It is to that issue, avoided by my colleagues, but pressed exclusively by all parties before this court, that I must now turn.

II

A

The question before us—that is, the legality of the FCC's action—is somewhat of a hybrid, exhibiting both constitutional and administrative law characteristics. As I see it, judicial review of the FCC's Order is most correctly viewed as involving two distinct tasks. First, the court is called upon to scrutinize the Commission's interpretation of the constitutional principles enunciated in *Red Lion* and its progeny. This task involves measuring the FCC's articulation of constitutional principles, as distinguished from its application of those principles to the facts. Our scope of review in this particular is plenary. [ ] Second, we are called upon to review the Commission's factual determinations. . . .

The parties have assumed that the Commission's findings of fact are subject to review under the "arbitrary and capricious" standard laid down in the APA, 5 U.S.C. section 706 (1985); [ ]. However, where, as here, factual determinations are intimately connected with the evaluation of constitutionality under the First Amendment, the Supreme Court has held (outside the agency context) that those findings should be reviewed independently. Bose Corp. v. Consumers Union of U.S., Inc., [ ] (and cases cited therein). On reflection, I believe that in this instance the parties' assumption is well-founded; the administrative law model of review indeed applies notwithstanding the presence of important First Amendment questions. Although the FCC's factual findings are closely intermingled with its ultimate conclusion as to the constitutionality *vel non* of the fairness doctrine, independent review by the judiciary seems inappropriate for several reasons.

First, the FCC's Order does not deny a constitutional claim. No one has urged that the fairness doctrine is constitutionally compelled. Rather, the FCC has determined, pursuant to its obligation to uphold the Constitution, that the First Amendment requires elimination of the fairness doctrine. That point is of pivotal importance because the decisional law of the Supreme Court indicates that independent appellate review of facts is appropriate only where the decision under review *denies* a constitutional claim. [ ]

This conclusion flows from the principle that independent review, where applicable, derives from the Constitution itself. Bose v. Consumers Union, 466 U.S. at 510 ("The requirement of independent review . . . is a rule of federal constitutional law"). Thus, where no constitutional rights are threatened by the findings at issue, the reason undergirding the unusual tack of independent appellate review of facts does not exist. . . .

Independent review of the Commission's findings also seems inappropriate because we have before us the predictive judgments of a federal agency concerning the (perceived) effects of its own policy. The Supreme Court has recognized that the FCC is possessed of substantial expertise with respect to the impact of the fairness doctrine on the communications marketplace. [ ] Indeed, the Court has accorded weight to factual findings underlying an FCC decision that broadcast regulation was inconsistent with the First Amendment. [CBS v. DNC] The present case is thus readily distinguishable from instances in which the Supreme Court has independently reviewed the case-specific findings of juries or trial judges. See e.g., Miller v. California, 413 U.S. 15 (1973) (independent review of jury determination that a specific publication or film is "patently offensive" and appeals to the "prurient interest"). . . . In view of the FCC's obvious expertise, we would be unwise (and unfaithful to the APA) to disregard the Commission's ultimate conclusions of fact with respect to the fairness doctrine's chilling effect; its interference with broadcasters' editorial discretion; and the explosive growth of media outlets.

Under these principles, the Commission's Order should be upheld. It is based on reasonable factual findings and embodies a correct statement of applicable constitutional principles. . . .

. . . To reiterate: I would hold only that the FCC's decision to eliminate the fairness doctrine correctly interprets *Red Lion* and is based, as the court's opinion effectively demonstrates, on an adequate factual record. Such a decision would therefore not automatically foreclose a future FCC (or Congress) from reestablishing the fairness doctrine in its present (or some modified) form. The fate of any future attempt to resurrect (or refashion) the fairness doctrine would depend, obviously, on the Supreme Court's articulation of applicable constitutional doctrine (e.g., *Red Lion*); but it would also be affected by the scope of review applied to the facts upon which the "new" fairness doctrine was sought to be justified. Of course, as we have just seen, the line of cases culminating in *Bose Corp.* indicates that factual findings underlying the *denial* of a First Amendment challenge would be subject to independent review. Although this situation is, again, not before us today, it bears mentioning that this additional burden imposed on proponents of allegedly unconstitutional government action (i.e., a "new" or "resurrected" fairness doctrine) represents the inevitable result of our system of constitutional supremacy.

I should hasten to add that this burden, while substantial, appears to be by no means hopelessly insurmountable. To the contrary, under the *Red Lion* framework (assuming, as I do, continued High Court allegiance to its teachings), the constitutionality of the fairness doctrine is linked in part to technological developments (and behavior) in the communications marketplace. Those developments obviously continue to unfold, with impacts that can only foggily be predicted. What is more, we have precious little experience in a *sans*-fairness doctrine regulatory environment. It remains to be seen whether the necessarily predictive judgments embodied in the Order will withstand the hard, true test of time. [   ]

In short, it is not at all inconceivable that detailed reconsideration by a future FCC or carefully considered Congressional findings, [   ], could persuade a future court that, notwithstanding the FCC's contrary findings vindicated by today's decision, some *in futuro* version of the fairness doctrine could be implemented consistent with First Amendment strictures.

C

As to the constitutional principles applicable to this case, the parties are congenially in accord (1) that *Red Lion* principles govern; and (2) that, under the *Red Lion* framework, government restrictions on broadcasters' speech are valid only if "narrowly tailored to further a substantial government interest, such as ensuring adequate and balanced coverage of public issues." Order at 5049 (quoting FCC v. League of Women Voters, 468 U.S. at 380). It is also by now well recognized that this standard affords broadcasters somewhat less First Amendment protection than that enjoyed by their print media counterparts. [   ]

But there consensus abruptly stops. Although the parties agree that *Red Lion* is king, they strenuously disagree over the proper interpretation of that seminal decision. For its part, the FCC argues that the constitutional question turns on whether enforcement of the fairness doctrine

(1) chills speech and results in the net reduction of the presentation of controversial issues of public importance and

(2) excessively infringes on the editorial discretion of broadcast journalists and involves unnecessary government intervention to the extent that it is no longer narrowly tailored to meet its objective.

[   ] The FCC believes that regulatory intervention through the vehicle of the fairness doctrine is not "narrowly tailored" if the number (and distribution) of media outlets ensures public access to diverse viewpoints. [   ] That is, if access to diverse viewpoints can be achieved without the fairness doctrine, then the doctrine is not "narrowly tailored" because it unnecessarily interferes with editorial decisions. Finally, the FCC interprets *Red Lion* to render the fairness doctrine unconstitutional if either of these tests (net reduction or not "narrowly tailored") is satisfied. [   ]

Petitioners' most vigorous attack is aimed at the proposition that the numerosity of media outlets and intrusive impact of the fairness doctrine may, without more, render the fairness doctrine unconstitutional. Petitioners contend that the relevant concern is the number of media outlets relative to the demand of broadcasters (expressed through license applications) for such outlets. More pertinently, petitioners direct our attention to the unique characteristic of broadcast regulation, namely the potential for interference occasioned by the fact that the broadcasters spectrum can physically accommodate only a finite number of users. The potential for signal interference among competing broadcasters, it is argued, necessitates an allocation system whereby regulatory authority assures to broadcasters exclusive use of their portions of the spectrum. As this system by its nature excludes some who wish to broadcast, the readmission of excluded speakers via the fairness doctrine is constitutionally permissible, petitioners maintain, as an adjunct to the licensing system.

To recap: as petitioners see it, the fairness doctrine is constitutionally permissible so long as *allocational scarcity* exists, namely, that demand for broadcast frequencies exceeds supply. [   ] The FCC, in contrast, asserts that the constitutionality of the doctrine depends on *numerical scarcity* in the sense that, without government intervention, the public is not provided with access to diverse viewpoints.

There is thus a rather pivotal difference in the perspectives vying for judicial approbation. As I see it, the FCC's position is much better founded; indeed, in my view, petitioners have fallen badly into error by misreading *Red Lion*. There is, to be sure, language in *Red Lion* with respect to the scarcity of the broadcast spectrum and the consequent tendency toward unrequited demand for frequencies. [   ] Under *Red Lion*, however, that sort of scarcity seems to constitute a necessary (rather than sufficient) condition of the fairness doctrine's legitimacy. That is, allocational scarcity accounts for the fundamental difference in First Amendment treatment of print and broadcast media. [   ] However, spectrum scarcity, without more, does not necessarily justify regulatory schemes which intrude into First Amendment territory. This point is made clear by the familiar cases in which the Court has upheld broadcast regulation on the ground that the regulation *furthered* substantial First Amendment interests, see *Red Lion,* [ ]; Columbia Broadcasting Co. v. FCC, 453 U.S. 367, 396 (1981); and by [CBS v. DNC], where the Court held that the FCC need not require licensees to accept all paid political advertisements because such a requirement unduly impinged upon broadcasters' rights and produced little public benefit. In short, petitioners conflate the Supreme Court's choice of a standard for evaluating broadcast regulation with the Court's application of its chosen standard to the interests assertedly advanced by a particular regulatory regime.

Petitioners' reliance on the concept of allocational scarcity is logically flawed as well. As part of their attack on numerical scarcity, petitioners contend that "[t]he *Red Lion* Court did not speak in terms of satisfaction, or hypothesize a point at which 'enough' diversity is present. . . . Only when supply and demand [for licenses] reach equipoise does the governmental interest change." [ ] The argument is an intriguing one; but I think, with all respect, that it focuses with undue exclusivity on the market for broadcast licenses, whereas the central concern of *Red Lion* is that the fairness doctrine "preserve an uninhibited marketplace of ideas". [ ] Indeed, a reading of *Red Lion* yields no evidence that the mere presence of excluded *broadcasters* is to be regarded as dispositive of the *public's* need for programming of a particular type. Especially since individual members of the listening or viewing public, such as disappointed broadcast license applicants, may express their viewpoints on controversial issues in any number of ways that do not involve applying for and receiving a broadcasting license, it seems odd (and inaccurate) to equate scarcity in licenses with scarcity in the marketplace of ideas. Indeed, petitioners' argument ultimately flies in the teeth of *Red Lion*'s admonition that "it is the right of viewers and listeners and not that of broadcasters, which is paramount." [ ]

In contrast, the FCC has correctly discerned that, under *Red Lion,* the constitutionality of the fairness doctrine is closely related to the incapacity of the communications marketplace to give expression to diverse voices. . . .

The governing constitutional doctrine therefore recognizes that the communications marketplace may be sufficiently responsive to the public's need for controversial issue programming so that government regulation is unnecessary. Cf. *Red Lion,* 395 U.S. at 397 (fairness doctrine constitutional in light of the fact that the increased carrying capacity of the broadcast spectrum has been devoted largely to uses unrelated to debate on controversial issues). As a corollary of that principle, the FCC also recognized that, where the communications marketplace itself provides a plethora of voices, the fairness doctrine is not only superfluous, it is positively harmful. This is of singular importance in the analysis. As the Court has stated time and again, regulatory schemes that tread unnecessarily on the editorial discretion of broadcasters contravene the First Amendment. [ ] Columbia Broadcasting System, Inc. v. FCC, 453 U.S. at 395. ("[T]he broadcasting industry is entitled under the First Amendment to exercise 'the widest journalistic freedom consistent with its public [duties].' ") quoting [CBS v. DNC].

The Commission is also correct in interpreting the Supreme Court's holdings as rendering the fairness doctrine constitutionally problematic where the "net effect" of the doctrine is a reduction in coverage of controversial public issues. . . . Obviously, as the fairness doctrine exists to *promote speech* on controversial issues, it seems manifest that the doctrine should not readily enjoy constitutional approbation if it ceases to promote and secure bedrock constitutional interests.

D

As the court's opinion ably demonstrates, the Commission's factual determinations (1) that the growth of broadcast outlets ensures the public's access to viewpoint diversity, and (2) that the fairness doctrine ultimately operates to reduce coverage of controversial issues, find reasonable support in the record. Rather than rehearse the salient points of the record in detail, it suffices for present purposes to highlight several points.

Significantly, petitioners do not dispute that, since the late '60s when *Red Lion* was handed down, the number of media sources has expanded dramatically. The number of full power TV stations has increased 54 percent, [ ], with the result that nearly 96 percent of U.S. households with television received 5 or more signals. Nearly two thirds of U.S. households received 9 or more signals. [ ] Similarly, the number of radio stations has increased 57 percent since the first year of the Nixon Administration, when *Red Lion* was first introduced to the world of constitutional law. [ ] As of 1987, listeners had access to an average of 6 radio stations in the smallest markets and a whopping 25 stations in the largest markets. [ ] As commuters and Walkman aficionados know, all news-all talk stations (or some variation thereof) abound in large markets.

The Commission also took account of the growth of various non-broadcast media, the most important of which is cable television. More than half of the nation's TV households currently subscribe to cable. [ ] The number is growing. . . . And, the proliferation of choice ushered in by cable is staggering. Over 94 percent of cable subscribers receive more than 12 channels; some cable systems have the capacity to offer more than 100 channels. [ ]

Petitioners are, nonetheless, unconvinced by all this. . . . They emphasize that the growth in media outlets has not reached many local markets. [ ] But, as Judge Williams' opinion for the court persuasively indicates, the data offered by petitioners in this respect fall short of drawing into question the impressive statistics marshalled by the FCC. No more need be said in these already overlong pages on that score.

Petitioners also contend that the increase in media sources has not resulted in significant increases in controversial issue programming. They point in particular to FM radio and UHF TV as examples of media sources that have grown rapidly without contributing significantly to viewpoint diversity. The FCC responds that petitioners offer little to back up their opinion-laden allegations. [ ] But, even assuming that UHF TV and FM radio programs are not particularly intensive in their coverage of controversial issues, I am satisfied that the FCC did not put all of its eggs in one part of the large communications-market basket. Rather, as we just saw, the Order points to growth in broadcast media and non-broadcast technologies such as cable and satellite television. [ ] The Commission has also indicated that these technologies are contributing to viewpoint diversity. For example, one well-known cable channel . . . is devoted solely to news; two cable channels are given over to coverage of Congress and related issues. [ ] We are told that the media stand ready and able to enter (and in some instances are entering) the courthouses of this blessed land, if the least dangerous branch decides to opt in favor of glasnost in its own house. In short, inasmuch as the Commission has relied on credible evidence concerning the growth and programming in many types of media, I cannot, in conscience, condemn as arbitrary and capricious its ultimate finding that the communications market as a whole provides "reasonable assurance" of public access to viewpoint diversity.

As to the FCC's finding that the fairness doctrine so chilled speech as to result in a net reduction in the coverage of controversial issues, the court quite correctly notes that, where government regulation imposes substantial (and, to a certain extent, unpredictable) consequences on speech, drawing an inference of some chilling effect hardly represents an heroic step in our First Amendment tradition. [ ] Of greater difficulty is the FCC's finding of a net reduction in controversial issue programming. Petitioners' main argument in this particular is that the Commission gave undue weight to testimony of chilling effect and insufficient weight to evidence that the doctrine stimulated speech.

. . .

. . . In view of the attention given by the Supreme Court to the net reduction issue, FCC v. League of Women Voters, 468 U.S. at 379 n. 12 (a finding that the fairness doctrine has the net effect of reducing speech would require reconsideration of *Red Lion*), and the principle that the interests of broadcasters, while important, are ultimately secondary to those of the viewing and listening public, our review should focus on the evidence adduced by the Commission in favor of its conclusion of a net reduction.

In this respect, my reading of the Order suggests that the Commission, based on its regulatory experience and testimony before the agency concerning chilling effects, reasonably determined that the fairness doctrine's predominant effect on speech was inhibitory. [ ] Specifically, the Commission found that the fairness doctrine chilled individual program decisions *and* induced broadcasters to adopt categorical policies against carrying editorials, political advertisements or nationally-produced public affairs programs. [ ] The Commission further noted that, by virtue of the fairness doctrine, many broadcasters were encouraged not to air controversial issue programming above that minimal amount required by the first part of the doctrine. [ ] The Commission was also entitled to take into account the fact that the doctrine, by requiring coverage only of "major" contrasting viewpoints, fell with particular severity on broadcasters who express unorthodox views, thus tending to deprive the public of "uninhibited, robust and wide-open" debate. [ ] Finally, the Commission pointed to the fact that "no broadcaster indicated to us that its station's coverage of controversial issues has increased as a result of the fairness doctrine." [ ]

These findings, taken together, reasonably support the Commission's ultimate conclusion that elimination of the fairness doctrine would unleash a substantial amount of controversial issue programming. . . .

E

A final criticism directed at the Order concerns the Commission's decision to eliminate the first part of the fairness doctrine. . . .

[Judge Starr rejected the FCC's severability analysis.] More plausible is the Commission's contention that, as the first part of the fairness doctrine is "largely duplicative" of the requirement that broadcasters cover issues responsive to the needs of their community, retention of Part One would produce "no added public benefit". [ ] This point is rather unilluminating, however, in light of the Commission's emphasis elsewhere on the distinctions between Part One of the fairness doctrine and the requirement of community issue programming. [ ] Indeed, petitioners point out that the FCC loosened the issue-responsive obligation in part because of a distinct obligation imposed under Part One. [ ] In light of the admitted difference between the two regulatory standards, I am of the view that the Commission's "largely duplicative" rationale is inadequate.

Despite these deficiencies, I nonetheless agree that the Commission reasonably eliminated Part One in light of the FCC's findings that the explosive growth in media outlets, combined with the removal of the deterrent to controversial public issue programming imposed by Part Two of the doctrine, will adequately ensure availability of such programs. [ ] The reasonableness of the Commission's decision to eliminate Part One is reinforced by the (inevitably) predictive quality of the FCC's reasoning. It is in this sense that I agree with Judge Williams that the Commission is entitled to conclude that elimination of Part One would not create an impermissible regulatory gap. . . .

Notes and Questions

1. The reference to the presidential veto is to an episode occurring when Congress passed the Fairness in Broadcasting Act of 1987 (S. 742). The Act read as follows:

> To clarify the congressional intent concerning, and to codify, certain requirements of the Communications Act of 1934 that ensure that broadcasters afford reasonable opportunity for the discussion of conflicting views on issues of public importance.
>
> *Be it enacted by the Senate and House of Representatives of the United States of America in Congress assembled,* That this Act may be cited as the "Fairness in Broadcasting Act of 1987".

SEC. 2 FINDINGS.

> The Congress finds that—
>
> (1) despite technological advances, the electromagnetic spectrum remains a scarce and valuable public resource;
>
> (2) there are still substantially more people who want to broadcast than there are frequencies to allocate;
>
> (3) a broadcast license confers the right to use a valuable public resource and a broadcaster is therefore required to utilize that resource as a trustee for the American people;
>
> (4) there is a substantial governmental interest in conditioning the award or renewal of a broadcast license on the requirement that the licensee ensure the widest possible dissemination of information from diverse and antagonistic sources by presenting a reasonable opportunity for the discussion of conflicting views on issues of public importance;
>
> (5) while new video and audio services have been proposed and introduced, many have not succeeded, and even those that are operating reach a far smaller audience than broadcast stations;
>
> (6) even when and where new video and audio services are available, they do not provide meaningful alternatives to broadcast stations for the dissemination of news and public affairs;
>
> (7) for more than thirty years, the Fairness Doctrine and its corollaries, as developed by the Federal Communications Commission on the basis of the provisions of the Communications Act of 1934, have enhanced free speech by securing the paramount right of the broadcast audience to robust debate on issues of public importance; and
>
> (8) the Fairness Doctrine (A) fairly reflects the statutory obligations of broadcasters under that Act to operate in the public interest, (B) was given statutory approval by the Congress in making certain amendments to that Act in 1959, and (C) strikes a reasonable balance among the First Amendment rights of the

public, broadcast licensees, and speakers other than owners of broadcast facilities.

SEC. 3 AMENDMENT TO THE COMMUNICATIONS ACT OF 1934.

(a) Section 315 of the Communications Act of 1934 (47 U.S.C.A. § 315) is amended—

(1) by redesignating subsections (a) through (d) as subsections (b) through (e), respectively; and

(2) by inserting before subsection (b) the following new subsection:

"(a)(1) A broadcast licensee shall afford reasonable opportunity for the discussion of conflicting views on issues of public importance.

"(2) The enforcement and application of the requirement imposed by this subsection shall be consistent with the rules and policies of the Commission in effect on January 1, 1987."

SEC. 4 EFFECTIVE DATE.

This Act and the amendment to the Communications Act of 1934 added by this Act shall take effect upon the date of enactment.

President Reagan vetoed the bill and issued the following statement explaining his veto:

I am returning herewith without my approval S. 742, the "Fairness in Broadcasting Act of 1987," which would codify the so-called "fairness doctrine." This doctrine, which has evolved through the decisional process of the Federal Communications Commission (FCC), requires Federal Officials to supervise the editorial practices of broadcasters in an effort to ensure that they provide coverage of controversial issues and a reasonable opportunity for the airing of contrasting viewpoints on those issues. This type of content-based regulation by the Federal Government is, in my judgment, antagonistic to the freedom of expression guaranteed by the First Amendment.

In any other medium besides broadcasting, such Federal policing of the editorial judgment of journalists would be unthinkable. The framers of the First Amendment, confident that public debate would be freer and healthier without the kind of interference represented by the "fairness doctrine," chose to forbid such regulations in the clearest terms: "Congress shall make no law . . . abridging the freedom of speech, or the press." More recently, the United States Supreme Court, in striking down a right-of-access statute that applied to newspapers, spoke of the statute's intrusion into the function of the editorial process and concluded that "[i]t has yet to be demonstrated how governmental regulation of this crucial process can be exercised consistent with First Amendment guarantees of a free press as they have evolved to this time." [*Tornillo*, p. 83, *supra*].

I recognize that 18 years ago the Supreme Court indicated that the "fairness doctrine" as then applied to a far less technologically advanced broadcast industry did not contravene the First Amendment. [*Red Lion*, p. 71, *supra*]. The Red Lion decision was based on the theory that usable broadcast frequencies were then so inherently scarce that government regulation of broadcasters was inevitable and the FCC's "fairness doctrine" seemed to be a reasonable means of promoting diverse and vigorous debate of controversial issues.

The Supreme Court indicated in Red Lion a willingness to reconsider the appropriateness of the "fairness doctrine" if it reduced rather than enhanced broadcast coverage. In a later case, the Court acknowledged the changes in the technological and economic environment in which broadcasters operate. It may now be fairly concluded that the growth in the number of available media outlets does indeed outweigh whatever justifications may have seemed to exist at the period during which the doctrine was developed. The FCC itself has concluded that the doctrine is an unnecessary and detrimental regulatory mechanism. After a massive study of the effects of its own rule, the FCC found in 1985 that the recent explosion in the number of new information sources such as cable television has clearly made the "fairness doctrine" unnecessary. Furthermore, the FCC found that the doctrine in fact inhibits broadcasters from presenting controversial issues of public importance, and thus defeats its own purpose.

Quite apart from these technological advances, we must not ignore the obvious intent of the First Amendment, which is to promote vigorous public debate and a diversity of viewpoints in the public forum as a whole, not in any particular medium, let alone in any particular journalistic outlet. History has shown that the dangers of an overly timid or biased press cannot be averted through bureaucratic regulation, but only through the freedom and competition that the First Amendment sought to guarantee.

S. 742 simply cannot be reconciled with the freedom of speech and the press secured by our Constitution. It is, in my judgment, unconstitutional. Well-intentioned as S. 742 may be, it would be inconsistent with the First Amendment and with the American tradition of independent journalism. Accordingly, I am compelled to disapprove this measure.

Was President Reagan's veto justified? There was no attempt to override because proponents of the bill were convinced that they did not have enough votes in the Senate for an override. As of late 1992 Congress had not passed a new fairness bill. This was due, at least in part, to a threatened veto by President Bush. However, the election of

President Clinton increases the likelihood that either Congress or the FCC will reinstitute the fairness doctrine.

2.   Under the majority's view, how might a new fairness doctrine come into being? Under Judge Starr's view, what would it take to bring a new fairness doctrine into being?

3.   On the constitutional side, what does Judge Starr's discussion of "scarcity" add to the discussion in *Red Lion*?

4.   After the decision in *TRAC* and the oral argument in *Meredith*, Congress had attached a requirement in the 1986 Appropriations Act that "funds appropriated to the Federal Communications Commission by this Act shall be used to consider alternative means of administration and enforcement of the Fairness Doctrine and report to the Congress by Sept. 30, 1987." Pursuant to that directive, the Commission issued an NOI. Alternatives to the General Fairness Doctrine Obligations of Broadcast Licensees, 2 F.C.C.Rcd. 1532 (1987).

The Commission issued its report on the same day it announced its decision in *Syracuse Peace Council*. Although some alternatives were considered preferable to the existing enforcement of the fairness doctrine, the Commission concluded that "the best alternative to the Doctrine and the one that best serves the First Amendment principles underlying the Doctrine, and consequently, our public interest objectives, would be an unregulated marketplace of ideas." Fairness Alternatives Report, 2 F.C.C.Rcd. 5272, 63 R.R.2d 488 (1987). A Petition for Reconsideration was denied. Fairness Doctrine Alternatives (Reconsideration), 3 F.C.C.Rcd. 2050, 64 R.R.2d 1069 (1988).

5.   If a statute similar to S. 742 should be enacted, how should a court treat its findings in a case challenging its constitutionality? Do the Congressional "findings" make the FCC's "findings" irrelevant?

6.   In a 1987 letter to Rep. John Dingell (D.–Mich.), then-FCC Chairman Dennis Patrick indicated that *Syracuse Peace Council* was limited to the facts of that case. Thus, technically, the Commission had not yet made a decision concerning enforcement of the personal attack and political editorial rules, the *Zapple* doctrine, or the application of the fairness doctrine to political campaigns and ballot issues.

However, in Arkansas AFL–CIO, 70 R.R.2d 369 (1992), the Commission concluded that *Syracuse Peace Council* does govern ballot issues and thus, licensees have no obligation to provide any specified amount of coverage to ballot issues. The decision was affirmed on appeal, 2–1. Arkansas AFL–CIO v. FCC, 980 F.2d 1197 (8th Cir.1993). However, the court of appeals has granted a rehearing *en banc*. Broadcasting, Mar. 23, 1983.

C. NEWS DISTORTION

There is no policy on distortion in the fairness doctrine, nor has Congress enacted specific legislation to address it. The distortion policy descends from the broadcaster's duty to "protect the public interest." The FCC's policy on distorting the news did not emerge until Hunger in America, 20 F.C.C.2d 143, 17 R.R.2d 674 (1969). The developments since then are traced in the following case.

GALLOWAY v. FEDERAL COMMUNICATIONS COMMISSION

United States Court of Appeals, District of Columbia Circuit, 1985.
778 F.2d 16, 59 R.R.2d 587, 12 Med.L.Rptr. 1443.

Before WRIGHT, MIKVA and FRIEDMAN, CIRCUIT JUDGES.

WRIGHT, CIRCUIT JUDGE.

Petitioner Carl Galloway, who was mentioned during a CBS News broadcast about insurance fraud, complained to the Federal Communications Commission that the broadcast had violated both the Commission's Personal Attack rule and its policy against deliberate news distortion. Petitioner asked the Commission to revoke the licenses of intervenor CBS's owned-and-operated stations. The Commission denied Galloway's request and he appeals to this court, challenging both the policies and their application. Because petitioner has failed to make the necessary showings on either his personal attack or deliberate distortion complaint, we affirm the Commission's ruling.

1. Background

On December 9, 1979, the CBS News program *60 Minutes* broadcast a story entitled "It's No Accident," about an allegedly widespread fraudulent insurance scheme. According to the program, doctors, lawyers and "victims" would conspire to submit reports of accidents that had never occurred (or were greatly exaggerated) and submit bills for medical treatment that had never been rendered. The program said that such schemes cost insurers more than $1 billion a year, that much of the cost was passed on to honest policyholders in the form of higher premiums, and that the insurance companies were not as vigorous as they might be in investigating fraudulent claims "because it's cheaper to settle than to investigate." [ ]

In the course of preparing the broadcast CBS sent an insurance investigator to a clinic suspected of participating in the fraudulent schemes. "[She] was instructed to tell the clinic that one month earlier she had been in a minor accident, had not been hurt, but needed back-dated full medical bills as the basis for an insurance claim." [ ] She received a bill listing 19 visits that never occurred for treatment that was never administered. In describing that bill CBS Correspondent Dan Rather said, "It was signed by Carl A. Galloway, M.D." [ ]

Although the clinic figured prominently in the broadcast, no other mention was made of Galloway.

Galloway sued CBS for libel in the state courts of California, claiming that his name had been forged on the fraudulent bill. Galloway lost at trial on a general jury verdict that is currently the subject of a separate appeal in the California courts. During discovery for the libel suit Galloway received a great deal of information, including film or tape that was shot for the broadcast but never aired ("outtakes"). This material formed the basis of his complaint to the FCC.

Galloway's FCC complaint alleged two separate violations by CBS. First, he said he had been the victim of a personal attack and had been denied an opportunity to reply. Second, he said that CBS "violated Commission policy by deliberately distorting, slanting, falsifying and staging" the broadcast at issue. We will consider these two issues separately.

. . .

III. The Deliberate Distortion Complaint
A. *The FCC Policy*

The FCC's policy on rigging, staging, or distorting the news was developed in a series of cases beginning in 1969.[2] In the first of these, Hunger In America, CBS had shown an infant it said was suffering from malnutrition, but who was actually suffering from another ailment. The Commission found that

> [r]igging or slanting the news is a most heinous act against the public interest—indeed, there is no act more harmful to the public's ability to handle its affairs. In all cases where we may appropriately do so, we shall act to protect the public interest in this important aspect. But in this democracy, no government agency can authenticate the news, or should try to do so.

Hunger In America, 20 F.C.C.2d 143, 151 (1969). As in all the subsequent cases, the FCC made a crucial distinction between deliberate distortion and mere inaccuracy or difference of opinion.

The Commission realized that news events can be "staged" by the participants as well as by reporters. The behavior of the subjects of news reports is often affected by the presence of television cameras, and in a real sense every news conference is a staged event. In the years since 1969 "media events" from protest demonstrations to "photo opportunities" have become more sophisticated and more pervasive. The technological imperatives of TV news may also require a certain

---

2. See Hunger In America, 20 F.C.C.2d 143 (1969); WBBM–TV, 18 F.C.C.2d 124 (1969) (allegations that college pot party was staged for camera crew); Democratic National Convention Television Coverage, 16 F.C.C.2d 650 (1969) (concerning aspects of coverage of demonstrations outside the 1968 convention in Chicago); Hon. Harley O. Staggers, 25 Rad.Reg.2d (P & F) 413 (1972) (policy statement in response to a congressional subcommittee investigating the staging of news events).

amount of stage managing, shooting "reverses."[3] These were not the kinds of practices that concerned the Commission. "The Commission viewed its proper area of concern to be with those activities which are not a matter of journalistic judgment or a grey area, but rather constitute the deliberate portrayal of a 'significant "event" which did not in fact occur but rather is "acted out" at the behest of news personnel.' " Hon. Harley O. Staggers, 25 Rad.Reg.2d (P & F) 413, 414 (1972).

The key elements of this standard are, first, that the distortion or staging be deliberately intended to slant or mislead. It is not enough to dispute the accuracy of a news report, [ ], or to question the legitimate editorial decisions of the broadcaster, [ ]. The allegation of deliberate distortion must be supported by "extrinsic evidence," that is, evidence other than the broadcast itself, such as written or oral instructions from station management, outtakes, or evidence of bribery. [ ]

Second, the distortion must involve a significant event and not merely a minor or incidental aspect of the news report. The Commission has refused to investigate "inaccurate embellishments concerning peripheral aspects" of news reports or "attempts at window dressing which concerned the *manner* of presenting the news" as long as "the essential facts of the news stories to which these presentational devices related were broadcast in an accurate manner." [ ] "[T]he real criterion with respect to staging is whether the public is deceived about a matter of significance." [ ] In one of its early descriptions of news staging and distortion, the Commission said:

> For example, the licensee's newsmen should not, upon arriving late at a riot, ask one of the rioters to throw another brick through a store window for its cameras. First, if the window is already broken, it is staging a news event—one which did not in fact occur, but is acted out at the request of the news personnel; the licensee could fairly present such a film only with the full disclosure of its nature.

WBBM–TV, 18 F.C.C.2d 124, 132–133 (1969). More recently, however, the Commission tolerates such practices unless they "affect[ ] the basic accuracy of the events reported." WPIX, Inc., [68 FCC2d at 386]; see also Oscar B. White, 87 FCC2d 954, 959–960 (1981). As with the Personal Attack Rule, the Commission's practice in this respect has given its policy against news distortion an extremely limited scope. But within the constraints of the Constitution, Congress and the Commission may set the scope of broadcast regulation; it is not the role of this court to question the wisdom of their policy choices.

3. "Because documentary interviews are normally filmed by a single camera, the film crew typically will train the camera on the individual being interviewed during a question and answer series, and then run through a second 'take', known as a 'reverse', with the camera focused on the interviewer in order to get film footage of his questioning". [ ]

B. *The Specific Allegations of Distortion*

1. *The Johnson interview.* The *60 Minutes* broadcast included tape CBS purportedly made when "we observed [insurance investigator Milton Crawford] interrogating insurance claimant Montanette Johnson." At first Johnson is seen telling Crawford that she was involved in an accident. Then Rather says, "Crawford suspects Johnson is lying. * * * After some hard questioning, Johnson changed her story." Johnson then admits that she had filed a fraudulent claim, "[b]ecause somebody told me that if I did it that I would get paid a certain amount of money." [ ]

Crawford actually "interrogated" Johnson at least twice in succession for CBS cameras, and both times she at first professed the legitimacy of her claim and later (without being confronted with contradictory evidence or the like, but simply being asked again, "Now was it true that you were involved in an accident?" and "Were you really involved in an accident on that date?") she confessed her participation in the fraud. [ ] Interviews of another woman, not broadcast, followed a similar pattern. [ ] Galloway alleges that this "clearly shows that what CBS maintained were spontaneous interrogations were, in reality, staged interviews performed for the benefit of and at the behest of CBS news personnel. * * * They were simply giving CBS another 'take' for the 'docudrama' CBS had previously scripted." [ ]

The Commission disposed of this allegation in a footnote, in which it described this matter as an exercise of "editorial judgment," lacking sufficient evidence of deliberate distortion. [ ] We think this is mistaken. The Commission is unlikely to find better circumstantial evidence that an interview is staged, and intervenor CBS never explicitly denied that these "interrogations" were staged. The interrogation was clearly an " 'event' which did not in fact occur but is 'acted out' at the behest of news personnel." [ ] And "all staging as [so] defined * * * involves distortion." [ ]

On appeal the FCC no longer argues that the evidence of distortion is insufficient. Instead, it asserts that the distortion is not significant. "Galloway did not allege that any of the statements made by the interviewee in the broadcast were false or that the broadcast misrepresented her participation in an insurance fraud scheme. * * * Whether or not this individual 'confessed' to involvement in a fraudulent scheme because of 'hard questioning' or for other reasons is not, however, a significant matter." Brief for respondents at 17. Since Ms. Johnson actually *did* participate in the fraud and *did* confess, even if not in precisely the manner portrayed, the "basic accuracy of the events reported," [ ], has not been distorted. Whatever we may think of this playacting as a journalistic practice, it does not violate FCC rules as currently applied.

2. *The Petty Interview.* One of those interviewed for the broadcast was Robert Petty, an attorney who once participated in insurance fraud and now faced disbarment. Rather asked Petty, "If I were an

attorney and I sought to specialize in these kinds of cases, could I make a quarter of a million dollars a year, half-million dollars a year?" [ ] During the filming, Petty's answer began, "So long as you were success-ful," and after discussing the dangers inherent in maintaining a fraudu-lent scheme concluded, "It's simply not worth it." [ ] Rather asked the question again for a reverse shot, and this time Petty's (off-camera) answer was "Quite easily." [ ] In the actual broadcast, CBS used a shot of Petty responding to a completely different question, saying simply, "Yes."

Galloway alleged that CBS had substituted an affirmative answer for a negative one. We think Petty's answer . . . was clearly affirma-tive, notwithstanding his warnings about the risks involved. The decision not to include Petty's cautionary remarks is more "a matter of editorial discretion . . . than an act of deliberate distortion." [ ] While the substitution of an answer to another question may fairly be considered distortion *per se,* when it does not affect the "basic accuracy" of the answer it is not "significant" enough to violate FCC rules.

. . .

4. *Anonymous doctor interview.* During the broadcast Rather interviewed an unidentified doctor who said he had once been involved in fraudulent insurance claims. In the narration Rather said, "This doctor... confided that he used to conspire with 15 different lawyers. He has never been in jail, has never been suspended from practice; indeed, his medical business is booming, and he is respected throughout his profession." [ ]

The statement *was* somewhat misleading in that it implied the doctor had never been caught. In fact, as the outtakes show, the doctor had struck a plea bargain for turning state's evidence. (It was only when confronted with this fact that he "confided" in Dan Rather.) It is technically accurate, however, that the doctor was never in jail or suspended from practice. . . .

C. *Repeal by Non-enforcement*

Galloway argues that even if the decision in his case is consistent with the Commission's stated policies, the Commission's threshold re-quirements for complaints "are so excessive that, as a practical matter, they are unreachable and have produced a *de facto* nullification of a valid Act of Congress." These arguments about the Commission's hostility to the Fairness Doctrine owe more to ideology than to the law.

First, this court has upheld the FCC policy of requiring a substan-tial prima facie case before proceeding against a broadcaster. See American Security Council Education Foundation v. FCC, 607 F.2d 438 (D.C.Cir.1979) (*en banc*). This policy reflects an appropriate respect for First Amendment values. Second, it is difficult to determine precisely what "Act of Congress" is being "nullifi[ed]." The Commission's poli-cies on staging and distortion are *not* part of the Fairness Doctrine, but simply an attempt to particularize the statutory duty of broadcasters to "operate in the public interest." 47 U.S.C. § 315(a) (1982). Perhaps the broad public interest standard would justify a stricter policy, but neither the language nor the legislative history of the statute demand it. Congress has shown concern with the danger of distortion in television news,[5] but it has never enacted more particular regulation of the practice. This court will not presume to do so.

IV. Conclusion

Whatever one may think of the production techniques employed by *60 Minutes,* especially in the Johnson and Petty interviews, these techniques are not violations of FCC rules. The Commission's decision on the complaint is therefore

Affirmed.

Notes and Questions

1. What justifications might be offered for the juxtaposition of questions with answers to different questions?

2. Which of the matters discussed in the case are attributable to news judgment? Which to technical problems of the medium?

3. In Gen. William Westmoreland's libel suit against CBS (to be discussed in Chapter XII), in violation of internal CBS guidelines, the producer gave only friendly interviewees some idea in advance of the questions to be asked, allowed one friendly interviewee to be interviewed a second time so that he could come across better, and may have photographed friendly witnesses from a distance, giving them a "halo" effect, while zooming in close on unfriendly witnesses so that their images looked more like mug shots and they could be seen perspiring. Should government be involved in investigating these practices or in imposing sanctions for their use?

---

5. See, e.g., Inquiry Into Alleged Rigging of Television News Programs, H.R.Rep. No. 96, 92d Cong., 2d Sess. (1972):

When film and sound recording of an actual event is presented, the public has a right to expect that the events have been filmed and recorded as they actually took place, unless there is an appropriate disclosure to the contrary. If this is not done, then the public's attention and interest is being gained under false pretenses . . . [and] people are given manufactured evidence upon which to base their conclusions on matters which vitally affect their lives and those of their children.

Id. at 3 (statement of Rep. Staggers); [ ].

Chapter VII

LEGAL CONTROL OF BROADCAST PROGRAMMING: NONPOLITICAL SPEECH

In Chapter VI we examined legal controls on broadcast programming that were concerned primarily with political speech. We now turn to other content regulation of broadcasting. Here the restrictions often take the form of direct bans on speech. As we examine each case ask yourself whether these restrictions are more, or less, justifiable than those covered in the previous chapter.

A. DRUGS

YALE BROADCASTING CO. v. FEDERAL COMMUNICATIONS COMMISSION

United States Court of Appeals, District of Columbia Circuit, 1973.
478 F.2d 594.
Certiorari denied 414 U.S. 914, 94 S.Ct. 211, 38 L.Ed.2d 152 (1973).

Before DANAHER, SENIOR CIRCUIT JUDGE, and ROBINSON and WILKEY, CIRCUIT JUDGES.

WILKEY, CIRCUIT JUDGE:

The source of this controversy is a Notice issued by the Federal Communications Commission regarding "drug oriented" music allegedly played by some radio stations. This Notice and a subsequent Order, the stated purposes of which were to remind broadcasters of a preexisting duty, required licensees to have knowledge of the content of their programming and on the basis of this knowledge to evaluate the desirability of broadcasting music dealing with drug use. Appellant, a radio station licensee, argues first that the Notice and the Order are an unconstitutional infringement of its First Amendment right to free speech. . . .

. . .

Despite all its attempts to assuage broadcasters' fears, the Commission realized that if an Order can be misunderstood, it will be misunderstood—at least by some licensees. To remove any excuse for misunderstanding, the Commission specified examples of how a broadcaster could obtain the requisite knowledge. A licensee could fulfill its obligation through (1) pre-screening by a responsible station employee, (2) monitoring selections while they were being played, or (3) considering and responding to complaints made by members of the public. The Order made clear that these procedures were merely suggestions, and

313

were not to be regarded as either absolute requirements or the exclusive means for fulfilling a station's public interest obligation.

Having made clear our understanding of what the Commission has done, we now take up appellant's arguments seriatim.

III. AN UNCONSTITUTIONAL BURDEN ON FREEDOM OF SPEECH

Appellant's first argument is that the Commission's action imposes an unconstitutional burden on a broadcaster's freedom of speech. This contention rests primarily on the Supreme Court's opinion in Smith v. California,[12] in which a bookseller was convicted of possessing and selling obscene literature. The Supreme Court reversed the conviction. Although the State had a legitimate purpose in seeking to ban the distribution of obscene materials, it could not accomplish this goal by placing on the bookseller the procedural burden of examining every book in his store. To make a bookseller criminally liable for all the books sold would necessarily "tend to restrict the books he sells to those he has inspected; and thus the State will have imposed a restriction upon the distribution of constitutionally protected as well as obscene literature. . . ."

Appellant compares its own situation to that of the bookseller in *Smith* and argues that the Order imposes an unconstitutional burden on a broadcaster's freedom of speech. The two situations are easily distinguishable.

Most obviously, a radio station can only broadcast for a finite period of twenty-four hours each day; at any one time a bookstore may contain thousands of hours' worth of readable material. Even if the Commission had ordered that stations pre-screen all materials broadcast, the burden would not be nearly so great as the burden imposed on the bookseller in *Smith*. As it is, broadcasters are not even required to pre-screen their maximum twenty-four hours of daily programming. Broadcasters have specifically been told that they may gain "knowledge" of what they broadcast in other ways.

A more subtle but no less compelling answer to the appellant's argument rests upon *why* knowledge of drug oriented music is required by the Commission. In *Smith*, knowledge was imputed to the purveyor in order that a criminal sanction might be imposed and the dissemination halted. Here the goal is to assure the broadcaster has adequate knowledge. . . .

We say that the licensee must have *knowledge* of what it is broadcasting; the precise *understanding* which may be required of the licensee is only that which is reasonable. No radio licensee faces any realistic possibility of a penalty for misinterpreting the lyrics it has chosen or permitted to be broadcast. If the lyrics are completely obscure, the station is not put on notice that it is in fact broadcasting

12. 361 U.S. 147 (1959).

material which would encourage drug abuse. If the lyrics are meaningless, incoherent, the same conclusion follows. The argument of the appellant licensee, that so many of these lyrics are obscure and ambiguous, really is a circumstance available to some degree in his defense for permitting their broadcast, at least until their meaning is clarified. Some lyrics or sounds are virtually unintelligible. To the extent they are completely meaningless gibberish and approach the equivalent of machinery operating or the din of traffic, they, of course, do not communicate with respect to drugs or anything else, and are not within the ambit of the Commission's order. Speech is an expression of sound or visual symbols which is intelligible to some other human beings. At some point along the scale of human intelligibility the sounds produced may slide over from characteristics of free speech, which should be protected, to those of noise pollution, which the Commission has ample authority to abate.[15]

We not only think appellant's argument invalid, we express our astonishment that the licensee would argue that before the broadcast it has no knowledge, and cannot be required to have any knowledge, of material it puts over the airwaves. We can understand that the individual radio licensees would not be expected to know in advance the content or the quality of a network program, or a free flowing panel discussion of public issues, or other audience participation program, and certainly not a political broadcast. But with reference to the broadcast of that which is frequently termed "canned music," we think the Commission may require that the purveyors of this to the public make a reasonable effort to know what is in the "can." No producer of pork and beans is allowed to put out on a grocery shelf a can without knowing what is in it and standing back of both its content and quality. The Commission is not required to allow radio licensees, being freely granted the use of limited air channels, to spew out to the listening public canned music, whose content and quality before broadcast is totally unknown.

Supposedly a radio licensee is performing a public service—that is the raison d'etre of the license. If the licensee does not have specific knowledge of what it is broadcasting, how can it claim to be operating in the public interest? Far from constituting any threat to freedom of speech of the licensee, we conclude that for the Commission to have been less insistent on licensees discharging their obligations would have verged on an evasion of the Commission's own responsibilities.

By the expression of the above views we have no desire whatsoever to express a value judgment on different types of music, poetry, sound, instrumentation, etc., which may appeal to different classes of our most diverse public. "De gustibus non est disputandum." But what we are saying is that whatever the style, whatever the expression put out over the air by the radio station, for the licensee to claim that it has no responsibility to evaluate its product is for the radio station to abnegate

15. Cf. Noise Control Act of 1972, Pub.L. No. 92–574, 86 Stat. (1972).

completely what we had always considered its responsibility as a licensee. All in all, and quite unintentionally, the appellant-licensee in its free speech argument here has told us a great deal about quality in this particular medium of our culture.

. . .

For the reasons given above, the action of the Federal Communications Commission is

Affirmed.

Notes and Questions

1. A motion for a rehearing *en banc* was denied over the objection of Chief Judge Bazelon, who commented that:

> . . . the Order restated its basic threat: "the broadcaster could jeopardize his license by failing to exercise licensee responsibility in this area." As we have recognized, "licensee responsibility" is a nebulous concept. It could be taken to mean—as the panel opinion takes it—only that "a broadcaster must 'know' what it is broadcasting." On the other hand, in light of the earlier Notice, and in light of the renewed warnings in the Order about the dangers of "drug-oriented" popular songs, broadcasters might have concluded that "responsibility" meant "prohibition."

. . .

This case presents several other questions of considerable significance: Is the popular song a constitutionally protected form of speech? [23] Do the particular songs at which these directives were aimed have a demonstrable connection with illegal activities? If so, is the proper remedy to "discourage or eliminate" the playing of such songs? Can the FCC assert regulatory authority over material that could not constitutionally be regulated in the printed media? [25]

Clearly, the impact of the Commission's order is ripe for judicial review. And, on that review, it would be well to heed Lord Devlin's recent warning:

> If freedom of the press . . . [or freedom of speech] perishes, it will not be by a sudden death. . . . It will be a long time dying from a debilitating disease caused by a series

23. Popular songs might be considered mere entertainment, or even noise pollution. Yale Broadcasting Co. v. FCC, at 598, 599. On the other hand, historians and sociologists have noted that the popular song has been an important medium of political, moral, and aesthetic expression in American life.

25. See Brandywine–Main Line Radio, Inc. v. FCC, 473 F.2d 16 (D.C.Cir.1972) (Chief Judge Bazelon, dissenting) (application of the Fairness Doctrine). Unlike the "Fairness Doctrine" cases, there can be no assertion here that the chilling effect is incidental to providing access to the media for viewpoints that would contribute to a fuller debate on public issues. The question is thus presented whether the rationale of the "Fairness Doctrine," or any other realities of the electronic media, warrant intrusion on broadcasters' free speech rights in this case.

of erosive measures, each of which, if examined singly, would have a good deal to be said for it.

2. The Supreme Court denied *certiorari*, 414 U.S. 914 (1973). Justice Brennan would have granted the writ and set the case for argument. Justice Douglas dissented along the lines sketched by Chief Judge Bazelon. He noted that the Commission majority apparently had intended to ban drug-related lyrics from the air and that at a Congressional hearing the Chairman testified that if a licensee were playing songs that the Commission thought promoted the use of "hard drugs," "I know what I would do, I would probably vote to take the license away." Even though drug lyrics might not cause great concern if banned, "next year it may apply to comedy programs, and the following year to news broadcasts." He concluded that:

> The Government cannot, consistent with the First Amendment, require a broadcaster to censor its music any more than it can require a newspaper to censor the stories of its reporters. Under our system the Government is not to decide what messages, spoken or in music, are of the proper "social value" to reach the people.

3. Could Congress ban pro-drug broadcasts—whether of songs or of normal speech? Are your views here consistent with your views about Congressional power to ban cigarette commercials, p. 274, *supra?*

4. Could Congress ban pro-drug messages in the print media? What about pro-cigarette messages? In 1985 the American Medical Association recommended extending the ban on cigarette commercials to all media. We will return to the issue of banning commercials for certain products later in this chapter.

5. In 1985 the Parents Music Resource Center proposed that record companies place warning labels on records with lyrics that contain "explicit sexual language, profanity, violence, the occult and the glorification of drugs and alcohol." Broadcasting, Sept. 26, 1985 at 28. Some record companies agreed to a voluntary system of warning labels. What if the Commission were to ban the playing of records with warning labels? What if the Commission merely indicated a belief that playing records with those labels was against the public interest?

B. OBSCENITY AND INDECENCY

Obscenity as a class of speech has long been viewed as unprotected by the First Amendment, even though the Supreme Court did not address the issue until 1957. In Roth v. United States, 354 U.S. 476 (1957), the Court held that even though it was "expression," obscenity was outside the protection of the First and Fourteenth Amendments.

The current definition of obscenity, the *Miller* standard, was handed down by the Supreme Court in Miller v. California, 413 U.S. 15, 1 Med.L.Rptr. 1441 (1973):

(a) whether "the average person, applying contemporary community standards" would find that the work, taken as a whole, appeals to the prurient interest, [ ]; (b) whether the work depicts or describes, in a patently offensive way, sexual conduct specifically defined by the applicable state law; and (c) whether the work, taken as a whole, lacks serious literary, artistic, political, or scientific value.

In order for something to be declared obscene, all three parts of the test must be met.

Since obscenity is beyond the protection of the First Amendment, both state and federal government are free to regulate it. However, statutes that are not limited to material covered by the *Miller* standard are usually considered unconstitutionally overbroad. For example, in Erznoznik v. Jacksonville, 422 U.S. 205, 1 Med.L.Rptr. 1508 (1975), the Court struck down an ordinance forbidding the showing of nudity on drive-in theatre screens visible from the public streets. When its captive audience justification proved unsuccessful, the city also asserted that the ordinance was justified as a protection of children. This also failed because the restriction was "broader than permissible. The ordinance is not directed against sexually explicit nudity, nor is it otherwise limited. Rather, it sweepingly forbids display of films containing any uncovered buttocks or breasts, irrespective of contexts or pervasiveness. Thus, it would bar a film containing a picture of a baby's buttocks, the nude body of a war victim, or scenes from a culture in which nudity is indigenous. . . . Clearly all nudity cannot be deemed obscene even as to minors." In appropriately drafted statutes, it is possible to protect minors from obscenity even though such a statute could not apply to the general public. See Ginsberg v. New York, 390 U.S. 629, 1 Med.L.Rptr. 1424 (1968) for a discussion of the states' power to regulate minors' access to obscene material.

The subject of obscenity did not become a problem on radio and television until the 1960s. In the earlier years of these media, the licensees apparently had no practical reason to want to test the limits of permissible communication and were unsure what the Commission might legally do to licensees who stepped over the line.

In the 1934 Act, § 326, the prohibition on censorship, also contained a passage forbidding the use of obscene or indecent speech in broadcasting. In 1948 that ban was removed from § 326 and added to the general criminal law in 18 U.S.C.A. § 1464:

> Whoever utters any obscene, indecent, or profane language by means of radio communication shall be fined not more than $10,-000 or imprisoned not more than two years, or both.

Several other sections empower the Commission to impose sanctions for violation of § 1464.

In 1964 the Commission considered renewal of stations belonging to the Pacifica Foundation. Five programs had provoked complaints: two poets reading their own works; one author reading from his novel; a recording of Edward Albee's "Zoo Story"; and a program "in which eight homosexuals discussed their attitudes and problems." All were late at night except one of the poetry readings. The Commission indicated that it was "not concerned with individual programs" but with whether there had been a pattern of programming inconsistent with the public interest. Although it found nothing to bar renewal, the Commission discussed the five programs, claiming it would be "useful" to the "industry and the public."

The Commission found three of the programs were well within the licensee's judgment under the public interest standard. The Commission recognized that provocative programming might offend some listeners. To rule such programs off the air, however, would mean that "only the wholly inoffensive, the bland, could gain access to the radio microphone or TV camera." The remedy for offended listeners was to turn off the program. The two poetry readings raised different questions. One did not measure up to the licensee's standards for presentation, but it had not been carefully screened because it had come from a reputable source. The other reading, involving 28 poems, was broadcast at 7:15 p.m. because the station's editor admitted he had been lulled by the poet's "rather flat, monotonous voice" and did not catch unidentified "offensive words" in the 19th poem. The errors were isolated and thus caused no renewal problem. Pacifica Foundation, 36 F.C.C. 147, 1 R.R.2d 747 (1964). For a history of Pacifica's struggle in 1964, including the fact that no broadcaster came to its defense, see Barton, The Lingering Legacy of Pacifica: Broadcasters' Freedom of Silence, 53 Journ.Q. 429 (1976).

Another episode involved a taped interview on a noncommercial FM station with Jerry Garcia, leader of a musical group known as the Grateful Dead. Garcia apparently used "various patently offensive words as adjectives, introductory expletives, and as substitutes for 'et cetera.'" The Commission imposed a forfeiture of $100 for "indecency" and apparently hoped for a court test of its powers. Eastern Educational Radio (WUHY–FM), 24 F.C.C.2d 408, 18 R.R.2d 860 (1970). The licensee paid the fine, and the case was over.

Next came charges of obscenity leveled at "topless radio," midday programs consisting of "call-in talk shows in which masters of ceremonies discuss intimate sexual topics with listeners, usually women." The format quickly became quite popular. The Commission responded to complaints by ordering its staff to tape several of the shows and to present a condensed tape of some of the most offensive comments. The next day, Chairman Burch spoke to the National Association of Broadcasters condemning the format. Two weeks later the Commission issued a Notice of Apparent Liability proposing a forfeiture of $2,000 against one licensee. Sonderling Broadcasting Corp. (WGLD–FM), 27 R.R.2d 285 (F.C.C.1973). The most troublesome language was apparently:

> Female Listener: . . . of course I had a few hangups at first about—in regard to this, but you know what we did—I have a

craving for peanut butter all that [sic] time so I used to spread this on my husband's privates and after a while, I mean, I didn't even need the peanut butter anymore.

Announcer: (Laughs) Peanut butter, huh?

Listener: Right. Oh, we can try anything—you know—any, any of these women that have called and they have, you know, hangups about this, I mean they should try their favorite—you know like—uh. . . .

Announcer: Whipped cream, marshmallow . . ..

In addition, the host's conversation with a complaining listener was thought to be suffused with "leering innuendo." The Commission thought this program ran afoul of both the "indecency" and "obscenity" standards of § 1464. On the other hand, the Commission disclaimed any intention to ban the discussion of sex entirely:

We are emphatically not saying that sex *per se* is a forbidden subject on the broadcast medium. We are well aware that sex is a vital human relationship which has concerned humanity over the centuries, and that sex and obscenity are not the same thing. In this area as in others, we recognize the licensee's right to present provocative or unpopular programming which may offend some listeners, Pacifica Foundation, 36 F.C.C. 147, 149 (1964). Second, we note that we are not dealing with works of dramatic or literary art as we were in *Pacifica*. We are rather confronted with the talk or interview show where clearly the interviewer can readily moderate his handling of the subject matter so as to conform to the basic statutory standards which, as we point out, allow much leeway for provocative material. . . . The standards here are strictly defined by the law: The broadcaster must eschew the "obscene or indecent."

Again the Commission sought a test: "we welcome and urge judicial consideration of our action." Commissioner Johnson dissented on several grounds, including the view that the Commission had no duty to act in these cases and should leave the matter to possible prosecution by Justice Department. Sonderling denied liability but paid the fine. Two citizen groups asked the Commission to reconsider on the grounds that listeners' rights to hear such programs had been disregarded by the Commission's action. The Commission reaffirmed its action. 41 F.C.C.2d 777, 27 R.R.2d 1508 (1973). It indicated that it had based its order "on the pervasive and intrusive nature of broadcast radio, even if children were left completely out of the picture." It went on, however, to point out that children were in the audience in these afternoon programs and there was some evidence that the program was not intended solely for adults. "The obvious intent of this reference to children was to convey the conclusion that this material was unlawful, and that it was even more clearly unlawful when presented to an audience which included children."

The citizen groups appealed but lost. Illinois Citizens Committee for Broadcasting v. Federal Communications Commission, 515 F.2d 397, 31 R.R.2d 1523 (D.C.Cir.1974). The court refused to allow the petitioners to make certain procedural arguments that it thought were open only to the licensee itself. On the merits:

> The excerpts cited by the Commission contain repeated and explicit descriptions of the techniques of oral sex. And these are presented, not for educational and scientific purposes, but in a context that was fairly described by the FCC as "titillating and pandering." The principles of Ginzburg v. United States, 383 U.S. 463 (1966) are applicable, for commercial exploitation of interests in titillation is the broadcaster's sole end. It is not a material difference that here the tone is set by the continuity provided by the announcer rather than, as in *Ginzburg*, by the presentation of the material in advertising and sale to solicit an audience. We cannot ignore what the Commission took into account—that the announcer's response to a complaint by an offended listener and his presentation of advertising for auto insurance are suffused with leering innuendo. Moreover, and significantly, "Femme Forum" is broadcast from 10 a.m. to 3 p.m. during daytime hours when the radio audience may include children—perhaps home from school for lunch, or because of staggered school hours or illness. Given this combination of factors, we do not think that the FCC's evaluation of this material infringes upon rights protected by the First Amendment.

> The FCC found Sonderling's broadcasts obscene   . . . ..

>   . . .

> Petitioners object that the Commission's determination was based on a brief condensation of offensive material and did not take into account the broadcast as a whole, as would seem to be required by certain elements of both the *Memoirs* and the *Miller* tests. The Commission's approach is not inappropriate in evaluating a broadcasting program that is episodic in nature—a cluster of individual and typically disconnected commentaries, rather than an integrated presentation. It is commonplace for members of the radio audience to listen only to short snatches of a broadcast, and programs like "Femme Forum" are designed to attract such listeners.

> We conclude that, where a radio call-in show during daytime hours broadcasts explicit discussions of ultimate sexual acts in a titillating context, the Commission does not unconstitutionally infringe upon the public's right to listening alternatives when it determines that the broadcast is obscene.

The court explicitly did not rely upon the Commission's argument that it had latitude to hold things "indecent" that are not obscene.

A motion for rehearing *en banc* was denied over the lengthy dissent of Chief Judge Bazelon, 515 F.2d 407, 33 R.R.2d 118 (1984). He was much concerned about the ability of the Commission, by "raised eyebrow" and the Chairman's speech, virtually to end a popular format. He saw this as "flagrant and illegal censorship." He also found four areas of error committed by the panel.

INTRODUCTION TO THE PACIFICA CASE

Two points should be made before reading the following case. The first involves the notion of "nuisance" in law. Activities that may be socially desirable are often called nuisances if located in the wrong place. This might include a factory that emits smoke in an amount that would be acceptable in a factory district but is unacceptable in a residential district. The legal goal is to encourage the factory either to conform to the needs of its surroundings or to relocate to a factory area.

The second point involves a conflict within the Court about the legitimacy of regulations based on the content of the communication. In Police Department of Chicago v. Mosley, 408 U.S. 92 (1972), the Court invalidated an ordinance that barred picketing outside schools unless the picketing was related to a labor-management dispute concerning the school. "Once a forum is opened up to assembly or speaking by some groups, government may not prohibit others from assembling or speaking on the basis of what they intend to say."

In Young v. American Mini Theatres, Inc., 427 U.S. 50, 1 Med. L.Rptr. 1151 (1976), Detroit adopted a zoning ordinance requiring that theaters that specialized in showing sexually explicit movies had to be separated from one another by a minimum distance. The Court upheld the ordinance 5–4, but there was no majority opinion. Justice Stevens, for the plurality of four, said that the *Mosley* statement must be kept in context. Even though the First Amendment did not permit "total suppression of erotic materials that have some arguably artistic value, it is manifest that society's interest in protecting this type of expression is of a wholly different, and lesser, magnitude than the interest in untrammeled political debate . . .. [F]ew of us would march our sons and daughters off to war to preserve the citizen's right to see 'Specified Sexual Activities' exhibited in the theaters of our choice."

The plurality then concluded that the record supported the city council's conclusion that unfortunate effects followed from the clustering of such enterprises in one area.

Justice Powell provided the crucial fifth vote on the ground that this case involved "an example of innovative land-use regulation, implicating First Amendment concerns only incidentally and to a limited extent." The ordinance did not "restrict in any significant way the viewing of these movies by those who desire to see them."

The four dissenters considered the decision "a drastic departure from established principles of First Amendment law." These principles require that regulations concerning the time, place and manner of communicating "be content-neutral except in the limited context of a captive or juvenile audience."

As we will see, this conflict reappears in *Pacifica*.

FEDERAL COMMUNICATIONS COMMISSION
v. PACIFICA FOUNDATION

Supreme Court of the United States, 1978.
438 U.S. 726, 98 S.Ct. 3026, 57 L.Ed.2d 1073, 43 R.R.2d 493, 3 Med.L.Rptr. 2553.

[George Carlin, a "satiric humorist," recorded a 12–minute monologue entitled "Filthy Words" before a live audience in a California theater. The theme was "the words you couldn't say on the public, ah, airwaves." Carlin then proposed a basic list: "The original seven words were shit, piss, fuck, cunt, cocksucker, motherfucker, and tits. Those are the ones that will curve your spine, grow hair on your hands and (laughter) maybe, even bring us, God help us, peace without honor (laughter) um, and a bourbon." Carlin then discussed "shit" and "fuck" at length, including the various phrases that use each word. The following passage gives some idea of the format:

> Now the word shit is okay for the man. At work you can say it like crazy. Mostly figuratively. Get that shit out of here, will ya? I don't want to see that shit anymore. I can't *cut* that shit, buddy. I've had that shit up to here. I think you're full of shit myself. (laughter) He don't know shit from Shinola. (laughter) You know that? (laughter) Always wondered how the Shinola people felt about that? (laughter) Hi, I'm the new man from Shinola. (laughter) Hi, how are ya? Nice to see ya. (laughter) How are ya? (laughter) Boy, I don't know, whether to shit or wind my watch. (laughter) Guess I'll shit on my watch. (laughter) Oh, *the* shit is going to hit *de* fan. (laughter) Built like a brick shit-house. (laughter) Up, he's up shit's creek. (laughter) He's had it. (laughter) He hit me, I'm sorry. (laughter) Hot shit, holy shit, tough shit, eat shit. (laughter) Shit-eating grin. Uh, whoever thought of that was ill. (murmur laughter) He had a shit-eating grin! He had a what? (laughter) Shit on a stick. (laughter) Shit in a handbag. I always like that.

One weekday afternoon at 2 p.m., Pacifica's FM station in New York City played the monologue during a discussion about society's attitude toward language. The station warned that the monologue included language that might offend some listeners. A man who apparently did not hear the warning heard the broadcast while driving with his young son, and complained to the Commission. In response to an inquiry from the Commission, Pacifica responded that Carlin was a "significant social satirist" who "like Twain and Sahl before him, examines the language of ordinary people." Apparently, no one else complained about the broadcast.

The Commission ruled that Pacifica's action was subject to administrative sanction. Instead of imposing a formal sanction, it put the order in the file for possible use if subsequent complaints were received. The Commission asserted four reasons for treating broadcasting differently from other media: access by unsupervised children; since radio receivers are in the home, privacy interests are entitled to extra deference; unconsenting adults may tune in without a warning that offensive language is being used; and scarcity of spectrum space requires government to license in the public interest. Further facts are stated in the opinions.]

MR. JUSTICE STEVENS delivered the opinion of the Court (Parts I, II, III, and IV–C) and an opinion in which THE CHIEF JUSTICE and MR. JUSTICE REHNQUIST joined (Parts IV–A and IV–B).

This case requires that we decide whether the Federal Communications Commission has any power to regulate a radio broadcast that is indecent but not obscene.

     . . .

     . . . [T]he Commission found a power to regulate indecent broadcasting in two statutes: 18 U.S.C. § 1464, which forbids the use of "any obscene, indecent, or profane language by means of radio communications," and 47 U.S.C. § 303(g), which requires the Commission to "encourage the larger and more effective use of radio in the public interest."

The Commission characterized the language used in the Carlin monologue as "patently offensive," though not necessarily obscene, and expressed the opinion that it should be regulated by principles analogous to those found in the law of nuisance where the "law generally speaks to *channeling* behavior more than prohibiting it. . . . [T]he concept of 'indecent' is intimately connected with the exposure of children to language that describes, in terms patently offensive as measured by contemporary community standards for the broadcast medium, sexual or excretory activities and organs, at times of the day when there is a reasonable risk that children may be in the audience." 56 F.C.C.2d, at 98.[5]

     . . . In summary, the Commission stated: "We therefore hold that the language as broadcast was indecent and prohibited by 18 U.S.C. 1464."

After the order issued, the Commission was asked to clarify its opinion by ruling that the broadcast of indecent words as part of a live newscast would not be prohibited. . . . The Commission noted that its "declaratory order was issued in a specific factual context," and

---

5. Thus, the Commission suggested, if an offensive broadcast had literary, artistic, political, or scientific value, and were preceded by warnings, it might not be indecent in the late evening, but would be so during the day, when children are in the audience.

declined to comment on various hypothetical situations presented by the petition.[7] . . .

The United States Court of Appeals for the District of Columbia reversed, with each of the three judges on the panel writing separately.

Having granted the Commission's petition for certiorari, 434 U.S. 1007, we must decide: (1) whether the scope of judicial review encompasses more than the Commission's determination that the monologue was indecent "as broadcast"; (2) whether the Commission's order was a form of censorship forbidden by § 326; (3) whether the broadcast was indecent within the meaning of § 1464; and (4) whether the order violates the First Amendment of the United States Constitution.

I

The general statements in the Commission's memorandum opinion do not change the character of its order. Its action was an adjudication. . . . The specific holding was carefully confined to the monologue "as broadcast."

. . . Accordingly, the focus of our review must be on the Commission's determination that the Carlin monologue was indecent as broadcast.

II

The relevant, statutory questions are whether the Commission's action is forbidden "censorship" within the meaning of 47 U.S.C. § 326 and whether speech that concededly is not obscene may be restricted as "indecent" under the authority of 18 U.S.C. § 1464. The questions are not unrelated, for the two statutory provisions have a common origin. . . .

The prohibition against censorship unequivocally denies the Commission any power to edit proposed broadcasts in advance and to excise material considered inappropriate for the airwaves. The prohibition, however, has never been construed to deny the Commission the power to review the content of completed broadcasts in the performance of its regulatory duties.[9]

During the period between the original enactment of the provision in 1927 and its re-enactment in the Communications Act of 1934, the

---

7. The Commission did, however, comment that:

" '[I]n some cases, public events likely to produce offensive speech are covered live, and there is no opportunity for journalistic editing.' Under these circumstances we believe that it would be inequitable for us to hold a licensee responsible for indecent language . . . .. We trust that under such circumstances a licensee will exercise judgment, responsibility, and sensitivity to the community's needs, interests, and tastes." [   ]

9. Zechariah Chafee, defending the Commission's authority to take into account program service in granting licenses, interpreted the restriction on "censorship" narrowly: "This means, I feel sure, the sort of censorship which went on in the seventeenth century in England—the deletion of specific items and dictation as to what should go into particular programs." 2 Z. Chafee, Government and Mass Communications 641 (1947).

courts and the Federal Radio Commission held that the section deprived the Commission of the power to subject "broadcasting matter to scrutiny prior to its release," but they concluded that the Commission's "undoubted right" to take note of past program content when considering a licensee's renewal application "is not censorship."

Not only did the Federal Radio Commission so construe the statute prior to 1934; its successor, the Federal Communications Commission, has consistently interpreted the provision in the same way ever since. [   ]   And, until this case, the Court of Appeals for the District of Columbia has consistently agreed with this construction.   .   .   .

Entirely apart from the fact that the subsequent review of program content is not the sort of censorship at which the statute was directed, its history makes it perfectly clear that it was not intended to limit the Commission's power to regulate the broadcast of obscene, indecent, or profane language.   .   .   .

There is nothing in the legislative history to contradict this conclusion.   .   .   .

We conclude, therefore, that § 326 does not limit the Commission's authority to impose sanctions on licensees who engage in obscene, indecent, or profane broadcasting.

III

The only other statutory question presented by this case is whether the afternoon broadcast of the "Filthy Words" monologue was indecent within the meaning of § 1464.[13]   Even that question is narrowly confined by the arguments of the parties.

The Commission identified several words that referred to excretory or sexual activities or organs, stated that the repetitive, deliberate use of those words in an afternoon broadcast when children are in the audience was patently offensive, and held that the broadcast was indecent.   Pacifica takes issue with the Commission's definition of indecency, but does not dispute the Commission's preliminary determination that each of the components of its definition was present. Specifically, Pacifica does not quarrel with the conclusion that this afternoon broadcast was patently offensive.   Pacifica's claim that the broadcast was not indecent within the meaning of the statute rests entirely on the absence of prurient appeal.

The plain language of the statute does not support Pacifica's argument.   The words "obscene, indecent, or profane" are written in the disjunctive, implying that each has a separate meaning.   Prurient appeal is an element of the obscene, but the normal definition of

---

13.   In addition to § 1464, the Commission also relied on its power to regulate in the public interest under 47 U.S.C. § 303(g).   We do not need to consider whether § 303 may have independent significance in a case such as this. The statutes authorizing civil penalties incorporate § 1464, a criminal statute.   See 47 U.S.C. §§ 312(a)(6), 312(b)(2), and 503(b)(1)(E). But the validity of the civil sanctions is not linked to the validity of the criminal penalty.   The legislative history of the provisions establishes their independence.   .   .   .

"indecent" merely refers to nonconformance with accepted standards of morality.

Pacifica argues, however, that this Court has construed the term "indecent" in related statutes to mean "obscene" as that term was defined in Miller v. California, 413 U.S. 15 (1973). Pacifica relies most heavily on the construction this Court gave to 18 U.S.C. § 1461 in Hamling v. United States, 418 U.S. 87 (1974). See also United States v. Twelve 200–foot Reels of Film, 413 U.S. 123, 130 n. 7 (1973) (18 U.S.C. § 1462) (dicta). . . .

The reasons supporting *Hamling*'s construction of § 1461 do not apply to § 1464. Although the history of the former revealed a primary concern with the prurient, the Commission has long interpreted § 1464 as encompassing more than the obscene. The former statute deals primarily with printed matter enclosed in sealed envelopes mailed from one individual to another; the latter deals with the content of public broadcasts. It is unrealistic to assume that Congress intended to impose precisely the same limitations on the dissemination of patently offensive matter by such different means.[17]

Because neither our prior decisions nor the language or history of § 1464 supports the conclusion that prurient appeal is an essential component of indecent language, we reject Pacifica's construction of the statute. When that construction is put to one side, there is no basis for disagreeing with the Commission's conclusion that indecent language was used in this broadcast.

IV

Pacifica makes two constitutional attacks on the Commission's order. First, it argues that the Commission's construction of the statutory language broadly encompasses so much constitutionally protected speech that reversal is required even if Pacifica's broadcast of the "Filthy Words" monologue is not itself protected by the First Amendment. Second, Pacifica argues that inasmuch as the recording is not obscene, the Constitution forbids any abridgment of the right to broadcast it on the radio.

A

The first argument fails because our review is limited to the question whether the Commission has the authority to proscribe this

---

17. This conclusion is re-enforced by noting the different constitutional limits on Congress' power to regulate the two different subjects. Use of the postal power to regulate material that is not fraudulent or obscene raises "grave constitutional questions." Hannegan v. Esquire, Inc., 327 U.S. 146, 156 (1946). But it is well settled that the First Amendment has a special meaning in the broadcasting context. See, e.g., FCC v. National Citizens Committee for Broadcasting, 436 U.S. 775 (1978); Red Lion Broadcasting Co., Inc. v. FCC, 395 U.S. 367 (1969); Columbia Broadcasting System, Inc. v. Democratic National Committee, 412 U.S. 94 (1973). For this reason, the presumption that Congress never intends to exceed constitutional limits, which supported *Hamling*'s narrow reading of § 1461, does not support a comparable reading of § 1464.

particular broadcast. As the Commission itself has emphasized, its order was "issued in a specific factual context." 59 F.C.C.2d, at 893. That approach is appropriate for courts as well as the Commission when regulation of indecency is at stake, for indecency is largely a function of context—it cannot be adequately judged in the abstract.

The approach is also consistent with Red Lion Broadcasting Co., Inc. v. FCC, 395 U.S. 367 (1969). . . .

It is true that the Commission's order may lead some broadcasters to censor themselves. At most, however, the Commission's definition of indecency will deter only the broadcasting of patently offensive references to excretory and sexual organs and activities.[18] While some of these references may be protected, they surely lie at the periphery of First Amendment concern. Cf. Bates v. State Bar, 433 U.S. 350, 380–381 (1977). Young v. American Mini Theatres, Inc., 427 U.S. 50, 61 (1976). The danger dismissed so summarily in Red Lion, in contrast, was that the broadcasters would respond to the vagueness of the regulations by refusing to present programs dealing with important social and political controversies. Invalidating any rule on the basis of its hypothetical application to situations not before the Court is "strong medicine" to be applied "sparingly and only as a last resort." Broadrick v. Oklahoma, 413 U.S. 601, 613 (1973). We decline to administer that medicine to preserve the vigor of patently offensive and excretory speech.

B

When the issue is narrowed to the facts of this case, the question is whether the First Amendment denies government any power to restrict the public broadcast of indecent language in any circumstances.[19] For if the government has any such power, this was an appropriate occasion for its exercise.

The words of the Carlin monologue are unquestionably "speech" within the meaning of the First Amendment. It is equally clear that the Commission's objections to the broadcast were based in part on its content. The order must therefore fall if, as Pacifica argues, the First Amendment prohibits all governmental regulation that depends on the content of speech. Our past cases demonstrate, however, that no such absolute rule is mandated by the Constitution.

---

18. A requirement that indecent language be avoided will have its primary effect on the form, rather than the content, of serious communication. There are few, if any, thoughts that cannot be expressed by the use of less offensive language.

19. Pacifica's position would of course deprive the Commission of any power to regulate erotic telecasts unless they were obscene under Miller v. California, 413 U.S. 15 (1973). Anything that could be sold at a newsstand for private examination could be publicly displayed on television.

We are assured by Pacifica that the free play of market forces will discourage indecent programming. "Smut may," as Judge Leventhal put it, "drive itself from the market and confound Gresham," 556 F.2d at 35; the prosperity of those who traffic in pornographic literature and films would appear to justify his skepticism.

The classic exposition of the proposition that both the content and the context of speech are critical elements of First Amendment analysis is Mr. Justice Holmes' statement for the Court in Schenck v. United States:

> "We admit that in many places and in ordinary times the defendants in saying all that was said in the circular would have been within their constitutional rights. But the character of every act depends upon the circumstances in which it is done. . . . The most stringent protection of free speech would not protect a man in falsely shouting fire in a theatre and causing a panic. It does not even protect a man from an injunction against uttering words that may have all the effect of force. . . . The question in every case is whether the words used are used in such circumstances and are of such a nature as to create a clear and present danger that they will bring about the substantive evils that Congress has a right to prevent." 249 U.S. 47, 52.

Other distinctions based on content have been approved in the years since *Schenck*. The government may forbid speech calculated to provoke a fight. See Chaplinsky v. New Hampshire, 315 U.S. 568 (1942). It may pay heed to the " 'commonsense differences' between commercial speech and other varieties." Bates v. State Bar, 433 U.S. 350, 381 (1977). It may treat libels against private citizens more severely than libels against public officials. See Gertz v. Robert Welch, Inc., 418 U.S. 323 (1974). Obscenity may be wholly prohibited. Miller v. California, 413 U.S. 15 (1973). And only two Terms ago we refused to hold that a "statutory classification is unconstitutional because it is based on the content of communication protected by the First Amendment." Young v. American Mini Theatres, 427 U.S. 50, 52 (1976).

The question in this case is whether a broadcast of patently offensive words dealing with sex and excretion may be regulated because of its content. Obscene materials have been denied the protection of the First Amendment because their content is so offensive to contemporary moral standards. Roth v. United States, 354 U.S. 476 (1957). But the fact that society may find speech offensive is not a sufficient reason for suppressing it. Indeed, if it is the speaker's opinion that gives offense, that consequence is a reason for according it constitutional protection. For it is a central tenet of the First Amendment that the government must remain neutral in the marketplace of ideas. If there were any reason to believe that the Commission's characterization of the Carlin monologue as offensive could be traced to its political content—or even to the fact that it satirized contemporary attitudes about four-letter words [22]—First Amendment protection might

---

22. The monologue does present a point of view; it attempts to show that the words it uses are "harmless" and that our attitudes toward them are "essentially silly." [ ] The Commission objects, not to this point of view, but to the way in which it is expressed. The belief that these words are harmless does not necessarily confer a First Amendment privilege to use them while proselytizing, just as the conviction that obscenity is harmless does not license one to communicate that conviction by the

be required. But that is simply not this case. These words offend for the same reasons that obscenity offends.[23] Their place in the hierarchy of First Amendment values was aptly sketched by Mr. Justice Murphy when he said, "such utterances are no essential part of any exposition of ideas, and are of such slight social value as a step to truth that any benefit that may be derived from them is clearly outweighed by the social interest in order and morality." Chaplinsky v. New Hampshire, 315 U.S. 568, 572 (1942).

Although these words ordinarily lack literary, political, or scientific value, they are not entirely outside the protection of the First Amendment. Some uses of even the most offensive words are unquestionably protected. See, e.g., Hess v. Indiana, 414 U.S. 105 (1973). Indeed, we may assume, *arguendo,* that this monologue would be protected in other contexts. Nonetheless, the constitutional protection accorded to a communication containing such patently offensive sexual and excretory language need not be the same in every context. It is a characteristic of speech such as this that both its capacity to offend and its "social value," to use Mr. Justice Murphy's term, vary with the circumstances. Words that are commonplace in one setting are shocking in another. To paraphrase Mr. Justice Harlan, one occasion's lyric is another's vulgarity. Cf. Cohen v. California, 403 U.S. 15, 25.

In this case it is undisputed that the content of Pacifica's broadcast was "vulgar," "offensive," and "shocking." Because content of that character is not entitled to absolute constitutional protection under all circumstances, we must consider its context in order to determine whether the Commission's action was constitutionally permissible.

C

We have long recognized that each medium of expression presents special First Amendment problems. Joseph Burstyn, Inc. v. Wilson, 343 U.S. 495, 502–503 (1952). And of all forms of communication, it is broadcasting that has received the most limited First Amendment protection. Thus, although other speakers cannot be licensed except under laws that carefully define and narrow official discretion, a broadcaster may be deprived of his license and his forum if the Commission decides that such an action would serve "the public interest, convenience, and necessity." Similarly, although the First Amendment protects newspaper publishers from being required to print the replies of those whom they criticize, Miami Herald Publishing Co. v. Tornillo, 418 U.S. 241, it affords no such protection to broadcasters; on

indiscriminate distribution of an obscene leaflet.

23. The Commission stated: "Obnoxious, gutter language describing these matters has the effect of debasing and brutalizing human beings by reducing them to their mere bodily functions . . . ." 56 F.C.C.2d, at 98. Our society has a tradition of performing certain bodily functions in private, and of severely limiting the public exposure or discussion of such matters. Verbal or physical acts exposing those intimacies are offensive irrespective of any message that may accompany the exposure.

the contrary, they must give free time to the victims of their criticism. Red Lion Broadcasting Co. v. FCC, 395 U.S. 367 (1969).

The reasons for these distinctions are complex, but two have relevance to the present case. First, the broadcast media have established a uniquely pervasive presence in the lives of all Americans. Patently offensive, indecent material presented over the airwaves confronts the citizen, not only in public, but also in the privacy of the home, where the individual's right to be let alone plainly outweighs the First Amendment rights of an intruder. Rowan v. Post Office Department, 397 U.S. 728 (1970). Because the broadcast audience is constantly tuning in and out, prior warnings cannot completely protect the listener or viewer from unexpected program content. To say that one may avoid further offense by turning off the radio when he hears indecent language is like saying that the remedy for an assault is to run away after the first blow. One may hang up on an indecent phone call, but that option does not give the caller a constitutional immunity or avoid a harm that has already taken place.[27]

Second, broadcasting is uniquely accessible to children, even those too young to read. Although Cohen's written message might have been incomprehensible to a first grader, Pacifica's broadcast could have enlarged a child's vocabulary in an instant. Other forms of offensive expression may be withheld from the young without restricting the expression at its source. Bookstores and motion picture theaters, for example, may be prohibited from making indecent material available to children. We held in Ginsberg v. New York, 390 U.S. 629 (1968), that the government's interest in the "well being of its youth" and in supporting "parents' claim to authority in their own household" justified the regulation of otherwise protected expression. Id., at 640 and 639.[28] The ease with which children may obtain access to broadcast material, coupled with the concerns recognized in *Ginsberg*, amply justify special treatment of indecent broadcasting.

It is appropriate, in conclusion, to emphasize the narrowness of our holding. This case does not involve a two-way radio conversation between a cab driver and a dispatcher, or a telecast of an Elizabethan comedy. We have not decided that an occasional expletive in either setting would justify any sanction or, indeed, that this broadcast would justify a criminal prosecution. The Commission's decision rested entirely on a nuisance rationale under which context is all-important. The concept requires consideration of a host of variables. The time of

---

27. Outside the home, the balance between the offensive speaker and the unwilling audience may sometimes tip in favor of the speaker, requiring the offended listener to turn away. See Erznoznik v. Jacksonville, 422 U.S. 205 (1975).

28. The Commission's action does not by any means reduce adults to hearing only what is fit for children. Cf. Butler v. Michigan, 352 U.S. 380, 383 (1957). Adults who feel the need may purchase tapes and records or go to theatres and nightclubs to hear these words. In fact, the Commission has not unequivocally closed even broadcasting to speech of this sort; whether broadcast audiences in the late evening contain so few children that playing this monologue would be permissible is an issue neither the Commission nor this Court has decided.

day was emphasized by the Commission. The content of the program in which the language is used will also affect the composition of the audience,[29] and differences between radio, television, and perhaps closed-circuit transmissions, may also be relevant. As Mr. Justice Sutherland wrote, a "nuisance may be merely a right thing in the wrong place—like a pig in the parlor instead of the barnyard." Euclid v. Ambler Realty Co., 272 U.S. 365, 388 (1926). We simply hold that when the Commission finds that a pig has entered the parlor, the exercise of its regulatory power does not depend on proof that the pig is obscene.

The judgment of the Court of Appeals is reversed.

Mr. Justice Powell, with whom Mr. Justice Blackmun joins, concurring.

I join Parts I, II, III, and IV(C) of Mr. Justice Stevens' opinion, and with its conclusion that the Commission's holding in this case does not violate the First Amendment. . . .

. . . Because I do not subscribe to all that is said in Part IV, however, I state my views separately.

I

It is conceded that the monologue at issue here is not obscene in the constitutional sense. See 56 F.C.C.2d 94, 98 (1975); Brief for Petitioner 18. Nor, in this context, does its language constitute "fighting words" within the meaning of Chaplinsky v. New Hampshire, 315 U.S. 568 (1942). Some of the words used have been held protected by the First Amendment in other cases and contexts. [ ] I do not think Carlin, consistently with the First Amendment, could be punished for delivering the same monologue to a live audience composed of adults who, knowing what to expect, chose to attend his performance. See Brown v. Oklahoma, 408 U.S. 914 (1972) (Powell, J., concurring in result). And I would assume that an adult could not constitutionally be prohibited from purchasing a recording or transcript of the monologue and playing or reading it in the privacy of his own home. Cf. Stanley v. Georgia, 394 U.S. 557 (1969).

But it also is true that the language employed is, to most people, vulgar and offensive. It was chosen specifically for this quality, and it was repeated over and over as a sort of verbal shock treatment. The Commission did not err in characterizing the narrow category of language used here as "patently offensive" to most people regardless of age.

The issue, however, is whether the Commission may impose civil sanctions on a licensee radio station for broadcasting the monologue at two o'clock in the afternoon. The Commission's primary concern was

---

29. Even a prime-time recitation of Chaucer's Miller's Tale would not be likely to command the attention of many children who are both old enough to understand and young enough to be adversely affected by passages such as "And prively he caughte hire by the queynte." G. Chaucer, *The Miller's Tale* 1.3276 (c. 1386).

to prevent the broadcast from reaching the ears of unsupervised children who were likely to be in the audience at that hour. In essence, the Commission sought to "channel" the monologue to hours when the fewest unsupervised children would be exposed to it. See 56 F.C.C.2d at 98. In my view, this consideration provides strong support for the Commission's holding.

The Court has recognized society's right to "adopt more stringent controls on communicative materials available to youths than on those available to adults." Erznoznik v. City of Jacksonville, [ ]. This recognition stems in large part from the fact that "a child . . . is not possessed of that full capacity for individual choice which is the presupposition of First Amendment guarantees." Ginsberg v. New York, supra, at 649–650 (Stewart, J., concurring in result). Thus, children may not be able to protect themselves from speech which, although shocking to most adults, generally may be avoided by the unwilling through the exercise of choice. At the same time, such speech may have a deeper and more lasting negative effect on a child than an adult. For these reasons, society may prevent the general dissemination of such speech to children, leaving to parents the decision as to what speech of this kind their children shall hear and repeat:

> "[C]onstitutional interpretation has consistently recognized that the parents' claim to authority in their own household to direct the rearing of children is basic in the structure of our society. 'It is cardinal with us that the custody, care and nurture of the child reside first in the parents, whose primary function and freedom include preparation for obligations the state can neither supply nor hinder.' Prince v. Massachusetts, [321 U.S. 158, 166 (1944)]. The legislature could properly conclude that parents and others, teachers for example, who have this primary responsibility for children's well-being are entitled to the support of laws designed to aid discharge of that responsibility." Ginsberg v. New York, supra, at 639.

The Commission properly held that the speech from which society may attempt to shield its children is not limited to that which appeals to the youthful prurient interest. The language involved in this case is as potentially degrading and harmful to children as representations of many erotic acts.

In most instances, the dissemination of this kind of speech to children may be limited without also limiting willing adults' access to it. Sellers of printed and recorded matter and exhibitors of motion pictures and live performances may be required to shut their doors to children, but such a requirement has no effect on adults' access. See Ginsberg v. New York, supra, at 634–635. The difficulty is that such a physical separation of the audience cannot be accomplished in the broadcast media. During most of the broadcast hours, both adults and unsupervised children are likely to be in the broadcast audience, and the broadcaster cannot reach willing adults without also reaching children. This, as the Court emphasizes, is one of the distinctions between the broadcast and other media to which we often have adverted as justifying a different treatment of the broadcast media for First Amendment purposes. [ ] In my view, the Commission was entitled to give substantial weight to this difference in reaching its decision in this case.

A second difference, not without relevance, is that broadcasting— unlike most other forms of communication—comes directly into the home, the one place where people ordinarily have the right not to be assaulted by uninvited and offensive sights and sounds. . . . The Commission also was entitled to give this factor appropriate weight in the circumstances of the instant case. This is not to say, however, that the Commission has an unrestricted license to decide what speech, protected in other media, may be banned from the airwaves in order to protect unwilling adults from momentary exposure to it in their homes.[2] Making the sensitive judgments required in these cases is not easy. But this responsibility has been reposed initially in the Commission, and its judgment is entitled to respect.

II

As the foregoing demonstrates, my views are generally in accord with what is said in Part IV(C) of Mr. Justice Stevens' opinion. I therefore join that portion of his opinion. I do not join Part IV(B), however, because I do not subscribe to the theory that the Justices of this Court are free generally to decide on the basis of its content which speech protected by the First Amendment is most "valuable" and hence deserving of the most protection, and which is less "valuable" and hence deserving of less protection. Compare ante, at 15–19; Young v. American Mini Theatres, 427 U.S. 50, 63–73 (1976) (opinion of Stevens, J.), with id., at 73 n. 1 (Powell, J., concurring).[3] In my view, the result in this case does not turn on whether Carlin's monologue, viewed as a whole, or the words that comprise it, have more or less "value" than a candidate's campaign speech. This is a judgment for each person to make, not one for judges to impose upon him.[4]

The result turns instead on the unique characteristics of the broadcast media, combined with society's right to protect its children from speech generally agreed to be inappropriate for their years, and with the interest of unwilling adults in not being assaulted by such

---

2. It is true that the radio listener quickly may tune out speech that is offensive to him. In addition, broadcasters may preface potentially offensive programs with warnings. But such warnings do not help the unsuspecting listener who tunes in at the middle of the program. In this respect, too, broadcasting appears to differ from books and records, which may carry warnings on their faces, and from motion pictures and live performances, which may carry warnings on their marquees.

3. The Court has, however, created a limited exception to this rule in order to bring commercial speech within the protection of the First Amendment. See Ohralik v. Ohio State Bar Association, 436 U.S. 447 (1978).

4. For much the same reason, I also do not join IV(A). I had not thought that the application *vel non* of overbreadth analysis should depend on the Court's judgment as to the value of the protected speech that might be deterred. . . .

offensive speech in their homes. Moreover, I doubt whether today's decision will prevent any adult who wishes to receive Carlin's message in Carlin's own words from doing so, and from making for himself a value judgment as to the merit of the message and words. . . .

MR. JUSTICE BRENNAN, with whom MR. JUSTICE MARSHALL joins, dissenting.

I agree with Mr. Justice Stewart that, under Hamling v. United States, 418 U.S. 87 (1974) and United States v. 12 200–ft. Reels of Film, 413 U.S. 123 (1973), the word "indecent" in 18 U.S.C. § 1464 must be construed to prohibit only obscene speech. . . .

I

For the second time in two years, see Young v. American Mini Theatres, 427 U.S. 50 (1976), the Court refuses to embrace the notion, completely antithetical to basic First Amendment values, that the degree of protection the First Amendment affords protected speech varies with the social value ascribed to that speech by five Members of this Court. See opinion of Mr. Justice Powell . . . .. Yet despite the Court's refusal to create a sliding scale of First Amendment protection calibrated to the Court's perception of the worth of a communication's content, and despite our unanimous agreement that the Carlin monologue is protected speech, a majority of the Court nevertheless finds that, on the facts of this case, the FCC is not constitutionally barred from imposing sanctions on Pacifica for its airing of the Carlin monologue. This majority apparently believes that the FCC's disapproval of Pacifica's afternoon broadcast of Carlin's "Dirty Words" recording is a permissible time, place, and manner regulation. . . .

A

Without question, the privacy interests of an individual in his home are substantial and deserving of significant protection. In finding these interests sufficient to justify the content regulation of protected speech, however, the Court commits two errors. First, it misconceives the nature of the privacy interests involved where an individual voluntarily chooses to admit radio communications into his home. Second, it ignores the constitutionally protected interests of both those who wish to transmit and those who desire to receive broadcasts that many—including the FCC and this Court—might find offensive.

. . . . I believe that an individual's actions in switching on and listening to communications transmitted over the public airways and directed to the public at-large do not implicate fundamental privacy interests, even when engaged within the home. Instead, because the radio is undeniably a public medium, these actions are more properly viewed as a decision to take part, if only as a listener, in an ongoing public discourse. See Note, Filthy Words, the FCC, and the First Amendment: Regulating Broadcast Obscenity, 61 Va.L.Rev. 579, 618 (1975). Although an individual's decision to allow public radio communications into his home undoubtedly does not abrogate all of his privacy interests, the residual privacy interests he retains vis-a-vis the communication he voluntarily admits into his home are surely no greater than those of the people present in the corridor of the Los Angeles courthouse in *Cohen* who bore witness to the words "Fuck the Draft" emblazoned across Cohen's jacket. Their privacy interests were held insufficient to justify punishing Cohen for his offensive communication.

Even if an individual who voluntarily opens his home to radio communications retains privacy interests of sufficient moment to justify a ban on protected speech if those interests are "invaded in an essentially intolerable manner," Cohen v. California, supra, at 21, the very fact that those interests are threatened only by a radio broadcast precludes any intolerable invasion of privacy; for unlike other intrusive modes of communication, such as sound trucks, "[t]he radio can be turned off," Lehman v. City of Shaker Heights, 418 U.S. 298, 302 (1974)—and with a minimum of effort. . . . Whatever the minimal discomfort suffered by a listener who inadvertently tunes into a program he finds offensive during the brief interval before he can simply extend his arm and switch stations or flick the "off" button, it is surely worth the candle to preserve the broadcaster's right to send, and the right of those interested to receive, a message entitled to full First Amendment protection. . . .

The Court's balance, of necessity, fails to accord proper weight to the interests of listeners who wish to hear broadcasts the FCC deems offensive. It permits majoritarian tastes completely to preclude a protected message from entering the homes of a receptive, unoffended minority. No decision of this Court supports such a result. Where the individuals comprising the offended majority may freely choose to reject the material being offered, we have never found their privacy interest of such moment to warrant the suppression of speech on privacy grounds. . . .

B

Most parents will undoubtedly find understandable as well as commendable the Court's sympathy with the FCC's desire to prevent offensive broadcasts from reaching the ears of unsupervised children. Unfortunately, the facial appeal of this justification for radio censorship masks its constitutional insufficiency.

Because the Carlin monologue is obviously not an erotic appeal to the prurient interests of children, the Court, for the first time, allows the government to prevent minors from gaining access to materials that are not obscene, and are therefore protected, as to them. It thus ignores our recent admission that "[s]peech that is neither obscene as to youths nor subject to some other legitimate proscription cannot be suppressed solely to protect the young from ideas or images that a legislative body thinks unsuitable for them." [*Erznoznik*] [3] The Court's

---

3. It may be that a narrowly drawn regulation prohibiting the use of offensive language on broadcasts directed specifically at younger children constitutes one of refusal to follow its own pronouncements is especially lamentable since it has the anomalous subsidiary effect, at least in the radio context at issue here, of making completely unavailable to adults material which may not constitutionally be kept even from children. . . .

In concluding that the presence of children in the listening audience provides an adequate basis for the FCC to impose sanctions for Pacifica's broadcast of the Carlin monologue, the opinions of my Brother Powell and my Brother Stevens both stress the time-honored right of a parent to raise his child as he sees fit—a right this Court has consistently been vigilant to protect. See Wisconsin v. Yoder, 406 U.S. 205 (1972); Pierce v. Society of Sisters, 268 U.S. 510 (1925). Yet this principle supports a result directly contrary to that reached by the Court. *Yoder* and *Pierce* hold that parents, *not* the government, have the right to make certain decisions regarding the upbringing of their children. As surprising as it may be to the individual Members of the Court, some parents may actually find Mr. Carlin's unabashed attitude toward the seven "dirty words" healthy, and deem it desirable to expose their children to the manner in which Mr. Carlin defuses the taboo surrounding the words. Such parents may constitute a minority of the American public, but the absence of great numbers willing to exercise the right to raise children in this fashion does not alter the right's nature or its existence. Only the Court's regrettable decision does that.[4]

C

As demonstrated above, neither of the factors relied on by both the opinion of my Brother Powell and the opinion of my Brother Stevens— the intrusive nature of radio and the presence of children in the listening audience—can, when taken on its own terms, support the FCC's disapproval of the Carlin monologue. These two asserted justifications are further plagued by a common failing: the lack of principled limits on their use as a basis for FCC censorship. No such limits come readily to mind, and neither of the opinions constituting the Court serve to clarify the extent to which the FCC may assert the privacy and children-in-the-audience rationales as justification for expunging from

the "other legitimate proscription[s]" alluded to in *Erznoznik*. This is so both because of the difficulties inherent in adapting the *Miller* formulation to communications received by young children, and because such children are "not possessed of that full capacity for individual choice which is the presupposition of the First Amendment guarantees." Ginsberg v. New York, 390 U.S. 629, 649–650 (1968) (Stewart, J., concurring). I doubt, as my Brother Stevens suggests, ante, at 17 n. 20, that such a limited regulation amounts to a regulation of speech based on its content, since, by hypothesis, the only persons at whom the regulated communication is directed are incapable of evaluating its content. To the extent that such a regulation is viewed as a regulation based on content, it marks the outermost limits to which content regulation is permissible.

4. The opinions of my Brothers Powell and Stevens rightly refrain from relying on the notion of "spectrum scarcity" to support their result. As Chief Judge Bazelon noted below, "although scarcity has justified *increasing* the diversity of speakers and speech, it has never been held to justify censorship." See Red Lion Broadcasting Co. v. FCC, 395 U.S. 367, 396 (1969).

the airways protected communications the Commission finds offensive. . . .

   . . . The opinions of both my Brother Powell and my Brother Stevens take the FCC at its word, and consequently do no more than permit the Commission to censor the afternoon broadcast of the "sort of verbal shock treatment," opinion of Mr. Justice Powell, involved here. To insure that the FCC's regulation of protected speech does not exceed these bounds, my Brother Powell is content to rely upon the judgment of the Commission while my Brother Stevens deems it prudent to rely on this Court's ability accurately to assess the worth of various kinds of speech.[6] For my own part, even accepting that this case is limited to its facts, I would place the responsibility and the right to weed worthless and offensive communications from the public airways where it belongs and where, until today, it resided: in a public free to choose those communications worthy of its attention from a marketplace unsullied by the censor's hand.

II

. . .

   . . . The idea that the content of a message and its potential impact on any who might receive it can be divorced from the words that are the vehicle for its expression is transparently fallacious. A given word may have a unique capacity to capsule an idea, evoke an emotion, or conjure up an image. Indeed, for those of us who place an appropriately high value on our cherished First Amendment rights, the word "censor" is such a word. Mr. Justice Harlan, speaking for the Court, recognized the truism that a speaker's choice of words cannot surgically be separated from the ideas he desires to express when he warned that "we cannot indulge the facile assumption that one can forbid particular words without also running a substantial risk of suppressing ideas in the process." Cohen v. California, 403 U.S., at 26. Moreover, even if an alternative phrasing may communicate a speaker's abstract ideas as effectively as those words he is forbidden to use, it is doubtful that the sterilized message will convey the emotion that is an essential part of so many communications.

. . .

   The Court apparently believes that the FCC's actions here can be analogized to the zoning ordinances upheld in Young v. American Mini Theatres, supra. For two reasons, it is wrong. First, the zoning ordinances found to pass constitutional muster in *Young* had valid goals other than the channeling of protected speech. [ ] No such

---

6. Although ultimately dependent upon the outcome of review in this Court, the approach taken by my Brother Stevens would not appear to tolerate the FCC's suppression of any speech, such as political speech, falling within the core area of First Amendment concern. The same, however, cannot be said of the approach taken by my Brother Powell, which, on its face, permits the Commission to censor even political speech if it is sufficiently offensive to community standards. A result more contrary to rudimentary First Amendment principles is difficult to imagine.

goals are present here. Second, . . . the ordinances do not restrict the access of distributors or exhibitors to the market or impair the viewing public's access to the regulated material. [ ] Again, this is not the situation here. Both those desiring to receive Carlin's message over the radio and those wishing to send it to them are prevented from doing so by the Commission's actions. Although, as my Brethren point out, Carlin's message may be disseminated or received by other means, this is of little consolation to those broadcasters and listeners who, for a host of reasons, not least among them financial, do not have access to, or cannot take advantage of, these other means.

. . .

III

It is quite evident that I find the Court's attempt to unstitch the warp and woof of First Amendment law in an effort to reshape its fabric to cover the patently wrong result the Court reaches in this case dangerous as well as lamentable. Yet there runs throughout the opinions of my Brothers Powell and Stevens another vein I find equally disturbing: a depressing inability to appreciate that in our land of cultural pluralism, there are many who think, act, and talk differently from the Members of this Court, and who do not share their fragile sensibilities. It is only an acute ethnocentric myopia that enables the Court to approve the censorship of communications solely because of the words they contain.

. . . The words that the Court and the Commission find so unpalatable may be the stuff of everyday conversations in some, if not many, of the innumerable subcultures that comprise this Nation. Academic research indicates that this is indeed the case. [ ] As one researcher concluded, "[w]ords generally considered obscene like 'bullshit' and 'fuck' are considered neither obscene nor derogatory in the [black] vernacular except in particular contextual situations and when used with certain intonations." [ ] Cf. Keefe v. Geanakos, 418 F.2d 359, 361 (1st Cir.1969) (finding the use of the word "motherfucker" commonplace among young radicals and protestors).

Today's decision will thus have its greatest impact on broadcasters desiring to reach, and listening audiences comprised of, persons who do not share the Court's view as to which words or expressions are acceptable and who, for a variety of reasons, including a conscious desire to flout majoritarian conventions, express themselves using words that may be regarded as offensive by those from different socio-economic backgrounds.[8] . . .

8. Under the approach taken by my Brother Powell, the availability of broadcasts *about* groups whose members comprise such audiences might also be affected. Both news broadcasts about activities involving these groups and public affairs broadcasts about their concerns are apt to contain interviews, statements, or remarks by group leaders and members which may contain offensive language to an extent my Brother Powell finds unacceptable.

MR. JUSTICE STEWART, with whom MR. JUSTICE BRENNAN, MR. JUSTICE WHITE, and MR. JUSTICE MARSHALL join, dissenting.

.   .   .

The statute pursuant to which the Commission acted, 18 U.S.C. § 1464, makes it a federal offense to utter "any obscene, indecent, or profane language by means of radio communication." The Commission held, and the Court today agrees, that "indecent" is a broader concept than "obscene" as the latter term was defined in Miller v. California, 413 U.S. 15, because language can be "indecent" although it has social, political, or artistic value and lacks prurient appeal. 56 F.C.C.2d, at 97–98. But this construction of § 1464, while perhaps plausible, is by no means compelled. To the contrary, I think that "indecent" should properly be read as meaning no more than "obscene." Since the Carlin monologue concededly was not "obscene," I believe that the Commission lacked statutory authority to ban it. Under this construction of the statute, it is unnecessary to address the difficult and important issue of the Commission's constitutional power to prohibit speech that would be constitutionally protected outside the context of electronic broadcasting.

.   .   .

Notes and Questions

1. There are now products available to control what programs can be seen on a television set. Using a weekly schedule, a parent can enter the day, time, channel number and duration of time of each program the parent wishes a child to be able to see. If the set is turned to a channel that is not cleared for that day and time, no picture or sound will appear. A key permits changes to be made. If this were standard equipment on all television sets (and radios), might it meet some of the concerns in *Pacifica*?

2. Is the "risk" of tuning in an offensive program on radio or television any greater than the risk of encountering offensive language on a person's clothing in a public place, as in Cohen v. California, 403 U.S. 15 (1971)? What about offensive films visible from the street while being shown at an outdoor movie theatre, *Erznoznik*, p. 318, *supra*? If averting your eyes is an adequate remedy in these cases, why is turning off the radio or television set not adequate here? Is the fact that one may occur in the home relevant?

3. It is easier to warn viewers that an adult, or possibly offensive, program is being presented when television is involved. In some countries, such programs carry a white dot in a corner of the picture so that a viewer can know the nature of the programming instantly. Would this solve our problems so far as television is concerned? Is there a similar technique that can be used for radio? Is it enough that certain stations become known as likely to present certain kinds of material offensive to some? What more could the licensee have done

here to warn adult listeners? See Glasser and Jassem, Indecent Broadcasts and the Listener's Right of Privacy, 24 J. Broadcasting 285 (1980).

4. It has long been agreed that Congress has preempted the matter of obscenity on radio and television—both of which are within "radio communication." Thus, a state may not impose its movie censorship scheme on films shown on television.

5. In a clarification sought by the Radio Television News Directors Association (RTNDA), the Commission announced that its decision in the Pacifica case was not meant to impinge on the coverage of news events in which offensive speech is sometimes uttered without a chance for editing: "Under these circumstances we believe that it would be inequitable for us to hold a licensee responsible for indecent language." Pacifica Foundation, 59 F.C.C.2d 892, 36 R.R.2d 1008 (1976). What if there is time for editing the dialogue but to do so would change the impact of the event? Can this be handled by an announcer who says "At this point the speaker launched into a stream of obscenities"?

Vice President Nelson Rockefeller used a finger gesture generally considered "obscene" when replying in kind to a heckler during a campaign rally. Most newspapers ran the photograph, but some did not. Would the decision be different for television stations? Are the considerations different for the 6 p.m. and the 11 p.m. news? Does the fact that it was in the course of a live news event make a difference?

6. Shortly after *Pacifica* the Commission rejected a petition to deny renewal to a television station. The petitioners had contended that the station had broadcast programs in which obscenities had been used and also carried programs with unacceptable themes, such as a "Masterpiece Theatre" episode that was said to approve of adultery. The Commission stated that its role in reviewing programs at renewal time "is and must be limited to determining whether the licensee's *overall* programming has served its service area, and not whether a particular program is 'appropriate' for broadcast." Nor can the subjective views of groups of listeners be considered.

Turning to the relevance of *Pacifica,* the Commission stated that it "affords no general prerogative to intervene in any case where words similar or identical to those in *Pacifica* are broadcast over a licensed radio or television station. We intend strictly to observe the narrowness of the *Pacifica* holding." The FCC noted that in *Pacifica,* the Commission had stressed the "repetitive occurrence" of the words and that Justice Powell had stressed the same feature in his opinion. "It was certainly not our intent . . . to inhibit coverage of diverse and controversial subjects by licensees, whether in news and public affairs or in dramatic or other programming contexts." WGBH Educational Foundation, 69 F.C.C.2d 1250, 43 R.R.2d 1436 (1978).

7. Shortly after *Pacifica,* a primary election for governor was held in Georgia. J. B. Stoner, a legally qualified candidate, speaking under § 315, made broadcast messages using the word "nigger." Black groups asked the Commission to bar such language as indecent under

the *Pacifica* principle. The Broadcast Bureau rejected the request. First, it ruled that the word was not "language that describes in the broadcast medium, sexual or excretory activities and organs, at times of the day when there is reasonable risk that children may be in the audience," quoting the Commission's language in *Pacifica*. Also, the Commission had already announced that "we intend strictly to observe the narrowness of the Pacifica holding." Even if the Commission were to find the word obscene or indecent, under § 315 the candidate could not be prevented from using the word during his "use" of the licensee's facilities. Julian Bond, 69 F.C.C.2d 943, 43 R.R.2d 1015 (Bd.Bur.1978).

8. During the 1980 Presidential campaign, one radio commercial began as follows: A man says "Bullshit!" After a woman says "What?," the man's voice replies: "Carter, Reagan, and Anderson. It's all Bullshit! Bullshit!" Then the party's candidate says "Too bad people have to use such strong language, but isn't that what you think too? That's why we started an entirely new political party, the Citizens Party." The FCC, which received many complaints and inquiries, responded that the precedents were quite clear that no censorship was possible—at least unless a candidate created a clear and present danger of riot or violence.

The campaign director said that for six months the media had been covering only the three major candidates "despite the fact that they have little to say of substance about the problems of the nation." He observed that "It's a sad commentary on the media that we received more attention as a result of using that word than we've received in the last six months combined."

9. In 1983 *Hustler* magazine publisher Larry Flynt was reported to be intending to use clips from X-rated films in television ads supporting his presidential candidacy. This caused Sen. Jeremiah Denton (R–Ala.) to introduce legislation to allow broadcasters to refuse to air pornographic political announcements despite the no-censorship provision of § 315. Subsequently the FCC indicated that it would not apply the no-censorship provision to obscene or indecent political announcements. The issue never arose as Flynt chose not to run.

10. In 1992, the Commission was asked to rule that allegedly indecent anti-abortion political ads for federal candidates could be channelled to the safe harbor time period. Initially, the Mass Media Bureau held that channelling these ads—which contained graphic pictures of aborted fetuses—would violate the candidates' right of access under § 312(a)(7). Vincent A. Pepper, Esq. 71 R.R.2d 214 (M.Med.Bur.1992) WAGA–TV, one of the parties filing the original petition, then obtained an order from a U.S. District Court restraining a campaign ad for congressional candidate Daniel Becker to the safe harbor time period. Becker's appeal to the Eleventh Circuit was denied. Meanwhile, the FCC issued a ruling leaving a decision on channelling the Becker ad to the good faith judgment of WAGA–TV. The Commission also issued an

NOI on the general question of channelling graphic anti-abortion advertisements to the safe harbor time period. Broadcasting, Nov. 9, 1992 at
48.

11. Following *Pacifica* the Commission's enforcement of the indecency
provisions of § 1464 was essentially nonexistent. In the mid–1980s
citizen groups put increasing pressure on the Commission actively to
enforce § 1464.

Finally, in April 1987 the Commission took action against three
broadcast stations and one amateur radio operator. One station had
broadcast excerpts from the play, "Jerker." The play was running in
Los Angeles and had previously run in New York. Much of the play
consists of telephone conversations between two homosexuals dying of
AIDS in which they share their sexual fantasies. In an interview with
the play's director that preceded the excerpts, the play was characterized as "blazingly erotic." The Commission rejected arguments by
Pacifica that the excerpts should be considered in the context of the
play's message—"the need to affirm life in the face of death." "Notwithstanding the licensee's assertion, we do not believe the context
dilutes or ameliorates the patently offensive manner in which the
sexual activity was described." Pacifica Foundation, Inc., 2 F.C.C.Rcd.
2698, 62 R.R.2d 1191 (1987).

A second station had aired a song that in the Commission's view
"contained a number of patently offensive references to sexual organs
and activities as measured by contemporary community standards for
the broadcast medium." The Regents of the University of California, 2
F.C.C.Rcd. 2703, 62 R.R.2d 1199 (1987).

The complaint against the third station centered on "The Howard
Stern Show." The show is an example of a new radio format that is
often referred to as "shock radio." Characterized by humor that is full
of sexual innuendo and ridicule, it is considered offensive and tasteless
by its opponents. At the same time, it is successful in the ratings. For
example, Stern's show had moved from number 16 to three in the
Philadelphia market. The following excerpts were cited by the Commission as examples of the programming they found indecent:

Excerpt 1

Howard Stern:	"God, my testicles are like down to the floor. Boy, Susan, you could really have a party with these. I'm telling you honey."
Ray:	"Use them like Bocci balls."

Excerpt 2

Howard Stern:	"Let me tell you something, honey. These homos you are with are all limp."
Ray:	"Yeah. You've never even had a real man."
Howard Stern:	"You've probably never been with a man with a full erection."

Excerpt 3

Susan: "No, I was in a park in New Rochelle, N.Y."

Howard Stern: "In a park in New Rochelle? On your knees?"

Susan: "No, no."

Ray: "And squeezing someone's testicles, probably."

Excerpt 5

As part of a discussion of lesbians

Howard Stern: "I mean to go around porking other girls with vibrating rubber products and they want the whole world to come to a standstill."

Excerpt 6

Howard Stern: "Have you ever had sex with an animal?"

Caller: "No."

Howard Stern: "Well, don't knock it. I was sodomized by Lambchop, you know that puppet Sherri Lewis holds?"

Howard Stern: "Baaaaah. That's where I was thinking that Sherri Lewis, instead of like sodomizing all the people at the Academy to get that shot on the Emmys she could've had Lambchop do it."

Infinity Broadcasting Corp. of Pennsylvania, 2 F.C.C.Rcd. 2705, 62 R.R.2d 1202 (1987). Several stations toned down "shock radio" shows as a result of the Commission's actions.

Because the application of the indecency provisions of § 1464 in these cases represented a departure from previous Commission Policy, the stations were warned, but no further action was taken. At the same time, in a public notice, the Commission announced its intent to expand its enforcement of § 1464. New Indecency Enforcement Standards to be Applied to All Broadcast and Amateur Radio Licensees, 2 F.C.C.Rcd. 2726, 62 R.R.2d 1218 (1987).

Rather than limiting enforcement of § 1464 to the seven "dirty words" contained in the Carlin dialogue, the Commission announced it would "apply the *generic* definition of broadcast indecency advanced in *Pacifica,* which is: 'Language or material that depicts or describes, in terms patently offensive as measured by contemporary community standards for the broadcast medium, sexual or excretory activities or organs.'"

The Commission also announced a change in the times during which programming would be subject to the indecency provisions of § 1464. ". . . [I]ndecency will be actionable when there is a reasonable risk that children may be in the audience, but . . . this benchmark is not susceptible to a uniform standard. . . . [D]espite prior assumptions that children were not in the broadcasting audience at 10:00 p.m., recent evidence for the markets involved indicates that there is still a reasonable risk that children may be in the listening audience at [those] hours. . . ." Thus, as was the case in both the new Pacifica case and the Regents of the University of California case, programs after 10 p.m. could still be subject to the indecency provisions of § 1464 if there was evidence that children were in the audience.

Shortly thereafter Pacifica asked the Commission for a declaratory ruling on whether planned readings from James Joyce's *Ulysses* over its New York City station would violate the Commission's new indecency standards. In its request Pacifica did not identify the source of the readings. Claiming that such a ruling would constitute a prior restraint, the Commission's staff refused to issue a ruling. Pacifica carried the readings as planned but also filed an appeal. Broadcasting, June 22, 1987 at 48.

In response to various Petitions for Clarification and Petitions for Reconsideration, including ones from the three broadcast licensees involved in the original decision, the Commission issued a further opinion and order on indecency. Infinity Broadcasting Corporation of Pennsylvania (Indecency Policy Reconsideration), 3 F.C.C.Rcd. 930, 64 R.R.2d 211 (1987). The FCC began by rejecting a request by Morality in Media that some "sexually explicit, yet non-obscene material" be absolutely prohibited. Such a prohibition would in the Commission's opinion be unconstitutional because the Supreme Court decision in *Pacifica* authorized only "the imposition of reasonable time, place and manner restrictions on the broadcast of indecent material in order to advance the government's interest in protecting children." In a footnote the Commission indicated that it would rely on parents to supervise their children after midnight, thus creating a "safe harbor" for broadcasts of indecent—but not obscene—programs. Although the footnote did not indicate when the "safe harbor" would end, the FCC's general counsel suggested at a press conference that 6 a.m. was the appropriate time. In a concurrence, Commissioner Dennis suggested that the "safe harbor" start at the conclusion of prime time.

Next the Commission declined to define "patently offensive" or exempt material with "serious literary, artistic, political or scientific value."

> 14. "Patently offensive" is a phrase that must, of necessity, be construed with reference to specific facts. We cannot and will not attempt to provide petitioners with a comprehensive index or thesaurus of indecent words or pictorial depictions that will be considered patently offensive. There is no way to construct a definitive list that would be both comprehensive and not over-inclusive in the abstract, without reference to the specific context. All we hold here, therefore, is that, in the three cases before us, we properly found the material identified as indecent to be patently offensive.

> 15. Our approach here is consistent with that of the courts, which have likewise never attempted to identify with the degree of certainty requested by petitioners the complete and definitive range of material that falls within the generic, legal definitions of

certain categories of speech. [The Commission cited obscenity law as a specific example where the term "patently offensive" had passed constitutional muster.]

. . .

17. The merit of a work is also one of the many variables that make up a work's "context," as the Court implicitly recognized in *Pacifica* when it contrasted the Carlin monologue to Elizabethan comedies and works of Chaucer. But merit is simply one of many variables, and it would give this particular variable undue importance if we were to single it out for greater weight or attention than we give other variables. We decline to do so in deciding the three cases before us. We must, therefore, reject an approach that would hold that if a work has merit, it is *per se* not indecent. At the same time, we must reject the notion that a work's "context" can be reviewed in a manner that artificially excludes merit from the host of variables that ordinarily comprise context. The ultimate determinative factor in our analysis, however, is whether the material, when examined in context, is patently offensive. . . .

After reviewing the three specific cases and concluding that the broadcasts in each case were indecent, the Commission did clarify the definition of the phrase, "contemporary community standards," as used in the definition of indecency. The standard is that of "an average broadcast viewer." Thus, the Commission will use a national standard for indecency as opposed to the local standard for obscenity prescribed by *Miller.*

Finally, the FCC turned to a request that it defer to the reasonable, good faith judgment of a licensees when determining whether they have violated § 1464:

. . . Although we acknowledge that the statute requires a broadcaster to make judgments as to whether certain material would violate the statute, the fact that the decision may not be an easy one cannot excuse the broadcaster from having to exercise its judgment, any more than it can excuse the Commission from exercising its enforcement responsibilities. We note, however, that it is standard procedure for the Commission, in deciding whether to impose a sanction for violation of the law and, if so, what those sanctions should be, to give weight to the reasonable determinations of licensees endeavoring to comply with the law. Because licensees demonstrating reasonable judgment have no cause to fear the imposition of unjustified sanctions, we reject the petitioners' contentions that the editorial decisions of broadcasters will be inappropriately chilled by continuation of this approach.

The Commission's decision was appealed by various trade organizations and public interest groups.

ACTION FOR CHILDREN'S TELEVISION v. FEDERAL COMMUNICATIONS COMMISSION

United States Court of Appeals, District of Columbia Circuit, 1988.
852 F.2d 1332, 65 R.R.2d 45, 15 Med.L.Rptr. 1907.

Before ROBINSON, RUTH B. GINSBURG, and SENTELLE, CIRCUIT JUDGES.

GINSBURG, CIRCUIT JUDGE.

. . .

IV.

The FCC acknowledges a change of regulatory course: The Commission now measures broadcast material against the generic definition of indecency, while formerly "no action was taken unless material involved the repeated use, for shock value, of words similar or identical to those satirized in the Carlin 'Filthy Words' monologue." [*Indecency Policy Reconsideration*] Petitioners charge that the Commission has failed to supply an adequate explanation for the change. [ ] Specifically, petitioners say that the Commission deliberately narrowed the former standard to make it reasonably certain and to afford broadcasters ample breathing space. [ ] The new standard, they contend, is "inherently vague" and was installed without any evidence of a problem justifying a thickened regulatory response. [ ]

The explanation offered by the Commission, in its *Reconsideration Order*, is that it found the deliberately-repeated-use-of-dirty-words policy "unduly narrow as a matter of law" and inconsistent with its obligation responsibly to enforce Section 1464. [ ] The former approach permitted the unregulated broadcast of any material that did not contain Carlin's "filthy words," no matter how the material might affect children exposed to it. It made no legal or policy sense, the FCC said, to regulate the Carlin monologue but not "material that portrayed sexual or excretory activities or organs in as patently offensive a manner . . . simply because it avoided certain words." [ ]

We find the FCC's explanation adequate. Short of the thesis that *only* the seven words are properly designated indecent—an argument petitioners disavow—some more expansive definition must be attempted. The FCC rationally determined that its former policy could yield anomalous, even arbitrary, results. No reasonable formulation tighter than the one the Commission has announced has been suggested in this review proceeding. The difficulty, or "abiding discomfort," we conclude, is not the absence of "reasoned analysis" on the Commission's part, but the "[v]agueness . . . inherent in the subject matter." [ ] We turn next to that issue.

V.

Petitioners charge that the term "indecent" is inherently unclear, and that the FCC's generic definition of indecency adds nothing significant in the way of clarification. The Commission's definition, petitioners therefore contend, provides broadcasters no meaningful guide identifying the category of material subject to regulation; accordingly, petitioners urge, the definition should be ruled unconstitutionally vague. In our view the Supreme Court's disposition of *Pacifica* stops "what the Constitution calls an 'inferior court' " from addressing this question on the merits. [ ]

The generic definition of indecency now employed by the FCC is virtually the same definition the Commission articulated in the order reviewed by the Supreme Court in [*Pacifica*]. However, the Court did not address, specifically, whether the FCC's definition was on its face unconstitutionally vague. The Court did hold the Carlin monologue indecent within the meaning of Section 1464. 438 U.S. at 741. We infer from this holding that the Court did not regard the term "indecent" as so vague that persons "of common intelligence must necessarily guess at its meaning and differ as to its application." . . .

. . . [I]f acceptance of the FCC's generic definition of "indecent" as capable of surviving a vagueness challenge is not implicit in *Pacifica*, we have misunderstood Higher Authority and welcome correction.

VI.

Intervenors ACLU *et al.* argue that the FCC's generic definition of indecency is substantially overbroad. As we read *Pacifica*, only two members of the five-member majority thought it in order to rule on overbreadth, so we proceed to address that issue on the merits. The ACLU's challenge is predicated on the absence of redemption from indecency status for material that has "serious merit." We hold that "serious merit" need not, in every instance, immunize indecent material from FCC channeling authority.

. . . According to intervenors, a proper definition of indecency would include the requirement that the "work, taken as a whole, lacks serious literary, artistic, political, or scientific value." [ACLU Brief, quoting *Miller*] . . .

. . .

Indecent but not obscene material, we reiterate, qualifies for First Amendment protection whether or not it has serious merit. Children's access to indecent material, however, may be regulated, because "even where there is an invasion of protected freedoms 'the power of the state to control the conduct of children reaches beyond the scope of its authority over adults. . . .' " [ ] Channeling is designed to protect unsupervised children. [ ] Some material that has significant social value may contain language and descriptions as offensive, from the perspective of parental control over children's exposure, as material lacking such value.[13] Since the overall value of a work will not

13. The Carlin monologue itself may be an example of indecent material possessing significant social value. . . .

necessarily alter the impact of certain words or phrases on children, the FCC's approach is permissible under controlling case law: merit is properly treated as a factor in determining whether material is patently offensive, but it does not render such material *per se* not indecent. [ ] The FCC's definition, therefore, is not vulnerable to the charge that it is substantially overbroad.

VII.

We have upheld the FCC's generic definition of indecency in light of the sole purpose of that definition: to permit the channeling of indecent material, in order to shelter children from exposure to words and phrases their parents regard as inappropriate for them to hear. [ ] Petitioners press two linked objections to the FCC's "current thinking" that 12:00 midnight is the hour after which indecent material may be broadcast without sanctions.[15] The FCC's channeling decision is arbitrary and capricious, petitioners contend, because it is not based on adequate factual or analytic foundation. [ ] Tied to and coloring that contention, petitioners charge that the Commission's action regarding channeling violates the First Amendment because it reduces adults to seeing and hearing material fit only for children.

We agree that, in view of the curtailment of broadcaster freedom and adult listener choice that channeling entails, the Commission failed to consider fairly and fully what time lines should be drawn. We therefore vacate, in the *Pacifica Foundation* and *Regents of the University of California* cases, the FCC's ruling that the broadcast under review was actionable, and we remand those cases to the agency for thoroughgoing reconsideration of the times at which indecent material may be aired.

[The court affirmed the FCC's ruling in *Infinity* because the programming at issue was broadcast between 6 and 10 a.m. The court could find no rational distinction between those early morning programs and the Carlin broadcast in the earlier Pacifica case, which was aired in the early afternoon.]

Each of the April 29, 1987 rulings reported an FCC finding that the broadcast occurred at a time of day when there was a reasonable risk that children may have been in the audience. In *Pacifica Foundation*, involving a 10:00–11:00 p.m. broadcast, the Commission relied on ratings data indicating that "approximately 112,200 children age 12–17 are in the Los Angeles metro survey area radio audience per average quarter hour between 7 p.m. and midnight on Sunday night." [ ] In

---

Other examples that come readily to mind include descriptions of the doings of Gargantua and Pantagruel in Rabelais' classic, certain passages in the works of Joyce, words and phrases found in the writings of D.H. Lawrence, James Baldwin, and Frank Harris.

15. Petitioners do not challenge the FCC's requirement that programs containing indecent material be preceded by appropriate warnings. [ ] That aspect of the Commission's channeling regulation is not affected by this decision.

Regents of the University of California, involving a program aired after 10:00 p.m., available data indicated that

> approximately 1,200 children between 12 and 17 years of age are still in the radio audience per average quarter hour in the Santa Barbara area between 7 p.m. and midnight on Saturday evenings. There are approximately 4,900 children within this age group within the City of Santa Barbara itself and 27,800 in the county.
> [ ]

Even were we to treat each of the two rulings solely as an *ad hoc* adjudication, we would regard the evidence on which the Commission rested its channeling decisions as insubstantial, and its findings more ritual than real. It is familiar law that an agency treads an arbitrary course when it fails to "articulate any rational connection between the facts found and the choice made." [ ] We conclude the Commission followed such a course here.

In each instance under inspection the cited population figures appear to estimate the number of teens in the *total* radio audience. There is no indication of the size of the predicted audience for the specific radio stations in question. [ ] More troubling, the FCC ventures no explanation why it takes teens 12–17 to be the relevant age group for channeling purposes. In the Commission's 1976 legislative proposal, cited to the Supreme Court in the FCC's *Pacifica* brief, the Commission would have required broadcasters to minimize the risk of exposing to indecent material children *under* age 12. The FCC reasoned: "Age 12 was selected since it is the accepted upper limit for children's programming in the industry and at the Commission . . . ." [ ] We cannot tell from the record before us whether the Commission is now spreading the focus of its concern to children over 12. [ ] If it is thus widening its sights, that apparent change in policy warrants explanation. If, on the other hand, the FCC continues to consider children under 12 as the age group of concern, it should either supply information on the listening habits of children in that age range, or explain how it extrapolates relevant data for that population from the available ratings information.

[Noting that in the Santa Barbara case only 4 percent of the teens living in that area were estimated to be in the radio listening audience, the court questioned whether that "amounts to a 'reasonable risk' for channeling purposes."]

We do not, however, remand solely for reconsideration of the individual rulings. In the *Reconsideration Order* the FCC offered some advice to broadcasters:

> [W]hereas previously we indicated that 10:00 p.m. was a reasonable delineation point, we now indicate that 12:00 midnight is our current thinking as to when it is reasonable to expect that it is late enough to ensure that the risk of children in the audience is minimized and to rely on parents to exercise increased supervision

over whatever children remain in the viewing and listening audience.

64 R.R.2d at 219 n. 47. The Commission next listed several competing interests, . . ., and said that its approach accommodated them. As noted by Commissioner Dennis, however, "the arguments the majority gives in support of midnight as the critical hour may well be equally true if applied to an earlier hour." [ ] We agree that the FCC's midnight advice, indeed its entire position on channeling, was not adequately thought through.

At oral argument . . . General Counsel for the FCC suggested that if this Court found the midnight safe harbor problematic, we could disregard it and permit the Commission to make future channeling decisions on a case-by-case basis. However, the FCC itself has recognized that "the effect of that approach may well be to cause broadcasters to forego the broadcast of certain protected speech altogether, rather than to channel it to late night hours." [ ] In common with the Commission, we are constrained to agree with that assessment. Facing the uncertainty generated by a less than precise definition of indecency *plus* the lack of a safe harbor for the broadcast of (possibly) indecent material, broadcasters surely would be more likely to avoid such programming altogether than would be the case were one area of uncertainty eliminated. We conclude that, in view of the constitutionally protected expression interests at stake, the FCC must afford broadcasters clear notice of reasonably determined times at which indecent material safely may be aired.

It is within our authority to instruct the FCC to establish a safe harbor by means of a rulemaking proceeding. [ ] We call attention, however, to the clear statement made by one Commissioner: "The fact is the Commission has no scientific body of information that conclusively establishes one time as more appropriate than another as the critical hour after which to permit broadcast of indecent speech. What is necessary is a notice of proposed rulemaking to establish a record." [ ] The inadequate record relevant to channeling made in the cases the Commission adjudicated lends support to that Commissioner's view.

The FCC noted that a channeling decision must accommodate these competing interests:

> (1) the government, which has a compelling interest in protecting children from indecent material; (2) parents, who are entitled to decide whether their children are exposed to such material if it is aired; (3) broadcasters, who are entitled to air such material at times of day when there is not a reasonable risk that children may be in the audience; and (4) adult listeners, who have a right to see and hear programming that is inappropriate for children but not obscene.

[ ] . . . [T]he first two interests identified by the FCC coalesce; the government's role is to facilitate parental supervision of children's

listening. . . . Thus, the FCC must endeavor to determine what channeling rule will most effectively promote parental—as distinguished from government—control.

A securely-grounded channeling rule would give effect to the government's interest in promoting parental supervision of children's listening, without intruding excessively upon the licensee's range of discretion or the fare available for mature audiences and even children whose parents do not wish them sheltered from indecent speech. Such a rule would present a clearly-stated position enabling broadcasters to comprehend what is expected of them and to conform their conduct to the legal requirement.

CONCLUSION

Broadcast material that is indecent but not obscene is protected by the First Amendment; the FCC may regulate such material only with due respect for the high value our Constitution places on freedom and choice in what people say and hear. We have concluded that, under governing precedent, the FCC's definition of indecent broadcast material, though vagueness is inherent in it, is not constitutionally defective, and that the Commission's declaratory order in [*Infinity*] must be affirmed. But we have also found that the FCC has not implemented its authority to channel such material in a reasonable manner. We therefore vacate in part the reconsideration order under review and return [*Pacifica*] and [*Regents of the University of California*] to the Commission for redetermination, after a full and fair hearing, of the times at which indecent material may be broadcast.

It is so ordered.

Notes and Questions:

1. In April 1988, prior to the circuit court's decision *in Action for Children's Television*, the Commission had issued its first indecency decisions since the new policy was announced. It dismissed five indecency complaints including one involving the reading of selections from James Joyce's *Ulysses* over Pacifica's New York station.

2. Two months later, however, the Commission had voted 2–1 to fine KZKC–TV $2,000 for broadcasting the movie, "Private Lessons," during prime time. In dissent, Commissioner Dennis argued that proof of unsupervised children in the audience should be required before finding a station in violation of § 1464. Media Central, the licensee of KZKC–TV, announced that it would fight the ruling. After the remand in *Action for Children's Television,* the Commission decided to delay any action in the KZKC–TV case until after the hearing mandated by the circuit was concluded.

3. In October, 1988, however, Congress passed a requirement that the FCC enforce its anti-indecency policy 24 hours a day. The Commission expressed concern that the resulting rules would "actually hinder rather than advance [the FCC's] enforcement effort because we think a

court might enjoin the commission's effort altogether." Broadcasting, Oct. 3, 1988 at 28. Nevertheless, the FCC complied with the requirement and passed the 24–hour–a–day ban. The ban's Jan. 27, 1989, effective date was then stayed by the court of appeals. Broadcasting, Jan. 30, 1989 at 58.

4. Both proponents and opponents of the 24–hour–a–day ban had hoped that the Supreme Court might provide support for their position in a case involving "dial-a-porn," prerecorded pornographic messages available to telephone callers for a small per-call fee. In 1988 Congress had attempted to abolish dial-a-porn by making it a crime to provide obscene or indecent commercial telephone messages in interstate commerce. The Supreme Court unanimously held the statute unconstitutional insofar as it proscribed material that was not obscene:

> Sexual expression which is indecent but not obscene is protected by the First Amendment, and the government does not submit that the sale of such materials to adults could be criminalized solely because they are indecent. The government may, however, regulate the content of constitutionally protected speech in order to promote a compelling interest if it chooses the least restrictive means to further the articulated interest. We have recognized that there is a compelling interest in protecting the physical well-being of minors. This interest extends to shielding minors from the influence of literature that is not obscene by adult standards. [   ] The government may serve this legitimate interest, but to withstand constitutional scrutiny, "it must do so by narrowly drawn regulations designed to serve those interests without unnecessarily interfering with First Amendment freedoms." [   ]

The government argued that a total ban on dial-a-porn was the only effective way to prevent it from reaching minors, because enterprising youngsters would find some way to avoid lesser restrictions such as codes, scrambling procedures, or access by credit card only. The Court refused to defer to Congress's view on that point, noting that both the FCC and the court of appeals had concluded that the lesser restrictions would be "feasible and effective" in preventing access by children. Sable Communications, Inc. v. Federal Communications Commission, 492 U.S. 115, 16 Med.L.Rptr. 1961 (1989).

The Court in *Sable* did not make any specific reference to the pending dispute over broadcast indecency. In August 1989, 17 media groups, relying heavily on *Sable* and the earlier decision of the court of appeals, filed briefs challenging the constitutionality of the 24–hour ban on indecent broadcast speech.

The Commission then asked the court of appeals to remand the case involving the 24–hour ban to the Commission to give it a chance to build a record justifying the ban. In September 1989, over the opposition of the media challengers, the court of appeals remanded the case to the Commission for a "full and fair" inquiry on the ban.

In late 1989 the Commission issued an NOI soliciting public comment on the validity of a total ban on broadcast indecency. The FCC asserted two government interests served by indecency regulation: "protecting children from exposure to indecent material" and "assisting parents in supervising their children." The Commission asked for comments as to whether the 24–hour ban would advance these interests.

17. The more difficult issue is whether a record can be developed to demonstrate that a 24–hour ban is a sufficiently limited means of restricting children's access to indecent broadcasts. In order to develop such a record, we need to compile information on many interrelated subjects, such as: (1) children's access to the broadcast media as well as their actual viewing and listening habits; (2) the feasibility of alternative means of restricting children's access to broadcasts, including time channeling alone or in conjunction with parental supervision, ratings or warning devices or alternative broadcast technologies; and (3) the availability of indecent material for adults through non-broadcast means.

Noting the court's criticism in *ACT I* of the reliance on data regarding children ages 12 to 17 even though the Commission's 1976 legislative proposal defined children as 12 or younger, the Commission started the NOI by adopting a definition of children as ages 17 and younger. The Commission then asked for information on both children's access to the broadcast media as well as their actual listening and viewing habits. Included in this was information regarding VCR use, specifically: "(1) the availability of VCR equipment to children; (2) the ability of children to use VCR equipment; and (3) children's actual use of the equipment for delayed viewing."

The Commission then asked for comments on alternatives to a 24–hour ban, "including: (1) channeling indecent broadcasts to a time of day when children most likely will not be exposed to them, including reliance on parental supervision to protect children; (2) program rating codes or pre-broadcast warning devices; and (3) feasible technologies that can be used to keep indecent broadcasts from children."

The only specific technology suggested was the Second Audio Program (SAP) channel which allows TVs equipped with a decoder to receive a different audio track for a program, The Commission asked whether putting the indecent audio on the SAP channel would sufficiently restrict access to children or would the decoders become so common as to make the SAP broadcast as accessible as regular broadcast signals. The FCC also asked whether a locking device for the SAP channel would be feasible.

Finally, the Commission asked for comments on whether a 24–hour ban would impermissibly infringe an adult's First Amendment rights:

> . . . . [W]e seek comment on whether non-broadcast alternatives, including cable with a lock-box capacity, videocassettes, audiocas-

settes, records, motion pictures, theatres and nightclubs, provide adults with sufficient access to visual and audio indecency. Do the costs associated with each alternative reduce its practical availability to adults? Are there differences in the types of alternatives available for video versus audio indecency?

Enforcement of Prohibitions Against Broadcast Indecency in 18 U.S.C. § 1464, R.R. Current Service 53:475 (1989).

In July 1990, the Commission unanimously adopted a report supporting a 24–hour–a–day ban on indecency for both radio and television. In its report the Commission argued that because children are part of the broadcast audience 24 hours a day, time channeling would be ineffective in promoting the government's interest in protecting children from indecent programming. The Commission also rejected the use of technological restrictions such as limiting indecency to the SAP channel.

Given the ineffectiveness of less restrictive means of protecting children, the Commission concluded that the 24–hour ban would be a narrowly tailored way of serving a compelling government. Thus, according to the Commission, the ban was constitutional under the test adopted by the Supreme Court in *Sable*, p. 353, *supra*.

In a concurrence, Commissioner Quello expressed concern over the lack of empirical evidence regarding the viewing habits of children 12 years old and under. Given the fact the courts have never upheld a total ban on indecency in any medium, Quello felt that the additional evidence was needed. Broadcasting, July 16, 1990 at 30.

The Commission's action was reversed on appeal. Action for Children's Television v. Federal Communications Commission, 932 F.2d 1504, 69 R.R.2d 179, 18 Med.L.Rptr. 2153 (D.C.Cir.1991). The court found the reversal mandated by *ACT I*:

> Our holding in *ACT I* that the Commission must identify some reasonable period of time during which indecent material may be broadcast necessarily means that the Commission may not ban such broadcasts entirely. The fact that Congress itself mandated the total ban on broadcast indecency does not alter our view that, under *ACT I*, such a prohibition cannot withstand constitutional scrutiny. While "we do not ignore" Congress' apparent belief that a total ban on broadcast indecency is constitutional, it is ultimately the judiciary's task, particularly in the First Amendment context, to decide whether Congress has violated the constitution. [ ] . . .

> Nothing else in the intervening thirty-four months has reduced the precedential force *ACT I*. Indeed, the Supreme Court's decision in *Sable*, striking down a total ban on indecent commercial telephone messages, affirmed the protected status of indecent speech and reiterated the strict constitutional standard that government efforts to regulate the content of speech must satisfy. [ ]

The court's decision essentially placed the Commission in the position it had been in after *ACT I*, but prior to the appropriations rider. In other words the Commission was once again directed to initiate a proceeding to determine "'the times at which indecent material may be broadcast,' to carefully review and address the specific concerns we raised in *ACT I*: among them, the appropriate definitions of 'children' and 'reasonable risk' for channeling purposes, the paucity of station- or program-specific audience data expressed as a percentage of the relevant age group population, and the scope of the government's interest in regulating indecent broadcasts.

A petition for *certiorari* was denied, 112 S.Ct. 1281 (1992).

5. The Public Telecommunications Act of 1992, Pub.Law 102–356, included a provision requiring the FCC to promulgate regulations prohibiting the broadcasting of indecent programming between the hours of 6 a.m. and 12 midnight. Public radio and television stations that go off the air before or at midnight will be allowed to broadcast indecent programming between 10 p.m. and midnight. The FCC promulgated the rules in Broadcast Indecency, 71 R.R.2d 1116 (1993). Will these new rules pass constitutional muster? What evidence is needed to support the new regulations?

6. In 1992 the Commission fined 3 Infinity Broadcasting stations $200,000 each for broadcasts of the "Howard Stern Show." Sagitarius Broadcasting, 71 R.R.2d 989 (1992). This is the largest fine ever for indecent programming.

7. In *Video 44*, p. 141, *supra*, the Review Board had designated the question of obscene programming as an issue. The Commission in turn eliminated it as an issue, holding that initial determinations on obscenity should be left to local officials. The Commission indicated that it would take appropriate action in cases where a licensee was convicted of violating an obscenity statute.

Acting on a Petition for Reconsideration, the Commission reversed itself on the obscenity issue:

> 11. Although it may be preferable, in most cases, to deal with questions of obscenity in the context of a previously adjudicated prosecution in a local judicial district, we are persuaded, on reflection, that we should retain the ability to pursue a range of options when allegations of a violation of Section 1464 are raised against a licensee. Those options include not only referring complaints against licensees to the U.S. Department of Justice for a possible criminal prosecution for obscenity under Section 1464, *e.g., Pacifica Foundation, Inc.*, 2 F.C.C.Rcd. at 2701 para. 26, but also undertaking our own action and exercising one of the many administrative sanctions available to us. *E.g.*, 47 U.S.C. §§ 303(m) (suspension of license), 312(a) (revocation of license), 312(b) (cease and desist order) & 503(b) (forfeiture). . . .

However, the Commission still refused to examine the specific obscenity allegations against Video 44 because they were first presented in the context of a renewal proceeding. Such allegations must be presented shortly after the broadcast in question and may not be held until the end of the license term. Video 44, 3 F.C.C.Rcd. 757, 64 R.R.2d 378 (1988).

In *Monroe Communications*, p. 142, *supra*, the court of appeals held that the Commission had not adequately justified its contemporaneous complaint requirement. The FCC had argued that the rule "would guarantee the Commission flexibility in responding to the obscenity allegations in a responsible manner; would enable the Commission to put the licensee on notice that its broadcasts were unacceptable, thus minimizing the chilling effect on a broadcaster's disposition to air protected speech that might result from allowing allegations of obscenity to be raised for the first time in the context of comparative renewal hearings, and would ensure that allegations of obscenity are judged by contemporary community standards, as required by [*Miller*], rather than the standards of a later period."

The court dismissed the first argument because allegations of obscene broadcasts were clearly relevant to the public interest and no other factor bearing on the public interest was subject to a contemporaneous complaint requirement. The chilling effect argument was rejected because the court did not see how the threat of eventual nonrenewal was any more chilling than the threat of an immediate forfeiture or license revocation. Finally, the court found the argument that the requirement would ensure adherence to *Miller* to "make[ ] no sense whatsoever." Adjudications of obscenity, whether by the courts or the FCC, always require a determination at a later date of what the standards were at the time of the allegedly obscene broadcast. The court instructed the FCC either to consider the obscenity complaints against Video 44 or to better justify its refusal to do so.

In *Video 44*, p. 142, *supra*, the Commission found it unnecessary to address the obscenity complaints because it had already decided to award the license to a competing applicant.

8. As the Commission indicated in *Video 44*, it had referred the Pacifica broadcast of "Jerker" to the Justice Department for a possible obscenity prosecution. The Justice Department declined to take any action.

C. SAFETY—VIOLENCE AND PANIC

The 1980s saw an increase in lawsuits asserting that mass media are legally liable for personal injuries that can be traced in one way or another to a broadcast. These cases, which have not yet produced definitive results, raise some of the most hotly disputed questions in all of media liability. The examples that follow suggest the range of situations that might give rise to controversy. The cases tend to fall into two main categories—those in which the content of the program has an immediate impact on the recipient and those in which the recipient engages in conduct that hurts third parties. Both types of cases raise questions about tort law and the First Amendment.

The most extensive suit raising this question arose out of a television drama entitled "Born Innocent."

OLIVIA N. v. NATIONAL BROADCASTING CO.

California Court of Appeal, First District, 1981.
126 Cal.App.3d 488, 178 Cal.Rptr. 888, 7 Med.L.Rptr. 2359.

Before: CALDECOTT, P.J., CHRISTIAN and POCHE, JJ.

CHRISTIAN, J.:

Olivia N. appeals from a judgment of nonsuit terminating her action against the National Broadcasting Company and the Chronicle Broadcasting Company. Appellant sought damages for physical and emotional injury inflicted by assailants who had seen a television broadcast of a film drama.

[The case was originally dismissed before trial, but the appellate court held that improper procedure below had deprived the plaintiff of her right to a jury trial. After a jury was empaneled on the remand and plaintiff had made an opening statement, the trial judge dismissed the case on the ground that the only basis for recovery would be a showing that NBC intended that violence follow its presentation of the drama. Since plaintiff did not make that claim, the case was dismissed.]

At 8 p.m. on September 10, 1974, NBC telecast nationwide, and Chronicle Broadcasting Company broadcast locally, a film entitled "Born Innocent."

> The subject matter of the television film was the harmful effect of a state-run home upon an adolescent girl who had become a ward of the state. In one scene of the film, the young girl enters the community bathroom of the facility to take a shower. She is then shown taking off her clothes and stepping into the shower, where she bathes for a few moments. Suddenly, the water stops and a look of fear comes across her face. Four adolescent girls are standing across from her in the shower room. One of the girls is carrying a "plumber's helper," waving it suggestively by her side. The four girls violently attack the younger girl, wrestling her to the floor. The young girl is shown naked from the waist up, struggling as the older girls force her legs apart. Then the television film shows the girl with the plumber's helper making intense thrusting motions with the handle of the plunger until one of the four says "That's enough." The young girl is left sobbing and naked on the floor. [ ]

It is alleged that on September 14, 1974, appellant, aged 9, was attacked and forcibly "artificially raped" with a bottle by minors at a San Francisco beach. [ ] The assailants had viewed and discussed the "artificial rape" scene in "Born Innocent," and the film allegedly caused the assailants to decide to commit a similar act on appellant. Appellant offered to show that NBC had knowledge of studies on child violence and should have known that susceptible persons might imitate the crime enacted in the film. Appellants alleged that "Born Innocent" was particularly likely to cause imitation and that NBC televised the film without proper warning in an effort to obtain the largest possible viewing audience. Appellant alleged that as a proximate result of respondents' telecast, she suffered physical and psychological damage.

Appellant contends that where there is negligence liability could constitutionally be imposed despite the absence of proof of incitement as defined in Brandenburg v. Ohio, 395 U.S. 444, 447 (1969). Appellant argues in the alternative that a different definition of "incitement" should be applied to the present circumstances.

"Analysis of this appeal commences with recognition of the overriding constitutional principle that material communicated by the public media, including fictional material such as the television drama here at issue, is generally to be accorded protection under the First Amendment to the Constitution of the United States. [ ]" First Amendment rights are accorded a preferred place in our democratic society. [ ] First Amendment protection extends to a communication, to its source and to its recipients. [ ] "[A]bove all else, the First Amendment means that government has no power to restrict expression because of its message, its ideas, its subject matter, or its content." . . .

. . .

The electronic media are also entitled to First Amendment protection. . . .

Appellant does not seek to impose a prior restraint on speech; rather, she asserts civil liability premised on traditional negligence actions for a television broadcast is obvious. "The fear of damage awards . . . may be markedly more inhibiting than the fear of prosecution under a criminal statute." New York Times Co. v. Sullivan, 376 U.S. 254, 277 (1964). Realistically, television networks would become significantly more inhibited in the selection of controversial materials if liability were to be imposed on a simple negligence theory. "[T]he pall of fear and timidity imposed upon those who would give voice to public criticism is an atmosphere in which the First Amendment cannot survive." New York Times v. Sullivan [ ]. . . .

Although the First Amendment is not absolute, the television broadcast of "Born Innocent" does not, on the basis of the opening statement of appellant's attorney, fall within the scope of unprotected speech. Appellant concedes that the film did not constitute an "incitement" within the meaning of [Brandenburg]. Notwithstanding the pervasive effect of the broadcasting media (see FCC v. Pacifica Foundation (1978) 438 U.S. 726, 748; Note, The Future of Content Regulation in Broadcasting (1981) 69 Cal.L.Rev. 555, 580–581) and the unique access afforded children [*Pacifica*], the effect of the imposition of liability could reduce the U.S. adult population to viewing only what is fit for children. [ ] Incitement is the proper test here. [ ] In areas outside of obscenity the United States Supreme Court has "consistently held that the fact that protected speech may be offensive to some does not justify its suppression. See, e.g., Cohen v. California, 403 U.S. 15 (1971)." [ ] . . . The television broadcast which is the subject of this action concededly did not fulfill the incitement requirements of *Brandenburg*. Thus it is constitutionally protected.

Appellant would distinguish between the fictional presentation of "Born Innocent" and news programs and documentaries. But that distinction is too blurred to protect adequately First Amendment values. "Everyone is familiar with instances of propaganda through fiction. What is one man's amusement, teaches another's doctrine." [ ] If a negligence theory is recognized, a television network or local station could be liable when a child imitates activities portrayed in a news program or documentary. Thus, the distinction urged by appellant cannot be accepted. [ ] . . . "Among free men, the deterrents ordinarily to be applied to prevent crime are education and punishment for violations of the law, not abridgment of the rights of free speech . . .." [ ] The trial court's determination that the First Amendment bars appellant's claim where no incitement is alleged must be upheld.

[*Pacifica* was held inapplicable to anything other than regulation of indecency.]

Notes and Questions

1. Is there any possible showing that should entitle plaintiff to a judgment against NBC? What if the plaintiff could show that NBC officials had been warned by psychologists that the program was likely to provoke imitation? Is it significant that there was only one reported case of imitation? What if plaintiff could show only that the attackers heard about the program from friends but that none of them saw it? Is it relevant that the show was presented at 8 p.m.?

2. Is there a difference between the "Born Innocent" program and a news broadcast that reports the details of a recent case of torture in the city—which is then imitated by persons unknown?

3. *Direct Harm.* During a 1979 broadcast of "The Tonight Show," a Hollywood stunt man showed how to stage a hanging that appeared real but was not. A few hours after the program, a 14–year–old boy was found hanging in front of his television set, which was on, and tuned to the local outlet that had carried that show. The plaintiff's attorney alleged that "the entire tenor of the scene was such as to challenge a teenaged boy to imitate the hanging." The trial judge dismissed the complaint in 1980.

The dismissal was affirmed in DeFilippo v. National Broadcasting Co., 446 A.2d 1036 (R.I.1982). The court concluded that "incitement" was required and that it could not be shown here. Plaintiff was apparently the only viewer who tried the stunt and those on the program had warned viewers that this was not something to try at home. To permit recovery here "would invariably lead to self-censorship by broadcasters in order to remove any matter that may be emulated and lead to a law suit."

4. *Indirect Harm. Olivia N.* is only one of a number of cases in which a victim has claimed that a broadcast caused listeners or viewers to engage in conduct that led to plaintiff's injury.

In one such case later relied on by the plaintiff in *Olivia N.*, a radio station catering to teenagers broadcast clues as to the whereabouts of a disc jockey and offered a cash prize to the first listener to reach him. Two teenagers reached the correct location but were not the first to arrive. While following the disc jockey to his next stop, the two drivers vied for position on the freeway and thereby caused a fatal accident. The court held that the station owed the decedent a duty of care and had violated it. Weirum v. RKO General, Inc., 15 Cal.3d 40, 123 Cal.Rptr. 468, 539 P.2d 36 (1975). Without relying on the fact that the contest was a boost for the station, the court easily rejected the station's First Amendment claim as "clearly without merit. The issue here is civil accountability for the foreseeable results of a broadcast which created an undue risk of harm to decedent. The First Amendment does not sanction the infliction of physical injury merely because achieved by word, rather than act." Is this sound? The court in *Olivia N.* distinguished *Weirum* on the ground that the station in that case actively encouraged the conduct leading to the accident. No such encouragement was present in "Born Innocent."

5. *The Zamora Case.* In Florida, 15–year–old Ronald Zamora was convicted of murdering his 83–year–old neighbor and was sentenced to a long prison term. He sued all three networks claiming that between the ages of 5 and 15 he had become involuntarily addicted to, and "completely subliminally intoxicated" by, extensive viewing of television violence. He claimed that the networks had "impermissibly stimulated, incited and instigated" him to duplicate the atrocities he viewed on television. He alleged further that he had developed a sociopathic personality, had become desensitized to violent behavior and had become a danger to himself and others. The trial judge dismissed the complaint. Zamora v. Columbia Broadcasting System, 480 F.Supp. 199 (S.D.Fla.1979).

The judge refused to impose any tort obligation on the networks because he concluded that courts lack "the legal and institutional capacity to identify isolated depictions of violence, let alone the ability to set the standard for media dissemination of items containing 'violence' in one form or the other. Airway dissemination is, and to some extent should be, regulated but not on the basis or by the [tort] procedure suggested by the plaintiffs."

To the extent plaintiff was arguing for the regulation of programming that would adversely affect "susceptible" viewers, the judge indicated that the "imposition of such a generally undefined and undefinable duty would be an unconstitutional exercise by this Court in any event." Plaintiffs "would place broadcasters in jeopardy for televising Hamlet, Julius Caesar, Grimm's Fairy Tales; more contemporary offerings such as All Quiet On The Western Front, and even The Holocaust, and indeed would render John Wayne a risk not acceptable by any but the boldest broadcasters."

The judge observed, however, that "One day, medical or other sciences with or without the cooperation of programmers may convince the F.C.C. or the Courts that the delicate balance of First Amendment rights should be altered to permit some additional limitations in programming." But this case did not present such an occasion.

The judge implied that the plaintiff's approach in the "Born Innocent" case was stronger because of its claim that a specific program stimulated the harmful conduct. Is that a sound distinction? Note that the *Zamora* suit involves direct harm because the viewer is the one claiming that his life has been ruined by the programming. There is no reason, however, to think that the judge would have been any more receptive to a suit by the heirs of the dead neighbor against the networks.

6. Is the plaintiff's case stronger in general if more recipients are affected? If half the viewers faint in front of their screens after viewing a particularly gory shot of a murder victim presented during a news program, is the case any different from one in which a few "susceptible" viewers faint? Is there any reason to distinguish the cases in which direct harm occurs from those in which indirect harm occurs? Can you imagine a case in which the "average" viewer would be induced to engage in antisocial behavior that harmed others?

7. *Mass Hysteria.* Another substantive problem involves programs that frighten the listening public. At 11 p.m. on Oct. 30, 1974, a radio station in Rhode Island presented a contemporary version of the famous H.G. Wells's "War of the Worlds," that had been presented on the same night in 1938. A meteorite was reported to have fallen in a sparsely populated community killing several people; later "black-eyed, V-shaped mouthed, glistening creatures dripping saliva" were reported to have emerged from what turned out to be a capsule, and other landings were reported. What steps would you expect the licensee to take before presenting such a program—or is it inappropriate to present such material at any time? Telephone calls from frightened, and later from angry, listeners flooded the station, police and other public service departments.

The licensee had taken several steps before the program to inform state public safety officials in the listening area of the station. The state police in turn sent notices to all their stations in the area alerting them to the program. Approximately once an hour from noon until 10 p.m. the licensee broadcast the following promotional announcement: "Tonight at 11 p.m., WPRO invites you to listen to a spoof of the 1930s a special Halloween classic presentation. . . ." The last was made about an hour before the program. Three announcements were made during the program—after 47, 48 and 56 minutes. The reason for the timing was said to be that the first 30 to 35 minutes of the show involved what appeared to be a meteor crashing in a remote spot and the arrival of creatures was not reported until 30 minutes into the program.

The Commission told the licensee that it had not met its responsibility to operate in a manner consistent with the public interest. The warnings were inadequate because "it is a well known fact that the radio audience is constantly changing. The only way to assure adequately that the public would not be alarmed in this case would be an introductory statement repeated at frequent intervals throughout the program." One Commissioner dissented because intrusion into presentations of drama should be made with "utmost caution" and the licensee's precautions "were not in my opinion unreasonable." Capital Cities Communications, Inc., 54 F.C.C.2d 1035, 34 R.R.2d 1016 (1975).

Would the Commission's suggestions impinge on the dramatic effect sought by the licensee? Is that relevant? Can you think of other ways to meet the Commission's concern? Recall the greater ease of warning an unwilling audience about possibly offensive programs over television as opposed to radio. Is that distinction applicable here?

8. During the Persian Gulf War, a St. Louis disk jockey played an old Civil Defense alert, causing listeners to believe a nuclear attack was in progress. The disk jockey was suspended, and the station issued an apology. Broadcasting, Feb. 4, 1991 at 29. The licensee was subsequently fined $25,000. Broadcasting, July 29, 1991 at 69. Letter to KSHE–FM, 6 F.C.C.Rcd. 2289, 69 R.R.2d 155 (1991).

9. After the St. Louis incident, as well as incidents in Pasadena and Providence the Commission issued an NPRM seeking comments on a new hoax rule. The Pasadena case involved a radio station airing a call from a man who supposedly had killed his girlfriend. A police investigation of the "murder" ensued and the hoax was only exposed when viewers of a "Unsolved Mysteries" (NBC) story on the "crime" notified police of the similarities between the caller and a disc jockey who had subsequently been hired by the station.

In the Providence hoax, a station's news director announced that the station's morning man had been shot just outside the station. The news director then refused to disclose the hoax even when ordered to by the station's general manager. The news director and morning man were both fired. Broadcasting, July 29, 1991 at 68.

In 1992 the FCC adopted a rule prohibiting "licensees from knowingly engaging in hoaxes involving a false report of a crime or catastrophe when it is foreseeable that the report will, and does in fact, result in substantial public harm." Broadcast Hoaxes, 70 R.R.2d 1383 (1992).

D. CHILDREN'S PROGRAMMING

Over the years, groups have expressed special concern about programs aimed at children. Some have been concerned primarily with commercials and others have been concerned about the content of the programs themselves. Still others have been concerned that there is too little children's programming. All of these concerns and conflicts became more heated in the late 1970s. As we consider each situation, note the different approaches being considered. Sometimes it is prohibiting certain content; sometimes it involves mandatory programming; and sometimes it is conditional in the sense that a broadcaster who presents one kind of content may be obligated to present other types of programs. Also note that occasionally the FCC invokes the aid of private groups such as the National Association of Broadcasters (NAB) to alter a practice within the industry.

1. PROGRAM CONTENT

Most of the concern about the impact of television on children has stressed the role of violence and sexual innuendo. Although some groups have been concerned about these matters as far as adults are concerned, more seem concerned about their impact on children. Under Butler v. Michigan, 352 U.S. 380 (1957), it is unlawful for government to impose a complete ban on printed matter that is legally protected as to adults, simply to keep the material from children. Might that rule be different with television or radio? Does *Pacifica* suggest differences?

a. Government Action

Although the Surgeon General has issued reports on the relationship between violence and television, and other academic studies have addressed the same issue primarily in connection with children, the Commission has never attempted to regulate the area in any substantive way. It has been asked several times but each time has refused.

In 1972, for example, the Commission was asked to analogize the area to cigarette smoking because of the actions of the Surgeon General in the two areas. George Corey, 37 F.C.C.2d 641, 25 R.R.2d 437 (1972). The complainant sought to have three Boston stations carry a public service notice at appropriate times: "Warning: Viewing of violent television programming by children can be hazardous to their mental health and well being." The Commission rejected the request on two grounds. First, it stated any action should come by rule rather than moving against a few stations. Second, the Commission rejected the contention that the fairness doctrine was applicable to violent programming. The cigarette episode was discussed:

However, it could not reasonably or logically be concluded that the mere viewing of a person smoking a cigarette during a movie being broadcast on television constitutes a discussion of a controversial issue of public importance thus raising a fairness doctrine obligation.   Similarly, we cannot agree that the broadcast of violent episodes during entertainment programs necessarily constitutes the presentation of one side of a controversial issue of public importance.   It is simply not an appropriate application of the fairness doctrine to say that an entertainment program—whether it be Shakespeare or an action-adventure show—raises a controversial issue if it contains a violent scene and has a significant audience of children.   Were we to adopt your construction that the depiction of a violent scene is a discussion of one side of a controversial issue of public importance, the number of controversial issues presented on entertainment shows would be virtually endless (e.g., a scene with a high-powered car; or one showing a person taking an alcoholic drink or cigarette; depicting women in a soft, feminine, or light romantic role).   Finally, we note that there are marked differences in the conclusiveness of the hazard established in this area as against cigarette smoking.   [   ]

The real thrust of your complaint would appear to be not fairness in the discussion of controversial issues but the elimination of violent TV children's programming because of its effect on children.   That issue is being considered particularly by appropriate Congressional committees and agencies such as HEW.   [   ]   It is a difficult, complex, and sensitive matter.   But whatever its resolution, there is no basis for the action along the line proposed by you.

In its Report on the Broadcast of Violent, Indecent, and Obscene Material, 51 F.C.C.2d 418, 32 R.R.2d 1367 (1975), the Commission explained to Congress that the violence area was unlike the obscenity area because of the totally different statutory framework involved.   In the absence of any prohibitions on violence in programming, "industry self-regulation is preferable to the adoption of rigid governmental standards."   The Commission took this position for two reasons.   First, it feared the constitutional questions that would emerge from such an intrusion into program content.   Second, the judgments concerning the suitability of certain programming for children are "highly subjective."   A speech by Chairman Wiley was quoted to the effect that slapstick comedy, an episode in Peter Pan when Captain Hook is eaten by a crocodile, and the poisoning of Snow White by the witch, all raise judgmental questions for which there is no objective standard.

One surge of interest has been concentrated on advertisers.   A pilot study indicated that 10 percent of those surveyed had considered not buying a product because it was advertised on a program they thought excessively violent.   The president of a leading advertising agency announced that it counseled clients to consider the negative aspects of placing commercials in violent programs.   Editor & Publisher, June 12,

1976 at 5. The FCC chairman also suggested that advertisers consider the commercial implications of such programs. See also Broadcasting, June 14, 1976 at 32, 42.

Several detailed studies of the impact of television on children are collected in 20 J. Broadcasting 1—68 (1976). See also, D. Cater and S. Strickland, *TV Violence and the Child—The Evolution and Fate of the Surgeon General's Report*, (1975).

b. *Private Action*

The NAB is a private voluntary organization whose membership includes the three major networks, well over half the television stations in the country and some 3,000 radio broadcasters. The NAB promulgated codes and standards that members had to follow if they wished to retain membership. The codes addressed such matters as how many minutes of commercials were appropriate in an hour; what types of commercials should not be accepted; what material should not be shown on the screen; and how subjects such as suicide or astrology or religion should be treated. We shall see examples from the NAB Code shortly.

A broadcaster that adhered to the code could display the NAB seal. The NAB maintained a staff that advised members about the propriety of their behavior under the codes.

In 1975 the result of the interaction of the network officials, the FCC chairman and the NAB was the promulgation of the "family viewing policy" as an amendment to the NAB's Television Code. Under the policy, programs of a violent or sexually-oriented nature were wholly barred from the time slots before 9 p.m. (8 p.m. Central Time). This required moving some programs that had been popular in earlier prime-time slots and also involved decisions about which programs were affected in the first place. The entire story of the development and early enforcement of the family viewing policy is traced at length in G. Cowan, *See No Evil: The Backstage Battle over Sex and Violence on Television* (1979). The policy was challenged in court as being the result of illegal government pressure. Writers Guild of America West, Inc. v. American Broadcasting Co., Inc., 609 F.2d 355 (9th Cir.1979), certiorari denied 449 U.S. 824 (1980). After years of litigation complicated by jurisdictional issues, all parties in the case agreed to a settlement in 1984. The Family Viewing Policy had not been enforced for years.

In 1990 Congress passed an exemption to the antitrust laws for "any joint discussion, consideration, review, action, or agreement by or among persons in the television industry for the purpose of, and limited to, developing and disseminating voluntary guidelines designed to alleviate the negative impact of violence in telecast material." The exemption will sunset Dec. 1, 1993. P.L. 101–650 (1990).

2. Too Few Programs for Children

There has long been concern that too few programs are written expressly for children. Although the prime time access rule was motivated in part by hopes that this type of programming would result, the rule had no such effect. Following a petition in 1970 from Action for Children's Television (ACT) to require children's programming, the FCC spent much of the 1970s trying to decide how to react. In 1974 it issued a Policy Statement asking licensees to "make a meaningful effort" to increase overall programming for children; to air "a reasonable amount" of programming designed to educate and inform children, not simply to entertain them; to address the needs of both preschool and school-age children; and to air these programs on weekdays as well as weekends.

The Commission concluded in 1979 that over a five-year period, the amount of children's programming per station had increased less than one hour per week (from 10.5 to 11.3 hours) and that this was totally accounted for by new programming from independent stations. Network affiliates had not increased their programming at all. No significant increase in education or informational programs was detected. Few licensees sought to develop age-specific programs for children. Finally, although only 8 percent of children's television viewing occurred on weekends, almost half the programs for children were presented on weekends.

The staff concluded that "the small numbers of children and their limited appeal to advertisers, combined with the small outlets in most markets, create incentives for the commercial television system to neglect the specific needs of the child audience." Age-specific programming would be even less attractive to broadcasters because of the further splitting of an already small market.

In Children's Television Programming and Advertising Practices, 75 F.C.C.2d 138 (1979), the FCC announced a proposed rulemaking in which it listed five options. These were to rescind the *1974 Policy Statement* and rely on program sources other than commercial broadcasting; to maintain or modify the policy statement; to institute mandatory programming requirements; to develop renewal guidelines; or to increase the number of video outlets.

The Commission completed the proceeding in 1983. Mandatory children's programming obligations for television stations were rejected. The FCC found that the amount and variety of children's programming available was substantial and diverse. It noted that establishment of quotas might be impermissible content-based regulation and would create difficult definitional problems. Such quotas would also preclude the establishment of experimental children's services and efforts at specialization. Although no quotas were created, each licensee has the obligation to consider the needs of all significant elements of the community. A licensee at renewal time must demonstrate the attention devoted to the needs of children in its viewing audience, but may consider the alternative program sources available to children in its area. Children's Television Programming, 55 R.R.2d 199 (1984). On appeal, the D.C. Circuit affirmed the Commission's position that alternatives such as public broadcasting and cable could be considered in assessing the need for children's programming. "To be sure, Congress did not intend noncommercial broadcasting to 'relieve commercial broadcasters of their responsibilities to present public affairs and public service programs, and in general to program their stations in the public interest,' [ ]. But that does not mean that the Commission must require commercial broadcasters to pursue those responsibilities in disregard of the fact that some gaps in the public interest may have been filled by that source while other needs remain entirely unmet." The court did not read the Commission's Order as relieving broadcasters of the obligation, under the public interest standard, to present age-specific programming. Action for Children's Television v. Federal Communications Commission, 756 F.2d 899, 57 R.R.2d 1406, 11 Med. L.Rptr. 2080 (D.C.Cir.1985).

An effort by citizen groups to deny license renewals to television stations that had no regularly scheduled children's programming failed in Washington Association for Television and Children v. Federal Communications Commission, 712 F.2d 677, 54 R.R.2d 293 (D.C.Cir. 1983). The Commission's policy statement did not require regular scheduling, and the Commission did not have to prefer a station that presented regularly scheduled cartoons to one that presented educational specials.

3. COMMERCIALS IN CHILDREN'S PROGRAMS

Efforts to eliminate all sponsorship of children's programs have been rejected by the Commission. The court of appeals affirmed on the ground that the FCC's refusal to adopt the ban "was a reasoned exercise of its broad discretion." The Commission had taken some steps, such as ordering a clear separation between programming and advertising on children's programs and prohibiting "host selling"— program hosts, personalities or characters endorsing products—and this could not be held insufficient as a matter of law. Action for Children's Television v. Federal Communications Commission, 564 F.2d 458, 40 R.R.2d 1577, 2 Med.L.Rptr. 2120 (D.C.Cir.1977).

The Commission had, however, established commercial guidelines limiting the amount of advertising that could be broadcast during children's shows. These guidelines were eliminated as part of *Deregulation of Television*, p. 703, *supra*. In *Action For Children's Television*, *supra*, the court of appeals held that the Commission provided inadequate justification for the elimination of the children's commercialization guidelines.

Another innovative attempt to address the question of commercials in children's programming occurred when Public Advocates, Inc., and ACT petitioned the Commission to require television licensees and cable companies to insert an inaudible electronic signal at the beginning and end of every advertisement aimed at children. The signal would allow parents to attach a device to their television sets which would blank out the advertisements. After a rulemaking proceeding, the Commission decided against such a requirement. The obvious effect of such a requirement would be to reduce the value of the advertising that in turn would diminish the economic base for children's programming. In essence it would be a milder form of the ban on advertising aimed at children that the Commission had rejected several years earlier. Children's Advertising Detector Signal, 100 F.C.C.2d 163, 57 R.R.2d 935 (1985). Is advertising the only effective way to finance children's programming?

The Commission has also declined to require the networks to provide instructional programs to educate children about television advertising. The Commission was concerned about the impact of the First Amendment and § 326 on an order requiring programs with certain content. The issue was not so critical that, under the first part of the fairness doctrine, a licensee who ignored the issue would be acting unreasonably. Finally, because commercials being shown did not meaningfully discuss the issue, it did not come within the second part of the fairness doctrine. Council on Children, Media and Merchandising, 65 F.C.C.2d 421, 40 R.R.2d 1718 (1977).

In 1983 ACT and the National Association for Better Broadcasting (NABB) filed complaints against various licensees alleging violations of the Commission policy against "program length commercials." These complaints focused on a new marketing strategy for children's television, basing shows on toys that were already on the market. Among the shows at issue were "He–Man and the Masters of the Universe," "G.I. Joe: A Real American Hero," "Dungeons and Dragons," "Rubik the Amazing Cube," "Monchhichi's," "The Shirt Tales," "Strawberry Shortcake and Care Bears Family TV Fun Festival" and "Pac–Man."

According to ACT and NABB, these shows were created for the sole purpose of selling the toys that were featured in the show. As further evidence of this allegation, ACT cited an arrangement offered by Telepictures Corporation whereby broadcasters could receive a share of the profits derived from the sale of "Thunder Cats" toys in return for carrying the "Thunder Cats" cartoon show.

The Commission rejected the complaints. "[O]nly when the program segment is 'so interwoven with, and in essence auxiliary to the sponsor's advertising . . . to the point that the entire program constitutes a single, commercial promotion for the sponsor's products or services'" will an entire program be considered a commercial. Because the toys featured in the shows were not being advertised during those shows, the Commission did not find an interweaving of commercials and program content sufficient to constitute a program length commercial.

> The fact that programming may serve commercial goals, however, in and of itself, is not controlling. If the existence of commercial rewards from associated products were the criteria for imposing restrictions upon children's programming, then no program-related product licensing would be possible and even popular educational programs such as "Sesame Street" and critically acclaimed commercial television programs like those in the "Peanuts" series would have to be eliminated from broadcast station schedules. We see no sensible or administratively practical method of making distinctions among programs based on the subjective intentions of the program producers or on the product licensing/program production sequence. Considering that ACT's, NABB's, and the Commission's primary intention is to prevent harm to children, we must consider what, if any, possible harm might result from product-based programming. There is, however, no evidence before us to demonstrate that exposure to programming based on products harms the child audience. Action for Children's Television, 58 R.R.2d 61 (F.C.C.1985).

In a related proceeding, the Commission rejected ACT's petition for rule making pertaining to profit-sharing arrangements in the broadcasting of children's programming. ACT asserted that profit-sharing arrangements such as that offered by Telepictures for "Thunder Cats" would induce licensees to select programs for financial as opposed to public interest reasons. The Commission concluded that such a danger was extremely speculative and did not warrant an NOI or NPRM, but stressed that licensees should not allow profit sharing or product tie-ins to detract from the "'bedrock obligation of every broadcaster to be responsive to the needs and interests of its community, including the specialized needs of children in that community.'" Commissioner Rivera dissented, believing that profit sharing and product tie-ins raised enough questions to justify further study. Children's Programming (Profit–Sharing Arrangements), 100 F.C.C.2d 709 58 R.R.2d 90 (1985).

NABB appealed the Commission's decision as it applied to NABB's complaint against KCOP–TV in Los Angeles. NABB argued that because "He–Man and the Masters of the Universe" was provided to the station on a barter basis whereby the station furnished only two minutes of non-prime time for each show, the show was being obtained for "token payment." According to NABB this meant that under § 317 of the Communications Act the station had to identify the show's distributors as sponsors of the program. The Commission had rejected NABB's argument by ruling that § 317 applies only when a broadcast is "so interwoven with, and in essence auxiliary to the sponsor's advertising . . . to the point that the entire program constitutes a single commercial promotion for the sponsor's products or services."

The court of appeals overruled the Commission, holding that § 317 is not limited to purely commercial broadcasts. National Association for Better Broadcasting v. Federal Communications Commission, 830 F.2d 270, 63 R.R.2d 1501 (D.C.Cir.1987).

Still another controversy over product tie-ins erupted when several companies announced plans for interactive children's television shows. By transmitting inaudible signals the shows will cause specially designed toys to react. ACT filed a petition with the Commission asking that the toys be declared against the public interest.

In response to these various petitions and remands, the FCC issued a combined NOI/NPRM. Revision of Programming and Commercialization Policies, Ascertainment Requirements, and Program Log Requirements for Commercial Television Stations, 2 F.C.C.Rcd. 7463 (1987). In the NOI/NPRM the Commission asked for comments pertaining to commercialization guidelines for children's shows as well as definitions of what constitutes commercial matter. It also asked for comments on the new toys designed to interact with specific children's shows.

Although this specific NOI/NPRM did not request comments on the sponsorship identification questions raised by barter deals for children's shows, the Commission indicated in a footnote that as a result of the remand in *NABB,* it would address those issues in the near future. Subsequently the FCC asked parties to the case to file comments.

In 1990 Congress passed a children's television bill. On weekdays commercial television stations are limited to 12 minutes of commercial matter per hour during children's programming. On weekends the limit is 10.5 commercial minutes per hour during children's programming. The act also requires the FCC to include service to children as a factor in television renewal decision.

The Act required the FCC to complete a proceeding implementing these requirements within 6 months. The three primary issues addressed by the proceeding were the standards to be used in setting commercial limits for children's programming, guidelines for evaluating at renewal time broadcasters' service to children, and the definition of program-length commercials.

IN THE MATTER OF POLICIES AND RULES CONCERNING
CHILDREN'S TELEVISION PROGRAMMING
REVISION OF PROGRAMMING AND COMMERCIALIZATION
POLICIES, ASCERTAINMENT REQUIREMENTS, AND
PROGRAM LOG REQUIREMENTS FOR COMMERCIAL
TELEVISION STATIONS

Federal Communications Commission, 1991.
6 F.C.C.Rcd. 2111, 68 R.R.2d 1615.

[For the purposes of implementing the commercial limits set forth in the Act, the Commission defined children's programming as "programs originally produced and broadcast primarily for an audience of children 12 years old and under." Commercial matter was defined as "air time sold for the purposes of selling a product," but the FCC added a number of clarifications:]

5.   By requiring that air time be "sold," we mean that the advertiser must give some valuable consideration either directly or indirectly to the broadcaster or cablecaster as an inducement for airing the material. Without such a qualification, it would be difficult to distinguish mention of logos or brand name a writer or producer used to advance creative objectives. We also clarify that although our proposed definition only referred to air time sold "for purposes of selling a product," commercial matter also encompasses advertising for services.

6.   We also find that the scope of Section 317 of the Communications Act, 47 USC § 317, which governs when the sponsors of broadcast material must be identified, is not coterminous with the scope of commercial matter. In particular we hold that material is not necessarily "commercial matter" for purposes of the Children's Television Act simply because Section 317 requires a sponsorship identification. . . . For example, nonprofit organizations purchasing air time for a public service message must identify themselves as sponsors under Section 317, even though such a message is not commercial material.

7.   We accordingly find that the bare sponsorship identification announcement required under Section 317 and our implementing rules, where such material is not otherwise commercial in nature, will not be deemed commercial matter under our definition here. Thus, public service messages sponsored by nonprofit organizations that promote not-for-profit activities will not be considered commercial matter for purposes of applying the commercial limits. Similarly, air time sold for purposes of presenting educational and informational material, including "spot" announcements, which the only sponsorship mention a "sponsored by," is not commercial matter. The addition of product mentions or advertising to such an identification announcement, however, would constitute commercial matter. Moreover, where a station or cable operator promotes one of its upcoming programs and mentions that program's sponsor, even though not required to do so under

Section 317, the mention of the sponsor will constitute commercial matter for purposes of determining whether the commercial limits have been exceeded. In such a case, the mention of the sponsor is not required under the Rule and is thus clearly intended to promote the sponsor. Thus, if such a station or cable operator's promo (1) mentions that the upcoming program is "brought to you by" a sponsor, or (2) promotes a product or service related to the program or program sponsor, or (3) mentions a prize furnished by the program sponsor, the mention of the sponsor or the sponsor's product or services, not being required under our sponsorship identification rules, will be considered commercial matter. Promotions of upcoming programs which do not contain such sponsor-related mentions will not be deemed commercial matter.

[The Commission decided that it would count commercial minutes by the hour as opposed to by the program. Where a half-hour of children's programming is both preceded and followed by adult programming, the FCC applies the limits on a proportionate basis. The limits are not applied to children's programming segments less than a half hour in length.

Commercial limits also apply to cable operators with regard to local origination channels and cable network programs. They do not, however, apply to retransmissions of broadcast channels or access channels. (These distinctions are discussed in more detail in Chapter IX).]

III. Programming Renewal Review Requirements

14. The Children's Television Act requires that, in reviewing television license renewal applications, we consider whether the licensee has served "the educational and informational needs of children through the licensee's overall programming, including programming specifically designed to serve such needs." . . . In light of the legislative intent, we will implement this programming provision by reviewing a licensee's renewal application to determine whether, over the course of its license term, it has served the educational and informational needs of children in its overall programming, including programming specifically designed to serve such needs.

A. Age Range of "Children"

15. The Act does not define "children" for purposes of the educational and informational programming renewal review requirement. . . . After reviewing the variety of positions taken in the record, we find that the different policies underlying the Act's programming provision necessitate a broader conception of "children" than we used for commercial limits. While it is primarily younger children who need protection from commercial matter that they do not fully comprehend, older as well as younger children have unique needs and can benefit from programming directed to them. Teenagers are undergoing a transition to adulthood. They are still very influenced by adult role models and peers, including those portrayed on television. They are

generally inexperienced and yet face many crucial decisions concerning sex, drugs, and their own identities. To fully comply with the Act's directive that licensees demonstrate responsiveness to the needs of the child audience, we believe that we must interpret the programming renewal review requirement to apply to programs originally produced and broadcast for an audience of children 16 years of age and under.

. . .

18. The *Notice* asked whether the Act requires broadcasters to target particular segments of the child audience. The legislative history, we find, permits but does not require such targeting to satisfy our renewal review. Imposing such a requirement would contravene the legislative intent to afford broadcasters maximum flexibility in determining the "mix" of programming they will present to meet children's special needs. Requiring each broadcaster to serve all age groups in order to pass our renewal review would probably result in less expensive and lower quality programming, possibly engendering what INTV describes as "sameness and mediocrity." We thus decline to adopt suggestions that broadcasters program to all ages or to each subset of children within the under 16 range. Stations may select the age groups they can most effectively serve.

B. *Standard*

1. *Programming*

19. Although we stated the desire to avoid any *de facto* system of "precensorship" and to leave it to licensees to interpret the meaning of educational and informational programming, the *Notice* asked those commenters desiring a delineation of the Act's programming renewal review requirement to address what definition of "educational and informational" programming we might use. The *Notice* specifically referred to a description by Senator Inouye, as programming which furthers a child's intellectual, emotional and social development. After further reflection, we believe that a general definition of "educational and informational" programming for children would provide needed guidance to the industry as well as to Commission staff administering the statute, and would give licensees sufficient flexibility to exercise their discretion in serving children's needs. We also encourage licensees to use the assessment criteria proposed in the *Notice* in determining how to meet the educational and informational needs of children in their communities.

. . .

21. We believe that a definition based on Senator Inouye's view, described above, or based on McGannon's formulation—content that serves children's cognitive/intellectual or social/emotional needs—is closer to the spirit of the Act and to our desire to stimulate, and not dictate, programming responsive to children's needs. Thus, programming that furthers the positive development of the child in any respect, including the child's cognitive/intellectual or emotional/social needs,

can contribute to satisfying the licensee's obligation to serve the educational and informational needs of children.

22.　The *Notice* proposed to require each licensee to assess the needs of children given (1) the circumstances within the community, (2) other programming on the station, (3) programming aired on other broadcast stations within the community, and (4) other programs for children available in the broadcaster's community of license. Licensees would then air programs intended to meet "the educational and informational needs of children" responding to this assessment. In order to avoid unnecessary burdens, we are not requiring use of the proposed assessment criteria. We do, however, adopt them as permissive guidelines for exercise of licensee discretion in applying this definition. These factors can serve to make licensees' decisionmaking process more objective and may make it easier for licensees to justify programming decisions that are questioned. We therefore encourage their use. We are concerned with licensee responsiveness to children's needs, not with the precise methodology they use to assess those needs. We thus do not adopt proposals for structured assessment procedures. Licensees will retain reasonable discretion to determine the manner in which they assess the educational and informational needs of children in their communities, provided that they are able to demonstrate the methodology they have used.

.　.　.

24.　The Act imposes no quantitative standards and the legislative history suggests that Congress meant that no minimum amount criterion be imposed. Given this strong legislative directive direction, and the latitude afforded broadcasters in fulfilling the programming requirement, we believe that the amount of "specifically designed" programming necessary to comply with the Act's requirement is likely to vary according to other circumstances, including but not limited to, type of programming aired and other nonbroadcast efforts made by the station. We thus decline to establish any minimum programming requirement for licensees for renewal review independent of that established in the Act.

25.　At the request of numerous parties, we clarify that short segment programming, including vignettes and PSAs, may qualify as specifically designed educational and informational programming for children. Such material is well suited to children's short attention spans and can often be locally produced with acceptable production quality. It thus may be a particularly appropriate way for a local broadcaster to respond to specific children's concerns. Whether or not short segment programming fully satisfies the requirement to air programming "specifically designed" to meet children's needs depends on the entire context of the licensee's programming and nonbroadcast efforts directed at children. We also clarify that qualifying programming need not be locally produced and need not be live action, as opposed to animation. We can see no reason in the statute's purpose or legislative history for these restrictions. As the legislative history also indicates, general audience programming can contribute, as part of the licensee's overall programming, to serving children's needs pursuant to the Act. It does not by definition, however, satisfy the additional requirement that licensees air some programming "specifically designed" to serve the educational and informational needs of children.

. . .

2. Nonbroadcast efforts

27. Section 103(b) of the Act permits the Commission, in evaluating compliance with the broadcaster's obligation to demonstrate at renewal time that it served the educational and informational needs of children, to consider "in addition" to its programming (1) "any special nonbroadcast efforts . . . which enhance the educational and informational value" of programming meeting such needs and (2) any "special efforts" to produce or support programming broadcast by another station in the licensee's market that is specifically designed to meet such needs. . . .

28. For nonbroadcast efforts to contribute to satisfying the Act's programming renewal review requirement, they must enhance the "educational and informational value" to children of television programming broadcast either by the licensee or by another station in the community. Thus, however, praiseworthy, community outreach efforts unrelated to television programming will not qualify. Similarly, we do not believe that support for children's radio programming, as some urge, although a very laudable objective, qualifies under Section 103(b)(2) as support for another licensee's programming. . . . For efforts to be credited toward satisfying the Act's programming renewal review requirements, they must somehow enhance or support educational and informational television programming for children.

26. If a station produces or buys children's programs broadcast on another station, so as to qualify under Section 103(b)(2) of the Act, we hold that both stations may rely on such programming in their renewal applications. The extent of support, measured in both time and money, given to another station's programming will determine the weight afforded it. . . .

. . .

V. Program-Length Children's Commercials

A. Definition

40. We find that the definition of program-length children's commercial proposed in the *Notice*—a program associated with a product in which commercials for that product aired—strikes the best balance between the important interests involved. This definition protects children from the confusion and deception the intermixture of related program and commercial material may inflict upon them, and still preserves the creative freedom and practical revenue sources that make

children's programming possible. For the reasons given below, we adopt this definition.

41. ACT maintains . . . that the Commission should establish a rebuttable presumption that if there is less than a two-year time span between the introduction of a television program and a related product or *vice versa*, this is *prima facie* evidence that the show is a program-length commercial. We do not find that this is a viable definition. We agree with numerous commenters that it would jeopardize highly acclaimed children's shows such as Sesame Street and Disney programs that have products associated with them. As CTW, the producer of Sesame Street, states, a program's relationship to products is not necessarily indicative of commercial content. According to CTW, ACT's proposal would inhibit the simultaneous introduction of any new CTW program series and associated products, such as books, magazines, games and computer software whose purpose is to extend the educational benefits of the series. We fear that such a definition would stifle creativity by restricting the sources that writers could draw upon for characters, would limit revenues from merchandising which are an important source of production funding, and would ignore the educational role toys or other related products can play in child development.

. . .

44. The definition of children's program-length commercial that we are now adopting—a program associated with a product, in which commercials for that product are aired—is clear, easy to understand and apply, and narrowly tailored. It directly addresses a fundamental regulatory concern, that children who have difficulty enough distinguishing program content from unrelated commercial matter, not be all the more confused by a show that interweaves program content and commercial matter. Removal of related commercial matter should help alleviate this confusion. Our definition also would cover programs in which a product or service is advertised within the body of the program and not separated from program content as children's commercials are required to be. Contrary to ACT's view, we find that our definition clarifies the manner in which our traditional definition of program-length commercial applies to children's programs. We have previously so held. Given the First Amendment context of this issue, our approach is a restrained one. Should abuses occur, however, we will not hesitate to revisit this issue. We also note that our definition harmonizes with, and codifies to some degree, existing policies with respect to host-selling and adequate separation of commercial from program material in children's programs.[147]

147. Our policy against "host-selling" prohibits the use of program talent to deliver commercials. Action for Children's Television, 50 FCC2d 1, 8, 16–17 (1974). The policy applies to endorsements or selling by animated cartoon characters as well as "live" program hosts. [ ] "Host-selling" is a special application of our more general policy with respect to separation of commercial and program material. The separation policy is an attempt to aid children in distinguishing advertising from

45. In addition, a program will be considered a program-length commercial if a product associated with the program appears in commercial spots not separated from the start or close of the program by at least 60 seconds of unrelated material. It is reasonably likely that a young viewer will tune in immediately before or stay tuned immediately after a program, and that in such circumstances an adjacent spot would have the same effect as if the spot were included in the program itself. We do not find record evidence justifying extending this Rule beyond 60 seconds, or further expanding our host-selling policy, as ACT requests. In light of the short attention spans of children, particularly younger children most likely to confuse program and commercial material, we believe that a 60–second separation is adequate.

. . .

Notes and Questions

1. In an omitted portion of *Children's Television Programming*, the FCC denied ACT's petition regarding interactive children's programs, p. 371, *supra*, on the ground that there was no evidence that any interactive toys were currently for sale.

2. In 1992 the FCC audited 141 television stations and 27 cable systems. Eight television stations and three cable systems were cited for running too much commercial matter during children's programming. Broadcasting, July 13, 1992 at 38.

E. MISCELLANEOUS CONSTRAINTS

1. LOTTERIES

Another specific substantive limitation has been 18 U.S.C.A. § 1304, prohibiting broadcast of "any advertisement of or information concerning any lottery . . .." What is the basis for this statute? As with the specific obscenity statute, the Commission has taken the view that it has responsibility for enforcement. This has been bolstered by the provisions in the Communications Act that provide for revocation of license and for forfeitures against those who violate § 1304: §§ 312(a)(6), 312(b), 503(b)(1)(E). Remember the United Television case discussed in Chapter IV.

A lottery is defined as anything containing three elements: chance, consideration and a prize. If all three are present, the broadcaster cannot air any information either as an advertisement or public service announcement concerning the lottery, and even news coverage is limited to situations where the lottery is truly newsworthy.

Until recently it was irrelevant whether the beneficiary of the lottery was a commercial enterprise or a non-profit one. This was

---

program material. It requires that broadcasters separate the two types of content by use of special measures such as "bumpers" (*e.g.*, "And now its time for a commercial break." "And now back to the [title of the program]"). Action for Children's Television, 50 FCC2d at 14–16. . . .

changed by the Charity Games Advertising Clarification Act of 1988, which expanded the exceptions to § 1304. The Commission also amended its rules to conform to these changes. Broadcasters may now advertise lotteries "if they are conducted by: (a) not-for-profit organizations; (b) governmental organizations; or (c) commercial entities, provided the lottery is clearly occasional and ancillary to the primary business of the commercial organization." Broadcast of Lottery Information (Charity Games), 67 R.R.2d 996 (1990). However, state law has not been preempted, leaving states free to restrict or prohibit lottery advertising. Thus, in many states the restrictions on broadcasters have effectively remained unchanged.

What constitutes chance as opposed to skill is up to the interpretation of the Commission. Guessing the number of beans in a jar has been held to be chance, but betting on horse races is viewed as skill. A golf tournament would be viewed as skill, but a hole-in-one contest would be chance. The distinction is supposed to be whether some difference in ability significantly improves a contestant's chances of winning. Where elements of both chance and skill are present—for example, a tie among all those who correctly answer contest questions is broken by a coin flip—then, assuming there is consideration and a prize, the contest is a lottery.

Consideration exists when an entrant must provide something of value to enter the contest. The most obvious examples of consideration are entry fees or purchase requirements. Sometimes, however, a significant expenditure of effort will be viewed as "shoe-leather" consideration. Thus, having to visit an automobile showroom is not consideration, but being required to take a test drive is. Similarly, having to be present at a drawing is not consideration as long as the drawing is held at a previously announced time. If, however, one must be present for a long period of time, then it is consideration.

The most common method of circumventing this lottery element is to allow people who have not provided consideration also to enter the contest. This is why so many giveaways advertise no purchase necessary or allow contestants to submit facsimiles of proofs of purchase. However, in order to avoid having the contest declared a lottery, those who do not provide consideration must have an equal chance of winning. Sometimes the question of what constitutes an equal chance presents a difficult problem. For example, in contests where people have to match the insides of soft drink bottle caps, the Commission has determined that a non-purchaser who sends in a self-addressed, stamped envelope must receive six bottle caps because people usually buy soft drinks in six-packs.

If the consideration does not go to the promoter, it is not a lottery. Thus, in the soft drink example above, the postage required to obtain the caps does not constitute consideration because the money goes to the Post Office, not the soft drink company. Similarly, a broadcaster could hold a contest inside a county fair without the admission fee constituting consideration, as long as the broadcaster did not receive any of the admissions proceeds.

The easiest element of a lottery to ascertain is the prize. If any contestant receives a benefit as a result of entering the contest, then there is a prize. Prizes usually take the form of money, merchandise, services or discounts.

As a number of Washington, D.C., area radio stations discovered, licensees can be held responsible under § 1304 even in cases where they don't know they are promoting a lottery. A 1975 "Dial–a–Discount" promotion for Allyn's Pants Ranch allowed customers to spin a wheel to determine how much of a discount would be applied to a pants purchase. The licensees were under the impression that the spin occurred prior to purchase, which meant there was no consideration. In support of this position they submitted written "procedure rules" for the promotion and affidavits from various store personnel that no purchase was necessary. However, Commission investigators who visited the stores were told that a purchase was required. Also, the original broadcast announcements contained the statement, "After you purchase any pair of pants . . . you get to dial your own discount." The Commission determined that the promotion required, at the very least, an agreement to purchase. The agreement alone was sufficient to supply the element of consideration.

With regard to the argument that § 1304 requires "knowingly" broadcasting lottery information, the Commission construed that to mean the announcements were knowingly broadcast, not that the licensee knew it was a lottery. Rather, the licensee is required to exercise reasonable diligence in determining whether any promotion is a lottery. Relying on the assurances of the store or advertising agency is not considered reasonable diligence. Metromedia, Inc., 38 R.R.2d 785 (1976).

When states began running their own lotteries, new questions arose concerning the ban on lottery information. After an early case that somewhat limited the scope of § 1304, New York State Broadcasters Association v. United States, 414 F.2d 990 (2d Cir.1969), the issue came to a head in New Jersey. During three consecutive news broadcasts each Thursday, the day of the drawing in the state lottery, a licensee wanted to announce: "The winning state lottery number drawn today is . . .." The Commission in a declaratory ruling concluded that such a statement would violate § 1304, even though it was presented as a news item. A main argument was that this was "news" only to those who held tickets. Experience had shown that the lottery's telephone lines were greatly overloaded on Thursdays as people called to learn the winning number. On a typical Thursday, there were 2,750,000 ticket-holders. On appeal, the court, sitting *en banc*, unanimously reversed the Commission's ban on such broadcasts. New Jersey State Lottery Commission v. United States, 491 F.2d 219 (3d Cir.1974). The court concluded that the Commission had misconstrued § 1304 by interpreting it to ban "news." Although the information here was of transitory value, the court noted that on Thursdays more people in New Jersey care about this information than care about any given stock market quotation. Thus, the size of the interested group could not be the test of news. Broadcasters should be free to decide what is news and what news will serve the public unless their decision is beyond the realm of reason. The court was also influenced by the no-censorship language of § 326, which reinforced its view that § 1304 should be limited to advertising and information meant to make a particular lottery more attractive to participants.

The government's petition for *certiorari* was granted to resolve the apparent conflict between the decisions of the Second and Third Circuits. After argument, but before decision, Congress passed a statute providing that § 1304 shall not apply to "an advertisement, list of prizes, or information concerning a lottery conducted by a State acting under the authority of State law . . . broadcast by a radio or television station licensed to a location in that State or an adjacent State which conducts such a lottery." 18 U.S.C.A. § 1307(a)(2). On the government's motion, the Court, over a dissent by Justice Douglas, vacated the judgment of the Third Circuit and remanded for its consideration of whether the case had become moot. United States v. New Jersey State Lottery Commission, 420 U.S. 371 (1975).

On remand, the court noted that states adjacent to New Jersey (and to intervenor New Hampshire) did not have state lotteries, so that broadcasters in those states were not permitted by § 1307 to broadcast information about the New Jersey (or New Hampshire) lottery. The concern about limited dissemination of "news" still existed and the case was not moot. The court reaffirmed its earlier decision rejecting the Commission's interpretation of § 1304. The result is reported in New Jersey State Lottery Commission v. United States, 519 F.2d 1398 (3d Cir.1975). The opinion is reported in 34 R.R.2d 825 (1975).

Recently, a district court declared the adjacent state restriction unconstitutional as applied to a North Carolina radio station. The station, located near the Virginia border, sought a declaratory judgment so that it could accept advertising for the Virginia State Lottery.

The court found that the application of the restriction to the station failed the third part of the *Central Hudson* test which requires the regulation to directly advance a substantial government interest. (We will discuss the *Central Hudson* test later in this chapter.) Because the vast majority of the station's listeners were in Virginia and those listeners in Virginia were heavily exposed to Virginia broadcast stations—for whom the lottery advertising was legal—the court found that prohibiting the radio station from broadcasting lottery advertising failed "materially to protect North Carolina residents from the harms which may result from lottery advertising." Edge Broadcasting Co. v. United States, 732 F.Supp. 633, 17 Med.L.Rptr. 1649, 67 R.R.2d 981

(E.D.Va.1990). The decision was upheld on appeal. Edge Broadcasting Co. v. United States, 956 F.2d 263 (4th Cir.1992). The Supreme Court has granted *certiorari.*

Under the Charity Games Advertising Clarification Act of 1988, p. 379, *supra,* the adjacent states restriction was eliminated for states that have state-run lotteries. Regardless of whether a state has a state-run lottery, it does not apply to lotteries run by other government organizations or by non-profit or commercial organizations.

The only other significant case in this area involved whether so-called "give-away" programs on radio and television ran afoul of § 1304 as lotteries. The Supreme Court construed the statute narrowly and held that requiring contestants to listen to the program did not constitute a "valuable consideration." Thus, the Commission had no basis for prohibiting the programs. Federal Communications Commission v. American Broadcasting Co., 347 U.S. 284 (1954).

2. CONTESTS

The stations themselves, however, are permitted to run their own contests so long as they are not fraudulent, are not broadcast only during rating periods to increase the figures ("hypoing"), and do not disturb public safety. The Commission has rejected an effort to ban contests that involve no skill, such as those in which listeners tune in to know how much money is in the jackpot in case they are telephoned. The complaint was that this type of contest "bribed" listeners and tended to force other stations to compete by imitation rather than by making improvements in programming. The Commission refused to act, because it was not convinced that the problem required attention or that it was empowered to deal with such a situation. Broadcast of Station Contests, 37 R.R.2d 260 (F.C.C.1976). Does this kind of situation warrant action? Under what authority?

Although contests are not prohibited, they are subject to strict standards of honesty. 47 C.F.R. § 73.1216 provides:

> A licensee that broadcasts or advertises information about a contest it conducts shall fully and accurately disclose the material terms of the contest, and shall conduct the contest substantially as announced or advertised. No contest description shall be false, misleading, or deceptive with respect to any material terms.

When determining whether or not a contest is deceptive, the Commission is not limited to considering the promotional announcements as a complete package but can also look at individual announcements or even misleading phrases. For example, referring to a prize as a '$479 cash prize jackpot" when it consisted of $30 in cash and $449 in non-cash prizes was held deceptive even though other promotional announcements made it clear that the jackpot was not all cash. Musical Heights, Inc., 40 R.R.2d 1016 (F.C.C.1977).

Note that the § 73.1216 requires that disclosure be full as well as accurate. Omission of relevant details can be viewed as seriously as deceptive statements. This applies to both the rules of the contest and the prizes to be awarded. Any ambiguity is decided against the licensee. Consider the following promotional announcement:

THIS SOUND COULD MEAN 4 DAYS AND 3 NIGHTS FOR YOU AND YOUR COMPANION IN YOUR CHOICE OF *LAS VEGAS, SAN JUAN, FT. LAUDERDALE OR ACAPULCO, MEXI-CO. SECRET SOUNDS* ARE COMING THIS FRIDAY TO 99 WIBZ. EACH DAY FOR FIFTEEN DAYS WIBZ WILL BROAD-CAST A *SECRET SOUND* . . . LISTEN EACH DAY AND IDENTIFY EACH SOUND, THEN ON MAY 7TH SEND IN A LIST OF THE *SECRET SOUNDS* AS YOU HAVE IDENTIFIED THEM. WE WILL SELECT THE 25 ENTRIES THAT COME THE CLOSEST TO BEING CORRECT THEN THOSE 25 PEOPLE WILL RECEIVE *4* DAYS AND *3* NIGHTS IN YOUR CHOICE OF *LAS VEGAS, SAN JUAN, FT. LAUDERDALE OR ACAPULCO. SE-CRET SOUNDS* STARTS THIS FRIDAY ON *WIBZ.* THE SOUNDS WILL BE BROADCAST NUMEROUS TIMES DURING THE DAY WITH A DIFFERENT SOUND EACH DAY FOR 15 DAYS. IT'S EASY . . . SIMPLY LISTEN AND WIN ON *WIBZ 99—STILL THE BEST ROCK!* (SORRY ONLY THOSE OVER 23 YEARS OF AGE ELIGIBLE.)

The Commission held that the above announcement was deceptive and misleading because it created the impression that transportation was included when in fact it was not. An official admonishment was placed in the station's files for consideration with the next renewal application. Randy Jay Broadcasting Co., 39 R.R.2d 937 (1977).

Often, where there has been deception as to the prizes to be awarded, stations have been required to provide the promised prizes. More serious violations—a "find the disc jockey" contest where the disc jockey was in another part of the country, a contest requiring winners to call during a specified time period when the phone was left off the hook, or a treasure hunt where the treasure was not hidden until the last day of the contest—have led to forfeitures and revocations.

In 1966 the Commission issued a Policy Statement entitled "Contests and Promotions Which Adversely Affect the Public Interest." 2 F.C.C.2d 464, 6 R.R.2d 671 (1966). Among the specific examples cited as contests that "adversely affect the public interest" were the following.

A contest which resulted in a vast accumulation of scrap metal in a certain location, blocking access to nearby commercial establishments.

A contest which led listeners to choose names at random from the telephone directory and to call the persons listed at all hours of the day and night causing great annoyance and effectively blocking use of their telephones for normal purposes.

Contests which, by requiring the participants to travel to a specified place in a very short time, have caused traffic violations and endangered life.

The broadcast of "scare" announcements or headlines which either are untrue or are worded in such a way as to mislead and frighten the public; e.g., a sudden announcement delivered in a tone of excitement to the effect that "amoebas" were invading a certain city, implying that the amoebas were dangerous creatures.

In 1985, as part of its ongoing attempt to remove "regulatory underbrush," the Commission rescinded the *1966 Policy Statement.* "[M]ost important by far in our conclusion to delete the policy is that it is simply unwarranted and unnecessary—the raison d'etre of this 'underbrush' proceeding. While the stated purposes for the policy of public safety, etc. are important, the examples cited therefor and the resultant policy constitute regulatory overkill. To issue a Public Notice cautioning all broadcast licensees against engaging in such an obvious hoax as 'amoebas' invading a city is simply an overreaction." The Commission concluded that alternative remedies were adequate to protect the public interest in these areas. These alternative remedies include civil suits (remember *Weirum,* p. 361, *supra*) and criminal statutes prohibiting disturbing the peace, maintaining a public nuisance, and making harassing phone calls. The Commission did note, however, that despite the elimination of the *1966 Policy Statement,* a broadcast of something similar to "War of the Worlds" without adequate cautionary language would still be a violation of the general duty to program in the public interest. Unnecessary Broadcast Regulation, 57 R.R.2d 939 (1985).

Broadcasts of Telephone Conversations. Some of the most common promotional contests involve telephoning a viewer or listener and broadcasting the conversation. Section 73.1206 of the Commission's rules sets very strict guidelines for broadcasting phone conversations. If the conversation is live, the party answering the phone must give consent *before* the licensee can start to broadcast it. If the conversation is to be recorded for later broadcast, consent must be given before the recording can start. In response to broadcasters' complaints that this rule destroys all spontaneity, the Commission reexamined the rule and concluded that the loss of spontaneity was outweighed by the substantial privacy interests protected by the notice requirements. Broadcast of Telephone Conversations, 65 R.R.2d 444 (1988). Broadcasting telephone conversations may also raise invasion of privacy questions. We will discuss these issues in Chapter XIII.

3. Payola and Plugola

Perhaps the biggest scandal ever to occur in broadcasting was the quiz show scandal of the late 1950s. At that time big money quiz shows such as "The $64,000 Question," "Tic Tac Dough" and "Twenty One" constituted one of the most popular forms of prime-time programming. However, in 1959 the nation was shocked when Charles Van Doren, a popular contestant and leading money winner on "Twenty One," testified before a House subcommittee that the shows were fixed. At approximately the same time, evidence surfaced that many disc jockeys and program directors were accepting bribes to play specific records on their stations. This latter practice became known as "payola."

Congressional and Commission reaction was swift. Section 317 of the Communications Act was amended, and two new sections, 508 and 509, were added to the Communications Act.

Section 317

(a)(1) All matter broadcast by any radio station for which any money, service or other valuable consideration is directly or indirectly paid, or promised to or charged or accepted by, the station so broadcasting, from any person, shall, at the time the same is so broadcast, be announced as paid for or furnished, as the case may be, by such person: *Provided,* That "service or other valuable consideration" shall not include any service or property furnished without charge or at a nominal charge for use on, or in connection with, a broadcast unless it is so furnished in consideration for an identification in a broadcast of any person, product, service, trademark, or brand name beyond an identification which is reasonably related to the use of such service or property on the broadcast.

Section 508 requires employees, program producers and program suppliers to notify broadcasters of any payments given or received for the purpose of inducing the inclusion of specific material in broadcast programming.

Section 509

(a) It shall be unlawful for any person, with intent to deceive the listening or viewing public—

    (1) To supply to any contestant in a purportedly bona fide contest of intellectual knowledge or intellectual skill any special and secret assistance whereby the outcome of such contest will be in whole or in part prearranged or predetermined.

    (2) By means of persuasion, bribery, intimidation, or otherwise, to induce or cause any contestant in a purportedly bona fide contest of intellectual knowledge or intellectual skill to refrain in any manner from using or displaying his knowledge

or skill in such contest, whereby the outcome thereof will be in whole or in part prearranged or predetermined.

After the passage of these new provisions, the Commission issued notices that they would be strictly enforced.

Technically, payola is accepting or receiving money or other valuable consideration for the inclusion of material in a broadcast *without* disclosing that fact to the audience, while plugola is promoting goods or services in which someone responsible for selecting the material broadcast has a financial interest. The Commission has adopted several rules governing payola and plugola. In essence, these rules are aimed at preventing the public from being deceived as to the commercial nature of sponsored material. We will return to the most important of these rules, the sponsorship identification requirement, shortly.

The structure of the radio industry has changed dramatically since the original payola scandal. In the late 1950s, most radio programming was done by the individual stations. Now many stations have their music programmed by syndicated programmers who supply the music on record or tape as well as directions as to the order of play. Syndicators have even more control of programming with the hundreds of stations that are carrying satellite-delivered programming. How can the Commission control potential payola problems with these syndicators?

In 1980, after lengthy proceedings, the Commission concluded that plugola was best handled on a case-by-case basis and that "it would be difficult to frame a rule that covered the important elements of this complex subject without either going too far in regulating licensees or leaving important loopholes in the effectiveness of the rule." The Commission also noted that relatively few plugola complaints had been filed in the the late 1970s. Plugola Practices, 46 R.R.2d 1421 (F.C.C. 1980).

However, after four people were indicted in early 1988 for payola, the Commission issued a reminder to broadcast licensees that payola could result not only in criminal charges, but in administrative sanctions against the stations involved. The Commission then attempted to clarify the licensees' obligations in this area:

Both Section 317(c) of the Act and § 73.1212(b) of the Commission's Rules require that each licensee "exercise reasonable diligence to obtain from its employees, and from other persons with whom it deals" information to enable the licensee to comply with the sponsorship identification requirements of Section 317 of the Act. The "reasonable diligence" standard can require a higher duty of care by stations whose formats or other circumstances make them more susceptible to payola. Thus, for example, we would expect stations that report to record charting services to demonstrate greater diligence to prevent improper conduct by its principals and employees than would a station with an all-news format. It may fall short of "reasonable diligence" if the licensee of such a reporting station does nothing more than require its employees to execute affidavits stating that they will not violate laws and regulations prohibiting payola.

The Commission also indicated a willingness to give informal opinions to licensees concerning specific practices or situations. Payola and Undisclosed Promotion, 64 R.R.2d 1338 (1988).

4. ADVERTISING AND COMMERCIAL PRACTICES

Broadcasters are of course subject to advertising regulation aimed at the mass media in general. However, as we saw in our discussion of cigarette advertising, p. 274, *supra*, broadcast advertising is also subject to special restrictions not applicable to other media.

a. *Sponsorship Identification*

One such restriction is the sponsorship identification requirement that is part of the measures taken in response to the payola scandal. The Commission has interpreted § 317 to require that every advertisement must contain material specifying that it was paid for, and by whom. 47 C.F.R. § 73.1212. This information is obvious in most cases—a commercial for a specific brand of automobile is assumed to have been purchased by the manufacturer or dealers association promoted in the commercial. But it does restrict one specific form of advertising, "teasers." A teaser is an advertisement that withholds specific information to arouse the public's interest, e.g., "On August 2, automotive history will be made." Obviously, ads of this nature violate the sponsorship identification rules.

b. *Commercial Speech Doctrine*

Traditionally, special restrictions on broadcast advertising were not seen as raising serious constitutional problems. Although the special status of broadcasting contributed to the lack of constitutional protection, the primary reason was that commercial speech was viewed as outside the protection of the First Amendment. However, as a result of a series of Supreme Court decisions during the past decade, commercial speech now enjoys considerable First Amendment protection.

Thus far, the effect of the new commercial speech doctrine on broadcast advertising restrictions has not yet been fully determined. In addition, to the inevitable reliance on *Red Lion* and the scarcity rationale, several arguments for allowing more extensive restrictions on the broadcast media have been advanced. Relying on *Pacifica*, advocates of regulation argue that the greater impact of broadcasting, its unique accessibility to children and its intrusion into the home all mandate less constitutional protection for broadcast advertising. Oth-

ers contend that the restricted format of broadcast advertising—30–
or 60–second commercials—makes it inherently deceptive and misleading.

Recently there has been a lot of pressure for a ban on alcoholic
beverages on electronic media similar to the cigarette advertising ban.
Due to the changes in the commercial speech doctrine, the constitutionality of such a ban is in doubt. The test that would have to be applied to any such restriction originated in Central Hudson Gas & Electric Corp. v. Public Service Commission of New York, 447 U.S. 557
(1980).

> In commercial speech cases, then, a four-part analysis has
> developed. At the outset, we must determine whether the expres-
> sion is protected by the First Amendment. For commercial speech
> to come within that provision, it at least must concern lawful
> activity and not be misleading. Next, we ask whether the asserted
> governmental interest is substantial. If both inquiries yield posi-
> tive answers, we must determine whether the regulation directly
> advances the governmental interest asserted, and whether it is not
> more extensive than is necessary to serve that interest.

The likelihood of a ban on alcoholic beverage advertising being
found constitutional increased dramatically as a result of a 1986 Supreme Court decision. The case involved a selective ban on casino
advertising in Puerto Rico.

In 1948 Puerto Rico legalized certain forms of casino gambling in
an effort to encourage tourism. Although local residents were not
banned from using the casinos, the legislature provided that casinos
were not to advertise to the local public. Over the years, the focus of
the regulation became one of identifying the primary audience of the
advertisement in question. This meant that casinos might advertise
within Puerto Rico if their primary audience was tourists rather than
residents. In Posadas De Puerto Rico Associates v. Tourism Company
of Puerto Rico, 478 U.S. 328, 13 Med.L.Rptr. 1033 (1986), the Court,
5–4, rejected a casino's facial challenge to the statute and the regulations.

> For the majority, Justice Rehnquist began by noting that the case
> involved "pure commercial speech which does 'no more than propose a
> commercial transaction.'" He then applied the four-part test of *Cen-*
> *tral Hudson*. First, the regulation concerned a lawful activity and was
> not misleading or fraudulent. Second, the "reduction of demand for
> casino gambling by the residents of Puerto Rico" was a "substantial"
> government interest. Third, the regulation "directly advanced" the
> government's asserted interest:

> The Puerto Rico Legislature obviously believed . . . that advertis-
> ing of casino gambling aimed at the residents of Puerto Rico would

serve to increase the demand for the product advertised. We think the legislature's belief is a reasonable one. . . .

The Court rejected the casino's argument that the regulation was underinclusive because other types of gambling could be advertised to residents. The restrictions do in fact directly advance the government's interest in this case. Furthermore, the legislature's concern might have been casino gambling rather than horse racing, cockfighting and the lottery, which might "have been traditionally part of the Puerto Rican's roots."

Fourth, the restrictions were "no more extensive than necessary to serve the government's interest." The casino argued that the First Amendment required the government to reduce demand for casino gambling "not by suppressing commercial speech that might *encourage* such gambling, but by promulgating additional speech designed to *discourage* it." The Court disagreed:

> We think it is up to the legislature to decide whether or not such a "counterspeech" policy would be as effective in reducing the demand for casino gambling as a restriction on advertising. The legislature could conclude, as it apparently did here, that residents of Puerto Rico are already aware of the risks of casino gambling, yet would nevertheless be induced by widespread advertising to engage in such potentially harmful conduct. Cf. Capital Broadcasting Co. v. Mitchell, 333 F.Supp. 582, 585 (D.C.C.1971) (three-judge court) ("Congress has convincing evidence that the Labelling Act of 1965 had not materially reduced the incidence of smoking") affirmed 405 U.S. 1000 (1972); Dunagin v. City of Oxford, Miss., 718 F.2d 738, 751 (5th Cir.1983) (en banc) (". . . The state's concern is not that the public is unaware of the dangers of alcohol. . . . The concern instead is that advertising will unduly promote alcohol despite known dangers"), cert. denied 467 U.S. 1259 (1984).

This led the Court to conclude that the *Central Hudson* test had been met and that the lower courts had properly rejected the First Amendment claim.

The casino argued that cases like Bigelow v. Virginia, 421 U.S. 809, 1 Med.L.Rptr. 1919 (1975), dictated protection here. The Court disagreed. In *Bigelow*, the underlying activity (abortion) itself was protected. Here, though, the legislature "surely could have prohibited casino gambling" by residents altogether.

Finally, the casino argued that once the government chose to legalize casino gambling for residents, the First Amendment barred it from using restrictions on advertising to reduce demand for the activity. The Court disagreed:

> In our view, [the casino] has the argument backwards. . . . [I]t
> is precisely *because* the government could have enacted a wholesale
> prohibition of the underlying conduct that it is permissible for the
> government to take the less intrusive step of allowing the conduct,
> but reducing the demand through restrictions on advertising. It
> would surely be a Pyrrhic victory for casino owners . . . to gain
> recognition of a First Amendment right . . . only to thereby force
> the legislature into banning casino gambling by residents altogeth-
> er. It would just as surely be a strange constitutional doctrine
> which would concede to the legislature the authority to totally ban
> a product or activity, but deny to the legislature the authority to
> forbid the stimulation of demand for the product or activity
> through advertising. . . . Legislative regulation of products or
> activities deemed harmful, such as cigarettes, alcoholic beverages,
> and prostitution, has varied from outright prohibition on the one
> hand, [   ], to legalization of the product or activity with restrictions
> on stimulation of its demand on the other hand, [   ]. To rule out
> the latter intermediate kind of response would require more than
> we find in the First Amendment.

Justice Brennan, joined by Justices Marshall and Blackmun, dissented. None of the differences between commercial and other speech
"justify protecting commercial speech less extensively where, as here,
the government seeks to manipulate behavior by depriving citizens of
truthful information concerning lawful activities." Regulation of
speech based on "fear that recipients will act on the information
provided, . . . should be subject to strict judicial scrutiny." The
majority improperly used the "relaxed standards" normally applied to
commercial speech in its First Amendment analysis. It was incumbent
on the government to "*prove* that the interests it seeks to further are
real and substantial." Here there was no showing that "serious harmful effects" would result if local residents gambled in casinos.

Even if a substantial government interest had been shown, Justice
Brennan found no showing that the advertising regulation would meet
concerns about corruption or organized crime. Finally, he objected that
Puerto Rico could "seek directly to address the specific harms" by
monitoring casino operations to guard against the influences of crime,
by vigorously enforcing its criminal laws to combat crime and prostitution, by putting limits on the size of the bets, or by promulgating
additional speech. Contrary to the majority's view, it is not "up to the

legislature" to decide whether the government's interest can be met by less intrusive means:

> Rather, it is incumbent upon the government to *prove* that more limited means are not sufficient to protect its interests, and for a *court* to decide whether or not the government has sustained this burden. [ ] In this case, nothing suggests that the Puerto Rico Legislature ever considered the efficacy of measures other than suppressing protected expression. More importantly, there has been no showing that alternative measures would inadequately safeguard the Commonwealth's interest in controlling the harmful effects allegedly associated with casino gambling. Under these circumstances, Puerto Rico's ban on advertising clearly violates the First Amendment.

Justice Brennan also rejected the majority's argument that banning speech was "less intrusive" than banning the activity itself. Once Puerto Rico made it legal for residents to gamble in casinos, the decision to ban truthful speech about that activity raised "serious" First Amendment questions. "I do not agree that a ban on casino advertising is 'less intrusive' than an outright prohibition of such activity. . . . [T]he 'constitutional doctrine' which bans Puerto Rico from banning advertisements concerning lawful casino gambling is not so strange a restraint—it is called the First Amendment."

Justice Stevens also dissented, joined by Justices Marshall and Blackmun. His focus was on the operation of the Puerto Rico regulatory scheme which he found to discriminate between publications and to involve aspects of prior restraint.

What does this case suggest about future efforts to limit advertising of alcoholic beverages or of cigarettes or of legal prostitution? The lower court cases are cited in the majority opinion. What about banning advertising for motion pictures that could be banned as obscene, but which are permitted by the state? What about banning advertising for any spectator sport that charges more than $20 for a seat, on the ground that citizens should be discouraged from spending their money on such expensive events? What about a requirement of equal time for messages aimed at discouraging the consumption of alcoholic beverages?

In Board of Trustees v. Fox, 492 U.S. 469 (1989), the Court held that the fourth prong of the *Central Hudson* analysis does not require that the regulation be the least restrictive means of effectively protecting the state's interest. In an opinion by Justice Scalia, the Court acknowledged that it had frequently said commercial speech restrictions could be no more extensive than "necessary" to serve the state's substantial interests, and that strictly speaking, such regulations are not "necessary" if less restrictive means are available. Indeed, in *Central Hudson* itself, the Court said "if the governmental interest could be served as well by a more limited restriction on commercial speech, the excessive restrictions cannot survive."

But Justice Scalia said "the reason of the matter requires something short of a least-restrictive-means standard." Otherwise, he said, restrictions on commercial speech would be even harder to justify than time-place-and-manner restrictions on core political speech, which need only be "tailored":

What our decisions require is a " 'fit' between the legislature's ends and the means chosen to accomplish those ends," [   ]—a fit that is not necessarily perfect, but reasonable; that represents not necessarily the single best disposition but one whose scope is "in proportion to the interest served," [   ], that employs not necessarily the least restrictive means but, as we have put it in the other contexts discussed above, a means narrowly tailored to achieve the desired objective. Within those bounds we leave it to governmental decisionmakers to judge what manner of regulation may best be employed.

We reject the contention that the test we have described is overly permissive. It is far different, of course, from the "rational basis" test used for Fourteenth Amendment equal protection analysis. [   ] There it suffices if the law could be thought to further a legitimate governmental goal, without reference to whether it does so at inordinate cost. Here we require the government goal to be substantial, and the cost to be carefully calculated. Moreover, since the State bears the burden of justifying its restrictions, [   ], it must affirmatively establish the reasonable fit we require. By declining to impose, in addition, a least-restrictive-means requirement, we take account of the difficulty of establishing with precision the point at which restrictions become more extensive than their objective requires, and provide the legislative and executive branches needed leeway in a field (commercial speech) "traditionally subject to governmental regulation." [   ] Far from eroding the essential protections of the First Amendment, we think this disposition strengthens them. "To require a parity of constitutional protection for commercial and noncommercial speech alike could invite dilution, simply by a leveling process, of the force of the Amendment's guarantees with respect to the latter kind of speech."

The case involved a regulation of the State University of New York prohibiting commercial solicitations, such as "Tupperware parties" in dormitories. The Court remanded the case to determine whether the regulation had been applied in a manner that restricted noncommercial as well as commercial speech, and if not, whether it was overbroad nonetheless because of its potential applicability to noncommercial speech.

Justice Blackmun, joined by Justices Brennan and Marshall, dissented. They would have held the regulation overbroad on its face and therefore would not have reached the least-restrictive-means issue.

In the *Central Hudson* case the Commission "acknowledged that the ban is not a perfect vehicle for conserving energy." After *Fox* that admission obviously is not fatal to the Commission's case. Would the Court defer to the Commission's determination that the restriction was a reasonable though imperfect way of dampening unnecessary growth in energy consumption?

c.   The NAB Codes

As we have seen, indirect regulation of the content of broadcast programs was possible through the NAB Codes. The adherence was even greater because of the membership of the three major networks. Because they abided by the Television Code, even affiliates that did not themselves belong would be carrying only material acceptable under the Code whenever they carried network programming.

Among the provisions of the code were several restrictions on advertising. Advertising of products such as hard liquor and contraceptives were prohibited. Limits on the total number of advertising minutes per hour were part of the code as was a ban on single 30–second advertisements for two or more unrelated products ("split 30s"). In 1979 the Justice Department brought an action against the NAB charging that certain of the commercial time restrictions violated the antitrust laws. In 1982 Judge Greene declared the prohibition against split 30s to be an antitrust violation. As a result the NAB negotiated a consent decree with the Justice Department that prohibited the NAB from adopting any rule respecting the quantity, placement, or format of advertising or other nonprogram material. In addition, although not as a requirement of the settlement, the NAB cancelled the advertising standards of the Television and Radio Codes and dissolved the Code Boards of Directors. Broadcasting and Government, Jan. 1, 1985 at 138–139.

In 1983 Alberto–Culver filed an action against NAB, CBS, Inc., and several group owners alleging that they were still conspiring to prevent the broadcast of multiple product ads. Alberto–Culver negotiated a settlement with each of the broadcasters named in the case, and the suit was dismissed.

d.   Commercial Practices

The Commission has long taken an interest in the commercial practices of broadcast licensees. Recall the White Mountain Broadcasting case where renewal was denied for "double billing." In 1985, as part of another "regulatory underbrush" proceeding, the Commission eliminated many of these rules and issued an NPRM proposing deletion of others. Among the regulations deleted were those covering distortion of audience ratings, selection of sports announcers, conflicts of interest, promotion of nonbroadcast business of a station, concert promotion announcements, and false, misleading or deceptive advertisements. As in the other "underbrush" proceedings, the Commission argued that the policies eliminated "either relate to areas which often are not within this Commission's area of expertise and where either alternate remedies exist to deter the activity addressed by the particular policy or where marketplace forces will correct the particular abuse." Unnecessary Broadcast Regulation, 57 R.R.2d 913 (1985). The court of appeals rejected a petition for review of the Commission's order. Telecommunications Research and Action Center v. Federal Communications Commission, 800 F.2d 1181, 61 R.R.2d 61 (D.C.Cir. 1986).

The regulations proposed for deletion in that proceeding were subsequently eliminated. They applied to fraudulent billing practices, network clipping and joint sales practices. Unnecessary Broadcast Regulation, 59 R.R.2d 1500 (1986).

In addition, the Commission no longer hears complaints regarding distortion of a station's ratings or inaccurate signal coverage maps. It did state that the filing of a misleading coverage map would imply unacceptable character and could place a station's renewal at risk. Unnecessary Broadcast Regulation (Advertising Misrepresentations), 54 R.R.2d 705 (F.C.C.1983).

5. OTHER CONSTRAINTS

a. Sports Blackouts

In 1973 Congress passed a statute to resolve the clamor raised by the refusal of professional football teams to permit televising of a home game that was being televised to other parts of the country (47 U.S.C.A. § 331). It provided that professional sports telecasts could not be barred if all the tickets had been sold 72 hours before game time, and spelled out the conditions under which the rights to telecast could be made available. The statute expired by its own terms in 1975. A permanent anti-blackout statute was blocked in 1976, but the National Football League agreed to follow the expired statute.

b. Other Underbrush

We considered some of the policies eliminated in the regulatory underbrush proceedings earlier in this chapter. Policies aimed at discouraging liquor advertisements in dry areas, restrictions on broadcasts of foreign language programs, broadcast of astrology information, music format service agreements, repetitious broadcasts, call-in polls, private interest broadcasts, the use of sirens and sound effects, and rules regarding harassing and threatening phone calls resulting from broadcasts were all eliminated. Unnecessary Broadcast Regulation, 54

R.R.2d 1043 (F.C.C.1983). The FCC also eliminated restrictions on horse racing programming and advertising. Unnecessary Broadcast Regulation, 56 R.R.2d 976 (F.C.C.1984).

Chapter VIII

NONCOMMERCIAL BROADCASTING

A. DEVELOPMENT OF PUBLIC BROADCASTING

Virtually all of our attention so far has been devoted to commercial broadcasting. Most of the litigation and regulation has involved commercial broadcasters, and, in terms of viewers, commercial broadcasting is the preeminent part of the picture. But it is not the only part. AM broadcasting developed too early for the Commission to be able to consider reserving spots for noncommercial educational stations. In allocating FM and television, however, the Commission was able to plan in advance and reserved certain spots for educational broadcasters. These are usually operated by academic institutions, by governmental groups, or by groups organized by private citizens. Although an academic institution may operate a station only in a community where it operates a bona fide fulltime school, a private or governmental organization may qualify for a station in any community as long as it demonstrates an educational goal and a commitment to the advancement of an educational program. A station run by a sectarian academic institution may be eligible for a reserved educational spot in the community in which the school is located. If an organization's central purpose is religious, it is not eligible for a reserved channel. We will return to the issue of religious broadcasting later in this chapter.

Although many of the Commission's rules apply equally to commercial and noncommercial licensees, there are some differences. For example, the duopoly and multiple ownership rules are not applicable to noncommercial licensees. In 1988 the Commission amended its public file requirements for non-commercial licensees to conform them to the requirements for commercial licensees. Issues–Programs List for Public Broadcasting Licensees, 3 F.C.C.Rcd. 1032, 64 R.R.2d 667 (1988).

The development of public broadcasting and several questions it raises are considered in the following case.

ACCURACY IN MEDIA, INC. v. FEDERAL COMMUNICATIONS COMMISSION

United States Court of Appeals, District of Columbia Circuit, 1975.
521 F.2d 288, 35 R.R.2d 241.
Certiorari denied 425 U.S. 934, 96 S.Ct. 1664, 48 L.Ed.2d 175 (1976).

Before BAZELON, CHIEF JUDGE, LEVENTHAL, CIRCUIT JUDGE and WEIGEL, UNITED STATES DISTRICT JUDGE for the Northern District of California.

BAZELON, CHIEF JUDGE.

Accuracy in Media, Inc. (AIM) filed two complaints with the FCC against the Public Broadcasting Service (PBS) concerning two programs distributed by PBS to its member stations. AIM alleged that the programs, dealing with sex education and the American system of criminal justice, were not a balanced or objective presentation of each subject and requested the FCC to order PBS to rectify the situation. The legal basis for AIM's complaints was the Fairness Doctrine and 47 U.S.C. § 396(g)(1)(A) (1970). On its initial hearing of the matter, the FCC concluded that the PBS had not violated the Fairness Doctrine and invited comments from interested parties on its authority to enforce whatever standard of program regulation was contained in § 396(g)(1)(A). AIM does not seek the review of the Commission's decision on the Fairness Doctrine issue.

Section 396(g)(1)(A) is part of the Public Broadcasting Act of 1967, an act which created the Corporation for Public Broadcasting (CPB) and authorized it to fund various programming activities of local, non-commercial broadcasting licensees. Section 396(g)(1)(A) qualifies that authorization in the following language:

> In order to achieve the objectives and to carry out the purposes of this subpart, as set out in subsection (a) of this section, the Corporation is authorized to—
>
>> (A) facilitate the full development of educational broadcasting in which programs of high quality, obtained from diverse sources, will be made available to noncommercial educational television or radio broadcast stations, with strict adherence to objectivity and balance in all programs or series of programs of a controversial nature. . . .

AIM contends that since the above-mentioned PBS programs were funded by the CPB, pursuant to this authorization, the programs must contain "strict adherence to authorization and balance," a requirement AIM contends is more stringent than the standard of balance and fairness in overall programming contained in the Fairness Doctrine. AIM alleges that the two relevant programs did not meet this more stringent standard of objectivity and balance.

After consideration of the comments received on the matter, invited in its preliminary decision discussed above, the Commission concluded that it had no jurisdiction to enforce the mandate of § 396(g)(1)(A) against CPB. . . .

I. THE ORGANIZATION OF PUBLIC BROADCASTING IN THE UNITED STATES

Resolution of the issues raised by AIM's petition requires an understanding of the operation of the public broadcasting system. There are three tiers to this operation, each reflecting a different scheme of governmental regulation. The basic level is comprised of the local, noncommercial broadcasting stations that are licensed by the FCC and, with a few exceptions, subject to the same regulations as commercial licenses. Through the efforts of former Commissioner Frieda Hennock, the FCC has reserved exclusive space in its allocation of frequencies for such noncommercial broadcasters. Other than this specific reservation, noncommercial licensees are still subject to the same renewal process and potential challenges as their commercial counterparts.

Such was the state of the public broadcasting system until the passage of the Educational Television Facilities Act in 1962. The Act added the element of government funding to public broadcasting by establishing a grant program for noncommercial facilities. This second level of the system was reorganized and expanded by the Public Broadcasting Act of 1967 which created the Corporation for Public Broadcasting (CPB). The Corporation, the product of a study made by the Carnegie Commission on Educational Television, was established as a funding mechanism for virtually all activities of noncommercial broadcasting. In setting up this nonprofit, private corporation, the Act specifically prohibited CPB from engaging in any form of "communication by wire or radio."

The third level of the public broadcasting system was added in 1970 when CPB and a group of noncommercial licensees formed the Public Broadcasting Service (PBS) and National Public Radio. The Public Broadcasting Service operates as the distributive arm of the public television system. As a nonprofit membership corporation, it distributes national programming to approximately 150 educational licensees via common carrier facilities. This interconnection service is funded by the Corporation (CPB) under a contract with PBS; in addition, much of the programming carried by PBS is either wholly or partially funded by CPB. National Public Radio provides similar services for noncommercial radio. In 1974, CPB and the member licensees of PBS agreed upon a station program cooperative plan [14] to insure local control and origination of noncommercial broadcasting funded by CPB. Though PBS is the national coordinator under this scheme, it is not a "network" in the commercial broadcasting sense, and does not engage in "communication by wire or radio," except to the extent that it contracts for interconnection services.

II. FCC JURISDICTION OVER THE CORPORATION FOR PUBLIC BROADCASTING

With the structure of the public broadcasting system in view, we turn to AIM's contention that the FCC should enforce the mandate of

14. The Station Program Cooperative (SPC) is a unique concept in program selection and financing for public television stations. Though the idea of public broadcasting as a "fourth network" had been proposed at various times, the 1974 plan reversed this trend toward centralization. Under the SPC, certain programming will be produced only if the individual local stations decide together to fund the production. The local licensees will be financed through the CPB and other sources; the funding of specific programs will be by a 4 to 5 ratio (station funds to national cooperative funds). The aim of this cooperative is to reinforce the existing licensee responsibility for programming discretion. Through this plan the local stations will eventually assume the responsibility for support of the cooperative and the Corporation will concentrate on new programming development. [ ]

§ 396(g)(1)(A) against the CPB. Since the Section is clearly directed to the Corporation and its programming activities, we have no doubt that the Corporation must respect the mandate of the Section. However, we conclude that nothing in the language and legislative history of the Federal Communications Act or the Public Broadcasting Act of 1967 authorizes the FCC to enforce that mandate against the CPB.

Section 398 of the Communications Act expresses the clear intent of Congress that there shall be no direct jurisdiction of the FCC over the Corporation. That section states that nothing in the 1962 or 1967 Acts "shall be deemed (1) to amend any other provision of, or requirement under this Act; or (2) to authorize any department, agency, officer, or employee of the United States to exercise any direction, supervision or control over educational television or radio broadcasting, or over the Corporation or any of its grantees or contractors . . . .." Since the FCC is obviously an "agency . . . of the United States" and since any enforcement of § 396(g)(1)(A) would necessarily entail "supervision" of the Corporation, the plain words of subsection (2) preclude FCC jurisdiction. . . .

Congress desired to establish a program funding agency which would be free from governmental influence or control in its operations. Yet, the lawmakers feared that such complete autonomy might lead to biases and abuses of its own. The unique position of the Corporation is the synthesis of these competing influences. Reference to the legislative history of the 1967 Act shows a deep concern that governmental regulation or control over the Corporation might turn the CPB into a Government spokesman. Congress thus sought to insulate CPB by removing its "programming activity from governmental supervision." . . .

. . .

AIM maintains that this view of FCC jurisdiction to enforce § 396(g)(1)(A) renders the section nugatory and hence ignores the Congressional sentiment that biases and abuses within the public broadcasting system should be controlled. We do not view our holding on the FCC's jurisdiction as having that effect. Rather, we take notice of the carefully balanced framework designed by Congress for the control of CPB activities.

The Corporation was established as nonprofit and non-political in nature and is prohibited from owning or operating "any television or radio broadcast station, system or network, community antenna system, or interconnection, or production facility." Numerous statutory safeguards were created to insure against partisan abuses.[28] Ultimately,

---

28. Other statutory checks on the Corporation include: restricting the Board membership to no more than eight out of fifteen members from the same political party, § 396(c)(1). The composition of the Board was an important issue during de-bate and the decision to make the Board bipartisan was a significant addition to the original Carnegie Commission proposal. The Act also requires that the CPB's accounts be audited annually by an independent accountant, § 396(*l*)(1)(A), and *may* be

Congress may show its disapproval of any activity of the Corporation through the appropriation process.[29] This supervision of CPB through its funding is buttressed by an annual reporting requirement.[30] Through these statutory requirements and control over the "purse-strings," Congress reserved for itself the oversight responsibility for the Corporation.

A further element of this carefully balanced framework of regulation is the accountability of the local noncommercial licensees under established FCC practice, including the Fairness Doctrine in particular. This existing system of accountability was clearly recognized in the 1967 legislative debates as a crucial check on the power of the CPB.. . .

. . .

The framework of regulation of the Corporation for Public Broadcasting we have described—maximum freedom from interference with programming coupled with existing public accountability requirements—is sensitive to the delicate constitutional balance between First Amendment rights of the broadcast journalist and the concerns of the viewing public struck in Columbia Broadcasting System, Inc. v. Democratic National Committee, 412 U.S. 94 (1973). There the Supreme Court warned that "only when the interests of the public are found to outweigh the private journalistic interests of the broadcasters" will governmental interference with broadcast journalism be allowed. The Court on the basis of this rule rejected a right of access to broadcast air time greater than that mandated by the Fairness Doctrine as constituting too great a "risk of an enlargement of Governmental control over the content of broadcast discussion of public issues."

It is certainly arguable that FCC application of the standard—whatever that standard may be—of § 396(g)(1)(A) could "risk [an] enlargement of Government control over the content of broadcast discussion of public issues" in the following two ways: whereas the existing Fairness Doctrine requires only that the presentation of a controversial issue of public importance be balanced in *overall* programming, § 396(g)(1)(A) might be argued to require balance of controversial issues within each individual program. Administration of such a standard would certainly require a more active role by the FCC in oversight of programming. Furthermore, whereas the FCC has at present carefully avoided anything but the most limited inquiry into the factual accuracy of programming, § 396(g)(1)(A) by use of the term "objective" could be read to expand that inquiry and thereby expand FCC oversight of programming. Both of these potential enlargements of government control of programming, whether directed against the CPB, PBS or individual noncommercial licensees, threaten to upset the

audited by the General Accounting Office, § 396(*l*)(2)(A).

29. Section 396(k) assures that most of the CPB's operating budget be derived

through the Congressional appropriation process.

30. 47 U.S.C. § 396(i) (1970).

constitutional balance struck in *CBS.* We will not presume that Congress meant to thrust upon us the substantial constitutional questions such a result would raise. We thus construe § 396(g)(1)(A) and the scheme of regulation for public broadcasting as a whole to avoid such questions.

. . . We hold today only that the FCC has no function in this scheme of accountability established by § 396(g)(1)(A) and the 1967 Act in general other than that assigned to it by the Fairness Doctrine. Therefore, we deny the petition for review and affirm the Commission's decision rejecting jurisdiction over the Corporation for Public Broadcasting.

So ordered.

Notes and Questions

1. What is the difference between the fairness doctrine and AIM's reading of § 396(g)(1)(A)? Why does the court think that one would call for more Commission intervention in programming than the other?

2. The court suggests that PBS, although thought of by many as a "fourth network," does not properly fit such a description. Why not?

3. Despite the ruling in the AIM case, the Commission retains several controls over public noncommercial broadcasters. The primary power is to be found in the licensing process. Recall the denial of renewal to the eight Alabama stations, p. 126, *supra.* A fundamental dispute over the proper role of educational stations emerged when WNET in New York was challenged on its application for renewal: Commissioner Hooks dissented from the approval on the ground that the station was programming for a small elite minority and essentially neglecting the needs of larger groups in the community that would benefit from language, vocational and remedial programs. Elite programming is defended on the ground that the noncommercial stations do not get enough money from public sources and must solicit funds from their communities. It is thought that a station that presents culturally high-level programs for the wealthier segments of the community will have better success at raising the funds necessary to keep the station going. Is this a problem? How might the situation be changed?

4. Concern about adequate funding for public broadcasting has increased during the past few years because of decreases in federal funding. In 1981 Congress created the Temporary Commission on Alternative Financing for Public Telecommunications (TCAF). Chaired by Commissioner Quello of the FCC, TCAF was directed as part of its investigation of alternative funding to oversee an 18–month experiment allowing some public broadcasters to sell advertising. Nine public television stations participated in the experiment. Although the advertising experiment generated significant income for the participants, it was not extended.

TCAF recommended to Congress that advertising not be allowed but that enhanced underwriting (allowing identification of contributors to include product identifications and slogans) be given explicit approval. What are the risks of allowing advertising on noncommercial stations? What other funding mechanisms should be considered? Congress did not include any provision for further advertising experiments in the latest CPB funding authorization.

5. In keeping with these recommendations and the Public Broadcasting Amendments Act of 1981, the Commission reconsidered its 1982 ruling prohibiting the inclusion of brand names in donor acknowledgements. Under the new rules, "donor acknowledgements utilized by public broadcasters may include (1) logograms or slogans which identify and do *not* promote, (2) location, (3) value neutral descriptions of a product line or service, (4) brand and trade names and product or service listings." Noncommercial Educational Broadcasting Stations, 97 F.C.C.2d 255, 55 R.R.2d 1190 (1984).

6. Another approach to helping public television stations raise badly needed funds was contained in an NPRM released in 1985. The Commission proposed to permit noncommercial and commercial licensees in the same community to exchange channels and amend the TV Table of Assignments accordingly without allowing third parties to apply for the channels in question. In essence, this would have allowed commercial licensees to exchange less desirable channels for more attractive noncommercial channels, e.g. a UHF for a VHF. The commercial licensees would pay the noncommercial licensees for this exchange. 50 Fed.Reg. 11909 (March 8, 1985). The general reaction to this proposal was negative. In September 1988, as part of an appropriations bill, Congress passed a one-year prohibition on swapping commercial UHFs for noncommercial VHFs. The FCC has not taken any further action on this proposal.

7. Section 399(b) required public broadcasters to make and retain for 60 days (to allow inspection by government or public) audio tapes for all programs "in which any issue of public importance is discussed." It was declared unconstitutional in an *en banc* decision, 5–4. Community–Service Broadcasting of Mid–America, Inc. v. Federal Communications Commission, 593 F.2d 1102, 43 R.R.2d 1675, 4 Med.L.Rptr. 1257 (D.C.Cir.1978). The majority relied on equal protection grounds—that no similar burden was imposed on commercial broadcasters. Several members of the majority also expressed varying degrees of certainty that such a provision imposed on all broadcasters would violate the First Amendment. The dissenters thought that the statutory requirement of "objectivity and balance" justified the special obligation of § 399(b).

8. In 1986 the board of the Corporation for Public Broadcasting began considering a controversial proposal to conduct a content analysis of public television programming. The avowed purpose of the proposed study was to evaluate the objectivity and balance of CPB–funded programming. After 10 months of often-heated debate, the board voted to table the proposal. Broadcasting, Mar. 9, 1987 at 88.

9. The Public Telecommunications Act of 1992, p. 356, *supra,* imposed a requirement on the CPB Board of Directors to provide a reasonable opportunity for members of the public to comment on the "quality, diversity, creativity, excellence, innovation, objectivity, and balance of public broadcasting services, including all public broadcasting programming of a controversial nature." Based on this information the directors must take such steps in awarding programming grants as are necessary to facilitate objectivity and balance in programming of a controversial nature.

B. CONTENT REGULATION OF PUBLIC BROADCASTING

One of the more troublesome questions in the 1967 Act involved § 399's restrictions on editorializing, p. 86, *supra.* What arguments might be made against such a provision? What arguments to sustain it?

In 1982 a district judge declared unconstitutional the ban on editorializing by stations accepting CPB grants. The Supreme Court, 5–4, affirmed.

FEDERAL COMMUNICATIONS COMMISSION v. LEAGUE OF WOMEN VOTERS OF CALIFORNIA

Supreme Court of the United States, 1984.
468 U.S. 364, 104 S.Ct. 3106, 82 L.Ed.2d 278, 10 Med.L.Rptr. 1937.

JUSTICE BRENNAN delivered the opinion of the Court.

[The background of the case and an excerpt from an earlier part of Justice Brennan's opinion appear at page 86, *supra.*]

III

We turn now to consider whether the restraint imposed by § 399 satisfies the requirements established by our prior cases for permissible broadcast regulation. Before assessing the government's proffered justifications for the statute, however, two central features of the ban against editorializing must be examined, since they help to illuminate the importance of the First Amendment interests at stake in this case.

A

First, the restriction imposed by § 399 is specifically directed at a form of speech—namely, the expression of editorial opinion—that lies at the heart of First Amendment protection. In construing the reach of the statute, the FCC has explained that "although the use of noncommercial educational broadcast facilities by licensees, their management or those speaking on their behalf for the propagation of the licensee's own views on public issues is not permitted, such prohibition should not be construed to inhibit any *other* presentations on controversial issues of public importance." As we recently reiterated in NAACP v. Claiborne Hardware Co., 458 U.S. 886 (1982), "expression on public issues 'has always rested on the highest rung of the hierarchy of First Amendment values.'" Id., at 913 (quoting Carey v. Brown, 447 U.S. 455, 467 (1980)). And we have emphasized that:

> "The freedom of speech and of the press guaranteed by the Constitution embraces at least the liberty to discuss publicly and truthfully all matters of public concern without previous restraint or fear of subsequent punishment. . . . Freedom of discussion, if it would fulfill its historic function in this nation, must embrace all issues about which information is needed or appropriate to enable the members of society to cope with the exigencies of their period." Thornhill v. Alabama, 310 U.S. 88, 101–102 (1940).

The editorial has traditionally played precisely this role by informing and arousing the public, and by criticizing and cajoling those who hold government office in order to help launch new solutions to the problems of the time. Preserving the free expression of editorial opinion, therefore, is part and parcel of "our profound national commitment . . . that debate on public issues should be uninhibited, robust, and wide-open." New York Times v. Sullivan, 376 U.S. 254, 270 (1964). As we recognized in Mills v. Alabama, supra, the special place of the editorial in our First Amendment jurisprudence simply reflects the fact that the press, of which the broadcasting industry is indisputably a part, United States v. Paramount Pictures, Inc., 334 U.S. 131, 166 (1948), carries out a historic, dual responsibility in our society of reporting information and of bringing critical judgment to bear on public affairs. Indeed, the pivotal importance of editorializing as a means of satisfying the public's interest in receiving a wide variety of ideas and views through the medium of broadcasting has long been recognized by the FCC; the Commission has for the past 35 years actively encouraged commercial broadcast licensees to include editorials on public affairs in their programming. Because § 399 appears to restrict precisely that form of speech which the Framers of the Bill of Rights were most anxious to protect—speech that is "indispensable to the discovery and spread of political truth"—we must be especially careful in weighing the interests that are asserted in support of this restriction and in assessing the precision with which the ban is crafted. Whitney v. California, 274 U.S. 357, 375 (1927) (Brandeis, J., concurring).

Second, the scope of § 399's ban is defined solely on the basis of the content of the suppressed speech. A wide variety of non-editorial speech "by licensees, their management or those speaking on their behalf," In re Complaint of Accuracy in Media, Inc., supra, 45 F.C.C.2d, at 302, is plainly not prohibited by § 399. Examples of such permissible forms of speech include daily announcements of the station's program schedule or over-the-air appeals for contributions from listeners. Consequently, in order to determine whether a particular statement by station management constitutes an "editorial" proscribed by § 399, enforcement authorities must necessarily examine the content of the message that is conveyed to determine whether the views expressed concern "controversial issues of public importance." Ibid.

As Justice Stevens observed in Consolidated Edison Co. v. Public Service Commission, 447 U.S. 530 (1980), however, "[a] regulation of speech that is motivated by nothing more than a desire to curtail expression of a particular point of view on controversial issues of general interest in the purest example of a 'law . . . abridging the freedom of speech, or of the press.' A regulation that denies a group of persons the right to address a selected audience on 'controversial issues of public policy' is plainly such a regulation." Id., at 546 (concurring opinion); accord id., at 537–540 (majority opinion). Section 399 is just such a regulation, for it singles out noncommercial broadcasters and denies them the right to address their chosen audience on matters of public importance. . . .

B

In seeking to defend the prohibition on editorializing imposed by § 399, the Government urges that the statute was aimed at preventing two principal threats to the overall success of the Public Broadcasting Act of 1967. According to this argument, the ban was necessary, first, to protect noncommercial educational broadcasting stations from being coerced, as a result of federal financing, into becoming vehicles for government propagandizing or the objects of governmental influence; and, second, to keep these stations from becoming convenient targets for capture by private interest groups wishing to express their own partisan viewpoints.[16] By seeking to safeguard the public's right to a balanced presentation of public issues through the prevention of either governmental or private bias, these objectives are, of course, broadly consistent with the goals identified in our earlier broadcast regulation cases. But, in sharp contrast to the restrictions upheld in *Red Lion* or in Columbia Broadcasting System, Inc. v. FCC, which left room for editorial discretion and simply required broadcast editors to grant others access to the microphone, § 399 directly prohibits the broadcaster from speaking out on public issues even in a balanced and fair manner. The Government insists, however, that the hazards posed in the "special" circumstances of noncommercial educational broadcasting are so great that § 399 is an indispensable means of preserving the public's First Amendment interests. We disagree.

(1)

When Congress first decided to provide financial support for the expansion and development of noncommercial educational stations, all

---

16. The Government also contends that § 399 is intended to prevent the use of taxpayer monies to promote private views with which taxpayers may disagree. This argument is readily answered by our decision in Buckley v. Valeo, 424 U.S. 1, 90–93 (1976) (per curiam). As we explained in that case, virtually every congressional appropriation will to some extent involve a use of public money as to which some taxpayers may object. Id., at 91–92. Nevertheless, this does not mean that those taxpayers have a constitutionally protected right to enjoin such expenditures. Nor can this interest be invoked to justify a congressional decision to suppress speech.

concerned agreed that this step posed some risk that these traditionally independent stations might be pressured into becoming forums devoted solely to programming and views that were acceptable to the Federal government. That Congress was alert to these dangers cannot be doubted. It sought through the Public Broadcasting Act to fashion a system that would provide local stations with sufficient funds to foster their growth and development while preserving their tradition of autonomy and community-orientation. . . .

The intended role of § 399 in achieving these purposes, however, is not as clear. The provision finds no antecedent in the Carnegie Report, which generally provided the model for most other aspects of the Act. It was not part of the Administration's original legislative proposal. And it was not included in the original version of the Act passed by the Senate. The provision found its way into the Act only as a result of an amendment in the House. Indeed, it appears that, as the House Committee Report frankly admits, § 399 was added not because Congress thought it was essential to preserving the autonomy and vitality of local stations, but rather "out of an abundance of caution." H.R.Rep. No. 572, 90th Cong., 1st Sess. 20 (1967). [ ] [18]

More importantly, an examination of both the overall legislative scheme established by the 1967 Act and the character of public broadcasting demonstrates that the interest asserted by the Government is not substantially advanced by § 399. First, to the extent that federal financial support creates a risk that stations will lose their independence through the bewitching power of governmental largesse, the elaborate structure established by the Public Broadcasting Act already operates to insulate local stations from governmental interference. Congress not only mandated that the new Corporation for Public Broadcasting would have a private, bipartisan structure, see §§ 396(c)–(f), but also imposed a variety of important limitations on its powers. The Corporation was prohibited from owning or operating any station, § 396(g)(3), it was required to adhere strictly to a standard of "objectivity and balance" in disbursing federal funds to local stations, § 396(g)(1)(A), and it was prohibited from contributing to or otherwise supporting any candidate for office, § 396(f)(3).

The Act also established a second layer of protections which serve to protect the stations from governmental coercion and interference. Thus, in addition to requiring the Corporation to operate so as to "assure the maximum freedom [of local stations] from interference with

---

18. Of course, as the Government points out, Congress has consistently retained the basic proscription on editorializing in § 399, despite periodic reconsiderations and modifications of the Act in 1973, 1978, and 1981. Brief for the United States 25–27; see also n. 7, supra. A reviewing court may not easily set aside such a considered congressional judgment. At the same time, "[d]eference to a legislative finding cannot limit judicial inquiry when First Amendment rights are at stake.. . . . Were it otherwise, the scope of freedom of speech and of the press would be subject to legislative definition and the function of the First Amendment as a check on legislative power would be nullified." Landmark Communications, Inc. v. Virginia, 435 U.S. 829, 843–844 (1978).

or control of program content or other activities," § 396(g)(1)(D), the Act expressly forbids "any department, agency, officer, or employee of the United States [from] exercis[ing] any direction, supervision, or control over educational television or radio broadcasting, or over the Corporation or any of its grantees or contractors . . .," § 398(a). . . . The principal thrust of the amendments, therefore, has been to assure long-term appropriations for the Corporation and, more importantly, to insist that it pass specified portions of these funds directly through to local stations to give them greater autonomy in defining the uses to which those funds should be put. Thus, in sharp contrast to § 399, the unifying theme of these various statutory provisions is that they substantially reduce the risk of governmental interference with the editorial judgments of local stations without restricting those stations' ability to speak on matters of public concern.[19]

Even if these statutory protections were thought insufficient to the task, however, suppressing the particular category of speech restricted by § 399 is simply not likely, given the character of the public broadcasting system, to reduce substantially the risk that the Federal Government will seek to influence or put pressure on local stations. An underlying supposition of the Government's argument in this regard is that individual noncommercial stations are likely to speak so forcefully on particular issues that Congress, the ultimate source of the stations' Federal funding, will be tempted to retaliate against these individual stations by restricting appropriations for all of public broadcasting. But, as the District Court recognized, the character of public broadcasting suggests that such a risk is speculative at best. There are literally hundreds of public radio and television stations in communities scattered throughout the United States and its territories, see CPB, 1983–84 Public Broadcasting Directory 20–50, 66–86 (Sept. 1983). Given that central fact, it seems reasonable to infer that the editorial voices of these stations will prove to be as distinctive, varied, and idiosyncratic as the various communities they represent. More importantly, the editorial focus of any particular station can fairly be expected to focus largely on issues affecting only its community.[20] Accordingly, absent some showing by the Government to the contrary, the risk that local

---

19. Furthermore, the risk that federal coercion or influence will be brought to bear against local stations as a result of federal financing is considerably attenuated by the fact that CPB grants account for only a portion of total public broadcasting income. CPB, Public Broadcasting Income: Fiscal Year 1982, at Table 2 (Final Report, Dec. 1983) (noting that federal funds account for 23.4% of total income for all public broadcasting stations). The vast majority of financial support comes from state and local governments, as well as a variety of private sources, including foundations, businesses, and individual contributions; indeed, as the CPB recently noted, "[t]he diversity of support in America for public broadcasting is remarkable," CPB, 1982 Annual Report 2 (1982). Given this diversity of funding sources and the decentralized manner in which funds are secured, the threat that improper federal influence will be exerted over local stations is not so pressing as to require the total suppression of editorial speech by these stations.

20. This likelihood is enhanced with respect to public stations because they are required to establish community advisory boards which must reasonably reflect the "diverse needs and interests of the communities served by such station[s]." § 396(k)(9)(A). . . .

editorializing will place all of public broadcasting in jeopardy is not sufficiently pressing to warrant § 399's broad suppression of speech.

Indeed, what is far more likely than local station editorials to pose the kinds of dangers hypothesized by the Government are the wide variety of programs addressing controversial issues produced, often with substantial CPB funding, for national distribution to local stations. . . .

Furthermore, the manifest imprecision of the ban imposed by § 399 reveals that its proscription is not sufficiently tailored to the harms it seeks to prevent to justify its substantial interference with broadcasters' speech. Section 399 includes within its grip a potentially infinite variety of speech, most of which would not be related in any way to governmental affairs, political candidacies or elections. Indeed, the breadth of editorial commentary is as wide as human imagination permits. But the Government never explains how, say, an editorial by local station management urging improvements in a town's parks or museums will so infuriate Congress or other Federal officials that the future of public broadcasting will be imperiled unless such editorials are suppressed. Nor is it explained how the suppression of editorials alone serves to reduce the risk of governmental retaliation and interference when it is clear that station management is fully able to broadcast controversial views so long as such views are not labelled as its own.
[ ]

The Government appears to recognize these flaws in § 399, because it focuses instead on the suggestion that the source of governmental influence may well be state and local governments, many of which have established public broadcasting commissions that own and operate local noncommercial educational stations.[22] The ban on editorializing is all the more necessary with respect to these stations, the argument runs, because the management of such stations will be especially likely to broadcast only editorials that are favorable to the state or local authorities that hold the purse strings. The Government's argument, however, proves too much. First, § 399's ban applies to the many private noncommercial community organizations that own and operate stations that are not controlled in any way by state or local government. Second, the legislative history of the Public Broadcasting Act clearly indicates that Congress was concerned with "assur[ing] complete freedom from any *Federal Government influence.*" [ ] Consistently with this concern, Congress refused to create any federally owned stations and it expressly forbid the CPB to own or operate any television or radio stations, § 396(g)(3). By contrast, although Congress was clearly aware in 1967 that many noncommercial educational stations were

---

22. As the Government points out in its Brief, at least two-thirds of the public television broadcasting stations in operation are licensed to (a) state public broadcasting authorities or commissions, in which commission members are often appointed by the governor with the advice and consent of the state legislature, (b) state universities or educational commissions, or (c) local school boards or municipal authorities.
[ ]

owned by state and local governments, it did not hesitate to extend Federal assistance to such stations, it imposed no special requirements to restrict state or local control over these stations, and, indeed, it ensured through the structure of the Act that these stations would be as insulated from Federal interference as the wholly private stations.

Finally, although the Government certainly has a substantial interest in ensuring that the audiences of noncommercial stations will not be led to think that the broadcaster's editorials reflect the official view of the government, this interest can be fully satisfied by less restrictive means that are readily available. To address this important concern, Congress could simply require public broadcasting stations to broadcast a disclaimer every time they editorialize which would state that the editorial represents only the view of the station's management and does not in any way represent the views of the Federal Government or any of the station's other sources of funding. Such a disclaimer—similar to those often used in commercial and noncommercial programming of a controversial nature—would effectively and directly communicate to the audience that the editorial reflected only the views of the station rather than those of the government. . . .

In sum, § 399's broad ban on all editorializing by every station that receives CPB funds far exceeds what is necessary to protect against the risk of governmental interference or to prevent the public from assuming that editorials by public broadcasting stations represent the official view of government. The regulation impermissibly sweeps within its prohibition a wide range of speech by wholly private stations on topics that do not take a directly partisan stand or that have nothing whatever to do with federal, state, or local government.

(2)

Assuming that the Government's second asserted interest in preventing noncommercial stations from becoming a "privileged outlet for the political and ideological opinions of station owners and management," Brief at 34, is legitimate, the substantiality of this asserted interest is dubious. The patent over- and underinclusiveness of § 399's ban "undermines the likelihood of a genuine [governmental] interest" in preventing private groups from propagating their own views via public broadcasting. First National Bank of Boston v. Bellotti, supra, 435 U.S., at 793. If it is true, as the government contends, that noncommercial stations remain free, despite § 399, to broadcast a wide variety of controversial views through their power to control program selection, to select which persons will be interviewed, and to determine how news reports will be presented, Brief at 41, then it seems doubtful that § 399 can fairly be said to advance any genuinely substantial governmental interest in keeping controversial or partisan opinions from being aired by noncommercial stations. . . .

In short, § 399 does not prevent the use of noncommercial stations for the presentation of partisan views on controversial matters; instead, it merely bars a station from specifically communicating such views on its own behalf or on behalf of its management. If the vigorous expression of controversial opinions is, as the Government assures us, affirmatively encouraged by the Act, and if local licensees are permitted under the Act to exercise editorial control over the selection of programs, controversial or otherwise, that are aired on their stations, then § 399 accomplishes only one thing—the suppression of editorial speech by station management. It does virtually nothing, however, to reduce the risk that public stations will serve solely as outlets for expression of narrow partisan views. What we said in Columbia Broadcasting System, Inc. v. Democratic National Committee, supra, applies, therefore, with equal force here: the "sacrifice [of] First Amendment protections for so speculative a gain is not warranted. . . ." 412 U.S., at 127.

Finally, the public's interest in preventing public broadcasting from becoming forums for lopsided presentations of narrow partisan positions is already secured by a variety of other regulatory means that intrude far less drastically upon the "journalistic freedom" of noncommercial broadcasters. [ ] The requirements of the FCC's fairness doctrine, for instance, which apply to commercial and noncommercial stations alike, ensure that such editorializing would maintain a reasonably balanced and fair presentation of controversial issues. Thus, even if the management of a noncommercial educational station were inclined to seek to further only its own partisan views when editorializing, it simply could not do so. . . . Since the breadth of § 399 extends so far beyond what is necessary to accomplish the goals identified by the Government, it fails to satisfy the First Amendment standards that we have applied to this area.

We therefore hold that even if some of the hazards at which § 399 was aimed are sufficiently substantial, the restriction is not crafted with sufficient precision to remedy those dangers that may exist to justify the significant abridgement of speech worked by the provision's broad ban on editorializing. The statute is not narrowly tailored to address any of the government's suggested goals. Moreover, the public's "paramount right" to be fully and broadly informed on matters of public importance through the medium of noncommercial educational broadcasting is not well served by the restriction, for its effect is plainly to diminish rather than augment "the volume and quality of coverage" of controversial issues. *Red Lion,* supra, at 393. Nor do we see any reason to deny noncommercial broadcasters the right to address matters of public concern on the basis of merely speculative fears of adverse public or governmental reactions to such speech.

IV

Although the Government did not present the argument in any form to the District Court, it now seeks belatedly to justify § 399 on the basis of Congress' Spending Power. Relying upon our recent decision in Regan v. Taxation With Representation, 461 U.S. 540 (1983), the Government argues that by prohibiting noncommercial educational stations that receive CPB grants from editorializing, Congress has, in the proper exercise of its Spending Power, simply determined that it "will not subsidize public broadcasting station editorials." Brief of the United States 42. In *Taxation With Representation,* the Court found that Congress could, in the exercise of its Spending Power, reasonably refuse to subsidize the lobbying activities of tax-exempt charitable organizations by prohibiting such organizations from using tax-deductible contributions to support their lobbying efforts. . . .

. . .

Of course, if Congress were to adopt a revised version of § 399 that permitted noncommercial educational broadcasting stations to establish "affiliate" organizations which could then use the station's facilities to editorialize with non-federal funds, such a statutory mechanism would plainly be valid under the reasoning of *Taxation With Representation.* Under such a statute, public broadcasting stations would be free, in the same way that the charitable organization in *Taxation With Representation* was free, to make known its views on matters of public importance through its non-federally funded, editorializing affiliate without losing federal grants for its non-editorializing broadcast activities. [ ] But in the absence of such authority, we must reject the Government's contention that our decision in *Taxation With Representation* is controlling here.

V

In conclusion, we emphasize that our disposition of this case rests upon a narrow proposition. We do not hold that the Congress or the FCC are without power to regulate the content, timing, or character of speech by noncommercial educational broadcasting stations. Rather, we hold only that the specific interests sought to be advanced by § 399's ban on editorializing are either not sufficiently substantial or are not served in a sufficiently limited manner to justify the substantial abridgement of important journalistic freedoms which the First Amendment jealously protects. Accordingly, the judgment of the District Court is affirmed.

JUSTICE REHNQUIST, with whom THE CHIEF JUSTICE and JUSTICE WHITE join, dissenting.

All but three paragraphs of the Court's lengthy opinion in this case are devoted to the development of a scenario in which the government appears as the "Big Bad Wolf" and appellee Pacifica as "Little Red Riding Hood." In the Court's scenario the Big Bad Wolf cruelly forbids Little Red Riding Hood from taking to her grandmother some of the food that she is carrying in her basket. Only three paragraphs are used to delineate a truer picture of the litigants, wherein it appears that some of the food in the basket was given to Little Red Riding Hood by the Big Bad Wolf himself, and that the Big Bad Wolf had told Little Red Riding Hood in advance that if she accepted his food she would have to abide by his conditions. Congress in enacting § 399 of the

Public Broadcasting Act, 47 U.S.C. (Supp. V) § 399, has simply determined that public funds shall not be used to subsidize noncommercial, educational broadcasting stations which engage in "editorializing" or which support or oppose any political candidate. I do not believe that anything in the First Amendment to the United States Constitution prevents Congress from choosing to spend public monies in that manner. Perhaps a more appropriate analogy than that of Little Red Riding Hood and the Big Bad Wolf is that of Faust and Mephistopheles; Pacifica, well aware of § 399's condition on its receipt of public money, nonetheless accepted the public money and now seeks to avoid the conditions which Congress legitimately has attached to receipt of that funding.

. . .

The Court's three-paragraph discussion of why § 399, repeatedly reexamined and retained by Congress, violates the First Amendment is to me utterly unpersuasive. Congress has rationally determined that the bulk of the taxpayers whose monies provide the funds for grants by the CPB would prefer not to see the management of local educational stations promulgate its own private views on the air at taxpayer expense. Accordingly Congress simply has decided not to subsidize stations which engage in that activity.

. . .

This is not to say that the government may attach *any* condition to its largess; it is only to say that when the government is simply exercising its power to allocate its own public funds, we need only find that the condition imposed has a rational relationship to Congress' purpose in providing the subsidy and that it is not primarily "aimed at the suppression of dangerous ideas." Cammarano v. United States, 358 U.S. 498, 513 (1959), quoting Speiser v. Randall, 357 U.S. 513, 519 (1958). In this case Congress' prohibition is directly related to its purpose in providing subsidies for public broadcasting, and is plainly rational for Congress to have determined that taxpayer monies should not be used to subsidize management's views or to pay for management's exercise of partisan politics. Indeed, it is entirely rational for Congress to have wished to avoid the appearance of government sponsorship of a particular view or a particular political candidate. Furthermore, Congress' prohibition is strictly neutral. In no sense can it be said that Congress has prohibited only editorial views of one particular ideological bent. Nor has it prevented public stations from airing programs, documentaries, interviews, etc. dealing with controversial subjects, so long as management itself does not expressly endorse a particular viewpoint. And Congress has not prevented station management from communicating its own views on those subjects through any medium other than subsidized public broadcasting.

For the foregoing reasons I find this case entirely different from the so-called "unconstitutional condition" cases, wherein the Court has stated that the government "may not deny a benefit to a person on a basis that infringes his constitutionally protected interests—especially his interest in freedom of speech." Perry v. Sinderman, 408 U.S. 593, 597 (1972). In those cases the suppressed speech was not content-neutral in the same sense as here, and in those cases, there is at best only a strained argument that the legislative purpose of the condition imposed was to avoid *subsidizing* the prohibited speech. Speiser v. Randall, supra, is illustrative of the difference. In that case California's decision to deny its property tax exemption to veterans who would not declare that they would not work to overthrow the government was plainly directed at suppressing what California regarded as speech of a dangerous content. And the condition imposed was so unrelated to the benefit to be conferred that it is difficult to argue that California's property tax exemption actually subsidized the dangerous speech.

Here, in my view, Congress has rationally concluded that the bulk of taxpayers whose monies provide the funds for grants by the CPB would prefer not to see the management of public stations engage in editorializing or the endorsing or opposing of political candidates. Because Congress' decision to enact § 399 is a rational exercise of its spending powers and strictly neutral, I would hold that nothing in the First Amendment makes it unconstitutional. Accordingly, I would reverse the judgment of the District Court.

Justice White: Believing that the editorializing and candidate endorsement proscription stand or fall together and being confident that Congress may condition use of its funds on abstaining from political endorsements, I join Justice Rehnquist's dissenting opinion.

JUSTICE STEVENS, dissenting.

The court jester who mocks the King must choose his words with great care. An artist is likely to paint a flattering portrait of his patron. The child who wants a new toy does not preface his request with a comment on how fat his mother is. Newspaper publishers have been known to listen to their advertising managers. Elected officials may remember how their elections were financed. By enacting the statutory provision that the Court invalidates today, a sophisticated group of legislators expressed a concern about the potential impact of government funds on pervasive and powerful organs of mass communication. One need not have heard the raucous voice of Adolph Hitler over Radio Berlin to appreciate the importance of that concern.

As Justice White correctly notes, the statutory prohibitions against editorializing and candidate endorsements rest on the same foundation. In my opinion that foundation is far stronger than merely "a rational basis" and it is not weakened by the fact that it is buttressed by other provisions that are also designed to avoid the insidious evils of government propaganda favoring particular points of view. The quality of the interest in maintaining government neutrality in the free market of ideas—of avoiding subtle forms of censorship and propaganda—outweigh the impact on expression that results from this statute. Indeed, by simply terminating or reducing funding, Congress could curtail much more expression with no risk whatever of a constitutional transgression.

. . .

Although appellees originally challenged the validity of the entire statute, in their amended complaint they limited their attack to the prohibition against editorializing. In its analysis of the case, the Court assumes that the ban on political endorsements is severable from the first section and that it may be constitutional.[3] In view of the fact that the major difference between [the restrictions on editorializing and] the ban on political endorsements is based on the content of the speech, it is apparent that the entire rationale of the Court's opinion rests on the premise that it may be permissible to predicate a statutory restriction on candidate endorsements on the difference between the content of that kind of speech and the content of other expressions of editorial opinion.

The Court does not tell us whether speech that endorses political candidates is more or less worthy of protection than other forms of editorializing, but it does iterate and reiterate the point that "the expression of editorial opinion" is a special kind of communication that "is entitled to the most exacting degree of First Amendment protection." [   ].[4]

Neither the fact that the statute regulates only one kind of speech, nor the fact that editorial opinion has traditionally been an important kind of speech, is sufficient to identify the character or the significance of the statute's impact on speech. Three additional points are relevant. First, the statute does not prohibit Pacifica from expressing its opinion through any avenue except the radio stations for which it receives federal financial support. It eliminates the subsidized channel of communication as a forum for Pacifica itself, and thereby deprives Pacifica of an advantage it would otherwise have over other speakers, but it does not exclude Pacifica from the marketplace for ideas. Second, the statute does not curtail the expression of opinion by individual commentators who participate in Pacifica's programs. Third, and of greatest significance for me, the statutory restriction is completely neutral in its operation—it prohibits all editorials without any distinc-

---

3. The Court actually raises the wrong severability issue. The serious question in this regard is whether the entire public funding scheme is severable from the prohibition on editorializing and political endorsements. The legislative history of the statute indicates the strength of the congressional aversion to these practices. . . .

4. Thus, once again the Court embraces the obvious proposition that some speech is more worthy of protection than other speech—that the right to express editorial opinion may be worth fighting to preserve even though the right to hear less worthy speech may not—a proposition that several members of today's majority could only interpret "as an aberration" in Young v. American Mini Theaters, 427 U.S. 50, 87 (1976) (dissenting opinion) ("The fact that the 'offensive' speech here may not address 'important' topics—'ideas of social and political significance,' in the Court's terminology, *ante*, does not mean that it is less worthy of constitutional protection." Ibid.)

tion being drawn concerning the subject matter or the point of view that might be expressed.[5]

II

The statute does not violate the fundamental principle that the citizen's right to speak may not be conditioned upon the sovereign's agreement with what the speaker intends to say. On the contrary, the statute was enacted in order to protect that very principle—to avoid the risk that some speakers will be rewarded or penalized for saying things that appeal to—or are offensive to—the sovereign.[7] The interests the statute is designed to protect are interests that underlie the First Amendment itself.

In my judgment the interest in keeping the Federal Government out of the propaganda arena is of overriding importance. That interest is of special importance in the field of electronic communication, not only because that medium is so powerful and persuasive, but also because it is the one form of communication that is licensed by the Federal Government.[8] When the government already has great potential power over the electronic media, it is surely legitimate to enact statutory safeguards to make sure that it does not cross the threshold that separates neutral regulation from the subsidy of partisan opinion.

The Court does not question the validity of the basic interests served by § 399. Instead, it suggests that the statute does not substantially serve those interests because the Public Broadcasting Act oper-

---

5. Section 399's ban on editorializing is a content based restriction on speech, but not in the sense that the majority implies. The majority speaks of "editorial opinion" as if it were some sort of special species of opinion, limited to issues of public importance. The majority confuses the typical content of editorials with the meaning of editorial itself. An editorial is, of course, a statement of the *management's* opinion on any topic imaginable. The Court asserts that what the statute "forecloses is the expression of editorial opinion on 'controversial issues of public importance.'" The statute is not so limited. The content which is prohibited is that the station is not permitted to state its opinion with respect to any matter. In short, it may not be an on-the-air advocate if it accepts government funds for its broadcasts. The prohibition on editorializing is not directed at any particular message a station might wish to convey. . . .

Paradoxically, section 399 is later attacked by the majority as essentially being underinclusive because it does not prohibit "controversial" national programming that is often aired with substantial federal funding. . . . Next, § 399's ban on editorializing is attacked by the majority on overinclusive grounds—because it is content-neu-

tral—since it prohibits a "potentially infinite variety of speech, most of which would not be related in any way to governmental affairs, political candidacies or elections." . . .

7. . . .

Moreover, the statute will also protect the listener's interest in not having his tax payments used to finance the advocacy of causes he opposes. The majority gives extremely short shrift to the Government's interest in minimizing the use of taxpayer monies to promote private views with which the taxpayers may disagree. The Court briefly observes that the taxpayers do not have a constitutionally protected right to enjoin such expenditures and then leaps to the conclusion that given the fact that the funding scheme itself is not unconstitutional, this interest cannot be used to support the statute at issue. The conclusion manifestly does not follow from the premise, and this interest is plainly legitimate and significant.

8. We have consistently adhered to the following guiding principles applicable to First Amendment claims in the area of broadcasting, and they bear repeating at some length: [quoting from *Red Lion*].

ates in many other respects to insulate local stations from governmental interference. In my view, that is an indication of nothing more than the strength of the governmental interest involved here—Congress enacted many safeguards because the evil to be avoided was so grave. Organs of official propaganda are antithetical to this nation's heritage and Congress understandably acted with great caution in this area. It is no answer to say that the other statutory provisions "substantially reduce the risk of government interference with the editorial judgments of the local stations without restricting the stations' ability to speak out on matters of public concern." [ ] The other safeguards protect the stations from interference with judgments that they will necessarily make in selecting programming, but those judgments are relatively amorphous. No safeguard is foolproof; and the fact that funds are dispensed according to largely "objective" criteria certainly is no guarantee. Individuals must always make judgments in allocating funds, and pressure can be exerted in subtle ways as well as through outright fund-cutoffs.

Members of Congress, not members of the Judiciary, live in the world of politics. When they conclude that there is a real danger of political considerations influencing the dispensing of this money and that this provision is necessary to insulate grantees from political pressures in addition to the other safeguards, that judgment is entitled to our respect.

The magnitude of the present danger that the statute is designed to avoid is admittedly a matter about which reasonable judges may disagree.[10] Moreover, I would agree that the risk would be greater if other statutory safeguards were removed. It remains true, however, that Congress has the power to prevent the use of public funds to subsidize the expression of partisan points of view, or to suppress the propagation of dissenting opinions. No matter how great or how small the immediate risk may be, there surely is more than a theoretical possibility that future grantees might be influenced by the ever present tie of the political purse strings, even if those strings are never actually pulled. . . .

III

The Court describes the scope of § 399's ban as being "defined solely on the basis of the content of the suppressed speech," [ ], at 18, and analogizes this case to the regulation of speech we condemned in *Consolidated Edison Co. v. Public Serv. Comm'n,* 447 U.S. 530 (1980).

10. The majority argues that the Government's concededly substantial interest in ensuring that audiences of educational stations will not perceive the station to be a government propaganda organ can be fully satisfied by requiring such stations to broadcast a disclaimer each time they editorialize stating that the editorial "does not in any way represent the views of the Federal Government. . . ." [ ] This solution would be laughable were it not so Orwellian: the answer to the fact that there is a real danger that the editorials are really government propaganda is for the government to require the station to tell the audience that it is not propaganda at all!

This description reveals how the Court manipulates labels without perceiving the critical differences behind the two cases.

In *Consolidated Edison* the class of speakers that was affected by New York's prohibition consisted of regulated public utilities that had been expressing their opinion on the issue of nuclear power by means of written statements inserted in their customers' monthly bills. Although the scope of the prohibition was phrased in general terms and applied to a select group of speakers, it was obviously directed at spokesmen for a particular point of view. The justification for the restriction was phrased in terms of the potential offensiveness of the utilities' messages to their audiences. It was a classic case of a viewpoint-based prohibition.

In this case, however, although the regulation applies only to a defined class of noncommercial broadcast licensees, it is common ground that these licensees represent heterogeneous points of view.[12] There is simply no sensible basis for considering this regulation a viewpoint restriction—or, to use the Court's favorite phrase, to condemn it as "content-based"—because it applies equally to station owners of all shades of opinion. Moreover, the justification for the prohibition is not based on the "offensiveness" of the messages in the sense that that term was used in *Consolidated Edison*. Here, it is true that taxpayers might find it offensive if their tax monies were being used to subsidize the expression of editorial opinion with which they disagree, but it is the fact of the subsidy—not just the expression of the opinion—that legitimates this justification. Furthermore, and of greater importance, the principal justification for this prohibition is the overriding interest in forestalling the creation of propaganda organs for the Government.

I respectfully dissent.

Notes and Questions

1. How realistic are the fears of the dissenting justices? President Nixon once vetoed the CPB budget because of dissatisfaction with CPB programming. Are noncommercial licensees likely to be influenced by the "power of the purse?" If, indeed, prohibitions on specific forms of speech are unconstitutional, how can noncommercial licensees be insulated from government control?

2. In response to a complaint by Sen. James F. Buckley (R.-N.Y.), the Commission held that § 312(a)(7) was equally applicable to commercial and noncommercial stations. However, only those noncommercial stations using channels specifically reserved for noncommercial broadcasting are prohibited from charging for the time they must make avail-

---

12. That does not necessarily mean, however, "that the editorial voices of these stations will prove to be as distinctive, varied, and idiosyncratic as the various communities they represent," [ ], given the potential effects of government funding, [ ].

able. Senator James F. Buckley, 63 F.C.C.2d 952, 38 R.R.2d 1255
(1976).

3. From a First Amendment perspective, the crucial difference between commercial and noncommercial broadcasting involves the question of the licensee's ability to control content and to reject programming. In *League of Women Voters*, the Court was faced with the
problem of indirect control of PBS stations through the CPB funding
mechanism. Consider, however, that more than 140 PBS stations are
under some form of government ownership. What effect should that
have on the ability of those licensees to control content and reject
programming? Consider the following case.

MUIR v. ALABAMA EDUCATIONAL TELEVISION COMMISSION

United States Court of Appeals, Fifth Circuit, en banc, 1982.
688 F.2d 1033, 52 R.R.2d 935, 8 Med.L.Rptr. 2305.
Certiorari denied 460 U.S. 1023, 103 S.Ct. 1274, 75 L.Ed.2d 495 (1983).

[In this case, decided by the old Fifth Circuit before it was split, 22
judges participated in the decision. Judge Hill's opinion, referred to by
all as the majority opinion, has the implicit support of 10 judges.
Judge Garwood states that he concurs in the majority opinion and then
adds some thoughts of his own. Judge Rubin and the three judges who
join him say that they join only the result reached by the majority
because they reach their conclusion on a different basis. Yet, they join
in the views expressed by Judge Garwood (who says that he joins the
majority opinion). That makes 15. However, subsequent cases have
held that Judge Rubin's opinion, as opposed to Judge Hill's, is the
majority opinion. See e.g., Schneider v. Indian River Community
College Foundation, Inc., 875 F.2d 1537 (11th Cir.1989). The seven
dissenters write three opinions. Judge Garwood's opinion is placed
earlier in the sequence to make matters easier to understand. The
opinions in this case offer enough food for thought to match the size of
the bench.]

Before BROWN, CHARLES CLARK, RONEY, GEE, TJOFLAT, HILL, FAY, RUBIN,
VANCE, KRAVITCH, FRANK M. JOHNSON, HENDERSON, REAVLEY, POLITZ,
HATCHETT, ANDERSON, RANDALL, TATE, SAM D. JOHNSON, THOMAS A. CLARK,
WILLIAMS and GARWOOD, CIRCUIT JUDGES.

JAMES C. HILL, CIRCUIT JUDGE:

I. *Introduction*

The two appeals before this Court on consolidated rehearing raise
the important and novel question of whether individual viewers of
public television stations, licensed by the Federal Communications
Commission to state instrumentalities, have a First Amendment right
to compel the licensees to broadcast a previously scheduled program
which the licensees have decided to cancel. For the reasons below we
find that the viewers do not have such a right.

Both cases before us concern the decisions of the licensees not to broadcast the program "Death of a Princess." In Muir v. Alabama Educational Television Commission, 656 F.2d 1012 (5th Cir.1981), the District Court for the Northern District of Alabama denied the plaintiff viewers' motion for a preliminary injunction requiring the defendant licensee, Alabama Educational Television Commission (AETC), to broadcast the program. The district court found (1) that the likelihood of success on the merits criterion for an injunction had not been shown; (2) that the First Amendment protects the right of broadcasters, private and public, to make programming decisions free of interference; and (3) that viewers have no First Amendment right of access to the Alabama educational television network sufficient to compel the showing of "Death of a Princess." The court granted summary judgment for AETC.

In Barnstone v. University of Houston, 514 F.Supp. 670 (S.D.Tex. 1980), the District Court for the Southern District of Texas reached a different conclusion and granted the injunction requested by the plaintiff viewers and ordered the defendant licensee, University of Houston, to broadcast the program. The court held that KUHT–TV, the television station operated by the university, was a public forum and as such it could not deny access to speakers—here, the producers of "Death of a Princess"—who wished to be heard in the public forum, unless its reasons for doing so could withstand the rigorous scrutiny to which "prior restraints" are traditionally subjected.

On appeal a panel of this court affirmed the District Court's decision in *Muir*. The panel held that the plaintiffs had no constitutional right to compel the broadcast of "Death of a Princess," and that AETC's refusal to broadcast the program was a legitimate exercise of its statutory authority as a broadcast licensee and was protected by the First Amendment. In *Barnstone* another panel of this court found that the decision in *Muir* required that the panel reverse the judgment of the District Court for the Southern District of Texas and dissolve the injunctive relief which had been granted the plaintiffs.

We directed both cases be consolidated and reheard en banc. We now affirm the judgment of the District Court for the Northern District of Alabama in *Muir* and reverse the judgment of the District Court for the Southern District of Texas in *Barnstone*.

II. *Factual Background*

The *Muir* case arose when AETC decided not to broadcast "Death of a Princess," which had been scheduled for broadcast on May 12, 1980 at 8:00 p.m. The program, one of thirteen in the series "World," is a dramatization of the investigation by the program's director, producer, and co-author into the motivations and circumstances which were said to have led to the July 1977 execution for adultery of a Saudi Arabian princess and her commoner lover.

AETC, organized under Ala.Code 1975, § 16–7–1, is responsible for "making the benefits of educational television available to and promoting its use by inhabitants of Alabama" and has "the duty of controlling and supervising the use of channels reserved by the Federal Communications Commission to Alabama for noncommercial, educational use." Ala.Code 1975, § 16–7–5. AETC operates a statewide network of nine noncommercial, educational television stations licensed by the Federal Communications Commission under the Communications Act of 1934 (47 U.S.C. §§ 151, et seq.). AETC is funded through state legislative appropriations from the Special Education Trust Fund, matching federal grants through the Corporation for Public Broadcasting (CPB), and private contributions.

AETC is a member of the Public Broadcasting Service (PBS), a nonprofit corporation distributing public, non-commercial television programs to its members by satellite. AETC is also a member of the Station Program Cooperative (SPC), a program funding and acquisition mechanism operated by PBS. Membership in SPC entitles licensees to participate in the selection and funding of national public television programs distributed by PBS. Only those licensees who contribute to a program's cost have a right to broadcast it. Those who contribute are free to broadcast or not to broadcast the program.

PBS's acquisition of the program series "World" was funded by 144 public television licensees, including AETC, through the SPC. During the week prior to the scheduled broadcast of "Death of a Princess" AETC received numerous communications from Alabama residents protesting the showing of the program. The protests expressed fear for the personal safety and well-being of Alabama citizens working in the Middle East if the program was shown. On May 10 AETC announced its decision not to broadcast the film as scheduled.

Appellants Muir, Buttram, and Faircloth, residents of Alabama who had planned to watch "Death of a Princess," brought this action on May 12, 1980 under the First and Fourteenth Amendments and 42 U.S.C. § 1983, seeking to compel AETC to broadcast the film, and preliminary and permanent injunctions against AETC's making "political" decisions on programming. The *Barnstone* case arose in a factual context similar to that of *Muir.* The University of Houston is a co-educational institution of higher learning funded and operated by the State of Texas. See Tex.Educ.Code Ann. §§ 111.01 et seq. The university funds and operates KUHT–TV, a public television station licensed to the university by the F.C.C. As a member of the SPC, KUHT–TV contributed to the funding of the "World" program series. KUHT–TV scheduled "Death of a Princess" for broadcast on May 12, 1980 at 8:00 p.m.

On May 1, 1980 KUHT–TV announced that it had decided not to broadcast the program. This decision was made by Dr. Patrick J. Nicholson, University of Houston Vice–President for Public Information and University Relations. Dr. Nicholson had never previously made a programming decision such as this, though as the university official charged with the responsibility of operating KUHT–TV he had the power to do so. In a press release announcing the cancellation Dr. Nicholson gave the basis of his decision as "strong and understandable objections by the government of Saudi Arabia at a time when mounting crisis in the Middle East, our long friendship with the Saudi government and U.S. national interest all point to the need to avoid exacerbating the situation." Dr. Nicholson also expressed a belief that the program was not balanced in a "responsible manner." [5]

Upon learning of Dr. Nicholson's decision, on May 8, 1980, plaintiff Barnstone brought a suit to require KUHT–TV to air "Death of a Princess." Ms. Barnstone argued that as a subscriber to and regular viewer of KUHT–TV her First and Fourteenth Amendment rights were violated by the decision to cancel the program.

III.   *The First Amendment Does Not Prohibit Governmental Expression*

The central argument advanced by the plaintiffs on appeal is that their First Amendment rights were violated when the defendants, as state actors, denied the plaintiffs an opportunity to view "Death of a Princess" on the public television stations operated by the defendants. We are thus called upon to determine whether the First Amendment rights of viewers impose limits on the programming discretion of public television stations licensed to state instrumentalities.

The First Amendment operates to protect private expression from infringement by government. Such protection applies both to the right to speak and the right to hear and is operative in a variety of contexts. The amendment prohibits government from controlling or penalizing expression which has been singled out by government because of the expression's viewpoint. The First Amendment also prohibits government from taking certain actions which impermissibly constrict the flow of information or ideas.

The plaintiffs emphasize that the protection of the First Amendment extends only to private expression and not to governmental expression. They assert that the amendment serves only to confer duties on government—not rights. While this argument of the plaintiffs may be essentially correct it in no way resolves the issue before us. To find that the government is without First Amendment protection is

---

5. In addition to the reasons cited in the press release, the District Court, upon consideration of Dr. Nicholson's testimony, found four other reasons why the cancellation decision may have been made. First, Dr. Nicholson testified that he considered the program to be "in bad taste." Second, Dr. Nicholson expressed concern that some members of the public might believe that the "docu-drama" was a true documentary. Third, Dr. Nicholson testified that the University of Houston had previously entered into a contract with the Saudi Arabian royal family to instruct a particular princess. Finally, Dr. Nicholson testified that he had been in charge of fund raising activities for the university from 1957–1978 and that a significant percentage of the university's private contributions came from major oil companies and from individuals in oil related companies.

not to find that the government is prohibited from speaking or that private individuals have the right to limit or control the expression of government. Even without First Amendment protection government may "participate in the marketplace of ideas," and "contribute its own views to those of other speakers." Community Service Broadcasting v. F.C.C., 593 F.2d 1102, 1110 n. 17 (D.C.Cir.1978). As Justice Stewart aptly noted in Columbia Broadcasting Systems, Inc. v. Democratic National Committee, 412 U.S. 94, 139, n. 7 (1973) (Stewart, J., concurring) (hereinafter CBS), "[g]overnment is not restrained by the First Amendment from controlling its own expression . . . '[t]he purpose of the First Amendment is to protect the private expression and nothing in the guarantee precludes the government from controlling its own expression or that of its agents.' " [12]

Our essential task thus does not center on determining whether AETC and the University of Houston are vested with a First Amendment right to make the programming decisions which they make regarding "Death of a Princess." In the absence of a violation of constitutional right inhering in the plaintiffs, AETC and the University of Houston are free to make whatever programming decisions they choose, consistent with statutory and regulatory requirements. The fundamental question before us is whether in making the programming decisions at issue here, the defendants violated the First Amendment rights of the plaintiffs.

IV.　*The Regulatory Framework Enacted by Congress*

Our inquiry into the constitutional issue at hand is aided by a brief review of the broadcast legislation enacted by Congress. . . .

. . .

The picture which emerges from the regulatory scheme adopted by Congress is one which clearly shows broadcast licensees endowed with the privilege and responsibility of exercising free programming control of their broadcasts, yet also charged with the obligation of making programming decisions which protect the legitimate interests of the public. The right to the free exercise of programming discretion is, for private licensees, not only statutorily conferred but also constitutionally protected. *CBS*. Under the existing statutes public licensees such as AETC and the University of Houston possess the same rights and obligations to make free programming decisions as their private counterparts; however, as state instrumentalities, these public licensees are without the protection of the First Amendment. This lack of constitutional protection implies only that government could possibly impose

---

12. Government expression, being unprotected by the First Amendment, may be subject to legislative limitation which would be impermissible if sought to be applied to private expression. Yet there is nothing to suggest that, absent such limitation, government is restrained from speaking any more than are the citizens. Freedom of expression is the norm in our society, for government (if not restrained) and for the people. Freedom of speech is not good government because it is in the First Amendment; it is in the First Amendment because it is good government.

restrictions on these licensees which it could not impose on private licensees. The lack of First Amendment protection does not result in the lessening of any of the statutory rights and duties held by the public licensees. It also does not result in individual viewers gaining any greater right to influence the programming discretion of the public licensees.

V. *KUHT–TV and AETC Are Not Public Forums*

It is clear that Congress did not deem it necessary for viewers to be accorded a right of access to television broadcast stations in order for the public's First Amendment interests in this medium to be fully realized. Indeed it is clear that Congress concluded that the First Amendment rights of public television viewers are adequately protected under a system where the broadcast licensee has sole programming discretion but is under an obligation to serve the public interest. In spite of this Congressional scheme the District Court in *Barnstone* found that KUHT–TV was a public forum because it was operated by the government for public communication of views on issues of political and social significance. The court held that as a public forum the station could not deny access to speakers who wished to be heard in the forum, unless the requirements for prior restraint were satisfied. 514 F.Supp. at 689–91.

The plaintiffs now urge that we affirm the District Court's ruling that public television stations are public forums. The plaintiffs, unlike the District Court, however, do not argue for a public right of access to the stations. Instead the plaintiffs contend that as public forums the stations are prohibited by the First Amendment from making programming decisions motivated by hostility to the communicative impact of a program's message and stemming from a specific viewpoint of the broadcaster.

We find both the holding of the District Court and the argument of the plaintiffs to be incorrect. The Supreme Court has recently rejected the theory adopted by the District Court that because a government facility is "specifically used for the communication of information and ideas" it is *ipso facto* a public forum. United States Postal Service v. Council of Greenburgh Civic Ass'ns, 453 U.S. 114 (1981).[22] A facility is a public forum only if it is designed to provide a general public right of access to its use, or if such public access has historically existed and is not incompatible with the facility's primary activity.

. . .

In the cases in which a public facility has been deemed a public forum the speakers have been found to have a right of access because they were attempting to use the facility in a manner fully consistent with the "pattern of usual activity" and "the general invitation extend-

---

22. The Court in *United States Postal Service* ruled that mailboxes are not public forums.

ed." The pattern of usual activity for public television stations is the statutorily mandated practice of the broadcast licensee exercising sole programming authority. The general invitation extended to the public is not to schedule programs, but to watch or decline to watch what is offered.[25] It is thus clear that the public television stations involved in the cases before us are not public forums. The plaintiffs have no right of access to compel the broadcast of any particular program.

Our holding today is consistent with the Supreme Court's ruling in *CBS* that television stations operated by private broadcast licensees provide no public right of access. . . .

The plaintiffs stress that they do not argue for the creation of a public right of access to public television stations. They contend that, even without a public right of access, the stations are public forums and as such cannot make programming decisions based on communicative impact of a program. We find this contention to be untenable. It is the right of public access which is the essential characteristic of a public forum and the basis which allows a speaker to challenge the state's regulation of the forum. The gravamen of a speaker's public forum complaint is the invalid and discriminatory denial of his right of access to the forum. If a speaker does not have a right of access to a facility, that facility by definition is not a "public forum" and the speaker is without grounds for challenge under the public forum doctrine.

VI. *The Decision to Cancel Death of a Princess Was Not Governmental Censorship*

The plaintiffs argue that even if we decline to characterize KUHT–TV and AETC as public forums we should nonetheless find that the defendants violated the plaintiffs' First Amendment rights by "censoring" "Death of a Princess." The plaintiffs contend that censorship, in violation of the First Amendment, occurs when state officials in charge of state operated public television stations decide to cancel a scheduled program because of the officials' opposition to the program's political content.

There is no question that "the First Amendment means that government has no power to restrict expression because of its message, its ideas, its subject matter, or its content. . . . The essence of this forbidden censorship is content control." Police Dept. of Chicago v. Mosley, 408 U.S. 92, 95–96 (1972). . . .

We are not convinced that editorial decisions of public television stations owned and operated by the state must, or should, be viewed in

---

25. Similarly producers of television programs are extended no invitation to air their programs on the public television stations. Producers are, of course, free to submit their programs to the stations with a request that they be broadcast, but they have no right to compel the broadcast. The decision whether to broadcast a program remains entirely with the licensee. The District Court for the Southern District of Texas thus erred in finding that the producers of "Death of a Princess" had a right of access to station KUHT–TV to broadcast the film.

the same manner and subjected to the same restrictions as state regulatory activity affecting speech in other areas. Standard First Amendment doctrine condemns content control by governmental bodies where the government sponsors and financially supports certain facilities through the use of which others are allowed to communicate and to exercise their own right of expression. Government is allowed to impose restrictions only as to "time, place, or manner" in the use of such public access facilities—public forums. As we observed earlier, however, the First Amendment does not prohibit the government, itself, from speaking, nor require the government to speak. Similarly, the First Amendment does not preclude the government from exercising editorial control over its own medium of expression. [ ]

The plaintiffs concede that state officials operating public television stations can exercise some editorial discretion. They contend, however, that in exercising this discretion the officials must be "carefully neutral as to which speakers or viewpoints are to prevail in the marketplace of ideas." The plaintiffs further contend that if the officials restrict a program due to the political content of the program then the restriction is presumptively unconstitutional. The plaintiffs suggest that we adopt the evidentiary standard established by the Supreme Court in Mt. Healthy City School Dist. v. Doyle, 429 U.S. 274 (1977). Under this standard the initial burden would be on the plaintiffs to show that unconstitutional motivations were a "substantial" or "motivating" factor in the defendants' decisions to cancel "Death of a Princess." Once this burden is met by the plaintiffs the duty shifts to the defendants to show that the decisions would have been the same if the improper factor had not been considered.

The plaintiffs' analysis fails to recognize a number of essential differences between typical state regulation of private expressive activity and the exercise of editorial discretion by state officials responsible for the operation of public television stations. When state officials operate a public television station they must necessarily make discriminating choices. As the Supreme Court pointed out in CBS, 412 U.S. at 124, "[f]or better or worse, editing is what editors are for; and editing is selection and choice of material." In exercising their editorial discretion state officials will unavoidably make programming decisions which can be characterized as "politically motivated." All television broadcast licensees are required, under the public interest standard, to cover political events and to provide news and public affairs programs dealing with the political, social, economic and other issues which concern their community. [ ] The licensees are thus required to make the inherently subjective determination that their programming decisions are responsive to the needs, problems and interests of the residents of the area they serve. Red Lion, 395 U.S. at 380. A general proscription against political programming decisions would clearly be contrary to the licensees' statutory obligations, and would render virtually every programming decision subject to judicial challenge.

The plaintiffs seek to draw a distinction between a decision not to show a program and a decision to cancel a previously scheduled program. They suggest that while it is a proper exercise of editorial discretion for a licensee initially to decide not to schedule a program, it is constitutionally improper for the licensee to decide to cancel a scheduled program because of its political content. In support of their view the plaintiffs cited decisions holding that school officials may be free initially to decide which books to place in their school libraries but that a decision to remove any particular book may be subject to constitutional challenge. We are not persuaded, however, that the distinction urged upon us is valid or that the school library cases are applicable.

The decision to cancel a scheduled program is no less editorial in nature than an initial decision to schedule the program. [ ] Both decisions require the licensee to determine what will best serve the public interest, and, as we noted earlier, such a determination is inherently subjective and involves judgments which could be termed "political."

School libraries are distinguishable from broadcast stations in a number of important ways. There are limited hours in a day for broadcasting, and broadcast licensees are constantly required to make sensitive choices between available programs. Cf. Board of Education v. Pico, 457 U.S. 853, 875, n. 1, (1982) ("The school's finite resources—as well as the limited number of hours in the day—require that educational officials make sensitive choices between subjects to be offered. . . .") (Blackmun, J., concurring in part). The maintenance of one volume on a library shelf does not (absent space limitations) preempt another. In broadcast, only one transmission of information, entertainment, or other message can occur at any one time. A library constantly and simultaneously proffers a myriad of written materials. As discussed in Part IV, hereinabove, the Congress has undertaken its careful analysis and balancing of conflicting interests involved in broadcasting and in public broadcasting, and the judicial branch should pay careful attention. [ ] There have been no comparable deliberations or enactments by that branch with respect to libraries. More specifically, there is no counterpart, vis-a-vis libraries, to the Federal Communications Commission's "Fairness Doctrine." When a television broadcaster finds that it has scheduled a program espousing one view, it may have unwittingly encumbered its limited broadcast hours with a requirement that equal time be devoted to other viewpoints which might touch upon an issue of limited interest in its viewing area. But the maintenance of one volume espousing one side of an issue does not invoke government regulation requiring that shelf space be made available for all other views. Finally, a school would be expected to furnish only one library for its student population. The residents of a state may expect a choice of a number of television stations, often with the publicly owned facility attracting the smallest number of viewers.

The right to cancel a program is, furthermore, far more integral a part of the operation of a television station than the decision to remove a book from a school library. Libraries typically have at least the opportunity to review a book before acquiring it, therefore, there may be "few legitimate reasons why a book, once acquired, should be removed from a library not filled to capacity." [ ] In comparison, television stations frequently do not have the chance to see a program until after the station's schedule has been printed, and there are numerous legitimate reasons why a station may decide to cancel a program it has initially scheduled. Indeed FCC regulations specifically require that licensees retain the power to reject any program which the licensee has already contracted for if the licensee determines that the program is "unsatisfactory or unsuitable or contrary to the public interest." 47 C.F.R. § 73.658.

We conclude that the defendants' editorial decisions to cancel "Death of a Princess" cannot be properly characterized as "censorship." Had the states of Alabama and Texas sought to prohibit the exhibition of the film by another party then indeed a question of censorship would have arisen. Such is not the case before us. The states have not sought to forbid or curtail the right of any person to show or view the film. In fact plaintiff Barnstone has already viewed the film at an exhibition at Rice University in Houston. The state officials in charge of AETC and KUHT–TV have simply exercised their statutorily mandated discretion and decided not to show a particular program at a particular time. There is a clear distinction between a state's exercise of editorial discretion over its own expression and a state's prohibition or suppression of the speech of another.

VII. *The Plaintiffs Can Seek Remedial Relief From the FCC*

Our holding that the defendants did not violate the plaintiffs' First Amendment rights does not preclude the plaintiffs from challenging the propriety of the defendants' programming decision with the FCC. Our decision is limited to the constitutional issue presented. We offer no opinion as to whether or not the actions of AETC and the University of Houston comport with their statutory and regulatory obligation.

. . .

VIII. *Conclusion*

The decisions of AETC and the University of Houston to cancel "Death of a Princess" did not violate the First Amendment rights of the plaintiffs. The plaintiffs have no constitutional right to compel the broadcast of the program. Accordingly, we find that the District Court for the Northern District of Alabama properly awarded summary judgment to AETC. We also find that the District Court for the Southern District of Texas erred in issuing its order requiring KUHT–TV to broadcast the program.

. . .

GARWOOD, CIRCUIT JUDGE, concurring.

I concur in the majority opinion, and append these remarks only to point up two additional interrelated matters I believe significant.

First, plaintiffs are not attacking governmental "public" broadcasting as such. Nor do they seek to require its operation to be on a pure "open forum" basis—like an empty stage available to all comers—where each citizen can cause the broadcast of his or her program of choice, with their inevitable selectivity determined by completely content neutral factors such as lot, or first come first served or the like. Rather, plaintiffs seek to become a *part* of governmental "public" broadcasting essentially as it is, except they want it to broadcast this particular program of their choice. However, there is simply no way for them—together with all others who might wish to assert similar rights for their favorite "dramatization"—to become a part of *such* "conventional" (as distinguished from pure "open forum") governmental broadcasting *except* on the basis of governmental selection of the individual programs.

As the majority opinion convincingly demonstrates, in television broadcasting not only is selection inevitable, but it is likewise inevitable that in numerous instances it will be largely based on factors that are not content neutral and on considerations that involve sympathy for or hostility to the program's "message" on the part of the party having the power of selection. This is *not* to say that program selection influenced by "message" sympathy or hostility on the part of governmental television stations is a desirable phenomenon, or even one which is wholly consistent with the values underlying the First Amendment. But such a characteristic is part and parcel of the operation of the conventional (not pure "open forum") governmental television stations of which plaintiffs seek to avail themselves. They are not entitled to have a special exception made in their favor so that for this particular program *they* are entitled to make the selection and require that these conventionally operated governmental stations broadcast it.

. . .

In the second place, plaintiffs do not assert that the stations in question have, on the basis of their agreement or disagreement with the different points of view involved or for similar "political" type reasons, structured their programming so that it constitutes a one-sided or slanted presentation of any matter of public concern, importance or controversy, whether relevant to the "message" of plaintiffs' desired program or otherwise.[3] So far as any such matters are concerned, plaintiffs' complaint is made essentially in a vacuum—they claim that merely because on one particular occasion a "political" type decision was made *not* to air one specific program plaintiffs wished to see, they therefore have a right to a court order directing these conventionally

---

3. And plaintiffs do not contend their particular (or some similar) program must be shown to fairly balance the presentation on this subject matter which the stations have improperly slanted by showing some other program or programs.

operated government stations to promptly air this precise program. We have rejected this claim. This is not to say, however, that no private citizen has a right to question the programming of governmental "public" television stations under any circumstances, or that the remedy of complaint to the F.C.C. will always be adequate.

A private citizen has no constitutional right to force a conventionally operated governmental "public" television station to enter with its broadcasting a particular propaganda war by showing a specific program selected by the citizen. Whether it is proper for such a governmental station to enter that kind of a war at all, or whether if it does so it may nevertheless present only one side while refusing, for reasons of a "political" nature, to broadcast any competing view, are questions of a different nature that are not now before us.

RUBIN, CIRCUIT JUDGE, with whom POLITZ, RANDALL and WILLIAMS, CIRCUIT JUDGES, join, specially concurring.

While I join in the result reached by the majority, I reach my conclusion on a different basis. Therefore, I join in the views expressed by Judge Garwood and add:

The sensitive and important issues in these cases cannot be resolved simply by attempting to decide whether a television station operated by a state agency is, or is not, a public forum. That term is but a label, developed to describe a location the use of which is open to the public. It does not express a definition but a conclusion. . . .

The issue directly presented can be stated simply: whether an individual viewer has a right to compel a television station operated by a state agency to broadcast a single program previously scheduled by an employee of the agency that a higher-ranking state official has decided, because of its content, to cancel. This pretermits the factual questions whether the program was canceled for what the dissent calls "legitimate reasons" and whether the official's objection to the content of the program and to its political implications was in either of these cases the sole reason for canceling "Death of a Princess" or merely the decisive one. Although these are not unimportant inquiries, they do not focus on the crucial issue: how does the first amendment control state action when the state is operating a television station?

Determination of the constitutional limitations that result because a television licensee is a state agency rather than a private agency must take into account not only the rights of viewers but a number of other considerations. The license is federally bestowed. The state agency licensee has both a statutory duty to comply with the rules and regulations governing the use of its license and, like other licensees, the statutory right to determine the way in which it shall fulfill that duty. Those state employees who are charged with operation of the station, whether high or low in the managerial hierarchy, may have some right to free expression, which may be stronger if, for example, they function in an academic environment devoted to freedom of inquiry. Those who want access to the medium in order not to view and listen but to disseminate a message must also be considered. Viewers also have an interest in the content of programs, not only because of their "right to see" but also because the state agency is financed at least in part by viewers as taxpayers.

These interests are all entitled to consideration and some or all of them may be accorded constitutional protection. . . .

Even the fact that the state is engaged in television broadcasting does not fully define the constitutional limitations on its actions, for such broadcasting might be designed to serve differing purposes. Licensing is not destiny. That the state is the licensee does not predetermine the station's function. The state may elect the station's mission, so long as this mission is consistent with the station's license and the Constitution. The prerogatives of managers, editors, and programmers, the rights of access of those who seek exposure, and the rights of viewers, as well as the prerogatives of the licensee itself as a state agency, are at least in part determined by this mission.

All, or in other instances a part, of a station's programs might be devoted to providing a medium for the communication of competing views. Some channels on cable television networks and some viewer or listener call-in programs on television and radio stations are of this kind. Some television stations are devoted entirely to educational purposes, designed solely for pedagogy. Others may be operated to furnish a varied menu of entertainment having greater cultural and educational value than the programs available on commercial stations. While the record is not clear, it appears that the two stations involved in these cases were of this sort. Neither station has been shown to have been a magazine of the air, a forum for all views, or a dispassionate communicator on issues of the day. Each appears to serve instead a diet that differs from commercial television primarily in appeal to a somewhat more sophisticated audience, the absence of commercials, and efforts to raise funds from viewers.

The function of a state agency operating an informational medium is significant in determining first amendment restrictions on its actions. State agencies publish alumni bulletins, newsletters devoted to better farming practices, and law reviews; they operate or subsidize art museums and theater companies and student newspapers. The federal government operates the Voice of America and Radio Free Europe and Radio Liberty, publishes "journals, magazines, periodicals, and similar publications" that are "necessary in the transaction of the public business," including newspapers for branches of the Armed Forces, and pays the salaries of many federal officials who, like the President's Press Secretary, communicate with the public through the media. The first amendment does not dictate that what will be said or performed or published or broadcast in these activities will be entirely content-neutral. In those activities that, like television broadcasting to the general public, depend in part on audience interest, appraisal of audience interest and suitability for publication or broadcast inevitably involves judgment of content.

If the state is conducting an activity that functions as a market-place of ideas, the Constitution requires content neutrality. Thus, a state university may not override editorial freedom for student newspapers. If, however, the state's activity is devoted to a specific function rather than general news dissemination or free exposition of ideas, the state may regulate content in order to prevent hampering the primary function of the activity, just as it may to some degree restrict the content of material distributed or displayed on military establishments, in prisons, on public buses, or in public hospitals.

All of the opinions in Board of Educ. v. Pico, 457 U.S. 853 (1982) recognize such a distinction either implicitly or expressly.[18] . . .

. . .

While the Mobile and Houston television stations are operated by state agencies, neither station is designed to function as a marketplace of ideas, a medium open to all who have a message, whatever its nature. The staff of each station had made an initial programming decision based in part on their assessment of the content of "Death of a Princess." Had the initial decision been not to use the program, the argument might have been made that this too was censorship and violated the potential viewers' right to see. If a decision is initially made at one level to use a program and is then reversed at a higher level, the content assessment involved is more apparent, but it is not necessarily converted thereby from legitimate programming into forbidden censorship.

Judicial reassessment of the propriety of a programming decision made in operating a television station involves not only interference with station management but also reevaluation of all the content-quality-audience reaction factors that enter into a decision to use or not to use a program by a medium that cannot possibly, by its very nature, accommodate everything that every viewer might desire. With deference to the dicta observations made in the *Pico* plurality opinion, our reexamination of such a decision cannot logically be confined to occasions when higher officials overrule subordinates. If it is forbidden censorship for the higher official to cancel a program, it is equally censorship for the lower officials to decide initially to reject a program.

The Constitution is categoric but it does not command the theoretical. The state's discretion is confined by the functions it may perform as a broadcast licensee, and the purpose to which it has dedicated its license. Moreover, these cases involve only one program, not a licensee policy or practice of, for example, favoring only one political party, or of broadcasting racially or religiously discriminatory views. Neither com-

---

18. Seven justices filed opinions in *Pico*. The Court divided four-four on the constitutional issue of the extent to which the first amendment limits the discretion of a school board to remove books from a school library. Justice White concurred in the judgment of the Court but did not reach this issue. [ ]

plaint even alleges that either station has a policy of curtailing access to ideas. Each seeks only to compel the defendant station to show a single program. Judicial intervention might be required if these or other licensees should adopt or follow policies or practices that transgress constitutional rights. But, one call, even if it is ill-advised, does not constitute a policy or practice, and judicial intervention does not appear required or warranted for a single programming decision.

For these reasons, although I cannot agree with all of the majority opinion, particularly its discussion of the application of the public forum doctrine, I concur in the result.

KRAVITCH, CIRCUIT JUDGE, dissenting:

I agree with the analysis in Judge Johnson's thorough and well-reasoned dissent, with one exception: his statement that the government's decision to withdraw a program becomes presumptively unconstitutional once a plaintiff has shown that the decision was made because of the program's "substantive content." In my view, in addition to "substantive content," there must be shown an improper motivation, an intent to "restrict[ ] access to the political ideas or social perspectives discussed. . . ." Board of Education v. Pico, 457 U.S. 853, 879 (1982) (Blackmun, J., concurring). In this regard I agree with Judge Reavley. I do not join Judge Reavley's dissent, however, because his standard suggests that intent to suppress must be the *sole* factor before the withdrawal violates the First Amendment. The *Pico* plurality explicitly stated that an improper motive is a "decisive factor" and makes the withdrawal unconstitutional if it is a "substantial factor." Id. at ___ & n. 22 (plurality opinion of Brennan, J., Marshall, J., and Stevens, J.). The improper motivation need not be the only factor in the withdrawal decision. For these reasons I write separately.

FRANK M. JOHNSON, JR., CIRCUIT JUDGE, with whom HATCHETT, ANDERSON, TATE and THOMAS A. CLARK, CIRCUIT JUDGES, join, dissenting:

I dissent because I am convinced that the majority has committed a serious error in applying the law to these cases. The clearly defined issue in these appeals is whether the executive officers of a state operated public television station may cancel a previously scheduled program because it presents a point of view disagreeable to the religious and political regime of a foreign country. The majority opinion permitting cancellation on these grounds flies completely in the face of the First Amendment and our tradition of vigilance against governmental censorship of political and religious expression.

. . .

The majority of the Court . . . has affirmed *Muir* and reversed *Barnstone* in an opinion which grants state authorities unlimited discretion to regulate the content of public television within their control. Because state law and FCC licensing grant defendants full broadcasting authority over these stations in their respective areas, the majority's decision confers unrestricted control over a monopoly market. [ ] By finding no other restriction on state operated television than that imposed by federal regulation, the Court has elevated "the Communications Act above the Constitution." [ ] Moreover, the Court has abdicated its duty in an area in which the plaintiffs have no comparable remedy.

The freedom of expression protected by the First Amendment encompasses the rights of both speakers and listeners . . .. The proper inquiry for this Court, then, should not be whether the Communications Act grants state broadcasters editorial discretion, but whether the action of state officials in these cases abridged free expression protected by the First Amendment. [ ]

Our system of constitutional protection clearly reflects the free discussion of public issues on the basis of the political, religious, or ideological content of the message. Freedom of expression concerning public issues "is at the heart of the First Amendment's protection." [ ] Self-government suffers when those in power suppress competing views on public issues. [ ] As a result, federal courts have consistently struck down content-based restrictions on the discussion of public issues. [ ]

. . .

The majority opinion completely ignores the critical issue in these cases by concluding that "[t]he state officials in charge of AETC and KUHT–TV have simply exercised their statutorily mandated discretion and decided not to show a particular program at a particular time." The very simple answer to that position is that FCC regulation is designed neither to preempt judicial scrutiny nor to redress state censorship as alleged in these cases.

Federal regulation of the broadcast media, for the most part, reflects the government's attempt to balance the allocation of a scarce resource with the First Amendment interests of private broadcasters and the public. [ ] The fact that state operated television stations are entitled to exercise editorial discretion, however, does not absolve them of their First Amendment responsibilities. "The First Amendment protects the press *from* governmental interference; it confers no analogous protection *on* the Government." CBS, Inc. v. FCC, 395 U.S. at 390 (First Amendment protects against governmental monopolization of the free marketplace of ideas). The majority commits fundamental error when it permits state broadcasters to ride on the coattails of their private counterparts. Even when the majority admits that state broadcasters "are without the protection of the First Amendment," it offers no principled reason why this "implies only that government could possibly impose restrictions on these licensees which it could not impose on private licensees."

In addition, while it is true that the FCC hears complaints similar to those raised in these cases, it is also true that the FCC routinely denies relief. A brief review of the cases cited by the majority reveals that the FCC steadfastly refuses to depart from its "longstanding policy of deferring to licensee discretion." . . .

Complaints regarding individual cancellation decisions are regularly denied. [ ]

Thus it is clear that the majority's deference to the FCC in these cases that present important constitutional questions amounts to nothing more than ". . . a promise to the ear . . ." which will most certainly be broken "to the hope." [ ] Relying on the system of FCC regulation, the majority has granted state broadcasters immunity from constitutional scrutiny. . . . Because the FCC does not distinguish between private and public broadcasters in its regulation of the airwaves, [ ], it provides no protection from the kind of state censorship alleged in these cases.

The concurring opinions of Judges Rubin and Garwood erroneously suggest that official censorship may only be found when the state operates a medium which is "content neutral," [ ], or which is a "public forum." [ ] In all other cases, the concurrences suppose, the state must be given unbridled authority to discriminate among different viewpoints, even if the state chooses to suppress a particular point of view solely on the basis of the political content of the message. Otherwise, the opinions caution, any citizen would have the "right" to force the state operated televisions in this case to broadcast any program of his choosing.

These suppositions erroneously ignore the proper considerations a Court may give the editorial process.

In the recent case of Board of Educ. v. Pico, 457 U.S. 853 (1982), both the plurality and Justice Blackmun recognized the presence of enforceable First Amendment rights, even within the context of a highly discretionary state function. As Justice Blackmun wrote, concurring: "In my view, we strike a proper balance here by holding that school officials may not remove books for the *purpose* of restricting access to the political ideas or social perspectives discussed in them, when that action is motivated simply by the officials' disapproval of the ideas involved." Id. at 899–80, (Blackmun, J., concurring). Unlike Judges Hill and Rubin, I find allegations of censorship in the context of state operated television broadcasting entitled to much greater scrutiny than similar allegations involving school board regulation of students' reading material. Public television stations "provide educational, cultural, and discussion programs which serve the general community." [ ] AETC is specifically charged with the duty "of making the benefits of educational television available to and promoting its use by inhabitants of Alabama . . .." Ala.Code 1975, § 16–7–5. Viewed in the context of these stations' purposes and the framework of existing regulation, the editorial discretion of a state broadcaster is more circumscribed than that of a school board member. Moreover, the facts of both *Muir* and *Barnstone* reveal dramatic departures from established editorial practice in direct response to the urgings or implied threats of a foreign government.

Finally, the concurring opinions would appear to recognize official censorship by state television broadcasters when that censorship is conducted as a "policy or practice" of the state. Neither opinion, however, advances a principled distinction between censorship which is a "policy or practice" and that which is an individual overt act of suppression. It is clear to me that the First Amendment does not prohibit censorship only when it reaches the level of state "policy." To do so would be to allow the state to abrogate the fundamental concept of individual civil liberty. [ ]

It is the judiciary which is the ultimate arbiter of the fundamental rights involved in these cases. Courts may not abdicate their duty by reference to a system of administrative regulation, or because they would prefer that the plaintiffs take their complaints elsewhere. We must review the allegations of state censorship in the context of television broadcasting according to applicable legal standards. The standard for evaluating the allegations of abridgment in these cases must be that which was articulated in Mt. Healthy School Dist. v. Doyle, 429 U.S. 274, 287 (1977). Once the plaintiff demonstrates that the government has silenced a message because of its substantive content, the government's decision becomes presumptively unconstitutional. The government should then be allowed to demonstrate that it would have taken the same action on the basis of legitimate reasons. Finally, the plaintiff should be given a full opportunity to refute the government's assertion.

. . .

REAVLEY, CIRCUIT JUDGE, dissenting:

I cannot join the majority or concurring opinions for the reason that each of these television stations does far more than transmit expressions of the state. Our desire to free non-profit public broadcasting from judicial interference is no justification for pretending that the state is not relaying messages into the idea marketplace. I must conclude that the state encounters the First Amendment requirement of neutrality for reasons generally discussed in my original panel concurrence. Barnstone v. University of Houston, KUHT–TV, 660 F.2d 137, 138 (5th Cir.1981).

On the other hand, I would not go so far as Judge Johnson does to make the state's decision presumptively unconstitutional whenever a program is not shown "because of its substantive content." State operated television stations should be given more latitude, even to choose on the basis of substantive content, in their program selection. They should be entitled to pursue excellence, to build viewing audiences, to respond to what viewers want, and to consider the effect of their programs upon that audience. Bona fide programming decisions would not, for me, violate First Amendment neutrality. Only if the decision to show or not to show were based upon viewpoint alone, in juxtaposition to the personal viewpoint of the programming authority or state superiors, entirely aside from any opinion as to program value or effect, would I regard neutrality abused and court action justifiable.

Notes and Questions

1. Judge Garwood points out that the plaintiffs did not "attack governmental 'public' broadcasting as such." Are there any grounds for such an attack? What are the justifications for allowing government organizations, such as AETC or the University of Houston, to be broadcast licensees?

2. Given the difficulty of finding alternative funding and the difficulty of insulating recipients of government funding from interference— either direct or indirect—in their programming policies, what changes should be made in the public broadcasting scheme?

3. Because many of these stations are run by state and local governments, which also provide some of the financing, an additional set of problems has emerged with regard to the power of the state to impose restrictions more stringent than those imposed by Congress. In State of Maine v. University of Maine, 266 A.2d 863 (Me.1970), the state-run educational television system was partially financed from state funds. A statute ordered that no facilities "supported in whole or in part by state funds shall be used directly or indirectly for the promotion, advertisement or advancement of any political candidate . . . or for the purpose of advocating or opposing any specific program, existing or proposed, of governmental action which shall include, but shall not be limited to, constitutional amendments, tax referendums or bond issues."

The court concluded that the limitations ran counter to federal demands that a licensee operating in the public interest may not flatly ban all such programming. The role of state funding gave the state no added power in this area. Although the state "has a valid surviving power to protect its citizens in matters involving their health and safety or to protect them from fraud and deception, it has no such valid interest in protecting them from the dissemination of ideas as to which they may be called upon to make an informed choice."

4. Both the majority in *League of Women Voters* and Judge Hill in *Muir* relied in part on the protection against one-sided programming afforded by the fairness doctrine. How much protection against pro-government bias can necessarily be expected from the FCC when its members are political appointees? Now that the doctrine has been eliminated, does the analysis change? Are there stronger arguments for retaining it with respect to noncommercial broadcasting?

C. RELIGIOUS BROADCASTING

As noted earlier, religious institutions may be eligible for reserved educational channels. The test used by the Commission to decide whether an institution is eligible for a reserved spot is "whether the primary thrust is educational, albeit with a religious aspect to the educational activity. Recognizing that some overlap in purposes is, or can be, involved, we look to the application as a whole to determine which is the essential purpose and which is incidental." Bible Moravian Church, Inc., 28 F.C.C.2d 1, 21 R.R.2d 492 (1971) (rejecting an application for a reserved educational spot).

Religious institutions that do not meet the educational qualifications are able to apply for other spots as noncommercial licensees. In such instances, the rules applicable to other broadcasters are applicable to religious broadcasters as well. In addition, the Commission will apply the 'fair break' doctrine by inquiring as to "whether the applicant, whatever his own views, is likely to give a 'fair break' to others who do not share them." Noe v. Federal Communications Commission, 260 F.2d 739, 742 (D.C.Cir.1958). The Commission has made one major exception to its general rules in allowing a religious broadcaster to consider an applicant's religion for employment, but only to "those persons hired to espouse a particular religious philosophy over the air."

In its early days of reallocating frequencies, when there were no spots reserved for educational broadcasting, the Radio Commission had occasion to consider the value of a station emphasizing religious programming. It decided that such programming was usually aimed at too narrow a base of listeners and this "discriminated against" the rest of the listeners. "In rare cases it is possible to combine a general public-service station and a high-class religious station in a division of time which will approximate a well-rounded program. In other cases religious stations must accept part time on inferior channels or daylight assignments . . .." Great Lakes Broadcasting Co., 3 F.R.C.Ann.Rep. 32 (1929), modified on other grounds 37 F.2d 993 (D.C.Cir.1930), certiorari dismissed 281 U.S. 706 (1930). As the spectrum has expanded, religious broadcasting has gained a more secure footing.

Some have argued that religious programming provides too narrow a base to justify the allocation of a license. An effort to persuade the Commission of this failed in 1975. Multiple and Religious Ownership of Educational Stations, 54 F.C.C.2d 941, 34 R.R.2d 1217 (1975). Two persons requested a "freeze" on all grants of reserved educational FM and television channels to religious institutions pending a study of their value. The Commission thought this would violate its obligation of "neutrality" toward sectarian applicants. The Commission concluded that no new policies were needed and decided to continue ad hoc enforcement of its existing policies such as the fairness doctrine and "the principle that a broadcast station may not be used solely to promote the personal or partisan objectives of the broadcaster."

One effect of this petition was to demonstrate the support for religious stations. Periodically, a rumor surfaces that this petition—incorrectly attributed to famous atheist Madalyn Murray O'Hair—is again being considered by the Commission. Each time this happens, the Commission is flooded with calls and letters opposing the petition.

As we saw in Chapter VI with the fairness complaint against the program "In Search of Noah's Ark," the Commission has never declared the fairness doctrine "applicable to issues involving the interpretation of religious doctrine." This position was challenged in 1965 by Madalyn Murray O'Hair, who requested time on several Hawaiian radio stations to discuss "freethought." She argued that the various church services carried by these stations entitled her to time to discuss her contrasting views. The Commission rejected her complaint on the grounds that "mere broadcast of church services, devotionals and prayers is not the presentation of a controversial issue within the meaning of the Fairness Doctrine." Madalyn Murray, 40 F.C.C. 647 (1965).

At what point do religious statements become statements on issues of public controversy? Would a sermon against abortion shown as part of a televised church service raise a fairness doctrine problem? What about references to the need for eliminating "smut" from the airwaves, or a suggestion that viewers should boycott companies that advertise on shows that do not reflect traditional Christian values? Traditionally, the Commission has tended to avoid these questions by deferring to the licensee's determination of whether it was a presentation on an issue of public importance. With the growing number of religious programs and even networks for broadcasting and cable, these issues assume greater importance.

Chapter IX

CABLE TELEVISION

Our discussion until this point has been addressed solely to broadcasting. Some programs reached the public through radios and others through television sets. In this chapter and the next we will examine other forms of communication that do not necessarily involve broadcasting—though the end product does emerge through the television set. It is important to recognize at the outset that although broadcasting and the television set have been joined, new technology permits the television set to be used for communications that have not been broadcast. The most obvious example is the use of video cassette players and recorders, which permit the owner of a television set to buy or rent a video cassette at a store and play it on a television set at home—all without any use of the spectrum. That activity much more closely resembles the showing of movies at home than anything else.

A. DEVELOPMENT

Cable television, the first of the "new" communication technologies, involves the transmission of electrical signals over wires to television sets in homes or elsewhere. The technique involves a studio, called the "head-end," and either coaxial or fiber optic cables that physically connect the head-end with every television set in the system. The cable is capable of carrying such a wide range of electrical signals that it can simultaneously carry signals sufficient for 55 or more television channels. (As the signals are carried along the cable they become weaker and must be amplified along the way.) As a result of the video compression technology that has been a byproduct of HDTV development, p. 56, *supra,* some cable systems are expected to offer up to 500 channels by 1994.

It is possible to transmit certain signals in scrambled forms that require decoders, but others can be received by all users. It is also possible, as Warner Communications first showed with QUBE in Columbus, Ohio, to run a system in which the users are able to send signals back to the head-end: voting on a question asked on a program, ordering merchandise or telling a quarterback what plays to call in a semiprofessional football game.

The programming sent out from the head-end can come from many sources. System owners might send out a variety of motion pictures they have bought or rented; they might send camera crews out to cover local high school football games; they might present live programs from their own studios; they might carry programs prepared by others specially for cable that they receive by wire or by satellite; or they might seek to transmit over their systems the signals and programs broadcast by television stations. This last source of programming raises serious questions of the relationship between cable and over-the-air television. So long as the cable system carries only programming from other sources, cable television is simply another competitor of broadcasting, along with movies, phonograph records, books and other communications sources. In fact, however, cable has been intimately involved with broadcasting since its inception—and that has produced substantial conflict.

Cable transmission was first used in the 1950s to provide television reception in remote locations that otherwise would have received none. For example, a community in the mountains of West Virginia could construct an antenna on high ground to receive the signals of nearby television stations and transmit them through cable to households in the community. Such systems were called CATV for "community antenna television." Because cable was the only means of bringing television service to these remote areas, television broadcasters welcomed the additional viewers.

It was soon realized, however, that cable could do more than merely provide television service to remote areas. In 1961 a cable operator began serving San Diego, a city already served by three VHF network affiliates. The cable operator erected an antenna capable of picking up signals from Los Angeles, 100 miles away. In addition to the three networks received locally, cable offered four independent stations that served Los Angeles with sports, old motion pictures and reruns of network shows. The San Diego experience demonstrated that the three channels offered by over-the-air signals were not enough to satisfy an ordinary audience and that viewers were willing to pay for more diversified programming through importation of distant signals. In effect, cable television service filled in the uneven pattern of FCC station allocation. Because cable offered a service alternative to that offered by local, over-the-air stations, television broadcasters began to view cable transmission as a competitive threat.

The spread of color television also provided a new impetus to cable development. VHF signals tend to bounce off large obstacles rather than bend around them. Hence a tall building can act like a weak transmitter, rebroadcasting the television signal at the same frequency as the station from which the signal originates. The result is interference, barely noticeable on a black-and-white set, but more pronounced on a color set. Cable provides the residents of large cities something that an over-the-air television signal cannot—a high-quality color picture. Thus, cable television invaded large cities, despite the presence of a full complement of VHF signals.

Finally, cable began to originate programming not available to viewers of network or independent television. Cable systems offered entertainment programming, sports events and special programs designed to meet the interests of discrete groups. Communication satellites made nationwide distribution of this programming economically feasible. The discovery that viewers were willing to pay a few dollars more per month for programming not available on over-the-air television led to the development of pay cable service.

Pay cable involves the cable distribution of non-broadcast programming for which the subscriber is charged an additional program or channel fee beyond the regular monthly fee for over-the-air television channels, access and local origination channels, and advertiser-supported cable programming services. The systems for distributing pay cable vary technically. The simplest method is to distribute the programming on one or more channels of a cable television system in garbled form. System subscribers who wish to receive the additional programming are supplied with a device that converts the programming transmission so that it can be understood. It is technically possible, but more expensive, to use systems that permit a separate charge to be made for each program viewed. These either require the subscriber to purchase a ticket for each program in advance, which when inserted into a decoding device in the subscriber's home provides access to the programming, or to utilize the return communications capacity of a cable system or a telephone connection to activate a central computer facility that releases the programming through the subscriber's decoding device (an addressable converter) and performs the billing functions.

Most cable systems utilize a fee structure known as "tiering." A relatively low monthly fee gives the subscriber access to the local over-the-air television stations as well as any community access or local origination channels. Access channels carry programming produced by citizens or community groups, and local origination consists of local news, sports and public affairs programming produced by the cable operator. Sometimes advertiser-supported services such as the Entertainment and Sports Programming Network (ESPN), the Cable News Network (CNN) and over-the-air signals imported from other parts of the country are included.

An additional monthly fee gives the subscriber access to other specialized programming services ranging from children's programs to adult entertainment. These services are usually bundled together in groups called "tiers." Thus, the subscriber must sometimes take several unwanted program services to obtain one desired service. Usually a higher tier includes all the programming available in lower tiers.

The range of programming available via cable has grown greatly. Among the services now available are programming directed to racial and religious groups, all-news and all-sports channels, live coverage of Congress, children's programming, "superstations" (to be discussed later in this chapter), movie and entertainment channels, adult movies and cultural programming.

In the late 1970s and early 1980s, new programming services were constantly beginning, but by the mid-1980s, a shakeout in the industry had begun. CBS shut down CBS Cable after losing $30 million on the new service in its first year. The RCA and Rockefeller Center entry, The Entertainment Channel, was discontinued after posting a $35 million loss in its first nine months.

In 1983 Ted Turner agreed to pay ABC and Westinghouse $12.5 million each to shut down Satellite News Channel, which was the main competitor to Turner's Cable News Network and CNN Headline News. Group W and ABC promised not to compete in the cable news business for at least three years.

The late 1980s and early 1990s have brought another wave of new cable channels. Many of these are new services produced by existing cable programmers. For example, TNT and the Cartoon Network belong to Turner Broadcasting, while the Sci–Fi Channel belongs to USA Network.

Thus, cable has provided a variety of services. It began as a way of bringing to a community programming that would have been available but for geographical barriers. Then it imported programs from communities beyond the reach of normal reception. Later it became a service for those who wished to improve reception of their local signals. These features have been combined with each other as well as with the origination of new programming on cable. Now it is possible to obtain the origination without any of the other features—and this origination may be local or part of a network that programs specially for cable subscribers.

By 1993 cable systems had been installed in 55.8 million (60.6 percent) of the nation's 92.1 million television homes. Systems varied in size from a few hundred homes to some in larger cities with hundreds of thousands of subscribers. The largest multiple system operators (MSOs) owned hundreds of systems. Pay cable reached 43.5 million of these subscribers. The pay systems ranged from Home Box Office, with 16 million subscribers, to specialized services with only a few thousand subscribers.

B. JURISDICTION

1. FCC JURISDICTION

When the first CATV systems emerged in the late 1950s, rural television stations became concerned about their local dominance. Their requests that the FCC assume jurisdiction over the activities of these new enterprises were rejected on the ground that the problem was trivial and no different from a request for protection against motion picture theaters or publishers, who also compete with broadcasting.

In 1962, however, the FCC changed direction and began to deny cable systems permission to carry broadcast signals that might adversely affect local television. The Commission had two main concerns. First, it believed that if cable systems were allowed to import distant signals, this would fragment the audience available to local stations, erode their revenue bases, affect their programming and perhaps cause the stations to leave the air—to the public's detriment.

The second concern was that a cable system's use of retransmitted broadcast programming, for which the cable system had paid nothing, gave it an unfair competitive advantage over local television stations because the latter had to pay considerable sums to those who held the copyrights on particular programs. We will discuss the relationship between copyright law and cable regulation later in this chapter.

These two concerns—for fragmentation and program costs—led the FCC to embark on a series of regulations designed to keep cable systems subservient to over-the-air broadcasting. Recall that this was the period of weak UHF stations, for whom audience fragmentation might well have been fatal.

One of the restrictions imposed was a ban on importing distant signals (those from outside the market area) into a top–100 market unless the cable system could prove that the importation would not hurt UHF development in that market. This restriction resulted in the first court challenge to the FCC's authority to regulate cable. United States v. Southwestern Cable Co., 392 U.S. 157 (1968). The Commission relied on § 2(a) of the Communications Act: "The provisions of this Act shall apply to all interstate and foreign communication by wire or radio . . . ." 47 U.S.C.A. § 152(a). Southwestern argued that "§ 152(a) does not independently confer regulatory authority upon the Commission, but instead merely prescribes the forms of communication to which the Act's other provisions may separately be made applicable." Since there were no specific cable provisions in the Act, Southwestern contended the Commission had no authority to regulate cable.

The Court rejected that argument as an overly restrictive reading of the Act. Relying on *National Broadcasting Co.*, p. 65, *supra*, the Court held that Congress had delegated "not niggardly but expansive powers" over electronic media to the Commission and that a broad reading of the Act was required:

> Moreover, the Commission has reasonably concluded that regulatory authority over CATV is imperative if it is to perform with appropriate effectiveness certain of its other responsibilities. Congress has imposed upon the Commission the "obligation of providing a widely dispersed radio and television service," with a fair, efficient, and equitable distribution" of service among the "several States and communities." 47 U.S.C. § 307(b). . . . The Commission has concluded, and Congress has agreed, that these obligations require for their satisfaction the creation of a system of local broadcasting stations, such that "all communities of appreciable size [will] have at least one television station as an outlet for local self-expression." In turn the Commission has held that an

appropriate system of local broadcasting may be created only if two subsidiary goals are realized. First, significantly wider use must be made of the available ultra-high-frequency channels. Second, communities must be encouraged "to launch sound and adequate programs to utilize the television channels now reserved for educational purposes." These subsidiary goals have received the endorsement of Congress.

The Commission has reasonably found that the achievement of each of these purposes is "placed in jeopardy by the unregulated explosive growth of CATV." [ ] Although CATV may in some circumstances make possible "the realization of some of the [Commission's] most important goals," [ ], its importation of distant signals into the service areas of local stations may also "destroy or seriously degrade the service offered by a television broadcaster," [ ], and thus ultimately deprive the public of the various benefits of a system of local broadcasting stations. In particular, the Commission feared that CATV might, by dividing the available audiences and revenues, significantly magnify the characteristically serious financial difficulties of UHF and educational television broadcasters. The Commission acknowledged that it could not predict with certainty the consequences of unregulated CATV, but reasoned that its statutory responsibilities demand that it "plan in advance of foreseeable events, instead of waiting to react to them." [ ] We are aware that these consequences have been variously estimated, but must conclude that there is substantial evidence that the Commission cannot "discharge its overall responsibilities without authority over this important aspect of television service." [ ]

The Commission has been charged with broad responsibilities for the orderly development of an appropriate system of local television broadcasting. The significance of its efforts can scarcely be exaggerated, for broadcasting is demonstrably a principal source of information and entertainment for a great part of the Nation's population. The Commission has reasonably found that the successful performance of these duties demands prompt and efficacious regulation of community antenna television systems. We have elsewhere held that we may not, "in the absence of compelling evidence that such was Congress' intention . . . prohibit administrative action imperative for the achievement of an agency's ultimate purposes." [ ] There is no such evidence here, and we therefore hold that the Commission's authority over "all interstate . . . communication by wire or radio" permits the regulation of CATV systems.

There is no need here to determine in detail the limits of the Commission's authority to regulate CATV. It is enough to emphasize that the authority which we recognize today under § 152(a) is restricted to that reasonably ancillary to the effective performance of the Commission's various responsibilities for the regulation of television broadcasting. The Commission may, for these purposes, issue "such rules and regulations and prescribe such restrictions and conditions, not inconsistent with law," as "public convenience, interest, or necessity requires." 47 U.S.C. § 303(r). We express no views as to the Commission's authority, if any, to regulate CATV under any other circumstances or for any other purposes.

Although *Southwestern Cable* established that the Commission did have jurisdiction over cable, it left unanswered the boundaries of that jurisdiction. The next challenge arose from the promulgation in the late 1960s of rules requiring larger cable systems to originate a certain amount of programming from their own resources. This requirement was upheld, 5–4, by the Supreme Court in United States v. Midwest Video Corp. (*Midwest Video I*), 406 U.S. 649 (1972), on the ground that the regulation was "reasonably ancillary" to the FCC's obligations to regulate over-the-air television. Because cable operators had become enmeshed with television broadcasting, the FCC could require them to engage in the functional equivalent of broadcasting. Chief Justice Burger concurred but noted that the FCC's regulations "strain[ed] the outer limits of even the open-ended and pervasive jurisdiction that has evolved by decisions of the Commission and the Courts." Ironically, less than two years later, the FCC eliminated the origination requirement because it concluded that quality local programming could not be obtained by government mandate.

Instead, the Commission issued rules requiring new cable systems to allocate four of their 20 channels to public, educational, local government and leased access. The systems had to make equipment available for studio use by the public and could not control who might use the facilities or what they might say. Charges for use of the facilities were controlled. The court of appeals invalidated the regulations. Once again the Court was asked to define the limits of the Commission's jurisdiction.

This time the Court held, 6–3, that the Commission had exceeded its authority. Section 3(h) of the Communications Act (17 U.S.C.A. § 153(h)) prohibits the Commission from treating broadcasters as common carriers. The access-channel requirements "plainly impose common-carrier obligations on cable operators." The Court concluded that, given Congress' express disapproval of common-carrier status for broadcasters, imposing such status on cable could not be construed as "reasonably ancillary to the effective performance of [the FCC's] various responsibilities for the regulation of television broadcasting." Federal Communications Commission v. Midwest Video Corporation (*Midwest Video II*), 440 U.S. 689, 45 R.R.2d 58, 4 Med.L.Rptr. 2345 (1979).

The mandatory access rules had also been challenged on First Amendment grounds. The Court chose not to address that issue at that time. As we will discuss later in this chapter, the Cable Communications Policy Act of 1984 authorizes the imposition of access channel requirements and for larger systems mandates leased access. However, as we will see in the notes following Preferred Communications, Inc. v. City of Los Angeles, *infra,* in two separate district court decisions access channel requirements instituted pursuant to these provisions have been declared unconstitutional.

In the early 1980s there were no serious challenges to the Commission's jurisdiction over cable, perhaps because the Commission changed its regulatory posture towards cable. As we will discuss later in this chapter, the Commission had begun to eliminate its regulations governing cable in the late 1970s.

2. PREEMPTION

Cable, unlike broadcasting, is regulated by both state and federal government. State and local jurisdiction was originally based primarily on the cable operator's use of the city streets and other rights of way. As we have seen, federal jurisdiction grew out of the FCC's jurisdiction over broadcasting. Gradually a conflict arose over where the line between state and federal jurisdiction should be drawn.

The majority of cable operators preferred to have state and local jurisdiction restricted as much as possible. They believed that some cities were making impossible demands in return for their franchises and imposing heavy burdens on the cable operators once the franchises were awarded. There were also serious fears that franchise renewal in cable would not carry the same renewal expectancy that is present in broadcasting (discussed in Chapter IV).

At the same time the FCC was gradually asserting the right to preempt more and more state and local regulation. As these issues reached the courts, the Commission's position was generally being upheld. In 1984 the Commission received strong support for its asserted right to preempt in a case in which it was not directly involved.

CAPITAL CITIES CABLE, INC. v. CRISP

Supreme Court of the United States, 1984.
467 U.S. 691, 104 S.Ct. 2694, 81 L.Ed.2d 580, 56 R.R.2d 263, 10 Med.L.Rptr. 1873.

[In 1980 the Oklahoma Attorney General decided that the state's ban on the advertising of alcoholic beverages applied to advertisements carried by out-of-state broadcast stations when retransmitted by Oklahoma cable television systems. Because the definition of alcoholic beverages did not include beer, and there was little, if any, electronic media advertising of hard liquors, the statute was only applied to electronic media advertising of wine. Capital Cities Cable filed a suit seeking a declaratory judgment that application of the law violated the Supremacy Clause and First Amendment to the Federal Constitution. The district court found the ban a violation of the First Amendment, but the decision was reversed by the court of appeals.]

JUSTICE BRENNAN delivered the opinion of the Court.

The question presented in this case is whether Oklahoma may require cable television operators in that State to delete all advertisements for alcoholic beverages contained in the out-of-state signals that they retransmit by cable to their subscribers. Petitioners contend that Oklahoma's requirement abridges their rights under the First and Fourteenth Amendments and is pre-empted by federal law. Because we conclude that this state regulation is pre-empted, we reverse the judgment of the Court of Appeals for the Tenth Circuit and do not reach the First Amendment question.

. . .

II

Petitioners and the FCC contend that the federal regulatory scheme for cable television systems administered by the Commission is intended to pre-empt any state regulation of the signals carried by cable system operators. Respondent apparently concedes that enforcement of the Oklahoma statute in this case conflicts with federal law, but argues that because the State's advertising ban was adopted pursuant to the broad powers to regulate the transportation and importation of intoxicating liquor reserved to the States by the Twenty-first Amendment, the statute should prevail notwithstanding the conflict with federal law. . . .

. . . Under the Supremacy Clause, U.S. Const., Art. VI, cl. 2, the enforcement of a state regulation may be pre-empted by federal law in several circumstances: first, when Congress, in enacting a federal statute, has expressed a clear intent to pre-empt state law, [ ]; second, when it is clear despite the absence of explicit pre-emptive language, that Congress has intended, by legislating comprehensively, to occupy an entire field of regulation and has thereby "left no room for the States to supplement" federal law, [ ]; and, finally, when compliance with both state and federal law is impossible, [ ], or when the state law "stands as an obstacle to the accomplishment and execution of the full purposes and objectives of Congress." [ ]

And as we made clear in Fidelity Federal Savings and Loan Ass'n v. De La Cuesta, 458 U.S. 141 (1982):

> "Federal regulations have no less pre-emptive effect than federal statutes. Where Congress has directed an administrator to exercise his discretion, his judgments are subject to judicial review only to determine whether he has exceeded his authority or acted arbitrarily. When the administrator promulgates regulations intended to pre-empt state law, the court's inquiry is similarly limited: 'If [h]is choice represents a reasonable accommodation of conflicting policies that were committed to the agency's care by the statute, we should not disturb it unless it appears from the statute or its legislative history that the accommodation is not one that Congress would have sanctioned.' " [ ]

The power delegated to the FCC plainly comprises authority to regulate the signals carried by cable television systems. In United States v. Southwestern Cable Co., 392 U.S. 157 (1968), the Court found that the Commission had been given "broad responsibilities" to regulate all aspects of interstate communication by wire or radio by virtue of § 2(a) of the Communications Act of 1934, 47 U.S.C. § 152(a), and that this comprehensive authority included to regulate cable communications systems. [ ] We have since explained that the Commission's authority extends to all regulatory actions "necessary to ensure the achievement of the Commission's statutory responsibilities." FCC v. Midwest Video Corp., 440 U.S. 689, 706 (1979). Accord, United States v. Midwest Video Corp., 406 U.S. 649, 665–667 (1972). Therefore, if the FCC has resolved to pre-empt an area of cable television regulation and if this determination "represents a reasonable accommodation of conflicting policies" that are within the agency's domain, [ ], we must conclude that all conflicting state regulations have been precluded.

A

In contrast to commercial television broadcasters, which transmit video signals to their audience free of charge and derive their income principally from advertising revenues, cable television systems generally operate on the basis of a wholly different entrepreneurial principle. In return for service fees paid by subscribers, cable operators provide their customers with a variety of broadcast and nonbroadcast signals obtained from several sources. Typically, these sources include over-the-air broadcast signals picked up by a master antenna from local and nearby television broadcasting stations, broadcast signals from distant television stations imported by means of communications satellites, and nonbroadcast signals that are not originated by television broadcasting stations, but are instead transmitted specifically for cable systems by satellite or microwave relay. Over the past twenty years, pursuant to its delegated authority under the Communications Act, the FCC has unambiguously expressed its intent to pre-empt any state or local regulation of this entire array of signals carried by cable television systems.

The Commission began its regulation of cable communication in the 1960s. At that time, it was chiefly concerned that unlimited importation of distant broadcast signals into the service areas of local television broadcasting stations might, through competition, "destroy or seriously degrade the service offered by a television broadcaster," and thereby cause a significant reduction in service to households not served by cable systems. . . .

. . . In marking the boundaries of its jurisdiction, the FCC determined that, in contrast to its regulatory scheme for television broadcasting stations, it would not adopt a system of direct federal licensing for cable systems. Instead, the Commission announced a program of "deliberately structured dualism" in which state and local authorities were given responsibility for granting franchises to cable operators within their communities and for overseeing such local incidents of cable operations as delineating franchise areas, regulating the construction of cable facilities, and maintaining rights of way. [ ] At the same time, the Commission retained exclusive jurisdiction over all operational aspects of cable communication, including signal carriage and technical standards. . . . The Commission has also made clear that its exclusive jurisdiction extends to cable systems' carriage of specialized, non-broadcast signals. . . .

Although the FCC has recently relaxed its regulation of importation of distant broadcast signals to permit greater access to this source of programming for cable subscribers, it has by no means forsaken its regulatory power in this area. [ ] Indeed, the Commission's decision to allow unfettered importation of distant broadcast signals rested on its conclusion that "the benefits to existing and potential cable households from permitting the carriage of additional signals are substantial. Millions of households may be afforded not only increased viewing options, but also access to a diversity of services from cable television that presently is unavailable in their communities." 79 F.C.C.2d, at 746. [ ] . . . Clearly, the full accomplishment of such objectives would be jeopardized if state and local authorities were now permitted to restrict the ability of cable operators to provide these diverse services to their subscribers.

Accordingly, to the extent it has been invoked to control the distant broadcast and nonbroadcast signals imported by cable operators, the Oklahoma advertising ban plainly reaches beyond the regulatory authority reserved to local authorities by the Commission's rules, and trespasses into the exclusive domain of the FCC. To be sure, Oklahoma may, under current Commission rules, regulate such local aspects of cable systems as franchisee selection and construction oversight, [ ], but, by requiring cable television operators to delete commercial advertising contained in signals carried pursuant to federal authority, the State has clearly exceeded that limited jurisdiction and interfered with a regulatory area that the Commission has explicitly pre-empted.

B

Quite apart from this generalized federal pre-emption of state regulation of cable signal carriage, the Oklahoma advertising ban plainly conflicts with specific federal regulations. These conflicts arise in three principal ways. First, the FCC's so-called "must-carry" rules require certain cable television operators to transmit the broadcast signals of any local television broadcasting station that is located within a specified 35–mile zone of the cable operator or that is "significantly viewed" in the community served by the operator. [ ] These "must-carry" rules require many Oklahoma cable operators, including petitioners, to carry signals from broadcast stations located in nearby states such as Missouri and Kansas. [ ] In addition, under Commission regulations, the local broadcast signals that cable operators are required to carry must be carried "in full, without deletion or alteration of any portion. . . ." [ ] Because, in the Commission's view, enforcement of these non-deletion rules serves to "prevent a loss of revenues to local broadcasters sufficient to result in reduced service to the public," they have been applied to commercial advertisements as well as to regular programming. [ ] Consequently, those Oklahoma cable operators required to carry out-of-state broadcast signals in full, including any wine commercials, are subject to criminal prosecution under Oklahoma law as a result of their compliance with federal regulations.

Second, current FCC rulings permit, and indeed encourage, cable television operators to import out-of-state television broadcast signals and retransmit those signals to their subscribers. [ ] For Oklahoma cable operators, this source of cable programming includes signals from television broadcasting stations located in Kansas, Missouri and Texas, as well as the signals from so-called "superstations" in Atlanta and Chicago. [ ] It is undisputed that many of these distant broadcast signals retransmitted by petitioners contain wine commercials that are lawful under federal law and in the states where the programming originates. Nor is it disputed that cable operators who carry such signals are barred by Commission regulations from deleting or altering any portion of those signals, including commercial advertising. [ ] Under Oklahoma's advertising ban, however, these cable operators must either delete the wine commercials or face criminal prosecution. Since the Oklahoma law, by requiring deletion of a portion of these out-of-state signals, compels conduct that federal law forbids, the State ban clearly "stands as an obstacle to the accomplishment and execution of the full purposes and objectives" of the federal regulatory scheme. [ ]

Finally, enforcement of the state advertising ban against Oklahoma cable operators will affect a third source of cable programming over which the Commission has asserted exclusive jurisdiction. Aside from relaying local television broadcasting in accordance with the "must-carry" rules, and distant broadcast signals, cable operators also transmit specialized nonbroadcast cable services to their subscribers. This source of programming . . . includes such advertiser-supported national cable programming as the Cable News Network (CNN) and the Entertainment and Sports Programming Network (ESPN). Although the Commission's "must-carry" and non-deletion rules do not apply to such nonbroadcast cable services, the FCC, as noted earlier, [ ], has explicitly stated that state regulation of these services is completely precluded by federal law.

Petitioners generally receive such signals by antenna, microwave receiver, or by satellite dish and retransmit them by wire to their subscribers. But unlike local television broadcasting stations that transmit only one signal and receive notification from their networks concerning advertisements, cable operators simultaneously receive and channel to their subscribers a variety of signals from many sources without any advance notice about the timing or content of commercial advertisements carried on those signals. [ ] As the record of this case indicates, developing the capacity to monitor each signal and delete every wine commercial before it is retransmitted would be a prohibitively burdensome task. [ ] . . . Accordingly, if the state advertising ban is enforced, Oklahoma cable operators will be compelled either to abandon altogether their carriage of both distant broadcast signals and specialized non-broadcast cable services or run the risk of criminal prosecution. As a consequence, the public may well be deprived of the wide variety of programming options that cable systems make possible.

Such a result is wholly at odds with the regulatory goals contemplated by the FCC. Consistent with its congressionally defined charter to "make available, so far as possible, to all the people of the United States a rapid, efficient, Nation-wide and world-wide wire and radio communication service . . .," 47 U.S.C. § 151, the FCC has sought to ensure that "the benefits of cable communications become a reality on a nationwide basis." [ ] With that end in mind, the Commission has determined that only federal pre-emption of state and local regulation can assure cable systems the breathing space necessary to expand vigorously and provide a diverse range of program offerings to potential cable subscribers in all parts of the country. While that judgment may not enjoy universal support, it plainly represents a reasonable accommodation of the competing policies committed to the FCC's care and we see no reason to disturb the agency's judgment. And, as we have repeatedly explained, when federal officials determine, as the FCC has here, that restrictive regulation of a particular area is not in the public interest, "States are not permitted to use their police power to enact such a regulation." [ ]

C

Although the FCC has taken the lead in formulating communications policy with respect to cable television, Congress has considered the impact of this new technology, and has, through the Copyright Revision Act of 1976, 90 Stat. 2541, 17 U.S.C. § 101 et seq., acted to facilitate the cable industry's ability to distribute broadcast programming on a national basis. Prior to the 1976 revision, the Court has determined that the retransmission of distant broadcast signals by cable systems did not subject cable operators to copyright infringement liability because such retransmissions were not "performances" within the meaning of the 1909 Copyright Act. [ ] In revising the Copyright Act, however, Congress concluded that cable operators should be required to pay royalties to the owners of copyrighted programs retransmitted by their systems on pain of liability for copyright infringement. At the same time, Congress recognized that "it would be impractical and unduly burdensome to require every cable system to negotiate [appropriate royalty payments] with every copyright owner" in order to secure consent for such retransmission. [ ] Section 111 of the 1976 Act codifies the solution devised by Congress. It establishes a program of compulsory copyright licensing that permits cable systems to retransmit distant broadcast signals without securing permission from the copyright owner and, in turn, requires each system to pay royalty fees to a central royalty fund based on a percentage of its gross revenues. To take advantage of this compulsory licensing scheme, a cable operator must satisfy certain reporting requirements, § 111(d)(1) and (2)(A), pay specified royalty fees to a central fund administered by the Register of Copyrights, § 111(d)(2)(B)–(D), and (3), and refrain from deleting or altering commercial advertising on the broadcast signals it transmits, § 111(c)(3). Failure to comply with these conditions results in forfeiture of the protections of the compulsory licensing system.

In devising this system, Congress has clearly sought to further the important public purpose framed in the Copyright Clause, U.S. Const., Art. I, § 8, of rewarding the creators of copyrighted works, and of "promoting broad public availability of literature, music, and the other arts," [ ]. Compulsory licensing not only protects the commercial value of copyrighted works but also enhances the ability of cable systems to retransmit such programs carried on distant broadcast signals, thereby allowing the public to benefit by the wider dissemination of works carried on television broadcast signals. By requiring cable operators to delete commercial advertisements for wine, however, the Oklahoma ban forces these operators to lose the protections of compulsory licensing. Of course, it is possible for cable systems to comply with the Oklahoma ban by simply abandoning their importation of the distant broadcast signals covered by the Copyright Act. But such a loss of viewing options would plainly thwart the policy identified by both Congress and the FCC of facilitating and encouraging the importation of distant broadcast signals.

III

[Oklahoma argued that even if normal pre-emption analysis invalidated the ban, it was valid because of the Twenty-first Amendment. "States enjoy broad power under § 2 of the Twenty-first Amendment to regulate the importation and use of intoxicating liquor within their borders." The Court decided that the state interest in regulating liquor was outweighed by the substantial "federal objective of ensuring widespread availability of diverse cable services throughout the United States." In reaching this conclusion the Court was heavily influenced by the extremely limited approach that Oklahoma had taken to further its asserted interest. Oklahoma had only banned electronic media advertising of wine. There was no direct regulation of consumption or even a ban on other alcoholic beverage advertising.]

IV

We conclude that the application of Oklahoma's alcoholic beverage advertising ban to out-of-state signals carried by cable operators in that State is pre-empted by federal law and that the Twenty-first Amendment does not save the regulation from pre-emption. The judgment of the Court of Appeals is

Reversed.

Notes and Questions

1. How does the balance between state and federal regulation set out here differ from the balance established in broadcast regulation? Why have these differences developed? Is either model preferable to the other?

2. By deciding the case on preemption grounds, the Court avoided having to address the First Amendment question concerning regulation of alcoholic beverage advertising. Recall our discussion of this issue in Chapter VII.

3. THE 1984 POLICY ACT

The FCC's increasingly aggressive policy of preemption had already led the National League of Cities (NLC) to pursue legislative relief. However, lengthy negotiations between NLC and the National Cable Television Association (NCTA) had not produced a compromise satisfactory to both constituencies. Perhaps given new impetus by Court decisions such as *Crisp,* a compromise bill was drafted and presented to Congress with the backing of both groups. In late 1984 this bill was enacted into law as the Cable Communications Policy Act of 1984.

One of the provisions of the Cable Act amended § 2 of the Communications Act of 1934 to include within the FCC's jurisdiction "cable service to all persons engaged within the United States in providing such service, and to the facilities of cable operators which relate to such service, as provided in Title VI." 47 U.S.C.A. § 152. Thus, the Commission no longer has to derive its jurisdiction over cable from its jurisdiction over broadcasting, and courts will no longer have to determine whether a Commission rule is reasonably ancillary to its jurisdiction over broadcasting.

Title VI, "Cable Communications," contains the specific provisions governing cable. 47 U.S.C.A. §§ 521–559. The following are some of the most important provisions.

Franchising. Under the Cable Act, franchising is still the province of state and local governments with certain restrictions. The most important of these is the prohibition on regulating cable service as a common carrier. At the same time, anyone wishing to offer cable service must obtain a franchise. 47 U.S.C.A. § 541. Franchising authorities are prohibited from specifying video programming or other information services in requests for proposals. 47 U.S.C.A. § 544.

Franchise Fees. Section 622 of the Act prohibits franchising authorities from charging more than five percent of gross revenues as a franchise fee. In the case of existing franchises money used to support community access channels will not be covered by the five percent limit. 47 U.S.C.A. § 542. The Commission eliminated its rule limiting franchise fees to three percent (five percent with a waiver).

Concentration Rules.   The Cable Act essentially codified existing FCC crossownership restrictions.   A television broadcast licensee may not own a cable system within its primary signal coverage area.   47 U.S.C.A. § 533(a).   Similarly, a common-carrier was not permitted to own a cable system within its telephone service area.   The latter restriction does not apply to rural areas.   47 U.S.C.A. § 533(b).   What is the reason for this exemption?

In the early 1990s, the Commission reexamined both the network-cable and the cable-telephone company crossownership rules.   The new network-cable crossownership rules permit networks to own cable systems as long as a network's cable systems do not exceed 10 percent of the homes passed by cable nationwide or 50 percent of the homes passed by cable within any ADI.   An ADI, Area of Dominant Influence, is comprised of those communities located within the primary coverage area of a television station as defined by the FCC.   Network–Cable Cross–Ownership, 70 R.R.2d 1531 (1992).

NBC and INTV have filed petitions for reconsideration.   NBC claims that the new ownership limits still make it almost impossible for networks to enter the cable business.   It is not cost-effective for a network to buy individual cable systems.   Rather, the only effective way for networks to enter the cable business is to merge with or invest in major MSO's.   This is precluded by the new rules.

In contrast, INTV argues that the new rules will result in "dangerous levels of horizontal concentration in local broadcast markets." INTV also claims that "negative must carry" is "hopelessly inadequate" to protect against anticompetitive behavior.   Finally, according to INTV, the network-cable crossownership rules, together with the changes in the financial interest and syndication rules will result in off-network programming going directly to network-owned cable systems, as opposed to independent broadcast stations.   Broadcasting, Sept. 14, 1992 at 42.

The FCC also relaxed the cable-telephone company crossownership rules by authorizing telephone companies to transmit video programming on a common-carrier basis.   Telephone companies cannot exercise any editorial control over video programming carried under the new "video dialtone" rules, and must offer their transmission capacity on a nondiscriminatory basis.   However, they can own up to a five percent interest in video programmers.   They can also provide nonregulated and enhanced services including billing and collection, order processing, equipment, and video processing services.   The FCC, which had previously determined that the cross-ownership rules do not apply to long-distance carriers, also affirmed an earlier holding that neither a telephone company offering video dialtone services, nor its customer programmers are subject to the franchising requirements of the Communications Act.   Telephone–Cable Cross–Ownership, 7 F.C.C.Rcd. 5785 (1992).

The Commission is permitted to issue further ownership restrictions, but state regulation is preempted. Some states previously had more restrictive crossownership rules. For example, in Massachusetts, crossownership of cable and a newspaper, daily or weekly, was prohibited.

Renewals. One of the great fears of cable operators was nonrenewal. Specific guidelines for franchise renewal are set out in great detail in § 626 of the Communications Act. 47 U.S.C.A. § 546. A denial of renewal must be based on a finding that the operator failed to comply substantially with the existing franchise agreement; that the quality of the operator's service was unreasonable in light of community needs; that the operator lacks necessary technical, financial or legal ability to fulfill the promises made in its proposal; or that the operator's proposal is not reasonable in terms of meeting the future needs of the community. This appears to create a strong renewal expectancy. The full impact of this section will, of course, not be clear until it has been in effect for several years.

Rate Regulation. The new law allows regulation only of rates of basic cable service, and then only in the absence of effective competition. 47 U.S.C.A. § 543. This provision is viewed as a major victory for cable operators, who have long argued that rate regulation was unnecessary due to competition from other communication technologies. Opponents of the provision contended that cable is effectively a monopoly and thus, cable rates are not subject to adequate pressure from competition.

The Commission initially defined effective competition as the availability of three or more off-the-air television signals in the market. The Commission rejected the suggestion of some parties that the availability of the three major networks be part of the definition. Cable Communications Act Rules, 58 R.R.2d 1 (1985).

The court of appeals held that the standard for measuring signal availability was insufficiently justified and remanded that issue for further proceedings. American Civil Liberties Union v. Federal Communications Commission, 823 F.2d 1554, 63 R.R.2d 729 (D.C.Cir.1987), certiorari denied 485 U.S. 959 (1988).

On remand, the Commission modified the definition of effective competition. A cable system was subject to effective competition only if three or more off-air signals were available in all geographic areas served by that system. The three signals did not have to be the same ones for all parts of the cable system's service area. A presumption of availability was created if the station's predicted coverage met a certain minimum standard or the station was "significantly viewed" in that community. However, the presumption could be rebutted by actual engineering data. Cable Communications Policy Act Rules (Signal Availability Standard), 3 F.C.C.Rcd. 2617, 64 R.R.2d 1276 (1988).

Three years later, the Commission revisited this area and concluded that in at least some cases cable rates had increased unreasonably.

Under the three-signal definition of effective competition, less than four percent of all cable systems were subject to rate regulation. The FCC decided, therefore, to change the definition once again. Under the new definition a cable system was subject to effective competition if (1) six unduplicated over-the air broadcast signals were available in the entire cable community or (2) an independently owned, competing multichannel video service was available to at least 50 percent of the homes and subscribed to by at least 10 percent of the homes passed by the cable system. Effective Competition, 6 F.C.C.Rcd. 4545 (1991).

The Cable Act has not eliminated jurisdictional disputes between the Commission and local authorities. For example, in 1985 the Commission promulgated rules establishing technical standards for cable signal quality and preempting local cable authorities from imposing standards of their own. Technical and Operational Requirements of Part 76 Cable Television, 102 F.C.C.2d 1372, 59 R.R.2d 569 (1985). The Commission's standards applied only to "cable channels devoted to delivering standard broadcast television service," Class I channels, but the preemption of local standards applied to all cable service.

On appeal, the court upheld the preemption of Class I channels, but found that in preempting standards for all other cable service without imposing any standards of its own, the Commission was in apparent conflict with § 626 of the Cable Act. One of the factors a franchisor is required to consider in a renewal proceeding is "the quality of the operator's service, including signal quality. . . ." 47 U.S.C.A. § 546(c)(1)(B):

> The Cable Act thus requires franchisors to consider the quality of a cable operator's signal when considering his renewal application. And a franchisor's determination that the operator's signal quality has been inadequate must be the product of reasoned decision-making. Petitioner argues that franchising authorities cannot evaluate reasonably a cable operator's signal quality without referring to objective technical standards; otherwise franchising authorities and cable operators alike would be cast into an endless series of subjective disputes over whether the Section 626 renewal criterion of "signal quality" has been satisfied. We agree.

The court, finding the failure to consider the apparent conflict to be arbitrary and capricious, vacated the preemption of technical standards for non-Class I channels. City of New York v. Federal Communications Commission, 814 F.2d 720, 62 R.R.2d 914 (D.C.Cir.1987).

The various petitioners that had brought the original action sought *certiorari* with regard to the Class I channels ruling. The Supreme Court granted *certiorari* and affirmed the lower court ruling. The Court relied heavily on § 624 of the Cable Act. "In [§ 624], Congress specified that the local franchising authority could regulate 'services, facilities, and equipment' in certain respects, and could enforce those requirements, but § 624(e) of the Act grants the Commission the power to 'establish technical standards relating to the facilities and equipment of cable systems which a franchising authority may require in the franchise.'" The Court concluded that there was nothing to indicate that the Commission's decision was contrary to what Congress intended. City of New York v. Federal Communications Commission, 486 U.S. 57, 64 R.R.2d 1423 (1988).

In response to the remand on Class II, III and IV signals, the Commission issued a new NPRM. In it the FCC proposed to extend the signal quality standards for Class I signals to Class II, III and IV signals. Technical and Operational Requirements of Part 76, Cable Television, 53 Fed.Reg. 40920 (Oct. 11, 1988). A further NPRM was issued in 1991. Cable Television Technical and Operational Requirements, 6 F.C.C.Rcd. 3673 (1991).

C. FRANCHISING

Cable systems operate under franchise authority granted by a municipality, though state agencies also may grant permission to operate. See, e.g., Clear Television Cable Corp. v. Board of Public Utility Commissioners, 85 N.J. 30, 424 A.2d 1151 (1981). A franchise gives the cable operator access to city streets and other rights-of-way within a defined area for specific periods of time. Franchises usually are awarded after competitive bidding by several companies in response to a request for proposals outlining the requirements of the franchising authority. In practice they are almost always exclusive. After a franchise is awarded, a franchise agreement is signed specifying services the system must provide, construction schedules and franchise fees. Many also specify fees the operators may charge subscribers, although much of this rate regulation has now been preempted by the FCC.

For a while the competition among cable operators for city franchises was incredibly intense. At the height of the franchising process, operators were willing to promise almost anything to obtain a franchise. For example, in 1981 Denver attracted bids from three firms, one offering a 215-channel system including a 107-channel home network. The three offered basic home services for monthly fees ranging from nothing to $3.95.

Unfortunately, once they had obtained the franchises, many of these operators discovered that cable was not necessarily the gold mine they had anticipated. Some of these operators asked the cities to renegotiate the franchise agreements, eliminating some of the promised services. Others sold the franchises. One company that found itself in that position, Warner Amex Cable Communications, ended up building a 56-channel system in Milwaukee in lieu of the 108-channel system originally agreed upon. Broadcasting, Oct. 29, 1984 at 10.

From the 1970s into the early 1980s, when franchising competition was at its peak, cities were able to demand far more than large numbers of channels. Access channels, studios, mobile vans, financial contributions to access foundations and free wiring of public buildings were commonly sought—and offered. In many cities, cable companies ended up providing benefits totally unrelated to cable service. These benefits ranged from building new libraries to planting trees along the roads.

A slightly more subtle approach to winning the franchise competition was a practice known as "rent-a-citizen." Prominent local citizens were given shares in the local subsidiary of a company seeking the franchise. If the company was granted the franchise, these shares suddenly acquired great value. Obviously, this meant that these prominent citizens would exert all their influence towards having that company awarded the franchise.

In addition, the cable company would try to persuade the city that these citizens would provide local ownership, thus guaranteeing that the cable company would always be looking out for the city's best interests. The reality was that these citizens never had a controlling interest in even the local subsidiary. Their influence was minimal. Furthermore, the arrangement between the company and the local stockholders almost always included a buy-back arrangement providing that after a few years the local citizens would sell the stock back to the company for a healthy profit.

Spurred on by cable industry hype and franchising fever, the cities kept increasing the cost of obtaining franchises. Gradually, the FCC increased its limitations on state and municipal regulation of cable. Among the more important restrictions imposed by the Commission were a prohibition of rate regulation of premium services and a ceiling on franchise fees. Further restrictions were under consideration when the Cable Communications Policy Act of 1984 was enacted.

During this period, there were no serious challenges to the cities' authority to extract everything possible from the cable companies by running what was, in essence, an auction, with the franchise going to the highest bidder. Probably, most companies were loath to start fights with the cities for fear of being denied the franchises. As a result, serious questions remained unanswered. What is the connection between a city's control of public rights of way and authority over cable programming? Is awarding a franchise based in part on programming promises a violation of the First Amendment? If there is room for more than one company's cables, does awarding an exclusive franchise violate the First Amendment?

These issues were raised in a suit against the city of Los Angeles. The case arose when Preferred Communications requested a cable franchise after refusing to participate in the city's competitive franchising process. When denied the franchise, Preferred sued, alleging the franchising process violated the First Amendment. The suit was dismissed for failure to state a claim upon which relief could be granted, and Preferred appealed. [Note: When a suit is dismissed for failure to state a claim upon which relief can be granted, it means that even if every fact in dispute is assumed to be in the plaintiff's favor, the plaintiff would still lose the case. Thus, the issue on appeal is not should the plaintiff have won the case, but rather, has the plaintiff at least indicated a chance of winning the case. If the plaintiff wins the appeal, the case will then proceed further.]

The court of appeals framed the issue in the case as follows:

Can the City, consistent with the First Amendment, limit access by means of an auction process to a given region of the City to a single cable television company, when the public utility facilities and other public property in that region necessary to the installation and operation of a cable television system are physically capable of accommodating more than one system?

The court, in a sweeping opinion, concluded that the city could not. Preferred Communications, Inc. v. City of Los Angeles, 754 F.2d 1396, 57 R.R.2d 1396 (9th Cir.1985).

The Supreme Court affirmed, but on narrower grounds.

CITY OF LOS ANGELES v. PREFERRED COMMUNICATIONS, INC.

Supreme Court of the United States, 1986.
476 U.S. 488, 106 S.Ct. 2034, 90 L.Ed.2d 480, 60 R.R.2d 792, 12 Med.L.Rptr. 2244.

JUSTICE REHNQUIST delivered the opinion of the Court.

Respondent Preferred Communications, Inc., sued petitioners City of Los Angeles (City) and the Department of Water and Power (DWP) in the United States Court for the Central District of California. The complaint alleged a violation of respondent's rights under the First and Fourteenth Amendments, and under §§ 1 and 2 of the Sherman Act, by reason of the City's refusal to grant access to DWP's poles or underground conduits used for power lines. The Court of Appeals for the Ninth Circuit affirmed with respect to the Sherman Act, but reversed as to the First Amendment claim. [ ] We granted certiorari with respect to the latter issue, [ ].

Respondent's complaint against the City and DWP alleged, *inter alia,* the following facts: Respondent asked Pacific Telephone and Telegraph (PT & T) and DWP for permission to lease space on their utility poles in order to provide cable television service in the South Central area of Los Angeles. [ ] These utilities responded that they would not lease the space unless respondent first obtained a cable television franchise from the City. [ ] Respondent asked the City for a franchise, but the City refused to grant it one, stating that respondent had failed to participate in an auction that was to award a single franchise in the area. [ ][1]

1. California authorizes municipalities to limit the number of cable television operators in an area by means of a "franchise or license" system, and to prescribe "rules and regulations" to protect customers of such operators. [ ] Congress has recently endorsed such franchise systems. [ ] Pursuant to the authority granted by the State, the City has adopted a provision forbidding the construction or operation of

The complaint further alleged that cable operators are First Amendment speakers, [ ], that there is sufficient excess physical capacity and economic demand in the south central area of Los Angeles to accommodate more than one cable company, [ ], and that the City's auction process allowed it to discriminate among franchise applicants based on which one it deemed to be the "best." [ ] Based on these and other factual allegations, the complaint alleged that the City and DWP had violated the Free Speech Clause of the First and Fourteenth Amendments, §§ 1 and 2 of the Sherman Act, the California Constitution, and certain provisions of state law. [ ]

The City did not deny that there was excess physical capacity to accommodate more than one cable television system. But it argued that the physical scarcity of available space on public utility structures, the limits of economic demand for the cable medium, and the practical and esthetic disruptive effect that installing and maintaining a cable system has on the public right-of-way justified its decision to restrict access to its facilities to a single cable television company. [ ]

. . .

. . . [The Court of Appeals] held that, taking the allegations in the complaint as true, [ ], the City violated the First Amendment by refusing to issue a franchise to more than one cable television company when there was sufficient excess physical and economic capacity to accommodate more than one. [ ] The Court of Appeals expressed the view that the facts alleged in the complaint brought respondent into the ambit of cases such as [*Miami Herald*], rather than of cases such as [*Red Lion*], and *Members of City Council v. Taxpayers for Vincent,* 466 U.S. 789 (1984). [ ]

We agree with the Court of Appeals that respondent's complaint should not have been dismissed, and we therefore affirm the judgment of that court; but we do so on a narrower ground than the one taken by it. The well-pleaded facts in the complaint include allegations of sufficient excess physical capacity and economic demand for cable

a cable television system within city limits unless a franchise is first obtained. [ ] A City ordinance provides that franchises are to be allotted by auction to the bidder offering "the highest percentage of gross annual receipts" derived from the franchise and "such other compensation or consideration . . . as may be prescribed by the Council in the advertisement for bids and notice of sale." [ ]

In October 1982, the City published an advertisement soliciting bids for a cable franchise in the South Central area of Los Angeles. The advertisement indicated that only one franchise would be awarded, and it established a deadline for the submission of bids. [ ] It also set forth certain nonfinancial criteria to be considered in the selection process, including the de-gree of local participation in management or ownership reflecting the ethnic and economic diversity of the franchise area, the capacity to provide 52 channels and two-way communication, the willingness to set aside channels for various public purposes and to provide public access facilities, the willingness to develop other services in the public interest, the criminal and civil enforcement record of the company and its principals, the degree of business experience in cable television or other activities, and the willingness to engage in creative and aggressive affirmative action. [ ] Respondent did not submit a bid in response to this solicitation, and the franchise was eventually awarded to another cable operator.

television operators in the area which respondent sought to serve.[2] The City, while admitting the existence of excess physical capacity on the utility poles, the rights-of-way and the like, justifies the limit on franchises in terms of minimizing the demand that cable systems make for the use of public property. The City characterizes these uses as the stringing of "nearly 700 miles of hanging and buried wire and other appliances necessary for the operation of its system." [ ] The City also characterizes them as "a permanent visual blight," [ ], and adds that the process of installation and repair of such a system in effect subjects City facilities designed for other purposes to a servitude which will cause traffic delays and hazards and esthetic unsightliness. Respondent in its turn replies that the City does not "provide anything more than speculations and assumptions," and that the City's "legitimate concerns are easily satisfied without the need to limit the right to a single speaker." [ ]

We of course take the well-pleaded allegations of the complaint as true for the purpose of a motion to dismiss, [ ]. Ordinarily such a motion frames a legal issue such as the one which the Court of Appeals undertook to decide in this case. But this case is different from a case between private litigants for two reasons: first, it is an action of a municipal corporation taken pursuant to a city ordinance that is challenged here, and, second, the ordinance is challenged on colorable First Amendment grounds. The City has adduced essentially factual arguments to justify the restrictions on cable franchising imposed by its ordinance, but the factual assertions of the City are disputed at least in part by the respondent. We are unwilling to decide the legal questions posed by the parties without a more thoroughly developed record of proceedings in which the parties have an opportunity to prove those disputed factual assertions upon which they rely.

We do think that the activities in which respondent allegedly seeks to engage plainly implicate First Amendment interests. Respondent alleges:

> The business of cable television, like that of newspapers and magazines, is to provide its subscribers with a mixture of news, information and entertainment. As do newspapers, cable companies use a portion of their available space to reprint (or retransmit) the communications of others, while at the same time providing some original content. [ ]

Thus, through original programming or by exercising editorial discretion over which stations or programs to include in its repertoire, respondent seeks to communicate messages on a wide variety of topics and in a wide variety of formats. We recently noted that cable

---

2. They also include allegations that the City imposes numerous other conditions upon a successful applicant for a franchise. It is claimed that, entirely apart from the limitation of franchises to one in each area, these conditions violate respondent's First Amendment rights. The Court of Appeals did not reach these contentions, and neither do we.

operators exercise "a significant amount of editorial discretion regarding what their programming will include." [*Midwest Video II*] Cable television partakes of some of the aspects of speech and the communication of ideas as do the traditional enterprises of newspaper and book publishers, public speakers and pamphleteers. Respondent's proposed activities would seem to implicate First Amendment interests as do the activities of wireless broadcasters, which were found to fall within the ambit of the First Amendment in [*Red Lion*], even though the free speech aspects of the wireless broadcasters' claim were found to be outweighed by the government interests in regulating by reason of the scarcity of available frequencies.

Of course, the conclusion that respondent's factual allegations implicate protected speech does not end the inquiry. "Even protected speech is not equally permissible in all places and at all times." [ ] Moreover, where speech and conduct are joined in a single course of action, the First Amendment values must be balanced against competing societal interests. See, *e.g,* [*Vincent; O'Brien*]. We do not think, however, that it is desirable to express any more detailed views on the proper resolution of the First Amendment question raised by the respondent's complaint and the City's responses to it without a fuller development of the disputed issues in this case. We think that we may know more than we know now about how the constitutional issues should be resolved when we know more about the present uses of the public utility poles and rights-of-way and how respondent proposes to install and maintain its facilities on them.

. . .

We affirm the judgment of the Court of Appeals reversing the dismissal of respondent's complaint by the District Court, and remand the case to the District Court so that petitioners may file an answer and the material factual disputes between the parties may be resolved.

It is so ordered.

JUSTICE BLACKMUN, with whom JUSTICE MARSHALL and JUSTICE O'CONNOR join, concurring.

I join the Court's opinion on the understanding that it leaves open the question of the proper standard for judging First Amendment challenges to a municipality's restriction of access to cable facilities. Different communications media are treated differently for First Amendment purposes. [ ] In assessing First Amendment claims concerning cable access, the Court must determine whether the characteristics require a new analysis. As this case arises out of a motion to dismiss, we lack factual information about the nature of cable television. Recognizing these considerations, [ ], the Court does not attempt to choose or justify any particular standard. It simply concludes that, in challenging Los Angeles' policy of exclusivity in cable franchising, respondent alleges a cognizable First Amendment claim.

Notes and Questions

1. What relevant facts might be developed on remand—and how might they help clarify the legal issues?

2. Might some standard between the current newspaper standard and the current broadcasting standard be a useful resolution of the issue? If so, what should that standard be? In considering this question, look at the Cable Communications Policy Act of 1984. Which provisions, if any, should be declared unconstitutional?

3. *Preferred* had been expected to resolve a number of cases involving constitutional challenges to the cable franchising process. The Supreme Court's refusal to set a specific First Amendment standard for cable has meant that the lower courts have had to proceed with little guidance. The results have been inconsistent as can be seen from the cases in the following notes.

4. In Central Telecommunications, Inc. v. TCI Cablevision, Inc., 800 F.2d 711 (8th Cir.1986) the court held:

> [T]he evidence reveals that the City's cable television market is currently a natural monopoly which, under present technology, offers room for only one operator at a time. Thus, we hold that the City could properly offer a de facto exclusive franchise in order to create competition for its cable television market.

TCI had asserted a First Amendment defense to allegations that it had engaged in illegal monopolistic practices aimed at keeping exclusive control of the local cable market. In essence, TCI argued that exclusive franchises were unconstitutional and therefore Central Telecommunications had not been deprived of any protectable interest by TCI's conduct. The Supreme Court denied *certiorari*. 480 U.S. 910 (1987).

5. Similarly, a district court judge rejected Erie Telecommunications, Inc.'s First Amendment attack on the franchise-fee and access-channel provisions of its franchise agreement with the City of Erie. According to the judge, "In its effort to preserve an uninhibited marketplace of ideas, government is entrusted with protecting the First Amendment rights of cable television viewers." Erie Telecommunications, Inc. v. City of Erie, 659 F.Supp. 580, 62 R.R.2d 1467 (W.D.Pa.1987).

On appeal, the court never reached the First Amendment issue. As part of the franchise agreement, Erie Telecommunications had executed a Mutual Release and Covenant in which it had agreed to release the city from any and all claims related to the franchise agreement. The court held that this precluded the cable company's raising any challenges to the agreement. Erie Telecommunications, Inc. v. City of Erie, Pennsylvania, 853 F.2d 1084, 65 R.R.2d 1 (3d Cir.1988).

6. In Chicago Cable Communications v. Chicago Cable Commission, 879 F.2d 1540, 66 R.R.2d 1222 (7th Cir.1989), cert. denied 493 U.S. 1044 (1990), the Commission fined a group of three cable franchisees for failing to honor the local origination clause of the franchises. That

clause required 4 1/2 hours per week of local programming geared to Chicago. The violation was said to have occurred when the group presented local programming that had been prepared by a suburban affiliate even though the group said that it selected programs that it believed would be interesting to its Chicago customers.

Among other defenses, the group contended that the First Amendment prevented the content control inherent in the clause and its enforcement. The district court enforced the fine, and the court of appeals affirmed. The court adhered to an earlier cable decision in which it said that "there are enough differences between cable television and the non-television media to allow more government regulation of the former." In deciding to adopt the *O'Brien* analysis, p. 22, *supra,* the court said that it was not abandoning First Amendment scrutiny because of the natural monopoly characteristics of cable. "Rather, each medium of expression must be assessed by standards properly suited to it."

The court concluded that the government had met its burdens of establishing the elements of the *O'Brien* test. Promotion of "community self-expression can increase direct communications between residents by featuring topics of local concern. Encouragement of 'localism' certainly qualifies as an important or substantial interest." The court approvingly quoted the district court's statement that the "important qualities of localism (community pride, cultural diversity, *etc.*) may not be furthered enough simply by the availability of local broadcast television stations for retransmission over cable systems, but may require original cable programming specifically concerning the locality and directed at that locality's residents." An additional interest fostered by the requirement was providing jobs for residents: "Production of programming in the City provides career opportunities as well as potential internships for students studying communications at local schools." These were enough to satisfy *O'Brien* 's second prong.

As to the congruence between means and ends, the court relied on Supreme Court language to the effect that "so long as the neutral regulation promotes a substantial government interest that would be achieved less effectively absent the regulation," an incidental burden on speech is permissible. Here on the one hand was a requirement of only 4 1/2 hours per week with no requirement of any specific kind of programming. "As long as the particular episode is geared to Chicago—be it sports, politics, news, weather, entertainment, *etc.*—[the group] has full discretion over what it may desire to transmit. This restriction on [the group's] control in meeting the minimal [local origination] requirements does not divest it of discretion, for, as in *Midwest Video*, the cable operator here still retains the ultimate decision" over which programs to present.

On the other hand, cable "is an economically scarce medium. Unlike the traditional forms of print media, a cable programmer enjoys a virtual monopoly over its area, without the threat of an alternative provider. As a result the government, which serves as the representative of the cable customers, is duty-bound to recognize the effects of 'medium scarcity' by ensuring that the few programmers who are granted a franchise make optimum use of it. [ ] With this in mind, it is within the City's rights, arguably its responsibilities, to proffer some requirements guaranteeing that the cable customers are, to the extent possible, accorded a range of programming from the franchisee, since the cable viewing public has no other channel to which to turn."

7. However, in Century Federal, Inc. v. City of Palo Alto, California, 648 F.Supp. 1465, 61 R.R.2d 1348 (N.D.Cal.1986), the court ruled that a franchising process under which the cities of Palo Alto, Menlo Park and Atherton, intended to grant only one franchise was unconstitutional on its face. In reaching this conclusion, the court applied the test first set out in *O'Brien,* p. 22, *supra.* The test, which is used when the restriction on speech resulting from a regulation is incidental to the purpose of the regulation, has two parts: "If such regulations '[1] further an important or substantial governmental interest; . . . and [2] if the incidental restriction on alleged First Amendment freedoms is no greater than is essential to the furtherance of that interest,' [ ] (bracketed numbers added), then the regulations are valid."

The court found that four of the five "substantial" interests asserted by the cities to support its grant of a *de facto* exclusive franchise were based on the idea that cable is a natural monopoly. "Essentially, the Cities argue that if there is a reasonable probability that their service area will economically support only one CTV operator, then they should be able to choose, at the outset, that operator who will provide the highest quality service and use the offer of an exclusive franchise as a plum to bargain for certain concessions, e.g., access channels, that they might not be able to acquire if an operator knew that it would have to compete with other cable providers." The court found that rationale unacceptable as an asserted government interest under *O'Brien.* "The paternalistic role in the First Amendment that the Cities envision for government is simply inconsistent with the purpose and goals of the First Amendment."

The cities' final asserted interest, minimizing disruption of the public domain, was not found to be furthered by the franchising process. The court reasoned that if multiple cable systems were installed simultaneously, there would be no more disruption of the public domain than if a single system were installed.

The court took care to point out that it was not holding that cities "necessarily have to open their cable facilities to all comers regardless of size, shape, quality or qualifications." It was holding only that the cities had not offered evidence of a substantial government interest that justified granting a *de facto* exclusive franchise.

8. Later, in further proceedings in the same case, the court held also that the cities' access channel, universal service and state-of-the-art technology requirements were unconstitutional. Citing *Tornillo* and

Pacific Gas, the court found the access channels to be an impermissible intrusion into the editorial functions of the cable operator. Freedom of speech necessarily implies " 'a concomitant freedom *not* to speak public-ly, one which serves the same ultimate end as freedom of speech in its affirmative aspect.' [*Pacific Gas*]." Requiring service to an entire community as a prerequisite to serving any part of the community infringed that right not to speak.

Finally, turning to the cities' requirement for state-of-the-art tech-nology, the court applied the *O'Brien* test. The cities' assertion that the important government interest served by the regulation was pre-venting disruption of the public domain for system improvements was dismissed as overly speculative. Century Federal, Inc. v. City of Palo Alto, California, 63 R.R.2d 1736 (N.D.Cal.1984).

9. In still a third proceeding in the case, the court also struck down the franchise fee, performance bond requirement and security fund requirement mandated by the franchising process. The court empha-sized that other similar users of the public rights of way such as Pacific Bell and Pacific Gas and Electric were not subject to the same fees and requirements. Thus, under Minneapolis Star & Tribune Co. v. Minne-sota Commissioner of Revenue, 460 U.S. 575, 9 Med.L.Rptr. 1369 (1983) (a case involving a state tax on newsprint and ink used in publications of a certain circulation value), "the government had an unusually heavy burden of justification." The court found that the city had not met that burden. Century Federal, Inc. v. City of Palo Alto, California, 65 R.R.2d 875 (N.D.Cal.1988).

10. Similarly, in Group W Cable, Inc. v. Santa Cruz, 669 F.Supp. 954, 63 R.R.2d 1656 (N.D.Cal.1987), Group W successfully challenged Santa Cruz's refusal to renew its franchise. Applying *O'Brien,* the court held that the city's grant of an exclusive franchise to a competing company violated the First Amendment. Relying on *Miami Herald,* the court also struck down franchising provisions requiring public access chan-nels and state-of-the-art technology.

11. In 1990 in the *Preferred* remand, the district court ruled on a number of motions for summary judgment by both parties. In making the rulings the court divided the various franchise requirement into two categories: restrictions imposing an incidental burden on speech, which are subject to the *O'Brien* test, and restrictions "intended to curtail expression," which are subject to the highest level of judicial scrutiny. The court defined this to mean that the government had to show that the challenged regulation "is a precisely drawn means of serving a compelling state interest."

The court held that the limit of one cable operator in any franchise area was an incidental burden. Nevertheless, it was unconstitutional as a matter of law because the one operator requirement was too restrictive a method of achieving the city's substantial interests in minimizing disruption and visual blight.

A requirement of participation of local individuals and/or groups in the ownership and operation of the cable system was held non-incidental "as it, at the very least, indirectly bans speech by favoring speakers 'responsive to the needs of the South Central area residents' over others." The court then found the government's interest in localism compelling, and thus the requirement was held constitutional.

Mandatory public, educational and governmental ("PEG") access channels were also held a non-incidental burden on speech. The city asserted two compelling interests in access channels: "(1) to protect the First Amendment interests of various parties by promoting the avail-ability of diverse sources of information over a cable system; and (2) providing groups and individuals historically excluded from the elec-tronic media with access to the medium of cable communications."

Although these were held to be compelling interests, the require-ment was still found unconstitutional. The reason was that the city failed to explain why eight channels were necessary to achieve these interests.

The court also found unconstitutional the city's use of overall character as a factor in awarding a cable franchise. Because the character inquiry was not limited to past criminal or civil liability, but in fact included consideration of whether the applicant had ever "initi-ated litigation against a franchising authority or ha[d] a franchising authority instigated litigation against it," the court found the require-ment a non-incidental burden on speech. The requirement was not narrowly tailored to serve the city's asserted interest in protecting its citizens from fraud because it allowed the city to take into account whether the applicant had ever brought "legitimate challenges to franchise ordinances invoking first amendment rights."

The state-of-the-art-technology requirement was also found a non-incidental burden on speech after the city asserted as one of its purposes "promoting universal availability of educational opportuni-ties." The promotion of certain forms of speech over others, here educational speech, made the requirement non-incidental. Because the city failed to support its conclusion that this requirement would pro-mote its interests with empirical evidence, the court found that they were not compelling interests.

The court also found provisions allowing the city to purchase the franchise at below-market value and to require continued service after the expiration or revocation of the franchise unconstitutional under *O'Brien*. Again applying *O'Brien*, it upheld provisions prohibiting transfer of the franchise without the city's consent and requiring universal service. Finally, it struck down a five-year franchise term because the city failed to offer evidence why such a short franchise term was needed. Preferred Communications, Inc. v. City of Los Angeles, 67 R.R.2d 366 (CD Cal.1990).

12. A few months later, the court issued still another series of rulings on motions for summary judgment. Among the more important of

these were the following: The five percent franchise fee was held to be an incidental burden on speech. The court further held that the fee furthered the substantial government interest "in receiving compensation from private individuals who benefit from the commercial exploitation of that property" in a narrowly tailored fashion. Thus, under *O'Brien*, the fee requirement is constitutional.

However, the Court found the city's requirement of a $10,000 filing fee, a $500 good faith deposit and a $60,000 processing fee (this last fee to be paid only by the winning applicant) to be unconstitutional. The city had justified these fees as necessary to cover the costs of the franchising process. Because the fees were calculated to cover the original franchising process, some of which had subsequently been declared unconstitutional, the city was, in effect, requiring the applicants to pay for the expenses of an unconstitutional review process.

A requirement that the cable operator provide "public access production facilities, equipment and staff available for noncommercial programming purposes" was found unconstitutional because the city's answer and subsequent briefs did not address the allegations in Preferred's complaint regarding this issue even though the city had the burden of proving the requirement's constitutionality. More specific equipment requirements were struck down because the city's asserted interest was to further the development of PEG programs and the court had already found the PEG requirement unconstitutional, p. 467, *supra*.

Finally, a requirement that the cable franchisee create a cable advisory board, every aspect of which would be subject to the city's approval, was found unconstitutional. The city justified the board as a means of furthering localism. Finding that the board constituted a direct burden on speech, the court held that, to be constitutional, it had to be a precisely drawn means of furthering the compelling localism interests. Because there was nothing in the requirement limiting the board's role to advising the cable company on local interests, the requirement, in the court's opinion, was not precisely drawn and, thus, unconstitutional. Preferred Communications, Inc. v. City of Los Angeles, 68 R.R.2d 121 (CD Cal.1990).

13. One problem raised by holdings such as *Century Federal* is the effect on existing franchisees who have complied with access channel, universal service and state-of-the-art technology requirements in return for exclusive franchises. Suddenly, a second company is allowed to cable only the most lucrative sections of a city without the expense of access channels and state-of-the-art technology. Not only is the first company deprived of the exclusive franchise it bargained for, but the second company has a major competitive edge. In Sacramento, after a district court decision prohibiting an exclusive franchise, the city granted additional franchises, which do not contain universal service requirements. The original franchisee filed suit claiming that the grant of these additional franchises violated its franchise agreement. The case was settled out of court.

D. SIGNAL CARRIAGE RULES AND COPYRIGHT PROBLEMS

All of the major challenges to the Commission's jurisdiction over cable resulted from the Commission's various signal carriage rules. Each of these rules was designed to protect local broadcasting from cable competition.

1. LEAPFROGGING AND SUPERSTATIONS

One of the earliest restrictions, called the anti-leap-frogging rule, provided that when it was permissible to import distant signals, the system had to select from among those nearest to the city in which the system was operating. The FCC deleted this rule in 1976. One result was the emergence of the so-called "superstation"—an independent television station that makes its programs available to cable systems throughout the country, via satellite transmission.

The most famous superstation is Turner Broadcasting's Channel 17 in Atlanta, which has access to 200 live sporting events each year. By early 1993, the station was distributing its programs nationwide to more than 13,000 cable systems with more than 50 million subscribers. The satellite company charged the cable systems 10 cents per subscriber per month. The cable systems made the programs available as part of their basic monthly charge to attract subscribers.

Channel 17 has prospered by increased charges for advertising on its programs that are now reaching up to 30 million more viewers than previously. In addition, Turner began substituting national commercials for local commercials in the feed he sends Southern Satellite Systems, Inc., the company that distributes Channel 17 nationally. Thus, there are now two versions of Channel 17. One is broadcast in Atlanta; the other is distributed to cable systems throughout the country. Current estimates are that 40 percent of the local commercials are replaced. We will discuss the copyright implications of this practice later in this chapter. Program suppliers have increased charges to Channel 17 because the program is reaching a much larger audience than it did before, and cable distribution may result in reduced licensing fees or even preclude sales to local stations in cities receiving the cable program.

Other superstations followed, but they lag behind the Atlanta enterprise, which had a two-year head start. Some, using wires or microwaves instead of satellites, became regional stations.

2. COPYRIGHT PROBLEMS

One of the major factors influencing the Commission in its decisions governing signal carriage has been the application of copyright law to the retransmission of broadcast signals by cable operators. The question has always been whether or not cable operators should have to compensate either the broadcasters or the program producers for retransmission and, if so, how the compensation should be determined.

The issue first reached the Supreme Court in Fortnightly Corp. v. United Artists Television, Inc., 392 U.S. 390, 13 R.R.2d 2061 (1968). The case involved a West Virginia cable operator who was retransmitting the signals of five broadcast television stations. The stations were all located between 50 and 85 miles from the cable system. Fortnightly provided no other service.

United Artists, which owned the copyright to various shows that were aired over the five broadcast stations, claimed that the retransmission constituted infringement of its copyrights. The Court held that retransmission was not a "performance," and thus, there was no infringement. The Court was unable to find a real distinction between a viewer's antenna system and the cable company's equipment. Both were designed to improve reception of the broadcast signals.

When cable systems started using microwaves to import signals from around the country, there was some question whether this would change the copyright issue. The Supreme Court decided that the fact that there was no way a non-cable subscriber could receive these signals using existing technology did not make a difference. "When a television broadcaster transmits a program, it has made public for simultaneous viewing and hearing the contents of that program. The privilege of receiving the broadcast electronic signals and of converting them into the sights and sounds of the program inheres in all members of the public who have the means of doing so. The reception and rechanneling of these signals for simultaneous viewing is essentially a viewer function, irrespective of the distance between the broadcast station and the ultimate viewer." Teleprompter Corporation v. Columbia Broadcasting System, Inc., 415 U.S. 394, 29 R.R.2d 1011 (1974).

These copyright rulings greatly increased the importance to local broadcasters of the FCC signal carriage rules. The increased coverage afforded the imported signals was of minimal value to them, since their local advertisers had little or no interest in reaching consumers in other parts of the country. Meanwhile, the imported signals fragmented the local audiences, reducing the number of viewers they could offer to local advertisers.

There also was an apparent inequity in the system. Broadcasters had to pay royalties or license fees for much of their programming. Cable operators were paying nothing to distribute the exact same programming and were collecting a fee for doing so. The Copyright Act of 1976 attempted to remedy this seemingly unfair situation.

In the 1976 copyright statute, retransmission of broadcast signals by cable systems is defined as copyright infringement. However, the simultaneous retransmission, "secondary transmission," of broadcast signals is governed by a complex compulsory licensing scheme. Section 111 provides, in effect, that cablecasters need pay no royalties for programs on "local" (or "must-carry") stations that they were required to carry until September 1985. (We will discuss the must-carry rules later in this chapter.) Cablecasters are permitted to carry the copyrighted programs of "distant" (or "may-carry") stations without the owner's consent in return for the payment of a compulsory royalty fee. This fee is fixed by statute and depends on the size of the cable system and whether the distant station is commercial or educational.

The Act represented a compromise between the interests of broadcasters and cable operators. Although cable operators now had to pay for the right to retransmit broadcast programming, broadcasters were still unable to withhold the right to carry the programming.

Because of this inability to refuse transmission consent, certain stations found themselves unwilling superstations. As previously noted, the added audience resulting from the cable distribution is of little value to the broadcaster. The only way to benefit is to sell to national advertisers as opposed to local or regional advertisers. Meanwhile, there are several disadvantages to being a superstation, although Turner, for one, found them outweighed by the advantages. Program acquisition costs increase as a result of the increased audience. In addition, certain sports programming is unavailable because the importation of that programming into other areas of the country will violate agreements between the syndicator and the league or conference. For example, WTBS was unable to carry baseball playoff games involving the Atlanta Braves, even though the station that carries a team during the regular season is normally entitled to carry that team's playoff games. Importation of the games on WTBS into other markets would have conflicted with an agreement between the networks and professional baseball giving the networks exclusivity outside the markets of the teams participating in the playoffs.

A second controversy involves distribution of the royalties collected each year. Demands from the various claimants, such as program producers and syndicators, sports leagues, music groups, broadcast licensees themselves, and others, greatly exceed 100 percent. In September 1980 the Tribunal allocated the 1978 revenues, giving 75 percent to program producers and syndicators, and 3.25 percent to commercial television broadcasters. This means that total copyright payments to all commercial television for programs carried during 1978 by cable systems amounted to $476,000.

The enactment of the Copyright Act of 1976 was soon followed by a change in the Commission's attitude toward cable. In 1980 the FCC repealed the distant signal limitations and syndicated program exclusivity rule. We will discuss the syndicated exclusivity rule later in this chapter. The Commission argued that there was no real evidence that repeal of the rules would seriously harm broadcasters. Furthermore, the new copyright act now provided compensation for the retransmission of those programs. Finally, with regard to syndicated program exclusivity, the viewers' interest in "time-diversity"—seeing programs when they wanted—was more compelling than the local station's interest in the exclusive programming. Deletion of the old rule would not reduce the supply of programs for television. The deletion of the rules was upheld in Malrite T.V. of New York v. Federal Communications Commission, 652 F.2d 1140 (2d Cir.1981), certiorari denied 454 U.S. 1143 (1982).

As a result of the FCC's repeal of the distant signal rules, the Tribunal raised the rates cable operators had to pay for distant signals starting March 15, 1983. Large cable systems became liable for a compulsory license fee of 3.75 percent of their basic revenues for each distant signal added since June 24, 1981, the date on which the repeal of the distant signal rules became effective. This increase was upheld in National Cable Television Association, Inc. v. Copyright Royalty Tribunal, 724 F.2d 176, 55 R.R.2d 387 (D.C.Cir.1983). In response, some cable operators dropped distant signals to reduce their copyright liability. Superstations were the major casualties.

As a result of these changes, fee distribution has also become more complicated. There are now three funds at stake: the basic royalties, the 3.75 percent fund which contains the fees for distant signals added after June 24, 1981, and the syndex fund which contains a surcharge adopted as a result of the repeal of the syndicated program exclusivity rules.

The Copyright Royalty Tribunal issued a decision in 1987 on the distribution of about $100 million in 1984 cable television royalties. The NAB received 5 percent of the "basic" fund and the "3.75" fund, but only 0.7 percent of the "syndex" fund. The distribution of the 1985 funds was settled with the claimants receiving the same percentages as were awarded in 1984.

As a result of the FCC's adoption of new syndication exclusivity rules, p. 484, *infra*, the CRT drastically reduced the application of the syndex surcharge. Essentially, it applies only to retransmission of stations that were covered by the old rules but not the new ones. Broadcasting, July 23, 1990 at 80.

Broadcasters maintain that cable's contribution to the fund is tiny when compared with the fact that commercial television broadcasters spend some 35 percent of their budgets on program acquisition. Cable operators claim the current fees, after the recent rate hikes, are already prohibitive. Meanwhile, the FCC has asserted that any economic problem for the broadcasters derives from the Copyright Act or the Tribunal's allocation—and relief must come from those sources.

For years, the compulsory license and royalty provision has been under attack in Congress. The decisions in *Quincy Cable* and *Century Communications* (to be discussed later in this chapter) have only intensified the pressure. The problem is that the 1976 Act did not contemplate the changes in FCC rules that have permitted the growth of superstations and increased carriage of distant signals. The result is that an increasing amount of cable programming is coming from distant sources, leaving the program suppliers with less control over geographical distribution of their products. Complaints have also been heard from major sports leagues because, for example, an Atlanta baseball game may be shown on a Boston area cable system at the same time another game is being played in Boston. In 1985 the Atlanta Braves and New York Yankees agreed to pay the other major league teams a special annual fee based on the subscriber base of the superstations that carry their games. The other teams whose games are carried by superstations have followed suit.

The National Basketball Association tried a different approach to this problem by limiting to 20 the number of games allowed on a local signal received by more than five percent of the cable subscribers located outside the team's local market. Superstation WGN, which had already contracted to carry more than 20 games, successfully sued the NBA, claiming the rule was an unreasonable restraint of trade in violation of antitrust law. Chicago Professional Sports Limited Partnership and WGN Continental Broadcasting v. National Basketball Association, 961 F.2d 667 (7th Cir.1992), certiorari denied 113 S.Ct. 409 (1992).

Broadcasters have argued that the compulsory license should be abolished and replaced by a negotiated agreement between the cable system and the originating broadcaster (who, under contract, would need the consent of the copyright owner). This need not lead to individual negotiations—the matter could be handled the way song writers grant licenses and collect royalties, through such groups as ASCAP and BMI that grant bulk licenses for a fee and then distribute the proceeds according to a formula.

Further complicating the issue was a 1986 district court holding that the Copyright Office had incorrectly defined "gross receipts" in calculating the amounts paid by cable operators under the terms of the compulsory license. Cablevision Company v. MPAA, 641 F.Supp. 1154 (D.D.C.1986). According to the court, the Copyright Office's definition included money received for transmitting nonbroadcast signals, even though the only purpose of the compulsory license fee is to compensate copyright owners for the retransmission of distant broadcast signals. The effect of the decision would have been to reduce the total amount paid by cable operators by 40–50 percent.

On appeal, the decision was reversed. Acknowledging that § 111 of the Copyright Act is "not a model of clarity," the court found the Copyright Office's definition of gross receipts to be the most reasonable one. The court remanded the case for a determination of Cablevision's liability for copyright infringement. Cablevision Systems Development Co. v. Motion Picture Association of America, Inc., 836 F.2d 599, 64 R.R.2d 1031 (D.C.Cir.1988), certiorari denied, 487 U.S. 1235 (1988).

One of the requirements for coverage by the compulsory copyright license for secondary transmissions is that the signal be transmitted unaltered. In 1985 the court of appeals upheld a ruling that Ted Turner's practice of substituting national commercials for local ones, p. 469, *supra*, does not cause Southern Satellite Systems, Inc. (SSS) to forfeit the compulsory license. The court held that Turner's microwave feed to SSS, which already contains the national commercials, is a primary transmission. Because SSS transmits this signal unaltered, it is covered by the compulsory license. Hubbard Broadcasting, Inc. v. Southern Satellite Systems, Inc., 777 F.2d 393, 59 R.R.2d 392 (8th Cir.1985), certiorari denied 479 U.S. 1005 (1986).

3. THE ANTI-SIPHONING RULES

After an erratic early history, the Commission began to regulate pay systems' programs. The first major challenge of these regulations involved subscription television (STV). In defending the regulations, the Commission noted that they were the result of a two-year test in Hartford, Conn. The rules generally barred STV from showing any sports that were regularly carried on conventional television and also restricted showing of feature films that were more than three but less than 10 years old. Also, commercials were barred, and no more than 90 percent of the programming could be movies and sports. The Commission decided that although it had the authority to allocate scarce channels to a pay service, such a service would not be justifiable unless it presented programs that were not readily available on conventional television. A second concern was that revenues from subscription operations might be sufficient to permit pay systems to bid away the most popular programs on conventional television, thus reducing the quality of conventional programming. These regulations were upheld in National Ass'n of Theatre Owners v. Federal Communications Commission, 420 F.2d 194 (D.C.Cir.1969), certiorari denied 397 U.S. 922 (1970).

The next major development was the promulgation of similar restrictions for pay cable origination. These regulations, similar to those just mentioned for STV, were overturned in a lengthy opinion in Home Box Office, Inc. v. Federal Communications Commission, 567 F.2d 9 (D.C.Cir.), certiorari denied 434 U.S. 829 (1977). In the consolidated proceeding, involving 15 cases, the Commission's pay cable regulations, previously aimed at preventing cable from "siphoning" programs from "free" commercial television, were now said to be intended to prevent the "migration" of such programs from "free" television to cable.

The Court in *Home Box Office* found that the connection between the perceived threat to broadcasting and the anti-siphoning rules was insufficient to justify them under the "reasonably ancillary to broadcasting" standard. Therefore, they held the rules were beyond the Commission's jurisdiction.

Although the lack of jurisdiction alone would necessitate rejection of the Commission's action, the court decided to consider the merits of the rules.

Here the court found insufficient evidence to support the claim that pay cable would bar popular programs to the conventional audience. Rather, the court assumed that pay cable would sell these programs for use by conventional broadcasters. The court was more concerned about the problem of the poor because pay cable would demand exclusive rights—at least for first presentation. But the court concluded that it was not clear that the popularity of films declined "with an increase in the interval between first theater exhibition and first television broadcast." The conclusion was that as to movies, at least, migration would not hurt the poor "very much." Also, the court noted that the Commission's exclusion of advertising on pay cable hurt the poor because it prevented cablecasters from experimenting with a combined revenue system that allowed lower program fees together with some advertising. But all this was speculation; the record was silent and could not support these restrictions on cable.

Addressing the constitutional question, the court started by rejecting the contention that cable's First Amendment rights were governed by *Red Lion*, p. 71, *supra*. This left the question of what constituted permissible restrictions on cable. "The absence in cable television of the physical restraints of the electromagnetic spectrum does not, however, automatically lead to the conclusion that no regulation of cable television is valid."

The court drew a distinction between regulation aimed at suppression of free speech and regulation where the restriction on speech is incidental to the purpose of the regulation. Having done so the court applied the *O'Brien* test, p. 22, *supra*. This was the first case applying *O'Brien* to cable regulation.

Applying the test to the anti-siphoning rules, the court found them "grossly overbroad." For example, the rules restricted the exhibition on cable of many films that were clearly unsuitable for broadcast television. Furthermore, there was no real evidence that siphoning was a serious threat to broadcasting. "Where the First Amendment is concerned, creation of such a rebuttable presumption of siphoning without clear record support is simply impermissible."

4. MUST-CARRY RULES

One of the earliest signal carriage rules was a requirement that cable systems retransmit the signal of any local television station or "significantly viewed" station that requested carriage. Cable systems were allowed to request a waiver of the rule where it created hardship, but the process was a slow one, and few waivers were granted. The "must-carry" rules imposed a special hardship on the smaller systems as most of the channels could be occupied by must-carry channels. Due to overlapping signals, some systems were forced to carry several affiliates of the same network or similarly duplicative stations to the exclusion of other non-duplicative services.

As with the other rules, the purpose was to protect local broadcasters, especially UHF stations, whose picture quality was noticeably inferior to that provided by cable. There was also concern that people would remove their television antennas upon subscribing to cable, or at the least fail to maintain them, putting broadcasters not carried by the cable system at a great competitive disadvantage.

After the compulsory license scheme was enacted in the Copyright Act of 1976, many believed that it was a trade-off for the must-carry rules. Although the legislative history on this issue is inconclusive, many cable operators were reluctant to challenge the must-carry rules for fear of losing the compulsory license.

However, in 1980 Turner Broadcasting System petitioned the Commission to institute rulemaking proceedings to delete the must-carry rules. TBS argued that the rules violated the First Amendment rights of cable operators and furthermore, that, at the least, extensive changes in the broadcast and cable industries since the promulgation of the rules required a re-examination of the rules. The Commission denied the TBS petition.

Meanwhile, the FCC ordered Quincy Cable Television, Inc., operator of a cable system in Quincy, Wash., to carry the signals of various Spokane, Wash., television stations and fined it $5,000 for failing to do so. Quincy Cable's appeal of the order and the fine was consolidated with TBS's appeal resulting in what may be one of the most important decisions involving cable television.

In Quincy Cable TV, Inc. v. Federal Communications Commission, 768 F.2d 1434, 58 R.R.2d 977 (D.C.Cir.1985), the court concluded that the must-carry rules, as drafted, violated the First Amendment.

The court thought that the Commission's rules created "undifferentiated protectionism." The Commission had failed in its attempt to strike a balance between the competing interests of controlling a new technology that allegedly threatened long-established values, such as serving community needs through a locally-oriented press, and the regulatory throttling of the number and variety of outlets for free expression.

Under pressure from Congress, the Commission drafted a new set of must-carry rules. Must Carry Rules, 1 F.C.C.Rcd. 864, 61 R.R.2d 792 (1986). When a large number of petitions for reconsideration were filed, the Commission stayed the new rules. In 1987 some relatively minor changes in the new rules were announced. Must Carry Rules (Reconsideration), 2 F.C.C.Rcd. 3593, 62 R.R.2d 1251. A First Amendment challenge to the revised rules quickly followed.

CENTURY COMMUNICATIONS CORPORATION v. FEDERAL COMMUNICATIONS COMMISSION

United States Court of Appeals, District of Columbia Circuit, 1987.
835 F.2d 292, 64 R.R.2d 113, 14 Med.L.Rptr. 2049.
Certiorari denied 486 U.S. 1032, 108 S.Ct. 2015, 100 L.Ed.2d 602 (1988).

Before WALD, CHIEF JUDGE, MIKVA, CIRCUIT JUDGE, and McGOWAN, SENIOR CIRCUIT JUDGE.

WALD, CHIEF JUDGE:

Two years ago, in Quincy Cable TV, Inc. v. Federal Communications Commission, 768 F.2d 1434 (D.C.Cir.1985), cert. denied sub nom. National Association of Broadcasters v. Quincy Cable TV, Inc., 106 S.Ct. 2889 (1986), we struck down as violative of the first amendment the FCC's "must-carry" rules. . . . Today, we revisit this distinctive corner of first amendment jurisprudence, to evaluate the constitutional validity of the scaled-down must-carry rules adopted by the FCC following our decision in *Quincy Cable TV.* Although the FCC has eliminated the more extreme demands of its initial set of regulations, its arguments in this case leave us unconvinced that the new must-carry rules are necessary to advance any substantial governmental interest, so as to justify an incidental infringement of speech under the test set forth in United States v. O'Brien, 391 U.S. 367 (1968). Accordingly, we invalidate as incompatible with the first amendment this latest incarnation of the FCC's must-carry rules.

I.   Facts

. . .

In 1985, this circuit faced for the first time the question whether the broad must-carry rules which had been in existence for nearly two decades were in harmony with the first amendment. Judge Wright's opinion for a unanimous panel in *Quincy Cable TV* held that they were not. As a threshold matter, we observed that our first amendment review of regulations burdening cable television was not governed by those cases, such as [*Red Lion*] and [*League of Women Voters*], upholding regulations on broadcast television. In reaching that conclusion, we noted "the Supreme Court's oft-repeated suggestion that the First Amendment tolerates far more intrusive regulation of broadcasters than of other media precisely because of the inescapable physical limitations on the number of voices that can simultaneously be carried over the electromagnetic spectrum." [*Quincy Cable TV* at 1448]. Wire-carried media like cable, of course, have no such limitations, and thus we found that the "scarcity rationale" that the Supreme Court has used to justify broadcast television regulations to offer no succor to those seeking to establish the constitutional validity of cable television regulations. *Id.* at 1448–50.

Quincy Cable TV did not, however, establish the precise degree of first amendment protection enjoyed by cable operators. Although our opinion noted that some parallels existed between the must-carry regulations and regulations impinging on editorial discretion that had been invalidated in the past, [   ], it pointedly declined to "definitively decide" whether cable operators enjoy the heightened protection accruing to newspapers or whether the must-carry regulations were more appropriately evaluated under the test, set forth in [*O'Brien*]. Rather, we concluded that the must-carry rules would fail even the *O'Brien* test's requirement of a substantial governmental interest furthered by means no greater than are essential to the furtherance of that interest.

The reasons for our invalidation of the 1985 must-carry rules under the *O'Brien* test were twofold. First, we concluded that the Commission had not adequately substantiated its assertion that a substantial governmental interest existed. In *Quincy Cable TV* we stated that, even accepting the view that the preservation of free local television was an important regulatory goal, our review of the FCC's reports and regulations suggested that the problem the sweeping must-carry rules purported to prevent—the destruction of free, local television—was merely a "fanciful threat," unsubstantiated by the record or by two decades of experience with cable TV. [ ] In general, we noted, "the mere abstract assertion of a substantial governmental interest, standing alone, is insufficient to justify the subordination of First Amendment freedoms." [ ] Second, even if the interest had been deemed substantial, the broadly-drafted must-carry rules represented a fatally overinclusive response to the problem. We observed in this vein that the rules indiscriminately protected every local broadcaster, regardless of whether it was in fact threatened, and regardless of the quantity of local service available in the community and the degree to which the cable operator in question already carried local outlets. [ ] We did, however, note that our decision in no way foreclosed the Commission from adopting new must-carry rules consonant with the *O'Brien* test. [ ]

. . . [I]n November 1986, 16 months after *Quincy Cable TV* had been handed down, the agency released a new, more limited set of must-carry rules designed to accommodate *Quincy Cable TV*'s concerns. . . .

The most salient feature of the new rules was that the Commission substantially altered its stated justification for imposing must-carry rules at all. No longer did the Commission argue . . . that the rules were needed for the indefinite future to ensure viewer access to local broadcast stations. Rather, the Commission now argued that must-carry rules were needed to guarantee such access during a shorter-term transition period during which viewers could become accustomed to an existing and inexpensive but largely unknown piece of equipment known as the "input-selector device."

Such devices, if hooked up to a television, allow viewers at any given time to select, simply by flicking a switch, between shows offered by their cable system and broadcast television shows offered off-the-air. These devices, the most-common of which is known in the cable industry as an "A/B switch," are about the size of a standard light-switch, and work by being hooked up to a roof-top, attic or television-top antenna. . . .

The Commission estimated that it would take approximately five years for the public to become acclimated to the existence of these switches, and accordingly, its interim rules should be in place for that same five years. [ ] At that point, the need for ongoing must-carry rules to ensure viewer access to local broadcast stations would be obviated. . . .

Because the Commission envisioned these switches as guaranteeing effective viewer choice between local and cable shows, it ultimately added to the new must-carry regime the requirement that cable systems offer subscribers, for pay, input-selector devices that could be hooked up to their TVs. . . . The Commission, observing that relatively few consumers knew about the switch-and-antenna mechanism and noting that the long history of must-carry rules had created a public "misperception" that "broadcast signals will always be available as part of their basic cable service," [ ], also promised to require cable operators to educate the viewing public about the availability of the switch-and-antenna mechanism. [ ]

In addition to thus offering a new and more limited justification for must-carry rules, the Commission also substantially limited the sweep of the new rules in a number of respects. It set forth limits on how many channels a cable carrier must devote to must-carry: carriers with 20 channels or less were not required to carry any must-carry stations; carriers with between 21 and 26 stations could be required to carry up to 7 channels of must-carry stations; and carriers with 27 or more channels could be required to devote up to 25% of their system to must-carry signals. [ ] It also limited the pool of potential must-carry channels to those satisfying a "viewing standard" generally demonstrating a minimum viewership of the channel in question. . . . The Commission also authorized cable operators to refuse to carry more than one station affiliated with the same commercial network. [ ] Finally, the Commission limited the number of noncommercial stations required to be carried, stating that when the cable system had fewer than 54 channels and an eligible noncommercial station or translator existed, the cable operator must devote at least one channel to a noncommercial station; and that when the cable system had 54 or more stations, it must devote two must-carry channels to such endeavors. [ ]

. . .

II. Opinion

A. *The Appropriate Level of First Amendment Scrutiny*

A threshold question for our first amendment analysis is what standard of review to apply. . . .

. . .

The precise level of first amendment protection due a cable television operator is clearly an issue of much moment to the industry and ultimately to viewers. However, having closely analyzed the rationale for and workings of the new must-carry rules, we conclude that we again need not resolve this vexing question. Like the original must-carry regime invalidated in *Quincy Cable TV,* the new, scaled-back edition fails to satisfy even the less-demanding first amendment test of [*O'Brien*] whose use here is advocated by the FCC. . . .

B. *An* O'Brien–*Test Analysis of the New Regulations*

In [*O'Brien*], the Supreme Court stated:

[W]e think it clear that a government regulation is sufficiently justified if it is within the constitutional power of the Government; if it furthers an important or substantial government interest; if the governmental interest is unrelated to the suppression of free expression; and if the incidental restriction on alleged First Amendment freedoms is no greater than is essential to the furtherance of that interest.

[ ] Typically, analysis under [*O'Brien*] begins with an appraisal of whether the interest said to be served by a governmental measure is substantial. If it is, we proceed to the more delicate fact-bound issue of whether the means chosen are congruent with the desired end, or whether they are too broadly tailored to pass muster. [ ]

In this endeavor we are mindful of the fact that it is a first amendment test we are applying. Although at times an *O'Brien* inquiry into an agency regulation may appear to resemble an exercise in administrative law analysis, the Supreme Court has often noted that the substantial deference due in the administrative context has little relevance when first amendment freedoms are even incidentally at stake. [ ]

. . .

1. *The Substantiality of the Governmental Interest*

It may well be that upon a suitable record showing, the justification offered by the FCC, that interim regulations are needed to keep local broadcasts accessible to viewers while the new switch-and-antenna technology takes hold, would satisfy the *O'Brien* standard. [ ] The difficulty is that here, as in *Quincy Cable TV*, the FCC's judgment that transitional rules are needed is predicated not upon substantial evidence but rather upon several highly dubious assertions of the FCC, from which we conclude that the need for a new saga of must-carry rules is more speculative than real. [ ] Such speculative fears alone have never been held to justify trenching on first amendment liberties.

The agency's first questionable contention is that consumers are not now aware and cannot be expected to become aware in fewer than five years that the installation of an A/B switch could preserve their choice of programs: . . ..

The FCC, however, adduces scant evidence for its judgment of a widespread "misperception" among cable subscribers that the only means of access to off-the-air signals is through cable service. It puts forth no attitudinal surveys, or polls, suggesting the likely pace of consumer adaptation to the A/B switch technology. Nor does it offer analogies illustrating how swiftly consumers have incorporated previous electronic innovations. Such evidence might have shown what the FCC simply assumes here: that upon the disappearance of must-carry regulations, consumers would collectively fail to install with any dispatch the switches and antennas necessary to gain access to local broadcast stations, conceivably imperiling the survival of these stations and thereby depriving viewers of diverse broadcasting offerings.

. . .

Even were we to accept, however, the Commission's view that consumer ignorance cannot be readily eradicated, we have a second fundamental problem with the Commission's judgment that its interim must-carry rules are needed to advance a substantial governmental interest sufficient to support burdening cable operators' first amendment rights. The Commission relies heavily on its assumption that in the absence of must-carry rules, cable companies would drop local broadcasts. Experience belies that assertion. As cable operators reported to the Commission during rulemaking proceedings, [   ], during the 16 months that elapsed between *Quincy Cable TV* and the reimposition of the modified must-carry rules, cable companies generally did not drop the local broadcast signals that they had been carrying prior to *Quincy Cable TV.*

The FCC responds that this constitutes "only limited direct evidence," and that in any event some cable companies did drop individual broadcast stations, [   ]. One might also speculate on behalf of the FCC that the inaction of cable companies after *Quincy Cable TV* may have partially resulted from their expectation that some new must-carry rules would inevitably emerge. Nevertheless, given *Quincy Cable TV*'s vigorous denunciation of the breadth of the old must-carry rules, one can hardly assume that cable companies expected the FCC to reintroduce anything like the old sweeping must-carry requirements. Also undercutting the FCC's fearful assumption is the fact that both the Federal Trade Commission and the Department of Justice have concluded, in separate reports, that the absence of must-carry would not harm local broadcasting. [   ]

For these reasons, we conclude that the FCC has not demonstrated that the new must-carry rules further a substantial governmental interest, as the rules must to outweigh the incidental burden on first amendment interests conceded by all parties here. As we stated in *Quincy Cable TV,* "[a]t least in those instances in which both the existence of the problem and the beneficial effects of the agency's response to that problem are concededly susceptible of some empirical demonstration, the agency must do something more than merely posit the existence of the disease sought to be cured." [   ] The FCC error in this case was its failure to go that extra step here.

2. *The Congruence Between Means and Ends*

The second prong of the *O'Brien* test focuses on the congruence between the means chosen by the agency and the end it seeks to achieve. In this case, even were we convinced that the interest in whose name the FCC purports to act was more than a "fanciful threat," [ ], the new must-carry regulations, because of their lengthy duration, are too broad to pass muster even under the *O'Brien* test.

If any interim period of must-carry rules is, in fact, necessary, the FCC adduces literally no evidence that this period must last for fully five years. Such a period is strikingly long in an industry that the FCC itself characterizes as "rapidly evolving." [ ] In the absence of any empirical support for the new must-carry rules, the FCC falls back on what it terms a "sound predictive judgment," [ ], that it will take about five years for consumers to learn about the switch-and-antenna mechanism, and thus that a five-year transition period is needed during which the agency will provide consumer education.

We are, however, unpersuaded. In large part our reluctance to countenance reimposing must-carry rules for five years based on a "sound predictive judgment" that is never explained reflects our perceptions about consumer aptitude stated earlier. Such a guess about consumer instincts hardly presents the sort of issue where, "if complete factual support . . . for the Commission's judgment or prediction is not possible," we should defer to the Commission's expert judgment. [ ] It is wholly unclear to us why it should take five years to inform consumers that with the installation of a $7.50 switch and a television antenna they can view more local channels. The FCC report does nothing to shed light on this matter.

Additionally, we are skeptical—and the FCC's report says nothing to relieve this skepticism—that any consumer education campaign will have much impact so long as viewers can continue to rely on must-carry to get their fix of local broadcasts. It is entirely likely that not until the waning few months of the five-year must-carry regime would the FCC's admonitions about the need for switches and antennas begin to sink in, much as the existence of switches and antennas has largely gone unnoticed in a consumer population already accessed to local television as a result of must-carry in recent years. Opting for a five-year interim period therefore merely delays the inevitable, but almost certainly brief, period during which TV owners will learn of, purchase, and install the requisite equipment. We therefore find it difficult to defer blindly to the Commission's unproven belief that half a decade is necessary.

III. Conclusion

Our decision today is a narrow one. We hold simply that, in the absence of record evidence in support of its policy, the FCC's reimposition of must-carry rules on a five-year basis neither clearly furthers a substantial governmental interest nor is of brief enough duration to be considered narrowly tailored so as to satisfy the *O'Brien* test for incidental restrictions on speech. We do not suggest that must-carry rules are *per se* unconstitutional, and we certainly do not mean to intimate that the FCC may not regulate the cable industry so as to advance substantial governmental interests. But when trenching on first amendment interests, even incidentally, the government must be able to adduce either empirical support or at least sound reasoning on behalf of its measures. As in *Quincy Cable TV*, we reluctantly conclude that the FCC has not done so in this case, but instead has failed to " 'put itself in a position to know' " whether the problem that its regulations seek to solve " 'is a real or fanciful threat.' " *Quincy Cable TV*, [ ]. Accordingly, we have no choice but to strike down this latest embodiment of must-carry.

Notes and Questions

1. In both *Quincy Cable* and *Century Communications*, the court emphasized that it was not holding must-carry rules *per se* unconstitutional. What further changes in the rules could the Commission make that would allow them to pass constitutional muster?

2. One reaction of the Commission to the elimination of the must-carry rules has been a suggestion that Congress consider eliminating the compulsory license for cable retransmission. In conjunction with that suggestion, the Commission issued a Notice of Inquiry aimed at developing a record on the effects of the compulsory license. Compulsory Copyright License for Cable Retransmission, 2 F.C.C.Rcd. 2387 (1987).

In late 1988, the Commission voted to recommend to Congress that the compulsory copyright license for cable retransmission of broadcast signals be eliminated. Chairman Dennis Patrick and Patricia Diaz Dennis voted to recommend elimination for both local and distant signals, while James Quello dissented with regard to local signals. Recall that since early 1987, the Commission had been operating with only three members. Compulsory Copyright License for Cable Retransmission, 4 F.C.C.Rcd. 6711, 66 R.R.2d 1259 (1988).

3. The results of an FCC survey conducted at the request of Congress were released in 1988. Two hundred and eighty of the 912 TV stations that responded reported a total of 1,533 incidences of being dropped or denied carriage since the elimination of the must-carry rules. Meanwhile, 869 of the 4,303 cable systems responding reported 1,820 incidences. Shortly thereafter the National Cable Television Association (NCTA) released the results of its own survey. According to the survey, 98 percent of those stations that would have qualified for must-carry status under the rules struck down in *Century Communications* remained on cable systems. The survey also showed 94 percent of cable systems had not dropped stations or denied stations carriage. Broadcasting, Sept. 26, 1988 at 80.

5. EXCLUSIVITY

a. *Network Exclusivity*

To protect the local station when it was carrying network programs, the FCC promulgated exclusivity rules (formerly called non-duplication rules) to prevent cable from carrying an imported distant signal that was offering the same network program as the local network affiliate. First, the FCC required the cable system to black out the distant signal if the program was being broadcast on the same day as it was being presented by the local affiliate. Later, the FCC changed the rule to require black-out only if the two showings were at the same hour.

In the mid–1970s the Commission modified the black-out requirement, permitting cable systems to show the local station's signal (and its commercials) simultaneously on both the local channel and the channel that normally carries the distant signal, even though the local station might suffer if the local audience stays with the distant station after the program is over.

b. *Syndication Exclusivity*

Another regulation protecting local stations had provided that cable systems in large markets could not carry distant signals showing programs to which a local station had acquired exclusive future local rights. The obvious concern underlying the syndicated program exclusivity rule was that the increased availability of the program would fragment the audience for the show. As previously noted, p. 471, *supra*, this was repealed in 1980.

As an outgrowth of the must-carry proceedings, the Commission issued a combined NOI/NPRM proposing to reinstitute the syndicated exclusivity rule, expand the network exclusivity rule, and relax or delete the territorial exclusivity rule (one of the chain broadcasting rules discussed in Chapter V). Amendment of Parts 73 and 76 of the Commission's Rules Relating to Program Exclusivity in the Cable and Broadcast Industries, 2 F.C.C.Rcd. 2393 (1987):

> The public's *long-run* interests, we believe, will best be served by facilitating a competitive market that is not skewed in favor of any competitor. This, in turn, can only serve to encourage as full and diverse a supply of creative programming as the public is willing to pay for. Not only do the links between demand and production appear to be weakened, but the current regulatory scheme appears to put broadcasters at a disadvantage in competing with other media for product from which the programming producers can receive full value. Such a situation would be the antithesis of the fair competition on a level playing field that this Commission has attempted to provide in all of its industry regulation.

In 1988 the Commission announced new syndication exclusivity rules and expanded the network exclusivity rules. The new rules allow stations to enforce exclusivity contracts against cable systems retransmitting distant signals with duplicative programming. Syndicators may also enforce exclusivity in all markets for the first year after their initial sale to a television station. Contracts in existence prior to the imposition of the new rules cannot be used to enforce exclusivity unless there is explicit language covering the reimposition of syndication exclusivity. Program Exclusivity in the Cable and Broadcast Industries, 64 R.R.2d 1818 (1988).

In addition, stations are allowed to negotiate national exclusivity. This provision, which is particularly valuable for superstations, includes a blanket exemption from the territorial exclusivity rule. Thus, a superstation such as WTBS can obtain national rights to a syndicated program and preclude any other broadcast station in the country from carrying that program.

Cable systems with fewer than 1,000 subscribers are exempted from the new rules as are programs carried on stations generally available off the air.

Network exclusivity was also expanded. The old provision that limited protection to simultaneously aired duplicative network programming was eliminated. Network affiliates are allowed to demand protection against all duplicative network programming.

Various cable companies and satellite retransmitters appealed the new rules.

UNITED VIDEO, INC. v. FEDERAL COMMUNICATIONS COMMISSION

United States Court of Appeals, District of Columbia Circuit, 1989.
890 F.2d 1173, 66 R.R.2d 1865.

Before WALD, CHIEF JUDGE, and EDWARDS and SILBERMAN, CIRCUIT JUDGES.

WALD, CHIEF JUDGE:

A syndicated television program is a program marketed from its supplier to local television stations by means other than a television network. In 1988, the FCC reinstated its "syndicated exclusivity" rules. These rules allow the supplier of a syndicated program to agree with a broadcast television station that the station shall be the exclusive presenter of the program in its local broadcast area. A broadcast station with exclusive rights to a syndicated program can forbid any cable television station from importing the program into its local broadcast area from a distant station.

Petitioners, mostly cable television companies whose distant signal offerings will be restricted under the new rules, challenge the rules as arbitrary and capricious, and as violative of the Copyright Act of 1976, the Cable Act of 1984, and the First Amendment. We find that the Commission's action is within its authority and is not arbitrary and capricious. Accordingly we deny the petition for review.

I. BACKGROUND

This Court has had several opportunities to examine the checkered history of the regulation of cable television by the Federal Communications Commission. . . . *See e.g.,* [*Century Communications*]; [*Quincy Cable*]; [*Home Box Office*]. As a prelude to our analysis in this case, we review briefly highlights from the history of syndicated exclusivity regulation ("syndex").

The volatile relationship between cable and broadcast television has traditionally hinged on the ability of cable television stations to receive the signal that a broadcast station sends over the air, and to retransmit that signal to subscribers via a cable. This retransmission is not a "broadcast," for it is not a dissemination of radio communications intended to be received by the public. [ ] The Communications Act forbids a broadcast station from rebroadcasting another broadcast station's signal without permission, 47 USC § 325(a), but does not forbid cable retransmission.

Prior to the 1976 revision of the copyright laws, two Supreme Court decisions held that the distinction between broadcasting and cable transmission had important copyright law implications. [*Fortnightly*] held that when a cable company posted an antenna high on a hilltop, and ran a cable from the antenna into its subscribers' homes, it did nothing significantly different than an individual television owner does when she puts an antenna on her own roof, and runs a cable from it to her television inside. In particular, the cable company's retransmission was not a "performance" of the television program, and so did not violate the copyright on it. [*Teleprompter*] extended this reasoning to cases where the cable brought a program to a distant market. Accordingly, cable companies were free, as far as copyright law was concerned, to pick up signals aired by broadcasters and retransmit them throughout the country.

The distress felt by originating broadcasters whose signals were retransmitted in this way was matched only by the anger of local broadcasters in the receiving end communities, who watched the cable companies importing into their local markets the very programs that they were themselves showing, and to which they had purchased exclusive broadcast rights. [ ] Even before the *Fortnightly* decision validated this practice against copyright claims, the FCC decided that it was an unfair form of competition. Beginning in 1965, the Commission promulgated exclusivity rules that protected local broadcasters from the importation into their markets of distant signals that duplicated signals to which they had purchased exclusive rights. [ ] These rules provided nonduplication protection for both network and syndicated programs. In 1966, the Commission expanded the rules . . . and required all cable systems to notify the Commission before carrying any distant signal. [ ]

The Commission for some time attempted to review every importation of a distant signal into any of the top one hundred local television markets for consistency with "the establishment and healthy maintenance of television broadcast service in the area." [ ] This proved to be an administrative impossibility, however, and the Commission sought a more workable scheme. In 1972, the Commission adopted an industry "consensus agreement," that provided comprehensive regulation of the relationship between broadcast and cable television. [ ] The consensus agreement included syndex rules. [ ]

In 1976, Congress finally got around to addressing the question of the copyright liability of cable companies that carried distant signals. Congress provided, in the Copyright Revision Act of 1976, a compulsory licensing scheme whereby cable companies paid an administratively-set fee for such carriage. Subsequently, in 1980, the FCC decided that, given the new copyright regime, syndex protection was no longer in the public interest, although network exclusivity was retained. [ ] The Commission stated that the elimination of syndex would cause no significant harm to broadcast stations.

Broadcast stations petitioned the Commission for a reconsideration of its negative position on syndex in 1984, but the Commission refused to budge, saying that there had been no change in circumstances that would justify a change in its position. [ ] In 1987, however, the Commission began another review of its 1980 decision to eliminate syndex, and in 1988 it promulgated the rules challenged in this case. *In the Matter of Amendment of Parts 73 and 76 of the Commission's Rules Relating to Program Exclusivity in the Cable and Broadcast Industries,* 3 F.C.C.Rcd. 5299 [64 R.R.2d 1818] (1988), *on reh'g,* 4 F.C.C.Rcd. 2711 [66 R.R.2d 44] (1989) (rules codified at 47 C.F.R. §§ 73.-658, 76.92–76.97, 76.151–76.163). The Commission decided that its 1980 decision reflected an imperfect understanding of the role cable was to assume in the ensuing decade as a full competitor to broadcast television. The Commission found that with the enormous growth in cable's audience and advertising revenues, the lack of syndex was harming broadcast stations, and might have been significantly affecting the supply of syndicated programs. The Commission decided to reinstate syndex in view of the changes in the cable television industry that occurred between 1980 and 1988.

II. ARBITRARINESS AND CAPRICE

A. The Commission's Factual Findings

The Commission's decision to reinstate syndex rests on its finding that syndex rules will promote diversity in syndicated programming. In the report accompanying the rules, the Commission found that unrestricted importation of distant signals (*i.e.*, no syndex protection) leads to duplication of programming in local broadcasting areas; this duplication lessens the value of syndicated programs to broadcast stations; that loss of value in turn lowers the price syndicated program suppliers will receive for their programs; and all of this ultimately reduces the incentive for syndicated program suppliers to produce programs, which translates into a reduction in the diversity of programming available to the public. [ ] On the basis of this scenario the Commission concluded that syndex rules should be reinstated in order to promote diversity of programming.

The petitioners challenge the FCC's rule as arbitrary and capricious, for want of support in the rulemaking record. Our review on such a claim is narrow: the court must not substitute its judgment for that of the agency, but it must ensure that the agency has examined the relevant data and articulated a satisfactory explanation for its action, including a "rational connection between the facts found and the choice made." [ ] Since this action represents a change in agency policy, the court must also ensure that the agency supplied a "reasoned analysis indicating that its prior policies and standards are being deliberately changed, not casually ignored." [ ] We will examine each of the links in the Commission's alleged causal chain.

1. Duplication

The petitioners do not challenge the Commission's finding that unrestricted importation of distant signals leads to duplication of programming between broadcast and cable channels. . . .

2. Lessening of Value of Syndicated Programs to Local Broadcast Stations

The petitioners hotly contest the Commission's finding that program duplication lessens the value of syndicated programs purchased by local broadcast stations. However, the Commission's report cites substantial evidence from which it could reasonably draw this conclusion. The Commission discusses two related ways in which duplication lessens the value of syndicated programs: audience diversion and the loss of exclusivity as a competitive tool.

The Commission found that duplication of programming diverts a substantial portion of the broadcast audience to cable. The evidence was strongest regarding diversion caused by a cable station's *simultaneous* transmission of a program being aired by a broadcast channel, for such diversion can be gauged by ratings information. . . .

The Commission reasonably inferred that diversion lessened the value of the programming by lowering advertising revenues. The petitioners contest this finding, claiming it is based on a single study, which they attack as faulty. However, the report makes clear that the Commission relied on the study for only a rough approximation of the decrease in advertising revenue. More important was the hardly controversial conclusion that the amount that advertisers will pay depends on the size of the audience that a program attracts. [ ] This statement needs no detailed study to support it.

. . . .

The Commission's report does not specify quite so clearly how it reached the conclusion that *non-simultaneous* transmission of duplicative programming (including transmission of different episodes of the same program) also causes audience diversion. The one sentence explicitly devoted to this question in the report says that "the quantity of non-simultaneous duplication documented in the record in this proceeding, taken as a whole, presents compelling evidence that substantial diversion is taking place." [ ] This sentence suggests that the Commission has simply assumed diversion from the conceded fact of non-simultaneous duplication. The Commission points to no specific empirical support for this statement in the record.

While it is intuitively reasonable to assume that simultaneous duplication causes diversion, the question of non-simultaneous duplication seems more varied and complex. . . . If the Commission had relied solely on its assumption of audience diversion as evidence that non-simultaneous duplication lessens the value of programs to broadcast stations, we might well have felt obliged to require some supplementation or further explanation of its reasoning.

However, the Commission relies on more solid evidence that duplication makes programming less valuable. The evidence is that all stations, broadcast and cable, want exclusivity. . . . The reason, as the FCC notes in its report, is that exclusivity gives stations the opportunity to promote themselves as the only presenter of a certain program. If a broadcaster spends money promoting a duplicated program, some of the value of the expenditure will be captured by the cable company that is importing the same program. Syndex will give the local broadcaster a competitive tool that it can use both to call attention to the particular program and to "alert viewers to the general attractiveness of the broadcaster's whole range of programming." [ ] The strong desire of all stations for complete exclusivity is evidence that even non-simultaneous duplication lessens the value of programming, whether because of audience diversion or for other reasons.

While the Commission's report may leave something to be desired in its detail on the dangers of non-simultaneous duplication, we do not think its conclusion that even this type of duplication lessens the value of programming for broadcast stations can be called arbitrary or capricious. The record as a whole shows that both broadcast and cable companies want complete exclusivity; the Commission did not act without reason in concluding that exclusivity must be a valuable commodity, and conversely that lack of exclusivity diminishes the value of a program.

B. Effects on Program Supply

The weakest link in the FCC's causal chain is its claim that reinstating syndex will affect the supply of syndicated programming.

And indeed, throughout the rule making proceeding, the Commission has always conceded that there is no direct, empirical evidence that syndex will actually increase program diversity, explaining that such evidence would be particularly difficult to obtain empirically. [ ]

We do not think that the absence of empirical evidence is fatal to the Commission's claim. Courts reviewing an agency's selection of means to accomplish policy goals are "not entitled to insist on empirical data for every proposition on which the selection depends." [ ] In [*Century Communications*], which struck down the FCC's must-carry regulations, this Court noted that an agency contention may be "so obvious or commonsensical that it needs no empirical support to stand up." [ ]

We think the Commission's conclusion about the link between lack of program diversity and lowered broadcast revenues due to lack of exclusivity is sufficiently in accord with accepted economic theory that it can stand without empirical support, particularly since we agree with the Commission that it would be very difficult for it to show the degree to which programs are currently *not* being produced because of the lack of syndex protection. . . . [T]he FCC has assumed only that increasing the value of programs to broadcast companies will increase the amount paid for them, and that these higher prices will improve product supply. The Commission explains that "[p]rogram suppliers, like other business people, respond to incentives. . . . Incentives to develop new programs are greatest when program suppliers are able to sell their programs wherever there are viewers (or advertisers) willing to pay for them." [ ] These claims, unlike the ones made by the FCC in *Century Communications*, do not "beg[ ] incredulity," 835 F.2d at 302; rather they are reasonable.

. . .

Having tested each link in the Commission's causal chain, we find that it used valid reasoning to conclude that syndex rules will increase the diversity of programming options available to the public. Its imposition of syndex was adequately supported by the rulemaking record.

C. Change in Agency Course

The petitioners complain that the Commission has not adequately explained why it is reinstating syndex rules only eight years after abandoning them, and only four years after reaffirming its decision to abandon them. However, the Commission's report, which examines in great detail its 1980 decision to eliminate syndex, meets this circuit's standard that an agency changing course must "supply a reasoned analysis indicating that its prior policies and standards are being deliberately changed, not casually ignored." [*Action for Children's Television*]

The Commission's report reviews in detail the history of the regulation of cable, including, in particular, the 1980 decision to eliminate syndex rules. [ ] The report notes several ways in which the Commission now feels the 1980 decision to have been inadequate. First, the report discusses how circumstances have changed since 1980. The principal change has been the unforeseen emergence of cable television as a full competitor to broadcast television. As the report documents, cable's audience and advertising revenues have increased dramatically and unexpectedly since 1980. In 1980, cable served 19% of television households, but in 1988 it served 51%, a percentage the FCC projected would rise to 60% by 1996. [ ] In 1980, the Commission had predicted that cable penetration would never go beyond 48%. [ ] Cable advertising revenues were $45.5 million in 1980, but they grew to over $1 billion in 1980; cable's share of total television advertising revenue climbed from less than 0.5% to more than 6%. [ ] This unexpected growth, the Commission notes, substantially undermines its 1980 findings that repeal of syndex would not cause significant audience diversion or otherwise harm broadcast stations.

The Commission also faults its earlier studies for focusing on the effects repeal of syndex would have on individual stations, rather than its effects on the competitive process and the incentive for production of new programs. . . .

. . .

The Commission in its report also acknowledges that the absence of syndex provides consumers with the benefit of "time and episode diversity." A cable station, free of syndex restraints, may import a different episode of a program than the one aired by a broadcast station, or the same episode at a different time of day. The Commission suggests, however, that this diversity must be balanced against the lack of diversity engendered by duplication, and by the reduced incentive for the production of new programs. The Commission also suggests that market forces will allow duplication where viewers value it sufficiently, since stations with exclusive rights to a program can always sell the right to duplicate it. Finally, the Commission notes that the value of cable in providing time diversity has been lessened by the significant increase in the penetration of video cassette recorders (up from 1.5% of television households in 1979 to 58.1% today), since VCRs allow viewers to provide time diversity for themselves. [ ]

The Commission's report *in toto* suggests it undertook a thoroughgoing review of the syndex question and came to a new result with full awareness of its prior choices. . . . Accordingly, we reject the petitioners' claim that the Commission's rules are arbitrary and capricious.

III. THE COMMISSION'S AUTHORITY

[Petitioners also argued that the syndex rules were an attempt to impose copyright liability and as such preempted by the Copyright Act of 1976. The court rejected this argument relying on both the text and legislative history of the Copyright Act as well as the fact that the previous syndex rules were in effect when the 1976 Act was passed.]

B.   The Cable Act

The Cable Communications Policy Act of 1984 amended the Communications Act to explicitly grant the FCC a power it had previously only inferred from its general authority to regulate television: the power to regulate cable television. [ ] However, the Act also set some limits on that power, and in particular it provided:

(1) Any Federal agency, State, or franchising authority may not impose requirements regarding the provision or content of cable television services, except as expressly provided in this subchapter.

. . .

47 U.S.C. § 544(f). The petitioners claim that this section forbids syndex rules.

The Commission argues that the legislative history of Section 544(f) shows that the term "requirements," as used in the section, refers only to *affirmative* requirements, that is, to rules that a cable station *must* carry a certain program or channel or type of program or channel, and does not prohibit negative requirements, that is, rules prohibiting cable stations from carrying certain signals. . . .

. . .

However, having consulted the legislative history, we cannot agree with the Commission's contention that, as used in Section 544(f), the word "requirements" was meant to distinguish between affirmative and negative obligations. Some "negative" rules would probably fall under Section 544(f)'s bar. For instance, a local franchising authority's attempt to *prohibit* the carriage of HBO would likely implicate the same Congressional concerns as an attempt to *require* carriage of HBO. We therefore think Section 544(f) would bar such a prohibition.

On the other hand, not every "affirmative" regulation implicates Section 544(f). Suppose, for instance, a cable company bidding for a local franchise indicated that it was planning to provide service on only Mondays, Tuesdays, and Wednesdays. If the local franchising authority decided that it would award the franchise only to a cable company that agreed to provide service seven days a week, it would not be, in the words of the House report, "dictat[ing] the specific programming to be provided over a cable system" even though the regulation would be affirmative in nature.

In short, we think that the affirmative/negative distinction suggested by the Commission fails to capture what Congress meant by the term "requirements" in Section 544(f). Rather, the examples given in the House report suggest that the key is whether a regulation is content-based or content-neutral. Section 544(f), one must note, does not simply forbid "requirements"; it forbids "requirements regarding the *provision* or *content* of cable services" (emphasis added). The House report suggests that Congress thought a cable company's owners, not government officials, should decide what sorts of programming the company would provide. But it does not suggest a concern with regulations of cable not based on the content of cable programming, and do not require that particular programs or types of programs be provided. Such regulations are not requirements "regarding the provision or content" of cable services.

Syndex is clearly different from a requirement or prohibition of the carriage of a particular program or channel. Although it will certainly affect the content of cable programming, it is content-neutral. . . .

We do not mean to suggest that the concept of content neutrality, as developed in First Amendment cases, can be freely imported into all cases construing the Communications Act. In this case, however, the history reviewed above explicitly shows that Congress's concern in enacting Section 544(f) was with content-based rules. We think it plain that Congress did not intend Section 544(f) to forbid syndex. . . .

. . .

C. The First Amendment

The petitioners argue that syndex rules, like the must-carry rules that this Court struck down in [*Century Communications*], cannot survive even the relaxed First Amendment scrutiny of [*O'Brien*]. However, the Commission was correct to find that the rules are not subject to such scrutiny.

The petitioners repeatedly claim that syndex restrains the expression of fully protected speech which has been paid for and authorized under the compulsory licensing scheme of Section 111 of the Copyright Act. [ ] The fact is, however, that because of the provisions of Section 111, cable companies will *not* be able to obtain a compulsory license to transmit a program if transmission would violate the syndex rules. As explained above, Congress deliberately chose to withhold a compulsory license from those transmissions that the FCC decides to prohibit for reasons of communications policy. The petitioners are therefore in the position of claiming that they have a First Amendment right to express themselves using the copyrighted materials of others.

. . .

In the present case, the petitioners desire to make commercial use of the copyrighted works of others. There is no First Amendment right to do so. Although there is some tension between the Constitution's copyright clause and the First Amendment, the familiar idea/expression dichotomy of copyright law, under which ideas are free but their particular expression can be copyrighted, has always been held to give adequate protection to free expression. [ ]

. . .

IV. CONCLUSION

"While the deregulation of the cable television industry raises serious policy questions, . . . these questions are best left to the agencies that were created, in large part, to resolve them." [*Malrite*] The Commission has considered anew the question of how to balance the rights of broadcast and cable television companies so as best to serve the public interest in receiving diverse programming. Congress decided that this question should be resolved by the agency, and on the record before us we uphold its resolution.

The petition for review is denied.

6. *Access Channel Requirements*

The elimination of the Commission's access channel requirements in *Midwest Video II,* p. 445, *supra,* did not eliminate mandatory access channels. Filling the vacuum were state and municipal requirements. Most cities demanded access channels and studios as a prerequisite for obtaining a cable franchise. Often these demands were more extensive than the FCC's had been.

In the Cable Communications Policy Act of 1984, Congress provided express authorization for access channel requirements. Section 611 states that access channels for public, educational and governmental use ("PEG channels") can be required as part of a franchise proposal or a proposal for renewal. 47 U.S.C.A. § 531. Furthermore, a federal requirement to set aside some channels for commercial use by persons unaffiliated with the operator is imposed on all systems with 36 or more activated channels. The number of channels that must be set aside varies according to the size of the system. 47 U.S.C.A. § 532.

The Court in *Midwest Video II* chose not to address the question of whether mandatory access channels violate the First Amendment. Recall, however, from our discussion of franchising that since then several district courts have addressed this question with inconsistent results. As with other questions involving cable and the First Amendment, the primary problem is determining the appropriate First Amendment standard.

The conflict over access channels has another side—produced by the requirement that the cable operator not censor any access material. More than 1,200 of the nation's 8,000 systems offer some form of public access, and an estimated 40,000 hours of public access programming is produced each week. In cities in which access channels exist, they may be opposed by citizens who are offended by what is presented. Some examples from two channels fully devoted to public access in Austin, Texas, are reported in Schwartz, Austin Gets an Eyeful: Sacrilege and the Klan, Channels, Mar./Apr. 1985, at 42–43:(a) in front of a crucifix "a man in a Charles Manson mask dances and chants incoherently about sex and religion;" (b) a Ku Klux Klan leader interviews a man who had been imprisoned for fire-bombing school buses during Detroit's busing controversy; and (c) a Halloween program in which a slimy monster comes out of a nearby lake and kills everything in its path. Some groups wanted to end access, particularly because of the Klan programs.

Apparently, indecency is rarely a problem on the public access channels. "Shows containing nudity are usually more expensive to film and are often shown on other channels, known as leased-access channels, where time is sold for a fee of about $100 a half-hour and commercials are allowed." N.Y. Times, April 13, 1987, at 19. The regulation of indecency is discussed later in this chapter.

Operators of the public access channels are permitted to schedule programs. The Austin channels, for example, extended their hours. One result was that the group that put the Manson program on was moved from 10:30 p.m. to 1 a.m. In San Francisco, the operators scheduled a Klan program for 3:30 p.m. on Tuesdays and sandwiched it between programs produced by Chinese for Affirmative Action, the Anti–Defamation League, and Jewish Community Relations. San Francisco Chronicle, Dec. 29, 1986, at A6.

Apart from the suits by cable operators seeking to be free of the access requirement, suits are beginning to come from the other direction. In Kansas City, Mo., the Klan failed to get on the access channel. The city had insisted that the franchisee provide an access channel. When the Klan requested access, the operator refused because the show was not locally produced. The Missouri Klan then offered to provide a program featuring interviews with local advocates of white supremacy. The operator agreed to air the show. Before the Klan members could be trained in using the equipment and producing the show, the city council passed legislation converting the channel to a community programming channel under operator control. The operator offered the Klan a guest appearance on a hosted half-hour talk show. The Klan rejected the offer because it had no control over the program. The operator refused to permit the Klan to air its own program.

The ACLU brought suit. One claim was that the city council's action was intended "to suppress the 'racialist' viewpoint" of the Klan. A second argument was that the city, by granting only one cable franchise, has incurred a constitutional obligation to require the operator to provide an access channel. In 1989, the city council reinstated the access channel, and the case was dropped.

E. CONTENT REGULATION

Because of the early view that cable television was merely an enhancement of broadcast television, many of the same restrictions on content that were developed for broadcasting are applicable to cable. At the same time there are very few cases involving these restrictions.

1. POLITICAL SPEECH

Many of the political access rules have also been applied to origination cablecasting. The equal opportunities provision applicable to cable is essentially identical to that which governs broadcasting. There is also an equivalent lowest-unit-rate provision. 47 C.F.R. § 76.205.

The Commission has also adopted regulations applying the fairness doctrine, including the personal attack and political editorial rules, to origination cablecasting. 47 C.F.R. § 76.209. In 1983 the Commission instituted proceedings aimed at eliminating the fairness doctrine for cable. As of the end of 1992, no action had been taken in these proceedings.

One political access provision that is not applicable to cable is the reasonable access requirement of § 312(a)(7). In its 1991 political access NPRM, p. 251, *supra*, the FCC proposed extending that requirement to cable. In its final order, however, the Commission concluded that Congress never intended § 312(a)(7) to apply to cable.

Because the cable operators are not responsible under these rules for secondary transmissions or mandated access channels, and because many of the premium cable channels do not carry any political programming, there have been no real tests of the application of the rules. Also contributing to the lack of cases is the limited size of the audience for many cable programs.

2. NONPOLITICAL SPEECH

Among the restrictions on nonpolitical speech are a prohibition on cablecasting lottery information and a requirement for sponsorship identification. These provisions mirror the broadcasting rules. Also, the ban on cigarette advertising applies to cable.

However, most of the controversy surrounding restrictions on cable programming has involved attempts to ban indecent programs or nudity. The following case is typical of cases involving such restrictions.

CRUZ v. FERRE

United States Court of Appeals, Eleventh Circuit, 1985.
755 F.2d 1415, 57 R.R.2d 1452.

Before HATCHETT and CLARK, CIRCUIT JUDGES, and STAFFORD, CHIEF DISTRICT JUDGE, Northern District of Florida.

STAFFORD, DISTRICT JUDGE. This cause involves a challenge to the constitutionality of a Miami ordinance regulating the distribution of obscene and indecent material through cable television. . . .

. . .

. . . The relevant portions of this ordinance provide:

"Section 1. No person shall by means of a cable television system knowingly distribute by wire or cable any obscene or indecent material.

"Section 2. The following words have the following meanings:

. . .

"(f) The test of whether or not material is 'obscene' is (i) whether the average person, applying contemporary community standards, would find that the work, taken as a whole, appeals to the prurient interest; (ii) whether the work depicts or describes, in a patently offensive way, sexual conduct specifically defined by the applicable state law; and (iii) whether the work, taken as a whole, lacks serious literary, artistic, political or scientific value.

"(g) 'Indecent material' means material which is a representation or description of a human sexual or excretory organ or function which the average person, applying contemporary community standards, would find to be patently offensive."

. . .

First Amendment

The United States Supreme Court has long recognized that the First Amendment's prohibition against any "law . . . abridging the freedom of speech" applies to the states and their subdivisions through the Fourteenth Amendment. Gitlow v. New York, 268 U.S. 652 (1925). The Court has recognized only limited categories of speech that fall outside of the First Amendment's protection. . . . In Miller v. California, 413 U.S. 15 (1973), the Court reaffirmed that obscene material is unprotected by the First Amendment and set forth the current permissible limits of regulation. However, the Miller court "acknowledge[d] . . . the inherent dangers of undertaking to regulate any form of expression. State statutes designed to regulate obscene materials must be carefully limited." Id. at 23–24.

Appellees did not challenge the Miami ordinance's definition of "obscene" material or the city's constitutional authority to regulate obscenity on cable television. (The ordinance's definition of obscenity is in fact closely derived from the test set forth in *Miller.)* Rather, appellees challenged the provisions of the ordinance which attempt to regulate "indecent" materials. The ordinance's definition of indecent materials goes beyond the *Miller* definition of obscenity in two significant respects. First the ordinance does not require that the challenged materials, "taken as a whole, appeal to the prurient interest in sex." [ ] Second, the ordinance does not inquire whether the materials, "taken as a whole, do not have serious literary, artistic, political, or scientific value." [ ] Therefore, if materials falling within the ordinance's definition of "indecent" are to be regulated, the city's authority to do so must be found somewhere other than in the Supreme Court's obscenity cases.

Appellant's primary argument on appeal is that authority for the city's regulation is found in the Supreme Court decision FCC v. Pacifica Foundation, 438 U.S. 726 (1978). . . . Five members of the Court concluded that broadcasting of indecency could be regulated by the FCC under certain circumstances. The Court noted that "of all forms of communication, it is broadcasting that has received the most limited First Amendment protection." Id. at 748. The Court found two factors regarding broadcasting to be of particular relevance to the case with which it was presented. First, the Court found relevance in the fact that "the broadcast media have established a uniquely pervasive presence in the lives of all Americans" and that "[p]atently offensive, indecent material presented over the airwaves confronts the citizen, not only in public, but also in the privacy of the home, where the individual's right to be left alone plainly outweighs the First Amendment rights of an intruder." Id. Second, the Court found that "broadcasting is uniquely accessible to children, even those too young to read." Id. at 749. The Court was concerned with "[t]he ease with which children may obtain access to broadcast material," and also recognized "the government's interest in the 'well-being of its youth' and in supporting 'parents' claim to authority in their own household'. . . ." Id. at 749–50 (quoting Ginsberg v. New York, 390 U.S. 629, 639–640 (1968)).

The *Pacifica* Court, however, made a point of "emphasiz[ing] the narrowness of our holding." 438 U.S. at 750. The Court suggested that factors such as the time of day of the broadcast, the content of the program, and the composition of the audience might affect whether a particular broadcast could be regulated. Id. Moreover, the Court wrote that "differences between radio, television, and perhaps closed-circuit transmissions, may also be relevant." Id.

The district court after "a careful consideration of *Pacifica,*" found *Pacifica* to be "inapplicable to the facts herein." [ ] After describing the cable television medium, the district court contrasted the cable medium with broadcast television. A cablevision subscriber must make the affirmative decision to bring Cablevision into his home. By using the monthly program guides, the Cablevision subscriber may avoid the unpleasant surprises that sometimes occur in broadcast programming. Additionally, the district court noted, the ability to protect children is provided through the use of a free "lockbox" or "parental key" available from Cablevision. [ ]

. . .

Although we recognize the complicated and uncertain area of constitutional interpretation which we are entering and the importance of the interests asserted by the city, we are persuaded that *Pacifica* cannot be extended to cover the particular facts of this case. *Pacifica,* it must be remembered, focused upon broadcasting's "pervasive presence," [ ]. The Court's concern with the pervasiveness of the broadcast media can best be seen in its description of broadcasted material as an "intruder" into the privacy of the home. Cablevision, however, does not "intrude" into the home. The Cablevision subscriber must affirmatively elect to have cable service come into his home. Additionally, the subscriber must make the additional affirmative decision whether to purchase any "extra" programming services, such as HBO. The subscriber must make a monthly decision whether to continue to subscribe to cable, and if dissatisfied with the cable service, he may cancel his subscription. The Supreme Court's reference to "a nuisance rationale," id. at 750, is not applicable to the Cablevision system, where there is no possibility that a non-cable subscriber will be confronted with materials carried only on cable. One of the keys to the very existence of cable television is the fact that cable programming is available only to those who have the cable attached to their television sets.[6]

Probably, the more important justification recognized in *Pacifica* for the FCC's authority to regulate the broadcasting of indecent materials was the accessibility of broadcasting to children. "The ease with which children may obtain access to broadcast material . . . justif[ies] special treatment of indecent broadcasting." Id. at 750. This interest, however, is significantly weaker in the context of cable television because parental manageability of cable television greatly exceeds the ability to manage the broadcast media. Again, parents must decide whether to allow Cablevision into the home. Parents decide whether to select supplementary programming services such as HBO. These services publish programming guides which identify programs containing "vulgarity," "nudity," and "violence." Additionally, parents may obtain a "lockbox" or "parental key" device enabling parents to prevent children from gaining access to "objectionable" channels of programming. Cablevision provides these without charge to subscribers.

Pacifica represents a careful balancing of the First Amendment rights of broadcasters and willing adult listeners against the FCC's interests in protecting children and unwilling adults. The Court held that, under the particular facts of *Pacifica*, the balance weighed in favor of the FCC. Because we determine that, under the facts of the instant case the interests of the City of Miami are substantially less strong than those of the FCC in *Pacifica*, we believe that we must hold *Pacifica* to be inapplicable to this case.

   . . .

Even if we were to find the rationale of *Pacifica* applicable to this case, we would still be compelled to strike the ordinance as facially overbroad. As the district judge noted, the ordinance "prohibits far too broadly the transmission of indecent materials through cable television. The ordinance's prohibition is wholesale, without regard to the time of day or other variables indispensable to the decision in *Pacifica*." [ ] The ordinance totally fails to account for the variables identified in *Pacifica*: the time of day; the context of the program in which the material appears; the composition of the viewing audience. In ignor-

---

6. Appellants seem to want to extend Justice Stevens' "pig in the parlor" analogy. See Brief of Appellants at 16 ("it makes no difference whether the pig enters the parlor through the door of broadcast, cable, or amplified speech: government is entitled to keep the pig out of the parlor"). It seems to us, however, that if an individual voluntarily opens his door and allows a pig into his parlor, he is in less of a position to squeal.

ing these variables, the ordinance goes far beyond the realm of permissible regulation envisioned by the *Pacifica* Court.

However noble may have been the city's intentions, we are constrained to recognize the limitations imposed by the Constitution and the opinions of the Supreme Court. The city's attempt through the challenged ordinance to regulate indecency on its cable television system exceeds these limitations.

[The court also upheld the district court's determination that the enforcement provisions of the ordinance violated due process. These provisions authorized the city manager to initiate complaints, conduct hearings on complaints, determine the admissibility of evidence and make findings based on the hearing and impose sanctions. "[C]oncentrating the functions of complainant, jury, judge and 'executioner' in one person" created a "risk of arbitrary or capricious governmental action [which] under these circumstances is intolerably high."]

For the reasons stated herein, we hold that the findings of the district court were correct as a matter of law. Accordingly, we affirm.

Notes and Questions

1. What is the difference between buying a television set, certainly a prerequisite to bringing broadcast service into the home, and subscribing to cable? What if basic cable service is provided free of charge? Would a statute banning nudity on basic cable then be subject to the *Pacifica* rationale?

2. A similar Utah statute was struck down on similar grounds. Community Television of Utah, Inc. v. Wilkinson, 611 F.Supp. 1099, 11 Med.L.Rptr. 2217 (D.Utah 1985). The Cable Television Programming Decency Act authorized the filing of nuisance actions against anyone who continuously and knowingly distributed indecent material over cable television. Material was defined as indecent if it was "presented in a patently offensive way for the time, place and manner, and context in which the material is presented." The court held that the statute was unconstitutionally vague and overbroad.

The decision was upheld on appeal. The court adopted the lower court's reasoning without adding any of its own. One judge specially concurred to indicate that he felt *Pacifica* should be the standard used in evaluating cable indecency statutes. However, he found the Utah Cable Television Programming Decency Act unconstitutionally vague and overbroad under even the more relaxed *Pacifica* standard. Jones v. Wilkinson, 800 F.2d 989, 61 R.R.2d 1, 13 Med.L.Rptr. 1913 (10th Cir.1986). The Supreme Court summarily affirmed without opinion. 480 U.S. 926 (1987).

3. The Cable Communications Policy Act provides that anyone who "transmits over any cable system any matter which is obscene or otherwise unprotected by the Constitution of the United States shall be fined not more than $10,000 or imprisoned not more than two years." 47 U.S.C.A. § 559. Could someone be prosecuted for indecent program-

ming under this statute? As a result of this provision, the Commission eliminated its regulation banning obscene or indecent cable programming. Cable Communications Act Rules, 58 R.R.2d 1 (1985).

4. The Act also provides that cable operators must, upon request, sell or lease lock-out devices to subscribers. 47 U.S.C.A. § 544(2)(a).

F.　THE CABLE TELEVISION CONSUMER PROTECTION AND COMPETITION ACT OF 1992

On October 5, 1992 Congress overrode President Bush's veto and enacted the Cable Television Consumer Protection and Competition Act of 1992. The 1992 Cable Act requires the FCC to conduct numerous rulemaking proceedings by October 5, 1993. In addition, as this book goes to press, several lawsuits challenging the constitutionality of various provisions of the 1992 Act are pending. Thus, at this time it is difficult to predict the exact form that cable regulation will take. The following is a brief discussion of the more important provisions of the 1992 Act. Subsequent developments will be covered in the annual supplements to this casebook.

Renewals. Franchisees are now required to submit specific written notices to invoke renewal proceedings. Franchising authorities must commence renewal proceedings within six months of receiving this written notice. Submission of a renewal notice does not preclude a franchise authority from revoking a franchise for cause during the renewal process. 47 U.S.C.A. § 546.

Transfers. The Act prohibits transfers of cable systems within 36 months of acquisition or initial construction. The Commission is permitted to waive this requirement "in the cases of default, foreclosure, or other financial distress." 47 U.S.C.A. § 537. Note the similarity between this provision and the FCC's original antitrafficking rules governing broadcast license transfers, p. 140, *supra.*

Government Immunity. The Act limits law suits against franchising authorities or other governmental bodies arising out of the regulation of cable service to injunctive or declaratory relief. Essentially this provision protects franchising authorities and other governmental bodies from any liability for monetary damages. 47 U.S.C.A. § 555.

Concentration Rules. The Act prohibits cable operators from holding multichannel multipoint distribution service (MMDS) licenses or offering satellite master antenna television (SMATV) service in any portion of a franchise area served by that cable operator. This provision does not apply to MMDS and SMATV services owned by the cable operator on October 5, 1992. We will discuss MMDS and SMATV in Chapter X.

Also, by October 5, 1993, the FCC is to have conducted a rulemaking proceeding establishing reasonable limits on the number of subscribers a cable operator is authorized to reach and on the number of channels that can be occupied by a program supplier in which the cable operator has an attributable interest. In the same proceeding the FCC must also consider the "necessity and appropriateness of imposing limitations on the degree to which multichannel video programming distributors may engage in the creation or production of video programming." 47 U.S.C.A. § 533(f)(1).

Must Carry. The 1992 Act has two separate must-carry provisions. § 614 sets out the must-carry rules for commercial television stations, while § 615 sets out the must-carry rules for noncommercial television stations. Under § 614 cable systems with 300 or fewer subscribers are exempt. Other cable systems with 12 or fewer channels must carry a minimum of three local broadcast signals. Systems with more than 12 channels must carry all local broadcast stations up to a maximum of one third of the total number of the system's channels. If the number of local commercial television stations exceeds the maximum number of must-carry signals, the cable operator is permitted to choose which stations will be carried subject to the following restrictions. First, no low power station can be carried unless all local commercial stations are carried. Second, if a cable operator chooses to carry a broadcast network affiliate, the operator must carry the affiliate of that network that is closest to the principal headend of the cable system.

Notwithstanding these requirements, systems are not required to carry local commercial television stations that substantially duplicate the programming of another local commercial television station carried by the system. Also, cable systems are not required to carry local commercial television stations whose programming is predominately sales presentations or program length commercials.

Section 614 requires the Commission to issue regulations implementing these new must-carry rules by April 5, 1993. In addition, by July 2, 1993, the Commission must complete a proceeding to determine whether stations whose programming is predominately sales presentations or program length commercials are serving the public interest, convenience and necessity. If the Commission determines that one or more of such stations do serve the public interest, convenience and necessity, the Commission must designate such stations as local commercial stations for must-carry purposes. Those stations found not to serve the public interest, convenience and necessity will be given a reasonable period of time to change their programming, and will not be denied renewal expectancy solely because of the Commission's determination regarding their programming. 47 U.S.C.A. § 534.

Section 615 sets out the carriage requirements for qualified noncommercial educational television stations. Cable systems with 12 or fewer channels must carry one local noncommercial educational television station. Stations with 13 to 36 channels must carry all local noncommercial educational television stations up to a maximum of three. Systems with more than 36 channels must carry all local noncommercial educational television stations. In the event that there are no local noncommercial educational television stations, a cable system must import one noncommercial educational television station.

These must-carry requirements do not apply to any station whose signal is considered a distant signal for copyright purposes unless the station pays any increase in copyright costs attributable to the carriage of that station. 47 U.S.C.A. § 535.

Retransmission Consent. The Act creates a new alternative to must carry that permits a commercial television station to waive its must-carry right in return for the right to require the station's consent before a cable system can carry its signal. In essence this requires each station to determine the value of its signal to nearby cable systems. The assumption is that the more attractive stations will choose retransmission consent in order to force cable systems to pay for the right to carry them. Lower-rated stations will be likely to opt for must carry. This section requires the FCC to issue regulations establishing the procedure for making this choice by April 5, 1993. Stations will have until October 5, 1993, to make its initial choice between must carry and retransmission consent. Every three years thereafter stations will have the right to change their status. 47 U.S.C.A. § 325.

Channel Positioning. Every station carried under the provisions of § 614, must be carried on either the channel number on which the station is broadcast, "the channel on which it was carried on July 19, 1985, or on the channel on which it was carried on January 1, 1992, at the election of the station." Stations can be carried on other channels only with their consent. The Commission has been given the authority to resolve any channel positioning disputes. 47 U.S.C.A. § 534.

Rate Regulation. Recall that prior to the 1992 Act, only a small percentage of cable systems were subject to rate regulation and even then the only rates regulated were those for basic cable service. The 1992 makes several major changes in the area of rate regulation. As was the case prior to the 1992 Act, rate regulation is precluded for cable systems subject to effective competition, p. 455, *supra*. However, the 1992 Act sets out the following requirements for effective competition. Either "fewer than 30 percent of the households in the franchise area subscribe to the cable service of a cable system," or the franchise area must be served by at least two "unaffiliated multichannel video programmers" offering comparable video programming to at least half of the households in that area and at least 15 percent of the households in the franchise area must subscribe to programming services offered by "multichannel video programming distributors other than the largest multichannel video programming distributors," or at least 50 percent of the households in the area must be served by a multichannel video programming distributor operated by the franchising authority for that area.

By April 5, 1993, the Commission must issue regulations that will ensure in those franchise areas where there is not effective competition reasonable rates for basic cable service. The goal of these regulations is to protect subscribers of cable systems that are not subject to effective competition from rates for basic service that exceed the rates that would be charged if there was effective competition. The actual rate regulation will be done by the franchising authority. A franchise authority that regulates rates in a manner inconsistent with the Commission's regulation will have its jurisdiction revoked. In that case, the Commission will regulate rates for basic cable service for that franchise area.

The 1992 Act also establishes limitations on rates for other cable program services. Previously these were not subject to any regulation. The Commission must now issue regulations regarding unreasonable rates by April 5, 1993. These regulations must set out criteria for identifying unreasonable rates, procedures for receiving, considering and resolving complaints, and procedures for reducing rates found to be unreasonable.

In addition, the Act places severe restrictions on the practice of tiering, p. 441, *supra*. Cable systems must offer a separate basic service, subscription to which is required for access to any other programming tier. At a minimum this tier must include all must-carry stations, any PEG channels required by the franchise agreement, and any other television station carried by the cable system except for stations retransmitted by a "satellite carrier beyond the local service area of such station." Requiring subscribers to subscribe to any channel or tier other than the basic tier as a prerequisite to purchasing video programming offered on a per channel or per programming basis is prohibited. Systems that cannot comply with this provision due to technological limitations are exempted until the technological limitation is eliminated as a result of equipment upgrades. This exemption expires 10 years after the enactment of the 1992 Cable Act. 47 U.S.C.A. § 543.

Indecency. The Act permits cable operators to "enforce prospectively a written and published policy of prohibiting programming that the cable operator reasonably believes describes or depicts sexual or excretory activities or organs in a patently offensive manner as measured by contemporary community standards." By February 2, 1993, the Commission is to have promulgated regulations requiring cable operators to place all indecent programming intended for carriage on leased access channels on a single leased access channel. These regulations must also require cable operators to block this channel absent a written request for access from the subscriber. Furthermore, under these regulations, cable programmers will be required to identify indecent programming to cable operators. Finally, by April 5, 1993, the FCC is to have promulgated regulations enabling cable operators to prohibit obscene or sexually explicit material on PEG channels. 47 U.S.C.A. § 532.

Access channels. The Act gives the FCC authority to establish "maximum reasonable rates" that a cable operator can charge for leased access channels. By April 5, 1993, the Commission is to have established rules for determining maximum reasonable rates for leased access channels. 47 U.S.C.A. § 532. In addition, the Act gives cable operators the right to use up to one third of any leased access channels required under § 612 (47 U.S.C.A. § 532) of the Communications Act for "the provision of programming from a qualified minority programming source or from any qualified educational programming source." The Act defines qualified minority programming source as "a programming source which devotes substantially all of its programming to coverage of minority viewpoints, or to programming directed at members of minority groups, and which is over 50 percent minority-owned." A qualified educational programming source is defined as "a programming source which devotes substantially all of its programming to educational or instructional programming that promotes public understanding of mathematics, the sciences, the humanities, and the arts and has a documented annual expenditure on programming exceeding $15,000,000." 47 U.S.C.A. § 532(i).

Customer Service Standards. One of the most common complaints about cable television has been in the area of customer service. The 1992 Act gives franchising authorities the right to establish and enforce customer service requirements. Furthermore, by April 5, 1993, the FCC is to have established standards for customer service requirements. These standards must include: "(1) cable system office hours and telephone availability; (2) installations, outages, and service calls; and (3) communications between the cable operator and the subscriber (including standards governing bills and refunds)." 47 U.S.C.A. § 552.

Technical Standards. By October 5, 1993, the "Commission shall prescribe regulations which establish minimum technical standards relating to cable systems' technical operation and signal quality." Franchising authorities that wish to impose more stringent standards than the Commissions are authorized to apply to the Commission for a waiver. 47 U.S.C.A. § 544(e).

Equipment Compatibility. Many cable systems use scrambling or encryption systems and devices such as converter boxes and remote control devices that effectively disable advanced features built into television receivers and videocassette recorders. For example, when a cable system uses a converter box to decode some or all channels, channel selection must be made through the converter. Whatever channel is selected will be delivered to the television and/or VCR on a single specified channel (usually either channel three or four). Because the channel selection uses the converter's tuner as opposed to the television or VCR's tuner, features that utilize those tuners are rendered unusable. Among these are the ability to watch one channel while recording another or to record two consecutive programs that appear on different channels.

The 1992 Act requires the Commission to submit to Congress by October 5, 1993 a report on "means of assuring compatibility between televisions and video cassette recorders and cable systems, consistent with the need to prevent theft of cable service." Within 180 days of the submission of this report, the FCC must promulgate whatever regulations are necessary to assure such compatibility. 47 U.S.C.A. § 544A.

Chapter X

NEW COMMUNICATIONS TECHNOLOGIES

As we discussed in Chapter IX, at one time cable was seen as the ultimate communications technology. At the height of the franchising battles, operators were promising that cable would provide everything to everybody. Not only were those promises unfulfilled, but cable is no longer even the "new" technology. A proliferation of new delivery systems such as multi-point distribution service (MDS), direct broadcast satellites (DBS) and satellite master antenna television (SMATV) are fighting for their share of the communications marketplace.

As each of these services has developed, new regulatory questions have arisen. The FCC does not have complete freedom in developing regulatory frameworks for new technologies. Rather, the Commission must work within the context of the Communications Act. Originally, the Act provided two basic models for regulation. One is the "broadcast" model we studied in Chapters II–VIII. The second is the "common-carrier" model to be discussed below. If a communications technology does not fit either of these models, the authority of the Commission to regulate it is questionable. This was a major issue in the regulation of cable. In *Midwest Video I*, p. 445, *supra*, the Commission's jurisdiction over cable was upheld as being ancillary to its jurisdiction over broadcasting. However, the exact limits of this jurisdiction were never clear, a problem that was apparently solved by the Cable Communications Policy Act of 1984.

Common carriers are regulated under Title II of the Communications Act. The key element of common carrier regulation is that the "content is separated from the conduit." In other words, unlike broadcasters, common carriers have no editorial discretion. Instead, they must provide, in a non-discriminatory manner, the facilities for transmission of the customer's message. National Association of Regulatory Utility Commissioners v. Federal Communications Commission (NARUC I), 525 F.2d 630 (D.C.Cir.), certiorari denied 425 U.S. 992 (1976). Telephone and telegraph companies are examples of common carriers.

There are a number of other important distinctions between broadcasters and common carriers. The federal government has preempted state regulation of broadcasting. In contrast, common carriers are regulated on both the state and federal levels. Interstate service is regulated by the Federal Communications Commission, while intrastate service is regulated by state agencies.

Sometimes, however, the Commission will decide to preempt the states and regulate a service on a strictly federal basis. When the

Commission decides to preempt state regulation, it does not necessarily imply that the Commission will choose to regulate to the same extent. Instead, the FCC may choose to "preempt and forbear." This means that the Commission will eliminate the state regulations without substituting any of its own because the Commission believes as a matter of policy that no regulation is the proper regulation for that area.

The regulations most commonly subject to preemption are entry requirements and rate regulation. When a common carrier wishes to provide a service, it is usually required to demonstrate a need for the service. Some states require that, in addition to showing need, an applicant demonstrate that current carriers are either unable to or unwilling to provide the additional needed service. These requirements can effectively bar any new entrants into a given type of service.

Because common carriers often enjoy either a natural or government-created monopoly, they are often subject to rate regulation by either the FCC or appropriate state agencies. Rate regulation is usually eliminated when there is a finding of sufficient effective competition in the services provided.

Traditionally, the Commission has assigned services to the two regulatory models based on the method of transmission. Thus, STV is under the broadcast model while until recently Multipoint Distribution Service (MDS) was a common carrier, because STV is transmitted through the broadcast portion of the spectrum, but MDS utilizes the microwave portion, which has always been viewed as a point-to-point medium. This led to seemingly anomalous results. For example, STV operators leasing their facilities to a movie service would be subject to different regulations than MDS operators leasing their facilities to the same movie service. In fact, a third regulatory scheme would obtain when the same movie service was carried over cable. Although many of these anomalies still exist, the Commission has started to take a new approach, imposing regulations based on the service provided as opposed to the method of transmission. In some cases, for example MDS, the Commission is now leaving the initial choice of regulatory model up to the licensee. In other words, licensees can decide for themselves which regulatory model would be most appropriate for the type of service they wish to offer.

Still another major concern for the Commission is that it not favor one service or technology over another. This attempt at regulatory neutrality has come to be called the "level playing field." As we will see, a level playing field can be very difficult to create. Nevertheless, it is an important issue as most of the regulatory battles involving new communications technologies are grounded firmly in economics. Although the rhetoric may concentrate on the public interest or even the First Amendment, the real issue in almost every case is which service will gain some competitive advantage.

Obviously, the flood of new communications technologies has presented the FCC with serious problems as it tries to fit them into the traditional regulatory models. Let us now turn to some of these new communication technologies and examine how the Commission has attempted to resolve these problems.

A. MULTIPOINT DISTRIBUTION SERVICE (MDS)

MDS transmits microwave signals over super-high frequencies within a range of about 25 miles. The signal is received by a small microwave antenna, usually located on a rooftop. The signal can then be converted to a broadcast frequency and shown on a vacant VHF channel. Originally, MDS was intended to be used to transmit data. However, some operators found that a more profitable use was distribution of video programming to hotels and other multi-unit buildings. As the cost of converters and antenna systems dropped it even became feasible to distribute programming to single-family dwellings. In some urban areas in which cable is not available, MDS has been distributing HBO programming.

In an early decision, the Commission preempted state and local regulation that serves to hinder the development of MDS. Orth–O–Vision, Inc., 69 F.C.C.2d 657, 44 R.R.2d 329 (1978), recon., 82 F.C.C.2d 178, 48 R.R.2d 503 (1980), affirmed sub nom. New York State Commission on Cable Television v. Federal Communications Commission, 669 F.2d 58, 50 R.R.2d 1201 (2d Cir.1982). In essence, the case preempted state and local government attempts to impose entry restrictions.

In 1983 the FCC reallocated eight of the 28 instructional television fixed service (ITFS) microwave channels to MDS, making multichannel multipoint distribution service (MMDS) available. ITFS (MDS Reallocation), 54 R.R.2d 107 (1983). MMDS operators may also obtain extra channel capacity by leasing an ITFS operator's excess capacity.

The Commission decided to use a lottery system to award licenses for the ITFS channels reallocated to MDS. In 1985 the Court of Appeals for the District of Columbia Circuit ordered the FCC either to postpone the MDS lottery scheduled for that time until rulemaking on women's preferences was completed or to protect women applicants until the rulemaking was completed. The Commission postponed the lottery. The next month the Commission voted to give women no preference in MDS lotteries and rescheduled the lottery. The Commission's decision was affirmed in *Pappas*, p. 110, *supra*.

For many years MDS was regulated as a common carrier because, as we previously discussed, it was viewed by the Commission as a point-to-point service. Finally, in 1987 the Commission changed its regulations to permit MDS operators to choose the regulatory model to be used for them based on the service provided. 47 C.F.R. § 21.900–.908. The reason for the change was the Commission's recognition that MDS was often being used to deliver broadcast-type services. This was especially true of MMDS.

Initially, there had been some ownership restrictions on MMDS, the most important of which was that a single operator could not acquire a license for more than four of the eight MDS channels in a market. (Remember that an operator could still exceed four channels by leasing other channels from ITFS operators.) The purpose of this restriction was to promote competition between MMDS operators. However, recently, the Commission concluded that competition from other multichannel service providers such as cable was so strong that for even a single MMDS operator to survive in a given market it was necessary that the operator have access to as many channels as possible. Therefore, the Commission voted to eliminate the ownership restrictions. Wireless Cable Service, 68 R.R.2d 429 (1990).

As a result of the FCC's action, the maximum number of channels that an MMDS system can transmit was increased to 24. However, MMDS systems may soon be able to transmit 100 channels by utilizing the new video compression technology, p. 59, *supra.*

B. DIRECT BROADCAST SATELLITES (DBS)

DBS is a system of broadcasting directly from studio to home via satellite. The technology involves the usual transmission to a satellite and the return to earth, where the signal is collected by a receiving dish two or three feet in diameter placed on the roof of the home of the subscriber.

The first communications satellites were not suitable for DBS because their relatively weak signals could only be received by very large, expensive dishes. By the late 1970s, however, the technology had improved to the point where a commercial DBS system appeared feasible. It was now possible to build higher-powered satellites, which would allow the use of small, inexpensive dishes for home reception.

At the 1979 World Administrative Radio Conference (WARC–79) the 12 GHz band was allocated to DBS. Decisions on specific orbital locations and frequency assignments were left for the 1983 Regional Administrative Radio Conference (RARC–83). In the interim the Commission opened proceedings on domestic DBS service. As a result of those proceedings, the Commission decided to adopt interim DBS regulations pending the outcome of RARC–83. These interim DBS regulations authorizing domestic DBS service were adopted in July 1982. Three months later the Commission granted Satellite Television Corporation's (STC) application to construct an experimental DBS system offering subscription television service to the Eastern portion of the United States. Both the Interim DBS Regulations and the grant of STC's application were appealed.

NATIONAL ASSOCIATION OF BROADCASTERS v.
FEDERAL COMMUNICATIONS COMMISSION

United States Court of Appeals, District of Columbia Circuit, 1984.
740 F.2d 1190, 56 R.R.2d 1105.

Before TAMM, MIKVA and DAVIS, CIRCUIT JUDGES.

MIKVA, CIRCUIT JUDGE:

Of the technological innovations currently revolutionizing the communications field, the most recent, and potentially the most significant, is direct broadcast satellite service (DBS). DBS involves the transmission of signals from the earth to highpowered, geostationary satellites which then beam television signals directly to individual homes equipped to receive them. Use of satellites massively extends the range of a broadcast's voice by freeing it from the atmospheric limitations that traditionally limit terrestrial broadcasters to narrow broadcast areas; a single DBS signal will eventually be capable of reaching the entire continental United States. For this reason and others, DBS promises several significant advantages over existing television technology: high-quality service to individuals in rural or remote areas where conventional broadcasting is inefficient; the addition of many more channels even in urban areas already receiving several television signals; "narrowcasting" of programs to specialized tastes through the ability to aggregate small, widely dispersed audiences; the development of higher quality visual and audio signals through use of high-definition-television signals; and television transmission of non-entertainment programming, such as medical data and educational information.

The regulatory approach to DBS taken by the Federal Communications Commission . . . is as novel as the technology with which it is concerned. In essence, the Commission has chosen to deregulate DBS even before the service is born. . . . We find that, on the whole, the FCC has done a commendable job in assuring that regulation in the communications field not impede new technologies that offer substantial public benefits. . . . We also find, however, that in its zeal to promote this new technology, the FCC gave short shrift to certain of its statutory obligations, and we therefore vacate part of the Interim DBS regulations; in addition, our approval of other parts is qualified by several guidelines to which the Commission must hew in its continuing oversight of this nascent technology.

. . .

Analysis

I. *The FCC's Power to Approve Non–local Broadcast Service*

DBS technology is inherently unsuitable for the provision of traditional local broadcast service. The satellites involved cannot presently be located with the requisite precision nor economically equipped with a sufficiently large antenna to provide a spot beam capable of covering only a traditional size local community. [ ] Moreover, many of the benefits of DBS—including narrowcasting and provision of service to less densely populated areas—could not practically be realized by a "local" DBS system. . . .

Petitioner NAB argues that the FCC does not have the power to approve a technology that will sever broadcast services from their traditional link to a particular community. NAB seeks to rest this Luddite argument on section 307(b) of the [Communications Act], which provides:

> the Commission shall make such *distribution of licenses*. . . *among the several States and communities* as to provide a fair, efficient, and equitable distribution of radio service to each of the same.

47 U.S.C. § 307(b) (emphasis added). NAB reads this provision to require that broadcast licenses indeed *be* "distributed" among the "States" and "communities;" NAB thus concludes that the Act mandates a system of *local* broadcast licensing and service with which STC's authorization, and DBS in general, is "fundamentally irreconcilable."

We do not think it necessary to ascribe to the framers of the Act an intent so shortsighted as to preclude new technology that offers the promise of substantial public benefit. The plain language of the Act does not compel such impracticable consequences. . . . The ultimate touchstone for the FCC is . . . the distribution of service, rather than of licenses or of stations; the constituency to be served is people, not municipalities. Moreover, the Commission also has an obligation to "encourage the larger and more effective use of radio in the public interest." 47 U.S.C. § 303(g). . . . Just as we have held that the Act does not bestow a vested right on any particular *licensee* to retention of its license, [ ], so too we now hold that the Act does not entrench any particular *system* of broadcasting: existing systems, like existing licensees, have no entitlement that permits them to deflect competitive pressure from innovative and effective technology.

In so holding we do not denigrate the importance of local programming to a national broadcasting system that is designed to serve the public interest. [ ] We need not define the outer limits of the Commission's authority to make this country's broadcasting system a regional or national one, however, for two reasons. First, the *DBS Order* does not by its terms eliminate local programming. Second, the Commission explicitly found that DBS will merely supplement the existing local broadcast system, rather than replace it, [ ], and we find no error in that finding. We therefore need not decide how far the Commission may go toward the elimination of local programming to hold that not *every* communications service approved by the Commission need be tied to a local community.

. . .

II. *Applicability to DBS of Broadcast Restrictions*

The most innovative of the steps taken by the FCC with respect to DBS was the Commission's decision, in the service of a "flexible regulatory approach" designed to stimulate DBS technology, not to apply to DBS the major regulatory restrictions traditionally imposed on broadcasters. Central to this approach was the Commission's refusal to extend the broadcast restrictions of Title III of the [Communications Act] to all DBS systems.

. . .

Among the statutory restraints that broadcasters currently face are section 312(a)(7), which requires that qualified candidates for federal office be provided reasonable access to broadcast facilities, and section 315, which provides that, if one political candidate is allowed to use a station, other qualified candidates must be given an equal opportunity to respond. Because DBS is likely to be a particularly attractive medium at least for presidential candidates, the question of how these broadcast restraints apply to DBS is of great moment.

The *DBS Order* established the following classificatory scheme for purposes of applying the Act's broadcasting rules. Those DBS applicants which propose to provide service (whether in the form of free or pay-TV) direct to homes and to "retain [ ] control over the content of the transmissions" will be treated as broadcasters. A DBS satellite owner can choose instead to operate as a common carrier, in which case satellite transmission services would have to be offered indiscriminately to the public pursuant to tariff under the provisions of Title II of the Act; a satellite owner who chooses the common carrier option will not be treated as a broadcaster. Also not treated as a broadcaster under the *DBS Order* are those who lease satellite space from a DBS common carrier and who use the leased channels to distribute programming via satellite to individual homes. These lessees, who neither own nor operate a DBS satellite, are referred to as "customer-programmers" of DBS common carriers, and it is they who control the content of the programming transmitted by a DBS common carrier.

. . .

We recognize the Commission's authority to approve services on an experimental basis in an effort to gather important market data to be used in the completion of a regulatory framework. [ ] Moreover, as other parts of this opinion will confirm, that discretion is particularly capacious when the Commission is dealing with new technologies unforeseen at the time the Communications Act was passed. But that discretion is not boundless: the Commission has no authority to experiment with its statutory obligations. We conclude that the Commission has engaged in precisely such forbidden statutory experimentation in exempting from Title III the customer-programmers of DBS common carriers.

Section 3(*o*) of the Communications Act defines "broadcasting" as "the dissemination of radio communications intended to be received by the public, directly or by the intermediary of relay stations." 47 U.S.C. § 153(*o*). We have previously held that the test for whether a particular activity constitutes broadcasting is whether there is "an intent for *public* distribution" and whether the programming is "of interest to the *general* . . . audience." . . .

When DBS systems transmit signals directly to homes with the intent that those signals be received by the public, such transmissions rather clearly fit the definition of broadcasting; radio communications are being disseminated with the intent that they be received by the public. That remains true even if a common carrier satellite leases its channels to a customer-programmer who does not own any transmission facilities; in such an arrangement, someone—either the lessee or the satellite owner—is broadcasting. Despite the argument of some intervenors and the suggestion of the government . . ., it also remains true regardless of whether a DBS system is advertiser or subscriber funded. . . .   While the FCC may be coming increasingly to the view that subscription services are not "broadcasting", [ ], a view not yet passed upon by the courts, the *DBS Order* must rise or fall upon the FCC's articulated policies at the time of the order. And as the *Order* itself recognizes, these policies did not distinguish free-TV from pay-TV for purposes of defining "broadcasting." [ ] The FCC therefore cannot justify its exemption of some DBS systems from broadcast restrictions by pointing to the fact that those systems are subscriber rather than advertiser funded. [ ]

The irrationality of the Commission's view of the statute, which makes ownership the touchstone of broadcasting, is illustrated by the following example. If a DBS owner broadcasts programming directly to homes, it is subject to regulation as a broadcaster; if that owner sends its programs via leased channels on another satellite, the very same programming will be immune from broadcast regulation. Through a general system of cross-leasing, all DBS systems could therefore escape Title III. Nothing in the statutory definition allows the Commission to elevate form over function in this way nor suggests that the definition of broadcasting turns on whether the provider of the service leases satellite facilities from a common carrier or owns the satellite outright. . . .

. . .

Very real practical consequences could therefore follow from the FCC's exemption of common carrier DBS lessees from broadcast restrictions—consequences at odds with the basic objectives of the Communications Act. Under the *DBS Order,* a federal candidate who wanted access to a DBS system that was operated as a common carrier could not force either the satellite owner or its channel lessees to provide that access, for both would be immune from the Act's broadcast restraints; the candidate would instead have to rely on his or her purchasing power, as well as on the whim of the channel programmer, to receive access and an opportunity to respond to opponents. It was to avoid this very result, in which a speaker "who could afford the cost" could purchase enough time on a broadcast station operated as a common carrier to dominate American thought and American politics without any regulatory restraints, that Congress imposed restraints such as the equal opportunity rule upon broadcasters. [ ]

We therefore reject the central rationale upon which the Commission relied to exempt customer-programmers of DBS common carriers from the statutory constraints under which broadcasters must operate: the fact that Congress did not in 1934 contemplate DBS does not give the Commission a blank check to regulate DBS in any way it deems fit. . . .

The Commission's other rationales for its treatment of customer-programmers provide even less persuasive reasons for the Commission's departure from the statute's plain language. The claim that imposition of Title III obligations on channel lessees "merely would serve to duplicate the more pervasive" common carrier obligations of Title II, [ ], is clearly wrong, as Title II merely requires a carrier to accept all applicants for service on a non-discriminatory basis and thus offers no surrogate for Title III requirements such as reasonable access or equal opportunity. A common carrier *cannot* guarantee political candidates reasonable access to airtime or an equal opportunity to respond to opponents, for the sine qua non of a common carrier is the obligation to accept applicants on a non-content oriented basis. [The court also rejected an analogy to MDS. When the Commission decided not to apply broadcast regulations to MDS, it had not contemplated MDS being used to supply subscription television. Since the time the Commission had authorized the use of MDS for subscription television, no court had passed on the validity of exempting MDS programmer-customers from broadcast regulations.]

. . .

A final reason for exempting DBS customer-programmers from broadcast regulation, a reason not directly invoked by the FCC but raised by intervenors in the companion case, [ ], must also be rejected. These intervenors argue that the Commission never regulates *programmers* but only station *licensees*; examples of non-regulated programmers are said to be television networks, which provide programming over the facilities of affiliated broadcast stations, subscription television programmers, who perform similar functions on stations of television licensees, and pay television programmers such as Home Box Office, whose services are carried via satellites to cable television systems. However, the Commission previously *has* applied broadcast restraints to programmers and has been upheld in doing so. Columbia Broadcasting System, Inc. v. FCC, 629 F.2d 1, 26 (D.C.Cir.1980) (affirming Commission's authority to apply reasonable access requirements of Section 312(a)(7) to major broadcast networks) [affirmed by the Supreme Court].

The reason the FCC does not *ordinarily* regulate programmers is a simple one: the Commission applies the statute directly to the entities responsible for program selection and transmission—the broadcast licensees. This approach is consistent with the Act's philosophy, for where a programmer operates through a broadcast licensee who must comply with the statute's broadcast restrictions, as is the case with STV programmers, the networks, and cable, the Act's objectives are met. But when both the customer-programmer *and* the common-carrier through which the former's signals are carried are immunized from broadcast regulation, as they are in the *DBS Order*, the statutory scheme is completely negated.

To avoid this result, we vacate that part of the *DBS Order* that exempts customer-programmers of DBS common carriers from the statutory requirements imposed on broadcasters. . . .

We also do not suggest that all uses of DBS constitute broadcasting; activity that would provide non-general interest, point-to-point service, where the format is of interest to only a narrow class of subscribers and does not implicate the broadcasting objectives of the Act, need not be regulated as broadcasting. . . .

. . .

III. *The FCC's Refusal to Apply its Ownership Restrictions to DBS*

In addition to refusing to impose statutory broadcast restrictions on customer-programmers of DBS common carrier, the FCC also declined to apply to DBS Commission regulations that seek to assure that control of the media is lodged in diverse hands. . . .

The interim DBS rules temporarily suspend for DBS both the multiple channel and the cross-ownership rules. . . .

The refusal to apply the cross-ownership rules to DBS is not at issue in this case. However, petitioner NAB argues that it was arbitrary and capricious for the FCC to relax temporarily the multiple-channel rule for DBS while leaving that same rule in place for terrestrial licensees.

At least at this early stage in the development of DBS, we reject that argument: DBS and traditional television broadcasting are not sufficiently similar in their technology, marketability, capitalization requirements, or other relevant factors that identical regulatory treatment of the two is required. Unlike conventional television systems, DBS systems are extraordinarily capital intensive and have high fixed costs; one applicant estimated that preoperational and first year expenditures alone would be $600 million. [ ] Weighing in against these costs are significant risks which the FCC has found to be associated with the new technology: (i) a lengthy delay (approaching five years) between issuance of a construction permit and initiation of service; (ii) reliance on unproven and developing technology; (iii) an uncertain and rapidly changing marketplace; (iv) operational and marketing problems associated with the provision of service and distribution of home receiving equipment over vast geographic areas. [ ]

These differences led several potential applicants to comment that no "responsible business organization" would enter the DBS field "without control over the programming of more than one channel." [ ] Such multiple-channel control allows counter programming, in which a satellite owner can offer movies on one channel, for example, sports on another, and cultural and children's programs on the third—thereby potentially attracting substantially more viewers than would be possible were only a single channel available. Based on the comments of some applicants that the ability to counterprogram was necessary to justify investment in DBS, the FCC concluded that, at least for the time being, it was unwise to impose ownership restrictions comparable to those existing in other areas. However, the FCC expressly reserved the right to impose ownership restrictions if actual operational experience with DBS systems demonstrated the need for increased regulatory intervention.

. . .

In this case, we conclude that the Commission acted within its discretion in suspending the multiple-channel restrictions. . . .

. . .

CONCLUSION

When technology as novel as DBS confronts a statute as broadly drafted as the Communications Act of 1934, the administering agency has substantial leeway in its efforts to harmonize the two. We conclude that, on the whole, the Commission has exercised this leeway in a reasonable manner. We therefore vacate only that portion of the *DBS Order* that makes broadcast restrictions inapplicable to some DBS systems and, with the caveats noted above, affirm the rest of that Order. We also affirm in its entirety the *STC Decision*.

It is so ordered.

Notes and Questions

1. Subsequent to the court of appeals decision, STC attempted to find a partner to help finance its DBS operation. When none of the negotiations proved successful, STC abandoned its DBS plans entirely.

2. The first DBS system began operating in 1983, utilizing medium-powered communications satellites. United Satellite Communications, Inc. (USCI) began five-channel service to central Indiana. The consumer response was far less than USCI had envisioned, and the service was discontinued in 1985. The future of DBS is still hard to determine because authorization for high-powered satellites allowing inexpensive receiving equipment was not granted until late 1988.

In 1991 Hughes Aircraft announced that it will begin DBS service in 1994. Hughes, through a newly formed subsidiary, DirecTv, Inc., plans to launch two satellites and use them to transmit hundreds of channels to subscribers. By mid–1992 no firm program deals had been signed, but the president of DirecTv has indicated that he expects a mix of cable networks, broadcast superstations, sports, movies and narrow interest programming. Broadcasting, July 27, 1992 at 48.

3. At RARC–83, orbital slots and frequencies were awarded. A frequency band from 12.2 to 12.7 GHz was set aside for DBS. Meanwhile, further questions of satellite use and allocation were negotiated at the 1985 World Administrative Radio Conference, which has become known as Space–WARC, p. 42, *supra*.

4. Given the court's opinion in NAB v. FCC, would the Commission's exemption of MDS customer-programmers from broadcast regulation be able to withstand a legal challenge? What distinctions between the new MMDS subscription television systems and DBS might allow a different result?

5. Concerned that the decision in *NAB* would indeed apply to other common carrier services, including MMDS and SCAs, the Commission decided to reexamine its method of classifying STV and other subscription video programming services. In Subscription Video, 2 F.C.C.Rcd. 1001, 62 R.R.2d 389 (1987), the FCC changed from a content-based approach to service classification, known as the *"Functional Music test,"* to an intent-based approach.

The Commission based the change on the language of the Communications Act of 1934. "The [Act] defines 'broadcasting' as the 'dissemination of radio communications intended to be received by the public, directly or by the intermediary of relay stations.' 47 U.S.C.A. § 153(*o*). Thus, the words of the statute clearly indicate that broadcast classification turns on the *intent* of the purveyor of radio communications that its service be received by the public."

Arguing that the intent of subscription service purveyors is to limit access to their signals, the Commission concluded that subscription services could not be classified as broadcasting. The Commission cited the need for special reception equipment and/or decoders to receive the service and the private contractual relationship between purveyors of subscription programming and their audiences as "indicia of an intent that the communications service not be received by the public."

By reclassifying subscription services as non-broadcast services, the Commission removed them from the application of various broadcast rules, including § 315, § 312(a)(7), the fairness doctrine and the FCC's broadcast equal opportunity rules.

At the same time the Commission decided that switching from conventional broadcast program service to STV service will not constitute a "major change." Thus, stations who switch will not be subject to the notice and hearing requirements of § 309.

The court of appeals upheld both actions, 2–1. The majority found that the Communication Act definition of "broadcasting" was sufficiently ambiguous as to allow the Commission's interpretation. Nor did the apparent inconsistency between the Commission's decision and the court's decision in *NAB* make the decision arbitrary and capricious. The FCC had conducted a properly noticed rulemaking and supplied a reasoned explanation for the change in its approach. National Association for Better Broadcasting v. Federal Communications Commission, 849 F.2d 665, 64 R.R.2d 1570 (D.C.Cir.1988).

Chief Judge Wald dissented, arguing that the legislative history of the Act makes it clear that services such as the ones at issue were intended to be treated as "broadcasting." She quoted former Commissioner Rivera: "It looks like broadcasting, smells like broadcasting, tastes like broadcasting, has all the benefits of broadcasting, but it's not regulated like broadcasting?" Many of her concerns echoed those of the court in *NAB*. For example, the absence of reasonable access and equal opportunities in her view invites unfair political propagandizing.

Judge Wald also found fault with treating a switch to STV as a minor change: "A regular TV station could convert to STV in the first year of its license and be exempt from Title III regulation for almost five years until its renewal came up. In areas served by only one channel, this could mean an end to free television. What more 'major change' could there be for those unable to afford subscription TV?"

C. SATELLITE MASTER ANTENNA TELEVISION (SMATV)

SMATV involves setting up one or more earth stations on a large building or complex and distributing by wire or cable the various programming received. The distinction between SMATV and cable television is that no city streets or rights of way are used. This prevents cities from subjecting SMATV operators to a franchising process. It also limits SMATV systems to large apartments and hotels where enough subscribers can be reached without crossing city streets.

In some ways SMATV resembles MMDS in that multiple channels are distributed to receiving systems most of which are set up on rooftops. However, there are some distinctions. SMATV uses large expensive earth stations to receive the programming directly from satellites, whereas MMDS receives the satellite feeds at some central location and then redistributes them by microwave to the customer. Since the more expensive satellite receiving equipment must be located at each building served by SMATV, it is only viable for large buildings. In contrast, a single earth station facility allows MMDS to serve all buildings in an approximately 25–mile radius. Because the equipment needed at a customer's location is relatively inexpensive, a small microwave antenna and a converter, MMDS can economically serve single-family homes.

However, SMATV does have some advantages over MMDS. An SMATV system can offer essentially unlimited channels because the transmission from central facility to actual customers is through wires.

MMDS is limited to the number of separate microwave channels available. Recall that until 1983 that limit was essentially a single channel.

SMATV's freedom from franchising requirements has long concerned cable operators, who argue that it gives SMATV an unfair competitive advantage. Cable companies must compete through a long and expensive process and often are required to pay franchise fees and make expensive concessions for the right to do business, but SMATV operators can just set up a dish and start delivering service. Furthermore, cable companies are required to offer service to everyone within their franchise areas. SMATV operators are free to choose their customers.

To counter this perceived inequity, cable operators tried to persuade state and local governments to regulate SMATV by imposing strict entry requirements similar to those applied to cable television. In 1983 Earth Satellite Communications, Inc., (ESCOM) was enjoined from constructing an SMATV system in East Orange, N.J., for failure to comply with the New Jersey Cable Television Act. ESCOM responded by filing a petition with the FCC asking it to preempt state and local entry regulation of SMATV. The Commission acted favorably on the ESCOM petition. The FCC's action was then appealed by the New York State Commission on Cable Television.

NEW YORK STATE COMMISSION ON CABLE TELEVISION v. FEDERAL COMMUNICATIONS COMMISSION

United States Court of Appeals, District of Columbia Circuit, 1984.
749 F.2d 804, 57 R.R.2d 363.

Before TAMM, WILKEY, and EDWARDS, CIRCUIT JUDGES.

TAMM, CIRCUIT JUDGE. . . .

. . .

II.

. . .

B. *The Commission's Authority*

. . .

In its preemption order the Commission based its authority over SMATV upon the federal interest in "the unfettered development of interstate transmission of satellite signals." [ ] This development would be frustrated, the Commission found, if each state could impose its own entry restrictions upon systems that were part of the national satellite network. [ ] The Commission chose not to impose entry restrictions of its own, believing that open entry policies in the satellite field would create a more diverse and competitive telecommunications environment. [ ]

Petitioners do not challenge the general authority of the Commission to preempt state and local regulation of cable television in appropriate circumstances. Rather, they contend that, in this particular instance, because the Commission has failed to show that preemption is necessary "to ensure the achievement of the Commission's statutory responsibilities," FCC v. Midwest Video Corp., 440 U.S. 689, 706 (1979), it has acted beyond its authority. To support this contention, petitioners advance two closely related arguments. First, they contend that preemption of state and local regulation of SMATV is a reversal of well-established policy and therefore "presumptively" contrary to the achievement of the Commission's statutory responsibilities. Second, petitioners contend that the policies underlying the Communications Act cannot be advanced by the Commission's determination to allow SMATV to enter the telecommunications marketplace unregulated. We reject both of these arguments and conclude that the Commission's action is not only consistent with prior Commission policy, but also a " 'reasonable accommodation of conflicting policies' that are within the agency's domain." [ ]

1. The Allocation of Regulatory Responsibilities Between
    the Commission and State and Local Governments

During the past 12 years, the Commission has given local jurisdictions significant control over the franchising of traditional cable systems. Petitioners contend that the Commission's refusal to give state and local governments the same authority over SMATV as they have over traditional cable is a reversal of well-established policy. Careful review of Commission precedent, however, reveals that the petitioners' argument ignores the critical distinction the Commission has made between cable television systems that use public rights-of-way and systems, like SMATV, that are operated solely on private property.

The Commission recognized in 1972 that direct federal licensing of the thousands of cable systems operating in large and small communities throughout the country would place "an unmanageable burden on the Commission." . . . The Commission therefore created a "deliberately structured dualism" whereby local government would be responsible for selecting franchises, pursuant to minimum standards established by the Commission, while the Commission retained exclusive authority over all operational aspects of cable communication, including technical standards and signal carriage. [ ]

. . . Although the Commission recognized that "the essentially local service offered by cable television, at least in its formative stages, could best be developed through local participation and enforcement," it cautioned that "the developing duplicative and burdensome overregulation of cable television" was of increasing concern. [ ]

Following a comprehensive study of the effect of dual regulation upon the cable industry, the Commission in 1975 recognized the need for clarification of local governments' regulatory responsibilities. . . . The Commission made explicit its intention to preempt

local regulation whenever necessary "to assure the orderly development of this new technology into the national communications structure." [ ]

Under this dual regulatory framework, the Commission has consistently retained exclusive authority over these elements of cable television that do not involve the use of public rights-of-way. The Commission has retained exclusive authority over the licensing of the satellites
that transmit SMATV signals, [ ], and the earth stations that receive
the satellite signals. [ ] The Commission has preempted regulation
of pay television programming services and rates, [ ], and the carriage
of television broadcast signals. [ ] As the Supreme Court stated in its
unanimous *Crisp* decision, "[o]ver the past twenty years, pursuant to its
delegated authority under the Communications Act, the FCC has unambiguously expressed its intent to preempt any state or local regulation
of this entire array of signals carried by cable television systems." [ ]

A case similar to this appeal, Orth–O–Vision, Inc., 69 F.C.C.2d 657
(1978), recon., 82 F.C.C.2d 178 (1980), affirmed sub nom. New York
State Commission on Cable Television v. FCC, 669 F.2d 58 (2d Cir.1982),
clearly demonstrates the Commission's willingness to preempt state
regulation of systems that do not involve the use of public rights-of-
way. . . .

. . .

In affirming the Commission's preemption, the Second Circuit
found that by denying franchises, municipalities could curtail the
development of MDS. [ ] Since the Commission's policy of advancing
the development of MDS was within its statutory authority, the Commission properly preempted conflicting state entry regulation. [ ]

. . . The Commission's preemption of a cable system, which, like
the system involved in this appeal, does not use public rights-of-way,
plainly refutes petitioners' contention that the Commission has arbitrarily reversed well-established policy.

2. Commission Reliance on Market Forces to Regulate SMATV

In a general challenge to the Commission's decision not to impose
entry regulations upon SMATV, petitioners contend that the Commission has failed to show that its open entry policy is necessary for the
achievement of its statutory responsibilities. Franchise cable television
and SMATV have flourished under local regulation, they claim, and no
federal interest would be promoted by allowing SMATV to compete
unregulated with traditional cable.

Although the Commission does not have unbridled discretion to use
the marketplace to regulate an industry under its control, "the public
interest touchstone of the Communications Act, beyond question, permits the FCC to allow the marketplace to substitute for direct Commission regulation in appropriate circumstances." [ ] Indeed, the Com-

mission has increasingly come to rely upon market forces to regulate the entry and operation of new cable television systems. [   ]

Petitioners advance no credible argument to show that the market is an inappropriate tool for the Commission to choose in this instance to effectuate its statutory mandate. Competition, petitioner NYSCCT argues, will have a grave impact upon the existing cable franchises. The Commission's determination that SMATV should be allowed to serve residents of multi-unit dwellings cannot be challenged as contrary to the purposes of the Communications Act merely because some harm will be visited upon existing and developed franchises. Measuring the public interest standard of the Communications Act with sole reference to the impact Commission action would have upon a developed technology ensures a regulatory regime frozen into maintaining the status quo. We cannot read into the Communications Act a congressional intent to so prevent innovative technologies from conferring substantial benefits upon the viewing public. We therefore conclude that the Commission's present reliance on market forces to regulate the entry of SMATV into the cable television marketplace is consistent with its statutory mandate.

. . .

C. *The Reasonableness of the Commission's Exercise of Authority*

Having established the preemption of state regulation of SMATV is within the Commission's statutory authority, we now consider whether in exercising its authority the Commission acted arbitrarily or capriciously. [   ] As this court recently stated in Wold Communications, Inc. v. FCC, 735 F.2d 1465, 1476 (D.C.Cir.1984), the proper inquiry under the arbitrary and capricious standard is "whether a reasonable person, considering the matter on the agency's table, could arrive at the judgment the agency made." [   ] Our discussion of the Commission's authority forecloses extensive inquiry into the rationality of its decision. A finding that the Commission has the power to preempt state regulation means that preemption is necessary for the full accomplishment of lawful Commission objectives. Establishing this logical relationship between the action taken—preemption—and the Commission policy involves, at least to a certain extent, the determination that the Commission has not acted arbitrarily or capriciously. Furthermore, the nature of this preemption action obviates extensive analysis of the facts upon which the determination was reached: the parties do not so much dispute the factual circumstances surrounding the cable industry as the kind of regulation that should or should not be imposed upon the existing and emerging cable systems. Yet, if the Commission has chosen rationally among competing policies, we cannot reverse because we would have chosen other means of effectuating the congressional mandate. . . .

Petitioner NYSCCT claims that there is inadequate evidence in the record to justify the Commission's conclusion that state and local regulations actually impede the growth of SMATV. The petitioner's comments to the Commission, however, betray the weakness of its contention. The petitioner argued that "[t]he principal evil of allowing private cable to exist outside the regulatory scheme for cable is the impact upon territorial cable television." [ ] Since the dominant theme of the petitioner's opposition to the preemption order is the alleged need to stifle SMATV development, the Commission rationally determined that federal preemption was necessary to effectuate its policy of enhancing the diversity of cable programming. [ ]

Petitioners contend with only slightly more force that the Commission acted arbitrarily by failing to consider the impact preemption and deregulation would have upon the traditional cable industry. Petitioner NYSCCT estimated that the unregulated entry of SMATV into the New York City marketplace would cost franchise cable systems between $348 million and $793 million over the lifetime of the franchises. To replace the revenue lost from those subscribers who would choose SMATV, the franchise systems would have to increase their rates of their remaining subscribers from $7.00 to $11.00 per month.

The Commission found NYSCCT's analysis unpersuasive for several reasons. First, the Commission stated that it is "not an economic guarantor of competitive communications technologies which may offer similar services to subscribers." [ ] Second, the Commission noted that NYSCCT's arguments had been raised and answered in the Orth-O–Vision proceedings. Finally, the Commission predicted that, in states such as New York where cable franchises have mandatory access to multi-unit dwellings, franchise cable and SMATV could co-exist or at least compete for the same subscribers. [ ]

The Commission's response, while terse, was reasonably commensurate with the persuasive force of the petitioner's argument. Petitioner's "economic analysis" purports to document the degree of SMATV penetration into the cable television marketplace. Instead of doing so, it simply assumes that SMATV will replace franchise cable in every apartment of every multi-unit dwelling. Moreover, the data provided by the petitioner, viewed in the most positive light, merely show what the Commission already recognizes: the unregulated entry of SMATV into the cable television marketplace will have a competitive impact upon franchise cable. Petitioner's argument does not relate to the Commission's evaluation of the *facts* ; it merely involves a recharacterization of the petitioner's basic quarrel with the Commission's *policy* of allowing SMATV to compete with franchise cable. We have already determined that the Commission has the statutory authority to adopt the policy of preventing local governments from enforcing entry regulations that have the purpose or the effect of restricting SMATV's competitive position. Evidence purporting to document the degree of SMATV penetration into the cable television marketplace does nothing to undermine the rationality of this decision. [ ]

. . . .

For the foregoing reasons, the Commission's order is affirmed.

Notes and Questions

1. The Commission's stated rationale for preempting state and local regulation of SMATV was to prevent such regulation from inhibiting the development of SMATV service to the public. Could it be argued, however, that the Commission's action served to give SMATV an unfair regulatory advantage over cable television? Which is more important, regulatory parity or service to the public? Would it make a difference if, as a result of SMATV competition, some cable systems failed, leaving many people with no service at all?

2. The court of appeals has ordered the FCC to justify treating SMATV systems as though they are cable systems even though they do not use public rights-of-way. The FCC had ruled that "wholly private" SMATVs did not need a franchise but that "external, quasi-private" SMATVs did need a franchise. Analyzing the case in equal protection terms, the court was "unable to imagine *any* basis" for the distinction. The FCC was ordered to explain it. The court deferred facing First Amendment questions until it is confronted with an as-applied claim, rather than the facial challenge in this case. Beach Communications, Inc. v. Federal Communications Commission, 959 F.2d 975, 70 R.R.2d 773 (D.C.Cir.1992). The Supreme Court has granted *certiorari*.

3. Compare DBS, MMDS and SMATV. Are they sufficiently dissimilar as to require different regulatory approaches? If so, what differences justify that conclusion?

D. HOME SATELLITE DISHES

In 1979 the Commission decided to eliminate a licensing requirement for receive-only satellite dishes. Regulation of Domestic Receive–Only Satellite Earth Stations, 74 F.C.C.2d 205, 46 R.R.2d 698 (1979). Over the next few years, the cost of receive-only satellite dishes dropped from more than $10,000 to under $1,000. As a result of this deregulation and sudden affordability, a rapidly increasing number of people have bought dishes for their homes. The dishes give them access to the hundreds of video signals being transmitted by communications satellites. Among these signals are many of the cable programming services and programming fed by the broadcast networks to their affiliates. In addition, a lot of unedited video, e.g. news feeds, can be picked up by the dishes.

The dishes became controversial because the dish owners were paying nothing for the programming. The cable programming companies argued that the dish owners were pirates, stealing the signals. The dish owners and their trade association, Society of Private and Commercial Earth Stations (SPACE), claimed that they were willing to pay for the service, but the programming companies refused to sell to them. From a legal standpoint, it was unclear whether § 605 of the Communications Act, which prohibited unauthorized reception of some signal transmissions, applied to home satellite dishes.

A compromise solution to the controversy was included in the Cable Communications Policy Act of 1984. Section 605, now redesignated § 705, of the Communications Act was amended to authorize receipt of any non-encrypted signal for private viewing, unless a system for marketing the programming service for private viewing has been established.

Many cable programming services began scrambling their signals to prevent any unauthorized reception. In 1986, acting upon requests from Congress and NTIA, the Commission announced a Notice of Inquiry to examine the issues raised by scrambling as well as the question of Commission authority to set standards for scrambling and regulate rates for satellite programming.

After gathering extensive comments, the Commission concluded that "government intervention into the home satellite dish marketplace, whether by the Commission or through legislation, is neither necessary or wise." Scrambling of Satellite Television Signals, 2 F.C.C.Rcd. 1669, 62 R.R.2d 687 (1987). This conclusion was based on the finding that scrambling served a legitimate public interest—"to protect programmers from commercial theft and to allow them to recover compensation from all who view their copyrighted product." The Commission also found that marketplace forces were creating a *de facto* technical standard for encryption equipment and that competitive distribution and marketing systems appeared to be developing.

The Commission did note that the home satellite dish (HSD) programming industry was at a very early stage of development. Therefore the Commission directed its staff to monitor the HSD industry and submit quarterly reports to Congress.

In 1988 the Commission issued its second report on scrambling satellite television signals.

INQUIRY INTO THE SCRAMBLING OF SATELLITE TELEVISION SIGNALS AND ACCESS TO THOSE SIGNALS BY OWNERS OF HOME SATELLITE DISH ANTENNAS

Federal Communications Commission, 1988.
3 F.C.C.Rcd. 1202, 64 R.R.2d 910.

By the Commission: CHAIRMAN PATRICK issuing a statement.

I. INTRODUCTION

. . .

4. The last two years have witnessed substantial progress in the HSD marketplace. The Videocipher II (VCII) decoder has emerged as a *de facto* industry standard. HSD households need acquire only one decoder to receive satellite cable programming. VC II decoders are now widely available, and as consumers turn to the integrated receiver decoder (IRD), the incremental cost of decoding capacity will fall from $395, the current retail price of a stand-alone VC II unit.

5. Since the *First Report* was completed, many additional channels have scrambled their signals, all using the VC II decoding system. . . . As the number of services with scrambled signals has increased, more and more discounted program packages have come onto the market. . . . Additionally, programming clearinghouses have developed. They are primarily equipment distributors who buy subscriptions to various services in bulk and take advantage of the sales incentive plans (in essence, commissions) offered by the premium programmers in particular. This allows them to put together packages at rates below the *a la carte* prices of the components of the package, and to offer "one-stop shopping" to customers.

6. HSD households currently have access to a wide variety of programming. Many satellite services are unscrambled and may be received without violating federal law.[4] Packages of scrambled services are available from a variety of sources at prices comparable to or below those paid by cable subscribers. Additional options are likely to become available as the HSD market continues to mature. . . .

7. These positive developments have occurred without government intervention. Market forces pushed the industry to a *de facto* scrambling standard. This provides consumers with the ability to receive all satellite cable services via a single decoder. . . .

8. Market incentives are also spurring the industry . . . to take private action against "piracy"—the use of altered decoders to descramble satellite programming without payment. Piracy is the biggest single problem facing the industry today. In this area, there *is* a role for the government to play.

9. Property rights in goods and services sold are an important prerequisite for markets to function well. For that reason, it is appropriate to note that theft of satellite program services is covered by the criminal penalties of Section 705 of the Communications Act, as well as subject to its civil remedies. . . .

10. Unchecked piracy poses a severe threat to HSD programming distribution. We therefore believe that it is important to enforce the criminal provisions of Section 705. Indeed, the Congress may wish to consider increasing the penalties now contained in that section.

11. Our [*First Report*] found that scrambling protects programmers from commercial theft of their services and allows them to recover compensation from all who view their copyrighted product. This mechanism is important for both premium and basic cable channels, since the basic services rely to a significant extent on subscription fees to finance their program acquisition and production activities. Recovering compensation from *all* viewers of copyrighted video product is not only a question of equity. A regime in which HSD households

4. Under Section 705 of the Communications Act (codified at 47 U.S.C. § 605), HSD households may view without authorization any unscrambled satellite cable services that do not have HSD marketing plans in place. At this point, none of the services that do not plan to scramble have such marketing plans.

subscribe to programming also enhances efficiency, since those households are provided with the means by which they can convey their preferences to programmers and can acquire the services that they desire. By maintaining the incentives to produce programming, scrambling serves the public interest.

12. With respect to the provision of broadcast programming via satellite to HSD's, certain legal and policy questions remain unresolved. It is not clear whether the cable compulsory license applies to HSD viewing. The legal questions are questions of copyright law. They are before the courts and the Congress. . . .

13. We continue to believe that government regulatory intervention in the HSD market is not needed. This does *not* mean that most or all market participants are satisfied with their current positions. That issue is not before the Commission. . . . It *does* mean that some decisions and adjustments—such as the choice of a scrambling standard and the expansion of decoder supply—are, in this case, better accomplished by market forces than regulation. It means that when programming is widely available from multiple sources, we see no case for regulatory intervention to increase the number of distributors *per se*. We do not at this point rule out the possibility that cable operators could be exercising market power to maintain some HSD programming prices at artificially high levels. We simply note that our investigation disclosed no persuasive evidence of the exercise of such market power. Should such power exist, it could be addressed through antitrust enforcement. . . .

. . .

II. VIDEOCIPHER II ISSUES

. . .

24. VC II piracy refers to the decoding of scrambled programming without the authorization of the programmer and without payment for the programming. This is accomplished by altering legitimate decoders with illicit chips. Piracy (a term that has gained currency in the industry, although "theft of services" is probably a better description of this activity) is the single most important problem facing the HSD industry. If it is not solved, programmers will be unable to obtain payment from many HSD viewers of their copyrighted material and their incentives to serve the HSD market will be correspondingly weakened. This could lead programmers to adopt a more secure (and more expensive) encryption system. It is likely that cable operators would absorb the cost of more expensive decoders but the average HSD household probably would not be able to do so. (The Videocipher I, predecessor of the VC II, is a more technically sophisticated system. Videocipher I decoders were to have had a retail price of $3500. [ ]) Unchecked piracy could therefore halt satellite-to-home program distribution.

25. The private chips now being distributed all apparently make use of a procedure known as "cloning." In this case, a "master" decoder is legally authorized to receive all scrambled services (by payment of regular subscription fees to the programmers). Then, information on the "master" decoder's authorization is extracted. That information is programmed into pirate chips that are then sold. Buyers of the pirate chips can then attach them to *their* decoders, and those decoders will be authorized to receive all services for which the "master" decoder has a current subscription. If [General Instrument Corp. (GIC)] or law enforcement officials find the master and it is deauthorized, all of the clones lose their service.

26. GIC has taken a variety of measures to combat piracy. It has redesigned the VC II module to make it physically harder to alter (by coating key components with epoxy) and revised the module's software. A new decoding chip is under development, which makes use of very large scale integration (VLSI) techniques. This chip will include all of the secure processes within it. The current module design requires that information relating to the secure processes be transmitted electronically to certain separate chips within the module. These chips can be replaced with fairly standard components that, when suitably programmed, enable pirates to extract information regarding the secure processes. This is the basis for the cloning procedure. The new VLSI chip will eliminate these transmissions of information and will itself be extremely hard to "read." GIC has also undertaken a series of electronic countermeasures (ECM), which consist of deauthorizing decoders that GIC has reason to believe have been altered.

. . .

29. In the fall of 1987, the [Satellite Broadcasting and Communications Association] formed an anti-piracy task force, with the cooperation of the Motion Picture Association of America (MPAA). The task force held a series of meetings in December of 1987 to formulate a strengthened industry anti-piracy campaign. One development that apparently impressed the attendees was GIC's frankness in admitting the scope of the piracy problem. Some saw this as a change by GIC from an earlier stance. GIC's acknowledgement that no scrambling system (particularly an inexpensive one such as the VC II) can be absolutely secure was seen as particularly significant.

30. The plan of action that came out of these meetings has three components. The first is a continuing program of ECM by GIC. GIC is also reviewing the internal security at all VC II manufacturing and design sites. The second component is a public relations campaign to inform consumers and dealers about the penalties for piracy and about actions taken against pirates. It will include an information kit to be distributed to dealers, with sample advertisements that could be run locally, suggestions on attracting local press coverage, and instructions on how to report suspected pirates. Also telephone "hot lines" have been set up for reporting pirate activity.

31. Law enforcement is the third component of the plan. The range of such activities has been described above. The industry is clearly eager for additional efforts by federal authorities to enforce Section 705. In particular, it is felt that criminal indictments (and convictions) are a key step in the anti-piracy struggle. The United States Attorneys have limited resources available and a wide range of law enforcement activities. Major felonies receive a higher priority than VC II piracy. While it is not our place to advise the Department of Justice on the allocation of enforcement resources, we wish to reiterate our judgment that VC II piracy is deplorable and a serious matter. As we noted above, unchecked piracy would threaten the very viability of HSD program distribution. While an adequate legal prohibition is in place, if the Congress wished to underline the importance of stopping piracy, it might wish to consider raising the relatively modest criminal penalties in Section 705.[14]

. . .

III. PROGRAM DISTRIBUTION AND PRICING

34. During the past year, a wide variety of discounted program packages have become available to HSD households. [ ] Many of them are sold on a nationwide basis, and may be ordered via toll free telephone numbers. Thus, consumers who wish to subscribe to satellite program services have no trouble doing so.

35. Prices for HSD program packages are comparable to or below cable subscriber rates. By this admittedly limited standard, HSD rates are not unreasonable. With respect to two important segments of the program market—premium services and superstations—structural factors also support the conclusion that HSD prices are reasonable. In the case of premium services, the "big ticket" items of the satellite programming market, rivalry between satellite cable programmers has been particularly vigorous. Furthermore, the satellite cable programmers—HBO and Showtime—face competition from a non-cable premium channel and from cassette rentals. Under the current regime, entry into superstation distribution is extremely easy. Established superstation distributors not only compete with each other but also are constrained by potential entry.

36. Some have suggested that cable multiple system operators have exercised market power to force programmers to keep HSD wholesale rates artificially high. The purpose, it is argued, is to limit competition to cable distribution. Such allegations are made primarily with respect to basic cable services. Our investigation revealed no

---

14. The maximum penalty for a first offense is a fine of $25,000 and one year of imprisonment. For each subsequent offense, the maximum is a $50,000 fine and two years imprisonment, 47 U.S.C. § 605(d)(2). In contrast, the maximum penalty for knowingly trafficking in counterfeit labels for phonograph records or motion pictures is a fine of $250,000 and five years imprisonment, 18 U.S.C. § 2318. Penalties for fraud and related activity in connection with "access devices" (for example, credit cards) include fines and maximum prison terms of 10, 15, or 20 years, depending on the specific infraction. 18 U.S.C. § 1029.

specific evidence of the exercise of cable market power in the HSD programming market. Moreover, it appears that the observed pricing pattern could also be explained by efficiency factors. These and other considerations . . . lead us to recommend against direct or indirect government regulation of HSD program prices.

. . .

HSD Household Access to Programming

62. HSD households have access to virtually every satellite-delivered program service, but important questions remain unresolved with respect to the provision of television broadcast programming to those households. . . .

63. Satellites can also be used to relay broadcast program material, but those transmissions—whether they be "superstations" or "network feeds"—have a different status. The term "superstation" has come to mean a television broadcast station whose signal has been uplinked by an independent carrier and retransmitted via satellite to subscribers, primarily cable systems. Historically, superstations have been independent television stations, but within the last two years, carriers have begun to uplink the signals of network stations as well. Superstations are now widely available to HSD households, but there is some controversy regarding the status of HSD sales under copyright law.

64. There are thus two ways in which satellite transmissions could, in principle, be used to extend the reach of the three commercial networks to unserved areas. As part of our analysis of the HSD programming market, we sought information on the extent of these "white areas," *i.e.*, areas without local network service off-air or via cable. Precise data on the extent of white areas are unavailable. While estimates vary, the consensus appears to be that 800,000 to 1 million households are in these areas. This is roughly equivalent to one percent of television households.

65. The three major commercial broadcast networks, as well as PBS, make use of satellite feeds to transmit programming to their television station affiliates for those affiliates to broadcast. The network feeds include programming for immediate broadcast, programming for delayed broadcast, material that requires editing and other additional processing prior to broadcast, internal network communications, and other material. The commercial networks all plan to scramble these network feeds and do not intend to market them to HSD households (or any other customers). The networks view these feeds as private communications, but at this point are not trying to prevent HSD households from receiving them.

66. With respect to the network feeds, we concluded that they were not broadcasting but private communications. Thus, the prohibition of unauthorized reception in Section 705 of the Communications Act applies to them, and the networks are legally entitled to scramble

their feeds and to refrain from providing them to HSD households. We also recognized the networks' interest in protecting the exclusivity provisions that are a foundation of the network-affiliate distribution system that well serves the overwhelming majority of television households. Some parties proposed that the networks should provide "clean" feeds to unserved households. The networks opposed these suggestions, and, because of unresolved legal and economic problems, we declined to endorse these proposals. While not presenting them as a panacea, we noted that expanded use of television translators could provide some extension of service.

67. The Public Broadcasting Service also uses satellite feeds to transmit programming to its affiliates. PBS is currently experimenting with a new digital audio system that would allow it to transmit in stereo or to provide audio in more than one language. This type of signal processing entails scrambling the signal. PBS has indicated that it will maintain a clean (unscrambled) feed of its national program service at all times, so HSD households without VC II decoders will be able to receive that service. HSDs with VC II decoders will be able to receive the scrambled feeds as well, without any payment or the need for individual authorization of their decoders. PBS will, however, maintain the privacy of its commercial, non-broadcast satellite transmissions.

68. The superstation route for bringing commercial network programming to unserved areas appears more promising than provision of network feeds, but difficulties remain. They center on the status under copyright law of HSD reception of superstations. The Copyright Act of 1976 conferred on *cablesystems* a compulsory license to retransmit television broadcast stations. It is unclear whether this license also applies to reception by HSD households. This controversy affects all superstations—network or independent—and the carriers involved have taken varying approaches to the situation. Five carriers are involved. Three of them uplink independent stations only. . . . Netlink uplinks three network affiliates, two independents, and a PBS affiliate, all from Denver, Colorado. SBN uplinks three network affiliates. . . . It appears that all five now believe that the compulsory license does apply to HSD sales. . . .

69. Netlink is also selling to the HSD market, but it is seeking the permission of the relevant networks and network affiliates for its carriage, and it is marketing its network stations only to unserved areas. Netlink has secured an agreement with NBC to provide this service, and it is pursuing negotiations with ABC and CBS for similar agreements. SBN is marketing its package of network affiliates nationwide on an unrestricted basis. It has been sued by all three networks, two of their affiliate associations, and one individual affiliate. We know of no outstanding lawsuits that challenge the provision of independent superstations to HSD households, nor are we aware of any legal challenges to Netlink's provision of network stations.

70. The agreement with NBC allows Netlink to transmit NBC's Denver station to HSD households without access to a local NBC affiliate off-air or via cable. Potential customers certify to Netlink that local service is not available, and local NBC affiliates have the right to review the roster of customers to ensure that they meet the lack-of-local-access criterion. Neither NBC nor its Denver station receive any compensation for permitting signal retransmission under this plan. It is important to recall that, for programming not produced by NBC or its local station, permission of the relevant copyright holders will also be required for these retransmissions.

71. Netlink currently offers the ABC and CBS stations in Denver on the same terms that the NBC station is offered. Customers interested in the services of the three commercial networks only pay $2.00 per month for one, two, or three services, depending on how many network affiliates are locally available. . . .

72. Congressman Kastenmeier has introduced a bill, HR 2848, that would extend explicitly the compulsory copyright license to include the retransmission of certain television broadcast stations to HSD customers. HR 2848, the "Satellite Home Viewer Copyright Act of 1987," sets an initial fee of $0.12 per subscriber per month for each channel. The House Subcommittee on Courts, Civil Liberties, and the Administration of Justice held hearings on HR 2848 on January 27, 1988. Representatives of all three networks testified at the hearing and affirmed their desire to reach unserved households with network programming. A representative of the ABC Affiliate Association stated that ABC had been working with Netlink and expected to conclude an agreement in the near future. A representative of the CBS Television Network indicated that CBS and its affiliates endorsed the idea of distributing a CBS station to unserved households via satellite, without making any statement regarding Netlink as the distributor for such a service.

73. The network representatives also emphasized the importance they place on maintaining the exclusivity provisions of the network-affiliate distribution system. Two network representatives suggested that exclusivity was important for meeting affiliates' public interest obligations, and one of them referred explicitly to the promotion of localism.

. . .

IV. CONCLUSIONS

. . .

80. Accordingly, it is ordered, that this proceeding on satellite television signal scrambling is terminated.

81. It is further ordered, that the Secretary shall forward copies of this *Second Report* to the appropriate Committees and Subcommittees of the House of Representatives and the Senate.

[Chairman Patrick issued a concurring statement to emphasize that "the advent of scrambling has promoted the public interest by strengthening protection for the property rights that are a prerequisite for markets to operate efficiently."]

Notes and Questions

1. Some of the questions raised by the Scrambling of Satellite Signals Inquiry were settled by the Satellite Home Viewer Act of 1988. The bill extended the compulsory copyright license to satellite carriers retransmitting independent stations. In addition satellite carriers retransmitting network stations to dish owners who cannot otherwise receive network programming are covered. 17 U.S.C.A. § 111.

2. The Satellite Home Viewer Act directed the Commission to conduct several inquiries. One of these was to determine "the need for a universal encryption standard that permits decryption of satellite cable programming intended for private viewing." After conducting the required inquiry, the Commission concluded that a mandatory encryption standard would not serve the public interest. The Commission found that there was little need for one because the VC II system had established itself as the *de facto* standard. Furthermore, a mandatory standard would have several negative effects: it would limit technological innovation, increase piracy by restricting technological responses to theft of signals, and it would cause extensive delays in implementing new equipment because of the lengthy standards setting process. Satellite Cable Programming (Universal Encryption Standard), 67 R.R.2d 967 (1990).

3. In another inquiry mandated by the Satellite Home Viewer Act, the FCC found that there was no "pattern of discrimination by satellite carriers among the various distributors who market superstation and network station programming." However, the Commission did find differences in the rates charged to home dish distributors and cable operators raising the possibility that unlawful rate discrimination was taking place. After adopting the test for unlawful discrimination used in proceedings under Section 202(a) of the Communications Act (47 U.S.C.A. § 202(a)), the Commission issued a further notice on this issue. "The test in Section 202(a) has three components: (1) whether the services in question are like services; (2) whether discrimination has occurred; and (3) whether such discrimination is just and reasonable." Superstation and Network Station Programming (Discrimination in Distribution), 67 R.R.2d 675 (1990).

Following that inquiry the Commission issued a report concluding that "there are significant disparities in some of the prices charged by some carriers to home dish distributors as compared to the prices charged to cable companies and other customers for superstation and network station programming. Some of these disparities are not justified by the cost of providing service as documented in this proceeding." However, the Commission left the final determination of whether or not these constitute violations of the Communications Act to hearings on specific complaints filed by the National Rural Telecommunications Cooperative. At the same time the Commission noted that the Satellite Home Viewer Act provides aggrieved parties a private right of action in federal court under the Copyright Act. Superstation and Network Station Programming (Discrimination in Distribution), 69 R.R.2d 436 (1991).

4. As part of the 1992 Cable Act, p. 501, *supra,* The Commission has been directed to "establish regulations governing program carriage agreements and related practices between cable operators or other multichannel video programming distributors and video programming vendors." The primary purpose of these regulations is to ensure that cable MSOs do not use their market power to limit the access of other multichannel video systems to programming. The FCC is required to complete the rulemaking proceeding by October 5, 1993. 47 U.S.C.A. § 535.

5. Still another provision of the Satellite Home Viewer Act directed the FCC to extend the syndicated exclusivity rules to satellite carriers to the extent it was feasible. After conducting an inquiry into the matter, the FCC concluded that it was not technically or economically feasible to subject satellite carriers to the syndicated exclusivity rules. Among the reasons cited for this conclusion were the inability of the VC II or even the VC II Plus decoders to selectively delete programs in over 200 markets and the much smaller subscriber base (53,900,000 cable subscribers versus 678,000 HSD subscribers) from which to recover the developmental costs of implementing syndicated exclusivity. Syndicated Exclusivity Requirements for Satellite Carriers, 68 R.R.2d 1172 (1991).

6. In July 1988 the Commission issued a notice warning those either engaged in the unauthorized interception of satellite signals or in providing equipment for unauthorized interception that such conduct could result in serious civil and criminal penalties. In the notice the Commission announced that it was in the process of issuing citations to several vendors who appeared to be marketing illegal decoders. Theft of Satellite Programming, 65 R.R.2d 36 (1988).

7. Despite increased enforcement efforts by the FCC, the large black market in decoders continued to flourish. In another attempt to thwart pirates, General Instrument developed still another decoder, the VideoCipher–RS. The new decoder has a slot for insertion of a TvPass security card. The card allows the security codes to be changed in the event the original code is broken. By late 1992, HBO and Showtime had converted to the new system with other programming services expected quickly to follow suit.

E. SUBSIDIARY COMMUNICATION AUTHORIZATIONS

It may seem odd to consider part of an AM or FM radio signal a new communications technology, but due to longstanding Commission restrictions, few radio stations used their subcarriers prior to the mid–

1980s. A subcarrier is a secondary transmission that can be "piggy-backed" on the primary signal. These subcarriers can be heard only through the use of special receivers.

Until 1983 the use of subcarriers was limited to broadcast-related services such as stereo-enhancement, background music for stores and elevators, foreign language programming, and commodities reports. AM subcarriers could also be used for utility-load management. In 1983 the Commission authorized FM licensees to use their subcarriers for any purpose they wished. The new, expanded authorization allows for such uses as entertainment programming, data transmission and paging.

At the same time the Commission increased the width of the FM baseband from 75 to 99 khz, making two subcarriers rather than one possible for each station. The FCC eliminated a requirement that FM subcarriers be frequency modulated and that subcarriers operate only during the hours when main-channel programming is carried. The Commission no longer requires a formal application for subcarrier operation.

All of these changes left the Commission with an important question: What regulatory model should be applied to the newly authorized subcarrier services? When subcarriers were limited to broadcast-related services, it was clear that the broadcast model applied. But services such as paging and data-transmission had traditionally been regulated as common carriers. The Commission took the novel approach of requiring the licensee to determine which regulatory model to apply. In other words, a licensee wishing to offer a subcarrier service must decide which model is most appropriate for the service in question.

If the licensee plans to provide a fixed service, this determination must be made in accordance with the test laid down in *NARUC I*, p. 506, *supra*. If the licensee plans to provide a land mobile service, the regulatory status will be determined by § 331(c) of the Communications Act. 47 U.S.C.A. § 332 (1982).

Most of the controversy surrounding the expanded use of subcarriers focused on the use of subcarriers for paging. Radio Common Carriers (RCCs) had been providing paging services for a number of years and obviously did not welcome the competition. They argued that the Commission was favoring FM broadcasters over RCCs. Meanwhile, broadcasters contended that the Commission was favoring the RCCs.

The controversy provides another good illustration of the difficulty the Commission faces when it attempts to establish regulatory parity between two competing services. The idea of a level playing field is good in theory, but difficult to put into practice. Consider the following facts about RCCs and FM subcarriers.

Due to height and power limitations imposed on RCCs, an RCC cannot serve as large an area as a full-power Class C FM. On the other hand, a full-power Class A FM cannot serve as large an area as an RCC. RCCs can put up multiple towers—an option denied FMs by the duopoly rule—giving them better coverage in large cities because tall buildings can block line-of-sight transmissions. In less populated areas, the extra height of some FM towers gives them a coverage advantage.

Given these circumstances, how can the FCC establish regulatory parity? It is impossible to make both service providers subject to identical regulations because of the other services offered by FM broadcasters. The duopoly rule cannot be eliminated for subcarriers alone, and forcing RCCs to suddenly divest themselves of all but one transmitter in a market would impose great hardship. Even if it were possible to establish identical regulation, would that be the solution? Does equal regulation translate into regulatory parity? Among other problems, suddenly imposing equal regulation fails to take into account the effect of previous regulation. For example, allowing needs-showing requirements to apply equally to RCCs and FM subcarriers would ignore the effects of the earlier prohibition on FM subcarriers offering paging services. But does preempting the needs-showing requirements for subcarriers really level the playing field? Obviously, this is not an easy question to answer.

The Commission decided on reconsideration to preempt state entry requirements that might hinder the development of subcarrier service. Concern over the needs-showing requirements, p. 507, *supra,* imposed on paging services by more than 20 states, was the primary motivation for the preemption. FM Subsidiary Communications Authorizations, 55 R.R.2d 1607 (1984). On appeal, the Commission's preemption order was reversed. The court of appeals held that the order went beyond the scope of the Commission's jurisdiction. The mere fact that state regulation might limit entry of FCC licensees was not viewed by the court as sufficient to justify FCC intervention. People of State of California v. Federal Communications Commission, 798 F.2d 1515, 60 R.R.2d 1720 (D.C.Cir.1986).

In a 1984 decision, the Commission similarly freed AM subcarriers from the limitations placed on their use. AM Carrier Signals, 56 R.R.2d 1292 (1984).

F. ELECTRONIC PUBLISHING

Electronic publishing puts pages of information, both text and images, on television sets or other display tubes. Teletext is a one-way system with signals flowing only from the computer to the screen. It operates by sending a continuous cycle of information to home television screens during the regular vertical blanking interval (VBI) of a television signal (the black horizontal line that appears when the vertical hold is not properly adjusted). A user chooses the desired "page" of information from a published index, and instructs the receiver terminal to "grab" the page as it goes by. When the user is finished, the page is released from the screen. Teletext can be delivered by either broadcasting or cable.

Another system, called "videotex," is a two-way system in which the computer holds a much larger data base and the user signals which information is sought. The selected pages are then transmitted to the user. This system requires telephone lines or cable.

When the Commission authorized teletext service in 1983, several important questions had to be answered. Teletext Transmission, 53 R.R.2d 1309 (1983). Again, it was necessary to determine an appropriate regulatory model. As in the SCA proceeding, the Commission opted to place the onus on the licensee to decide this based on the nature of the service to be provided.

The Commission also decided that, even in the case of broadcast-related services, teletext would be exempt from content restrictions such as § 315 and the fairness doctrine. In response to petitions for reconsideration filed by various parties, the Commission reaffirmed its position, Teletext Transmission (Reconsideration), 57 R.R.2d 842 (1985):

14. . . . First, we dispute the contrary implications of some petitioners and reaffirm our intention to pursue continued enforcement of these content-related broadcast laws, policies and rules until and unless they are altered by ourselves or other competent authority. This, however, in no way alters or diminishes our authority and responsibility to interpret and apply these as necessary when novel questions and circumstances arise. This is particularly true as in this situation where new services are being authorized that could not be, or were not, contemplated when Congress passed related statutory provisions nor when this Commission enacted rules and policies designed to give force to these provisions. Our attention is further focused in this area where the changing nature of the industry due both to competitive and technological flux requires us to give primary concern to the First Amendment implications of our actions. . . .

15. . . . In this context we view our decision here as no way inconsistent with the court's views in NAB v. FCC, 740 F.2d 1190 (D.C.Cir.1984), for the reasons detailed below. We consider teletext clearly as an ancillary service not strictly related to the traditional broadcast mode of mass communication. First, the very definition of teletext confined the service to traditional print and textual data transmission. [ ] Thus, although these data will be transmitted at some point through the use of the electromagnetic spectrum, its primary and overriding feature will be its historical and cultural connection to the print media, especially books, magazines and newspapers. Users of this medium will not be listening or viewing teletext in any traditional broadcasting sense, but instead will be *reading* it, and thus be able to skip, scan and select the desired material in ways that are incomparable to anything in the history of broadcasting and broadcast regulation. In this light,

we believe that the content regulations created for traditional broadcast operations are simply out of place in this new print-related textual data transmission medium. . . .

The Commission continued the analogy to print media by noting that modern newspapers are often written and edited in one location and then transmitted by satellite to other locations for printing. Relying on *Miami Herald*, p. 83, *supra*, the Commission concluded that application of content restrictions to teletext would serve "neither the letter nor the purpose of the First Amendment."

The Commission's decision was appealed by the Telecommunications Research and Action Center and the Media Access Project. As we discussed in Chapter VI, the most significant aspect of the decision was the court of appeals' determination that the fairness doctrine was not codified by the 1959 amendments to § 315 of the Communications Act. However, the opinion also illustrates the difficulty of determining how much latitude the Commission has in developing regulatory frameworks for new technologies.

TELECOMMUNICATIONS RESEARCH AND ACTION CENTER v. FEDERAL COMMUNICATIONS COMMISSION

United States Court of Appeals, District of Columbia Circuit, 1986.
801 F.2d 501, 61 R.R.2d 330, 13 Med.L.Rptr. 1881.
Rehearing denied 806 F.2d 1115, 61 R.R.2d 1342, 13 Med.L.Rptr. 1896.
Certiorari denied 482 U.S. 919, 107 S.Ct. 3196, 96 L.Ed.2d 684 (1987).

Before: BORK, SCALIA, and MacKINNON, CIRCUIT JUDGES.

BORK, CIRCUIT JUDGE:

Petitioners challenge the Federal Communications Commission's decision not to apply three forms of political broadcast regulation to a new technology, teletext. Teletext provides a means of transmitting textual and graphic material to the television screens of home viewers.

. . .

The case before us presents the question whether the Commission erred in determining that these three political broadcast provisions do not apply to teletext. Because we find that the Commission acted reasonably with respect to section 312(a)(7) and the fairness doctrine, but erroneously held section 315 not to apply to teletext, we affirm in part and reverse in part, and remand to the Commission for further proceedings.

I.

The technologically novel element of teletext service is its utilization of an otherwise unused portion of the television broadcast signal. Television signals are not continuous but are sent in pulses. The human eye retains the image from one pulse to the next so that the picture is perceived as uninterrupted. The time between the pulses of regular television broadcasting ("main signal" transmission) is known as the "vertical blanking interval," and can be used for pulses that constitute teletext transmission. As treated by the Commission in the docket now before us, "teletext" refers exclusively to such over-the-air transmissions, and not to transmission of text and graphics by way of cable or telephone. Main signal operators now control and operate teletext, though the FCC has authorized the operation of teletext "on a franchise basis" or through the "leas[ing] of space to multiple users." [ ] The Commission, however, admonished licensees "that they remain responsible for all broadcast related teletext provided via the station's facilities, whether produced in-house or obtained from outside sources." [ ]

To receive teletext, the viewer must have a device to decode the signal carrying the textual information and graphics. Currently, viewers may purchase teletext decoders in retail stores selling television sets. In the future, at least some television manufacturers will build decoding equipment into selected television models. Broadcasters of teletext thus have no control over who obtains the ability to decode teletext signals.

. . .

On November 27, 1981, the FCC released a Notice of Proposed Rulemaking to explore possible authorization for television stations to operate teletext systems. [ ] The Commission announced its goal "to provide a regulatory environment that is conducive to the emergence and implementation of new technology and new uses of the [broadcast] spectrum." [ ] The Commission added that "[i]n the case of teletext, the available evidence appears to indicate that the forces of competition and the open market are well suited to obtaining the kinds and amounts of service that are most desirable in terms of the public interest." [ ] The Notice therefore proposed that "teletext . . . be treated as an anciallary [sic] service" and that "[s]tations . . . not be required to observe service guidelines or other performance standards." [ ]

In its *Report and Order,* [ ], the Commission addressed the applicability of political broadcast requirements to teletext and concluded that "as a matter of law, . . . sections [312(a)(7) and 315] need not be applied to teletext service," and that applying these provisions would be "both unnecessary and unwise as a matter of policy." [ ] Moreover, the Commission "conclude[d] that the Fairness Doctrine should not be applied to teletext services." [ ] Thus the *Report and Order* sought to adopt an approach of non-regulation of teletext under any of the political broadcasting provisions administered by the FCC.

The Commission noted that section 312(a)(7) guarantees federal candidates only " 'reasonable access' " to "a broadcasting station" and considered what access would be "reasonable" when dealing with "variant broadcast services" such as teletext. . . . [T]he FCC suggested that by providing a candidate access to the broad television audience attracted to the station's regular broadcast operation a licensee satisfied its section 312(a)(7) duties even if the broadcaster at the same time denied access to the more limited audience viewing the "ancillary or subsidiary" teletext service. [   ]

In contrast, the Commission found section 315 wholly inapposite to teletext. Noting that a broadcast "use" triggered section 315's substantive obligations, that a "use" required "a personal appearance by a legally qualified candidate by voice or picture," and that the textual and graphics nature of teletext made it "inherently not a medium by which a candidate [could] make a personal appearance," the Commission held that teletext could not trigger the requirements of section 315. [   ] The Commission also reasoned that teletext differed from "traditional broadcast programming" because it does not have the powerful audiovisual capabilities of main-channel broadcasting, and therefore, does not pose the danger of "abuse" of these powerful sound and image "uses" that Congress envisioned in enacting section 315. [   ]

The Commission reserved its most elaborate analysis for the fairness doctrine. It began with the contention that the fairness doctrine is a Commission-made policy, and that Congress did not codify the fairness doctrine when it added language recognizing that policy in the course of a 1959 amendment to section 315. [   ] Thus, the 1959 amendment does not compel extension of the fairness doctrine to "new services . . . which did not even exist" at the time, and applications of the doctrine to serve the public interest rests in the Commission's "sound judgment and discretion." [   ]

The Commission then determined that it should not apply the fairness doctrine to teletext, "primarily [because of] a recognition that teletext's unique blending of the print medium with radio technology fundamentally distinguishes it from traditional broadcast programming." [   ] Noting that "scarcity" of broadcasting frequencies provided the first amendment justification of the fairness doctrine's application to traditional broadcast media, the Commission posited an "[i]mplicit . . . assumption that . . . power to communicate ideas through sound and visual images . . . is significantly different from traditional avenues of communication because of the immediacy of the medium." [   ] In other words, because scarcity inheres in all provisions of goods and services, including the provision of information through print media, the lessened first amendment protection of broadcast regulation must also rely upon the powerful character of traditional broadcasting. Because teletext "more closely resembles . . . other print communication media such as newspapers and magazines," the Commission found the "scarcity" rationale, as reinterpreted, insufficient to justify regulating teletext.

The Commission also reasoned that teletext, as a print medium in an "arena of competition . . . includ[ing] all other sources of print material," would not encounter the same degree of scarcity, in the usual sense, as the sound and visual images of regular programming. [   ] Thus, the Commission felt it constitutionally suspect to apply the fairness doctrine to teletext. And, in light of its obligation to "encourage, not frustrate, the [ ] development" of new services like teletext, the FCC decided, therefore, to heed concerns of commenters that teletext services might not prove "viable if . . . burdened by Fairness Doctrine obligations" and to exempt teletext from the fairness doctrine. [ ]

. . .

II.

In the Commission's view the regulation of teletext's "unique blend of the print medium with radio technology" raises first amendment problems not associated with the regulation of traditional broadcasting. Thus, the argument goes, existing Supreme Court precedent upholding political content regulation of traditional broadcasting does not necessarily justify the application of such regulation to the new medium of teletext. While not concluding that this application to a "print medium" like teletext would violate the first amendment, the Commission suggested that its application of that regulation would be sufficiently suspect to justify not imputing to Congress an intent to apply "section 315 and similar statutory provisions, and . . . associated rules and policies, to the teletext medium." [ ] To appreciate the Commission's argument, a brief discussion of the case law will be useful.

[The court then reviewed *Red Lion* and the Supreme Court's reliance on the "scarcity rationale" to uphold the constitutionality of political broadcast regulation.]

The Commission believes, however, that the regulation of teletext falls not within the permissive approach of *Red Lion*, but rather within the strict first amendment rule applied to content regulation of the print media. [*Tornillo*]. . . If the Commission's view is correct, and *Tornillo* rather than *Red Lion* applies to teletext, that service is entitled to greater first amendment protections than ordinary broadcasting and it would be proper, at a minimum, to construe political broadcasting provisions narrowly to avoid constitutionally suspect results.

The Commission has offered two grounds for its view that *Tornillo* rather than *Red Lion* is pertinent. Both reasons relate to the textual nature of teletext service. First, the Commission read an "immediacy" component into the scarcity doctrine:

> Implicit in the "scarcity rationale . . . is an assumption that broadcasters, through their access to the radio spectrum, possess a power to communicate ideas through sound and visual images in a manner that is significantly different from traditional avenues of communication because of the immediacy of the medium.

[ ] Second, the Commission held that the print nature of teletext "more closely resembles, and will largely compete with, other print communication media such as newspapers and magazines." [ ] Un-

der this analysis, scarcity of alternative first amendment resources does not exist with respect to teletext. We address these points in turn.

With respect to the first argument, the deficiencies of the scarcity rationale as a basis for depriving broadcasting of full first amendment protection, has led some to think that it is the immediacy and the power of broadcasting that causes its differential treatment. Whether or not that is true, we are unwilling to endorse an argument that makes the very effectiveness of speech the justification for according it less first amendment protection. More important, the Supreme Court's articulation of the scarcity doctrine contains no hint of any immediacy rationale. The Court based its reasoning on the physical scarcity of broadcasting frequencies, which, it thought, permitted attaching fiduciary duties to the receipt of a license to use a frequency. This "immediacy" distinction cannot, therefore, be employed to affect the ability of the Commission to regulate public affairs broadcasting on teletext to ensure "the right of the public to receive suitable access to social, political, esthetic, moral, and other ideas and experiences." *Red Lion,* [ ].

The Commission's second distinction—that a textual medium is not scarce insofar as it competes with other "print media"—also fails to dislodge the hold of *Red Lion.* The dispositive fact is that teletext is transmitted over broadcast frequencies that the Supreme Court has ruled scarce and this makes teletext's content regulable. . . .

. . .

. . . [N]either we nor the Commission are free to seek new rationales to remedy the inadequacy of the [scarcity] doctrine in this area. The attempt to do that has led the Commission to find "implicit" considerations in the law that are not really there. The Supreme Court has drawn a first amendment distinction between broadcast and print media on a premise of the physical scarcity of broadcast frequencies. Teletext, whatever its similarities to print media, uses broadcast frequencies, and that, given *Red Lion,* would seem to be that.

The Commission, therefore, cannot on first amendment grounds refuse to apply to teletext such regulation as is constitutionally permissible when applied to other, more traditional, broadcast media. We now turn to the consideration of the particular regulation at issue in this case.

III.

Section 312(a)(7) states that "[t]he Commission may revoke any station license or construction permit . . . for willful or repeated failure to allow reasonable access to or to permit purchase of reasonable amounts of time for the use of a broadcasting station by a legally qualified candidate for Federal elective office on behalf of his candidacy." 47 U.S.C. § 312(a)(7) (1982). The question here is the rationality of the Commission's decision about the applicability of this provision to teletext.

At the outset, we state what we understand the Commission's decision to be. In introducing its legal analysis, the Commission stated: "As discussed below, we have concluded that, as a matter of law, . . . sections [312(a)(7) and 315] need not be applied to teletext service." [ ] The Commission stated that "the statutory requirement of affording reasonable access is adequately satisfied by permitting federal candidates access to a licensee's regular broadcast operation; it does not require access to ancillary or subsidiary service offerings like teletext." The *Report and Order's* analysis of section 312(a)(7) concluded by stating that the Commission "perceive[d] no legal requirement that licensees grant federal candidates access to their teletext offerings." [ ] Finally, in rejecting reconsideration of this issue in its *Memorandum Opinion and Order,* the FCC asserted: "Guided as we are in such matters by a reasonableness standard, we find that a broadcaster could satisfy the 'reasonable access' rights of a candidate without use of teletext." [ ] We find it clear, therefore, that the Commission believes that a broadcaster cannot be deemed to have acted unreasonably under the statute on the ground that he or she adopts a policy refusing to permit any access to teletext. We now turn to our analysis of the Commission's conclusion on this point.

The scope of review in this case is quite narrow. In Columbia Broadcasting System, Inc. v. FCC, 453 U.S. 367, 386 (1981) ("CBS"), the Supreme Court stated that, in enacting section 312(a)(7), Congress "[e]ssentially . . . adopted a 'rule of reason' and charged the Commission with its enforcement." The Court also asserted that Congress "did not give guidance on how the Commission should implement the statute's access requirement." *Id.* . . . Thus, we approach the question of the agency's construction of section 312(a)(7) with significant "judicial deference," *CBS,* 453 U.S. at 390, and we must uphold that construction if it is a "reasonable" one. [ ] We now examine whether the "Commission's action represents a reasoned attempt to effectuate the statute's access requirement." *CBS,* 453 U.S. at 390.

. . .

Contrary to Petitioners' assertions, there is, we believe no conflict between the Commission's section 312(a)(7) policy, as approved by the Supreme Court in *CBS,* and the decision made in the teletext docket. When the Supreme Court approved the Commission's policy of proscribing "blanket rules" or "uniform policies" concerning access, this meant only that broadcasters could not adopt policies that would effectively nullify the statute's rule of reason approach to granting access to federal candidates. This does not, and could not, suggest, however, that no rules may be applied in the determination of what access is reasonable under the statute. Reasonableness does not mean that an impressionistic judgment must be made in every case. . . . In the context of section 312(a)(7), Congress has empowered the Commission to establish rules and regulations to guide broadcasters in their determination of what access is reasonable, *see CBS,* 453 U.S. at 386 (citing 47 U.S.C.

§ 303(r)), and, while the Commission has principally developed standards on a case-by-case basis, it has also identified some of the extreme cases in which the reasonableness or unreasonableness of a practice is clear.

The Court in fact approved the use of per se rules by assenting to the Commission's policy limiting the applicability of section 312(a)(7) to the period after a campaign commences, a limitation nowhere found in the statute. . . . In the teletext decision, that is all the Commission did; it merely adopted a rule of per se reasonableness as to a minor portion of the station's operations because it believed the reasonableness of that exclusion to be clear.

. . .

Nor do we think that the Supreme Court's approving description of Commission policy "requir[ing] [broadcasters] to tailor their responses to accommodate, as much as reasonably possible, a candidate's stated purpose in seeking air time," CBS, [ ], detracts from our conclusion. Petitioners argue that permitting licensees to refuse access to teletext allows broadcasters to ignore a candidate's desire both to provide "the public with detailed campaign information" and to discuss a complex set of campaign issues, and that this relieves the broadcaster of the need for the individualized tailoring of his or her response to the candidate's request. [ ] Implicit in the Commission's decision that a broadcaster need not provide access to teletext, however, is the conclusion that such purposes as discussion of complex issues may be satisfied by resort to the main channel. We cannot say that the Commission's conclusion is irrational. Complex campaign issues have been treated for years in television broadcasting, well before teletext, and we do not see, nor have petitioners directed us to, any evidence that carries the petitioners' burden of showing that main channel access cannot be tailored to satisfy, as much as reasonably possible, a candidate's desire for air time for such purposes. Accordingly, we affirm the Commission's decision with respect to section 312(a)(7).

IV.

. . .

. . . Even applying the considerable deference we owe the agency, however, we are unable to conclude that the agency's construction of the statute is a rational one, for it is plainly at odds with the language and intent of [§ 315]. See CBS, [ ]. We believe that the agency erred in concluding that the teletext does not constitute "traditional broadcast services" within the contemplation of the statute and that teletext is incapable of a "use" as that statutory term has evolved.

In section 153(o) of the Communications Act of 1934, Congress defined the term "broadcasting" to mean "dissemination of radio communications intended to be received by the public." 4 U.S.C. § 153(o) (1982). The Commission appears to have suggested that teletext transmissions are neither "radio communications" nor "intended to be received by the public." First, the Commission argued that the print nature of teletext differentiates it from more traditional types of electromagnetic transmissions, and that Congress, therefore, could not have intended to cover such a service under section 315. Second, the Commission distinguished teletext from "traditional broadcasting" in that teletext is an "ancillary" service. We address these points in turn.

The Commission's attempt to distinguish teletext from traditional broadcasting because of teletext's textual and graphic nature conflicts with the plain intent of Congress. The proper starting place for statutory interpretation is with "the language employed by Congress." [ ] On this question it is also the terminal point, for the definition of "radio communication" unmistakably includes such transmissions as teletext. In section 153(b) of the Act, Congress defined "radio communication" as

> the transmission by radio of *writing, signs, signals, pictures,* and sounds *of all kinds,* including all instrumentalities, facilities, apparatus, and services (among other things, the receipt, forwarding, and delivery of communications) incidental to such transmission.

47 U.S.C. § 153(b) (1982) (emphasis added). The text could hardly be clearer. Teletext falls squarely within this definition. Teletext involves "print and textual transmission" and that is plainly covered.

The Commission's attempt to distinguish teletext from the "traditional broadcast mode of mass communication" by calling it an "ancillary" service, [ ], departs without explanation from well-established precedent. Teletext and main channel broadcasting are merely different time intervals within the broadcast spectrum. Teletext is "ancillary" to main channel broadcasting only in the sense that it will probably not attract nearly as many viewers. But the Commission has explicitly held that the "number of actual or potential viewers is not significant" in determining whether some constitutes "broadcasting." [ ] What matters is "an intent for *public* distribution." *Functional Music, Inc. v. FCC,* 274 F.2d 543, 548 (D.C.Cir.1958) (emphasis in original), *cert. denied,* 361 U.S. 813 (1959). Under the *Functional Music* test, recently reaffirmed by this court in National Association of Broadcasters v. FCC, [ ], an intent for public distribution exists when the licensee's "programming can be, and is, of interest to the *general . . .* audience." [ ] The Commission has made no attempt to distinguish or repudiate this test, and no one disputes that teletext can and does carry programming, including news, sports, weather, and information about community events, of interest to a general audience. Given our conclusion about "radio communication," it is obvious that teletext service meets the statutory definition of "broadcasting" and that the Commission therefore erred in deciding that obligations applicable to "broadcasting stations" do not apply to teletext.

We reach a similar conclusion with respect to the Commission's efforts to establish as a matter of law that a candidate cannot "use" teletext within the meaning of section 315. In a careful analysis of the legislative history, Judge Maris concluded that Congress clearly intended section 315 to apply "only to the personal use of [transmission] facilities by the candidates themselves." [ ] The Commission has accordingly defined a "use" as follows:

> In the case of *spots*, if a candidate makes any appearance in which he is identified or identifiable by voice or picture, even if it is only to identify sponsorship of the spot, the whole announcement will be considered a use. In the case of a *program*, the entire program is a use if "the candidate's personal appearance(s) is substantial in length, integrally involved in the program, and indeed the focus of the program, and where the program is under the control and direction of the candidate."

1978 Political Broadcasting Primer, 69 F.C.C.2d at 2245 (emphasis in original). If, as the Commission urges in support of its conclusion that teletext is exempt from section 315, the teletext services were utterly incapable of a "use" thus defined, we might still doubt the rationality of a conclusion that one could not "use" teletext under section 315. Defining a "use" as a personal appearance by "voice or picture" suggests an approach under which the Commission defines "use" according to the qualities of the medium being used. In the case of traditional broadcasting, that "use" took on an audio-visual character consistent with that of the medium. Given the textual nature of teletext, it appears to be an unexplained departure from the Commission's past practice for it not to redefine "use" to account for the nature of the new medium. Such a redefinition would allow for "use" of teletext broadcasting when there was transmission of personal statements, reprints of speeches, policy papers by the candidate, and the like. These represent clear examples of a candidate's making a personal use of the teletext broadcasting medium and appear to fall within the meaning of section 315. At a minimum, the Commission would have to address whether the existence of personal "textual uses" of teletext might necessarily follow from the Commission's previous treatment of "uses" and then either redefine "use" to include such a situation or explain why it feels it can reasonably do so under the statutory scheme.

We also have a more particular objection to the Commission's reasoning. The Commission asserted that a "use" was not possible because teletext could not reproduce a "voice or picture" of a candidate. In this, the Commission ignored the fact that teletext is capable of high-resolution graphics and can transmit a recognizable image of a candidate using that capability. The transmission of a "drawing or other pictorial representation" of a candidate, if "identified or identifiable," will satisfy "the requirement for an appearance by voice or picture of a candidate." Carter/Mondale Reelection Committee, Inc., 80 F.C.C.2d 285, 286 (Broadcast Bureau 1980). Thus, even under the current definition, teletext cannot be found utterly incapable of a "use" under section 315. Because the Commission did not acknowledge or in any way deal with this inconsistent precedent, its ruling cannot be deemed the product of reasoned decisionmaking.

Accordingly, we reverse the Commission's decision with respect to section 315 and remand for further proceedings consistent with this opinion. We now turn to an examination of the Commission's treatment of the fairness doctrine.

V.

. . .

Because the fairness doctrine derives from the mandate to serve the public interest, the Commission is not bound to adhere to a view of the fairness doctrine that covers teletext. "An agency's view of what is in the public interest may change, either with or without a change in circumstances." *Greater Boston Corp. v. FCC*, [ ]. To the extent that the Commission's exemption of teletext amounts to a change in its view of what the public interest requires, however, the Commission has an obligation to acknowledge and justify that change in order to satisfy the demands of reasoned decisionmaking. . . .

The Commission has offered two justifications for its refusal to apply the fairness doctrine to teletext. First, the Commission relies on its theory about the textual nature of teletext and the first amendment implications flowing from this distinction between teletext and other, more traditional modes of broadcasting. . . .

The second justification is more substantial. The Commission decided, and petitioners have not disputed, that the burdens of applying the fairness doctrine might well impede the development of the new technology and that "the likelihood of licensees' embarking upon . . . endeavors [like teletext] will be substantially affected" by the agency's policy. [ ] Accordingly, the Commission explicitly concluded that "the public interest is better served by not subjecting teletext to Fairness Doctrine obligations." [ ]

We believe the Commission acted rationally in so concluding. Petitioners have not challenged the Commission's assertions about the negative impact the application of the fairness doctrine would have upon the development of teletext. Moreover, the Commission's view that encouragement of new technologies is not only rational, but is explicit in the Communications Act of 1934. *See* 47 U.S.C. § 303(g) (1982). In effect, the Commission posited an absence of fairness doctrine burdens and made predictions about the marginal encouragement to the development of teletext and the marginal diminution, if any, in the presentation of opposing viewpoints on controversial matters of public importance. In weighing the public interest implications of the two marginal effects, the Commission concluded that the balance favored forbearance from applying the fairness doctrine, and, absent a showing, not even attempted here, that this conclusion was arbitrary and capricious, we cannot disturb the Commission's decision on this point. Accordingly, with respect to the fairness doctrine, we affirm the decision of the Commission.

To summarize: we reverse and remand the Commission's decision for further proceedings consistent with this opinion as it concerns section 315 of the Communications Act of 1934, and we affirm the Commission's decision with respect to section 312(a)(7) and the fairness doctrine.

It is so ordered.

MacKINNON, CIRCUIT JUDGE, concurring in part and dissenting in part:

. . . I would thus allow reasonable access to teletext by legally qualified candidates for federal elected office on behalf of their candidacies. I would also hold that the fairness doctrine is applicable. . . . In my opinion this would not impede the development of teletext.

Notes and Questions

1. As previously noted, in *Subscription Video,* p. 517, *supra,* the Commission subsequently substituted an intent-based approach to service classification for the *Functional Music* test and redefined subscription programming services as nonbroadcast services. However, the FCC specifically declined to redefine subscription teletext in a similar fashion.

2. At the time of the Commission's original authorization of teletext service, the most controversial part of the ruling was the decision to allow cable systems to remove the teletext portion of the signal from any broadcast transmissions they carried. The importance of the Commission's failure to mandate carriage of teletext was reduced, however, by the *Quincy Cable* and *Century Communications* decisions.

Despite the Commission's ruling, *Quincy Cable* and *Century Communications* cable operators are not free to remove all teletext from the (VBI) of secondary transmissions of broadcast signals. In WGN Continental Broadcasting Co. v. United Video, Inc., 693 F.2d 622, petition for rehearing denied 693 F.2d 628 (7th Cir.1982), the court of appeals held that under some circumstances, stripping teletext constitutes a copyright violation. According to the court, main-channel programming and program-related teletext constitute a single, copyrighted work. Deletion of the teletext not only is infringement, but it removes the signal from the protection of the compulsory license normally applicable to secondary transmissions.

The extent of the protection afforded teletext providers by *WGN* is difficult to determine. It is not at all clear what constitutes program-related teletext. Closed-captioning and subtitles are obviously program-related material, as is provision of more detailed information concerning the subject of the main-channel programming, e.g., where to buy an advertised product. What about announcements of upcoming programs? The court thought they were also program-related material.

A second problem with *WGN* is its holding that deletion constitutes infringement. This relatively novel holding was based on a single case, Gilliam v. American Broadcasting Companies, Inc., 538 F.2d 14 (2d Cir.1976), and the facts in that case were markedly different. *Gilliam* involved a complaint by the British comedy group, Monty Python, that during a broadcast, ABC deleted material from one of their movies in a way that seriously damaged the artistic value of the movie.

Due in part to the limited teletext service available at this time, *WGN* has yet to be tested further in the courts.

Chapter XI

COPYRIGHT AND TRADEMARK

There are several ways to protect a creative work product, but historically this protection was first achieved through copyright law. Copyright and trademark law provide protection for intellectual property—something akin to the protection of a patent for an invention. Copyright protects a literary or artistic creation, such as the script of a television program. Specifically, it protects the *expression* of ideas and facts rather than the *facts* or *ideas* themselves, because it is generally in the public interest to encourage dissemination of the latter. Trademark law, on the other hand, protects words or symbols associated with a company or product, such as the call letters of a broadcasting station or the name of a television show.

The right to own, to control and to profit from one's creative work is, of course, essential to people who make their living in the communications media.

As we shall see, a great deal of expression is in the *public domain*—not owned by any one owner—and can be used freely by anyone without permission. When one wants to use copyrighted work, however (with some exceptions to be noted later), one needs permission.

The laws of copyright are thus restraints on freedom of expression, but they are not generally condemned for being so.

Article I, § 8, of the Constitution of the United States gives Congress the power "to promote the progress of science and useful arts by securing for limited times to authors and inventors the exclusive right to their respective writings and discoveries . . .." The first Congress utilized that authority to adopt copyright legislation, and it has been with us in some form ever since. The framers of the Constitution could hardly have envisioned the wide range of media with which copyright must today be concerned: broadcast, cable, print, computer, videorecording, photocopying, jukeboxes, etc.

The copyright statute is found in Title 17 of the United States Code, §§ 101–118.

A. THE NATURE OF COPYRIGHT

1. BACKGROUND

The origins of copyright are interwoven with the history of English licensing procedures. One technique for controlling the printing press in England was to organize printers into a group that became known as the Stationers Company. The Crown granted to that company a monopoly of all printing, with the power to seek out and suppress material published by non-members who violated the monopoly. The Crown's goal was to thwart seditious libel and other objectionable material. The printers, for their part, seized on the monopoly situation to control reproduction of whatever they printed. The result was the licensed printers' right to control copies based on the censorship of the 16th and 17th centuries. When licensing was discontinued in 1695, the rights of the printers were undermined. They petitioned Parliament to adopt protections resembling what they had had under the licensing schemes. In 1709 Parliament responded with the Statute of Anne, which set the pattern for copyright legislation both in England and in this country. The Stationers Company remained, but its new role was to register printed material, which would serve to protect that material against unauthorized copying.

The first U.S. Congress adopted a similar procedure: printed matter could be protected by filing a copy with the newly established copyright office, headed by the "Register of Copyrights." The types of writings protected and the period of protection have been expanded since the 1790 statute, which protected only books, maps and charts for 14 years plus renewal for a second 14–year term.

Under the 1909 statute, published works were protected by federal law while unpublished works were protected under state law. Under the new legislation, all protection is in a single national framework.

In 1976 the copyright statute enacted in 1909 was replaced with new legislation that preserves the basic philosophical strands of copyright law, including the denial of copyright for federal government documents. Changes have been made in legal technicalities or to accommodate media that emerged after 1909 and did not easily fit within the old framework. The "new" statute, which is found in Title 17 of the United States Code, went into effect Jan. 1, 1978.

2. SUBJECT MATTER

Section 102 of the 1976 copyright statute sets out the basic pattern of protection when it states that protection subsists in "original works of authorship fixed in any tangible medium of expression, now known or later developed, from which they can be perceived, reproduced or otherwise communicated, either directly or with the aid of a machine or device." The types of "original works of authorship" that can be protected by copyright include:

> (1) literary works; (2) musical works, including any accompanying words; (3) dramatic works, including any accompanying music; (4) pantomimes and choreographic works; (5) pictorial, graphic, and sculptural works; (6) motion pictures and other audiovisual works; and (7) sound recordings.

Although one can copyright the way one *expresses* facts and ideas, one cannot copyright those facts and ideas themselves. As the statute says:

In no case does copyright protection for an original work of authorship extend to any idea, procedure, process, system, method or operation, concept, principle, or discovery, regardless of the form it which it is described, explained, illustrated, or embodied in such work. 17 U.S.C.A. § 102.

In a variety of cases, courts have had to decide whether specific works were (a) protected subject matter under the statute or (b) ideas or facts that were not protected. Sometimes works fall into the latter category because, while they required effort, or "sweat of the brow," they did not necessarily require creativity—thus they may not be considered to be "*original*." Such a work, for example, may present only factual information that is not the kind of subject matter that can be copyrighted.

One case in which a court had to consider whether the subject matter was protectable under the copyright statute was a case involving an author's theory that a crew member had sabotaged the German dirigible Hindenburg in New Jersey in 1937—supposedly causing its explosion and crash to please a Communist girlfriend. Two other authors developed similar explanations for the disaster, and a suit resulted. Hoehling v. Universal City Studios, Inc., 618 F.2d 972 (2d Cir.), certiorari denied 449 U.S. 841 (1980). The court began its discussion by placing copyright in its broader context:

> A grant of copyright in a published work secures for its author a limited monopoly over the expression it contains. The copyright provides a financial incentive to those who would add to the corpus of existing knowledge by creating original works. Nevertheless, the protection afforded the copyright holder has never extended to history, be it documented fact or explanatory hypothesis. The rationale for this doctrine is that the cause of knowledge is best served when history is the common property of all, and each generation remains free to draw upon the discoveries and insights of the past. Accordingly, the scope of copyright in historical accounts is narrow indeed, embracing no more than the author's original expression of particular facts and theories already in the public domain. As the case before us illustrates, absent wholesale usurpation of another's expression, claims of copyright infringement where works of history are at issue are rarely successful.

The court asserted that although plaintiff had a valid copyright on his book, to prove "infringement" he had to prove that defendants had "improperly appropriated" his "expression." Although plaintiff admitted that his idea was not copyrightable, he correctly argued that "his 'expression' of *his* idea is copyrightable." The court analyzed that claim as follows:

> He relies on Learned Hand's opinion in [Sheldon v. Metro–Goldwyn Pictures Corp., 81 F.2d 49 (2d Cir.), certiorari denied 298 U.S. 669 (1936)] holding that *Letty Lynton* infringed *Dishonored Lady* by copying its story of a woman who poisons her lover, and

Augustus Hand's analysis in Detective Comics, Inc. v. Bruns Publications, Inc., 111 F.2d 432 (2d Cir.1940), concluding that the exploits of "Wonderman" infringed the copyright held by the creators of "Superman," the original indestructible man. Moreover, Hoehling asserts that, in both these cases, the line between "ideas" and "expression" is drawn, in the first instance, by the fact finder.

Sheldon and *Detective Comics,* however, dealt with works of fiction, where the distinction between an idea and its expression is especially elusive. But, where, as here, the idea at issue is an interpretation of an historical event, our cases hold that such interpretations are not copyrightable as matter of law. In Rosemont Enterprises, Inc. v. Random House, Inc., 366 F.2d 303 (2d Cir.1966), cert. denied, 385 U.S. 1009 (1967), we held that the defendant's biography of Howard Hughes did not infringe an earlier biography of the reclusive alleged billionaire. Although the plots of the two works were necessarily similar, there could be no infringement because of the "public benefit in encouraging the development of historical and biographical words and their public distribution." Id. at 307; accord, Oxford Book Co. v. College Entrance Book Co., 98 F.2d 688 (2d Cir.1938). To avoid a chilling effect on authors who contemplate tackling an historical issue or event, broad latitude must be granted to subsequent authors who make use of historical subject matter, including theories or plots. Learned Hand counseled in Myers v. Mail & Express Co., 36 C.O.Bull 487, 479 (S.D.N.Y.1919), "[t]here cannot be any such thing as copyright in the order of presentation of the facts, nor, indeed, in their selection."

The court went further, however, and asserted that it may not even be possible to protect even some fictitious episodes:

The remainder of Hoehling's claimed similarities relate to random duplications of phrases and sequences of events. For example, all three works contain a scene in a German beer hall, in which the airship's crew engages in revelry prior to the voyage. Other claimed similarities concern common German greetings of the period, such as "Heil Hitler," or songs, such as the German National anthem. These elements, however, are merely *scenes a faire,* that is, "incidents, characters or settings which are as a practical matter indispensable, or at least standard, in the treatment of a given topic." [ ] Because it is virtually impossible to write about a particular historical era or fictional theme without employing certain "stock" or standard literary devices, we have held that *scenes a faire* are not copyrightable as a matter of law. See Reyher v. Children's Television Workshop, 533 F.2d 87, 91 (2d Cir.), cert. denied, 429 U.S. 980 (1976).

Finally, the court brought these several aspects of the case together and recognized that breaking the copyrighted work up into many little parts created a new danger:

All of Hoehling's allegations of copying, therefore, encompass material that is non-copyrightable as a matter of law, rendering summary judgment entirely appropriate. We are aware, however, that in distinguishing between themes, facts, and *scenes a faire* on the one hand, and copyrightable expression on the other, courts may lose sight of the forest for the trees. By factoring out similarities based on non-copyrightable elements, a court runs the risk of overlooking wholesale usurpation of a prior author's expression. A verbatim reproduction of another work, of course, even in the realm of nonfiction, is actionable as copyright infringement. See Wainwright Securities, Inc. v. Wall Street Transcript Corp., 558 F.2d 91 (2d Cir.1977), cert. denied, 434 U.S. 1014 (1978). Thus, in granting or reviewing a grant of summary judgment for defendants, courts should assure themselves that the works before them are not virtually identical. In this case, it is clear that all three authors relate the story of the Hindenburg differently.

In works devoted to historical subjects, it is our view that a second author may make significant use of prior work, so long as he does not bodily appropriate the expression of another. Rosemont Enterprises, Inc., *supra*, 366 F.2d at 310. This principle is justified by the fundamental policy undergirding the copyright laws—the encouragement of contributions to recorded knowledge. The "financial reward guaranteed to the copyright holder is but an incident of this general objective, rather than an act in itself." Berlin v. E.C. Publications, Inc., 329 F.2d 541, 543–44 (2d Cir.), cert. denied, 379 U.S. 822 (1964). Knowledge is expanded as well by granting new authors of historical works a relatively free hand to build upon the work of their predecessors.

The meaning of the words "original works of authorship" and "fixed," as used in § 102 of the 1976 Copyright Act, were critical to a case involving the telecasting of a parade. Production Contractors, Inc. v. WGN Continental Broadcasting Co., 622 F.Supp. 1500, 12 Med. L.Rptr. 1708 (N.D.Ill.1985). The plaintiff (PCI) planned, organized and promoted a parade on Michigan Avenue in Chicago. It sold exclusive Chicago area television broadcasting rights in the parade to the American Broadcasting Company, owner of WLS–TV in Chicago, designating WLS as the "Official Television Station of the 1985 McDonald's Charity Christmas Parade."

Knowing that another station, WGN–TV, planned to televise the parade, PCI sought a declaratory judgment concerning rights to broadcast the parade. The federal district court held that the parade itself was not a *work of authorship*. It said "[T]here is no case law supporting the proposition that the promotion and production of a parade is a work of authorship entitled to copyright protection." Further, the court held that "[T]he telecast of the parade is a work of authorship fixed simultaneously with its transmission only for purposes of copyright protection from videotaping, tape-delays, or secondary transmissions," none of which applied to WGN–TV, which planned to use its own equipment. The court granted summary judgment for WGN–TV.

Problems involving "exclusive" rights continue to arise in television, despite the basic premise that facts, ideas, information and events cannot be copyrighted—only the *expression* of them can. During the July 4, 1986, festivities at the Statue of Liberty, for example, there was disagreement over the extent of coverage by other networks of events for which ABC was the "official" network. Those differences were resolved without litigation.

A Supreme Court decision, Feist Publications, Inc. v. Rural Telephone Service Co., Inc., 111 S.Ct. 1282 (1991), illustrates the principle that facts cannot be copyrighted. Rural Telephone Service, which provides telephone service to several communities in Kansas, publishes a telephone directory. It refused to license its white pages listings to Feist for a larger telephone directory covering 11 telephone service areas. Feist extracted the information from Rural's directory and used it in their own, altering some of the listings and using others identical to the listings in Rural's directory. Rural sued for copyright infringement. The Supreme Court decided in favor of Feist Publications.

Justice O'Connor wrote for the Court that "This case concerns the interaction of two well-established propositions. The first is that facts are not copyrightable; the other, that compilations of facts generally are. Each of these propositions possesses an impeccable pedigree. . . . [I]t is beyond dispute that compilations of facts are within the subject matter of copyright. Compilations were expressly mentioned in the Copyright Act of 1909, and again in the Copyright Act of 1976. . . . There is undeniable tension between these two propositions. . . . The key to resolving the tension lies in understanding why facts are not copyrightable. The *sine qua non* of copyright is originality. To qualify for copyright protection, a work must be original to the author."

"[T]he copyright in a factual compilation is thin," she wrote. "Notwithstanding a valid copyright, a subsequent compiler remains free to use the facts contained in [another's] publication to aid in preparing a competing work, so long as the competing work does not feature the same selection and arrangement." The Court has rejected, she said, "sweat of the brow" arguments that would give protection to factual compilations on the basis of hard work rather than originality. "Rural expended sufficient effort to make the white pages directory useful," she wrote, "but insufficient creativity to make it original," concluding that the names, towns and telephone numbers copied by Feist were not original to Rural and were therefore not protected by copyright.

3. OWNERSHIP OF COPYRIGHT

The authors of a work are the initial copyright owners unless the work is a "work made for hire." This is defined as

(1) a work prepared by an employee within the scope of his or her employment; or

(2) a work specifically ordered or commissioned for use as a contribution to a collective work, as a part of a motion picture or other audiovisual work, as a translation, as a supplementary work, as a compilation, as an instructional text, as a test, as answer material for a test, or as an atlas, if the parties expressly agree in a written instrument signed by them that the work shall be considered a work made for hire. 17 U.S.C.A. § 101.

In the case of a "work made for hire," the original ownership belongs to the employer or person who commissioned the work. As is the case with any property right, ownership of a copyright can be left to the owner's heirs or sold.

In Community for Creative Non–Violence v. Reid, 490 U.S. 730 (1989), the Supreme Court was asked to avoid the rigors of section 101(2) by expansively interpreting the term "employee" in section 101(1). It declined. Reid had created a sculpture for CCNV in conformance with CCNV's concept and general design ideas. The parties did not discuss copyright ownership in advance. After the sculpture was finished, each filed a competing copyright claim. The trial judge held that CCNV owned the copyright, but the Court of Appeals for the District of Columbia reversed, holding that it was not a work for hire and therefore copyright was owned by Reid.

The Supreme Court unanimously affirmed. CCNV did not claim the sculpture was a specially commissioned work under subsection (2); there was no written agreement to that effect, and even if there had been, a sculpture is not one of the types of works to which the subsection applies. Instead, CCNV argued that Reid should be considered an "employee" for purposes of subsection (1), on the ground that CCNV had retained the right to control Reid's product and had actually exercised such control. The Court, however, held that the legislative history of the Act required the term to be understood in light of the general common law of agency, which takes into account many factors in addition to control of the work. It concluded Reid was not an employee because he was engaged in a skilled occupation, supplied his own tools, worked in his own studio, was retained for a brief time for the project in question and no others, had control of his own working hours and the employment and compensation of assistants, and was not treated as an employee for purposes of benefits, social security and payroll taxes, worker's compensation or unemployment taxes.

The Court refused to allow the interpretation given to section 101(1) by the Second Circuit, which had held that freelancers were "employees" if the hiring party had actually wielded control during the creation of the work. See Aldon Accessories Ltd. v. Spiegel, Inc., 738 F.2d 548 (2d Cir.), cert. denied 469 U.S. 982 (1984). Many publishing and communications companies headquartered in New York apparently had relied on that interpretation and therefore failed to obtain contractual assignments from their freelance contributors. As a result, some industry sources said the CCNV decision put in question the ownership of millions of dollars in literary and entertainment properties, and might affect 40 percent of all existing copyrights. See Scardino, "The Media Business: A Copyright Ruling Opens a Costly Can of Worms," New York Times, June 12, 1989, at D12.

The decision also generated concern among publishing, communications and entertainment companies because of its effect on termination of copyrights. Licenses and transfers granted by authors generally may be terminated after 35 or 40 years by the authors or their survivors; companies that find themselves holding licenses rather than authorship as a result of *CCNV v. Reid* now have to worry about having their interests terminated altogether.

Magazine publishers often commission freelance photographers or artists to illustrate specific articles. Sometimes they reuse the articles and/or illustrations in books, calendars, special anniversary editions, etc. After the decision in *CCNV v. Reid*, how may publishers protect their interest in future use of these illustrations? What is their potential liability for past reuses that may be infringing after *CCNV v. Reid*?

See Chapter XIII for a discussion of Baltimore Orioles v. Major League Baseball Players, in which it was decided that owners of baseball teams hold exclusive rights to games. In the court's view, the players, paid as team employees, create works for hire by their participation in games.

4. RIGHTS OF COPYRIGHT OWNER(S)

Section 106 states the nature of the protection extended to the copyright owner:

> Subject to sections 107 through 118, the owner of copyright under this title has the exclusive right to do and to authorize any of the following:
>
> (1) to reproduce the copyrighted work in copies or phonorecords;
>
> (2) to prepare derivative works based upon the copyrighted work;
>
> (3) to distribute copies or phonorecords of the copyrighted work to the public by sale or other transfer of ownership, or by rental, lease, or lending;
>
> (4) in the case of literary, musical, dramatic, and choreographic works, pantomimes, and motion pictures and other

audiovisual works, to perform the copyrighted work publicly; and

(5) in the case of literary, musical, dramatic, and choreographic works, pantomimes, and pictorial, graphic, or sculptural works, including the individual images of a motion picture or other audiovisual work, to display the copyrighted work publicly. 17 U.S.C.A. § 106.

It is possible for a copyright owner to sell some rights and retain others. A famous novelist, for example, might first sell the rights to publish excerpts of a forthcoming novel to a national magazine, next sell the right to publish the hardcover first edition of the book to a publishing house, then sell the right for publication of a later paperback edition to another publishing house, and, finally, sell the right to make a movie based on the book to a studio.

It is important to note that the only protections accorded copyright are statutory and are listed in § 106. An unlicensed use that does not conflict with one of the exclusive rights enumerated in § 106 is not an infringement. Beyond that, § 106 is explicitly made subject to a series of limitations listed in §§ 107–118. We will discuss the most important of these limitations, fair use, later in this chapter.

One limitation on the § 106 rights that is not mentioned in the copyright statute is the first sale doctrine. A judicially-created rule, the doctrine provides that copyright owners who sell copies of their copyrighted works have no further control over the sale or lease of those particular copies. The original copyright owners' other rights remain unimpaired.

Under the first sale doctrine, for example, a video store can buy videotapes and then rent them to the public. However, under a 1984 amendment to § 109(b)(1) of the Copyright Act, phonograph records cannot be rented (except by nonprofit libraries or nonprofit educational institutions) without the permission of the copyright holders. The rationale is that there would be little or no purpose in renting a record other than to copy it. In contrast, one can presume that customers may rent videotapes to view them without illegally copying them. For a more complete discussion of the doctrine, see United States v. Atherton, 561 F.2d 747 (9th Cir.1977).

5. DURATION OF COPYRIGHT

Under the 1909 Act, copyright protection lasted for 28 years with the opportunity for one 28–year renewal. Under the 1976 Act, it lasts for the life of the author plus 50 years. With joint authors it is 50 years from the last surviving author's death. Anonymous works, pseudonymous works and "works made for hire" are protected for 75 years from publication or 100 years from creation, whichever comes first. 17 U.S.C.A. § 302.

6. STATUTORY FORMALITIES

Under the Copyright Act of 1976, any work is protected as soon as it is "fixed in a tangible medium." However, to retain this protection certain statutory formalities should be observed. Originally every copy was required to carry notice consisting of the full word copyright, the accepted abbreviation "copr.," or the internationally accepted symbol; but the Berne Convention Implementation Act, Public Law 100–568, eliminated the requirement that domestic authors display a copyright notice, substituting the word "may" for "shall" in 17 U.S.C.A. 401(a). (For discussion of the Berne Convention, see the discussion of international protection, *infra.*)

One requirement for obtaining *full* copyright protection is to register the work with the Register of Copyrights. Registration is a prerequisite for filing a copyright infringement suit and involves filling out a form, paying a small fee and providing a few copies of the work.

Forms and current fee schedules are available from the Copyright Office, Library of Congress, Washington, D.C. 20559.

7. PREEMPTION OF STATE LAW

The Copyright Act of 1976 preempted all state law governing rights equivalent to copyright protection. As previously noted, this eliminated common-law copyright protection for unpublished works. It does not, however, mean that other state laws, such as those relating to defamation, cannot be applied to copyrighted works.

Sometimes, however, determining what constitutes a non-equivalent right is not easy. In Chapter XIII, in the discussion of the right of privacy, we will see the Supreme Court decision in Zacchini v. Scripps–Howard Broadcasting Co., which recognized a "right of publicity" for Hugo Zacchini, an entertainer known for his "human cannonball" act. Zacchini's 15–second act at a fair grounds was videotaped by a television station and broadcast on the evening news. The Court held that the broadcast posed a substantial threat to the economic value of the performance and that the performer was entitled to damages in an invasion of privacy suit.

Zacchini's act was not copyrighted. Had he "fixed" it by having it filmed or taped himself, he could have copyrighted it.

Notice the similarities between copyright law and this special application of privacy law in protecting one's right to control one's own creation or performance.

It is difficult to generalize from *Zacchini* because so few entertainers' acts are so short that they can be recorded in substantial portion by news media and because this area of privacy law is so undeveloped.

8. INTERNATIONAL PROTECTION

Many countries—but not the United States—signed an agreement in 1886 in Berne, Switzerland, giving international copyright protection. That agreement, widely referred to as the Berne Convention, established the International Union for the Protection of Literary and Artistic Works. Although it was a member of an overlapping international treaty, the United States took more than a century to consider joining the other Berne Convention countries but finally did so after Congress passed the Berne Convention Implementation Act of 1988 and President Reagan signed it. Membership took effect March 1, 1989.

It was hoped that membership in the treaty would help to curb international piracy of original works by Americans—at least in the 79 other countries that were members when the U.S. joined. International piracy has continued, however, to be a problem, particularly in developing countries with active commercial sectors. The U.S. Trade Representative has reported, for instance, that "Pirates issued their own Chinese version of the *Encyclopedia Britannica* in Taiwan before the legitimate edition could be published, kept selling it despite court rulings and, with amazing *chutzpah,* warned consumers 'to watch out for fakes.'" The Washington Post, Nov. 5, 1989 at C3.

The Berne Convention includes, in Article VI, a Moral Rights Clause adopted in 1928. That clause provides that, "independently of the author's copyright, and even after assignment of the said copyright, the author shall retain the right to claim authorship of the work, as well as the right to object to deformation, mutilation, or other modification of the said work with may be prejudicial to his honor or his reputation." Despite the fact that Congress asserted in the Berne Convention Implementation Act that the moral rights clause should *not* be explicitly enforced in American courts, experts viewed the Berne membership as a "moral statement" of the importance of protecting intellectual property and were optimistic that authors and creators whose works were altered would be better able to protect their works from alteration than they had been previously. New York Times, March 10, 1989 at B–7.

B. ALLEGED OR ACTUAL INFRINGEMENTS

Infringements, real or imagined, can take a variety of forms. In some instances permission to use all or part of the copyrighted material may have been given, but the copyright holder may allege that the user has exceeded the permission. That may happen when the material is disseminated more widely (perhaps in another country) than originally envisioned, when the material used is more extensive than the copyright holder envisioned or when the purpose of the dissemination or the context in which the material is presented is not what the copyright holder expected.

More frequently, the problem may be that material is used with no permission having been granted at all. In some such instances, the material has been attributed correctly to the copyright holder (which still does not give the user any right to use it without permission); in other instances the material has not been attributed.

In cases involving such literary or artistic creative work as musical or dramatic presentations, the problem may involve the question of whether the user's reproduction of the copyright holder's work actually constituted a "performance" of it.

In other cases, such as those in which two writers or two composers have created similar works, the key question will be whether one author copied the other's work. The plaintiff in such a case attempts to prove that the defendant had access to the copyrighted work and that there is a *substantial similarity* between the copyrighted work and the defendant's work.

Copyright protection extends only to copying the work in question. If someone *independently creates* a similar work, there is no copyright infringement. Thus, in any copyright suit the plaintiff must show that the defendant had access to the plaintiff's work. However, as former Beatle George Harrison learned, plaintiff does not have to prove that defendant intentionally or even consciously copied it. Bright Tunes Music Corp. v. Harrisongs Music, Ltd., 420 F.Supp. 177 (S.D.N.Y.1976).

Two cases illustrate problems of protection of commercial rights to ideas—specifically excluded from copyright coverage under Section 102. When copyright protection is unavailable, plaintiffs sometimes sue under contract law. In one of the cases, Murray v. NBC, 844 F.2d 988, 15 Med.L.Rptr. 1285 (2d Cir.1988), a plaintiff claimed that, four years before "The Cosby Show" premiered on NBC, he had proposed to the network an idea for a half-hour situation comedy starring Cosby to be titled "Father's Day." Unable to sue for copyright infringement, the plaintiff sued for misappropriation, conversion, breach of contract and violation of the Lanham Act (on the theory that the program's origin was falsely designated). The court of appeals held that the plaintiff's idea for a program about an intact, middle-class black family was not novel and could not be protected.

In the second case, humorist Art Buchwald announced in 1988 that he was suing Paramount Pictures for $5 million, claiming that the Eddie Murphy movie "Coming to America" was based on a screen treatment Buchwald sold to Paramount in 1983 as a vehicle for Murphy. Buchwald's lawyer said that under the 1983 sale agreement, Buchwald is entitled to a lump sum payment and a share of the net profits from the movie. Like plaintiff Murray, Buchwald sued for breach of contract. Murphy's manager was quoted as saying that so many people were claiming authorship of "Coming to America" that "It's like Zabar's. You [had] better take a number and get in line [to sue]." Mentioning four other suits claiming the idea for the same film, the manager said, "I ought to throw a cocktail party for all these people." New York Times, Nov. 22, 1988 at C19. Buchwald won his breach of contract suit in California Superior Court, Los Angeles

County. The court held that evidence demonstrating similarity between Buchwald's screen treatment and "Coming to America," together with evidence of Paramount's unlimited access to Buchwald's idea, warranted a finding that the movie was "based upon" Buchwald's work. Buchwald v. Paramount Pictures Corp., 17 Med.L.Rptr. 1257 (1990). He was awarded damages in the amount of $250,000 plus 19 percent of the profits, but Paramount Pictures denied that there had been any profits, and Buchwald's attorney then alleged that Paramount's accounting was bogus. Subsequently a California court awarded Buchwald $150,000 and a co-plaintiff $750,000 in the suit. Art Buchwald v. Paramount Pictures, 1990 WL 357611 (1992). By that time the *New York Times* reported (March 17, 1992 at C13) that legal costs on behalf of Buchwald exceeded $2.5 million. Paramount decided in August 1992 to appeal, and the appeal process was expected to add another year or more to the protracted battle. The Washington Post, Aug. 26, 1992 at C–4.

1. REMEDIES

The Copyright Act of 1976 provides numerous remedies for copyright infringement. Sections 502–503 provide for an injunction against further infringement as well as destruction of all existing infringing materials. Under § 504, the copyright owner may elect to receive either the damages actually suffered plus any additional profits of the infringer or statutory damages of not less than $250 or more than $10,000. The court may also at its discretion award costs and attorney's fees.

In the case of willful infringement for commercial advantage or private financial gain, criminal sanctions are also available. Section 506 provides for fines of up to $50,000 and imprisonment for up to two years, depending on the type of work infringed and the prior record of the defendant.

2. FAIR USE

As previously noted, the grant of rights to the owner of the copyright is conditioned on a series of limitations expressed in §§ 107–118. These include permitting libraries to make single photocopies of articles and permitting persons to make phonograph records of music without permission upon payment of certain royalties. As we saw earlier, p. 470, *supra*, § 111 deals with cable television. Probably the most important of these limitations is found in § 107, dealing with the question of fair use. Until the 1976 statute fair use had been left to develop as a judicially created exception to the rights of the copyright owner. There was great controversy over whether to recognize the defense explicitly and, if so, how to do it. The result is § 107:

> Notwithstanding the provisions of section 106, the fair use of a copyrighted work, including such use by reproduction in copies or

phonorecords or by any other means specified by that section, for purposes such as criticism, comment, news reporting, teaching (including multiple copies for classroom use), scholarship, or research, is not an infringement of copyright. In determining whether the use made of a work in any particular case is a fair use the factors to be considered shall include—

(1) the purpose and character of the use, including whether such use is of a commercial nature or is for nonprofit educational purposes;

(2) the nature of the copyrighted work;

(3) the amount and substantiality of the portion used in relation to the copyrighted work as a whole; and

(4) the effect of the use upon the potential market for or value of the copyrighted work.　17 U.S.C.A. § 107.

The following case involves two special fair use questions. One is the application of fair use to historical works. Remember our earlier discussion of historical works, p. 552, *supra.* The other question is whether fair use can be used if the copyrighted work was unpublished at the time of infringement. The case is also an excellent illustration of how courts approach fair use cases in general.

HARPER & ROW PUBLISHERS, INC. v. NATION ENTERPRISES

Supreme Court of the United States, 1985.
471 U.S. 539, 105 S.Ct. 2218, 85 L.Ed.2d 588, 11 Med.L.Rptr. 1969.

Justice O'Connor delivered the opinion of the Court.

This case requires us to consider to what extent the "fair use" provision of the Copyright Revision Act of 1976, 17 U.S.C. § 107 (hereinafter the Copyright Act), sanctions the unauthorized use of quotations from a public figure's unpublished manuscript. In March 1979, an undisclosed source provided The Nation magazine with the unpublished manuscript of "A Time to Heal: The Autobiography of Gerald R. Ford." Working directly from the purloined manuscript, an editor of The Nation produced a short piece entitled "The Ford Memoirs—Behind the Nixon Pardon." The piece was timed to "scoop" an article scheduled shortly to appear in Time magazine. Time had agreed to purchase the exclusive right to print prepublication excerpts from the copyright holders. . . .

I

. . . . The memoirs were to contain "significant hitherto unpublished material" concerning the Watergate crisis, Mr. Ford's pardon of Former President Nixon and "Mr. Ford's reflections on this period of history, and the morality and personalities involved." . . . In addition to the right to publish the Ford memoirs in book form, the agreement gave petitioners the exclusive right to license prepublication excerpts, known in the trade as "first serial rights." . . . . [A]s the memoirs were nearing completion, petitioners negotiated a prepublication licensing agreement with Time, a weekly news magazine. Time agreed to pay $25,000, $12,500 in advance and an additional $12,500 at publication, in exchange for the right to excerpt 7,500 words from Mr. Ford's account of the Nixon pardon. The issue featuring the excerpts was timed to appear approximately one week before shipment of the full length book version to bookstores. Exclusivity was an important consideration; Harper & Row instituted procedures designed to maintain the confidentiality of the manuscript, and Time retained the right to renegotiate the second payment should the material appear in print prior to its release of the excerpts.

[Mr. Navasky received a copy of the manuscript.] Mr. Navasky knew that his possession of the manuscript was not authorized and that the manuscript must be returned to his "source" to avoid discovery. [ ] He hastily put together what he believed was a "real hot news story" composed of quotes, paraphrases and facts drawn exclusively from the manuscript. [ ] Mr. Navasky attempted no independent commentary, research or criticism, in part because of the need for speed if he was to "make news" by "publish[ing] in advance of publication of the Ford book." [ ] The 2,250 word article . . . appeared on April 3, 1979. As a result of The Nation's article, Time canceled its piece and refused to pay the remaining $12,500.

II

We agree with the Court of Appeals that copyright is intended to increase and not to impede the harvest of knowledge. But we believe the Second Circuit gave insufficient deference to the scheme established by the Copyright Act for fostering the original works that provide the seed and substance of this harvest. The rights conferred by copyright are designed to assure contributors to the store of knowledge a fair return for their labors. [ ]

Article I, § 8, of the Constitution provides that:

"The Congress shall have Power . . . to Promote the Progress of Science and useful Arts, by securing for limited Times to Authors and Inventors the exclusive Right to their respective Writings and Discoveries."

As we noted last Term, "[this] limited grant is a means by which an important public purpose may be achieved. It is intended to motivate the creative activity of authors and inventors by the provision of a special reward, and to allow the public access to the products of their genius after the limited period of exclusive control has expired." Sony v. Universal Studios, 464 U.S. 417 (1984). "The monopoly created by copyright thus rewards the individual author in order to benefit the public." [ ] This principle applies equally to works of fiction and nonfiction. The book at issue here, for example, was two years in the making, and began with a contract giving the author's copyright to the publishers in exchange for their services in producing and marketing the work. In preparing the book, Mr. Ford drafted essays and word portraits of hundreds of taped interviews that were later distilled to chronicle his personal viewpoint. It is evident that the monopoly granted by copyright actively served its intended purpose of inducing the creation of new material of potential historical value.

Section 106 of the Copyright Act confers a bundle of exclusive rights to the owner of the copyright. Under the Copyright Act, these rights—to publish, copy, and distribute the author's work—vest in the author of an original work from the time of its creation. In practice, the author commonly sells his rights to publishers who offer royalties in exchange for their services in producing and marketing the author's work. The copyright owner's rights, however, are subject to certain statutory exceptions. Among these is § 107, which codifies the traditional privilege of other authors to make "fair use" of an earlier writer's work. In addition, no author may copyright facts or ideas. The copyright is limited to those aspects of the work—termed "expression"—that display the stamp of the author's originality.

Creation of a nonfiction work, even a compilation of pure fact, entails originality. . . . The copyright holders of "A Time to Heal" complied with the relevant statutory notice and registration procedures. Thus, there is no dispute that the unpublished manuscript of "A Time to Heal," as a whole was protected by § 106 from unauthorized reproduction. Nor do respondents dispute that verbatim copying of excerpts of the manuscript's original form of expression would constitute infringement unless excused as fair use. [ ] Yet copyright does not prevent subsequent users from copying from a prior author's work those constituent elements that are not original—for example, quotations borrowed under the rubric of fair use from other copyrighted works, facts, or materials in the public domain—as long as such use does not unfairly appropriate the author's original contributions. [ ] Perhaps the controversy between the lower courts in the case over copyrightability is more aptly a dispute over whether The Nation's appropriation of unoriginal and uncopyrightable elements encroached on the originality embodied in the work as a whole. Especially in the realm of factual narrative, the law is currently unsettled regarding the ways in which uncopyrightable elements combine with the author's original contributions to form protected expression. . . .

We need not reach these issues, however, as The Nation has admitted to lifting verbatim quotes of the author's original language totalling between 300 and 400 words and constituting some 13% of The Nation article. In using generous verbatim excerpts of Mr. Ford's unpublished manuscript to lend authenticity to its account of the forthcoming memoirs, The Nation effectively arrogated to itself the right of first publication, an important marketable subsidiary right. For the reasons set forth below, we find that this use of the copyrighted manuscript, even stripped to the verbatim quotes conceded by The Nation as to be copyrightable expression, was not a fair use within the meaning of the Copyright Act.

III

A

Fair use was traditionally defined as "a privilege in others than the owner of the copyright to use the copyrighted material in a reasonable manner without his consent." [ ] The statutory formulation of the defense of fair use in the Copyright Act of 1976 reflects the intent of Congress to codify the common-law doctrine. Section 107 requires a case-by-case determination whether a particular use is fair, and the statute notes four nonexclusive factors to be considered. This approach was "intended to restate the [pre-existing] judicial doctrine of fair use, not to change, narrow, or enlarge it in any way." H.R.Rep. No. 94–1476, p. 66 (1976) (hereinafter House Report).

"[T]he author's consent to a reasonable use of his copyrighted works ha[d] always been implied by the courts as a necessary incident of the constitutional policy of promoting the progress of science and the useful arts, since a prohibition of such use would inhibit subsequent writers from attempting to improve upon prior works and thus . . . frustrate the very ends sought to be attained." . . .

. . .

Perhaps because the fair use doctrine was predicated on the author's implied consent to "reasonable and customary" use when he released his work for public consumption, fair use traditionally was not recognized as a defense to charges of copying from an author's as yet unpublished works. Under common-law copyright, "the property of the author . . . in his intellectual creation [was] absolute until he voluntarily part[ed] with the same." [ ] This absolute rule, however, was tempered in practice by the equitable nature of the fair use doctrine. In a given case, factors such as implied consent through *de facto* publication or performance or dissemination of a work may tip the balance of equities in favor of prepublication use. [ ] But it has never been seriously disputed that "the fact that the plaintiff's work is unpublished . . . is a factor tending to negate the defense of fair use." . . .

The Copyright Revision Act of 1976 represents the culmination of a major legislative reexamination of copyright doctrine. Among its other innovations, it eliminated publication "as a dividing line between common law and statutory protection," [ ], extending statutory protection to all works from the time of their creation. It also recognized for the first time a distinct statutory right of first publication, which had previously been an element of the common-law protections afforded unpublished works. . . .

Though the right of first publication, like the other rights enumerated in § 106, is expressly made subject to the fair use provision of § 107, fair use analysis must always be tailored to the individual case. The nature of the interest at stake is highly relevant to whether a given use is fair. From the beginning, those entrusted with the task of revision recognized the "overbalancing reasons to preserve the common law protection of undisseminated works until the author or his successor chooses to disclose them." [ ] The right of first publication implicates a threshold decision by the author whether and in what form to release his work. First publication is inherently different from other § 106 rights in that only one person can be the first publisher; as the contract with Time illustrates, the commercial value of the right lies primarily in exclusivity. Because the potential damage to the author from judicially enforced "sharing" of the first publication right with unauthorized users of his manuscript is substantial, the balance of equities in evaluating such a claim of fair use inevitably shifts.

. . .

. . . The author's control of first public distribution implicates not only his personal interest in creative control but his property interest in exploitation of prepublication rights, which are valuable in themselves and serve as a valuable adjunct to publicity and marketing. See Belushi v. Woodward, 598 F.Supp. 36 (DC 1984) (successful marketing depends on coordination of serialization and release to public); Marks, Subsidiary Rights and Permissions, in What Happens in Book Publishing, 230 (C. Grannis ed. 1967) (exploitation of subsidiary rights is necessary to financial success of new books). Under ordinary circumstances, the author's right to control the first public appearance of his undisseminated expression will outweigh a claim of fair use.

B

Respondents, however, contend that First Amendment values require a different rule under the circumstances of this case. The thrust of the decision below is that "[t]he scope of [fair use] is undoubtedly wider when the information conveyed relates to matters of high public concern." . . . Respondents explain their copying of Mr. Ford's expression as essential to reporting the news story it claims the book itself represents. In respondents' view, not only the facts contained in Mr. Ford's memoirs, but "the precise manner in which [he] expressed himself was as newsworthy as what he had to say." [ ] Respondents argue that the public's interest in learning this news as fast as possible outweighs the right of the author to control its first publication.

The Second Circuit noted, correctly, that copyright's idea/expression dichotomy "strike[s] a definitional balance between the First Amendment and the Copyright Act by permitting free communication of facts while still protecting an author's expression." [ ] No author may copyright his ideas or the facts he narrates. . . . As this Court long ago observed: "[T]he news element—the information respecting current events contained in the literary production—is not the creation of the writer, but is a report of matters that ordinarily are *public juris;* it is history of the day." International News Service v. Associated Press, [ ]. But copyright assures those who write and publish factual narratives such as "A Time to Heal" that they may at least enjoy the right to market the original expression contained therein as just compensation for their investment.

. . . The promise of copyright would be an empty one if it could be avoided merely by dubbing the infringement a fair use "news report" of the book.

Nor do respondents assert any actual necessity for circumventing the copyright scheme with respect to the types of works and users at issue here.[6] Where an author and publisher have invested extensive resources in creating an original work and are poised to release it to the public, no legitimate aim is served by preempting the right of first publication. . . .

In our haste to disseminate news, it should not be forgotten that the Framers intended copyright itself to be the engine of free expression. . . .

It is fundamentally at odds with the scheme of copyright to accord lesser rights in those works that are of greatest importance to the public. Such a notion ignores the major premise of copyright and injures author and public alike. . . .

. . .

IV

. . . [W]hether The Nation article constitutes fair use under § 107 must be reviewed in light of the principles discussed above. The factors enumerated in the section are not meant to be exclusive: "[S]ince the doctrine is an equitable rule of reason, no generally applicable definition is possible, and each case raising the question must be decided on its own facts." [ ] The four factors identified by Congress as especially relevant in determining whether the use was fair are: (1) the purpose and character of the use; (2) the nature of the copyrighted work; (3) the substantiality of the portion used in relation to the copyrighted work as a whole; (4) the effect on the potential market for or value of the copyrighted work. We address each one separately.

Purpose of the Use. The Second Circuit correctly identified news reporting as the general purpose of The Nation's use. News reporting is one of the examples enumerated in § 107 to "give some idea of the sort of activities the courts might regard as fair use under the circumstances." . . . The fact that an article arguably is "news" and therefore a productive use is simply one factor in a fair use analysis.

. . . The Nation has every right to seek to be the first to publish information. But The Nation went beyond simply reporting uncopyrightable information and actively sought to exploit the headline value

---

6. It bears noting that Congress in the Copyright Act recognized a public interest warranting specific exemptions in a number of areas not within traditional fair use, see, e.g., 17 U.S.C. § 115 (compulsory license for records); § 105 (no copyright in government works). No such exemption limits copyright in personal narratives written by public servants after they leave government service.

of its infringement, making a "news event" out of its unauthorized first publication of a noted figure's copyrighted expression.

The fact that a publication was commercial as opposed to non-profit is a separate factor that tends to weigh against a finding of fair use. "[E]very commercial use of copyrighted material is presumptively an unfair exploitation of the monopoly privilege that belongs to the owner of the copyright." [*Sony*] In arguing that the purpose of news reporting is not purely commercial, The Nation misses the point entirely. The crux of the profit/nonprofit distinction is not whether the sole motive of the use is monetary gain but whether the user stands to profit from exploitation of the copyrighted material without paying the customary price.

In evaluating character and purpose we cannot ignore The Nation's stated purpose of scooping the forthcoming hardcover and Time abstracts. The Nation's use had not merely the incidental effect but the *intended purpose* of supplanting the copyright holder's commercially valuable right of first publication. Also relevant to the "character" of the use is "the propriety of the defendant's conduct." [　] The trial court found that The Nation knowingly exploited a purloined manuscript. Unlike the typical claim of fair use, The Nation cannot offer up even the fiction of consent as justification. Like its competitor newsweekly, it was free to bid for the right of abstracting excerpts from "A Time to Heal." . . .

Nature of the Copyrighted Work. Second, the Act directs attention to the nature of the copyrighted work. "A Time to Heal" may be characterized as an unpublished historical narrative or autobiography. The law generally recognizes a greater need to disseminate factual works than works of fiction or fantasy. . . . Some of the briefer quotes from the memoir are arguably necessary adequately to convey the facts: for example, Mr. Ford's characterization of the White House tapes as the "smoking gun" is perhaps so integral to the idea expressed as to be inseparable from it. But The Nation did not stop at isolated phrases and instead excerpted subjective descriptions and portraits of public figures whose power lies in the author's individualized expression. Such use, focusing on the most expressive elements of the work, exceeds that necessary to disseminate the facts.

The fact that a work is unpublished is a critical element of its "nature." Our prior discussion establishes that the scope of fair use is narrower with respect to unpublished works. . . .

In the case of Mr. Ford's manuscript, the copyrightholders' interest in confidentiality is irrefutable; the copyrightholders had entered into a contractual undertaking to "keep the manuscript confidential" and required that all those to whom the manuscript was shown also "sign an agreement to keep the manuscript confidential." While the copyrightholders' contract with Time required Time to submit its proposed article seven days before publication, The Nation's clandestine publication afforded no such opportunity for creative or quality control. It was hastily patched together and contained "a number of inaccuracies." A use that so clearly infringes the copyrightholder's interests in confidentiality and creative control is difficult to characterize as "fair."

Amount and Substantiality of the Portion Used. Next, the Act directs us to examine the amount and substantiality of the portion used in relation to the copyrighted work as a whole. In absolute terms, the words actually quoted were an insubstantial portion of "A Time to Heal." The district court, however, found that "[T]he Nation took what was essentially the heart of the book." [ ] We believe the Court of Appeals erred in overruling the district judge's evaluation of the qualitative nature of the taking. See, e.g., Roy Export Co. Establishment v. Columbia Broadcasting System, Inc., [ ] (taking of 55 seconds out of one hour and twenty-nine minute film deemed qualitatively substantial). A Time editor described the chapters on the pardon as "the most interesting and moving parts of the entire manuscript." . . .

As the statutory language indicates, a taking may not be excused merely because it is insubstantial with respect to the *infringing* work. As Judge Learned Hand cogently remarked, "[N]o plagiarist can excuse the wrong by showing how much of his work he did not pirate." [*Sheldon*] Conversely, the fact that a substantial portion of the infringing work was copied verbatim is evidence of the qualitative value of the copied material, both to the originator and to the plagiarist who seeks to profit from marketing someone else's copyrighted expression.

Stripped to the verbatim quotes, the direct takings from the unpublished manuscript constitute at least 13% of the infringing article. See [*Meeropol*] (copyrighted letters constituted less than 1% of infringing work but were prominently featured). The Nation article is structured around the quoted excerpts which serve as its dramatic focal points. In view of the expressive value of the excerpts and their key role in the infringing work, we cannot agree with the Second Circuit that the "magazine took a meager, indeed an infinitesimal amount of Ford's original language." [ ]

Effect on the Market. Finally, the Act focuses on "the effect of the use upon the potential market for or value of the copyrighted work." This last factor is undoubtedly the single most important element of fair use. . . . [O]nce a copyrightholder establishes with reasonable probability the existence of a causal connection between the infringement and a loss of revenue, the burden properly shifts to the infringer to show that this damage would have occurred had there been no taking of copyrighted expression. Petitioners established a prima facie case of actual damage that respondent failed to rebut. The trial court properly awarded actual damages and accounting of profits.

. . .

It is undisputed that the factual material in the balance of The Nation's article, besides the verbatim quotes at issue here, was drawn exclusively from the chapters on the pardon. The excerpts were employed as featured episodes in a story about the Nixon pardon—precisely the use petitioners had licensed to Time. The borrowing of these verbatim quotes from the unpublished manuscript lent The Nation's piece a special air of authenticity—as Navasky [*The Nation*'s editor] expressed it, the reader would know it was Ford speaking and not The Nation. Thus, it directly competed for a share of the market for prepublication excerpts. . . .

V

. . . In sum, the traditional doctrine of fair use, as embodied in the Copyright Act, does not sanction the use made by The Nation of these copyrighted materials. Any copyright infringer may claim to benefit the public by increasing public access to the copyrighted work. But Congress has not designed, and we see no warrant for judicially imposing, a "compulsory license" permitting unfettered access to the unpublished copyrighted expression of public figures.

The Nation conceded that its verbatim copying of some 300 words of direct quotation from the Ford manuscript would constitute an infringement unless excused as a fair use. Because we find that The Nation's use of these verbatim excerpts from the unpublished manuscript was not a fair use, the judgment of the Court of Appeals is reversed and remanded for further proceedings consistent with this opinion.

It is so ordered.

JUSTICE BRENNAN, with whom JUSTICE WHITE and JUSTICE MARSHALL join, dissenting.

The Court holds that The Nation's quotation of 300 words from the unpublished 200,000–word manuscript of President Gerald R. Ford infringed the copyright in that manuscript, even though the quotations related to a historical event of undoubted significance—the resignation and pardon of President Richard M. Nixon. Although the Court pursues the laudable goal of protecting "the economic incentive to create and disseminate ideas," this zealous defense of the copyright owner's prerogative will, I fear, stifle the broad dissemination of ideas and information copyright is intended to nurture. Protection of the copyright owner's economic interest is achieved in this case through an exceedingly narrow definition of the scope of fair use. The progress of arts and sciences and the robust public debate essential to an enlightened citizenry are ill served by this constricted reading of the fair use doctrine. [   ] I therefore respectfully dissent.

I

A

This case presents two issues. First, did The Nation's use of material from the Ford manuscript in forms other than direct quotation from that manuscript infringe Harper & Row's copyright. Second, did the quotation of approximately 300 words from the manuscript infringe the copyright because this quotation did not constitute "fair use" within the meaning of § 107 of the Copyright Act. The Court finds no need to resolve the threshold copyrightability issue. The use of 300 words of quotation was, the Court finds, beyond the scope of fair use and thus a copyright infringement. Because I disagree with the Court's fair use holding, it is necessary for me to decide the threshold copyrightability question.

. . .

The "originality" requirement now embodied in § 102 of the Copyright Act is crucial to maintenance of the appropriate balance between these competing interests. Properly interpreted in the light of the legislative history, this section extends copyright protection to an author's literary form but permits free use by others of the ideas and information the author communicates. . . .

It follows that infringement of copyright must be based on a taking of literary form, as opposed to the ideas or information contained in a copyrighted work. Deciding whether an infringing appropriation of literary form has occurred is difficult for at least two reasons. First, the distinction between literary form and information or ideas is often elusive in practice. Second, infringement must be based on a *substantial* appropriation of literary form. This determination is equally challenging. Not surprisingly, the test for infringement has defied precise formulation. In general, though, the inquiry proceeds along two axes: *how closely* has the second author tracked the first author's particular language and structure of presentation; and *how much* of the first author's language and structure has the second author appropriated.

. . .

The Language. Much of the information The Nation conveyed was not in the form of paraphrase at all, but took the form of synopsis of lengthy discussions in the Ford manuscript. In the course of this summary presentation, The Nation did use occasional sentences that closely resembled language in the original Ford manuscript. But these linguistic similarities are insufficient to constitute an infringement. . . .

At most The Nation paraphrased disparate isolated sentences from the original. A finding of infringement based on paraphrase generally requires far more close and substantial a tracking of the original language than occurred in this case.

The Structure of Presentation. The article does not mimic Mr. Ford's structure. The information The Nation presents is drawn from scattered sections of the Ford work and does not appear in the sequence in which Mr. Ford presented it. . . . Also, it is difficult to suggest that a 2,000–word article could bodily appropriate the structure of a 200,000–word book. Most of what Mr. Ford created, and most of the history he recounted, was simply not represented in The Nation's article.

When The Nation was not quoting Mr. Ford, therefore, its efforts to convey the historical information in the Ford manuscript did not so closely and substantially track Mr. Ford's language and structure as to constitute an appropriation of literary form.

II

The Nation is thus liable in copyright only if the quotation of 300 words infringed any of Harper & Row's exclusive rights under § 106 of the Act. . . . The question here is whether The Nation's quotation was a noninfringing fair use within the meaning of § 107.

. . .

With respect to a work of history, particularly the memoirs of a public official, the statutorily-prescribed analysis cannot properly be conducted without constant attention to copyright's crucial distinction between protected literary form and unprotected information or ideas. The question must always be: was the subsequent author's use of *literary form* a fair use within the meaning of § 107, in light of the purpose for the use, the nature of the copyrighted work, the amount of literary form used, and the effect of this use of literary form on the value of or market for the original.

Limiting the inquiry to the propriety of a subsequent author's use of the copyrighted owner's literary form is not easy in the case of a work of history. Protection against only substantial appropriation of literary form does not ensure historians a return commensurate with the full value of their labors. . . . Copyright thus does not protect that which is often of most value in a work of history and courts must resist the tendency to reject the fair use defense on the basis of their feeling that an author of history has been deprived of the full value of his or her labor. A subsequent author's taking of information and ideas is in no sense piratical because copyright law simply does not create any property interest in information and ideas.

The urge to compensate for subsequent use of information and ideas is perhaps understandable. An inequity seems to lurk in the idea that much of the fruit of the historian's labor may be used without compensation. This, however, is not some unforeseen by-product of a statutory scheme intended primarily to ensure a return for works of the imagination. Congress made the affirmative choice that the copyright laws should apply in this way. . . .

. . . Application of the statutorily prescribed analysis with attention to the distinction between information and literary form leads to a straightforward finding of fair use within the meaning of § 107.

The Purpose of the Use. The Nation's purpose in quoting 300 words of the Ford manuscript was, as the Court acknowledges, news reporting. . . .

. . .

The Court concedes the validity of the news reporting purpose but then quickly offsets it against three purportedly countervailing considerations. First, the Court asserts that because The Nation publishes for profit, its publication of the Ford quotes is a presumptively unfair commercial use. Second, the Court claims that The Nation's stated desire to create a "news event" signalled an illegitimate purpose of supplanting the copyright owner's right of first publication. Third, The Nation acted in bad faith, the Court claims, because its editor "knowingly exploited a purloined manuscript."

The Court's reliance on the commercial nature of The Nation's use as "a separate factor that tends to weigh against a finding of fair use," is inappropriate in the present context. Many uses § 107 lists as paradigmatic examples of fair use, including criticism, comment and *news reporting,* are generally conducted for profit in this country, a fact of which Congress was obviously aware when it enacted § 107. To negate any argument favoring fair use based on news reporting or criticism because that reporting or criticism was published for profit is to render meaningless the congressional imprimatur placed on such uses.

Nor should The Nation's intent to create a "news event" weigh against a finding of fair use. Such a rule, like the Court's automatic presumption against news reporting for profit, would undermine the congressional validation of the news reporting purpose. . . . The record suggests only that The Nation sought to be the first to reveal the information in the Ford manuscript. The Nation's stated purpose of scooping the competition should under those circumstances have no negative bearing on the claim of fair use. Indeed the Court's reliance on this factor would seem to amount to little more than distaste for the standard journalistic practice of seeking to be the first to publish news.

The Court's reliance on The Nation's putative bad faith is equally unwarranted. No court has found that The Nation possessed the Ford manuscript illegally or in violation of any common law interest of Harper & Row; all common law causes of action have been abandoned or dismissed in this case. Even if the manuscript had been "purloined" by someone, nothing in this record imputes culpability to The Nation. On the basis of the record in this case, the most that can be said is that The Nation made use of the contents of the manuscript knowing the copyright owner would not sanction the use.

. . .

The Nature of the Copyrighted Work. . . .

The Court acknowledges that "[t]he law generally recognizes a greater need to disseminate factual works than works of fiction or fantasy," and that "some of the briefer quotations from the memoir are arguably necessary to convey the facts," ibid. But the Court discounts the force of this consideration, primarily on the ground that "the fact that a work is unpublished is a crucial element of its 'nature.'" At this point the Court introduces into analysis of this case a categorical presumption against prepublication fair use. ("Under ordinary circumstances, the author's right to control the first public appearance of his undisseminated expression will outweigh a claim of fair use.")

This categorical presumption is unwarranted on its own terms and unfaithful to congressional intent. Whether a particular prepublication use will impair any interest the Court identifies as encompassed within the right of first publication, will depend on the nature of the copyrighted work, the timing of prepublication use, the amount of expression used and the medium in which the second author communicates. Also, certain uses might be tolerable for some purposes and not others. . . .

. . .

The Amount and Substantiality of the Portion Used. More difficult questions arise with respect to judgments about the importance to this case of the amount and substantiality of the quotations used. . . .

. . .

At least with respect to the six particular quotes of Mr. Ford's observations and reflections about President Nixon, I agree with the Court's conclusion that The Nation appropriated some literary form of substantial quality. I do not agree, however, that the substantiality of the expression taken was clearly excessive or inappropriate to The Nation's news reporting purpose.

Had these quotations been used in the context of a critical book review of the Ford book, there is little question that such a use would be fair use within the meaning of § 107 of the Act. The amount and substantiality of the use—in both quantitative and qualitative terms— would have certainly been appropriate to the purpose of such a use. It is difficult to see how the use of these quoted words in a news report is less appropriate. . . .

. . .

The Effect on the Market. The Court correctly notes that the effect on the market "is undoubtedly the single most important element of fair use," and the Court properly focuses on whether The Nation's use adversely affected Harper & Row's serialization potential and not merely the market for sales of the Ford work itself. Unfortunately, the Court's failure to distinguish between the use of information and the appropriation of literary form badly skews its analysis of this factor.

The Nation's publication indisputably precipitated Time's eventual cancellation. But that does not mean that The Nation's use of the 300 quoted words caused this injury to Harper & Row. Wholly apart from these quoted words, The Nation published significant information and ideas from the Ford manuscript. If it was this publication of information, and not the publication of the few quotations, that caused Time to abrogate its serialization agreement, then whatever the negative effect on the serialization market, that effect was the product of wholly legitimate activity.

. . .

Balancing the Interests. Once the distinction between information and literary form is made clear, the statutorily prescribed process of weighing the four statutory fair use factors discussed above leads naturally to a conclusion that The Nation's limited use of literary form was not an infringement. . . .

III

The Court's exceedingly narrow approach to fair use permits Harper & Row to monopolize information. This holding "effect[s] an important extension of property rights and a corresponding curtailment in the free use of knowledge and of ideas." International News Service v. Associated Press, 248 U.S. at 263 (Brandeis, J. dissenting). The Court has perhaps advanced the ability of the historian—or at least the public official who has recently left office—to capture the full economic value of information in his or her possession. But the Court does so only by risking the robust debate of public issues that is the "essence of self-government." Garrison v. Louisiana, 379 U.S., at 74–75. The Nation was providing the grist for that robust debate. The Court imposes liability upon The Nation for no other reason than that The Nation succeeded in being the first to provide certain information to the public. I dissent.

Notes and Questions

1. How would the analysis change if *The Nation's* article had appeared a week after the book was published? A week after the *Time* publication?

2. During the oral argument counsel for *The Nation* asserted that "There are two words to describe what *The Nation* was doing: news reporting." Does the majority accept that view?

3. Although most commentators have concluded that the 1976 statute did not change the prior law of fair use, it seems safer to consider cases decided since then. A sampling of post–1976 fair use cases follows.

a. In Sony Corp. v. Universal City Studios, Inc., 464 U.S. 417 (1984), discussed in more detail later in this chapter, the Court, 5–4, held that home recording of broadcast television programs constitutes a fair use. "[A]lthough every commercial use of copyrighted material is presumptively an unfair exploitation of the monopoly privilege," a different rule applies for noncommercial uses. Here, plaintiff must show "either that the particular use is harmful, or that if it should become widespread, it would adversely affect the potential market for the copyrighted work. Actual present harm need not be shown . . .. Nor is it necessary to show with certainty that future harm will result. What is necessary is a showing by a preponderance of the evidence that *some* meaningful likelihood of future harm exists. If the intended use is for commercial gain, that likelihood may be presumed. But if it is for a noncommercial purpose, the likelihood must be demonstrated."

Two critical findings of the trial court led the majority to deny protection. "First, Sony demonstrated a significant likelihood that substantial numbers of copyright holders who license their works for broadcast on free television would not object to having their broadcasts time-shifted by private viewers. And second, respondents failed to demonstrate that time-shifting would cause any likelihood of nonminimal harm to the potential market for, or the value of, their copyrighted works." These led the Court to conclude that time-shifting, by far the most common use of the recorders, was fair use.

b. In Pacific and Southern Co., Inc. v. Duncan, 744 F.2d 1490, 56 R.R.2d 1620, 11 Med.L.Rptr. 1135 (11th Cir.1984), certiorari denied 471 U.S. 1004 (1985), plaintiff television station WXIA–TV presented four copyrighted local news programs daily. It audiotaped and videotaped each program. It retained the audiotape and the written transcript of the program for an indefinite time; it erased the videotape after seven days. WXIA did not market clips of its own stories, though it honored requests for tapes when made.

Defendant, doing business as TV News Clips, taped the news programs of television stations and tried to sell copies of the clips to those persons or groups covered by the news reports. The copies were not copyrighted and stated "for personal use only not for rebroadcast." Defendant erased tapes after one month.

The court of appeals found a valid copyright even though the only fixed copy was defendant's. The plaintiff's tapes satisfied the requirement that the work be fixed for a period of "more than transitory duration." On the fair use question, the court turned to the four factors. The commercial nature of defendant's practices "militates quite strongly against a finding of fair use." Moreover, defendant's use "is neither productive nor creative in any way. It does not analyze the broadcast or improve it at all. . . . TV News Clips only copies and sells." Since the court treated each story on the news as a "coherent narrative," it found that the defendant had taken the entire work. The fourth factor also cut against defendant since it "uses the broadcasts for a purpose that WXIA might use for its own benefit." The potential market is undermined.

The second factor might be seen to favor defendant because of the importance to society of access to the news. "But the courts should also take care not to discourage authors from addressing important topics for fear of losing their copyright protections."

Defendant argued that every copyright must further the ends of the copyright clause and that this one did not because of WXIA's systematic destruction of videotapes. (Although the defendant treated this as a First Amendment argument, the court thought it should be addressed under fair use.) Not every copyright holder "must offer benefits to society, for the copyright is an incentive rather than a command. And, *a fortiori,* a copyright holder need not provide the most complete public access possible. WXIA provides complete access for seven days and permanent access to everything except the visual images broadcast live from within the studio. The public benefits from this creative work; therefore, enforcing the copyright statute in this case does not violate the Copyright Clause."

The court held that the district court had abused its discretion by refusing to issue an injunction after finding an infringement.

c. In Diamond v. Am–Law Publishing Corp., 745 F.2d 142 (2d Cir.1984), defendant *American Lawyer* published a story reporting that a formal grievance had been filed against plaintiff lawyer. He wrote defendant demanding an apology and a retraction. The editor invited the plaintiff to write a letter stating that no grievance had been filed. Plaintiff then sent a long letter making that point and also attacking the reporting practices of the defendant. The letter stated that "You are authorized to publish this letter but only in its entirety." Defendant published excerpts from the letter that made the point about the grievance but omitted, without showing any deletions, the parts attacking the defendant.

Plaintiff obtained a copyright on the letter and sued for infringement. The trial court's grant of summary judgment for defendant and its award of $15,000 in attorney's fees and costs were affirmed on appeal.

Fair use was established as a matter of law. The nonuse or editing of the letter did not put the copyrighted work in an unfair or distorted light. The omissions involved an unrelated matter and did not mislead the public about the contents of the entire letter. (Even if it did, it was not clear that this made it a copyright violation.) In any event, the use here was for comment or news reporting, uses protected under § 107. The claim that too little was used differed from the usual claim and did not help the plaintiff. Finally, plaintiff could show no present or future use of the letter that had been adversely affected by defendant's use.

d. Defendant wrote a book about Julius and Ethel Rosenberg: their trial, conviction and execution for conspiring to transmit national defense information to the Soviet Union. The book quoted verbatim from 28 copyrighted letters written by the Rosenbergs while in prison— a total of 1,957 words. The plaintiffs, sons of the Rosenbergs, claimed the copyright in the letters, which had been published as the book, *Death House Letters.* The trial judge dismissed the claim but was reversed on appeal.

The court noted that although the letters represented less than 1 percent of the defendant's book, they were featured prominently in promotional literature for the book. Several questions of fact had to be resolved before the fair use question could be answered: the purpose for which the letters were used in the defendant's book, the need for verbatim copying of the letters and the effect of their use on the future market for *Death House Letters*. The fact that *Death House Letters* had been out of print for 20 years did not necessarily mean that the letters had no future market. The possibilities of republication, and sale of motion picture rights, might have been affected by their use in defendant's book. Meeropol v. Nizer, 560 F.2d 1061, 2 Med.L.Rptr. 2269 (2d Cir.1977), certiorari denied 434 U.S. 1013 (1978).

e.   In Salinger v. Random House, Inc., 811 F.2d 90, 13 Med.L.Rptr. 1954 (2d Cir.1987), author J.D. Salinger sought an injunction to stop publication by Random House and author Ian Hamilton of an unauthorized biography entitled *J.D. Salinger: A Writing Life*. The biography drew heavily from approximately 70 copyrighted letters written by Salinger many years ago, and Salinger alleged that their use was a copyright infringement.

The letters had been deposited by their recipients in several university libraries, where Hamilton had access to them. Reacting to Salinger's demand, Hamilton substantially revised his book after it had been set in type, rewriting or paraphrasing most of the previously quoted material from the letters so that he quoted no more than 10 percent of any one letter and, in most cases, no more than 10 words from any one letter.

The district court held that the vast majority of the material taken from the letters—the *information* in them—was not copyrightable: "For the biographer to report in his own words Salinger's ideas drawn from the letters or the fact that Salinger was depressed, elated, or angry, does not violate the copyright."

Salinger's attorneys had argued that the doctrine of fair use could not apply to unpublished works like Salinger's letters, and there was little case precedent involving unpublished works; but the district court held that "plaintiff's argument that there may be no fair use of an unpublished work is exaggerated and unreasonable." Calling Hamilton's use of Salinger's copyright material "minimal and insubstantial," the court refused to enjoin publication.

The court of appeals reversed, holding that "[t]he taking is significant not only from a quantitative standpoint but from a qualitative one as well," and enjoined distribution of the biography.

The court of appeals relied heavily on *Harper & Row* for its fair use analysis because it was "the court's first delineation of the scope of fair use as *applied to unpublished works*" (emphasis added).

In considering the application of the four fair-use factors to Hamilton's use of the Salinger letters, the court started by categorizing the purpose of the use alternatively as "criticism," "scholarship" or "research." All of these categories are viewed as appropriate to a fair use. The court went on, however, to reject specifically the district court's assertion that a biographer is entitled to an especially generous application of the defense. The district court had argued that this was necessary because of the special dilemma faced by a biographer ("to the extent he departs from the words of the letters, he distorts, sacrificing both accuracy and vividness of description"). The court of appeals, however, recognized no need to take the *expression* contained in the letters.

Although acknowledging that Salinger disavowed any intention to publish the letters during his lifetime, the court wrote that Salinger was entitled to protect his *opportunity* to sell them—an opportunity estimated by Salinger's literary agent to be worth more than $500,000. Note, however, that Salinger's interest was essentially one of privacy not profit—a situation quite different from that in *Harper & Row,* where economic gain was the plaintiff's principal concern.

In its analysis of the nature of the work, the court of appeals' opinion emphasized the insulation of unpublished works like Salinger's letters from fair use, quoting from the Supreme Court's opinion in *Harper & Row* that "the scope of fair use is narrower with respect to unpublished works." The Supreme Court denied *certiorari,* 484 U.S. 890 (1987).

f. The Second Circuit again addressed the fair use doctrine in New Era Publications International v. Henry Holt & Co., 873 F.2d 576, 16 Med.L.Rptr. 1559 (2d Cir.1989). The case involved a biography by Russell Miller entitled *Bare–Faced Messiah: The True Story of L. Ron Hubbard.* The book contended that Hubbard and the Church of Scientology, which he founded, had glorified Hubbard's image over a period of 30 years through various embellished and distorted accounts of Hubbard's life and activities in Hubbard's own writings and in information put out by the church.

Miller relied in part on information from court records, official documents, interviews and newspaper stories, but in many instances the evidence of alleged discrepancies and distortions came from Hubbard's own unpublished works, such as letters and diaries. Copyright in these works was held by New Era under license from the Church of Scientology, to which Hubbard had bequeathed the rights upon his death.

New Era sought to enjoin publication of the biography in the United States. The case was decided by Judge Leval, who had decided the *Salinger* case. He believed *Bare–Faced Messiah* should be protected as fair use but conceded that "given *Salinger* 's strong presumption against fair use for unpublished materials, I cannot conclude that the Court of Appeals would accord fair use protection to all of Miller's quotations, or that the biography as a whole would be considered non-infringing." he concluded that the book contained 44 passages that would not qualify as fair use under *Salinger.*

Nevertheless, Leval exercised his equitable discretion to deny the injunction. He conceded that injunctive relief is common in copyright cases, but said those typically involve "piracy of artistic creations motivated exclusively by greed." This case was different:

[A]n injunction would . . . suppress an interesting, well-researched, provocative study of a figure who, claiming both scientific and religious credentials, has wielded enormous influence over millions of people. . . . The abhorrence of the First Amendment to prior restraint is so powerful a force in shaping so many areas of our law, it would be anomalous to presume casually its appropriateness for all cases of copyright infringement. . . .

In the past, efforts to suppress critical biography through the copyright injunction have generally not succeeded because courts (sometimes straining) have found fair use. [ ] The conflict between freedom of speech and the injunctive remedy was thus avoided. Since *Salinger*, however, the issue is inescapable.

He concluded that New Era's damage remedy was adequate to protect its copyright interests with far less harm to First Amendment interests. 695 F.Supp. 1493 (S.D.N.Y.1988).

The Second Circuit affirmed, but only on the ground of laches. (Under the doctrine of laches, if without sufficient justification a plaintiff has delayed bringing an action, and that delay harms the defendant, then the action will be dismissed.) New Era had taken no steps to protect its rights until the book was in print, even though it had known for several years that it was being prepared. "The prejudice suffered by Holt as the result of New Era's unreasonable and inexcusable delay in bringing action invokes the bar of laches." Judge Miner wrote an extended opinion, however, in which the majority rejected Judge Leval's analysis on both the fair use and First Amendment points.

As to fair use, the court said Leval's analysis was too generous to Holt, and as a result the book was a more serious infringement than Leval had concluded. Leval had suggested that use of an author's words to make a point about his character ought to be viewed more favorably than use of an author's words to display the distinctiveness of his writing style. He also urged a distinction between uses to merely "enliven" the text and uses that are necessary to communicate significant points about the subject. The court of appeals rejected both of those suggestions and also disagreed with Leval's conclusion that Miller's book would not affect the market for an authorized biography of Hubbard, which New Era said it planned to commission.

As for Leval's First Amendment concerns, the court was not persuaded "that any first amendment concerns not accommodated by the Copyright Act are implicated in this action. Our observation that the fair use doctrine encompasses all claims of first amendment in the copyright field [ ] has never been repudiated. See, e.g., [*Harper & Row*]. An author's expression of an idea, as distinguished from the idea itself, is not considered subject to the public's 'right to know.' [ ]."

Chief Judge Oakes concurred, but would have affirmed on the merits as well as on the laches ground. He believed there was no proof that *Bare-Faced Messiah* would impair the future market value of

Hubbard's writings, that the public interest in encouraging biographical work justified denying the injunction, and that "a non-injunctive remedy provides the best balance between the copyright interests and the First Amendment interests at stake in this case."

Although Henry Holt Co. had prevailed on the laches ground, it took the unusual step of requesting rehearing *en banc* to challenge the panel's conclusions on the fair use issue. The request was denied, 7–5, but it provoked a heated exchange of opinions among the judges of the Second Circuit. 884 F.2d 659, 16 Med.L.Rptr. 2224 (1989).

In the main opinion for the dissenters, Judge Newman said they feared the panel majority opinion would create "misunderstanding on the part of authors and publishers as to the copyright law of this Circuit—misunderstanding that risks deterring them from entirely lawful writings in the fields of scholarly research, biography, and journalism."

They said denial of the rehearing, "does not mean that this Circuit is committed to the language of the panel opinion . . .." They specifically challenged the portion of the panel opinion refusing to distinguish between copying to enliven text and copying to make a point about the author's character. They also questioned the panel's suggestion that injunctive relief should normally be granted when infringement is threatened. "We do not believe that anything we have said in this opinion concerning fair use or injunctive relief is contrary to the views of a majority of the judges of this court," the dissenters concluded.

Judge Miner wrote a separate opinion to comment on Judge Newman's opinion:

> First, the panel majority opinion is consistent with settled law and leaves no room for misunderstanding. Second, a dissent from a denial of rehearing en banc lacks the authority to dispel misunderstanding in any event. Third, whether or not "this Circuit is committed to the language of the panel opinion," it surely is not committed to the language of the appended dissenting opinion.

On the merits, Judge Miner again rejected the proposed distinction between copying to enliven the copier's prose and copying where necessary to report a fact. He said those considerations were irrelevant once the Court decided—as the panel did in *New Era*—that the purpose-of-use factor favored the copier anyway. "Moreover, I question whether judges, rather than literary critics, should decide whether literary material is used to enliven text or demonstrate truth. It is far too easy for one author to use another's work on the pretext that it is copied for the latter purpose rather than the former."

On the appropriateness of injunctive relief, Judge Miner said, "All now agree that injunction is not the automatic consequence of infringement and that equitable considerations always are germane to the determination of whether an injunction is appropriate." He said the statement that "the copying of 'more than minimal amounts' of unpub-

lished expressive material calls for an injunction barring the unauthorized use" with the words, "under ordinary circumstances."

g.   A year later the Second Circuit was presented with another fair use
question involving a biography of L. Ron Hubbard in New Era Publications International v. Carol Publishing Group, 904 F.2d 152, 17 Med.
L.Rptr. 1913 (2d Cir.1990).   An injunction had been issued against the
publication of *A Piece of Blue Sky: Scientology, Dianetics and L. Ron
Hubbard Exposed* by Jonathan Caven–Atack.   New Era had argued
that the book contained 121 passages drawn from 48 of Hubbard's
published works.   After finding that the copyright on one of the works
quoted had expired, the district court analyzed the other disputed
passages using the four fair use factors.   According to the district court,
the purpose and character of the use "strongly" favored New Era
because "many of the passages lack any allowable fair use purpose."
The nature of the copyrighted work also favored New Era because
many of the quoted passages "are expressive rather than factual."   The
amount used in relation to the copyrighted work as a whole was still a
third factor favoring New Era because the disputed passages constituted a "small, but significant element of" the book.   The court found that
the fourth factor, the effect of the use on the market for the copyrighted work, did not favor either party.   The court then issued a permanent
injunction listing the 103 infringing passages from 43 published works
that had to be deleted before the biography could be published.   729
F.Supp. 992 (S.D.N.Y.1990).

The court of appeals lifted the injunction, finding that the disputed
passages were a fair use.   With regard to the purpose and character of
the use, the court held that critical biographies "fit 'comfortably within'
[the] statutory categories 'of uses illustrative of uses that can be fair.'
[*Salinger*]" Although the work was intended to be published for profit,
the court distinguished it from *Harper & Row* :

> However, what the Court [in *Harper & Row*] went on to consider
> was the infringer's knowing exploitation of the copyrighted materi-
> al—obtained in an underhanded manner—for an undeserved eco-
> nomic profit.   [   ]   The present case, by contrast, does not involve
> "an attempt to rush to the market just ahead of the copyright
> holder's imminent publication," as occurred in *Harper & Row.
> Salinger* [   ].   Instead . . . the author uses Hubbard's works for
> the entirely legitimate purpose of making his point that Hubbard
> was a charlatan and the Church a dangerous cult. To be sure, the
> author and appellant want to make a profit in publishing the book.
> But the author's use of material "to enrich" his biography is
> protected fair use, "not-withstanding that he and his publisher
> anticipate profits."   *Id.*

The nature of the copyrighted work also favored Carol because all
of the works quoted were published works.   Further, the court of
appeals found that the works were factual and "the scope of fair use is
greater with respect to factual than non-factual works."

With regard to the third factor, the amount and substantiality of the portion used in relation to the copyrighted work, the court of appeals found that the quoted passages did not constitute too great a percentage of the works from which they were taken. Neither did they "take essentially the heart of Hubbard's works." Thus, the third factor favored Carol from both a quantitative and a qualitative standpoint.

Finally, in analyzing the effect of the biography on Hubbard's works as well as an authorized biography that New Era argued it intended to publish, the court of appeals first noted that:

> even assuming that the book discourages potential purchasers of the authorized biography, this is not necessarily actionable under the copyright laws. Such potential buyers might be put off because the book persuaded them (as it clearly hopes to) that Hubbard was a charlatan, but the copyright laws do not protect that sort of injury. Harm to the market for a copyrighted work or its derivatives caused by a "devastating critique" that "diminished sales by convincing the public that the original work was of poor quality" is not "within the scope of copyright protection." [   ]

In distinguishing this case from *New Era v. Henry Holt*, the court again focused on the published nature of the works:

> . . . *New Era* involved the publication of previously unpublished material, "particularly from [Hubbard's] early diaries and journals." [   ] Arguably, then, the unfavorable biography in *New Era* threatened economic harm to the authorized biography, even though it fulfilled a different function, because it contained material whose market value (1) had not yet been realized by the copyright holder, and (2) might be entirely misappropriated by the infringing publication. Here, by contrast, the works quoted from all are published, and the book will not tap any sources of economic profit that would otherwise go to the authorized biography.

Having found all four fair use factors to favor Carol, the court of appeals concluded that the book's use of the quoted passages was a fair use and ordered the injunction lifted.

h. Note that one of the considerations in determining fair use is whether the use is of an educational nature. Clearly, however, the fact that a use is educational does not give one free license to use another's copyrighted property and to infringe on another's ability to profit from his work. Recording of broadcast programming for classroom use presents particular problems which were addressed by a committee composed of representatives from both industry and education. Committee members agreed upon a set of "Guidelines for Off–Air Recording of Broadcast Programming for Educational Purposes." Copyright L.Rep. p. 20, 157 (Dec. 30, 1981).

1. The guidelines were developed to apply only to off-air recording by non-profit educational institutions.

2. A broadcast program may be recorded off-air simultaneously with broadcast transmission (including simultaneous cable retransmission) and retained by a non-profit educational institution for a period not to exceed the first forty-five (45) consecutive calendar days after date of recording. Upon conclusion of such retention period, all off-air recordings must be erased or destroyed immediately. "Broadcast programs" are television programs transmitted by television stations for reception by the general public without charge.

3. Off-air recordings may be used once by individual teachers in the course of relevant teaching activities, and repeated once only when instructional reinforcement is necessary, in classrooms and similar places devoted to instruction within a single building, cluster or campus, as well as in the homes of students receiving formalized home instruction, during the first ten (10) consecutive school days in the forty-five (45) day calendar day retention period. "School days" are school session days—not counting weekends, holidays, vacations, examination periods, or other scheduled interruptions—within the forty-five (45) calendar day retention period.

4. Off-air recordings may be made only at the request of and used by individual teachers, and may not be regularly recorded in anticipation of requests. No broadcast program may be recorded in anticipation of requests. No broadcast program may be recorded off-air more than once at the request of the same teacher, regardless of the number of times the program may be broadcast.

5. A limited number of copies may be reproduced from each off-air recording to meet the legitimate needs of teachers under these guidelines. Each such additional copy shall be subject to all provisions governing the original recording.

6. After the first ten (10) consecutive school days, off-air recordings may be used up to the end of the forty-five (45) calendar day retention period only for teacher evaluation purposes, i.e., to determine whether or not to include the broadcast program in the teaching curriculum, and may not be used in the recording institution for student exhibition or any other non-evaluation purpose without authorization.

7. Off-air recordings need not be used in their entirety, but the recorded programs may not be altered from their original content. Off-air recordings may not be physically or electronically combined or merged to constitute teaching anthologies or compilations.

8. All copies of off-air recordings must include the copyright notice on the broadcast program as recorded. Educational institutions are expected to establish appropriate control procedures to maintain the integrity of these guidelines.

It is too early to tell exactly how these guidelines will be treated by the courts, because they are not part of the Copyright Act. They were, however, entered into the Congressional Record, and they are expected to carry weight with the courts.

4. In 1986 Congress passed the Electronic Communications Privacy Act prohibiting unauthorized interception of network satellite feeds—and thus providing another kind of protection for the creators of works transmitted by electronic means. See discussion of the Electronic Communications Privacy Act in Chapter XIII.

5. The disputes—beginning in the 1980s—over "colorization" of old black and white films and the compression of films (speeding them up almost imperceptibly) in order to shorten their showing time (and thus allow more time for television commercials) raise new questions about what can be done to copyrighted works once they have been sold.

In March 1988 actors Jimmy Stewart and Burt Lancaster—along with the directors of such films as "The Last Picture Show," "The Sound of Music" and "High Noon"—went to Capitol Hill to lobby for the protection of films from what they called "desecration" through colorization.

One proposal was that "colorized" classic films would not be shown under their original titles after being colorized. That provision was dropped, however, and Senate and House conferees agreed to less strict requirements for special labels on colorized films. The provisions were included in a 1989 appropriations bill for the Interior Department and related agencies. Congressional Quarterly, Aug. 13, 1988 at 2296.

Unwilling to pass a strong anti-colorizing statute, Congress enacted a compromise version, the National Film Preservation Act of 1988, 2 U.S.C.A. §§ 178–178L. It allows the Librarian of Congress to select 25 American films each year that are "culturally, historically or esthetically significant" and to require those films to be labeled if they are altered. In such instances a warning label, similar to the one on cigarettes, is placed on video copies of such films: "This is a colorized version of a film originally marketed and distributed to the public in black and white. It has been altered without the participation of the principal director, screenwriter and other creators of the original film." A related issue is the compression of films—"lexiconning" or speeding them up imperceptibly to shorten their showing time and thus allow more time for television commercials. Here, too, the creators argue that the film's artistic integrity is violated.

The National Film Preservation Act established the 13–member National Film Preservation Board, representing writers, directors, producers, critics and scholars, to participate in the selection of the 25 films per year. Critic Caryn James, in a 1990 article critical of the law and its ambiguities, said the "coldest, hardest fact of all" is that "a labeling requirement won't stop anyone from coloring or editing a film." New York Times, Nov. 8, 1990 at C15. The act was originally due to expire in one year but has been extended through 1996.

The "Film Disclosure Act," proposed in the House of Representatives in 1991 was still before Congress in 1992. It would require copyright owners to label all movies when "materially altered" for the home video market, commercial exhibition or for transmission over cable, satellite or broadcast television. In addition to the concerns about colorization, proponents of the proposed legislation expressed concern over "panning and scanning" (a technique that attempts to make up for the loss of visual information from both sides of a wide-screen picture), adding new footage, substituting alternate takes to "soften up" the movie for family viewing, and substituting substantially different musical soundtracks. The Washington Post, May 17, 1992 at G1.

C. MUSIC LICENSING

The frequent use of copyrighted musical works by the electronic media requires special treatment. It would be difficult for individual music composers and performers to police the use of their own works, so performing rights societies have been organized for the protection of copyright holders. The groups include the American Society of Composers, Authors and Publishers (ASCAP), Broadcast Media, Inc. (BMI) and SESAC, Inc. (formerly the Society of European State Authors and Composers).

Getting permission to use copyrighted music is especially complicated. One must be concerned with both synchronization rights and performance rights. Synchronization rights allow the combining of the copyrighted music with a video to create a single work. Performance rights allow one to show the video work to others.

Whether you need to obtain the performance rights as well as the synchronization rights depends how you intend to use your video piece. If you intend to show it on broadcast television, performance rights are unnecessary. Because of the practical realities of the licensing system, broadcasters have little or no choice but to obtain blanket licenses from the major licensing societies. This means the broadcaster must either pay for a blanket license giving the right to all music licensed by that organization or refrain from using any material licensed by that organization. Even if the material is supplied by a network or syndicator and that supplier has rights to the material, the broadcaster must have the blanket license.

Thus, because the broadcaster has obtained the performing rights for almost any copyrighted piece of music, you will not need to obtain them. If you do the synchronizing, however, you must still obtain these rights.

This licensing scheme has survived several legal challenges, one of them in the case below. Performance and synchronization rights can be obtained either from the individual authors or from music licensing organizations. If you plan to use a record, the label will designate which organization (BMI, ASCAP or SESAC) licenses that piece of music.

The following case illustrates some of the music licensing problems.

BUFFALO BROADCASTING COMPANY, INC. v. AMERICAN SOCIETY OF COMPOSERS, AUTHORS AND PUBLISHERS

United States Court of Appeals, Second Circuit, 1984.
744 F.2d 917.
Certiorari denied 469 U.S. 1211, 105 S.Ct. 1181, 84 L.Ed.2d 329 (1985).

JON O. NEWMAN, CIRCUIT JUDGE:

Once again we consider the lawfulness under section 1 of the Sherman Antitrust Act of the blanket license offered by the American Society of Composers, Authors and Publishers (ASCAP) and Broadcast Music, Inc. (BMI). The license permits the licensee to perform publicly any musical composition in the repertory of the licensor. In this litigation the blanket license is challenged by a class of licensees comprising all owners of "local" television stations in the United States, i.e., stations not owned by any of the three major television networks, ABC, CBS, and NBC. After a bench trial . . . the blanket license was held to be an unreasonable restraint of trade. [ ] ASCAP and BMI were enjoined from licensing to local television stations non-dramatic music performing rights for any "syndicated" program. For reasons that follow, we conclude that the evidence was insufficient as a matter of law to show that the blanket license is an unlawful restraint of trade in the legal and factual context in which it currently exists. We therefore reverse the judgment of the District Court.

Background

I. The Parties

The five named plaintiffs own and operate one or more local television stations. They represent a class of owners of local television stations in the United States who obtain music performing rights pursuant to license agreements with ASCAP and/or BMI. The class does not include the three major television networks, ABC, CBS, and NBC, each of which owns five television stations. The class includes approximately 450 owners who, because of multiple holdings, own approximately 750 local television stations. . . .

Defendant ASCAP is an unincorporated membership association of composers, authors, and publishers of music, formed in 1914. It has approximately 21,000 writer and 8,000 publisher members. It holds non-exclusive licenses for the non-dramatic performing rights to more than three million musical compositions. BMI is a non-profit corporation organized in 1939 by radio broadcasters. It has approximately 38,000 writer and 22,000 publisher affiliates. Its repertory, for which it holds non-exclusive licenses for non-dramatic performing rights, includes more than one million compositions. The eleven individual defendants represent two classes of defendants that include all persons from whom ASCAP and BMI have obtained the non-exclusive right to license non-dramatic music performing rights to others.

II.   Music, Rights, and Licenses

The subject matter of this litigation is music transmitted by television stations to their viewer-listeners. Television music is classified as either theme, background, or feature. Theme music is played at the start or conclusion of a program and serves to enhance the identification of the program. Background music accompanies portions of the program to heighten interest, underscore the mood, change the pace, or otherwise contribute to the overall effect of the program. Feature music is a principal focus of audience attention, such as a popular song sung on a variety show.

More particularly, we are concerned with the licensing of non-dramatic performing rights to copyrighted music, that is, the right to "perform" the music publicly by transmitting it, whether live or on film or tape, to television audiences.[1] This performance right is created by the Copyright Act as one of the exclusive rights enjoyed by the copyright owner. 17 U.S.C.A. § 106(4) (1982). Also pertinent to this litigation is the so-called synchronization right, or "synch" right, that is, the right to reproduce the music onto the soundtrack of a film or a videotape in synchronization with the action. The "synch" right is a form of the reproduction right also created by statute as one of the exclusive rights enjoyed by the copyright owner. Id. § 101.

Music performed by local television stations is selected in one of three ways. It may be selected by the station itself, or by the producer of a program that is sold to the station, or by a performer spontaneously. The stations select music for the relatively small portion of the program day devoted to locally produced programs. The vast majority of music aired by television stations is selected by the producers of programs supplied to the stations. In some instances these producers are the major television networks, but this litigation is not concerned with the performing rights to music on programs supplied to the local stations by the major networks because the networks have blanket licenses from ASCAP and BMI and convey performing rights to local stations when they supply network programs. Apart from network-produced programs, the producers of programs for local stations are "syndicators" supplying the stations with "syndicated" programs. Most syndicated programs are feature length movies or one-hour or half-hour films or videotapes produced especially for television viewing by motion picture studios, their television production affiliates, or

---

1. A non-dramatic performing right is the right to perform a musical composition other than in a dramatic performance, which the ASCAP blanket license defines as "a performance of a musical composition on a television program in which there is a definite plot depicted by action and where the performance of the musical composition is woven into and carries forward the plot and its accompanying action." See *3 Nimmer on Copyright* § 10.-10[E] (1984).

independent television program producers. However, the definition of "syndicated program" that was stipulated to by the parties also includes live, non-network television programs offered for sale or license to local stations.[2] These syndicated programs are the central focus of this litigation. The third category of selected music, songs chosen spontaneously by a performer, accounts for a very small percentage of the music aired by the stations. These spontaneous selections of music can occur on programs produced either locally or by the networks or by syndicators.

Syndicators wishing to include music in their programs may either select pre-existing music (sometimes called "outside" music) or hire a composer to compose original music (sometimes called "inside" music). Most music on syndicated programs, up to 90% by plaintiffs' estimate, is inside music commissioned through the use of composer-for-hire agreements between the producer and either the composer alone or the composer and a corporation entitled to contract for a loan of the composer's services. Composer-for-hire agreements are normally standard form contracts. The salary paid to the composer, sometimes called "up front money," varies considerably from a few hundred dollars to several thousand dollars. The producer for whom a "work made for hire" was composed is considered by the Act to be the author and, unless the producer and composer have otherwise agreed, owns "all of the rights comprised in the copyright." [ ] However, composer-for-hire agreements for syndicated television programs typically provide that the producer assigns to the composer and to a music publishing company the performing right to the music composed pursuant to the agreement.[3]

When the producer wishes to use outside music in a film or videotape program, it must obtain from the copyright producer the "synch" right in order to record the music on the soundtrack of the film or tape. "Synch" rights vary in price, usually within a range of $150 to $500. When the producer wishes to use inside music, as is normally the case, it need not obtain the "synch" right because it already owns this right by virtue of the "work made for hire" provision of the Act.

Whether the producer decides to use outside or inside music, it need not acquire the television performing right since neither the making of the program nor the selling of the program to a television station is a "performance" of the music that would require a performing right. The producer is therefore free either to sell the program without the performing right and leave it to the station to obtain that right, or to obtain the performing right from the copyright proprietor,

2. The stipulation defines "syndicated program" as "a theatrical motion picture, pre-recorded television program or live television program which is offered for sale or license to a television station to be broadcast by that station as a non-network program."

3. The assignment of performing rights from the producer to the composer and publishing company is typically not an assignment of all performing rights, but the exceptions are not pertinent to this litigation.

usually the composer and a publishing company, and convey that music performing right to the station along with the performing rights to all other copyrighted components of the program. If the producer obtains the music performing right from the copyright proprietor and conveys it to the station, the transaction is known as "source licensing" or "clearance at the source." If the station obtains the music right directly from the copyright proprietor, the transaction is known as "direct licensing."

The typical arrangement whereby local television stations acquire music performing rights in syndicated and all other programs is neither source licensing nor direct licensing. Instead, the stations obtain from ASCAP and BMI a blanket license permitting television performance of all of the music in the repertories of these organizations. The license is conveyed for a fee normally set as a percentage of the station's revenue. That fee, after deduction of administrative expenses, is distributed to the copyright proprietors on a basis that roughly reflects the extent of use of the music and the size of the audience for which the station "performed" the music. The royalty distribution is normally divided equally between the composer and the music publishing company.

In addition to offering stations a blanket license, ASCAP and BMI also offer a modified form of the blanket license known as a "program" or "per program" license. The program license conveys to the station the music performing rights to all of the music in the ASCAP or BMI repertory for use on the particular program for which the license is issued. The fee for a program license is a percent of the revenue derived by the station from the particular program, i.e., the advertising dollars paid to sponsor the program.

The blanket license contains a "carve-out" provision exempting from the base on which the license fee is computed the revenue derived by the station from any program presented by motion picture or transcription for which music performing rights have been licensed at the source by the licensor, i.e., ASCAP or BMI. The program license contains a more generous version of this provision, extending the exemption to music performing rights licensed at the source *either* by ASCAP/BMI *or* by the composer and publisher. Thus, for film and videotaped syndicated programs, a station can either obtain a blanket license for all of its music performing rights and reduce its fee for those programs licensed at the source by ASCAP/BMI, or obtain program licenses for each of its programs that use copyrighted music and avoid the fee for those programs licensed at the source by either ASCAP/BMI or by the composers and publishers.

III. Prior Litigation

[The opinion recounts previous litigation concerning the licensing of music performing rights back to a 1941 antitrust suit brought against ASCAP and BMI. That suit was settled by consent decrees that imposed some limitations on ASCAP and BMI but permitted them to obtain exclusive licenses for music performing rights from their members and affiliates. The consent decree was amended in 1950; there were suits in 1951 and 1961. CBS sued ASCAP in 1969, challenging the legality of blanket licenses taken by local television stations from ASCAP and BMI. The Supreme Court eventually held that the blanket license was not a *per se* violation of § 1 of the Sherman Anti–Trust Act, BMI, Inc. v. CBS, Inc., 441 U.S. 1 (1979). On remand, the United States Court of Appeals for the Second Circuit agreed that the blanket license had not been proven to be a restraint of trade. CBS, Inc. v. ASCAP, 620 F.2d 930 (2d Cir.1980), certiorari denied 450 U.S. 970 (1981) which the opinion subsequently refers to as "*CBS-remand.*" The local stations began this litigation in 1978.]

. . . We think the initial and, as it turns out, dispositive issue on the merits is whether the blanket licensing of performing rights to the local television stations has been proven to be a restraint of trade. [ ] Arguably the answer is *a fortiori* after the Supreme Court's decision and our decision on remand in the CBS litigation. The Supreme Court noted that "the necessity for and advantages of a blanket license for [television and radio networks] may be far less obvious than is the case when the potential users are individual television or radio stations. . . ." 441 U.S. at 21[ ]. And on remand we upheld the blanket license against the claim of a network. However, for several reasons, it does not follow that the local stations lose simply because the CBS network lost. First, the Supreme Court's observation concerned the relative pro-competitive effects of the blanket license for a network compared to local stations. Even though the pro-competitive effects may be greater when the licensees are local stations, those pro-competitive effects do not necessarily outweigh the anti-competitive effects. Second, the Supreme Court's comparative statement does not determine the threshold issue of whether the blanket licensing of performing rights to local television stations is a restraint at all. The fact that CBS did not prove that blanket licensing of networks restrained competition does not necessarily mean that blanket licensing of local stations may not be shown to be a restraint. Finally, in *CBS-remand* we reviewed the District Judge's ruling that no restraint had been proved; here, we review a ruling that the local stations proved the existence of a restraint.

. . .

In reaching the conclusion that plaintiffs had proven the lack of realistically available alternatives to the blanket license, Judge Gagliardi gave separate consideration to three possibilities: the program license, . . . direct licensing, and source licensing. We consider each in turn.

Program License. Judge Gagliardi based his conclusion that a program license is not realistically available to the plaintiffs essentially on two circumstances: the cost of a program license and the reporting requirements that such a license imposes on a licensee. "The court therefore concludes that the per program license is too costly and

burdensome to be a realistic alternative to the blanket license." [ ]
Without rejecting any subsidiary factual finding concerning the availability of a program license, we reject the legal conclusion that it is not
a realistic alternative to the blanket license.

. . .

. . . [T]he only valid test of whether the program license is "too
costly" to be a realistic alternative is whether the price for such a
license, in an objective sense, is higher than the value of the rights
obtained. But plaintiffs presented no evidence that the price of the
program license is "high" in terms of value received. . . .

. . .

. . . The fact that very few stations have elected to take program licenses is not evidence that they are priced beyond an objectively
reasonable price range. It may simply reflect, as defendants believe,
that the blanket license has virtues of convenience that make it a
legitimate object of customer preference.

. . .

[The conclusion that the program license is not realistically available because of the burdens of required record-keeping that accompany
its use] is similarly flawed by the lack of evidence . . . ..

. . .

Direct Licensing. The District Court concluded that direct licensing is not a realistic alternative to the blanket license without any
evidence that any local station ever offered any composer a sum of
money in exchange for the performing rights to his music. . . .
Judge Gagliardi concluded . . . that direct licensing could not occur
without the intervention of some agency to broker the numerous
transactions . . . .. We have no quarrel with [that] proposition. . . .

However, we see no evidentiary support for the . . . proposition . . . that no one would undertake the brokering function for
direct licensing . . . ..

Source Licensing. As Judge Gagliardi noted, the "current availability and comparative efficiency of source licensing have been the
focus of this lawsuit." [ ] The availability of source licensing is
significant to the inquiry as to whether the blanket license is a
restraint because so much of the stations' programming consists of
syndicated programs for which the producer could, if so inclined,
convey music performing rights. Most of these syndicated programs
use composer-for-hire music. As to such music, the producer starts out
with the rights of the copyright, including the performing right, by
operation of law, 17 U.S.C. § 201(b), unless the hiring agreement
otherwise provides. Thus it becomes important to determine whether
the stations can obtain from the producer the music performing right,

along with all of the other rights in a syndicated program that are conveyed to the stations when the program is licensed. . . .

  . . .

Judge Gagliardi properly declined to give any probative weight to the plaintiffs' transparent effort to assemble in the midst of litigation evidence that they had seriously tried to obtain source licensing. . . . Nevertheless the District Court concluded that source was not a realistic alternative . . .. [But we conclude that plaintiffs have simply failed to produce sufficient evidence to support a conclusion that the blanket license is a restraint of trade.]

  . . .

The Claimed Lack of Necessity. Plaintiffs earnestly advance the argument that the blanket license, as applied to syndicated programming, should be declared unlawful for the basic reason that it is unnecessary. In their view, the blanket license is suspect because, where it is used, no price competition occurs among songs when those who need performing rights decide which songs to perform. The resulting absence of price competition, plaintiffs urge, is justifiable only in some contexts such as night clubs, live and locally produced programming of television stations, and radio stations, which make more spontaneous choices of music than do television stations.

There are two fundamental flaws in this argument. First, it has not been shown on this record that the blanket license, even as applied to syndicated television programs, is not necessary. If all the plaintiffs mean is that a judicial ban on blanket licensing for syndicated television programs would not halt performance of copyrighted music on such programs and that some arrangement for the purchase of performing rights would replace the blanket license, we can readily agree. . . . But a licensing system may be "necessary" in the practical sense that it is far superior to other alternatives in efficiency . . ..

  . . .

  . . . Even if the evidence showed that most of the efficiencies of the blanket license could be achieved under source licensing, it would not follow that the blanket license thereby becomes unlawful. . . .

  . . . [W]e hold that the local television stations have not presented evidence in this case permitting a conclusion that the blanket license is a restraint of trade in violation of section 1.

The judgment of the District Court is therefore reversed.

[Judge Winter wrote a separate opinion, concurring.]

Notes and Questions

1. If the court of appeals had upheld the district court ruling that ASCAP and BMI blanket licenses to local television stations constituted an unreasonable restraint of trade under section 1 of the Sherman Anti–Trust Act, the performing societies could have lost $80 million in

annual local television performing rights revenues. That represents about 25 percent of the performing rights societies' total annual revenues. The Entertainment and Sports Lawyer, Winter 1985 at 10.

2. Do you agree with the court of appeals' conclusion that there was no violation of the Sherman Act, or would you be more inclined to agree with the district court? Does it seem reasonable to conclude that direct licensing and source licensing are viable alternatives to blanket licensing just because the plaintiffs had been unable to prove that they were not?

3. ASCAP, BMI and other music licensing organizations negotiate with stores that wish to play music for their customers. Even playing radio stations in commercial establishments can require copyright permission. The key question is whether or not playing the radio constitutes a performance.

In Twentieth Century Music Corp. v. Aiken, 422 U.S. 151 (1975), the owner of a fast-service food shop in Pittsburgh known as "George Aiken's Chicken" was sued for copyright infringement because he played a radio with four ceiling speakers in his shop each day. Included in the broadcasts were copyrighted musical compositions which plaintiffs complained were being "performed." The Supreme Court held that there was no performance:

> The practical unenforceability of a ruling that all of those in Aiken's position are copyright infringers is self-evident. One has only to consider the countless business establishments in this country with radio or television sets on their premises—bars, beauty shops, cafeterias, car washes, dentists' offices, and drive-ins—to realize the total futility of any evenhanded effort on the part of copyright holders to license even a substantial percentage of them . . . . Secondly, to hold that all in Aiken's position "performed" these musical compositions would be to authorize the sale of an untold number of licenses for what is basically a single public rendition of a copyrighted work. The exaction of such multiple tribute would go far beyond what is required for the economic protection of copyright owners . . . .

By contrast, in Sailor Music v. Gap Stores, Inc., 668 F.2d 84 (2d Cir.1981), certiorari denied 456 U.S. 945 (1982), it was held that use of music companies' copyrighted works by radio in Gap stores (average size 3,500 square feet) *did* constitute copyright infringement. Because they exceeded the "outer limit" of size, the Gap stores were enjoined from use of the works.

4. The National Cable Television Association, Community Antenna Television Association and the Disney Channel filed suit in 1990 against BMI alleging antitrust violations. The plaintiffs said that the cable industry and its members confront "a cartelized industry in which non-negotiable demands for license fees and terms have been made by the cartel" and are "enforced through punitive copyright infringement litigation." The suit challenges the 50–year practice by

BMI of granting, for a price, blanket licenses for public performance of the works of the composers and publishers it represents. In other litigation, American Television & Communications and 16 other cable companies sued BMI and nine affiliates, alleging Sherman Antitrust Act violations. They alleged that BMI and its members are succeeding "in their anticompetitive scheme because of the monopolistic and illegal stranglehold" that they have on the performance rights to music. BMI countersued. The ,U.S. District Court for the District of Columbia decided in 1991 that the Disney Channel and Black Entertainment Television had infringed BMI's copyrights and levied a judgment of $1.98 million against the Disney Channel and $225,000 against BET. National Cable Television Association, Inc. v. Broadcast Music, Inc., 772 F.Supp. 614 (D.D.C.1991). The Disney Channel and Black Entertainment subsequently reached new licensing agreements with BMI. Billboard, Dec. 14, 1991 at 75.

D. PROBLEMS OF NEW TECHNOLOGIES

Perhaps the biggest problem Congress faced in drafting the Copyright Act of 1976 was providing for new technologies. As a result the courts are now having to answer difficult questions concerning the application of copyright law to these new technologies.

For example, in Sony Corp. v. Universal City Studios, Inc., p. 576, *supra,* the Court, held 5–4, that the use of videotape recorders did not infringe the copyrights of the producers of the programs that were copied. The majority began by noting that the "monopoly privileges that Congress may authorize are neither unlimited nor primarily designed to provide a special private benefit. Rather, the limited grant is a means by which an important public purpose may be achieved. It is intended to motivate the creative activity of authors and inventors by the provision of a special reward, and to allow the public access to the products of their genius after the limited period of exclusive control has expired."

The Court also observed that the clause assigned Congress the primary responsibility for defining the scope of protection. "Because the task involves a difficult balance between the interests of authors and inventors in the control and exploitation of their writings and discoveries on the one hand, and society's competing interest in the free flow of ideas, information, and commerce on the other hand, our patent and copyright statutes have been amended repeatedly."

In this case, dealing with a new technology, the majority stressed that the "judiciary's reluctance to expand the protections afforded by the copyright without explicit legislative guidance is a recurring theme. [ ] Sound policy, as well as history, supports our consistent deference to Congress when major technological innovations alter the market for copyrighted materials."

Recall from Chapter IX another major copyright controversy involving new technologies—cable television liability for the retransmission of broadcast television programming.

E. TRADEMARKS

Trademarks and servicemarks, like copyright, protect intellectual property. Instead of protecting an entire movie script, an entire book or an entire magazine, as a copyright may, trademarks and servicemarks protect "identifying symbols"—words, names, symbols or devices.

The distinction between trademarks and servicemarks is that trademarks are symbols that identify goods whereas servicemarks are symbols that identify services. Because the law governing trademarks and servicemarks is essentially the same, we will use "trademark" to represent both.

Federal registration of trademarks is authorized under Congressional legislation. Unlike copyright and patents, trademarks are not specifically mentioned in the Constitution. The governing statute is the Federal Trademark Act of 1946, known as the Lanham Act after the late Rep. Fritz Garland Lanham. Registrations are filed with the United States Patent and Trademark Office.

Whether a term is eligible for trademark protection depends on how it is classified. For example, Miller Brewing was denied trademark protection for the term "LITE" because it was viewed as a descriptive term for a type of beer. "A term for which trademark protection is claimed will fit somewhere in the spectrum which ranges through (1) generic or common descriptive and (2) merely descriptive to (3) suggestive and (4) arbitrary or fanciful." Miller Brewing Co. v. G. Heileman Brewing Co., Inc., 561 F.2d 75, 79 (7th Cir.1977). Generic terms—those that describe a kind of good—can never become trademarks. Merely descriptive terms—those that describe a characteristic or ingredient—can become trademarks only by acquiring a secondary meaning "distinctive of the applicant's goods." Suggestive terms—ones that suggest rather than describe a characteristic or ingredient—can become trademarks without proof of a secondary meaning. Arbitrary or fanciful terms—ones that in no way suggest or describe a characteristic or ingredient of the product—can also become trademarks without proof of secondary meaning. Arbitrary or fanciful terms are better protected than suggestive terms because there is always a danger that a suggestive term will be viewed as a descriptive term, thus requiring proof of a secondary meaning.

Groups of letters, even an individual letter, can function as a trademark. If one uses an individual letter, the typestyle or design of the letter must be distinctive.

It is also possible to register titles, characters, names and "other distinctive features" of radio or television programs under § 45 of the

Lanham Act. Section 43(a) of the Lanham Act permits protection of unregistered names of performers or sports teams, etc.

Cartoon characters and literary characters can be protected under either copyright or trademark, depending on the use. For example, a "Superman" cartoon would be copyrighted, but "Superman" products would be trademarked.

Manufacturers, for obvious reasons, want to protect their exclusive rights to use names and symbols associated with their products. Sometimes, if they are not sufficiently vigilant in their protection of their trademarks, the trademarks enter the *public domain* and can be used by anyone. Aspirin and cellophane are examples of trademarks that lost trademark protection because people came to use them as generic terms for the product as opposed to the name of a specific brand. The owners of the registered trademarks Xerox® and Kleenex®, knowing that people sometimes misuse their trademarks as though they were generic names, are among those that advertise in such magazines as *Editor & Publisher* and *Broadcasting,* emphasizing that their names are protected and should be capitalized.

Trademark owners particularly concerned about the problem emphasize the ® symbol next to their names or go to considerable lengths to emphasize that their names are brand names, as in broadcast commercials referring to "Sanka Brand" coffee.

Like copyright holders, trademark owners do not have unlimited, exclusive rights to the use of their trademarks. Trademark owners are protected against uses that could cause confusion between their products and other similar products (trademark infringement) as well as uses on dissimilar products that might cause deterioration of the distinctive aspect of the trademarks (trademark dilution). Such cases, however, can be difficult to win. For example, although the Boston Athletic Association registered the trademark "Boston Marathon" and licensed one television station to broadcast the race, it was unable to get an injunction prohibiting another station from also televising the event, because it failed to show sufficient evidence of relevant customer confusion. WCVB–TV v. Boston Athletic Association, 926 F.2d 42, 18 Med.L.Rptr. 1710 (1st Cir.1991).

Noncommercial uses of trademarks are generally considered protected by the First Amendment. For example, an injunction prohibiting the publication of a parody of the L.L. Bean Catalogue pursuant to Maine's anti-dilution statute was found to violate the First Amendment. L.L. Bean, Inc. v. Drake Publishers, Inc., 811 F.2d 26, 13 Med.L.Rptr. 2009 (1st Cir.1987). L.L. Bean had argued that the parody, *L.L. Beam's Back–To–School–Sex–Catalog,* would tarnish the goodwill and reputation associated with Bean's trademark:

It offends the Constitution, however, to invoke the anti-dilution statute as a basis for enjoining the noncommercial use of a trademark by a defendant engaged in a protected form of expression . . ..

If the anti-dilution statute were construed as permitting a trademark owner to enjoin the use of his mark in a noncommercial context found to be negative or offensive, then a corporation could shield itself from criticism by forbidding the use of its name in commentaries critical of its conduct. The legitimate aim of the anti-dilution statute is to prohibit the unauthorized use of another's trademark in order to market incompatible products or services. The Constitution does not, however, permit the range of the anti-dilution statute to encompass the unauthorized use of a trademark in a noncommercial setting such as an editorial or artistic context.

Similarly, in Lucasfilm Ltd. v. High Frontier, 622 F.Supp. 931 (D.D.C.1985), the court rejected an infringement suit brought by the owners of the trademark "Star Wars" against public interest groups using the term in commercial advertisements discussing President Reagan's Strategic Defense Initiative.

Broadcasters may protect their stations' call letters by trademark. For years, under an assumption that the government owned the call letters, individuals could not trademark them, but the FCC protected them. After the FCC ended such protection, the issue of call letters arose in an appeal before the Trademark Trial and Appeal Board of the Patent and Trademark Office, U.S. Department of Commerce. WSM, Inc., an AM radio station, had used the call letters "WSM" since 1925 and claimed use of the call letters as a servicemark. The Examining Attorney in the Patent and Trademark Office had refused to register the letters as a servicemark on the assumption that the station did not own the call letters because they were used only with FCC approval. The Trademark Trial and Appeal Board reversed:

> The Examining Attorney has apparently misunderstood the nature of the relationship between the FCC and applicant. . . . It is clear that the FCC is not the owner of the call letters used by the broadcasters which it regulates. The right to broadcast is what the agency licenses to broadcasters. . . . In the case at hand the applicant obtained whatever rights it has in its service mark by adopting it and using it to identify its broadcasting services. The FCC neither selected the mark for applicant nor used it to identify any services. . . . [A]s long as applicant uses the mark to identify its services which are lawfully rendered in commerce applicant is the owner of its service mark [and is therefore entitled to register it].

WSM, Inc., 225 U.S. Patent Quarterly 883 (1985).

Today, although it is possible to trademark call letters, problems still can arise when two stations have call letters which look or sound similar. An example involves a trademark infringement alleged by station WMEE(FM) of Fort Wayne, Ind., which in 1984 complained after a station in Decatur, Ind., whose signal overlapped with that of WMEE, changed its call letters from WADM to WMCZ(FM). On the request of WMEE, a federal district court judge issued a preliminary injunction prohibiting the new WMCZ from identifying itself by those call letters. Furthermore, the judge ordered WMCZ to air a disclaimer differentiating itself from WMEE. The judge, who said the two calls were "overwhelmingly phonetically and rhythmically similar," said that, "[i]mplicit in the FCC's relinquishment of its role as arbiter of call letter disputes is the conclusion that, when local courts resolve call letter disputes, the law of that local forum and circuit would apply." Pathfinder Communications Corp. v. Midwest Communications Co., 593 F.Supp. 281 (N.D.Ind.1984).

The issue of ownership of the word "olympic" was argued in San Francisco Arts and Athletics, Inc. v. United States Olympic Committee, 479 U.S. 1052 (1987). The Olympic Committee had sought to bar a gay rights group from sponsoring an athletic competition called the Gay Olympics. In a 5–4 decision, the Court held that Congress had granted the Olympic Committee exclusive commercial use of the word "olympic." The gay rights group had argued that by allowing "olympics" for handicapped children, police officers and others, but not for gays, the committee had enforced its trademark rights in a biased way, but Justice Powell, in the majority opinion, said that because the committee was not a government agency, it could not violate someone's constitutionally protected right to equal protection under the law. An attorney for the gay rights group said they would carry the fight to use the word "olympics" to Congress. New York Times, June 26, 1987 at A14.

The underlying purpose of the special protection given the word "olympic" appears to be more of an attempt to maintain dignity or "officialness" of the internationally-sanctioned games, than to protect their commercial value.

The 1988 Trademark Law Revision Act, amending the Lanham Act, overhauled the trademark system. Under its provisions, the term of registration and renewal was reduced from 20 to 10 years. The amendments also permit a company to receive trademark protection for as much as three years before it actually sells a product or service with that mark. Companies formerly could register trademarks only when they had put them into use. Language in Section 43(a) of the Act includes a provision making misrepresentations about another's product or service—so-called product disparagement—actionable.

The latter provision is directed at some forms of comparative advertising in which rival advertisers have sometimes been accused of maligning their competitors' goods or services. As a result of compromise with media organizations worried about threats to free speech, it applies only to business advertising and promotion and not to political advertising or editorial commentary. New York Times, Oct. 21, 1988 at B6.

As the Trademark Review Commission of the United States Trademark Association has reported,

> Trademark owners have increasingly been subjected to uses of their trademarks by others which ridicule, parody, insult, or defame. The ENJOY COCAINE imitation of the Coca–Cola slogan, the "L.L. Beam's Back–To–School–Sex–Catalog," and the slogan MUTANT OF OMAHA with a logo resembling Mutual of Omaha's Indian head logo are but a few examples. Many of these are merely tasteless and a few amuse, but a number of them cross the legal line and become injurious to the trademark owner. . . .

77 The Trademark Reporter 433–34 (1987).

A lengthy and thorough examination of trademark strategy from a marketing viewpoint appears in Journal of Marketing, vol. 55, no. 3, July 1991 at 46.

Chapter XII

DEFAMATION

In this chapter and those that follow we will consider the range of legal arguments for prohibiting certain communications because of their substantive content. In each case we will consider, among other points, the justifications offered for restriction and the value of the communication. The justifications are as diverse as the situations to which they are applied. Arguments for limiting speech and press to protect privacy are unlikely to resemble the arguments based on national security.

Even if the speech is determined to be subject to governmental control, there is the further question of what types of sanctions may be imposed. Among the array are criminal prosecutions, civil damage remedies and bans on speech imposed by administrative techniques or by court injunction. Again, particular sanctions are used for specific kinds of speech. Even when speech is found to be defamatory, for example, it is regulated after the fact and is not enjoined. On the other hand, speech held to invade privacy has been barred from publication. In sum, the sanctions available are as diverse as the justifications offered to restrict the speech in the first place.

We begin our survey of restraints on communication with the state's interest in granting redress to persons whose reputations have been hurt by false statements. We start with defamation law in part because it was one of the earliest legal actions available against journalists and in part because even today it poses a significant legal danger for broadcasters. It is certainly the most extensively litigated area of media law.

Harm to reputation is one of the earliest injuries recognized by virtually every legal system. Early societies were undoubtedly concerned that the failure to provide legal recourse to those whose reputations had been impugned would lead to breaches of the peace. Although that concern has eased as civilization has advanced, states may still be concerned about the potential for violence. Beyond that, however, traditional values emphasize the importance of an individual's good name. Whatever the justifications, the action for defamation has long had a place in the common law.

English law has redressed and punished attacks on reputation since the feudal days. During the 16th century, the authorities began using the law of defamation to punish political criticism of the government and its officials. These attacks were referred to as seditious libel.

Although it is doubtful that the English law of seditious libel was transplanted in this country, it seems clear that the tort law that provided damage remedies to individuals did cross the Atlantic. After independence, defamation law continued to be enforced. The First Amendment's statement that "Congress shall make no law . . . abridging the freedom of speech, or of the press . . ." had no apparent impact upon defamation law until the mid–1960s. Because defamation law was a creature of state law—the power to regulate defamation law was not delegated to Congress—the First Amendment had no immediate effect on the states' administration of that law.

Even after it became clear that the First Amendment applied to the states through the Fourteenth Amendment, these provisions were thought inapplicable to false statements that adversely affected an individual's reputation. The Supreme Court did not tie defamation and the First Amendment together until the seminal case of New York Times Co. v. Sullivan, decided in 1964. That case not only brought major change to the law of defamation, but also provided a philosophy that has led to many other recent developments in mass media law. We shall consider the impact of this case on defamation law shortly.

A. THE STATE LAW OF DEFAMATION

Before we can appreciate the significance of the constitutional developments, however, we must understand the common-law world of defamation. The constitutional developments have not created a totally new legal area; rather they have altered some of the pre-existing state rules and left the remaining ones in place. States remain free to protect reputation in whatever manner they see fit so long as they do so consistently with the First Amendment.

A second reason for inquiring into state law is that state law itself has a significant number of protections for those who are sued for defamation. It is often possible for a defendant to win a defamation case under the state's traditional rules without ever having to rely upon the protection of the First Amendment.

Why might a defendant who could win a case under First Amendment principles try to win that case under state rules? There are several practical explanations. Perhaps the major one is that, as a matter of procedure, the state defenses may permit a defendant to win the case earlier in the litigation (such as on a motion to dismiss, rather than on a motion for summary judgment or perhaps only after a trial is held). It is often faster and cheaper for a media defendant to succeed on state law grounds than to rely exclusively on the more glorious, but perhaps less expeditious, ground of the First and Fourteenth Amendments.

The point is that we must understand the basic operation of traditional state defamation law as well as the Constitution. We turn first to the state law and then to the impact of constitutional law.

1. THE REPUTATION ELEMENT

a. Definition

The essence of the action for defamation is the claim that defendant has uttered a false statement that has harmed the plaintiff's reputation. The modern view is that a statement is defamatory if it harms the plaintiff's reputation by lowering the plaintiff in the estimation of the community or by deterring others from associating or dealing with the plaintiff. It is easy to think of statements that will fit such a broad definition. It obviously covers charges that plaintiff committed a crime or that the plaintiff was inept in his or her chosen trade or profession. It is enough that the published statement be of the sort that would lead a segment of the community to think less of the plaintiff. That segment need not be large.

When the false statement is transmitted by electronic media, obviously, there is usually a large audience, but there need not be.

Most cases have involved charges of volitional behavior by plaintiff—committing a crime, lacking skill or writing an article. The broad sweep of the definition, however, extends to accusations that the plaintiff was of illegitimate birth, had been raped or was in dire financial straits. Even though the plaintiff cannot be blamed for a condition, the courts have nonetheless bowed to reality and recognized that these kinds of charges may in fact cause others to shun, or refrain from associating with, the plaintiff. Judges "take the world as we find it" even if the segment of the community that thinks less of the plaintiff can be characterized as "wrong-thinking"—as they would be in the illegitimacy and rape examples.

At the same time, there is a limit to that principle. Consider, for example, a false charge that the mob's gunman missed his target. Were the gunman to sue and assert that his reputation had been tarnished among the underworld, it is unlikely that a court would entertain the charge. Is it appropriate to redress a claim based on an audience segment that is criminal rather than simply wrong-thinking?

b. Corporations

Until now, the discussion has been directed to the question of protecting the reputation of a human being. Not infrequently, however, defamatory statements are made about corporations. It is generally held that corporations also have reputations that they may vindicate through actions for defamation. Generally the corporation must be attacked in a way that affects its credit or, if it is a corporation organized for profit, its profit-making ability.

A non-profit corporation may also be defamed if the charge is one that tends to interfere with its ability to obtain financial support from the public. A corporation that relies on public donations may be able to sue for defamation if the charge would interfere with its ability to obtain such funds.

c.   Ambiguity

Statements are often ambiguous. In such cases the prevailing rule is to have the judge decide whether any of the statement's possible meanings can reasonably be understood to have a defamatory impact. If the judge decides that at least one of the possible meanings would be defamatory, it then becomes a function of the jury to decide the meaning that was in fact conveyed.

It should be noted here that the Supreme Court in one discussion of ambiguous statements resolved the question itself. The case arose from a tumultuous city council meeting involving the plaintiff, a local real estate developer, in a negotiation with the city council. Members of the audience characterized the plaintiff's bargaining position as "blackmail." The defendant newspaper accurately reported the meeting and included the blackmail charges—sometimes without quotation marks. The state courts granted plaintiff a judgment against the newspaper.

Justice Stewart concluded for the majority that "as a matter of constitutional law, the word 'blackmail' in these circumstances was not" defamatory:

> It is simply impossible to believe that a reader who reached the word "blackmail" in either article would not have understood exactly what was meant; it was Bresler's public and wholly legal negotiating proposals that were being criticized. No reader could have thought that either the speakers at the meeting or the newspaper articles reporting their words were charging Bresler with the commission of a criminal offense. On the contrary, even the most careless reader must have perceived that the word was no more than rhetorical hyperbole . . ..

Justice White dissented. He could not "join the majority claim of superior insight with respect to how the word 'blackmail' would be understood by the ordinary reader in Greenbelt, Maryland." Greenbelt Cooperative Publishing Association v. Bresler, 398 U.S. 6, 1 Med.L.Rptr. 1589 (1970).

Another problem arises when part of a story has a defamatory impact but another part of the story negates that impact. The lead-in to a story may be defamatory, but the story as a whole may be harmless. Normally, courts consider how a reasonable reader would respond.

Statements may be defamatory even though the thrust of the accusations is not clear from the words used. In such indirect defamation cases, plaintiffs' complaints must show the court how the plaintiffs have been defamed. The description of how plaintiffs do this involves the use of three technical words. If the plaintiffs themselves are not directly named, they must show by "colloquium" that the statements were "of and concerning" them. If it is still not clear how the plaintiffs have been defamed, they must plead extrinsic facts that would permit a defamatory meaning to be applied to defendants' words. Such an allegation of extrinsic facts is called the "inducement." Finally we have "innuendo." Where the statements are not clearly defamatory on their face, it is the function of the innuendo to assert the meanings that plaintiffs attach to the passages and any additions by colloquium and inducement. The innuendo is not a fact but is the plaintiffs' assertion of how the passages would be understood by those who heard the defendants' words and knew the additional unstated facts.

An example may help clarify the matter. Let us assume a defendant says, "The man who lives in the house two doors east of my house was the only person in the Smith home between 7 and 8 p.m. last night." If the plaintiff thinks that this statement defames him and wishes to sue, his pleading must establish how he has been defamed. For colloquium he might allege, "I am the only man who lives in the house two doors east of the speaker's house." This ties the plaintiff to the statement but does not clarify its defamatory nature. The defamation is clarified if the plaintiff alleges as inducement that the Smith house was burglarized between 7 and 8 p.m. that night. The plaintiff will then assert that the innuendo is that he is being accused of the crime of burglary.

d. *"Of and Concerning Plaintiff"*

In order for a defamatory statement to affect the plaintiff adversely, the reader must connect that statement with the plaintiff. As we said above, the plaintiff must show that the statement objected to was "of and concerning" him. Sometimes this is a problem because of the ambiguity of the statement or because the plaintiff is only indirectly identified. In those cases our discussion about ambiguous statements will help resolve the case. If readers could plausibly believe that the plaintiff was referred to, then a jury will decide whether the statement was in fact so understood.

e. *Groups*

Another aspect of this problem involves statements that attack large groups of people. In such cases is it possible for an individual member of that group to assert that the statement hurt his personal reputation? At the extreme, an attack on all lawyers in the United States or on all clergymen would be held to be such a general broadside that no individual lawyer or clergyman could sue. The same would be true of broadside attacks on racial, religious or ethnic groups.

At the other extreme it is generally accepted that a charge made against a small group may defame all members of that group. For example, a television newscast may assert that "the officers" of a corporation have embezzled funds. There are only four officers of the corporation. Each of them may be found to have been defamed. Even if the statement had said "one of the officers of the corporation" had embezzled funds, the group is small enough so that all four officials are put under a shadow and can sue.

As the group grows larger the impact of the statement may depend on the number accused. In one case, a defamatory charge was made against one unidentified member of a 21–member police force. All 21 sued. The court dismissed the case. It feared that allowing the action would permit a suit by an entire baseball team over a report that one member was disciplined for brawling. Such a result "would chill communication to the marrow." But suppose the charge had been against "all but one" of the members of that police force. Such a statement may reflect on each member of the force though the same charge made against only one of the 21 might not. Arcand v. Evening Call Publishing Co., 567 F.2d 1163, 3 Med.L.Rptr. 1748 (1st Cir.1977).

All states deny damage actions to large groups, but a few have attempted to use criminal statutes to prevent or punish such charges against racial or ethnic groups. We will discuss this later in this chapter.

f. Opinions—A Special Problem

At common law there was much confusion about whether opinion, as distinguished from fact, could be the basis for a defamation action. Because a strongly expressed unfavorable opinion could easily lower a person's reputation in the eyes of others, the courts usually held that such a statement could form the basis of a defamation action even though it could not be found to be true or false. Occasionally, the courts held that although truth was a defense to defamation, that did not mean that a statement could be defamatory only if it could be shown to be false. Courts held that those sued for publishing defamatory opinions might invoke the defense of fair comment—the privilege of stating opinions that they actually held and did not express solely for the purpose of hurting the object of the attack. We will discuss fair comment later in this chapter.

Much of this confusion is disappearing, largely as a result of a passage in Gertz v. Robert Welch, Inc., 418 U.S. 323, 1 Med.L.Rptr. 1633 (1974), reprinted at p. 634, *infra*: "Under the First Amendment there is no such thing as a false idea. However pernicious an opinion may seem, we depend for its correction not on the conscience of judges and juries but on the competition of other ideas." 418 U.S. at 339–40, 1 Med.L.Rptr. at 1640.

The states have moved sharply to clarify their own law without waiting for further prodding by the Supreme Court. In Rinaldi v. Holt, Rinehart & Winston, Inc., 42 N.Y.2d 369, 397 N.Y.S.2d 943, 366 N.E.2d 1299, 2 Med.L.Rptr. 2169, certiorari denied 434 U.S. 969 (1977), an author had strongly attacked a judge's decisions and competence. The court relied on the *Gertz* dictum: "The expression of opinion, even in the form of pejorative rhetoric, relating to fitness for judicial office or to performance while in judicial office, is safeguarded. . . . Plaintiff may not recover from defendants for simply expressing their opinion of his judicial performance, no matter how unreasonable, extreme or erroneous these opinions might be." In his writing, the author "set forth the basis for his belief that plaintiff is incompetent and should be removed. Based upon the facts stated and public debate provoked by the statements, each reader may draw his own conclusions as to whether Newfield's views should be supported or challenged."

In cases arising from statements during political campaigns, the courts have concluded that the statements must have been understood by the electorate as opinion. One letter to the editor accused the plaintiff of "contrived public opinion polls, unfounded statements, emphatic denials, committees no one ever heard of, attacks on straw men and a lot of slick, big-time expensive political public relations." It also charged him with an "amateurish job of chicanery."

The court concluded that "distasteful as this letter may have been to Block, it sounds remarkably similar to the usual and ordinary kind of political rhetoric which is all too often composed of equal parts of bombast, hyperbole, and billingsgate." The reader could only conclude that Block was being accused of "being a city slicker who is trying to bamboozle the good citizens of Palm Springs with the old snake-oil routine . . .. As such it is a statement of opinion, not fact." *Desert Sun Publishing Co. v. Superior Court,* 97 Cal.App.3d 49, 158 Cal.Rptr. 519, 5 Med.L.Rptr. 1881 (1979).

In *Ollman v. Evans,* 713 F.2d 838, 9 Med.L.Rptr. 1969 (D.C.Cir. 1983), rehearing en banc 750 F.2d 970, 11 Med.L.Rptr. 1433 (1984), certiorari denied 471 U.S. 1127 (1985), a political science professor who had been nominated to head the University of Maryland's Department of Politics and Government sued nationally-syndicated columnists Evans and Novak after their column characterized him as an "outspoken proponent of political Marxism." The column quoted Professor Bertell Ollman's writings and asked, "What is the true measurement of Ollman's scholarship? Does he intend to use the classroom for indoctrination? Will he indeed be followed by other Marxist professors? Could the department in time be closed to non-Marxists, following the tendency at several English universities?"

The professor sued for defamation, and the defendants sought summary judgment on the ground that the statements were all statements of opinion. The federal district court's granting of summary judgment was first remanded by the court of appeals; on rehearing *en banc* the court affirmed the granting of the summary judgment in a 6–5 vote, reflecting the lack of consensus on the court. Even among the six judges voting to affirm there was no consensus. Judge Starr wrote the principal opinion, but three of his colleagues joined a concurring opinion by Judge Bork. Judge Starr adopted a four-part test: (1) whether the allegedly libelous statement has a "precise core of meaning" or is indefinite or ambiguous, (2) whether the statement is objectively verifiable, (3) whether the content of the statement suggests that the statement has factual content and (4) whether the broader context—for example the kind of writing—signals the reader that it is likely to be opinion.

As to the first part, Judge Starr suggested that a precise statement, like an accusation of a crime, is more likely to be libelous than a "loosely definable" or vague one. As for the second part, he said "a reader cannot rationally view an unverifiable statement as conveying actual facts." On the third point, Judge Starr wrote that "[t]he degree to which a statement is 'laden with factual content' or can be read to imply facts depends upon the article or column, taken as a whole, of which the statement is a part." Finally, the judge wrote that courts should examine the broader social context into which the statement fits and pointed out that different types of writing have widely varying social conventions that signal to the reader the likelihood of a statement's being either fact or opinion. He wrote also that the placement of an item in a newspaper should be considered. Referring to Loeb v. Globe Newspaper Co., 489 F.Supp. 481, 6 Med.L.Rptr. 1235 (D.Mass. 1980), he pointed out that an article in that case was on the editorial page, but that "if the statement had appeared on the front page where news is reported, it would most likely have been treated as a statement of fact."

Judge Bork wrote a concurring opinion in which he argued that "the law as enunciated by the Supreme Court" makes no sharp dichotomy between fact and opinion. He wrote that "[a]ny . . . rigid doctrinal framework is inadequate to resolve the sometimes contradictory claims of the libel laws and the freedom of the press." Judge Bork was influenced by the political nature of Ollman's role: "Whatever the merits of his scholarship, he was also a political man who publicly tried to forward his political goals. He had entered the political arena. . . . That being so, he must accept the hanging and jostling of political debate, in ways that a private person need not, in order to keep the political arena free and vital."

The *Ollman* four-part test was subsequently used in Janklow v. Newsweek, Inc., 788 F.2d 1300, 12 Med.L.Rptr. 1961 (8th Cir.1986), in which the governor of South Dakota sued the news magazine for allegedly defamatory statements in an article about the alleged "feud" between the governor and American Indian activist Dennis Banks. The court, rehearing *en banc,* found the statements imprecise and unverifiable, presented in a forum where spirited writing is expected and involving criticism of a public official's motives and intentions, and thus to be a protected statement of opinion. The court used both Judge Starr's four-part test and Judge Bork's concept of a public, political arena.

In Milkovich v. Lorain Journal Co., the Supreme Court rejected the *Ollman* approach.

MILKOVICH v. LORAIN JOURNAL CO.

Supreme Court of the United States, 1990.

497 U.S. 1, 110 S.Ct. 2695, 111 L.Ed.2d 1, 17 Med.L.Rptr. 2009.

[Milkovich was coach of the Maple Heights high school wrestling team, which was involved in a brawl with a competing team. The Ohio High School Athletic Association (OHSAA) censured Milkovich and placed his team on probation. Parents of some of the team members sued to enjoin OHSAA from enforcing the probation, contending OH-SAA's investigation and hearing violated due process. Milkovich and the school's superintendent, Scott, testified at the hearing on the suit, both denying that Milkovich had incited the brawl through his behavior toward the crowd and a meet official. The judge granted the restraining order sought by the parents. A sports columnist who had attended both the meet and the court hearing wrote about the hearing in a column published the next day in the defendant newspaper. The headline was "Maple beat the law with the 'big lie.'" The theme of the column was that Milkovich and Scott in their testimony at the hearing misrepresented Milkovich's role in the altercation and thereby prevented the team from receiving the punishment it deserved. The concluding paragraphs of the column were as follows:

"Anyone who attended the meet, whether he be from Maple Heights, Mentor [the opposing school] or impartial observer, knows in his heart that Milkovich and Scott lied at the hearing after each having given his solemn oath to tell the truth.

"But they got away with it.

"Is that the kind of lesson we want our young people learning from their high school administrators and coaches?

"I think not."

Milkovich and Scott both sued the newspaper, alleging that the column accused them of perjury and thus was libellous per se. After 15 years of litigation and several appeals, the Ohio Court of Appeals held in Milkovich's case that the column was constitutionally protected opinion and granted the newspaper's motion for summary judgment. The Supreme Court reversed.]

CHIEF JUSTICE REHNQUIST delivered the opinion of the Court.

[The opinion reviewed the various constitutional limitations imposed on state libel law in the series of cases beginning with New York Times v. Sullivan. The Court also mentioned its decision in Hustler Magazine, Inc. v. Falwell, p. 681, infra, an emotional distress case holding that the First Amendment precluded recovery for an ad parody that "could not reasonably have been interpreted as stating actual facts about the public figure involved."]

Respondents would have us recognize, in addition to the established safeguards discussed above, still another First Amendment-based protection for defamatory statements which are categorized as "opinion" as opposed to "fact." For this proposition they rely principally on the following dictum from our opinion in *Gertz* :

> "Under the First Amendment there is no such thing as a false idea. However pernicious an opinion may seem, we depend for its correction not on the conscience of judges and juries but on the competition of other ideas. But there is no constitutional value in false statements of fact." [ ]

Judge Friendly appropriately observed that this passage "has become the opening salvo in all arguments for protection from defamation actions on the ground of opinion, even though the case did not remotely concern the question." Cianci v. New Times Publishing Co. [ ]. Read in context, though, the fair meaning of the passage is to equate the word "opinion" in the second sentence with the word "idea" in the first sentence. Under this view, the language was merely a reiteration of Justice Holmes' classic "marketplace of ideas" concept. [ ]

Thus, we do not think this passage from *Gertz* was intended to create a wholesale defamation exemption for anything that might be labeled "opinion." Not only would such an interpretation be contrary to the tenor and context of the passage, but it would also ignore the fact that expressions of "opinion" may often imply an assertion of objective fact.

If a speaker says, "In my opinion John Jones is a liar," he implies a knowledge of facts which lead to the conclusion that Jones told an untruth. Even if the speaker states the facts upon which he bases his opinion, if those facts are either incorrect or incomplete, or if his assessment of them is erroneous, the statement may still imply a false assertion of fact. Simply couching such statements in terms of opinion does not dispel these implications; and the statement, "In my opinion Jones is a liar," can cause as much damage to reputation as the statement, "Jones is a liar." As Judge Friendly aptly stated: "[It] would be destructive of the law of libel if a writer could escape liability for accusations of [defamatory conduct] simply by using, explicitly or implicitly, the words 'I think.' " See *Cianci* [ ]. It is worthy of note that at common law, even the privilege of fair comment did not extend to "a false statement of fact, whether it was expressly stated or implied from an expression of opinion." Restatement (Second) of Torts, supra, § 566 Comment a.

Apart from their reliance on the *Gertz* dictum, respondents do not really contend that a statement such as, "In my opinion John Jones is a liar," should be protected by a separate privilege for "opinion" under the First Amendment. But they do contend that in every defamation case the First Amendment mandates an inquiry into whether a statement is "opinion" or "fact," and that only the latter statements may be actionable. They propose that a number of factors developed by the lower courts (in what we hold was a mistaken reliance on the *Gertz* dictum) be considered in deciding which is which. But we think the

" 'breathing space' " which " 'freedoms of expression require in order to survive,' " [   ] is adequately secured by existing constitutional doctrine without the creation of an artificial dichotomy between "opinion" and fact.

Foremost, we think *Hepps* stands for the proposition that a statement on matters of public concern must be provable as false before there can be liability under state defamation law, at least in situations, like the present where a media defendant is involved.[6] Thus, unlike the statement, "In my opinion Mayor Jones is a liar," the statement, "In my opinion Mayor Jones shows his abysmal ignorance by accepting the teachings of Marx and Lenin," would not be actionable. *Hepps* ensures that a statement of opinion relating to matters of public concern which does not contain a provably false factual connotation will receive full constitutional protection.

Next, the *Bresler–Letter Carriers–Falwell* line of cases provide protection for statements that cannot "reasonably [be] interpreted as stating actual facts" about an individual. [   ] This provides assurance that public debate will not suffer for lack of "imaginative expression" or the "rhetorical hyperbole" which has traditionally added much to the discourse of our Nation. [   ]

The New York Times–Butts and Gertz culpability requirements further ensure that debate on public issues remains "uninhibited, robust, and wide-open." [   ] Thus, where a statement of "opinion" on a matter of public concern reasonably implies false and defamatory facts regarding public figures or officials, those individuals must show that such statements were made with knowledge of their false implications or with reckless disregard of their truth. Similarly, where such a statement involves a private figure on a matter of public concern, a plaintiff must show that the false connotations were made with some level of fault as required by Gertz. Finally, the enhanced appellate review required by Bose Corp., provides assurance that the foregoing determinations will be made in a manner so as not to "constitute a forbidden intrusion of the field of free expression." [   ]

We are not persuaded that in addition to these protections, an additional separate constitutional privilege for "opinion" is required to insure the freedom of expression guaranteed by the First Amendment. The dispositive question in the present case then becomes whether or not a reasonable factfinder could conclude that the statements in the . . . column imply an assertion that petitioner Milkovich perjured himself in a judicial proceeding. We think this question must be answered in the affirmative. As the Ohio Supreme Court itself observed, "the clear impact in some nine sentences and a caption is that [*Milkovich*] 'lied at the hearing after . . . having given his solemn

---

6. In *Hepps* the Court reserved judgment on cases involving non media defendants, [   ] and accordingly we do the same. Prior to *Hepps* of course, where public-official or public-figure plaintiffs were involved, the *New York Times* rule already required a showing of falsity before liability could result. [   ]

oath to tell the truth.'" [ ] This is not the sort of loose, figurative or hyperbolic language which would negate the impression that the writer was seriously maintaining petitioner committed the crime of perjury. Nor does the general tenor of the article negate this impression.

We also think the connotation that petitioner committed perjury is sufficiently factual to be susceptible of being proved true or false. A determination of whether petitioner lied in this instance can be made on a core of objective evidence by comparing, *inter alia*, petitioner's testimony before the OHSAA board with his subsequent testimony before the trial court. As the [Ohio Supreme Court noted in the case of the superintendent] "[w]hether or not H. Don Scott did indeed perjure himself is certainly verifiable by a perjury action with evidence adduced from the transcripts and witnesses present at the hearing. Unlike a subjective assertion the averred defamatory language is an articulation of an objectively verifiable event." 25 Ohio St. 3d, at 252, 496 N.E.2d, at 707. So too with petitioner Milkovich.

The numerous decisions discussed above establishing First Amendment protection for defendants in defamation actions surely demonstrate the Court's recognition of the Amendment's vital guarantee of free and uninhibited discussion of public issues. But there is another side to the equation; we have regularly acknowledged the "important social values which underlie the law of defamation," and recognize that [s]ociety has a pervasive and strong interest in preventing and redressing attacks upon reputation." *Rosenblatt v. Baer.* [ ] Justice Stewart [concurring] in that case put it with his customary clarity:

"The right of a man to the protection of his own reputation from unjustified invasion and wrongful hurt reflects no more than our basic concept of the essential dignity and worth of every human being—a concept at the root of any decent system of ordered liberty.

"The destruction that defamatory falsehood can bring is, to be sure, often beyond the capacity of the law to redeem. Yet, imperfect though it is, an action for damages is the only hope for vindication of redress the law gives to a man whose reputation has been falsely dishonored." [ ]

We believe our decision in the present case holds the balance true. The judgment of the Ohio Court of Appeals is reversed and the case remanded for further proceedings not inconsistent with this opinion.

Reversed.

[Justice Brennan, joined by Justice Marshall, dissented. He said the Court addressed the opinion issue "cogently and almost entirely correctly," and agreed that the lower courts had been under a "misimpression that there is a so-called opinion privilege wholly in addition to the protections we have already found to be guaranteed by the First Amendment . . .." But he disagreed with the application of agreed principles to the facts. ". . . I find that the challenged statements cannot reasonably be interpreted as either stating or implying defamatory facts about petitioner. Under the rule articulated in the majority opinion, therefore, the statements are due 'full constitutional protection.' "

He characterized the columnist's assumption that Milkovich lied as "patently conjecture" and asserted that conjecture is as important to the free flow of ideas and opinions as "imaginative expression" and "rhetorical hyperbole," which the majority agreed are protected. He gave several examples:

> Did NASA officials ignore sound warnings that the Challenger Space Shuttle would explode? Did Cuban–American leaders arrange for John Fitzgerald Kennedy's assassination? Was Kurt Waldheim a Nazi officer? Such questions are matters of public concern long before all the facts are unearthed, if they ever are. Conjecture is a means of fueling a national discourse on such questions and stimulating public pressure for answers from those who know more.

The dissent argued that the language of the column itself made clear to readers that the columnist was engaging in speculation, personal judgment, emotional rhetoric, and moral outrage. "No reasonable reader could understand [the columnist] to be impliedly asserting—as fact—that Milkovich had perjured himself."]

Notes and Questions

1. Why does the Constitution require protection of rhetorical hyperbole but not opinion? Is rhetorical hyperbole less likely to damage reputation? A more valuable form of speech?

2. The majority says "the statement, 'In my opinion Mayor Jones shows his abysmal ignorance by accepting the teachings of Marx and Lenin,' would not be actionable." If the mayor does not accept the teachings of Marx and Lenin, why is the statement not actionable? Does the Court mean only that the statement that the mayor is abysmally ignorant is not actionable if the rest of the statement is true?

3. Would the statements at issue in *Ollman* be actionable under the *Milkovich* principles?

4. The procedural history of the *Milkovich* case, described at length in omitted portions of the majority opinion, illustrates the persistence and endurance that libel litigation sometimes demands of its participants. The column was published in 1974. Milkovich and Scott filed separate suits. The Milkovich case went to trial, but the judge directed a verdict for the defendants on the ground that Milkovich was required to show actual malice and had failed to do so. The Ohio Court of Appeals reversed, holding that there was sufficient evidence of actual malice. The Ohio Supreme Court and the U.S. Supreme Court denied review. On remand, the trial court granted defendants' motion for summary judgment on the ground that the column was constitutionally protected as opinion, and alternatively, that Milkovich was a public figure and

had failed to make out a *prima facie* case of actual malice. The court of appeals this time affirmed both determinations, but the Ohio Supreme Court reversed, holding that Milkovich was neither a public official nor public figure and that the column was not opinion. The U.S. Supreme Court denied review.

Two years later, Scott's case reached the Ohio Supreme Court. Some judges had been replaced in the interval, and the court now held that the column was constitutionally protected opinion, affirming summary judgment against Scott. Scott v. News–Herald, 25 Ohio St.3d 243, 496 N.E.2d 699 (1986).

The trial court in Milkovich granted summary judgment on the opinion ground, and the Ohio Court of Appeals affirmed on the authority of the *Scott* decision. The Ohio Supreme Court denied review, but Milkovich finally won U.S. Supreme Court review 16 years after the column appeared.

5. The decision left the Milkovich case unresolved. In a footnote dismissing arguments that independent state grounds precluded Supreme Court review of the opinion issue, the Court recognized that the Ohio courts still might hold for the defendants on the ground that the state constitution protects opinion or on the ground that Milkovich is a public official or public figure and cannot show actual malice. The Ohio appellate court to which the case was then remanded found that the Ohio Constitution does not afford greater protection to opinion than does the federal Constitution, but it remanded the case to the trial court to determine if the column was written with some level of *Gertz* fault. 591 N.E.2d 394 (1990). An appeal to the Supreme Court of Ohio was dismissed on application of appellant Milkovich in 1991.

6. In 1990, the Supreme Court vacated and remanded a lower court's decision in Immuno AG. v. Moor–Jankowski, 74 N.Y.2d 548, 549 N.Y.S.2d 938, 549 N.E.2d 129, 17 Med.L.Rptr. 1161 (1989) for further reconsideration in light of *Milkovich*. Immuno AG, an Austrian pharmaceutical company that performs tests on animals, had sued Moor–Jankowski, editor of the *Journal of Medical Primatology*, published in New York, over a letter to the editor from an animal rights activist concerned about a proposed research facility using chimpanzees for research. When the *Journal* had published the letter, it had included an editor's note saying that Immuno's lawyers had challenged the accuracy of the letter and identifying the writer as an animal rights activist. New York's highest court decided that the state's constitution offers more protection for freedom of the press than does the U.S. Constitution—and dismissed the case. Judge Judith Kaye, writing for the majority, said "We look to our state law because of the nature of the issue in controversy—liberty of the press—where this state has its own exceptional history and rich tradition." 18 Med.L.Rptr. 1625 (1991). The Supreme Court denied *certiorari* 111 S.Ct. 2261 (1991).

7. The *Milkovich* distinction between fact and opinion was also an issue in Unelko Corp. v. Rooney, in which the maker of a car wind-

shield treatment product sued Andy Rooney of "60 Minutes" for saying the product "Rain–X" "didn't work." Although Rooney's comment was held to imply an assertion of objective fact and, under *Milkovich*, was not shielded from liability, the U.S. Court of Appeals for the Ninth Circuit upheld a grant of summary judgment for Rooney due to the manufacturer's failure to demonstrate falsity. 912 F.2d 1049, 17 Med. L.Rptr. 2317 (9th Cir.1990).

g. *Vagueness*

Some courts have found language too imprecise to form the basis of a defamation action. An accusation that William F. Buckley, Jr., was a "fellow traveler" of fascist causes was too "loosely definable" and too "variously interpretable" to be actionable as a defamation. The court suggested that there might be a difference between that vague charge and a more specific charge that plaintiff was a member of a particular party or group that subscribed to that type of belief. Buckley v. Littell, 539 F.2d 882, 1 Med.L.Rptr. 1762 (2d Cir.1976), certiorari denied 429 U.S. 1062 (1977).

Similarly, a charge that a police union's collective bargaining efforts involved the "inroad of communism" was held too vague to support a suit. National Association of Government Employees, Inc. v. Central Broadcasting Corp., 379 Mass. 220, 396 N.E.2d 996, 5 Med. L.Rptr. 2078 (1979). The court thought it clear from the context and words used that no hearer in the community after even brief reflection would understand the speaker to be charging plaintiff with complicity in the "horrors distinctive of a totalitarian regime."

h. *"Libel–Proof" Plaintiffs*

Courts have long assumed that plaintiffs whose reputations were already bad prior to the publication of a libel should be treated differently than those who had previously had good reputations— whatever damages were suffered from incrementally lowering the reputation were unlikely to be significant. The doctrine was that "a libel-proof plaintiff is not entitled to burden a defendant with a trial in which the most favorable result the plaintiff could achieve is an award of nominal damages." Jackson v. Longcope, 394 Mass. 577, 476 N.E.2d 617 (1985). In *Jackson*, a convicted multiple murderer was challenging a statement that he had raped and strangled all of his victims. In another example, *Penthouse* magazine publisher Robert Guccione was held to be "libel proof" in connection with a 1983 article in *Hustler* that alleged that he was "married and has a live-in girlfriend." At the time the article appeared, Guccione had been divorced four years, but he had earlier lived with his girlfriend for 13 years while married to someone else. Guccione v. Hustler Magazine, Inc., 800 F.2d 298, 13 Med.L.Rptr. 1316 (2d Cir.1986), certiorari denied 479 U.S. 1091 (1987).

The extent to which plaintiffs may be found to be libel-proof in the future, however, is unpredictable after the decision of the Supreme

Court of the United States in Masson v. New Yorker Magazine, Inc., 501 U.S. ___ (1991), which appears as a principal case at p. 1656, *infra.* In *Masson,* the Supreme Court noted that the court below had relied on the "incremental harm" doctrine—looking at the extent to which statements for which the plaintiff had sued damaged him beyond the extent to which he might have been damaged by statements for which he had not sued. The Supreme Court said that "[W]e reject any suggestion that the incremental harm doctrine is compelled as a matter of First Amendment protection for speech. The question of incremental harm does not bear upon whether a defendant has published a statement with knowledge of falsity or reckless disregard of whether it was false or not."

2. LIBEL AND SLANDER—THE DAMAGE QUESTION

So far we have been discussing the general subject of "defamation." Included within defamation are the subcategories of libel and slander. Historically, slanders were oral defamations and were handled by the common-law courts; libels were written defamations that, because of the development of printing, became a major concern of the crown. After the end of the days of the Star Chamber, a criminal court, oral and written defamations were redressed by the common-law courts. Those courts, however, preserved some distinctions between the two that have survived to our day.

The critical distinction relates to what types of damages a plaintiff must show in order to be allowed to bring an action for defamation. Two types of damages are central to this discussion. "Special damages" are specific identifiable losses that the plaintiff can prove he has sustained and can trace to the defendant's defamatory statement. "General damages" are damages to reputation that the plaintiff is presumed or proven to have sustained as a result of the defendant's statement. The jury is permitted to speculate on the extent of injury based on the words used, the medium used and the predicted response of the community.

The common law courts have treated libel as substantially more serious than slander. The distinction arose when relatively few people could read and the written word inspired awe and thus was more credible. A writing may be given more weight because it requires more thought and planning than a spontaneous oral utterance. Furthermore, the writing is more lasting and is likely to reach a larger audience than most, if not all, slanders. Thus, libels as a class were more likely to cause harm than slanders, and courts declared that plaintiffs in libel cases were able to recover general damages without any showing of special damages. Therefore, a plaintiff proceeding under libel has always been at least as well off as, and often better off than, a plaintiff suing for slander for precisely the same words.

If an action is for slander, plaintiff must prove "special damages" unless the defamatory thrust fits into at least one of four categories.

These categories are: the imputation of a serious crime involving moral turpitude; imputation of an existing loathsome disease; a charge that attacks the plaintiff's competence or honesty in business, trade or profession; or a charge of unchastity in a woman. Such a spoken charge is called "slander per se" and permits an action enabling the plaintiff to claim general damages to reputation without proving actual pecuniary harm. Here the jury may conclude that publication of the charge caused substantial harm in the community, and can measure damages according to the number and identity of those who learned of the charge, and their presumed reaction based on the seriousness and credibility of the charge. If a plaintiff can also establish special damages, these could be recovered in addition to any general damages.

If the slander is not within the four categories, then an action must be supported by proof of special damages, such as losing a job or a business deal.

The distinction between libel and slander has blurred with the development of new modes of communication. Until this century, it was likely that a written defamation would reach more people than an oral one. But with the development of radio and then of television, the odds have shifted. In analyzing new technologies should we stick to the traditional oral-written line or should we develop an approach that treats all modes of mass communication as libel and other modes of communication as slander? In a few states, legislation has resolved the matter. For example, California provides that broadcasting is slander. In the states that are resolving the question by common law, the tendency has been to treat broadcasting as libel.

The resulting libel-slander rules have sometimes permitted a plaintiff to recover enormous amounts in general damages. At other times they have barred a plaintiff from recovering anything whatever, because special damages were required but could not be proven although serious general harm seemed likely.

In addition to the critical distinction between general and special damages, two other classifications loom large in defamation law: nominal damages and punitive damages. Although nominal damages are unimportant in most tort actions, they may be central in defamation cases. The award of a symbolic amount such as six cents usually shows that the jury found the attack to be false but also found the words not to have hurt, either because the speaker was not credible or the plaintiff's strong reputation blunted the harm (or his reputation was so low nothing could really hurt it). For an example, see the suit by Quentin Reynolds against the Hearst Corporation and one of its columnists, upholding a jury award of $1 in compensatory damages and $175,000 in punitive damages against the various defendants. Reynolds v. Pegler, 223 F.2d 429 (2d Cir.), certiorari denied 350 U.S. 846 (1955) (Black, J., dissenting).

A few states declare that punitive damages, which are to punish defendants for serious misbehavior, are never recoverable. Most states allow them in appropriate cases.

3. THE BASIS FOR LIABILITY—THE TROUBLE SPOT

Before one person is liable in tort law for hurting another, commonly, but not universally, some "fault" must be ascribed to the actor's conduct. For example, a plaintiff cannot win an automobile accident case simply by showing that the defendant's car hit the plaintiff. Instead, plaintiff must show that the defendant driver was "at fault" in his behavior. (It is, of course, different in so-called "no-fault" states, which emphasize the harm to plaintiff rather than the fault of the defendant.)

In defamation, the common law long took the view that fault played no part in the tort. In other words, historically, plaintiffs had only to show that the defendants' statements hurt the plaintiffs' reputations and prove whatever damages were required by the libel-slander rules. It was irrelevant that the defendants did not realize that their statements could hurt the plaintiffs or anyone.

Thus, a newspaper lost a case in which it published a birth announcement that was a hoax—the couple had been married only three months. Those who read the article and who knew the fact of plaintiff's recent marriage would have given the story a meaning the newspaper never intended. Even if the newspaper had tried unsuccessfully to check the story but failed to learn about the hoax, it would not have mattered. The common law asserted that defendants in defamation cases were subject to "strict liability"—a liability that was not based on fault. The peril to free speech is readily apparent today. But the response in earlier times was that the remedy was accuracy and refusal to write about things that were not known first hand.

As we shall see, this troubling aspect of the common law has become the focus of constitutional developments.

For the electronic media, the problem of determining liability can be particularly difficult in instances of live or near-live transmissions. In a Massachusetts case, a candidate for public office alleged that he had been libeled when the host of a radio talk show failed to take advantage of a seven-second delay to terminate the remarks of an anonymous caller. Pacella v. Milford Radio Corp., 18 Mass.App.Ct. 6, 462 N.E.2d 355 (1984), affirmed without opinion by an evenly divided court, 394 Mass. 1051, 476 N.E.2d 595, certiorari denied 474 U.S. 844 (1985). Under the common law, the candidate might have won. The common-law tradition was that media were responsible for libelous statements they transmitted, whether they originated them or not, and whether they were careful or not. Several states adopted a model statute giving broadcasters greater protection. As we shall see in the discussion of constitutional privilege, p. 623, *infra,* however, a different standard is imposed in cases involving public figures today. Thus, in the Pacella case, the court held that the broadcaster was not responsible because it had not been shown that failure to stop the allegedly libelous statement demonstrated "reckless disregard of truth or falsity," language to which we will return later in this chapter.

Traditionally, the plaintiff's action for defamation has been easy to establish. The plaintiff had to prove the publication to a third person of a statement of and concerning plaintiff that injured his reputation, and then had to meet whatever damage showing was required under the relevant libel-slander rules. These elements shown, it was up to the defendant to present a defense.

4. COMMON LAW DEFENSES

Several common law libel defenses are typically recognized in state law. They include truth, the privilege accorded participants in certain official proceedings, the privilege accorded to those who quote accurately from such proceedings and the privilege of criticism, sometimes called "fair comment." These defenses were used by libel defendants under strict liability prior to the New York Times v. Sullivan decision. We will discuss them first and then look at the important constitutional privilege of absence of malice in a separate section.

a. Truth

The most obvious defense, but one rarely used, is to prove the essential truth of the defamatory statement. Most states recognize truth as a complete defense regardless of the speaker's motives. Because the action is intended to compensate those whose reputations are damaged incorrectly, if the defendant has spoken the truth, the reputational harm is deemed to provide no basis for an action. A minority of states have required the truth to have been spoken with "good motives" or for "justifiable ends" or both, but in the wake of *New York Times* and its progeny, such requirements may not be constitutional.

The defendant need not prove literal truth but must establish the "sting" of his charge. Thus, if the defendant has charged the plaintiff with stealing $25,000 from a bank, truth will be established even if the actual amount was only $12,000. If the defendant cannot prove any theft whatever but can prove the plaintiff is a bigamist, this information will not support his defense of truth, but it may help mitigate damages to show that the plaintiff's reputation is already in low esteem for other reasons and, thus he has suffered less harm than might otherwise have occurred.

These matters can raise troublesome questions. In Hovey v. Iowa State Daily Publication Board, Inc., 372 N.W.2d 253, 12 Med.L.Rptr. 1035 (Iowa 1985), the defendant newspaper reported on a violent episode that took place while the female plaintiff was serving as a bartender at an American Legion Hall. One customer knocked the only other customer unconscious and forced the plaintiff to perform oral sex upon him. The man was charged with "sexual abuse." The newspaper, however, reported that the man had been charged with "raping a bartender." Another paragraph reported that he had been charged with "second degree sexual abuse, willful injury, and first degree robbery." The article also stated that bond for the "rape" and robbery charges had been set at $50,000.

The court rejected the plaintiff's claim that "rape" referred only to "forcible genital sexual intercourse." It agreed with the defendant that "rape" was broad enough to include "any forced sex act, including oral sex." The court referred to general dictionaries and to recent revisions in the Iowa criminal code that had subsumed rape into the crime of sexual abuse in 1978.

Finally, after adopting the substantial truth test, the court concluded that the "difference between the truth and the reported truth was not material enough for the inaccuracy to be actionable."

Truth is little used as a defense because the defense may be very expensive to establish. A defendant relying on truth almost always bears the legal costs of a full-dress trial as well as the sometimes major expense of investigating the matter and gathering enough evidence to ensure the outcome.

b. State Privileges

Not only were there disadvantages to the defense of truth, there were attractive alternatives. Over the centuries the law of defamation has developed several privileges to protect those who utter defamations. Some privileges are "absolute" in the sense that if the occasion gives rise to an absolute privilege, there will be no liability even if the speaker deliberately lied about the plaintiff. The most significant example is the federal and state constitutional privilege afforded legislators who may not be sued for defamation for any statement made during debate. High executive officials, judges and participants in judicial proceedings also have an absolute privilege to speak freely on matters relevant to their obligations. No matter how such a speaker abuses the privilege by lying, no tort liability will flow. See Barr v. Matteo, 360 U.S. 564 (1959). The main circumstance that gives absolute privilege to the media occurs when broadcasters are required to grant equal opportunity to all candidates for the same office. If a candidate commits defamation, the broadcaster is not liable for the defamation. See *WDAY*, p. 235, *supra*.

Most common law privileges serve individuals and do not specifically affect media—with two important exceptions. The first involves the conditional privilege to make fair and accurate reports of governmental proceedings. Under general defamation law, one who repeats another's statement is responsible for the truth of what he repeats. Thus, if X states that "Y told me that Z is a murderer," and Z sues X for defamation, X will be treated as the publisher who is responsible for his own statement. In order to prevail on the defense of truth, X must prove that Z is in fact a murderer—it is not enough for X to prove that in fact Y told him that Z was a murderer. The general reason underlying this view is the reluctance to protect gossip.

It was not long, however, before the courts and the legislatures began to realize that sometimes speakers should be encouraged to repeat others' statements. The federal and state constitutions had already provided that members of the legislative branch could quote others in debate with absolute protection against legal sanctions.

The major example of the value of repetition was found in the reporting of how government was functioning and what government officials were saying. Thus, observers were to be encouraged to report what legislators said on the floor or in the committee as well as events in court. It would put reporters in a hopeless situation to be able to report safely only the truthful statements of government officials or of witnesses at a trial. As a result of these considerations, a privilege developed, sometimes called the privilege of "record libel," under which reports of what occurs in governmental proceedings are privileged even if some of those quoted have spoken falsely—so long as the report is accurate or a fair summary of what transpired.

The second major common law privilege of value to the media was the privilege of fair comment upon matters of public interest. When the privilege was applied in cases of literary and artistic criticism it caused little confusion. Problems raised by such comment are discussed in the classic Cherry v. Des Moines Leader, 114 Iowa 298, 86 N.W. 323 (1901) in which a reviewer scathingly described a performance by the Cherry sisters. But at the turn of the century cases arose in which the privilege of fair comment was claimed with regard to other matters of public interest, including the conduct of politicians. This was not the privilege of reporting what certain public officials were doing in their official capacity. Rather the privilege claimed would permit citizens to criticize and argue about the conduct of their officials, and these cases presented the problem of distinguishing between facts and opinion. In the literary criticism area the application of the privilege could depend upon the accuracy of the "facts" because they were usually readily apparent. When dealing with politics, however, the "facts" were often elusive. This new problem created a judicial split.

Most state courts decided that in order for criticism of government officials and others to be privileged, the facts upon which the comments were based had to be true. A minority of courts, including Coleman v. MacLennan, 78 Kan. 711, 98 P. 281 (1908), disagreed. They decided that facts relating to matters of public interest could not form the basis for a defamation case even if the facts were incorrect, so long as the speaker honestly believed them to be true.

It was from this disagreement among the states that the constitutional developments sprang.

B. CONSTITUTIONAL PRIVILEGE

So long as state law controlled, publishers and broadcasters could try to persuade state courts and legislatures to alter the defamation rules. As we have seen, their success varied in different states. Early efforts to gain further protection in defamation cases by invoking federal constitutional law to limit state power did not fare well.

In *Near*, p. 25, *supra*, the case that perhaps first reinforced the protection of the press in this country, the majority observed, "But it is recognized that punishment for the abuse of the liberty accorded to the press is essential to the protection of the public, and that the common-law rules that subject the libeler to responsibility for the public offense, as well as for the private injury, are not abolished by the protection extended in our Constitution."

In *Chaplinsky*, p. 23, *supra*, the Court said:

There are certain well-defined and narrowly limited classes of speech, the prevention and punishment of which have never been thought to raise any Constitutional problem. These include the lewd and obscene, the profane, the libelous, and the insulting or "fighting" words—those that by their very utterance inflict injury or tend to incite an immediate breach of the peace. It has been well observed that such utterances are no essential part of any exposition of ideas, and are of such slight social value as a step to truth that any benefit that may be derived from them is clearly outweighed by the social interest in order and morality.

This language was often quoted approvingly. Justice Frankfurter, writing for a 5–4 majority in Beauharnais v. Illinois, 343 U.S. 250 (1952), to sustain a state criminal libel law, relied on *Chaplinsky* for the proposition that libelous utterances were not "within the area of constitutionally protected speech."

This sequence set the stage for the following case from Alabama, a state that had long followed the majority rule that there was no privilege for incorrect facts, even in stories of public importance.

NEW YORK TIMES CO. v. SULLIVAN

Together with Abernathy v. Sullivan.

Supreme Court of the United States, 1964.
376 U.S. 254, 84 S.Ct. 710, 11 L.Ed.2d 686, 1 Med.L.Rptr. 1527.

[This action was based on a full-page advertisement in *The New York Times* on behalf of several individuals and groups protesting a "wave of terror" against blacks involved in non-violent demonstrations in the South. Plaintiff, one of three elected commissioners of Montgomery, the capital of Alabama, was in charge of the police department. When he demanded a retraction, as state law required, *The Times* instead responded that it failed to see how he was defamed. He then filed suit against *The Times* and four clergymen whose names appeared as sponsors—although they denied having authorized this—in the ad. Plaintiff alleged that the third and the sixth paragraphs of the advertisement libelled him:

> "In Montgomery, Alabama, after students sang 'My Country, 'Tis of Thee' on the State Capitol steps, their leaders were expelled from school, and truckloads of police armed with shotguns and tear-gas ringed the Alabama State College Campus. When the entire student body protested to state authorities by refusing to re-register, their dining hall was padlocked in an attempt to starve them into submission."

> . . .

> "Again and again the Southern violators have answered Dr. King's peaceful protests with intimidation and violence. They have bombed his home almost killing his wife and child. They have assaulted his person. They have arrested him seven times— for 'speeding,' 'loitering' and similar 'offenses.' And now they have charged him with 'perjury'—a *felony* under which they could imprison him for *ten years*. . . ."

Plaintiff claimed that he was libelled in the third paragraph by the reference to the police, since his responsibilities included supervision of the Montgomery police. He asserted that the paragraph could be read as charging the police with ringing the campus and seeking to starve the students by padlocking the dining hall. As to the sixth paragraph, he contended that the word "they" referred to his departments since arrests are usually made by the police and the paragraph could be read as accusing him of committing the acts charged. Several witnesses testified that they read the statements as referring to plaintiff in his capacity as commissioner.

The defendants admitted several inaccuracies in these two paragraphs; the students sang "The Star Spangled Banner," not "My Country, 'Tis of Thee"; nine students were expelled, not for leading the demonstration, but for demanding service at a lunch counter in the county courthouse; the dining hall was never padlocked; police at no time ringed the campus though they were deployed nearby in large numbers; they were not called to the campus in connection with the demonstration; Dr. King had been arrested only four times; and officers disputed his account of the alleged assault. Plaintiff proved that he had not been commissioner when three of the four arrests occurred and that he had nothing to do with procuring the perjury indictment.

The trial judge charged that the statements were libel *per se*, that the jury should decide whether they were made "of and concerning" the plaintiff, and, if so, general damages were to be presumed. Although noting that punitive damages required more than carelessness, he refused to charge that they required a finding of actual intent to harm or "gross negligence and recklessness." He also refused to order the jury to separate its award of general and punitive damages. The jury returned a verdict for $500,000—the full amount demanded. The Alabama Supreme Court affirmed, holding that malice could be found in several aspects of *The Times*'s conduct.

The Supreme Court began by disposing of the assertion that the Fourteenth Amendment is directed against State action and not private action, holding that "[t]he test is not the form in which state power has been applied but, whatever the form, whether such power has in fact been exercised." It also rejected the argument that constitutional guarantees were inapplicable because the statements were part of an advertisement.]

Justice Brennan delivered the opinion of the Court.

. . .

II.

. . .

The question before us is whether [Alabama's] rule of liability, as applied to an action brought by a public official against critics of his official conduct, abridges the freedom of speech and of the press that is guaranteed by the First and Fourteenth Amendments.

Respondent relies heavily, as did the Alabama courts, on statements of this Court to the effect that the Constitution does not protect libelous publications. Those statements do not foreclose our inquiry here. None of the cases sustained the use of libel laws to impose sanctions upon expression critical of the official conduct of public officials. . . . In deciding the question now, we are compelled by neither precedent nor policy to give any more weight to the epithet "libel" than we have to other "mere labels" of state law. NAACP v. Button, 371 U.S. 415, 429 (1963). Like insurrection, contempt, advocacy of unlawful acts, breach of the peace, obscenity, solicitation of legal business, and the various other formulae for the repression of expression that have been challenged in this Court, libel can claim no talismanic immunity from constitutional limitations. It must be measured by standards that satisfy the First Amendment.

The general proposition that freedom of expression upon public questions is secured by the First Amendment has long been settled by our decisions. . . . Mr. Justice Brandeis, in his concurring opinion in Whitney v. California, 274 U.S. 357, 375–376 (1927), gave the principle its classic formulation:

"Those who won our independence believed . . . that public discussion is a political duty; and that this should be a fundamental principle of the American government. . . . Believing in the power of reason as applied through public discussion, they eschewed silence coerced by law—the argument of force in its worst form. Recognizing the occasional tyrannies of governing majorities, they amended the Constitution so that free speech and assembly should be guaranteed."

Thus we consider this case against the background of a profound national commitment to the principle that debate on public issues should be uninhibited, robust, and wide-open, and that it may well include vehement, caustic, and sometimes unpleasantly sharp attacks on government and public officials. [ ] The present advertisement, as an expression of grievance and protest on one of the major public issues of our time, would seem clearly to qualify for the constitutional protection. The question is whether it forfeits that protection by the falsity of some of its factual statements and by its alleged defamation of respondent.

. . .

Injury to official reputation affords no more warrant for repressing speech that would otherwise be free than does factual error. Where judicial officers are involved, this Court has held that concern for the dignity and reputation of the courts does not justify the punishment as criminal contempt of criticism of the judge or his decision. Bridges v. California, 314 U.S. 252 (1941). . . . There is no force in respondent's argument that the constitutional limitations implicit in the history of the Sedition Act apply only to Congress and not to the States. It is true that the First Amendment was originally addressed only to action by the Federal Government, and that Jefferson, for one, while denying the power of Congress "to control the freedom of the press," recognized such a power in the States. [ ] But this distinction was eliminated with the adoption of the Fourteenth Amendment and the application to the States of the First Amendment's restrictions. [ ]

What a State may not constitutionally bring about by means of a criminal statute is likewise beyond the reach of its civil law of libel . . . .

[The Court quoted James Madison, suggesting the need for breathing space in public discussion, and the fear that even speakers of the truth will be chilled when the law is too restrictive.]

The constitutional guarantees require, we think, a federal rule that prohibits a public official from recovering damages for a defamatory falsehood relating to his official conduct unless he proves that the statement was made with "actual malice"—that is, with knowledge that it was false or with reckless disregard of whether it was false or not. An oft-cited statement of a like rule, which has been adopted by a number of state courts, is found in the Kansas case of Coleman v. MacLennan, 78 Kan. 711, 98 P. 281 (1908). . . .

Such a privilege for criticism of official conduct is appropriately analogous to the protection accorded a public official when *he* is sued for libel by a private citizen. In Barr v. Matteo, 360 U.S. 564, 575 (1959), this Court held the utterance of a federal official to be absolutely privileged if made "within the outer perimeter" of his duties. The States accord the same immunity to statements of their highest officers, although some differentiate their lesser officials and qualify the privilege they enjoy. But all hold that all officials are protected unless actual malice can be proved. The reason for the official privilege is said to be that the threat of damage suits would otherwise "inhibit the fearless, vigorous, and effective administration of policies of government" and "dampen the ardor of all but the most resolute, or the most irresponsible, in the unflinching discharge of their duties." Barr v. Matteo, supra, 360 U.S., at 571. Analogous considerations support the privilege for the citizen-critic of government. It is as much his duty to criticize as it is the official's duty to administer. . . .

We conclude that such a privilege is required by the First and Fourteenth Amendments.

III.

We hold today that the Constitution delimits a State's power to award damages for libel in actions brought by public officials against critics of their official conduct. Since this is such an action, the rule requiring proof of actual malice is applicable. While Alabama law apparently requires proof of actual malice for an award of punitive damages, where general damages are concerned malice is "presumed." Such a presumption is inconsistent with the federal rule. . . . Since the trial judge did not instruct the jury to differentiate between general and punitive damages, it may be that the verdict was wholly an award of one or the other. But it is impossible to know, in view of the general verdict returned. Because of this uncertainty, the judgment must be reversed and the case remanded. [ ]

Since respondent may seek a new trial we deem that considerations of effective judicial administration require us to review the evidence in the present record to determine whether it could constitutionally support a judgment for respondent. . . .

Applying these standards, we consider that the proof presented to show actual malice lacks convincing clarity which the constitutional standard demands, and hence that it would not constitutionally sustain the judgment for respondent under the proper rule of law. The case of the individual petitioners requires little discussion. Even assuming that they could constitutionally be found to have authorized the use of their names on the advertisement, there was no evidence whatever that they were aware of any erroneous statements or were in any way reckless in that regard. The judgment against them is thus without constitutional support.

As to the Times, we similarly conclude that the facts do not support a finding of actual malice. . . .

. . .

We also think the evidence was constitutionally defective in another respect: it was incapable of supporting the jury's finding that the allegedly libelous statements were made "of and concerning" respondent. Respondent relies on the words of the advertisement and the testimony of six witnesses to establish a connection between it and himself. . . . There was no reference to respondent in the advertisement, either by name or official position. . . .

This proposition has disquieting implications for criticism of governmental conduct. For good reason, "no court of last resort in this country has ever held, or even suggested, that prosecutions for libel on government have any place in the American system of jurisprudence." City of Chicago v. Tribune Co., 307 Ill. 595, 601, 139 N.E. 86, 88 (1923). The present proposition would sidestep this obstacle by transmuting criticism of government, however impersonal it may seem on its face, into personal criticism, and hence potential libel, of the officials of whom the government is composed. . . . We hold that such a proposition may not constitutionally be used to establish that an otherwise impersonal attack on governmental operations was a libel of an official responsible for those operations. Since it was relied on exclusively here, and there was no evidence to connect the statements with respondent, the evidence was constitutionally insufficient to support a finding that the statements referred to respondent.

The judgment of the Supreme Court of Alabama is reversed and the case is remanded to that court for further proceedings not inconsistent with this opinion.

Reversed and remanded.

MR. JUSTICE BLACK, with whom MR. JUSTICE DOUGLAS joins, concurring.

I concur in reversing this half-million-dollar judgment against the New York Times Company and the four individual defendants. In reversing the Court holds that "the Constitution delimits a State's power to award damages for libel in actions brought by public officials against critics of their official conduct." I base my vote to reverse on the belief that the First and Fourteenth Amendments not merely "delimit" a State's power to award damages to "public officials against critics of their official conduct" but completely prohibit a State from exercising such a power. The Court goes on to hold that a State can subject such critics to damages if "actual malice" can be proved against them. "Malice," even as defined by the Court, is an elusive, abstract concept, hard to prove and hard to disprove. The requirement that malice be proved provides at best an evanescent protection for the right critically to discuss public affairs and certainly does not measure up to the sturdy safeguard embodied in the First Amendment. Unlike the Court, therefore, I vote to reverse exclusively on the ground that the Times and the individual defendants had an absolute, unconditional constitutional right to publish in the Times advertisement their criticisms of the Montgomery agencies and officials. . . .

. . .

We would, I think, more faithfully interpret the First Amendment by holding that at the very least it leaves the people and the press free to criticize officials and discuss public affairs with impunity. . . . An unconditional right to say what one pleases about public affairs is what I consider to be the minimum guarantee of the First Amendment.[6]

I regret that the Court has stopped short of this holding indispensable to preserve our free press from destruction.

MR. JUSTICE GOLDBERG, with whom MR. JUSTICE DOUGLAS joins, concurring in the result.

. . .

In my view, the First and Fourteenth Amendments to the Constitution afford to the citizen and to the press an absolute, unconditional privilege to criticize official conduct despite the harm which may flow from excesses and abuses. . . .

. . .

. . . It may be urged that deliberately and maliciously false statements have no conceivable value as free speech. That argument, however, is not responsive to the real issue presented by this case, which is whether that freedom of speech which all agree is constitutionally protected can be effectively safeguarded by a rule allowing the imposition of liability upon a jury's evaluation of the speaker's state of mind. If individual citizens may be held liable in damages for strong words, which a jury finds false and maliciously motivated, there can be little doubt that public debate and advocacy will be constrained. And if newspapers, publishing advertisements dealing with public issues, thereby risk liability, there can also be little doubt that the ability of minority groups to secure publication of their views on public affairs and to seek support for their causes will be greatly diminished. . . .

. . .

If the government official should be immune from libel actions so that his ardor to serve the public will be dampened and "fearless, vigorous, and effective administration of policies of government" not be inhibited, [ ], then the citizen and the press should likewise be immune from libel actions for their criticism of official conduct. . . .

6. Cf. Meiklejohn, Free Speech and Its   Relation to Self–Government (1948).

The conclusion that the Constitution affords the citizen and the press an absolute privilege for criticism of official conduct does not leave the public official without defenses against unsubstantiated opinions or deliberate misstatements. "Under our system of government, counterargument and education are the weapons available to expose these matters, not abridgment . . . of free speech. . . ." Wood v. Georgia, 370 U.S. 375, 389 (1962). The public official certainly has equal if not greater access than most private citizens to media of communication. . . .

. . .

Notes and Questions

1. What is the justification for the majority position?

2. The majority twice observes that deliberate falsity is used in argument. Why is such behavior not protected here?

3. Do you consider either of the concurring opinions preferable to the majority approach? Would it be desirable to enable a public official to have a jury assess the truth of charges against him—without seeking damages?

4. Commenting after the *Times* case, Professor Kalven speculated on the case's future:

> The closing question, of course, is whether the treatment of seditious libel as the key concept for development of appropriate constitutional doctrine will prove germinal. It is not easy to predict what the Court will see in the *Times* opinion as the years roll by. It may regard the opinion as covering simply one pocket of cases, those dealing with libel of public officials, and not destructive of the earlier notions that are inconsistent only with the large reading of the Court's action. But the invitation to follow a dialectic progression from public official to government policy to public policy to matters in the public domain, like art, seems to me to be overwhelming. If the Court accepts the invitation, it will slowly work out for itself the theory of free speech that Alexander Meiklejohn has been offering us for some fifteen years now.

Kalven, The New York Times Case: A Note on "The Central Meaning of the First Amendment," 1964 Sup.Ct.Rev. 191, 221. Does his prediction seem sound? Keep it in mind as we consider the cases decided since *Times*.

5. The majority in the *New York Times* case did not explicitly condemn the concurring approaches. A few months later, in Garrison v. Louisiana, 379 U.S. 64, 1 Med.L.Rptr. 1548 (1964), the Court, in an opinion by Justice Brennan, extended the *Times* rule to cases of criminal libel and also held that truth must be a defense in cases brought by public officials. The majority explained its refusal to protect deliberate falsity:

Although honest utterance, even if inaccurate, may further the fruitful exercise of the right of free speech, it does not follow that the lie, knowingly and deliberately published about a public official, should enjoy a like immunity. At the time the First Amendment was adopted, as today, there were those unscrupulous enough and skillful enough to use the deliberate or reckless falsehood as an effective political tool to unseat the public servant or even topple an administration. [ ] That speech is used as a tool for political ends does not automatically bring it under the protective mantle of the Constitution. For the use of the known lie as a tool is at once at odds with the premises of democratic government and with the orderly manner in which economic, social, or political change is to be effected. Calculated falsehood falls into that class of utterances which "are no essential part of any exposition of ideas, and are of such slight social value as a step to truth that any benefit that may be derived from them is clearly outweighed by the social interest in order and morality. . . ." [ ] Hence the knowingly false statement and the false statement made with reckless disregard of the truth, do not enjoy constitutional protection.

6. The next major case was Rosenblatt v. Baer, 383 U.S. 75, 1 Med. L.Rptr. 1558 (1966). Plaintiff Baer had been hired to be Supervisor of a public recreation facility owned by Belknap County, N.H. Defendant, in his weekly newspaper column, noted that a year after plaintiff's discharge the facility was doing much better financially. The column could be understood as charging either inefficiency or dishonesty. In reversing plaintiff's state court judgment, the Supreme Court said that the vague language could be read as an attack on government—and that Baer could not sue unless he showed that he had been singled out for attack. Justice Brennan's majority opinion said that it is clear that the public official designation from *New York Times* applies all the way down the hierarchy of government employees "who have, or appear to the public to have, substantial responsibility for or control over the conduct of governmental affairs."

7. The Supreme Court next considered two cases together, Curtis Pub. Co. v. Butts, and Associated Press v. Walker, 388 U.S. 130, 1 Med. L.Rptr. 1568 (1967). In *Butts*, the defendant magazine had accused the plaintiff athletic director of disclosing his game plan to an opposing coach before their game. Although he was on the staff of a state university, Butts was paid by a private alumni organization. In *Walker*, the defendant news service reported that the plaintiff, a former United States Army general who resigned to engage in political activity, had personally led students in an attack on federal marshals who were enforcing a desegregation order at the University of Mississippi.

In both cases, lower courts had affirmed substantial jury awards against the defendants and had refused to apply the *Times* doctrine on the ground that public officials were not involved. The Supreme Court divided several ways on several issues, affirming *Butts*, 5–4, and reversing *Walker*, 9–0. Chief Justice Warren wrote the pivotal opinion in which he concluded that both men were "public figures" and that the standard developed in *New York Times* should apply to "public figures" as well:

> To me, differentiation between "public figures" and "public officials" and adoption of separate standards of proof for each has no basis in law, logic, or First Amendment policy. Increasingly in this country, the distinctions between governmental and private sectors are blurred. . . . [A]lthough they are not subject to the restraints of the political process, "public figures," like "public officials," often play an influential role in ordering society. And surely as a class these "public figures" have as ready access as "public officials" to mass media of communication, both to influence policy and to counter criticism of their views and activities. Our citizenry has a legitimate and substantial interest in the conduct of such persons, and freedom of the press to engage in uninhibited debate about their involvement in public issues and events is as crucial as it is in the case of "public officials." The fact that they are not amenable to the restraints of the political process only underscores the legitimate and substantial nature of the interest, since it means that public opinion may be the only instrument by which society can attempt to influence their conduct.

He found that on the merits the standard had not been met in *Walker*. In *Butts*, he found that defendant's counsel had deliberately waived the *Times* doctrine and he also found evidence establishing reckless behavior. He thus voted to reverse *Walker* and affirm *Butts*.

Justices Brennan and White agreed with the Chief Justice in *Walker* but found no waiver in *Butts* and would have reversed both cases. They agreed with the Chief Justice that *Butts* had presented enough evidence to come within the *Times* standard but thought that errors in the charge required a new trial.

Justices Black and Douglas adhered to their position, urged that the *Times* rule was too weak and voted to reverse both cases.

The remaining four justices, led by Justice Harlan, argued that the *Times* standard should not apply to public figures because criticism of government was not involved:

> We consider and would hold that a "public figure" who is not a public official may also recover damages for a defamatory falsehood whose substance makes substantial danger to reputation apparent, on a showing of highly unreasonable conduct constituting an extreme departure from the standards of investigation and reporting ordinarily adhered to by responsible publishers. . . .

Applying that standard Justice Harlan concluded that Walker had failed to establish a case, but that Butts had shown that the *Saturday Evening Post* ignored elementary precautions in preparing a potentially damaging story. Together with the Chief Justice's vote, there were five votes to affirm *Butts*.

8. In St. Amant v. Thompson, 390 U.S. 727, 1 Med.L.Rptr. 1586 (1968), the defendant, a candidate for public office, read on television a series of statements he had received from Mr. Albin, a member of a Teamsters' Union local. The statements, made under oath, falsely implied that the plaintiff, a deputy sheriff, had taken bribes. The defendant had not checked the facts stated by Albin, nor had he investigated Albin's reputation for veracity. The state court ruled that these failures to inquire further sufficed to meet the required standard of reckless disregard for the truth. The Supreme Court reversed and concluded that the standard of "reckless disregard" had not been met. It recognized that the term could receive no single "infallible definition" and that its outer limits would have to be developed in "case-to-case adjudication, as is true with so many legal standards for judging concrete cases, whether the standard is provided by the Constitution, statutes or case law." There "must be sufficient evidence to permit the conclusion that the defendant in fact entertained serious doubts as to the truth of his publication" in order for recklessness to be found.

9. Next the Court unanimously extended the *Times* rationale to candidates because "it can hardly be doubted that the constitutional guarantee has its fullest and most urgent application precisely to the conduct of campaigns for political office." Monitor Patriot Co. v. Roy, 401 U.S. 265, 1 Med.L.Rptr. 1619 (1971) and Ocala Star–Banner Co. v. Damron, 401 U.S. 295, 1 Med.L.Rptr. 1624 (1971).

10. A plurality of the Court took the next step in Rosenbloom v. Metromedia, Inc., 403 U.S. 29, 1 Med.L.Rptr. 1597 (1971), involving a broadcaster's charge that a magazine distributor sold obscene material and was arrested in a police raid. Justice Brennan, joined by Chief Justice Burger and Justice Blackmun, held that the *Times* standard should be extended to "all discussion and communication involving matters of public or general concern, without regard to whether the persons involved are famous or anonymous." The arrest and the distributor's subsequent claims against the police were thought to fit this category, and the *Times* standard was applied. In reaching that position, Justice Brennan concluded that the focus on the plaintiff's status begun in the *Times* case bore "little relationship either to the values protected by the First Amendment or to the nature of our society. . . . Thus, the idea that certain 'public' figures have voluntarily exposed their entire lives to public inspection, while private individuals have kept theirs carefully shrouded from public view is, at best, a legal fiction." Discussion of a matter of public concern must be protected even when it involves an unknown person. If the states fear that private citizens will be unable to respond to adverse publicity, "the solution lies in the direction of ensuring their ability to respond, rather than in stifling public discussion of matters of public concern," a reference to possible use of a right for people attacked in the media to reply. 403 U.S. at 47.

Justice White concurred on the narrow ground that the press is privileged to report "upon the official actions of public servants in full detail." Justice Black provided the fifth vote against liability for the reasons stated in his earlier opinions. Justices Harlan, Stewart and Marshall dissented on various grounds, but they agreed that the private plaintiff should be required to prove no more than negligence in this case. Justice Douglas did not participate.

Because there was no majority opinion from the Court in *Rosenbloom*, the case provided little guidance for future defamation cases. Three years later, in Gertz v. Robert Welch, Inc., the Court handed down a major libel decision, considered by many to be the most important since *Sullivan*. As you will see, *Gertz* attempts to clarify the difference between public and private figure libel plaintiffs. It also lifts from many private figure plaintiffs—depending on the state in which they sue—the burden of proving "actual malice" to collect compensatory damages.

GERTZ v. ROBERT WELCH, INC.

Supreme Court of the United States, 1974.
418 U.S. 323, 94 S.Ct. 2997, 41 L.Ed.2d 789, 1 Med.L.Rptr. 1633.

[Plaintiff, an attorney, was retained to represent the family of a youth killed by Nuccio, a Chicago policeman. In that capacity, plaintiff attended the coroner's inquest and filed an action for damages but played no part in a criminal proceeding in which Nuccio was convicted of second degree murder. Respondent publishes *American Opinion*, a monthly outlet for the views of the John Birch Society. As part of its efforts to alert the public to an alleged nationwide conspiracy to discredit local police, the magazine's editor engaged a regular contributor to write about the Nuccio episode. The article that appeared charged a frame-up against Nuccio and portrayed plaintiff as a "major architect" of the plot. It also falsely asserted that he had a long police record, was an official of the Marxist League for Industrial Democracy, and was a "Leninist" and a "Communist-fronter." The editor made no effort to verify the story.

Gertz filed an action for libel in District Court because of the diversity of citizenship. The trial judge first ruled that Gertz was not a public official or public figure and that under Illinois law there was no defense. The jury awarded $50,000. On further reflection, the judge decided that since a matter of public concern was being discussed, the *Times* rule should apply, and he granted the defendant judgment notwithstanding the jury's verdict. He thus anticipated the plurality's approach in Rosenbloom v. Metromedia, Inc. The court of appeals, relying on the intervening decision in *Rosenbloom*, affirmed because of the absence of "clear and convincing" evidence of "actual malice." Gertz appealed.]

Mr. Justice Powell delivered the opinion of the Court.

. . .

II

The principal issue in this case is whether a newspaper or broadcaster that publishes defamatory falsehoods about an individual who is neither a public official nor a public figure may claim a constitutional privilege against liability for the injury inflicted by those statements. The Court considered this question on the rather different set of facts presented in Rosenbloom v. Metromedia, Inc., 403 U.S. 29 (1971). . . .

. . .

In his opinion for the plurality in Rosenbloom v. Metromedia, Inc., [ ], Mr. Justice Brennan took the *New York Times* privilege one step further. He concluded that its protection should extend to defamatory falsehoods relating to private persons if the statements concerned matters of general or public interest. . . .

. . .

III

We begin with the common ground. Under the First Amendment there is no such thing as a false idea. However pernicious an opinion may seem, we depend for its correction not on the conscience of judges and juries but on the competition of other ideas. But there is no constitutional value in false statements of fact. Neither the intentional lie nor the careless error materially advances society's interest in "uninhibited, robust, and wide-open" debate on public issues. . . .

Although the erroneous statement of fact is not worthy of constitutional protection, it is nevertheless inevitable in free debate. . . . And punishment of error runs the risk of inducing a cautious and restrictive exercise of the constitutionally guaranteed freedoms of speech and press. Our decisions recognize that a rule of strict liability that compels a publisher or broadcaster to guarantee the accuracy of his factual assertions may lead to intolerable self-censorship. Allowing the media to avoid liability only by proving the truth of all injurious statements does not accord adequate protection to First Amendment liberties. . . . The First Amendment requires that we protect some falsehood in order to protect speech that matters.

The need to avoid self-censorship by the news media is, however, not the only societal value at issue. If it were, this Court would have embraced long ago the view that publishers and broadcasters enjoy an unconditional and indefeasible immunity from liability for defamation.

The legitimate state interest underlying the law of libel is the compensation of individuals for the harm inflicted on them by defamatory falsehood. . . . Some tension necessarily exists between the need for a vigorous and uninhibited press and the legitimate interest in redressing wrongful injury. . . .

The *New York Times* standard defines the level of a constitutional protection appropriate to the context of defamation of a public person.

Those who, by reason of the notoriety of their achievements or the vigor and success with which they seek the public's attention, are properly classed as public figures and those who hold governmental office may recover for injury to reputation only on clear and convincing proof that the defamatory falsehood was made with knowledge of its falsity or with reckless disregard for the truth. This standard administers an extremely powerful antidote to the inducement to media self-censorship of the common-law rule of strict liability for libel and slander. And it exacts a correspondingly high price from the victims of defamatory falsehood. Plainly many deserving plaintiffs, including some intentionally subjected to injury, will be unable to surmount the barrier of the *New York Times* test. Despite this substantial abridgment of the state law right to compensation for wrongful hurt to one's reputation, the Court has concluded that the protection of the *New York Times* privilege should be available to publishers and broadcasters of defamatory falsehood concerning public officials and public figures. [ ] We think that these decisions are correct, but we do not find their holdings justified solely by reference to the interest of the the press and broadcast media in immunity from liability. Rather, we believe that the *New York Times* rule states an accommodation between this concern and the limited state interest present in the context of libel actions brought by public persons. For the reasons stated below, we conclude that the state interest in compensating injury to the reputation of private individuals requires that a different rule should obtain with respect to them.

Theoretically, of course, the balance between the needs of the press and the individual's claim to compensation for wrongful injury might be struck on a case-by-case basis. As Mr. Justice Harlan hypothesized, "it might seem, purely as an abstract matter, that the most utilitarian approach would be to scrutinize carefully every jury verdict in every libel case, in order to ascertain whether the final judgment leaves fully protected whatever First Amendment values transcend the legitimate state interest in protecting the particular plaintiff who prevailed." Rosenbloom v. Metromedia, Inc., 403 U.S., at 63 (footnote omitted). But this approach would lead to unpredictable results and uncertain expectations, and it could render our duty to supervise the lower courts unmanageable. Because an *ad hoc* resolution of the competing interests at stake in each particular case is not feasible, we must lay down broad rules of general application. Such rules necessarily treat alike various cases involving differences as well as similarities. Thus it is often true that not all of the considerations which justify adoption of a given rule will obtain in each particular case decided under its authority.

With that caveat we have no difficulty in distinguishing among defamation plaintiffs. The first remedy of any victim of defamation is self-help—using available opportunities to contradict the lie or correct the error and thereby to minimize its adverse impact on reputation. Public officials and public figures usually enjoy significantly greater access to the channels of effective communication and hence have a more realistic opportunity to counteract false statements than private individuals normally enjoy.[9] Private individuals are therefore more vulnerable to injury, and the state interest in protecting them is correspondingly greater.

More important than the likelihood that private individuals will lack effective opportunities for rebuttal, there is a compelling normative consideration underlying the distinction between public and private defamation plaintiffs. An individual who decides to seek governmental office must accept certain necessary consequences of that involvement in public affairs. He runs the risk of closer public scrutiny than might otherwise be the case. And society's interest in the officers of government is not strictly limited to the formal discharge of official duties. As the Court pointed out in Garrison v. Louisiana, 379 U.S., at 77, the public's interest extends to "anything which might touch on an official's fitness for office . . .. Few personal attributes are more germane to fitness for office than dishonesty, malfeasance, or improper motivation, even though these characteristics may also affect the official's private character."

Those classed as public figures stand in a similar position. Hypothetically, it may be possible for someone to become a public figure through no purposeful action of his own, but the instances of truly involuntary public figures must be exceedingly rare. For the most part those who attain this status have assumed roles of especial prominence in the affairs of society. Some occupy positions of such persuasive power and influence that they are deemed public figures for all purposes. More commonly, those classed as public figures have thrust themselves to the forefront of particular public controversies in order to influence the resolution of the issues involved. In either event, they invite attention and comment.

Even if the foregoing generalities do not obtain in every instance, the communications media are entitled to act on the assumption that the public officials and public figures have voluntarily exposed themselves to increased risk of injury from defamatory falsehood concerning them. No such assumption is justified with respect to a private individual . . .. Thus, private individuals are not only more vulnerable to injury than public officials and public figures; they are also more deserving of recovery.

For these reasons we conclude that the States should retain substantial latitude in their efforts to enforce a legal remedy for defamatory falsehood injurious to the reputation of a private individual. The extension of the *New York Times* test proposed by the *Rosenbloom* plurality would abridge this legitimate state interest to a degree that

---

9. Of course, an opportunity for rebuttal seldom suffices to undo harm of defamatory falsehood. Indeed, the law of defamation is rooted in our experience that the truth rarely catches up with a lie. But the fact that the self-help remedy of rebuttal, standing alone, is inadequate to its task does not mean that it is irrelevant to our inquiry.

we find unacceptable. And it would occasion the additional difficulty of forcing state and federal judges to decide on an *ad hoc* basis which publications address issues of "general or public interest" and which do not—to determine, in the words of Mr. Justice Marshall, "what information is relevant to self-government." Rosenbloom v. Metromedia, Inc., 403 U.S., at 79. We doubt the wisdom of committing this task to the conscience of judges. . . .

We hold that, so long as they do not impose liability without fault, the States may define for themselves the appropriate standard of liability for a publisher or broadcaster of defamatory falsehood injurious to a private individual. This approach provides a more equitable boundary between the competing concerns involved here. It recognizes the strength of the legitimate state interest in compensating private individuals for wrongful injury to reputation, yet shields the press and broadcast media from the rigors of strict liability for defamation. . . .

IV

Our accommodation of the competing values at stake in defamation suits by private individuals allows the States to impose liability on the publisher or broadcaster of defamatory falsehood on a less demanding showing than that required by *New York Times*. This conclusion is not based on a belief that the considerations which prompted the adoption of the *New York Times* privilege for defamation of public officials and its extension to public figures are wholly inapplicable to the context of private individuals. Rather, we endorse this approach in recognition of the strong and legitimate state interest in compensating private individuals for injury to reputation. But this countervailing state interest extends no further than compensation for actual injury. For the reasons stated below, we hold that the States may not permit recovery of presumed or punitive damages, at least when liability is not based on a showing of knowledge of falsity or reckless disregard for the truth.

The common law of defamation is an oddity of tort law, for it allows recovery of purportedly compensatory damages without evidence of actual loss. Under the traditional rules pertaining to actions for libel the existence of injury is presumed from the fact of publication. Juries may award substantial sums as compensation for supposed damage to reputation without any proof that such harm actually occurred. The largely uncontrolled discretion of juries to award damages where there is no loss unnecessarily compounds the potential of any system of liability for defamatory falsehood to inhibit the vigorous exercise of First Amendment freedoms. Additionally, the doctrine of presumed damages invites juries to punish unpopular opinion rather than to compensate individuals for injury sustained by the publication of a false fact. More to the point, the States have no substantial interest in securing for plaintiffs such as this petitioner gratuitous awards of money damages far in excess of any actual injury.

We would not, of course, invalidate state law simply because we doubt its wisdom, but here we are attempting to reconcile state law with a competing interest grounded in the constitutional command of the First Amendment. It is therefore appropriate to require that state remedies for defamatory falsehood reach no farther than is necessary to protect the legitimate interest involved. It is necessary to restrict defamation plaintiffs who do not prove knowledge of falsity or reckless disregard for the truth to compensation for actual injury. We need not define "actual injury," as trial courts have wide experience in framing appropriate jury instructions in tort actions. Suffice it to say that actual injury is not limited to out-of-pocket loss. Indeed, the more customary types of actual harm inflicted by defamatory falsehood include impairment of reputation and standing in the community, personal humiliation, and mental anguish and suffering. Of course, juries must be limited by appropriate instructions, and all awards must be supported by competent evidence concerning the injury, although there need be no evidence which assigns an actual dollar value to the injury.

We also find no justification for allowing awards of punitive damages against publishers and broadcasters held liable under state-defined standards of liability for defamation. In most jurisdictions jury discretion over the amounts awarded is limited only by the gentle rule that they not be excessive. Consequently, juries assess punitive damages in wholly unpredictable amounts bearing no necessary relation to the actual harm caused. And they remain free to use their discretion selectively to punish expressions of unpopular views. Like the doctrine of presumed damages, jury discretion to award punitive damages unnecessarily exacerbates the danger of media self-censorship, but, unlike the former rule, punitive damages are wholly irrelevant to the state interest that justifies a negligence standard for private defamation actions. They are not compensation for injury. Instead, they are private fines levied by civil juries to punish reprehensible conduct and to deter its future occurrence. In short, the private defamation plaintiff who establishes liability under a less demanding standard than that stated by *New York Times* may recover only such damages as are sufficient to compensate him for actual injury.

V

Notwithstanding our refusal to extend the *New York Times* privilege to defamation of private individuals, respondent contends that we should affirm the judgment below on the ground that petitioner is either a public official or a public figure. There is little basis for the former assumption. Several years prior to the present incident, petitioner had served briefly on housing committees appointed by the mayor of Chicago, but at the time of publication he had never held any remunerative governmental position. Respondent admits this but argues that petitioner's appearance at the coroner's inquest rendered him a "de facto public official." Our cases recognize no such concept.

Respondent's suggestion would sweep all lawyers under the *New York Times* rule as officers of the court and distort the plain meaning of the "public official" category beyond all recognition. We decline to follow it.

Respondent's characterization of petitioner as a public figure raises a different question. That designation may rest on either of two alternative bases. In some instances an individual may achieve such pervasive fame or notoriety that he becomes a public figure for all purposes in all contexts. More commonly, an individual voluntarily injects himself or is drawn into a particular public controversy and thereby becomes a public figure for a limited range of issues. In either case such persons assume special prominence in the resolution of public questions.

Petitioner has long been active in community and professional affairs. He has served as an officer of local civic groups and of various professional organizations, and he has published several books and articles on legal subjects. Although petitioner was consequently well known in some circles, he had achieved no general fame or notoriety in the community. None of the prospective jurors called at the trial had ever heard of petitioner prior to this litigation, and respondent offered no proof that this response was atypical of the local population. We would not lightly assume that a citizen's participation in community and professional affairs rendered him a public figure for all purposes. Absent clear evidence of general fame or notoriety in the community, and pervasive involvement in the affairs of society, an individual should not be deemed a public personality for all aspects of his life. It is preferable to reduce the public-figure question to a more meaningful context by looking to the nature and extent of an individual's participation in the particular controversy giving rise to the defamation.

In this context it is plain that petitioner was not a public figure. He played a minimal role at the coroner's inquest, and his participation related solely to his representation of a private client. He took no part in the criminal prosecution of Officer Nuccio. Moreover, he never discussed either the criminal or civil litigation with the press and was never quoted as having done so. He plainly did not thrust himself into the vortex of this public issue, nor did he engage the public's attention in an attempt to influence its outcome. We are persuaded that the trial court did not err in refusing to characterize petitioner as a public figure for the purpose of this litigation.

We therefore conclude that the *New York Times* standard is inapplicable to this case and that the trial court erred in entering judgment for respondent. Because the jury was allowed to impose liability without fault and was permitted to presume damages without proof of injury, a new trial is necessary. We reverse and remand for further proceedings in accord with this opinion.

It is so ordered.

MR. JUSTICE BLACKMUN, concurring.

[Although I joined the *Rosenbloom* plurality opinion,] I am willing to join, and do join, the Court's opinion and its judgment for two reasons:

1. By removing the specters of presumed and punitive damages in the absence of *New York Times* malice, the Court eliminates significant and powerful motives for self-censorship that otherwise are present in the traditional libel action. By so doing, the Court leaves what should prove to be sufficient and adequate breathing space for a vigorous press. What the Court has done, I believe, will have little, if any, practical effect on the functioning of responsible journalism

2. The Court was sadly fractionated in *Rosenbloom*. A result of that kind inevitably leads to uncertainty. I feel that it is of profound importance for the court to come to rest in the defamation area and to have a clearly defined majority position that eliminates the unsureness engendered by *Rosenbloom*'s diversity. If my vote were not needed to create a majority, I would adhere to my prior view. A definitive ruling, however, is paramount. [ ]

For these reasons, I join the opinion and the judgment of the Court.

Mr. Chief Justice Burger, dissenting.

. . .

Agreement or disagreement with the law as it has evolved to this time does not alter the fact that it has been orderly development with a consistent basic rationale. In today's opinion the Court abandons the traditional thread so far as the ordinary private citizen is concerned and introduces the concept that the media will be liable for negligence in publishing defamatory statements with respect to such persons. Although I agree with much of what Mr. Justice White states, I do not read the Court's new doctrinal approach in quite the way he does. I am frank to say I do not know the parameters of a "negligence" doctrine as applied to the news media. Conceivably this new doctrine could inhibit some editors, as the dissents of Mr. Justice Douglas and Mr. Justice Brennan suggest. But I would prefer to allow this area of law to continue to evolve as it has up to now with respect to private citizens rather than embark on a new doctrinal theory which has no jurisprudential ancestry.

The petitioner here was performing a professional representative role as an advocate in the highest tradition of the law, and under that tradition the advocate is not to be invidiously identified with his client. The important public policy which underlies this tradition—the right to counsel—would be gravely jeopardized if every lawyer who takes an "unpopular" case, civil or criminal, would automatically become fair game for irresponsible reporters and editors who might, for example, describe the lawyer as a "mob mouthpiece" for representing a client with a serious prior criminal record, or as an "ambulance chaser" for representing a claimant in a personal injury action.

I would reverse the judgment of the Court of Appeals and remand for reinstatement of the verdict of the jury and the entry of an appropriate judgment on that verdict.

Mʀ. Jᴜsᴛɪᴄᴇ Dᴏᴜɢʟᴀs, dissenting.

. . .

. . . The standard announced today leaves the States free to "define for themselves the appropriate standard of liability for a publisher or broadcaster" in the circumstances of this case. This of course leaves the simple negligence standard as an option with the jury free to impose damages upon a finding that the publisher failed to act as "a reasonable man." With such continued erosion of First Amendment protection, I fear that it may well be the reasonable man who refrains from speaking.

Since in my view the First and Fourteenth Amendments prohibit the imposition of damages upon respondent for this discussion of public affairs, I would affirm the judgment below.

Mʀ. Jᴜsᴛɪᴄᴇ Bʀᴇɴɴᴀɴ, dissenting.

I agree with the conclusion, expressed in Part V of the Court's opinion, that, at the time of publication of respondent's article, petitioner could not properly have been viewed as either a "public official" or "public figure"; instead, respondent's article, dealing with an alleged conspiracy to discredit local police forces, concerned petitioner's purported involvement in "an event of public or general interest." . . .

. . .

[Justice Brennan restated the views he expressed in *Rosenbloom.*]

. . . Under a reasonable-care regime, publishers and broadcasters will have to make pre-publication judgments about juror assessment of such diverse considerations as the size, operating procedures, and financial condition of the newsgathering system, as well as the relative costs and benefits of instituting less frequent and more costly reporting at a higher level of accuracy. [ ] Moreover, in contrast to proof by clear and convincing evidence required under the *Times* test, the burden of proof for reasonable care will doubtless be the preponderance of the evidence. . . .

The Court does not discount altogether the danger that jurors will punish for the expression of unpopular opinions. This probability accounts for the Court's limitation that "the States may not permit recovery of presumed or punitive damages, at least when liability is not based on a showing of knowledge of falsity or reckless disregard for the truth." [ ] But plainly a jury's latitude to impose liability for want of due care poses a far greater threat of suppressing unpopular views than does a possible recovery of presumed or punitive damages. Moreover, the Court's broad-ranging examples of "actual injury," including impairment of reputation and standing in the community, as well as personal humiliation, and mental anguish and suffering, inevitably allow a jury bent on punishing expression of unpopular views a formidable weapon for doing so. Finally, even a limitation of recovery to "actual injury"—however much it reduces the size or frequency of recoveries—will not provide the necessary elbowroom for First Amendment expression. . . .

. . .

Mr. Justice White, dissenting.

. . .

The impact of today's decision on the traditional view of libel is immediately obvious and indisputable. No longer will the plaintiff be able to rest his case with proof of a libel defamatory on its face or proof of a slander historically actionable *per se*. In addition, he must prove some further degree of culpable conduct on the part of the publisher, such as intentional or reckless falsehood or negligence. And if he succeeds in this respect, he faces still another obstacle: recovery for loss of reputation will be conditioned upon "competent" proof of actual injury to his standing in the community. This will be true regardless of the nature of the defamation and even though it is one of those particularly reprehensible statements that have traditionally made slanderous words actionable without proof of fault by the publisher or of the damaging impact of his publication. The Court rejects the judgment of experience that some publications are inherently capable of injury, and actual injury so difficult to prove, that the risk of falsehood should be borne by the publisher, not the victim. . . .

. . .

These are radical changes in the law and severe invasions of the prerogatives of the States. . . .

. . .

The central meaning of *New York Times,* and for me the First Amendment as it relates to libel laws, is that seditious libel—criticism of government and public officials—falls beyond the police power of the State. . . .

. . .

The Court evinces a deep-seated antipathy to "liability without fault." But this catch-phrase has no talismanic significance and is almost meaningless in this context where the Court appears to be addressing those libels and slanders that are defamatory on their face and where the publisher is no doubt aware from the nature of the material that it would be inherently damaging to reputation. He publishes notwithstanding, knowing that he will inflict injury. With this knowledge, he must intend to inflict that injury, his excuse being that he is privileged to do so—that he has published the truth. But as it turns out, what he has circulated to the public is a very damaging falsehood. Is he nevertheless "faultless?" Perhaps it can be said that the mistake about his defense was made in good faith, but the fact remains that it is he who launched the publication knowing that it could ruin a reputation.

In these circumstances, the law has heretofore put the risk of falsehood on the publisher where the victim is a private citizen and no grounds of special privilege are invoked. The Court would now shift this risk to the victim, even though he has done nothing to invite the calumny, is wholly innocent of fault, and is helpless to avoid his injury. I doubt that jurisprudential resistance to liability without fault is sufficient ground for employing the First Amendment to revolutionize the law of libel, and in my view, that body of legal rules poses no realistic threat to the press and its service to the public. The press today is vigorous and robust. To me, it is quite incredible to suggest that threats of libel suits from private citizens are causing the press to refrain from publishing the truth. I know of no hard facts to support that proposition, and the Court furnishes none.

The communications industry has increasingly become concentrated in a few powerful hands operating very lucrative businesses reaching across the Nation and into almost every home. Neither the industry as a whole nor its individual components are easily intimidated, and we are fortunate that they are not. Requiring them to pay for the occasional damage they do to private reputation will play no substantial part in their future performance or their existence.

In any event, if the Court's principal concern is to protect the communications industry from large libel judgments, it would appear that its new requirements with respect to general and punitive damages would be ample protection.

. . .

For the foregoing reasons, I would reverse the judgment of the Court of Appeals and reinstate the jury's verdict.

Notes and Questions

1. Why did the majority adhere to the *Times* rule for public officials? Public figures? Some have argued that *Gertz* was a public figure and that the case should have been analyzed along the lines of *Butts* and *Walker*.

2. Why does the majority in *Gertz* prefer its approach to the plurality's approach in *Rosenbloom*?

3. What criteria might be relevant in deciding whether a broadcaster has been at fault in broadcasting a false statement?

4. If a private citizen proves fault, why can he not recover traditional damages for defamation?

5. The Supreme Court has not decided finally whether libel plaintiffs may recover punitive damages, but *Dun & Bradstreet* (see note 15 below) indicates that some can.

6. *Three Attempts to Apply Gertz.* The first significant application of *Gertz* occurred in Time, Inc. v. Firestone, 424 U.S 448, 1 Med.L.Rptr. 1665 (1976), in which *Time* magazine reported, perhaps incorrectly, that a member of "one of America's wealthier families" had received a divorce because of his wife's adultery. The divorce decree was probably based on either "extreme cruelty" or "lack of domestication" but the judge was not explicit. The state court upheld the wife's defamation award of $100,000. *Time* argued that the "actual malice" standard should apply for two reasons. First, it asserted that the plaintiff was a public figure, but the majority disagreed: "Respondent did not assume any role of especial prominence in the affairs of society, other than perhaps Palm Beach society, and she did not thrust herself to the forefront of any particular public controversy in order to influence the resolution of the issues involved in it." The Court rejected the argument that because the case was of great public interest, the respondent must have been a public figure: "Dissolution of a marriage through judicial proceedings is not the sort of 'public controversy' referred to in *Gertz*, even though the marital difficulties of extremely wealthy individuals may be of interest to some portion of the reading public." Moreover, plaintiff was compelled to go to court to seek relief in a marital dispute and her involvement was not voluntary. The fact that she held "a few" press conferences during the case did not change her otherwise private status. She did not attempt to use them to influence the outcome of the trial or to thrust herself into an unrelated dispute.

The second claim was that negligent errors in the reporting of judicial proceedings should never lead to liability. Justice Rehnquist's opinion for the Court rejected the contention:

> It may be that all reports of judicial proceedings contain some informational value implicating the First Amendment, but recognizing this is little different from labeling all judicial proceedings matters of "public or general interest," as that phrase was used by the plurality in *Rosenbloom*. Whatever their general validity, use of such subject matter classifications to determine the extent of constitutional protection afforded defamatory falsehoods may too often result in an improper balance between the competing interests in this area.

Plaintiff had withdrawn her claim of damages to reputation before trial, but the Court held that the award could be sustained on proof of anxiety and concern over the impact of the adultery charge on her young son. The Court vacated the judgment for lack of consideration of fault by either the jury or any of the state courts. Justices Powell and Stewart, though joining the majority, asserted that the grounds of divorce were so unclear in this "bizarre case" that there was "substantial evidence" that *Time* was not negligent. Justice White, believing that the state courts had found negligence, would have affirmed the award. Justice Brennan dissented on the ground that reports of judicial proceedings should not lead to liability unless the errors are deliberate or reckless. He also thought the damage limits of *Gertz* had been "subverted" by the recovery allowed here with no showing of reputational harm. Justice Marshall, dissenting, thought that plaintiff was a public figure; he also doubted the existence of negligence. Justice Stevens took no part.

The Florida Supreme Court ordered a new trial, but plaintiff dropped the case, saying that she had been vindicated.

Recall that under the common law "record libel" privilege, reports of governmental proceedings were privileged if they were fair and accurate reports of what had happened—even if the speaker being quoted had committed a defamation. Under the common law privilege, *Time'*s report, if incorrectly reporting the basis of the divorce decree, would not have been protected. For this reason *Time* had to assert a constitutional privilege.

7. Neutral reportage. One federal case suggests the possibility of a First Amendment privilege that differs from the *Times–Gertz* variety. In the case, Edwards v. National Audubon Society, Inc., 556 F.2d 113, 2 Med.L.Rptr. 1849 (2d Cir.), certiorari denied sub nom. Edwards v. New York Times Co., 434 U.S. 1002 (1977), Devlin, a *Times* nature reporter, was following the continuing dispute between the Audubon Society and the chemical industry over the impact of various pesticides on birds. Based in part on the fact that annual bird counts conducted by the Audubon Society showed increasing numbers, some scientists retained by the industry argued that pesticides were not harmful. The Society believed that the higher numbers were due to more watchers with more skill using better observation areas.

An editorial in a Society publication asserted that whenever members heard a scientist use the bird count in an argument "you are in the presence of someone who is being paid to lie, or is parroting something he knows little about." The reporter called the Society and, the jury found, was told the names of five scientists that Society officials had in mind. The reporter then wrote a story accurately reporting the dispute and stating that a Society official had said that the scientists referred to in the editorial included five the reporter then named. In a suit by the scientists, the court held that an accurate report of this nature could not constitutionally lead to a libel judgment against the newspaper.

> At stake in this case is a fundamental principle. Succinctly stated, when a responsible, prominent organization like the National Audubon Society makes serious charges against a public figure, the First Amendment protects the accurate and disinterested reporting of those charges, regardless of the reporter's private views regarding their validity. [ ] What is newsworthy about such accusations is that they were made. We do not believe that the press may be required under the First Amendment to suppress newsworthy statements merely because it has serious doubts regarding their truth. Nor must the press take up cudgels against dubious charges in order to publish them without fear of liability

for defamation. [ ] The public interest in being fully informed about controversies that often rage around sensitive issues demands that the press be afforded the freedom to report such charges without assuming responsibility for them.

   . . .

It is clear here, that Devlin reported Audubon's charges fairly and accurately. He did not in any way espouse the Society's accusations: indeed, Devlin published the maligned scientists' outraged reactions in the same article that contained the Society's attack. The *Times* article, in short, was the exemplar of fair and dispassionate reporting of an unfortunate but newsworthy contretemps. Accordingly, we hold that it was privileged under the First Amendment.

What are the limits of the *Edwards* principle? Are there times when the public should be informed of charges that are not made by a "responsible, prominent organization"? What is the test for whether a report of a particular charge is "newsworthy"? What level of error in the report, if any, should deprive the reporter of the privilege? Should it be restricted to public figures?

Some courts have rejected the neutral reportage defense as inconsistent with *St. Amant*, since *Edwards* would allow one who reports a story that he knows to be false or has serious doubts about, to be protected from liability.

One can only conjecture about whether the neutral reportage privilege retains much vitality. In the 1970s and 1980s, some courts adopted the standard and some flatly rejected it. An example of the former is Barry v. Time, Inc., 584 F.Supp. 1110 (N.D.Cal.1984). An example of the latter is Postill v. Booth Newspapers, Inc., 118 Mich. App. 608, 325 N.W.2d 511 (1982).

Note that the record libel privilege discussed earlier is a state privilege that can be limited by state statutes and decisions. In New York, for example, the relevant statute requires "official proceedings" before a privilege comes into play—and the New York courts have not expanded that privilege. Thus, in *Edwards,* the state statute did not apply.

8. In Wolston v. Reader's Digest Association, Inc., 443 U.S. 157, 5 Med.L.Rptr. 1273 (1979), defendant published a book in 1974 that included plaintiff's name on a list of "Soviet agents identified in the United States." A footnote said that the list consisted of agents "who were convicted of espionage or falsifying information or perjury and/or contempt charges following espionage indictments or who fled to the Soviet bloc to avoid prosecution."

Plaintiff had been convicted of contempt of court in 1958 for failing to appear before a grand jury investigating Soviet espionage. He was never indicted for any of the listed offenses. At the time, plaintiff did not attempt to debate the propriety of his behavior. During the six weeks between his failure to appear and his sentencing, plaintiff's case was the subject of 15 stories in Washington and New York newspapers. "This flurry of publicity subsided" following the sentencing and plaintiff "succeeded for the most part in returning to the private life he had led" prior to the subpoena.

When plaintiff sued for libel, the lower courts held that in both 1958 and 1974 he was a public figure and that summary judgment was properly granted against him because he had presented no evidence of actual malice. (In the Supreme Court, plaintiff abandoned the argument that even if he was a public figure in 1958, he was no longer in 1974.)

The Supreme Court reversed. For the majority, Justice Rehnquist reviewed the "self-help" and the "assumption of risk" explanations developed in *Gertz* to support the public-private distinction, and concluded that the second was the more important.

Justice Rehnquist concluded that plaintiff had neither "voluntarily thrust" nor "injected" himself into the forefront of the controversy surrounding the investigation of Soviet espionage in the United States:

> It would be more accurate to say that petitioner was dragged unwillingly into the controversy. The government pursued him in its investigation. . . .
>
> Petitioner's failure to appear before the grand jury and citation for contempt no doubt were "newsworthy," but the simple fact that these events attracted media attention also is not conclusive of the public figure issue. A private individual is not automatically transformed into a public figure just by becoming involved in or associated with a matter that attracts public attention. . . .
>
> Nor do we think that petitioner engaged the attention of the public in an attempt to influence the resolution of the issues involved. . . . He did not in any way seek to arouse public sentiment in his favor and against the investigation. Thus, this case is not a case where a defendant invites a citation for contempt in order to use the contempt citation as a fulcrum to create public discussion about the methods being used in connection with an investigation or prosecution. . . . In short, we find no basis whatsoever for concluding that petitioner relinquished, to any degree, his interest in the protection of his own name.
>
> This reasoning leads us to reject the further contention of respondents that any person who engages in criminal conduct automatically becomes a public figure for purposes of comment on a limited range of issues relating to his conviction. [ ] We declined to accept a similar argument in Time, Inc. v. Firestone.

Justice Rehnquist concluded that, "[t]o hold otherwise would create an 'open season' for all who sought to defame persons convicted of a crime."

Justice Blackmun, joined by Justice Marshall, concurred in the result. He would hold that even if plaintiff had acquired public figure status in 1958, "he clearly had lost that distinction" by 1974. Although plaintiff had not pressed that argument in the Supreme Court, Justice Blackmun, noting that the lower courts had decided the point, thought it still open as a basis for decision.

Justice Blackmun recognized that his view put a more difficult burden on historians than on contemporary commentators:

> This analysis implies, of course, that one may be a public figure for purposes of contemporaneous reporting of a controversial event, yet not be a public figure for purposes of historical commentary on the same occurrence. Historians, consequently, may well run a greater risk of liability for defamation. Yet this result, in my view, does no violence to First Amendment values. While historical analysis is no less vital to the marketplace of ideas than reporting current events, historians work under different conditions than do their media counterparts.

Justice Brennan dissented. He thought plaintiff a public figure for the limited purpose of comment on his connection with espionage in the 1940s and 1950s. He remained a public figure in 1974 because the issue of Soviet espionage "continues to be a legitimate topic of debate today . . .." But he found enough evidence of "actual malice" to warrant a trial under the *Times* standard.

The next case was decided on the same day as *Wolston.*

9. Hutchinson v. Proxmire, 443 U.S. 111, 5 Med.L.Rptr. 1279 (1979), arose from Senator Proxmire's awarding of one of his Golden Fleece awards—made to government agencies that he believed engaged in wasteful spending. In this case he awarded it to agencies that had funded the plaintiff-scientist's research work on aggression in animals. The Senator had uttered the alleged defamation in several forums, including a speech prepared for delivery on the Senate floor; advance press releases; a newsletter sent to 100,000 people; and a television interview program. The Court first decided that in this case Article I, Section 6 of the Constitution—the so-called Speech or Debate Clause—protected only a speech delivered on the floor.

The Court then turned to the First Amendment issue. Chief Justice Burger concluded that neither the fact that plaintiff had successfully applied for federal funds nor that he had access to media after Senator Proxmire's charges, "demonstrates that Hutchinson was a public figure prior to the controversy . . .."

> On this record Hutchinson's activities and public profile are much like those of countless members of his profession. His published writings reach a relatively small category of professionals concerned with research in human behavior. To the extent the subject of his published writings became a matter of controversy, it was a consequence of the Golden Fleece Award. Clearly those

charged with defamation cannot, by their own conduct, create their own defense by making the claimant a public figure. See Wolston v. Reader's Digest, Inc., [   ].

Hutchinson did not thrust himself or his views into public controversy to influence others. Respondents have not identified such a particular controversy; at most, they point to concern about general public expenditures. But that concern is shared by most and relates to most public expenditures; it is not sufficient to make Hutchinson a public figure. . . .

. . .

In a footnote, the Chief Justice observed that "[t]he Court has not provided precise boundaries for the category of 'public official'; it cannot be thought to include all public employees, however."

Justice Brennan was the sole dissenter. He believed that "public criticism by legislators of unnecessary governmental expenditures, whatever its form, is a legislative act shielded by the Speech and Debate Clause." He did not reach the public figure question.

Senator Proxmire subsequently made a public retraction, before television cameras, of his comments about Hutchinson.

10. *Public and Private Figures.* Businessmen accused of connections with organized crime tend to be held to be public figures. One case involved an attorney who represented persons alleged to have criminal connections and who was said to have "contributed down payments of up to $25,000 on grass transactions. Charges against him were dismissed because he cooperated with further investigations." Although recognizing that "mere newsworthiness" is not sufficient, the court first concluded that the issue of "drug trafficking" was "a real dispute, the outcome of which affects the general public or some segment of it." As to plaintiff's part in it, the court noted that sometimes one can be a public figure without voluntary actions. "For example, sports figures are generally considered public figures because of their positions as athletes or coaches. [   ] If a position itself is so prominent that its occupant unavoidably enters the limelight, then a person who voluntarily assumes such a position may be presumed to have accepted public figure status." Marcone v. Penthouse International, Ltd., 754 F.2d 1072, 11 Med.L.Rptr. 1577 (3d Cir.1985).

11. In Dameron v. Washington Magazine, Inc., 779 F.2d 736, 12 Med.L.Rptr. 1508 (D.C.Cir.1985), cert. denied 476 U.S. 1141 (1986), plaintiff had been the only air traffic controller on duty in 1974 when a plane approaching Dulles crashed into Mt. Weather. The episode received much attention: plaintiff testified in hearings and a claim under the Federal Torts Claims Act was litigated. In that case the court dismissed claims based on controller negligence. In 1982 a plane crashed into the Potomac River. Part of the story on the 1982 crash in defendant's city magazine was a sidebar on earlier plane crashes and

their causes. In that list the 1974 crash was attributed to "controller" failure. Plaintiff sued for libel.

The court held that although plaintiff had not injected himself into any controversy, persons "can become involved in public controversies and affairs without their consent or will. Air-controller Dameron, who had the misfortune to have a tragedy occur on his watch, is such a person. We conclude that Dameron did become an involuntary public figure for the limited purpose of discussions of the Mt. Weather crash."

Although the Supreme Court had said that "the instances of truly involuntary public figures must be exceedingly rare," the court thought that "within the very narrow framework represented by the facts of this case, such has been Dameron's fate."

12. *Proving Actual Malice.* One case on proving "actual malice" raised the issue of what types of questions the plaintiff could ask the media defendants during the pretrial effort to obtain evidence for the trial. The normal rule in civil cases is that any evidence that would be admissible at the trial may be obtained by "discovery" beforehand— usually either by deposition (oral testimony given by a prospective witness with only the lawyers for the parties present) or by interrogatories (written answers to written questions). This exchange of information allows the parties to know the strengths and weaknesses of their cases and avoids surprises at trial.

In Herbert v. Lando, 441 U.S. 153, 4 Med.L.Rptr. 2575 (1979), Anthony Herbert, an admitted public figure, sued the producer and reporter of the television program "60 Minutes" and the CBS network for remarks on the program about his behavior while in military service in Vietnam. During his deposition, Barry Lando, the producer, generally responded, but he refused to answer some questions about why he made certain investigations and not others, what he concluded about the honesty of certain people he interviewed for the program, and about conversations he had with Mike Wallace, the reporter, in preparation for the segment. Lando contended that these thought processes and internal editorial discussions were protected from disclosure by the First Amendment. The Supreme Court disagreed.

Justice White, for the Court, understood the defendants to be arguing that "the defendant's reckless disregard of truth, a critical element, could not be shown by direct evidence through inquiry into the thoughts, opinions, and conclusions of the publisher but could be proved only by objective evidence from which the ultimate fact could be inferred." This was a barrier of some substance "particularly when defendants themselves are prone to assert their good-faith belief in the truth of their publications, and libel plaintiffs are required to prove knowing or reckless falsehood with 'convincing clarity.'"

Justice White concluded that permitting plaintiffs "to prove their cases by direct as well as indirect evidence is consistent with the balance struck by our prior decisions." He "found it difficult to believe that error-avoiding procedures will be terminated or stifled simply because there is liability for culpable error and because the editorial process will itself be examined in the tiny percentage of instances in which error is claimed and litigation ensues."

Justice Powell concurred in the opinion of the Court but wrote separately to emphasize that trial judges must consider First Amendment interests as well as the private interests of plaintiffs in deciding how much pretrial discovery to allow.

Three justices dissented in separate opinions.

On remand, Herbert's $44 million libel suit was dismissed by the court of appeals, which said that CBS had presented sufficient evidence to defend its overall view of him and that a libel action cannot be based on minor subsidiary statements that merely support the story's overall conclusion. 781 F.2d 298, 12 Med.L.Rptr. 1593 (2d Cir.1986).

This case indirectly suggests problems when a reporter is asked to identify the source of a story. That subject is discussed at length in Chapter XIV.

13. *Appellate Review.* In Bose Corp. v. Consumers Union, 466 U.S. 485, 10 Med.L.Rptr. 1625 (1984), the Supreme Court held in favor of the publisher of *Consumer Reports* magazine in a product disparagement suit filed by the manufacturer of loudspeakers criticized in the magazine. The magazine said that Bose 901 speakers produced sounds that "tended to wander about the room" and that a violin "appeared to be 10 feet wide and a piano stretched from wall to wall."

The Supreme Court held that appeals courts, when reviewing findings of actual malice in libel cases and other cases governed by New York Times v. Sullivan, must exercise their own judgment in determining whether actual malice was shown with convincing clarity. Thus, the court of appeals decision in favor of Consumers Union was affirmed.

14. In Levine v. CMP Publications, Inc., 738 F.2d 660 (5th Cir.1984), the majority concluded that *Bose* did not apply to private plaintiff cases. *Bose* is criticized in Monaghan, Constitutional Fact Review, 85 Colum.L.Rev. 229 (1985).

15. A case involving the libel of a judicial candidate in Ohio provided an opportunity for the Supreme Court to clarify the decision in *Bose* regarding independent appellate review—and simultaneously provided parallels to *Butts*. Daniel Connaughton was an unsuccessful candidate for municipal judge in Hamilton, Ohio, in 1983. A local newspaper, the *Journal News*, supported his opponent, who was the incumbent. A week prior to the election, the newspaper ran a front-page story quoting a grand jury witness as saying that Connaughton had used "dirty tricks" and offered her and her sister jobs and a trip to Florida "in appreciation" for their help in the investigation of the director of court services who had worked for the incumbent. At a libel trial in federal district court, the jury found by a preponderance of the evidence that the story in question was defamatory and false, and by clear and convincing proof that the story was published with actual malice, and

awarded Connaughton $5,000 in compensatory damages and $195,000 in punitive damages.

The Court of Appeals affirmed. It separately considered the evidence supporting each of the jury's special verdicts, concluding that the findings were not clearly erroneous. It did not attempt to make an independent evaluation of the credibility of conflicting oral testimony concerning facts underlying the finding of actual malice but identified 11 subsidiary facts that the jury "could have" found and held that such findings would not have been clearly erroneous, and, based on its independent review, held that when considered cumulatively they provided clear and convincing evidence of actual malice. Harte–Hanks Communications appealed to the Supreme Court. Although the latter held that a showing of "highly unreasonable conduct constituting an extreme departure from the standards of investigation and reporting ordinarily adhered to by responsible publishers" cannot alone support a verdict in favor of a public figure plaintiff in a libel action, that the rule applied by the Court of Appeals nonetheless was supportive of the court's ultimate conclusion that the *Journal News* acted with actual malice. The Court said that a reviewing court in a public figure libel case must "exercise independent judgment and determine whether the record establishes actual malice with convincing clarity" to ensure that the verdict is consistent with *New York Times* and subsequent cases. Harte–Hanks Communications, Inc. v. Connaughton, 491 U.S. 657, 16 Med.L.Rptr. 1881 (1989).

16. *Truth and Falsity.* Although the Court's focus was on the fault requirement, questions still lingered about who had the burden of proof on the question of truth or falsity. In Philadelphia Newspapers, Inc. v. Hepps, 475 U.S. 767, 12 Med.L.Rptr. 1977 (1986), the Court, 5–4, held that the plaintiff had the burden of proving falsity at least in cases brought by private plaintiffs where the speech was of public concern. For the majority, Justice O'Connor concluded that to "ensure that true speech on matters of public concern is not deterred, we hold that the common-law presumption that defamatory speech is false cannot stand when a plaintiff seeks damages against a media defendant for speech of public concern." (Two of the five joining the majority opinion rejected the limitation to "media" defendants.) Even though this burden would "insulate from liability some speech that is false, but unprovably so," that result is essential to avoid the "chilling" effect that would otherwise accompany true speech on matters of public concern.

The majority asserted that its conclusion added "only marginally to the burdens" on libel plaintiffs because a jury is more likely to accept a "contention that the defendant was at fault in publishing the statements at issue if convinced that the relevant statements were false. As a practical matter, then, evidence offered by plaintiffs on the publisher's fault . . . will generally encompass evidence of the falsity of the matters asserted." The majority reserved the question of the quantity of proof of falsity that a plaintiff must present.

Justice Stevens, for the dissenters, thought the majority result "pernicious." He posited a situation in which a defendant, knowing that the plaintiff could not prove the statement false, deliberately lied about the plaintiff. This situation might occur due to the passage of time, the loss of critical records, or the absence of an eyewitness. The majority's analysis was an "obvious blueprint for character assassination." In his view, as long as publishers are protected by the fault requirement, "there can be little, if any, basis for a concern that a significant amount of true speech will be deterred unless the private person victimized by a malicious libel can also carry the burden of proving falsity."

In a footnote, Justice Stevens asserted that if the issue were brought before the Court, he "would be inclined to the view that public figures should not bear the burden of disproving the veracity of accusations made against them with 'actual malice' as the *New York Times* Court used that term." In his opinion, the contrary remarks in several cases were not necessary to the decisions in those cases, and the actual malice rule is enough protection.

17. In Anderson v. Liberty Lobby, Inc., 477 U.S. 242, 12 Med.L.Rptr. 2297 (1986), the Supreme Court held, 6–3, that the standard for considering summary judgment motions must take into account the burden the plaintiff will have to meet at trial. Because the plaintiff in the case was held to be a public figure, the Court held that on the summary judgment motion, the judge must decide "whether the evidence in the record could support a reasonable jury finding either that the plaintiff has shown actual malice by clear and convincing evidence or that the plaintiff has not."

In response to the argument that at the summary judgment stage the plaintiff need show only enough to prevail on a "preponderance of the evidence" standard, the Court responded that it "makes no sense to say that a jury could reasonably find for either party without some benchmark as to what standards govern its deliberations and within what boundaries its ultimate decision must fall, and these standards and boundaries are in fact provided by the applicable evidentiary standards."

The Court denied that its holding denigrated the role of the jury. "Credibility determinations, the weighing of the evidence, and the drawing of legitimate inferences from the facts are jury functions, not those of a judge, whether he is ruling on a motion for summary judgment or for a directed verdict."

In a footnote, the Court addressed footnote 9 in *Hutchinson*, p. 649, *supra*, in which the Court had suggested that proof of actual malice "does not readily lend itself to summary disposition." That sentence "was simply an acknowledgment of our general reluctance" to grant special procedural protections to the media in addition to the substantive standards announced in cases like *Times* and *Gertz*. This was not relevant here because the Court in *Liberty Lobby* was announcing a general approach to all civil cases—that the summary judgment standard was to be the same as the one that the plaintiff must meet at the trial itself.

Justice Brennan dissented out of concern that the majority's decision "may erode the constitutionally enshrined role of the jury, and also undermine the usefulness of summary judgment procedure." On the latter point, he was concerned that the decision would confuse the lower courts.

Justice Rehnquist, joined by Chief Justice Burger, also dissented. He offered some examples that he thought showed that the majority's decision would have no effect on a large class of cases. His examples follow:

(1) On a summary judgment motion, "the plaintiff concedes that his only proof of malice is the testimony of witness A. Witness A testifies at his deposition that the reporter who wrote the story in question told him that she, the reporter, had done absolutely no checking on the story and had real doubts about whether or not it was correct as to the plaintiff. The defendant's examination of witness A brings out that he has a prior conviction for perjury." Justice Rehnquist said that summary judgment must be denied if the majority meant what it said about the jury judging credibility.

(2) At trial, after plaintiff's case the defendant moves for a directed verdict. The trial testimony repeats the deposition testimony except that now the trial judge has seen A's demeanor—"and noticed that he fidgets when answering critical questions, his eyes shift from the floor to the ceiling, and he manifests all other indicia traditionally attributed to perjurers." Justice Rehnquist asserted that no directed verdict may be entered.

(3) The defense puts on its case which includes three disinterested witnesses who were present at the alleged conversation. Each "categorically denies that the reporter made the claimed statement" to A. Justice Rehnquist asserted that a directed verdict must be denied to the defendant.

The lesson he drew was that the standard does not matter in a credibility case. Even in cases based on documentary evidence he asserted that inferences from the documents are "as much the prerogative of the finder of fact as inferences as to the credibility of witnesses." He thought the line between "evidence which should satisfy reasonable men, and the evidence which should satisfy reasonable men beyond a reasonable doubt, . . . in the long run . . . is too thin for day to day use" (quoting Judge Learned Hand). If that was true, it was even more true where the standard was convincing clarity.

18. One of the most highly publicized libel cases in recent years, Tavoulareas v. Washington Post Co., 817 F.2d 762, 13 Med.L.Rptr. 2377 (D.C.Cir.1987), resulted from a *Washington Post* story alleging that Mobil Oil Corporation President and Chief Executive Officer William

Tavoulareas had "set up" his son Peter in the shipping business and diverted some of Mobil's shipping business to him.

There was evidence that a copy editor at the *Post* had questioned the story, but the newspaper ran it anyway, believing, according to testimony, that it was true. A reporter's statement that "it is not every day you knock off" someone like Tavoulareas also was part of the evidence. The trial court jury held in favor of Tavoulareas, the trial judge voided the jury's $2.05 million award to Tavoulareas, a panel decision of the appeals court reinstated the jury's original verdict, and then the full bench of the court affirmed the trial judge's decision to void the award.

The court concluded that the article was substantially true and that Tavoulareas had failed to prove actual malice. It held that Tavoulareas was a limited purpose public figure.

The Supreme Court denied *certiorari*. 484 U.S. 870 (1987).

19. Singer Wayne Newton's libel suit against NBC also received widespread media attention, particularly when he won a $19.2 million trial verdict in a federal court in Las Vegas in 1986, but a Federal appeals court overturned the verdict four years later. Newton had charged that three NBC news broadcasts in 1980–81 falsely linked him to organized crime figures. A three-judge panel of the United States Court of Appeals for the Ninth Circuit, in overturning the award, found there was insufficient evidence to show that NBC had either prior knowledge of falsity or reckless disregard of the truth. Newton v. National Broadcasting Co., 913 F.2d 652, 18 Med.L.Rptr. 1001 (9th Cir.1990). The same court later denied a petition for rehearing, 930 F.2d 662 (1991).

20. A 1991 case presented the Supreme Court with the question of whether a journalist's use of quotation remarks around words that are not provably the plaintiff's should be treated as reckless disregard for the truth under the actual malice standard.

MASSON v. NEW YORKER MAGAZINE, INC.

Supreme Court of the United States, 1991.
501 U.S. ___, 111 S.Ct. 2419, 115 L.Ed. 2d 447, 18 Med.L.Rptr. 2241.

JUSTICE KENNEDY delivered the opinion of the Court.

In this libel case, a public figure claims he was defamed by an author who, with full knowledge of the inaccuracy, used quotation marks to attribute to him comments he had not made. The First Amendment protects authors and journalists who write about public figures by requiring a plaintiff to prove that the defamatory statements were made with what we have called "actual malice," a term of art denoting deliberate or reckless falsification. We consider in this opinion whether the attributed quotations had the degree of falsity required to prove this state of mind, so that the public figure can defeat a motion for summary judgment and proceed to a trial on the merits of the defamation claim.

I

Petitioner Jeffrey Masson trained at Harvard University as a Sanskrit scholar, and in 1970 became a professor of Sanskrit & Indian Studies at the University of Toronto. He spent eight years in psychoanalytic training, and qualified as an analyst in 1978. Through his professional activities, he came to know Dr. Kurt Eissler, head of the Sigmund Freud Archives, and Dr. Anna Freud, daughter of Sigmund Freud and a major psychoanalyst in her own right. The Sigmund Freud Archives, located at Maresfield Gardens outside of London, serves as a repository for materials about Freud, including his own writings, letters, and personal library.

In 1980, Eissler and Anna Freud hired petitioner as Projects Director of the Archives. After assuming his post, petitioner became disillusioned with Freudian psychology. In a 1981 lecture before the Western New England Psychoanalytical Society in New Haven, Connecticut, he advanced his theories of Freud. Soon after, the Board of the Archives terminated petitioner as Projects Director.

Respondent Janet Malcolm is an author and a contributor to respondent The New Yorker, a weekly magazine. She contacted petitioner in 1982 regarding the possibility of an article on his relationship with the Archives. He agreed, and the two met in person and spoke by telephone in a series of interviews. Based on the interviews and other sources, Malcolm wrote a lengthy article. One of Malcolm's narrative devices consists of enclosing lengthy passages in quotation marks, reporting statements of Masson, Eissler, and her other subjects.

During the editorial process, Nancy Franklin, a member of the fact-checking department at The New Yorker, called petitioner to confirm some of the facts underlying the article. According to petitioner, he expressed alarm at the number of errors in the few passages Franklin discussed with him. Petitioner contends that he asked permission to review those portions of the article which attributed quotations or information to him, but was brushed off with a never-fulfilled promise to "get back to [him]." [ ] Franklin disputes petitioner's version of their conversation. [ ]

The New Yorker published Malcolm's piece in December 1983, as a two-part series. In 1984, with knowledge of at least petitioner's general allegation that the article contained defamatory material, respondent Alfred A. Knopf, Inc., published the entire work as a book, entitled In the Freud Archives.

Malcolm's work received complimentary reviews. But this gave little joy to Masson, for the book portrays him in a most unflattering light. According to one reviewer,

"Masson the promising psychoanalytic scholar emerges gradually, as a grandiose egotist—mean-spirited, self-serving, full of braggadocio, impossibly arrogant, and in the end, a self destructive fool. But it is not Janet Malcolm who calls him such: his own words reveal this psychological profile—a self-portrait offered to us through the efforts of an observer and listener who is, surely, as wise as any in the psychoanalytic profession." Coles, Freudianism Confronts Its Malcontents, Boston Globe, May 27,1984, pp. 58, 60.

Petitioner wrote a letter to the New York Times Book Review calling the book "distorted." In response, Malcolm stated:

"Many of [the] things Mr. Masson told me (on tape) were discreditable to him, and I felt it best not to include them. Everything I do quote Mr. Masson as saying was said by him, almost word for word. (The 'almost' refers to changes made for the sake of correct syntax.) I would be glad to play the tapes of my conversation with Mr. Masson to the editors of The Book Review whenever they have 40 or 50 short hours to spare.) [ ]

Petitioner brought an action for libel under California law in the United States District Court for the Northern District of California. During extensive discovery and repeated amendments to the complaint, petitioner concentrated on various passages alleged to be defamatory, dropping some and adding others. The tape recordings of the interviews demonstrated that petitioner had, in fact, made statements substantially identical to a number of the passages, and those passages are no longer in the case. We discuss only the passages relied on by petitioner in his briefs to this Court.

Each passage before us purports to quote a statement made by petitioner during the interviews. Yet in each instance no identical statement appears in the more than 40 hours of taped interviews. Petitioner complains that Malcolm fabricated all but one passage; with respect to that passage, he claims Malcolm omitted a crucial portion, rendering the remainder misleading.

(a) *Intellectual Gigolo.* Malcolm quoted a description by petitioner of his relationship with Eissler and Anna Freud as follows: " 'Then I met a rather attractive older graduate student and I had an affair with her. One day, she took me to some art event, and she was sorry afterward. She said, "Well, it is very nice sleeping with you in your room, but you're the kind of person who should never leave the room—you're just a social embarrassment anywhere else, though you do fine in your own room." And you know, in their way, if not in so many words, Eissler and Anna Freud told me the same thing. They like me well enough "in my own room." They loved to hear from me what creeps and dolts analysts are. I was like an intellectual gigolo— you get your pleasure from him, but you don't take him out in public. . . .' " [ ]

The tape recordings contain the substance of petitioner's reference to his graduate student friend, [   ], but no suggestion that Eissler or Anna Freud considered him, or that he considered himself, an " 'intellectual gigolo.' " Instead, petitioner said:

> "They felt, in a sense, I was a private asset but a public liabili-
> ty . . .. They liked me when I was alone in their living room,
> and I could talk and chat and tell them the truth about things and
> they would tell me. But that I was, in a sense, much too junior
> within the hierarchy of analysis for these important training
> analysts to be caught dead with me." [   ]

(b) *"Sex, Women, Fun."* Malcolm quoted petitioner as describing his plans for Maresfield Gardens, which he had to occupy after Anna Freud's death:

> " 'It was a beautiful house, but it was dark and somber and dead.
> Nothing ever went on there. I was the only person who ever came.
> I would have renovated it, opened it up, brought it to life. Mares-
> field Gardens would have been a center of scholarship, but it would
> also have been a place of sex, women, fun. It would have been like
> the change in *The Wizard of Oz*, from black-and-white into color.' "
> [   ]

The tape recordings contain a similar statement, but in place of the reference to "sex, women, fun," and The Wizard of Oz, petitioner commented;

> "[I]t is an incredible storehouse. I mean, the library, Freud's
> library alone is priceless in terms of what it contains: all his books
> with his annotations in them; the Schreber case annotated, that
> kind of thing. It's fascinating." [   ]

Petitioner did talk, earlier in the interview, of his meeting with a London analyst:

> "I like him. So, and we got on very well. That was the first time
> we ever met and you know, it was buddy-buddy, and we were to
> stay with each other and [laughs] we were going to have a great
> time together when I lived in the Freud house. We'd have great
> parties there and we were [laughs]—. . .   going to really, we
> were going to live it up." [   ]

(c) *"It Sounded Better."* Petitioner spoke with Malcolm about the history of his family, including the reasons his grandfather changed the family from Moussaieff to Masson, and why petitioner adopted the abandoned family name as his middle name. The article contains the passage:

> " 'My father is a gem merchant who doesn't like to stay in any one
> place too long. His father was a gem merchant, too—a Bessarabi-
> an gem merchant, named Moussaieff, who went to Paris in the
> twenties and adopted the name Masson. My parents named me

Jeffrey Lloyd Masson, but in 1975 I decided to change my middle name to Moussaieff—it sounded better.' " [   ]

In the most similar tape recorded statement, Masson explained at considerable length that his grandfather had changed the family name from Moussaieff to Masson when living in France, "[j]ust to hide his Jewishness." Petitioner had changed his last name back to Moussaieff, but his then wife Terry objected that "nobody could pronounce it and nobody knew how to spell it, and it wasn't the name that she knew me by." Petitioner had changed his name to Moussaieff because he "just liked it." "[I]t was sort of part of analysis: a return to the roots, and your family tradition and so on." In the end, he had agreed with Terry that "it wasn't her name after all," and used Moussaieff as a middle instead of a last name. [   ]

[Several more examples are given.]

Malcolm submitted to the District Court that not all of her discussions with petitioner were recorded on tape, in particular conversations that occurred while the two of them walked together or traveled by car, while petitioner stayed at Malcolm's home in New York, or while her tape recorder was inoperable. She claimed to have taken notes of these unrecorded sessions, which she later typed, then discarding the handwritten originals. Petitioner denied that any discussion relating to the substance of the article occurred during his stay at Malcolm's home in New York, that Malcolm took notes during any of their conversations, or that Malcolm gave any indication that her tape recorder was broken.

Respondents moved for summary judgment. The parties agreed that petitioner was a public figure and so could escape summary judgment only if the evidence in the record would permit a reasonable finder of fact, by clear and convincing evidence, to conclude that respondents published a defamatory statement with actual malice as defined by our cases. [*Liberty Lobby*] The District Court analyzed each of the passages and held that the alleged inaccuracies did not raise a jury question. The court found that the allegedly fabricated quotations were either substantially true, or were " 'one of a number of possible rational interpretations' of a conversation or event that 'bristled with ambiguities,' " and thus were entitled to constitutional protection, 686 F.Supp. 1396, 1399 (1987) (quoting [*Bose*]). The court also ruled that the "he had the wrong man" passage involved an exercise of editorial judgment upon which the courts could not intrude. [   ]

The Court of Appeals affirmed, with one judge dissenting. 895 F.2d 1535 (CA9 1989). The court assumed for much of its opinion that Malcolm had deliberately altered each quotation not found on the tape recordings, but nevertheless held that petitioner failed to raise a jury question of actual malice, in large part for the reasons stated by the District Court. In its examination of the "intellectual gigolo" passage, the court agreed with the District Court that petitioner could not demonstrate actual malice because Malcolm had not altered the substantive content of petitioner's self-description, but went on to note that it did not consider the "intellectual gigolo" passage defamatory, as the quotation merely reported Kurt Eissler's and Anna Freud's opinions about petitioner. In any event, concluded the court, the statement would not be actionable under the " 'incremental harm branch' of the 'libel-proof' doctrine," id., at 1541 (quoting [*Herbert*]).

The dissent argued that any intentional or reckless alteration would prove actual malice, so long as a passage within quotation marks purports to be a verbatim rendition of what was said, contains material inaccuracies, and is defamatory 895 F.2d, at 1562–1570. We granted certiorari, 498 U.S. 808 (1990), and now reverse.

II

A

Under California law, "[l]ibel is a false and unprivileged publication by writing . . . which exposes any person to hatred, contempt, ridicule, or obloquy, or which causes him to be shunned or avoided, or which has a tendency to injure him in his occupation." Cal. Civ. Code Ann. § 45 (West 1982). False attribution of statements to a person may constitute libel, if the falsity exposes that person to an injury comprehended by the statute. [ ] It matters not under California law that petitioner alleges only part of the work at issue to be false. "[T]he test of libel is not quantitative; a single sentence may be the basis for an action in libel even though buried in a much longer text," though the California courts recognize that "[w]hile a drop of poison may be lethal, weaker poisons are sometimes diluted to the point of impotency." [ ]

The First Amendment limits California's libel law in various respects. When, as here, the plaintiff is a public figure he cannot recover unless he proves by clear and convincing evidence that the defendant published the defamatory statement with actual malice, i. e., with "knowledge that it was false or with reckless disregard of whether it was false or not." [*Sullivan*]. Mere negligence does not suffice. Rather the plaintiff must demonstrate that the author "in fact entertained serious doubts as to the truth of his publication," [*St. Amant*], or acted with a "high degree of awareness of . . . probable falsity," [*Garrison*].

Actual malice under the *New York Times* standard should not be confused with the concept of malice as an evil intent or a motive arising from spite or ill will. See [*Greenbelt*]. We have used the term actual malice as a shorthand to describe the First Amendment protections for speech injurious to reputation and we continue to do so here. But the term can confuse as well as enlighten. In this respect, the phrase may be an unfortunate one. See [*Connaughton*]. In place of the term actual malice, it is better practice that jury instructions refer to publication of a statement with knowledge of falsity or reckless disregard as to truth or falsity. The definitional principle must be remembered in the case before us.

B

In general, quotation marks around a passage indicate to the reader that the passage reproduces the speaker's words verbatim. They inform the reader that he or she is reading the statement of the speaker, not a paraphrase or other indirect interpretation by an author. By providing this information, quotations add authority to the statement and credibility to the author's work. Quotations allow the reader to form his or her own conclusions, and to assess the conclusions of the author, instead of relying entirely upon the author's characterization of her subject.

A fabricated quotation may injure reputation in at lease two senses, either giving rise to a conceivable claim of defamation. First, the quotation might injure because it attributes an untrue factual assertion to the speaker. An example would be a fabricated quotation of a public official admitting he had been convicted of a serious crime when in fact he had not.

Second, regardless of the truth or falsity of the factual matters asserted within the quoted statement, the attribution may result in injury to reputation because the manner of expression or even the fact that the statement was made indicates a negative personal trait or an attitude the speaker does not hold. John Lennon once was quoted as saying of the Beatles, "We're more popular than Jesus Christ now." [ ] Supposing the quotation had been a fabrication, it appears California law could permit recovery for defamation because, even without regard to the truth of the underlying assertion, false attribution of the statement could have injured his reputation. Here, in like manner, one need not determine whether petitioner is or is not the greatest analyst who ever lived in order to determine that it might have injured his reputation to be reported as having so proclaimed.

A self-condemnatory quotation may carry more force than criticism by another. It is against self-interest to admit one's own criminal liability, arrogance, or lack of integrity, and so all the more easy to credit when it happens. This principle underlies the elemental rule of evidence which permits the introduction of admissions, despite their hearsay character, because we assume "that persons do not make statements which are damaging to themselves unless satisfied for good reason that they are true." [ ]

Of course, quotations do not always convey that the speaker actually said or wrote the quoted material. "Punctuation marks, like words, have many uses. Writers often use quotations marks, yet no reasonable reader would assume that such punctuation automatically implies the truth of the quoted material." *Baker v. Los Angeles Examiner*, 42 Cal. 3d, at 263, 721 P.2d, at 92. In *Baker*, a television reviewer printed a hypothetical conversation between a station vice president and writer/producer, and the court found that no reasonable reader would conclude the plaintiff in fact had made the statement attributed to him. [ ] Writers often use quotations as in *Baker*, and a reader will not reasonably understand the quotation to indicate reproduction of a conversation that took place. In other instances, an acknowledgement that the work is so-called docudrama or historical fiction or that it recreates conversations from memory, not from recordings, might indicate that the quotations should not be interpreted as the actual statements of the speaker to whom they are attributed.

The work at issue here, however, as with much journalistic writing, provides the reader no clue that the quotations are being used as a rhetorical device or to paraphrase the speaker's actual statements. To the contrary, the work purports to be nonfiction, the result of numerous interviews. At least a trier of fact could so conclude. The work contains lengthy quotations attributed to petitioner, and neither Malcolm nor her publishers indicate to the reader that the quotations are anything but the reproduction of actual conversations. Further, the work was published in The New Yorker, a magazine which at the relevant time seemed to enjoy a reputation for scrupulous factual accuracy. These factors would, or at least could, lead a reader to take the quotations at face value. A defendant may be able to argue to the jury that quotations should be viewed by the reader as nonliteral or reconstructions, but we conclude that a trier of fact in this case could find that the reasonable reader would understand the quotations to be nearly verbatim reports of statements made by the subject.

C

The constitutional question we must consider here is whether, in the framework of a summary judgment motion, the evidence suffices to show that respondents acted with the requisite knowledge of falsity or reckless disregard as to truth or falsity. This inquiry in turn requires us to consider the concept of falsity; for we cannot discuss the standards for knowledge or reckless disregard without some understanding of the acts required for liability. We must consider whether the requisite falsity inheres in the attribution of words to the petitioner which he did not speak.

In some sense, an alteration of a verbatim quotation is false. But writers and reporters by necessity alter what people say, at the very least to eliminate grammatical and syntactical infelicities. If every alteration constituted the falsity required to prove actual malice, the practice of journalism, which the First Amendment standard is designed to protect, would require a radical change, one inconsistent with our precedents and First Amendment principles. Petitioner concedes this absolute definition of falsity in the quotation context is too stringent, and acknowledges that "minor changes to correct for grammar or syntax" do not amount to falsity for purposes of proving actual malice. [ ] We agree, and must determine what, in addition to this technical falsity, proves falsity for purposes of the actual malice inquiry.

Petitioner argues that, excepting correction of grammar or syntax, publication of a quotation with knowledge that it does not contain the words the public figure used demonstrates actual malice. The author will have published the quotation with knowledge of falsity, and no more need be shown. Petitioner suggests that by invoking more forgiving standards the Court of Appeals would permit and encourage the publication of falsehoods. Petitioner believes that the intentional manufacture of quotations does not "represen[t] the sort of inaccuracy that is commonplace in the forum of robust debate to which the *New York Times* rule applies, [*Bose*], and that protection of deliberate falsehoods would hinder the First Amendment values of robust and well-informed public debate by reducing the reliability of information available to the public.

We reject the idea that any alteration beyond correction of grammar or syntax by itself proves falsity in the sense relevant to determining actual malice under the First Amendment. An interviewer who writes from notes often will engage in the task of attempting a reconstruction of the speaker's statement. That author would, we may assume, act with knowledge that at times she has attributed to her subject words other than those actually used. Under petitioner's proposed standard, an author in this situation would lack First Amendment protection if she reported as quotations the substance of a subject's derogatory statements about himself.

Even if a journalist has tape recorded the spoken statement of a public figure, the full and exact statement will be reported in only rare circumstances. The existence of both a speaker and a reporter; the translation between two media, speech and the printed word; the addition of punctuation; and the practical necessity to edit and make intelligible a speaker's perhaps rambling comments, all make it misleading to suggest that a quotation will be reconstructed with complete accuracy. The use or absence of punctuation may distort a speaker's meaning, for example, where that meaning turns upon a speaker's emphasis of a particular word. In other cases, if a speaker makes an obvious misstatement, for example by unconscious substitution of one name for another, a journalist might alter the speaker's words but preserve his intended meaning. And conversely, an exact quotation out of context can distort meaning, although the speaker did use each reported word.

In all events, technical distinctions between correcting grammar and syntax and some greater level of alteration do not appear workable for we can think of no method by which courts or juries would draw the line between cleaning up and other changes, except by reference to the meaning a statement conveys to a reasonable reader. To attempt narrow distinctions of this type would be an unnecessary departure from First Amendment principles of general applicability, and, just as important, a departure from the underlying purposes of the tort of libel as understood since the latter half of the 16th century. From then until now, the tort action for defamation has existed to redress injury to the plaintiff's reputation by a statement that is defamatory and false. See [*Milkovich*]. As we have recognized, "[t]he legitimate state interest underlying the law of libel is the compensation of individuals for the harm inflicted on them by defamatory falsehood." [*Gertz*] If an author alters a speaker's words but effects no material change in meaning, including any meaning conveyed by the manner or fact of expression, the speaker suffers no injury to reputation that is compensable as a defamation.

These essential principles of defamation law accommodate the special cases of inaccurate quotations without the necessity for a discrete body of jurisprudence directed to this subject alone. Last Term, in [*Milkovich*], we refused "to create a wholesale defamation exemption for anything that might be labeled 'opinion.'" [ ] We recognized that "expressions of 'opinion' may often imply an assertion of objective fact." [ ] We allowed the defamation action to go forward in that case, holding that a reasonable trier of fact could find that the so-called expressions of opinion could be interpreted as including false assertions as to factual matters. So too in the case before us, we reject any special test of falsity for quotations, including one which would draw the line at correction of grammar or syntax. We conclude, rather, that the exceptions suggested by petitioner for grammatical or syntactical corrections serve to illuminate a broader principle.

The common law of libel takes but one approach to the question of falsity, regardless of the form of the communication. [ ] It overlooks minor inaccuracies and concentrates upon substantial truth. As in other jurisdictions, California law permits the defense of substantial truth, and would absolve a defendant even if she cannot "justify every word of the alleged defamatory matter; it is sufficient if the substance of the charge be proved true, irrespective of slight inaccuracy in the details." [ ] In this case, of course, the burden is upon petitioner to prove falsity. See [*Hepps*]. The essence of that inquiry, however, remains the same whether the burden rests upon plaintiff or defendant. Minor inaccuracies do not amount to falsity so long as "the substance, the gist, the sting, of the libelous change be justified." [ ] Put another way, the statement is not considered false unless it "would have a different effect on the mind of the reader from that which the pleaded truth would have produced." [ ] Our definition of actual malice relies upon this historical understanding.

We conclude that a deliberate alteration of the words uttered by a plaintiff does not equate with knowledge of falsity for purposes of [*Sullivan* and *Gertz*], unless the alteration results in a material change in the meaning conveyed by statement. The use of quotations to attribute words not in fact spoken bears in a most important way on that inquiry, but it is not dispositive in every case.

Deliberate or reckless falsification that comprises actual malice turns upon words and punctuation only because words and punctuation express meaning. Meaning is the life of language. And, for the reasons we have given, quotations may be a devastating instrument for conveying false meaning. In the case under consideration, readers of In the Freud Archives may have found Malcolm's portrait of petitioner especially damning because so much of it appeared to be a self-portrait, told by petitioner in his own words. And if the alterations of petitioner's words gave a different meaning to the statements, bearing upon their defamatory character, then the device of quotations might well be critical in finding the words actionable.

D

The Court of Appeals applied a test of substantial truth which, in exposition if not in application, comports with much of the above discussion. The Court of Appeals, however, went one step beyond protection of quotations that convey the meaning of a speaker's statement with substantial accuracy and concluded "that an altered quotation is protected so long as it is a "rational interpretation" of an actual statement drawing this standard from our decisions in Time, Inc. v. Pape, 401 U. S. 279 (1971), and [*Bose*]. Application of our protection for rational interpretation in this context finds no support in general principles of defamation law or in our First Amendment jurisprudence. Neither *Time, Inc. v. Pape*, nor *Bose Corp.*, involved the fabrication of quotations, or any analogous claim, and because many of the quotations at issue might reasonably be construed to state or imply factual assertions that are both false and defamatory, we cannot accept the reasoning of the Court of Appeals on this point.

In *Time, Inc. v. Pape*, we reversed a libel judgment which arose out of a magazine article summarizing a report by the United States Commission on Civil Rights discussing police civil rights abuses. The article quoted the Commission's summary of facts surrounding an incident of police brutality, but failed to include the Commission's qualification that these were allegations taken from a civil complaint. The Court noted that "the attitude of the Commission toward the factual verity of the episodes recounted was anything but straightforward," and distinguished between a "direct account of events that speak for themselves," 401 U. S., at 285, 286, and an article descriptive of what the Commission had reported. *Time, Inc. v. Pape* took into account the difficult choices that confront an author who departs from direct quotation and offers his own interpretation of an ambiguous source. A fair reading of our opinion is that the defendant did not publish a falsification sufficient to sustain a finding of actual malice.

In *Bose Corp.*, a Consumer Reports reviewer had attempted to describe in words the experience of listening to music through a pair of loudspeakers, and we concluded that the result was not an assessment of events that speak for themselves, but " 'one of a number of possible rational interpretations' of an event 'that bristled with ambiguities' and descriptive challenges for the writer." [ ] We refused to permit recovery for choice of language which, though perhaps reflecting a misconception, represented "the sort of inaccuracy that is commonplace in the forum of robust debate to which the *New York Times* rule applies." [ ]

The protection for rational interpretation serves First Amendment principles by allowing an author the interpretive license that is necessary when relying upon ambiguous sources. Where, however, a writer uses a quotation, and where a reasonable reader would conclude that the quotation purports to be a verbatim repetition of a statement by the speaker, the quotation marks indicate that the author is not involved in an interpretation of the speaker's ambiguous statement, but attempting to convey what the speaker said. This orthodox use of a quotation is the quintessential "direct account of events that speak for themselves." *Time, Inc. v. Pape, supra,* at 285. More accurately, the quotation allows the subject to speak for himself.

The significance of the quotations at issue, absent any qualification, is to inform us that we are reading the statement of petitioner, not Malcolm's rational interpretation of what petitioner has said or thought. Were we to assess quotations under a rational interpretation standard, we would give journalists the freedom to place statements in their subjects' mouths without fear of liability. By eliminating any method of distinguishing between the statements of the subject and the interpretation of the author, we would diminish to a great degree the trustworthiness of the printed word, and eliminate the real meaning of quotations. Not only public figures but the press doubtless would suffer under such a rule. Newsworthy figures might become more wary of journalists, knowing that any comment could be transmuted and attributed to the subject, so long as some bounds of rational interpretation were not exceeded. We would ill serve the values of the First Amendment if we were to grant near absolute, constitutional protection for such a practice. We doubt the suggestion that as a general rule readers will assume that direct quotations are but a rational interpretation of the speaker's words, and we decline to adopt any such presumption in determining the permissible interpretations of the quotations in question here.

III

A

We apply these principles to the case before us. On summary judgment, we must draw all justifiable inferences in favor of the nonmoving party, including questions of credibility and of the weight to be accorded particular evidence. [*Liberty Lobby*] So we must assume, except where otherwise evidenced by the transcripts of the tape recordings, that petitioner is correct in denying that he made the statements attributed to him by Malcolm, and that Malcolm reported with knowledge or reckless disregard of the differences between what petitioner said and what was quoted.

Respondents argue that, in determining whether petitioner has shown sufficient falsification to survive summary judgment, we should consider not only the tape recorded statements but also Malcolm's typewritten notes. We must decline that suggestion. To begin with, petitioner affirms in an affidavit that he did not make the complained of statements. The record contains substantial additional evidence, moreover, evidence which, in a light most favorable to petitioner, would support a jury determination under a clear and convincing standard that Malcolm deliberately or recklessly altered the quotations.

First, many of the challenged passages resemble quotations that appear on the tapes, except for the addition or alteration of certain phrases, giving rise to a reasonable inference that the statements have been altered. Second, Malcolm had the tapes in her possession and was not working under a tight deadline. Unlike a case involving hot news, Malcolm cannot complain that she lacked the practical ability to compare the tapes with her work in progress. Third, Malcolm represented to the editor-in-chief of The New Yorker that all the quotations were from the tape recordings. Fourth, Malcolm's explanations of the time and place of unrecorded conversations during which petitioner allegedly made some of the quoted statements have not been consistent in all respects. Fifth, petitioner suggests that the progression from typewritten notes, to manuscript, then to galleys provides further evidence of intentional alteration. Malcolm contests petitioner's allegations, and only a trial on the merits will resolve the factual dispute. But at this stage, the evidence creates a jury question whether Malcolm published the statements with knowledge or reckless disregard of the alterations.

B

We must determine whether the published passages differ materially in meaning from the tape recorded statements so as to create an issue of fact for a jury as to falsity.

(a) *"Intellectual Gigolo."* We agree with the dissenting opinion in the Court of Appeals that "[f]airly read, intellectual gigolo suggests someone who forsakes intellectual integrity in exchange for pecuniary or other gain." [ ] A reasonable jury could find a material difference between the meaning of this passage and petitioner's tape-recorded statement that he was considered "much too junior within the hierarchy of analysis, for these important training analysts to be caught dead with [him]."

The Court of Appeals majority found it difficult to perceive how the "intellectual gigolo" quotation was defamatory, a determination supported not by any citation to California law, but only by the argument that the passage appears to be a report of Eissler's and Anna Freud's opinions of petitioner. [ ] We agree with the Court of Appeals that the most natural interpretation of this quotation is not an admission that petitioner considers himself an intellectual gigolo but a statement that Eissler and Anna Freud considered him so. It does not follow, though, that the statement is harmless. Petitioner is entitled to argue that the passage should be analyzed as if Malcolm had reported falsely that *Eissler* had given this assessment (with the added level of complexity that the quotation purports to represent petitioner's understanding of Eissler's view). An admission that two well-respected senior colleagues considered one an "intellectual gigolo" could be as or more damaging than a similar self-appraisal. In all events, whether the "intellectual gigolo" quotation is defamatory is a question of California law. To the extent that the Court of Appeals bases its conclusion in the First Amendment, it was mistaken.

The Court of Appeals relied upon the "incremental harm" doctrine as an alternative basis for its decision. As the court explained it, "[t]his doctrine measures the incremental reputational harm inflicted by the challenged statements beyond the harm imposed by the nonactionable remainder of the publication." [ ] The court ruled, as a matter of law, that "[g]iven the . . . many provocative, bombastic statements indisputably made by Masson and quoted by Malcolm, the additional harm caused by the 'intellectual gigolo' quote was nominal or nonexistent, rendering the defamation claim as to this quote nonactionable." [ ]

This reasoning requires a court to conclude that, in fact, a plaintiff made the other quoted statements, cf. [*Liberty Lobby*]. As noted by the dissent in the Court of Appeals, the most "provocative, bombastic statements" quoted by Malcolm are those complained of by petitioner, and so this would not seem an appropriate application of the incremental harm doctrine. 895 F. 2d, at 1566.

(b) *"Sex, Women, Fun."* This passage presents a closer question. The "sex, women, fun" quotation offers a very different picture of petitioner's plans for Maresfield Gardens than his remark that "Freud's library alone is priceless." [ ] Petitioner's other tape-recorded remarks did indicate that he and another analyst planned to have great parties at the Freud house and, in a context that may not even refer to Freud house activities, to "pass women on to each other." We cannot conclude as a matter of law that these remarks bear the same substantial meaning as the quoted passage's suggestion that petitioner would make the Freud house a place of "sex, women, fun."

(c) *"It Sounded Better."* We agree with the District and the Court of Appeals that any difference between petitioner's tape-recorded statement that he "just liked" the name Moussaieff, and the quotation that "it sounded better" is, in context, immaterial. Although Malcolm did not include all of petitioner's lengthy explanation of his name change, she did convey the gist of that explanation: Petitioner took his abandoned family name as his middle name. We agree with the Court of Appeals that the words attributed to petitioner did not materially alter the meaning of his statement.

[Several more examples are analyzed.]

C

Because of the Court of Appeals' disposition with respect to Malcolm, it did not have occasion to address petitioner's argument that the District Court erred in granting summary judgment to The New Yorker Magazine, Inc., and Alfred A. Knopf, Inc. on the basis of their respective relations with Malcolm or the lack of any independent actual malice. These questions are best addressed in the first instance on remand.

The judgment of the Court of Appeals is reversed, and the case is remanded for further proceedings consistent with this opinion.

It is so ordered.

JUSTICE WHITE, with whom JUSTICE SCALIA joins, concurring in part and dissenting in part.

. . .

As this case comes to us, it is to be judged on the basis that in the instances identified by the court, the reporter, Malcolm, wrote that Masson said certain things that she knew Masson did not say. By any definition of the term, this was "knowing falsehood": Malcolm asserts that Masson said these very words, knowing that he did not. The issue, as the Court recognizes, is whether Masson spoke the words attributed to him, not whether the fact, if any, asserted by the attributed words is true or false. In my view, we need to go no further to conclude that the defendants in this case were not entitled to summary judgment on the issue of malice with respect to any of the six erroneous quotations.

That there was at least an issue for the jury to decide on the question of deliberate or reckless falsehood, does not mean that plaintiffs were necessarily entitled to go to trial. If, as a matter of law, reasonable jurors could not conclude that attributing to Masson certain words that he did not say amounted to libel under California law, i.e., "expose[d] [Masson] to hatred, contempt, ridicule, or obloquy, or which causes him to be shunned or avoided, or which has a tendency to injure him in his occupation," [　], a motion for summary judgment on this ground would be justified. I would suppose, for example, that if Malcolm wrote that Masson said that he wore contact lenses, when he said nothing about his eyes or his vision, the trial judge would grant summary judgment for the defendants and dismiss the case. The same would be true if Masson had said "I was spoiled as a child by my Mother," whereas, Malcolm reports that he said "I was spoiled as a child by my parents." But if reasonable jurors should conclude that the deliberate misquotation was libelous, the case should go to the jury.

This seems to me to be the straightforward, traditional approach to deal with this case. Instead, the Court states that deliberate misquotation does not amount to *New York Times* malice unless it results in a material change in the meaning conveyed by the statement. This ignores the fact that under *New York Times*, reporting a known falsehood—here the knowingly false attribution—is sufficient proof of malice. The falsehood, apparently, must be substantial; the reporter may lie a little, but not too much.

This standard is not only a less manageable one than the traditional approach, but it also assigns to the courts issues that are for the jury to decide. For a court to ask whether a misquotation substantially alters the meaning of spoken words in a defamatory manner is a far different inquiry than whether reasonable jurors could find that the misquotation was different enough to be libelous. In the one case, the court is measuring the difference from its own point of view; in the other it is asking how the jury would or could view the erroneous attribution.

The Court attempts to justify its holding in several ways, none of which is persuasive. First, it observes that an interviewer who takes notes of any interview will attempt to reconstruct what the speaker said and will often knowingly attribute to the subject words that were not used by the speaker. [ ] But this is nothing more than an assertion that authors may misrepresent because they cannot remember what the speaker actually said. This should be no dilemma for such authors, or they could report their story without purporting to quote when they are not sure, thereby leaving the reader to trust or doubt the author rather than believing that the subject actually said what he is claimed to have said. Moreover, this basis for the Court's rule has no application where there is a tape of the interview and the author is in no way at a loss to know what the speaker actually said. Second, the Court speculates that even with the benefit of a recording, the author will find it necessary at times to reconstruct, [ ], but again, in those cases why should the author be free to put his or her reconstruction in quotation marks, rather than report without them? Third, the Court suggests that misquotations that do not materially alter the meaning inflict no injury to reputation that is compensable as defamation. [ ] This may be true, but this is a question of defamation or not, and has nothing to do with whether the author deliberately put within quotation marks and attributed to the speaker words that the author knew the speaker did not utter.

As I see it, the defendants' motion for summary judgment based on lack of malice should not have been granted on any of the six quotations considered by the Court in Part III-B of its opinion. I therefore dissent from the result reached with respect to the "It Sounded Better" quotation dealt with in paragraph (c) of Part III-B, but agree with the Court's judgment on the other five misquotations.

Notes and Questions

1. Suppose at trial the jury finds (1) that the "intellectual gigolo" quote deliberately and materially altered the meaning of what Masson actually said, but that the resulting misquotation was not defamatory; (2) other passages in the article were false and defamatory, but there was no evidence that Malcolm knew those were false or had serious doubts as to their truth. Would these findings meet the Court's requirement that there be a deliberate alteration that "results in a material change in the meaning conveyed by the statement"? Why did the Court stop short of requiring a finding that the changed meaning is defamatory? Does its analysis of specific quotations suggest that the latter is in fact the test?

2. In a case described as the "mirror image" of *Masson,* Donald Diesen, a former county attorney, claimed to have been libeled by articles in the *Duluth News–Tribune* concerning his record in prosecuting cases of domestic abuse. He said the newspaper got the details right but the gist wrong (in contrast to *Masson,* in which he said Malcolm had gotten the gist right but the details wrong). Although a trial court awarded Diesen $785,000 in damages, the Minnesota Supreme Court reversed, holding that true statements, or statements of opinion on matters of public concern, cannot give rise to a cause of action for defamation by implication. Diesen v. Hessburg, 455 N.W.2d 446, 17 Med.L.Rptr. 1849 (1990), cert. denied 111 S.Ct. 1071 (1991).

3. When *Masson* came before the U.S. Court of Appeals for the Ninth Circuit on remand from the Supreme Court, the court held that *The New Yorker* and Malcolm must stand trial for the alleged defamation caused by the altering of the quotations. A publisher which, in investigating a story's accuracy, learns facts casting doubt as to that accuracy, "may not ignore those doubts, even though it had no duty to conduct the investigation in the first place," the court said. In its first opinion on the case in 1989, the Ninth Circuit had applied the incremental harm doctrine, saying the "intellectual gigolo" quote was not actionable because any harm rendered by the quote was nominal or non-existent in view of the unchallenged or verifiably accurate statements made by Masson. The Supreme Court had rejected the applicability of the incremental harm doctrine pursuant to the First Amendment but left open the possibility that the doctrine could be recognized under state law. The Ninth Circuit declined to apply the doctrine, saying, "We believe the California Supreme Court would agree." Masson v. The New Yorker Magazine, Inc., 960 F.2d 896, 20 Med.L.Rptr. 1009 (9th Cir.1992).

C. REMEDIES FOR DEFAMATION

1. INJUNCTIONS

Injunctions are generally unavailable for reasons discussed in Chafee's Government and Mass Communication 91–92 (1947): "One man's judgment is not to be trusted to determine what people can read. . . . So our law thinks it better to let the defamed plaintiff take his damages for what they are worth than to intrust a single judge (or even a jury) with the power to put a sharp check on the spread of possible truth." Furthermore, there are gradations of partial truth that are too subtle for a blanket injunction.

2. REPLY

If the plaintiff completes the obstacle course we have described, damages are the only available remedy of any importance. The right of reply mentioned by Justice Brennan in *Rosenbloom* and *Gertz* would allow the victim of the defamation to respond in his own words in the offending publication, but states rarely require this, and such a requirement has constitutional problems. As to the role of reply in broadcasting, see Chapters III and VI.

3. RETRACTION

The common law itself had some rules that tended to reduce the amount of damages recoverable in defamation. They were called "partial" defenses since they did not defeat liability but only reduced the size of the award. At common law if the defendant voluntarily retracted the statement, that fact was admissible to show that the plaintiff had not been damaged as badly as he claimed. It might also show that the defendant had not acted maliciously in the first place. Some states have enacted retraction statutes that grant further protection to mass media defendants. These apply only to media with immediacy of dissemination because of the requirement that the retraction be published promptly and with the same prominence as the defamation. It would be meaningless to make the retraction privilege available to media such as books and motion pictures, and the effectiveness of retraction varies even among those media that are covered in most states. It is generally thought, for example, that a retraction in the same space in a newspaper is more likely to reach the audience that read the original defamation than would most retractions over radio or television of an electronic media defamation.

The statutes vary in covering those who defame innocently, carelessly or maliciously. What they have in common is a requirement that the prospective plaintiff demand a retraction shortly after the defamation. If the publisher complies within a similar period of time, then the plaintiff may recover only his special damages, and no general damages. If the retraction is not published within the time limit, the plaintiff may recover whatever damages the common law allows—subject now to the damage limitations of *Gertz*.

California law limits libel plaintiffs suing newspapers to special damages unless they demand retractions. In Burnett v. National Enquirer, Inc., 144 Cal.App.3d 991, 193 Cal.Rptr. 206, 9 Med.L.Rptr. 1921 (1983), one of the issues was whether the defendant *National Enquirer* was protected because it had run a retraction: "An item in this column on March 2 erroneously reported that Carol Burnett had an argument with Henry Kissinger at a Washington restaurant and became boisterous, disturbing other guests. We understand these events did not occur and we are sorry for any embarrassment our report may have caused Miss Burnett." The *Enquirer* argued that it was a newspaper, but the California Court of Appeal held that it was a magazine, and thus the trial court did not err in not limiting the damage award on that basis.

4. SETTING THE RECORD STRAIGHT

The Libel Reform Project of the Annenberg Washington Program of Northwestern University in 1988 proposed dramatic reforms in libel law. Under the proposal, plaintiffs would give up the possibility of collecting damages in exchange for a "no-fault" trial at which the only issue would be the truth or falsity of the allegedly defamatory statement. Defendants would no longer have the protection of the absence of malice defense. Proponents of the proposal emphasize the need to simplify the law and curtail mushrooming litigation costs. Opponents stress that the absence of malice defense is, by the Supreme Court's own rulings, inherent in the First Amendment and is therefore not something that can be bargained away as a part of reform.

D. CRIMINAL LIBEL AND GROUP LIBEL

1. CRIMINAL LIBEL

Criminal libel is not generally available although it is part of the law in most states. The New York State Constitution, for example, provides that, "In all criminal prosecutions or indictments for libels, the truth may be given in evidence to the jury; and if it shall appear to the jury that the matter charged as libelous is true, and was published with good motives and for justifiable ends, the party shall be acquitted; and the jury shall have the right to determine the law and the fact." McKinney's Const. Art. 1, § 8.

Criminal libel had already fallen into disuse before *Garrison*, p. 630, *supra*. The strictures placed on the action in that case diminished still further its usefulness. The role of the action is even more doubtful when it is used by prosecutors on behalf of famous or powerful persons who do not wish to bring a civil action themselves. This was the situation in 1976 when a state court declared the California criminal libel law unconstitutional because of its limitations on the defense of truth and its presumption of malice. Because some states have taken the same path and others are not enforcing statutes, criminal libel no longer appears to be a serious risk to the media.

Recall *R.A.V.*, p. 23, *supra*, in which the Supreme Court in 1992 struck down as unconstitutionally overbroad a St. Paul ordinance making it a crime to engage in speech or behavior likely to arouse "anger or alarm" on the basis of "race, color, creed, religion or gender."

2. GROUP LIBEL STATUTES

The main concern in the debate over group libel has been the hazards of unrestricted hate propaganda. Curbs on group defamation have been advocated to reduce friction among racial, religious and ethnic groups. As early as 1917 some states enacted criminal group libel laws for that purpose. The Nazi defamation of minority groups, and conspicuous racial tensions in the United States, brought renewed attention to group libel laws in the 1940s and 1950s.

The most common method of confronting group libel has been the enactment of criminal laws directed specifically at the problem. Such laws typically prohibit communications that are abusive or offensive toward a group or that tend to arouse hatred, contempt or ridicule of the group. Penalties have ranged from a fine of $50 or 30 days imprisonment, to $10,000 or two years in prison.

Beauharnais v. Illinois, 343 U.S. 250 (1952), is the only Supreme Court decision to review the constitutionality of group libel legislation. The Court, 5–4, affirmed a conviction under Illinois's 1917 group libel statute. The law prohibited publications portraying "depravity, criminality, unchastity, or lack of virtue of a class of citizens, of any race, color, creed, or religion" that subjected those described to "contempt, derision, or obloquy or which is productive of breach of the peace or riots." Beauharnais, the president of an organization called the "White Circle League," had distributed leaflets calling on the Mayor and City Council to halt the "further encroachment, harassment and invasion of white people, their property, neighborhoods and persons, by the Negro."

Justice Frankfurter's opinion for the Court treated the statute as "a form of criminal libel law" and accepted the *dictum* of *Chaplinsky*, p. 23, *supra*, that libel was one of those "well-defined and narrowly limited classes of speech, the prevention and punishment of which has never been thought to raise any constitutional problem." He traced the history of violent and destructive racial tension in Illinois and concluded that it would "deny experience" to say that the statute was without reason. He disposed of the First Amendment question in a single paragraph near the end of his opinion.

> Libelous utterances not being within the area of constitutionally protected speech, it is unnecessary, either for us or for the State courts, to consider the issue behind the phrase "clear and present danger." Certainly no one would contend that obscene speech, for example, may be punished only upon a showing of such circumstances. Libel, as we have seen, is in the same class.

Of the four dissenters, only Justices Black and Douglas addressed the First Amendment problems that the majority had cast aside by excluding the whole area of libel from First Amendment protection. Justice Black analyzed the decision as extending the scope of the law of criminal libel from "the narrowest of areas" involving "purely private feuds" to "discussions of matters of public concern." This was an invasion of the First Amendment's absolute prohibition of laws infringing the freedom of public discussion. Justice Douglas concurred in Justice Black's opinion and wrote separately to emphasize that he would have required a demonstration that the "peril of speech" was "clear and present." He agreed with Justice Black that allowing a legislature to regulate "within reasonable limits" the right of free speech was "an ominous and alarming trend." Only a half-dozen states retain group defamation statutes.

Group libel statutes also raise practical objections. Group libel prosecutions normally involve issues on which the community is sharply divided. The incidence as well as the outcome of prosecutions may thus depend on which segments of the community are represented in the office of the prosecuting attorney and on the jury. Moreover, a defendant could use the trial to promote his views and might well benefit regardless of the result: an acquittal would validate his viewpoint, while a conviction would make him a martyr whose civil liberties have been violated. These difficulties have led most commentators and many representatives of minority groups to oppose group libel litigation.

E. PRACTICAL CONSIDERATIONS FOR MEDIA DEFENDANTS

1. HEADING OFF LIBEL SUITS

Recent research among libel plaintiffs suggests that many of them, unhappy though they may be when they realize that something harmful and erroneous has been published about them, are not immediately inclined to sue the media. Too frequently, people who have been defamed become angry enough to sue only after they have been treated curtly or even rudely when they tried to get the errors corrected.

Keeping this in mind, media attorneys and managers are today trying harder to prepare their employees for better handling of complaints. Such complaints should be taken seriously, and the complainer should be handled with courtesy and care. Usually, that means that the complaint should be referred to a senior staff member trained in handling such complaints.

Apologies and retractions, when appropriate, can help to head off law suits before they occur. That is normally to the advantage of both the potential plaintiff and the media defendant. Defendants will, of course, have to use care in making apologies or retractions; should the potential plaintiff become an actual plaintiff, the admission may be used against the defendant in court. Publication of the correct information without embellishment is sometimes the best approach.

Professors Randall Bezanson, Gilbert Cranberg and John Soloski of the University of Iowa have contributed to the understanding of libel plaintiffs through a major study and a number of publications. See, R. Bezanson, G. Cranberg and J. Soloski, Libel Law and the Press: Myth and Reality (1987).

2. MEGAVERDICTS

Much has been written in the last decade about the dollar size of libel suits and about jury verdicts for millions of dollars sometimes characterized as "megaverdicts" or "monster verdicts." To some extent the media play into the hands of plaintiffs seeking publicity through multi-million dollar suits, because such amounts are the stuff of which headlines are made. Among the suits receiving extraordinary attention were actress Carol Burnett's suit against the *National Enquirer* and Army General William Westmoreland's suit against CBS. A jury awarded Carol Burnett $1.6 million in damages. Westmoreland sued CBS for $120 million. These cases are hardly typical, but large damage awards are not imaginary either. What press headlines usually fail to point out is how many of these large damage awards are reversed or reduced by appellate courts. For many years no damage award over $500,000 was ever upheld.

Most of those that claimed big headlines were subsequently reduced. In the Carol Burnett case, for example, the original award was reduced to $200,000. With the possibility of a new trial on the damage amount, Burnett and *National Enquirer* settled out of court for an undisclosed amount rumored to be about $400,000—still only one-fourth the amount of the original award. The Westmoreland case, on the other hand, ended with no money changing hands between the litigants (but with each side reportedly having incurred millions of dollars in legal fees).

In Brown & Williamson Tobacco Corp. v. Jacobson, 827 F.2d 1119, 14 Med.L.Rptr. 1497 (7th Cir.1987), cert. denied 485 U.S. 993 (1988), the Supreme Court let stand a $3.05 million damage award against CBS and Walter Jacobson. The award was four times as large as any previous libel award ever upheld by the federal appellate courts.

Jacobson, an anchorman on CBS-owned station WBBM–TV, Chicago, in delivering a nightly editorial segment titled "Walter Jacobson's Perspective," commented on the cigarette industry. While discussing attempts by cigarette manufacturers to attract young people to smoking, Jacobson referred to cigarette manufacturers as "slicksters" trying to link smoking with "pot, wine, beer, and sex." He said that "Viceroy slicksters" were "not slicksters, they're liars." The statement was held to be fact rather than opinion.

Although Jacobson's remarks related to a report by the Federal Trade Commission about cigarette manufacturers' advertising strategy aimed at young people, the court held that the remarks were not protected by a privilege of fair reporting because of significant inaccuracies. Brown & Williamson, the manufacturer of Viceroys, attempted to prove that Jacobson's charges were false by introducing every Viceroy advertisement published between 1975 and 1982. An executive of one of their advertising agencies, Ted Bates and Company, testified that Brown & Williamson had never asked the agency to utilize a "pot," wine, beer and sex strategy in developing advertisements. The claim that Viceroy had used such strategies was false. Furthermore, Jacobson had said the FTC had said Viceroy had done these things, but the FTC had not. Jacobson used the term "children" to refer to the objects of the strategy rather than "young smokers" and "starters"—the terms used in the FTC report.

Acknowledging that Brown and Williamson was, for purpose of libel litigation, a public figure, the court held that the destruction of critical documents concerning the broadcast, and demonstration that the reporter knew a researcher had been unable to find actual "pot, wine, beer, and sex" ads was sufficient to warrant a finding that the broadcast was made with actual malice. The court found that Jacobson's researcher had intentionally destroyed critical documents including an 18-page sample script for Jacobson's remarks and the researcher's annotated copy of the FTC report. The court said that, "... [h]e destroyed various documents that in all likelihood would have established that both he and Jacobson were aware that the 'tobacco industry hooks children' Perspective was false at the time that it was delivered."

The trial jury awarded the plaintiff company $3 million in compensatory damages and $2.5 million in punitive damages. That had subsequently been reduced, but the court of appeals reinstated an award of $1 million in compensatory damages, $2 million in punitive damages against CBS, and $50,000 in punitive damages against Jacobson. In doing so, the court noted that the broadcaster's audience was 2.5 million, that the network's net worth exceeded $1 billion and that the reporter's net worth exceeded $5 million. The court also noted that Brown & Williamson's attorney's fees were $1,360,000 prior to post-trial motions.

The concern over high damage awards is not, of course, unique to media defendants. Many non-media businesses have expressed concern over rapidly escalating damage awards, and some have argued that they should be capped. In one high profile case, Cleopatra Haslip had been awarded $1.04 million in punitive damages in a health insurance case; when the insurance company appealed to the Supreme Court claiming a violation of the due process clause of the Fourteenth Amendment, a coalition of 19 media groups filed an *amicus* brief arguing that "Punitive damages awards in libel cases involving matters of public concern are irreconcilable with the requirements of the First Amendment." Med.L.Rptr. News Notes, June 26, 1990. A wide variety of nonmedia professional groups filed *amicus* briefs as well. The Supreme Court, however, held that the award in *this* case did *not* violate the Fourteenth Amendment—leaving the door open to the possibility of finding that an excessive award in some future case could be overturned on due process grounds. Pacific Mutual Life Insurance Co. v. Haslip, 499 U.S. ___, 111 S.Ct. 1032 (1991).

Huge damage awards in a few media cases since *Brown & Williamson* have been highly publicized. The largest jury award was one for $58 million against WFAA–TV in Dallas; the station had been sued by former district attorney Vic Feazell in a case involving television reports alleging the taking of payments to quash drunken driving cases. Feazell and WFAA's owner, A.H. Belo Corporation, subsequently settled for an undisclosed sum. In another case, Attorney Richard A. Sprague was awarded $2.5 million in compensatory damages and $31.5 million in punitive damages by a 1990 jury in a libel suit after *The*

Philadelphia Inquirer alleged improprieties in his conduct as a prosecutor; the trial judge refused to overturn or reduce the verdict, and the newspaper said it would appeal. The New York Times, Sept. 20, 1992 at 1–34.

A New York appellate court affirmed a damage award of nearly $15.5 million in Prozeralik v. Capital Cities Communications, Inc., 593 N.Y.S.2d 662, 21 Med.L.Rptr. 1073 (1993). Restaurant owner John Prozeralik sued the owner of Buffalo TV station WKBW after it broadcast reports linking him with organized crime. He had been falsely identified as the victim of an abduction and beating.

3. LIBEL INSURANCE

When a court awards damages against a media defendant in a libel suit, it is legally irrelevant whether that defendant carries libel insurance. As a practical matter, of course, it is extremely important. Media employers are often reluctant to be candid about their insurance, even with their own employees. Certainly employers do not want their employees to take unnecessary risks, and media employers typically value their reputations for accuracy so they do not want to lose libel suits even if they do carry insurance. Media libel insurance policies typically provide for a deductible amount that is paid by the insured before the insurance coverage comes into play. The higher the deductible, the lower the premiums that the employer pays for the insurance. Media employers who could afford to sustain losses of $50,000 or $100,000 on each damage award against them or who can afford the legal expenses might elect to be "self-insured" for those amounts and to carry insurance policies with the $50,000 or $100,000 deductible clause to cover them for any awards or expenses greater than those amounts. The increasing size of trial court awards for libel damages has, inevitably, led to an increase in libel insurance premiums; that increase in the premiums in turn has a negative effect on virtually every insured media organization—not just those that are sued.

Libel insurance policies are offered through some trade associations like the National Association of Broadcasters.

4. DEFENSE COSTS

Even the media defendants who win their cases in trial or appellate courts may spend large sums of money defending themselves. In major cases some defendants have spent several million dollars defending themselves. While vindication in court may seem ideal, the cost of lawyers and the cost in terms of one's own employees' time may make it tempting to settle out of court with the plaintiff—even where there is a substantial likelihood that the defendant would ultimately prevail should the case be decided by an appellate court. A media defendant who developed the reputation of settling out of court too easily could become a target for nuisance suits brought by plaintiffs who do not really expect to win but hope defendants will buy them off by settling out of court without ever going to trial. Some major media organizations have adopted the position of never settling out of court for just that reason, but such a posture is difficult to maintain in an instance where the media organization really did publish a false statement, particularly where the plaintiff is a private figure who does not need to prove actual malice and who has real damages. The defendant's own insurance carrier may apply pressure to settle, and the size of the verdicts of recent years makes the risk of going to trial all the greater and increases the temptation to settle out of court.

5. EVIDENCE AND WITNESSES

Attorneys representing media clients sometimes have a difficult choice to make: if they scare the journalists too much about possible libel suits, they may create their own chilling effect; but if they ignore the subject, the journalists may fall into traps that can make the defense of a libel suit more troubling. Plaintiffs who are public officials or public figures will, of course, be seeking evidence that the defendant published with knowledge of falsity or with a high degree of awareness of probable falsity. Internal memos or margin notes written on copy expressing doubts about the facts in a story can be just the kind of evidence the plaintiff will seek. Newsroom conversations about doubts—even doubts in one's own mind—may be discoverable (see discussion of *Herbert*, p. 782, *infra*).

In an age in which libel litigation is common, journalists publishing material that may damage a person's reputation would be wise to think of the story subject as a potential plaintiff and to be as sure of their facts as possible. Just as such nationally-known journalists as Dan Rather and Mike Wallace have been called to discuss their stories from the witness stand, younger journalists may have to do the same and should be unafraid to do so if they have followed accepted journalistic practices. (The latter can present interesting questions, because professional standards in journalism vary. Codes of ethics—like the code of The Society of Professional Journalists—may be of some use. Principles such as getting at least two independent sources before disseminating damaging information may be widely followed but still are not provably a part of a universally accepted code of conduct for the journalist.)

F. INFLICTION OF EMOTIONAL DISTRESS

When Rev. Jerry Falwell sued *Hustler* magazine publisher Larry Flynt in a highly publicized case, he sued for libel and invasion of privacy and a separate but related tort—infliction of emotional distress. The possibility that public figure libel plaintiffs, frustrated by their inability to win libel suits under *New York Times,* would sue in great numbers for infliction of emotional distress was a serious concern for the media as the Falwell case went to the Supreme Court.

The case resulted from a *Hustler* magazine ad parody that included a fake interview with Falwell that implied that he was a "hypocritical incestuous drunkard."

In pre-trial discovery, Larry Flynt identified himself as Christopher Columbus Cornwallis I.P.Q. Harvey H. Apache Pugh and testified that the parody was written by Yoko Ono and Billy Idol. In answers to other questions, he testified that he had been attempting to characterize Falwell as a liar and hypocrite and to "assassinate" his character. Flynt's attorneys subsequently claimed that Flynt was unable to give a correct account of the events.

HUSTLER MAGAZINE, INC. v. FALWELL

Supreme Court of the United States, 1988.
485 U.S. 46, 108 S.Ct. 876, 99 L.Ed.2d 41, 14 Med.L.Rptr. 2281.

CHIEF JUSTICE REHNQUIST delivered the opinion of the Court.

Petitioner Hustler Magazine, Inc., is a magazine of nationwide circulation. Respondent Jerry Falwell, a nationally known minister who has been active as a commentator on politics and public affairs, sued petitioner and its publisher, petitioner Larry Flynt, to recover damages for invasion of privacy, libel, and intentional infliction of emotional distress. The District Court directed a verdict against respondent on the privacy claim, and submitted the other two claims to a jury. The jury found for petitioners on the defamation claim, but found for respondent on the claim for intentional infliction of emotional distress and awarded damages. We now consider whether this award is consistent with the First and Fourteenth Amendments of the United States Constitution.

The inside front cover of the November 1983 issue of Hustler Magazine featured a "parody" of an advertisement for Campari Liqueur that contained the name and picture of respondent and was entitled "Jerry Falwell talks about his first time." This parody was modeled after actual Campari ads that included interviews with various celebrities about their "first times." Although it was apparent by the end of each interview that this meant the first time they sampled Campari, the ads clearly played on the sexual double entendre of the general subject of "first times." Copying the form and layout of these Campari ads, Hustler's editors chose respondent as the featured celebrity and drafted an alleged "interview" with him in which he states that his "first time" was during a drunken incestuous rendezvous with his mother in an outhouse. The Hustler parody portrays respondent and his mother as drunk and immoral, and suggests that respondent is a hypocrite who preaches only when he is drunk. In small print at the bottom of the page, the ad contains the disclaimer, "ad parody—not to be taken seriously." The magazine's table of contents also lists the ad as "Fiction; Ad and Personality Parody."

Soon after the November issue of Hustler became available to the public, respondent brought this diversity action in the United States District Court for the Western District of Virginia against Hustler Magazine, Inc., Larry C. Flynt, and Flynt Distributing Co. Respondent stated in his complaint that publication of the ad parody in Hustler entitled him to recover damages for libel, invasion of privacy, and intentional infliction of emotional distress. The case proceeded to trial.[1] At the close of the evidence, the District Court granted a directed verdict for petitioners on the invasion of privacy claim. The jury then found against respondent on the libel claim, specifically finding that the ad parody could not "reasonably be understood as describing actual facts about [respondent] or actual events in which [he] participated." [ ] The jury ruled for respondent on the intentional infliction of emotional distress claim, however, and state that he should be awarded $100,000 in compensatory damages, as well as $50,000 each in punitive damages from petitioners. Petitioners' motion for judgment notwithstanding the verdict was denied.

On appeal, the United States Court of Appeals for the Fourth Circuit affirmed the judgment against petitioners. Falwell v. Flynt, 797 F.2d 1270 (CA4 1986). The court rejected petitioners' argument that the "actual malice" standard of New York Times Co., [ ], must be met before respondent can recover for emotional distress. The court agreed that because respondent is concededly a public figure, petitioners are "entitled to the same level of first amendment protection in the claim for intentional infliction of emotional distress that they received in [respondent's] claim for libel." [ ] But this does not mean that a literal application of the actual malice rule is appropriate in the context of an emotional distress claim. In the court's view, the New York Times decision emphasized the constitutional importance not of the falsity of the statement or the defendant's disregard for the truth, but of the heightened level of culpability embodied in the requirement of "knowing . . . or reckless" conduct. Here the New York Times standard is satisfied by the state-law requirement, and the jury's finding, that the defendants have acted intentionally or recklessly.[3] The Court of Appeals then went on to reject the contention that because the jury found that the ad parody did not describe actual facts about respondent, the ad was an opinion that is protected by the First Amendment. As the court put it, this was "irrelevant," as the issue is "whether [the ad's] publication was sufficiently outrageous to constitute intentional infliction of emotional distress." Id., at 1276.[4] Petitioner then filed a petition for rehearing en banc, but this was denied by a

---

1. While the case was pending, the ad parody was published in Hustler magazine a second time.

3. Under Virginia law, in an action for intentional infliction of emotional distress a plaintiff must show that the defendant's conduct (1) is intentional or reckless; (2) offends generally accepted standards of de-

cency or morality; (3) is causally connected with the plaintiff's emotional distress; and (4) caused emotional distress that was severe. [ ]

4. The Court below also rejected several other contentions that petitioners do not raise in this appeal.

divided court. Given the importance of the constitutional issues involved, we granted certiorari.

This case presents us with a novel question involving First Amendment limitations upon a State's authority to protect its citizens from the intentional infliction of emotional distress. We must decide whether a public figure may recover damages for emotional harm caused by the publication of an ad parody offensive to him, and doubtless gross and repugnant in the eyes of most. Respondent would have us find that a State's interest in protecting public figures from emotional distress is sufficient to deny First Amendment protection to speech that is patently offensive and is intended to inflict emotional injury, even when that speech could not reasonably have been interpreted as stating actual facts about the public figure involved. This we decline to do.

At the heart of the First Amendment is the recognition of the fundamental importance of the free flow of ideas and opinions on matters of public interest and concern. "[T]he freedom to speak one's mind is not only an aspect of individual liberty—and thus a good unto itself—but also is essential to the common quest for truth and the vitality of society as a whole." Bose Corp. v. Consumers Union of United States, Inc., 466 U.S. 485, 503–504 (1984). We have therefore been particularly vigilant to ensure that individual expressions of ideas remain free from governmentally imposed sanctions. The First Amendment recognizes no such thing as a "false" idea. Gertz v. Robert Welch, Inc., 418 U.S. 323, 339 (1974). As Justice Holmes wrote, "[W]hen men have realized that time has upset many fighting faiths, they may come to believe even more than they believe the very foundations of their own conduct that the ultimate good desired is better reached by free trade in ideas—that the best test of truth is the power of the thought to get itself accepted in the competition of the market. . . ." Abrams v. United States, 250 U.S. 616, 630 (1919) (dissenting opinion).

The sort of robust political debate encouraged by the First Amendment is bound to produce speech that is critical of those who hold public office or those public officials who are "intimately involved in the resolution of important public questions or, by reason of their fame, shape events in areas of concern to society at large." Associated Press v. Walker, decided with Curtis Publishing Co. v. Butts, 388 U.S. 130, 164 (1967) (Warren, C.J., concurring in result). Justice Frankfurter put it succinctly in Baumgartner v. United States, 322 U.S. 665, 673–674 (1944), when he said that "[o]ne of the prerogatives of American citizenship is the right to criticize public men and measures." Such criticism, inevitably, will not always be reasoned or moderate; public figures as well as public officials will be subject to "vehement, caustic, and sometimes unpleasantly sharp attacks." New York Times, supra, at 270. "[T]he candidate who vaunts his spotless record and sterling integrity cannot convincingly cry 'foul!' when an opponent or an industrious reporter attempts to demonstrate the contrary." Monitor Patriot Co. v. Roy, 401 U.S. 265, 274 (1971).

Of course, this does not mean that any speech about a public figure is immune from sanction in the form of damages. Since New York Times Co. v. Sullivan, supra, we have consistently ruled that a public figure may hold a speaker liable for the damage to reputation caused by publication of a defamatory falsehood, but only if the statement was made "with knowledge that it was false or with reckless disregard of whether it was false or not." Id., at 279–280. False statements of fact are particularly valueless; they interfere with the truth-seeking function of the marketplace of ideas, and they cause damage to an individual's reputation that cannot easily be repaired by counterspeech, however persuasive or effective. See Gertz, 418 U.S., at 340, 344, n. 9. But even though falsehoods have little value in and of themselves, they are "nevertheless inevitable in free debate," id., at 340, and a rule that would impose strict liability on a publisher for false factual assertions would have an undoubted "chilling" effect on speech relating to public figures that does have constitutional value. "Freedoms of expression require 'breathing space.' " Philadelphia Newspapers, Inc. v. Hepps, 475 U.S. 767, 772 (1986) (quoting New York Times, 376 U.S., at 272). This breathing space is provided by a constitutional rule that allows public figures to recover for libel or defamation only when they can prove both that the statement was false and that the statement was made with the requisite level of culpability.

Respondent argues, however, that a different standard should apply in this case because here the State seeks to prevent not reputational damage, but the severe emotional distress suffered by the person who is the subject of an offensive publication. Cf. Zacchini v. Scripps–Howard Broadcasting Co., 433 U.S. 562 (1977) (ruling that the "actual malice" standard does not apply to the tort of appropriation of a right of publicity). In respondent's view, and in the view of the Court of Appeals, so long as the utterance was intended to inflict emotional distress, was outrageous, and did in fact inflict serious emotional distress, it is of no constitutional import whether the statement was a fact or an opinion, or whether it was true or false. It is the intent to cause injury that is the gravamen of the tort, and the State's interest in preventing emotional harm simply outweighs whatever interest a speaker may have in speech of this type.

Generally speaking the law does not regard the intent to inflict emotional distress as one which should receive much solicitude, and it is quite understandable that most if not all jurisdictions have chosen to make it civilly culpable where the conduct in question is sufficiently "outrageous." But in the world of debate about public affairs, many things done with motives that are less than admirable are protected by the First Amendment. In Garrison v. Louisiana, 379 U.S. 64 (1964), we held that even when a speaker or writer is motivated by hatred or ill-will his expression was protected by the First Amendment:

"Debate on public issues will not be uninhibited if the speaker must run the risk that it will be proved in court that he spoke out of hatred; even if he did speak out of hatred, utterances honestly believed contribute to the free interchange of ideas and the ascertainment of truth." Id., at 73.

Thus, while such a bad motive may be deemed controlling for purposes of tort liability in other areas of the law, we think the First Amendment prohibits such a result in the area of public debate about public figures.

Were we to hold otherwise, there can be little doubt that political cartoonists and satirists would be subjected to damages awards without any showing that their work falsely defamed its subject. Webster's defines a caricature as "the deliberately distorted picturing or imitating of a person, literary style, etc. by exaggerating features or mannerisms for satirical effect." Webster's New Unabridged Twentieth Century Dictionary of the English Language 275 (2d ed. 1979). The appeal of the political cartoon or caricature is often based on exploration of unfortunate physical traits or politically embarrassing events—an exploration often calculated to injure the feelings of the subject of the portrayal. The art of the cartoonist is often not reasoned or evenhanded, but slashing and one-sided. One cartoonist expressed the nature of the art in these words:

> "The political cartoon is a weapon of attack, of scorn and ridicule and satire; it is least effective when it tries to pat some politician on the back. It is usually as welcome as a bee sting and is always controversial in some quarters." Long, The Political Cartoon: Journalism's Strongest Weapon. The Quill, 56, 57 (Nov. 1962).

Several famous examples of this type of intentionally injurious speech were drawn by Thomas Nast, probably the greatest American cartoonist to date, who was associated for many years during the post Civil War era with Harper's Weekly. In the pages of that publication Nast conducted a graphic vendetta against William M. "Boss" Tweed and his corrupt associates in New York City's "Tweed Ring." It has been described by one historian of the subject as "a sustained attack which in its passion and effectiveness stands alone in the history of American graphic art." M. Keller, The Art and Politics of Thomas Nast 177 (1968). Another writer explains that the success of the Nast cartoon was achieved "because of the emotional impact of its presentation. It continuously goes beyond the bounds of good taste and conventional manners." C. Press, The Political Cartoon 251 (1981).

Despite their sometimes caustic nature, from the early cartoon portraying George Washington as an ass down to the present day, graphic depictions and satirical cartoons have played a prominent role in public and political debate. Nast's castigation of the Tweed Ring, Walt McDougall's characterization of presidential candidate James G. Blaine's banquet with the millionaires at Delmonico's as "The Royal Feast of Belshazzar," and numerous other efforts have undoubtedly had an effect on the course and outcome of contemporaneous debate. Lincoln's tall, gangling posture, Teddy Roosevelt's glasses and teeth, and

Franklin D. Roosevelt's jutting jaw and cigarette holder have been memorialized by political cartoons with an effect that could not have been obtained by the photographer or the portrait artist. From the viewpoint of history it is clear that our political discourse would have been considerably poorer without them.

Respondent contends, however, that the caricature in question here was so "outrageous" as to distinguish it from more traditional political cartoons. There is no doubt that the caricature of respondent and his mother published in Hustler is at best a distant cousin of the political cartoons described above, and a rather poor relation at that. If it were possible by laying down a principled standard to separate the one from the other, public discourse would probably suffer little or no harm. But we doubt that there is any such standard, and we are quite sure that the pejorative description "outrageous" does not supply one. "Outrageousness" in the area of political and social discourse has an inherent subjectiveness about it which would allow a jury to impose liability on the basis of the jurors' tastes or views, or perhaps on the basis of their dislike of a particular expression. An "outrageousness" standard thus runs afoul of our longstanding refusal to allow damages to be awarded because the speech in question may have an adverse emotional impact on the audience. See NAACP v. Claiborne Hardware Co., 458 U.S. 886, 910 (1982) . . .. And, as we stated in FCC v. Pacifica Foundation, 438 U.S. 726 (1978):

> "[T]he fact that society may find speech offensive is not a sufficient reason for suppressing it. Indeed, if it is the speaker's opinion that gives offense, that consequence is a reason for according it constitutional protection. For it is a central tenet of the First Amendment that the government must remain neutral in the marketplace of ideas." Id., at 745–746.

. . .

Admittedly, these oft-repeated First Amendment principles, like other principles, are subject to limitations. We recognized in Pacifica Foundation, that speech that is " 'vulgar,' 'offensive,' and 'shocking' " is "not entitled to absolute constitutional protection under all circumstances." 438 U.S., at 747. In Chaplinsky v. New Hampshire, 315 U.S. 568 (1942), we held that a state could lawfully punish an individual for the use of insulting " 'fighting' words—those which by their very utterance inflict injury or tend to incite an immediate breach of the peace." Id., at 571–572. These limitations are but recognition of the observation in Dun & Bradstreet, Inc. v. Greenmoss Builders, Inc., 472 U.S. 749, 758 (1985), that this Court has "long recognized that not all speech is of equal First Amendment importance." But the sort of expression involved in this case does not seem to us to be governed by any exception to the general First Amendment principles stated above.

We conclude that public figures and public officials may not recover for the tort of intentional infliction of emotional distress by reason of publications such as the one here at issue without showing in addition that the publication contains a false statement of fact which was made with "actual malice," i.e., with knowledge that the statement was false or with reckless disregard as to whether or not it was true. This is not merely a "blind application" of the New York Times standard, see Time, Inc. v. Hill, 385 U.S. 374, 390 (1967), it reflects our considered judgment that such a standard is necessary to give adequate "breathing space" to the freedoms protected by the First Amendment.

Here it is clear that respondent Falwell is a "public figure" for purposes of First Amendment law. The jury found against respondent on his libel claim when it decided that the Hustler ad parody could not "reasonably be understood as describing actual facts about [respondent] or actual events in which [he] participated." App. to Pet. for Cert. Cl. The Court of Appeals interpreted the jury's finding to be that the ad parody "was not reasonably believable," 797 F.2d, at 1278, and in accordance with our custom we accept this finding. Respondent is thus relegated to his claim for damages awarded by the jury for the intentional infliction of emotional distress by "outrageous" conduct. But for reasons heretofore stated this claim cannot, consistently with the First Amendment, form a basis for the award of damages when the conduct in question is the publication of a caricature such as the ad parody involved here. The judgment of the Court of Appeals is accordingly

Reversed.

JUSTICE KENNEDY took no part in the consideration or decision of this case.

JUSTICE WHITE, concurring in the judgment.

As I see it, the decision in New York Times v. Sullivan, 376 U.S. 254 (1964), has little to do with this case, for here the jury found that the ad contained no assertion of fact. But I agree with the Court that the judgment below, which penalized the publication of the parody, cannot be squared with the First Amendment.

Notes and Questions

1. Attempts at humor have resulted in a variety of suits against radio stations for intentional infliction of emotional distress. Some, like Falwell's suit, involve a potential loss of reputation and therefore are tied to libel litigation. In other cases, pranks are alleged to cause distress even though no loss of reputation is alleged.

A California case exemplifies actions against broadcasters for intentional infliction of emotional distress. A superior court in Los Angeles held for the defendant in Raye v. Letterman, 14 Med.L.Rptr. 2047 (Cal.Super.1987). David Letterman had said, "I saw the most terrifying commercial on television last night, featuring Martha Raye, actress, condom user." The court noted that Martha Raye is well known for a denture product commercial in which she is introduced as "Martha Raye, actress, denture wearer," and that a parody/satire of the line could not reasonably be understood as statement of fact and thus could not be defamatory.

4. A 1991 New York case provides a broadcast example of a situation that, like the Falwell ad parody, prompted a suit for defamation, invasion of privacy, and intentional infliction of emotional distress. Plaintiff Mark Glickman sued talk show host Howard Stern after the latter broadcast a Halloween television skit with the plaintiff's wife, Susan Glickman. Stern and other members of his staff and crew went to Bayside, Queens, wearing Halloween masks. Susan Glickman and a friend were driving by in Susan's automobile when they recognized Stern and said "hello." Stern asked if he could come back to Susan's house for a "rubdown," and she readily agreed. At the Glickman residence, she changed into a negligee, and she and another woman gave the men "rubdowns." During the taping someone handed Stern a framed wedding portrait of the Glickman's, and it was held up to the camera for a few seconds. Stern remarked, "Mark's a lucky dude, swear to God; you're a good-looking girl; swear to God; poor Mark." The taped skit was subsequently broadcast during a segment titled "trick or treat." Stern had said at the beginning of the telecast: "We went trick-or-treating and all I'm gonna say is that this is the best eleven minutes of tape that you'll ever see ... wait till you see this— this is a married woman!" The trial court held that the statements made during the broadcast could be considered gross or vulgar but, taken in context, could not be understood to be anything more than purely nonsensical entertainment and were therefore not defamatory. The court further held that the "newsworthiness" exemption to the state's law protecting people from appropriation of their names and likenesses for commercial purposes is not limited to "legitimate" news broadcasts, so the plaintiff could not prevail on his privacy claim. The court further held that he could not prevail on his intentional infliction of emotional distress claim because it was grounded on the same facts as his unsuccessful defamation claim. Glickman v. Stern, 19 Med. L.Rptr. 1769 (N.Y.Sup.Ct., N.Y.County, 1991).

Chapter XIII

PRIVACY

Defamation, which we discussed in the last chapter, and invasion of privacy, which we discuss in this one, are sometimes treated together in law courses as related rights to protect one's dignity. In defamation, we balance the right of freedom of expression against the right of individuals to protect their reputations. In privacy, we balance the right of freedom of expression against the right of individuals to be let alone. Although many people tend to think of privacy as a basic human right and many assume that it is constitutional, the word privacy never appears in the Constitution. Compared to defamation, privacy is a relatively new legal concept with many facets.

Concerns for privacy in the 1980s have been diverse—involving such varied issues as the dissemination of personal credit information via computerized systems, electronic eavesdropping, the protection of newsrooms from police searches, release of personal information about individuals by the government and a right to know what is in one's own academic records. Some of these issues we will address elsewhere in this book, because they are related to other topics; the protection of newsrooms from police searches, for example, is dealt with in Chapter XIV because the "privacy" of the newsroom is directly related to the confidentiality of journalists' sources and their notes. Other privacy issues are beyond the scope of this book.

In this chapter we will be concerned primarily with invasion of privacy as a tort—a civil wrong or injury. Although the recognition of privacy torts varies from state to state, scholars generally have recognized four different torts or branches of invasion of privacy. One of these relates to the newsgathering stage of the communications process: intruding on the plaintiff's physical solitude. It is akin to the tort of trespass. The other three torts or branches of invasion of privacy relate to the publication stage of the communications process. They are publication of embarrassing private (true) facts; putting the plaintiff in a false light in the public eye; and appropriation of another's name or likeness for commercial or trade purposes. Of the four branches, the "false-light" tort comes closest to the tort of defamation, because it is the only one that involves falsity.

Because of the similarities between defamation and false-light invasion of privacy, some of the traditional defenses in defamation are sometimes applicable to this branch of invasion of privacy—including truth. Truth is obviously not a defense for publication of embarrassing private facts, because the fact that an embarrassing publication is true just makes it all the more embarrassing. Because the applicability of defenses varies with the branch of invasion of privacy being considered, we shall touch on defenses at several different points in this chapter.

A. INTRUSION ON THE PLAINTIFF'S PHYSICAL SOLITUDE

As indicated above, intrusion on the plaintiff's physical solitude is the only one of the four branches of privacy that comes up in the context of *newsgathering* rather than in the context of dissemination. In the absence of any Supreme Court decision involving such an invasion of privacy by the mass media, we will look here at some cases decided by the lower courts as examples.

The major divisions of this branch of invasion of privacy reflect the type of consent problem involved. Within each subsection we consider the types of invasions that plaintiff may complain about. The most traditional are trespass (unpermitted entry) on land and theft of personal property. The claim is that the physical zone of privacy that surrounds each of us has been intruded upon—usually in an effort to obtain information that would otherwise not be available.

1. INTRUSIONS WITHOUT EXPRESS CONSENT

a. *Trespass*

For centuries, the act of intentionally entering the land of another without consent has made the entrant liable for trespass. The civil damages include any actual harm done to the property and some damages for the symbolic invasion of the owner's or occupier's legal interest. If accompanied by ill will or spite or a desire to harm the owner, perhaps punitive damages as well are awarded. Comparable rules apply to a person who legally enters land but then remains on it against the wishes of the owner or occupier of the land.

In one clear case, the plaintiff alleged that his wife had committed suicide during the day; that when he returned to the house that evening he discovered that the screen over the kitchen window had been cut and that a photograph of his wife that had been on a table in the living room that morning had been taken. Although the plaintiff failed to prove that the defendant's reporters had committed the trespass, the court indicated that the only problem in the case was one of identification. The trespass and theft could not be defended even if there had been great public interest in the photograph. Metter v. Los Angeles Examiner, 35 Cal.App.2d 304, 95 P.2d 491 (1939).

Sometimes reporters may claim they have authority to enter properties even though owners have not expressly consented. Two Florida cases present examples.

In Florida Publishing Co. v. Fletcher, 340 So.2d 914, 2 Med.L.Rptr. 1088 (Fla.1976), the plaintiff alleged that after she had left town on a trip, a fire broke out in her house that killed her 17–year–old daughter; that after the daughter's body was removed from the floor a silhouette was revealed; that defendant newspaper's photographer took a photograph of the silhouette; and that plaintiff first learned of the tragedy by reading the story in a newspaper and seeing the accompanying photographs. In her claim for trespass, the depositions revealed that police and fire officials, as was their standard practice, invited press photographers and reporters to enter the house; that the media representatives entered through an open door without objection; and that they entered quietly and did no damage to the property. The fire marshal wanted a clear picture of the silhouette to show that the body had been on the floor before the heat of the fire damaged the room. After the official took one picture, he ran out of film and asked the newspaper photographer to take pictures for the official investigation. He did so and also made copies for his own paper, which published them.

The defendant moved for summary judgment on the trespass claims. Affidavits from various government and media sources stated that entering private property and inviting the press in this type of situation was common practice. Plaintiff filed only her own affidavit and none from media or other experts. She conceded that it was proper for the police and fire officials to enter and also admitted that no one had objected to the entry of the press. The trial judge granted summary judgment because the affidavits "attest to the fact that it is common usage, custom, and practice for news media to enter private premises and homes to report on matters of public interest or a public event."

The Florida Supreme Court agreed that implied consent covered the case. Research showed that implied consent by custom and usage "do not rest upon the previous nonobjection to entry by the particular owner of the property in question but rest upon custom and practice generally." In addition to the fact that here the press entered in response to an express invitation from public officials, the court stressed that this was the first case presenting the question. "This, in itself, tends to indicate that the practice has been accepted by the general public since it is a widespread practice of longstanding." One judge dissented on jurisdictional grounds. The Supreme Court denied *certiorari*, 431 U.S. 930 (1977).

Compare Green Valley School, Inc. v. Cowles Florida Broadcasting, Inc., 327 So.2d 810 (Fla.App.1976). State officials planned a midnight raid, under a properly issued warrant, to search the premises of a controversial local private boarding school. The head of the party of 50 raiders invited reporters and photographers from several local media organizations to accompany the party. The defendant television station presented an extensive report of the raid on the evening news the following night, suggesting that the raid had turned up evidence of mistreatment of the students, rampant sexual misbehavior and use of drugs. The school sued the station for defamation and trespass.

The trial judge granted summary judgment to the station on the trespass claim. The court of appeals reversed, addressing the question entirely in the following passage.

> To uphold appellees' assertion that their entry upon appellant's property at the time, manner, and circumstances as reflected by this record was as a *matter of law* sanctioned by "the request of and with the consent of the State Attorney" and with the "common usage and custom in Florida" could well bring to the citizenry of this state the hobnail boots of a Nazi stormtrooper equipped with glaring lights invading a couple's bedroom at midnight with the wife hovering in her nightgown in an attempt to shield herself from the scanning TV camera. In this jurisdiction, a law enforcement officer is not as a *matter of law* endowed with the right or authority to invite people of his choosing to invade private property and participate in a midnight raid of the premises.

On the same day that it decided *Fletcher,* the Florida Supreme Court dismissed an appeal in the Green Valley case, indicating that it found no conflict between the results in the two cases. Can they be reconciled?

As soon as we move from private residential property to premises that are usually open to the public for some purpose, the questions get more difficult.

In Le Mistral, Inc. v. Columbia Broadcasting System, 61 A.D.2d 491, 402 N.Y.S.2d 815, 3 Med.L.Rptr. 1913 (1978), CBS, as owner and operator of WCBS–TV in New York City, directed reporter Rich and a camera crew to visit restaurants that had been cited for health code variations. Plaintiff was on the list. The crew entered plaintiff's restaurant with cameras "rolling" and using bright lights that were necessary to get the pictures. The jury found CBS liable for trespass and awarded plaintiff $1,200 in compensatory damages and $250,000 in punitive damages. After the verdict (in a passage approved on appeal), the trial judge stated:

> The instructions given to the crew, whether specific to this event or as standing operating procedure, were to avoid seeking an appointment or permission to enter any of the premises where a story was sought, but to enter unannounced catching the occupants by surprise; "with cameras rolling" in the words of CBS' principal witness, Rich. From the evidence the jury was entitled to conclude that following this procedure the defendant's employees burst into plaintiff's restaurant in noisy and obtrusive fashion and following the loud commands of the reporter, Rich, to photograph the patrons dining, turned their lights and camera upon the dining room. Consternation, the jury was informed, followed. Patrons waiting to be seated left the restaurant. Others, who had finished eating, left without waiting for their checks. Still others hid their faces behind napkins or table cloths or hid themselves beneath tables. (The reluctance of the plaintiff's clientele to be video taped was

never explained, and need not be. Patronizing a restaurant does not carry with it an obligation to appear on television). [The] president of the plaintiff and manager of its operations, refused to be interviewed, and as the camera continued to "roll" he pushed the protesting Miss Rich and her crew from the premises. All told, the CBS personnel were in the restaurant not more than ten minutes, perhaps as little as one minute, depending on the testimony the jury chose to credit. The jury by its verdict clearly found the defendant guilty of trespass and from the admissions of CBS' own employees they were guilty of trespass. The witness Rich sought to justify her crew's entry into the restaurant by calling it, on a number of occasions, a "place of public accommodation", but, as she acknowledges, they did not seek to avail themselves of the plaintiff's "accommodation"; they had no intention of purchasing food or drink.

The trial judge upheld the determination of liability but set aside both damage awards because he had erroneously barred a defense witness from testifying as to CBS's motive and purpose in entering the premises. On appeal, the court held that its review of the record "demonstrates an adequate basis to justify the compensatory damage award rendered by the jury and, accordingly, such award must stand." As to punitive damages, the court agreed that the judge had erred in excluding the testimony because all "circumstances immediately connected with the transaction tending to exhibit or explain the motive of the defendant are admissible." One judge thought it clear that the defendants were "not motivated by actual malice or such an intentional disregard of plaintiff's rights as would justify the imposition of punitive damages. [ ] The defendant was merely pursuing a newsworthy item in the overly aggressive but good faith manner that characterizes the operation of the news media today. . . . In this sensitive and evolving First Amendment area, I would permit this precedent-setting opinion to stand as a warning to all newsgatherers that future trespasses may well be met with an award of punitive damages."

CBS, dissatisfied with the decision, sought to appeal to New York's highest court to argue that no trespass had been committed and also that, in any event, punitive damages were improper. That court ultimately refused to hear the case for jurisdictional reasons.

The case is complicated by the disruptive presence of the television cameras. If newspaper reporters had entered the restaurant, would they have been trespassers from the moment they entered—or only from the moment they refused to leave? If, while the newspaper reporters were leaving, they continued watching the scene and making mental notes of what they saw, would that be improper? If the court is suggesting that the premises were open only to those seriously considering purchasing food or drink, why should it matter whether the entry was disruptive?

Under traditional law, the owner could prevent entry by posting a notice on the front door stating that no reporters are permitted on the premises. But today it is possible that the courts of New York would develop a special rule allowing reporters to enter "newsworthy" premises—at least so long as they are not disruptive. Further, the courts might develop some First Amendment privilege to allow reporters to enter certain types of "private" premises—at least until they are explicitly asked to leave. All of this is most unclear. See Watkins, Private Property vs. Reporter Rights—A Problem in Newsgathering. 54 Journ.Q. 690 (1977).

In order for plaintiffs to claim damages for trespass or theft of property, they must own or occupy the property. If the property has been abandoned—the former owners have indicated a desire to relinquish their control over it—then no civil damages can be brought. An example of this situation may have occurred in 1975 when it was revealed that a reporter had been sifting through the garbage cans outside the house of Secretary of State Henry Kissinger. A reporter who went on the land to reach the garbage cans would have been a trespasser. If the cans were on the public sidewalk, the only claim would be interference with personal property—the garbage. But if, as seems likely, the property has been abandoned, no civil liability would be possible. Commenting on the episode in an editorial, *Editor & Publisher* (July 19, 1975 at 6) attacked the practice: "Pawing through someone else's garbage is a revolting exercise and doing it in the name of journalism makes it none the less so." Do you agree?

b. Other Intrusions Without Consent

We turn now to alleged invasions of privacy that do not fit into the trespass mold. These involve issues of how far persons may use cameras or high-technology equipment to obtain information about a subject; wiretapping; and secretly recording conversations to which the person is a party.

Galella v. Onassis, 487 F.2d 986, 1 Med.L.Rptr. 2425 (2d Cir.1973), involved aggressive efforts by a "paparazzo" photographer to obtain photographs of the widow and children of President John Kennedy. Galella brought his power boat close to Mrs. Onassis as she was swimming, jumped out of bushes as she was walking past, jumped into her son's path to take a photograph of him riding his bicycle, and invaded the children's private schools. Those acts that reasonably put the subject in fear of personal safety would create tort liability under longstanding rules. But those that involved annoyance presented harder questions.

Mrs. Onassis claimed that when she went through the streets to go shopping or to visit a friend, or walked alone in Central Park, she was engaged in private activities that should not be the subject of any unwanted photography. The court disagreed. Mrs. Onassis was "a public figure and thus subject to news coverage" although the First

Amendment provided no "wall of immunity protecting newsmen" from liability for torts committed while gathering news. The court balanced Mrs. Onassis's concern about intrusion with the legitimate interests of photography by ordering Galella to stay 25 feet from Mrs. Onassis at all times; not to block her movement in public places; and not to do "any act foreseeably or reasonably calculated" to place Mrs. Onassis in jeopardy or frighten her. Any further restriction on his taking and selling photographs of her would be improper.

Galella was subsequently charged with criminal contempt for violating the order, but he avoided paying a $120,000 fine for contempt by agreeing not to take any more pictures of Mrs. Onassis.

In 1979 a TV camera crew trailed a man as he was trying to pay a ransom to persons who had kidnapped his wife. Despite his pleas, the crew followed the man, apparently along public ways. The episode attracted much press discussion after the FBI said the action had "put that woman's life in danger." An editorial in *Editor & Publisher*, July 28, 1979 at 6, asserted that although the TV crew might have considered its actions "enterprising reporting . . . it was more like sheer stupidity. . . . It is this sort of arrogance and brashness that gets media in trouble with the public."

After the woman was released, the couple sued the station for endangering the woman's life. Since no harm actually occurred in the case the suit might be difficult. Should the husband be able to sue for mental anguish he suffered as a result of the crew's actions? Criminal liability might be possible if it was shown that the crew learned of the man's movements by making unauthorized interceptions of messages on a nonbroadcast frequency in violation of what was then § 605 of the Communications Act (now § 705), 47 U.S.C.A. § 605. Should the law impose a sanction against reporters whose gathering efforts in fact lead to harm because kidnappers panic or get angry because their instructions apparently are not being followed?

Where solitude is invaded, the courts speak of the subject's reasonable expectations of privacy as the guide to available protection. Thus, one who leaves his curtains open, knowing that persons in the building across the street can look inside his apartment, can claim no reasonable expectation of privacy. But if the only vantage point from which the inside of the apartment can be seen is a hilltop two miles away, a court might well find that a reporter who set up a powerful telescope on that hill and looked through the open window has invaded privacy.

Similarly, a person inside a dwelling can make no reasonable claim of invasion of privacy if he shouts at his spouse and is overheard by others outside. But if he speaks in a normal or hushed voice—and is overheard because a highly sensitive microphone in the next apartment or across the street has picked up the communication, a court would probably find an invasion.

Wiretapping and other forms of intercepting messages frequently have been involved in litigation. For a thorough discussion of the issue, see Middleton, "Journalists and Tape Recorders: Does Participant Monitoring Invade Privacy?" 2 Comm/Ent L.J. 287 (Winter 1979–80). Although some early cases did impose tort liability in these cases, the major development occurred when Congress passed The Omnibus Crime Control and Safe Streets Act of 1968, 18 U.S.C.A. §§ 2510–2520. The basic provision subjects to criminal liability "any person" who without a warrant "willfully intercepts" any "wire or oral communication." Section 2520 provides that violators are liable for compensatory and punitive damages. Some exclusions apply, but none specially to reporters.

Revisions in 18 U.S.C.A. §§ 2510–2520 were made in 1986, in the Electronic Communications Privacy Act. Section 2511 now provides, in part, that any person who, unless authorized by one or both parties to the communication, intentionally intercepts, uses or discloses any "wire, oral, or electronic communication" is subject to punishment.

The Electronic Communications Act also prohibits unauthorized interception of network satellite feeds—specifically news and sports backhauls. The legislation reaffirmed existing prohibitions against interception of scrambled broadcast signals. The House accepted the Senate version of the bill, under which government can seek an injunction for a first offense, and repeat offenders can be fined up to $500. For intentional or malicious interference with communications and weather satellites, possible penalties are prison terms up to 10 years and fines up to $250,000.

Two television cases exemplify litigation of the 1980s. In one, a woman who was alleged to have traded sexual favors for a light sentence by an Ohio judge agreed to be interviewed by ABC in her home, but she refused to appear on camera. The network made surreptitious video and voice recordings, and she sued. Although the court held that there was no criminal or tortious purpose, it held that the plaintiff was entitled to try to prove in court that ABC intended to injure her. Boddie v. American Broadcasting Companies, Inc., 731 F.2d 333, 10 Med.L.Rptr. 1923 (6th Cir.1984). In the other, ABC had surreptitiously recorded a meeting between congressional investigators and a cancer insurance salesman—with the consent of the investigators. The court ruled that ABC must show that its *only* purpose was to aid Congress or that it must demonstrate that it had no injurious purpose in secretly recording the encounter. Benford v. American Broadcasting Companies, Inc., 502 F.Supp. 1159, 6 Med.L.Rptr. 2489 (D.Md.1980), affirmed 661 F.2d 917 (4th Cir.1981), certiorari denied 454 U.S. 1060 (1981). For discussion of such problems, see Spellman, "Tort Liability of the News Media for Surreptitious Recording," Journalism Quarterly, Summer 1985 at 289.

In Ribas v. Clark, 38 Cal.3d 355, 212 Cal.Rptr. 143, 696 P.2d 637 (1985), a woman with marital difficulties had a friend listen in on a telephone call with her husband; the court awarded no common law damages, but there was a statutory penalty. The court quoted a law review comment:

> There is a qualitative as well as a quantitative difference between secondhand repetition by the listener and simultaneous dissemination to a second auditor, whether that auditor be a tape recorder or a third party. In the former situation the speaker retains control over the extent of his immediate audience. Even though that audience may republish his words, it will be done secondhand, after the fact, probably not in entirety, and the impact will depend upon the credibility of the teller. Where electronic monitoring is involved, however, the speaker is deprived of the right to control the extent of his own firsthand dissemination. . . . In this regard participant monitoring closely resembles third-party surveillance; both practices deny the speaker a most important aspect of privacy of communication—the right to control the extent of first instance dissemination of his statements.

Florida has a statute that reaches participant monitoring by barring persons "not acting under color of law" from intercepting a wire or oral communication unless all parties to the communication had given their prior consent. An important lawsuit arose from a general attack on the statute by reporters who claimed that the use of concealed recording equipment was essential to investigative reporting for three reasons: it aided accuracy of reporting; persons being interviewed would not be candid if they knew they were being recorded; and the recording provided corroboration in case of suit for defamation.

The Florida Supreme Court upheld the statute's constitutionality. The statute allows "each party to a conversation to have an expectation of privacy from interception by another party to the conversation. It does not exclude any source from the press, intrude upon the activities of the news media in contacting sources, prevent the parties to the communication from consenting to the recording, or restrict the publication of any information gained from the communication. First Amendment rights do not include a constitutional right to corroborate news gathering activities when the legislature has statutorily recognized the private rights of individuals."

In response to the argument that secret recording may be the only way to get credible information about crime, the court stated that protection against intrusion might protect even a person "reasonably suspected of committing a crime." Shevin v. Sunbeam Television Corp., 351 So.2d 723, 3 Med.L.Rptr. 1312 (Fla.1977).

Based on the briefs and without argument, the Supreme Court dismissed the appeal by the press for want of a substantial federal question, 435 U.S. 920 (1978). Three justices dissented.

The Florida court had relied to some extent on the case of Dietemann v. Time, Inc., 449 F.2d 245, 1 Med.L.Rptr. 2417 (9th Cir.1971). In that case, two reporters obtained access to plaintiff's home to find out whether he was a medical quack. While plaintiff was diagnosing the alleged ailment of one reporter, the other secretly took photographs with a hidden camera. The entire conversation was transmitted to confederates outside by means of a transmitter hidden in one reporter's purse. In this part of the case, the court concluded that California would impose liability for invasion of privacy:

> [One who invites others to his home] does not and should not be required to take the risk that what is heard and seen will be transmitted by photograph or recording, or in our modern world, in full living color and hi-fi to the public at large or to any segment of it that the visitor may select. A different rule could have a most pernicious effect upon the dignity of man and it would surely lead to guarded conversations and conduct where candor is most valued, e.g., in the case of doctors and lawyers.

> The defendant claims that the First Amendment immunizes it from liability for invading plaintiff's den with a hidden camera and its concealed electronic instruments because its employees were gathering news and its instrumentalities "are indispensable tools of investigative reporting." We agree that newsgathering is an integral part of news dissemination. We strongly disagree, however, that the hidden mechanical contrivances are "indispensable tools" of newsgathering. Investigative reporting is an ancient art; its successful practice long antecedes the invention of miniature cameras and electronic devices. The First Amendment has never been construed to accord newsmen immunity from torts or crimes committed during the course of newsgathering. The First Amendment is not a license to trespass, to steal, or to intrude by electronic means in the precincts of another's home or office. It does not become such a license simply because the person subjected to the intrusion is reasonably suspected of committing a crime.

> Defendant relies upon the line of cases commencing with New York Times Co. v. Sullivan, 376 U.S. 254 (1964) . . . to sustain its contentions that (1) publication of news, however tortiously gathered, insulates defendant from liability for the antecedent tort.
> . . .

> As we previously observed, publication is not an essential element of plaintiff's cause of action. Moreover, it is not the foundation for the invocation of a privilege. Privilege concepts developed in defamation cases and to some extent in privacy actions in which publication is an essential component are not relevant in determining liability for intrusion conduct antedating publication. [ ] Nothing in *New York Times* or its progeny suggests anything to the contrary. Indeed, the Court strongly indicates that there is no First Amendment interest in protecting news media from calculated misdeeds. [ ]

2. CONSENT HAS BEEN OBTAINED

We turn now to cases in which the reporter contends that what might otherwise be a tort is not because the plaintiff consented to the conduct in question. The basic legal principle is not in doubt. Occasionally, the cases involve such neat situations as a plaintiff who signs a written consent. Usually, the cases are more complex.

In Cassidy v. American Broadcasting Companies, Inc., 60 Ill.App.3d 831, 17 Ill.Dec. 936, 377 N.E.2d 126, 3 Med.L.Rptr. 2449 (1978), an undercover policeman was sent to a massage parlor. After paying $30 he was escorted to a room to watch "de-luxe lingerie modeling." On entering the warm room he observed camera lights. He asked, "What are we on, TV?" The model replied, "Yes, we're making a movie." As plaintiff reclined on the bed watching the model change her lingerie several times, he made suggestive remarks and advances. He then arrested the model for solicitation. The entire scene was in fact being photographed from an adjacent room by a local television station through a two-way mirror. The manager of the parlor had asked the defendant to film the episode to show that police were harassing him.

Plaintiff's suit failed because, among other reasons, the plaintiff apparently did not intend his conduct to be private because he knew that someone might be making a movie of his conduct. He testified his actions were in the line of duty as an officer and that if the model wished to sell him a completed film he would use it as evidence in his investigation. Plaintiff had no expectation of privacy.

Although plaintiff had not explicitly consented to being filmed, his conduct after being informed that a film was being made amounted to consent. But should the same rule apply if a jury could reasonably find that the model made her statement jokingly or sardonically so that a reasonable person in plaintiff's position would not have believed what she said?

The most common problems reporters face in consent cases appear to involve consents that are obtained by some type of misrepresentation. Since reporters often investigate alleged misdeeds they are unlikely to get consent to do interviews, go to certain places or record interviews if they identify themselves as reporters. In such cases, what is the role of consent?

In *Dietemann*, the reporters posed as a couple seeking medical advice from the plaintiff, who lived a quiet life and did not advertise or even have a telephone. They went to his gate and rang the bell. When plaintiff appeared, the reporters falsely said that they had been sent by a certain person and wanted to see plaintiff because the female visitor had a lump in her breast that she wanted diagnosed. Plaintiff admitted the pair to his den and made his diagnosis. On this part of the case the court observed:

Plaintiff's den was a sphere from which he could reasonably expect to exclude eavesdropping newsmen. He invited two of defendant's employees to the den. One who invites another to his home or office takes a risk that the visitor may not be what he seems, and that the visitor may repeat all he hears and observes when he leaves. But he does not and should not be required to take the risk that what is heard and seen will be transmitted by photograph or recording. . . .

Why does plaintiff take the risk that a visitor may not be who he claims to be, or that a visitor may repeat what he hears inside, but not take the risk that secret recordings and photographs are being made? Is it that the plaintiff does in fact intend to deal with the persons who are standing before him—whatever names they give or whatever reasons they give for coming?

Courts generally rule that consent to enter one section of land does not authorize entering any other part; and that consent to do one thing, such as reading the gas meter, does not authorize removal of the gas meter. In these cases, it is apparent that the actor has exceeded the consent. In *Dietemann,* however, the plaintiff gave consent to enter the land and come to the den—and that is precisely what the reporters did. His misunderstanding about identity did not lead him to consent to one thing but to be hit with another. (A person who wants legal protection against someone who is told a secret and then reveals it may obtain it by entering into a contract in which the recipient makes legally enforceable promises about his future behavior.)

If misrepresenting identity doesn't raise major legal problems, it does raise ethical questions that are much discussed among journalists. The matter is reviewed at length in Zimmerman, "By Any Other Name . . .," *Washington Journalism Review* (Nov./Dec. 1979) at 32.

The matter received much attention in 1979 when the Pulitzer prize for local investigative reporting was denied to a newspaper that uncovered massive official corruption after it bought and ran a bar in Chicago under a false name. At about the same time, a reporter posed as a Congressman to obtain a seat at the signing of the Egyptian–Israeli peace treaty. The reporter said that the episode involved telling "only one lie." *Editor & Publisher,* June 9, 1979 at 6, responded, "But *how many lies* are too many? Are we getting back to the no-holds-barred philosophy that the story should be gotten at any cost?" Noting that the press complains loudly when someone impersonates a newsman, the editorial continued, "We believe that newsmen's impersonations of others in order to get a story [are] equally damaging to their believability and should be scrupulously avoided." Some have suggested that if reporters will lie to get a story, readers may believe that they would also lie in writing the story if they thought the matter important enough.

The argument the other way, of course, stresses that uncovering crime or other misbehavior is very hard—that it would have been virtually impossible to have demonstrated the corruption in Chicago without setting up the fake business. A recent example involved a reporter who got a job as a guard at the Three Mile Island nuclear plant after the malfunctioning and then took photographs while on the job. His goal was to show how easy it was to get a job—his asserted background and references were never checked—and to show how lax security was inside the plant. Are there other ways to obtain this information? How important is it to obtain the information? Does such behavior damage the credibility of the press?

For a former *New York Times* reporter's analysis of some of these ethical issues, see T. Goldstein, *News At Any Cost: How Journalists Compromise Their Ethics to Shape the News*, 1985.

Although civil actions by persons deceived in these cases may not be likely, some of the cases may well involve potential criminal liability—particularly cases involving impersonation of government officials or lying to government officials.

Should different principles apply if reporters knowingly accept material improperly obtained by others? In one case, aides to a United States Senator removed numerous documents from his files, copied them and passed the copies to columnists who knew how they had been obtained. The court held that the columnists had committed no tort:

> If we were to hold appellants liable for invasion of privacy on these facts, we would establish the proposition that no one who receives information from an intruder, knowing it has been obtained by improper intrusion, is guilty of a tort. In an untried and developing area of tort law, we are not prepared to go so far. A person approached by an eavesdropper with an offer to share in the information gathered through the eavesdropping would perhaps play the nobler part should he spurn the offer and shut his ears. However, it seems to us that at this point it would place too great a strain on human weakness to hold one liable in damages who merely succumbs to temptation and listens. Pearson v. Dodd, 410 F.2d 701 (D.C.Cir.) certiorari denied 395 U.S. 947 (1969).

Should the result change if a reporter had said to the aide "I'd sure love to see your file on" a particular matter—and three days later the aide presented the file?

Defenses. As discussed above, consent (if not exceeded) can be a defense for a suit for an intrusion on physical solitude. Such defamation defenses as truth and absence of malice have no relevance because neither falsity nor its cause is part of an intrusion suit. It should be noted specifically that newsworthiness is *not* a defense for intrusion: the fact that the public wants news is no justification for violating another's rights in order to obtain it.

3.　Other Civil Liability

A New York case, Ramirez v. Time, 134 A.D.2d 970, 521 N.Y.S.2d 355, 12 Med.L.Rptr. 2230 (1987) illustrates a possibility of civil liability for misconduct in newsgathering beyond the liability for intrusion on a plaintiff's physical solitude. Dr. Janice Runkle, the veterinarian at Belmont Park raceway, mysteriously disappeared in New York on or about July 27, 1981, and her body was found a few days later in Illinois. A *Time* magazine reporter left a false message on her answering machine to the effect that he had an eyewitness who had seen her alive on July 28, 1981.

Relying on the reporter's message, representatives of Dr. Runkle's estate went to the reporter's office in the Time–Life Building in New York City and talked to him for several hours—only to discover near the end of the discussions that the message was apparently nothing but a ruse.

Dr. Runkle's estate sued the magazine and reporter for defamation and for fraud, despite the fact that New York law permits no recovery for defamation of the dead. Defendants moved for dismissal. New York law requires the following elements in a cause of action for fraud: representation of a material existing fact, falsity, scienter, deception and injury, as well as detrimental reliance by the party to whom the misrepresentation was made. Appellate court held that there was no significant injury to the plaintiff directly springing from the misrepresentation and granted the motion to dismiss.

Ramirez is not, of course, a privacy case, but it does illustrate the possibility of other civil actions against journalists resulting from misconduct during newsgathering.

4.　Criminal Liability

At several points during the foregoing discussion of civil liability, we have had occasion to touch on related criminal sanctions. In this section we draw together the likely sources of criminal liability that may confront newsgatherers.

At the outset, federal and state governments have statutes punishing such acts as the theft of government property and the concealment or removal of official records and documents. See, e.g., 18 U.S.C.A. §§ 641, 2071. In addition, conspiracy to commit criminal acts is also a crime. Other statutes directly relate to property or information in specific areas, such as national security or nuclear energy. Knowingly receiving stolen property may also be criminal even though the recipient had nothing to do with the original theft.

Other crimes involving direct harm to government may include impersonating an officer not obeying a lawful order of a police officer or bribing a government employee. The latter was involved when a news photographer paid a prison guard to take secret photographs of the accused killer known as "Son of Sam."

The government also uses criminal legislation to support the civil law in protecting individual property and privacy. We have seen some in operation already, such as the criminal punishment for intercepting communications whether by wiretapping or otherwise. Breaking into a home and stealing a photograph from the table would involve several criminal offenses as well as tort liability. Other protections are available. In one episode, a publisher was charged with extortion by allegedly threatening to write untrue stories about people in the community unless they supplied information for forthcoming stories or agreed to advertise in the paper.

In one case, reporters covering a demonstration at a construction site for a nuclear plant in Oklahoma were convicted of trespassing on private property. The utility, Public Service Company of Oklahoma (PSO), did not want extensive coverage of the marchers—as had occurred at an earlier demonstration. This time, PSO warned all reporters that they would be arrested if they entered the fenced property at any point not permitted by PSO. PSO then set up a viewing area that reporters might use on its otherwise closed property. It was not clear in advance whether the demonstration or any confrontation would be visible from that point.

Several reporters used the viewing area. Others followed the demonstrators and entered the land when the demonstrators went through the fence. These reporters were the ones convicted of trespass. Each was fined $25.

The Oklahoma Court of Criminal Appeals held that the First Amendment does not shield newspersons from state criminal prosecution in their newsgathering function and affirmed the convictions. Stahl v. State, 665 P.2d 839, 9 Med.L.Rptr. 1945 (Okl.Crim.1983), certiorari denied 464 U.S. 1069 (1984).

B. INVASION OF PRIVACY BY PUBLICATION

As indicated above, there are several ways the media may invade privacy through the publication or dissemination of information rather than through its gathering.

The idea that a right of privacy from the media should be legally protected can be traced to a law review article by Louis D. Brandeis and his law partner, Samuel D. Warren, The Right to Privacy, 4 Harv. L.Rev. 193 (1890), often considered the most influential law review article ever published. The authors, reacting to the editorial practices of Boston newspapers, made clear their concerns:

> The press is overstepping in every direction the obvious bounds of propriety and of decency. Gossip is no longer the resource of the idle and of the vicious, but has become a trade, which is pursued with industry as well as effrontery. To satisfy a prurient taste the details of sexual relations are spread broadcast in the columns of the daily papers. To occupy the indolent, column upon column is

filled with idle gossip, which can only be procured by intrusion upon the domestic circle.

Working with a variety of rather remote precedents from other areas of law, the authors developed an argument that courts should recognize an action for invasion of privacy by media publication.

The theory was rejected in the first major case to consider it. In Roberson v. Rochester Folding Box Co., 171 N.Y. 538, 64 N.E. 442 (1902), the defendants, a flour company and a box company, obtained a good likeness of the plaintiff, a pretty girl, and reproduced it on their advertising posters. Plaintiff said she was humiliated and suffered great distress. The court, 4–3, rejected a common law privacy action on grounds that suggested concern about innovating after so many centuries; an inability to see how the doctrine, once accepted, could be judicially limited to appropriate situations; and skepticism about finding liability for behavior that might actually please some potential "victims." The Warren and Brandeis article was discussed at length, but the court concluded that the precedents relied upon were too remote to sustain the proposed rights.

The outcry was immediate. At its next session, the New York legislature created a statutory right of privacy (New York Civil Rights Law, §§ 50 and 51). The basic provision was that "a person, firm or corporation that uses for advertising purposes, or the purposes of trade, the name, portrait or picture of any living person without having first obtained the written consent of such person, or if a minor or his or her parent or guardian, is guilty of a misdemeanor." The other section provided for an injunction and created an action for compensatory and punitive damages. The meaning of "advertising purposes" was clear, but the phrase "purposes of trade" was not self-explanatory. Eventually it came to mean that an accurate story carried as editorial (non-advertising) content did not violate the statute.

Other states, perhaps learning from the New York experience, slowly began to develop a common law right to privacy that was not influenced by statutory language and not limited to advertising invasions. In addition to an action for commercial use of one's name, the courts also developed actions for truthful uses of plaintiff's name that were thought to be outside the areas of legitimate public concern. The action for invasion of privacy by publication of true editorial material began to take hold during the 1920s and early 1930s.

Courts in the late 1930s became more attentive to the Supreme Court's expanding protection of expression. Operating on a common-law level, they tended to expand protection for the media by taking a narrow view of what were legitimately private areas.

For the embarrassing private facts tort, the courts allowed a defense of newsworthiness to be expanded, because they were reluctant to impose normative standards of what should be newsworthy. Instead, they leaned toward a descriptive definition of newsworthiness that protected whatever editors had decided would interest their readers.

By the 1960s some doubted whether the action for invasion of privacy had any remaining vitality.

It was precisely, during the last part of the 1960s and the beginning of the 1970s, however, that privacy as a general social value was perceived to be threatened in different ways by the encroachment of computers, data banks and electronic devices, as well as the media. The concept of privacy also expanded as the Supreme Court dealt with birth control, abortion and other problems in the context of a right of privacy. This was bound to have an impact on the media aspects of privacy as well.

One result of the new thinking was to broaden the area of privacy protection.

1. PUTTING THE PLAINTIFF IN A FALSE LIGHT

As indicated earlier, the tort of putting the plaintiff in a false light in the public eye is the privacy tort closest to defamation, because both involve publication of falsity. There is a critical difference between the two, however: the publication that results in a successful defamation action is *harmful* as well as false. The publication that results in a successful false light invasion of privacy action may not be harmful in the sense of harming the plaintiff's reputation. It may be just the opposite—a publication that falsely portrays the plaintiff to be better than he is in real life (i.e., a hero) or simply *different* than he is in real life.

In one example, a group used the plaintiff's name without authorization on a petition to the governor to veto a bill. Although falsely stating that plaintiff had signed the petition would not be defamatory, the court found the situation actionable because it cast plaintiff in a false light.

The first two Supreme Court decisions involving alleged invasions of privacy by the mass media both happened to be false light cases. They were Time, Inc. v. Hill, 385 U.S. 374, 1 Med.L.Rptr. 1791 (1967) and Cantrell v. Forest City Publishing Co., 419 U.S. 245, 1 Med.L.Rptr. 1815 (1974).

In 1952 James Hill and his family were held hostage in their Pennsylvania home for 19 hours by escaped convicts who apparently treated them decently. The incident received nationwide coverage. Thereafter the Hills moved to Connecticut, sought seclusion, and refused to make public appearances. A novel—*The Desperate Hours*—modeled partially on the event was published the following year. In 1955 *Life* magazine in a short article announced that a play and motion picture were being made from the novel, which they said was "inspired" by the Hill episode. The play, "a heartstopping account of how a family rose to heroism in a crisis," would enable the public to see the Hill story "re-enacted." Photographs showed actors performing scenes from the play at the house at which the original events had occurred.

The Hills claimed the story was inaccurate because the novel and play showed convicts committing violence on the father and uttering a "verbal sexual insult" at the daughter.

Suit was brought under the New York statute requiring plaintiff to show the article was being used for advertising purposes or purposes of trade. A truthful article, no matter how unpleasant for the Hills, would not have been actionable. The state courts had previously indicated that falsity would show that the article was really for the purposes of trade and not for public enlightenment. The state courts allowed recovery after lengthy litigation.

The Supreme Court, in a plurality opinion, decided that the privilege to comment on matters of public interest had constitutional protection and could not be lost by the introduction of falsity unless actual malice could be proved. Thus, the Hill family lost.

The decision should be viewed in the context of what was happening in the court's defamation decisions in the same period. This was only three years after the Court had decided, in *New York Times*, p. 623, *supra*, that public officials would be required to prove actual malice in defamation cases. By 1967 thinking, the members of the Hill family were public figures—having become so involuntarily as the result of having been part of a newsworthy event. And 1967 was the same year in which the Court extended the actual malice rule of *New York Times* to public figures like Wally Butts and former Army Gen. Edwin Walker.

One should not miss the irony that the attorney who represented the Hill family before the Supreme Court was a man with a strong sense of privacy and considerable distaste for the media: then former Vice President, not-yet-President Richard M. Nixon.

The next false-light privacy case decided by the Supreme Court was Cantrell v. Forest City Publishing Co. A reporter for *The Cleveland Plain Dealer* had written a prize-winning story about a bridge collapse that had killed 44 people, including Melvin Cantrell. Some months later the reporter returned to the Cantrell home for a follow-up on how the family coped with the disaster. Although Mrs. Cantrell was not present, her children were. The reporter's story failed to make clear that Mrs. Cantrell had been absent, and a reader presumably would have concluded just the opposite from the story, which said she "will talk neither about what happened nor about how they are doing. She wears the same mask of non-expression she wore at the funeral. She is a proud woman. Her world has changed. She says that after it happened, the people in town offered to help them out with money and they refused to take it." The family sought damages on a false-light privacy theory.

The Court, in an opinion by Justice Stewart, held that the First Amendment did not protect deliberate or reckless falsity. He also observed that because the actual malice standard was met in this case, it was not an appropriate case in which to consider the hypothetical question of whether private figure plaintiffs like the Cantrells *had* to prove actual malice or might merely be asked to prove simple negligence. As Justice Stewart put it, it was not an appropriate occasion to "consider whether a State may constitutionally apply a more relaxed standard of liability for a publisher . . . of false statements injurious to a private individual under a false-light theory of privacy, or whether the constitutional standard announced in Time, Inc. v. Hill applies to all false-light cases."

Justice Douglas was the sole dissenter in *Cantrell*: "Those who write the current news seldom have the objective, dispassionate point of view—or the time—of scientific analysts. They deal in fast-moving events and the need for 'spot reporting.' . . . [I]n matters of public import such as the present news reporting, there must be freedom from damages lest the press be frightened into playing a more ignoble role than the Framers visualized."

The stories that resulted in the *Cantrell* and *Hill* cases purported to tell the truth. A different sort of false light problem arises in the context of "docudramas," which openly mix fact and fiction. Actress Elizabeth Taylor held a nationally-publicized news conference to say she would sue ABC if it dared to broadcast a docudrama based on her life. The network cancelled the docudrama.

However, in Hicks v. Casablanca Records, 464 F.Supp. 426 (S.D.N.Y.1978), a motion picture and novel about an incident in the life of mystery-writer Agatha Christie was held to be protected under the First Amendment so long as it was not presented to be taken as true.

A particular problem for broadcasters is contextual false light, in which something truthful becomes misleading because of the context in which it is used. Broadcasters must be especially careful of juxtaposing pictures with unrelated audio and of using file footage which viewers may mistake as current.

See p. 681, *supra,* for a discussion of the *Hustler* case, in which Rev. Jerry Falwell sued for libel, invasion of privacy and intentional infliction of emotional distress.

Defenses. Many of the same defenses that can be used by media defendants in defamation cases might also be argued to have application in a false-light privacy case. *Truth* would be a strong defense. Qualified privilege might be offered as a defense if one had quoted accurately from a record of an official proceeding. Privileged criticism or fair comment might work as a defense if the publication alleged to put the plaintiff in a false light was actually a statement of opinion rather than a statement of fact. If the plaintiff is a public official or public figure, absence of malice could be a strong defense. To a large extent, the applicability of the libel defenses in privacy cases is yet to be determined in the courts and there would be special problems in applying some of those to contextual false light.

2. Publication of Embarrassing Private Facts

Publication of embarrassing private facts (which we address in this section) and appropriation of another's name or likeness for commercial or trade purposes (which we address in the next section) are the two branches of invasion of privacy that have to do with truthful publication—either by electronic media or by print—that interferes with someone's right to be let alone. Redundant though it may seem, it may be helpful to think of the former as publication of embarrassing private *true* facts.

a. Categories

The cases of publication of embarrassing private facts fall into a small number of categories—those dealing with sexual matters, commission of crime, poverty, idiosyncratic qualities and other embarrassing stories.

The important point is not whether the state cases are decided "correctly." The area is so new and unformed that the cases do not fit into a neat pattern—except that plaintiffs rarely win. The results are given in capsule form at the end of each case, without reasons, simply to satisfy curiosity—not to suggest the proper resolution. Below, we will explore approaches to this very troublesome area. The law aside, prospective reporters and news directors should consider how the facts of each story should be handled.

Sexual Matters. 1. In a study of official misconduct at a county home, a newspaper reported that among the misconduct was the involuntary sterilization of a named 18–year–old young woman seven years earlier. Howard v. Des Moines Register and Tribune Co., 283 N.W.2d 289, 5 Med.L.Rptr. 1667 (Iowa 1979), certiorari denied 445 U.S. 904 (1980) (case dismissed).

2. Television cameras went to the scene of a report that a man was threatening harm to his housekeeper's sister. The crew arrived and began filming as police led the stark-naked man from the house. In a news report the following evening, plaintiff's "buttocks and genitals were visible to television viewers for a time period of approximately eight-to-nine-tenths of one second." Taylor v. KTVB Inc., 96 Idaho 202, 525 P.2d 984 (1974) (case remanded to determine defendant's reasons for using the film; settled out of court).

3. A television station reported the identity of a deceased rape victim. Cox Broadcasting Corp. v. Cohn, 420 U.S. 469, 1 Med.L.Rptr. 1819 (1975). The case is included later in this chapter.

4. Plaintiff was kidnapped by her estranged husband and taken to an apartment. He forced her to disrobe and then beat her. Police came. Following the suicide of the husband, police hurried plaintiff from the apartment nude "save for a mere towel." Photographers on

the scene took photographs and turned them over to defendant newspaper, which ran several of them. Cape Publications, Inc. v. Bridges, 423 So.2d 426, 8 Med.L.Rptr. 2535 (Fla.App.1982), certiorari denied 464 U.S. 893 (1983) (judgment for $10,000 reversed on appeal and case dismissed).

5. A group of Pittsburgh Steeler fans urged a photographer from *Sports Illustrated* to take pictures of them. The photographer did so. From among many photographs available for use, the editors chose one that showed the plaintiff with his fly open. Neff v. Time, Inc., 406 F.Supp. 858 (W.D.Pa.1976) (case dismissed).

6. A newspaper columnist included the following item: "More education stuff: The students at the College of Alameda will be surprised to learn that their student body president, Toni Diaz, is no lady, but is in fact a man whose real name is Antonio.

"Now I realize, that in these times, such a matter is no big deal, but I suspect his female classmates in P.E. 97 may wish to make other showering arrangements." The plaintiff, who had had sex change surgery, won a $775,000 judgment at the trial court. But it was reversed on appeal, and the parties settled the case shortly thereafter. Diaz v. Oakland Tribune, Inc., 139 Cal.App.3d 118, 188 Cal.Rptr. 762, 9 Med.L.Rptr. 1121 (1983).

7. During an assassination attempt on President Ford in San Francisco, Oliver Sipple knocked the arm of the assailant as she sought to aim a second shot at the President. Sipple was the object of extensive media attention, including stories that identified him as homosexual. Sipple, asserting that relatives who lived in the Midwest did not know of his orientation, sued the *San Francisco Chronicle*. The newspaper defended in part on the argument that privacy was not involved because Sipple had marched in gay parades and had acknowledged that at least 100 to 500 people in San Francisco knew he was homosexual. The newspaper argued that his sexual orientation was relevant to the story because, although some stereotyped gays as sissies, Sipple was an ex-marine who acted heroically. The court held that the newspaper articles' references to Sipple's homosexuality did not constitute unlawful public disclosure of private facts, because Sipple's sexual orientation was well known and the articles about him were of legitimate public interest. Sipple v. Chronicle Publishing Co., 154 Cal. App.3d 1040, 201 Cal.Rptr. 665, 10 Med.L.Rptr. 1690 (1984).

Prison and Criminal Behavior. 8. Plaintiff was arrested for drunk driving. At the police station, he was "hitting and banging on his cell door, hollering and cursing from the time of his arrest" until five hours later. A local broadcaster taped some of the noise and played excerpts from it on the radio. Holman v. Central Arkansas Broadcasting Co., Inc., 610 F.2d 542, 5 Med.L.Rptr. 2217 (8th Cir.1979) (case dismissed).

9. A newspaper reproduced the front page of a 1952 edition as part of its regular feature called "Page from Our Past." The page

contained an article about the cattle theft trial of three brothers who asserted that the 25–year–old matter was no longer of public concern and that they had been law-abiding and hard working citizens of the community, and had ultimately received full pardons. Roshto v. Hebert, 439 So.2d 428, 9 Med.L.Rptr. 2417 (La.1983). (Judgment for plaintiffs reversed on appeal and case dismissed.)

Poverty. 10. A newspaper article included a front-page photograph of the plaintiff's home. The photograph was one of a series on the newspaper's hometown and its environs. The caption read, "one of Crowley's stately homes, a bit weatherworn and unkempt, stands in the shadow of a spreading oak." Jaubert v. Crowley Post–Signal, Inc., 375 So.2d 1386, 5 Med.L.Rptr. 2084 (La.1979) (case dismissed).

Idiosyncrasies. 11. *The New Yorker* magazine did one of its extensive profiles on a man who, 27 years earlier, had been an 11–year–old child prodigy who had lectured to mathematicians. For the last 20 years, however, he had lived as unobtrusively as possible. The profile reported that the plaintiff was living in a hall bedroom in Boston's "shabby south end," that his room was untidy, that he had a curious laugh, that he collected street car transfers, and that he was interested at the moment in the lore of the Okamakammessett Indians. The article was "merciless in its dissection of intimate details of its subject's personal life" and a "ruthless exposure of a once public character who has since sought and has now been deprived of the seclusion of private life." Sidis v. F–R Publishing Corp., 113 F.2d 806, 1 Med.L.Rptr. 1775 (2d Cir.), certiorari denied 311 U.S. 711 (1940) (case dismissed).

12. *Sports Illustrated* planned an article about a California beach reputed to be the world's most dangerous site for body surfing. Plaintiff, known as the most daring surfer at the site, was interviewed and was referred to in the story as one who extinguished cigarettes in his mouth, ate spiders and other insects, dove head first down a flight of stairs, had never learned to read, and was perceived by other surfers as "abnormal." (Although plaintiff had once consented to be interviewed, he withdrew the consent when he learned the shape the story would take. The court rejected the defense of consent.) Virgil v. Time, Inc., 527 F.2d 1122, 1 Med.L.Rptr. 1835 (9th Cir.1975), certiorari denied 425 U.S. 998 (1976) (affirming denial of summary judgment, two justices dissenting).

Embarrassment or Ridicule. 13. A newspaper article reported that the basketball team at the state university was in trouble because four named players, of the eight who were returning, "are on academic probation and in danger of flunking." Bilney v. Evening Star Newspaper Co., 43 Md.App. 560, 406 A.2d 652 (1979) (case dismissed).

14. Plaintiff was a janitor who found $240,000 that had fallen from an armored car. He returned it (and received a reward of $10,000), to the scorn of his neighbors and his children's friends. When their hostile reaction was reported, he received many congratulatory

messages, including one from President John Kennedy. The full story was reported in a periodical and reprinted in a college English textbook. Johnson v. Harcourt, Brace, Jovanovich, Inc., 43 Cal.App.3d 880, 118 Cal.Rptr. 370 (1974) (case dismissed).

Suicide. 15. Electronic journalists faced a particularly difficult decision involving ethics and privacy when the Pennsylvania state treasurer, R. Budd Dwyer, shot himself during a news conference in January 1987. Several stations, after warning viewers, showed the entire suicide—Dwyer putting a .357 Magnum pistol into his mouth and pulling the trigger. Others showed an edited version period. Enraged viewers complained that children, home from school because of a snowstorm, saw the videotape before parents could switch the channel. The incident points up the difficulty of balancing full disclosure in news coverage against respect for the privacy of a suicide victim's family and viewers' sensitivities. Editor & Publisher, Jan. 31, 1987, at 9.

b. Legal Analysis

As the law has been developing, the plaintiff must show that the information made public was in fact "private," that the disclosure would be "highly offensive to a reasonable person" and that the revelation was not newsworthy. We look at each element in turn.

Private Information. The courts have not been very attentive to this aspect of the matter—perhaps because in most cases the information is clearly something that the plaintiff has held closely and did not want bandied about. Our examples ranged from one extreme to the other. The plaintiff in the sex-change case had not publicized the surgery. On the other hand, private facts are unlikely to exist as to the exterior of a home, when someone at a football game with his fly open poses for a professional photographer, or when someone at a police station shouts so loudly that others cannot help but hear what is said.

Between these extremes we have cases like that of Oliver Sipple, whose sexual orientation was not a secret among his friends and his immediate community, and who was willing to march in gay parades, but who wanted the information kept inside San Francisco. Although some cases should be eliminated on the ground that the information published had not been "private" at the time of the publication, most do seem to involve matters that most people would attempt to keep secret.

"Highly Offensive to a Reasonable Person." This formulation has received much more attention. Although the specific language is taken from the Restatement of Torts (Second) § 652D, similar expressions have been used in the cases during this tort's development. The single most important consideration appears to be the substance of the statement. In some cases it appears difficult to argue that the revelation would be highly offensive to a reasonable person—as in the case of the janitor who returned the money he found, even though some members

of plaintiff's community criticized his behavior. It would also apply to the "weatherworn and unkempt" house. Perhaps a similar analysis would apply to the cases involving idiosyncrasies—the body surfer and the child prodigy. Even though the article about the prodigy was described as "merciless in its dissection of intimate details of its subject's personal life," perhaps what was revealed would not be highly offensive to a reasonable person. That some people may wish to keep private some of their quirks is not the same as saying that reasonable people would find the revelation of that information to be highly offensive.

It is no coincidence that the cases commonly involve sexual, health and financial topics that are generally thought to involve the most intimate matters. Another area has involved revelations about rehabilitated criminals. As we shall see, simply showing that the revelation would be highly offensive to a reasonable person does not guarantee that the defendant will be held liable for an invasion of privacy. It is, however, an essential first step.

Note that no complex damage rules, such as exist in defamation, have emerged in privacy. The plaintiff who can successfully demonstrate an invasion of privacy will recover damages measured by the emotional harm suffered. Obviously, damages here cannot rehabilitate the plaintiff in the way that damages in defamation might pay for the reputational harm caused by the false statement.

"Newsworthiness" or *"Legitimate Concern" Defense.* In addition to requiring that the publicized matter be private and "highly offensive to a reasonable person," the courts demand that the matter be "not of legitimate concern to the public." Most litigation has revolved around this or similar phrases, such as claims that the article in question was "newsworthy" or that it was of "general or public concern." It should be emphasized at the outset that this requirement exists under state common law and has been applied with greater or lesser rigor in every major state case in which a privacy claim has been raised.

As noted in the introduction to this section, there was a period in which the courts seemed to treat "newsworthy" or "of legitimate concern" as descriptive terms. Any article appearing in a newspaper would meet that requirement because if an editor chose to include it, it must be newsworthy. Such an approach would soon eliminate the privacy action. More recently, the courts have shifted and now attempt to develop normative guidelines to determine when the information might be of "legitimate concern to the public."

Although the public figure definitions in libel are not used in privacy, an important distinction here too is between voluntary and involuntary public figures. It should not be surprising that those who seek the public limelight should be thought to have a lesser claim to privacy protection than those brought into the glare of publicity simply because they are either the unfortunate victims of an accident or crime or are otherwise swept up in an event. But even involuntary subjects are not immune. As a comment to the *Restatement* puts it:

> These persons are regarded as properly subject to the public interest, and publishers are permitted to satisfy the curiosity of the public as to its heroes, leaders, villains and victims, and those who are closely associated with them. As in the case of the voluntary public figure, the authorized publicity is not limited to the event that itself arouses the public interest, and to some extent includes publicity given to facts about the individual that would otherwise be purely private.

One should note the categorization of voluntary and involuntary public figures and private figures in post-*Gertz* libel law. In libel one assumes that one must be *voluntary* to be public. In privacy, however, one can be *involuntarily* drawn into the public eye, and the courts do not necessarily distinguish between matters of public interest and matters in which the public is interested.

Our examples include a variety of plaintiffs. The body surfer has voluntarily brought himself into the public eye by his prowess, his continued attendance at a particular beach, and his engaging in a particular type of activity. Sidis, who may have been a voluntary public figure at age 11 and in his teens, later sought obscurity—but the public has a legitimate concern with what happens to prodigies in later life. Is there a similar concern with criminals? Others "voluntarily" become public figures on the spur of the moment—as when Sipple knocked the arm of the President's assailant or when Johnson returned the money he found in the street. Most of our examples, however, involved involuntary public figures—those who wished to keep their sterilization private, and in no other way had been voluntarily in the public spotlight.

Although courts sometimes suggest that the distinction is relevant to the decision, the difference is at most a matter of degree and more often may control the question of whether the editor will choose to name the person in the story. As a practical matter, a voluntary public figure who is involved in an accident or other misfortune is much more likely to be named in any story that results from the episode than is a previously anonymous person. Those who seek the limelight risk having their names used in unwanted contexts. But this does not mean that every aspect of their lives, or that no aspects of the lives of involuntary figures, may be revealed. The *Restatement* seeks to draw a line in the following comment:

> Permissible publicity to information concerning either voluntary or involuntary public figures is not limited to the particular events that arouse the interest of the public. That interest, once aroused by the event, may legitimately extend, to some reasonable degree, to further information concerning the individual and to facts about him, which are not public and which, in the case of one who had not become a public figure, would be regarded as an

invasion of his purely private life. Thus the life history of one accused of murder, together with such heretofore private facts as may throw some light upon what kind of person he is, his possible guilt or innocence, or his reasons for committing the crime, are a matter of legitimate public interest. . . . On the same basis the home life and daily habits of a motion picture actress may be of legitimate and reasonable interest to the public that sees her on the screen.

The extent of the authority to make public private facts is not, however, unlimited. There may be some intimate details of her life, such as sexual relations, which even the actress is entitled to keep to herself. In determining what is a matter of legitimate public interest, account must be taken of the customs and conventions of the community; and in the last analysis what is proper becomes a matter of the community mores. The line is to be drawn when the publicity ceases to be the giving of information to which the public is entitled, and becomes a morbid and sensational prying into private lives for its own sake, with which a reasonable member of the public, with decent standards, would say that he had no concern. The limitations, in other words, are those of common decency, having due regard to the freedom of the press and its reasonable leeway to choose what it will tell the public, but also due regard to the feelings of the individual and the harm that will be done to him by the exposure. Some reasonable proportion is also to be maintained between the event or activity that makes the individual a public figure and the private facts to which publicity is given. Revelations that may properly be made concerning a murderer or the President of the United States would not be privileged if they were to be made concerning one who is merely injured in an automobile accident.

A 1986 case decided by the Supreme Court of Oregon demonstrates the problems in balancing "newsworthiness" and "legitimate concern" against concerns over material which is "highly offensive to a reasonable person." Anderson v. Fisher Broadcasting Companies, Inc., 300 Or. 452, 712 P.2d 803, 12 Med.L.Rptr. 1604 (1986), involved television coverage of the scene of an automobile accident. A camera crew for KATU–TV in Portland videotaped events at the scene, including shots of the plaintiff bleeding and in pain while receiving emergency treatment. The tape was never used as part of a news broadcast, but the station later used a brief excerpt in promotional spots advertising a special news report about a new system for dispatching emergency medical help.

Plaintiff Richard Anderson sued for general damages for mental anguish, and said he was pictured in a condition "offensive to a reasonable person" and not of legitimate public concern. The broadcaster claimed the use of the plaintiff's picture occurred in advertising another news program and that such use was constitutionally privileged.

The Oregon Supreme Court found it unnecessary to reach the constitutional issue. The court held that "[g]enerally, Oregon decisions have not allowed recovery for injury to a stranger's feelings as such, unless the infliction of psychic distress was the object of defendant's conduct or the conduct violated some legal duty apart from causing the distress."

Further, the court said:

What is "private" so as to make its publication offensive likely differs among communities, between generations, and among ethnic, religious, or other social groups, as well as among individuals. Likewise, one reader's or viewer's "news" is another's tedium or trivia. The editorial judgment of what is "newsworthy" is not . . . properly a community standard. Even when some editors themselves vie to tailor "news" to satisfy popular tastes, others may believe that the community should see or hear facts or ideas that the majority finds uninteresting or offensive.

The court concluded that in Oregon, ". . . [t]he truthful presentation of facts concerning a person, even facts that a reasonable person would wish to keep private and that are not 'newsworthy,' does not give rise to common law tort liability for damages for mental or emotional distress, unless the manner or purpose of defendant's conduct is wrongful in some respect apart from causing the plaintiff's hurt feelings," and reinstated the judgment of the circuit court for the defendant television station.

Sometimes members of the family of someone portrayed in the media sue for invasion of privacy. Such was the case when a former employee entered a Louisville company armed with an assault rifle and shot 20 people, killing seven of them, before killing himself. A photographer for the Louisville *Courier–Journal* took a photograph of one the victims, Richard Barger, but Barger was not identified in the caption. The widow and children sued, alleging intentional infliction of emotional distress and invasion of privacy. The trial court dismissed the action, holding that because the photograph did not disclose the identity of the members of Barger's family, "their right of privacy was clearly not invaded by the publication of the photograph." The court also said that Barger "involuntarily became a legitimate subject of public interest." The family acknowledged that the crime was of legitimate public interest but asserted that "the publishing of a photograph depicting the condition of Richard Barger's body was a matter of private concern only for the family." The newspaper said that "This is nothing more than a claim based on 'good taste,' a claim which the courts have time and again refused to accept." The Kentucky Court of Appeals affirmed the trial court's dismissal, the Kentucky Supreme Court denied a petition for review, Kentucky Court of Appeals (unpublished), 20 Med.L.Rptr. 1189 (1991), cert. denied 112 S.Ct. 1763 (1992).

c. *Constitutional Privilege Defense*

The Supreme Court of the United States has not been called upon frequently in this area because the state courts, operating at common law, have tended to protect the press. Because they have prevailed under state law, the media defendants rarely have needed recourse to the Supreme Court to assert constitutional rights. In *Cox,* the case of the naming of a deceased rape victim, however, the state court ruled that the plaintiffs were entitled to a judgment. The broadcaster's appeal led to the first Supreme Court decision in this area.

COX BROADCASTING CORP. v. COHN

Supreme Court of the United States, 1975.
420 U.S. 469, 95 S.Ct. 1029, 43 L.Ed.2d 328, 1 Med.L.Rptr. 1819.

[Mr. Cohn's 17–year–old daughter was raped in Georgia and did not survive the occurrence. In Georgia it was a misdemeanor for "any news media or any other person to print and publish, broadcast, televise or disseminate through any other medium of public dissemination . . . the name or identity of any female who may have been raped. . . ." Ga.Code Ann. § 26–9901. Similar statutes exist in a few other states. The girl was not identified at the time. Eight months later, appellant's reporter, Wassell, also an appellant, attended a hearing for the six youths charged with the rape and murder. He learned the girl's name by inspecting the indictment in the courtroom. His report naming the girl was telecast.

The Georgia Supreme Court held that the complaint stated a common law action for damages for invasion of the father's own privacy. Defendant's First Amendment argument was rejected on the ground that the statute was an authoritative declaration that Georgia considered a rape victim's name not to be a matter of public concern. The court could discern "no public interest or general concern about the identity of the victim of such a crime as will make the right to disclose the identity of the victim rise to the level of First Amendment protection."

On appeal, the Supreme Court first decided that the decision below was a "final" judgment so as to give the court jurisdiction. The Court then turned to the First Amendment issue.]

Mr. Justice White delivered the opinion of the Court.

. . .

Georgia stoutly defends both § 26–9901 and the State's common-law privacy action challenged here. Her claims are not without force, for powerful arguments can be made, and have been made, that however it may be ultimately defined, there *is* a zone of privacy surrounding every individual, a zone within which the State may protect him from intrusion by the press, with all its attendant publicity.

Indeed, the central thesis of the root article by Warren and Brandeis, The Right to Privacy, 4 Harv.L.Rev. 193, 196 (1890), was that the press was overstepping its prerogatives by publishing essentially private information and that there should be a remedy for the alleged abuses.

More compellingly, the century has experienced a strong tide running in favor of the so-called right of privacy. . . .

. . . . Because the gravamen of the claimed injury is the publication of information, whether true or not, the dissemination of what is embarrassing or otherwise painful to an individual, it is here that claims of privacy most directly confront the constitutional freedoms of speech and press. The face-off is apparent, and the appellants urge upon us the broad holding that the press may not be made criminally or civilly liable for publishing information that is neither false nor misleading but absolutely accurate, however damaging it may be to reputation or individual sensibilities.

. . .

Rather than address the broader question whether truthful publications may ever be subjected to civil or criminal liability consistently with the First and Fourteenth Amendments, or to put it another way, whether the State may ever define and, protect an area of privacy free from unwanted publicity in the press, it is appropriate to focus on the narrower interface between press and privacy that this case presents, namely, whether the State may impose sanctions on the accurate publication of the name of a rape victim obtained from public records— more specifically, from judicial records which are maintained in connection with a public prosecution and which themselves are open to public inspection. We are convinced that the State may not do so.

In the first place, in a society in which each individual has but limited time and resources with which to observe at first hand the operations of his government, he relies necessarily upon the press to bring to him in convenient form the facts of those operations. Great responsibility is accordingly placed upon the news media to report fully and accurately the proceedings of government, and official records and documents open to the public are the basic data of governmental operations. Without the information provided by the press most of us and many of our representatives would be unable to vote intelligently or to register opinions on the administration of government generally. With respect to judicial proceedings in particular, the function of the press serves to guarantee the fairness of trials and to bring to bear the beneficial effects of public scrutiny upon the administration of justice. See Sheppard v. Maxwell, 384 U.S. 333, 350 (1966).

Appellee has claimed in this litigation that the efforts of the press have infringed his right to privacy by broadcasting to the world the fact that his daughter was a rape victim. The commission of crime, prosecutions resulting from it, and judicial proceedings arising from the prosecution, however, are without question events of legitimate concern to the public and consequently fall within the responsibility of the press to report the operations of government.

The special protected nature of accurate reports of judicial proceedings has repeatedly been recognized. This Court, in an opinion written by Mr. Justice Douglas, has said:

> "A trial is a public event. What transpires in the court room is public property. If a transcript of the court proceedings had been published, we suppose none would claim that the judge could punish the publisher for contempt. And we can see no difference though the conduct of the attorneys, of the jury, or even of the judge himself, may have reflected on the court. *Those who see and hear what transpired can report it with impunity.* There is no special perquisite of the judiciary which enables it, as distinguished from other institutions of democratic government, to suppress, edit, or censor events which transpire in proceedings before it." Craig v. Harney, 331 U.S. 367, 374 (1947) (emphasis added).

. . .

The developing law surrounding the tort of invasion of privacy recognizes a privilege in the press to report the events of judicial proceedings. The Warren and Brandeis article, supra, noted that the proposed new right would be limited in the same manner as actions for libel and slander where such a publication was a privileged communication: "the right to privacy is not invaded by any publication made in a court of justice . . . and (at least in many jurisdictions) reports of any such proceedings would in some measure be accorded a like privilege."

. . .

Thus, even the prevailing law of invasion of privacy generally recognizes that the interests in privacy fade when the information involved already appears on the public record. The conclusion is compelling when viewed in terms of the First and Fourteenth Amendments and in light of the public interest in a vigorous press. The Georgia cause of action for invasion of privacy through public disclosure of the name of a rape victim imposes sanctions on pure expression—the content of a publication—and not conduct or a combination of speech and non-speech elements that might otherwise be open to regulation or prohibition. See United States v. O'Brien, 391 U.S. 367, 376–377 (1968). The publication of truthful information available on the public record contains none of the indicia of those limited categories of expression, such as "fighting" words, which "are no essential part of any exposition of ideas, and are of such slight social value as a step to truth that any benefit that may be derived from them is clearly outweighed by the social interest in order and morality." Chaplinsky v. New Hampshire, 315 U.S. 568, 572 (1942) (footnote omitted).

By placing the information in the public domain on official court records, the State must be presumed to have concluded that the public interest was thereby being served. Public records by their very nature are of interest to those concerned with the administration of government, and a public benefit is performed by the reporting of the true contents of the records by the media. The freedom of the press to publish that information appears to us to be of critical importance to our type of government in which the citizenry is the final judge of the proper conduct of public business. In preserving that form of government the First and Fourteenth Amendments command nothing less than that the States may not impose sanctions on the publication of truthful information contained in official court records open to public inspection.

We are reluctant to embark on a course that would make public records generally available to the media but forbid their publication if offensive to the sensibilities of the supposed reasonable man. Such a rule would make it very difficult for the media to inform citizens about the public business and yet stay within the law. The rule would invite timidity and self-censorship and very likely lead to the suppression of many items that would otherwise be published and that should be made available to the public. At the very least, the First and Fourteenth Amendments will not allow exposing the press to liability for truthfully publishing information released to the public in official court records. If there are privacy interests to be protected in judicial proceedings, the States must respond by means which avoid public documentation or other exposure of private information. Their political institutions must weigh the interests in privacy with the interests of the public to know and of the press to publish.[26] Once true information is disclosed in public court documents open to public inspection, the press cannot be sanctioned for publishing it. In this instance as in others reliance must rest upon the judgment of those who decide what to publish or broadcast. See Miami Herald Pub. Co. v. Tornillo, 418 U.S., at 258.

Appellant Wassell based his televised report upon notes taken during the court proceedings and obtained the name of the victim from the indictments handed to him at his request during a recess in the hearing. Appellee has not contended that the name was obtained in an improper fashion or that it was not on an official court document open to public inspection. Under these circumstances, the protection of freedom of the press provided by the First and Fourteenth Amendments bars the State of Georgia from making appellants' broadcast the basis of civil liability.[27]

Reversed.

26. We mean to imply nothing about any constitutional questions which might arise from a state policy not allowing access by the public and press to various kinds of official records, such as records of juvenile court proceedings.

27. Appellants have contended that whether they derived the information in question from public records or instead through their own investigation, the First and Fourteenth Amendments bar any sanctions from being imposed by the State because of the publication. Because appellants have prevailed on more limited grounds, we need not address this broader challenge to the validity of § 26–9901 and of Georgia's right of action for public disclosure.

MR. CHIEF JUSTICE BURGER concurs in the judgment.

MR. JUSTICE POWELL, concurring.

. . .

MR. JUSTICE DOUGLAS, concurring.

On the merits, . . . there is no power on the part of the government to suppress or penalize the publication of "news of the day."

MR. JUSTICE REHNQUIST, dissenting.

Because I am of the opinion that the decision which is the subject of this appeal is not a[reviewable] "final" judgment or decree, . . . I would dismiss this appeal for want of jurisdiction.

Notes and Questions

1. What issues does the majority opinion avoid deciding? Why do you think the majority took the approach it did?

2. On the importance of the passage of time, consider this comment to Restatement, Second § 652D:

> The fact that there has been a lapse of time, even of considerable length, since the event that has made the plaintiff a public figure, does not of itself defeat the authority to give him publicity or to renew publicity when it has formerly been given. Past events and activities may still be of legitimate interest to the public, and a narrative reviving recollection of what has happened even many years ago may be both interesting and valuable for purposes of information and education. Such a lapse of time is, however, a factor to be considered, with other facts, in determining whether the publicity goes to unreasonable lengths in revealing facts about one who has resumed the private, lawful and unexciting life led by the great bulk of the community. . . . Again the question is to be determined upon the basis of community standards and mores. Although lapse of time may not impair the authority to give publicity to a public record, the pointing out of the present location and identity of the individual raises a quite different problem.

Is this passage consistent with the Cox case? Does it help analyze the problem of Sidis, the child prodigy? Consider *Roshto,* p. 710, *supra.*

3. The principal opinion in *Howard,* the involuntary sterilization case, p. 708, *supra,* responded to the argument that plaintiff's name was unnecessary as follows:

> Here the disclosure of plaintiff's involuntary sterilization was closely related to the subject matter of the news story. It documented the article's theme of maladministration and patient abuses at the Jasper County Home. . . .
>
> In the sense of serving an appropriate news function, the disclosure contributed constructively to the impact of the article. It offered a personalized frame of reference to which the reader

could relate, fostering perception and understanding. Moreover, it lent specificity and credibility to the report.

In this way the disclosure served as an effective means of accomplishing the intended news function. It had positive communicative value in attracting the reader's attention to the article's subject matter and in supporting expression of the underlying theme.

Examined in the light of the first amendment, we do not believe the disclosure could reasonably be held to be devoid of news value. [ ]

Assuming, as plaintiff argues, the newspaper had a right to print an article that documented extrastatutory involuntary sterilizations at the Jasper County Home, the editors also had a right to buttress the force of their evidence by naming names. We do not say it was necessary for them to do so, but we are certain they had a right to treat the identity of victims of involuntary sterilizations as matters of legitimate public concern. . . .

This is a far cry from embarrassing people by exposing their medical conditions or treatment when identity can add nothing to the probity of the account. [ ]

The disclosure of plaintiff's identity in this case could not reasonably be viewed as the spreading of gossip solely for its own sake. . . .

Would *Cox* reach the same result?

4. In *Virgil*, p. 710, *supra*, involving the body surfer, the publisher, citing *Cox*, argued in its brief that the First Amendment protected almost all true statements from liability:

A press which must depend upon a governmental determination as to what facts are of 'public interest' in order to avoid liability for their truthful publication is not free at all. . . . A constitutional rule can be fashioned which protects all the interests involved. This goal is achieved by providing a privilege for truthful publications which is defeasible only when the court concludes as a matter of law that the truthful publication complained of constitutes a clear abuse of the editor's constitutional discretion to publish and discuss subjects and facts which in his judgment are matters of public interest.

The court rejected the argument and adopted the view of the *Restatement (Second) of Torts*, that liability may be imposed if the matter published is "not of legitimate concern to the public." Then the court relied on a passage from the *Restatement* that was quoted earlier in this section—that "in the last analysis what is proper becomes a matter of the community mores."

In libel and obscenity cases juries utilize community standards, and the court thought they should do so here, too, "subject to close judicial scrutiny to ensure that the jury resolutions comport with First Amendment principles." What is the difference between *Time'*s position and that adopted by the court? Is the court's view consistent with *Cox*? Over the dissents of Justices Brennan and Stewart, the Supreme Court denied *certiorari* in *Virgil*. 425 U.S. 998 (1976). The case was remanded for trial.

On remand, the trial judge held that the magazine was entitled to summary judgment. First, the judge concluded that the facts revealed were not "highly offensive." Even if they were, the facts were "included as a legitimate journalistic attempt to explain Virgil's extremely daring and dangerous style of body surfing at the Wedge. There is no possibility that a juror would conclude that the personal facts were included for any inherent morbid, sensational, or curiosity appeal they might have." Virgil v. Sports Illustrated, 424 F.Supp. 1286, 2 Med. L.Rptr. 1271 (S.D.Cal 1976).

5. Although the courts have tended to take this area case-by-case, editors complain that such an approach breeds intolerable uncertainty. An editor must decide today what might happen in court in several years—and the standards are said to be vague. What will be found "highly offensive to a reasonable person" or to violate "community standards and mores"? Juries given these questions may punish unpopular broadcasters and publishers.

Compare this situation with that confronting an editor in the defamation area. There the editor, with advice from lawyers, must decide whether the *Times* or *Gertz* rule applies and then decide whether the publication's conduct meets that standard. And truth is always a defense. Do you see a sharp difference between the editor's position there and where the case involves privacy?

6. As we saw in *Hustler*, p. 681, *supra*, infliction of emotional distress is a tort related to both defamation and invasion of privacy. In *Hustler*, Falwell argued that his emotional distress resulted from untruths in the ad parody, so we discussed that case in the context of defamation law. Other plaintiffs allege that emotional distress is inflicted on them by dissemination of *truthful* information, and those cases are much closer to invasion of privacy by publication of embarrassing private facts than they are to defamation. An example is Hyde v. City of Columbia, 637 S.W.2d 251 (Mo.App.1982), certiorari denied 459 U.S. 1226 (1983). Sandra Hyde sued for negligent infliction of emotional distress after city police disclosed, and a local newspaper published, her name and address in a news story about her escape from an unknown kidnapper. Following the publication, the assailant terrorized her on seven different occasions. The trial judge dismissed the petition, but an appellate court ordered the petition reinstated. The court said, "We determine . . . that the name and address of an abduction witness who can identify an assailant still at large before arrest is a matter of such trivial public concern compared with the high

probability of risk to the victim by their publication, that a news medium owes a duty in such circumstances to use reasonable care not to give likely occasion for a third party [assailant still at large] to do injury to the plaintiff by the publication." Eventually the case was settled out of court.

7. A rare successful privacy case has resulted in an award of $1,500 actual and $25,000 punitive damages, affirmed by the South Carolina Supreme Court. Hawkins v. Multimedia, Inc., 288 S.C. 569, 344 S.E.2d 145, 12 Med.L.Rptr. 1878 (1986). In a sidebar article to a story on teenage pregnancies, defendant's newspaper identified plaintiff as the teenage father of an illegitimate child. The majority of the article focused on the teenage mother. After the mother identified plaintiff as the father, the reporter called plaintiff twice to obtain comments. The first time she spoke with plaintiff's mother. The second time she spoke with the reluctant plaintiff for three or four minutes. "In neither call did the reporter request permission to identify or quote [plaintiff]."

Over defendant's objection, the trial judge charged that a minor cannot consent to an invasion of privacy. The appellate court did not reach the issue because it found that defendant had failed to establish consent in the first place. Although plaintiff did not hang up immediately, he was "very shy." He never agreed to the use of his name.

The court rejected defense arguments that the article was of "general interest" because that defense requires "legitimate" public interest. "Public or general interest does not mean mere curiosity, and newsworthiness is not necessarily the test." This issue was properly submitted to the jury.

Finally, the trial judge refused the defendant's charge that "malice must be shown by clear and convincing evidence." The appellate court concluded that malice "need not be shown to recover for invasion of privacy." It is relevant only for punitive damages. The proper burden for punitive damages was not raised at trial and could not be raised on appeal.

The Supreme Court denied *certiorari.*

Compare this result with that in *Howard*, pp. 708 and 720, *supra.*

8. A case involving *The Florida Star* brought the problem of identification of rape victims to the Supreme Court for a second time. The small weekly newspaper inadvertently violated its own policy by printing a victim's name in a weekly "Police Reports" section. A jury award of $100,000 to the plaintiff was upheld on appeal in the state courts, and the award, had it been upheld by the Supreme Court, could have bankrupted the *Star.*

THE FLORIDA STAR v. B.J.F.

Supreme Court of the United States, 1989.
491 U.S. 524, 109 S.Ct. 2603, 105 L.Ed.2d 443, 16 Med.L.Rptr. 1801.

JUSTICE MARSHALL delivered the opinion of the Court.

Florida Stat. § 794.03 (1987) makes it unlawful to "print, publish, or broadcast . . . in any instrument of mass communication" the name of the victim of a sexual offense. Pursuant to this statute, appellant The Florida Star was found civilly liable for publishing the name of a rape victim which it had obtained from a publicly released police report. The issue presented here is whether this result comports with the First Amendment. We hold that it does not.

I

The Florida Star is a weekly newspaper which serves the community of Jacksonville, Florida, and which has an average circulation of approximately 18,000 copies. A regular feature of the newspaper is its "Police Reports" section. That section, typically two to three pages in length, contains brief articles describing local criminal incidents under police investigation.

On October 20, 1983, appellee B.J.F. reported to the Duval County, Florida, Sheriff's Department (the Department) that she had been robbed and sexually assaulted by an unknown assailant. The Department prepared a report on the incident which identified B.J.F., by her full name. The Department then placed the report in its press room. The Department does not restrict access either to the press room or to the reports made available therein.

A Florida Star reporter-trainee sent to the press room copied the police report verbatim, including B.J.F.'s full name, on a blank duplicate of the Department's forms. A Florida Star reporter then prepared a one-paragraph article about the crime, derived entirely from the trainee's copy of the police report. The article included B.J.F.'s full name. It appeared in the "Robberies" subsection of the "Police Reports" section on October 29, 1983, one of fifty-four police blotter stories in that day's edition. The article read:

> "[B.J.F.] reported on Thursday, October 20, she was crossing Brentwood Park, which is in the 500 block of Golfair Boulevard, enroute to her bus stop, when an unknown black man ran up behind the lady and placed a knife to her neck and told her not to yell. The suspect then undressed the lady and had sexual intercourse with her before fleeing the scene with her 60 cents, Timex watch and gold necklace. Patrol efforts have been suspended concerning this incident because of a lack of evidence."

In printing B.J.F.'s full name, The Florida Star violated its internal policy of not publishing the names of sexual offense victims.

On September 26, 1984, B.J.F. filed suit in the Circuit Court of Duval County against the Department and The Florida Star, alleging that these parties negligently violated § 794.03. Before trial, the Department settled with B.J.F. for $2,500. The Florida Star moved to dismiss, claiming, *inter alia*, that imposing civil sanctions on the newspaper pursuant to § 794.03 violated the First Amendment. The trial judge rejected the motion. [ ]

At the ensuing day-long trial, B.J.F. testified that she had suffered emotional distress from the publication of her name. She stated that she had heard about the article from fellow workers and acquaintances; that her mother had received several threatening phone calls from a man who stated that he would rape B.J.F. again; and that these events had forced B.J.F. to change her phone number and residence, to seek police protection, and to obtain mental health counseling. In defense, The Florida Star put forth evidence indicating that the newspaper had learned B.J.F.'s name from the incident report released by the Department, and that the newspaper's violation of its internal rule against publishing the names of sexual offense victims was inadvertent.

At the close of B.J.F.'s case, and again at the close of its defense, The Florida Star moved for a directed verdict. On both occasions, the trial judge denied these motions. He ruled from the bench that § 794.03 was constitutional because it reflected a proper balance between the First Amendment and privacy rights, as it applied only to a narrow set of "rather sensitive . . . criminal offenses." [ ] At the close of newspaper's defense, the judge granted B.J.F.'s motion for a directed verdict on the issue of negligence, finding the newspaper *per se* negligent based upon its violation of § 794.03. [ ] This ruling left the jury to consider only the questions of causation and damages. The judge instructed the jury that it could award B.J.F. punitive damages if it found that the newspaper had "acted with reckless indifference to the rights of others." [ ] The jury awarded B.J.F. $75,000 in compensatory damages and $25,000 in punitive damages. Against the actual damage award, the judge set off B.J.F.'s settlement with the Department.

The First District Court of Appeal affirmed in a three-paragraph *per curiam* opinion. [ ] In the paragraph devoted to the Florida Star's First Amendment claim, the court stated that the directed verdict for B.J.F. had been properly entered because, under § 794.03, a rape victim's name is "of a private nature and not to be published as a matter of law." [ ] The Supreme Court of Florida denied discretionary review.

The Florida Star appealed to this court. We noted probable jurisdiction, [ ], and now reverse.

II

The tension between the right which the First Amendment accords to a free press, on the one hand, and the protections which various statutes and common-law doctrines accord to personal privacy against the publication of truthful information, on the other, is a subject we have addressed several times in recent years. Our decisions in cases involving government attempts to sanction the accurate dissemination of information as invasive of privacy, have not, however, exhaustively considered this conflict. On the contrary, although our decisions have without exception upheld the press' right to publish, we have emphasized each time that we were resolving this conflict only as it arose in a discrete factual context.

The parties to this case frame their contentions in light of a trilogy of cases which have presented, in different contexts, the conflict between truthful reporting and state-protected privacy interests. In [*Cox*], we found unconstitutional a civil damages award entered against a television station for broadcasting the name of a rape-murder victim which the station had obtained from courthouse records. In *Oklahoma Publishing Co. v. District Court*, 430 U.S. 308 [2 Med.L.Rptr. 1456] (1977), we found unconstitutional a state court's pretrial order enjoining the media from publishing the name or photograph of an 11-year-old boy in connection with a juvenile proceeding involving that child which reporters had attended. Finally, in [*Smith v. Daily Mail*, p. 30, *supra*], we found unconstitutional the indictment of two newspapers for violating a state statute forbidding newspapers to publish, without written approval of the juvenile court, the name of any youth charged as a juvenile offender. The papers had learned about a shooting by monitoring a police band radio frequency, and had obtained the name of the alleged juvenile assailant from witnesses, the police, and a local prosecutor.

Appellant takes the position that this case is indistinguishable from [*Cox*]. [ ] Alternatively, it urges that our decisions in the above trilogy, and in other cases in which we have held that the right of the press to publish truth overcame asserted interests other than personal privacy, can be distilled to yield a broader First Amendment principle that the press may never be punished, civilly or criminally, for publishing the truth. [ ] Appellee counters that the privacy trilogy is inapposite, because in each case the private information already appeared on a "public record," [ ], and because the privacy interests at stake were far less profound than in the present case. [ ] In the alternative, appellee urges that [*Cox*] be overruled and replaced with a categorical rule that publication of the name of a rape victim never enjoys constitutional protection. [ ]

We conclude that imposing damages on appellant for publishing B.J.F.'s name violates the First Amendment, although not for either of the reasons appellant urges. Despite the strong resemblance this case bears to [*Cox*], that case cannot fairly be read as controlling here. The name of the rape victim in that case was obtained from courthouse records that were open to public inspection . . . . [ ] Significantly, one of the reasons we gave in [*Cox*] for invalidating the challenged damages award was the important role the press plays in subjecting trials to public scrutiny and thereby helping guarantee their fairness. [ ] That role is not directly compromised where, as here, the information in question comes from a police report prepared and disseminated at a time at which not only had no adversarial criminal proceedings begun, but no suspect had been identified.

Nor need we accept appellant's invitation to hold broadly that truthful publication may never be punished consistent with the First Amendment. Our cases have carefully eschewed reaching this ultimate question, mindful that the future may bring scenarios which prudence counsels our not resolving anticipatorily. [ ] Indeed, in [*Cox*], we pointedly refused to answer even the less sweeping question "whether truthful publications may ever be subjected to civil or criminal liability" for invading "an area of privacy" defined by the State. [ ] Respecting the fact that press freedom and privacy rights are both "plainly rooted in the traditions and significant concerns of our society," we instead focused on the less sweeping issue of "whether the State may impose sanctions on the accurate publication of the name of a rape victim obtained from public records—more specifically, from judicial records which are maintained in connection with a public prosecution and which themselves are open to public inspection." [ ] We continue to believe that the sensitivity and significance of the interests presented in clashes between First Amendment and privacy rights counsel relying on limited principles that sweep no more broadly than the appropriate context of the instant case.

In our view, this case is appropriately analyzed with reference to such a limited First Amendment principle. It is the one, in fact, which we articulated in *Daily Mail* in our synthesis of prior cases involving attempts to punish truthful publication: "[I]f a newspaper lawfully obtains truthful information about a matter of public significance then state officials may not constitutionally punish publication of the information, absent a need to further a state interest of the highest order." [ ] According the press the ample protection provided by that principle is supported by at least three separate considerations, in addition to, of course, the overarching " 'public interest, secured by the Constitution, in the dissemination of truth.' " [ ] The cases on which the *Daily Mail* synthesis relied demonstrate these considerations.

First, because the *Daily Mail* formulation only protects the publication of information which a newspaper has "lawfully obtain[ed]," [ ], the government retains ample means of safeguarding significant interests upon which publication may impinge, including protecting a rape victim's anonymity. To the extent sensitive information rests in private hands, the government may under some circumstances forbid its nonconsensual acquisition, thereby bringing outside of the *Daily Mail* principle the publication of any information so acquired. To the extent sensitive information is in the government's custody, it has even greater power to forestall or mitigate the injury caused by its release. The government may classify certain information, establish and enforce procedures ensuring its redacted release, and extend a damages remedy against the government or its officials where the government's mishandling of sensitive information leads to its dissemination. Where information is entrusted to the government, a less drastic means than punishing truthful publication almost always exists for guarding against the dissemination of private facts. [ ]

A second consideration undergirding the *Daily Mail* principle is the fact that punishing the press for its dissemination of information which is already publicly available is relatively unlikely to advance the interests in the service of which the State seeks to act. It is not, of course, always the case that information lawfully acquired by the press is known, or accessible, to others. But where the government has made certain information publicly available, it is highly anomalous to sanction persons other than the source of its release. We noted this anomaly in [*Cox*]: "By placing the information in the public domain on official court records, the State must be presumed to have concluded that the public interest was thereby being served." [ ] The *Daily Mail* formulation reflects the fact that it is a limited set of cases indeed where, despite the accessibility of the public to certain information, a meaningful public interest is served by restricting its further release by other entities, like the press. As *Daily Mail* observed in its summary of *Oklahoma Publishing*, "once the truthful information was 'publicly revealed' or 'in the public domain' the court could not constitutionally restrain its dissemination." [ ]

A third and final consideration is the "timidity and self-censorship" which may result from allowing the media to be punished for publishing certain truthful information. [ ] [*Cox*] noted this concern with overdeterrence in the context of information made public through official court records, but the fear of excessive media self-suppression is inapplicable as well to other information released, without qualification, by the government. A contrary rule, depriving protection to those who rely on the government's implied representations of the lawfulness of dissemination, would force upon the media the onerous obligation of sifting through government press releases, reports, and pronouncements to prune out material arguably unlawful for publication. This situation could inhere even where the newspaper's sole object was to reproduce, with no substantial change, the government's rendition of the event in question.

Applied to the instant case, the *Daily Mail* principle clearly commands reversal. The first inquiry is whether the newspaper "lawfully obtain[ed] truthful information about a matter of public significance." [ ] It is undisputed that the news article describing the assault on B.J.F. was accurate. In addition, appellant lawfully obtained B.J.F.'s name. Appellee's argument to the contrary is based on the fact that under Florida law, police reports which reveal the identity of the victim of a sexual offense are not among the matters of "public record" which the public, by law, is entitled to inspect. [ ] But the fact that state officials are not required to disclose such reports does not make it unlawful for a newspaper to receive them when furnished by the government. Nor does the fact that the Department apparently failed to fulfill its obligation under § 794.03 not to "cause or allow to be . . . published" the name of a sexual offense victim make the newspaper's ensuing receipt of this information unlawful. Even assuming the Constitution permitted a State to proscribe *receipt* of information, Florida has not taken this step. It is clear, furthermore, that the news article concerned "a matter of public significance," [   ], in the sense in which the *Daily Mail* synthesis of prior cases used that term. That is, the article generally, as opposed to the specific identity contained within it, involved a matter of paramount public import: the commission, and investigation, of a violent crime which had been reported to authorities. [   ]

The second inquiry is whether imposing liability on appellant pursuant to § 794.03 serves "a need to further a state interest of the highest order." [   ] Appellee argues that a rule punishing publication furthers three closely related interests: the privacy of victims of sexual offenses; the physical safety of such victims, who may be targeted for retaliation if their names become known to their assailants; and the goal of encouraging victims of such crimes to report these offenses without fear of exposure. [   ]

At a time in which we are daily reminded of the tragic reality of rape, it is undeniable that these are highly significant interests, a fact underscored by the Florida Legislature's explicit attempt to protect these interests by enacting a criminal statute prohibiting much dissemination of victim identifies. We accordingly do not rule out the possibility that, in a proper case, imposing civil sanctions for publication of the name of a rape victim might be so overwhelmingly necessary to advance these interests as to satisfy the *Daily Mail* standard. For three independent reasons, however, imposing liability for publication under the circumstances of this case is too precipitous a means of advancing these interests to convince us that there is a "need" within the meaning of the *Daily Mail* formulation for Florida to take this extreme step. [   ]

First is the manner in which appellant obtained the identifying information in question. As we have noted, where the government itself provides information to the media, it is most appropriate to assume that the government had, but failed to utilize, far more limited means of guarding against dissemination than the extreme step of punishing truthful speech. That assumption is richly borne out in this case. B.J.F.'s identity would never have come to light were it not for the erroneous, if inadvertent, inclusion by the Department of her full name in an incident report made available in a press room open to the public. Florida's policy against disclosure of rape victims' identifies, reflected in § 794.03, was undercut by the Department's failure to abide by this policy. Where, as here, the government has failed to police itself in disseminating information, it is clear under [*Cox*], *Oklahoma Publishing*, and *Landmark Communications* that the imposition of damages against the press for its subsequent publication can hardly be said to be a narrowly tailored means of safeguarding anonymity. [ ] Once the government has placed such information in the public domain, "reliance must rest upon the judgment of those who decide what to publish or broadcast," [ ], and hopes for restitution must rest upon the willingness of the government to compensate victims for their loss of privacy, and to protect them from the other consequences of its mishandling of the information which these victims provided in confidence.

That appellant gained access to the information in question through a government news release made it especially likely that, if liability were to be imposed, self-censorship would result. Reliance on a news release is a paradigmatically "routine newspaper reporting techniqu[e]." [ ] The government's issuance of such a release, without qualification, can only convey to recipients that the government considered dissemination lawful, and indeed expected the recipients to disseminate the information further. Had appellant merely reproduced the news release prepared and released by the Department, imposing civil damages would surely violate the First Amendment. The fact that appellant converted the police report into a news story by adding the linguistic connecting tissue necessary to transform the report's facts into full sentences cannot change this result.

A second problem with Florida's imposition of liability for publication is the broad sweep of the negligence *per se* standard applied under the civil cause of action implied from § 794.03. Unlike claims based on the common law tort of invasion of privacy, [ ], civil actions based on § 794.03 require no case-by-case findings that the disclosure of a fact about a person's private life was one that a reasonable person would find highly offensive. On the contrary, under the *per se* theory of negligence adopted by the courts below, liability follows automatically from publication. This is so regardless of whether the identity of the victim has otherwise become a reasonable subject of public concern— because, perhaps, questions have arisen whether the victim fabricated an assault by a particular person. Nor is there a scienter requirement of any kind under § 794.03, engendering the perverse result that truthful publications challenged pursuant to this cause of action are less protected by the First Amendment than even the least protected defamatory falsehoods: those involving purely private figures, where liability is evaluated under a standard, usually applied by a jury, of ordinary negligence. [ ] We have previously noted the impermissibility of categorical prohibitions upon media access where important First Amendment interests are at stake. [ ] More individualized adjudication is no less indispensable where the State, seeking to safeguard the anonymity of crime victims, sets its face against publication of their names.

Third, and finally, the facial underinclusiveness of § 794.03 raises serious doubts about whether Florida is, in fact, serving, with this statute, the significant interests which appellee invokes in support of affirmance. Section 794.03 prohibits the publication of identifying information only if this information appears in an "instrument of mass communication," a term the statute does not define. Section 794.03 does not prohibit the spread by other means of the identities of victims of sexual offenses. An individual who maliciously spreads word of the identity of a rape victim is thus not covered, despite the fact that the communication of such information to persons who live near, or work with, the victim may have consequences equally devastating as the exposure of her name to large numbers of strangers. [   ]

When a State attempts the extraordinary measure of punishing truthful publication in the name of privacy, it must demonstrate its commitment to advancing this interest by applying its prohibition evenhandedly, to the smalltime disseminator as well as the media giant. Where important First Amendment interests are at stake, the mass scope of disclosure is not an acceptable surrogate for injury. A ban on disclosures effected by "instrument[s] of mass communication" simply cannot be defended on the ground that partial prohibitions may effect partial relief. [   ] Without more careful and inclusive precautions against alternative forms of dissemination, we cannot conclude that Florida's selective ban on publication by the mass media satisfactorily accomplishes its stated purpose.

III

Our holding today is limited. We do not hold that truthful publication is automatically constitutionally protected, or that there is no zone of personal privacy within which the State may protect the individual from intrusion by the press, or even that a State may never punish publication of the name of a victim of a sexual offense. We hold only that where a newspaper publishes truthful information which it has lawfully obtained, punishment may lawfully be imposed, if at all, only when narrowly tailored to a state interest of the highest order, and that no such interest is satisfactorily served by imposing liability under § 794.03 to appellant under the facts of this case. The decision below is therefore

Reversed.

JUSTICE SCALIA, concurring in part and concurring in the judgment.

I think it is sufficient to decide this case to rely upon the third ground set forth in the Court's opinion, [   ]: that a law cannot be regarded as protecting an interest "of the highest order," [   ] and thus as justifying a restriction upon truthful speech, when it leaves appreciable damage to that supposedly vital interest unprohibited. In the present case, I would anticipate that the rape victim's discomfort at the dissemination of news of her misfortune among friends and acquaintances would be at least as great as her discomfort at its publication by the media to people to whom she is only a name. . . .

This law has every appearance of a prohibition that society is prepared to impose upon the press but not upon itself. Such a prohibition does not protect an interest "of the highest order." For that reason, I agree that the judgment of the court below must be reversed.

JUSTICE WHITE, with whom THE CHIEF JUSTICE and JUSTICE O'CONNOR join, dissenting.

"Short of homicide, [rape] is the 'ultimate violation of self.' " [ ] For B.J.F., however, the violation she suffered at a rapist's knifepoint marked only the beginning of her ordeal. A week later, while her assailant was still at large, an account of this assault—identifying by name B.J.F. as the victim—was published by The Florida Star. As a result, B.J.F. received harassing phone calls, required mental health counseling, was forced to move from her home, and was even threatened with being raped again. Yet today, the Court holds that a jury award of $75,000 to compensate B.J.F. for the harm she suffered due to the Star's negligence is at odds with the First Amendment. I do not accept this result.

The Court reaches its conclusion based on an analysis of three of our precedents and a concern with three particular aspects of the judgment against appellant. I consider each of these points in turn, and then consider some of the larger issues implicated by today's decision.

I

The Court finds its result compelled, or at least supported in varying degrees, by three of our prior cases: [*Cox, Oklahoma Publishing, Daily Mail*]. I disagree. None of these cases requires the harsh outcome reached today.

. . . While there are similarities [to *Cox*], critical aspects of that case make it wholly distinguishable from this one. First, in [*Cox*], the victim's name had been disclosed in the hearing where her assailants pled guilty; and, as we recognized, judicial records have always been considered public information in this country. [ ] In fact, even the earliest notion of privacy rights exempted the information contained in judicial records from its protections. [ ] Second, unlike the incident report at issue here . . . the judicial proceedings at issue in [*Cox*] were open as a matter of state law. . . .

These facts . . . were critical to our analysis in [*Cox*]. . . .

[*Cox*] stands for the proposition that the State cannot make the press its first line of defense in withholding private information from the public—it cannot ask the press to secrete private facts that the State makes no effort to safeguard in the first place. In this case, however, the State has undertaken "means which avoid [but obviously, not altogether prevent] public documentation or other exposure of private information." No doubt this is why the Court frankly admits that "[*Cox*] . . . cannot fairly be read as controlling here." [ ]

. . .

. . . I cannot agree that [*Cox, Oklahoma Publishing, Daily Mail*] require—or even substantially support—the result reached by the Court today.

II

We are left, then, to wonder whether the three "independent reasons" the Court cites for reversing the judgment for B.J.F. support its result. [ ]

The first of these relied on by the Court is the fact "appellant gained access to [B.J.F.'s name] through a government news release." [ ] "The government's issuance of such a release, without qualification, can only convey to recipients that the government considered dissemination lawful," the court suggests. [ ] So described, this case begins to look like the situation in *Oklahoma Publishing*, where a judge invited reporters into his courtroom, but then tried to forbid them from reporting on the proceedings they observed. But this case is profoundly different. Here the "release" of information provided by the government was not, as the Court says, "without qualification." As the Star's own reporter conceded at trial, the crime incident report that inadvertently included B.J.F.'s name was posted in a room that contained signs making it clear that the names of rape victims were not matters of public record, and were not to be published. [ ] The Star's reporter indicated that she understood that she "[was not] allowed to take down that information" (*i.e.*, B.J.F.'s name) and that "[was] not supposed to take the information from the police department." [ ] Thus, by her own admission the posting of the incident report did not convey to the Star's reporter the idea that "the government considered dissemination lawful"; the Court's suggestion to the contrary is inapt.

Instead, Florida has done precisely what we suggested, in [*Cox*], that States wishing to protect the privacy rights of rape victims might do: "respond [to the challenge] by means which *avoid* public documentation or other exposure of private information." [ ] By amending its public records statute to exempt rape [victims'] names from disclosure, [ ] and forbidding its officials from releasing such information, [ ], the State has taken virtually every step imaginable to prevent what happened here. This case presents a far cry, then, from [*Cox*] or *Oklahoma Publishing*, where the State asked the news media not to publish information it had made generally available to the public: here, the State is not asking the media to do the State's job in the first instance. Unfortunately, as this case illustrates, mistakes happen: even when States take measures to "avoid" disclosure, sometimes rape victim's names are found out. As I see it, it is not too much to ask the press, in instances such as this, to respect simple standards of decency and refrain from publishing a victim's name, address, and/or phone number.

Second, the Court complains that appellant was judged here under too strict a liability standard. The Court contends that a newspaper might be found liable under the Florida courts' negligence *per se*

theory without regard to a newspaper's scienter or degree of fault. [   ]
The short answer to this complaint is that whatever merit the Court's
argument might have, it is totally inapposite here, where the jury
found that appellant acted with "reckless indifference towards the
rights of others," [   ], a standard far higher than the *Gertz* standard the
Court urges as a constitutional minimum today. [   ] B.J.F. proved the
Star's negligence at trial—and, actually, far more than simple negligence; the Court's concerns about damages resting on a strict liability
or mere causation basis are irrelevant to the validity of the judgment
for appellee.

But even taking the Court's concerns in the abstract, they miss the
mark. Permitting liability under a negligence *per se* theory does not
mean that defendants will be held liable without a showing of negligence, but rather, that the standard of care has been set by the
legislature, instead of the courts. The Court says that negligence *per se*
permits a plaintiff to hold a defendant liable without a showing that
the disclosure was "of a fact about a person's private life . . . that a
reasonable person would find highly offensive." [   ] But the point
here is that the legislature—reflecting popular sentiment—has determined that disclosure of the fact that a person was raped is categorically a revelation that reasonable people find offensive. And as for the
Court's suggestion that the Florida courts' theory permits liability
without regard for whether the victim's identity is already known, or
whether she herself has made it known—these are facts that would
surely enter into the calculation of damages in such a case. In any
event, none of these mitigating factors was present here; whatever the
force of the arguments generally, they do not justify the Court's ruling
against B.J.F. in this case.

Third, the Court faults the Florida criminal statute for being
underinclusive: § 794.03 covers disclosure of rape [victims'] names in
"instrument[s] of mass communication," but not other means of distribution, the Court observes. [   ] But our cases which have struck down
laws that limit or burden the press due to their underinclusiveness
have involved situations where a legislature has singled out one segment of the news media or press for adverse treatment, [   ]. Here, the
Florida law evenhandedly covers all "instrument[s] of mass communication" no matter their form, media, content, nature or purpose. It
excludes neighborhood gossips, [   ], because presumably the Florida
Legislature has determined that neighborhood gossips do not pose the
danger and intrusion to rape victims that "instrument[s] of mass
communication" do. Simply put: Florida wanted to prevent the widespread distribution of rape [victims'] names, and therefore enacted a
statute tailored almost as precisely as possible to achieving that end.

Moreover, the Court's "underinclusiveness" analysis itself is "underinclusive." After all, the lawsuit against the Star which is at issue
here is not an action for violating the statute which the Court deems
underinclusive, but is, more accurately, for the negligent publication of
appellee's name. [   ] The scheme which the Court should review,

then, is not only § 794.03 (which, as noted above, merely provided the standard of care in this litigation), but rather, the whole of Florida privacy tort law. As to the latter, Florida does recognize a tort of publication of private facts. Thus, it is quite possible that the neighborhood gossip whom the Court so fears being left scott-free to spread news of a rape victim's identity would be subjected to the same (or similar) liability regime under which appellant was taxed. The Court's myopic focus on § 794.03 ignores the probability that Florida law is more comprehensive than the Court gives it credit for being.

Consequently, neither the State's "dissemination" of B.J.F.'s name, nor the standard of liability imposed here, nor the underinclusiveness of Florida tort law require setting aside the verdict for B.J.F. And as noted above, such a result is not compelled by our cases. I turn, therefore, to the more general principles at issue here to see if they recommend the Court's result.

III

At issue in this case is whether there is any information about people, which—though true—may not be published in the press. By holding that only "a state interest of the highest order" permits the State to penalize the publication of truthful information, and by holding that protecting a rape victim's right to privacy is not among those state interests of the highest order, the Court accepts appellant's invitation, [ ], to obliterate one of the most note-worthy legal inventions of the 20th-Century; the tort of the publication of private facts. [ ] Even if the Court's opinion does not say as much today, such obliteration will follow inevitably from the Court's conclusion here. If the First Amendment prohibits wholly private persons (such as B.J.F.) from recovering from the publication of the fact that she was raped, I doubt that there remain any "private facts" which persons may assume will not be published in the newspapers, or broadcast on television.

Of course, the right to privacy is not absolute. Even the article widely relied upon in cases vindicating privacy rights, Warren & Brandeis, The Right to Privacy, 4 Harv. L. Rev., at 193, recognized that this right inevitably conflicts with the public's right to know about matters of general concern—and that sometimes, the latter must trump the former. [ ] Resolving this conflict is a difficult matter, and I do not fault the Court for attempting to strike an appropriate balance between the two, but rather, for according too little weight to B.J.F.'s side of equation, and too much on the other.

I would strike the balance rather differently. Writing for the Ninth Circuit, Judge Merrill put this view eloquently:

"Does the spirit of the Bill of Rights require that individuals be free to pry into the unnewsworthy private affairs of their fellowmen? In our view it does not. In our view, fairly defined areas of privacy must have the protection of law if the quality of life is to continue to be reasonably acceptable. The public's right to know is, then, subject to reasonable limitations so far as concerns the private facts of its individual members." [   ]

Ironically, this Court, too, had occasion to consider this same balance just a few weeks ago, in *United States Department of Justice* v. *Reporters Committee for Freedom of the Press*, 489 U.S. 749[16 Med. L.Rptr. 1545] (1989). There, we were faced with a press request, under the Freedom of Information Act, for a "rap sheet" on a person accused of bribing a Congressman—presumably, a person whose privacy rights would be far less than B.J.F.'s. Yet this Court rejected the media's request for disclosure of the "rap sheet," saying:

> "The privacy interest in maintaining the practical obscurity of rap-sheet information will always be high. When the subject of such a rap sheet is a private citizen and when the information is in the Government's control as compilation, rather than as a record of 'what the government is up to,' the privacy interest . . . is . . . at its apex while the . . . public interest in disclosure is at its nadir." [   ]

The Court went on to conclude that disclosure of rap sheets "categorical[ly]" constitutes an "unwarranted" invasion of privacy. [   ] The same surely must be true—indeed, much more so—for the disclosure of a rape victim's name.

I do not suggest that the Court's decision today is radical departure from a previously charted course. The Court's ruling has been foreshadowed. In *Time, Inc.* v. *Hill*, [   ], we observed that—after a brief period in this century where Brandeis' view was ascendant—the trend in "modern" jurisprudence has been to eclipse an individual's right to maintain private any truthful information that the press wished to publish. More recently, in [*Cox*], we acknowledged the possibility that the First Amendment may prevent a State from ever subjecting the publication of truthful but private information to civil liability. Today, we hit the bottom of the slippery slope.

I would find a place to draw the line higher on the hillside: a spot high enough to protect B.J.F.'s desire for privacy and peace-of-mind in the wake of a horrible personal tragedy. There is no public interest in publishing the names, addresses, and phone numbers of persons who are the victims of crime—and no public interest in immunizing the press from liability in the rare cases where a State's efforts to protect a victim's privacy have failed. Consequently, I respectfully dissent.

Notes and Questions

1. Why is the *Star* 's case not precisely covered by *Cox* ?

2. Why is the *Star* 's case not precisely covered by *Daily Mail* ?

3. How might the *Star* 's case have been analyzed in a state in which there was no statute?

4.   How might the *Star*'s case have been analyzed if the *Star* had learned about the name from an eyewitness rather than as the result of a mistake in the sheriff's office?

5.   What might change if it turned out that the *Star* got the name from a sheriff's deputy who violated a statute in revealing the name?

6.   Does state law or the First Amendment protect a broadcaster that identifies a rape victim in a case in which a man arrested on a rape charge claims that the warden beat him up? (The alleged rape victim is the warden's daughter.) Does *Florida Star* address this?

What analysis in a case in which the rape victim is the daughter of a man who is a strong proponent of criminal rehabilitation and early paroles? What if the rapist had been recently paroled after serving time for rape?

What analysis in a case in which a statute provides that an accused rapist is not to be identified unless and until he is brought to trial?

7.   The decision in *Florida Star* led to a petition seeking review of a case involving an alleged invasion of privacy by a television statement which disclosed the identity of a rape victim. Ross v. Midwest Communications Inc., 870 F.2d 271, 16 Med.L.Rptr. 1463 (5th Cir.1989), cert. denied 493 U.S. 935. Marla Ross was raped in 1983 by an assailant who was never apprehended. Police assured her her name would be held in strict confidence. In a documentary about the possible innocence of a man accused of another rape, Minneapolis television station WCCO–TV mentioned Ross as "Marla" and showed a photograph of the house in which she lived at the time of the rape. A federal district court granted summary judgment for the television station, holding that the details of the rape were a matter of legitimate public interest, and the U.S. Court of appeals for the Fifth Circuit affirmed. In his petition for review following the *Florida Star* case, Ross's attorney told the Supreme Court that its decision in *Florida Star* "shattered the fragile confidence rape survivors possessed in law enforcement promises that their identities would not be disclosed." Med.L.Rptr. News Notes, Sept. 26, 1989. The Supreme Court denied *certiorari* on Oct. 30. 493 U.S. 935 (1989).

8.   The highly publicized sexual assault charges against William Kennedy Smith, along with decisions by a London tabloid, an American supermarket tabloid (*The Globe*), *The New York Times* and NBC to identify Patricia Bowman, the woman who made the allegations against him, raised anew the concerns about the proper ways of treating complainants in sexual assault cases prior to any court determination that they are, in fact, victims. Public disclosure of Bowman's history, particularly in a profile of her in the *Times*, generated a national controversy over identification of rape complainants.

The day after NBC first used Bowman's name, *The New York Times* published its profile of her, including comments by unnamed sources that she had had a poor academic record and "a little wild streak" in high school, had borne a child out of wedlock, and frequented expensive bars in Palm Beach. The story was accompanied by an editor's note saying that *The Times* ordinarily did not publish rape victims' names, "but editors said yesterday that NBC's broadcast took the matter out of their hands." See Butterfield and Tabor, Leap up Social Ladder for Woman in Rape Inquiry, New York Times, April 17, 1991 at A17. (In later editions the headline was changed to "Woman in Florida Rape Inquiry Fought Adversity and Sought Acceptance").

The *Times* story set off a furor within the newspaper's own staff and around the country. A week later *The Times* ran an editor's note saying it had not intended to challenge the veracity of the woman's accusations and that the story should have included such a statement. See New York Times, April 26, 1991 at A3. The same issue of the *Times* contained a story reporting that 100 *Times* employees had signed a petition objecting to the original story about the woman and that a staff meeting of *Times* editors with 300 staffers "quickly turned confrontational." The story quoted one of the *Times* editors who approved the story as saying *Times* editors expected much of the mainstream press to follow its lead in identifying the woman, but that most news organizations did not do so. Glaberson, "Times Article Naming Rape Accuser Ignites Debate on Journalistic Values," New York Times, April 26, 1991 at A12.

A local prosecutor in Florida filed misdemeanor charges against *The Globe*, which is published in Boca Raton. The publication was charged with violating the criminal statute on which B.J.F.'s civil suit was based in the Florida Star case. The statute provided a $500 fine and up to 60 days in jail for publishing a rape victim's name. The prosecutor was said to be studying whether the statute could be invoked against out-of-state media such as *The New York Times* and NBC. Weekly Newspaper Charged with Violating Law on Rape, New York Times, May 9, 1991 at A18. He also asked a state circuit court for a declaratory judgment as to the constitutionality and extra-territorial applicability of the statute, which had been on the books for 80 years but had not previously been employed in a criminal prosecution. Suro, Ruling is Sought on Rape Name Law, New York Times, April 19, 1991 at B6.

A state court judge dismissed the criminal proceeding against *The Globe,* holding the statute unconstitutional on its face and as applied. The judge determined that *The Globe* had obtained the victim's name by lawful means through interviews with public officials, Palm Beach patrons and others, and by reading other media. He believed *Daily Mail, Landmark Communications* and *Florida Star* all precluded the enforcement of the statute. Florida v. The Globe Communications Corp., No. 91–111008MM A02, Palm Beach County Court, Oct. 24, 1991. The state appealed this decision, and the appeal was transferred to Miami.

After Smith's acquittal on the rape charge, Patricia Bowman appeared on the ABC News television program "Prime Time Live" without the "blue dot" that had hidden her face except during inadvertant glitches during the television coverage of the trial. Her appearance pushed the program to its highest rating ever on Thursday night. It normally finished third behind "L.A. Law" and "Knots Landing" but was in first place on the night of the Bowman appearance. New York Times, Dec. 21, 1991 at 47.

NBC similarly identified the accuser of boxer Mike Tyson. The executive producer of NBC News said that not naming her would open NBC up to criticism from people who would say, "How come you used Bowman's name, but not this one's?" USA Today, Feb 3, 1992 at 3D. In an interview on NBC Today two months later, Bowman made a personal appeal to NBC News President Michael Gartner to stop the policy of naming alleged rape victims. She called the policy "frightening" and said disclosure inhibits victims from coming forward. An NBC spokesperson said the network had no plans to change the policy of making decisions on naming rape victims on a case-by-case basis. The spokesperson said Gartner believes "the more we tell our viewers, the better informed they'll be in making up their own minds about the issues involved." USA Today, Apr. 29, 1992 at 3D.

d. *Enjoining Violations of Privacy*

Many commentators have observed that damages in defamation are a more adequate remedy than in truthful invasion of privacy cases. In defamation the award of damages, especially special damages, may compensate the plaintiff for a loss of reputation that has in fact injured him financially. Even a judgment for nominal damages may have a vital symbolic function. In privacy, however, once the invasion has occurred the embarrassing truth is out and a judgment or an award of money does not resurrect a sullied reputation or undo other harm caused by the publication. Counterattack and counterspeech are not useful here.

Thus, courts have looked more seriously at alternatives in privacy suits and have been somewhat more responsive to a plea for an injunction to prevent the utterance of the invasion in the first place. Often the plaintiff learns about the invasion only after actual broadcast or publication, but in some situations prevention is feasible. Because the privacy action is so recent in origin, it lacks a long history like that of defamation. In the latter, the injunction came to be totally rejected.

The Supreme Court has never passed on the constitutionality of injunctions in this area. Despite three cases taken on appeal, the Court has yet to come to grips with the issue. In the first, a famous baseball player persuaded the New York courts to enjoin the publication of an unauthorized biography that contained false dialogue. Spahn v. Julian Messner, Inc., 21 N.Y.2d 124, 286 N.Y.S.2d 832, 233 N.E.2d 840 (1967). The defendants compromised and settled their dispute while it was being appealed to the Supreme Court.

The second chance came in a case involving a motion picture about conditions in a Massachusetts institution for the criminally insane. The state court barred showing of the picture except to selected groups because of the producer's invasion of the privacy of the inmates, assertedly in violation of an agreement he signed in order to get permission to make the film. Commonwealth v. Wiseman, 356 Mass. 251, 249 N.E.2d 610 (1969). The Supreme Court denied *certiorari* to Frederick Wiseman, the producer, 398 U.S. 960 (1969), over the lengthy dissent of Justice Harlan, joined by Justices Douglas and Brennan:

> Petitioners seek review in this Court of a decision of the Massachusetts Supreme Judicial Court enjoining the commercial distribution to general audiences of the film "Titticut Follies." Petitioners' film is a "documentary" of life in Bridgewater State Hospital for the criminally insane. Its stark portrayal of patient routine and treatment of the inmates is at once a scathing indictment of the inhumane conditions that prevailed at the time of the film and an undeniable infringement of the privacy of the inmates filmed, who are shown nude and engaged in acts that would unquestionably embarrass an individual of normal sensitivity. . . .
>
> The balance between these two interests, that of the individual's privacy and the public's right to know about conditions in public institutions, is not one that is easily struck, particularly in a case like that before us where the importance of the issue is matched by the extent of the invasion of privacy. . . .

In 1991 the judge revised the order to require only that names and addresses of inmates be kept confidential. At the Boston Film Festival in September 1991, the film was shown to a general audience for the first time since its suppression in 1967. See "Judge Lifts Bar on 'Titticut Follies' Film," News Media and the Law, Fall 1991, at 36.

The third Supreme Court case involved a claim by a former patient trying to enjoin her analyst from publishing a book the analyst had written about the patient's treatment. Although names and other facts were changed in the book, plaintiff alleged that she and her family were easily identifiable. The state courts granted a preliminary injunction enjoining all distribution until the litigation concluded. The defendants, including the book's publisher, sought *certiorari*, claiming that the injunction against publishing concededly true statements of medical and scientific importance violated the First Amendment. The Court granted *certiorari*, Roe v. Doe, 417 U.S. 907 (1974), and heard oral arguments. It then decided not to decide the case by dismissing the writ of *certiorari* as having been "improvidently granted." 420 U.S. 307 (1975). The complication of the confidential relationship between the parties and the murky record caused by the use of the names "Doe" and "Roe" might have dissuaded the Court from deciding the case.

The case then went to trial on the merits. The trial judge found that the plaintiff was entitled to a remedy because of defendant's violation of an implied agreement to treat the plaintiff in confidence. He awarded damages for the harm plaintiff suffered from the release of 220 copies of the book before the preliminary injunction was issued. He also permanently enjoined distribution of the remaining stock. Doe v. Roe, 93 Misc.2d 201, 400 N.Y.S.2d 668 (1977). By subsequent order, the remaining volumes were destroyed.

In 1976 a television crew entered an institution for the care of neglected children and filmed some of the children. Questions "which could fairly be described as leading or suggestive were directed to the children with respect to drugs, assaults, etc. to which the children responded." The institutions director sought to enjoin the televising of the film. The trial judge denied a preliminary injunction and vacated his temporary restraining order, but granted a stay pending appeal. The appellate court concluded after viewing the film that they were "not persuaded that its sole or even its chief object is to provide information which could lead to a correction of the conditions it claims exists." Nonetheless, nothing in the film warranted a ban on its showing. If appropriate, the defendants could be "called to account" after the fact. Quinn v. Johnson, 51 A.D.2d 391, 381 N.Y.S.2d 875 (1976). At this point, the case was resolved when the broadcaster decided that it could blur the faces of the children to make them unrecognizable. One newspaper noted, "Here was a case where the large principle against prior restraint or censorship was upheld; and yet, where a humane judgment could be made at the same time. Nothing in the First Amendment prevents the exercise of good taste and compassion." New York Times, May 10, 1976 at 26.

How might one analyze the competing interests in these invasion of privacy cases when the issue becomes one of a remedy for a true statement that is adjudged an invasion? How do these cases square with concern about prior restraint?

3. APPROPRIATION

The fourth branch of invasion of privacy is appropriation of another's name or likeness for commercial or trade purposes. Its major impact is on the field of advertising, because news reports have generally been held not to be "for commercial or trade purposes." But see Zacchini v. Scripps–Howard Broadcasting, *infra*. As is the case with other branches of invasion of privacy, truth is not a defense. A manufacturer who advertises that John Smith uses his product may not be able to defend himself merely by proving that John Smith does use his product, although that is important for other reasons.

What must be demonstrated to avoid a successful appropriation action is consent. This usually comes in the form of a written "release" since many states require that consent to appropriation be written.

Indeed, it is common for advertising agencies and even news organizations to have standard release forms available for use. Many release forms are limited in that they restrict the uses that can be made of a particular name or likeness or the period of time during which the use will be permitted. Numerous appropriation cases have been the result of using a picture in a manner not covered by the original release.

Determining what constitutes commercial or trade purposes has not always proved easy for the courts. In one case, a television station that telephoned a couple during the program "Dialing for Dollars," and aired the ensuing conversation found itself liable for appropriation. Jeppson v. United Television, Inc., 580 P.2d 1087, 3 Med.L.Rptr. 2513 (Utah 1978). Does the following case offer any guidance?

ZACCHINI v. SCRIPPS–HOWARD BROADCASTING CO.

Supreme Court of the United States, 1977.
433 U.S. 562, 97 S.Ct. 2849, 53 L.Ed.2d 965, 2 Med.L.Rptr. 2089.

MR. JUSTICE WHITE delivered the opinion of the Court.

Petitioner, Hugo Zacchini, is an entertainer. He performs a "human cannonball" act in which he is shot from a cannon into a net some 200 feet away. Each performance occupies some 15 seconds. In August and September 1972, petitioner was engaged to perform his act on a regular basis at the Geauga County Fair in Burton, Ohio. He performed in a fenced area, surrounded by grandstands, at the fair grounds. Members of the public attending the fair were not charged a separate admission fee to observe his act.

On August 2, a freelance reporter for Scripps–Howard Broadcasting Co., the operator of a television broadcasting station and respondent in this case, attended the fair. He carried a small movie camera. Petitioner noticed the reporter and asked him not to film the performance. The reporter did not do so on that day; but on the instructions of the producer of respondent's daily newscast, he returned the following day and videotaped the entire act. This film clip, approximately 15 seconds in length, was shown on the 11 o'clock news program that night, together with favorable commentary.[1]

Petitioner then brought this action for damages, alleging that he is "engaged in the entertainment business," that the act he performs is one "invented by his father and . . . performed only by his family for the last fifty years," that respondent "showed and commercialized the film of his act without his consent," and that such conduct was an "unlawful appropriation of plaintiff's professional property." App. 4–5.

1. The script of the commentary accompanying the film clip read as follows: [Indent] "This . . . now . . . is the story of a *true spectator* sport . . . the sport of human cannonballing . . . in fact, the great *Zacchini* is about the only human cannonball around, these days . . . just happens that, *where* he is, is the Great Geauga County Fair, in Burton . . . and believe me, although it's not a *long* act, it's a thriller . . . and you really need to see it *in person* . . . to appreciate it. . . ." (Emphasis in original.)

Respondent answered and moved for summary judgment, which was granted by the trial court.

. . .

. . . Insofar as the Ohio Supreme Court held that the First and Fourteenth Amendments of the United States Constitution required judgment for respondent, we reverse the judgment of that court.

. . .

Even if the judgment in favor of respondent must nevertheless be understood as ultimately resting on Ohio law, it appears that at the very least the Ohio court felt compelled by what it understood to be federal constitutional considerations to construe and apply its own law in the manner it did. In this event, we have jurisdiction and should decide the federal issue; for if the state court erred in its understanding of our cases and of the First and Fourteenth Amendments we should so declare, leaving the state court free to decide the privilege issue solely as a matter of Ohio law. [ ] If the Supreme Court of Ohio "held as it did because it felt under compulsion of federal law as enunciated by this Court so to hold, it should be relieved of that compulsion. It should be freed to decide . . . these suits according to its own local law." [ ]

The Ohio Supreme Court relied heavily on Time, Inc. v. Hill, 385 U.S. 374 (1967), but that case does not mandate a media privilege to televise a performer's entire act without his consent. Involved in Time, Inc. v. Hill was a claim under the New York "Right of Privacy" statute that Life Magazine, in the course of reviewing a new play, had connected the play with a long-past incident involving petitioner and his family and had falsely described their experience and conduct at that time. The complaint sought damages for humiliation and suffering flowing from these nondefamatory falsehoods that allegedly invaded Hill's privacy. The Court held, however, that the opening of a new play linked to an actual incident was a matter of public interest and that Hill could not recover without showing that the Life report was knowingly false or was published with reckless disregard for the truth—the same rigorous standard that had been applied in New York Times Co. v. Sullivan, [ ].

Time, Inc. v. Hill, which was hotly contested and decided by a divided Court, involved an entirely different tort from the "right of publicity" recognized by the Ohio Supreme Court. . . .

The differences between these two torts are important. First, the State's interests in providing a cause of action in each instance are different. "The interest protected" in permitting recovery for placing the plaintiff in a false light "is clearly that of reputation, with the same overtones of mental distress as in defamation." Prosser, supra, 48 Calif.L.Rev., at 400. By contrast, the State's interest in permitting a "right of publicity" is in protecting the proprietary interest of the individual in his act in part to encourage such entertainment. As we later note, the State's interest is closely analogous to the goals of patent and copyright law, focusing on the right of the individual to reap the reward of his endeavors and having little to do with protecting feelings or reputation. Second, the two torts differ in the degree to which they intrude on dissemination of information to the public. In "false light" cases the only way to protect the interests involved is to attempt to minimize the publication of the damaging matter, while in "right of publicity" cases the only question is who gets to do the publishing. An entertainer such as petitioner usually has no objection to the widespread publication of his act as long as he gets the commercial benefit of such publication. Indeed, in the present case petitioner did not seek to enjoin the broadcast of his act; he simply sought compensation for the broadcast in the form of damages.

. . .

Moreover, *Time, Inc. v. Hill, New York Times, Metromedia, Gertz,* and *Firestone* all involved the reporting of events; in none of them was there an attempt to broadcast or publish an entire act for which the performer ordinarily gets paid. It is evident, and there is no claim here to the contrary, that petitioner's state-law right of publicity would not serve to prevent respondent from reporting the newsworthy facts about petitioner's act. Wherever the line in particular situations is to be drawn between media reports that are protected and those that are not, we are quite sure that the First and Fourteenth Amendments do not immunize the media when they broadcast a performer's entire act without his consent. The Constitution no more prevents a State from requiring respondent to compensate petitioner for broadcasting his act on television than it would privilege respondent to film and broadcast a copyrighted dramatic work without liability to the copyright owner, [ ], or to film and broadcast a prize fight, [ ], or a baseball game, [ ], where the promoters or the participants had other plans for publicizing the event. There are ample reasons for reaching this conclusion.

The broadcast of a film of petitioner's entire act poses a substantial threat to the economic value of that performance. As the Ohio court recognized, this act is the product of petitioner's own talents and energy, the end result of much time, effort, and expense. Much of its economic value lies in the "right of exclusive control over the publicity given to his performance"; if the public can see the act free on television, it will be less willing to pay to see it at the fair.[12] The effect of a public broadcast of the performance is similar to preventing petitioner from charging an admission fee. . . . Moreover, the broadcast of petitioner's entire performance, unlike the unauthorized use of another's name for purposes of trade or the incidental use of a

---

12. It is possible, of course, that respondent's news broadcast increased the value of petitioner's performance by stimulating the public's interest in seeing the act live. In these circumstances, petitioner would not be able to prove damages and thus would not recover. But petitioner has alleged that the broadcast injured him to the extent of $25,000, App. 5, and we think the State should be allowed to authorize compensation of this injury if proved.

name or picture by the press, goes to the heart of petitioner's ability to earn a living as an entertainer. Thus, in this case, Ohio has recognized what may be the strongest case for a "right of publicity"—involving, not the appropriation of an entertainer's reputation to enhance the attractiveness of a commercial product, but the appropriation of the very activity by which the entertainer acquired his reputation in the first place.

Of course, Ohio's decision to protect petitioner's right of publicity here rests on more than a desire to compensate the performer for the time and effort invested in his act; the protection provides an economic incentive for him to make the investment required to produce a performance of interest to the public. This same consideration under-lies the patent and copyright laws long enforced by this Court. . . .

There is no doubt that entertainment, as well as news, enjoys First Amendment protection. It is also true that entertainment itself can be important news. Time, Inc. v. Hill. But it is important to note that neither the public nor respondent will be deprived of the benefit of petitioner's performance as long as his commercial stake in his act is appropriately recognized. Petitioner does not seek to enjoin the broad-cast of his performance; he simply wants to be paid for it. Nor do we think that a state-law damages remedy against respondent would represent a species of liability without fault contrary to the letter or spirit of Gertz v. Robert Welch, Inc., [ ]. Respondent knew exactly that petitioner objected to televising his act but nevertheless displayed the entire film.

We conclude that although the State of Ohio may as a matter of its own law privilege the press in the circumstances of this case, the First and Fourteenth Amendments do not require it to do so.

Reversed.

MR. JUSTICE POWELL, with whom MR. JUSTICE BRENNAN and MR. JUSTICE MARSHALL join, dissenting.

Disclaiming any attempt to do more than decide the narrow case before us, the Court reverses the decision of the Supreme Court of Ohio based on repeated incantation of a single formula: "a performer's entire act." The holding today is summed up in one sentence:

"Wherever the line in particular situations is to be drawn between media reports that are protected and those that are not, we are quite sure that the First and Fourteenth Amendments do not immunize the media when they broadcast a performer's entire act without his consent."

I doubt that this formula provides a standard clear enough even for resolution in this case.[1] In any event, I am not persuaded that the

---

1. Although the record is not explicit, it is unlikely that the "act" commenced abruptly with the explosion that launched petitioner on his way, ending with the

landing in the net a few seconds later. One may assume that the actual firing was preceded by some fanfare, possibly stretch-ing over several minutes, to heighten the

Court's opinion is appropriately sensitive to the First Amendment values at stake, and I therefore dissent.

Although the Court would draw no distinction, I do not view respondent's action as comparable to unauthorized commercial broadcasts of sporting events, theatrical performances, and the like where the broadcaster keeps the profits. There is no suggestion here that respondent made any such use of the film. Instead, it simply reported on what petitioner concedes to be a newsworthy event, in a way hardly surprising for a television station—by means of film coverage. The report was part of an ordinary daily news program, consuming a total of 15 seconds. It is a routine example of the press fulfilling the informing function so vital to our system.

The Court's holding that the station's ordinary news report may give rise to substantial liability has disturbing implications, for the decision could lead to a degree of media self-censorship. [ ] Hereafter whenever a television news editor is unsure whether certain film footage received from a camera crew might be held to portray an "entire act," he may decline coverage—even of clearly newsworthy events—or confine the broadcast to watered-down verbal reporting, perhaps with an occasional still picture. The public is then the loser. This is hardly the kind of news reportage that the First Amendment is meant to foster. [ ]

In my view the First Amendment commands a different analytical starting point from the one selected by the Court. Rather than begin with a quantitative analysis of the performer's behavior—is this or is this not his entire act?—we should direct initial attention to the actions of the news media: what use did the station make of the film footage? When a film is used, as here, for a routine portion of a regular news program, I would hold that the First Amendment protects the station from a "right of publicity" or "appropriation" suit, absent a strong showing by the plaintiff that the news broadcast was a subterfuge or cover for private or commercial exploitation.[4]

. . . In a suit like the one before us, however, the plaintiff does not complain about the fact of exposure to the public, but rather about its timing or manner. He welcomes some publicity, but seeks to retain control over means and manner as a way to maximize for himself the monetary benefits that flow from such publication. But having made

audience's anticipation: introduction of the performer, description of the uniqueness and danger, last-minute checking of the apparatus, and entry into the cannon, all accompanied by suitably ominous commentary from the master of ceremonies. If this is found to be the case on remand, then respondent could not be said to have appropriated the "entire act" in its 15-second newsclip—and the Court's opinion then would afford no guidance for resolution of the case. Moreover, in future cases involving different performances, similar difficulties in determining just what constitutes the "entire act" are inevitable.

4. This case requires no detailed specification of the standards for identifying a subterfuge, since there is no claim here that respondent's news use was anything but bona fide. [ ] I would point out, however, that selling time during a news broadcast to advertisers in the customary fashion does not make for "commercial exploitation" in the sense intended here. [ ]

the matter public—having chosen, in essence, to make it newsworthy—
he cannot, consistent with the First Amendment, complain of routine
news reportage. Cf. Gertz v. Robert Welch, Inc., [   ] (clarifying the
different liability standards appropriate in defamation suits, depending
on whether or not the plaintiff is a public figure).

Since the filmclip here was undeniably treated as news and since
there is no claim that the use was subterfuge, respondent's actions were
constitutionally privileged. I would affirm.

[Mr. Justice Stevens dissented on the ground that he could not tell
whether the Ohio Supreme Court had relied on federal constitutional
issues in deciding the case. He would have remanded the case to that
court "for clarification of its holding before deciding the federal constitutional issue."]

Notes and Questions

1.   On remand, the Ohio Supreme Court took advantage of the opportunity afforded by the majority opinion and decided that nothing in the
Ohio Constitution protected the behavior of the media defendant.   The
case was remanded for trial. Zacchini v. Scripps–Howard Broadcasting
Co., 54 Ohio St.2d 286, 376 N.E.2d 582, 3 Med.L.Rptr. 2444 (1978).

2.   How important is it that the majority treats the 15 seconds as the
"entire act"?

3.   Does this case involve an aspect of "privacy"? Does it resemble the
Cox Broadcasting case in that both involved lawfully obtained information of interest or concern to the public? Can you explain why the
defendant in *Cox Broadcasting* did not have to pay while the defendant
in *Zacchini* might have to pay?

4.   After *Zacchini*, what would happen in a case in which a street
artist who survives on contributions from passersby—a mime, an accor-
dionist, a dancer—is photographed by the local television station and
shown in a story about summer diversions on the streets of the city? Is
the street artist's claim as strong as Zacchini's?

5.   *Right of publicity*. The Zacchini case is an example of an offshoot
of appropriation known as right of publicity. This particular right was
once defined as follows:

> The distinctive aspect of the common-law right of publicity is
> that it recognizes the commercial value of the picture or represen-
> tation of a prominent person or performer and protects his proprie-
> tary interest in the profitability of his public reputation or persona.
> Ali v. Playgirl, Inc., 447 F.Supp. 723, 3 Med.L.Rptr. 2540 (S.D.N.Y.
> 1978).

Unlike the traditional tort of appropriation, right of publicity is
exclusively the province of well-known individuals. Also, whereas the
original tort was at least partially rooted in the concept of the right to
be let alone and not to be exploited for commercial or trade purposes,
this new variation seems only concerned with who should reap the

financial benefits. In essence it is a property right, as opposed to a personal right in some states. Thus, Johnny Carson was able to sue a manufacturer of portable toilets that were marketed under the name, "Here's Johnny." Carson v. Here's Johnny Portable Toilets, Inc., 698 F.2d 831, 9 Med.L.Rptr. 1153 (6th Cir.1983), reversing 498 F.Supp. 71 (E.D.Mich.1980). Similarly, the estate of Elvis Presley won a claim against the producers of THE BIG EL SHOW, an imitation of Presley's performances. Estate of Presley v. Russen, 513 F.Supp. 1339 (D.N.J. 1981).

In some cases it is not even the true name or likeness of a person, but rather some character or role that is at issue. In Groucho Marx Productions, Inc. v. Day and Night Co., Inc., 523 F.Supp. 485, 7 Med.L.Rptr. 2030 (S.D.N.Y.1981), reversed on other grounds 689 F.2d 317, 8 Med.L.Rptr. 2201 (2d Cir.1982), the court held that the play, "A Day in Hollywood, a Night in the Ukraine," appropriated the Marx brothers' characters. In this context, a suit for appropriation has become a new method of protecting creative work—even characters created by comedians. Is this a right equivalent to copyright? Should it be preempted by the federal copyright statute, especially in this context? How does it differ from copyright?

6. Baltimore Orioles, Inc. v. Major League Baseball Players Association, 805 F.2d 663, 13 Med.L.Rptr. 1625 (7th Cir.1986), certiorari denied 480 U.S. 941 (1987), raises the question of professional baseball players' right of publicity in the context of televised games. The court of appeals held that the team owners' copyright in videotaped telecasts preempts the players' right of publicity in their performances because the performances are fixed in tangible form and because the players' rights of publicity are equivalent to rights embraced in copyright.

7. In another case, Stephano v. News Group Publications, 64 N.Y.2d 174, 485 N.Y.S.2d 220, 474 N.E.2d 580, 11 Med.L.Rptr. 1303 (1984), a model sued for invasion of privacy under New York State's statute prohibiting appropriation for "advertising or trade purposes." The model had posed in a "bomber jacket" for a 1981 article on men's fall fashions for *New York* magazine. Contending that he had agreed to model for one article only, he sued, claiming a breach of his "right of publicity" because one of the photos was used in a "Best Bets" magazine column, giving an approximate price for the jacket and listing several stores at which it would be available. The New York Court of Appeals held that the magazine's use of the photo in the "Best Bets" column was of general public interest and that it was not used for advertising or trade purposes as defined by New York law. Despite the unusual result in *Zacchini*, the principle seems clear that the media will usually win such cases unless their claims of newsworthiness or public interest are exceptionally weak. Stephano's suit was *not*, of course, a copyright action, but the similarities to copyright—attempting to control or profit from what one perceives as one's property—are worth noting.

8. As noted in the *Hustler* case, p. 681, *supra*, the Rev. Jerry Falwell's suit against *Hustler* magazine alleged invasion of privacy as well as libel. Falwell alleged, in his privacy claim, that the "ad" constituted an unauthorized use of his name or likeness for trade purposes under the Virginia invasion of privacy statute. The court of appeals, noting that there were no decisions of the Virginia courts construing the statute, but that it was substantially similar to the New York statute, held that because the jury found that the parody in Falwell's case was not believable and because it contained a disclaimer, publication of the parody did not constitute a use of Falwell's name and likeness for purposes of trade.

9. When advertising agency Young & Rubicam contacted the agent of singer Bette Midler to ask whether she would be interested in doing a television commercial for the Ford Motor Company, the agent declined on Midler's behalf. The agency subsequently sought out Ula Hedwig, who had been a backup singer for Midler for 10 years, to do a sound-alike rendition of Midler's recording of "Do You Want to Dance." After the commercial aired, Midler sued under both copyright law and privacy law. The U.S. Court of Appeals for the Ninth Circuit held that the deliberate, unconsented imitation of the distinctive voice of a professional singer in order to sell a product constitutes an unlawful appropriation of identity under California law. Midler v. Ford Motor Co., 849 F.2d 460, 15 Med.L.Rptr. 1620 (9th Cir.1988), cert. denied 112 S.Ct. 1513 (1992). In March 1992, the Supreme Court denied *certiorari* in the case and a companion case, leaving in place an award to Midler of $400,000 in compensatory damages. Media Law Reporter News Notes, March 31, 1992.

10. The "New Kids on the Block" sued *USA Today* and *Star* magazine for violating their right of publicity—along with trademark infringement and misappropriation, when the "New Kids" trademark was used in articles which asked readers to participate, via a "900" telephone number, in a survey to determine the group's most popular member. The U.S. District Court for the Central District of California held that the use of the trademark was related to newsgathering and was not mere commercial exploitation, so the First Amendment barred the claims. The court of appeals affirmed. The New Kids on the Block v. News America Publishing, Inc., 971 F.2d 302, 20 Med.L.Rptr. 1468 (1992).

11. *Descendability*. Personal rights such as those protected by defamation and invasion of privacy law terminate at death. Thus, for example, one can publish defamatory statements about deceased individuals with impunity (unless the same statement also defames people who are still alive). Because the right of publicity is a property right, a great controversy has developed as to whether it survives the death of its creator.

Currently, there seem to be three distinct approaches being taken by various courts. One is that the right terminates upon death. Under this view, as soon as people die, their names, likenesses and characterizations are available for anyone to use without legal liability. At the other extreme is the position that death has no effect on the right of publicity. In jurisdictions adhering to this view, the consent of whoever owns the property in question (perhaps the individual's heirs or someone who has purchased the right) is always necessary. Finally, there is an intermediate approach that holds the right of publicity to survive death only if it was commercially exploited during the person's lifetime.

If the right of publicity continues beyond death (either because it always does or because it was commercially exploited during the person's lifetime), the next question is how long it lasts. A state statute might stipulate a specific number of years, or the right of publicity might last as long as it continues to be exploited by the individual's heirs or forever. State statutes that provide for survivability do so for varying periods of time ranging from 50 years after death in California to 10 years after death in Tennessee.

Chapter XIV

SPECIAL PROBLEMS OF ELECTRONIC MEDIA JOURNALISTS

Whereas defamation and invasion of privacy problems can arise in the context of entertainment programming on the electronic media (as well as in the context of electronic journalism), the special problems we consider in this chapter are ones that are typically limited to news and documentary programming. Among the problems are protection of government interests, news coverage of the administration of justice, journalist's privilege and newsgathering from public sources.

A. THE PROTECTION OF GOVERNMENT INTERESTS

In the discussion in Chapter I of abridgment of freedom of the press, we examined the question of prior restraint on dissemination of messages. In *Near*, p. 25, *supra*, we saw an example of a restraint imposed on a publication that had, in part, accused public officials in Minneapolis of involvement in bootlegging and gambling. In *New York Times*, p. 26, *supra*, we saw the federal government's Vietnam era attempt to restrain publication of the "Pentagon Papers," the secret study of U.S. decision-making in Southeast Asia. Recall that the Supreme Court found that the heavy burden of showing justification for the imposition of a prior restraint was met in neither case. In *The Progressive*, p. 26, *supra*, we saw the federal government's attempt to stop dissemination of the "secret of the H-bomb." That case, recall, ended with publication of the "secret" in publications other than *The Progressive*, and the case never reached the Supreme Court.

There are a variety of other contexts in which the government may want to use prior restraint or some other means to discourage or stop dissemination of messages that may present problems for the government, its officials, or its citizens.

For example, a 1972 case exemplifies the problems of authors who have had access to national security information. United States v. Marchetti, 466 F.2d 1309, 1 Med.L.Rptr. 1051 (4th Cir.1972), involved an injunction obtained by the government against publication of Marchetti's book about the Central Intelligence Agency, his former employer. At the time Marchetti joined, he promised not to divulge any classified information unless specifically authorized in writing by the director, and when he resigned from the CIA he signed a loyalty oath. The court upheld the restraint, and the Supreme Court denied *certiorari*, 409 U.S. 1063 (1972).

Sometimes the government's interest is with the protection of the private rights of its citizens—as in an instance in which a judge may seek to restrain dissemination of information in order to protect the fair trial rights of an accused individual.

Recall also from Chapter I the discussion of *Landmark Communications*, p. 30, *supra*, and *Daily Mail*, p. 30, *supra*, both of which involved attempts to protect a state or public interest through discouraging or restraining publication of facts that most electronic media journalists would certainly consider to be news.

Our long legal tradition against censorship and the difficulty of justifying such a restraint in court discourage most attempts to protect public or private interests through such restraints. Instead, as we have seen in defamation and privacy, we usually rely on the ability of persons who are damaged to sue *after* the dissemination has taken place.

B. PRESS COVERAGE OF THE ADMINISTRATION OF JUSTICE

Press coverage of the administration of justice poses special problems both for the press and for the courts. It is easy to generalize about the openness of the judicial system and about Americans' distaste for secret courts, and it is easy to generalize about our proud tradition of protecting the fairness of civil and criminal trials. The generalizations too often ignore the reality: the First Amendment right to freedom of the press and the Sixth Amendment right to a fair trial sometimes appear to give rise to conflict.

As journalists tell the story of a crime or arrest prior to trial, they inevitably influence opinions in the area, and it can be difficult—perhaps even impossible—to find jurors who can ignore press reports and come to a fair verdict based solely on evidence presented in court. On the other hand, if judges try to shape or stop news coverage of the administration of justice, they may be interfering with the First Amendment rights of journalists.

1. BACKGROUND

The judicial branch has been the object of considerable litigation as to which of its functions are to be open to public scrutiny. A specific constitutional provision, held to be solely for the benefit of the accused and not addressed to the press, is basic to our discussion. The Sixth Amendment to the United States Constitution provides: "In all criminal prosecutions, the accused shall enjoy the right to a speedy and public trial, by an impartial jury of the State and district wherein the crime shall have been committed. . . ."

Problems arise primarily in the context of press and public interest in dramatic criminal cases involving either sensational crimes or prominent persons, and less frequently in the context of highly-publicized civil lawsuits like General Westmoreland's against CBS. The resulting problems between journalists and lawyers/judges over pre-trial and trial news accounts have been referred to as "fair trial-free press" by the bar and "free press-fair trial" by the press.

In several Supreme Court cases of the 1960s, criminal convictions were reversed because the Court found that prejudicial press coverage had resulted in possible unfairness. Judges, realizing their responsibilities to protect defendants from such unfairness, reached for means of protection—ordering the press not to report certain information, closing pre-trial hearings to the press, keeping cameras out of the courtrooms, closing trials, etc. The press viewed such steps as intrusions on First Amendment rights. The Supreme Court decided cases involving these issues in the 1970s and 1980s.

The Supreme Court confronted the problem at the constitutional level in *Irvin v. Dowd*, 366 U.S. 717, 1 Med.L.Rptr. 1178 (1961). Defendant Leslie Irvin had been arrested in Indiana following a series of murders attributed to the "Mad Dog Killer." He was convicted and sentenced to death; his appeal included 46 exhibits indicating that, as Justice Clark put it, ". . . a barrage of newspaper headlines, articles, cartoons and pictures were unleashed against him during the six or seven months preceding his trial."

Typically in such appeals, newspaper headlines and stories receive greater emphasis than broadcast news accounts because of the easier availability of the former. The majority opinion in *Irvin* did, however, note that in the area "radio and TV stations . . . also carried extensive newscasts covering the same incidents."

Prominent in the telling evidence of trouble at the trial was the fact that the panel of potential jurors included 430 persons, of whom 268 were excused by the court itself as having fixed opinions as to the guilt of Irvin. At least 370 of the prospective jurors entertained some opinion as to Irvin's guilt. Finding a "pattern of deep and bitter prejudice," the Court vacated the conviction and remanded the case for retrial, at which Irvin was convicted again.

Another troubling case occurred when Wilbert Rideau was arrested in Louisiana for bank robbery, kidnapping and murder. The sheriff invited a film crew from the local television station to film the sheriff's "interview" with Rideau. During the 20–minute interrogation, Rideau confessed to the crimes. The station showed the interview three times. After a requested change of venue was denied, Rideau was convicted and sentenced to death. The Supreme Court overturned the conviction, noting that after drawing a jury from people who could have been exposed to the confession, any "court proceedings . . . could be but a hollow formality." The Court implied that nothing could have overcome the effects of the television film and that specific proof of juror prejudice was not necessary under such circumstances. Rideau v.

Louisiana, 373 U.S. 723, 1 Med.L.Rptr. 1183 (1963). (Rideau was ultimately retried and convicted a second time.)

Perhaps the most famous of the 1960s cases in this area was Sheppard v. Maxwell, 384 U.S. 333, 1 Med.L.Rptr. 1220 (1966). Dr. Sam Sheppard was accused of the 1954 murder of his pregnant wife, Marilyn, and tried in the light of national publicity. He was convicted and spent a number of years in prison before his attorney, a young, relatively unknown F. Lee Bailey, successfully carried Sheppard's appeal to the Supreme Court. Mr. Justice Clark delivered the opinion of the Court:

> Much of the material printed or broadcast during the trial was never heard from the witness stand, such as the charges that Sheppard had purposely impeded the murder investigation and must be guilty since he had hired a prominent criminal lawyer; that Sheppard was a perjurer; that he had sexual relations with numerous women; that his wife had characterized him as a "Jekyll–Hyde"; that he was "a bare-faced liar" because of his testimony as to police treatment; and finally, that a woman convict claimed Sheppard to be the father of her illegitimate child. As the trial progressed, the newspapers summarized and interpreted the evidence, devoting particular attention to the material that incriminated Sheppard, and often drew unwarranted inferences from testimony. At one point, a front-page picture of Mrs. Sheppard's blood-stained pillow was published after being "doctored" to show more clearly an alleged imprint of a surgical instrument.

> Nor is there doubt that this deluge of publicity reached at least some of the jury. On the only occasion that the jury was queried, two jurors admitted in open court to hearing the highly inflammatory charge that a prison inmate claimed Sheppard as the father of her illegitimate child. Despite the extent and nature of the publicity to which the jury was exposed during trial, the judge refused defense counsel's other requests that the jurors be asked whether they had read or heard specific prejudicial comment about the case, including the incidents we have previously summarized. In these circumstances, we can assume that some of this material reached members of the jury. [ ]

>   . . .

> The carnival atmosphere at trial could easily have been avoided since the courtroom and courthouse premises are subject to the control of the court. . . .

Concluding that the trial court judge had failed to protect the defendant's rights adequately, the Court ordered Sheppard released unless the state gave him a new trial. Ohio retried him, and Sheppard (unlike Irvin or Rideau) was acquitted at the second trial.

Some would argue that the overturned convictions of Irvin, Rideau and Sheppard reflected the strong protection of defendants' rights by the Warren Court. A 1975 case, Murphy v. Florida, 421 U.S. 794, 1 Med.L.Rptr. 1232 (1975), in which a criminal conviction was upheld, could be seen simply as reflecting the Court's changing attitudes toward defendants, but that analysis would fail to recognize that the circumstances of *Murphy* were quite different from those of the earlier cases. In *Murphy* the jurors in defendant's robbery trial had learned through news stories about some or all of Jack "Murph the Surf" Murphy's earlier convictions for murder, securities theft and the 1964 theft of the Star of India sapphire from a New York museum. The majority stated that qualified jurors need not be totally ignorant of the facts surrounding the case. The Court found in the *voir dire*— the examination of the potential jurors—no showing of hostility to the defendant. Four of the six jurors volunteered that defendant's past was irrelevant. Only 20 of the 78 persons examined were excused because of an opinion of guilt. (Note that this is quite unlike *Irvin*.) "This may indeed be 20 more than would occur in the trial of a totally obscure person, but it by no means suggests a community with sentiment so poisoned against the petitioner as to impeach the indifference of jurors who displayed no animus of their own." Only Justice Brennan dissented.

2. So-Called Remedies for the Fair Trial–Free Press Problem

a. The Standard Remedies

Although the judge's failure to maintain proper decorum during the trial was viewed as his major error in *Sheppard*, the Court devoted extensive consideration to the behavior of the media and suggested techniques by which the judge might better have insulated the trial. Some of those suggestions are included below. Note that most of the "remedies" have limitations or drawbacks that preclude their being used widely.

Cautioning Police, Prosecutors, etc. Cutting off information at its source is an obvious way of trying to curtail dissemination by the news media, and prosecutors sometimes are the sources of news stories about confessions and probable guilt, but gags on police and attorneys may be challenged by those gagged on the ground that they interfere with the First Amendment rights of the police and attorneys to express themselves. Furthermore, to the extent that the process of newsgathering may be protected by the First Amendment (see discussion of *Richmond Newspapers* later in this section), such restrictive orders may be unconstitutional.

In 1991 the Supreme Court of the United States reversed a judgment against Attorney Dominic P. Gentile, who had held a press conference the day after his client was indicted on criminal charges. The client was acquitted by a jury six months later, and the Disciplinary Board of the State Bar of Nevada subsequently found that Gentile had violated a Nevada Supreme Court Rule prohibiting lawyers from making extrajudicial statements to the press that they know or reasonably should know would have a "substantial likelihood of materially prejudicing" a proceeding. The Nevada Supreme Court had affirmed, rejecting Gentile's contention that the rule violated his right to free speech.

The Supreme Court of the United States reversed, holding that the "substantial likelihood of material prejudice" test applied by Nevada and most other states satisfies the First Amendment but that the Nevada rule was nonetheless void for vagueness: its grammatical structure and the absence of clarifying interpretation failed to provide fair notice to lawyers. Gentile v. State Bar of Nevada, 501 U.S. ___, 111 S.Ct. 2720 (1991).

Encouraging the Use of Voluntary Guidelines. In the 1960s the American Bar Association responded to the fair trial-free press concern by creating a committee that came to be known as the Reardon Committee to recommend guidelines for pre-trial and trial news coverage. The committee recommended that, prior to trial, lawyers release no extrajudicial statements relating to (1) prior criminal record of the accused, (2) existence or contents of any confession, (3) performance of any examinations or tests or the defendant's refusal to undergo them, (4) identity, testimony or credibility of prospective witnesses, (5) possibility of a guilty plea to the charge or a lesser offense or (6) any opinion as to the accused's guilt or innocence. Other recommendations dealt with other facets of the fair trial-free press issue. Many journalists resented what they viewed as an attempt by the legal profession to tell them how to do their jobs and ignored the Reardon Committee's recommendations.

Guidelines of state bench-bar-press organizations may have fared somewhat better because they were generally adopted by joint committees of members of the journalism and legal professions. These guidelines typically suggest that journalists *think carefully* before revealing information that the Reardon Committee cautioned against, but they also express recognition of a right of the journalist to access to information about the criminal justice system.

The effectiveness of the guidelines is directly related to their voluntariness. Even in states in which the guidelines are followed with some regularity in routine cases, they tend to lose their effectiveness when sensational crimes are committed. There is also some danger that courts may use the guidelines in ways the journalists never envisioned. We will see examples of this later in this chapter.

Shielding Witnesses. Shielding witnesses from the press similarly may interfere with the witnesses' own First Amendment rights and may interfere with a press right to gather news. On the other hand, of course, witnesses are under no obligation to answer questions from journalists.

Granting a Continuance. Postponing ("continuing") the trial until publicity dies down may interfere with the defendant's right to a *speedy* trial. Also, when the trial finally *does* take place, it becomes a news event all over again.

Granting Change of Venue. Where news accounts in an area may have created a situation in which it is unlikely that the accused can obtain a fair trial, a judge can transfer a trial to another area less touched by the publicity. A constitutional problem may arise in some instances, because the Sixth Amendment provides for one's trial "by an impartial jury of the State and district wherein the crime shall have been committed." Furthermore, such changes of venue are costly and bothersome to both the prosecution and the defense. If news accounts have already been state-wide or national, the change is unlikely to do much to mitigate the damage. Even if the new site of the trial has been untouched by earlier news accounts, the scheduling of the trial there becomes a news event in that area, and the problem may begin anew, though with less attention because the victim(s) are not local people.

Granting Change of Venire. Rather than moving the trial, it is theoretically possible to import a panel of jurors—or veniremen—from another area where they are less likely to have formed opinions about the case. In practice this is extremely rare, and it too raises Sixth Amendment questions.

Relying on the Voir Dire. During the *voir dire*, the process under which the prospective jurors are screened, attempts are made to exclude from the jury those people whose previously formed opinions will preclude their reaching a fair verdict based on the evidence presented during the trial. The *voir dire* may be successful in keeping truly biased people off a jury, but it is less successful when potential jurors have heard a specific piece of information. Also, the criticism is made that it can tend to eliminate from the jury those potential jurors who follow the news in their community most closely and who form intelligent opinions based on what they read or hear.

Cautioning Journalists. If the court cautions journalists in advance of publication of prejudicial information, the warning can seem to imply a threat of punishment by the contempt powers and may smack of an unconstitutional form of prior restraint (see Chapter I). If the warning is made after prejudicial information has already been revealed, the warning is likely to be ineffective.

Cautioning Jurors. The Court in *Sheppard* was critical of the trial judge for failing to give the jurors sufficient instruction about not reading media accounts of the trial or listening to comment outside the courtroom. Despite the fact that most judges today can be expected to give careful instructions, and most have faith in jurors to follow those instructions, there are undoubtedly instances in which jurors fail to heed those instructions and do see prejudicial news accounts outside the courtroom.

Sequestering the Jury. Sequestering the jury—keeping them in a hotel during the trial—greatly reduces the risk of improper exposure to media accounts of the trial. Because the public reads about sequestration in some highly publicized cases, it seems to perceive sequestration as a more common practice than it is. Its high cost precludes its use in all but a few cases, and defense attorneys are sometimes reluctant even to suggest it because of uncertainty about the effect on the jury. As some say, jurors who are unhappy about being confined for the duration of a trial cannot take out their frustrations on the judge and just may take them out on the accused.

b. Restraints on Publication

Because the First Amendment has traditionally been seen as a protection for the freedom to publish, restraints on the publication of information are undoubtedly the least desirable and most constitutionally suspect of the theoretically-available remedies for the fair trial-free press problem. Two cases that illustrate the problem are *Dickinson*, p. 28, *supra*, and Nebraska Press Association v. Stuart, 427 U.S. 539, 1 Med.L.Rptr. 1064 (1976).

The press calls them gag orders; lawyers and judges call them restrictive orders or protective orders. By whatever name, such an order directs the press (and often others) not to disseminate information a judge thinks may prejudice jurors in a forthcoming or present trial. Violating such an order can result in a citation for contempt.

A major case involving a restrictive order is *Nebraska Press Association.* Six members of the Kellie family were found murdered in their rural home in 1975. A neighbor, Erwin Charles Simants, was an immediate suspect, and the crime attracted widespread news coverage by electronic and print media. Three days after the crime, the prosecutor and the defense attorney joined in asking the trial court to enter a restrictive order relating to "matters that may or may not be publicly reported or disclosed to the public" because of the "mass coverage of news media" and the "reasonable likelihood of prejudicial news which would make difficult, if not impossible, the impaneling of an impartial jury and tend to prevent a fair trial."

The county court entered such an order, also requiring the members of the press to observe the Nebraska Bar–Press Guidelines, a set of voluntary guidelines of the type mentioned above. Attempts by the media to get the restrictive order lifted were unsuccessful. Simants was convicted, but the case brought by the Nebraska Press Association and other media organizations continued to the Supreme Court.

Chief Justice Burger, writing for the majority, said that in order to determine whether the danger posed by the media justified the restrictive order, "we must examine the evidence before the trial judge when the order was entered to determine (a) the nature and extent of pretrial news coverage; (b) whether other measures would be likely to mitigate the effects of unrestrained pretrial publicity; (c) how effectively a restraining order would operate to prevent the threatened danger." Finding that the trial judge's conclusion as to the impact of publicity on prospective jurors was "of necessity speculative" because he was dealing with "factors unknown and unknowable," the Court concluded that "the heavy burden imposed as a condition to securing a prior restraint was not met . . ." The judgment of the Nebraska Supreme Court was therefore reversed.

If a trial judge waits until unrestrained pretrial news accounts seem dangerous enough to justify a restraint, would such an order then be unacceptable because it would be largely ineffective?

In Goldblum v. National Broadcasting Corp., 584 F.2d 904, 4 Med.L.Rptr. 1718 (9th Cir. 1978), plaintiff, former executive officer of Equity Funding Corp., was serving a sentence for fraudulent activity in connection with the corporation's insolvency. NBC produced a "docudrama" based on the case, using the names of plaintiff and the corporation. Plaintiff, alleging that the program was inaccurate, sought an injunction against the showing of the program on the ground that it might inflame public opinion against him, jeopardize his release on parole and adversely affect jury selection in any future criminal or civil cases arising out of the episode.

The district judge ordered NBC to produce the movie for review the day its presentation was scheduled. When NBC refused the judge ordered counsel for the network imprisoned until the film was produced. A few hours later a panel of the court of appeals granted an application for relief and freed the attorney. In a subsequent opinion, the court said that it found "no authority which is even a remote justification" for issuing a prior restraint on the theory that parole officials might become inflamed or that jury selection in some "wholly speculative criminal prosecution" might be adversely affected. The order to produce and the imprisonment were invalid.

In State v. Coe, 101 Wash.2d 364, 679 P.2d 353, 10 Med.L.Rptr. 1465 (1984), a trial judge's order holding a broadcaster in contempt for playing tapes that had been played in open court was reversed on appeal. The judge had ordered that the tapes not be played on the air because the defendant might be suicidal. The appellate court majority held that the state permitted those cited for contempt to violate the order and then challenge it if the order was "patently invalid or 'void' as outside the court's power."

Recall from Chapter I *Noriega*, in which a temporary restraint was imposed on CNN to stop the network from broadcasting taperecorded telephone calls between Noriega and members of his defense team.

Gag Orders on Litigants. A special problem arises when the media are themselves parties to litigation and want to report on the case.

Part of the problem, in fact, is that the courts treat the press like any other litigant. In Seattle Times Co. v. Rhinehart, 467 U.S. 20, 10 Med.L.Rptr. 1705 (1984), the Supreme Court held that a protective order by a trial court in the state of Washington did not violate the First Amendment even though it prohibited the *Seattle Times* newspaper from publishing certain information related to a libel case against them. The information in question had been obtained by the newspaper as part of the discovery process prior to the libel trial, and the Court reasoned that there was a sufficient showing of good cause for the order and that the rights of a litigant do not necessarily include the right to disseminate information obtained through the "legislative grace" of the discovery process. Although most journalists and attorneys representing media clients consider it a disturbing trend, lower courts in other cases have also affirmed orders gagging litigants or trial participants.

Gags on Grand Jurors. In another attempt to cut off information at its source, a Florida law prohibited grand jury witnesses from disclosing their testimony. When a journalist was himself a grand jury witness, the statute effectively became a restraint on publication. In a 1990 case, the Supreme Court found the statute to violate the First Amendment. Michael Smith, a reporter for the *Charlotte Herald–News* in Charlotte County, Fla., had been called to testify before a special grand jury about information he had obtained while writing a series of newspaper stories about alleged improprieties committed by the Charlotte County state attorney's office and sheriff's department. He had been warned that any disclosure of his testimony would violate the Florida statute. Writing for a unanimous court, Chief Justice Rehnquist acknowledged various state interests in keeping grand jury testimony secret but concluded that they were insufficient "to overcome [Smith's] First Amendment right to make a truthful statement of the information he had acquired on his own." Butterworth v. Smith, 494 U.S. 624, 17 Med.L.Rptr. 1569 (1990).

c. Denials of Access to the Courtroom and Conditional Access

As judges faced the reality that other means of solving the fair trial-free press problems were either undesirable or ineffective, some turned to excluding the press and public from the courtroom during pretrial hearings or during trials themselves, or granted access to the courtroom only on the acceptance of conditions.

Journalists, of course, are also members of the public. But more, they see themselves as the eyes and ears of the public—surrogates for those who cannot attend a hearing or trial. They brought the first major challenge to closed pretrial hearings.

Gannett Co. v. DePasquale, 443 U.S. 368, 5 Med.L.Rptr. 1337 (1979), presented the question of whether members of the public are constitutionally entitled to attend a pretrial hearing. The issue arose out of a murder prosecution in upstate New York. The murder victim disappeared in 1976 after last having been seen fishing with two men. The victim's truck was found in Michigan, and the two young men were arrested there. Newspapers in New York State reported the arrest and police theories of the crime. Brought back to New York, the two men moved to suppress statements they had made to Michigan police, claiming the statements were given involuntarily. They also moved to suppress the gun that had been found as a result of the confession in Michigan.

The motions came before Judge Daniel DePasquale, and defense counsel asked the judge to close the hearing because "the unabated buildup of adverse publicity" had jeopardized the ability of the defendants to receive a fair trial. Neither the prosecutor nor the Gannett reporter in the courtroom objected. The judge removed press and public from the courtroom. The next day the reporter complained to the judge, but the hearing had concluded and the judge refused to release a transcript. Three days later counsel for Gannett appeared and asked that the ruling be vacated and that a transcript of the hearing be provided. The judge refused, the New York Court of Appeals upheld the judge's action, and the Supreme Court affirmed, 5–4, in an opinion by Justice Stewart.

Justice Stewart concluded that the Sixth Amendment's provision that "the accused shall enjoy the right to a speedy and public trial by an impartial jury" extended no rights whatever to the public. He said the right to a public trial is a personal right of the accused. He also said that any First and Fourteenth Amendment rights of Gannett to attend a criminal trial were not violated because the trial judge made an appraisal of the situation and concluded that, under the circumstances of this particular case, any right to attend the proceeding was outweighed by the defendants' right to a fair trial.

Four justices—Brennan, White, Marshall and Blackmun—all joined in a dissent emphasizing their belief (1) that the Sixth Amendment should be read to define trials as including suppression hearings because of the critical importance of such hearings, and (2) that the Sixth Amendment guarantee of a public trial extended to the public as well as to the accused.

After the *Gannett* decision, many thought the matter was left to each state. The decision caused considerable confusion, with its references to both pretrial hearings and trials, and there was speculation that the majority opinion had been drafted as a dissenting opinion before one of the justices was persuaded to join it as the majority opinion.

Following the decision, news directors, editors and professional associations circulated "Gannett cards" among their reporters. The cards, worded so that a reporter can read them on the spot should a judge be considering a closure, ask that such a decision be delayed until the reporter's media employer has an opportunity to be represented by legal counsel to argue on behalf of the right of the media and public to observe the proceedings.

Months before the Supreme Court's decision in *Gannett,* a trial judge in Hanover County, Va., closed a murder trial—setting the stage for Richmond Newspapers, Inc. v. Virginia, 448 U.S. 555, 6 Med.L.Rptr. 1833 (1980).

The defendant had been convicted of second-degree murder, and his conviction had been overturned on appeal because improper evidence had been admitted. The second and third trials resulted in mistrials. At the start of the fourth trial, defense counsel moved to exclude the press and public from the courtroom. He did not want witnesses to compare stories or information to leak out and be learned by the jurors, who had not been sequestered. The prosecutor offered no objection, and the judge closed the courtroom.

The newspaper appealed the reporter's exclusion, and the Supreme Court eventually held that the trial should have been open. The vote was 7–1, but the reasoning behind the decision is difficult to explain because the seven justices in the majority wrote six opinions and there was no majority opinion. Chief Justice Burger wrote the plurality opinion, stressing that *Gannett* had involved "pretrial" proceedings while this case involved a trial. He traced at length the history of public trials that ran back at least to the 13th century in England, mentioning as reasons for openness the greater likelihood that witnesses would tell the truth, the therapeutic value of having open criminal trials as an outlet for community concern, hostility, and emotion, and the opportunity for understanding the system and its workings in a particular case.

The Chief Justice then recognized a First Amendment right to attend criminal trials. Writing that it was not crucial whether the right be called a "right of access" or a "right to gather information," he said "The explicit, guaranteed rights to speak and to publish concerning what takes place at a trial would lose much meaning if access to observe the trial could, as it was here, be foreclosed arbitrarily." This recognition of a right to gather information is significant because the far more traditional view of the First Amendment had been that it protected one's right to disseminate information one had already obtained, not one's right to obtain information.

Although some confusion about closures of either pretrial hearings or trials remained after *Richmond,* many fewer judges closed courtrooms. In Globe Newspaper Co. v. Norfolk County Superior Court, 457 U.S. 596, 8 Med.L.Rptr. 1689 (1982), however, the Supreme Court had to examine *The Boston Globe's* challenge to a state statute providing for automatic closure of rape and other sexual assault trials during the testimony of minors who are victims. Justice Brennan wrote for the six-member majority, "We agree with respondent that the first interest—safe-guarding the physical and psychological well-being of a minor—is a compelling one. But as compelling as that interest is, it does not justify a mandatory-closure rule, for it is clear that the circumstances of the particular case may affect the significance of the interest. A trial court can determine on a case-by-case basis whether closure is necessary to protect the welfare of a minor victim."

In such closure decisions, the First Amendment requires that any such restriction on access to criminal trials be necessitated by compelling state interest and be narrowly tailored to serve that interest.

In Press–Enterprise Co. v. Superior Court (I), 464 U.S. 501, 10 Med.L.Rptr. 1161 (1984), the Supreme Court dealt with the issue of the closing of the *voir dire* examination of potential jurors. Holding that such proceedings in criminal trials are presumptively open to the public, the Court said that closure would be justified only where there is an overriding interest, where the closure is narrowly tailored and where alternatives to closure have been considered. The court found no support for the trial court's conclusion that an open proceeding would have threatened the prospective jurors' interests in privacy in this case. (The problem was compounded, from the press's point of view, by the fact that the trial court had refused to release the transcript of the *voir dire* as well.)

In Waller v. Georgia, 467 U.S. 39, 10 Med.L.Rptr. 1714 (1984), the Supreme Court addressed the problem of a closure of pretrial suppression hearings over the objection of the defendant. The case involved allegations of racketeering and gambling, and a pretrial hearing was held to consider suppression of wiretaps and evidence seized during searches at the defendants' homes. The hearing was closed when the prosecution moved for closure alleging that unnecessary "publication" of information obtained under the wiretaps would render the information inadmissible as evidence, and that the wiretap evidence would "involve" the privacy interests of some persons who were indicted but were not then on trial, and some who were not then indicted. Citing *Press–Enterprise (I)*, the court held the closure of the suppression hearing was unjustified, noting that the entire seven-day hearing had been closed even though the tapes were played for less than 2½ hours.

Concern for the *voir dire* process arose again in Press–Enterprise Co. v. Superior Court (II), 478 U.S. 1, 13 Med.L.Rptr. 1001 (1986). The case involved a preliminary hearing in the case of Robert Diaz, a nurse charged with murdering 12 patients. Acting on a motion from the defense, the magistrate had closed the hearing, noting that the case had attracted national publicity and that "only one side may get reported in the media."

The hearing continued for 41 days, during which much of the testimony was medical and scientific. The record of the hearing was sealed. The California Supreme Court held that if a defendant established a "reasonable likelihood of substantial prejudice," the burden shifted to the prosecution or the media to show by a preponderance of evidence that there was no such reasonable probability of prejudice. The Supreme Court of the United States reversed.

Chief Justice Burger, writing for a seven-member majority, said that, "The considerations that led the Court to apply the First Amendment right of access to criminal trials in *Richmond Newspapers* and *Globe* and the selection of jurors in *Press–Enterprise I* lead us to conclude that the right of access applies to preliminary hearings as conducted in California."

He wrote:

> Since a qualified First Amendment right of access attaches to preliminary hearings in California . . ., the proceedings cannot be closed unless specific, on the record findings are made demonstrating that "closure is essential to preserve higher values and is narrowly tailored to serve that interest." . . .
>
> . . . [The] risk of prejudice does not automatically justify refusing public access to hearings on every motion to suppress. Through voir dire, cumbersome as it is in some circumstances, a court can identify those jurors whose prior knowledge of the case would disable them from rendering an impartial verdict. And even if closure were justified for the hearings on a motion to suppress, closure of an entire 41–day proceeding would rarely be warranted. The First Amendment right of access cannot be overcome by the conclusory assertion that publicity might deprive the defendant of [the right to a fair trial]. And any limitation " 'must be narrowly tailored to serve that interest.' " [   ]

Justices Stevens and Rehnquist dissented. Justice Stevens wrote that "The constitutionally-grounded fair trial interests of the accused if he is bound over for trial, and the reputational interests of the accused if he is not, provide a substantial reason for delaying access to the transcript for at least the short term before trial."

The fact that nine out of 10 criminal prosecutions are concluded before they reach trial makes the decision in *Press–Enterprise II* particularly important to the news media.

Conditional Access. With a variety of precedents holding that trial court judges should not gag journalists and should not keep them or other members of the public out of the courtroom, it was perhaps inevitable that trial judges would seek another way of trying to solve fair trial-free press problems. A trial court judge in the State of Washington decided to use the voluntary bench-bar-media guidelines adopted in that state as a basis for granting access to his courtroom, allowing only reporters who agreed to abide by the guidelines into the room.

The Washington Supreme Court upheld the trial judge's order in Federated Publications, Inc. v. Swedberg, 96 Wash.2d 13, 633 P.2d 74, 7 Med.L.Rptr. 1865 (1981), certiorari denied 456 U.S. 984 (1982). Critics of bench-bar-press guidelines said that one of the envisioned dangers of such guidelines—their misuse by the courts—had become a reality. Early predictions of a trend toward such conditions on access to courtrooms proved premature, however. Adoption of amendments to state bench-bar-press guidelines, specifically precluding their use by courts for any purpose, lessened the likelihood that the guidelines, which media representatives had adopted in good faith, might be used against them in this way.

Conditional access also arises in juvenile proceedings. In many states, hearings in juvenile cases are confidential on the ground that they are primarily to rehabilitate and are clinical rather than punitive. The Supreme Court has said that a state may "continue, if it deems it appropriate, to provide and to improve provision for the confidentiality of records of police contracts and court action relating to juveniles." In re Gault, 387 U.S. 1, 25 (1967). In Mayer v. Florida, 523 So.2d 1171, 15 Med.L.Rptr. 2255 (1988), a newspaper reporter was held in contempt for writing about a child custody hearing.

d. *Denials of Access to Court Records*

Although there is a tradition of openness of court records, there are instances in which courts have withheld certain information during and sometimes after trials. Judges may bar release of the names of jurors in notorious cases to protect their privacy and impartiality. Or, as in *Press–Enterprise (I), supra*, part or all of a transcript may be withheld.

In one case, a trial court judge in Iowa, concerned about retaliation against jurors, ordered reporters not to print the names, addresses or phone numbers of jurors in a murder trial involving the widow of a slain motorcycle gang member. The judge also barred photographs of the jurors entering and leaving the courthouse. The press appealed the order, and it was overturned in light of *Nebraska Press*. Des Moines Register & Tribune Co. v. Osmundson, 248 N.W.2d 493, 2 Med.L.Rptr. 1321 (Iowa 1976).

If a judge cannot prevent the press from reporting the names of jurors that have become public, the next step might be to try to prevent the names from becoming public in a state in which jurors' names are not public property. This was approved in a criminal prosecution of major narcotics suspects in New York City. The trial judge gave prospective jurors numbers and never released their names and addresses. After conviction defendants appealed, asserting, as one ground, that the lack of names and addresses meant the defendants could not question neighbors and learn on their own about the prospective jurors. The court affirmed the convictions. United States v. Barnes, 604 F.2d 121 (2d Cir.1979), certiorari denied 446 U.S. 907 (1980). The court, in a decision called disturbing by *The New York Times* and others, said if an anonymous juror feels less pressure as the result of anonymity "this is as it should be—a factor contributing to his impartiality."

e. Use of the Contempt Power

Courts have long been concerned about efforts by the parties and press to influence judges to decide pending cases in a certain way. The traditional approach was that such efforts either influenced the judge or appeared to influence the judge—and that either view seriously impaired the functioning of the judicial branch. The technique for handling the problem was to hold the perpetrator in contempt of court and impose appropriate sanctions.

Contempt of court involves a variety of actions that obstruct the administration of justice. These include disturbance of a judicial proceeding by shouting in the courtroom, willful refusal to obey a court order to pay alimony, and refusal to answer a grand jury question after a judge has ordered the witness to do so. If a court were to punish a member of the press for contempt, it would be more likely to be for disobeying an order of the court (not to bring equipment into the courtroom, for instance), for interfering with the administration of justice by broadcasting or publishing something prejudicial (the power is generally *not* used in such instances but might be) or for refusing to answer a question about a secret source or secret notes. (We will discuss confidentiality in the next section of this chapter).

f. Restrictions on Cameras and Other Equipment

For most of the last half century, cameras and sound-recording equipment have been kept out of courtrooms—partially because of the canons of ethics of judges, partially because of Supreme Court decisions, and partially because of tradition. During those years electronic equipment has become less and less obtrusive, and television has become commonplace in most other places in which newsworthy events are taking place. Experimentation with cameras in the last 10 years has led to changes in the rules in many states, but some others still forbid them. To understand the situation, one must look at its history.

When Bruno Hauptmann was brought to trial for kidnapping and slaying the son of famous aviator Charles Lindbergh in 1932, journalists and photographers packed the courtroom. Hauptmann, found guilty and sentenced to death, may not have gotten a fair trial because of the adverse publicity. In response, the American Bar Association adopted Canon 35, banning radio and television broadcasting and still cameras from courtrooms, in 1937. The canon's successor, Canon 3A(7), was amended in 1982, reflecting changing state practices. The canon now says a judge should prohibit broadcasting, reporting and photographing, except when they are authorized by supervising appellate courts or other authorities and are consistent with fair trial rights— being unobtrusive, not distracting, and not interfering with the administration of justice.

In a Supreme Court case, Estes v. Texas, 381 U.S. 532, 1 Med. L.Rptr. 1187 (1965), defendant had been indicted in the Texas state courts for "swindling"—inducing farmers to buy nonexistent fertilizer tanks and then to deliver to him mortgages on the tanks. The nature of the charges and the large sums of money involved attracted national interest. Texas was one of two states that then permitted televised trials (the other, Colorado, required the defendant's permission). Over Estes's objection, the trial judge permitted televising of a two-day hearing before trial.

Estes was convicted, but the Supreme Court eventually reversed the conviction, 5–4. In his majority opinion Justice Clark concluded that the use of television at the trial involved "such a probability that prejudice will result that it is deemed inherently lacking in due process" even without any showing of specific prejudices. He was concerned about the impact on jurors, judges, parties, witnesses and lawyers.

Justice Harlan, who provided the crucial fifth vote for reversal, joined the majority opinion only to the extent that it applied to televised coverage of "courtroom proceedings of a criminal trial of widespread public interest," "a criminal trial of great notoriety" and "a heavily publicized and highly sensational affair." In such cases he was worried about the impact on jurors.

Despite the fact that there had not been five votes on the court for the notion that cameras were inherently unfair, the *Estes* decision was frequently and erroneously cited as standing for that principle during the years when cameras were almost universally banned from court-rooms. When some states began experimenting again with cameras, it was inevitable that the Supreme Court would again face this issue. The Court did so in Chandler v. Florida, 449 U.S. 560, 7 Med.L.Rptr. 1041 (1981), unanimously rejecting the view that televising a criminal trial over the objections of the defendant *automatically* rendered the trial unfair. (In Florida, only the consent of the trial judge was required to allow the trial to be televised.) The defendants had argued that the impact of television on the participants introduced potentially prejudicial, but unidentifiable, aspects into the trial. The majority, in an opinion by Chief Justice Burger, first concluded that *Estes* did not stand for the proposition that broadcasting was barred "in all cases and under all circumstances." Because of Justice Harlan's narrow views in that case, the ruling of *Estes* should apply only to cases of widespread interest. (On this point, two Justices insisted that *Chandler* overruled *Estes* and should say so.)

Then, Chief Justice Burger continued that the risk of prejudice from press coverage of a trial was not limited to broadcasting. "The risk of juror prejudice in some cases does not justify an absolute ban on news coverage of trials by the printed media; so also the risk of such prejudice does not warrant an absolute constitutional ban on all broad-cast coverage." A case attracts attention because of its intrinsic interest to the public. The "appropriate safeguard" against prejudice in such cases "is the defendant's right to demonstrate that the media's coverage of his case—be it printed or broadcast—compromised the ability of the particular jury that heard the case to adjudicate fairly." The Court also observed that the changes in technology since *Estes* supported the state's argument that it now be permitted to allow television in the courtroom.

Because the defendants in *Chandler*—two former city policemen accused of burglarizing a restaurant—showed no adverse impact from the televising, the convictions were upheld.

Notice that this case involved criminal defendants attacking their convictions. It did *not* involve a First Amendment claim by broadcasters to bring their equipment into the courtroom in a state that barred such entry. The Court did not discuss the impact of *Richmond Newspapers* or other First Amendment cases. As of the time *Chandler* was decided, over half the states were permitting television in the courtroom either on an experimental basis or on a permanent basis after a successful experiment had ended. In many of these states, the consent of a criminal defendant was required before entry could be allowed. Many states that barred entry or required consent of a party before entry have continued their practices after *Chandler*. Forty-four states now permit cameras in courtrooms, but rules vary, and some states continue to struggle with the issue.

In New York State, for example, cameras were permitted in appellate courts but not in trial courts prior to the beginning of an 18-month experiment with audiovisual equipment in trial courts that ended in 1989. Despite support from the state's governor and chief judge, legislative attempts to establish permanent rules allowing cameras in trial courts failed in 1989. A second experimental phase ended in 1991, again without agreement on permanent rules. Some legislators complained of media arrogance and of sensational coverage of the Amy Fisher case on Long Island. For more than a year, no cameras were permitted in trial courts. In June 1992, the legislature narrowly approved a third experimental phase to expire on Jan. 31, 1995. The third phase, viewed as "watered down" by some media observers, contains a provision under which some witnesses in criminal trials have their faces electronically obscured during testimony. The "experiment" could be extended indefinitely. New York Times, June 9, 1992 at B–4.

A three-year experiment with photographic and electronic media coverage of civil proceedings in federal courts began July 1, 1991, and is scheduled to end June 30, 1994. Approval of the experiment by the U.S. Judicial Conference was for two federal appeals courts (those chosen were the U.S. Circuit Courts of Appeals in New York and San Francisco) and up to six federal district courts. The district courts chosen were those in the Southern District of New York (New York City), the Western District of Washington (Seattle), the Eastern District of Pennsylvania (Philadelphia), the District of Massachusetts (Boston), the Eastern District of Michigan (Detroit, Ann Arbor, Bay City, Flint and Fort Huron), and the Southern District of Indiana (Indianapolis, Evansville, Muncie, New Albany and Terre Haute).

As part of efforts by 13 media organizations to open the Supreme Court to cameras, CBS News operated two cameras in the courtroom on a day the court was not in session in 1988. Three members of the Court, including Chief Justice Rehnquist, watched a demonstration and heard a presentation about the technology involved. The Chief Justice has made few public comments on the subject, but he did say he would give "sympathetic consideration" to a request for broadcast coverage of the Court when he was being questioned during the Senate hearing on his nomination as Chief Justice. Justice Scalia told an interviewer he thought a change would not happen soon. Broadcasting, Nov. 28, 1988 at 57.

Among the arguments in favor of cameras in courtrooms are educational value, the opportunity to let more people see the administration of justice, the "neutral" way the camera views the scene without necessity of human narration, the possibility that witnesses will testify more truthfully because others who know the truth may be watching, the creation of a video record for appellate purposes and the possibility of closed circuit viewing by spectators elsewhere in the courthouse.

Among arguments against cameras in courtrooms are the danger that excerpts of trials will be used sensationally, threats to the privacy or safety of the jurors, the possibility that participants (judge, lawyers, witnesses) may behave differently with cameras present, the fear that camera angles and choices of shots will influence viewers' perceptions of the scene, and the creation of disruption in the courtroom.

Courtroom Sketching. Where television has not been permitted in courtrooms, television news directors have resorted to sketches of the courtroom scene to provide a visual dimension to their reports of judicial proceedings. That practice came under attack during the pretrial proceedings involving the trial of the "Gainesville Eight," who were charged with conspiring to disrupt the 1972 Republican National Convention. The trial judge decreed that no sketches be drawn in the courtroom. On appeal, the court refused to accept "a sweeping prohibition of in-court sketching where there has been no showing whatsoever that sketching is any way obtrusive or disruptive." United States v. Columbia Broadcasting System, Inc., 497 F.2d 102, 1 Med.L.Rptr. 1351 (5th Cir.1974).

The Nixon Tapes in the Courts. As we will see later, the saga of the Nixon tapes reached its first significant stage when the Supreme Court ordered President Nixon to honor a subpoena from the Watergate special prosecutor to deliver tapes of a large group of conversations for use in the so-called Watergate trial. United States v. Nixon, 418 U.S. 683 (1974). In 1974 Congress passed the Presidential Recordings and Materials Preservation Act, directing the Administrator of General

Services to take custody of the former President's tapes and documents. The Administrator was directed to submit to Congress regulations governing access to Presidential materials of historical value. The act was upheld in Nixon v. Administrator of General Services, 433 U.S. 425, 2 Med.L.Rptr. 2025 (1977). That was chapter two.

The third episode took shape during the Watergate trial. The tape reels obtained from the President were played in the judge's chambers before trial. Some conversations were declared irrelevant or privileged and were not reproduced. The other conversations were rerecorded on new tapes designated Copy A for the district court and Copy B for the special prosecutor. Some, but not all, of the conversations on Copy A were admitted into evidence. Some, but not all, of these were played to the jury. Some were played in full; others only in part. "Deletions were effected not by modifying the exhibit itself, but by skipping deleted portions on the tape or by interrupting the sound transmission to the jurors' headphones." Written transcripts of the conversations being played to the jurors were provided to the jurors and others in the court—all of whom heard the tapes over headphones.

During the trial broadcasters approached Judge Sirica to obtain copies of the 22 hours of tapes played to the jury. After extensive proceedings he denied the request for immediate access to the tapes on the ground that the convicted defendants had appeals pending, and release of the tapes might prejudice their rights.

The court of appeals reversed, relying on the importance of the common-law privilege of inspecting and copying judicial records. The fear of prejudice to the defendants did not outweigh the public's right to access.

The Supreme Court reversed the court of appeals. Nixon v. Warner Communications, Inc., 435 U.S. 589, 3 Med.L.Rptr. 2074 (1978). Justice Powell, writing for the majority, began by discussing the asserted common-law right to inspect judicial records. Although he found some case support, the right was not absolute. "Every court has supervisory power over its own records and files and access has been denied where court files might have become a vehicle for improper purposes." Common-law rights to inspect had given way in cases in which the record might be used to "gratify private spite or promote public scandal" as in divorce cases; where the record contained libelous statements; and where the record contained "business information that might harm a litigant's competitive standing." Although he thought the cases showed that the decision was "one best left to the sound discretion of the trial court," Justice Powell was willing to assume that some right to inspect the tapes existed.

The Court then reviewed Nixon's arguments against disclosure. First, he argued that he had a property interest in his voice that the broadcasters should not be allowed to exploit for commercial gain. Second, he asserted a right of privacy. (The court of appeals had rejected that argument on the grounds that the passage of the Presidential Recordings Act contemplated release of the tapes at some time, and that presidential documents are not subject to ordinary privacy claims. The broadcasters added that the privacy claim was overridden by the fact that the tapes, with the nuances and inflections, would provide added understanding. Nixon disagreed on the ground that out of 22 hours of tapes, broadcasters and record makers would use fractions, necessarily taken out of context.) Third, Nixon argued that United States v. Nixon authorized use of the tapes only for the trial since they were obtained from a third party. Finally, he argued that it would be unseemly for the courts to "facilitate the commercialization" of the tapes for presentation "at cocktail parties" or in "comedy acts or dramatic productions." Justice Powell continued:

> At this point, we normally would be faced with the task of weighing the interests advanced by the parties in light of the public interest and the duty of the courts.[14] On respondents' side of the scales is the incremental gain in public understanding of an immensely important historical occurrence that arguably would flow from the release of aural copies of these tapes, a gain said to be not inconsequential despite the already widespread dissemination of printed transcripts. Also on respondents' side of the scales is the presumption—however gauged—in favor of public access to judicial records. On petitioner's side are the arguments identified above, which must be assessed in the context of court custody of the tapes. Underlying each of petitioner's arguments is the crucial fact that respondents require a court's cooperation in furthering their commercial plans. The court—as custodian of tapes obtained by subpoena over the opposition of a sitting President, solely to satisfy "fundamental demands of due process of law in the fair administration of criminal justice," United States v. Nixon, 418 U.S., at 713— has a responsibility to exercise an informed discretion as to release of the tapes, with a sensitive appreciation of the circumstances that led to their production. This responsibility does not permit copying upon demand. Otherwise, there would exist a danger that the court could become a partner in the use of the subpoenaed material "to gratify private spite or promote public scandal," [ ], with no corresponding assurance of public benefit.

Having set the stage, Justice Powell announced that the Court need not decide the case because of a "unique element that was neither advanced by the parties nor given appropriate consideration by the courts below." Although the parties argued that the Presidential Recordings Act did not cover these tapes, the Court found a Congressional intent to create an administrative procedure for processing all the Nixon documents, including these recordings. (Why might each party have argued against the Act's relevance?) "The presence of an alternative means of public access tips the scales in favor of denying

---

14. Judge Sirica's principal reason for refusing to release the tapes—fairness to the defendants, who were appealing their convictions—is no longer a consideration. All appeals have been resolved.

release." Questions concerning the regulations prepared by the Administrator of General Services were reserved "for future consideration in appropriate proceedings."

The broadcasters argued that even the presence of the Act could not destroy their constitutional claims to inspect the documents. First, the broadcasters relied on *Cox Broadcasting*, p. 716, *supra*, which barred damage liability against a broadcaster that named a rape victim whose name was obtained from official court records. The broadcasters argued that this gave them a right to copy anything displayed in open court. Justice Powell disagreed: the case gave the press only the right to copy records "open to the public." Here, reporters heard the tapes and were given transcripts, and could comment on each. *Cox Broadcasting* did not require that copies of the tapes "to which the public has never had *physical* access" be made available for copying. "The First Amendment generally grants the press no right to information about a trial superior to that of the general public."

In their second constitutional argument, the broadcasters relied on the Sixth Amendment's guarantee of a public trial, asserting that public understanding of the trial is incomplete if the public cannot hear the tapes that the jury heard. Justice Powell thought this proved too much—because it would require recording testimony of live witnesses at trials. Also, the guarantee is to avoid the use of "courts as instruments of persecution" and confers no special benefit on the press. Finally, the right to public trial does not require that the trial be broadcast or recorded for the public. The requirement "is satisfied by the opportunity of members of the public and the press to attend the trial and to report what they have observed. [ ] That opportunity abundantly existed here."

Although the lower court decision favoring the broadcasters was reversed, the Court did not decide how the district court should dispose of the tapes. Justices White and Brennan dissented in part on the reading of the Recordings Act and would have ordered the tapes delivered immediately to the Administrator. Justices Marshall and Stevens, in separate opinions, would have affirmed the court of appeals.

During 1980 a federal investigation of corruption among Congressmen (Abscam) produced several cases in which Congressmen took bribes from FBI agents posing as wealthy Arabs. The meetings were videotaped secretly and provided strong evidence at the trials—at which several Congressmen were convicted. After one early trial the networks sought and obtained permission to make copies of the tapes for showing on television. The argument against the showing was that this might prejudice trials still to come or retrials of those convicted if their appeals should succeed. The tapes were shown.

C. CONFIDENTIALITY IN NEWSGATHERING

The administration of justice depends upon access to information relevant to court disputes. When the only apparent way to obtain such information is by asking a journalist to reveal a confidential source or turn over unpublished notes, documents or outtakes, problems between the media and the courts can occur. Constitutional guarantees of a fair trial are meant to allow the parties a complete, objective hearing on the issues. What if a journalist refuses to divulge certain information? What about tapes in a television station's newsroom that shed light on an incident being considered by a court?

Journalists traditionally have sought recognition of a special privilege not to have to reveal their confidential sources, even when the identity of the source is part of the evidence sought by a court, a grand jury or a legislative committee; but confidential sources are just part of a larger problem. In addition to being asked to reveal sources, journalists have been asked for their notes, for documents and other evidence that they obtained in the course of newsgathering, for unpublished materials (negatives of photos not used and outtakes of television productions) and for testimony as to their thoughts during the newsgathering and editing processes. In addition, there have been attempts to gather evidence by police searches of newsrooms or by obtaining reporters' travel records or telephone records in an attempt to deduce their sources.

1. THE ROLE OF CONFIDENTIALITY

a. *Background*

It has been generally accepted that persons thought to have relevant information may be subpoenaed to testify as witnesses at certain governmental proceedings. Nevertheless, some relationships have been held to give rise to "privileges" permitting a party to withhold information he has learned in a confidential relationship. The most venerable of these relationships have been those of physician and patient, lawyer and client, and priest and penitent. In each of these the recipient may be prevented by the source from testifying as to information learned in confidence in that professional capacity.

Under common law, an assertion by journalists of a similar privilege from testifying was generally rejected. Critics of a privilege for journalists sometimes point out that professionals in medicine and law typically must meet certain educational requirements, be certified to practice and be subject to disciplinary action if they fail to adhere to professional standards. Journalists, on the other hand, have no minimum educational requirements, require no certification or license to be journalists, and are not subject to the same kinds of peer review to which doctors and lawyers are subject. So long as freedom of press belongs to everyone, not just to a few licensed to be journalists, professional standards are difficult to police. Although one likes to believe that the vast majority of journalists are ethical and truthful, such incidents as that involving the Janet Cooke Pulitzer Prize-winning story on the juvenile heroin addict (who turned out not to be a real child) in *The Washington Post* attract public attention and are sometimes pointed to by critics of a privilege for journalists.

Despite the rejection of the privilege at common law, it has made headway as a statutory protection. Since the first reporter's privilege statute was enacted in Maryland in 1896, half the states have enacted so-called "shield" laws. As we shall see, these statutes may have limited utility in certain situations.

In states without privilege statutes, reporters tried, with little success, to claim such a privilege under common law. Then, in 1958, columnist Marie Torre tried a different approach. She had reported that a CBS executive had made certain disparaging remarks about entertainer Judy Garland. Garland sued CBS for defamation and sought by deposition to get Torre to identify the executive. Torre attacked the effort as a threat to freedom of the press, refused to answer the question,and asserted that the First Amendment protected her refusal. The court, though seeing some constitutional implications, held that even if the First Amendment were to provide some protection, the reporter must testify when the information sought goes to the "heart" of the plaintiff's claim. Garland v. Torre, 259 F.2d 545, 1 Med.L.Rptr. 2541 (2d Cir.), certiorari denied 358 U.S. 910 (1958). Torre ultimately served 10 days in jail for criminal contempt.

After *Garland,* reporters continued to assert First Amendment claims, still with little success. In the late 1960s, the situation became more serious as the federal government began to serve subpoenas on reporters more frequently. The media asserted that this made previously willing sources of information unwilling because of fear that the courts would not protect the reporter or the source, and reporters would violate confidences when pressed by the government.

b. The Supreme Court Considers the Privilege

The first Supreme Court case to consider whether the First Amendment supports privileges claimed by reporters involved grand jury testimony. A grand jury is a group of citizens who receive evidence of alleged crimes brought to them by a prosecutor. If the grand jury believes that this evidence, uncontroverted by the accused, would justify conviction, it will return an "indictment"—a formal accusation of crime. This will set the criminal prosecution in operation. The Fifth Amendment to the United States Constitution provides that no one be brought to trial for "a capital, or otherwise infamous crime" unless first indicted by a grand jury. States need not, and some do not, use grand juries. (Where the grand jury is not used, the prosecutor instead files an "information" against the accused to get the case started.) Grand juries are able to subpoena witnesses, and all testimony before grand juries is supposed to be kept secret. In part, this confidentiality requirement is to prevent a stigma from attaching to those whom the grand jury refuses to indict.

The Supreme Court's decision in Branzburg v. Hayes, 408 U.S. 665, 1 Med.L.Rptr. 2617 (1972) was actually a decision in three cases, one of which involved a television reporter, Paul Pappas. Pappas recorded and photographed statements of Massachusetts Black Panther Party officials during a period of racial turmoil. He was allowed to enter the Party's headquarters to cover an expected police raid in return for his promise to disclose nothing he observed within. He stayed three hours, no raid occurred, and he wrote no story. He was summoned before the county grand jury but refused to answer any questions about what had taken place while he was there. When he was called a second time, he moved to quash the second summons. The motion was denied by the trial judge, who noted the absence of a statutory journalist's privilege in Massachusetts and denied the existence of a constitutional privilege. The Supreme Judicial Court of Massachusetts affirmed, and the case was appealed to the Supreme Court of the United States.

(The other two cases considered with *Pappas* involved print reporters. Paul Branzburg, a Kentucky newspaper reporter, had been called before a grand jury and directed to identify two individuals mentioned in an article he wrote about marijuana and hashish. Earl Caldwell, a *New York Times* reporter, had been subpoenaed to appear before a federal grand jury in California investigating the Black Panthers and to bring with him notes and tape recordings of interviews given to him for publication by the Panthers.)

The Supreme Court split 5–4. Justice White's opinion for the Court said, "The sole issue before us is the obligation of reporters to respond to grand jury subpoenas as other citizens do and to answer questions relevant to an investigation into the commission of a crime. . . . It is clear that the First Amendment does not invalidate every incidental burdening of the press that may result from the enforcement of civil or criminal statutes of general applicability. . . . A number of States have provided newsmen a statutory privilege of varying breadth, but the majority have not done so, and none has been provided by federal statute. Until now the only testimonial privilege for unofficial witnesses that is rooted in the Federal Constitution is the Fifth Amendment privilege against compelled self-incrimination. We are asked to create another by interpreting the First Amendment to grant newsmen a testimonial privilege that other citizens do not enjoy. This we decline to do. . . . The argument that the flow of news will be diminished by compelling reporters to aid the grand jury in a criminal investigation is not irrational, nor are the records before us silent on the matter. But we remain unclear how often and to what extent informers are actually deterred from furnishing information when newsmen are forced to testify before a grand jury. . . ."

The opinion invited legislative action: "At the federal level, Congress has freedom to determine whether a statutory newsman's privilege is necessary and desirable and to fashion standards and rules as narrow or broad as deemed necessary to deal with the evil discerned and, equally important, to refashion those rules as experience from time to time may dictate. There is also merit in leaving state legislatures free, within First Amendment limits, to fashion their own standards. . . ."

Accordingly, the Court affirmed the decision that Pappas must appear before the grand jury and made similar decisions in the cases of the print reporters.

Justice Powell, who provided the critical fifth vote for the majority, wrote a concurring opinion that was read by some as undercutting the majority opinion:

> I add this brief statement to emphasize what seems to me to be the limited nature of the Court's holding. The Court does not hold that newsmen, subpoenaed to testify before a grand jury, are without constitutional rights with respect to the gathering of news or in safeguarding their sources. Certainly, we do not hold, as suggested in Mr. Justice Stewart's dissenting opinion, that state and federal authorities are free to "annex" the news media as "an investigative arm of government." The solicitude repeatedly shown by this Court for First Amendment freedoms should be sufficient assurance against any such effort, even if one seriously believed that the media—properly free and untrammeled in the fullest sense of these terms—were not able to protect themselves.

>   . . . [T]he Court states that no harassment of newsmen will be tolerated. If a newsman believes that the grand jury investigation is not being conducted in good faith he is not without remedy. Indeed, if the newsman is called upon to give information bearing only a remote and tenuous relationship to the subject of the investigation, or if he has some other reason to believe that his testimony implicates confidential source relationships without a legitimate need of law enforcement, he will have access to the court on a motion to quash and an appropriate protective order may be entered. The asserted claim to privilege should be judged on its facts by the striking of a proper balance between freedom of the press and the obligation of all citizens to give relevant testimony with respect to criminal conduct. The balance of these vital constitutional and societal interests on a case-by-case basis accords with the tried and traditional way of adjudicating such questions. . . .

>   In short, the courts will be available to newsmen under circumstances where legitimate First Amendment interest require protection.

Justice Stewart, dissenting, wrote that "The Court's crabbed view of the First Amendment reflects a disturbing insensitivity to the critical role of an independent press in our society. . . . The right to gather news implies, in turn, a right to a confidential relationship between a reporter and his source."

Justice Stewart's dissent suggested three possible qualifications that might be incorporated into a qualified privilege for journalists: "[W]hen a reporter is asked to appear before a grand jury and reveal confidences, I would hold that the government must (1) show that there is probable cause to believe that the newsman had information that is clearly relevant to a specific probable violation of law; (2) demonstrate that the information sought cannot be obtained by alternative means less destructive of First Amendment rights; and (3) demonstrate a compelling and overriding interest in the information."

Outtakes. The problem of reporter's privilege arises most frequently in the context of material that has been published without attribution to a source, but the electronic media (and, less frequently, the print media) also face problems with "outtakes," parts of film or videotape that have been cut and not transmitted. The term might also refer to notes taken by a reporter that are not used in a story or even to perceptions or observations not even written down. Are government efforts to obtain this unpublished or unrecorded information different from the more conventional effort to get a reporter to identify a source of published information? Outtakes are essential when the goal is to try to judge the fairness of what was actually presented. This was the situation when a committee of the House of Representatives sought outtakes from a CBS documentary, "The Selling of the Pentagon," during the Vietnam War.

Unsolicited information. The courts are even less sympathetic when unsolicited information has been thrust on the reporter. See Lewis v. United States, 517 F.2d 236 (9th Cir.1975), upholding the contempt conviction of a manager of a radio station for refusing to produce the original of a "communique" he received from an underground group that claimed responsibility for a bombing. Does this situation differ greatly from those presented in *Branzburg*?

State Protection. Although there is still no federal shield law, about half of the states now have shield laws. Journalists might have been more effective in lobbying for such shield laws had they been in agreement about whether to lobby for absolute shield laws (that would be "airtight" but difficult to "sell" to legislators) or for qualified shield laws (that would be easier to sell but would be considerably weakened by the qualifications built into them). Some journalists, believing that the First Amendment should automatically protect confidentiality despite the Supreme Court decision in *Branzburg*, maintain that seeking shield laws from legislatures would be an inappropriate recognition of the legislators' right to pass such laws. Shield laws vary in detail but generally are statutory attempts to exempt journalists from divulging certain information—usually confidential sources or the information itself.

States also may find protection for confidentiality in their own state constitutions. In O'Neill v. Oakgrove Construction, Inc., 71 N.Y.2d 521, 528 N.Y.S.2d 1, 523 N.E.2d 277, 15 Med.L.Rptr. 1219 (1988), New York State's highest court held that the Gannett Newspapers in Rochester had a qualified privilege under the state constitution and the First Amendment to decline to produce unpublished photographs of a traffic accident scene. The photographs had been sought as part of a suit by a man injured when his car slid off a roadway under construction. The newspaper photographer had taken 58 photographs, of which one was published. Note that this is an example of the outtakes problem discussed above.

New York State's shield law was amended in 1990 to provide a qualified exemption from contempt charges for journalists who fail to disclose non-confidential news sources. Journalists in the state had pressed for the change following controversy over a television station was asked to provide tapes of an interview with a murder suspect that was taped before the subject became a suspect and with no promise of confidentiality. Med.L.Rptr. News Notes, April 3, 1990.

The Florida Supreme Court held that journalists in that state have no privilege to protect them against testifying in a court proceeding as to their eyewitness observations of a relevant event. The Miami Herald Publishing Co. v. Morejon, 561 So.2d 577, 17 Med.L.Rptr. 1920 (1990).

c. After Branzburg: Seeking Information From Journalists

Criminal Trials and Shield Laws. The conflict between the Sixth Amendment rights of defendants in criminal trials and First Amendment claims to testimonial privilege is illustrated in the Farber case.

Myron Farber, a reporter for *The New York Times,* began investigating a series of mysterious deaths that had occurred several years earlier at a hospital in New Jersey. His investigations led to a series of articles and to murder indictments against a physician. During the six-month-long murder trial, the defendant's attorney had subpoenas served on the reporter and the newspaper demanding that they produce certain documents relating to interviews with witnesses at the trial. Motions to quash the subpoenas were denied, but the trial judge did order that the documents be delivered to him for *in camera* inspection. Farber and the *Times* refused. Efforts to stay the order pending appeals were denied by the state appellate courts and Justices White and Marshall.

Farber and the *Times* refused to comply and were held in civil and criminal contempt. The civil contempt involved a fine of $5,000 per day on the *Times* and a flat $1,000 on Farber, who was sentenced to jail until he complied. The criminal penalties were $100,000 on the newspaper, and $1,000 on Farber plus six months in jail. On review, the

New Jersey Supreme Court affirmed, 5–2. Matter of Farber, 78 N.J. 259, 394 A.2d 330, 4 Med.L.Rptr. 1360 (1978).

The court rejected the argument that the First Amendment protected Farber's refusal because of the need to keep newsgathering and dissemination from being substantially impaired. It concluded that *Branzburg* "squarely held that no such First Amendment right exists." "Thus we do no weighing or balancing of societal interest in reaching our determination that the First Amendment does not afford appellants the privilege they claim."

The court held that the state constitutional provision affording a criminal defendant the right to compel witnesses to produce documents prevailed over the shield law. There is also a Sixth Amendment right under the U.S. Constitution to compulsory process. The Supreme Court of the United States denied *certiorari sub nom.* New York Times Co. v. New Jersey, 439 U.S. 997 (1978). Justice Brennan took no part in the decision.

Farber spent a total of 40 days in jail, and the *Times* was fined $285,000, part of which was refunded several years later when the governor of New Jersey pardoned both Farber and the *Times*. The physician was acquitted. The New Jersey Legislature subsequently strengthened its shield law by requiring more clearly that a showing of need must be made before the reporter can be required to reveal confidential information even to the trial judge in chambers, much less the litigants. The state's Supreme Court twice upheld the statute shortly thereafter.

In most confidentiality cases, it is the plaintiff or the prosecutor who seeks additional information from the journalist. *Farber* was unusual in that it was the defendant—a murder defendant at that—seeking the information. Under the Sixth Amendment, the defendant is entitled to compulsory process to seek information.

C.B.S., Inc. v. Superior Court, 85 Cal.App.3d 241, 149 Cal.Rptr. 421, 4 Med.L.Rptr. 1568 (1978), involved an arrangement between CBS and the Santa Clara County sheriff's department under which CBS was permitted to photograph meetings between undercover agents and two men. The meetings led to the arrest of both men for selling controlled substances, and CBS showed the arrest sequence on its program "60 Minutes." Before the criminal trial, the attorney for one defendant sought the CBS outtakes. CBS refused. The trial judge ordered the outtakes turned over to the defense.

On appeal, the court concluded that under state law, "where a criminal defendant has demonstrated a *reasonable possibility* that evidence sought to be discovered might result in his exoneration, he is entitled to its discovery." The court ordered the judge to conduct a preliminary screening of the film and to consider whether delivery of voice clips alone would satisfy the defendant's needs.

On remand, the tapes were made available to the parties. As a result, the prosecutor dropped the charges against the defendant who had sought the film. The defendant's attorney is reported to have said that the film clips showed that although the defendant was present, "he didn't participate" in the transaction, contrary to the officers' version. San Francisco Chronicle, Feb. 24, 1979 at 4.

In People v. Korkala, 99 A.D.2d 161, 472 N.Y.S.2d 310, 10 Med. L.Rptr. 1355 (1984), the state sought outtakes from an interview that interviewers from CBS's "60 Minutes" had held with the defendant. CBS had broadcast 22 minutes from interviews that were said to have lasted several hours. CBS argued that the New York shield law gave reporters an "absolute privilege" against having to turn over such information. The court disagreed on the ground that the statute covered only cases in which the source had an expectation of confidentiality. Here the defendant had spoken openly with others on the subject.

On the First Amendment issue, the court balanced and concluded that although relevance was clear, it was not yet clear that the information would actually be needed in the prosecution. That would depend on the tack taken by defendant at the trial. The court ordered that the outtakes be shown to the trial judge *in camera.* If the defense had taken a turn that made delivery relevant, then the judge could have ordered production of the relevant material.

CBS did not appeal further. It made the outtakes available to the judge, who viewed them in a CBS screening room. CBS asserted that if the judge were to order any material to be delivered to the prosecutor, CBS might again take legal action. N.Y. Times, Apr. 6, 1984, at 25.

A danger in this procedure is suggested by an episode involving a reporter on the *Sacramento Union* whose notes were demanded by a person accused of murder. "She refused, but allowed the judge to review a copy of them. . . . As it turned out, the judge ruled that the defense attorney was the only one capable of reviewing the notes. [The reporter] was ready to face contempt charges, but the judge avoided a showdown by turning over his copy of her notes to the defense." Feed/back, Winter 1985, at 28.

Civil cases. When we turn to civil cases the justifications change for insisting on a reporter's testimony. Since the case is not criminal, society's interest may be less direct, and no one's freedom or life is at stake. Instead, a private person or group is suing for injury to person, property, privacy or reputation.

A qualified privilege was found in Democratic National Committee v. McCord, 356 F.Supp. 1394 (D.D.C.1973). The Committee for the Reelection of the President (President Nixon's reelection committee) was defending several suits arising out of the Watergate break-in. To obtain evidence for use in the trials, the Committee caused subpoenas to be issued against a number of journalists. On motions to quash the subpoenas, a federal court held that since all other means had not been used to obtain the material before requesting it from reporters, and since the Committee had not shown clearly that the material was relevant to the trials, the subpoenas should not be issued. In so ruling, the court discussed "the right of the press to gather and publish, and that of the public to receive, news from . . . ofttimes confidential sources." The court also noted that the suits in question were civil, not criminal, and that the media were not parties to the suits.

The courts thus adapted to civil cases the thrust of Justice Stewart's dissent in *Branzburg,* in which he contended that three conditions be met before a journalist is forced to testify or submit material, p. 775, *supra.* A number of federal cases involving subpoenas to reporters in civil suits have followed the *McCord* approach.

The Reporter as Plaintiff. What if the reporter *is* a party in the case? Syndicated columnist Jack Anderson sued several officials of the Nixon administration for trying to harass him. The defendants asserted that the statute of limitations had run and denied the merits of the claims. As part of their defense, they asked plaintiff when and how he learned about the alleged harassment and also sought information on other aspects of his claims. Several of these questions required disclosure of confidential sources, but plaintiff refused to reveal them. The judge ordered Anderson to reveal the sources on the ground that they were central to the defenses being raised:

> Here the newsman is not being obliged to disclose his sources. Plaintiff's pledge of confidentiality would have remained unchallenged had he not invoked the aid of the Court seeking compensatory and punitive damages based on his claim of conspiracy. Plaintiff is attempting to use the First Amendment simultaneously as a sword and a shield. He believes he was wronged by a conspiracy that sought to retaliate against the sources and to undermine his reliability and professional standing before the public because what he said was unpopular with the conspirators. But when those he accuses seek to defend by attempting to discover who his sources were, so that they may find out what the sources knew, their version of what they told him and how they were hurt, plaintiff says this is off limits—a forbidden area of inquiry. He cannot have it both ways. Plaintiff is not a bystander in the process but a principal. He cannot ask for justice and deny it to those he accuses.

The judge rejected plaintiff's claim that the conflicting claims should be "balanced." This was "most unrealistic. Having chosen to become a litigant, the newsman is not exempt from those obligations imposed by the rule of law on all litigants." The choice was plaintiff's: reveal the sources or have the case dismissed. Anderson v. Nixon, 444 F.Supp. 1195, 3 Med.L.Rptr. 1687 (D.D.C.1978). The case was subsequently dismissed.

The Press as Defendant. One complex question that cuts across several areas we have discussed is whether media defendants in defamation cases are privileged to refuse to identify confidential sources who gave them allegedly defamatory information. The philosophy of New York Times v. Sullivan counsels that debate should be open and robust—but that the press should be liable for defamations that are deliberately or recklessly false. What if the public figure plaintiff must know the source of the story to prove that the falsehood was deliberate or reckless? On the other hand, if the plaintiff can expose confidential sources simply by the expedient of suing for libel, such sources may disappear. Is *Branzburg* relevant on this aspect of reporters' privilege?

Several courts struggled with this matter in the 1970s. (Recall that in the Judy Garland case, the newspaper was not sued.) In 1979 *Herbert*, p. 651, *supra*, shed some light on the question. Recall that the Supreme Court held that the First Amendment did not protect a journalist from having to testify about his thoughts, opinions and conclusions as he was researching and preparing a story, and about his intra-office communications with others working on the story. The Court stressed that a plaintiff operating under the *New York Times* standard had a difficult task and should be able to seek direct evidence of constitutional malice.

The Court's suggestion that relevant evidence should be available to the plaintiff would suggest that confidential sources not be protected. On the other hand, the Herbert case involved little or no potential for chilling confidential sources, because it involved only the professional journalist's thoughts and communications. The compelled revelation of confidential sources would raise a different question.

These cases present two different questions. The first is: When may courts order journalists to reveal confidential sources? Courts are reluctant to allow a person to sue a newspaper for libel and then immediately learn all the confidential sources that were involved in the creation of the story. Much more likely, whether under state law or the First Amendment, courts will require the plaintiff to show his need for the information. The role the source played in the story's development and the article will be crucial.

The second question is: What sanction should be imposed on a defendant who refuses to obey an order to disclose the identity of its confidential sources? Since *Herbert*, a few state and lower federal courts have begun to address both questions. The results in these cases appear to permit the defendant who refuses to obey an order still to prevail on the truth-falsity issue, or to prove that the damages claimed were not caused by the defamation. State shield laws may affect this question if they directly create a testimonial privilege for reporters that extends to cases where the reporter is a party.

Identifying Violators of Judicial Orders. Another issue of privilege arises when a judge or grand jury wants to learn who told a reporter information that was supposed to be secret. The problem is illustrated by the case of the late William Farr, a newspaper reporter who covered the lurid Manson trial in Los Angeles. To reduce potentially prejudicial publicity in that case, the trial judge ordered the attorneys and certain others not to speak about specific phases of the case. Farr reported certain facts that he could only have learned from a person covered by the judge's order. The judge demanded that Farr identify his source despite the California privilege statute: "A publisher, editor, reporter . . . cannot be adjudged in contempt by a court . . . for refusing to disclose the source of any information procured for publication and published in a newspaper. . . ." Farr stated that the information had come from forbidden sources including two of the six attorneys. Each attorney denied having been a source. The judge again asked Farr to identify the individuals. Farr refused and was held in contempt.

The statute was held inapplicable because the legislature had no power to prohibit the court from seeking to preserve the integrity of its own operations. The legislature's efforts to immunize persons from punishment for violation of court orders violated the separation of powers. To immunize Farr "would severely impair the trial court's discharge of a constitutionally compelled duty to control its own officers. The trial court was enjoined by controlling precedent of the United States Supreme Court to take reasonable action to protect the defendants in the Manson case from the effects of prejudicial publicity." Farr v. Superior Court, 22 Cal.App.3d 60, 99 Cal.Rptr. 342, 1 Med. L.Rptr. 2545 (1971). The Supreme Court of California denied a hearing and the Supreme Court of the United States denied *certiorari* 409 U.S. 1011 (1972).

In a later proceeding, Farr argued that a contempt citation upon him was essentially a sentence of imprisonment for life because he clearly would not comply. The court noted that an order committing a person until he complies with a court order is "coercive and not penal in nature." The purpose of this sanction is not to punish but to obtain compliance with the order. Where an individual demonstrates conclusively that the coercion will fail, the contempt power becomes penal and comes within a five-day maximum sentence set by California statute. The case was remanded to determine whether coercion could be justified. In re Farr, 36 Cal.App.3d 577, 111 Cal.Rptr. 649 (1974). Farr was released.

Disclosing Information to Other Bodies. Not only do courts ask journalists for information, so do legislatures and administrative agencies. In 1971 the House of Representatives Commerce Committee subpoenaed then-CBS president Frank Stanton, ordering him to produce portions of film shot for, but not shown on, the documentary, "The Selling of the Pentagon." When Stanton refused to give the outtakes to the Committee, it voted 25–13 to recommend that Congress issue a contempt citation. The House refused to do so.

Later Daniel Schorr, a former CBS journalist, obtained a copy of a "secret" report of the House Intelligence Committee concerning the Central Intelligence Agency. He gave the report to the *Village Voice,* which published it in 1976. When asked by the House Ethics Committee to name the ·person from whom he received the report, Schorr declined. The Committee did not vote to ask for a contempt citation.

The Justice Department in July 1985, subpoenaed the three major television networks, the Cable News Network and the national news magazines to turn over all video and audio tapes and photographs (including outtakes) of the 17–day hostage crisis at Beirut International Airport. Government lawyers said the evidence they hoped to gather would be used for presentation to a grand jury that would be asked to indict the hijackers. Despite protests that the request amounted to a "fishing expedition," most of the media turned over copies of at least some of their tapes and photographs.

The potential for a press-Congress confrontation was created when *Newsday* 's Timothy Phelps and National Public Radio's Nina Totenberg reported Professor Anita Hill's previously-confidential allegations about then-Supreme-Court-nominee Clarence Thomas in October 1991. A nearly five-month investigation to try to determine who leaked the accusation of sexual harassment failed to identify the person(s) who made the unauthorized disclosures. Special Counsel Peter E. Fleming subpoenaed Phelps and Totenberg, both of whom refused to answer questions. He sought the support of leaders of the Senate Rules Committee, but they declined to take any action—such as a contempt citation—to try to force the reporters to testify. New York Times, May 6, 1992 at A18.

In contrasting viewpoints, *The Los Angeles Times* editorialized that, "We said from the beginning that it was wrong to investigate the messengers. Reporters . . . properly cited First Amendment protections of press freedom in refusing to answer investigators' questions about their confidential sources. . . . At a time when waste is uppermost in the minds of voters, and when the deficit weights heavily on the country, the Senate investigators engaged in an expensive exercise aimed at extracting vengeance for some disgruntled Republicans," while Bruce Fein in the *ABA Journal* wrote, "In March, the chairman and ranking minority member of the Senate Rules Committee . . . meekly surrendered to journalistic claims of privilege in shutting down the Thomas–Hill leak investigation. The pernicious consequences are three-fold: Congress's fact-finding and deliberative process will be impaired; the executive branch will resist sharing classified or confidential information with the legislature; and the press will enjoy a *de facto* legal privilege to scuttle legislative investigations that is neither required by the First Amendment nor necessary for publicizing wrongdoing or waywardness." See "Four Months of Futility," Los Angeles Times, May 7, 1992 at B6, and ABA Journal, June 1992 at 54.

Department of Justice Guidelines. After *Branzburg*, the Attorney General of the United States in 1973 adopted guidelines to regulate the issuance of subpoenas to members of the news media. The main point was that, except for cooperating reporters, no subpoena could be issued to any member of the news media "without the express authorization of the Attorney General." In requesting such authorization, subordinates were told to do so in criminal cases only if there is reasonable ground to believe that a crime has occurred and that the information sought is essential to a successful investigation, particularly with respect to guilt or innocence, and only after efforts to obtain the information from alternative nonmedia sources have failed. In civil cases, the litigation must be "of substantial importance." Even subpoena authorization requests for publicly disclosed information "should be treated with care to avoid claims of harassment." All requests should be directed at limited subject matter, should cover a limited period of time, and "should avoid requiring production of a large volume of unpublished material."

After the Department of Justice in 1979 obtained records of a reporter's toll calls from the local telephone company, the press urged government attention to the problem. The result was the promulgation in 1980 of amendments to the subpoena guidelines to provide that discussions with the reporter should precede any subpoena to the telephone company where the appropriate Assistant Attorney General concludes that such disclosure would not jeopardize the investigation. Before any subpoena is issued, the "express authorization of the Attorney General" is required. Such authorization should not be requested from the Attorney General unless there is reason to believe a crime has been committed, the need is clear, and alternative investigation steps have been unsuccessfully explored. The reporter should be informed within 45 days (though that may be delayed another 45 days) and the information obtained shall be closely held to prevent unauthorized persons from learning what the records reveal. The amended guidelines, which may be altered by any successor Attorney General, are in 45 Fed.Reg. 76,436 (Nov. 19, 1980), are codified in 28 C.F.R. § 50.10, and are reprinted in 6 Med.L.Rptr. 2153 (1980).

d.   The Breach of Contract Problem: Journalists Willing to Provide Information

A Minnesota case presents a different problem. Thus far we have been primarily concerned with protecting the rights of journalists, but sources may also want to be protected. Dan Cohen sued two different newspaper companies after he was identified as the source of information he provided about the prior criminal conviction of a political candidate. Cohen had agreed to provide it on the explicit condition that he not be identified, but editors of the *Minneapolis Star and Tribune* and the *St. Paul Pioneer Press* overrode their reporters' promises not to identify Cohen. A trial court's award to him of $700,000 in damages was overturned by the Minnesota Supreme Court, and Cohen appealed to the Supreme Court of the United States.

COHEN v. COWLES MEDIA COMPANY

Supreme Court of the United States.

501 U.S. ___, 111 S.Ct. 2513, 115 L.Ed.2d 586, 18 Med.L.Rptr. 2273 (1991).

JUSTICE WHITE delivered the opinion of the Court.

The question before us is whether the First Amendment prohibits a plaintiff from recovering damages, under state promissory estoppel law, for a newspaper's breach of a promise of confidentiality given to the plaintiff in exchange for information. We hold that it does not.

During the closing days of the 1982 Minnesota gubernatorial race, Dan Cohen, an active Republican associated with Wheelock Whitney's Independent–Republican gubernatorial campaign, approached reporters from the St. Paul Pioneer Press Dispatch (Pioneer Press) and the Minneapolis Star and Tribune (Star Tribune) and offered to provide documents relating to a candidate in the upcoming election. Cohen made clear to the reporters that he would provide the information only if he was given a promise of confidentiality. Reporters from both papers promised to keep Cohen's identity anonymous and Cohen turned over copies of two public court records concerning Marlene Johnson, the Democratic–Farmer–Labor candidate for Lieutenant Governor. The first record indicated that Johnson had been charged in 1969 with three counts of unlawful assembly, and the second that she had been convicted in 1970 of petit theft. Both newspapers interviewed Johnson for her explanation and one reporter tracked down the person who had found the records for Cohen. As it turned out, the unlawful assembly charges arose out of Johnson's participation in a protest of an alleged failure to hire minority workers on municipal construction projects and the charges were eventually dismissed. The petit theft conviction was for leaving a store without paying for $6.00 worth of sewing materials. The incident apparently occurred at a time during which Johnson was emotionally distraught, and the conviction was later vacated.

After consultation and debate, the editorial staffs of the two newspapers independently decided to publish Cohen's name as part of their stories concerning Johnson. In their stories, both papers identified Cohen as the source of the court records, indicated his connection to the Whitney campaign, and included denials by Whitney campaign officials of any role in the matter. The same day the stories appeared, Cohen was fired by his employer.

Cohen sued respondents, the publishers of the Pioneer Press and Star Tribune, in Minnesota state court, alleging fraudulent misrepresentation and breach of contract. The trial court rejected respondents' argument that the First Amendment barred Cohen's lawsuit. A jury returned a verdict in Cohen's favor, awarding him $200,000 in compensatory damages and $500,000 in punitive damages. The Minnesota

Court of Appeals, in a split decision, reversed the award of punitive damages after concluding that Cohen had failed to establish a fraud claim, the only claim which would support such an award. 445 N. W. 2d 248, 260 (Minn. App. 1989). However, the court upheld the finding of liability for breach of contract and the $200,000 compensatory damage award. Id., at 262.

A divided Minnesota Supreme Court reversed the compensatory damages award. [ ] After affirming the Court of Appeals' determination that Cohen had not established a claim for fraudulent misrepresentation, the court considered his breach of contract claim and concluded that "a contract cause of action is inappropriate for these particular circumstances." [ ] The court then went on to address the question whether Cohen could establish a cause of action under Minnesota law on a promissory estoppel theory. Apparently, a promissory estoppel theory was never tried to the jury, nor briefed, nor argued by the parties; it first arose during oral argument in the Minnesota Supreme Court when one of the justices asked a question about equitable estoppel. [ ]

In addressing the promissory estoppel question, the court decided that the most problematic element in establishing such a cause of action here was whether injustice could be avoided only by enforcing the promise of confidentiality made to Cohen. The court stated the "[u]nder a promissory estoppel analysis there can be no neutrality towards the First Amendment. In deciding whether it would be unjust not to enforce the promise, the court must necessarily weigh the same considerations that are weighed for whether the First Amendment has been violated. The court must balance the interest in protecting a promise of anonymity." [ ] After a brief discussion, the court concluded that "in this case enforcement of the promise of confidentiality under a promissory estoppel theory would violate defendants' First Amendment rights." [ ]

We granted certiorari to consider the First Amendment implications of this case. [ ]

Respondents initially contend that the Court should dismiss this case without reaching the merits because the promissory estoppel theory was not argued or presented in the courts below and because the Minnesota Supreme Court's decision rests entirely on the interpretation of state law. These contentions do not merit extended discussion. It is irrelevant to this Court's jurisdiction whether a party raised below and argued a federal-law issue that the state supreme court actually considered and decided. [ ] Moreover, that the Minnesota Supreme Court rested its holding on federal law could not be made more clear than by its conclusion that "in this case enforcement of the promise of confidentiality under a promissory estoppel theory would violate defendants' First Amendment rights." [ ] It can hardly be said that there is no First Amendment issue present in the case when respondents have defended against this suit all along by arguing that the First

Amendment barred the enforcement of the reporters' promises to Cohen. We proceed to consider whether that Amendment bars a promissory estoppel cause of action against respondents.

The initial question we face is whether a private cause of action for promissory estoppel involves "state action" within the meaning of the Fourteenth Amendment such that the protections of the First Amendment are triggered. For if it does not, then the First Amendment has no bearing on this case. The rationale of our decision in New York Times Co. v. Sullivan [ ] and subsequent cases compels the conclusion that there is state action here. Our cases teach that the application of state rules of law in state courts in a manner alleged to restrict First Amendment freedoms constitutes "state action" under the Fourteenth Amendment. [ ] In this case, the Minnesota Supreme Court held that if Cohen could recover at all it would be on the theory of promissory estoppel, a state-law doctrine which, in the absence of a contract, creates obligations never explicitly assumed by the parties. These legal obligations would be enforced through the official power of the Minnesota courts. Under our cases, that is enough to constitute "state action" for purposes of the Fourteenth Amendment.

Respondents rely on the proposition that "if a newspaper lawfully obtains truthful information about a matter of public significance then state officials may not constitutionally punish publication of the information, absent a need to further a state interest of the highest order." Smith v. Daily Mail Publishing Co. [ ] That proposition is unexceptionable, and it has been applied in various cases that have found insufficient the asserted state interests in preventing publication of truthful, lawfully obtained information. See e. g., The Florida Star v. B. J. F., [ ]; Smith v. Daily Mail [ ]; Landmark Communications, Inc. v. Virginia, [ ].

This case however, is not controlled by this line of cases but rather by the equally well-established line of decisions holding that generally applicable laws do not offend the First Amendment simply because their enforcement against the press has incidental effects on its ability to gather and report the news. As the cases relied on by respondents recognize, the truthful information sought to be published must have been lawfully acquired. The press may not with impunity break and enter an office or dwelling to gather news. Neither does the First Amendment relieve a newspaper reporter of the obligation shared by all citizens to respond to a grand jury subpoena and answer questions relevant to a criminal investigation, even though the reporter might be required to reveal a confidential source. Branzburg v. Hayes, [ ]. The press, like others interested in publishing, may not publish copyrighted material without obeying the copyright laws. See Zacchini v. Scripps–Howard Broadcasting Co., [ ]. Similarly, the media must obey the National Labor Relations Act [ ] and the Fair Labor Standards Act [ ]; may not restrain trade in violation of the antitrust laws, [ ]; and must pay nondiscriminatory taxes. [ ] It is therefore beyond dispute that "[t]he publisher of a newspaper has no special immunity from the application of general laws. He has no special privilege to invade the rights and liberties of others." [ ] Accordingly, enforcement of such general laws against the press is not subject to stricter scrutiny than would be applied to enforcement against other persons or organizations.

There can be little doubt that the Minnesota doctrine of promissory estoppel is a law of general applicability. It does not target or single out the press. Rather, in so far as we are advised, the doctrine is generally applicable to the daily transactions of all the citizens of Minnesota.

Justice Blackmun suggests that applying Minnesota promissory estoppel doctrine in this case will "punish" Respondents for publishing truthful information that was lawfully obtained. [ ] This is not strictly accurate because compensatory damages are not a form of punishment, as were the criminal sanctions at issue in Smith. If the contract between the parties in this case had contained a liquidated damages provision, it would be perfectly clear that the payment to petitioner would represent a cost of acquiring newsworthy material to be published at a profit, rather than a punishment imposed by the State. The payment of compensatory damages in this case is constitutionally indistinguishable from a generous bonus paid to a confidential news source. In any event, as indicated above, the characterization of the payment makes no difference for First Amendment purposes when the law being applied is a general law and does not single out the press. Moreover, Justice Blackmun's reliance on cases like The Florida Star and Smith v. Daily Mail is misplaced. In those cases, the State itself defined the content of publications that would trigger liability. Here, by contrast, Minnesota law simply requires those making promises to keep them. The parties themselves, as in this case, determine the scope of their legal obligations and any restrictions which may be placed on the publication of truthful information are self-imposed.

Also, it is not at all clear that Respondents obtained Cohen's name "lawfully" in this case, at least for purposes of publishing it. Unlike the situation in The Florida Star, where the rape victim's name was obtained through lawful access to a police report, respondents obtained Cohen's name only by making a promise which they did not honor. The dissenting opinions suggest that the press should not be subject to any law, including copyright law for example, which in any fashion or to any degree limits or restricts the press' right to report truthful information. The First Amendment does not grant the press such limitless protection.

Nor is Cohen attempting to use a promissory estoppel cause of action to avoid the strict requirements for establishing a libel or defamation claim. As the Minnesota Supreme Court observed here, "Cohen could not sue for defamation because the information disclosed [his name] was true." [ ] Cohen is not seeking damages for injury to his reputation or his state of mind. He sought damages in excess of $50,000 for breach of a promise that caused him to lose his job and lowered his earning capacity. Thus this is not a case like Hustler Magazine, Inc. v. Falwell [ ], where we held that the constitutional libel standards apply to a claim alleging that the publication of a parody was a state-law tort of intentional infliction of emotional distress.

Respondents and *amici* argue that permitting Cohen to maintain a cause of action for promissory estoppel will inhibit truthful reporting because news organizations will have legal incentives not to disclose a confidential source's identity even when that person's identity is itself newsworthy. Justice Souter makes a similar argument. But if this is the case, it is no more than the incidental, and constitutionally insignificant, consequence of applying to the press a generally applicable law that requires those who make certain kinds of promises to keep them. Although we conclude that the First Amendment does not confer on the press a constitutional right to disregard promises that would otherwise be enforced under state law, we reject Cohen's request that in reversing the Minnesota Supreme Court's judgement we reinstate the jury verdict awarding him $200,000 in compensatory damages. [ ] The Minnesota Supreme Court's incorrect conclusion that the First Amendment barred Cohen's claim may well have truncated its consideration of whether a promissory estoppel claim had otherwise been established under Minnesota law and whether Cohen's jury verdict could be upheld on a promissory estoppel basis. Or perhaps the State Constitution may be construed to shield the press from a promissory estoppel cause of action such as this one. These are matters for the Minnesota Supreme Court to address and resolve in the first instance on remand. Accordingly, the judgement of the Minnesota Supreme Court is reversed, and the case is remanded for further proceedings not inconsistent with this opinion.

So ordered.

Justice Blackmun, with whom Justice Marshall and Justice Souter join, dissenting.

. . .

Contrary to the majority, I regard our decision in [*Hustler*] to be precisely on point. There, we found that the use of a claim of intentional infliction of emotional distress to impose liability for the publication of a satirical critique violated the First Amendment. There was no doubt that Virginia's tort of intentional infliction of emotional distress was "a law of general applicability" unrelated to the suppression of speech. Nonetheless, a unanimous Court found that, when used to penalize the expression of opinion, the law was subject to the strictures of the First Amendment. In applying that principle, we concluded, [ ] that "public figures and public officials may not recover for the tort of intentional infliction of emotional distress by reason of publications such as the one here at issue without showing in addition that the publication contains a false statement of fact which was made with 'actual malice.' " as defined by [*Sullivan*]. In so doing, we rejected the argument that Virginia's interest in protecting its citizens from emotional distress was sufficient to remove from First Amendment protection a "patently offensive" expression of opinion. [ ][2]

As in *Hustler*, the operation of Minnesota's doctrine of promissory estoppel in this case cannot be said to have a merely "incidental" burden on speech; the publication of important political speech is the claimed violation. Thus, as in *Hustler*, the law may not be enforced to punish the expression of truthful information or opinion.[3] In the instant case, it is undisputed that the publication at issue was true.

To the extent that truthful speech may ever be sanctioned consistent with the First Amendment, it must be in furtherance of a state interest "of the highest order." [Daily Mail]. Because the Minnesota Supreme Court's opinion makes clear that the State's interest in enforcing its promissory estoppel doctrine in this case was far from compelling [ ] I would affirm that court's decision.

I respectfully dissent.

JUSTICE SOUTER, with whom JUSTICE MARSHALL, JUSTICE BLACKMUN and JUSTICE O'CONNOR join, dissenting.

I agree with Justice Blackmun that this case does not fall within the line of authority holding the press to laws of general applicability where commercial activities and relationships, not the content of publication, are at issue. . . . "There is nothing talismanic about natural laws of general applicability," [ ], for such laws may restrict First Amendment rights just as effectively as those directed specifically at speech itself. Because I do not believe the fact of general applicability to be dispositive, I find it necessary to articulate, measure, and compare the competing interests involved in any given case to determine the legitimacy of burdening constitutional interests, and such has been the Court's recent practice in publication cases. [ ]

Nor can I accept the majority's position that we may dispense with balancing because the burden on publication is in a sense "self-imposed" by the newspaper's voluntary promise of confidentiality. [ ] This suggests both the possibility of waiver, the requirements for which

---

2. The majority attempts to distinguish *Hustler* on the ground that there the plaintiff sought damages for injury to his state of mind whereas the petitioner here sought damages "for a breach of a promise that caused him to lose his job and lowered his earning capacity." [ ] I perceive no meaningful distinction between a statute that penalizes published speech in order to protect the individual's psychological well being or reputational interest, and one that exacts the same penalty in order to compensate the loss of employment or earning potential. Certainly, our decision in *Hustler* recognized no such distinction.

3. The majority argues that, unlike the criminal sanctions we considered in *Smith*

v. Daily Mail Publishing Co., [ ], the liability at issue here will not "punish" respondents in the strict sense of that word. [ ] While this may be true, we have long held that the imposition of civil liability based on protected expression constitutes "punishment" of speech for First Amendment purposes. See, e.g., [*Pittsburgh Press, Gertz*]. Though they be civil, the sanctions we review in this case are no more justifiable as "a cost of acquiring newsworthy material," [ ], than were the libel damages at issue in *New York Times* a permissible cost of disseminating newsworthy material.

have not been met here [see *Curtis Publishing*], as well as a conception of First Amendment rights as those of the speaker alone, with a value that may be measured without reference to the importance of the information to public discourse. But freedom of the press is ultimately founded on the value of enhancing such discourse for the sake of a citizenry better informed and thus more prudently self-governed. . . .

The importance of this public interest is integral to the balance that should be struck in this case. There can be no doubt that the fact of Cohen's identity expanded the universe of information relevant to the choice faced by Minnesota voters in that State's 1982 gubernatorial election, the publication of which was thus of the sort quintessentially subject to strict First Amendment protection. [ ] The propriety of his leak to respondents could be taken to reflect on his character, which in turn could be taken to reflect on the character of the candidate who had retained him as an adviser. An election could turn on just such a factor; if it should, I am ready to assume that it would be to the greater public good, at least over the long run.

This is not to say that the breach of such a promise of confidentiality could never give rise to liability. One can conceive of situations in which the injured party is a private individual, whose identity is of less public concern than that of the petitioner; liability there might not be constitutionally prohibited. Nor do I mean to imply that the circumstances of acquisition are irrelevant to the balance, see, e.g., [*Florida Star*], although they may go only to what balances against, and not to diminish, the First Amendment value of any particular piece of information.

Because I believe the State's interest in enforcing a newspaper's promise of confidentiality insufficient to outweigh the interest in unfettered publication of the information revealed in this case, I respectfully dissent.

Notes and Questions

1. Note that the decision leaves the Minnesota Supreme Court free to decide that the potential interference with editorial autonomy, which it mistakenly thought would violate the First Amendment, does violate state policies underlying the equitable remedy of promissory estoppel. Should the state court have decided the case on that basis in the first instance?

The newspapers argued that the state court decision in fact rested on such a ground, and that the Supreme Court therefore lacked jurisdiction. The Supreme Court rejected the argument, noting that the state court had concluded that "in this case enforcement of the promise of confidentiality under a promissory estoppel theory would violate defendants' First Amendment rights." If the state court had substituted "free speech rights" for the last three words, would its decision have been reviewable by the Supreme Court?

2. Newspapers and other media often enter into contracts that restrict the dissemination of news. For example, some newspapers operate news services through which they make their reports available to other newspapers subject to many conditions, including payment of fees and observance of release times and publication dates. Networks make their programs, including news programs, available to affiliates under contracts that impose similar conditions. If an affiliate or a subscribing newspaper insisted on a constitutional right to publish without complying with those conditions, how would the dissenters distinguish that case from Cohen?

3. The majority opinion does not respond to Justice Blackmun's argument that the burden on speech arising from liability for breach of a promise is no more "incidental" than the burden arising from libel or intentional infliction of emotional distress. Is there a satisfactory answer to that argument? If all civil liability for publication were treated as imposing similar burdens on speech, what constitutional limitations on contract liability might be suggested by the libel analogy?

4. In the reporter's privilege cases, media argue that unless they are allowed to honor promises of confidentiality, sources will not be willing to rely on those promises and will stop communicating to reporters, thereby chilling the flow of information to the public. Would a similar chilling effect occur if courts held that promises of confidentiality were not enforceable?

5. On remand, the Minnesota Supreme Court held that Cohen was entitled to $200,000 in damages. Cohen v. Cowles Media Co., 19 Med.L.Rptr. 1858 (Minn.1992).

2. USE OF SEARCH WARRANTS AGAINST THE PRESS

Basically, law enforcement officials may choose from among three methods for obtaining relevant evidence. The first is simply to ask the person who probably has it to turn it over. The lack of formality simplifies and expedites the process. The drawback is that a possessor of information who decides not to cooperate may legally destroy or transfer possession of the material after learning that the police want it.

The second procedure is the subpoena, discussed above. Prosecutorial officials ask either the court or grand jury for authority to issue a subpoena for evidence sought in connection with an investigation, or act under delegated authority. The recipient may not legally destroy the material after being served with the subpoena. A recipient who thinks the subpoena asks something illegal may challenge it. A recipient who claims not to have the material or information being sought may make a statement to that effect under oath. It may be difficult to prove whether the person illegally destroyed the material after receiving the subpoena.

The third method, the search warrant, played the central role in a case involving *The Stanford Daily,* the campus newspaper at Stanford University. A magistrate must decide whether a police request for a search warrant establishes probable cause to believe that the material sought is at the named location. If the magistrate is persuaded, the police may execute the warrant by appearing at the specified location without prior notice and may search the premises until they find the identified material.

Police believed that *Stanford Daily* photographers had taken photographs that would aid in identifying persons who had assaulted policemen during a violent demonstration. The police obtained a search warrant and served it on the *Daily.* After the search, the *Daily* brought an action against the chief of police and other local officials, and the case, Zurcher v. Stanford Daily, 436 U.S. 547, 3 Med.L.Rptr. 2377 (1978), eventually reached the Supreme Court. Justice White wrote for the majority that valid warrants may be issued to search *any* property, and that even though the Fourth Amendment may protect the materials sought to be seized, nothing in the First Amendment bars searches of newspaper offices.

After the decision a few states enacted bans on the issuance of search warrants against the media, and Congress passed the Privacy Protection Act of 1980, making it unlawful for an official of any government to search or seize "any work product material possessed by a person reasonably believed to have a purpose to disseminate to the public a newspaper, book, broadcast, or other similar form of public communication, in or affecting interstate or foreign commerce," except in special circumstances.

Despite the protection afforded the media by the 1980 federal statute and similar provisions in state statutes, problems can still arise. Sheriff's deputies in Riverside County, Calif., confiscated unedited videotape of a drug raid from KESQ–TV in Cathedral City, Calif., in June 1988. The station had declined to furnish a copy of the tape, citing the California shield law, so deputies had obtained a search warrant from a municipal court judge, then gone to the station and demanded the tape. The News Media & The Law, Summer 1988 at 50.

Deputies in another California county confiscated videotapes from the Riverside office of KCBS–TV. Those tapes were of a raid by animal rights activists on a research lab. A San Bernardino County Superior Court judge had issued search warrants for the tapes but subsequently quashed them, and the tapes were ordered returned to the station 18 hours after they were taken. Editor & Publisher, Sept. 3, 1988 at 19.

Telephone Records. The government may learn about reporters' sources or activities in ways that do not involve search warrants or subpoenas. Reporters Committee for Freedom of the Press v. American Telephone & Telegraph Co., 593 F.2d 1030, 4 Med.L.Rptr. 1177 (D.C.Cir. 1978), involved government requests for records of long distance calls charged to (but perhaps not made to or from) certain telephone numbers. Reporters charged that the First and Fourteenth Amendments required that subscribers be given notice before AT&T honored the government's request for toll-call records. The court, 2–1, concluded that balancing was not appropriate because "Government access to third-party evidence in the course of a good faith felony investigation in no sense 'abridges' plaintiffs' information-gathering activities." The possibility of bad-faith investigations (to harass reporters) did not warrant prior judicial intervention unless the reporter could establish "a clear and imminent threat of such future misconduct." The dissenter would have afforded reporters the opportunity to have prior judicial decisions made on such requests on a case-by-case basis. *Certiorari* was denied, 440 U.S. 949, 4 Med.L.Rptr. 2536 (1979), Brennan, Marshall and Stewart, JJ., dissenting.

3. IMPLICATIONS FOR JOURNALISTS

No journalist would want to go through his career in constant fear of a subpoena or a jail term; that sort of "chill" would seriously damage the newsgathering process and the free flow of information to the public. On the other hand, journalists handling sensitive material or dealing with confidences would be foolish not to make themselves aware of the shield law protection or lack thereof in the state(s) in which they work. Journalists sometimes will find that their sources, particularly those in official positions who are experienced at dealing with the press, are themselves familiar with the state shield laws.

Legalities aside, identifiable sources and attributable quotes strengthen good news stories. That is enough reason not to promise confidentiality to every source who asks for such a promise. Even in those instances in which reporters believe pledges of confidentiality are the only way they can get information from a source, they should be certain they have authorization from their employers before making such promises. As we have seen from the cases, reporters and their employer publications or stations are often "in it together" when a court seeks evidence in their hands. News organizations are well advised to be sure that news directors, editors, reporters and others are aware of the organization's policy on confidential sources and information before promises are made or subpoenas are served.

Although journalists can reasonably expect their employers to be supportive when subpoena problems arise, legal problems can create stress. When reporters' notes are subpoenaed, who owns the notes— the reporters or their employers? Absent any formal understanding to the contrary, employers may assert that they have "bought" them as part of the reporters' work product when the reporters endorsed their pay checks, even though the employers do not normally ask for the notes. Journalists may be more likely to feel they have "sold" only their finished stories and that the notes are still their personal property. Should it make any difference whether the reporters have taken notes in notebooks from their employers' supply rooms or in notebooks they bought themselves?

Obviously, where sensitive material is concerned, journalists should be careful about what materials they create and where they store them. Generating photocopies of confidential materials or writing memos within the news organization that might reveal or tend to reveal confidential information are examples of creating additional pieces of paper that could be subject to subpoena and should therefore not be done unnecessarily. Despite the protection against newsroom searches afforded by 1980 Congressional action, journalists may prefer to keep their most confidential notes or documents away from their offices— even away from their homes—in safe deposit boxes, for instance. This is not to suggest that paranoia should be the order of the day, and most reporters will never face such problems, but caution is in order for those handling the most sensitive information.

Computers also raise questions. If the confidential information is stored in the computer, can the journalist be compelled to create a print-out? In the event of a newsroom search, could the journalist be compelled to give law enforcement agents the password?

Even where there is no subpoena or search, journalists will sometimes find themselves having to make difficult decisions about the release of unpublished (not necessarily confidential) information. Suppose, for example, a television newsperson takes several minutes of videotape at the scene of a fatal auto accident, but only a few seconds are used on the air. An insurance company, involved in subsequent litigation, asks the television station if it can buy the complete tape, because it believes the tape will show some details of the accident scene better than the official police photos. Should the station turn over the tape? Would doing so be a harmless extension of the station's usual role in disseminating the truth about events. Would the fact that the station last week turned over unaired tapes of a children's Halloween party play any part in the decision? Would accident victims or other news subjects be less cooperative with television cameramen if they thought the latter might give or sell tapes for non-journalistic purposes, including use in litigation?

These questions and others relating to the confidentiality problems are difficult to answer. Although it may at first be easy for journalists to say they would go to jail rather than to reveal a source or break a confidence, that becomes more difficult when relatives, neighbors and friends outside of journalism ask how journalists think they are "above the law" and not subject to the same obligations that other citizens have. And, although a few journalists have briefly become famous by going to jail and have written about the experience, the fact is that the experience is inconvenient and disruptive at the least and quite difficult at the worst.

Texas newspaper reporter Brian Karem spent 14 days in jail after he refused to disclose the names of confidential sources who assisted him in obtaining a jail house telephone interview with an accused murderer. Karem had been sentenced to six months in jail and fined $500 for contempt, but he was released when his source allowed her identity to be revealed. Jane Kirtley of the Reporters Committee for Freedom of the Press said it was the first time in more than 10 years that a journalist had had to spend more than a few days in jail for refusing to reveal confidential information. Med.L.Rptr. News Notes July 17, 1990.

D. NEWSGATHERING FROM PUBLIC SOURCES

Journalists obtain news from government sources and government-controlled places the same way they obtain news of other kinds—by cultivating sources, making phone calls, asking questions, observing. Sometimes government and the people in it are reluctant sources, and the journalist can use legal help in obtaining access to the information. The recognition by the Supreme Court in *Richmond Newspapers*, p. 762, *supra*, of a First Amendment right of the public to attend trials is still an unusual recognition of a constitutional protection for newsgathering; more typically, the First Amendment has been recognized only as a right to publish news that one already possesses. Because a constitutional right of newsgathering was far from clearly established, journalists and others interested in observing the workings of government lobbied successfully in the 1960s and later for legislation at both the federal and state levels to provide access to government information.

In this section we consider access to public records, access to public meetings and access to public places. Refer to the related discussion at p. 760, *supra*, on access to courtrooms and to Chapter XIII for a discussion of access to private places.

1. ACCESS TO PUBLIC RECORDS

a. *Freedom of Information Act*

As long as legislatures were the preeminent lawmakers in the country, persons concerned with government actions could follow the process. With the New Deal, however, vast numbers of administrative agencies and organizations emerged. Congress empowered most of them to promulgate their own internal rules, to issue substantive regulations, to enforce laws, to adjudicate some controversies and to take other action of great importance to citizens. The sheer number of regulations and orders being promulgated made it difficult to keep track of the process. In addition, some of the agencies were not open about their operations.

In 1946 Congress passed the Administrative Procedure Act to require all administrative agencies to follow certain procedures in the adoption of regulations and in their adjudicative hearings. Congress also sought to make the internal rules and procedures of agencies more readily available to the public.

For a variety of reasons, this first effort at openness was not notably successful. In 1967 Congress responded to growing criticism by adopting the first version of the Freedom of Information Act. The FOIA was amended in 1974 to expand its scope. 5 U.S.C.A. § 552.

Congress passed the Freedom of Information Reform Act in October 1986—adopting a number of changes the media had sought for years. The amendments were inserted by the Senate in an anti-drug bill and subsequently accepted by the House of Representatives. The changes reflected a compromise: Senate Republicans led by Sen. Orrin Hatch (R.–Utah) wanted amendments curtailing public access to law enforcement records and informant files, while Senate Democrats successfully negotiated changes in the Act's fee structure as part of the package. [H.R. 5484, 99th Cong., 2nd Sess., 132 Cong.Rec. S14033 (daily ed. Sept. 27, 1986)].

The FOIA applies to all federal government agencies except Congress, the courts, the government of the District of Columbia and courts martial or the military during wartime. The Act requires each agency to publish in the *Federal Register* a description of its organization and a list of its personnel through whom the public can obtain information. Each agency must also explain the procedures by which it will furnish information. Each agency must make available to the public staff manuals and internal instructions that affect members of the public, final opinions in adjudicated cases, and current indexes.

Agencies may set reasonable fees for finding and copying material requested by the public. These fees are to be waived when the information will be of benefit to the general public.

Agencies are supposed to respond quickly to requests for information. Should an agency not comply with the FOIA, a member of the public may ask a federal district court to enforce the Act. The court may review in private the material the agency wishes to withhold, but it is the agency that bears the burden of showing that the material may be withheld under one of the exemptions to the Act discussed below. If the court decides the information should be released, it can order the government to pay all costs associated with the court action. Additionally, the agency employee who authorized the improper withholding of the information may be punished.

The FOIA contains nine exemptions—categories of material that need not be made available to the public. Several of these exemptions were amended in 1974 and 1989 to require more material to be given to the public. The exemptions are:

(b) This section does not apply to matters that are—

(1)(A) specifically authorized under criteria established by an Executive order to be kept secret in the interest of national defense or foreign policy and (B) are in fact properly classified pursuant to such Executive order;

(2) related solely to the internal personnel rules and practices of an agency;

(3) specifically exempted from disclosure by statute (other than [the Privacy Act]), provided that such statute (A) requires that the matters be withheld from the public in such a manner as to leave no discretion on the issue, or (B) establishes particular criteria for withholding or refers to particular types of matters to be withheld;

(4) trade secrets and commercial or financial information obtained from a person and privileged or confidential;

(5) inter-agency or intra-agency memorandums or letters which would not be available by law to a party other than an agency in litigation with the agency;

(6) personnel and medical files and similar files the disclosure of which would constitute a clearly unwarranted invasion of personal privacy;

(7) records or information compiled for law enforcement purposes, but only to the extent that the production of such law enforcement records or information (A) could reasonably be expected to interfere with enforcement proceedings, (B) would deprive a person of a right to a fair trial or an impartial adjudication, (C) could reasonably be expected to constitute an unwarranted invasion of personal privacy, (D) could reasonably be expected to disclose the identity of a confidential source, including a State, local, or foreign agency or authority or any private institution which furnished information on a confidential basis, and, in the case of a record or information compiled by criminal law enforcement authority in the course of a criminal investigation or by an agency conducting a lawful national security intelligence investigation, information furnished by a confidential source, (E) would disclose techniques and procedures for law enforcement investigations or prosecutions, or would disclose guidelines for law enforcement investigations or prosecutions if such disclosure could reasonably be expected to risk circumvention of the law, or (F) could reasonably be expected to endanger the life or physical safety of any individual;

(8) contained in or related to examination, operating, or condition reports prepared by, on behalf of, or for the use of an agency responsible for the regulation or supervision of financial institutions; or

(9) geological and geophysical information and data, including maps, concerning wells.

[Any reasonably segregable portion of a record must be provided to any person requesting such record after deletion of the portions that are exempt under this subsection.]

Notes and Questions

1. Notice that nothing in the original Act gave any special rights to the press as opposed to the public generally. Is that surprising?

2. What appear to be the crucial limitations of the Act?

3. Each exemption has produced its share of litigation. Those causing the most difficulty appear to be the first, third, fifth and seventh exemptions. In some cases amendments have already altered interpretations when Congress disagreed with a judicial interpretation. The procedures under the Act can get quite complicated. The Reporters Committee for Freedom of the Press and other organizations have prepared publications on how to use the Act.

    The Supreme Court has had occasion to pass on several cases interpreting the Act. These are often technical in nature and not particularly useful for our purposes. Most recently, the Supreme Court held that names and other identifying information could be deleted from State Department documents, sought under the Freedom of Information Act, concerning Haitian nationals who had attempted to emigrate illegally to the U.S. The documents had been requested under the FOIA by a Florida lawyer, but the State Department had cited exemption six, which applies to privacy interests. State Department v. Ray, 112 S.Ct. 541, 19 Med.L.Rptr. 1641 (1991).

4. Critics of the Act argue that compliance with it costs the government and the taxpayers too much money, that it endangers some law enforcement personnel and informants, and that it is an example of too much government, but the Act appears to have weathered most of the attempts to weaken it.

5. The broadened definition of investigatory records after the 1986 amendments now covers any information compiled for law enforcement purposes and permits secrecy if public access "could reasonably be expected to cause" harm to law enforcement efforts. Previous language allowed secrecy only if disclosure "would" cause such harm.

    The amendments also exempt informant files from the FOI Act's disclosure requirements, except where the government has officially confirmed that a person is an informant. Also, when revealing information about an ongoing investigation would tip off the targets, government agencies are not required to disclose. Broadcasting, Nov. 3, 1986 at 76.

    See How to Use the Federal FOI Act, 6th Edition, published by the FOI Service Center, a project of The Reporters Committee for Freedom of the Press, at 6–7, 30–32.

6. The structure for fees and fee waivers included in the 1986 amendments provide that "news media," educational and scientific institutions are to be charged duplication fees for FOI Act requests only when the request exceeds 100 pages. These "non-commercial" requestors will also be exempt from charges for the first two hours of search time. Commercial requesters will normally be charged for both search time

and duplication charges, but they can request fee waivers if they can demonstrate that disclosure is in the public interest and would "contribute significantly to public understanding of the operations or activities of the government."

Under orders from Congress, the Office of Management and Budget (OMB) issued guidelines in March 1987 to help federal agencies develop fee schedules in accordance with the 1986 amendments.

Congress had not defined the term "news media," but OMB defined "Representatives of the News Media" to include persons gathering information for organizations that publish or broadcast news (defining "news" as information about current events). Examples of news media cited in the guidelines include "television or radio stations and publishers of periodicals (but only in those instances when they can qualify as disseminators of 'news') who make their products available for purchase or subscription by the general public."

7. Note that many materials the media seek are not mentioned in the Act—including records from search warrant proceedings. In the wake of the Pentagon procurement scandal of 1988, for example, KCST–TV and other media organizations sought documents from the search of Cubic Corp., a major San Diego employer and builder of flight simulators. In that instance and several others in other parts of the country, judges generally declined to allow public access to the documents because of the government's argument that disclosure would divulge the nature and scope of the investigation in its early stages. Harold W. Fuson, vice president and general counsel of Copley Press, Inc., was quoted as saying, "We are aware of a growing trend, particularly by federal authorities, to keep search warrants under wraps. This is as good a time as any to challenge that." Editor & Publisher, Aug. 6, 1988 at 15.

8. The Supreme Court of the United States held in 1989 that third party requests for law enforcement records or information about a private citizen (even one charged with or convicted of a crime) "can reasonably be expected to invade that citizen's privacy," and that the FBI's criminal identification or "rap sheet" records are therefore exempt from disclosure under the Freedom of Information Act. Justice Department v. Reporters Committee for Freedom of the Press, 489 U.S. 749, 16 Med.L.Rptr. 1545 (1989).

9. Computer technology presents quite different problems for requestors of information than existed when the Freedom of Information Act was passed. Receiving a computer tape of government data will do requestors little good if they do not have the computer software necessary to access the data. Government sometimes argues, however, that the purchase agreements it has made when it purchased computer software do not permit it to give free copies of the software to parties who are requesting the data. It has also been alleged that there are instances in which government has switched from one computer program to another, archived the old records, and then failed to save the

software necessary to access the data in its own archives—essentially rendering the data useless for government as well as for requestors. The Reporters Committee for Freedom of the Press issued a 30–page booklet about access to electronic records in 1990. Late in 1991, legislation was introduced in the Senate (S 1940) to permit the public to obtain government records in either paper format or in computer-readable format. The Electronic Freedom of Information Improvement Act would give requesters their option of format if the agency maintains the requested information in both formats. Bush administration officials criticized the legislation saying "scarce agency computer resources . . . may be consumed by increasingly sophisticated FOIA demands . . . ." BNA Washington Insider, May 1, 1992.

b.   *The Privacy Act*

The movement toward openness in government has been tempered by growing concern about the dangers to individual privacy resulting from the growing number of records and federal agencies keeping records. In response to these concerns, Congress passed the Privacy Act of 1974. 5 U.S.C.A. § 522a. One major part of the Act permits subjects of records to see their files, obtain copies and correct inaccuracies. Individuals are not required to give the agencies any reasons for wanting to see their files. Civil actions may be brought for improper refusals to provide the file and for improper refusals to make corrections.

The part of the Act of most interest to the press, however, is the part that restricts disclosure of the contents of records unless certain conditions are met:

(b) Conditions of disclosure.—No agency shall disclose any record which is contained in a system of records by any means of communication to any person, or to another agency, except pursuant to a written request by, or with the prior written consent of, the individual to whom the record pertains, unless disclosure of the record would be—

(1) to those officers and employees of the agency which maintains the record who have a need for the record in the performance of their duties;

(2) required under section 552 of this title [FOIA];

(3) for a routine use as defined . . .;

(4) to the Bureau of the Census for purposes of planning or carrying out a census or survey or related activity . . .;

(5) to a recipient who has provided the agency with advance adequate written assurance that the record will be used solely as a statistical research or reporting record, and the record is to be transferred in a form that is not individually identifiable;

(6) to the National Archives of the United States as a record which has sufficient historical or other value to warrant its continued preservation by the United States Government, or for evaluation by the Administrator of General Services or his designee to determine whether the record has such value;

(7) to another agency or to an instrumentality of any governmental jurisdiction within or under the control of the United States for a civil or criminal law enforcement activity if the activity is authorized by law, and if the head of the agency or instrumentality has made a written request to the agency which maintains the record specifying the particular portion desired and the law enforcement activity for which the record is sought;

(8) to a person pursuant to a showing of compelling circumstances affecting the health or safety of an individual if upon such disclosure notification is transmitted to the last known address of such individual;

(9) to either House of Congress, or, to the extent of matter within its jurisdiction, any committee or subcommittee thereof, any joint committee of Congress or subcommittee of any such joint committee;

(10) to the Comptroller General, or any of his authorized representatives, in the course of the performance of the duties of the General Accounting Office; or

(11) pursuant to the order of a court of competent jurisdiction.

c. State Open Records Statutes

Although they vary a great deal, state access to information statutes exist in every state and they are frequently parallel to the federal statute by beginning with a premise that all government records should be publicly available and then listing a series of exceptions or exemptions. These statutes are generally still new enough that they are subject to frequent amendment, and journalists are well advised to obtain copies of their open records statutes for their states to see just what is available.

d. Using the Statutes

Freedom of information legislation can sometimes be helpful to a journalist—or, for that matter, any other member of the public seeking information—but that is not to say that it is frequently relied upon by the average journalist covering government. Establishing a good relationship with friendly sources inside government is a much more common way of obtaining information than using the statutes. When, however, the information would otherwise be unavailable, the reporter needs to know how to use the statute.

Freedom of information requests often have to be put into writing. Persons requesting information are advised to make their requests as simple as possible, specify the records wanted as specifically as possible, cite the statute under which the records are sought, ask to whom an appeal should be addressed should access to the records be denied and either put a dollar limit on the amount they are willing to pay or ask to be advised of the cost before the request is filled.

Even with attempts to strengthen the federal and state statutes at various times, a number of problems remain. Among those most frequently cited are (1) charging excessive fees for the records, (2) delaying the filling of requests, (3) demanding unreasonable specificity in identifying the records sought, (4) contaminating otherwise releasable records by filing them with classified information and (5) applying the exemptions too broadly.

Regrettable though it may be, it is a fact of life that the level of compliance with the state statutes is sometimes a factor of the level of government from which information is sought. Small town officials are still heard to deny access to information and to respond to mention of their states' freedom of information laws by saying, "That's just some law passed in the state capital. What are they going to do to me about it?" With few penalties built into the state laws for non-compliance and enforcement, the freedom of information legislation still has a long way to go before it becomes very helpful from the journalists' point of view.

From government's viewpoint, one problem with freedom of information legislation has been so-called "reverse FOIA" lawsuits. At issue has been whether the exemptions in the statute are mandatory or discretionary. The Supreme Court held in Chrysler Corporation v. Brown, 441 U.S. 281, 4 Med.L.Rptr. 2441 (1979), that FOIA does *not* create a private right of action to stop an agency from releasing documents covered by exemptions. A submitter of confidential business information, however, might attempt to stop disclosure by asserting that release would constitute an abuse of an agency's discretion under the Trade Secrets Act, 18 U.S.C.A. § 1905.

2. Access to Public Meetings

Guidelines for access to meetings of Congress or its committees and access to information about Congressional proceedings are prescribed initially in the Constitution. (Art. I, § 5):

> Each House may determine the Rules of its Proceedings. . . . Each House shall keep a Journal of its Proceedings, and from time to time publish the same, excepting such Parts as may in their Judgment require Secrecy; and the Yeas and Nays of the Members of either House on any question shall, at the Desire of one fifth of those Present, be entered on the Journal.

From the earliest days, sessions of the full House or Senate have usually been open to the public. Senate sessions were occasionally closed for discussion of treaties or nominations, and in the 30 years between 1945 and 1975, the Senate held 17 closed sessions, devoted usually to foreign relations or defense questions. Guide to the Congress of the United States 73 (2d ed. 1976).

Although most sessions of the full House and Senate have been open, most committee meetings were closed unless hearings were being held. Since 1970 there has been a sharp increase in open committee meetings, extending first to mark-up sessions (in which a pending bill may be approved, amended or rewritten), and later to conference committee meetings in which representatives of the two houses try to reconcile two different versions of proposed legislation. In 1975 the House and Senate voted to require open conferences unless a majority of conferees from either chamber vote in public to close a session. Can such negotiations be conducted effectively in open sessions? Should all meetings of all committees and subcommittees be open?

A different problem arises out of the conduct of Congressional investigations. The power to legislate implies the power to inquire into subjects that may require legislation, and allows Congress to conduct investigations and hold hearings. Congress may compel the attendance of witnesses and the production of documents at these hearings under threat of citation for contempt. The arguments against open hearings do not involve national security or the inhibiting effect of publicity on legislative compromise. Rather they reflect a concern for the privacy of witnesses and those whose behavior is under scrutiny. The advent of television coverage of some Congressional hearings has made this concern more significant.

a.   The "Sunshine Act"

At the urging of Congressmen and Senators from Florida, which had had good experience with its "Sunshine Law," Congress in 1976 passed a federal "Government in the Sunshine Act." 5 U.S.C.A. § 552b. The statement of purpose accompanying the Act declares that "the public is entitled to the fullest practicable information regarding the decision-making processes of the Federal Government." The Act seeks to "provide the public with such information while protecting the rights of individuals and the ability of the Government to carry out its responsibilities."

Essentially, the Act provides that all federal agencies headed by boards of two or more persons appointed by the President—approximately 50 agencies—must hold "every portion of every meeting" open to the public unless there is a valid reason for closure. Adequate advance notice must be given of each meeting. If a meeting is closed because it falls within one of the 10 exemptions to be noted, the agency must make public a transcript or minutes of all parts of the meeting that do not contain exempt material. Meetings may be closed only after a publicly recorded vote of a majority of the full membership of the agency.

The exemptions apply where the agency "properly determines" that a portion of the meeting "is likely to" result in the disclosure of specified information. The exemptions include verbatim copies of several FOIA exemptions—(1) involving national defense or foreign policy; (2) involving internal rules and practices of the agency; (3) matters specifically exempted from disclosure by another statute; (4) trade secrets; (7) law enforcement investigatory records; and (8) involving financial institutions. In addition, another exemption tracks closely the "clearly unwarranted invasion of personal privacy" language of the sixth exemption of the FOIA. Given the similar goals of the two statutes, it is not surprising that they contain similar exemptions.

In addition, the Sunshine Act contains the following summarized exemptions not found in the FOIA:

(5) disclosures that "involve accusing any person of a crime, or formally censuring any person;"

(9) "premature disclosures" involving agencies that regulate currencies, securities, commodities, or financial institutions, where the disclosure would be likely to (i) lead to "significant financial speculation" in these items or (ii) "significantly endanger the financial stability of any financial institution" or where the disclosure would be likely to "significantly frustrate implementation of a proposed agency action."

(10) information concerning an agency's issuance of a subpoena or its participation in a civil action or proceeding.

b. State Open Meetings Statutes

Clearly, less governmental business is conducted by the state legislature than by the multitude of agencies created by the legislature or by the executive branch under legislative authorization. In an effort to bring these agencies and their decision-making processes under public scrutiny many state legislatures have adopted "open meeting" or "sunshine" laws. These statutes and their enforcement provisions vary greatly. Some statutes provide that actions improperly taken in closed meetings can be declared null and void. Journalists generally favor fines or other penalties for public officials who disregard the open meetings statutes.

3. ACCESS TO PUBLIC PLACES

In addition to keeping records and holding meetings, governments also control access to their own buildings and grounds and sometimes to privately-owned property as well. No general legislation covers these situations. Instead, each has been handled under regulations issued by the person in control or by specific governmental departments such as the Bureau of Prisons.

For example, in 1974 President Ford excluded all reporters from mingling with guests at White House receptions. In 1975 he announced new rules under which a small pool of reporters, carrying only notebooks, might circulate at such events "with the understanding that the pool reporters will respect the privacy of personal communications between myself or Mrs. Ford and our guests." Editor & Publisher, Sept. 13, 1975 at 15.

In 1979, when President Carter took a steamer trip down the Mississippi River, he set rules for reporters who wished to accompany him: that the White House must approve all photographs, that no photos be bought from tourists, and that national organizations not distribute photos taken by local photographers along the way. As a result, several organizations refused to send their staffs on the trip. New York Times, Aug. 15, 1979 at A18.

On Oct. 25, 1983, the United States began a military operation on the island nation of Grenada. Press representatives were excluded from entry to the island until October 27, when a limited number of reporters were transported to the island by military aircraft. By November 7 all travel restrictions had been lifted and the press had unlimited access to the island. After conditions had returned to normal, Larry Flynt, publisher of *Hustler* magazine, sued the Secretary of Defense and others for declaratory and injunctive relief. Damages were not sought. The district judge granted a government motion to dismiss the case on the ground of mootness. Because the district court's opinion had also discussed the merits and had dismissed the complaint with prejudice, the court vacated that opinion and ordered the dismissal solely on the ground of mootness. Flynt v. Weinberger, 762 F.2d 134, 11 Med.L.Rptr. 2118 (D.C.Cir.1985). The request for injunctive relief was clearly moot because the events had passed. The request for declaratory relief was also moot because the complaint was addressed solely to the constitutionality of the ban in Grenada. There was no "reasonable expectation" that the Grenada controversy would recur.

Judge Edwards, concurring, asserted that the court had no occasion to consider "whether it is unconstitutional for the government to ban the press from covering military actions where the sole or principal justification offered by the government is the safety of the press (and especially where an allegation is made that the government's actual motivation is to prevent unfavorable press coverage which might influence public opinion)." Since that issue was not encompassed in the complaint, there was no need to "decide whether this issue, if properly raised, would be moot."

For an extended consideration of this question, see Cassell, Restrictions on Press Coverage of Military Operations: The Right of Access, Grenada, and "Off–the–Record Wars," 73 Georgetown Law Journal 931 (1985). Cassell concludes that access "would undoubtedly allow the press to witness events that might otherwise go unreported and could thereby increase the flow of information to the public. Yet, the possibility that wide press access may lead to the imposition of censorship should certainly give one pause before concluding that access is an unmitigated blessing. . . . The press should explicitly consider the implications of its demand for access in terms of the possibility of a censorship overreaction. To do otherwise is to risk confirming Senator Hiram Johnson's observation that '[t]he first casualty when war comes is truth.' "

After the outcry over the episode, the Defense Department created a panel under Maj. Gen. Winant Sidle to consider alternatives. That panel proposed, and the Defense Department put into effect, a limited pool to cover the early stages of surprise military operations. The Defense Department picks the organizations to participate in the pool, but the organizations pick the specific reporters.

A 1987 communications seminar in Washington, D.C., explored some of the questions involved with space-age newsgathering via satellite photography and the problems of maintaining national security in the face of such technology. Broadcasting, May 11, 1987 at 97.

The Reporters Committee for Freedom of the Press published an 11–page report titled "Access to Places: A Guide for Reporters & Photographers Gathering News" as part of the Fall, 1986, issue of *The News Media & The Law*.

When U.S. troops were sent to Saudi Arabia in August 1990 following Iraq's invasion of Kuwait, the complaints about the pool arrangements surfaced again. Two pools were called nearly a week after the first U.S. troops arrived. One went to Saudi Arabia and the other pool members were sent to U.S. Navy ships in the area. The Secretary of Defense attributed the delay in sending the pools to Saudi objections to the media presence. Editor & Publisher, Aug. 18, 1990 at 11.

In the months leading up to the start of the air war in January 1991, the Pentagon came up with new regulations for combat pool reporters, including a requirement that the reporters pass a physical fitness test involving push-ups, sit-ups and a mile-and-a-half run. Requirements were adjusted according to age and sex, and reportedly few journalists had trouble with them. Editor & Publisher, Jan. 12, 1991 at 8. During the air war in January and February there were numerous press complaints about required "security review" of their stories and about allegations that their military escorts took them to unnewsworthy locations and sometimes picked the soldiers to be interviewed. There were also complaints that pool reports—particularly reports by print media reporters—sometimes took hours to be reviewed, even though broadcast journalists sometimes were able to send live transmissions with little or no interference from their military escorts. Even before the outbreak of hostilities, nine publications and four journalists brought suit against the Department of Defense charging unfair practices and seeking an injunction against implementing the press policies. The suit was filed by the New York-based Center for Constitutional Rights. Broadcasting, "Journalists in a War of Strict Press Rules," Jan. 28, 1991 at 22.

Press concerns over problems in war coverage continued long after the war ended. After eight months of talks with news organizations, the Pentagon issued a set of principles to give journalists greater access to military operations than they had in the Persian Gulf war. The guidelines say journalists "will be provided access to all major military units." The news organizations and the Pentagon could not agree on the critical issue of the military's "security review" of articles and broadcasts. New York Times, May 22, 1992 at A–15.

Access and Terrorism. Terrorist activity has shown the tension between the efforts of the press to gather news and the desire of law enforcement officials to isolate the terrorists and to prevent them from learning in advance what action the police are planning to take. The problem is, of course, aggravated if the terrorists have taken hostages whose lives are now in danger. Some have suggested that reporters covering such events receive training in psychology so that they understand the impact their coverage may have on the situation itself. Some police officials have proposed guidelines for handling future episodes, such as requiring that broadcast journalists be kept farther from the scene than are print reporters so that officials could brief the print press without risking the possibility that important information would reach the terrorists prematurely.

Many reporters have objected, obviously, to plans to keep them from the scene. They urge that the matter be left to the sense of responsibility of the reporters. One journalist has said that "suppressing news of terrorism would be a denial of democracy that could take more lives than it saves. It is unworkable and philosophically unthinkable." The Quill (Dec. 1977) at 23.

Access to Police and Fire Scenes. As for local situations, almost all states have statutes that authorize police to bar access and provide that failure to obey an order to remain outside is punishable as failing to obey lawful police orders. Press passes that frequently permit journalists to cross police or fire lines at the scene of an accident, crime, or tragedy are typically subject to the control of the police and do not give the reporter a privilege to disregard police orders directed to them.

Access to Prisons. In 1974 the Supreme Court decided two companion cases involving efforts to obtain information from inmates confined in prisons. Pell v. Procunier, 417 U.S. 817, 1 Med.L.Rptr. 2379 (1974), involved a ban on press interviews with named inmates in the California prison system. Saxbe v. Washington Post Co., 417 U.S. 843, 1 Med.L.Rptr. 2314 (1974) involved a similar ban in the federal prison system. The Court concluded in *Pell* that the security and penological considerations of incarceration were sufficient to justify rejection of the inmates' claims that the interview ban violated their First Amendment rights.

Justice Stewart, writing for the Court in *Pell* and in *Saxbe,* then turned to the claims raised by the press. He noted that "this regulation is not part of an attempt by the State to conceal the conditions in its prisons or to frustrate the press' investigation and reporting of those conditions." Reporters could visit the institutions and "speak about any subject to any inmates whom they might encounter." Interviews with inmates selected at random were also permitted and both the press and public could take tours through the prisons. "In short, members of the press enjoy access to California prisons that is not available to other members of the public." Indeed, the only apparent restriction was the one being challenged.

Relying in part on the logic of *Branzburg,* Justice Stewart said that ". . . [N]ewsmen have no constitutional right of access to prisons or their inmates beyond that afforded the general public." Four justices dissented.

A few years later the Supreme Court returned to the prison question in a slightly different context in Houchins v. KQED, Inc., 438 U.S. 1, 3 Med.L.Rptr. 2521 (1978). A suicide had occurred at a jail in Santa Rita, Calif. KQED, licensee of a television station in San Francisco, reported the story and quoted a psychiatrist as saying that conditions at part of the jail were responsible for the illnesses of some prisoners there. Earlier, a federal judge had ruled that conditions at part of the jail constituted cruel and unusual punishment. Houchins, the county sheriff, refused to admit a KQED camera crew to the jail, and no public tours of the jail were permitted.

KQED and the NAACP filed suit under 42 U.S.C.A. § 1983 claiming violation of their First Amendment rights. The NAACP claimed that information about the jail was essential to permit public debate on jail conditions in the county. After the suit was filed, the sheriff permitted monthly tours. Although he barred cameras and tape recorders, he allowed several reporters, including one from KQED, to tour. Tour members "were not permitted to interview inmates and inmates were generally removed from view."

KQED argued that the tours were unsatisfactory because advance scheduling prevented timely access and because photography and interviewing were barred. The sheriff defended his policy on grounds of "inmate privacy," the danger of creating "jail celebrities," and the concern that there would be a disruption of jail operations.

Chief Justice Burger announced the judgment of the Supreme Court and delivered an opinion joined by Justices White and Rehnquist. In it, he wrote, "The media are not a substitute for or an adjunct of government, and like the courts, they are 'ill-equipped' to deal with problems of prison administration. . . . The public importance of conditions in penal facilities and the media's role of providing information afford no basis for reading into the Constitution a right of the public or the media to enter these institutions, with camera equipment, and take moving and still pictures of inmates for broadcast purposes. This Court has never intimated a First Amendment guarantee of a right of access to all sources of information within government control."

Justices Marshall and Blackmun took no part in the case. Justice Stewart concurred in the judgment but thought KQED was entitled to some limited injunctive relief. Justices Stevens, Brennan and Powell dissented.

Does the sequence of Supreme Court decisions begun in *Richmond Newspapers*, p. 762, *supra*, and *Globe Newspaper*, p. 762, *supra*, have implications for any future cases in which journalists might seek access to prisons for the purpose of newsgathering?

Access to Voting Sites. Public concerns have been raised periodically about early network television predictions of winners on election days. Part of the fear was that, because of different time zones, predictions from the East would affect voting in the West. A law against such predictions would clearly be a prior restraint, but 24 states enacted laws regulating exit polling—thus trying to solve the problem through a denial of access to the areas immediately surrounding the voting places. The networks and other media organizations challenged such statutes. In Daily Herald Co. v. Munro, 838 F.2d 380, 14 Med. L.Rptr. 2332 (9th Cir.1988), the court of appeals ruled unanimously that exit polling is a form of speech protected by the First Amendment, not only because the broadcasting of results is speech, but because conducting the polls requires discussion between pollsters and voters. Federal courts in other jurisdictions have also blocked enforcement of exit polling laws. News Media & The Law, Summer 1988 at 51. Lyle Denniston, however, points out that the Supreme Court's decision in Burson v. Freeman, 504 U.S. ___, 112 S.Ct. 1846, 20 Med.L.Rptr. 1137 (1992), upholding a Tennessee law barring *campaigning* within 100 feet of the entrance to any polling place could lead to laws banning others in the same area. Says Denniston, "Politicians would invite constitutional trouble if they persuaded legislatures to put limits on press activity near polling places. But the Supreme Court's ruling in the Tennessee case suggests an alternative: passing laws to ban *everyone* but voters from the 'free zone' around the polls." "Are Exit Polls an Endangered Species?," Washington Journalism Review, Sept. 1992 at 50.

4. DISCRIMINATORY ACCESS TO INFORMATION

Our focus has been on the question of whether any statute or constitutional provision requires unwilling government officials to reveal information or to permit the press or public to gather information from government files, meetings, or areas under government control. (Occasionally, a statute like the Privacy Act bars willing officials from supplying information.) In such a situation, government officials want nobody to learn certain information.

A quite different question arises when government officials are willing to part with information that they are not required to divulge—but want to discriminate among the prospective gatherers. The government's interest in this situation is no longer that the material should remain confidential or that secrecy is needed, because the official is quite prepared to divulge the information. The claim of government secrecy has been replaced by the desire of a government official to play favorites in the disclosure process, either for personal or political reasons.

Reporters have no right to force unwilling private persons to reveal information. If the private sources do decide to speak, there is no reason why they cannot sell their stories to the highest bidders or give them first to reporters who are close friends. But government traditionally must not behave in a discriminatory fashion. Even though government officials may not be required by statute or constitution to reveal certain information, they do not have unlimited control over the method of dissemination.

The starting point in general is that unless an official can demonstrate some reason for treating two apparently similar persons differently, the one who is being treated less well is not receiving equal protection of the laws. Notice that this constitutional protection in the Fourteenth Amendment applies broadly to all government action. If a government welfare program were arbitrarily to pay more money to redheads than to other recipients, the others would be able to claim a denial of equal protection.

Not all distinctions are invidious. When press cards must be limited for some reasons, some government agencies may prefer media organizations that regularly cover the situations in which the cards will be needed. For example, if media representatives need press cards to get through police lines at emergencies, the police might give cards to media that regularly cover such events but not give cards to specialized newspapers or magazines that do not. Drawing these lines is sometimes difficult. The situation is explored in Los Angeles Free Press, Inc. v. City of Los Angeles, 9 Cal.App.3d 448, 88 Cal.Rptr. 605 (1970), certiorari denied 401 U.S. 982 (1971), Justices Black, Douglas and Brennan dissenting.

Sometimes gender differences between reporters have been asserted to justify unequal treatment. The question of admitting women sports reporters to men's locker rooms went to court when the New York Yankees refused to allow them in after games. (This was not a case of private discrimination because Yankee Stadium is located on property owned by the city and thus involved governmental action.) The judge ordered that the women be admitted when the men were admitted. The players' privacy could be protected in less restrictive ways than by totally excluding women reporters. "The other two interests asserted by defendants, maintaining the status of baseball as a family sport and conforming to traditional notions of decency and

propriety, are clearly too insubstantial to merit serious consideration."
Ludtke v. Kuhn, 461 F.Supp. 86, 4 Med.L.Rptr. 1625 (S.D.N.Y.1978).

Sometimes different treatment may be based on characteristics of
the individual. For example, in Sherrill v. Knight, 569 F.2d 124, 3
Med.L.Rptr. 1514 (D.C.Cir.1977), Sherrill, Washington correspondent
for *The Nation,* had credentials for the House and Senate press galler-
ies but was denied a White House press pass because of Secret Service
objections. He was said to be a security risk because he had assaulted
the press secretary to the governor of Florida and also faced assault
charges in Texas.

The Secret Service had been ordered by the trial court to formulate
"narrow and specific" standards for deciding who posed a sufficient
danger to the President to be denied a press card. Security officials
were the appellants in the court of appeals.

The court recognized that the safety of a President was a compelling, indeed overwhelming, interest that would justify restrictions on a
reporter's access to the White House. But simply telling the reporter
that he was barred "for reasons of security" did not meet the procedural safeguards that were required in this case. The court ordered the
Secret Service to "publish or otherwise make publicly known the actual
standard employed in determining whether an otherwise eligible journalist will obtain a White House pass." This did not lend itself to the
narrow specifications required by the trial judge. It is enough if the
Service is guided by the standard of whether the applicant "presents a
potential source of physical danger . . . so serious as to justify his
exclusion." In addition, a reporter who is barred must get notice of the
facts the Service is relying on and have a chance to rebut them.

Occasionally, the basis for the different treatment is to be found in
the nature of the media involved. Some states have barred journalists
with tape recorders from legislative chambers, though they have allowed reporters to use pencil and pad. These limits, which have rarely
been challenged, have usually been upheld.

Television has presented special problems. Earlier in this chapter,
we considered the question of television cameras in courtrooms. Television has also raised questions in connection with the coverage of
executions. In Garrett v. Estelle, 556 F.2d 1274, 2 Med.L.Rptr. 2265
(5th Cir.1977), certiorari denied 438 U.S. 914 (1978), the court upheld
Texas' refusal to allow cameras or tape recorders into the execution
chamber. The state was willing to allow press pool reporters into the
chamber and to permit other reporters to view the events over simultaneous closed-circuit television. The court held, following *Pell* and
Saxbe, that "the first amendment does not accompany the press where
the public may not go." There was no public right to entry or to film
the event.

The final argument was that Texas had already chosen to make
executions public by televising them over a closed circuit. Texas
responded that legislation closing executions had already been upheld,

Holden v. Minnesota, 137 U.S. 483 (1890), and that the limited televising of the execution should not be equated with making the event public. The court agreed that the closed circuit television was for those allowed to be present and should not be used to justify opening the event to the public.

Televising Congress. In early 1979 the House of Representatives began television coverage of its proceedings. The House decided to maintain control over the cameras and allow broadcasters to use whatever footage they wanted. The entire proceedings are available to subscribers to a special cable network. An early dispute involved the practice of blacking out the picture during votes. At these times the screen shows only the ongoing tally. Speaker O'Neill explained that since members may change their votes at the end of the 15–minute voting period only by "going to the well" and informing the clerk, they may be reluctant to do that with the cameras focused on them.

After a trial period the United States Senate voted in 1986 to permit television coverage of its proceedings. *The News Media & The Law* reported that four times between March and June, 1992, Congress closed its doors to cameras from C–SPAN and other broadcast journalists while giving print journalists unrestricted access to the same proceedings: "Legislators defending the actions claimed that broadcast journalists are traditionally barred from the meetings C–SPAN sought to cover, or that the presence of cameras would have caused proceedings to take more time because committee members would be 'playing to the camera.'" The News Media & The Law, Summer 1992 at 9.

Appendix A

THE CONSTITUTION OF THE UNITED STATES OF AMERICA

———

We the People of the United States, in Order to form a more perfect Union, establish Justice, insure domestic Tranquility, provide for the common defence, promote the general Welfare, and secure the Blessings of Liberty to ourselves and our Posterity, do ordain and establish this Constitution for the United States of America.

ARTICLE I.

SECTION 1. All legislative Powers herein granted shall be vested in a Congress of the United States, which shall consist of a Senate and House of Representatives.

SECTION 2. The House of Representatives shall be composed of Members chosen every second Year by the People of the several States, and the Electors in each State shall have the Qualifications requisite for Electors of the most numerous Branch of the State Legislature.

No Person shall be a Representative who shall not have attained to the Age of twenty five Years, and been seven Years a Citizen of the United States, and who shall not, when elected, be an inhabitant of that State in which he shall be chosen.

Representatives and direct Taxes shall be apportioned among the several States which may be included within this Union, according to their respective Numbers, which shall be determined by adding to the whole Number of free Persons, including those bound to Service for a Term of Years, and excluding Indians not taxed, three fifths of all other Persons. The actual Enumeration shall be made within three Years after the first Meeting of the Congress of the United States, and within every subsequent Term of ten Years, in such Manner as they shall by Law direct. The Number of Representatives shall not exceed one for every thirty Thousand, but each State shall have at Least one Representative; and until such enumeration shall be made, the State of New Hampshire shall be entitled to chuse three, Massachusetts eight, Rhode Island and Providence Plantations one, Connecticut five, New York six, New Jersey four, Pennsylvania eight, Delaware one, Maryland six, Virginia ten, North Carolina five, South Carolina five, and Georgia three.

When vacancies happen in the Representation from any State, the Executive Authority thereof shall issue Writs of Election to fill such Vacancies.

The House of Representatives shall chuse their Speaker and other Officers; and shall have the sole Power of Impeachment.

SECTION 3. The Senate of the United States shall be composed of two Senators from each State, chosen by the Legislature thereof, for six Years; and each Senator shall have one Vote.

Immediately after they shall be assembled in Consequence of the first Election, they shall be divided as equally as may be into three Classes. The Seats of the Senators of the first Class shall be vacated at the Expiration of the second Year, of the second Class at the Expiration of the fourth Year, and of the third Class at the Expiration of the sixth Year, so that one third may be chosen every second Year; and if Vacancies happen by Resignation, or otherwise, during the Recess of the Legislature of any State, the Executive thereof may make temporary Appointments until the next Meeting of the Legislature, which shall then fill such Vacancies.

No Person shall be a Senator who shall not have attained to the Age of thirty Years, and been nine Years a Citizen of the United States, and who shall not, when elected, be an Inhabitant of that State for which he shall be chosen.

The Vice President of the United States shall be President of the Senate, but shall have no Vote, unless they be equally divided.

The Senate shall chuse their other Officers, and also a President pro tempore, in the Absence of the Vice President, or when he shall exercise the Office of President of the United States.

The Senate shall have the sole Power to try all Impeachments. When sitting for that Purpose, they shall be on Oath or Affirmation. When the President of the United States is tried the Chief Justice shall preside: And no Person shall be convicted without the Concurrence of two thirds of the Members present.

Judgment in Cases of Impeachment shall not extend further than to removal from Office, and disqualification to hold and enjoy any Office of honor, Trust, or Profit under the United States: but the Party convicted shall nevertheless be liable and subject to Indictment, Trial, Judgment, and Punishment, according to Law.

SECTION 4. The Times, Places and Manner of holding Elections for Senators and Representatives, shall be prescribed in each State by the Legislature thereof; but the Congress may at any time by Law make or alter such Regulations, except as to the Places of chusing Senators.

The Congress shall assemble at least once in every Year, and such Meeting shall be on the first Monday in December, unless they shall by Law appoint a different Day.

SECTION 5. Each House shall be the Judge of the Elections, Returns, and Qualifications of its own Members, and a Majority of each shall constitute a Quorum to do Business; but a smaller Number may adjourn from day to day, and may be authorized to compel the Attendance of absent Members, in such Manner, and under such Penalties as each House may provide.

Each House may determine the Rules of its Proceedings, punish its Members for disorderly Behaviour, and, with the Concurrence of two thirds, expel a Member.

Each House shall keep a Journal of its Proceedings, and from time to time publish the same, excepting such Parts as may in their Judgment require Secrecy; and the Yeas and Nays of the Members of either House on any question shall, at the Desire of one fifth of those Present, be entered on the Journal.

Neither House, during the Session of Congress, shall, without the Consent of the other, adjourn for more than three days, nor to any other Place than that in which the two Houses shall be sitting.

SECTION 6. The Senators and Representatives shall receive a Compensation for their Services, to be ascertained by Law, and paid out of the Treasury of the United States. They shall in all Cases, except Treason, Felony and Breach of the Peace, be privileged from Arrest during their Attendance at the Session of their respective Houses, and in going to and returning from the same; and for any Speech or Debate in either House, they shall not be questioned in any other Place.

No Senator or Representative shall, during the Time for which he was elected, be appointed to any civil Office under the Authority of the United States, which shall have been created, or the Emoluments whereof shall have been increased during such time; and no Person holding any Office under the United States, shall be a Member of either House during his Continuance in Office.

SECTION 7. All Bills for raising Revenue shall originate in the House of Representatives; but the Senate may propose or concur with amendments as on other Bills.

Every Bill which shall have passed the House of Representatives and the Senate, shall, before it becomes a Law, be presented to the President of the United States; If he approve he shall sign it, but if not he shall return it, with his Objections to that House in which it shall have originated, who shall enter the Objections at large on their Journal, and proceed to reconsider it. If after such Reconsideration two thirds of that House shall agree to pass the Bill, it shall be sent, together with the Objections, to the other House, by which it shall likewise be reconsidered, and if approved by two thirds of that House, it shall become a Law. But in all such Cases the Votes of both Houses shall be determined by Yeas and Nays, and the Names of the Persons voting for and against the Bill shall be entered on the Journal of each House respectively. If any Bill shall not be returned by the President within ten Days (Sunday excepted) after it shall have been presented to him, the Same shall be a Law, in like Manner as if he had signed it, unless the Congress by their Adjournment prevent its Return, in which Case it shall not be a Law.

Every Order, Resolution, or Vote to which the Concurrence of the Senate and House of Representatives may be necessary (except on a question of Adjournment) shall be presented to the President of the United States; and before the Same shall take Effect, shall be approved by him, or being disapproved by him, shall be repassed by two thirds of the Senate and House of Representatives, according to the Rules and Limitations prescribed in the Case of a Bill.

SECTION 8. The Congress shall have Power To lay and collect Taxes, Duties, Imposts and Excises, to pay the Debts and provide for the common Defence and general Welfare of the United States; but all Duties, Imposts and Excises shall be uniform throughout the United States;

To borrow Money on the credit of the United States;

To regulate Commerce with foreign Nations, and among the several States, and with the Indian Tribes;

To establish an uniform Rule of Naturalization, and uniform Laws on the subject of Bankruptcies throughout the United States;

To coin Money, regulate the Value thereof, and of foreign Coin, and fix the Standard of Weights and Measures;

To provide for the Punishment of counterfeiting the Securities and current Coin of the United States;

To establish Post Offices and post Roads;

To promote the Progress of Science and useful Arts, by securing for limited Times to Authors and Inventors the exclusive Right to their respective Writings and Discoveries;

To constitute Tribunals inferior to the supreme Court;

To define and punish Piracies and Felonies committed on the high Seas, and Offences against the Law of Nations;

To declare War, grant Letters of Marque and Reprisal, and make Rules concerning Captures on Land and Water;

To raise and support Armies, but no Appropriation of Money to that Use shall be for a longer Term than two Years;

To provide and maintain a Navy;

To make Rules for the Government and Regulation of the land and naval Forces;

To provide for calling forth the Militia to execute the Laws of the Union, suppress Insurrections and repel Invasions;

To provide for organizing, arming, and disciplining, the Militia, and for governing such Part of them as may be employed in the Service of the United States, reserving to the States respectively, the Appointment of the Officers, and the Authority of training the Militia according to the discipline prescribed by Congress;

To exercise exclusive Legislation in all Cases whatsoever, over such District (not exceeding ten Miles square) as may, by Cession of particular States, and the Acceptance of Congress, become the Seat of the Government of the United States, and to exercise like Authority over all Places purchased by the Consent of the Legislature of the State in which the Same shall be, for the Erection of Forts, Magazines, Arsenals, dock-Yards, and other needful Buildings;—And

To make all Laws which shall be necessary and proper for carrying into Execution the foregoing Powers, and all other Powers vested by this Constitution in the Government of the United States, or in any Department or Officer thereof.

SECTION 9.   The Migration or Importation of such Persons as any of the States now existing shall think proper to admit, shall not be prohibited by the Congress prior to the Year one thousand eight hundred and eight, but a Tax or duty may be imposed on such Importation, not exceeding ten dollars for each Person.

The Privilege of the Writ of Habeas Corpus shall not be suspended, unless when in Cases of Rebellion or Invasion the public Safety may require it.

No Bill of Attainder or ex post facto Law shall be passed.

No Capitation, or other direct, Tax shall be laid, unless in Proportion to the Census or Enumeration herein before directed to be taken.

No Tax or Duty shall be laid on Articles exported from any State.

No Preference shall be given by any Regulation of Commerce or Revenue to the Ports of one State over those of another; nor shall Vessels bound to, or from, one State, be obliged to enter, clear, or pay Duties in another.

No Money shall be drawn from the Treasury, but in Consequence of Appropriations made by Law; and a regular Statement and Account of the Receipts and Expenditures of all public Money shall be published from time to time.

No Title of Nobility shall be granted by the United States: And no Person holding any Office of Profit or Trust under them, shall, without the Consent of the Congress, accept of any present, Emolument, Office, or Title, of any kind whatever, from any King, Prince or foreign State.

SECTION 10.   No State shall enter into any Treaty, Alliance, or Confederation; grant Letters of Marque and Reprisal; coin Money; emit Bills of Credit; make any Thing but gold and silver Coin a Tender in Payment of Debts; pass any Bill of Attainder, ex post facto Law, or Law impairing the Obligation of Contracts, or grant any Title of Nobility.

No State shall, without the Consent of the Congress, lay any Imposts or Duties on Imports or Exports, except what may be absolutely necessary for executing its inspection Laws: and the net Produce of all Duties and Imposts, laid by any State on Imports or Exports, shall be for the Use of the Treasury of the United States; and all such Laws shall be subject to the Revision and Controul of the Congress.

No State shall, without the Consent of Congress, lay any Duty of Tonnage, keep Troops, or Ships of War in time of Peace, enter into any Agreement or Compact with another State, or with a foreign Power, or engage in War, unless actually invaded, or in such imminent Danger as will not admit of delay.

ARTICLE II.

SECTION 1. The executive Power shall be vested in a President of the United States of America. He shall hold his Office during the Term of four Years, and, together with the Vice President, chosen for the same Term, be elected, as follows

Each State shall appoint, in such Manner as the Legislature thereof may direct, a Number of Electors, equal to the whole Number of Senators and Representatives to which the State may be entitled in the Congress: but no Senator or Representative, or Person holding an Office of Trust or Profit under the United States, shall be appointed an Elector.

The Electors shall meet in their respective States, and vote by Ballot for two Persons, of whom one at least shall not be an Inhabitant of the same State with themselves. And they shall make a List of all the Persons voted for, and of the Number of Votes for each; which List they shall sign and certify, and transmit sealed to the Seat of the Government of the United States, directed to the President of the Senate. The President of the Senate shall, in the Presence of the Senate and House of Representatives, open all the Certificates, and the Votes shall then be counted. The Person having the greatest Number of Votes shall be the President, if such Number be a Majority of the whole Number of Electors appointed; and if there be more than one who have such Majority, and have an equal Number of Votes, then the House of Representatives shall immediately chuse by Ballot one of them for President; and if no Person have a Majority, then from the five highest on the List the said House shall in like Manner chuse the President. But in chusing the President, the Votes shall be taken by States, the Representation from each State having one Vote; a quorum for this Purpose shall consist of a Member or Members from two thirds of the States, and a Majority of all the States shall be necessary to a Choice. In every Case, after the Choice of the President, the Person having the greatest Number of Votes of the Electors shall be the Vice President. But if there should remain two or more who have equal Votes, the Senate shall chuse from them by Ballot the Vice President.

The Congress may determine the Time of chusing the Electors, and the Day on which they shall give their Votes; which Day shall be the same throughout the United States.

No Person except a natural born Citizen, or a Citizen of the United States, at the time of the Adoption of this Constitution, shall be eligible to the Office of President; neither shall any Person be eligible to that Office who shall not have attained to the Age of thirty five Years, and been fourteen Years a Resident within the United States.

In Case of the Removal of the President from Office, or of his Death, Resignation, or Inability to discharge the Powers and Duties of the said Office, the Same shall devolve on the Vice President, and the Congress may by Law provide for the Case of Removal, Death, Resignation or Inability, both of the President and Vice President, declaring what Officer shall then act as President, and such Officer shall act accordingly, until the Disability be removed, or a President shall be elected.

The President shall, at stated Times, receive for his Services, a Compensation, which shall neither be encreased nor diminished during the Period for which he shall have been elected, and he shall not receive within that Period any other Emolument from the United States, or any of them.

Before he enter on the Execution of his Office, he shall take the following Oath or Affirmation:—"I do solemnly swear (or affirm) that I will faithfully execute the Office of President of the United States, and will to the best of my Ability, preserve, protect and defend the Constitution of the United States."

SECTION 2.   The President shall be Commander in Chief of the Army and Navy of the United States, and of the Militia of the several States, when called into the actual Service of the United States; he may require the Opinion, in writing, of the principal Officer in each of the executive Departments, upon any Subject relating to the Duties of their respective Offices, and he shall have Power to grant Reprieves and Pardons for Offences against the United States, except in Cases of Impeachment.

He shall have Power, by and with the Advice and Consent of the Senate, to make Treaties, provided two thirds of the Senators present concur; and he shall nominate, and by and with the Advice and Consent of the Senate, shall appoint Ambassadors, other public Ministers and Consuls, Judges of the supreme Court, and all other Officers of the United States, whose Appointments are not herein otherwise provided for, and which shall be established by Law: but the Congress may by Law vest the Appointment of such inferior Officers, as they think proper, in the President alone, in the Courts of Law, or in the Heads of Departments.

The President shall have Power to fill up all Vacancies that may happen during the Recess of the Senate, by granting Commissions which shall expire at the End of their next Session.

SECTION 3.   He shall from time to time give to the Congress Information of the State of the Union, and recommend to their Consideration such Measures as he shall judge necessary and expedient; he may, on extraordinary Occasions, convene both Houses, or either of them, and in Case of Disagreement between them, with Respect to the Time of Adjournment, he may adjourn them to such Time as he shall think proper; he shall receive Ambassadors and other public Ministers; he shall take Care that the Laws be faithfully executed, and shall Commission all the Officers of the United States.

SECTION 4.   The President, Vice President and all civil Officers of the United States, shall be removed from Office on Impeachment for, and Conviction of, Treason, Bribery, or other high Crimes and Misdemeanors.

ARTICLE III.

SECTION 1.   The judicial Power of the United States, shall be vested in one supreme Court, and in such inferior Courts as the Congress may from time to time ordain and establish.   The Judges, both of the supreme and inferior Courts, shall hold their Offices during good Behaviour, and shall, at stated Times, receive for their Services, a Compensation, which shall not be diminished during their Continuance in Office.

SECTION 2.   The judicial Power shall extend to all Cases, in Law and Equity, arising under this Constitution, the Laws of the United States, and Treaties made, or which shall be made, under their Authority;—to all Cases affecting Ambassadors, other public Ministers and Consuls;—to all Cases of admiralty and maritime Jurisdiction;—to Controversies to which the United States shall be a Party;—to Controversies between two or more States;—between a State and Citizens of another State;—between Citizens of different States;—between Citizens of the same State claiming Lands under Grants of different States, and between a State, or the Citizens thereof, and foreign States, Citizens or Subjects.

In all Cases affecting Ambassadors, other public Ministers and Consuls, and those in which a State shall be Party, the supreme Court shall have original Jurisdiction.   In all the other Cases before mentioned, the supreme Court shall have appellate Jurisdiction, both as to Law and Fact, with such Exceptions, and under such Regulations as the Congress shall make.

The Trial of all Crimes, except in Cases of Impeachment, shall be by Jury; and such Trial shall be held in the State where the said Crimes shall have been committed; but when not committed within any State, the Trial shall be at such Place or Places as the Congress may by Law have directed.

SECTION 3.   Treason against the United States, shall consist only in levying War against them, or in adhering to their Enemies, giving them Aid and Comfort.   No Person shall be convicted of Treason unless on the Testimony of two Witnesses to the same overt Act, or on Confession in open Court.

The Congress shall have Power to declare the Punishment of Treason, but no Attainder of Treason shall work Corruption of Blood, or Forfeiture except during the Life of the Person attainted.

ARTICLE IV.

SECTION 1. Full Faith and Credit shall be given in each State to the public Acts, Records, and judicial Proceedings of every other State. And the Congress may by general Laws prescribe the Manner in which such Acts, Records and Proceedings shall be proved, and the Effect thereof.

SECTION 2. The Citizens of each State shall be entitled to all Privileges and Immunities of Citizens in the several States.

A Person charged in any State with Treason, Felony, or other Crime, who shall flee from Justice, and be found in another State, shall on Demand of the executive Authority of the State from which he fled, be delivered up, to be removed to the State having Jurisdiction of the Crime.

No Person held to Service or Labour in one State, under the Laws thereof, escaping into another, shall, in Consequence of any Law or Regulation therein, be discharged from such Service or Labour, but shall be delivered up on Claim of the Party to whom such Service or Labour may be due.

SECTION 3. New States may be admitted by the Congress into this Union; but no new State shall be formed or erected within the Jurisdiction of any other State; nor any State be formed by the Junction of two or more States, or Parts of States, without the Consent of the Legislatures of the States concerned as well as of the Congress.

The Congress shall have Power to dispose of and make all needful Rules and Regulations respecting the Territory or other Property belonging to the United States; and nothing in this Constitution shall be so construed as to Prejudice any Claims of the United States, or of any particular State.

SECTION 4. The United States shall guarantee to every State in this Union a Republican Form of Government, and shall protect each of them against Invasion; and on Application of the Legislature, or of the Executive (when the Legislature cannot be convened) against domestic Violence.

ARTICLE V.

The Congress, whenever two thirds of both Houses shall deem it necessary, shall propose Amendments to this Constitution, or, on the Application of the Legislature of two thirds of the several States, shall call a Convention for proposing Amendments, which, in either Case, shall be valid to all Intents and Purposes, as Part of this Constitution, when ratified by the Legislatures of three fourths of the several States, or by Conventions in three fourths thereof, as the one or the other Mode of Ratification may be proposed by the Congress; Provided that no Amendment which may be made prior to the Year One thousand eight hundred and eight shall in any Manner affect the first and fourth Clauses in the Ninth Section of the first Article; and that no State, without its Consent, shall be deprived of its equal Suffrage in the Senate.

ARTICLE VI.

All Debts contracted and Engagements entered into, before the Adoption of this Constitution, shall be as valid against the United States under this Constitution, as under the Confederation.

This Constitution, and the Laws of the United States which shall be made in Pursuance thereof; and all Treaties made, or which shall be made, under the Authority of the United States, shall be the supreme Law of the Land; and the Judges in every State shall be bound thereby, any Thing in the Constitution or Laws of any State to the Contrary notwithstanding.

The Senators and Representatives before mentioned, and the Members of the several State Legislatures, and all executive and judicial Officers, both of the United States and of the several States, shall be bound by Oath or Affirmation, to support this Constitution; but no religious Test shall ever be required as a Qualification to any Office or public Trust under the United States.

ARTICLE VII.

The Ratification of the Conventions of nine States, shall be sufficient for the establishment of this Constitution between the States so ratifying the Same.

. . .

ARTICLES IN ADDITION TO, AND AMENDMENTS OF, THE CONSTITUTION OF THE UNITED STATES OF AMERICA, PROPOSED BY CONGRESS, AND RATIFIED BY THE SEVERAL STATES, PURSUANT TO THE FIFTH ARTICLE OF THE ORIGINAL CONSTITUTION.

AMENDMENT I [1791]

Congress shall make no law respecting an establishment of religion, or prohibiting the free exercise thereof; or abridging the freedom of speech, or of the press; or the right of the people peaceably to assemble, and to petition the Government for a redress of grievances.

AMENDMENT II [1791]

A well regulated Militia, being necessary to the security of a free State, the right of the people to keep and bear Arms, shall not be infringed.

AMENDMENT III [1791]

No Soldier shall, in time of peace be quartered in any house, without the consent of the Owner, nor in time of war, but in a manner to be prescribed by law.

AMENDMENT IV [1791]

The right of the people to be secure in their persons, houses, papers, and effects, against unreasonable searches and seizures, shall not be violated, and no Warrants shall issue, but upon probable cause, supported by Oath or affirmation, and particularly describing the place to be searched, and the persons or things to be seized.

AMENDMENT V [1791]

No person shall be held to answer for a capital, or otherwise infamous crime, unless on a presentment or indictment of a Grand Jury, except in cases arising in the land or naval forces, or in the Militia, when in actual service in time of War or public danger; nor shall any person be subject for the same offence to be twice put in jeopardy of life or limb; nor shall be compelled in any criminal case to be a witness against himself, nor be deprived of life, liberty, or property, without due process of law; nor shall private property be taken for public use, without just compensation.

AMENDMENT VI [1791]

In all criminal prosecutions, the accused shall enjoy the right to a speedy and public trial, by an impartial jury of the State and district wherein the crime shall have been committed, which district shall have been previously ascertained by law, and to be informed of the nature and cause of the accusation; to be confronted with the witnesses against him; to have compulsory process for obtaining Witnesses in his favor, and to have the Assistance of Counsel for his defence.

AMENDMENT VII [1791]

In Suits at common law, where the value in controversy shall exceed twenty dollars, the right of trial by jury shall be preserved, and no fact tried by a jury be otherwise re-examined in any Court of the United States, than according to the rules of the common law.

AMENDMENT VIII [1791]

Excessive bail shall not be required, nor excessive fines imposed, nor cruel and unusual punishments inflicted.

AMENDMENT IX [1791]

The enumeration in the Constitution, of certain rights, shall not be construed to deny or disparage others retained by the people.

AMENDMENT X [1791]

The powers not delegated to the United States by the Constitution, nor prohibited by it to the States, are reserved to the States respectively, or to the people.

AMENDMENT XI [1798]

The Judicial power of the United States shall not be construed to extend to any suit in law or equity, commenced or prosecuted against one of the United States by Citizens of another State, or by Citizens or Subjects of any Foreign State.

AMENDMENT XII [1804]

The Electors shall meet in their respective states and vote by ballot for President and Vice–President, one of whom, at least, shall not be an inhabitant of the same state with themselves; they shall name in their ballots the person voted for as President, and in distinct ballots the person voted for as Vice–President, and they shall make distinct lists of all persons voted for as President, and of all persons voted for as Vice–President, and of the number of votes for each, which lists they shall sign and certify, and transmit sealed to the seat of the government of the United States, directed to the President of the Senate;—The President of the Senate shall, in the presence of the Senate and House of Representatives, open all the certificates and the votes shall then be counted;—The person having the greatest number of votes for President, shall be the President, if such number be a majority of the whole number of Electors appointed; and if no person have such majority, then from the persons having the highest numbers not exceeding three on the list of those voted for as President, the House of Representatives shall choose immediately, by ballot, the President. But in choosing the President, the votes shall be taken by states, the representation from each state having one vote; a quorum for this purpose shall consist of a member or members from two-thirds of the states, and a majority of all the states shall be necessary to a choice. And if the House of Representatives shall not choose a President whenever the right of choice shall devolve upon them, before the fourth day of March next following, then the Vice–President shall act as President, as in the case of the death or other constitutional disability of the President—The person having the greatest number of votes as Vice–President, shall be the Vice–President, if such number be a majority of the whole number of Electors appointed, and if no person have a majority, then from the two highest numbers on the list, the Senate shall choose the Vice–President; a quorum for the purpose shall consist of two-thirds of the whole number of Senators, and a majority of the whole number shall be necessary to a choice. But no person constitutionally ineligible to the office of President shall be eligible to that of Vice–President of the United States.

AMENDMENT XIII [1865]

SECTION 1. Neither slavery nor involuntary servitude, except as a punishment for crime whereof the party shall have been duly convicted, shall exist within the United States, or any place subject to their jurisdiction.

SECTION 2. Congress shall have power to enforce this article by appropriate legislation.

AMENDMENT XIV [1868]

SECTION 1. All persons born or naturalized in the United States and subject to the jurisdiction thereof, are citizens of the United States and of the State wherein they reside. No State shall make or enforce any law which shall abridge the privileges or immunities of citizens of the United States; nor shall any State deprive any person of life, liberty, or property, without due process of law; nor deny to any person within its jurisdiction the equal protection of the laws.

SECTION 2. Representatives shall be apportioned among the several States according to their respective numbers, counting the whole number of persons in each State, excluding Indians not taxed. But when the right to vote at any election for the choice of electors for President and Vice President of the United States, Representatives in Congress, the Executive and Judicial officers of a State, or the members of the Legislature thereof, is denied to any of the male inhabitants of such State, being twenty-one years of age, and citizens of the United States, or in any way abridged, except for participation in rebellion, or other crime, the basis of representation therein shall be reduced in the proportion which the number of such male citizens shall bear to the whole number of male citizens twenty-one years of age in such State.

SECTION 3. No person shall be a Senator or Representative in Congress, or elector of President and Vice President, or hold any office, civil or military, under the United States, or under any State, who, having previously taken an oath, as a member of Congress, or as a member of any State legislature, or as an executive or judicial officer of any State, to support the Constitution of the United States, shall have engaged in insurrection or rebellion against the same, or given aid or comfort to the enemies thereof. But Congress may by a vote of two-thirds of each House, remove such disability.

SECTION 4. The validity of the public debt of the United States, authorized by law, including debts incurred for payment of pensions and bounties for services in suppressing insurrection or rebellion, shall not be questioned. But neither the United States nor any State shall assume or pay any debt or obligation incurred in aid of insurrection or rebellion against the United States, or any claim for the loss or emancipation of any slave; but all such debts, obligations and claims shall be held illegal and void.

SECTION 5. The Congress shall have power to enforce, by appropriate legislation, the provisions of this article.

AMENDMENT XV [1870]

SECTION 1. The right of citizens of the United States to vote shall not be denied or abridged by the United States or by any State on account of race, color, or previous condition of servitude.

SECTION 2. The Congress shall have power to enforce this article by appropriate legislation.

AMENDMENT XVI [1913]

The Congress shall have power to lay and collect taxes on incomes, from whatever source derived, without apportionment among the several States, and without regard to any census or enumeration.

AMENDMENT XVII [1913]

The Senate of the United States shall be composed of two Senators from each State, elected by the people thereof, for six years; and each Senator shall have one vote. The electors in each State shall have the qualifications requisite for electors of the most numerous branch of the State legislatures.

When vacancies happen in the representation of any State in the Senate, the executive authority of such State shall issue writs of election to fill such vacancies: *Provided,* That the legislature of any State may empower the executive thereof to make temporary appointments until the people fill the vacancies by election as the legislature may direct.

This amendment shall not be so construed as to affect the election or term of any Senator chosen before it becomes valid as part of the Constitution.

AMENDMENT XVIII [1919]

SECTION 1. After one year from the ratification of this article the manufacture, sale, or transportation of intoxicating liquors within, the importation thereof into, or the exportation thereof from the United States and all territory subject to the jurisdiction thereof for beverage purposes is hereby prohibited.

SECTION 2. The Congress and the several States shall have concurrent power to enforce this article by appropriate legislation.

SECTION 3. This article shall be inoperative unless it shall have been ratified as an amendment to the Constitution by the legislatures of the several States, as provided in the Constitution, within seven years from the date of the submission hereof to the States by the Congress.

AMENDMENT XIX [1920]

The right of citizens of the United States to vote shall not be denied or abridged by the United States or by any State on account of sex.

Congress shall have power to enforce this article by appropriate legislation.

AMENDMENT XX [1933]

SECTION 1. The terms of the President and Vice President shall end at noon on the 20th day of January, and the terms of Senators and Representatives at noon on the 3d day of January, of the years in which such terms would have ended if this article had not been ratified; and the terms of their successors shall then begin.

SECTION 2. The Congress shall assemble at least once in every year, and such meeting shall begin at noon on the 3d day of January, unless they shall by law appoint a different day.

SECTION 3. If, at the time fixed for the beginning of the term of the President, the President elect shall have died, the Vice President elect shall become President. If a President shall not have been chosen before the time fixed for the beginning of his term, or if the President elect shall have failed to qualify, then the Vice President elect shall act as President until a President shall have qualified; and the Congress may by law provide for the case wherein neither a President elect nor a Vice President elect shall have qualified, declaring who shall then act as President, or the manner in which one who is to act shall be selected, and such person shall act accordingly until a President or Vice President shall have qualified.

SECTION 4. The Congress may by law provide for the case of the death of any of the persons from whom the House of Representatives may choose a President whenever the right of choice shall have devolved upon them, and for the case of the death of any of the persons from whom the Senate may choose a Vice President whenever the right of choice shall have devolved upon them.

SECTION 5. Sections 1 and 2 shall take effect on the 15th day of October following the ratification of this article.

SECTION 6. This article shall be inoperative unless it shall have been ratified as an amendment to the Constitution by the legislatures of three-fourths of the several States within seven years from the date of its submission.

AMENDMENT XXI [1933]

SECTION 1. The eighteenth article of amendment to the Constitution of the United States is hereby repealed.

SECTION 2. The transportation or importation into any State, Territory, or possession of the United States for delivery or use therein of intoxicating liquors, in violation of the laws thereof, is hereby prohibited.

SECTION 3. This article shall be inoperative unless it shall have been ratified as an amendment to the Constitution by conventions in the several States, as provided in the Constitution, within seven years from the date of the submission hereof to the States by the Congress.

AMENDMENT XXII [1951]

SECTION 1. No person shall be elected to the office of the President more than twice, and no person who has held the office of President, or acted as President, for more than two years of a term to which some other person was elected President shall be elected to the office of the President more than once. But this Article shall not apply to any person holding the office of President when this Article was proposed by the Congress, and shall not prevent any person who may be holding the office of President, or acting as President, during the term within which this Article becomes operative from holding the office of President or acting as President during the remainder of such term.

SECTION 2. This article shall be inoperative unless it shall have been ratified as an amendment to the Constitution by the legislatures of three-fourths of the several States within seven years from the date of its submission to the States by the Congress.

AMENDMENT XXIII [1961]

SECTION 1. The District constituting the seat of Government of the United States shall appoint in such manner as the Congress may direct:

A number of electors of President and Vice President equal to the whole number of Senators and Representatives in Congress to which the District would be entitled if it were a State, but in no event more than the least populous State; they shall be in addition to those appointed by the States, but they shall be considered, for the purposes of the election of President and Vice President, to be electors appointed by a State; and they shall meet in the District and perform such duties as provided by the twelfth article of amendment.

SECTION 2. The Congress shall have power to enforce this article by appropriate legislation.

AMENDMENT XXIV [1964]

SECTION 1. The right of citizens of the United States to vote in any primary or other election for President or Vice President, for electors for President or Vice President, or for Senator or Representative in Congress, shall not be denied or abridged by the United States or any State by reason of failure to pay any poll or other tax.

SECTION 2. The Congress shall have power to enforce this article by appropriate legislation.

AMENDMENT XXV [1967]

SECTION 1. In case of the removal of the President from office or of his death or resignation, the Vice President shall become President.

SECTION 2. Whenever there is a vacancy in the office of the Vice President, the President shall nominate a Vice President who shall take office upon confirmation by a majority vote of both Houses of Congress.

SECTION 3. Whenever the President transmits to the President pro tempore of the Senate and the Speaker of the House of Representatives his written declaration that he is unable to discharge the powers and duties of his office, and until he transmits to them a written declaration to the contrary, such powers and duties shall be discharged by the Vice President as Acting President.

SECTION 4. Whenever the Vice President and a majority of either the principal officers of the executive department or of such other body as Congress may by law provide, transmit to the President pro tempore of the Senate and the Speaker of the House of Representatives their written declaration that the President is unable to discharge the powers and duties of his office, the Vice President shall immediately assume the powers and duties of the office as Acting President.

Thereafter, when the President transmits to the President pro tempore of the Senate and the Speaker of the House of Representatives his written declaration that no inability exists, he shall resume the powers and duties of his office unless the Vice President and a majority of either the principal officers of the executive department or of such other body as Congress may by law provide, transmit within four days to the President pro tempore of the Senate and the Speaker of the House of Representatives their written declaration that the President is unable to discharge the powers and duties of his office. Thereupon Congress shall decide the issue, assembling within forty-eight hours for that purpose if not in session. If the Congress, within twenty-one days after receipt of the latter written declaration, or, if Congress is not in session, within twenty-one days after Congress is required to assemble, determines by two-thirds vote of both Houses that the President is unable to discharge the powers and duties of his office, the Vice President shall continue to discharge the same as Acting President; otherwise, the President shall resume the powers and duties of his office.

AMENDMENT XXVI [1971]

SECTION 1. The right of citizens of the United States, who are eighteen years of age or older, to vote shall not be denied or abridged by the United States or by any State on account of age.

SECTION 2. The Congress shall have power to enforce this article by appropriate legislation.

AMENDMENT XXVII [1992]

No law varying the compensation for the services of the senators and representatives shall take effect until an election of representatives shall have intervened.

Appendix B

COMMUNICATIONS ACT OF 1934

48 Stat. 1064 (1934), as amended, 47 U.S.C.A. § 151 et seq.
(as of January 1, 1993)

TITLE I—GENERAL PROVISIONS
PURPOSES OF ACT; CREATION OF FEDERAL COMMUNICATIONS COMMISSION

Sec. 1. [47 U.S.C.A. § 151.]

For the purpose of regulating interstate and foreign commerce in communication by wire and radio so as to make available, so far as possible, to all the people of the United States a rapid, efficient, Nation-wide, and world-wide wire and radio communication service with adequate facilities at reasonable charges, for the purpose of the national defense, for the purpose of promoting safety of life and property through the use of wire and radio communication, and for the purpose of securing a more effective execution of this policy by centralizing authority heretofore granted by law to several agencies and by granting additional authority with respect to interstate and foreign commerce in wire and radio communication, there is hereby created a commission to be known as the "Federal Communications Commission," which shall be constituted as hereinafter provided, and which shall execute and enforce the provisions of this Act.

. . .

APPLICATION OF ACT

Sec. 2. [47 U.S.C.A. § 152.]

(a) The provisions of this Act shall apply to all interstate and foreign communication by wire or radio and all interstate and foreign transmission of energy by radio, which originates and/or is received within the United States, and to all persons engaged within the United States in such communication or such transmission of energy by radio, and to the licensing and regulating of all radio stations as hereinafter provided . . .. The provisions of this Act shall apply with respect to cable service to all persons engaged within the United States in providing such service, and to the facilities of cable operators which relate to such service as provided in title VI.

. . .

832

TITLE III—PROVISIONS RELATING TO RADIO
LICENSE FOR RADIO COMMUNICATION OR TRANSMISSION OF ENERGY

Sec. 301. [47 U.S.C.A. § 301.]

It is the purpose of this Act, among other things, to maintain the control of the United States over all the channels of interstate and foreign radio transmission; and to provide for the use of such channels, but not the ownership thereof, by persons for limited periods of time, under licenses granted by Federal authority, and no such license shall be construed to create any right, beyond the terms, conditions, and periods of the license. No person shall use or operate any apparatus for the transmission of energy or communications or signals by radio (a) from one place in any Territory or possession of the United States or in the District of Columbia to another place in the same Territory, possession, or district; or (b) from any State, Territory, or possession of the United States, or from the District of Columbia to any other State, Territory, or possession of the United States; or (c) from any place in any State, Territory, or possession of the United States, or in the District of Columbia, to any place in any foreign country or to any vessel; or (d) within any State when the effects of such use extend beyond the borders of said State, or when interference is caused by such use or operation with the transmission of such energy, communications, or signals from within said State to any place beyond its borders, or from any place beyond its borders to any place within said State, or with the transmission or reception of such energy, communications, or signals from and/or to places beyond the borders of said State; or (e) upon any vessel or aircraft of the United States; or (f) upon any other mobile stations within the jurisdiction of the United States, except under and in accordance with this Act and with a license in that behalf granted under the provisions of this Act.

. . .

GENERAL POWERS OF THE COMMISSION

Sec. 303. [47 U.S.C.A. § 303.]

Except as otherwise provided in this Act, the Commission from time to time, as public convenience, interest, or necessity requires shall:

(a) Classify radio stations;

(b) Prescribe the nature of the service to be rendered by each class of licensed stations and each station within any class;

(c) Assign bands of frequencies to the various classes of stations, and assign frequencies for each individual station and determine the power which each station shall use and the time during which it may operate;

(d) Determine the location of classes of stations or individual stations;

(e) Regulate the kind of apparatus to be used with respect to its external effects and the purity and sharpness of the emissions from each station and from the apparatus therein;

(f) Make such regulations not inconsistent with law as it may deem necessary to prevent interference between stations and to carry out the provisions of this Act: *Provided, however,* That changes in the frequencies, authorized power, or in the times of operation of any station, shall not be made without the consent of the station licensee unless, after a public hearing, the Commission shall determine that such changes will promote public convenience or interest or will serve public necessity, or the provisions of this Act will be more fully complied with;

(g) Study new uses for radio, provide for experimental uses of frequencies, and generally encourage the larger and more effective use of radio in the public interest;

(h) Have authority to establish areas or zones to be served by any station;

(i) Have authority to make special regulations applicable to radio stations engaged in chain broadcasting;

(j) Have authority to make general rules and regulations requiring stations to keep such records of programs, transmissions of energy, communications, or signals as it may deem desirable;

. . .

(m)(1) Have authority to suspend the license of any operator upon proof sufficient to satisfy the Commission that the licensee—

(A) has violated any provision of any Act, treaty, or convention binding on the United States, which the Commission is authorized to administer, or any regulation made by the Commission under any such Act, treaty, or convention; or

. . .

(D) has transmitted superfluous radio communications or signals or communications containing profane or obscene words, language, or meaning. . . .

. . .

(r) Make such rules and regulations and prescribe such restrictions and conditions, not inconsistent with law, as may be necessary to carry out the provisions of this Act, or any international radio or wire communications treaty or convention, or regulations annexed thereto, including any treaty or convention insofar as it relates to the use of radio, to which the United States is or may hereafter become a party.

(s) Have authority to require that apparatus designed to receive television pictures broadcast simultaneously with sound be capable of adequately receiving all frequencies allocated by the Commission to television broadcasting when such apparatus is shipped in interstate commerce, or is imported from any foreign country into the United States, for sale or resale to the public.

. . .

ALLOCATION OF FACILITIES; TERM OF LICENSES

Sec. 307. [47 U.S.C.A. § 307.]

(a) The Commission, if public convenience, interest, or necessity will be served thereby, subject to the limitations of this Act, shall grant to any applicant therefor a station license provided for by this Act.

(b) In considering applications for licenses, and modifications and renewals thereof, when and insofar as there is demand for the same, the Commission shall make such distribution of licenses, frequencies, hours of operation, and of power among the several States and communities as to provide a fair, efficient, and equitable distribution of radio service to each of the same.

. . .

(d) No license granted for the operation of a television broadcasting station shall be for a term longer than five years . . . and any license granted may be revoked as hereinafter provided. Each license granted for the operation of a radio broadcasting station shall be for a term of not to exceed seven years. Upon the expiration of any license, upon application therefor, a renewal of such license may be granted from time to time for a term of not to exceed five years in the case of television broadcasting licenses, for a term of not to exceed seven years in the case of radio broadcasting station licenses, and for a term of not to exceed five years in the case of other licenses, if the Commission finds that public interest, convenience, and necessity would be served thereby. . . .

(e) No renewal of an existing station license in the broadcast or the common carrier services shall be granted more than thirty days prior to the expiration of the original license.

APPLICATIONS FOR LICENSES . . .

Sec. 308. [47 U.S.C.A. § 308.]

. . .

(b) All applications for station licenses, or modifications or renewals thereof, shall set forth such facts as the Commission by regulation may prescribe as to the citizenship, character, and financial, technical, and other qualifications of the applicant to operate the station; the ownership and location of the proposed station and of the stations, if any, with which it is proposed to communicate; the frequencies and the power desired to be used; the hours of the day or other periods of time during which it is proposed to operate the station; the purposes for which the station is to be used; and such other information as it may require. . . .

. . .

ACTION UPON APPLICATIONS; FORM OF AND CONDITIONS ATTACHED TO LICENSES
Sec. 309.   [47 U.S.C.A. § 309.]

(a) Subject to the provisions of this section, the Commission shall determine, in the case of each application filed with it to which section 308 applies, whether the public interest, convenience, and necessity will be served by the granting of such application, and, if the Commission, upon examination of such application and upon consideration of such other matters as the Commission may officially notice, shall find that public interest, convenience, and necessity would be served by the granting thereof, it shall grant such application.

. . .

(d)(1) Any party in interest may file with the Commission a petition to deny any application. . . .

(2) If the Commission finds on the basis of the application, the pleadings filed, or other matters which it may officially notice that there are no substantial and material questions of fact and that a grant of the application would be consistent with subsection (a), it shall make the grant, deny the petition, and issue a concise statement of the reasons for denying the petition, which statement shall dispose of all substantial issues raised by the petition. If a substantial and material question of fact is presented or if the Commission for any reason is unable to find that grant of the application would be consistent with subsection (a), it shall proceed as provided in subsection (e).

(e) If, in the case of any application to which subsection (a) of this section applies, a substantial and material question of fact is presented or the Commission for any reason is unable to make the finding specified in such subsection, it shall formally designate the application for hearing on the ground or reasons then obtaining and shall forthwith notify the applicant and all other known parties in interest of such action and the grounds and reasons therefor, specifying with particularity the matters and things in issue but not including issues or requirements phrased generally. . . .

. . .

(h) Such station licenses as the Commission may grant shall be in such general form as it may prescribe, but each license shall contain, in addition to other provisions, a statement of the following conditions to which such license shall be subject: (1) The station license shall not vest in the licensee any right to operate the station nor any right in the use of the frequencies designated in the license beyond the term thereof nor in any other manner than authorized therein; (2) neither the license nor the right granted thereunder shall be assigned or otherwise transferred in violation of this Act; (3) every license issued under this Act shall be subject in terms to the right of use or control conferred by section 606 of this Act.*

. . .

LIMITATION ON HOLDING AND TRANSFER OF LICENSES
Sec. 310. [47 U.S.C.A. § 310.]

(a) The station license required hereby shall not be granted to or held by any foreign government or representative thereof.

(b) No broadcast or common carrier . . . license shall be granted to or held by—

(1) Any alien or the representative of any alien;

(2) Any corporation organized under the laws of any foreign government;

. . .

(d) No construction permit or station license, or any rights thereunder, shall be transferred, assigned, or disposed of in any manner, voluntarily or involuntarily, directly or indirectly, or by transfer of control of any corporation holding such permit or license, to any person except upon application to the Commission and upon finding by the Commission that the public interest, convenience, and necessity will be served thereby. Any such application shall be disposed of as if the proposed transferee or assignee were making application under section 308 for the permit or license in question; but in acting thereon the Commission may not consider whether the public interest, convenience, and necessity might be served by the transfer, assignment, or disposal of the permit or license to a person other than the proposed transferee or assignee.

SPECIAL REQUIREMENTS WITH RESPECT TO CERTAIN APPLICATIONS IN THE BROADCASTING SERVICE
Sec. 311. [47 U.S.C.A. § 311.]

. . .

(c)(1) If there are pending before the Commission two or more applications for a permit for construction of a broadcasting station, only one of which can be granted, it shall be unlawful, without approval of the Commission, for the applicants or any of them to effectuate an agreement whereby one or more of such applicants withdraws his or their application or applications.

(2) The request for Commission approval in any such case shall be made in writing jointly by all the parties to the agreement. Such request shall contain or be accompanied by full information with

* [Section 606 grants substantial powers to the President to utilize communications facilities during wartime or a national emergency.]

respect to the agreement, set forth in such detail, form, and manner as the Commission shall by rule require.

(3) The Commission shall approve the agreement only if it determines (A) that the agreement is consistent with the public interest, convenience, or necessity; and (B) no party to the agreement filed its application for the purpose of reaching or carrying out such agreement. If the agreement does not contemplate a merger, but contemplates the making of any direct or indirect payment to any party thereto in consideration of his withdrawal of his application, the Commission may determine the agreement to be consistent with the public interest, convenience, or necessity only if the amount or value of such payment, as determined by the Commission, is not in excess of the aggregate amount determined by the Commission to have been legitimately and prudently expended and to be expended by such applicant in connection with preparing, filing, and advocating the granting of his application.

. . .

ADMINISTRATIVE SANCTIONS
Sec. 312.   [47 U.S.C.A. § 312.]

(a) The Commission may revoke any station license or construction permit—

(1) for false statements knowingly made either in the application or in any statement of fact which may be required pursuant to section 308;

(2) because of conditions coming to the attention of the Commission which would warrant it in refusing to grant a license or permit on an original application;

(3) for willful or repeated failure to operate substantially as set forth in the license;

(4) for willful or repeated violation of, or willful or repeated failure to observe any provision of this Act or any rule or regulation of the Commission authorized by this Act or by a treaty ratified by the United States;

(5) for violation of or failure to observe any final cease and desist order issued by the Commission under this section;

(6) for violation of section 1304, 1343, or 1464 of title 18 of the United States Code;* or

* [Relevant provisions read as follows:

§ 1304. Broadcasting lottery information

Whoever broadcasts by means of any radio station for which a license is required by any law of the United States, or whoever, operating any such station, knowingly permits the broadcasting of, any advertisement of or information concerning any lottery, gift enterprise, or similar scheme, offering prizes dependent in whole or in part upon lot or chance, or any list of the prizes drawn or awarded by means of any such lottery, gift enterprise, or scheme, whether said list contains any part or all of such prizes, shall be fined not more than $1,000 or imprisoned not more than one year, or both.

(7) for willful or repeated failure to allow reasonable access to or to permit purchase of reasonable amounts of time for the use of a broadcasting station by a legally qualified candidate for Federal elective office on behalf of his candidacy.

(b) Where any person (1) has failed to operate substantially as set forth in a license, (2) has violated or failed to observe any of the provisions of this Act, or section 1304, 1343, or 1464 of title 18 of the United States Code, or (3) has violated or failed to observe any rule or regulation of the Commission authorized by this Act or by a treaty ratified by the United States, the Commission may order such person to cease and desist from such action.

(c) Before revoking a license or permit pursuant to subsection (a), or issuing a cease and desist order pursuant to subsection (b), the Commission shall serve upon the licensee, permittee, or person involved an order to show cause [at a hearing] why an order of revocation or a cease and desist order should not be issued. . . .

(d) In any case where a hearing is conducted pursuant to the provisions of this section, both the burden of proceeding with the introduction of evidence and the burden of proof shall be upon the Commission.

. . .

APPLICATION OF ANTITRUST LAWS; REFUSAL OF LICENSES AND PERMITS IN CERTAIN CASES
Sec. 313. [47 U.S.C.A. § 313.]

(a) All laws of the United States relating to unlawful restraints and monopolies and to combinations, contracts, or agreements in restraint of trade are hereby declared to be applicable to the manufacture and sale of and to trade in radio apparatus and devices entering into or affecting interstate or foreign commerce and to interstate or foreign

Each day's broadcasting shall constitute a separate offense.

§ 1343. Fraud by wire, radio, or television

Whoever, having devised or intending to devise any scheme or artifice to defraud, or for obtaining money or property by means of false or fraudulent pretenses, representations, or promises, transmits or causes to be transmitted by means of wire, radio, or television communication in interstate or foreign commerce, any writings, signs, signals, pictures, or sounds for the purpose of executing such scheme or artifice, shall be fined not more than $1,000 or imprisoned not more than five years, or both.

§ 1464. Broadcasting obscene language

Whoever utters any obscene, indecent, or profane language by means of radio communications shall be fined not more than $10,000 or imprisoned not more than two years, or both.

§ 1307. State-conducted lotteries

(a) The provisions of sections 1301, 1302, 1303, and 1304 shall not apply to an advertisement, list of prizes, or information concerning a lottery conducted by a State acting under the authority of State law—

(1) contained in a newspaper published in that State, or

(2) broadcast by a radio or television station licensed to a location in that State or an adjacent State which conducts such a lottery. . . .]

radio communications. Whenever in any suit, action, or proceeding, civil or criminal, brought under the provisions of any of said laws or in any proceedings brought to enforce or to review findings and orders of the Federal Trade Commission or other governmental agency in respect of any matters as to which said Commission or other governmental agency is by law authorized to act, any licensee shall be found guilty of the violation of the provisions of such laws or any of them, the court, in addition to the penalties imposed by said laws, may adjudge, order, and/or decree that the license of such licensee shall, as of the date the decree or judgment becomes finally effective or as of such other date as the said decree shall fix, be revoked and that all rights under such license shall thereupon cease: *Provided, however,* That such licensee shall have the same right of appeal or review, as is provided by law in respect of other decrees and judgments of said court.

(b) The Commission is hereby directed to refuse a station license and/or the permit hereinafter required for the construction of a station to any person (or to any person directly or indirectly controlled by such person) whose license has been revoked by a court under this section.

. . .

FACILITIES FOR CANDIDATES FOR PUBLIC OFFICE
Sec. 315.   [47 U.S.C.A. § 315.]

(a) If any licensee shall permit any person who is a legally qualified candidate for any public office to use a broadcasting station, he shall afford equal opportunities to all other such candidates for that office in the use of such broadcasting station: *Provided,* That such licensee shall have no power of censorship over the material broadcast under the provisions of this section. No obligation is imposed under this subsection upon any licensee to allow the use of its station by any such candidate. Appearance by a legally qualified candidate on any—

(1) Bona fide newscast,

(2) Bona fide news interview,

(3) Bona fide news documentary (if the appearance of the candidate is incidental to the presentation of the subject or subjects covered by the news documentary), or

(4) On-the-spot coverage of bona fide news events (included but not limited to political conventions and activities incidental thereto), shall not be deemed to be use of a broadcasting station within the meaning of this subsection. Nothing in the foregoing sentence shall be construed as relieving broadcasters, in connection with the presentation of newscasts, news interviews, news documentaries, and on-the-spot coverage of news events, from the obligation imposed upon them under this Act to operate in the public interest and to afford reasonable opportunity for the discussion of conflicting views on issues of public importance.

(b) The charges made for the use of any broadcast station by any person who is a legally qualified candidate for any public office in connection with his campaign for nomination for election, or election, to such office shall not exceed—

(1) During the 45 days preceding the date of a primary or primary runoff election and during the 60 days preceding the date of a general or special election in which such person is a candidate, the lowest unit charge of the station for the same class and amount of time for the same period; and

(2) At any other time, the charges made for comparable use of such station by other users thereof.

(c) For the purposes of this section:

(1) The term "broadcasting station" includes a community antenna television system.

(2) The terms "licensee" and "station licensee" when used with respect to a community antenna television system, mean the operator of such system.

(d) The Commission shall prescribe appropriate rules and regulations to carry out the provisions of this section.

MODIFICATION BY COMMISSION OF CONSTRUCTION PERMITS OR LICENSES

Sec. 316. [47 U.S.C.A. § 316.]

(a) Any station license or construction permit may be modified by the Commission either for a limited time or for the duration of the term thereof, if in the judgment of the Commission such action will promote the public interest, convenience, and necessity, or the provisions of this Act or of any treaty ratified by the United States will be more fully complied with. No such order of modification shall become final until the holder of the license or permit shall have been notified in writing of the proposed action and the grounds and reasons therefor, and shall have been given reasonable opportunity, in no event less than thirty days, to show cause by public hearing, if requested, why such order of modification should not issue. . . .

(b) In any case where a hearing is conducted pursuant to the provisions of this section, both the burden of proceeding with the introduction of evidence and the burden of proof shall be upon the Commission.

ANNOUNCEMENT WITH RESPECT TO CERTAIN MATTER BROADCAST

Sec. 317. [47 U.S.C.A. § 317.]

(a)(1) All matter broadcast by any radio station for which any money, service or other valuable consideration is directly or indirectly paid, or promised to or charged or accepted by, the station so broadcasting, from any person, shall, at the time the same is so broadcast, be announced as paid for or furnished, as the case may be, by such person: *Provided,* That "service or other valuable consideration" shall not include any service or property furnished without charge or at a nominal charge for use on, or in connection with, a broadcast unless it is so furnished in consideration for an identification in a broadcast of any person, product, service, trademark, or brand name beyond an identification which is reasonably related to the use of such service or property on the broadcast.

. . .

FALSE DISTRESS SIGNALS; REBROADCASTING . . .
Sec. 325.   [47 U.S.C.A. § 325.]

(a) No person within the jurisdiction of the United States shall knowingly utter or transmit, or cause to be uttered or transmitted, any false or fraudulent signal of distress, or communication relating thereto, nor shall any broadcasting station rebroadcast the program or any part thereof of another broadcasting station without the express authority of the originating station.

(b) Consent to retransmission of broadcasting station signals.

(1) Following the date that is one year after October 5, 1992, no cable system or other multichannel video programming distributor shall retransmit the signal of a broadcasting station, or any part thereof, except—

(A) with the express authority of the originating station; or

(B) pursuant to section 614 of this title, in the case of a station electing, in accordance with this subsection, to assert the right to carriage under such section.

(2) The provisions of this subsection shall not apply to—

(A) retransmission of the signal of a noncommercial broadcasting station;

(B) retransmission directly to a home satellite antenna of the signal of a broadcasting station that is not owned or operated by, or affiliated with, a broadcasting network, if such signal was transmitted by a satellite carrier on May 1, 1991;

(C) retransmission of the signal of a broadcasting station that is owned or operated by, or affiliated with, a broadcasting network directly to a home satellite antenna, if the household receiving the signal is an unserved household; or

(D) retransmission by a cable operator or other multichannel video programming distributor of the signal of a superstation if such signal was obtained from a satellite carrier and the originating station was a superstation on May 1, 1991.

. . .

(3)(A) Within 45 days after October 5, 1992, the Commission shall commence a rulemaking proceeding to establish regulations to govern the exercise by television broadcast stations of the right to grant retransmission consent under this subsection and of the right to signal carriage under section 614 of this title, and such other regulations as are necessary to administer the limitations contained in paragraph (2). The Commission shall consider in such proceeding the impact that the grant of retransmission consent by television stations may have on the rates for the basic service tier and shall ensure that the regulations prescribed under this subsection do not conflict with the Commission's obligation under section 623(b)(1) of this title to ensure that the rates for the basic service tier are reasonable. Such rulemaking proceeding shall be completed within 180 days after October 5, 1992.

(B) The regulations required by subparagraph (A) shall require that television stations, within one year after October 5, 1992, and every three years thereafter, make an election between the right to grant retransmission under this subsection and the right to signal carriage under section 614 of this title. If there is more than one cable system which services the same geographic area, a station's election shall apply to all such cable systems.

(4) If an originating television station elects under paragraph (3)(B) to exercise its right to grant retransmission consent under this subsection with respect to a cable system, the provisions of section 534 of this title shall not apply to the carriage of the signal of such station by such cable system.

(5) The exercise by a television broadcast station of the right to grant retransmission consent under this subsection shall not interfere with or supersede the rights under section 614 or 615 of this title of any station electing to assert the right to signal carriage under that section.

(6) Nothing in this section shall be construed as modifying the compulsory copyright license established in section 111 of Title 17 or as affecting existing or future video programming licensing agreements between broadcasting stations and video programmers.

. . .

CENSORSHIP . . .

Sec. 326. [47 U.S.C.A. § 326.]

Nothing in this Act shall be understood or construed to give the Commission the power of censorship over the radio communications or signals transmitted by any radio station, and no regulation or condition shall be promulgated or fixed by the Commission which shall interfere with the right of free speech by means of radio communication.

PROHIBITION AGAINST SHIPMENT OF
CERTAIN TELEVISION RECEIVERS

Sec. 330.   [47 U.S.C.A. § 330.]

(a) No person shall ship in interstate commerce, or import from any foreign country into the United States, for sale or resale to the public, apparatus described in paragraph (s) of section 303 unless it complies with rules prescribed by the Commission pursuant to the authority granted by that paragraph: *Provided,* That this section shall not apply to carriers transporting such apparatus without trading in it.

. . .

DIRECT BROADCAST SATELLITE SERVICE OBLIGATIONS
Sec. 335 [47 U.S.C.A. § 335.]

(a) The Commission shall, within 180 days after October 5, 1992, initiate a rulemaking proceeding to impose, on providers of direct broadcast satellite service, public interest or other requirements for providing video programming. Any regulations prescribed pursuant to such rulemaking shall, at a minimum, apply the access to broadcast time requirement of section 312(a)(7) of this title and the use of facilities requirements of section 315 of this title to providers of direct broadcast satellite service providing video programming. Such proceeding also shall examine the opportunities that the establishment of direct broadcast satellite service provides for the principle of localism under this chapter, and the methods by which such principle may be served through technological and other developments in, or regulation of, such service.

(b)(1) The Commission shall require, as a condition of any provision, initial authorization, or authorization renewal for a provider of direct broadcast satellite service providing video programming, that the provider of such service reserve a portion of its channel capacity, equal to not less than 4 percent nor more than 7 percent, exclusively for noncommercial programming of an educational or informational nature.

(2) A provider of such service may utilize for any purpose any unused channel capacity required to be reserved under this subsection pending the actual use of such channel capacity for noncommercial programming of an educational or informational nature.

(3) A provider of direct broadcast satellite service shall meet the requirements of this subsection by making channel capacity available to national educational programming suppliers, upon reasonable prices, terms, and conditions, as determined by the Commission under paragraph (4). The provider of direct broadcast satellite service shall not exercise any editorial control over any video programming provided pursuant to this subsection.

(4) In determining reasonable prices under paragraph (3)—

(A) the Commission shall take into account the nonprofit character of the programming provider and any Federal funds used to support such programming;

(B) the Commission shall not permit such prices to exceed, for any channel made available under this subsection, 50 percent of the total direct costs of making such channel available; and

(C) in the calculation of total direct costs, the Commission shall exclude—

(i) marketing costs, general administrative costs, and similar overhead costs of the provider of direct broadcast satellite service; and

(ii) the revenue that such provider might have obtained by making such channel available to a commercial provider of video programming.

. . .

TITLE V—PENAL PROVISIONS—FORFEITURES
FORFEITURES

Sec. 503. [47 U.S.C.A. § 503.]

. . .

(b)(1) Any person who is determined by the Commission, in accordance with paragraph (3) or (4) of this subsection, to have—

(A) willfully or repeatedly failed to comply substantially with the terms and conditions of any license, permit, certificate, or other instrument or authorization issued by the Commission;

(B) willfully or repeatedly failed to comply with any of the provisions of this Act or of any rule, regulation, or order issued by the Commission under this Act or under any treaty convention, or other agreement to which the United States is a party and which is binding upon the United States;

(C) violated any provision of section 317(c) or 509(a) of this Act; or

(D) violated any provision of sections 1304, 1343, or 1464 of Title 18, United States Code;

shall be liable to the United States for a forfeiture penalty. A forfeiture penalty under this subsection shall be in addition to any other penalty provided for by this Act; except that this subsection shall not apply to any conduct which is subject to forfeiture under . . . section 507 of this Act.

(2) The amount of any forfeiture penalty determined under this subsection shall not exceed $2,000 for each violation. Each day of a continuing violation shall constitute a separate offense, but the total forfeiture penalty which may be imposed under this subsection, for acts

or omissions described in paragraph (1) of this subsection and set forth in the notice or the notice of apparent liability issued under this subsection, shall not exceed:

(A) $20,000, if the violator is (i) a common carrier subject to the provisions of this Act, (ii) a broadcast station licensee or permittee, or (iii) a cable television operator; or

(B) $5,000, in any case not covered by subparagraph (A).

The amount of such forfeiture penalty shall be assessed by the Commission, or its designee, by written notice. In determining the amount of such a forfeiture penalty, the Commission or its designee shall take into account the nature, circumstances, extent, and gravity of the prohibited acts committed and, with respect to the violator, the degree of culpability, any history of prior offenses, ability to pay, and such other matters as justice may require.

. . .

PROHIBITED PRACTICES IN CASES OF CONTESTS OF INTELLECTUAL KNOWLEDGE, INTELLECTUAL SKILL OR CHANCE

Sec. 509. [47 U.S.C.A. § 509.]

(a) It shall be unlawful for any person, with intent to deceive the listening or viewing public—

(1) To supply to any contestant in a purportedly bona fide contest of intellectual knowledge or intellectual skill any special and secret assistance whereby the outcome of such contest will be in whole or in part prearranged or predetermined.

(2) By means of persuasion, bribery, intimidation, or otherwise, to induce or cause any contestant in a purportedly bona fide contest of intellectual knowledge or intellectual skill to refrain in any manner from using or displaying his knowledge or skill in such contest, whereby the outcome thereof will be in whole or in part prearranged or predetermined.

. . .

TITLE VI—CABLE COMMUNICATIONS
PURPOSES

Sec. 601. [47 U.S.C.A. § 521.]

The purposes of this title are to

(1) establish a national policy concerning cable communications;

(2) establish franchise procedures and standards which encourage the growth and development of cable systems and which assure that cable systems are responsive to the needs and interests of the local community;

(3) establish guidelines for the exercise of Federal, State, and local authority with respect to the regulation of cable systems;

(4) assure and encourage that cable communications provide and are encouraged to provide the widest possible diversity of information sources and services to the public;

(5) establish an orderly process for franchise renewal which protects cable operators against unfair denials of renewal where the operator's past performance and proposal for future performance meet the standards established by this title; and

(6) promote competition in cable communications and minimize unnecessary regulation that would impose an undue economic burden on cable systems.

. . .

DEFINITIONS

Sec. 602. [47 U.S.C.A. § 522.]

For purposes of this subchapter—

(1) the term "activated channels" means those channels engineered at the headend of a cable system for the provision of services generally available to residential subscribers of the cable system, regardless of whether such services actually are provided, including any channel designated for public, educational, or governmental use;

(2) the term "affiliate," when used in relation to any person, means another person who owns or controls, is owned or controlled by, or is under common ownership or control with, such person;

(3) the term "basic cable service" means any service tier which includes the retransmission of local television broadcast signals;

(4) the term "cable channel" or "channel" means a portion of the electromagnetic frequency spectrum which is used in a cable system and which is capable of delivering a television channel (as television channel is defined by the Commission by regulation);

(5) the term "cable operator" means any person or group of persons (A) who provides cable service over a cable system and directly or through one or more affiliates owns a significant interest in such cable system, or (B) who otherwise controls or is responsible for, through any arrangement, the management and operation of such a cable system;

(6) the term "cable service" means—

(A) the one-way transmission to subscribers of (i) video programming, or (ii) other programming service, and

(B) subscriber interaction, if any, which is required for the selection of such video programming or other programming service;

(7) the term "cable system" means a facility, consisting of a set of closed transmission paths and associated signal generation, reception, and control equipment that is designed to provide cable service which includes video programming and which is provided to multiple subscribers within a community, but such term does not include (A) a facility that serves only to retransmit the television signals of 1 or more

television broadcast stations; (B) a facility that serves only subscribers in 1 or more multiple unit dwellings under common ownership, control, or management, unless such facility or facilities uses any public right-of-way; (C) a facility of a common carrier which is subject, in whole or in part, to the provisions of subchapter II of this chapter, except that such facility shall be considered a cable system (other than for purposes of section 621(c) of this title) to the extent such facility is used in the transmission of video programming directly to subscribers; or (D) any facilities of any electric utility solely for operating its electric utility system;

(8) the term "Federal agency" means any agency of the United States, including the Commission;

(9) the term "franchise" means an initial authorization, or renewal thereof (including a renewal of an authorization which has been granted subject to section 626 of this title), issued by a franchising authority, whether such authorization is designated as a franchise, permit, license, resolution, contract, certificate, agreement, or otherwise, which authorizes the construction or operation of a cable system;

(10) the term "franchising authority" means any governmental entity empowered by Federal, State, or local law to grant a franchise;

(11) the term "grade B contour" means the field strength of a television broadcast station computed in accordance with regulations promulgated by the Commission.

(12) the term "multichannel video programming distributor" means a person such as, but not limited to, a cable operator, a multichannel multipoint distribution service, a direct broadcast satellite service, or a television receive-only satellite program distributor, who makes available for purchase, by subscribers or customers, multiple channels of video programming;

(13) the term "other programming service" means information that a cable operator makes available to all subscribers generally;

(14) the term "person" means an individual, partnership, association, joint stock company, trust, corporation, or governmental entity;

(15) the term "public, educational, or governmental access facilities" means—

(A) channel capacity designated for public, educational, or governmental use; and

(B) facilities and equipment for the use of such channel capacity;

(16) the term "service tier" means a category of cable service or other services provided by a cable operator and for which a separate rate is charged by the cable operator;

(17) the term "State" means any State, or political subdivision, or agency thereof;

(18) the term "usable activated channels" means activated channels of a cable system, except those channels whose use for the distribution of broadcast signals would conflict with technical and safety regulations as determined by the Commission; and

(19) the term "video programming" means programming provided by, a television broadcast station.

CABLE CHANNELS FOR PUBLIC, EDUCATIONAL OR GOVERNMENTAL USE

Sec. 611. [47 U.S.C.A. § 531.]

(a) A franchising authority may establish requirements in a franchise with respect to the designation or use of channel capacity for public, educational, or governmental use only to the extent provided in this section.

(b) A franchising authority may in its request for proposals require as part of a franchise, and may require as part of a cable operator's proposal for a franchise renewal, subject to section 626, that channel capacity be designated for public, educational, or governmental use,

. . .

(c) A franchising authority may enforce any requirement in any franchise regarding the providing or use of such channel capacity. Such enforcement authority includes the authority to enforce any provisions of the franchise for services, facilities, or equipment proposed by the cable operator, which relate to public, educational, or governmental use of channel capacity, whether or not required by the franchising authority pursuant to subsection (b).

. . .

(e) Subject to section 624(d), a cable operator shall not exercise any editorial control over any public, educational, or governmental use of channel capacity provided pursuant to this section.

. . .

CABLE CHANNELS FOR COMMERCIAL USE

Sec. 612. [47 U.S.C.A. § 532.]

(a) The purpose of this section is to assure that the widest possible diversity of information sources are made available to the public from cable systems in a manner consistent with growth and development of cable systems.

(b)(1) A cable operator shall designate channel capacity for commercial use by persons unaffiliated with the operator in accordance with the following requirements:

(A) An operator of any cable system with 36 or more (but not more than 54) activated channels shall designate 10 percent of such channels which are not otherwise required for use (or the use of which is not prohibited) by Federal law or regulation.

(B) An operator of any cable system with 55 or more (but not more than 100) activated channels shall designate 15 percent of such channels which are not otherwise required for use (or the use of which is not prohibited) by Federal law or regulation.

(C) An operator of any cable system with more than 100 activated channels shall designate 15 percent of all such channels.

(D) An operator of any cable system with fewer than 36 activated channels shall not be required to designate channel capacity for commercial use by persons unaffiliated with the operator, unless the cable system is required to provide such channel capacity under the terms of a franchise in effect on the date of the enactment of this title.

. . .

(c)(1) If a person unaffiliated with the cable operator seeks to use channel capacity designated pursuant to subsection (b) for commercial use, the cable operator shall establish, consistent with the purpose of this section, the price, terms, and conditions of such use which are at least sufficient to assure that such use will not adversely affect the operation, financial condition, or market development of the cable system.

(2) A cable operator shall not exercise any editorial control over any video programming provided pursuant to this section, or in any other way consider the content of such programming, except that an operator may consider such content to the minimum extent necessary to establish a reasonable price for the commercial use of designated channel capacity by an unaffiliated person.

. . .

(d) Any person aggrieved by the failure or refusal of a cable operator to make channel capacity available for use pursuant to this section may bring an action in the district court of the United States for the judicial district in which the cable system is located to compel that such capacity be made available. If the court finds that the channel capacity sought by such a person has not been made available in accordance with this section, or finds that the price, terms, or conditions established by the cable operator are unreasonable, the court may order such system to make available to such person the channel capacity sought, and further determine the appropriate price, terms, or conditions for such use consistent with subsection (c), and may award actual damages if it deems such relief appropriate. . . .

(e)(1) Any person aggrieved by the failure or refusal of a cable operator to make channel capacity available pursuant to this section may petition the Commission for relief under this subsection upon a showing of prior adjudicated violations of this section. . . . If the Commission finds that the channel capacity sought by such person has not been made available in accordance with this section, or that the price, terms, or conditions established by such system are unreasonable under subsection (c), the Commission shall, by rule and order, require such operator to make available such channel capacity under price, terms, and conditions consistent with subsection (c).

. . .

(h) Any cable service offered pursuant to this section shall not be provided, or shall be provided subject to conditions, if such cable service in the judgment of the franchising authority is obscene, or is in conflict with community standards in that it is lewd, lascivious, filthy, or indecent or is otherwise unprotected by the Constitution of the United States. This subsection shall permit a cable operator to enforce prospectively a written and published policy of prohibiting programming that the cable operator reasonably believes describes or depicts sexual or excretory activities or organs in a patently offensive manner as measured by contemporary community standards.

(i)(1) Notwithstanding the provisions of subsections (b) and (c) of this section, a cable operator required by this section to designate channel capacity for commercial use may use any such channel capacity for the provision of programming from a qualified minority programming source or from any qualified educational programming source, whether or not such source is affiliated with the cable operator. The channel capacity used to provide programming from a qualified minority programming source or from any qualified educational programming source pursuant to this subsection may not exceed 33 percent of the channel capacity designated pursuant to this section. No programming provided over a cable system on July 1, 1990, may qualify as minority programming or educational programming on that cable system under this subsection.

(2) For purposes of this subsection, the term "qualified minority programming source" means a programming source which devotes substantially all of its programming to coverage of minority viewpoints, or to programming directed at members of minority groups, and which is over 50 percent minority-owned, as the term "minority" is defined in section 309(i)(3)(C)(ii) of this title.

(3) For purposes of this subsection, the term "qualified educational programming source" means a programming source which devotes substantially all of its programming to educational or instructional programming that promotes public understanding of mathematics, the sciences, the humanities, and the arts and has a documented annual expenditure on programming exceeding $15,000,000. . . .

(4) Nothing in this subsection shall substitute for the requirements to carry qualified noncommercial educational television stations as specified under section 615 of this title.

(j)(1) Within 120 days following October 5, 1992, the Commission shall promulgate regulations designed to limit the access of children to indecent programming, as defined by Commission regulations, and which cable operators have not voluntarily prohibited under subsection (h) of this section by—

> (A) requiring cable operators to place on a single channel all indecent programs, as identified by program providers, intended for carriage on channels designated for commercial use under this section;

> (B) requiring cable operators to block such single channel unless the subscriber requests access to such channel in writing; and

> (C) requiring programmers to inform cable operators if the program would be indecent as defined by Commission regulations.

(2) Cable operators shall comply with the regulations promulgated pursuant to paragraph (1).

OWNERSHIP RESTRICTIONS

Sec. 613. [47 U.S.C.A. § 533.]

(a) It shall be unlawful for any person to be a cable operator if such person, directly or through one or more affiliates, owns or controls, the licensee of a television broadcast station and the predicted grade B contour of such station covers any portion of the community served by such operator's cable system.

(b)(1) It shall be unlawful for any common carrier, subject in whole or in part to Title II of this Act, to provide video programming directly to subscribers in its telephone service area, either directly or indirectly through an affiliate owned by, operated by, controlled by, or under common control with the common carrier.

> (2) It shall be unlawful for a cable operator to hold a license for multichannel multipoint distribution service, or to offer satellite master antenna television service separate and apart from any franchised cable service, in any portion of the franchise area served by that cable operator's cable system. The Commission—

>> (A) shall waive the requirements of this paragraph for all existing multichannel multipoint distribution services and satellite master antenna television services which are owned by a cable operator on October 5, 1992; and

>> (B) may waive the requirements of this paragraph to the extent the Commission determines is necessary to ensure that all significant portions of a franchise area are able to obtain video programming.

(c) The Commission may prescribe rules with respect to the ownership or control of cable systems by persons who own or control other media of mass communications which serve the same community served by a cable system.

(d) Any State or franchising authority may not prohibit the ownership or control of a cable system by any person because of such person's ownership or control of any media of mass communications or other media interests.

(e)(1) Subject to paragraph (2), a State or franchising authority may hold any interest in any cable system.

(2) Any State or franchising authority shall not exercise any editorial control regarding the content of any cable service on a cable system in which such governmental entity holds ownership interest (other than programming on any channel designated for educational or governmental use), unless such control is exercised through an entity separate from the franchising authority.

. . .

CARRIAGE OF LOCAL COMMERCIAL TELEVISION SIGNALS
Sec. 614. [47 U.S.C.A. § 534.]

(a) Each cable operator shall carry, on the cable system of that operator, the signals of local commercial television stations and qualified low power stations as provided by this section. Carriage of additional broadcast television signals on such system shall be at the discretion of such operator, subject to section 325(b) of this title.

(b)(1)(A) A cable operator of a cable system with 12 or fewer usable activated channels shall carry the signals of at least three local commercial television stations, except that if such a system has 300 or fewer subscribers, it shall not be subject to any requirements under this section so long as such system does not delete from carriage by that system any signal of a broadcast television station.

(B) A cable operator of a cable system with more than 12 usable activated channels shall carry the signals of local commercial television stations, up to one-third of the aggregate number of usable activated channels of such system.

(2) Whenever the number of local commercial television stations exceeds the maximum number of signals a cable system is required to carry under paragraph (1), the cable operator shall have discretion in selecting which such stations shall be carried on its cable system, except that—

(A) under no circumstances shall a cable operator carry a qualified low power station in lieu of a local commercial television station; and

(B) if the cable operator elects to carry an affiliate of a broadcast network (as such term is defined by the Commission by regulation), such cable operator shall carry the affiliate of such broadcast network whose city of license reference point . . . is closest to the principal headend of the cable system.

(3)(A) A cable operator shall carry in its entirety, on the cable system of that operator, the primary video, accompanying audio, and line 21 closed caption transmission of each of the local commercial television stations carried on the cable system and, to the extent technically feasible, program-related material in the vertical blanking interval or on subcarriers. Retransmission of other material in the vertical blanking interval or other nonprogram-related material (including teletext and other subscription and advertiser-supported information services) shall be at the discretion of the cable operator. Where appropriate and feasible, operators may delete signal enhancements, such as ghost-canceling, from the broadcast signal and employ such enhancements at the system headend or headends.

(B) The cable operator shall carry the entirety of the program schedule of any television station carried on the cable system unless carriage of specific programming is prohibited, and other programming authorized to be substituted, ...

(4)(A) The signals of local commercial television stations that a cable operator carries shall be carried without material degradation. The Commission shall adopt carriage standards to ensure that, to the extent technically feasible, the quality of signal processing and carriage provided by a cable system for the carriage of local commercial television stations will be no less than that provided by the system for carriage of any other type of signal.

(B) At such time as the Commission prescribes modifications of the standards for television broadcast signals, the Commission shall initiate a proceeding to establish any changes in the signal carriage requirements of cable television systems necessary to ensure cable carriage of such broadcast signals of local commercial television stations which have been changed to conform with such modified standards.

Notwithstanding paragraph (1), a cable operator shall not be required to carry the signal of any local commercial television that substantially duplicates the signal of another local commercial television station which is carried on its cable system, or to carry the signals of more than one local commercial television station affiliated with a particular broadcast network (as such term is defined by regulation). If a cable operator elects to carry on its cable system a signal which substantially duplicates the signal of another local commercial television station carried on the cable system, or to carry on its system the signals of more than one local commercial television station affiliated with a particular broadcast network, all such signals shall be counted toward the number of signals the operator is required to carry under paragraph (1).

(6) Each signal carried in fulfillment of the carriage obligations of a cable operator under this section shall be carried on the cable system channel number on which the local commercial

television station is broadcast over the air, or on the channel on which it was carried on July 19, 1985, or on the channel on which it was carried on January 1, 1992, at the election of the station, or on such other channel as is mutually agreed upon by the station and the cable operator. Any dispute regarding the positioning of a local commercial television shall be resolved by the Commission.

(7) Signals carried in fulfillment of the requirements of this section shall be provided to every subscriber of a cable system. Such signals shall be viewable via cable on all television receivers of a subscriber which are connected to a cable system by a cable operator or for which a cable operator provides a connection. If a cable operator authorizes subscribers to install additional receiver connections, but does not provide the subscriber with such connections, or with the equipment and materials for such connections, the operator shall notify such subscribers of all broadcast stations carried on the cable system which cannot be viewed via cable without a converter box, and shall offer to sell or lease such a converter box to such subscribers at rates in accordance with section (b)(3) of this title.

. . .

(10) A cable operator shall not accept or request monetary payment or other valuable consideration in exchange either for carriage of local commercial television stations in fulfillment of the requirements of this section or for the channel positioning rights provided to such stations under this section, except that—

(c)(1) If there are not sufficient signals of full power local commercial television stations to fill the channels set aside under subsection (b) of this section—

(A) a cable operator of a cable system with a capacity of 35 or fewer usable activated channels shall be required to carry one qualified low power station; and

(B) a cable operator of a cable system with a capacity of more than 35 usable activated channels shall be required to carry two qualified low power stations.

(2) A cable operator required to carry more than one signal of a qualified low power station under this subsection may do so, subject to approval by the franchising authority pursuant to section 611 of this title, by placing such additional station on public, educational, or governmental channels not in use for their designated purposes.

. . .

(g)(1) Pending the outcome of the proceeding under paragraph (2), nothing in this chapter shall require a cable operator to carry on any tier, or prohibit a cable operator to carry on any tier, the signal of any commercial television station or video programming service that is predominately utilized for the transmission of sales presentations or program length commercials.

(2) Within 270 days after October 5, 1992, the Commission, notwithstanding prior proceedings to determine whether broadcast television stations that are predominantly utilized for the transmission of sales presentations or program length commercials are serving the public interest, convenience, and necessity, shall complete a proceeding in accordance with this paragraph to determine whether broadcast television stations that are predominantly utilized for the transmission of sales presentations or program length commercials are serving the public interest, convenience, and necessity. . . . In the event that the Commission concludes that one or more of such stations are serving the public interest, convenience, and necessity, the Commission shall qualify such stations as local commercial television stations for purposes of subsection (a) of this section. In the event that the Commission concludes that one or more of such stations are not serving the public interest, convenience, and necessity, the Commission shall allow the licensees of such stations a reasonable period within which to provide different programming, and shall not deny such stations a renewal expectancy solely because their programming consisted predominately of sales presentations or program length commercials.

. . .

CARRIAGE OF NONCOMMERCIAL EDUCATIONAL TELEVISION
Sec. 615. [47 U.S.C.A. § 535.]

(a) In addition to the carriage requirements set forth in section 614 of this title, each cable operator of a cable system shall carry the signals of qualified noncommercial educational television stations in accordance with the provisions of this section.

(b)(1) Subject to paragraphs (2) and (3) and subsection (e) of this section, each cable operator shall carry, on the cable system of that cable operator, any qualified local noncommercial educational television station requesting carriage.

(2)(A) Notwithstanding paragraph (1), a cable operator of a cable system with 12 or fewer usable activated channels shall be required to carry the signal of one qualified local noncommercial educational television station; except that a cable operator of such system shall comply with subsection (c) of this section and may, in its discretion, carry the signals of other qualified noncommercial educational television stations.

(B) In the case of a cable system described in subparagraph (A) which operates beyond the presence of any qualified local noncommercial educational television station—

(i) the cable operator shall import and carry on that system the signal of one qualified noncommercial educational television station;

(ii) the selection for carriage of such a signal shall be at the election of the cable operator; and

(iii) in order to satisfy the requirements for carriage specified in this subsection, the cable operator of the system shall not be required to remove any other programming service actually provided to subscribers on March 29, 1990; except that such cable operator shall use the first channel available to satisfy the requirements of this subparagraph.

(3)(A) Subject to subsection (c) of this section, a cable operator of a cable system with 13 to 36 usable activated channels—

(i) shall carry the signal of at least one qualified local noncommercial educational television but shall not be required to carry the signals of more than three such stations, and

(ii) may, in its discretion, carry additional such stations.

(B) In the case of a cable system described in this paragraph which operates beyond the presence of any qualified local noncommercial educational television station, the cable operator shall import and carry on that system the signal of at least one qualified noncommercial educational television station to comply with subparagraph (A)(i).

(C) The cable operator of a cable system described in this paragraph which carries the signal of a qualified local noncommercial educational station affiliated with a State public television network shall not be required to carry the signal of any additional qualified local noncommercial educational television stations affiliated with the same network if the programming of such additional stations is substantially duplicated by the programming of the qualified local noncommercial educational television station receiving coverage.

(D) A cable operator of a system described in this paragraph which increases the usable activated channel capacity of the system to more than 36 channels on after March 29, 1990, shall, in accordance with the other provisions of this section, carry the signal of each qualified local noncommercial educational television station requesting carriage, subject to subsection (e) of this section.

(c) Notwithstanding any other provision of this section, all cable operators shall continue to provide carriage to all qualified local noncommercial educational television stations whose signals were carried on their systems as of March 29, 1990. The requirements of this subsection may be waived with respect to a particular cable operator and a particular such station, upon the written consent of the cable operator and the station.

(d) A cable operator required to add the signals of qualified local noncommercial educational television stations to a cable system under this section may do so, subject to approval by the franchising authority pursuant to section 611 of this title, by placing such additional stations on public, educational, or governmental channels not in use for their designated purposes.

(e) A cable operator of a cable system with a capacity of more than 36 usable activated channels which is required to carry the signals of three qualified local noncommercial educational television stations shall not be required to carry the signals of additional such stations the programming of which substantially duplicates the programming broadcast by another qualified local noncommercial educational television station requesting carriage. Substantial duplication shall be defined by the Commission in a manner that promotes access to distinctive noncommercial educational television services.

. . .

(i)(1) A cable operator shall not accept monetary payment or other valuable consideration in exchange for carriage of the signal of any qualified local noncommercial educational television station carried in fulfillment of the requirements of this section, except that such a station may be required to bear the cost associated with delivering a good quality signal or a baseband video signal to the principal headend of the cable system.

(2) Notwithstanding the provisions of this section, a cable operator shall not be required to add the signal of a qualified local noncommercial educational television station not already carried under the provisions of subsection (c) of this section, where such signal would be considered a distant signal for copyright purposes unless such station indemnifies the cable operator for any increased copyright costs resulting from carriage of such signal.

. . .

REGULATION OF CARRIAGE AGREEMENTS
Sec. 616 [47 U.S.C.A. § 536.]

(a) Within one year after October 5, 1992, the Commission shall establish regulations governing program carriage agreements and related practices between cable operators or other multichannel video programming distributors and video programming vendors. Such regulations shall—

(1) include provisions designed to prevent a cable operator or other multichannel video programming distributor from requiring a financial interest in a program service as a condition for carriage on one or more of such operator's systems;

(2) include provisions designed to prohibit a cable operator or other multichannel video programming distributor from coercing a video programming vendor to provide, and from retaliating against such a vendor for failing to provide, exclusive rights against other multichannel video programming distributors as a condition of carriage on a system;

(3) contain provisions designed to prevent a multichannel video programming distributor from engaging in conduct the effect of which is to unreasonably restrain the ability of an unaffiliated video programming vendor to compete fairly by discriminating in video programming distribution on the basis of affiliation or nonaffiliation of vendors in the selection, terms, or conditions for carriage of video programming provided by such vendors;

. . .

SALES OF CABLE SYSTEMS

Sec. 617 [47 U.S.C.A. § 617.]

(a) Except as provided in this section, no cable operator may sell or otherwise transfer ownership in a cable system within a 36–month period following either the acquisition or initial construction of such system by such operator.

(b) In the case of a sale of multiple systems, if the terms of the sale require the buyer to subsequently transfer ownership of one or more such systems to one or more third parties, such transfers shall be considered a part of the initial transaction.

. . .

(d) The Commission may, consistent with the public interest, waive the requirement of subsection (a) of this section, except that, if the franchise requires franchise authority approval of a transfer, the Commission shall not waive such requirements unless the franchise authority has approved the transfer. The Commission shall use its authority under this subsection to permit appropriate transfers in the cases of default, foreclosure, or other financial distress.

. . .

GENERAL FRANCHISE REQUIREMENTS

Sec. 621. [47 U.S.C.A. § 541.]

(a)(1) A franchising authority may award, in accordance with the provisions of this title, one or more franchises within its jurisdiction.

. . .

(3) In awarding a franchise or franchises, a franchising authority shall assure that access to cable service is not denied to any group of potential residential cable subscribers because of the

income of the residents of the local area in which such group resides.

. . .

(c) Any cable system shall not be subject to regulation as a common carrier or utility by reason of providing any cable service.

. . .

FRANCHISE FEES
Sec. 622. [47 U.S.C.A. § 542.]

(a) Subject to the limitation of subsection (b), any cable operator may be required under the terms of any franchise to pay a franchise fee.

(b) For any 12–month period, the franchise fees paid by a cable operator with respect to any cable system shall not exceed 5 percent of such cable operator's gross revenues derived in such period from the operation of the cable system.

. . .

REGULATION OF RATES
Sec. 623. [47 U.S.C.A. § 543.]

(a)(1) In general.—No Federal agency or State may regulate the rates for the provision of cable service except to the extent provided under this section and section 612 of this title. Any franchising authority may regulate the rates for the provision of cable service, or any other communications service provided over a cable system to cable subscribers, but only to the extent provided under this section. No Federal agency, State, or franchising authority may regulate the rates for cable service of a cable system that is owned or operated by a local government or franchising authority within whose jurisdiction that cable system is located and that is the only cable system located within such jurisdiction.

(2) Preference for competition.—If the Commission finds that a cable system is subject to effective competition, the rates for the provision of cable service by such system shall not be subject to regulation by the Commission or by a State or franchising authority under this section. If the Commission finds that a cable system is not subject to effective competition—

(b)(1) The Commission shall, by regulation, ensure that the rates for the basic service tier are reasonable. Such regulations shall be designed to achieve the goal of protecting subscribers of any cable system that is not subject to effective competition from rates for the basic service tier if such cable system were subject to effective competition.

. . .

(7)(A) Each cable operator of a cable system shall provide its subscribers a separately available basic service tier to which subscription is required for access to any other tier of service. Such basic tier shall, at a minimum, consist of the following:

(i) All signals carried in fulfillment of the requirements of sections 614 and 615 of this title.

(ii) Any public, educational, and governmental access programming required by the franchise of the cable system to be provided to subscribers.

(iii) Any signal of any television broadcast station that is provided by the cable operator to any subscriber, except a signal which is secondarily transmitted by a satellite carrier beyond the local service area of such station.

(B) A cable operator may add additional video programming signals or services to the basic service tier. Any such additional signals or services provided on the basic service tier shall be provided to subscribers at rates determined under the regulations prescribed by the Commission under this subsection.

(8)(A) A cable operator may not require the subscription to any tier other than the basic service tier required by paragraph (7) as a condition of access to video programming offered on a per channel or per program basis. A cable operator may not discriminate between subscribers to the basic service tier and other subscribers with regard to the rates charged for video programming offered on a per channel or per program basis.

(B) The prohibition in subparagraph (A) shall not apply to a cable system that, by reason of the lack of addressable converter boxes or other technological limitations, does not permit the operator to offer programming on a per channel or per program basis in the same manner required by subparagraph (A). This subparagraph shall not be available to any cable operator after—

(i) the technology utilized by the cable system is modified or improved in a way that eliminates such technological limitation; or

(ii) 10 years after October 5, 1992, subject to subparagraph (C).

(C) If, in any proceeding initiated at the request of any cable operator, the Commission determines that compliance with the requirements of subparagraph (A) would require the cable operator to increase its rates, the Commission may, to the extent consistent with the public interest, grant such cable operator a waiver from such requirements for such specified period as the Commission determines reasonable and appropriate.

(c)(1) Within 180 days after October 5, 1992, the Commission shall, by regulation, establish the following:

(A) criteria prescribed in accordance with paragraph (2) for identifying, in individual cases, rates for cable programming services that are unreasonable;

. . .

(*l*) As used in this section—

(1) The term "effective competition" means that—

(A) fewer than 30 percent of the households in the franchise area subscribe to the cable service of a cable system;

(B) the franchise area is—

(i) served by at least two unaffiliated multichannel video programming distributors each of which offers comparable video programming to at least 50 percent of the households in the franchise area; and

(ii) the number of households subscribing to programming services offered by multichannel video programming distributors other than the largest multichannel video programming distributor exceeds 15 percent of the households in the franchise area; or

(C) a multichannel video programming distributor operated by the franchising authority for that franchise area offers video programming to at least 50 percent of the households in that franchise area.

. . .

(2) require the provision of any service tier provided without charge (disregarding any installation or rental charge for equipment necessary for receipt of such tier); or

(3) regulate rates for the initial installation or the rental of one set of the minimum equipment which is necessary for the subscriber's receipt of basic cable service.

. . .

REGULATION OF SERVICES, FACILITIES, AND EQUIPMENT
Sec. 624. [47 U.S.C.A. § 544.]

(a) Any franchising authority may not regulate the services, facilities, and equipment provided by a cable operator except to the extent consistent with this title.

(b) In the case of any franchise granted after the effective date of this title, the franchising authority, to the extent related to the establishment or operation of a cable system—

(1) in its requests for proposals for a franchise (including requests for renewal proposals, subject to Section 626), may estab-

lish requirements for facilities and equipment, but may not establish requirements for video programming or other information services; and

(2) subject to Section 625, may enforce any requirements contained within the franchise—

(A) for facilities and equipment; and

(B) for broad categories of video programming or other services.

(c) In the case of any franchise in effect on the effective date of this title, the franchising authority may, subject to Section 625, enforce requirements contained within the franchise for the provision of services, facilities, and equipment, whether or not related to the establishment or operation of a cable system.

(d)(1) Nothing in this title shall be construed as prohibiting a franchising authority and a cable operator from specifying, in a franchise or renewal thereof, that certain cable services shall not be provided or shall be provided subject to conditions, if such cable services are obscene or are otherwise unprotected by the Constitution of the United States.

(2)(A) In order to restrict the viewing of programming which is obscene or indecent, upon the request of a subscriber, a cable operator shall provide (by sale or lease) a device by which the subscriber can prohibit viewing of a particular cable service during periods selected by that subscriber.

. . .

(e) Within one year after October 5, 1992, the Commission shall prescribe regulations which establish minimum technical standards relating to cable systems' technical operation and signal quality. The Commission shall update such standards periodically to reflect improvements in technology. A franchising authority may require as part of a franchise (including a modification, renewal, or transfer thereof) provisions for the enforcement of the standards prescribed under this subsection. A franchising authority may apply to the Commission for a waiver to impose standards that are more stringent than the standards prescribed by the Commission under this subsection.

(f)(1) Any Federal agency, State, or franchising authority may not impose requirements regarding the provision or content of cable services, except as expressly provided in this title.

. . .

CONSUMER ELECTRONICS EQUIPMENT COMPATIBILITY
Sec. 624a. [47 U.S.C.A. § 544a.]

. . .

(b)(1) Within 1 year after October, 1992, the Commission, in consultation with representatives of the cable industry and the consumer electronics industry, shall report to Congress on means of assuring compatibility between televisions and video cassette recorders and cable systems, consistent with the need to prevent theft of cable service, so that cable subscribers will be able to enjoy the full benefit of both the programming available on cable systems and the functions available on their televisions and video cassette recorders. Within 180 days after the date of submission of the report required by this subsection, the Commission shall issue such regulations as are necessary to assure such compatibility.

. . .

MODIFICATION OF FRANCHISE OBLIGATIONS
Sec. 625. [47 U.S.C.A. § 545.]

(a)(1) During the period a franchise is in effect, the cable operator may obtain from the franchising authority modifications of the requirements in such franchise—

(A) in the case of any such requirement for facilities or equipment, including public, educational, or governmental access facilities or equipment, if the cable operator demonstrates that (i) it is commercially impracticable for the operator to comply with such requirement, and (ii) the proposal by the cable operator for modification of such requirement is appropriate because of such commercial impracticability; or

(B) in the case of any such requirement for services, if the cable operator demonstrates that the mix, quality, and level of services required by the franchise at the time it was granted will be maintained after such modification.

. . .

RENEWAL
Sec. 626. [47 U.S.C.A. § 546.]

(a)(1) A franchising authority may, on its own initiative during the 6th month period which begins with the 36th month before the franchise expiration, commence a proceeding which affords the public in the franchise area appropriate notice and participation for the purpose of (A) identifying the future cable-related community needs and interests, and (B) reviewing the performance of the cable operator under the franchise during the then current franchise term. If the cable operator submits, during such 6–month period, a written renewal notice requesting the commencement of such a proceeding, the franchising authority shall commence such a proceeding not later than 6 months after the date such notice is submitted.

(2) The cable operator may not invoke the renewal procedures set forth in subsections (b) through (g) of this section unless—

(A) such a proceeding is requested by the cable operator by timely submission of such notice; or

(B) such a proceeding is commenced by the franchising authority on its own initiative.

(b)(1) Upon completion of a proceeding under subsection (a), a cable operator seeking renewal of a franchise may, on its own initiative or at the request of a franchising authority, submit a proposal for renewal.

(2) Subject to section 624, any such proposal shall contain such material as the franchising authority may require, including proposals for an upgrade of the cable system.

(3) The franchising authority may establish a date by which such proposals shall be submitted.

(c)(1) Upon submittal by a cable operator of a proposal to the franchising authority for the renewal of a franchise, the franchising authority shall provide prompt public notice of such proposal and, during the 4–month period which begins on the completion of any proceedings under subsection (a), renew the franchise or, issue a preliminary assessment that the franchise should not be renewed and, at the request of the operator or on its own initiative, commence an administrative proceeding after providing prompt public notice of such proceeding in accordance with paragraph (2) to consider whether—

(A) the cable operator has substantially complied with the material terms of the existing franchise and with applicable law;

(B) the quality of the operator's service including signal quality, response to consumer complaints, and billing practices, but without regard to the mix, quality, or level of cable services or other services provided over the system, has been reasonable in light of community needs;

(C) the operator has the financial, legal, and technical ability to provide the services, facilities, and equipment as set forth in the operator's proposal; and

(D) the operator's proposal is reasonable to meet the future cable-related community needs and interests, taking into account the cost of meeting such needs and interests.

. . .

(3) At the completion of a proceeding under this subsection, the franchising authority shall issue a written decision granting or denying the proposal for renewal based upon the record of such proceeding, and transmit a copy of such decision to the cable operator. Such decision shall state the reasons therefor.

(d) Any denial of a proposal for renewal shall be based on one or more adverse findings made with respect to the factors described in subparagraphs (A) through (D) of subsection (c)(1). . . .

DEVELOPMENT OF COMPETITION AND DIVERSITY
IN VIDEO PROGRAMMING DISTRIBUTION

Sec. 628. [47 U.S.C.A. § 548.]

(a) The purpose of this section is to promote the public interest, convenience, and necessity by increasing competition and diversity in the multichannel video programming market, to increase the availability of satellite cable programming and satellite broadcast programming to persons in rural and other areas not currently able to receive such programming, and to spur the development of communications technologies.

(b) It shall be unlawful for a cable operator, a satellite cable programming vendor in which a cable operator has an attributable interest, or a satellite broadcast programming vendor to engage in unfair methods of competition or unfair or deceptive acts or practices, the purpose or effect of which is to hinder significantly or to prevent any multichannel video programming distributor from providing satellite cable programming or satellite broadcast programming to subscribers or consumers.

(c)(1) Within 180 days after October 5, 1992, the Commission shall, in order to promote the public interest, convenience, and necessity by increasing competition and diversity in the multichannel video programming market and the continuing development of communications technologies, prescribe regulations to specify particular conduct that is prohibited by subsection (b) of this section.

(2) The regulations to be promulgated under this section shall—

(A) establish effective safeguards to prevent a cable operator which has an attributable interest in a satellite cable programming vendor or a satellite broadcast programming vendor from unduly or improperly influencing the decision of such vendor to sell, or the prices, terms, and conditions of sale of, satellite cable programming or satellite broadcast programming to any unaffiliated multichannel video programming distributor;

(B) prohibit discrimination by a satellite cable programming vendor in which a cable operator has an attributable interest or by a satellite broadcast programming vendor in the prices, terms, and conditions of sale or delivery of satellite cable programming or satellite broadcast programming among or between cable systems, cable operators, or other multichannel video programming distributors, or their agents or buying groups, ...

. . .

(C) prohibit practices, understandings, arrangements, and activities, including exclusive contracts for satellite cable programming or satellite broadcast programming between a cable operator and a satellite cable programming vendor or satellite broadcast programming vendor, that prevent a multichannel video programming vendor in which a cable operator has an attributable interest or any satellite broadcast programming vendor in which a cable operator has an attributable interest for distribution to persons in areas not served by a cable operator as of October 5, 1992; and

(D) with respect to distribution to persons in areas served by a cable operator, prohibit exclusive contracts for satellite cable programming or satellite broadcast programming between a cable operator and a satellite cable programming vendor in which a cable operator has an attributable interest or a satellite broadcast programming vendor in which a cable operator has an attributable interest, unless the Commission determines (in accordance with paragraph (4)) that such contract is in the public interest.

(3)(A) Nothing in this section shall require any person who is engaged in the national or regional distribution of video programming to make such programming available in any geographic area beyond which such programming has been authorized or licensed for distribution.

(B) Nothing in this section shall apply

(i) to the signal of any broadcast affiliate of a national television network or other television signal that is retransmitted by satellite but that is not satellite broadcast programming, or

(ii) to any internal satellite communication of any broadcast network or cable network that is not satellite broadcast programming.

(4) In determining whether an exclusive contract is in the public interest for purposes of paragraph (2)(D), the Commission shall consider each of the following factors with respect to the effect of such contract on the distribution of video programming in areas that are served by a cable operator:

(A) the effect of such exclusive contract on the development of competition in local and national multichannel video programming distribution markets;

(B) the effect of such exclusive contract on competition from multichannel video programming distribution technologies other than cable;

(C) the effect of such exclusive contract on the attraction of capital investment in the production and distribution of new satellite cable programming;

(D) the effect of such exclusive contract on diversity of programming in the multichannel video programming distribution market; and

(E) the duration of the exclusive contract.

. . .

CONSUMER PROTECTION AND CUSTOMER SERVICE
Sec. 632. [47 U.S.C.A. § 552.]

(a) A franchising authority may establish and enforce—

(1) customer service requirements of the cable operator; and

(2) construction schedules and other construction-related requirements, including construction-related performance requirements, of the cable operator.

(b) The Commission shall, within 180 days of enactment of the Cable Consumer Protection and Competition Act of 1992, establish standards by which cable operators may fulfill their customer service requirements. Such standards shall include, at a minimum, requirements governing—

(1) cable system office hours and telephone availability;

(2) installations, outages, and service calls; and

(3) communications between the cable operator and the subscriber (including standards governing bills and refunds).

(c)(1) Nothing in this subchapter shall be construed to prohibit any State or any franchising authority from enacting or enforcing any consumer protection law, to the extent not specifically preempted by this subchapter.

(2) Nothing in this section shall be construed to preclude a franchising authority and a cable operator from agreeing to customer service requirements that exceed the standards established by the Commission under subsection (b) of this section. Nothing in this subchapter shall be construed to prevent the establishment or enforcement of any municipal law or regulation, or any State law, concerning customer service that imposes customer service requirements that exceed the standards set by the Commission under this section, or that addresses matters not addressed by the Commission under this section.

UNAUTHORIZED RECEPTION OF CABLE SERVICE
Sec. 633. [47 U.S.C.A. § 553.]

(a)(1) No person shall intercept or receive or assist in intercepting or receiving any communications service offered over a cable system, unless specifically authorized to do so by a cable operator or as may otherwise be specifically authorized by law.

(2) For the purpose of this section, the term "assist in intercepting or receiving" shall include the manufacture or distribution of equipment intended by the manufacturer or distributor (as the case may be) for unauthorized reception of any communications service offered over a cable system in violation of subparagraph (1).

. . .

LIMITATION OF FRANCHISING AUTHORITY LIABILITY
Sec. 635a. [47 U.S.C.A. § 555a.]

(a) In any court proceeding pending on or initiated after October 5, 1992, involving any claim against a franchising authority or other governmental entity, or any official, member, employee, or agent of such authority or entity, arising from the regulation of cable service or from a decision of approval or disapproval with respect to a grant, renewal, transfer, or amendment of a franchise, any relief, to the extent such relief is required by any other provision of Federal, State, or local law, shall be limited to injunctive relief and declaratory relief.

(b) The limitation contained in subsection (a) of this section shall not apply to actions that, prior to such violation, have been determined by a final order of a court of binding jurisdiction, no longer subject to appeal, to be in violation of a cable operator's rights.

. . .

CRIMINAL AND CIVIL LIABILITY
Sec. 638. [47 U.S.C.A. § 558.]

Nothing in this title shall be deemed to affect the criminal or civil liability of cable programmers or cable operators pursuant to the Federal, State, or local law of libel, slander, obscenity, incitement, invasions of privacy, false or misleading advertising, or other similar laws, except that cable operators shall not incur any such liability for any program carried on any channel designated for public, educational, governmental use or any other channel obtained under Section 612 or under similar arrangements.

OBSCENE PROGRAMMING
Sec. 639. [47 U.S.C.A. § 559.]

Whoever transmits over any cable system any matter which is obscene or otherwise unprotected by the Constitution of the United States shall be fined not more than $10,000 or imprisoned not more than two years, or both.

UNAUTHORIZED PUBLICATION OR USE OF COMMUNICATIONS
Sec. 705. [47 U.S.C.A. § 605.]

(a) Except as authorized by Chapter 119, Title 18, no person receiving, assisting in receiving, transmitting, or assisting in transmitting, any interstate or foreign communication by wire or radio shall divulge or publish the existence, contents, substance, purport, effect, or meaning thereof, except through authorized channels of transmission or reception, (1) to any person other than the addressee, his agent, or attorney, (2) to a person employed or authorized to forward such communication to its destination, (3) to proper accounting or distributing officers of the various communicating centers over which the communication may be passed, (4) to the master of a ship under whom he is serving, (5) in response to a subpoena issued by a court of competent jurisdiction, or (6) on demand of other lawful authority. No person not being authorized by the sender shall intercept any radio communication and divulge or publish the existence, contents, substance, purport, effect, or meaning of such intercepted communication to any person. No person not being entitled thereto shall receive or assist in receiving any interstate or foreign communication by radio and use such communication (or any information therein contained) for his own benefit or for the benefit of another not entitled thereto. No person having received any intercepted radio communication or having become acquainted with the contents, substance, purport, effect, or meaning of such communication (or any part thereof) knowing that such communication was intercepted, shall divulge or publish the existence, contents, substance, purport, effect, or meaning of such communication (or any part thereof) or use such communication (or any information therein contained) for his own benefit or for the benefit of another not entitled thereto. This section shall not apply to the receiving, divulging, publishing, or utilizing the contents of any radio communication which is transmitted by any station for the use of the general public, which relates to ships, aircraft, vehicles or persons in distress, or which is transmitted by an amateur radio station operator or by a citizens band radio operator.

(b) The provisions of subsection (a) shall not apply to the interception or receipt by any individual, or the assisting (including the manufacture or sale) of such interception or receipt, of any satellite cable programming for private viewing if—

    (1) the programming involved is not encrypted; and

    (2)(A) a marketing system is not established under which—

        (i) an agent or agents have been lawfully designated for the purpose of authorizing private viewing by individuals; and

        (ii) such authorization is available to the individual involved from the appropriate agent or agents; or

    (B) a marketing system described in subparagraph (A) is established and the individuals receiving such programming have obtained authorization for private viewing under that system.

(c) For purposes of this section—

    (1) the term "satellite cable programming" means video programming which is transmitted via satellite and which is primarily intended for the direct receipt by cable operators for their retransmission to cable subscribers;

(2) the term "agent," with respect to any person, includes an employee of such person;

(3) the term "encrypt," when used with respect to satellite cable programming, means to transmit such programming in a form whereby the aural and visual characteristics (or both) are modified or altered for the purpose of preventing the unauthorized receipt of such programming by persons without authorized equipment which is designed to eliminate the effects of such modification or alteration;

(4) the term "private viewing" means the viewing for private use in an individual's dwelling unit by means of equipment, owned or operated by such individual, capable of receiving satellite cable programming directly from a satellite; and

(5) the term "private financial gain" shall not include the gain resulting to any individual for the private use in such individual's dwelling unit of any programming for which the individual has not obtained authorization for that use.

(d)(1) Any person who willfully violates subsection (a) shall be fined not more than $1,000 or imprisoned for not more than 6 months or both.

(2) Any person who violates subsection (a) willfully and for purposes of direct or indirect commercial advantage or private financial gain shall be fined not more than $25,000 or imprisoned for not more than 1 year, or both, for the first such conviction and shall be fined not more than $50,000 or imprisoned for not more than 2 years, or both, for any subsequent conviction.

(3)(A) Any person aggrieved by any violation of subsection (a) may bring a civil action in a United States district court or in any other court of competent jurisdiction.

(B) The court may—

(i) grant temporary and final injunctions on such terms as it may deem reasonable to prevent or restrain violations of subsection (a);

(ii) award damages as described in subparagraph (C); and

(iii) direct the recovery of full costs, including awarding reasonable attorneys' fees to an aggrieved party who prevails.

(C)(i) Damages awarded by any court under this section shall be computed, at the election of the aggrieved party, in accordance with either of the following subclauses;

(I) the party aggrieved may recover the actual damages suffered by him as a result of the violation and any profits of the violator that are attributable to the violation which are not taken into account in computing the actual damages; in determining the violator's profits, the party aggrieved shall be required to prove only the violator's gross revenue, and the violator shall be required to prove his deductible expenses and the elements of profit attributable to factors other than the violation; or

(II) the party aggrieved may recover an award of statutory damages for each violation involved in the action in a sum of not less than $250 or more than $10,000, as the court considers just.

(ii) In any case in which the court finds that the violation was committed willfully and for purposes of direct or indirect commercial advantage or private financial gain, the court in its discretion may increase the award of damages, whether actual or statutory, by an amount of not more than $50,000.

(iii) In any case where the court finds that the violator was not aware and had no reason to believe that his acts constituted a violation of this section, the court in its discretion may reduce the award of damages to a sum of not less than $100.

(4) The importation, manufacture, sale, or distribution of equipment by any person with the intent of its use to assist in any activity prohibited by subsection (a) shall be subject to penalties and remedies under this subsection to the same extent and in the same manner as a person who has engaged in such prohibited activity.

(5) The penalties under this subsection shall be in addition to those prescribed under any other provision of this title.

(6) Nothing in this subsection shall prevent any State, or political subdivision thereof, from enacting or enforcing any laws with respect to the importation, sale, manufacture, or distribution of equipment by any person with the intent of its use to assist in the interception or receipt of radio communications prohibited by subsection (a).

(e) Nothing in this section shall affect any right, obligation, or liability under Title 17, United States Code, any rule, regulation, or order thereunder, or any other applicable Federal, State, or local law.

Appendix C
FEDERAL COMMUNICATIONS COMMISSION

FEDERAL COMMUNICATIONS COMMISSION

INDEX

References are to Pages

†